W9-ABI-604

André Gide

André Gide

A Life in the Present

ALAN SHERIDAN

HARVARD UNIVERSITY PRESS
CAMBRIDGE, MASSACHUSETTS
1999

Printed in the United Kingdom

Library of Congress Catalog Card Number: 98–73544

ISBN 0–674–03527–5

To David Urmston

Contents

List of Illustrations   ix

Introduction   xi

1   Two Stars, Two Races, Two Provinces, Two Faiths   1

2   Childhood: Schooldays and Holidays (OCTOBER 1874 – OCTOBER 1880)   10

3   Youth: God and Love (OCTOBER 1880 – SEPTEMBER 1889)   28

4   André Walter: Puritan and Narcissist (OCTOBER 1889 – JUNE 1891)   54

5   The Ironic Narcissist: *Le Traité du Narcisse, Poésies d'André Walter, Le Voyage d'Urien, La Tentative amoureuse* (JUNE 1891 – OCTOBER 1893)   72

6   Liberation and . . . Engagement: 'J'écris . . . *Paludes*' (OCTOBER 1893 – JUNE 1895)   93

7   Marriage and Nomadism: *Les Nourritures terrestres, Saül, Le Prométhée mal enchaîné, Philoctète* (JUNE 1895 – OCTOBER 1898)   128

8   High Hopes Brought Low: *Le Roi Candaule* and *L'Immoraliste* (NOVEMBER 1898 – OCTOBER 1902)   165

9   The Barren Years: *Le Retour de l'Enfant prodigue* and *La Porte étroite* (OCTOBER 1902 – OCTOBER 1908)   195

10   The 'New' Gide and the Founding of the *NRF*: *Isabelle* and *Les Caves du Vatican* (OCTOBER 1908 – AUGUST 1914)   233

11   The War: De Profundis, Summer's Lease (AUGUST 1914 – NOVEMBER 1918)   280

12   The Post-War Years: *La Symphonie Pastorale* (NOVEMBER 1918 – DECEMBER 1921)   316

13   Gide, Homosexual Theorist and Father: *Corydon* and *Les Faux-Monnayeurs* (JANUARY 1922 – JULY 1925)   351

14 Heart of Darkness: *Voyage au Congo* and *L'Ecole des femmes*
    (JULY 1925 – DECEMBER 1930)   401

15 Gide, 'Fellow-traveller': *Oedipe*, *Perséphone* and *Les Nouvelles
    Nourritures* (JANUARY 1931 – JUNE 1936)   441

16 Retreat from Moscow, a Sense of Ending: *Retour de l'U.R.S.S.* and
    Geneviève (JUNE 1936 – SEPTEMBER 1939)   492

17 Another War: Retreat and Exile (SEPTEMBER 1939 – MAY 1945) 538

18 'The End of Life . . . A Rather Dull Last Act': *Thésée* and
    Ainsi soit-il (MAY 1945 – FEBRUARY 1951)   570

    Conclusion   621

    Notes and References   635

    Bibliography   655

    Family Trees: The Gide Family   676

                     The Rondeaux Family   677

    Index   679

List of Illustrations

Gide, aged eight, 1877 (Private Collection Danièle Allégret)

Gide's father, Paul Gide (Collection Catherine Gide/Gallimard, Paris)

Gide, aged three, with his mother, 1872 (Collection Catherine Gide/ Gallimard, Paris)

La Roque, drawing by Anna Shackleton, 1856 (Private Collection Danièle Allégret)

Anna Shackleton, c.1873 (Private Collection)

Gide, aged twenty-one, 1891 (Bibliothèque Littéraire Jacques Doucet/ Photo © Jean-Loup Charmet, Paris)

Gide at Biskra, 1893 (Photo © Collection Roger-Viollet, Paris)

Athman, aged fourteen, 1893 (Gallimard, Paris/Weidenfeld & Nicolson Archives)

Pierre Louÿs, c. 1894 (Photo © Martinie-Viollet/Roger-Viollet, Paris)

Paul Laurens

Henri Ghéon and André Gide in Asia Minor before 1914 (Collection Fond Ghéon, Corre-Macquin Family)

Eugène Rouart (Private Collection)

Francis Jammes, 1898 (Private Collection/Photo © Jean-Loup Charmet, Paris)

Jean Schlumberger (Private Collection)

Jacques Copeau at the Galerie Georges Petit, 1911 (Photo © Bibliothèque Nationale de France, Paris)

André Ruyters (Collection Catherine Gide/Gallimard, Paris)

Gide and Maria Van Rysselberghe at Weimar, 1903 (Collection Catherine Gide/Gallimard, Paris)

Cuverville, 1923, taken by Roger Martin du Gard (Archives Martin du Gard/Photo © Jean-Loup Charmet, Paris)

Madeleine Gide, in her bedroom at Cuverville, 1902 (Collection Catherine Gide/Gallimard, Paris)

Breakfast at Pontigny, 1923. Left to right: Roger Martin du Gard, Gide, and Dorothy Bussy (Archives Pontigny-Cerisy)

Marc Allégret, aged seventeen, 1917 (Private Collection Danièle Allégret)

Pontigny, 1923 (Archives Pontigny-Cerisy)

Villa Montmorency, interior (Photo © Lucien Hervé, Paris)

Villa Montmorency (Photo © Lucien Hervé, Paris)

Gide at Villa Montmorency, 1908 (Collection Catherine Gide/Gallimard, Paris)

Elisabeth Van Rysselberghe (Collection Catherine Gide/Gallimard, Paris)

Gide and Marc Allégret in the Congo, 1925 (Mission du Patrimoine – Archives Allégret/Photo © Jean-Loup Charmet)

Jef Last (Nederlands Letterkundig Museum/Photo © Cas Oorthuys/The Nederlands Photo Archives)

Robert Levesque, Ibiza, 1933 (Private Collection)

Gide and Pierre Herbart in Moscow, 1936 (Collection Anne-Marie Drouin/Photo © Jean-Loup Charmet)

Gide at the rue Vaneau, 1929 (Private Collection Danièle Allégret)

Gide and Maria Van Rysselberghe, at the rue Vaneau, 1938 (Photo © Gisèle Freund/John Hillelson Agency)

Gide speaking in Red Square, Moscow, 20 June 1936, on the occasion of Gorky's funeral. Left to right: Gide, Bulganin, Molotov, Stalin and Dimitrov (Photo: © Jean-Loup Charmet, Paris)

Gide and his daughter Catherine Lambert, Lake Maggiore, 1947 (Photo © Richard Heyd/Gallimard/Weidenfeld & Nicolson Archives)

Gide, his daughter Catherine, her husband Jean Lambert, their children and Marc Allégret, La Mivoie, 1951 (Private Collection Danièle Allégret)

Every effort has been made to contact all copyright holders. The publishers will be glad to make good in future editions any errors or omissions brought to their attention.

Introduction

At the time of his death in 1951, aged eighty-one, André Gide would have been on most lists of the ten most important novelists of the century, sharing the French representation only with Proust. For fifty years he had been France's best-known writer, but his name was also familiar the world over to millions who had never read any of his books. For Gide had long been a controversial figure, his life and his views on moral, political and religious matters being better known than his literary work. It was above all his status as 'sage' that brought him the Nobel Prize for Literature in 1947 – and brought it to him so late. (His closest friend, the 'uncontroversial' Roger Martin du Gard, twelve years his junior, had, to his own embarrassment, been awarded the prize ten years before.) Universal recognition came from another source, a year after Gide's death, when the Vatican Holy Office placed all his works, *opera omnia*, on the *Index librorum prohibitorum*, thus forbidding all Catholics, under pain of mortal sin, to read any of his works. The exact timing of the edict was due probably to bureaucracy's delays; a cynic might say that the Vatican made sure that it had the last word, that no reply would be forthcoming. It may not have looked like it in 1952, but even the Petrine See could be worn down by time. A posthumous Gide would have had the last laugh, if not the last word: a mere fourteen years later, the Index itself was abolished by the Second Vatican Council, that occasion of some moral improvement and much aesthetic devastation. The Index was not the first condemnation levelled at Gide's work. From the publication of *Retour de l'U.R.S.S* in 1936, the Soviet government and Communist Party placed a similar prohibition, *de facto* if not *de jure*, on the work of a man they had hitherto courted and fêted. In Paris, under the German occupation, Gide's works were given first a partial, then a total ban. In the circumstances, the accolade from Stockholm, that haven of liberal moderation, was a nice counter-balance.

Yet Gide did not set out to become a bestselling public figure: indeed he did everything possible to avoid it. As a young man, entering and emerging from the Mallarmé circle of Symbolist poets, he wrote for a small, discerning group of initiates. The *gloire* to which he and his young friends aspired was the recognition of artistic excellence, something that would probably be accorded posthumously: it was not what we understand by fame. Gide's first book, *Les Cahiers d'André Walter*, was published in 1891, when he was only twenty-one, at the author's (or, rather, his mother's) expense. (It was quite common at the time for publishers to charge printing costs to authors who would not otherwise be financially viable.) Supposedly the posthumous writings of its eponymous author, *Les Cahiers d'André Walter* did not even bear Gide's name. It was consciously intended to be the first Symbolist novel, almost a contradiction in terms. Gide sent a copy to Mallarmé and word got round as to the author's true identity. Apart from a few reviews by friends and a hundred or two copies sold, Gide's first book passed unnoticed. Over the next twenty years or more, Gide published some fifteen books, of varying length, always at his own expense, always to small sales and limited attention. What was to become his most influential book, *Les Nourritures terrestres*, sold only five hundred copies for the first twenty years of its existence. And yet, such was the nature of the French reading public at the time, Gide's standing and reputation grew with each year. He was known to those whose opinions mattered on such things and was already seen as one of France's most important writers.

Something of a breakthrough into a wider public occurred with *Les Caves du Vatican* in 1914, but the war that followed within weeks of its publication made its brilliant frivolity seem out of season. Gide wrote no more fiction until the war was over. In 1918, *Les Nourritures terrestres* was reissued, becoming at once a bestseller – and a sort of bible for generations of young people rebelling against limited family horizons. Over the next few years, most of Gide's earlier works were reprinted. In his fifties, he had finally achieved the position, in France and abroad, that was to remain exclusively his. On a purely literary level, this was to reach its height in what is incontrovertibly his masterpiece, *Les Faux-Monnayeurs:* here, in the spirit of the 1920s, he was able to recapture the pre-war light-hearted charm of *Les Caves du Vatican* and, at the same time, produce one of the century's great meditations on the art of fiction.

Gide's fame rested ultimately, of course, on his literary works. But, unlike many writers, he was no recluse: he had a need of friendship and a genius for sustaining it. At seventeen, during his year at the Ecole Alsacienne, he had become close friends with Pierre Louis, the future Pierre Louÿs and poet of *Les Chansons de Bilitis*, later to be set to music by Debussy. ('Bilitis' was an Arab girl whom Gide had passed on to Louÿs, after sharing her with his friend Paul Laurens for some weeks.) The following year, at the Lycée Henri IV, Gide sat next to a boy with literary ambitions who was to remain a lifelong friend: Léon Blum deserted literature for politics, eventually becoming French prime minister. At twenty-one, through Louÿs, Gide met a young student at Montpellier, Paul Valéry, who was to become France's greatest poet of the century: he, too, became a friend for life. Gide also met Maurice Barrès, the most influential French novelist of the day, Mallarmé, France's greatest living poet, and Oscar Wilde. It was through Mallarmé's celebrated *Mardis* that Gide made his *entrée* into the inner circle of the Paris literary world. In his modest apartment in the rue de Rome, near Saint-Lazare, the unworldly, other-worldly poet, standing by the fireplace in his sitting-/dining-room, held gatherings of celebrities and future celebrities spellbound.

In 1895, Gide married his first cousin and childhood sweetheart, Madeleine Rondeaux: the marriage was to remain unconsummated. Meanwhile, his circle of friends expanded: the poets Francis Jammes and Paul Claudel; Jacques Copeau, who, at this time, dreamed of being a writer, not the man of the theatre that he became; above all, Henri Ghéon, an impecunious doctor and writer, who became Gide's closest friend and companion on innumerable homosexual exploits, until, in 1916, 'God confiscated him' as a friend. Then there was Jean Schlumberger, like Gide the son of a rich Protestant family, like him too married: Gide helped him to find himself as a homosexual. In 1904, it was with Jean's younger brother, Maurice, then eighteen, that Gide and Ghéon began an extraordinary six-month long, three-cornered affair, celebrated not only *inter corpora*, but, fortunately for us, in letters, although the most revealing of those letters were excluded from the Gide–Ghéon correspondence, published in 1976, at the insistence of the then ultra-respectable ninety-year-old Maurice, *père de famille* and founder of the Banque Schlumberger.

In 1909, Gide and a group of friends, including Copeau, Ghéon and Schlumberger, started a literary monthly with the unprepossessing title, inherited from a previous attempt, of *La Nouvelle Revue Française*. It was merely the latest of many such 'little magazines', selling a few hundred copies to the cognoscenti; they seldom lasted longer than a year or two. After a few years, the review branched out into book publishing, and a young man, son of a theatrical impresario, was brought in, with family money, to act as a sort of business manager. He was Gaston Gallimard and he was to give his name to one of the most remarkable imprints of the century. As if that were not enough, 1913 saw the beginning of another offshoot of the *NRF,* this time led by Jacques Copeau – the Vieux Colombier; it was to become the most celebrated undertaking in the French theatre of the inter-war years.

The Great War found Gide helping to run the Foyer Franco-Belge, a charity organization formed to assist Belgian and French refugees from German-occupied territory. At his side were the poet Charles Du Bos and Maria Van Rysselberghe, the wife of a Belgian painter, who was to become one of Gide's closest friends. The years 1915–16 brought Gide to the depths of depression, a true 'dark night of the soul', during which, in the pages of his *Numquid et tu . . .?,* he struggled against what he saw as the two-pronged invasion of his spiritual territory by God (a Catholic God) and the Devil: the same God was winning victory after victory in the French literary world, converting some, bringing others back to the ecclesiastical bosom.

In 1917, the 'dark night' was banished by a dawn light appearing from a more familiar, Protestant source, in the person of Marc Allégret. It was Marc's father, Pastor Elie Allégret, a family friend, who had taken the eighteen-year-old Gide on his first trip to London and who acted as best man at his wedding. During much of the war, Pastor Allégret was in Africa working as a missionary, and Gide, known to his children as 'Oncle André', often stayed with his family, helping his wife financially and trying to broaden the outlook of the remaining children – by the end of the war, the two oldest sons were on active service. In 1917, the forty-seven-year-old Gide fell in love with the sixteen-year-old Marc, already in rebellion against his narrow Protestant upbringing; in his own way, he reciprocated Gide's feelings. In 1918, Gide in his turn took Marc on a long trip to England, most of which was spent at Grantchester, near Cambridge. It was in Cambridge that Gide first met Dorothy Bussy, wife of the French painter Simon Bussy and sister of Lytton Strachey. She fell instantly, passionately in love with Gide. At fifty-three, a plain, bespectacled lady, four years older than Gide, she had everything against her, but her passion endured to the end. She became Gide's chief translator.

Gide and Marc went back to England (and to Wales) in 1920, accompanied, this time, by Beth, Elisabeth Van Rysselberghe, the thirty-year-old daughter of Théo and Maria. By this time, Marc's attentions were turning to women. Beth, who, seven years before, in Germany, had had a brief affair with Rupert Brooke and wanted to have a child by him, was attracted to Marc. Gide found himself in another, rather different three-cornered relationship. In the end, Marc did not give Beth a child either. Three years later, that privilege fell to Gide, at his first and only attempt.

In 1924, Gide finally published *Corydon*, his 'Socratic dialogue' on homosexuality. It was a work that he had been thinking about for close on thirty years. Gide knew that, by publishing *Corydon*, he risked social ostracism, even in the Paris of the 1920s, and would cause further hurt to Madeleine, who, to spare her own feelings, had long since stopped reading most of what he wrote. He went ahead none the less, against the advice of all his friends. Perversely, we owe the publication of *Corydon* to what remained in Gide, and was always to remain in him, of the 'Protestant conscience': he felt impelled to 'bear witness' to the truth as he saw it, a truth, moreover, that concerned him at the very centre of his being.

In 1925, Gide and Marc set out on a ten-month-long trip to West Africa, at the official invitation of the French government. Marc, who did much of the initial research and information gathering, left hundreds of photographs and yards of film, which he later edited into a film. It was the beginning of his career as a film director. For Gide's part, the trip produced two books: *Voyage au Congo* and *Le Retour du Tchad*. They were a condemnation, not so much of political colonialism as of the lawless, exploitative role of the big rubber companies. Throughout the trip, sexual companions of both sexes were freely, abundantly available and Marc discovered his *penchant* for adolescent girls.

Gide's African experiences marked a new stage in his developing social conscience, which, in the 1930s, turned him into a Communist fellow-traveller. Like millions of others, he was taken in by the claims of the Soviet State and the Communist Party: a man of passionate sincerity, he always assumed, until evidence to the contrary, that others were speaking the truth. Hence his outrage when it was gradually borne in on him that they were not speaking the truth. The story of Gide's relations with the Communist Party during the years 1931–6 gives a fascinating insight into the Party mentality and the skill with which Communists like Louis Aragon and Ilya Ehrenburg manipulated eminent fellow-travellers like Gide. He was persuaded, sometimes tricked, into chairing mass meetings of front organizations; *Les Caves du Vatican* was serialized in the Party daily, *L'Humanité*; his collected works in Russian were being rapidly published, volume after volume.

On arrival in the Soviet Union in 1936, he spoke from the podium overlooking Red Square, with Stalin and Molotov at his side, at a ceremony hastily arranged to mark Gorky's death. In a dacha outside Moscow, he met Pasternak, Eisenstein and Isaac Babel – all three in disfavour. Babel and many others whom Gide was to meet during his visit, the most senior of whom was Bukharin, were to perish in the purges a year or two later – with millions of others less well known. Already beset by doubts about the Soviet Union, Gide wanted, desperately, to have his doubts dissipated. Even while writing *Retour de l'U.R.S.S.*, he was still trying to be fair to the 'Socialist Fatherland'. The Party did everything it could to stop him publishing his book, invoking the damaging effect it would have on the 'democratic forces' struggling to defeat fascism in Spain. Publication brought a campaign of vilification every bit as bad as anything he had suffered at the hands of Catholic bigots. The *Retour* was a world-wide bestseller, which went some way to compensate for the loss of Soviet royalties – Gide had been one of the rare authors published in the Soviet Union given the privilege of having access to his earnings in foreign currency. He was now even more of a public figure.

Gide, then, was, by general consent, one of the dozen most important writers of our century. Moreover, no writer of such stature had led such an interesting life, a life accessibly interesting to us as readers of his autobiographical writings, his journal, his voluminous correspondence and the testimony of others. It was the life of a man engaging not only in the business of artistic creation, but reflecting on that process in his journal, reading that work to his friends and discussing it with them; a man who knew and corresponded with all the major literary figures of his own country and with many in Germany and England; who found daily nourishment in the Latin, French, English and German classics, and, for much of his life, in the Bible; who engaged in commenting on the moral, political and sexual questions of the day; a man whose literary work was entangled, far more than one might expect, in his life. Gide could hardly be a better subject for a literary biography.

The works, however, are not to be treated as raw material of the biographer's own work: their autonomy must be respected. In that hybrid form, literary biography, the writer must be both literary critic and historian. Space forbids too lengthy analysis of each work, but it is the duty of the literary biographer to delineate the process by which the author transmutes the material of his life into the work, the formal structure of the work, its relation to other works and its reception at the time of publication. But the life, too, has its autonomy: it does not require justification by works. It is part of history and therefore our history; without history, we are not fully human, like individuals without memories. A life such as Gide's provides a unique angle of vision into the history and prehistory of our century, an experience, at second-hand, of what it was like, for one person, to live through the coming to birth of that century of unprecedented technological change, economic growth and collapse, the rise of socialism and fascism, two World Wars, a new concern for the colonial peoples and for women, and the astonishing hold over intellectuals, in a country so uniquely devoted to physical pleasure and intellectual attainment, of those then twin peaks of dogmatic authority and rigid uniformity, Rome and Moscow.

Perhaps I should admit at the outset that I have no theory about Gide. I have lost whatever faith I ever had in man's attempts to understand himself in general terms, whether these pertain to soul or psyche, societies or cultures. I have wasted too many long hours wrestling with such problems, hours that would have been better spent in the company of particular human creations. For me, such grand theories as theology, psychoanalysis, Marxism, etc., have turned out to be fictions, fictions that are less instructive and less entertaining than fictions that only pretend to tell the truth. I have scarcely more time for their younger, more sophisticated, but no more personable sisters, with their self-deprecating prefixes 'de-' and 'post-', that tease, half-seriously, with their own fictionality. This abandonment of general explanations does not preclude, of course, the holding of all manner of views about human activities, but these should arise out of the particular, indeed, perhaps, be confined to the particular. They should be constructed, and altered, bit by bit, without benefit of fashionable (or no longer fashionable) magic wands. I would hope that the reader of this book would acquire, in just such a way, bit by bit, an ever more complex view of Gide, just as one gets to know, and not to know, a friend. I may be accused of an old-fashioned dependence on chronology, of desperately clinging to dates, having abandoned the search for explanations. I admit to a liking for dates: when reading narratives like biographies, I do like to know what year it is. (Readers of this book will find the year in question at the top of each recto page.) Chronology, in itself, explains nothing, but it does provide a neutral framework for the narrative of a life, dates appearing like signposts that tell us how many miles we are from our destination, which, in a life, is the ultimate point of departure.

Critical works on Gide began early: by the time of his death there were over eighty. Since then, they have become a flood. More doctoral dissertations follow with each year. In 1968, Gide's surviving friends founded the Association des Amis d'André Gide. This admirable body publishes a quarterly *Bulletin* and an annual *Cahier.* Biographies of Gide have been another matter. To begin with, biography has not, until quite recently, been a very French form. It is one at which, by common consent, the English excel. As it happens, the first Gide biography off the mark was by an Englishman, a young friend of Dorothy Bussy's, working in the library of the British Museum. George Painter published his very short (192-page) *André Gide. A Critical and Biographical Study* in 1951. (Sixteen years later, after his longer, more satisfactory *Proust*, he reissued it in a revised, but still short version.) There is some achievement in appearing to get so much into so little, but, in fact, most of it gets left out. Painter had no English successors: the field was left to the French. In 1956–7, Jean Delay, physician, psychiatrist and friend of Gide, published his exhaustive two-volume, 1,250-page *La Jeunesse d'André Gide*, covering only the first twenty-six years of Gide's life. This particular relay was taken up in 1977 by Claude Martin, with his *La Maturité d'André Gide*, planned to appear in two volumes. The first even exceeded Delay's ratio of pages to years: seven years in 600 pages of text, plus a critical battery of a further eighty pages. A second volume, covering 1902–9, advertised in the first as forthcoming, never appeared. Meanwhile, in 1970, Pierre de Boisdeffre, at the time French Cultural Counsellor at the French Embassy in London, published the first volume of what was to be a complete, two-volume biography. The first volume, prudish, tendentious and sometimes inaccurate, took us up to 1907. As with Martin, no second Boisdeffre volume appeared. In 1986, a brief (180-page) *André Gide* by Jean-Jacques Thierry appeared: a shoddy, eccentric piece of work, surprising in someone who had helped to edit the Pléiade edition of the *Romans*. A much, much worse biography, *Gide: Le 'contemporain capital'*, by Eric Deschodt, was published in 1991. The most recent, *André Gide: Le Messager* by Pierre Lepage (1997), is competently written and tells the story of Gide's life year by year, devoting four or five skimpy pages to each, but, astonishing in the biography of a great writer, provides no analysis of the works. Few biographers of a major literary figure can have faced such scant competition.

The sources for a biography of Gide begin with his own *Journal, Si le grain ne meurt* (his account of his childhood and youth, ending with the death of his mother in 1895), other autobiographical works, including *Et nunc manet in te* and *Ainsi soit-il*, and the travel books (the two on Africa and the two on the Soviet Union). Then there is the correspondence, consisting of thousands of letters, most in the Bibliothèque Littéraire Jacques Doucet, many in the Bibliothèque Nationale, Paris, others elsewhere. Over thirty of the correspondences have been published so far, some in two volumes. Some of these have been published by the Presses Universitaires de Lyon, but most of the burden has been borne, with commendable *pietas* towards its founding-father, by Gallimard. The most important source from a third party is undoubtedly the *Cahiers de la Petite Dame,* in four volumes, published as *Cahiers André Gide* (nos 4–7), covering the period from 1918 to Gide's death in 1951. Other important sources are the journals of Gide's friends, especially those of Roger Martin du Gard (in three volumes, Gallimard, 1993), Jacques Copeau (in two volumes, Seghers, 1991) and Robert Levesque (Presses Universitaires de Lyon, 1995) and two books by friends, *Madeleine et André Gide* by Jean Schlumberger and *Notes sur André Gide* by Martin du Gard.

I refer to Gide's works by their original French titles – I use English titles only when referring to the translations as such. To my initial surprise, I felt the need to diverge, to a greater or lesser degree, from the work of Gide's translators.

I must acknowledge the assistance of many 'Amis d'André Gide', including Catherine Gide, Jean Lambert, Jean Meyer, Roger Kempf, Pierre Masson, Peter Fawcett and Patrick Pollard, and of the staff of the Bibliothèque Doucet. I should like to thank the estates and publishers of the writers quoted. I should also like to thank Juliet Annan, Helen Dore and Antonia Till, the three wise women of Wright's Lane. (I was tempted to call them *femmes savantes,* but thought better of it.) The Authors' Foundation provided a sum of money towards expenses incurred during the writing of this book.

I

Two Stars, Two Races,
Two Provinces, Two Faiths

'I have discovered quite by chance and without much believing in astrology that on 21 November precisely, my birthday, our earth leaves the influence of Scorpio to enter that of Sagittarius. Is it my fault if your God took such great care to have me born between two stars, the fruit of two races, two provinces and two faiths?'[1]

Throughout his life Gide made several references to an ancestry that he saw as combining the qualities of Catholic and Protestant, North and South, but this *Journal* entry for 2 December 1929, a few days after his sixtieth birthday, is, to my knowledge, his only reference to astrology. At the risk of raising the eyebrows of more serious readers, one might at this point look into what astrology has to say about those born on that particular cusp. On the Scorpio side, one would find such phrases as 'intelligent and creative', 'a tendency to frequent changes of sexual object', 'difficulty in coping with the responsibilities of your emotional needs'. Sagittarius introduces an even more recognizably Gidean picture: 'wanderer of the zodiac', 'devoted to the pursuit of wisdom through direct experience', 'scholar, teacher, traveller', 'unable to focus on any one activity or relationship', 'avoidance of emotional involvements because you value freedom above everything' – this of a man who rarely succeeded in combining love and sexual desire; who, two years after his first homosexual experience, seven months after his meeting with Wilde and Douglas in North Africa and his consequent initiation into the delights available there, married his first cousin and childhood soul-mate; who, past fifty, after twenty-seven years of unconsummated marriage and a year before the publication of *Corydon*, his homosexual tract, fathered a child on a woman who wanted one without the encumbrance of a relationship; who spent his life searching for a replacement for the Calvinist certainties of his youth and never succeeded for long; who never remained in one place for more than a few weeks and who would work in turn in every room in a house or apartment, when he was not tramping the garden, the surrounding countryside, or the streets; who, on finishing one work, often set about writing another to contradict the first.

Readers will make of this what they may, but my purpose in mentioning it at all is not to offer an astrological analysis of Gide's personality, but to indicate a central feature of that personality: a determination to see himself, whether or not he may legitimately be seen in this way, as being forever dual and therefore not to be confined within any one thing. But let us look again at the quotation from the *Journal* with which this chapter opens. It is hedged about with equivocation. Gide discovered the astrological signifi-cance of his birthday 'quite by chance': he cannot be accused of looking for it. Indeed he rejects (or accepts) both belief and disbelief in astrology: 'Without *much believing* in it'. However, the really significant point about Gide's remarks is that he was born not, as he says, on 21 November, but on the following day. Most of the commentators ignore this discrepancy. Pierre de Boisdeffre incorporates the astrological event, without attributing it to Gide, and corrects the date: 'On 22 November, young Mme Gide, *née* Juliette Rondeaux – gave birth to her first son . . . at a time when, in the heavens of the constellations, Scorpio yields to Sagittarius . . .' Jean Delay notes Gide's remark, but, with a dismissive rhetorical question ('Are we to believe that if André Gide had been born a few days earlier or later . . .?'), passes on to the more serious business of the two faiths, two provinces and two races. Jean-Jacques Thierry, who, apart from two books on Gide, appears to have devoted his entire *œuvre* to the Vatican and related matters, opens his *André Gide*: 'It is doubtless no accident that the future author of *Les Caves du Vatican* saw the light of day in Paris on the eve of the opening of the ecumenical council [of 1869].' He corrects Gide's 'mistake' without saying so, and attributes the quotation not to the *Journal*, but to *Prétextes*.

It seems to me that the 'mistake' was quite deliberate on Gide's part, astonishing none the less in someone so unrelentingly devoted to the truth. Incidentally, Gide himself shows no interest whatsoever in what being on the cusp of Scorpio and Sagittarius might signify. For him, the important thing was to be 'on the cusp', astrologically as well as in every other way. Learning that the shift from one planetary influence to another occurred 'precisely' on the 21st, he could not resist advancing his arrival in the world by a day: after all, what is a few hours? The fact is, of course, that he need not have bothered: the cusp is generally regarded as lasting three days anyway.

Perhaps Gide's most celebrated and most succinct affirmation of his inherited duality is the opening of a review of Maurice Barrès' *Les Déracinés* (*The Uprooted*), a novel in which the right-wing, nationalist writer and politician preaches the individual's need to be rooted in a particular region, 'in his soil and among his dead'. (It is worth noting that Barrès was a native of Lorraine, which, since 1871, had been incorporated in Germany.) Appearing in 1897, in the midst of the Dreyfus Affair, *Les Déracinés* questioned, by implication, the 'health' of uprooted people such as Jews. Availing himself of his knowledge of botany, Gide turns Barrès' argument against him, pointing out that uprooting, transplanting and cross-breeding are essential to the propagation of new, healthy species. In a letter of 1902 to his friend the poet Francis Jammes, Gide writes: 'You know how complicated I am, born of a crossing of races, situated at the crossroads of religions, sensing within me all the yearnings of Normans for the South, of Southerners for the North . . .'[2] Again, in 1920, in an article entitled 'Heredity', after evoking holidays spent in Normandy, with his mother's relations, and in Languedoc, with his father's, Gide remarks: 'Nothing could be more different than those two families; nothing more different than those two provinces of France, which have combined within me their contradictory influences . . .'[3]

So what of this 'crossing of races', these two diametrically opposed families? According to a note written by an earlier Gide living in Mulhouse, found in the papers of André Gide's father, the Gides descended from a Florentine family, the Guidos, who came to France in the late fifteenth century. They became Protestants and, with the loss of their religious liberties consequent on the revocation of the Edict of Nantes in 1685, many dispersed, some to Geneva, some to Berlin and some to Alsace. The largest group, however, remained at Nîmes. They prospered, becoming millers, glass-makers and lawyers. Gide's grandfather, Tancrède, born in 1800, was appointed a justice of the peace at Uzès at thirty, then a judge and, at thirty-nine, presiding judge. He devoted his retirement almost exclusively to charity work and Sunday-school teaching. He died in 1867, two years before André Gide's birth. He was a model Huguenot, 'austere, scrupulous to excess, unbending, carrying trust in God to a sublime degree. . . .'[4]

Tancrède Gide's elder son, Paul, André's father, was born in 1832, followed by his brother, Charles, fifteen years later. Paul attended the local school at Uzès, consistently coming top of his class in Greek, Latin and French. When he began his law studies his father insisted that he continue to live at home, fearing no doubt that if his son took up the life of a student at Aix, he would be less well taught and do less work than under parental supervision. No doubt, too, moral – and financial – considerations were not absent from his mind. As a result, Paul Gide attended the Aix law faculty only to sign on at the beginning of each academic year and to sit his examinations. On taking his *licence* (degree) at twenty-one, he was awarded the prize for Roman law and, two years later, won the gold medal for his doctoral thesis. After a period of teaching at Grenoble, he was summoned to Paris to stand in for the professor of Roman law. At thirty, he was appointed to a chair in his own right. An excellent teacher and respected scholar, he was nicknamed by his colleagues *vir probus*, a reference to his unimpeachable character and his specialization in Roman law; he wrote a number of works, including one on the status of women in Roman and modern law.

Juliette Rondeaux, who was to become Paul Gide's wife and André's mother, came from a Norman family that had lived in Rouen for five generations. The earliest known ancestor, Nicolas Rondeaux (1620–95), was a farmer, who, about 1650, set up business in Rouen as an apothecary. His second son, Marin (1649–1721), expanded the business and became an alderman of the city. When he was close on seventy, the now widowed Marin Rondeaux remarried; shortly afterwards he died, leaving an only son. Jean-Claude Rondeaux (1720–1805) was brought up by his young widowed mother and educated by the Jesuits at Rouen. He entered the law and, on being ennobled by Louis XV, took the name of Rondeaux de Sétry, adding a count's coronet to his coat-of-arms. In 1751, he married the eighteen-year-old daughter of a rich local manufacturer, Marie-Scholas-tique Desmonts. There were six children, the second of whom, Charles, was André Gide's great-grandfather.

Charles Rondeaux (1753–1820) inherited from his father a large fortune, a post at the Normandy Cour des Comptes and a love of the natural sciences. He was a Freemason and, consequently, a freethinker. He welcomed the Revolution of 1789, becoming mayor of Rouen three years later. However, he soon fell foul of the more extreme revolutionaries. While in prison, under threat of the guillotine, he wrote a *Tableau politique d'Athènes depuis sa fondation jusqu'au temps où cette ville passa sous la domination des Lacédémoniens*. Charles Rondeaux, like his father, married twice; his second wife, Marie-Anne Dufou, was a Protestant. From then on, all André Gide's maternal ancestors belonged to the French Reformed Church.

Charles Rondeaux's son Edouard (1789–1860), already a man of means, married into greater wealth. On his death, his fortune was calculated as being one-and-a-half million francs (approximately £60,000 or $300,000 at the time). His wife, Julie, was the daughter of a Protestant manufacturer of printed calico and, although Edouard was himself a sceptic, indeed something of a *bon vivant*, he had his children brought up in his wife's religion. Julie Rondeaux continued very much in the strict Protestant tradition of her own family. There were five children of the marriage: Charles (1820–90), Claire (1822–1901), Henry (1825–82), Emile (1831–90) and Juliette (1835–95), André Gide's mother. As far as the family was concerned, the problem child was Henry, the second son, and it was he who, indirectly, was responsible for its only scandal. One day – Henry was eighteen at the time – his mother happened to open a cupboard in her son's bedroom and fell back, fainting from the horror of what she saw there: an altar to the Virgin Mary. Apparently, Henry had, in spirit at least, become a Catholic, though he was not formally received into the Roman Church until six years later.

In the midst of these family troubles, when Juliette was fifteen, her mother took on a young Scottish woman as the child's governess. Anna Shackleton was the daughter of a foreman working for the British firm engaged in the construction of the Paris–Le Havre railway line. She was only nine years older than her pupil, but looked much younger than her twenty-four years. She was attractive and vivacious; she was also intelligent and well educated and could read German almost as fluently as English and French. But the fact that must have weighed more than any other in her favour was her Protestant background. In the event, her influence over her pupil lay not so much in a religious direction – there was no need of that – as in the cultural. She was a gifted artist and musician. The sensitivity of her piano-playing is attributed to her fictional counterpart, Miss Flora Ashburton, in *La Porte étroite*. Some of her drawings and watercolours have survived: they reveal above-average skill and technique. Pupil and governess soon became inseparable, with, on Juliette's side, an insistence on total devotion, which could take the form of jealousy, as when Anna spent too long writing to her pupil's nephew, Maurice Démarest. They would spend the winter at Rouen, in a large townhouse situated at the corner of the rue de Crosne and the rue de Fontenelle. Summer would be spent at La Roque-Baignard, in the Calvados, and at Cuverville, a few miles inland from the Channel resort of Etretat. Often the two young women were left to their own devices, much of their time being spent reading, widely and voraciously. But they were not humourless blue stockings. Anna Shackleton certainly felt that she did not always set her pupil a good example where matters of behaviour

were concerned. 'Someone wearing a *stiff collar* should have a certain dignity
in her character as well as in her bearing.'[5] By the time of that letter,
written in 1861, the widowed Mme Rondeaux was beginning to worry that
her daughter would not find a husband. There had been two or three offers
of marriage from sons of the better families in Rouen, but she had rejected
them all. Her prospects were not improved by the contrast between the shy,
rather plain French girl and the fun-loving, attractive Scot. 'It seemed to
many people that Anna Shackleton, herself still young and, what is more,
extremely pretty, might put her pupil in the shade. In any case, the young
Juliette Rondeaux was, it has to be admitted, a rather off-putting individual
[Gide is speaking of his mother!]. Not only did she constantly withdraw
into herself and keep in the background whenever she should have
shone, but she never missed an opportunity to push Miss Anna
forward.'[6]

In 1859, M. Roberty, the young Protestant pastor at Rouen, and his wife,
who was of Scottish origin, were invited to the Rondeaux house; they
became regular visitors and, before long, close friends. It was M. Roberty
who thought of introducing Juliette Rondeaux to Paul Gide, a young lawyer
of impeccable family background. However, it was to be three years before
the couple even met. No sooner were plans being hatched than Juliette's
father fell seriously ill; he died, a few months later, on 17 October 1860,
rejecting the ministrations of either a priest (at the instigation of his son
Henry) or of a Protestant pastor. At that time, not only was it unthinkable,
even among thrifty Huguenots, that the funeral baked-meats should 'coldly
furnish forth the marriage tables', but a couple of years were expected to
elapse between a parent's funeral and a daughter's wedding. There were
further complications: the bereavement and illness of the widow meant
that Juliette had to assume more and more responsibility for the running
of the household. This resulted in a thorough, godly reformation: most of
the staff, who, behind the scenes, had been involved in all manner
of 'immorality', were dismissed.

So it was not until 1862 that the two young people were finally brought
together. As André Gide himself put it, 'Juliette Rondeaux had long rejected
the most brilliant matches of Rouen society when, at last, to everyone's
surprise, she accepted a young, fortuneless professor of law from the South,
who would never have dared to ask for her hand had he not been urged to
do so by the excellent Pastor Roberty, who, knowing my mother's views,
introduced him to her.'[7] Or, as R.-G. Nobécourt, from a more Balzacian
perspective, tells us in his *Les Nourritures normandes d'André Gide*, 'Paul Gide

brought above all his merits, Juliette a great fortune, a share of her father's estate, which, in 1860, amounted to 250,000 francs [£10,000 or $50,000 at the time] in personal wealth and close on 150,000 francs [£6,000 or $30,000] in real estate.'

The marriage contract was signed at Rouen on 23 February 1863. Among the witnesses was Achille Flaubert, the Rondeauxs' family doctor and brother of the great novelist. The religious ceremony took place four days later: Paul Gide was twenty-nine, his wife twenty-seven. In Paris, the couple moved into an apartment at 19 rue de Médicis, a few minutes' walk from the rue Soufflot, where Claire Démarest, Juliette's sister, lived, and the Faculté de Droit, where the young professor taught. On 22 November 1869, some seven years after the marriage, Juliette Gide gave birth to a son, André Paul Guillaume. He was to be their only child.

'Two races' (*deux sangs*)? The terminology is very much of the time (1929) and, for all its retrospective connotations, has a certain innocence. But can the origins of one's parents, in the North and South of the same country, at a distance of under 500 miles, be so termed? Two races, two bloods? No more, surely, than in the case of someone born, say, of a Yorkshire (or New England) mother, and a Hampshire (or Virginian) father? 'Two provinces'? The paternal South was visited only once a year, at Easter, and could hardly have loomed as large in Gide's mind as Normandy, where the entire summer was spent, let alone Paris, of which he conveniently – and surely significantly – says nothing. Paris was where he had been born and educated; it was the place he came back to after his travels and set off from again, the place where he happened to be most of the time, where most of his writing got done and which was not, therefore, mythologizable. It was the median point, the all and therefore the nothing. 'Two faiths'? His mother's family, though originally Catholic, had been Protestant for three generations before his birth. Indeed it was largely on account of his mother's devotion to the Protestant faith that she had rejected so many otherwise eligible suitors – and it was precisely Paul Gide's association with the old Huguenot heartland in the South that made him such an attractive match. Without the services of the local Protestant pastor as go-between there would have been no Gide–Rondeaux marriage. What strikes one most about the two families is not their *difference* but their *similarity*, their very closeness, belonging as they both did to the tightly knit world of upper-middle-class Protestants whose incomes derived from trade or the liberal professions.

What we are confronted with in this series of dual origins is the creation of a personal mythology, an enduring, even obsessive attempt on Gide's part to understand himself in terms of dualities. A more likely origin of Gide's peculiarly dualistic thinking is to be found perhaps, not in such spurious oppositions as North/South, Catholic/Protestant, but *within* the Protestant, specifically Calvinist, mentality. The mental world of the Catholic was multiple rather than dualistic. The sensual, though fraught with danger, was not shunned, but actually incorporated into worship, pre-eminently in that Wagnerian *Gesamtkunstwerk*, the High Mass, with its drama, its spectacle, its music and even, not to be found at Bayreuth, an assault on the sense of smell. With the saints, there was a cast of hundreds, each highly individualized, each to be appealed to in some particular circumstance. Above them was 'Our Lady', to be appealed to in any circumstance, but especially where 'sins of impurity' were concerned. Above all was the celestial (as opposed to the Palestinian) Holy Family of Father, Son and oddly insubstantial, not to say androgynous, Holy Ghost (although, for most Catholics, the experiential Trinity was a blend of the two: Father, 'Our Lord', and 'Our Lady'). On earth, in the Church, the same multiplicity was to be found in the various orders of monks and nuns, and in the ascending ranks of clergy, each, of course, with its own distinctive costume. *Below*, everything was the Devil, omnipresent and omniscient, if not entirely omnipotent: all manner of devices, special prayers, acts of contrition, partial and plenary indulgences, and, in the last resort, that temporary hell, purgatory, had been set in train to outwit him and pay off the wages of sin. The mental universe of the Catholic, then, was multiple, often threefold (even the Devil had the world and the flesh added unto him to form another, infernal trinity). The total effect of all this was to arouse tension, of course, but it was also to reduce it by dispersal, to turn the poor sinner into a third party, an intermediary, a spectator almost, rather than an actor in the main of all.

The Protestant, the Calvinist at least, had none of this: no multiplicity, no hierarchy, just a single, terrible, internal drama played out between a fallen, guilt-ridden creature, never knowing for certain whether he was 'saved' or not, and his God. When Calvinists gathered together it was, typically, to address God in unison (in hymns), or to be addressed by the Word of God direct from Scripture or as interpreted by his minister in a sermon. Even in public, religion was essentially a private matter and, on the whole, the religious life took place in solitude, the soul wrestling with its conscience, without benefit of confessor or absolution. The Calvinist, then, lived in a dualistic, confrontational world of right/wrong, saved/unsaved, heaven/hell, God/I.

Gide himself put the matter with masterly succinctness in an often-quoted sentence in the *Journal* (22 June 1907): 'Je ne suis qu'un petit garçon qui s'amuse – doublé d'un pasteur protestant qui l'ennuie' ('I'm just a little boy amusing himself – coupled with a Protestant pastor who bores him.')[8] The story of Gide's life is of the child growing up to become an adult hedonist, or would-be hedonist, for the 'Protestant pastor', being within, was not easily disposed of: indeed, for over half of Gide's life, he stood there, in the background, disapproving. Gide finally got rid of him by turning him into a free moral conscience: once-Protestant countries have done the same.

From the original Calvinist opposition of 'little boy amusing himself' and 'Protestant pastor', a whole series of Gidean oppositions might be seen to stem: self/world, inner world/outer world, morality/pleasure, past/present, home/travel, mother (and wife)/male sexual partners, etc. The life and the work are shifting accommodations of one side of these oppositions with the other.

2

Childhood: Schooldays and Holidays

(OCTOBER 1874 – OCTOBER 1880)

Gide opens *Si le grain ne meurt* with one of his earliest and happiest memories. As usual with Gide's earliest and happiest memories, he is with his father. (It was the mother who was, and remained to the end, the killjoy.) The law professor and his son are standing on the balcony of their 'fourth- or fifth-floor apartment' throwing 'paper dragons' across the rue de Médicis into the Jardin du Luxembourg, where they get caught in the branches of the tall chestnut trees. Having lulled the reader into a false sense of security, Gide abruptly changes tack in the second paragraph. We are not, after all, going to be treated to the usual sequence of idyllic childhood memories. Without transition we move from an innocent game played with an adored father to Gide's first experience of 'sexuality'. He and the concierge's son – they were both five or six at the time – used to hide under the dining-table, which was covered by a cloth reaching to the floor. 'What are you doing under there?' the maid would ask after a while. 'Nothing. Just playing,' the boys would reply, rattling a couple of toys in the interest of verisimilitude. In fact, they were indulging, Gide explains, in what he later learnt to call 'bad habits'. What they did they did not do to each other, but each to himself. Gide does not remember which of them taught the other to do it: sometimes, he adds, children reinvent such things unaided. *Si le grain ne meurt* was published in 1926, though printed privately in thirteen copies, in 1920. *Corydon*, also printed privately (in 1911), in twelve undistributed copies, had been revised and published in 1924. It was a time when Gide was emerging not only as a major literary figure – that he had been for some time – but as one of the very few writers of note to state and argue their case as homosexuals. As Proust pertinently remarked, 'You can say whatever you like, so long as you don't say "I".' Gide insisted on saying 'I'. 'I am aware of the harm I am doing myself by recounting this and other things that follow . . . But my account has only one purpose: to tell the truth . . . In that age of innocence, when the soul is supposed to be all sweetness, light and purity, I see in myself nothing but ugliness, darkness and deceitfulness.'[1] Gide goes on to recount incidents calculated to under-mine any notion of innocent childhood. In the Luxembourg, with his Swiss maid, Marie Leuenberger, he refused to play with other children, but kept apart, observing them making their sandpies. Suddenly, when the maid's attention was distracted, he rushed over and trampled the sandpies under-foot. He describes how, at Uzès, he once bit into the exposed shoulder of one of his pretty Flaux cousins, who had bent down and proffered her cheek to be kissed. 'My cousin let forth a cry, I one of horror. She began to bleed. I spat out in disgust . . . I think everyone was so astonished that they forgot to punish me.'[2]

Much later, when the young André Gide was ten, he played, like other boys of his age, with toy soldiers. But, whereas his companions organized attacks in which a few score such soldiers were lined up and summarily killed by means of a toy cannon crammed full with gunpowder, young Gide's play took on a more literally destructive form. He would place the lead soldiers erect on a frying pan, which he then proceeded to heat up. Fascinated, he would watch them totter and fall flat on their faces. Then, Gide adds curiously, 'a little, shining, burning, denuded soul escaped from the tarnished uniform'.[3]

It would be wrong, I think, to derive from such incidents any theories as to Gide's 'perverse' or 'sadistic' character. One may not oneself recall performing at so early an age any act that might be called 'sexual', but there are many people who do. The sandpie incident is surely what any small boy is capable of – and the biting of the presumptuous cousin scarcely less so. Certainly the melting of the lead soldiers is of another order of interest, but it is hardly redolent of 'perversion' or 'sadism'. It expresses, rather, Gide's unconcern about material possessions and his desire for change, irritation that his toy soldiers should always be exactly the same, fascination with the forces of transformation at work in the material world, a desire too, perhaps, to free those mysteriously entrapped beings from their uniform lendings. In no ascertainable sense was he a sadist of any kind. Perversity, because lacking any precise or limited sense whatever, is more difficult to ascribe (or reject) in Gide's case. One motive behind the citing of these various incidents was undoubtedly to present himself as a 'perverse' child; at a time when he was striving to present himself to the world at large, and to the young in particular, as a rebel, it was an image of himself that he cultivated. It is surely significant that *Si le grain ne meurt*, the public *apologia pro vita sua*, says nothing of the nightmares that he suffered as a child, yet they were experiences that he never forgot. In a journal entry

for 1924 (though not published until 1939), he notes: 'When I was a child I
was easily scared; I had terrible nightmares from which I would wake
bathed in sweat ... Nowadays I can have horrible dreams, see myself
pursued by monsters, knifed, cut up into bits and pieces ... But it never
turns into a nightmare.'⁴ One can only imagine that what Gide does call
nightmares must have been of an abnormally frightening nature.

In 1875 – André was now six – the Gides moved to a new, more spacious
apartment on the second floor of 2 rue de Tournon, on a corner with the
rue Saint-Sulpice. André had a large room overlooking the courtyard, but
spent most of his free time in what he calls an '*antichambre*': it was there that
he would retreat when his mother, tired of his company, told him to go and
play with his friend Pierre, in other words, by himself. With nothing more
exciting to be done with 'Pierre', he usually ended up playing marbles with
him. Another toy that helped him to pass the long hours of loneliness was
a kaleidoscope. His cousins, too, had kaleidoscopes, but, whereas they
would try to get as many and varied images as possible, by shaking the
kaleidoscope vigorously, André would get greater satisfaction by staring at
a particular configuration for a long time, then, with the minimum of
movement, achieving a slight alteration in the image. Interestingly, however,
pure aesthetic pleasure eventually gave way, as in the case of the lead
soldiers, to scientific curiosity or a desire for change. At the risk of destroying
it forever, he would force the object to yield up its secret. He took it apart,
then, replacing only three or four of the many bits of glass, put it together
again. The resulting image was quite uninteresting compared with what it
had been, but, says Gide, how much greater pleasure he obtained from
satisfying his thirst for knowledge.

   The young André Gide was not just an only child; he was also a lonely
child, or at least a child who played alone. 'I had no friend,' Gide tells us
in *Si le grain ne meurt*. He then corrects himself: yes, there was one, but he
was not one he could play with. When André's Marie took him into the
Luxembourg, he would often meet a boy of his own age whom they
nicknamed 'Mouton' on account of his white sheepskin jacket. Mouton
was a quiet, gentle, rather sickly child who wore thick, tinted spectacles.
Since they could not play together, they were content to walk around the
gardens, hand in hand, saying nothing. After a while, Mouton no longer
appeared on their walks. The young Gide realized how attached he had
become to his strange friend. He was horrified to learn that Mouton was
going blind. 'I went to my room and cried, and for several days I would

keep my eyes shut for long periods, moving around without opening them, trying to feel what Mouton must have been feeling.'[5]

For the young André, quite the most mysterious, almost sacred room in the family apartment was his father's study, a huge, rather gloomy room that looked out on to the rue Saint-Sulpice. 'I entered it,' says Gide, 'as if it were a temple . . .' There his father spent most of the day when he was not at the law faculty. André's first introduction to the contents of his father's library took a curious form. Going over to the bookshelves, his father selected some large, ancient tome and, sitting next to his son, opened it on the arm of the chair. He then proceeded to trace the course taken by a bookworm through the pages of the book. 'Consulting some old text, the lawyer had admired those small, secret tunnels and said to himself: "Ah! That will amuse my son." And it amused me a great deal, not least because of the amusement that he himself seemed to derive from it.'[6] The same principle applied when his father started to read aloud to him. He chose books that he himself enjoyed: scenes from Molière, passages from the *Odyssey*, the adventures of Sinbad the Sailor and Ali-Baba. André's mother did not always approve of her husband's choice of reading matter: the child should not be entertained, but edified. Partly no doubt to accommodate her wishes, it was agreed that they should embark on a reading of the Book of Job. Whereupon Mme Gide decided to attend these readings, which took place, not in the professor's study, nor even in the *grand salon*, the drawing-room, where the furniture was kept under wraps, removed only on Wednesdays when Mme Gide 'received', but in a small sitting-room that was her preferred domain.

In those early readings are to be found two books that symbolized, indeed embodied, two more polarities that were to dominate Gide's life. Both were collections of stories, heteroclite in style, of uncertain provenance, but as starkly contrasting in every way as night and day, the *Arabian Nights* and, as one might say in the interest of symmetry, the *Judaic Days*. On the one hand, storytelling with a shameless acceptance of its fictionality, a hedonistic delight in its untruth, where the only hermeneutic revelation is postponed indefinitely in the interest of saving the storyteller's life; stories patently male in origin and intended for a male audience, yet attributed to a woman; stories recounted, in the Gidean household, in the male preserve of the library, by the father, a law professor, become for the duration of the narration, a pleasure-loving 'little boy amusing himself', to his son, in the absence of the mother–wife's moral authority, a situation that foreshadowed those other all-male, amoral Arabian nights to come. On the other hand, stories that claim to be the history of the world and of God's chosen people, the very Word of God himself, the one unquestionable Truth, where what was at stake was not only the storyteller's life, but the Eternal Life of the listener; stories as male in origin as the *Arabian Nights*, but without their carefree hedonism, fearful equally of God's wrath and Woman's wiles; stories that required the mother's presence and restrictive blessing in her own sitting-room. Who was responsible for the choice of the Book of Job, that most radically gloomy of the biblical texts – the mother, following her own natural inclination to the extremest gloom, or the father, with a touch of wry humour, determined to push the contrast with his own chosen readings to the limit? Gide does not say, does not even raise the question or appear to note the contrast. The ultimate irony is that although real-life Arabian nights continued to haunt his days, his reading of the Bible endured to the end, long surviving his belief in its divine inspiration.

Gide owed the awakening of his literary vocation, as reader, and therefore as writer, not, as with so many men and women, to the mother, but to the father. For a long time, too, his father was his only male companion. To a lesser degree, Gide probably played a similar role for his father. Paul Gide, it must be remembered, was not a Parisian and had no school or university friends. The readings in the study were, for both of them, a means of cultivating their friendship, away from the moral/female presence of the wife/mother. His father also introduced Gide to another of his lifelong pleasures: walking the streets of Paris for the sheer pleasure of it. This, too, offered an escape from the presence of the wife/mother. On certain summer evenings, after dinner, Paul Gide would turn to his son and ask: 'Is my little friend going to go for a walk with me?' André Gide adds: 'He never called me anything else but "son petit ami".' The wife/mother would see them to the door, never failing to deliver the usual admonition: 'You will be reasonable, won't you? Don't be too late back.' Again it was a case of *mutual* self-interest: Paul Gide was doing what *he* wanted to do, not carrying out some paternal duty. André was not just a companion on those innocent walks; he was also a necessary pretext without which the walks might have seemed less innocent, or at least a potential source of discord between husband and wife.

Playing some guessing game, father and son would walk up the rue de Tournon, cross the Luxembourg and end up at the Observatoire and its garden. At that time the buildings on either side of the avenue leading to the Observatoire had not yet been built. Instead of six-storey apartment buildings were improvised sheds where second-hand clothes merchants plied their trade and *vélocipèdes* were sold and hired.

Perched up on those strange, paradoxical machines, since replaced by bicycles, people swerved past us and disappeared into the darkness. We admired their boldness, their elegance. One could hardly make out the frame and the tiny rear wheel on which the balance of the aerial machine rested. The slim front wheel swayed from side to side; the rider seemed like some fantastic creature from another world. Night was falling, accentuating the lights, a little farther off, of a *café-concert*, whose music drew us on. One could no longer see the gaslights themselves, only the strange illumination of the chestnut trees above the fence. We drew nearer. The planks were not so well joined that one could not, here and there, peep through the gap between two of them: I could make out, over the dark, swarming mass of the audience, the magic spectacle of the stage on which some minor music-hall star was pouring out her sweet nothings.

Sometimes we had time to walk through the Luxembourg on our way home. Soon a drum roll would announce its closing. The last strollers were moving reluctantly towards the gates, with the attendants at their heels, and the broad paths that they were deserting filled behind them with mystery. On such nights I went to sleep drunk with shadows, sleep and strangeness.[7]

From the age of five André attended two small educational establishments run by a Mlle Fleur and a Mme Lackerbauer respectively. At Mlle Fleur's, in the rue de Vaugirard, he learnt to read and write. His most vivid memory of Mlle Fleur's was witnessing the preparations for a production of part of Racine's only comedy, *Les Plaideurs*: he could not imagine anything more exciting than dressing up and putting on a false beard. Mme Lackerbauer's establishment was memorable above all for a '*machine de Ramsden*', an old electrical contrivance whose purpose was none too clear, but which struck terror into the pupils on account of the notice that it bore forbidding anyone to touch it 'expressly on pain of death'. One day Mme Lackerbauer announced that she was going to operate the machine. The pupils all gathered around, convinced that she would instantly go up in smoke.

At seven, young André had private piano lessons at home from a Mlle de Goecklin. At the end of the lessons, his mother would join the teacher and play some piece for four hands, usually a transcription of the finale of a Haydn symphony, chosen, says Gide, because, being fairly fast, it did not require expressive playing. Throughout the piece, from beginning to end, Mme Gide would count time aloud. Later, André went to Mlle Goecklin's home for his lessons – on a piano that was always out of tune.

*

André Gide was eight when he attended his first 'proper' school, the mainly
Protestant Ecole Alsacienne, which had opened only three years before.
Unfortunately, the school year had already begun when his father took him
along to the school, thus isolating him at once as a curiosity. The situation
was made worse in his very first lesson. The master, M. Vedel, was explaining
synonyms, how a language may have two different words to denote the
same thing. Thus *coudrier* and *noisetier* refer to the same tree (the hazel). M.
Vedel went on to give other examples, soliciting yet others from his pupils.
He then turned to Gide and asked him to repeat what he had just said. 'I
did not answer. I did not know what I was supposed to say. But M. Vedel
was a kindly man: he repeated his definition with all the patience of the
true teacher, again proposed the same example, but when he again asked
me to repeat the synonym for "*coudrier*", I said not a word.' Gide was told
to go out into the yard and repeat twenty times that *coudrier* was the synonym
for *noisetier* and then to come back and repeat it before the class. 'My
stupidity had sent the whole class into paroxysms of delight . . . I did not
understand what was wanted of me, what was expected of me.' Gide was
awarded 'zero for conduct', as he was each week for the rest of the term.
He also came very near the bottom of the class. 'I was still asleep; I was
like something that had not yet been born.'[8] It was an odd way for one of
the greatest French writers of the twentieth century, a future laureate of the
Nobel Prize for Literature, to begin the study of his native language.

Before long Gide was in worse trouble. In the middle of a lesson, M.
Vedel suddenly paused in mid-sentence: 'Gide! You're looking rather red
in the face! I'd like a few words with you.' When confronted with what he
had been doing, André did not try to deny it; he was sent back to his bench
and the lesson continued. That evening Paul Gide received a letter from
the deputy head informing him that his son had been suspended from the
school for three months. Again Gide attributes his disgrace to his stupidity,
his mental somnolence: he had simply not realized that there was anything
particularly reprehensible about what he had been doing. Gide's mother
later told him that his father had been outraged by the letter and by the
severity of the punishment. No doubt a state *petit lycée* of the time would
have acted more leniently, but the Ecole Alsacienne prided itself on the
moral discipline that it tried to inculcate in its pupils. It was decided that
young André should see Dr Brouardel, a family friend and colleague, a
highly respected authority on medicine and the law. No doubt a few kindly
words of advice from him would put matters right. The boy's reception by
Dr Brouardel turned out to be more robust: 'I know what it's all about . . .

I don't need to examine you or question you today, my boy. But if, in due course, your mother sees fit to bring you back to me, in other words, if you haven't mended your ways . . .' The subtle-minded Paris professor of law and medicine stared dramatically at the boy and, without for a moment taking his eyes off him, pointed with outstretched arm to 'a panoply of Tuareg spearheads' decorating his office wall. 'Then those are the instruments we will have to resort to, those are what we use to operate on little boys like you!'[9] Fortunately, young Gide was not entirely convinced by the doctor's performance and did not, he claims, take the threat seriously. He was, however, deeply upset by his mother's very vocal reaction to the incident – and by his father's pained silence. At this distance it is probably difficult for most of us to appreciate the fear and horror with which masturbation was regarded until fairly recently. As late as 1970, Pierre de Boisdeffre, in his unfinished *Vie d'André Gide*, thought fit to steer a middle course. Trying to sound like a fairly broad-minded man of the world, he adds that, as we now know, 'masturbation among children and adolescents is not *automatically* the sign of a defect, it does not *inevitably* lead to suicide or imbecility (as many inexperienced educators then declared)'.[10] One cannot but applaud the courage shown by André Gide in his public admission, which, even in the relatively easygoing France of the 1920s, was received with shocked amazement.

There was another, unrelated episode that did not find its way into the final version of *Si le grain ne meurt*, but remained in Gide's unpublished notes for the book. It occurred a month earlier, during a written examination. Sitting at his desk, he suddenly realized that he was 'wetting his pants'. His hopes that the fact would pass unnoticed were dashed when an ever-widening pool began to appear on the floor. The assistant head, M. Brünig, was present at the examination and had seen what had happened. He later went over and had a word with the boy's parents, who had come to collect their son. On the way home, André was too ashamed to say anything: he fully expected a severe reprimand. When he finally burst into tears, his mother, to his great astonishment, kissed him and, smiling, promised to write M. Brünig a note apologizing on his behalf. Taking the two incidents together, what is interesting is that Gide the writer thought fit to suppress the incident for which Gide the child felt the more shame, even though his parents and teachers took the contrary view. There was some 'glamour' to be acquired by the middle-aged champion of youthful rebellion in describing the one incident, none in describing the other.

Attempts were made to amuse the banished schoolboy: Anna Shackleton, who was now living nearby, in the rue de Vaugirard, took him to see the preparations being made for the forthcoming Exposition Universelle of 1878. Marie, André's maid, would take him to the Musée du Luxembourg, then the museum of modern art. He was less interested in the anecdotal paintings, despite, or because of, Marie's painstaking explanations, than in the nudes (which shocked her). He was even more fascinated by the sculpture and could hardly be dragged away from a particular *Mercury*.

The three months' suspension came to an end and André returned to the Ecole Alsacienne, to all appearances cured of his *mauvaises habitudes*, only to fall victim, soon afterwards, to the measles. When he had recovered it was thought too late to send him back to school. The term was nearly over and it was decided to send André, with Anna Shackleton, to convalesce at La Roque, where the Gides usually began their summer holidays.

At the *rentrée* in October, it was decided that André would repeat the *classe de neuvième*. Thus last year's conspicuous new boy was this year's old hand: he gained rapidly in confidence, acquired a taste for school work and soon became one of the best pupils in the class. That autumn an incident occurred that also helped the young André Gide to emerge from his mental stupor. One evening, while his parents, Anna and his Aunt Démarest were playing bezique, his cousin, Albert Démarest, began to talk to him seriously, as if to a fellow adult – it would be about the time of André's ninth birthday. He quietly asked the boy if there was anything in life that interested him except himself; he was, Cousin Albert averred, well on the way to becoming a prime egoist. 'No one had ever spoken to me in that way before; Albert could have had no idea what a profound effect his words had on me and I only came to realize this myself later.'[11] For there was nothing self-important or censorious about Albert Démarest; he was in many ways the bohemian of the family. He was still an architect by profession, although, the following year, after the death of his father, he was to take up painting, his main passion in life, full-time. Indeed he was to paint the first portrait of Gide – at twenty-one. Clearly he had detected something in the boy that was worth cultivating and the interest shown in him by Albert elicited a response that his parents' attentions failed to do. Albert Démarest, twenty-one years André's senior, became his first real friend.

That winter was to be the severest in living memory. André was sent off to learn skating with Jules and Julien Jardinier, sons of a colleague of his father's, the younger being in André's class. They practised first on the pool in the Luxembourg, then moved on to the pond at Villebon in the Bois de Meudon or the grand canal at Versailles. André became passionately fond of the sport and even, for a time, skated his way to school, up the rue de Tournon, across the Luxembourg to the rue d'Assas. This at one time sickly child was not ill once during that coldest of winters; he even began to excel at gymnastics as well as in class.

It was during that school year that André fell passionately in love for the first time:

He was a Russian . . . delicate and extraordinarily pale; he had very fair, rather long hair and very blue eyes; he had a musical voice, made even more so by his slight accent. A certain poetic quality seemed to emanate from his whole person that derived, I think, from the fact that he felt weak and wanted to be liked. The other boys looked down on him and he seldom took part in their games; yet one glance from him made me feel ashamed of playing with the others; sometimes, I remember, I caught him looking at me during the break, and I would drop out of the game there and then and go over to him. The others used to tease me about it. I longed for someone to attack him so that I might fly to his defence.

They sat next to each other in the drawing lessons, when pupils were allowed to talk quietly to one another. The Russian boy's father, it seemed, was a famous scientist. One day, he stopped coming to school, but no one could tell André what had happened to his friend and he told no one of what was 'one of the first and deepest griefs in my life'.[12]

However, another *coup de foudre* was not long in coming. Every year the Gymnase Pascaud, which, in the absence of facilities of its own, the Ecole Alsacienne used for its gym lessons, gave a fancy-dress party for its clients' children. Young André became greatly excited at the prospect. His excitement was to be short-lived. Mme Gide conferred with Mme Jardinier, Julien's mother, on the matter of costume. The two women then consulted a catalogue from the Belle Jardinière department store: the costumes were listed in descending order of attractiveness (and price), from *petit marquis* to *pâtissier*. That settled the matter: Julien would go as a pastrycook. Never one to display the family's superior means before the less fortunate, Mme Gide agreed that André, too, should go as a pastrycook. When the great day came André was so dispirited by his costume that Mme Gide allowed him to take one of the kitchen saucepans and slipped a wooden spoon into his belt, 'with the idea that these accessories might brighten up the insipidness of my prosaic outfit'. On entering the ballroom he realized that he had not one fellow-*pâtissier*, but twenty. Moreover, the saucepan was too large and impeded his movements. Then, to make confusion worse confounded, he fell in love with a boy, a little older than himself, whose 'slimness, grace and volubility' dazzled him.

He was dressed as a little devil or clown, his slender body perfectly moulded in black tights covered in steel spangles. As people crowded round to look at him, he pranced and cavorted about, playing endless tricks, as if drunk with success and delight . . . I couldn't take my eyes off him. I would have liked to attract his attention and yet I was afraid to, because of my ridiculous get-up; I felt ugly and wretched. He stopped to take breath between two pirouettes, went up to a lady who must have been his mother, asked her for a handkerchief, with which he proceeded to wipe his forehead, for he was bathed in sweat . . . I went up to him and awkwardly offered him a few biscuits. He said 'Thank you', took one absentmindedly and at once turned on his heels. I left the ball shortly afterwards, broken-hearted, and, when I got home, I fell into such a fit of despair that my mother promised me that next year I could go as a Neapolitan *lazzarone*. Yes, I thought, that costume would at least suit me; perhaps the little devil would like it . . . So I went to the next ball as a *lazzarone* – but the little devil was not there.[13]

In October, young André Gide, now nearly ten, went into the *classe de huitième* (in France one proceeds up the school in reverse numerical order, ending in the *classe de premier*). It was decided that he would board in the home of his former master, M. Vedel. The Vedels lived in a house that had once been Sainte-Beuve's. A bust of 'that curious female saint, who looked astonishingly like a paternal old gentleman wearing a tasseled cap' stood at the end of a passage. 'M. Vedel had indeed told us that Sainte-Beuve was "a great critic"; but there are limits to a child's credulity.'[14] The Vedels took in five or six boarders. Gide shared a room on the second floor with 'a great apathetic, anaemic creature, incapable of mischief, called Roseau'. The only other fellow-boarder that Gide the middle-aged writer could remember was an American called Barnett. On the very first day at Vedel's Barnett amazed all his fellow-boarders by suddenly planting himself in the middle of the garden and, in full view of all, peeing into the air. He then turned up at the first lesson wearing a moustache, painted on in ink. 'His face was pockmarked, but extraordinarily open and laughing; he was bursting with joy and health, and a kind of inner turbulence was forever driving him to do weird and dangerous things . . .'[15]

With the end of the school year the Gides retired to their country house, the Château de La Roque-Baignard, near Pont-l'Evêque, in the department of Calvados. It had been bought, like all the Normandy houses in which André Gide was to live, by Edouard Rondeaux, his maternal grandfather. On the death of Gide's grandmother, in 1874, it passed to his mother, who, in turn, left it to him on her death. The former home of the Labbey de La Roque family, it was a substantial property, comprising eight farms, totalling 346 acres in all, and 370 acres of woodland. Indeed, with its meadows and rivers, its woods and moors, the estate was so large and varied that young Gide scarcely ever ventured outside it. However much he wandered over its expanse he was constantly discovering new, unfamiliar corners. The house stood on an island, surrounded by a pond and a broad, deep moat. Its oldest parts, a postern, a dovecote and the kitchen wing, dating from 1577, were built with 'an agreeable alteration of bricks and stone'. The main part, destroyed by revolutionaries in 1792 and rebuilt in 1803, possessed 'no other charm than the mantle of wisteria that covered it'. A wall, broad enough to be walked on with safety, linked the various wings of the house and enclosed the island from the moat. 'What joy it is, for a child, to live on an island, a tiny island, and one that he can escape from whenever he likes!' One of the child's greatest pleasures at La Roque was fishing – in the moat, where 'the trout were as heavy as salmon', and in the stream where they were 'of a more delicate flavour, but above all more timid and therefore more fun to catch'.[16] Fishing from a window overlooking a moat occurs in one of Gide's earliest works, *Paludes*, and again in *L'Immoraliste*. The estate of La Roque marched with that of Le Val-Richer, the two houses being separated by an expanse of almost impenetrable woodland. Le Val-Richer, the Blancmesnil of *Si le grain ne meurt*, was the property of the Guizot de Witt-Schlumberger family. It had once been a rich monastic establishment, but the twelfth-century abbey had long since been destroyed, leaving only the abbot's house, where the current owners lived. It was particularly associated with François Guizot, historian and French foreign minister at the time of the 1848 revolution. His grandson, François de Witt, who was exactly the same age as Gide, lived there and became the greatest friend of André's adolescent years. The writer Jean Schlumberger, the son of one of François de Witt's cousins, also lived here for a time; eight years Gide's junior, he was to become, in later life, one of his very closest friends.

La Roque was the La Morinière of *L'Immoraliste*; Cuverville was the Fongueusemare of *La Porte étroite*. André Gide's uncle, Emile Rondeaux, inherited the estate of Cuverville in the department of Caux on the death of his father in 1860, when he himself was not yet thirty. The white three-storey house, with its mansard roof and small-paned windows, was typical of many French eighteenth-century country houses. In front of the house was a broad, shaded lawn, surrounded by walls; beyond that was the farmyard, marked off by an avenue of beeches. To the west, behind the house, was the garden, its paths bordered by espaliered fruit trees. Beyond was the walled kitchen garden, which led, through 'a small gate with a secret mechanism', to a copse. It was here that Jérôme and Alissa in *La Porte étroite*, the fictional counterparts of Gide and Madeleine Rondeaux, would arrange to meet. The grounds amounted to 17 acres, to which were added 185 acres of farmland, together with six more farms, a further 142 acres in all.

In addition to his townhouse in Rouen and the estates of La Roque and Cuverville, André Gide's maternal grandfather, Edouard Rondeaux, acquired a third Normandy property at Amfreville-la-Mivoie, on the Seine a few miles upstream from Rouen. 'La Mi-Voie', bought in 1850 for 52,000 francs (about £2,000 or $10,000 at the time), was an exquisite eighteenth-century folly. When a very small child, André came here with his parents for the Easter holidays and in the early part of the summer. However, it was sold shortly afterwards, in 1874.

Gide's Uncle Emile, Edouard Rondeaux's third son, was a kindly, cultured, but somewhat indolent, indecisive man. He left the running of the family calico factory near Rouen to his younger brother, Henry, 'the Catholic', and seemed set for a carefree, bachelor existence. He spent long periods in Switzerland and Italy (he happened to be in Naples when Garibaldi and his Thousand Volunteers entered the city and would willingly recount the incident to anyone who would listen). At thirty-five, however, he met Mathilde Pochet, a highly attractive girl of twenty-one. She had been born in Mauritius and, with her exceptionally dark colouring which must have stood out among the pale-skinned Normans, she was often taken for a Creole. (In *La Porte étroite*, Gide describes her fictional counterpart, Aunt Lucile, unequivocally as 'a Creole'.) In fact, Mathilde's family was from Le Havre. Her mother died when she was very young and she was brought up, in great luxury, by an adoring father. With her exotic beauty, her cosmopolitan ways, her ostentatious elegance, her apparent disregard for the claims of gainful occupation and financial prudence, she was an object of constant disapproval among the Rondeauxs. She took little part in the everyday life of the household: she never appeared until after luncheon and, when she had not retired to her room, she was usually lying, provocatively *décolletée*, on a sofa or hammock. In *La Porte étroite*, the hero-narrator Jérôme expresses the younger Gide's equivocal feelings for her: 'I felt an odd kind of unease when I was with my aunt, a feeling compounded of inner turmoil, a sort of admiration and terror.'[17] Jérôme's '*malaise*' when alone with his Aunt Lucile reaches a climax in an incident that must have happened, or at least something very like it, to the young Gide. Jérôme goes into the *salon* to look for a book and finds Aunt Lucile alone, lying on a sofa. He immediately turns back to the door. 'Why away so fast?' his aunt asks. 'Jérôme! Are you afraid of me?'

My heart beating wildly, I went up to her; I forced myself to smile and hold out my hand. She took it in one of hers and with the other stroked my cheek.

'How badly your mother dresses you, my poor little fellow! . . . Sailor's collars are worn much more open!' she said, bursting one of my shirt buttons. 'There! Don't you look better like that?' and, taking out her little mirror, she drew my face down to hers, put her bare arm around my neck, her hand finding its way into my half-opened shirt, asked with a laugh if I was ticklish and continued downwards . . . I reacted so suddenly that I tore my shirt; my face burning with embarrassment . . . I fled; I ran out to the end of the garden and plunged my handkerchief into a little water tank, and put it to my forehead, washed and scrubbed my cheeks, my neck and any part of me that that woman had touched.[18]

Throughout Gide's childhood Cuverville was '*la maison des cousines*'. There were also two male cousins, Edouard and Georges, dismissively referred to as '*les garçons*', but they were younger and therefore of no account. It was the three *cousines* that interested the young André. They were very different from one another. Madeleine, the eldest, was two-and-a-half-years older than André, Jeanne one-and-a-half years older, Valentine, half-a-year younger. Writing *Si le grain ne meurt* in his mid-fifties, Gide thought fit to alter their names (though not those of *les garçons*). Madeleine assumed the name of Emmanuèle, her counterpart in his very first piece of 'fiction', *Les Cahiers d'André Walter*. (Throughout the *Journal*, too, she is referred to as 'Em'.) Jeanne is referred to as 'Suzanne', Valentine as 'Louise'. It is curious that Gide, who always claims that he 'invented nothing' in his fiction and who certainly 'made up' fewer characters and incidents than most novelists, should resort to fictitious names in supposedly factual accounts of his life. At first, André warmed to Madeleine least: she was 'too quiet for my taste'. When their games became too boisterous she would retire with a book. She never quarrelled and always gave in to others' wishes with good grace. She seemed to be in thrall to some secret sorrow. Jeanne was an altogether bolder spirit and André's favourite of the three. The two of them would often climb the huge cedar in front of the house from the top of which they could catch a glimpse of the sea, nearly 10 miles away, near the resort of Etretat. She shared André's passion for entomology: 'She would accompany me on my hunting expeditions and was not too disgusted at turning over bits of dung and carrion in search of necrophores, geotrupes and staphylinids.'[19] Valentine had a vivid imagination, 'an extraordinary sense of mystery', but was given to unpredictable moods. André and the three sisters were 'inseparable'.

We took our lessons together, played together; our tastes and characters were formed together; our lives were woven together; we shared each other's plans and yearnings, and when, at the end of each day, our parents separated us to take us off to bed, I used to think in my childish way 'that is how it has to be now, because unfortunately we are still children, but the time will come when we shall no longer be separated, even at night'.[20]

It was during the *grandes vacances* at Cuverville and during return visits to La Roque that the young Gide saw his cousins. They also met up again during the short Christmas and New Year holidays, this time at Rouen, where Emile Rondeaux and his family lived at 18 rue de Lecat, a fairly modest house in a somewhat gloomy street. The Gides stayed with Uncle Henry and his family in the large house where André's mother had spent much of her childhood. The ground floor was taken up by the shop that sold the calicos printed in the factory at Le Houlme, just outside Rouen, Henry Rondeaux's offices, the kitchen, stables, various storerooms and servants' quarters. There were three more floors, linked by a broad stairwell, lit overhead by a large roof light.

Easter brought the Gides to Uzès, the paternal heartland. They would travel by rail to Nîmes. There they would hire 'an old boneshaker' of a carriage for the last 15 miles of the journey. Scrawny-looking holm-oaks gave way to wheatfields and, in turn, to vineyards and olive groves. At the Pont Saint-Nicolas they crossed the Gardon, whose banks were covered with asphodels. In *Si le grain ne meurt*, Gide tries to imagine the reactions of his mother on first arriving from Rouen and the lush Normandy countryside in that sun-baked wilderness that seemed half a century behind the times.

It was Palestine, Judea. The rough *garrigue* was adorned with clumps of purple and white cistuses and the air was filled with the scent of lavender . . . As it passed our carriage disturbed numbers of huge grasshoppers, which spread their blue, red or grey wings and shot up into the air, becoming for a brief instant weightless butterflies, then falling again to the ground a little further off, their brightness gone, merging with the brushwood and stone . . . O little town of Uzès! If you were in Umbria, how the tourists would flock from Paris to see you![21]

The apartment in which Gide's father had grown up was on the second floor of the Hôtel de Trinquelage (*hôtel* refers here, of course, to a former aristocratic townhouse, not to an hotel in the more recent sense) on the boulevard de l'Esplanade. It was a large, imposing but uncomfortable apartment, in which all the rooms were *en suite*: if, for example, Uncle Charles wanted to go from the dining-room to his own room at the back of the house, he had to pass in turn through the drawing-room, the room occupied by André's parents, André's room and his mother's room. Since the death of Judge Tancrède Gide in 1867, his widow had continued to live in the apartment, accompanied only by her servant Rose and, for some years, by her younger son, Charles. By the time André was ten and old enough to take note of such things, his grandmother was an apparently ageless woman, with a heavily lined face – she was in fact seventy-eight and went on to live another fourteen years. She was also extremely deaf – indeed her hearing seemed to be getting worse with each year. Her sole occupation was knitting stockings.

Rose was almost as old as her mistress, but not as deaf. She was only able to go on working because old Mme Gide required so little. When Paul Gide and his family arrived, they brought their maid Marie with them to help in the household chores. After a while Mme Gide was persuaded to abandon the apartment in which she had lived for sixty years and moved to Montpellier, where her son Charles held a chair in the Law Faculty. Charles Gide was not to remain a lawyer: his fame as an economist eclipsed that of his nephew for a time. He was an early advocate of Christian Socialism and published several works, from his *Principes d'économie politique* of 1884 to *La Coöpération et les colonies communistes et coöpératives* of 1930. He ended his distinguished academic career with a chair at the Collège de France, dying in 1932 at the age of eighty-five. When André was ten, however, Uncle Charles was a surly, uncommunicative young man of twenty-two.

For Grandmother Gide, the Easter holidays must have been the high point of her year – this austere Southern Puritan would lavish every possible luxury upon her guests, at least as far as the dinner-table was concerned. André's mother had the greatest difficulty in persuading her that four dishes to a meal were enough for them. She took no notice and her daughter-in-law had to catch Rose before she went out to do the shopping and cancel three-quarters of the food ordered. 'Well, Rose, what happened to the spring chickens?' the old lady would ask. Her daughter-in-law intervened to explain that since there were lamb cutlets for lunch, they would have the chickens for dinner. 'Lamb cutlets!' the old lady expostulated. 'You need six of them to make a mouthful!' She would then go off and fetch some *fricandeaux* (pieces of pork, stuffed with truffles and preserved in lard). André's mother refused them on principle, not only for herself, but for her son, too. 'But you don't want him to die of hunger, do you?' his grandmother asked incredulously. 'For her,' Gide adds, 'any child who was not ready to burst was dying of hunger.'[22]

For young André the meals at Uzès seemed interminable, a terrible incursion into the daylight hours when he might be out-of-doors. His extramural activities were not those usually indulged in by boys of his age. Usually he ran off towards the rocks and climbed up to the *garrigue*, or heath, urged on by 'that strange love of the non-human and the arid that for so long made me prefer the desert to the oasis'.[23] There he would hunt for praying mantis and discover, under stones, scorpions, millipedes and centipedes. Later, his passion for entomology was given quasi-official recognition when Georges Pouchet, a professor at the Muséum d'Histoire Naturelle, better known as the Jardin des Plantes, left young André a collection of insects, consisting of twenty-four cork-lined boxes full of coleoptera (beetles), all classified, arranged and labelled. 'But it did not, as far as I remember, give me enormous pleasure,' says Gide. 'My own poor collection seemed too humiliated beside this treasure; and how much more precious to me was each of those insects that I had caught and pinned down myself.' He then adds, in a comment that is entirely typical of his constant preference for movement over stasis, for the present over the past: 'What appealed to me was not the collection, but the hunt.'[24]

It was probably Anna Shackleton who extended André's interest in insects to plants. He was allowed to accompany her on plant-collecting excursions organized by the Muséum. André started his own herbarium, but he tended rather to help Anna complete hers, which was remarkably comprehensive.

Not only had she managed, by patient effort, to find the finest examples of each variety, but they were marvellously presented: thin strips of gummed paper kept the most delicate little stalks in place; the natural bearing of the plant was scrupulously respected; the bud, the fully opened flower and the seed were placed side-by-side ... Sometimes the naming of some dubious variety required the most careful research and meticulous examination; Anna would bend over her microscope and, armed with pincers and tiny scalpels, delicately open the flower, spread out its organs under the objective and call me over to point out some peculiarity of the stamens . . .[25]

In Paris, then, Anna and André could attend lectures and go on organized expeditions. In La Roque, 'the herbarium reigned supreme': there, during the long summer months, they had the time – and the space – to indulge their passion. But La Roque was as nothing to Uzès, where a whole new botanical world opened up before them. 'The vegetation was so luxuriant we could hardly make our way through it. Anna marvelled at the many plants that were unknown to her or which, she admitted, she had never seen before in the wild.' Sometimes André's parents would go with them. His father took a delight in everything, oblivious, like the two botanists, of the passing hours, but his mother tried in vain to persuade them to make tracks for home at a reasonable hour. M. Gide and Anna, sensitive to the twilight beauty of the scene, were in no hurry and recited verses to one another. Mme Gide thought that 'it wasn't the time for that': 'Paul, you can recite that when we get home.'[26]

We left André's schooldays with him living in at the Vedels' house and repeating his *classe de neuvième* at the Ecole Alsacienne. In October 1880, not quite eleven, he entered the *classe de huitième*: he seemed, at last, to have entered a period of stability. Then, on the afternoon of 28 October, M. Vedel summoned André to his study. With him was Anna Shackleton; she had been deputed to tell André that his father had just died.

3

Youth: God and Love

Paul Gide was only forty-seven when he died. On the way home Anna recounted his last moments: it had been a very peaceful death. André said nothing, betraying no emotion until he saw his mother dressed entirely in black. He then threw himself into her arms and burst into tears. He soon recovered control of himself: the acknowledgement of feeling, let alone its outward expression, did not come easily to Gides and Rondeauxs. He then remarks, curiously perhaps, but with commendable honesty, that the pleasure of seeing his cousins again almost got the better of his grief. Fearing no doubt the effect of excessive emotion on her son's nervous disposition, Mme Gide decided that André would not attend the funeral: Madeleine and Jeanne would keep him company at home. Meanwhile, Paul Gide's funeral was proceeding with all the pomp reserved for those who have done the State some service. The pallbearers were the director of Higher Education, the inspector-general of the nation's law faculties, the dean of the Paris Law Faculty and Alexandre Ribot, lawyer, deputy and future prime minister. The entire teaching staff of the Paris Law Faculty, wearing red gowns, headed the *cortège*.

Paul Gide had been ill with persistent dysentery for most of the summer of 1880. 'In fact, it was intestinal tuberculosis and my mother knew this, I think; but, in those days, tuberculosis was an illness that people hoped to cure by ignoring it.'[1] He spent the last few days of his life confined to bed, reading, not the Bible, but Plato's *Symposium* (in the original Greek), a work that was later to have a quite special significance for his son.

André Gide was profoundly affected by his father's death – so profoundly that he could find no ready expression for his grief. In many respects, his parents had reversed the stereotypical roles of father and mother. His mother had been the authority figure; his father the accomplice in evasions of that authority. Despite the mystery and distance that seemed to envelop his father, André had adored him; indeed perhaps that very mystery and distance increased his love for him. But the loss of his father had another effect: it meant that he became the sole object of his mother's love – and rather overbearing solicitude. The chains forged by that love – and the compulsion to break them – would become all the stronger. In his unpublished notes for *Si le grain ne meurt* we find this: 'The first time my mother appeared wearing violet ribbons, after my father's death, I was scandalized. I said nothing, but the colour seemed indecent on her. It made her look younger.' Violet ribbons, a subtle enough gradation from the customary solemn black in one small item of what was certainly a very sober costume, indecent! Juliette Gide *veuve* was quite the last woman to wear anything unseemly or in the least conspicuous. The incident of the ribbons occurred when André was in the *classe de philo'* at the Lycée Henri IV, around the time of his nineteenth birthday, *eight years* after his father's death. Nor was it forgotten. Close on twenty years later it crops up, in suitably muted form, in *La Porte étroite*: 'One day, and I think it was quite long after my father's death, my mother had changed the black ribbon on her mourning hat for a mauve one. "*Maman!*" I cried. "That colour doesn't suit you at all!"' Next day, she was wearing the black ribbon again.'[2]

Soon after the funeral Mme Gide decided to leave Paris, taking her son with her, to spend several months at her childhood home in Rouen. André was only too pleased to abandon the discipline of M. Vedel and the Ecole Alsacienne for the relative freedom of Uncle Henry's house and private lessons with a tutor. Then, of course, he would be able to spend not only the summer, but also the winter close to his cousins. A tutor was engaged, a M. Huard (the 'M. Hubert' of Gide's slightly fictionalized autobiography): most memorable were the geography lessons, which consisted of the pupil testing his knowledge by writing the names of countries, cities, rivers, etc., on to blank maps. In his spare time, André started a magazine, which he printed himself on a copying machine. The magazine included poetry and prose by his three *cousines*, but his own contribution was confined to the selection of extracts from the French classics, Boileau and Buffon in particular. He also spent many hours at his uncle's cloth-printing factory at Le Houlme, where he took a particular interest in his cousin Fernand's pet rabbits.

With the summer, Mme Gide and her son moved on to La Roque, where a new tutor, a M. Romard (M. Gallin in *Si le grain ne meurt*) was engaged. This short-sighted theological student cared not at all for the countryside and, on their walks together, deprived André of any pleasure by singing extracts from popular operettas. André came to hate him and, as a result, refused to learn anything from him.

*

The new school year approached and Mme Gide was growing more and more anxious about her son's education: André had spent almost a year in semi-idleness. Her mind was made up: they would move to Montpellier and André would attend the *lycée* there. Uncle Charles, who had already initiated a fortnightly correspondence with his nephew, would provide some kind of paternal authority. Incidentally, Charles Gide's (unpublished) letters to his nephew are models of their kind and give a quite different impression of the man from André Gide's portrait of the hated, surly, uncommunicative uncle. They go out of their way to win the boy's respect and affection, referring to odd incidents likely to interest him. Even his comments on his nephew's academic shortcomings are diplomatic, not in the least authoritarian: 'Spelling can, I admit, be rather boring, but it's absolutely necessary to master it, if one is not to be regarded as an ignoramus.'

In Montpellier, Charles Gide and his wife occupied the second (top) floor of a house in which the owners, the Castelnau family, retained the ground and first floors. The Gides were also allowed access to the large garden, with its splendid views of the Esplanade in the foreground and of the mountains in the distance. André, his mother and the faithful Marie did not, however, move into Charles Gide's new apartment. They took rooms in an hotel and set about looking for rented accommodation. They found a furnished apartment in a dark, dirty street nearby. It was 'small, ugly, squalid', the furniture 'sordid'. Gide notes, with evident shock, that, in addition to their bedrooms, there was only one room, 'which served as both sitting-room and dining-room'. His own room overlooked a small 'garden' that was devoid of grass, trees or flowers. Beyond that was the seething world of 'shouting, singing, smells of oil, babies' nappies being dried, carpets shaken, chamber-pots emptied, squalling children and birds squawking in their cages'.[3] As if to underline their reduced circumstances, André and his mother dined two or three times a week with Uncle Charles. After the Paris apartment in the rue de Tournon and the Château de La Roque-Baignard, it seemed to the young André Gide that his father's death had entailed a collapse of the family fortunes, but, as so often with children, he dared not inquire too closely into such a matter and his fears remained unallayed.

'Small, ugly, wretched' as the rented apartment in the rue Salle-L'Evêque may have seemed, it was a haven of love and peace compared to the Lycée de Montpellier, which had changed little since Rabelais had been a pupil there in the early years of the sixteenth century. There were no desks: the pupils sat on rising steps, at the mercy of feet behind them, and wrote on their knees. But physical discomfort in the classroom was the least of young Gide's problems. During the first break, he was surrounded by a group of fellow-pupils and asked: '*T'es catholique, toi? Ou protescul?*' (The latter term being roughly translated as 'protarse', he was evidently among religious enemies.) He had not, until then, been aware that religious allegiance could be a source of conflict. He now learnt that the Protestant 'rich kids' were a hated minority among the largely proletarian Catholics – the better-off Catholics educated their sons in private schools run by religious orders.

The next occasion of difference between young Gide and his fellow-pupils occurred during a French lesson. Each pupil recited in turn, gabbling the verse as fast as possible, in a flat monotone, taking no account of metre or meaning. When Gide's turn came he read with all the skill he had acquired at home and at the Ecole Alsacienne. At first stunned into silence at the shock of hearing verse read in so 'pretentious' a fashion, no doubt made all the more singular by Gide's cultivated Parisian accent, the class soon erupted into loud, uncontrollable laughter. The general hilarity even affected the master, who could not resist a smile. 'The master's smile was my inevitable undoing. I don't know how I found the strength to keep going to the end of the piece, which, thank God, I knew by heart.' Then, to André's astonishment and to the utter amazement of the class, the master calmly announced that he was awarding Gide full marks. 'You may laugh,' he added, 'but let me tell you, gentlemen, that is how you should all recite verse.' This 'stupid success' aroused the hostility of all Gide's schoolmates. He was jeered at, beaten up, tracked down. As soon as school was over he took to his heels. He did not have far to go to reach home, but there was usually someone lying in wait for him. He invented long, roundabout routes: 'There were days when I got home in a terrible state, my clothes all torn and muddied, my nose bleeding, my teeth chattering, distraught with fear.'[4] Once a dead cat was rubbed in his face.

Not for the first, or last, time, illness came to young André's rescue. Smallpox was diagnosed, although, according to Jean Delay, it was probably chickenpox. After three weeks in bed, he was able to take a few tottering steps. Soon, as his mother reminded him, he would be back at school. He felt giddy. 'Supposing this giddiness were a little worse, I thought to myself, can I imagine what would happen? Oh, yes: my head would fall backwards, my knees would give way and I would suddenly collapse on the floor.' He proceeded to act out the scene. Marie came rushing in. Encouraged by the success of his performance, André became 'more skilled and definitely

more inventive'. He tried out other movements: 'Sometimes I invented
sudden, jerky ones; sometimes, on the contrary, they were long drawn out
and rhythmically repeated, as in a dance. I became very expert at these
dances and my repertoire soon became quite varied.'[5] The doctor was sent
for. He gave his expert diagnosis: 'Nerves, nothing but nerves.' Nevertheless,
he thought fit to consult two other specialists, thus increasing his own fee
by putting work the way of his friends and colleagues. André was examined
at length by all three doctors: fearing that the game was up, he redoubled
his histrionic efforts, even to the point of making his hand shake as he did
up a button on his jacket. In their collective wisdom, the doctors decided
that the child would benefit from some weeks spent at a spa. They knew
just the place . . . The terrible day when André would have to go back to
the *lycée* was postponed yet again.

Lamalou-les-Bains is a small watering-place near Béziers, some 40 miles
from Montpellier. The rheumatics frequented Lamalou-le-Bas, which, in
addition to the spa, had a casino and shops. Two-and-a-half miles up hill
was Lamalou-le-Haut, a more spartan hamlet, where the ataxics underwent
their *cure*. Locomotor ataxia, as its name implies, is a condition in which
one loses control of one's movements; it is caused by a degeneration of
nerve columns in the spinal cord. With softening of the brain, it was one
of the commonest manifestations of tertiary syphilis, which, in the late
nineteenth century, cut swathes through the Parisian *vie de bohème*. Quite
what effect a regime of bathing and cold showers was expected to have on
the ataxics is not clear. Since the three doctors of Montpellier presumably
did not imagine that the twelve-year-old André Gide was suffering from
tertiary syphilis, why Lamalou? Association of ideas, perhaps. What do the
child's sudden, apparently uncontrolled movements remind us of? Why,
those of ataxics, of course. And what do we do with ataxics? We send them
to take the waters at Lamalou. And so André Gide, his mother and Marie
found themselves in a village consisting almost entirely, the staff apart, of
middle-aged tertiary syphilitics. The bathing and the showers did no more
good to young André, of course, than to anyone else. However, removal from
Montpellier and its *lycée*, combined with freedom to roam the countryside
around, were remarkably beneficial.

We had just arrived. While *maman* and Marie were busy unpacking, I escaped. I
ran into the garden and made my way on and on into the narrow gorge; above
the schistose sides, tall trees formed a vault; a steaming rivulet, which passed
through the bathing establishment, and whose bed was carpeted with a thick, fluffy
rust, ran singing beside me; I was transfixed with surprise and, to give vent to my

delight, I remember walking along with my arms raised, in oriental fashion, as I had seen Sinbad do in an illustration in my beloved *Thousand and One Nights*.[6]

In due course, another consultation with the three doctors was arranged and the *cure* was declared a success.

With the new school year, Mme Gide decided to return to Paris and put her son back in the Ecole Alsacienne, after ten months' absence and very little schooling. He had been back at school only two weeks when 'I added headaches to my repertoire of nervous disorders; these were less obvious and, therefore, more practical for use in class.' Gide is keen to dispel any idea that the headaches at least were entirely feigned, although he admits that until they returned, in his forty-sixth year, and were recognized at once as those that he had suffered between twelve and twenty, he had long believed them to be more or less feigned. At this period he was also suffering from sudden tiredness and insomnia, often sleeping no more than three or four hours a night. But, in addition to these physical symptoms, the young Gide, precisely because his schooling had been so irregular, could not easily adapt to the monotonous rhythm of school life. He felt 'an unspeakable distaste for everything we did in class, for the class itself, for the entire regime of lessons, examinations, even the recreations; I could not bear sitting still on a bench, the boredom, the repetitiveness of it all.'[7]

Brouardel, the specialist who, it will be remembered, claimed to castrate masturbating young boys with Tuareg spearheads, had meanwhile become too exalted a figure to deal with young André's headaches. In the event, the treatment given by a Dr Lizart, an apparently kindly, harmless individual, was far more dangerous than the threat of Tuareg spearheads. The patient was given bromides for his headaches and chloral for the insomnia:

This for a brain scarcely formed! I hold him responsible for all my weakness of will and memory in later life. If one could sue the dead, I would take him to court. I can hardly contain my anger at the thought that every night, for weeks on end, half a glass of a solution of chloral (the bottle of nitrate crystals was put entirely at my disposal and I could take as much of it as I liked) . . . For weeks, for months on end, when I sat down at table, I found beside my plate a bottle of 'Laroze syrup – peel of bitter oranges and bromide of potassium'. At every meal I had to take first one, then two, then three spoonfuls (not teaspoons, but tablespoons) of it, and so on, in a rhythmical series of threes; and this treatment went on indefinitely and came to an end when the innocent patient was utterly stupefied.[8]

So, once again, André left the Ecole Alsacienne before the end of term, and Mme Gide, thinking the change might do him some good, took him off to Rouen. There he added another variant to his repertoire of illnesses. Although he does not use the term or, indeed, regard it as an illness, he was clearly suffering from anorexia. Sitting at table was 'a torture'. His mother, his Aunt Lucile, the maid Adèle and the cook Séraphine all busied them-selves around him, but the 'petits plats spéciaux' failed to tempt him. He would swallow a few mouthfuls with great difficulty, but he could not get very far. Every meal ended in tears.

The consolation of Rouen was, of course, his *cousines*. One day, just before Christmas, he left them to go back to the rue de Crosne. It was getting dark and he thought his mother would be expecting him. On arrival, he found the house empty. Quite on impulse, he decided to go back to the rue de Lecat and surprise his cousins. On the landing of the second floor he found the door of Aunt Mathilde's room wide open. As he slipped by, he caught a glimpse of his aunt, lying 'indisposed' on a sofa, Jeanne and Valentine leaning over her, fanning her. Madeleine did not seem to be there. He went up to her room on the top floor, knocked and, finding that the door was not completely shut, pushed it open. The room was so dimly lit, it took him a few seconds to realize that Madeleine was there, kneeling. 'Why have you come?' she said. 'You shouldn't have come back.' He went up to her and found that she was crying. For the first time André Gide understood the secret of Madeleine's sadness: her mother was having an affair.

Today I cannot imagine anything more cruel, for a young girl who was all purity, love and tenderness, than having to judge her own mother and condemn her conduct; and what increased her unhappiness was having to keep to herself and hide from a father she adored a secret that she had accidentally discovered and which was now tormenting her – a secret that was the talk of the town, which the servants laughed about and which took advantage of her two sisters' carefree innocence. Of course, I did not understand all this until later; but I felt that, within that little creature, already so dear to me, dwelt a great and intolerable grief, a pain that not all my love and all my life would be enough to cure . . . Till that day I had been wandering aimlessly; suddenly I had found the mystic east of my life.[9]

The scene is reproduced almost exactly in *La Porte étroite*, except that, as Jérôme passes his aunt's room, he sees not his two cousins, but a young army officer. Behind the fictional screen, the novel tells us more about the complexity of Gide's relationship with his cousin and future wife, more about the symbolic significance it had for him, than does the more circumspect autobiographical account written some ten or more years later:

That moment decided my life . . . I remained standing beside her; she remained kneeling; I could find no words to express the new rapture in my heart . . . Drunk with love, pity and a vague mixture of enthusiasm, abnegation, virtue, I called on God with all my strength and offered myself, no longer able to imagine any other aim in life than to protect that child against fear, against evil, against life. I finally knelt down beside her, my heart full of prayer . . .'[10]

What is made clear in this passage from *La Porte étroite* is that the sudden discovery of his 'mystic east', his new orientation, was, from the very beginning, in its very essence, both amatory (one cannot say sexual) and religious. Certainly that moment marked the beginning of André's *love* for his cousin: the thirteen-year-old boy was no longer, in a sense, a child. In another, of course, he was, and Madeleine, two years his senior, at an age where such a difference has its maximum effect, was already a young woman. But for young André Gide, Madeleine was not a 'young woman', but an 'angel', and love for an angel must be pure, *agape*, not *eros*. Madeleine was *agape*, selfless, pure, Christian love personified. That moment of awakening love was also the moment when, for the first time, it seems, André Gide felt an authentic upsurge of religious feeling. He was 'drunk with *love, pity . . . enthusiasm, abnegation, virtue*' (my italics). He 'called on God' and 'knelt down beside her'. His identification of the love between man and woman and the love between God and man was to dominate André Gide's first work, *Les Cahiers d'André Walter*, and was to return, from a more distant perspective, in *La Porte étroite*. As far as Gide's personal life was concerned, it occupied the adolescent void, one might say, that was to end, in his twenties, with his discovery of the *nourritures terrestres*, the earthly food of the material world and homosexual adventure. Meanwhile, Madeleine came to dominate André's life. They thought the same thoughts, read the same books: when reading he would write her initials beside any passage he wanted to share with her. In 1886 Aunt Mathilde left home, joining her lover, a Parisian lawyer, Talabart by name, and taking with her the youngest child of the marriage, Lucienne, whose very existence is ignored by the biographers of the Rondeaux family, Le Verdier and Nobécourt, and even by André Gide himself.

Mme Gide decided, in view of André's precarious health, that they would spend the rest of the winter on the Côte d'Azur. Some 'unfortunate inspiration' led them to Hyères, which turned out to be much further from the sea than it appeared on the map. To make matters worse, both André and Anna fell ill. A doctor was called and, as a result, André fell yet again into the clutches of some insane medical 'specialist', who duly persuaded Mme Gide that all her son's illness was due to flatulence: the boy's abdomen, it seemed, had 'alarming cavities' and 'a tendency to swell'. He should wear an orthopaedic bandage, which could be ordered from the doctor's cousin: this would impede the building-up of wind. 'I wore this ridiculous apparatus for a time; it impeded all my movements and proved all the more ineffective in flattening my stomach as I was already as thin as a rake.'[11]

Hyères had nothing to recommend it, although it was there that Gide experienced one of those childhood ecstasies, 'apparelled in celestial light', recollected in adult turmoil. Curiously, like the more famous episode described by Marcel Proust, the vision was of blossom, not the hawthorn of Combray, but the eucalyptus of Hyères. The resemblance goes no further. Proust's hawthorn hedge is rapidly turned into a succession of side chapels in a cathedral, the focus, the touchstone of a vanished time; in *Si le grain le meurt*, the eucalyptus is a passing incident, the occasion not for metaphorical transformations through a process of associational accretion, moving further and further away from the object, but for a concentration of the vision, the educated botanist's eye, upon the object.

The buds, of a verdigris colour, were covered with a kind of resinous bloom and looked like tiny closed caskets; one might have taken them to be seeds, were it not for their freshness; and suddenly the lid of one of the caskets would burst under the tumultuous pressure of the stamens; then, when the lid fell to the ground, the freed stamens would stand out to form a crown or a halo; at a distance, among the tangle of sharp, oblong, drooping leaves, that white, petalless flower looked like a sea-anemone.[12]

After some time, they moved on to Cannes. Even Mme Gide's disinclination to spend any more money than was strictly necessary – they were 'médiocrement installés' near the railway station, in the least agreeable district – could not rob young André of his delight in Cannes and the surrounding countryside. Proust's attention would have been caught by the endless movement of high-born fauna along the promenade. Gide ignores the princesses and grand-duchesses in favour of the madrepores and sea urchins at the bottom of some rock pool. For the young André Gide those months on the Côte d'Azur were more than a holiday – during the long summers at La Roque he had always had lessons from private tutors. On medical advice, Mme Gide had decided that André was not to over-exert himself in any way. Not only were there to be no lessons, he was not even allowed to practise on the hotel piano.

By May, André seemed sufficiently recovered for Mme Gide to contemplate a return to Paris. Of course, they would have to give up the apartment in the rue de Tournon, which had scarcely been occupied for two-and-a-half years: it was altogether too large for the two of them. At first, André imagined that the real reason was that they could no longer afford such an apartment – he remembered the miserable furnished flat at Montpellier. However, overhearing the conversations between his mother and his Aunt Démarest, he began to get excited by the prospect of change. Juliette Gide's sense of duty towards her means was more than countermanded by her sister's invocation of the higher duty to her standing. Certain streets were dismissed out of hand; one could only live on certain floors in a building; above all, there was the absolute necessity for a *porte-cochère*. Whether or not one actually had a carriage, horses and a coachman was beside the point: a building without a carriage-entrance was beneath consideration. 'It is not a question of convenience,' Aunt Claire would decree, 'but of propriety . . . In fact, it's quite simple, if you have no *porte-cochère*, I can tell you straight off the people who won't come to see you.' In the end, their joint choice fell upon a fourth-floor apartment at 6 rue de Commaille, appreciably larger, more beautiful, more pleasant, more luxurious than the old one. It also had the expensive privilege of looking out over a splendid garden. Clearly, the Gides were not ruined after all.

André did not, however, witness the move. On their return to Paris, Mme Gide sent her son to board in the home of a tutor. Henry Bauer (the M. Richard of *Si le grain ne meurt*) was a kindly, easy-going man, whose original vocation had been to become a Protestant pastor. Later, when he had passed his *agrégation*, he became a German teacher in a *lycée*. He lived in a small, two-storeyed house in the rue Raynouard, in the then suburban and relatively inexpensive area of Passy. With him were his wife, his two children, his sister-in-law (a general's widow, very conscious of having come down in the world) and her daughter. Soon after André joined the Bauer household they were joined by Henry Bauer's younger brother, Abel, a rather unprepossessing youth of eighteen. Though not exactly a simpleton, he was certainly slow-witted. He had an immediate crush on André, following him around wherever he went, trying desperately to attract his attention. One evening, on the terrace, Abel eventually plucked up the courage to ask: 'Will you be my friend?' Highly embarrassed, André muttered something that could be taken as assent. Next day, Abel took him to his room and, unlocking a doll's cupboard, took out a bundle of letters. Handing them to André, he said: 'There! You may read them all!' They were not, as André had supposed, love-letters, but a pathetic correspondence from his sister, full of complaints, references to overdue bills, requests for money. When

André had finished looking through them, Abel said: 'Now you know all my secrets. You'll tell me yours, won't you?' That introspective solitary, who was certainly possessed of secrets of greater moment than most thirteen-year-old boys, who, a few months before, had learnt of his aunt's infidelity and fallen in love with her daughter, and who would usually have found it all but impossible to tell a lie, replied, when confronted by the pathetic bundle of 'secrets' of a boy five years his senior, 'I don't have any.'

The school year came to an end and it was decided that M. Bauer would continue André's lessons during part of the summer holidays at La Roque and that a boy of André's age, Emile Ambresin, would act as a companion: it was unhealthy, Mme Gide believed, for a child to be left too much to himself. Inviting young Emile to La Roque also gave Mme Gide an occasion to exercise Christian charity. For the Ambresins were poor; better still, they were deserving poor and, which placed Emile beyond any kind of suspicion, his father was a pastor. Christian charity is not a simple matter. When Emile Ambresin (Armand Bavretel of *Si le grain ne meurt*) first entered the drawing-room at La Roque, he burst into tears: 'I was more than surprised, I was almost shocked by those tears; I thought he did not properly appreciate my mother's kindness . . . I was too young to understand how offensive the appearance of wealth may be in the eyes of poverty.'[13] It was through Emile Ambresin that André Gide first realized how privileged he himself was. 'I was privileged without knowing it, just as I was French and Protestant without knowing it; outside this magic circle everything seemed exotic to me.' Once, when Mme Gide had booked two seats for André and Emile for a matinee at the Opéra-Comique, André was horrified to discover that they were in the upper circle, much higher up than he was used to and 'surrounded by people who struck me as common'. He immediately went to the box office and demanded two tickets for the dress circle, paying the difference. 'Just as the house we lived in had to have a *porte-cochère* – or, rather, just as we owed it to ourselves to have a *porte-cochère*, as Aunt Claire said, so we owed it to ourselves always to travel first-class and at the theatre I could not imagine self-respecting people sitting anywhere but in the dress circle.'[14]

Years later, André Gide called on his old friend Emile. He found him in his room, lying on his unmade bed, dressed, though 'without a tie', unshaven. 'There was not the smallest object anywhere on which the eye could rest with any pleasure; its poverty, ugliness and darkness were so stifling that I asked him whether he would not come out with me.' Emile replied that he never went out any more. How could he, he asked, looking the way he did. Gide protested, to no avail, that he didn't care what he looked like. And what did he do all day? Nothing. He then explained that he no longer went out because he was capable only of doing harm to people. 'What do you think of suicide?' he suddenly asked André, who replied, in all honesty, that he believed it to be a praiseworthy course in certain cases. Some years after that last meeting, Gide learnt that Emile had thrown himself into the Seine. Something of the Ambresins and their lugubrious Twelfth Night parties went into the Vedels, and more than a little of Emile (and his death by drowning) into the Armand Vedel of *Les Faux-Monnayeurs*.

Mme Gide was determined that in October (we are now in 1883) André would go back to the Ecole Alsacienne and resume his normal schooling. André began at once to develop the old symptoms: headaches, tiredness, insomnia and extreme nervousness. After a few weeks, Mme Gide was forced to yield and André was handed back to the easygoing M. Bauer. For various reasons, Henry Bauer had decided to move into central Paris. The new accommodation did not allow boarders, so André arrived every morning at nine o'clock, had lunch with his tutor and returned home in the evening.

On 1 January 1884, André was walking home after going to wish Anna Shackleton a happy New Year. He was feeling particularly happy, at peace with himself and the world, 'blessed with all the unbounded wealth of the future'. Instead of turning into the rue Saint-Placide as usual, he walked down a small, parallel street (the rue Abbé-Grégoire), for no other reason than to make a change. It was nearly noon. One side of the narrow street was in bright sunlight, the other in shade. Half-way along he crossed from the sunlit side to the shady one.

I was feeling so happy that I sang as I walked and skipped along, looking up at the sky. Then, suddenly, I saw coming down towards me, as if in answer to my happiness, a little, fluttering, golden thing, like a shaft of sunlight cutting through the shade. Nearer and nearer it came, hovered for a moment, then settled on my cap, like the Holy Ghost. I put up my hand and a pretty canary nestled into it.[15]

The young Gide felt certain that the bird had been sent to him from heaven; he had been 'chosen'. As if one visitation from above were not enough, he was crossing the boulevard Saint-Germain one day, when he saw, in the middle of the street . . . a canary. He tried to catch it, but it kept eluding him. Finally, he managed to cover it with his cap, just as they were both about to be run over by a tram. When he reached home, André put his new acquisition in a huge cage that he had brought back from La Roque and which was already occupied by the first canary and a family of finches. As luck – or predestination – would have it, he now had two canaries of opposite sexes. Before long, they were joined by others, not from heaven, but by a more mundane process.

Anna Shackleton had not been well for at least a year. Four months after the New Year visit, André and his mother accompanied her to a private hospital in the rue Chalgrin, near the Etoile, where she was operated on for 'a tumour that had been disfiguring her and oppressing her for some time'. She died a week or so after the operation, on 14 May, 'in her own modest way, so quietly and discreetly that no one noticed that she was dying, only that she was dead'. She was fifty-eight and had been with the Rondeauxs for the last thirty-four years of her life. She had been Juliette Gide's closest friend and a second mother to André. Long afterwards, André Gide felt pain and guilt at the fact that he and his mother had not been with Anna at the end. 'For weeks, for months on end, I was haunted by the sense of aloneness she must have felt. I imagined, I heard that loving soul of hers utter its last despairing cry and sink back again, forsaken by all but God.'[16]

Before long, M. Bauer decided that his new lodgings were inadequate and set about looking for a new apartment. He was, in any case, rather given to the Aristotelian, peripatetic mode of teaching. 'It's a sin to stay indoors this fine weather!' he would say, and master and pupil would set off, continuing the lesson as best they could through the streets of Paris. Now their walks became longer and more frequent as M. Bauer combined the lessons with looking for a new home. Most mornings they would start by investigating the streets around the Gare Saint-Lazare and the Lycée Condorcet. 'These voyages of discovery were more instructive to me than the reading of many novels', let alone the lessons for which Mme Gide was paying. They never knew what sight might greet their eyes on crossing a threshold. In cases of extreme debauchery, M. Bauer would turn round hastily and say, 'Don't come in!' Nevertheless, André saw a great deal on these visits. It was an 'indirect initiation' into a side of life that he might otherwise not have encountered.[17]

As well as André M. Bauer had two other pupils: Adrien Giffard was attending classes at the Lycée Lakanal, Bernard Tissaudier at Condorcet. Adrien, Gide tells us, was one of those middling individuals, 'neither good nor bad, neither serious nor gay', whose purpose in life seemed to be to make up the numbers. The one unusual thing about him was that he was a compulsive smoker. Bernard was a Protestant and Mme Gide considered him well brought up. In the evenings, he and André would often walk part of the way home together from Bauer's. One evening, Mme Gide was sitting reading her newspaper when André noticed the expression on her face change dramatically. 'I hope your friend Tissaudier doesn't go through the passage du Havre when he comes out of the *lycée*,' she said. 'You ought to tell him to avoid it.' It seemed that the passage du Havre was '*extrêmement mal fréquenté*'. 'I understood more or less what "*mal fréquenté*" was supposed to mean, but my imagination, which was quite uninhibited by any notion of what was right and proper, immediately conjured up a picture of the passage du Havre . . . as a place of depravity, a Gehenna, a battlefield where morality lay slaughtered . . .' When they were next alone together, André asked Bernard: 'When you leave the *lycée*, you don't go down the passage du Havre, do you?' When his friend failed to answer, but instead asked why he wanted to know, André flung himself on his knees and, tears streaming down his cheeks, cried: 'Bernard! I implore you, don't, don't!' The astonished Bernard Tissaudier replied, with the utmost *désinvolture*, 'Do you imagine, then, that I don't know the profession?'

The word 'profession' [*métier*] sounded painfully in my ears; it cast a practical, vulgar light on something that I had hitherto regarded only as a highly charged mixture of the hideous and the poetic; I don't really think that it had ever occurred to me that the question of money had anything to do with debauchery, or that sensual pleasure [*volupté*] could be paid for . . .[18]

This incident had the effect of alerting the young André Gide to things that had hitherto eluded his attention. His Aunt Claire and Albert Démarest lived at 78 boulevard Saint-Germain, between the boulevard Saint-Michel and the place Maubert, almost opposite the Théâtre Cluny, a location much lower in social standing than one might have expected of Juliette Gide's sister, *porte-cochère* notwithstanding. Young André now noticed that, at dusk, the pavement in that part of the boulevard was frequented by several '*femmes en cheveux*', women not wearing hats. Tissaudier's word '*métier*' immediately came to mind. Should he get off the pavement in order to avoid them? 'Something in me almost always wins over fear: it is fear of cowardice.' Suddenly one of the women barred his way: shaking with emotion, he dodged sideways and hurried off. 'There's no need to be so frightened, my pretty lad!' the prostitute shouted after him, 'in a voice that was at once scolding, mocking, coaxing and playful'.

*

Years later, those questing creatures still inspired as much terror in me as vitriol-throwers ... I had a complete lack of curiosity about the opposite sex ... I entertained the flattering thought that my repugnance was disapproval, and attributed my aversion to virtue ... If I gave in, it was to vice [ie masturbation]; I took no notice at all of provocations from outside myself.[19]

Claire Démarest was Juliette Gide's elder and only sister – there were also three brothers – and, though thirteen years separated them, they had become intimate friends, especially since the deaths of their husbands within a year of each other. Claire Démarest lived with her younger son, Albert, her other two children being married. Every Sunday, the two sisters and their sons dined alternately in each other's apartments. They would spend Christmas and New Year at their old home in Rouen and saw a great deal of each other in the summer, in Normandy, where Claire Démarest had a property at Pont-de-l'Arche, some 40 miles from La Roque. The difference in age between the cousins – twenty years – was even greater than that between the sisters, yet they, too, had a very special relationship. Young André idolized Albert and, as we have seen, accepted criticism and advice from him that he would have accepted from no one else. 'His slightest remarks amused me enormously, perhaps because he said the very things I did not dare to say or even dare to think.'[20] Albert also had a great love of music and often, when their mothers were at one end of the drawing-room talking, he and André would go over to the piano and play duets. It was Albert, too, who had finally persuaded Juliette Gide to allow her son to open his father's huge bookcase, which had been kept locked, like some sanctuary, ever since they had moved into the rue de Commaille.

Albert Démarest was now a full-time painter, having inherited from his father enough money to live on. A big, athletic figure of a man, of great intelligence and charm, he nevertheless, at thirty-five, appeared to be unattached. What none of his family knew was that, for the past ten years, he had been living with a certain Marie, whom he had set up in a small apartment in the rue Denfert, and that there was now a daughter of the liaison.

By the summer of 1885, Mme Gide was clearly anxious about her son's spiritual welfare. Anna Shackleton had exerted an influence over him that she herself was incapable of. Soon André would be approaching his sixteenth birthday and his First Communion. He seemed to have put away childish things and was imbued with a new religious intensity. That, accompanied by an active, inquiring intelligence, presented its own dangers. This summer it was no longer a question of keeping André out of solitary mischief; a young Protestant companion like Bernard Tissaudier would not suffice, nor even a pastor's son like Emile Ambresin. Nothing short of an actual pastor could provide the spiritual guidance that Juliette Gide felt her son needed. Her choice fell on a certain Elie Allégret, a former missionary in the Congo. He was invited to spend some weeks at La Roque and returned there over the next few years. As a result he and his family became close friends of the Gides. Three years later, in October 1888, it was suddenly decided that André would accompany Pastor Allégret to London. This was the first time André had been abroad and the first time he had travelled anywhere without his mother. Not that she had any intention of being forgotten during the week of separation. The very day of his departure Mme Gide was writing to her son, somewhat apprehensively, it seems: 'And so you see, even in our life together, you are making personal memories of your own, independently of me' – a strange remark to a boy of close on nineteen. She hopes her son will 'thoroughly enjoy' the trip, but adds, inevitably, that she also hopes that he will show due appreciation of it.[21] And what was to be the highlight of his week in London? A night at Covent Garden, perhaps, or Irving at the Lyceum? Probably not with Pastor Allégret as his guide. A Richter concert at least? There is no record of what happened in that week until, at the very end of his life, in *Ainsi soit-il*, Gide describes the major event, which was also, presumably, the reason for going to London in the first place: Pastor Allégret 'took me to hear a preacher called Spurgeon, who was famous in his day and who, after the sermon, used to baptize adults in an *ad hoc* swimming-pool'. Not that André could have understood a word of that sermon: Anna Shackleton does not appear to have left him with much English. Indeed, when approached after the service by a young woman, he replied, without understanding her question, 'No, thank you.' She seemed none too pleased by his reply: apparently, she had asked him if he wanted to be saved.[22]

That summer of 1885, André also had a friend of his own age. The summer before he had become extremely friendly with his neighbour at the Château Val-Richer, François de Witt-Guizot (Lionel of *Si le grain ne meurt*).

Not content with meeting openly on Sundays, when I always went to Val-Richer for tea, we made real lovers' trysts, to which we hastened with beating hearts and trembling thoughts. We agreed on a hiding-place that would serve as a poste-restante; in order to decide where and when we would meet, we exchanged odd, mysterious, coded letters, which could be read only with the help of a key or grid.

The letter was put in a locked casket, hidden in moss, at the foot of an old apple tree, in a meadow on the edge of the wood, half-way between our two houses.[23]

The two swore eternal friendship and broke a cluster of clematis in two, exchanging the halves to be worn as talismans. One Sunday morning, as they were kneeling side by side at family prayers at Val-Richer, François suddenly took André's hand and held it tight for a while. As they parted, André tried to embrace him, but, to his great surprise, he resisted. 'No! Men don't embrace one another!' Not, Gide adds, that the slightest sexuality entered into their relationship: François was exceptionally ugly. Their love, for want of a better word, was chaste: it was also made more intense by a shared passion for matters spiritual. As well as comparing notes on their readings of such writers as Pascal, Bossuet and St Augustine, they would confess their moral lapses to one another. On the matter of masturbation, François took an altogether less serious view. Once, when André, flushed with pride, told his friend that he had resisted temptation for a whole week, François responded with a light-hearted '*Tant mieux!*' ('Good for you!'), and changed the subject. (This last anecdote did not appear in the published version of *Si le grain ne meurt*, but is to be found in the unpublished 'Cahiers d'Alençon', under November 1897.) On sexual matters generally the fifteen-year-old Gide was 'as ignorant as could be . . . I innocently asked him what one could possibly do with a woman.'

October found André and François in Paris and their friendship continued. It did not, however, survive much beyond the following summer. They went on seeing one another for some years to come, but a distinct cooling had set in. François was becoming increasingly aware of his superior social position and developed a devotion to the monarchist cause of the Duc d'Orléans.

André remained under the easygoing supervision of Henry Bauer for another term, then, in January 1886, he was moved to the altogether more serious Pension Keller, in the rue de Chevreuse, a few minutes away from the Ecole Alsacienne, to which, Mme Gide devoutly wished, her son would eventually return. Jacob Keller, a Protestant of Swiss origin, was an excellent teacher. In the eighteen months that André spent with him, he made spectacular progress, so much so that he more than made up for his lost years and was able, in October 1887, a month before his eighteenth birthday, to enter the *classe de rhétorique* at the Ecole Alsacienne.

During his second term at the Pension Keller, André also began to make rapid progress in his piano-playing. This was due entirely to the quality of a new teacher, Marc de La Nux, a native of the island of Réunion in the Indian Ocean and a cousin of the poet Leconte de Lisle. He had been something of a child prodigy. At eleven he came to France: he studied with Liszt, through whom he met Chopin. In 1890 his opera *Zaïre* was staged at the Paris Opéra. He was dark-skinned, tall, thin and, with his long, black hair, his outmoded clothes, with twice-encircled silk cravat, he seemed to belong to the generation of Romantics before his own. Indeed, says Gide, he bore a striking resemblance to Delacroix's self-portrait. His teaching technique was radically different from anything André had so far experienced. 'What a pianist M. de La Nux would have made of me if I had been sent to him earlier!' Gide exclaims with exasperation. He had never been able to memorize any piece: after a few weeks with M. de La Nux, he was able to play several Bach fugues from memory. André's twice-weekly lessons continued for four years. So close had his friendship with M. de La Nux become that, even after the lessons ceased, the young André Gide often visited his old teacher. Years afterwards, Gide learnt that de La Nux had told his mother that if she sacrificed the rest of her son's education to music, he could take over André's teaching on a full-time basis for little or no charge: André had, he assured her, the makings of a professional pianist. Mme Gide had refused de La Nux's proposal and made him promise never to tell her son of it lest it lead him to entertain vain ambitions about his future. Apparently, she had consulted her nephew, Albert Démarest, on the matter and it was through him, when it was too late to do anything about it, that André Gide learnt of his teacher's proposal. Some forty years later, André Gide repaid his teacher's faith in him, while proving the rightness of the view attributed to his mother, by immortalizing his by then forgotten master in the lovable character of the pianist and teacher La Pérouse in *Les Faux-Monnayeurs*.

One of Gide's most memorable musical experiences was a series of piano recitals in which the great Anton Rubinstein demonstrated the history of keyboard composition. André did not attend all the recitals, tickets being, as Mme Gide put it, '*hors de prix*'. The three they did go to were devoted to early music (Bach, Couperin, etc.), to Beethoven and to Schumann. Even here, at her most encouraging, however, Mme Gide managed to thwart André's desires in the interests of morality. André had very much wanted to go to the Chopin recital, but his mother had declared Chopin to be 'unhealthy'. Predictably, Chopin was to become the great musical love of Gide's life. His *Notes sur Chopin* is an interesting appeal to the pianist to conceal, rather than to display, his skill when playing Chopin, to *appear*, at least, to be improvising, to be 'constantly seeking, inventing, gradually discovering his thoughts'.

During his second year at the Pension Keller, André Gide also underwent instruction for his First Communion. Each week he joined ten or so other Protestant boys and girls in the apartment of Pastor Couve in the boulevard Saint-Michel. He was no doubt 'the worthiest man on the face of the earth', but, 'Heavens!, how boring his lessons were!'[24] It was M. Couve who had married André's parents twenty-three years before. So boring did this sensitive youth, his head filled with a somewhat highly charged mystical love of God, his cousin Madeleine and François de Witt find M. Couve's exposition of Protestant belief that he was tempted for the first (but not the last) time by Catholicism. However, when he put his problem to M. Couve, the pastor's fair, judicious exposition of Catholic doctrine was, if anything, even more boring than that of his own beliefs, thus, without realizing it, diverting any Romanizing tendency in his pupil. During the months preceding and following his First Communion, André experienced a degree of religious exaltation that, had he been a Catholic, would have been interpreted as a vocation to the priesthood.

For months on end, I lived in a kind of seraphic state – the state, I suppose, attained by saintliness . . . I had drawn up a time-table for myself and followed it strictly, for its very rigour gave me the greatest satisfaction . . . I rose at dawn and plunged into a tub of icy water . . . Then, before starting work, I read a few verses of Scripture . . . then I prayed. My prayer was like a perceptible movement of the soul towards a deeper penetration into the intimacy of God . . . Out of self-mortification I slept on bare boards; in the middle of the night I got up and knelt down again, not so much out of self-mortification as impatience for joy! I felt then that I had reached the highest point of happiness.[25]

It was a time when, for the young Gide, everything that mattered most to him was imbued with a religious spirit. He would spend his time with François de Witt discussing religious texts; he did the same, by almost daily letter, with Madeleine; music was another door that opened up celestial visions. He had also started to write a journal, thus establishing from the outset the self-reflective core of Gide's literary production. This totally self-absorbed youth had only one subject to write about, the state of his inner feelings. 'I disdained history and regarded events as impertinent intruders.'[26] The form of the journal, for even that apparently most artless literary form, that most unmediated means of turning reality into literature, requires a model, was suggested to Gide by a book recommended to him by Henry Bauer, *Fragments d'un journal intime* by the Swiss writer Henri-Frédéric Amiel (1821–81). Soon after reading it, André Gide began his own journal. The published version begins with the autumn of 1889, but more or less adapted extracts from earlier years were to appear in *Les Cahiers d'André Walter*, Gide's first publication completed before his twenty-first birthday. André Walter's '*cahiers*' were, very largely, André Gide's *cahiers*, an only partly fictional extension of André Gide's own journal. The freedom accorded the writer of 'fiction' allowed the young Gide to explore more deeply the matters touched on in the journal. But, of course, the opposite movement also operated. Not only was 'fiction' a thinly veiled transposition of 'reality', the writing of a journal can also become – some would say inevitably becomes – a form of fiction-writing, even though the use of fictional names for real people may be a trivial indication of this. The 'Em' of the *Journal*, the Alissa of *La Porte étroite* and the Emmanuèle of *Si le grain ne meurt* all had more in common, having sprung fully armed from Gide's head, than any had with the 'real' Madeleine Rondeaux who had not. Gide virtually says as much in *Et nunc manet in te*, that posthumous critique of his relationship with Madeleine. For the adolescent Gide, Madeleine was an 'imaginary figure, an ideal figure that I was inventing': 'It was as if there was nothing good inside me that did not come from her. My childish love became indistinguishable from my first feelings of religious fervour . . . It also seemed to me that, as I came nearer to God, I came closer to her . . .'[27] Of course, life for a seventeen-year-old boy cannot be all ascent on the wings of love, divine and incorporeally human, especially if that boy has become convinced that the flesh is, if not quite the work of the devil, at least his theatre of operations. The almost nightly descents into the hell of the flesh provide a kind of sub-text, in *Les Cahiers d'André Walter*, to the exalted daytime ascents.

And so André Gide took his First Communion and finished his second year at the Pension Keller. Now, at last, he was ready to go back to the Ecole Alsacienne, after an interruption of close on six years. There had, it is true, been attempts before, but these had never lasted more than a few weeks – headaches and other indispositions had seen to that. But the André Gide of October 1887, a month short of his eighteenth birthday, was a creature transformed. The intellectual supervision of Jacob Keller had unlocked the boy's intelligence and directed his considerable will-power in the direction of intellectual achievement. In those days, if one were specializing in *lettres*, that is, the arts subjects or humanities, and most pupils did, the penultimate

class in French secondary education was called the *classe de rhétorique*.
The curriculum consisted almost entirely of the Greek, Latin and French
languages and literatures. A *prof' de lettres* in charge of *rhétorique* taught all
those subjects, though there was the curious practice whereby a teacher
would teach Greek and French one year and Latin the next. The class thus
had two *professeurs titulaires*. At the end of the year, the pupils took the first
part of the *baccalauréat*. By then the average *lycée* pupil, aged about seventeen,
probably had a greater command of the Classics than did the average
graduate in Classics of an English university. As the supremacy of the
Classics declined in French education, as everywhere else, the curriculum
of the *classe de premier* widened and, eventually, the term '*rhétorique*' was
dropped. The next, and final year in French *lycées* was called the *classe de
philosophie*: it was considered quite natural by the architects of the French
educational system that the ultimate year should be devoted almost exclusively to a study of the ultimate in human thought. The *classe de philo'* survived
longer than *rhétorique* and was undoubtedly the bedrock on which the French
intelligentsia was based: it explains the extraordinary facility (in both
senses, good and bad) in the manipulation of ideas and the unmistakably
philosophical accent of French intellectuals in general. With Barthes,
Althusser, Foucault and Derrida, we have probably seen the last of that
particular tradition. The *classe de philo'*, too, is now on its way out.

In his new class at '*L'Alsa*' one pupil in particular attracted Gide's
attention. He was a year younger than Gide, but came consistently top in
French. Gide, timid as ever, longed to be his friend, but, after several weeks,
had still hardly spoken to him. His name was Pierre Louis. Then, one day,
their teacher, M. Dietz, announcing the results for French composition,
startled the entire class with: 'First, Gide; Second, Louis . . .' Gide looked
apprehensively at Louis, who, feigning indifference, continued to sharpen
a pencil. Gide blushed purple with embarrassment. Any hope of being
Louis' friend would now have to be abandoned: they would be deadly
rivals. After class, instead of going into the yard, Gide stayed in the corridor.
He took out of his pocket a copy of Heine's *Buch der Lieder*, which he could
now read in German. Suddenly, Pierre Louis appeared. 'What are you
reading?' he asked in the most natural way imaginable. Gide, struck dumb,
showed him the book. 'So you like poetry,' he said, with a smile. 'Yes, I
know those poems, but in German, I prefer Goethe.' Gide immediately set
to work reading Goethe. Later, when walking through the Bois de Meudon,
the two youths would recite passages from *Faust*, Part 2, to one another,
tears streaming down their cheeks. Pierre Louis lived with his half-brother,

Georges, in the rue Vavin, quite close to the Ecole Alsacienne. His mother had died when he was nine and his father, a retired lawyer, lived at Epernay, in Champagne. Georges, the son of their father's first marriage and twenty-three years Pierre's senior, was unmarried – though he did marry in 1900, aged fifty-three. He was a diplomat by profession and ended a distinguished career as French ambassador to Russia from 1909 to 1913.

The two youths each confessed to the other that he wrote poetry and that his vocation in life was to be a poet. Though Gide soon abandoned poetry in favour of prose, both proved to be very precocious writers. André Gide completed his first published work before his twenty-first birthday; Pierre Louis, changing his name to the less quotidian 'Louÿs', published, at twenty-four, his *Chansons de Bilitis*. Three years later, Debussy set the poems to music.

During their year at '*L'Alsa*' the two friends spent much of their time together, in and out of school. When one of them was ill, the other would come bearing gifts, usually books and his latest piece of writing. They walked the streets of Paris or the woods around the city; they went to concerts and plays. There were certainly insuperable divergences of taste. The temperamental differences were far greater. Louis' visits to the theatre were not confined to the Thursday afternoon performances of the classics at the national theatres. (In those days, French schools were closed on Thursday afternoons and open on Saturday mornings.) Like most Parisian schoolboys of his age, perhaps, he was obsessed with actresses, from Sarah Bernhardt (then forty-three) – '*Oh! Sarah! Sarah! Sarah la grâce! Sarah la jeunesse! Sarah la beauté! Sarah la divine!*' he begins an invocation in his (unpublished) diary for 16 January 1888 – to the humblest performer in some music hall. The year before he was writing: 'I'm seventeen, I'm a virgin and it can't go on much longer like this . . . I swear to God that May will not be out but . . . Oh! The first night and the first woman!' It is difficult to imagine André Gide swearing to God that he would lose his virginity by May or, for that matter, calling on Him to help him preserve it. Where woman was concerned, he had eyes only for Madeleine and his love for her was little more carnal than that of a Catholic youth for the Virgin Mary.

Mme Gide gave Louis her wholehearted approval. He seemed a very well brought up young man and would surely be a good influence on André. Mme Gide was usually suspicious of anything or anybody that aroused her son's enthusiasm. In April 1895 (André was then twenty-five!), she was writing to her brother-in-law, Charles Gide, alarmed by the deplorable

influence that 'this Goethe, of whom he speaks constantly' was having on
her son! One can only conclude that Louis' ability to charm straitlaced
middle-aged ladies (and to conceal his own depravity) was well in excess of
Juliette Gide's understanding of Goethe – one would be hard put to name
a less 'unhealthy' major writer.

The two friends passed the first part of their *baccalauréat* in July 1888 and
set off on their summer holidays. Louis was determined to make the best
of them: he would not rediscover his present '*ardeurs*' when he was seventy.
Gide went off, as usual, to La Roque. The big event of the holidays was the
arrival of the three Rondeaux sisters. That year had seen the legal separation
of their parents. Madeleine, now twenty, was particularly sensitive to her
father's plight. She and André were now, in a sense, closer than ever, each
sharing the other's sorrows and enthusiasms, both swept up in a great wave
of religious feeling that must have looked, to the outsider, like love, but
which, on both sides, excluded physical attraction. Indeed it would probably
be true to say that a degree of revulsion to the physical implications of love
operated on both sides. In *Les Cahiers d'André Walter* there is an entry for
October 1888 that certainly originated in Gide's own journal: 'I spent the
whole of today with her, but our looks did not seek each other out; I did
not move closer to you ... We shall pursue PARALLEL ways: there
was a time when that drove me to despair ...'[28] 'Nous cheminerons
PARALLÈLES': that is an astonishingly acute insight couched in a few
elegantly succinct words for an eighteen-year-old. He had certainly not at
this point in his life read Andrew Marvell's 'The Definition of Love':

> My love is of a birth as rare
> As 'tis for object strange and high:
> It was begotten by despair
> Upon impossibility ...
> As Lines so Loves *oblique* may well
> Themselves in every Angle greet:
> But ours so truly *parallel*,
> Though infinite can never meet.

There could be no finer *epitaphios* for the love of André and Madeleine
Gide, which was to continue its parallel courses for another fifty years.

André Gide and Pierre Louis returned to Paris for their *année de philosophie*,
but not to the Ecole Alsacienne. Georges Louis had moved from the rue
Vavin to Passy and arranged for his brother to attend the Lycée Janson-de-
Sailly. Gide entered the Lycée Henri IV, intellectually the most prestigious

lycée in Paris and therefore in France. Tucked away behind the Panthéon, in the heart of the Latin Quarter, 'H IV' (pron. 'ash catr'), as it was known to its familiars, had the history and allure of an Oxford or Cambridge college. It had been an important Augustinian priory and housed the remains of Descartes, Pascal and Racine. Before that, it had been a basilica, built in the sixth century by Clovis, the first of the Christian Frankish kings, to house the remains of himself, his wife Clotilde and their friend Ste Geneviève. However, none of this seems to have impressed the young André Gide. Indulging his individualism yet again, he decided, after a term, that the communal life of the *lycée* was not for him. But, this time, the symptoms were intellectual rather than physical: 'The study of philosophy seemed to me to require a state of quiet meditation that was incompatible with the atmosphere of the classroom . . .' He persuaded his mother that he would make greater progress having private lessons from M. Lyon, his philosophy teacher at the *lycée*. Not that M. Lyon had inspired him with any great love of philosophy: 'His teaching was the quintessence of dullness.'[29] What saved Gide's interest in philosophy was reading Burdeau's new translation of Schopenhauer's *The World as Will and Idea*, which he read 'from cover to cover and re-read with such intense application of mind that for many months I was impervious to everything happening around me'. It is easy to see why a philosopher whose principal dictum, 'the world is an idea [or representation]', should appeal to the young Gide. Then there was Schopenhauer's romantic pessimism, the view that the world of history, of conflict, was an illusion that brought nothing but pain, that man's salvation was to escape from it into a higher, essential reality, to which music and poetry were the purest means of access. Gide went on to appreciate Spinoza, Descartes and Leibnitz even more – and to make the decisive philosophical encounter of his life, with Nietzsche.

André Gide did make one important friend during his term at Henry IV. At the time Léon Blum had literary ambitions, like all the more intelligent *lycéens*. Though never a novelist or poet, he did become a literary and drama critic. His real career, of course, was to be in politics. While at the Ecole Normale Supérieure he became a socialist, converting an initially dubious Gide to the Dreyfus cause. Gide continued to see Pierre Louis regularly. He also met Pierre's new friends in the *classe de philo'* at Janson. One of these, Marcel Drouin, was recognized by all who knew him as a young man to be the most intellectually brilliant individual they had ever encountered. He was consistently top of his class, not only at Janson, but also, later, at the Ecole Normale; in the *agrégation*, at the end of his higher education, he came first throughout France. He was to remain a lifelong friend of André Gide if only because he became his brother-in-law, marrying Jeanne Rondeaux a few years after André married Madeleine. Through Louis, Gide met two other fellow-pupils with literary ambitions: Legrand, who, as Franc-Nohain, became a poet, and Maurice Quillot, who ended up, not as a writer, but as a milk producer. They were both Nivernais and it was at Nevers that Maurice Quillot founded a literary magazine, *Potache-Revue* (*potache* is slang for 'schoolkid'). They all wrote for the magazine, mainly under pseudonyms: Gide appeared as 'Zan-Bal-Dar' and 'Bernard Durval'.

Meanwhile, André had become much closer to his cousin, Albert Démarest, on whom he called almost every day at his studio in the rue de la Grande-Chaumière, off the boulevard du Montparnasse. At the beginning of André's *année de philosophie* Albert began a portrait of him posing, instrument in hand, as 'The Violinist'. At this time, but not for very long, Gide looked no more than his age – nineteen – sporting the air of a *fin-de-siècle* dandy: long hair and flowing *lavallière* cravat. During these sessions, Albert confided in his cousin, telling him of his disappointed hopes as an artist, of how his exuberant gaiety hid long-standing bitterness and, finally, of his liaison with Marie, which he had kept secret to spare his mother's feelings. For the young André Gide, Albert Démarest presented a persuasive counter-example: do at twenty what you really believe you want to do. Do not wait another twenty years, family and sensible advice notwithstanding. Through Albert, too, André was introduced into the social life that centred on the studio of Jean-Paul Laurens, Albert's teacher and *patron*. He became a good friend of the painter's son, Paul Laurens, whom he had known in one of his earlier classes at the Ecole Alsacienne.

Given young André's multifarious, non-philosophical activities – hours spent discussing literature with Pierre Louis and his friends, piano lessons and practice, long, frequent correspondence with his cousins, the writing of his journal, it was hardly surprising that he failed the second part of his '*bachot*' in July 1889. There was perhaps another reason: he was *too* interested in philosophy. As so often happens, the potentially more interesting minds work unevenly, concentrating on what most interests them, and striking the examiners, who probably do not share their views, as opinionated. Anyway, Gide already knew what he was going to do with his life and academic qualifications seemed irrelevant. However, under pressure from his mother, he agreed to spend some of the summer studying seriously and to retake the examination in October. But he also had other ideas about how he was going to spend the summer. His journal was already taking fictional form. It might be called *Allain*, after its hero, or *La Nouvelle Education sentimentale*. Allain was a Breton: accordingly, André was determined to set off, alone, for part of the summer at least, tramping through Brittany. His mother objected flatly: Switzerland would be much healthier. What is more, he should not be alone: he should join some Alpine Club, which would organize his time for him. André won the argument, but at the cost of an extraordinary compromise: he would go to Brittany alone, but his mother would follow in his footsteps, meeting up with him every two days at places arranged in advance.

André Gide took with him on the journey that was to be a stage in his own journey of self-discovery Flaubert's *roman de formation, L'Education sentimentale*, and Goethe's *bildungsroman, Wilhelm Meisters Lehrjahre*. They provided a sort of model. The holiday provided the scenery: the moors of Malestroit, the ponds of Couedèlo, the stagnant waters of Locmariaquer, the mists of Morbihan and the cliffs of Belle-Isle all appear in *Les Cahiers*. One evening, Gide arrived at a village inn. He was shown into a sparsely furnished, whitewashed room, in which a great many canvases were stacked against the wall. When he was left alone, he immediately went over to inspect the paintings. They struck him at the time as being of an almost childish, carefree exuberance; they were not like any paintings he had seen before. He was then taken into the dining-room and found himself in the company of three painters. It was their work that he had just seen. A year or more later he met one of them at Mallarmé's: it was Gauguin.

André Gide returned from Brittany and set about swotting for his '*bachot*'. In the event, he scraped through. At his mother's insistence he registered to take the *licence-ès-lettres* at the Sorbonne and agreed to have private lessons from M. Dietz, his old French teacher from the Ecole Alsacienne. But he had no intention of becoming a student. His days of apprenticeship were over: he was now a writer.

4

André Walter: Puritan and Narcissist

(OCTOBER 1889 – JUNE 1891)

Young writers need a garret. So, one autumn afternoon in 1889, André Gide and Pierre Louÿs climbed to the top floor of a house in the rue Monsieur-le-Prince to inspect a large, unfurnished room. Under the steeply sloping ceiling, 'a window, just waist-high, provides a view over the roofs of the Ecole de Médecine and the Latin Quarter, an expanse of grey houses as far as the eye can see, the Seine and Notre-Dame in the setting sun, and, in the far distance, Montmartre, barely visible in the rising evening mist'. Echoing Balzac's hero Rastignac, looking across Paris from the heights of Père Lachaise, they cried (or Gide, at least, thought): 'Et maintenant . . . à nous deux!'[1]

Of course, the entire episode was no more than a gesture. The two young men had no intention of living in a garret, still less of earning a living by what they might write in it. Louÿs would continue to eat and sleep in his brother's home in Passy; Gide would do likewise in his mother's more conveniently situated apartment in the rue de Commaille; after all, Gide was not yet twenty, or Louÿs nineteen. The purpose of the room, it seems, was for meetings of their *cénacle*, their group of literary friends. In the event nothing came of the idea; no other rooms were visited. Gide makes no mention of the incident in *Si le grain ne meurt*, but it is given prominence by opening the published version of the *Journal*.

The next step was the founding of a new review, to be called, with touching modesty, *Le Journal des Inconnus*. Did its contributors expect the circulation to be so low that they would remain unknown or would becoming known debar them from further participation in the review? The 'statutes' placed an age limit of twenty-five on contributors, a barrier that must have seemed as remote to those twenty-year-olds as fame, and therefore as little a threat. In addition to the two dominant figures, Gide and Louÿs, the editorial board consisted of Marcel Drouin, André Walckenaër (the great-nephew of Gide's Aunt Claire Démarest) and Léon Blum.

*

In January 1890, with a view to asking his advice, Gide and Louis called on the well-nigh decrepit Paul Verlaine in the Hôpital Broussais, where the poet stayed periodically for care and attention while trying to dry out. In fact, Verlaine was only forty-five and had another six years to live. He was at his most lucid at the time and talked to the two young men of Mallarmé, of Rimbaud and of his own work. He greatly impressed his visitors, but his down-to-earth description of the poet's craft must have come as a shock to the young aesthetes: 'It's like joinery, or rather *charcuterie*. Verses have to be rounded off like a blood sausage.'[2]

A few weeks later, André went to Rouen to give moral support to his *cousines*: their father, Emile Rondeaux, was obviously dying. Madeleine, who had always been devoted to her father, had drawn even closer to him, become more protective of him, since the discovery of her mother's adultery. André and Madeleine were alone with him at the last. This shared experience, the 'brother' comforting his 'sister' in her grief, brought them closer than ever, providing the perfect focus for their confused, half-understood amalgam of sexual love and fraternal affection. One does not have to be a Freudian to recognize the uniquely potent situation of a young woman kneeling beside her dying father, her hand clasped in that of her 'brother', 'lover' and future 'husband' (the inverted commas are appropriate in all three cases). André certainly saw that *Liebestod* as a sort of sanctified, if unofficial, betrothal; so, too, in a sense, despite all her hesitations and uncertainties, did Madeleine.

In his twenty-first year, then, André Gide had two overriding ambitions: to become a writer and to marry Madeleine. Indeed the two were indissolubly linked, since his book recounted his relationship with his cousin in a virtually untransposed way. It would be 'so noble, so moving, so insistent' that all objections to the marriage would fade and Madeleine could no longer refuse him. The only problem confronting André, then, was to get down to finishing it. And to do that he would have to leave Paris, with its endless conversations with Pierre Louÿs and his friends, its more exalted socializing with 'a few Society ladies . . . such as Mme Dolfus-Mieg, etc.' (a rather untypical note this, intended probably to impress his mother), trying to run the apartment in the rue de Commaille in his mother's absence ('Your errands have been done; money has been given to Marie; the builders are coming. Mercy me, how complicated living is and how curious I'd be to see what would happen if, just once, one didn't bother with any of all that'), not to mention writing long letters to his mother (from which these quotations come) every couple of days or so.

Finally, on 18 May, the young writer set off for a small hotel on the tiny lake at Pierrefonds, some 50 miles to the north-east of Paris. He was not to be left in peace for long: two days after his arrival, Pierre Louis turned up. André returned in haste to Paris and headed southwards and farther afield. Investigating the area around Grenoble, his choice fell on Menthon, a lakeside village near Annecy. He rented two rooms (to which a third was later added, at no extra cost) in a charming cottage surrounded with orchards. For the first time in his life he was entirely on his own: in Brittany, the previous summer, his mother had followed hard upon. Her presence was not so easily banished, however: long letters, often containing detailed accounts of expenditure, were sent off every two or three days, in response to equally long letters from her consisting almost entirely, it seems, of questions. Sometimes two would arrive in quick succession: 'In the first you ask me 24 questions – I counted them; my heart failed me to count those in the second. Not being able to answer all of them, I think it wiser not to answer any of them . . .'3 His main meals, even his breakfast, were provided for him, but there were certain things, like making a pot of tea, that he now had to do for himself. A delightful account of this operation, depicting André in the guise of some not very bright sorcerer's apprentice trying to remember the recipe for one of his mother's concoctions, takes up a good part of a letter to Madeleine's sister, Jeanne. It reveals not only a sense of comedy, but a capacity for self-mockery rare in so serious a young man and certainly absent from the book he was writing at the time.

There were certain home comforts, however, that the young André Gide could not do without: a piano was ordered from Annecy, no simple matter, as it turned out. Annecy itself boasted only one '*détestable*' instrument; anything worth playing (which for André, meant nothing less than a Gaveau or a Pleyel) had to be ordered from Grenoble or Geneva, with the attendant expense of its transportation. This Homeric enterprise, the getting of a piano from Grenoble to Menthon, which, in Gide's account (to his mother), seems to rival the assembling of the Greek forces before the walls of Troy, culminated in the carrying of the '*grand Cheval d'Ilios*' down the treacherous gravel path to the chalet, then up the steep, rickety stairs to his rooms. To be fair to Gide, a piano should not be classified, in his case, as a home comfort. Music was central to his existence and central, too, to the book that he was writing: Bach, Chopin and Schumann permeate its pages almost as much as Plato, Spinoza and Schopenhauer, or Homer, Dante and Flaubert.

Menthon turned out to be a place of literary associations. Renan had a house there. Rousseau had lived there for a time and Eugène Sue died there. Hippolyte Taine and his family were staying nearby: a great admirer of Taine, André Gide had just read *La Philosophie de l'art, de l'intelligence*, and *La Littérature anglaise*, but he did not pluck up courage to call on him. He did some climbing, four hours of it, and found it, the company of Schopenhauer notwithstanding, *assommant*, deadly boring. His presence in the village did not pass unnoticed: 'The inhabitants of Menthon have had some difficulty getting used to my hair [it was still very long, in the style of the early Romantics], my short trousers, etc. And, since M. Taine has taught them that man proceeded from the monkey, they take me for some intermediary species.'⁴ Apart from his mother and other members of his family, Gide's most frequent correspondent during this period was Pierre Louis. In February 1890, the initial infatuation was still in force, at least on Louis' part, if a letter from him to Jean Naville is to be believed: 'of all our friends . . . he is the one who has the greatest future and by a long chalk. If I have ever known a terrific fellow [*un type épatant*] it is he. Believe me, I would give a lot to have one day the prose that he has now.'⁵

Gide left Menthon on 5 July and, after a few days in Paris, went on to La Roque where he hoped to finish the book before the summer was out: in fact, he had set himself a deadline, 22 November, his twenty-first birthday. At La Roque he was alone with his mother until mid-August, when they were joined by Madeleine and her two sisters. The evenings were spent reading aloud, each in turn, Flaubert's *La Tentation de Saint Antoine*, Renan's *L'Avenir de la science* and Tolstoy's *Anna Karenina*. By the end of August, the first draft of *Allain* (or *Alain*, as *Les Cahiers d'André Walter* was still called at this stage) was finished. André left La Roque at once for Paris, where he handed over the manuscript, not to Pierre Louis, who had assumed that the honour would be his, but to his cousin Albert Démarest: only he could be depended on to come up with a sensitive, unbiased opinion. Albert's response was, on the whole, encouraging, but he was 'dismayed by my excessive pietism and the abundant Scriptural quotations. How abundant they were may be judged from what remains of them after I had followed his advice and cut two-thirds of them . . .'⁶ André Gide spent the rest of September implementing Cousin Albert's advice. The final version was typed professionally and Gide took it along to Didier Perrin, who had recently published Maurice Barrès' highly esteemed *L'Homme libre*. Perrin agreed to publish *Les Cahiers d'André Walter*, at the author's expense. Mme Gide, to her credit, agreed to foot the bill.

Only then, with publication guaranteed, did Gide finally inform Pierre

Louis that the book was finished. The response was typically exuberant: '*Alain* finished I feel as relieved as if I had done it myself.' But, he goes on, it was very cruel of Gide not to have shown it to him. He freely admits his annoyance that Gide has beaten him to it. 'It is true, of course, that you write very vulgar prose, while I wallow in the ethereal . . . And what about Art? You don't really care about it very much, do you? Well, we'll see how it turns out.'⁷ Gide did not hand over the manuscript to Louis but read it to him aloud.

Pierre Louis had another claim on the book: at the height of their friendship they had promised one another that in the first book to be published by each of them a page of the manuscript would be left blank, to be filled in by the other. In one of his letters, Louis reminds Gide of their promise: 'Oh! Almost nothing, half a page . . . like little girls who stick cut flowers in the arms of their Virgin in church . . .'⁸ Gide was to keep his promise, in a sense, with strict limitations on Louis' room for manoeuvre, in fact making use of Louis to serve his own ends. In the journal Gide adds: 'Arrive suddenly, unexpectedly . . . *or rather remain unknown*, but hear the work acclaimed – *for I shall not give my name.*'⁹ This is, of course, André Walter speaking of his novel *Allain*. Now André Walter is simultaneously writing *two* books: *Allain* and his *cahiers*. In the event, it is not *Allain* that is published, but the *cahiers*. In the real world, of course, there was no *Allain* and no 'André Walter'. The author of *Les Cahiers d'André Walter* was André Gide, but he could not claim credit for a book by a named but fictitious author. In fact, it was Gide who set up a situation in which he would 'remain unknown, but hear the work acclaimed – for I shall not give my name'. Rather than pose as André Walter's executor, presenting his friend's 'note-books' to the public, he excluded himself entirely from the game and made Pierre Louis (or 'Pierre Chrysis', as Louis sometimes signed himself at this period) the ostensible executor of the dead 'André Walter'. When *Les Cahiers d'André Walter* appeared in 1891, it bore no author's name and was subtitled '*œuvre posthume*'. Towards the end of the book, four weeks or so before André Walter dies, we read: 'ALLAIN. – The work must be finished. – But madness is imminent . . . Oh! To leave something, not to die completely; my notebook then, if Allain isn't finished or if I go mad too soon . . . Let Pierre C***, to whom I leave them, publish these notebooks . . . If he publishes my notebooks, let him keep *Allain*; one or the other.'¹⁰ 'Pierre Chrysis' chooses to publish the notebooks (he has no choice, of course, there being no *Allain*).

In the Preface, which was Louis' idea, 'Pierre Chrysis' tells us that André Walter was born on 20 December 1871 (two years after André Gide), in

Brittany, of a Breton Catholic mother and a 'Saxon' Protestant father, the product, as Gide saw himself to be, of a conjunction of 'two races'. The German influence, the Preface informs us, accounts for the author's metaphysical bent, while he derived his religious austerity from the mother. Of actual events in André Walter's life there is little to tell, the preface goes on: the drama of his life was 'played out in the soul'. After the death of his mother, he retired to Brittany to write. At his request, his friends ceased all communication with him. In under a year news reached them of his death from brain fever (meningitis), shortly before his twentieth birthday. In addition to the *cahiers* and the novel *Allain*, he left a number of other manuscripts, including poems, which may be published in due course. (The poems that Gide published in 1892 as *Les Poésies d'André Walter* had, in fact, not yet been written.)

So what manner of book was *Les Cahiers d'André Walter*, now shorn of two-thirds of its biblical quotations and much else? The book falls into two roughly equal halves. The *Cahier blanc*, white being the colour of purity, recounts the nineteen-year-old Walter's love for Emmanuèle, his cousin, who, after the death of her parents, was adopted and brought up by André's parents as his 'sister'. Like André Gide and Madeleine, André Walter and Emmanuèle spend much of their time reading together – the Greek and French classics, Shakespeare – and playing Chopin and Schumann on the piano. Their love, they felt, was already sanctified by God: their idea of a romantic carriage-ride through the night, sitting next to one another, a shawl covering their knees, is to read the Bible to one another. André's mother, however, regards the love between her son and niece to be no more than that appropriate between brother and sister, indeed André often addresses Emmanuèle as '*soeurette*', 'little sister'. André, however, is deter-mined to marry Emmanuèle, though she clearly shares many of her aunt's doubts and would certainly not oppose her wishes. André is ordered by his mother, who is close to death, to abandon his attentions. Possible suitors are considered and, before long, Emmanuèle is engaged to a certain 'T.'. ('T.' had particularly unpleasant associations for Gide, since the man with whom Madeleine's mother eloped was called Talabart.) On his mother's deathbed, André joins the betrothed couple, who are kneeling, hand-in-hand, beside the dying woman. (It will be remembered that, a few months before beginning this work, André Gide had knelt, hand-in-hand, with Madeleine, at her father's deathbed.) 'Rest in peace, mother,' André Walter writes. 'You have been obeyed.' Emmanuèle and T. marry and André goes off to Brittany to write his novel, *Allain*.

The *Cahier noir*, symbolizing the black of mourning and despair, begins. The only event referred to in this section is the death of Emmanuèle, although, even here, the author does his best to expunge it. 'The next page is left blank in the manuscript,' a comment in editorial parentheses tells us – blank, that is to say, except for a date: 4 August. A footnote informs us that 'Mme Emmanuèle T. died on the night of 31 July; André Walter did not learn of it until three days later.' Towards the end, André Walter senses the onset of madness and death: will he finish his book in time? Allain is already mad; will the author outlive his hero? A few days later, André Walter is hallucinating: Emmanuèle comes to visit him. He tells her that he thought she was dead; they both laugh. Outside it is snowing: everything is white (*blanc*, like the blank page in his book). The last words of *Les Cahiers* are: 'The snow is pure.' The ink has stopped flowing and the *Cahier noir* has reverted to the pure whiteness of silence and non-existence.

One would be forgiven for asking if *anything* happens in *Les Cahiers*. Well, a lot of writing and a lot of reading take place: the book is writing about writing and reading. In fictional terms, it is André Walter's notebook, in which he comments on the book *he* is writing, *Allain*, and on his reading. *Allain* may not exist, but André Walter's (that is, André Gide's) reading does. *Les Cahiers* is crammed full of comments on and quotations from Gide–Walter's reading. In addition to the remaining thirty or so quotations from the Bible, French literature of every period is strongly represented and there are quotations in Greek, Latin, Italian and German. There is even a quotation from *King Lear* but, and this says much about French education at the time, it is in French translation: Gide expected his readers to recognize and understand Aeschylus in Greek script, but clearly thought that a few such words as 'Through the sharp hawthorn blows the cold wind' would be met with blank incomprehension.

If nothing much *happens* in *Les Cahiers d'André Walter*, what, to keep to vernacular critical usage, is the book *about*? At the broadest, it is about Gide's state of mind in his late teens. More specifically it is about the young author's relationship with Madeleine and his mother. In the book, all three die. Mme Gide may not have appreciated being killed off by her son, but she would have endorsed entirely the view attributed to her that the 'fraternal' relationship between the two cousins was not a proper basis for marriage. Madeleine herself believed at the time that her mind was made up to refuse her cousin. She only conceded defeat five years later, at the age of twenty-eight, with rapidly vanishing alternative matrimonial prospects, and after the death of André's mother, who had come round to the view that the cousins' marriage would be the best course for both of them. *Les Cahiers d'André Walter* was 'a long declaration, a profession of love' but it makes clear that André Walter's love of Emmanuèle, like André Gide's for Madeleine, was pure and Platonic: by implication the marriage, too, would exclude physical congress. 'In order not to disturb her purity, I shall abstain from all caresses . . . even the most chaste . . . *lest she come to desire more, which I should not be able to give her* . . . To love by the soul alone a soul that loves you in the same way, so that both, becoming so similar through a slow education, come to know one another to the point of merging . . . So I do not desire you. *Your body embarrasses me and carnal possession appals me.*'[11]

But the flesh is not absent from *Les Cahiers*. In *Si le grain ne meurt*, Gide writes: 'My puritanical upbringing had turned the claims of the flesh into something monstrous . . . Yet the state of chastity, I had to admit, was an insidious and precarious one; since every other relief was denied me, I fell back into the vice of my early childhood . . . With a great deal of love, music, metaphysics and poetry, this was the subject of my book.'[12] It would be truer to say, perhaps, that it formed a subtext, a submerged subject visible only to those with eyes to see: clearly it did not strike Gide's mother as being one of the book's subjects, together with love, music, etc., or she would not have paid for its publication. Yet it is there, wrapped up in the religious language of temptation: 'You shut yourself up in your room, the enemy shuts himself up there with you.'[13] It is also there, more graphically, in the dreams of the deranged André Walter. Here the body reveals its 'other desires'. Walter peopled his loneliness with 'the subtle forms of children playing on the beach, whose beauty haunted me: I would like to have bathed with them and felt, beneath my hands, the softness of brown skins . . . I was overcome with fury that I was not one of them, one of those good-for-nothings of the open road, who spend all day prowling around in the sun, then at night lie down in a ditch, without care for the cold or rain; and, when they are feverish, plunge, completely naked, into the coolness of streams . . . *And who do not think.*'[14] They are not just a sexual fantasy: they represent amoral, unreflecting physicality and rootless, homeless freedom of movement. They are another avatar of one pole of Gide's psychological dualism, represented elsewhere by 'the little boy amusing himself', the Gide who became the sensualist traveller, forever moving on from one place, one encounter, to another. (Such passages are lifted, with little change, from Gide's own journal – which is why, when he began to publish entries from it, the earliest is dated 'autumn 1899'.) But if André Walter's dreams hold forth the earthly delights that were later to be enjoyed by André Gide in reality, with younger members of his own sex, there is also a negative, even terrifying side to André Walter's oneiric sexuality. In a passage unequivocally headed 'Nightmare', André Walter dreams of his dead beloved Emmanuèle:

She appeared before me, very beautiful, wearing a dress of orphrey, which reached to her feet . . . She was standing erect, her head to one side, a sickly smile on her face. A monkey hopped on to the scene; he raised the dress, swinging the fringes. And I was afraid to look; I wanted to avert my gaze, but, despite myself, I did look. Under the dress, there was nothing; it was black, black as a hole; I sobbed despairingly. Then, with both hands, she seized the hem of her dress and threw it back over her face. She turned herself inside-out, like a sack. And I could no longer see anything . . . I woke up out of sheer terror.[15]

Whether André Gide had such a nightmare or merely imagined it for fictional purposes is, of course, undecidable, although, given what we know of Gide's working methods on this book, he probably did not invent it. Either way, it could hardly be more startlingly revealing of Gide's fear of the female body as a sexual object. Emmanuèle (or Madeleine or Woman) appears first as a hieratic, almost religious figure: the unusual word 'orphrey' refers to gold embroidery applied to ecclesiastical vestments. Her smile, however, is equivocal, *mièvre* in French, meaning 'sickly', 'mawkish', 'nause-ating' even. The monkey, that reminder of our animal ancestry, reveals the female body to be a terrifying *black hole*, inspiring in the viewer a *horror vacui*, a fear of the void. Women are objects of spiritual love: they may be social, even intellectual companions, but they must remain clothed.

André Gide had finished *Les Cahiers d'André Walter* well before the self-imposed deadline of his twenty-first birthday. In due course, the proofs arrived; he spent days labouring over them. Finally, minutes before his twentieth year was up, the job was finished. Gide manages to make the proof-reading of his first book sound more arduous than the writing of it – and not, it would seem, to much avail. When, on 1 January 1891, the first copies arrived – he had joined his mother, who had decided to spend Christmas and the New Year at an hotel in Arcachon – he saw to his disgust that a lot of the printer's errors had survived. In the event, Perrin turned out to be no better a bookseller than a printer: the book went on sale in late February, but virtually no copies were sold. So, when the *de luxe* edition of 190 copies arrived from Bailly in April, Gide decided to pulp the entire Perrin printing, except for the complimentary copies that had already been sent out to the press and to influential literary figures. In the second *de luxe* edition, incidentally, and in all subsequent editions of the work, the Preface by 'Pierre Chrysis' was dropped: Gide's affections were already on the turn.

Gide planned to have a few copies refer to the hero's cousin not as 'Emmanuèle', but as 'Madeleine'. He presented one of these, in a special copy printed on rice paper, to Madeleine in person (she had meanwhile joined her aunt and cousin at the hotel), insisting that she read it that evening. It bore the dedication 'A ma bien-aimée Madeleine', followed by two quotations from the Song of Songs: 'Awake, O North Wind; And come thou South; Blow upon my garden that the spices thereof may flow out. Let my beloved come into his garden, and eat his pleasant fruits' and 'At our gates are all manner of pleasant fruits, new and old, which I have laid up for thee O my beloved' (Authorized Version, 4:16; 7:13). Madeleine did not read the book that evening; in fact, she refused to do so until André had left. In this way, she hoped to put off the inevitable proposal of marriage. When she did read *Les Cahiers*, she tells us in her (unpublished) diary, she was moved to tears. However, she felt that André had no right to publish for general consumption what was so clearly an account of their relationship, even to the point of having her own words repeated in it – not to mention her own name unchanged in some of the copies. Madeleine did not comment directly on the book, but rejected André's proposal of marriage. Gide refused to regard her refusal as final and said that he would bide his time. He had failed in both great aims: he had not leapt to fame as *the* writer of his generation and he had not won Madeleine's hand.

Sales of *Les Cahiers d'André Walter* may have been negligible, but the complimentary and review copies elicited a generally favourable response: Gide was now launched on a literary career. Many commentators adopted the usual procedure of assuming that a new, very young writer was speaking for 'youth' or at least manifesting some imminent tendency. Remy de Gourmont, in the Symbolist monthly *Mercure de France*, called the book a 'condensation of withdrawn, timorous youth'. Gide's own view of the book was complex. At the time of writing, he did not regard it as his first book, the beginning of a long literary career, but as his '*Summa*', the ultimate statement about himself and his position in the world. He could see nothing beyond it. Moreover, so convinced was he that he spoke not only for himself, but for a whole generation, that he was haunted by the fear that *someone else* might be writing a similar book and publish it before him. Later, Gide came to dislike it intensely. After being virtually unobtainable for some thirty-five years, a limited edition was published by G. Crès in 1925. In 1930, the same publisher reissued *Les Cahiers*, together with *Les Poésies d'André Walter*. For that edition, the now celebrated Gide wrote a Preface, by way of apology for a book that he could not open 'without pain and even mortification'. That edition, in turn, went out of print and the book was never republished in Gide's lifetime. Even now *Les Cahiers* is the only one of Gide's fictional works not to appear in Gallimard's collected Pléiade edition. In the 1930 Preface, Gide writes: 'My excuse is that at the time of André Walter I was not yet twenty. At that age I did not know how to write and, precisely perhaps because I felt within me new things to be said, I was groping my way. I was trying to bend the language to my will: I had not yet realized how much more one learns by bending oneself to its will . . .' He came to realize that one cannot write good French, whose prime virtue is its clarity, while trying to evoke the misty resonance of German. But there were 'more secret faults'. He was at the time 'an obstinate young puritan':[16] what the young Gide imagined to be sincere self-expression was merely the result of his puritanical upbringing, which, 'by teaching me to struggle against my inclinations, satisfied a taste for struggle and specious austerity'.[17] Such a struggle now struck him as pointless and the pride resulting from a victory pernicious; far better to give in to one's desires and to cease fighting oneself. Again, at the end of his life, he remarked to Jean Amrouche that *Les Cahiers* represented a struggle against what he saw as the two great enemies of the Christian faith, sex (*la sensualité*) and the critical spirit, the two things that he later came to value above everything else.[18]

In May 1890, André refused an invitation from his Uncle Charles to attend the celebrations for the 600th anniversary of the founding of the University of Montpellier, where Charles Gide was now professor of law: he was working on *Les Cahiers* at the time. Pierre Louis attended the celebrations as a member of the Sorbonne student body. There he met a nineteen-year-old law student: Paul-Ambroise Valéry was already a poet of astonishing precocity, if not yet the Paul Valéry that he was to become, the greatest French poet of the twentieth century and the only obvious successor to Mallarmé. The two struck up a close friendship that was subsequently continued by letter. Gide's relations with Louis were already strained; they were not improved by Louis' evident enthusiasm for '*le petit Montpelliérain*'. Nevertheless, Gide's curiosity was aroused – as was Valéry's in Gide's regard. On 10 December Gide arrived at his uncle's apartment in Montpellier, having arranged to meet Valéry the following day. In the fictional *Les Nourritures terrestres*, in a sort of litany of gardens, Gide recalls his first meetings with Valéry

at Montpellier, the botanical gardens. I remember, one evening, sitting there with Ambroise . . . on an ancient tomb, surrounded with cypresses; and we talked slowly, chewing rose petals. One night, from the Promenade du Peyrou, we saw the sea in the distance, silvered by the moon; nearby the cascades of the town's water tower could be heard; black swans fringed with white swam in the quiet pool.[19]

The 'ancient tomb' was reputedly that of Eliza, the daughter of Edward Young, the poet of *Night Thoughts*. It came to have especial significance for both young men. In March of that year, Valéry published his poem 'Narcisse parle', bearing as its epigraph words taken from the inscription on the grave: '*Narcissae placandis manibus*' (To appease Narcissa's shade – Narcissa being the name given to his daughter in Young's work).

As so often with Gide, a new 'best friend' emerged just as his interest in another was fading. Louis, who had been instrumental in bringing them together, would be supplanted by Valéry. Gide had found a friend whom he could respect, admire, treat as an equal, in a way he could no longer do with Louis. For his part, Valéry was as overwhelmed as Gide. 'I am in a state of ecstasy and delight with your friend Gide,' he wrote to Louis. 'What a rare, exquisite mind . . . I envy you such friendships.'[20] When Gide returned to Paris, a regular correspondence began. One of the most striking things, to the modern reader, is the open expression, on both sides, of an affection bordering on the amatory; sometimes, if only in jest, those early letters carry an overtly sexual reference, especially when the existence of the 'third party', Pierre Louis, introduces an element of jealousy. On 11 March, in a letter commenting on *Les Cahiers*, Valéry writes: 'Higher still. The icy peak. Everything . . . Your hand has pulled me up there. Thank you again. Then: "All this is thine – if thou wishest to *love* me. – Yes, lord."'[21] In the next letter Gide picks up on what is, after all, a biblical reference, and turns it to his own ends: '"If thou wishest to love me" – And you answer "yes" – it is an absolute that terrifies me . . . What do you yourself know of it? And until when? All affection makes me anxious . . . For I cannot rest in friendship, but always want it to be longer lasting, deeper and more trusting.'[22] Valéry does not respond specifically to Gide's probings, but he is no less affectionate in his reply and clearly does not regard them as anything untoward. The three-cornered relationship with Valéry and Louis sometimes brought out the worst in Gide. On 17 June, he wrote a letter to Valéry that consists almost entirely of a series of complaints against Louis. It is the tone, which we would find more suited to an amatory relationship, that surprises. 'Louis hurt me [*m'a meutri*] cruelly yesterday,' he writes. 'You know how feelings are with me . . . I was really dying to see him again [*le désir que j'avais de le revoir me brûlait vraiment le coeur*]; in friendship I am like a lover with a mistress . . .' Gide now slips in a few barbs at Louis' expense: 'We went out together and I spent the time (O such sweet intimacies!) listening to him pulling Huysmans to pieces . . .' (Huysmans was one of Valéry's favourite authors.) 'Then Louis talked about you; he holds it against you that you don't profess allegiance to Heredia and de Lisle.' Lest it be assumed that this almost suggestive tone was peculiar to Gide, the incipient homosexual, here is Paul Valéry's reply, perfectly at home in the mode: 'Dear heart, wounded like a drunken, bleeding bird, your letter has quite pained me . . . Louis is a child, you are both children . . . Allay his fever with the magic of your smiles and caresses . . . Then let us remain, all of us, in the green night to which I summon you, hand in hand, without a thought that we are others, but certain of our unity, of our perfect merging into a single person.'[23] There was nothing unusual about the tone adopted in these letters: it was one readily employed by educated men at the time.

The Gide/Louis relationship had now embarked on its long decline. Temperamentally, Gide's cult of seriousness and sincerity ran quite counter to Louis' cynicism and flippancy. Gide was seldom amused when Louis perpetrated one of his many practical jokes at his expense. There was the letter that arrived at La Roque addressed to 'Mlle Andrée Gide' and bearing a large seal on which the intertwined letters 'P.L' were inscribed. Inside was the message 'I love you' in several languages. On another occasion, Gide was told that a sick friend wanted to see him and, on arrival at the address given, was warmly received by a prostitute who set about trying to initiate him.[24] More seriously, Gide had begun to dislike the way in which Louis approached literature, that highly analytical, at times destructive, claustrophobic manner employed by a certain type of Parisian intellectual: 'Louis has made me hate books. Yet there is something other than books. Books are not *necessary*. And why do we have to have books?'[25] Gide, who never had to earn a living and spent most days of his life reading and writing (often about his reading), must have been sorely tried to talk of *hating* books. What we see here is the emergence of that other side of Gide, the impulse to move on, the lust for experience, which, with the hours spent with books, was to form one of his most enduring dualities.

It was largely through Louis that Gide entered the world of the Parisian literary *cénacles* and *salons*. In June 1890, Louis returned to Paris and set about obtaining all the right contacts for his various literary projects – he was still only nineteen. He believed in going to the top and so, without introduction, he called on Mallarmé, who was typically generous in his encouragement. The following week he attended the first of his *Mardis* at Mallarmé's apartment in the rue de Rome. By the close of the year, Louis had become friendly with two other poets, Henri de Régnier, a rising star of the younger generation, and José Maria de Heredia, whose Saturday afternoon *salon* at his apartment at 11 bis rue de Balzac, near the Champs-Elysées, had become one of the most brilliant of the time.

During much of 1890, while Louis had been practising self-promotion ('*auto-lançage*', his own term) in literary Paris, Gide had been away from the capital working on his first book. With the publication of *Les Cahiers*, Gide, too, was in a position to pursue his own promotion, though his way was a good deal less forceful than Louis'. Indeed it began almost by accident. On the morning of 31 January, Gide was at the back of Perrin's bookshop, standing beside the piles of his newly published book, when the young, much-acclaimed novelist Maurice Barrès came in. Idly leafing through a copy, Barrès remarked to Perrin that it was an 'astounding' ('*stupéfiant*') book and regretted that he had not met the author. Introductions were made at once, followed by an invitation to lunch with Barrès the following day. That evening Barrès took him to a literary banquet in honour of the Symbolist poet, Jean Moréas. Gide was struck at once by the similarities between the aims of the Symbolists and his own work. 'All their theories, all their professions of faith,' he wrote to Valéry, 'seem to me to be a direct apologia for my book when they are not sentences actually copied out of it. So I am a Symbolist . . .' Gide then makes the astonishing declaration: 'So Mallarmé for poetry, Maeterlinck for drama and – though beside those two I feel rather puny – I will add myself for the novel.'[26] The 'banquet Moréas' was presided over by Mallarmé, who, after toasting Jean Moréas, paid tribute to the '*cher absent* Verlaine'. The banquet over, some of the guests retired to the Café Voltaire, on the place de l'Odéon. No sooner were they inside than they were approached by an old man, unshaven, with dishevelled hair, a huge, filthy greatcoat draped around his shoulders, clearly much the worse for drink. It was none other than Verlaine: the '*cher absent*' had been no more than a few hundred yards away as Mallarmé was paying his tribute to him. He went straight up to Régnier and, grabbing hold of his immaculate waistcoat, their faces almost touching, blurted out:

'Toi, mon petit, je te reconnais! Tu t'appelles Henri de Régnier.' Régnier, always so *grand seigneur*, was clearly embarrassed, torn between pleasure at being recognized by the great man and disgust at the figure before him. Gide was later to see Verlaine in an even worse state, being teased by a group of children, like 'a great stag surrounded by a pack of hounds', outside the church of Saint-Etienne du Mont. His filthy top hat had fallen to the ground and he was holding up his muddy trousers with one hand, while lunging out at the children with the other. Staring at them fiercely, he answered their jeers with cries of '*Merde!*'

Two days after the 'banquet Moréas', Gide delivered a copy of *Les Cahiers d'André Walter* to Mallarmé's apartment. A few days later Mallarmé replied: 'Your book is a book of silences. You have succeeded in the most difficult of tasks: keeping silent; – in such a way that all the thoughts are between the lines.' This typically Mallarméan statement tells us more about the poet's own aesthetic ideal than about Gide's book, but it did consecrate *Les Cahiers* as a Symbolist work. Mallarmé went on to invite Gide to call on him the following Tuesday evening, just before eight, before anyone else. Seven years later, after Mallarmé's death, Gide wrote about the *Mardis* at 89 rue de Rome. The first thing to strike him, after the noise of the street, was 'the great silence'. Then Mallarmé spoke: his voice was 'soft, musical, unforgettable'. 'With him, one felt, one touched, for the first time, the reality of thought: what we were seeking, what we desired, what we worshipped in life, actually existed; a man, here, had sacrificed everything for *that*. For Mallarmé, literature was the purpose, yes, the very end of life.'[27] The famous *Mardis* took place in the sitting-/dining-room of Mallarmé's modest apartment, the acolytes sitting around the table, the master usually standing next to the stove. They consisted, in effect, of impromptu lectures, with very little discussion. It was not that Mallarmé set out to dominate his audience; he just did so by the sheer quiet brilliance of what he said. Many have attested to the extraordinary fertility of his ideas and to the clarity of his expression of them – he spoke far more lucidly than he wrote. Apart from the younger Symbolists, there were writers of an older generation – Leconte de Lisle, Catulle Mendès, Villiers de l'Isle-Adam, Anatole France and Maupassant. Maurras, Barrès, Dujardin, Maeterlinck, Claudel, Schwob, Laforgue and Debussy were constant visitors, while foreigners such as Wilde, Whistler, Arthur Symons, George Moore, Stefan George and Georg Brandes always dropped in when in Paris. Two weeks later, if he had not had a cold, Gide would have met Wilde there for the first time. As it was, it was not until the end of the year that the two met. Sometimes the little room was filled to capacity; at other times, only a few turned up and a more informal, relaxed atmosphere prevailed, when the disciples were joined by the poet's wife, Geneviève, the green parrots and the cat Lilith of the illustrious pedigree – she was the daughter of Théodore de Banville's cat and grand-daughter of Théophile Gautier's Eponine – and the inspiration of one of Baudelaire's poems. Yet this same man, the unchallenged intellectual leader of the Parisian avant-garde and one of the great French poets of all time, earned a living trying to teach recalcitrant schoolboys the rudiments of English. He had, by all accounts, a poor grasp of his subject, taught it badly, failed to keep discipline and was held in low esteem by his colleagues at the Lycée Condorcet. He only remained at his teaching post to avoid living by his pen: the very idea of writing for gain was, for him, demeaning. 'For us, followers of Mallarmé, the very idea that literature might "bring in" money was a shameful one,' Gide wrote years later. 'To get paid was, for us, tantamount to "selling oneself" in the worst sense. We were not to be bought.'[28] The *Mardis* lasted for ten years, from 1885 to 1895, when Mallarmé took early retirement from teaching, gave up his flat and retired to a small house at Valvins, near Fontainebleau. He died two years later, aged fifty-six.

Gide's next incursion into the literary world was to the home of José Maria de Heredia. On 7 March, having overcome his almost paralysing shyness, Gide agreed to accompany Louis and Régnier to the Saturday afternoon *salon*. Gide's reaction was not favourable. To begin with, Heredia in no way conformed to Gide's idea of what a poet should look like: he was short, stocky, with a square beard and very short hair. 'I was terribly disappointed at first'; there was 'no silence in him, no mystery, no subtlety in the stammering, trumpeting voice'. By four o'clock the smoking-room was full of 'diplomats, journalists, poets'; Mme Heredia and her daughters were receiving their own friends in the drawing-room. Occasionally, some brave soul dared to cross the boundary in one direction or another, through the half-open door. Fear of having to meet one of the hostesses and keep up a conversation with her kept Gide firmly in the smoky depths of the *fumoir*.[29] The contrast between Heredia and Mallarmé, between *Samedis* and *Mardis*, could hardly have been greater. The following day Gide wrote to Paul Valéry: 'I was really terrified of that fierce quarry, the "literary world". People eat each other furiously. Ah! The selfish hatred one feels in those souls . . . Everything becomes raw material for journalism and publicity – Heredia's drawing-room is like an advertising agency.' He then gets in a jab at the sociable, perfectly at ease Pierre Louis: 'I really admire Louis, who leaves one gathering only to go off to another and, at the end of the day, counts how many hands he has shaken.'[30] Yet, in his quieter, more nervous way, Gide, too, was extending his connections. By 8 October, he writes in his *Journal*, 'I now have about ten friends to whom I give my constant attention.'[31]

Gide and Louis had long planned to start a literary review. They were joined in the undertaking by Marcel Drouin and Maurice Quillot from the old *Potache-Revue* and by Léon Blum, Camille Mauclair, Henri de Régnier and Paul Valéry. Most of the work on the new review was done by the indefatigable Louis, whom we should now perhaps call Pierre Louÿs. It was he who persuaded such eminent elders as Mallarmé, Heredia, Leconte de Lisle, Verlaine, Maeterlinck and Moréas to contribute. *La Conque*, so named after an allusion to Triton's conch in a poem by Henri de Régnier, appeared on 15 March. Publication would be limited to twelve issues, of 100 copies each. (In the event only eleven issues appeared, at the rate of one a month.)

There were other friends, too, besides those associated with *La Conque*. Every Wednesday afternoon, when in Paris, Gide saw André Walkenaër. 'We talked tirelessly, inexhaustibly; Proust's way of writing reminds me of the texture of our conversation more than anything else I can think of. We discussed everything under the sun, and no hair was too fine for us to split.'[32] Incidentally, Gide also met Marcel Proust for the first time that year, on 1 May, at Gabriel Trarieux's. Proust, then not quite twenty, did not make a very good impression on Gide. Like many others Gide dismissed him as an Osric-like 'water-fly'. More important, Gide met that extraordinary scholar and polyglot, Marcel Schwob. Only two years older than Gide, he was already one of the first people in France to read Nietzsche. Schwob also introduced Gide to the work of Walt Whitman, whom he had just translated, Stevenson, Meredith and Ibsen.

Gide did not ignore the serious side of his nature during that year of *cénacles* and *salons*. In January, he resumed his Sunday-school teaching, which began at nine o'clock on Sunday mornings, before the service. Also in January he signed on at the Sorbonne for the philosophy degree and, although he did not attend lectures, he did continue his lessons with M. Dietz and read a quantity of philosophical works. With growing fascination, he read Taine's study of Carlyle, identifying readily enough with the Scottish Presbyterian who came under the sway of German Idealist philosophy. He went on to buy a French translation of Carlyle's *On Heroes and Hero Worship*. He read Stendhal's *Vie de Henri Brulard* and *Journal* which, as he later admitted, taught him a great deal, though Stendhal's sensibility was quite alien to him. In January, he bought a collected edition of Balzac's works in thirty volumes. He re-read *Louis Lambert*, but it was another year before he really got down to reading Balzac. He read *Crime and Punishment* (Dostoevsky was a crucial influence on his own work and, in 1923, he published his own study of the Russian novelist) and re-read *Anna Karenina*. In June he was studying Virgil, with the help of a couple of school textbooks, reading one of the eclogues each morning. Two of these, the second, which tells of the love of the shepherd Corydon for Alexis, and the tenth, recounting the consolation found by an unhappy lover in the natural beauties of Arcadia, he learnt by heart. Virgil provided Gide with the epigraphs to his next two prose works, *Le Traité du Narcisse* and *Le Voyage d'Urien* as well as the names of such characters as Tityre, Ménalque, Mopsus and, of course, Corydon, who gave his name to Gide's dialogue on homosexuality. In July he informed Valéry that he was reading '*tout Shakespeare et me passionne infiniment*'. On 29 June, he wrote to Valéry: 'Did you know that Laforgue lived at no. 2 in our street? I would have loved him. I cannot help being a little annoyed at him that he did not wait for me. Twenty-five! That's no age to die!' As André Walter, of course, Gide had killed himself off at twenty-one. He was now emerging from the gloom of a retarded adolescence: the irony of the mature Gide was already apparent behind the narcissistic stance.

5

The Ironic Narcissist: Le Traité du Narcisse, Poésies d'André Walter, Le Voyage d'Urien, La Tentative amoureuse

(JUNE 1891 – OCTOBER 1893)

André Walter had introduced André Gide to most of the leading literary figures of the day. One exalted admirer he had not yet met was Maurice Maeterlinck. Gide had already received a letter from him that was effusive even by the standards of the day: 'It is at certain moments, eternal, like *The Imitation*, like Marcus Aurelius, like the rare books that have an organic life, a life that one feels takes place *ab intro* as in the words of Jesus Christ for example . . . This great and noble book into which every soul that has not wished to fall at once will rediscover those immortalized struggles . . . Allow me humbly to shake your hand.'[1] Then, on 15 June, at the end of a short visit to Uzès, Gide read, in *L'Echo de Paris*, the latest instalment of Jules Huret's 'Enquête sur l'évolution littéraire'. In it Maeterlinck listed his literary preferences: Villiers de l'Isle-Adam, Mallarmé, Verlaine, Barrès, Henri de Régnier, Vielé-Griffin, Moréas, Baudelaire, Laforgue, *Les Cahiers d'André Walter*, Poe. Quite understandably, Gide felt an irresistible urge to visit the great Belgian. Certainly anyone reading Maeterlinck's work, so immaterial, so unphysical, so permeated with a sense of sickness and mortality, could be forgiven for thinking that he would not be long for this world.

By 18 July Gide was in Ghent. To his evident astonishment, Maeterlinck turned out to be a tall, well-built young man of twenty-nine, brimming with health and self-confidence. Gide and Maeterlinck spent much of the next two days together and got on extremely well. André was then joined by his mother and together they visited Bruges, Antwerp, Brussels, Amsterdam and The Hague. He spent much time in the museums of those cities, but there was nothing of modern cultural tourism about Gide's ten days or so in the Low Countries: often the contents of his own head are given more attention than the objects before his eyes. In his *Journal* he wrote:

Such boredom, such lugubrious lassitude overwhelms me as soon as I am in a new town that my only wish is to get away as soon as possible. I dragged myself through the streets feeling utterly miserable. However admirable those things may be, the idea of seeing them alone terrifies me . . . I sleep every afternoon, so as at least to dream a little. Or I read. [In fact, in the course of those ten days or so, he began and finished *War and Peace*.] The 'landscape', instead of distracting me from myself, always assumes desperately the form of my lamentable soul.[2]

Gide stopped off at Nancy to spend a few days with Marcel Drouin, then doing his military service before retreating to La Roque. Over the summer weeks, he read, wrote letters and returned to a work that was first mentioned as a project in the *Journal* a year before, *Le Traité du Narcisse*. Earlier in the year, the growing friendship between André Gide and Paul Valéry had been 'sanctified' by their visit to the tomb of 'Narcisse' at Montpellier. Shortly afterwards, Valéry wrote his 'Narcisse parle'. Meanwhile, Gide continued to work at his own *Narcissus*. Given the work's long and difficult gestation and Gide's claim to have spent 'the entire summer' of 1891 working on it, though much of it was already written by then, it may come as a surprise to learn that it amounts to only some 3,000 words or ten pages in its original edition. It represents nevertheless an important stage in Gide's development. In it, Gide finds the pure, restrained, cool, classical style that was to become his; the effusive, often unfocused, romantic, 'Germano-Belgian' French of *André Walter* has been left behind. Yet this treatise is arguably Gide's most Symbolist work. It is neither metaphysics nor fiction, though it has elements of both. It consists of three short sections, preceded and followed by two even shorter ones.

The introduction recounts a Gidean version of the myth: Narcissus, in search of a mirror, leans over the grey, illusory waters of the river of Time, where the years pass. What he sees is an endlessly repeated Present. He dreams of a crystalline Paradise of Primary Forms. Part I describes this Platonic Paradise, this 'Garden of Ideas', which is identified with the Garden of Eden. At the centre of the Garden is the 'logarithmic tree, Yghdrasil'. In its shade, leaning against its trunk, is the Book of Mystery, in which may be read 'the truth that one needs to know'. Also under the tree is an as yet androgynous, unsexed Adam. The eternal observer of a perfect world, he is bored; his existence is a form of slavery. He yearns to perform some gesture that might disturb the tyrannical harmony. He breaks a twig off the tree; a violent storm shakes the tree to the ground and disperses the pages of the sacred Book. Time is born. Adam splits in two, becoming a man and a woman. Hereafter, mankind would be tormented by the memory of the lost Paradise and poets would try to gather up what was left of the leaves of the sacred Book. Part II returns to Narcissus: 'Paradise is always to be recreated anew; it is not in some distant Thule. It lies under appearances . . .'³ Part III concerns the Poet, he who looks – and sees Paradise: 'For Paradise is everywhere . . . Appearances are imperfect: they stammer out the truths that they conceal; the Poet must understand those truths, without their being spelled out, then retell them . . .'⁴ Later editions of the *Traité* contain a footnote not in the original edition but written when the work was still in its earliest stages. It begins as yet another statement of Platonic Symbolism: 'Truths lie behind Forms – Symbols. Every phenomenon is the Symbol of a Truth. Its sole duty is to manifest it.' Gide then adds: 'Its sole sin: to prefer itself.' This clearly marks a departure from dominant Symbolist thinking in the name of that Gidean constant, *sincerity*. Most of the Symbolists took little account of some putative Truth behind the Symbol – the Symbol was an end in itself, was encouraged to prefer itself. For them, the Symbol might manifest the Truth, but the Truth must remain forever veiled within it: once the Symbol was there, any concern for Truth became superfluous, indeed a kind of unSymbolist vulgarity. Gide goes on: 'The artist, and the scientist, must not prefer himself to the Truth that he wishes to express: that is the whole of his morality . . . All things must be manifested, even the most pernicious [*funeste*].' Gide then quotes two of Jesus's sayings: 'Woe unto him through whom the offence arises' and 'Offences must arise'.⁵ That uncompromising assumption of the artist's role as scandal-bringer – and acceptance that he will become society's scapegoat as a result – is percipiently and pithily Gidean. The young writer was not yet of a stature to bring the 'offence', the scandal, for which he was later to become infamous, but, in the small compass of *Le Traité du Narcisse*, he had managed to introduce a number of minor scandals. He had upset his co-religionists by seeming to place the Adam of Judaeo-Christian revealed Truth on the same level as the Narcissus of Greek legend. On the other hand, the Symbolists would have been equally alarmed by Gide's insistence on the primacy of Truth over the Symbol and no doubt considered the beautiful myth of Narcissus defiled by contact with the Judaeo-Christian myth of Adam and the Garden of Eden.

The *Traité du Narcisse* first appeared in December 1891 in a private edition of twelve copies, the first five numbered copies going to Mallarmé, Louÿs, Valéry, Régnier and the author. The dedication was to Paul Valéry, in memory of their meeting at the tomb of 'Narcisse' at Montpellier, and the jacket bore the words 'Traité du' followed by a drawing of a narcissus, at the water's edge, by Pierre Louÿs. The text was published more widely in the review *Entretiens politiques et littéraires* for 1 January 1892. Later in the year, a first 'commercial' edition of eighty copies was published by the Librairie de l'Art Indépendant.

During the same summer that saw the completion of the *Traité*, Gide also composed, in a single week, most of the twenty poems that were later to be published as the *Poésies d'André Walter*. Perhaps the most obvious thing about these usually accomplished, controlled, often lighthearted poems, is that they could not have been written by André Walter: André Gide had left André Walter behind. *Les Poésies d'André Walter* appeared in May 1892, in an edition of 190 copies, with no reference to André Gide, though few of those who bothered to read them were in any doubt as to the identity of the author. André did not send Madeleine a copy. When, over a year later, she got hold of one, her response was uncharacteristically fierce: 'Read *Les Poésies d'André Walter*. Very boring and very bad. I assure you that you didn't take long to descend from the pedestal – Oh, a very small pedestal – on which *Les Cahiers* and *Narcisse* had perched you. Seriously, I was very disappointed. Why did you have that printed?'[6] Gide got a more complimentary reception from Stéphane Mallarmé: 'Very rare, my friend Gide, this poetic collection of André Walter. I have the impression of a harpsichord, shrill, but always well tuned . . .'[7]

Gide did not leave La Roque until he had finished *Le Traité du Narcisse*. Then, on 4 November, he left for Paris. 'With or without Louÿs,' he wrote to Valéry, he did the rounds of cafés and salons, 'shaking hands and putting on smiles'. He met 'l'esthète Oscar Wilde, ô admirable, admirable, celui-là'. Wilde was now thirty-seven; *The Picture of Dorian Gray* had been published, to the acclamation of the few and the outrage of the many, the year before. He was working on *Salomé* and, the following February, *Lady Windermere's Fan*, the first of the great comedies, was to be put on in London. His downfall was less than four years away. Wilde was staying at the residence of the British Ambassador, his friend Lord Lytton. Lytton, the son of a minor but successful writer, Bulwer Lytton, and himself a writer of sorts, was, despite a distinguished career in the diplomatic service, something of a bohemian. On his death, a few weeks after Wilde's departure, *The Times* carried an obituary on Lytton astonishing in its blend of outspoken censure and narrow-minded conventionality. The late ambassador's frequenting of 'French literary and artistic society of the semi-bohemian type' was criticized, as were his clothes, which were 'like nobody else's . . . certainly not English'! The conventions of polite society were 'as incomprehensible to him as to a child of some savage race'.

That autumn, Wilde was, according to *L'Echo de Paris*, 'le "great event" des salons littéraires'. 'Gide est amoureux d'Oscar Wilde,' Jules Renard wrote in his *Journal*. The word is either too general to be meaningful or too specific to be appropriate, but certainly Wilde had an immediate, powerful and long-lasting effect on Gide. Three years later, in North Africa, Wilde (with Douglas) was to be the main catalyst in Gide's physical discovery of homosexuality. What the mental encounter with Wilde, in the autumn of 1891, did was to accelerate an intellectual and emotional movement away from the Christian puritanism of his youth, and thus prepare the way for the later physical experiences. It is arguable that Gide would have found his way, intellectual and physical, without Wilde's help, but the sheer brilliance and bravado of Wilde's reversal of all the moral precepts to which Gide had clung so tenaciously must, to say the least, have accelerated the process. 'Do you know why Christ did not love his mother?' Wilde suddenly asked Gide at Heredia's one evening. 'Because she was a virgin!' he exclaimed with a great laugh.[8] On another occasion, he remarked to Gide: 'I don't like your lips; they are straight, like those of someone who has never lied. I want to teach you to lie, so your lips might become beautiful and twisted like those of an ancient mask.'[9] Wilde represented for Gide a sort of Mephistopheles to his Faust: the tempter's power of attraction was undeniable. In his unpublished notes, Gide described Wilde as 'always trying to insinuate inside you the *authorization of evil*'. Nietzsche was to exert over Gide's outlook a deeper, more integral influence, but the immediacy of impact of a man who declared that he had put his talent into his work and his genius into his life was overwhelming.

Gide left Paris on 28 December for Uzès to visit his sick grandmother. Away from Wilde's immediate hypnotic presence, he began to recover something of his old self, but the light, the excitement had gone out of his life. On Christmas Eve, he wrote to Valéry: 'Forgive my silence: since Wilde I exist only very little.'[10] The day of his arrival in the ancestral, Calvinist home, he wrote in his *Journal*: 'Lord, I have come back to Thee because I believe that all is vanity save knowing Thee . . . I have followed tortuous ways and thought to grow rich with false goods . . . I thought to grow rich and I find myself poor indeed. Lord, save me from evil . . .'[11]

*

On New Year's Day Gide wrote: 'Wilde, I believe, has done me nothing but harm. When I was with him, I forgot how to think. I had more varied emotions, but I was no longer able to order them . . .'[12] He hoped, by returning to his philosophical studies, shielded from Wilde's personal impact, to take hold of his mind once more. A few days later, he wrote to his somewhat neglected confidant, Albert Démarest: 'I want to ignore Paris and the literary world.' He now realizes that he was not strong enough to withstand the destructive effects of such a life. The Puritan has found his voice again: 'verbal facility' and 'mental agility' are the results of 'facile' and 'lightweight' thinking. 'Easy charm' and 'politeness to others' involve a gradual desertion of 'moral maxims'. 'I have really gone downhill since my book and I am now clinging to everything I can still find within myself to hoist me back to my former condition of gauche, unsociable worker . . .' One wonders what Albert might have made of such a confession. André had done nothing more, of course, than do less reading and writing than usual, and spend a great deal more time 'socializing'. Yet, he confesses, just as when he was a child, he is afraid of Albert's disapproval. 'That is because, after Madeleine, you are the person whose judgement matters most to me.' About the same time, Madeleine crops up again, this time in the *Journal*: again she is seen as the moral lodestar of his life. 'I thank thee, Lord, for the only feminine influence on my ravished soul, and it wishes for no other; Em. has always guided my soul towards the highest truths . . . If she came back to me, I would have no secrets from her.'[13]

But Madeleine did not come back to him, or not yet. He had heard nothing from her for a year, except for a New Year's message signed by her and her two sisters. When André needed her most, or at least felt that he needed her most, she remained silent.

Gide had gone to Uzès to recuperate from the life that he had been leading in Paris: the grand maternal home was about as far from Oscar Wilde as he could go. He spent five weeks in the South, including a week with Uncle Charles in Montpellier. Before returning to Paris he was planning a further escape. His choice fell on Munich. Germany had always been an important, if secondary, part of the young Gide's mental world. He had begun to learn German at school and, at home, his mother and Anna Shackleton spoke it fluently. With Madeleine, who had had a German governess and possessed an excellent command of the language, he had translated Heine and Schiller. In the last few years, German philosophy had, if anything, supplanted French literature at the centre of his mental universe. Then there was German music, from the greatest of all, Bach, to

the, for Gide, equivocal figure of Wagner. The previous summer, Pierre
Louÿs had spent a few weeks in Germany, mainly at Bayreuth, seeing
Parsifal no fewer than three times. Gide's Germanophilia was quite typical
of the young French intellectuals of his day. Indeed the French attitude to
Germany at this time developed largely along generational and political
lines. The older, conservative, Catholic wing, with vivid memories of the
humiliation wreaked on France in the Franco-Prussian war twenty years
before, was profoundly anti-German and it was from this Germanophobia
that the Dreyfus case was to emerge in a few years' time. The young radical,
anti-clerical intellectuals, on the other hand, steeped in German philosophy
from their *classe de philo*', excitedly reading Nietzsche as it appeared in
French, attending the first performances of plays by Hauptmann and Ibsen
(not German exactly, but '*nordique*') and the Concerts Lamoureux on Sunday
afternoons, with their heavy admixture of Wagnerian extracts, were as
profoundly Germanophile. Wagner, indeed, was the great divide. It was
one thing for the young to flock to privately financed concerts to listen to
Wagner; it was quite another when, in September 1891, Charles Lamoureux
was invited to conduct the first ever staging of a Wagner work at the State-
owned Opéra. Yet the innocuous *Lohengrin*, in French, with an all-French
cast, was seen, in certain quarters, as an insult to the nation, the return of
the hated Prussians to the streets of Paris. The opening night caused a riot:
warned of trouble, hundreds of uniformed police were in the surrounding
streets, scores of them in plainclothes in the auditorium itself. After the
performance, people were trampled underfoot, an elderly couple on their
way home afterwards were seized in a side street and nearly lynched, a
thousand suspects were held for identity checks. (Meanwhile, Covent
Garden had had several Wagner productions each season since 1875,
reaching its apotheosis, perhaps, in 1892, with a complete Ring cycle, *Tristan*
and *Tannhäuser* in German, under the baton of the thirty-one-year-old
Gustav Mahler.)

Gide's decision met with complete approval from the family: Germany
could have nothing but a beneficial effect on André and, in any case, it
would be an excellent opportunity to improve his German. Armed with
letters of recommendation from former colleagues of his father at the
Sorbonne, from Uncle Charles and from his mother, he arrived in Munich
on 8 March and lodged with 'three charming old ladies', in the Christoph-
strasse. If he followed up all his mother's introductions, he complained, he
would soon be leading the very life that he had left Paris to avoid. He
was presented to the great conductor Hermann Levi, who, in 1882, had

conducted the first performance of *Parsifal* at Bayreuth. Levi invited him to attend rehearsals at the Hof Theater, arranged for him to have violin lessons and took him to a social gathering of artists, writers and musicians at which quartets by Mozart and Schubert were played. Gide was greatly impressed. He went to no fewer than ten operas and plays in his first fortnight, including Lessing's *Nathan der Weise* at the Residenz Theater and, at the Hof Theater, *Tristan und Isolde, Tannhäuser* and Shakespeare's *Richard III*, which he took the trouble to read beforehand in German translation. All this theatregoing was very untypical of the usual, Parisian Gide. An inexhaustible reader, he had a lifelong suspicion, often verging on dislike, of the theatre. That most overtly 'artificial' of arts clearly offended his puritanical cult of sincerity and truth. Much later in life, especially under the influence of Jacques Copeau, he was to make a few forays into play-writing, but he was at ease on neither side of the footlights. During those weeks in Munich, he also visited the Glyptothek and the Pinakothek, the two main art collections, but, as always, he did a great deal of reading. This reading, of Goethe in particular, seems to have made a deeper impact on him than any number of operas or works of art. Goethe, of course, was not new to him. With Pierre Louis, he had read Part II of *Faust*. He went on to read *Werther* and *Wilhelm Meister*. During his stay in Munich, he read and re-read *Torquato Tasso, Iphigenie* and much of the poetry. What Gide learnt from Goethe, as he remarked years later, in an introduction to the Gallimard Pléiade edition of Goethe's plays, was that a certain serenity could be achieved, not by resolving conflicts, which would violate truthfulness, but, contradictorily, by cultivating them, by finding satisfaction in the struggle itself.

After four weeks in Munich, he left for Paris, stopping off, on the way, at Strasbourg and Nancy, where he spent a day with Marcel Drouin. In Paris, he took up his old life, with the same ill-grace. '*Paris m'exaspère*,' he wrote to Valéry on 26 April. 'In all this commotion one cannot do very much ... Mallarmé, Heredia, Régnier, then around them all the others; I am exhausted.'[14] Next day he attended his *conseil de révision*, the army medical examination, and was declared fit for military service. 'At first I was delighted; something will change at last,' he wrote to Paul Valéry. On 8 May he took the train back to Munich, where he was to spend the rest of the month. He went back, several times, to the Hof Theater. He took his violin lessons, managing a 'terribly difficult' Brahms sonata with his teacher, and studied German with Fräulein Steidl. He read and wrote long, sometimes acrimonious letters to his mother. André had only been in Munich four days when he was writing to her:

I have just received another terrible letter from you. Out of eight long pages 6½ are used to convince me of something . . . You have a way of taking people by the shoulder and pushing them in the direction you want them to go, saying 'Don't you think you'd do better to go that way?' . . . It all proves what an interest you take in what I do, but I prefer to make up my own mind about my actions . . .[15]

Mme Gide had tried to persuade her son to remain in Munich (and continue to improve his German). Two days later, Gide returned to the fray:

I gave myself a night of insomnia, thinking over whether I ought to get back to Paris soon or stay here until the end of June, and learn German frantically. *Despite* your terrible plea of yesterday, I have decided to stay here until 1 July and do nothing but German. I beg you, don't try too hard to demonstrate that I have come to the right decision . . . Let turbulent youth do as it please, and don't explain on every occasion why it is wrong.[16]

The problem was that André had more or less promised Jacques-Emile Blanche to be back in Paris by 1 June to allow him to finish a portrait of him. Mme Gide could not see that this was a good enough reason to abandon Munich and even suggested that her son was using the picture as an excuse to return to his 'idle life' in Paris. André's response begins gently, but soon gathers fury: 'What you say of life in Paris is (forgive me!) absurd and would be laughable were it not so infuriating. You say: so many months in Paris = so many months wasted . . . Time wasted!'[17] He then lists his Balzac reading: '*one novel a day*, that is *twenty-eight* novels . . . + four other volumes'. Moreover, between his two trips to Munich he practised the piano 'between four and five hours *each day*. I scrupulously noted the times' (Mme Gide was clearly unconvinced: in the margin of her son's letter she wrote: 'Si scrupuleusement noté?') Mme Gide had her own reasons for trying to postpone her son's arrival in Paris: her niece Madeleine was staying with her at the rue de Commaille. It would not be a good idea for the two young people to be under the same roof. André replies that, on arrival in Paris, he will probably stay in Auteuil, near Blanche's studio. This would cut down on travel to and from his sittings and, if no one knows he is back, enable him to get on with his work. This he did, though he made frequent visits to the rue de Commaille. For Madeleine, André's sudden arrival was 'un grand coup au coeur'.[18] 'You are still the same,' she goes on, 'and the same for me too. I still love you as much as ever. – So why the conflicts of last winter? Should I give in? Give up struggling against that affection, that fondness that fills me with a sort of lightness, of luminous, "winged" joy when I see you – hear you?' But, if she allowed herself to reveal her feelings of 'affection', of 'fondness', might they not be misinterpreted as encouragement to pursue his plans to marry her?

'Voyage sur l'Océan pathétique', the first part of a forthcoming work by Gide, occupied an entire issue of *La Wallonie*. Apparently, when Mallarmé saw the title of the projected work, *Voyage au Spitzberg*, he was very concerned. 'Ah! You gave me quite a fright,' he told Gide later. 'I was afraid that you had actually been there!' But Gide had not, after all, descended from Symbolist imagination to travel writing. He was still working on the book and reading widely among prose and verse likely to provide exotic material: the *Odyssey*, Friedrich von Humboldt's *Voyages aux Régions Equinoxiales du Nouveau Continent*, Loti's *Fantôme d'Orient*, Fromentin's *Un été dans le Sahara*, as well as Poe, Hugo and Balzac. The third and last part of the new work, 'Voyage vers une mer glaciale', appeared, later in the year, in *La Wallonie*. This last part was dedicated to his cousin, Georges Pouchet, 'qui y est allé'. André Gide might not have been there, but Georges Pouchet, professor of comparative anatomy, had – indeed he provided André with material for some of the landscape descriptions.

Determined to work, Gide spent most of the summer at La Roque. Three years later, when writing of sexual liberation in North Africa, he described the 'hell from which I was emerging' during those weeks: 'I thought I was going mad; I spent nearly the whole time I was there shut up in my room, where I ought to have been working and where I tried to work in vain . . . obsessed, haunted, hoping perhaps to find some escape in excess itself . . . to the point of utter exhaustion, until nothing remained before me but imbecility, madness.'[19] But the writing of *Le Voyage* did progress. 'Unbearable and horribly difficult at first, it soon amused me, and over the past ten days, I have lived in a state of delicious, joyful excitement . . .'[20] His reading did not abate, however. He returned to his biographies of Goethe and to Goethe's *Iphigenie*, which sent him back to Sophocles. He read Leibnitz and Fichte. His *Subjectif* also mentions Voltaire (*Zadig, Micromégas*), George Eliot (*Silas Marner*), Dumas *fils* (*L'Ami des femmes, Denise*) and Tolstoy (*The Power of Darkness*).

In August, he went off to Brittany, where he met up with Henri de Régnier. It was not to be just a holiday: he hoped to work on the second part of his new book 'among the moors and rocks of Belle-Isle' – and took with him a whole 'library' of books. It was here that an incident occurred that Henri de Régnier recounted to Léon Pierre-Quint in 1926: 'I can see him now at Belle-Isle . . . holding a copy of *Wilhelm Meister* or the Bible. I was teasing him: "Gide, why are you reading that here, at the seaside?"

I grabbed the book and flung it into the sea. I think he recovered it by diving in himself.'[21] Régnier, incidentally, was in the habit of referring to his friend as 'Ci-Gide' (*Ci-gît* is French for 'Here lies'). After a week, the friends set off to tour the Breton coast. The whole trip lasted three weeks.

André was back at La Roque on 10 September. Later in the month, he and his mother were joined by the Rondeaux *cousines*, then by Pastor Roberty and his daughter. The writing resumed, as did the reading: the reading aloud included Poe's *The Fall of the House of Usher*, Balzac's *Le Cousin Pons*, *Richard III*, *Martin Chuzzlewit*. Relations with Madeleine were still strained, despite the calm front put on for the benefit of relations and friends. By the time the *cousines* left, Madeleine let André know that he should give up, once and for all, any idea of marrying her: indeed each should feel quite free to marry someone else. Some days later, he wrote to her begging her not to break off all contact again, as she had previously done for a whole year. 'I know that my persistence worries you; I don't think that what I believe to be love may disappear or alter, and every effort made against it merely feeds it; but I shall silence it and wait . . .' (We do not have André's letters to Madeleine, these having been destroyed by her during André's escapade with Marc Allégret in England in 1918. What we do have are Madeleine's letters to André, found among his papers at his death, and a few drafts of letters from André to Madeleine. Both are so far unpublished in full, though extracts from them are included in *André Gide: Correspondance avec sa mère* and in Jean Schlumberger's *Madeleine et André Gide*.) On 17 October Madeleine replied at length:

Since Arcachon, when I realized that we really must separate and everything seemed to be dying inside me, even my religious faith, I have done my best not to think about you. This last visit to La Roque made me feel that I still loved you with as much infinite tenderness as ever. Our tastes, our feelings have remained profoundly similar, even when we seem to differ . . . I now realize that, although I may have had some influence over your heart, over your moral life, my mind has been developed, formed by you and that I owe you many intellectual joys unknown to many women . . . I have hope and belief in your future as a writer, I have confidence in your moral life, and if ever you were to change, if ever your life as a man were to deny your childhood, I feel that it would be as if a faith had disappeared from my heart.[22]

Madeleine goes on to say that she does not think that they should go on writing to one another; it would do neither of them any good: 'We are not, alas, brother and sister, and now that we know that we are not, I don't think that we can believe once again that we are. We have made each other very

happy for several years and if we are to suffer a little now, I think it will be
better than suffering a great deal later . . . Your sister who loves you . . .'²³
Behind the confident tone and apparent inflexibility of decision, the letter
suggests a quite understandable confusion. We must give up all this 'brother
and sister' nonsense, she says in effect. Then ends: 'Ta soeur qui t'aime'.
On a conventional, social level she knows that they are not brother and
sister: either they will get married or they will not, but they cannot, as
adults, have that emotionally charged but non-sexual relationship that they
had had since adolescence. In an obscure, intuitive, semi-formulated way,
she seemed to understand that André could not make her a proper husband.
She sensed the 'irremediable' suffering that would be hers if she did marry
him, that was hers when she did marry him: what did cause her anxiety
was André's moral life, the possibility that he might change, that his life as
a man might deny his childhood. André's response was vehement, destructive of all Madeleine's deliberately constructed phrases. He was 'appalled
at the idea that, out of fear of some imaginary unhappiness and to follow
some duty that you arbitrarily set yourself . . . you may cause certain,
irreparable unhappiness for both of us. But I love you, Madeleine! And if
I have not shouted it out to you, it is because I couldn't – so badly does the
word convey something so profound, so serious and so tender.' Madeleine
had advised André to marry . . . someone else. 'You mention marriage: do
you think I would marry? . . . Do you think that I shall forget you, now?
Do you think that you can forget me? . . . It is apart that our future seems
sad; and when I cry out to you, it is to our happiness that I cry out.'²⁴

Meanwhile, Mme Gide, observing the cousins, separately and together,
had come round to seeing a marriage as the best solution for both of them.
During André's absences in Munich, she had become increasingly aware
that her own moral influence over her son was rapidly diminishing. She
had helped, financially, to launch André's literary career: she had perhaps
not bargained for the kind of society that such a life would bring him into
contact with. Now he was confronted by the prospect of military service:
who knows what further temptations might be placed in his way? Madeleine
alone still seemed to have any moral influence over him.

On 15 November André Gide turned up at the barracks at Nancy to
begin his military service. He was already in deep depression over his failure
with Madeleine. His spirits were not raised by the prospect ahead. In May,
he had already been declared fit for service. Now, after a total of five
medicals, he was declared, after all, unfit: he had a weak chest and was
suspected of a predisposition to tuberculosis. He returned to Paris, went

out little – usually to fencing practice with Paul Laurens, painter and old
schoolfriend, and his brother Pierre – and by the end of December, he had
put the finishing touches to the new work.

Le Voyage d'Urien was published in May 1893 by the Librairie de l'Art
Indépendant, in an edition of 300 numbered copies. The title-page bore
the name of Maurice Denis as co-author. Denis was, in fact, the illustrator:
it was an extremely handsome piece of book production, on Holland paper,
of squarish format, with some thirty line drawings with very pale washes of
colour, distributed over the 109 pages. If Mallarmé had seen the final title
of the work, he would have realized that it was a true product of the
Symbolist imagination: *Voyage d'Urien* is clearly a pun on *voyage du rien*,
voyage of/into nothing. In case there had been any doubt on the matter, a
final 'Envoi' in verse tells us that it was all a dream: 'We never left the
chamber of our thoughts . . . We were reading.'

After a 'bitter night of thought, study and theological ecstasy', the as yet
unnamed hero goes down to the shore, where his companions await him.
They number twenty, but have little but their names to distinguish them
one from another – and even these, ranging from the familiar Alain, Eric,
Hector and Nathanaël, to the outlandish Aguisel, Lambègue, Paride and
Tradelineau, possess a mysterious homogeneity. Gide himself revealed what
it was in his interviews with Jean Amrouche: apparently, they all came from
a popular version of the Arthurian legend.

Urien and his companions make for the harbour, where their 'fabulous
ship', the *Orion*, awaits them. That evening, they and the crew, for these
twenty-one young philosophers are not sailors, but merely passengers, set
sail. They do not know where they are bound for. They pass floating islands,
rich with tropical vegetation. They bathe in water that is pink and green.
They arrive at a sandy beach: four of the young men disembark. The next
day they return, terrified by what they have seen: a 'prodigious city . . .
gold-coloured and Muslim, with fantastic minarets rising high into the sky;
staircase upon staircase led to hanging gardens, mauve palm trees shading
the terraces . . .'[25] But it is all a mirage, conjured up by sirens. The four
men flee at the sight of them. 'They were like women and very beautiful,'
says one of them. 'That is why I fled.' They arrive at the city of Queen
Haiatalnefous (the name comes from *The Thousand and One Nights*), peopled
entirely by beautiful women, who 'wanted our caresses and kept us for their
kisses'. On the first day, all the sailors succumb, then, one by one, the
companions, too, only twelve resisting. Meanwhile, a plague spreads through

the city; all those who have slept with the women are affected. The twelve watch their companions die, then flee from the stricken city and set sail. Such a brief summary of the plot of Part I brings out its implications rather more starkly than a reading of the exquisitely written text itself, with all its exotic description. Nevertheless, the homo-erotic bond between the young companions and the fear of women as diseased and fatal temptresses is evident, although, no doubt, much of this was lost on contemporary readers. One cannot help but note the similarity of the name 'Urien' to 'Uranism', one of the commonest terms at the time for homosexuality.

The second part, 'La Mer des Sargasses', takes Urien and his remaining companions into the 'sea of boredom'. So stagnant is the sea that it is almost overgrown with seaweed, through which the boat navigates as through a river or canal. On the seventh day, Urien sees his love, Ellis, sitting under an apple tree. This is the first mention of her in the book. She is wearing a polka-dot dress, holds a cerise-coloured parasol and is reading the *Prolegomena to all Future Metaphysics* (Kant)! At other times, incidentally, she is reading Leibnitz's *Théodicée* and *The Treatise on Contingency*. This philosophical bent does not, surprisingly, endear her to Urien/Gide: 'Exasperated, I snatched the book from her hand and . . . flung it into the river.' (Gide has obviously come to share Henri de Régnier's attitude to his younger self.) 'Don't you know,' Urien exclaims, 'that books are temptations? And we set out to perform glorious deeds.'[26] Later, Urien begins to have doubts about the true identity of 'Ellis'. He remembers that the woman he had once known was not fair-haired, like the woman before him, but dark. What is more, the pseudo-Ellis grows sick and ever paler, eventually fading away. In *Et nunc manet in te*, Gide wrote of Madeleine: 'In my first books, well before our marriage, I depicted her: Emmanuèle in *Les Cahiers d'André Walter*, Ellis in *Le Voyage d'Urien* . . . And, in my dreams, she constantly appeared to me as an unreachable, ungraspable figure; and the dream turned into a nightmare.'[27] So, even the insubstantial Ellis is a manifestation of Madeleine; the very fantastic nature of the narrative allows the writer to express his oneiric anxieties and fears. We are not far from André Walter's nightmare in which Emmanuèle appears to him in a dream, only to end up as nothing.

The third and last part takes Urien and his seven remaining friends to a 'Mer Glaciale', an Icy Sea. They arrive at the land of the Eskimos, who are ugly and small, 'their loves are devoid of tenderness; they are not voluptuous . . . they make love in the dark.'[28] Urien and his companions have escaped the physical infections of the 'Océan pathétique' and the mental death of the Mer des Sargasses, only to be confronted by a sort of spiritual deathliness, which takes the form of scurvy. The only cure for this scurvy is a special *eau-de-vie*: this water of life is stolen by one of their number, Eric, a Siegfried figure or Nietzschean *Übermensch*. They destroy the ship and construct a sleigh. Drawn by a reindeer, they set off across the ice into the night. They meet Ellis, but this time the true, dark-haired Ellis, Urien's 'sister'. 'Sad brother!' she says. 'Haven't you always dreamt me? . . . I await you beyond time, where the snows are eternal . . . Your journey is about to end . . . Cease looking to the past. There are still other lands, which you will not know . . . For everyone has his own way and each way leads to God . . .'[29] At which she rises up to heaven, her dress turning into a wedding-dress as she disappears in a dazzling white light. Urien and his friends move on and come to a huge block of ice in which are carved the words: *Hic desperatus* (Here lies the desperate man). Within the ice is the corpse of a man, clutching a piece of paper. They free the body from the ice, but find that the paper is completely blank. They are bitterly disappointed. 'If we had known at the outset that we would find this at our journey's end we might never have set out . . .'[30]

In his 1949 interview with Jean Amrouche Gide remarked of *Le Voyage d'Urien*: 'There was no Symbolist novel and I had the rather foolhardy pretension of supplying one.'[31] Gide had indeed written a piece of Symbolist fiction: 'novel' might be too definite a description, even for that most elastic of terms. The setting was unspecific in time and place; the characters were exotically named, but vague and undefined, having little notion of how they came to be where they were; moods, mental states, *états d'âme* – an 'in' phrase of the period – were conveyed almost entirely in the description of landscape. As so often with the Paris intelligentsia, theory had swept all before it: one figure, a truly great poet and inspiring intellectual leader, had given rise to a generalized imperative. If Mallarmé's poetry could be called 'Symbolist', then there must be Symbolist plays and Symbolist novels. In the event there were not to be many Symbolist novels – or, for that matter, Symbolist plays. Even *Pelléas et Mélisande* has survived only as Debussy's opera. Yet Gide, that indefatigable traveller, intellectually as well as physically, was not so easily caught by fashion. His flirtation with Symbolism was already coming to an end. The final 'Envoi' hints as much. The Symbolist dream, conceived in a life devoted almost exclusively to books, is not, after all, an autonomous monument to Beauty and therefore Truth. The whole book is 'nothing but a lie'. Is the old Gide, Gide the Puritan moralist, going to have the last word, after all? Not exactly. The author had wanted to 'look at life', but admits that, confronted by its terrifying complexity and fearing that poetry would have to be sacrificed to Truth, he had turned away, 'preferring to go on lying and to wait, – to wait, to wait . . .'[32] It is, after all, the future, not the past, that is beckoning. He was not to have long to wait; less than a year in fact. Meanwhile, *Le Voyage d'Urien* was a precise representation of Gide's mental state at the time. He was seeking to escape from the stifling puritanism of his childhood into life, freedom, etc. He had left André Walter behind, but his only instruments of escape, as yet, were books. Yet the irony of young men seeking life by reading is not lost on the author. There is, too, a quite new ironic distancing in the treatment of the Madeleine figure: though potentially frightening for the hero, the transformation of his 'sister' from brunette to blonde and back is handled lightly, even humorously.

Le Voyage d'Urien did not make André Gide's name, but it was warmly received by the small circle around Mallarmé. The Master himself was unstinting in his praise: 'With *Le Voyage d'Urien*, you have done something quite unique; it will remain, with Poe and a few others, part of my reading . . . This or that group of words, appearing unobtrusively [*sans faste*], remained, hauntingly, among the most beautiful ever written . . .'[33]

During the early months of 1893, Gide read and re-read two authors who were to have a crucial influence on him: Ibsen and the Goethe of the *Roman Elegies*. It was Marcel Schwob who turned him in the direction of Ibsen's plays. Ibsen, of course, was a highly fashionable figure in the 1890s, though in different, almost contradictory ways. In London, largely under the influence of Shaw, he was seen as an ally of socialists and other would-be social reformers; in Paris he was seen as an honorary Symbolist, providing exotic, Nordic settings and themes far removed from the experience of your average sensual Frenchman. Gide's Ibsen was neither of these: it was to be a long time before he showed any 'social' concern and the world Ibsen described, far from being exotic, was all too familiar. Indeed in those descriptions of a drab, guilt-ridden, joyless North, many of them written by the great Norwegian during his long Roman exile, Gide found a powerful expression of his own predicament. He had begun reading Goethe's *Roman Elegies* the previous summer. Now, in the first months of 1893, he made a deeper study of the poems. What his reading of the *Roman Elegies* did, above all, was to provide an aesthetic, almost ethical, justification of hedonism, an alternative ideal, a southern, Mediterranean, classical world of sunlight, sensuousness and unashamed joy. In a letter to Marcel Drouin, Gide speaks of the profound effect wrought on him by the *Roman Elegies*, then lets out this *cri de coeur*: 'I will have lived to the age of twenty-three completely virgin and utterly depraved, so crazed that I eventually sought everywhere some bit of flesh on which to press my lips. Laws, proprieties, ruthless self-discipline, the love of mystical affections have constituted all my joys – the greatest of them solitary and care-ridden – and gave to every pleasure in living the bitterness of sin.'[34] It was to be a few months yet before Gide lost his virginity. What became the North African experience did not come like a bolt from the blue: it was prepared for, awaited, sought after. In the early months of 1893, North Africa had not presented itself specifically as the setting for this *passage à l'acte*. For months, Gide and his equally virginal, but less tormented friend, the artist Paul Laurens, had talked, between fencing bouts, of a long trip to Italy.

For the time being, the closest André got to Italy was an improbable visit to Seville, for the Easter carnival with . . . his mother. During the 'interminable journey', André read the whole of *Little Dorrit* – holiday reading, even more inappropriate, it might be thought, than the choice of Mme Gide *mère* as companion at the Seville carnival! Of *Little Dorrit*, Gide wrote four pages in his *Cahier de lecture*. To Spain he devotes a few lines of the *Journal* and those on the immorality of bull-fighting. After the Holy Week festivities in Seville, André and his mother moved on to Granada. There, for the first time, outside books, outside *The Thousand and One Nights*, he encountered the Moorish world, the 'Alcazar' [*sic*], 'a garden like some Persian marvel', with its fountains, 'its marble walks, bordered with myrtle and cypress'.[35] Later, in a journal entry for 1910, when on a visit with Jacques Copeau, Gide remembered an evening in the Albaicin:

Nothing since, not even the songs of Egypt, has touched a more secret place in my heart: it was at night, in the huge hall of an inn, a gypsy boy singing; a chorus of men and women, in an undertone, then sudden pauses, punctuated that panting, excessive, painful song, in which one felt his soul expiring every time he caught his breath . . . Not Spanish, but gypsy and irreducibly so. Ah, to hear that song again, I would have crossed three Spains![36]

Back in Paris, Gide returns to the theme of the Puritan's struggle to enjoy life. This attack on morality is none the less addressed to God:

And now my prayer (for it is still a prayer): O God, let this over-narrow morality burst and let me live, oh, fully; and give me the strength to do so, oh without fear, and without always thinking that I am about to sin! It now takes as great an effort to let myself go as it used to take to resist doing so. That morality of privation has so thoroughly become my natural morality that the other is now very painful and difficult for me. I have to strive after pleasure. I find it painful to be happy.[37]

What turned out to be a most fortunate invitation arrived from the Laurens family to join them in their country house in the small Normandy coast town of Yport. André stayed there for four weeks in May and early June. His room was high up in a tower and had eight windows, looking out in every direction. The relaxed, friendly, slightly bohemian atmosphere of the Laurens was just what he needed at this time. He was particularly struck by the uncomplicated love between Paul and his mother, so different from the constant tensions and conflicts that existed in his relations with his own mother. He warmed particularly to Paul, the elder son of the painter Jean-Paul Laurens. From his art-school friends, Paul Laurens had acquired an easy self-assurance, a light-hearted manner that concealed a sensitive, shy young man. They would rise early, fence for a while, breakfast together, then set off on some expedition, or stay at home and work in the grounds, André writing, Paul painting.

While at Yport Gide made great progress with a new work, *La Tentative amoureuse*. After a brief stay in Rouen, he returned to Paris, where he remained until the end of June. He then retreated to La Roque, where he hoped to complete a work that, though short, had proved so difficult to bring to birth. Indeed, the work itself betrays authorial impatience. It is structured on the four seasons, but with the coming of autumn, the narrator declares, 'Madame, I'm getting bored with this story' and promptly polishes off the last two seasons at great speed. The idea for the work, which bore the more explicit subtitle 'Traité du vain désir', was first suggested by some lines from Calderón's play *La Vida es Sueño* (*Life is a Dream*), which appear as the epigraph: 'Desire is like a bright flame, and whatever touches it is turned to ashes, mere dust that is blown away by a puff of wind – let us think, therefore, only of what is eternal.' It is a sentiment that would have been endorsed by both the earlier, Puritan Gide and the later Symbolist Gide: it was, however, one that the new Gide, who was beginning to think that it was perhaps the 'eternal', not 'life', that was the dream, had outlived. Indeed the rather conventional sentiments of the epigraph seem to be contradicted by the beginning of the narrative itself, a violent rejection of all restrictions on desire. The narrative proper begins in full Symbolist, not to say pre-Raphaelite fashion: 'It was dawn. Laden with flowers, Luc came out of the wood, still shrouded in nocturnal darkness. Shivering slightly from the morning freshness, he sat down on a bank to await sunrise . . .'

Before long, a circle of dancing maidens, their hair dishevelled and damp from the grass, appear. They are gathering flowers, which they hold in their raised skirts. After bathing in the spring, they all go their separate ways. One, Rachel, comes back. Luc takes her by the hand and they go off together. Their love remains 'pure' until one day, Luc finds Rachel lying on his bed. Luc wanted love, but his 'sad upbringing' had made him 'afraid of carnal possession as of something bruised'. Nevertheless, they make love and love continues through the year, following the course of the four seasons, coming to birth in the spring, maturing in the summer and dying in the autumn; by the winter, it is dead and the two young people separate. Yet their love was always doomed. 'Why are you going away?' Rachel asks. 'Are you not my whole life?' 'But you . . . are not the whole of mine,' Luc answers. 'There are other things besides.'[38]

As so often with Gide, the narrative is not delivered directly, from narrator to reader, but at one remove. Often it takes a documentary form (letters, journals, etc.). Here the narrator recounts the story of Luc and Rachel to a listener, whom he addresses as 'Madame' and, towards the end of the book, as 'sister'. With the narrator himself, therefore, there are four characters in all, two contrasting couples: the central, entirely fictional pair of lovers, who fall in love, make love and fall out of love, and the framing, equivocally 'fictional' pair, whose love for one another, such as it was, is over by the time the story starts and is never consummated. In the *Journal*, paraphrasing George Eliot, Gide makes the interesting remark: 'In *La Tentative amoureuse*, I wanted to demonstrate the influence of a book on the person writing it, and during the very act of writing. For, as it emerges from us, it changes us, altering the course of our lives . . .'[39] Astonishingly, in this short work of under 5,500 words, Gide has done just that. The author began with a daydream of love consummated and ended with the reality of a love outworn. The relationship between 'Madame' and the narrator is not, like that of Luc and Rachel, that of tangents, touching for a brief moment, then moving ever further apart, but that of parallel lines, never meeting, but always side-by-side. (Gide repeats here the image of parallel lines from *Les Cahiers d'André Walter*.) Yet there is a distinct sense of the future, the almost immediate future to come, and he does not hide from 'Madame' that she will have no part in it. There is much in *La Tentative amoureuse* that seems dated, precious even, yet it is this that is left behind in the work itself, by the device of distancing the subject within an ironic frame of commentary that already suggests the light-hearted poise of Gide's next work, the astonishingly mature *Paludes*.

In August, Marcel Drouin came to stay for a few days at La Roque, prior to going to Germany to study. They talked endlessly, mainly about German philosophy and literature. Apart from that visit Gide spent most of the summer alone with his mother. On 1 September *La Tentative amoureuse* was finished to his satisfaction – or at least to as much satisfaction as it was likely to receive from him, given the rapid acceleration in his intellectual progress. He went off to spend another week with the Laurens at Yport. Madeleine again wrote to André asking him to join her and her sisters at Cuverville, where Mme Gide was now staying. 'We did hope to procure for you a little foretaste of the Sahara here,' she wrote, 'but since Saturday it has not stopped raining.' The planned visit to Italy with Paul Laurens had already turned into the more ambitious, more exotically exciting prospect of North Africa. André returned to the rue de Commaille with his mother, then, on 6 October, left Paris for Les Sources, Uncle Charles's country house near Nîmes. There he did get a foretaste of the delights to come. 'The wind is blowing from the South, from Africa,' he wrote to his mother. 'It is warm and enervating.'

But the young Gide was not anticipating a complete change in his *mode de vie*. In the same letter he asked his mother to send to the Hôtel Terminus, Marseille, the following items: 1) visiting cards, 2) a copy of *La Logique de Port-Royal*, 3) Goethe's *Elective Affinities* (in German) and 4) a Bible. These were only a few of the trunkfuls of books that were to accompany him on his adventures, but they are instructive as to his state of mind at this time. The Goethe comes as no surprise. The choice of the classic philosophical (Cartesian) justification for the austere Jansenist thinking of Port-Royal at a time when Gide was trying to emancipate himself from Christian moral teaching demonstrates that, as always, he is capable of self-contradiction. Only a few weeks before, he had written in his *Journal*: 'All my efforts this year have been directed towards the difficult task of freeing myself at last from everything useless and narrow with which an inherited religion had surrounded me, limiting my nature . . .' Then, more interestingly, he goes on: 'The Christian soul is always imagining battles within itself . . . For whichever side is defeated, it is always part of oneself – and one is worn out to no end. I have spent my entire youth setting two parts of myself, which wanted nothing more perhaps than to come to a mutual understanding, in opposition to one another.'[40] This goes some way to explaining the request for a Bible, but in *Si le grain ne meurt*, written some thirty years later by a publicly committed anti-Christian, we read, 'I declined to take my Bible with me.' This can hardly be seen as forgetfulness of some insignificant detail, since Gide goes on: 'This, which may seem a trifling matter, was of the greatest importance: up until that time not a day had gone by when I did not go to the Holy Book for moral sustenance and guidance. But it was precisely because that sustenance seemed to me to have become indispensable that I felt the need to deprive myself of it.'[41] I would not suggest that the older Gide is consciously falsifying the evidence: a more likely explanation would be that, as always, Gide was in two minds, that he had considered not taking a Bible with him and that, once back in the Puritan heartland, he changed his mind. What is more, once in North Africa, he may not have felt any need to consult his Bible and so deprived himself of it *de facto*, if not *de jure*. Incidentally, Mme Gide was delighted, and rather surprised, to hear from her son so soon – and in language so calculated to assuage any fears she may have had as to his moral welfare while away. She asked him not to let any thoughts of her own 'solitude' and 'isolation', caused by the absence of both dead husband and living son, spoil his trip in any way. She then systematically reports how she has dealt with all his requests, adding, typically: 'Paid your tailor 160f. You left me 150 for him, so you owe me 10f' (i.e. 8 shillings or $2 at the time).

From Les Sources André went on to pay his respects to his grandmother at Uzès. It was to be the last time he saw her: she was ninety-one and died, three months later, on 15 January 1894. She was so completely deaf that any conversation was impossible. Moreover, she seemed convinced, against all his denials, that André had come to tell her that he was getting married. He then went on to Marseille, where he met up with Paul Laurens. A cold that he had contracted at his uncle's grew worse: he was coughing quite badly. Doubts were raised as to the wisdom of his imminent departure: perhaps Paul should go off alone and he would join him later. But his fate cried out. Anyway, what better cure for a cold could there be than the Algerian heat? So, on 18 October 1893, the two friends, both twenty-three, set sail from Marseille for Tunis: 'It was not so much towards a new land as towards *that*, towards that Golden Fleece, that I was rushing . . . The élite of Greece did not tremble with more solemn enthusiasm on the Argo . . . Heat lightning quivered in the distance in the direction of Africa. Africa! I repeated the mysterious word over and over again; in my imagination it was big with terrors, with alluring horrors, and with expectations . . .'[42]

6

Liberation and . . . Engagement:
'J'écris . . . Paludes'

There they were on the strip of lowland that curved round the narrow channel we had just entered, silhouetted against the sky . . . I had of course expected to see camels at Tunis, but I had never imagined them to be so strange; and then, when our ship drew up alongside the quay, that shoal of golden fish it sent spurting and flying out of the water! And the crowd straight out of the Arabian Nights, which came hustling around to seize our luggage! We were at that stage of life when every novelty gives untold delight.[1]

Everything astonished the two innocents from Paris and, to begin with at least, they fell for every trap laid to relieve them of their money. On their first day a fourteen-year-old boy, 'Céci', attached himself to them and became their guide. As a result, everything cost them half as much as before (though it took the hard-headed Mme Gide to point out that Céci would still be taking his cut). They went native to the extent of buying and wearing haiks and burnouses. Every day they visited the souks, Paul painting, André reading and observing 'the strange, beautiful population' milling around them. They left the Hôtel du Louvre and moved into a small, three-room apartment. But André had not managed to throw off the cold that had been with him for several weeks. The sirocco was blowing and, at night, he slept badly, covered in sweat. On advice, the two decided to spend the 'bad season' at Biskra, an oasis town some 300 miles inland from the Algerian coast. In order to see something of wilder, southern Tunisia they decided to choose a long way round. They trusted their persons and belongings to 'two Maltese, who looked for all the world like a couple of Calabrian brigands', one a coachman, the other an interpreter, and set off in 'a large, very elegant landau, drawn by four horses'. They spent the first night in an army camp at Zaghouan and were attacked all night by 'ravenous fleas'. They moved on to the oasis town of Kairouan, where they were invited to a feast, given for French officers by the caliph. After another day's journey through the desert, they arrived at Sousse. But, though his letters to his mother give no inkling of his state, André's health was giving cause for concern. The truth is to be found in a confidential letter to Albert Démarest: 'One lung is already out of action, the other not much better . . . Breathless-ness, shivering, sweating, pain when breathing, a slight fever, great depression and my voice practically gone . . .' Paul called a doctor, who advised them not to continue with their cross-desert trek, but to sail back to Tunis and go on to Biskra by train.

During their few remaining days at Sousse, Paul Laurens went out painting and André, often shivering and enveloped in blankets, insisted on accompanying him. As they left their hotel they were besieged by Arab boys offering their services as porters. On one occasion, André went out after Paul, with the intention of joining him later. Before long, he was approached by Ali, one of the boys who hung around outside the hotel. André agreed to let him carry his shawl and overcoat. They walked as far as the dunes, where, in a hollow in the sand, the boy threw down his burden and, with a laugh, lay down on his back, his arms outstretched, staring. 'I was not so foolish as to misunderstand his invitation; but I did not respond at once. I sat down, not far from him, but not too near either, and stared back at him, waiting, very curious as to what he would do.' The writer of *Si le grain ne meurt* expresses surprise at his slowness to respond: 'Was I still hesitating on the threshold of what is called sin? No; my disappointment would have been too great if the adventure had ended with the triumph of my virtue – which I already loathed and despised. No; it really was curiosity that made me wait . . . And I saw his laughter slowly fade away, his lips close over his white teeth; an expression of disappointment, of sadness clouded his charming face.' Seeing that the young Frenchman did not respond to his hint, the boy got up and took his leave – or so Dorothy Bussy's English translation, published by Random House, in New York in 1935 and by Secker and Warburg, London, in 1951 – would have it. Between the words '"Goodbye, then," he said' and the next paragraph, we have: '[Omission]'. A publisher's note on the title-page verso of the British edition informs us that the translation first appeared in a limited edition of 1,500 copies in 1950, but that in this Standard Edition 'two short omissions have been made, with the consent of the author'. (These omissions were made good in the Penguin Modern Classics edition of 1977.) And what are the passages that the publishers considered might offend a wider readership – or risk prosecution? The first is:

But, grasping the hand that he held out to me, I pulled him back on to the ground. His laughter reappeared at once. He soon grew impatient with the complicated knots of the cords that served as a belt; taking a small dagger out of his pocket, he cut through the tangle at a stroke. The garment fell to the ground; he threw off his jacket and stood there, naked as a god. For a brief moment, he held up his skinny arms to the sky, then, laughing, let his body fall against mine. His skin may have been burning hot, but beneath my hands it seemed as cool as the shade. How beautiful the sand was! In the wonderful splendour of the evening, what rays of sunlight clothed my joy! . . .[2]

The omitted paragraph is not some expendable detail. It is quite central to Gide's account of his emancipation from his puritan upbringing; it is the first time he makes love with a boy. It represents the physical culmination of his emancipation. Yet, in this version, the boy appears to leave the scene. For all the reader knows, the narrator may have done no more than indulge in masturbation, imagining what he might have done with the boy. Any ambiguity could have been avoided and prudery satisfied if the first two sentences of the omitted paragraph had been retained, but, no, in the words of the preceding paragraph, 'virtue' appears to have triumphed after all, thus flatly contradicting the author's intentions. The second, much longer and no less important omission occurs near the end of *Si le grain ne meurt*, but I shall discuss it later.

The friends sailed from Sousse to Tunis, as advised, and set off for Biskra. There they took an apartment in a building now part of an hotel, that had once been a monastery. Indeed the apartment had been prepared to receive Cardinal Lavigerie, Primate of Africa, but the prelate had died the year before. They took on a fifteen-year-old servant boy, Athman, 'a veritable black pearl'. He slept in a third room, cleaned his employers' shoes, fetched whatever food they needed and, when Paul went out painting, carried the easel, paint-box, folding chair and sunshade. The boy soon became a friend and ate with the two young Frenchmen: André even started to teach him English. He charmed them with his gaiety, his simple enthusiasm and his picturesque French. He was no illiterate, however: he had only just left school, where he would have followed the same curriculum as in mainland France. He was very keen to give some outward sign of his status on becoming their servant, so, instead of giving his mother the money he earned, he would spend it on splendid multi-coloured waistcoats. Before long they were visited by several of Athman's young friends and relations. 'I perform with them most of the seven works of mercy,' André wrote to his mother, 'dressing them (I have got through three gandouras), feeding them (they often come and eat with us: I give them each a large piece of bread with a little butter or cheese and dates), warming them, etc . . .: so my fame is spreading and becoming legendary . . .'[3]

A piano arrived from Algiers and Mme Gide was asked to send more scores – Clementi, Beethoven, Schumann, Chopin, Brahms. André's reading continued unabated: Barbey d'Aurevilly, Sainte-Beuve and, of course, Goethe. Under the impact of so much exotic beauty around him, he began writing verse again. Then there were the long letters back and forth between André and his mother – and even between Paul and Mme Gide. An 'avalanche of letters', instructions on all moral, social and medical matters, arrived. 'I found your advice on how to take a shower . . . enormously irritating,' André wrote back. 'Just think a little that your advice arrives at least a fortnight after it is needed, if ever one did need advice from someone who was not on the spot – and who was never asked for it.'[4] Mme Gide took the rebuke in good part, with exaggerated apologies: 'Pour le tub, pardon humblement, excuse! . . . Je vois mon erreur! Très humbles excuses . . .'[5] In one letter, André asks his mother to send him 'a whole batch of TOYS . . . that can be used outside if possible . . . I am thinking particularly of kites: some are shaped like Japanese birds, they'd be perfect . . .'[6]

They were, he says, a way of winning over the Arab children and persuading them to model for Paul's pictures of local life: they certainly made him hugely popular. It was a trick Gide used all his life. When abroad, he often had some small toy in his pocket. Even as an old man, his friends would often find him in some street or square, sitting on the ground, talking to a group of children. He was always able to strike up an immediate rapport with them: the toys, of course, were merely adjuncts, pretexts. In those innocent days, such things were not looked at askance.

In his letters to his mother, André continued to play down his poor physical state, but Mme Gide became increasingly anxious about it. She insisted on his seeing the best doctor in Biskra and having his report sent on to her own doctor in Paris, a M. Miard. The result was a deluge of advice and medicaments. She even began to hint that her place might really be at her son's side. 'M. Miard is very surprised and *almost worried* that I am not going to Biskra,' she wrote.[7] Very soon, however, André and Paul had another, imperative reason for dissuading Mme Gide from joining them. Before leaving for North Africa, both virgins, they had decided that, once on the other side of the Mediterranean, they would acquire the state of sexual experience that any self-respecting Parisian male of twenty-four would regard as normal. Several weeks had passed and nothing had been done about the matter: André's single homosexual experience at Sousse does not seem to have persuaded him to give up the idea of sexual initiation with a woman. Then, one evening, the two friends were in a café in what the locals called ('by antiphrasis?' Gide wonders) *les rues Saintes*. For those streets were associated with girls of the Oulad Naïl tribe. It was the custom in that tribe for young girls to work as prostitutes for a few years in order to save enough money for a dowry; they would then marry. These girls were renowned for their beauty and for the splendour of their dress. In the café two such girls, Meriem and her cousin En Barka, were dancing: 'They danced in the antique manner of the Oulad, heads erect, motionless above the waist, their hands agile, their whole body shaken by the rhythmic stamping of their bare feet.' They were accompanied by a clarinettist, an old negro on castanets and a boy beating away on a drum. The boy, whose name turned out to be Mohammed, particularly attracted Gide's attention: 'How beautiful he was! Half naked under his rags, black and slender as a demon, open-mouthed and wild-eyed . . .' In *Si le grain ne meurt*, Gide then recounts a curious incident. Paul, who so far had seemed wholly heterosexual and, indeed, was to prove so thereafter, turned to André and whispered: 'Do you suppose he doesn't excite me more than Meriem?' André said nothing and the subject did not arise again. Some days later, Paul caught sight of Meriem and arranged a meeting. After spending the first part of the night with Paul, she got into André's bed at dawn. This 'treatment' proved more beneficial than any doctor's ministrations: he was overcome by 'a sense of extraordinary calm and wellbeing'. 'Meriem's skin was the colour of amber, her flesh firm, her figure well rounded, but still almost childlike, for she was barely sixteen.' However, Gide the middle-aged autobiographer adds: 'If that night I was valiant with Meriem, it was because, closing my eyes, I imagined I was holding Mohammed in my arms.'[8] One suspects, however, that the truth about Gide's state of mind at the time was a great deal more complicated than the older homosexual propagandist allows, for over a period of some weeks Meriem continued to divide her nights between the two friends. Did André, on each occasion, imagine that he was in Mohammed's arms? And why, after the revelatory experience in the sand dunes outside Sousse, did he make no attempt to contact Mohammed, or some other adolescent boy? Clearly, André Gide had some way to go yet before accepting, let alone proclaiming, what he calls his 'penchant naturel'. Incidentally, Gide makes some interesting comments on their *ménage à trois*. When he later told his cousin Albert Démarest of it, he was surprised to see how such an open-minded man could disapprove of an arrangement that, for Paul and him, had seemed so natural. 'We revelled in it, our friendship was strengthened by it, as by a new bond. Nor were we jealous of all the strangers to whom Meriem accorded or sold her favours. This was because we both looked upon the carnal act at that time with cynicism and, on this occasion at least, no feelings were involved . . .'[9]

A few days before the loss of the two male virginities André had spat blood. He himself did not attach much importance to the fact, but Paul was seriously alarmed and mentioned the incident in a letter to his parents. They, in turn, felt obliged to inform Mme Gide. Justifying her decision to join her son on the grounds that Paul was not in North Africa to act as a nurse, she made the necessary arrangements. André tried to get her to postpone her visit, but it was too late. His letter arrived after she and Marie, whose feelings for André were almost as maternal, had left. They arrived at Biskra on 7 January 1894. They were given the best rooms in the hotel: as it happened, these were immediately opposite those occupied by André and Paul on the other side of the courtyard. The day of their arrival, André and Paul had forgotten that Meriem was calling on them that night. Out of respect for his mother's feelings, André told Meriem not to come in and see him: she therefore spent the whole night with Paul. Early next morning, however, Mme Gide saw Meriem cross the terrace from Paul's room and then knock on her son's window to say goodbye. When André came to greet her, he saw his mother at the window opposite. Paul went off to paint. After taking her breakfast in her room, Mme Gide finally appeared.

I cannot remember her words exactly. I do remember that I was cruel enough to tell her, with some effort, both because I did not want the blame to fall on Paul alone and because I intended to safeguard the future:

'But you know: she doesn't come only for Paul. She's coming back.'

I remember her tears. She couldn't think of anything to say and could only cry . . . I felt she was inconsolably sad.[10]

With no words to contend with and disarmed by his mother's tears, André could not allow Meriem to come to the apartment again. His only other experience of the kind was with Meriem's cousin, En Barka: 'This new attempt failed miserably,' despite the girl's great beauty, indeed, 'her very beauty froze me'. Her beauty, of course, was that of a mature woman, whereas there was something 'almost childlike' about Meriem's body.

Meanwhile, 'spring touched the oasis' and André's health continued to improve. Mme Gide and Marie returned to France, leaving André and Paul to make a leisurely return through Italy.

I felt that I was beginning to live again; it even seemed as if I were living for the first time; I had left the valley of the shadow of death and was awakening to real life. Yes, I was entering upon a new existence where every joy would be welcome and none resisted . . . I heard, I saw, I breathed as I had never done before; and as the profusion of sounds, scents and colours flooded my empty heart, I felt it melt in gratitude.
'Take me, take me body and soul,' I cried, sobbing out my worship to some unknown Apollo. 'I am thine, obedient, submissive. Let all within me be light! Light and air! My struggle against thee has been in vain. But now I know thee. Thy will be done! I am in thy hands. Take me!'[11]

They landed in Syracuse, but it was clear that André's health had suffered a relapse. They pressed on to Messina, where they stayed for a few days in a luxurious hotel, hoping that André would recover. Naples found him 'sweating in the sun, shivering in the shade and only able to walk on perfectly flat ground'. He went on to Rome to consult a doctor, leaving Paul to see Pompeii alone. On 13 April, he called on M. Guillaume, director of the Villa Medici and a friend of the Laurens, who recommended a specialist in pulmonary infections. The doctor could find little by way of infection. When Paul Laurens joined him, they rented separate apartments at opposite ends of the via Gregoriana: in this way, Paul hoped to do more painting. André also rented a piano, visited the Pincio, but saw little more of the Eternal City than the nearby gardens of the Villa Medici. While Paul went off sightseeing, André read and wrote – mainly disparate passages and jottings, some of which were to find their way into his next two, very contrasted books, the 'negative' *Paludes*, a light-hearted satire on the Parisian literary world, and the 'positive', serious *apologia pro vita sua*, the apologia at least of what he hoped his new life would be, *Les Nourritures terrestres*.
In Rome, the social life of the two friends was provided by a few of the French students at the Villa Medici – a mixed blessing. One of the students introduced them to '*une putain de style*', whom they promptly baptized '*la dame*'. But André at least felt unable to avail himself of her: her 'distinguished air, elegance and affectation' disgusted him. 'I was beginning to realize that I was able to put up with Meriem only because she was a cynical little savage; with her, at least, one knew where one stood; in the way she talked and acted, there was nothing that aped love; with the other woman I profaned the most sacred feelings of my heart.'[12] When eating together, the

conversation always returned to 'over there', to Africa. 'Africa' returned in one curious way at least: for his breathlessness, the doctor recommended cigarettes containing *cannabis indica*, 'which gave me great relief', he told his mother.[13]

After five weeks in Rome, Paul left on a brief tour that would take in Orvieto, Perugia, Assisi and Arezzo. André thought it wiser to conserve his strength and join him a week or so later in Florence. In the event, André left Rome after a few days and therefore arrived in Florence first. He took rooms in a *pensione* overlooking the Arno. Despite the weather, which, at first, was no different to Rome's – bright, promising mornings, developing into violent thunderstorms by afternoon – Gide fell in love with Florence. 'After Rome, everything seems wonderful; I am moved just to know that I am in the city of the Medici and Savonarola,' he wrote to his mother.[14] It is a neat opposition, but one may well wonder what attractions the great preaching friar still held for a Gide struggling to shake off his puritan shackles. (Only a year before, Gide had seriously considered writing a life of Savonarola.)

Despite setbacks, his health, too, improved. He wandered the streets, and visited churches and museums: the many obvious treasures apart, he was particularly taken by the Santa Trinità bridge and by Cellini's *Perseus*, 'because they surprised me and produced within me an emotion that I was not expecting'. In the same letter to his mother, Gide writes: 'Who did I meet here? Oscar Wilde!! He looks older and ugly, but he is still an extraordinary storyteller.'[15] In a letter to Valéry, Gide tells us that Wilde was with Douglas – who had joined him from Egypt. Wilde had rented a large, two-roomed apartment overlooking the river, but was leaving the following day; he offered to let Gide and Laurens take over the apartment for the remaining two weeks. It was a tempting offer, but the *pensione* won out because it provided food. André took to tramping the surrounding countryside, leaving the city, its churches and museums to Paul. Before long, Mme Gide was writing to her son wearing her prudent housekeeper's hat and armed with a current statement of accounts, complete with details of incomings and outgoings. But André was in no hurry to return home, though the money from Paul's scholarship had run out. On 24 June Paul returned to Paris and André went on, via Pisa, Genoa and Turin, to Geneva. There he called on his aunt, Mme Charles Gide, who was staying with her sister; forewarned of André's arrival, she had arranged for a Dr Andreae, a great friend of her husband's, to call that afternoon. The good doctor concluded that André was suffering from nothing but 'nerves' and prescribed a water cure at Champel, nearby, to be followed by a winter in the mountains.

He had hardly been at Champel a week when Pierre Louÿs and Ferdinand Hérold called en route for Bayreuth. From reports of his illness, they expected to find him at death's door; they saw before them a transformed André Gide, brimming over with health. He read to them his 'Ronde de la grenade' ('Round of the Pomegranate'), a poem reminiscent of the Song of Songs, celebrating the 'Joys of the flesh, tender as grass, / Charming as hawthorn blossom', that later appeared in *Les Nourritures*. He then recounted his adventures with a sixteen-year-old Arab girl, urging them to follow his example. The imaginations of the evidently imperfect Wagnerites were so fired that they decided there and then to desert the formidable attractions of Brünnhilde for the more tangible charms of Meriem. André wrote at once to Athman, telling him that he had not forgotten the wonderful days at Biskra, that he would return the following year and that, in the meantime, he was to serve his two dear friends with the same devotion as he had served 'Monsieur Paul' and 'Monsieur André'. Before long, Pierre Louÿs and his friend were sharing Meriem's favours much as André and Paul had done. Ironically, too, their North African escapade may have been Wagner's loss, but it was music's gain. Pierre Louÿs wrote his *Chansons de Bilitis*, dedicated to Gide, with a special reference to 'M. b. A.', that is, Meriem Ben Atala, which have achieved greater celebrity in their setting by Louÿs' close friend, Debussy.

Since he had left Biskra only Florence had succeeded in challenging the small Algerian town in Gide's affections. On arrival at Champel, he wrote to his mother, telling her that he felt better already, but complaining, in terms and in a tone calculated to irritate her, that Switzerland was 'too chaste a country for my taste. As you know, I have already made an apologia of chastity and I am quite willing to do so again, but I don't like it when a country sets out to teach me it. On the contrary, I prefer it to invite me to indulge in sensuality and so allow me some merit in not listening to it often. The countryside here really isn't amorous enough . . .'[16] Mme Gide could not but have been reminded, painfully, of the amorous invitations to sensuality clearly accepted by her son at Biskra. 'Chastity?' she replied. 'Ah! What can I say, dear, dear child? What would *your father, your grandfather,* your uncle have said? Of course, they were not men to be swayed by the sophisms, excuses, explanations and prevarications of the world. Their moral sense would have remained intact, pure, lofty, uncompromised!'[17]

During the four weeks André spent in Switzerland, letters passed to and fro between Champel and La Roque almost daily, interspersed with the occasional, peremptory telegram. The question of money crops up intermittently. 'I gave you a summary of your financial situation in one of my recent letters, so I won't start all over again,' Mme Gide writes, then proceeds to do so: 'Between 1890 and 1893 (four years) you have spent the available part of the money you inherited from Aunt Briançon; this year you are *already* living off your inheritance from your grandmother,' etc., etc.[18] At one point Mme Gide hints that many of her son's problems would disappear if he had a proper career. 'At the moment, if I had a career, I would give my notice, or hang myself,' he replies. 'I am the happiest of men . . . Nothing is more uncertain than my life: what will become of me, what will I do, where will I go??? That is what makes life so wonderful for me.'[19]

The question as to who would go to La Roque and when was bandied back and forth. At one stage André committed the supreme blackmail of declaring that if he could not come on his terms, he would not come at all. 'It's all settled . . . *I'll see you at La Roque on 1 August,* and don't say there's no room for Rouart; *room must be found,* in the larder if necessary . . . If not, I'll go off to Madagascar at the next moon.'[20] (Eugène Rouart was the son of Henri Rouart, a friend of Manet and Degas and a well-known collector of modern French painting. Gide had met him at the Laurens' some eighteen months before and the two became close friends.) André got his way. At La Roque, Mme Gide set about preparing her household to receive her son and his prescribed guests: Madeleine Rondeaux and her two sisters, Paul Laurens and his brother Pierre, Marcel Drouin, Eugène Rouart and his dog (or bitch, rather) Ellis. All others – the Rondeaux brothers, Isabelle (Albert Démarest's sister) and her husband Edouard Widmer – were proscribed. When Mme Gide protested, in vain, that the Widmers had already been invited, André's reply was adamant: 'Too bad. Anyway, they will have to get used to being scandalized by me.'[21] André's intentions were not to keep his mother company over a long summer in Normandy, but to spend just two weeks at La Roque with those of his friends he felt closest to at that time and, more importantly, to see Madeleine in the best possible setting. In the event, André's designs did not succeed, though the occasion did sow the seeds of another marriage, that of Marcel Drouin and Jeanne Rondeaux. Madeleine could hardly recognize the confident man that her shy cousin had turned into. She did not doubt his affection and certainly reciprocated it, but she felt, rightly, that he did not love her in the way a future husband should. She seemed to be beyond persuasion; he more determined than ever that she should marry him. By the end of the fortnight at La Roque,

Madeleine was under the impression that André had abandoned his suit; in fact, meeting a categorical refusal, he merely pretended to do so, otherwise Madeleine would not have agreed to resume their correspondence.

After leaving La Roque, André did write to Madeleine, but received no response for two months. When it came, on 19 October, it consisted of fifty pages of beautiful handwriting, without a single crossing out, dated almost daily from 11 September. She enjoyed the weeks at La Roque, she says, but, of André's friends, she cared only for Drouin. On page 44, she asks whether the '*lettres-volume*' should be sent at all, or consigned to a drawer with others. She deals at some length with André's literary output so far, rejecting all of it, except 'certain pages of *Les Cahiers*', on account of its 'lack of naturalness'. 'Any work of art is sterile,' she then declares, 'if it does not depend upon the help of God.' On page 45 she finally comes to the main point:

I cannot leave you, dear André, without thanking you for the assurance you have given me of the constancy of your affection. Truly I have never entirely doubted it. I should also say what relief you have brought me by giving up any idea of marriage – for which I have always felt a moral terror, as my feelings moved ever further away from it. You cannot know how much I felt, on reading your letter, that a suffocating weight of anxiety had been lifted from me, forever. How much more I would have enjoyed La Roque if I had known this before! . . . But I regret nothing, not even the very unhappy days your disastrous obstinacy brought me . . . [All I wanted] was for our lives, which had been too close, to be disentangled. I thank God that this has now been done, and so simply.[22]

Despite his dislike of Switzerland, André had decided to follow medical advice and spend some months in the mountains, at La Brévine, near Neuchâtel. There, too, he hoped to finish *Paludes*. He would arrive there in mid-October. With disputes over the guest list at La Roque at an end, relations between mother and son improved. Over the next six or seven weeks he wandered over Switzerland and northern Italy. At Como, his hotel room overlooked the lake. On a particularly beautiful evening he hired a boat, complete with young oarsman. They rowed out on to the lake. Given the height, steepness and closeness of the mountains on either side, they were soon almost in darkness: 'We let fall our oars and sat there, motionless, in that marvellous serenity. The boy who was guiding me then came and sat beside me. "Come è bello!" I took his hand and we stayed for a long time like that, without saying a word . . . It was quite dark when we got back . . . Such evenings are unforgettable.' This idyllic episode comes not from the *Journal*, nor from *Si le grain ne meurt*, but from a letter . . . to his mother![23] Although André's account of the episode on Lake

Como may seem innocent enough, and would certainly have been taken as such by the letter's recipient, the episode itself was not at all 'innocent'. It does, in fact, appear in *Si le grain ne meurt*, though in a rather more unexpurgated version. Gide has just referred to his sexual encounter with Mohammed in Algiers, some four months later, in January 1895. The memory of that night, he says, haunted him whenever he went in search of pleasure. Between his first homosexual revelation at Sousse and that night with Mohammed in Algiers, his experiences with young men had occurred 'in passing, furtively as it were'. However, he goes on, there was one delicious occasion with 'a young boatman on Lake Como', when 'my ecstasy was wrapped in moonlight and the misty enchantment of the lake merged with the moist scents from its shores'.[24]

From Como, André moved on to Neuchâtel, where he took a room in a 'temperance' establishment, frequented by abstemious, impecunious old ladies. In the dining-room, they ate their frugal meals beneath a large notice bearing the words: 'The Lord is my Shepherd; I shall not want'. Below was a smaller notice advertising 'raspberry lemonade'. But his room had a splendid view of the lake and he went for long walks, along the lakeside and in the woods outside the town. To Marcel Drouin he wrote:

I have no time: I must work – it's a vital necessity (I'm speaking in Swiss) – every day four to six hours at the piano, three or four hours walking (I'd cut them out if I didn't think they were so good – anyway, my thoughts and imagination work best when I am walking) – one-and-a-half or two hours of hygiene (baths, washes, rubbings, exercises, etc.). Add to all that, quite apart from my work, writing letters to my mother and you'll see what is left for my, horribly stiff, translation of Novalis and for *Paludes*, which is getting nowhere . . .[25]

The same letter shows that, in addition to *Paludes*, he was also working on *Philoctète*, *Proserpine*, *La Mort de Mlle Claire* (to become *La Porte étroite*) and *Les Nourritures terrestres*. Notwithstanding all this, his reading continued unabated: Goethe and a life of Lessing; Strindberg and Ibsen. Every autumn he read 'Dickens, Turgenev, or Eliot, but especially Dickens'. He picked up Leibnitz where he had left off, and Fichte. Comments on his philosophical reading led to a new attempt to clarify his thoughts on the existence and nature of God. It might seem odd to us that, at this stage in his intellectual and emotional progress, he should devote the last four pages of his *Journal* for 1894 to theological concerns. He still believes in God, but his pantheistic, immanentist God is one that only the most modernist of Christian theologians could accept. The tortured guilt of the fallen creature has been left behind. God is to be found everywhere and to be worshipped by 'every part of me'. One should not set up an antagonism between two parts of one's nature, see oneself as an enemy of nature.

As the time approached for André to submit to the wintry rigours of La Brévine, Mme Gide began to doubt her son's resolution, fearing that he might take off for Egypt or Algeria. 'The experience of last year clearly showed, in my opinion, that hot climates are not at all as sedative for your nerves as the cold climate of the Alps,' she wrote. 'For once in your life have the manliness [*force virile*] to resist your enthusiasms and fancies . . .'[26] André responds firmly, but with a touch of humour: 'Please, don't try to force me with every possible trick . . . to spend this winter at La Brévine . . . If you want to put me off the idea just try to pass off my decision as a decision that you have taken and that I should be kind enough to follow.'[27]

Gide made an expedition to La Brévine to reconnoitre the terrain. He looked for accommodation at a couple of outlying farms, without success, and a night spent in 'a horrible little room' convinced him that the only hotel, the vaingloriously named Hôtel de Ville, would not do. The *hôtelière* then offered him 'a splendid apartment' consisting of four rooms, plus a servant's room on the floor above, for the ridiculously low rent of '6of a month, inclusive!!!!! with all meals provided for 3f a day!!!!!'[28] He then went off to spend a weekend with Maurice Quillot, who was now running a dairy at Montigny, near Dijon. During the fifteen-hour train journey, he read *Phèdre*, the *Symposium*, several chapters of a book on Goethe, some Lessing, Leibnitz . . . Quillot still clung to his literary ambitions and a large portrait of Maurice Barrès hung in his office. On the journey back to Neuchâtel Gide reflected on his good fortune, when compared to that of so many of his friends who were forced to earn a living: 'Only intense work can excuse my wealth in my own eyes. Wealth considered solely as a permission to work freely.'[29]

On the evening of 17 October, exposed to the bitterly cold wind, Gide travelled to La Brévine by *diligence-coupé*. The journey took over three hours. He arrived after ten, to be greeted as 'the new Lord of the Village' by the *hôtelière* and her staff. La Brévine turned out to be a small, inaccessible village, totally devoid of interest, set in a peat bog and surrounded by fir trees. Gide made inquiries of a few local people, expressing his intention of spending the winter there. This was greeted with 'the greatest stupefaction' by everyone. Gide made a couple of desultory social calls – on the local doctor and pastor, to whom he had a letter of introduction from Dr Andreae, but neither encouraged further meetings. The doctor informed him that the thermometer sometimes dropped for long periods to −30°C or more and that they had a lot of fog on account of the peat bogs. At this point, one cannot but wonder whether Dr Andreae of Geneva was not indulging in some practical joke at his patient's expense in prescribing a winter at La Brévine. Perhaps not, but he was trying to administer a shock, psychological and physical, to a young, highly nervous young man who seemed obsessed with North Africa. But Gide was in no way shaken in his resolve to spend the winter there. For him it was not a penance. That there was nothing to do there was an advantage: he wanted only to work, without distraction. It did have one, equivocal interest, however: Rousseau had lived there 125 years before – equivocal because Jean-Jacques does not seem to have taken to the place any more than Gide did. One has to have lived there, Gide writes in *Si le grain ne meurt*, to appreciate what Rousseau says of it in *Les Confessions*. 'Ill-will, spiteful talk, scowling looks, mocks and jeers – no, he invented none of them; I met with them all myself, even to the stones thrown at a stranger by a pack of village children.'[30]

Gide asked the pastor if he knew of some 'Athman of La Brévine who would clean my shoes, look after my skates, make tea, do little errands, make my fire, etc., etc.'. No village Athman materialized. Instead he was sent a Swiss girl of ample figure ('une plantureuse Suissesse'), called Augusta:

She used to talk to me a great deal about her fiancé; but one morning, while she was showing me his photograph, I rashly began to amuse myself by tickling her neck with my quill pen, when to my extreme embarrassment she suddenly collapsed into my arms. With great effort, I lifted her on to a sofa; then, as she still clung to me, I found myself tumbled on to her bosom between her open legs; seized with disgust, I cried out, 'I can hear voices!' and, pretending to be scared, I freed myself from her arms like another Joseph and went off to wash my hands.[31]

Augusta and her unwanted attentions apart, André Gide had little or no contact with the inhabitants of La Brévine. Attired in his new winter wardrobe of fur-lined coat, waterproof boots lined with sheepskin, fur hat, etc., he went for long walks through the fir trees, 'which seemed to introduce into the whole of nature a sort of moroseness and Calvinistic stiffness'. Before arriving he had had a piano sent from Neuchâtel and asked his mother to send him Bach scores – *The Well-Tempered Clavier, The Art of Fugue*; Chopin and Schumann, he felt, did not accord with La Brévine. Most days, he practised for two or more hours. Then there was his correspondence, especially with his mother. There were the usual altercations over money – and the usual complaints against La Brévine. 'For a hole, it's a real hole!!!'

he wrote on 26 October. 'Each day I exclaim ecstatically: God it's ugly!! . . . Everyone I meet is amazed to learn that I am spending the winter here. Some declare that I won't stay the course.'[32] He informs his mother of his plans to 'go off to Algiers for a month, Biskra for another month, then somewhere near Naples'. This meets with immediate disapproval: 'I feel quite demoralized to see this restless, unsettled, turbulent mood beginning to take hold of you and make you lose all feeling for anything other than this need for change, for novelty . . . If I were allowed to express *my wishes* on the matter, I would say that I am strictly opposed to a return to Biskra this year.'[33] Then there was the equivocal, unresolved status of his relationship with Madeleine, a constant source of anxiety for Mme Gide. André, believing that his mother was sabotaging his plans by interfering, wrote to her on 18 October: 'I beg you with all my heart to leave relations between Madeleine and me alone . . . One imprudent word from you can do us a lot of harm . . . I must warn you that if anyone upsets what is to me the dearest thing in the world, the worst consequences are possible . . .' He then adds an astonishing threat: 'Don't go against things. If you upset them, I don't know what I shall do, I don't think I could ever see you again.'[34] André now mooted the idea of returning to North Africa . . . with Madeleine and Mme Gide, his mother clearly acting as chaperone. By some strange, apparently contradictory thought process, he wanted to bring together, in irreconcilable disunion, the sensual, sexual delights of North Africa with his pure, quite unphysical love for Madeleine – which he did a year later . . . on his honeymoon. Mme Gide's response was predictable and, given the social conventions of the day, understandable. Madeleine was still of marriageable age (she was twenty-seven) and could not compromise her reputation and, by extension, that of her younger sisters, by appearing to consort with a man she was not engaged to.

Gide's main reason for staying in La Brévine was to finish *Paludes*. Long before it appeared, the work had been the subject of some speculation, many inquiries and a good deal of amusement in his circle of friends. On 11 November Pierre Louÿs, hearing, incorrectly, that *Paludes* was finished, wrote to Gide:

Why the devil is *Paludes* finished? Just like that, so quickly? It's very short, then? And anyway, it should never have been finished. P.S. I explain *Paludes* to the masses thus – am I wrong? Last winter I wrote to Gide: 'What are you doing?' Well, he was doing nothing, but he replied all the same: 'I'm writing *Paludes*.' And Régnier asked him: 'What are you doing these days, my dear fellow?' Well, he was still doing nothing, but he replied to Régnier: 'I'm writing *Paludes*!' – and the disciples wrote to him: 'What are you doing? Master, what are you doing?' Well, he was indulging in little acts of coitus with my future companion [Meriem]. But he replied gravely, in that voice that you know so well and with that gesture of the raised hand: 'I'm writing *Paludes*!' And so the idea occurred to him (*Paludes* being originally a volume of verse) to recount the situation of the gentleman who is writing *Paludes*. Send it to me.[35]

Gide did send him the first part, with a view to its publication in *La Revue Blanche*. (It appeared there in January 1895.) On 6 December, Gide wrote to Valéry, announcing that '*Paludes* was finished yesterday' and enclosing the manuscript. He asked Valéry to take it at once to Bailly, the publisher, and to show it to no one. However Louÿs, who had a rather proprietorial attitude to the book, believing that it would be dedicated to him – after all, he had dedicated *Les Chansons de Bilitis* to Gide – persuaded Valéry to lend it to him for a few hours. Gide must have been astonished to receive a wildly enthusiastic letter from him: '*Paludes* is extraordinarily good . . . A thousand times better than expected. But you're a filthy bastard, giving it to Valéry first, then forbidding him to show it to me.' Louÿs then embarks on a fantasy that must have caused Gide no little anxiety – and irritated him greatly. His only consolation, says Louÿs, is that Valéry has not yet read it. He is therefore the only person who has read it. It had to be thus and thus it should remain. He proposes to re-read it and burn it page by page, as he does so.[36]

Writing of this period in his life in *Si le grain ne meurt*, Gide describes his mental state after returning from North Africa as that of a 'Lazarus escaped from the tomb'. He felt possessed of 'the secret of a man who has come back to life' (*un secret de ressuscité*) and had 'a frantic desire to live'. Much of his previous existence had had the smell of mortality about it. Yet that sense of 'estrangement' would, he says, have driven him to suicide had he not been able to describe it, in ironic mode, in *Paludes*.[37] Certainly the ironic mode successfully conceals any mood of despair. The lightness of touch, the playful absurdity, the total lack of self-importance, indeed the witty gravity, are rare in a writer so young. They are unexpected, uncharacteristic even, in the Gide we thought we knew up to this time – though something of its *saugrenu* (the word, meaning preposterous, ridiculous, ludicrous, was Gide's own) is already to be found in the *Poésies d'André Walter* and in the second part of *Le Voyage d'Urien*.

The *saugrenu* begins with the title. '*Paludes*' is a neologism deriving from a passage in the first of Virgil's *Bucolics* that is quoted, or rather freely translated, on the first page. It refers to a *palus* (marsh), from which we have the French adjective *paludéen* (paludal). There is also in *paludes* an entirely appropriate suggestion of a verbal play on 'ludic', playful. The humour continues with the original subtitle, later dropped, 'Traité de la contingence', for this *jeu d'esprit* is in no sense a 'treatise'. It is, however, very much *about* contingency, about a world of banal, insignificant, apparently unconnected facts. As such it forms a pendant to the *Traité du Narcisse*, subtitled 'Théorie du Symbole', whose concern is the absolute. Indeed the 1891 edition of *Narcisse* announces a forthcoming 'petit traité de la contingence'. Then, in *Le Voyage d'Urien*, Ellis sits in the boat reading *Traité de la Contingence* – it had, of course, not yet been written and was no more than the working title of a project.

When *Les Caves du Vatican* was published in 1914, it was announced as a '*sotie* by the author of *Paludes*'. *Paludes* had thus become the prototype of a new category of Gidean fiction, in which the treatment was predominantly humorous. A *sotie* (from *sot*, foolish, stupid) was a genre of satirical farce current in the fifteenth and sixteenth centuries. In 1895, however, the word *sotie* had not yet occurred to Gide, but the notion was there, as witness the dedication: 'For my friend Eugène Rouart, I wrote this satire of what.' The connection with *Les Caves du Vatican* and the intuitive, intellectually uncertain nature of the writing are succinctly stated in one of Gide's interviews with Jean Amrouche: 'Quite frankly, the writing of *Paludes* gave me enormous pleasure and amusement, in a way that I have experienced since only with *Les Caves du Vatican*, but in a state of almost total unawareness.'[38] At the time, too, he admitted as much. 'Before I explain my book to others,' the preface begins, 'I am waiting for others to explain it to me.' But this uncertainty is seen as a positive virtue: 'To explain it beforehand would be to restrict its meaning; for though we may know what we intended to say, we do not know if that was all we said. – One always says more than THAT. – And what interests me most in my book is what I have put into it without being aware of it, – that unconscious part . . .'[39]

'Satire of what', then? In the first instance, *Paludes* is a satire of literary Paris in general, the world of the *salons* and *cénacles*, and, in particular, of the group of more-or-less Symbolist young writers who frequented Mallarmé's *Mardis*. Symbolism itself is not attacked, however, and there is no Mallarmé-figure in the book – though his name does crop up, once, in conversation. Indeed it was to Mallarmé that Gide addressed the first of six special 'lettered' copies (the one marked 'A'). Mallarmé repaid the compliment in a letter charged with bejewelled, quintessentially Mallarméan phrases that defy adequate translation: 'l'affabulation spirituelle approche la merveille' ('the witty construction of the plot verges on the marvellous'), 'génial, ce discret, terrible badinage à fleur d'âme' ('a work of genius, that discreet, terrible banter on the surface of the soul').[40]

Gide's relationship with Symbolism at this time was a complicated one: if *Paludes* is a critique of the Symbolists it is one directed from within rather than without. The treatment of his ostensible subject-matter may be critical, but its formal treatment of it is a move forward within the Symbolist tradition, towards what was to become 'modernism', rather than away from it. *Paludes*, then, may reject the Symbolist trappings, a mythological dream-world evoked in highly wrought 'poetic' prose. It is set in Paris, in the present, and nobody seems to do very much except call on friends. The writing is comic, ironic, deliberately unpoetic. Yet it is not a return to the realistic novel either. It has a truly Symbolist autonomy, self-referentiality, 'unreality', even. Nothing is 'described'. Most of the 'characters' – there are over forty 'names', ranging disconcertingly from the ordinary (Léon, Jules, Richard) to the preposterous (Hermogène, Amilcar, Ildevert, etc.) – make fleeting, walk-on appearances. In this short work, covering a period of only six days, from Tuesday to Sunday, plot is reduced to little more than the progress in the writing of *Paludes*. The work begins:

About five o'clock it got cooler; I shut my windows and began writing again.

At six my great friend Hubert arrived; he was on his way back from riding-school.

He said: 'Well, well! Are you working?'

I replied: 'I'm writing *Paludes*.'

'What's that?'

'A book.'[41]

For there are two *Paludes*: the one published under the name of André Gide, which we might call *Paludes I*, and the one being written by the first-person narrator (*Paludes II*, say), the first, in a sense, being named after the second. In a well-known passage of the *Journal*, written in the summer of 1893, Gide likens this fiction-within-the-fiction to the use of mirrors in paintings by Memling, Quintijn Metzys and Velázquez. (Readers of Michel Foucault will remember the brilliant analysis of Velázquez's *Las Meniñas* with which *Les Mots et les choses – The Order of Things –* opens.) Gide goes on to refer to the play-within-the-play in *Hamlet*, the puppet scenes in Goethe's *Wilhelm Meister* and the story read to Roderick in Poe's *The Fall of the House of Usher*. Yet, says Gide, none of these comparisons quite fits. A more accurate comparison would be with the heraldic device 'that consists in setting in the escutcheon a smaller one "in abyss" ["*en abyme*"]'.[42] The fiction-within-a-fiction was to reach its most splendid culmination, of course, some thirty years later, in *Les Faux-Monnayeurs*. As a result, much has been written by Gide's commentators on the '*mise-en-abyme*', as they invariably call it. Contrary to what might be supposed, however, the placing 'in abyss' refers, not to the escutcheon within the escutcheon, which is called 'inescutcheon', but simply to the placing of any 'charge' (i.e. motif) at the centre. Moreover, the commentators usually assume that what they erroneously call '*mise-en-abyme*' necessarily entails the use of a smaller escutcheon identical with the larger one, thus producing a progress to infinity. In fact, this is often not the case where 'inescutcheon' is used, though it may be. In any case, Gide could hardly have wished to suggest that *Paludes II* was identical with *Paludes I*: the characters of *Paludes I* often discuss *Paludes II*, usually with the effect of ridiculing it, and the few passages quoted from *Paludes II* are deliberately unappetizing. The relation between the two is, as we shall see, metaphorical, not literal – a very Symbolist device, this.

'What's that?' Hubert asks of *Paludes II*. The same question recurs throughout – and is given a variety of answers. It is 'the story of someone who cannot travel', 'the story of the neutral ground that belongs to every-body', 'it's about the normal man', 'the story of the third person, the person one is talking about, the person who lives within each of us and does not die with us', 'the story of the man who lies down', 'at this moment, *Paludes* is the story of Angèle's *salon*.'[43] More literally, *Paludes II* is about a bachelor, Tityre (the Gidean offspring of Virgil's shepherd, Tityrus), who lives in a tower, surrounded by a moat, in the middle of marshlands. Like Gide himself at La Roque, he can fish from his bedroom window. Through lack of skill and patience, and an abhorrence of doing anything that might be called 'an act', he soon gives up. Hungry, he is reduced to eating the bait, that is, worms (*vers*, also meaning verse), thus further demonstrating his impracticality.

At first sight an opposition seems to have been set up between the existence of Tityre in his tower and that of his narrator and his friends in Paris. Tityre lives alone in the country, never sees anyone, never goes anywhere, but remains, *Tityrus recubans*, staring out vacantly over the uninter-rupted view of the marshlands. The narrator and his friends are scarcely ever alone, spending their time bustling through the built-in streets of the city, from one small stuffy room to another. However, they do have a secret, metaphorical relationship, for the hustle and bustle of the Parisian *littérateurs* is as much a manifestation of unhealthy stagnation as Tityre's recumbent inaction. The urban social and literary whirl is, as it were, a whirlpool, a symbol of repetitive movement, turning endlessly on itself. The unnamed first-person narrator is very much of this world. What we know of *Paludes II* strikes only by its *saugrenu* quality, a trifle hardly worth the consideration given it by the characters of *Paludes I*, but then, they themselves do not seem worthy of our attention. In addition to the 'book' that he is writing, actually in the form of a diary ('Le Journal de Tityre'), the narrator also keeps a diary. (There are few works by Gide in which someone is not keeping a diary; here we have two.) This one, however, is original in that it consists of two parts; on one sheet the writer lists what he intends to do one week ahead, on another what he actually did. There is, of course, a wide discrepancy between the two, since, by the time he comes to do something, the diarist has forgotten what he originally intended to do. A comparison of the two affords him an element of surprise that would otherwise be absent from his repetitive, humdrum existence. He calls this a 'negative unforeseen' – there is little 'positive' unforeseen in his life. In the afterword to the second edition, Gide declares: 'I am not he who says *I* in *Paludes* and who bears no other name.'[44] On the other hand, he writes to Eugène Rouart on 20 May 1894: 'I'm working on *Paludes* . . . I put myself in it – indeed it's a satire on us.' Let us say, then, that the narrator is an aspect, at least, of the earlier, pre-Biskra André Gide. To complicate matters further, the narrator remarks of the central character of his own book: 'Tityre is me, and he isn't me . . .'[45]

Moreover, no positive alternative to that world is offered. When the narrator and Angèle finally bring themselves to escape from Paris and to travel, they get no further than Montmorency. The only escape is effected by Hubert and Roland, who go off to . . . Biskra. In the context, this seems like nothing more than a fashionable Parisian thing to do, yet André Gide could only write of the world of *Paludes* after his experiences at Biskra and in North Africa. He could only write of North Africa after writing *Paludes*. *Paludes* is a sort of prelude to *Les Nourritures terrestres*.

So the narrator's attempt to escape fails miserably. 'With *Paludes* finished, God only knows how I am going to occupy myself,' he complains. 'I thought of taking up my old subject, POLDERS, again . . .' The main body of *Paludes* ends symmetrically with its beginning:

At six o'clock, my great friend Gaspard arrived.
He was on his way back from fencing practice. He said:

'Well, well! Are you working?'
I replied: 'I'm writing *Polders* . . .'[46]

The very form of the book reflects, in its frivolous circularity, the world it satirizes. A polder, it should be said, is a piece of land that has been reclaimed from the sea, a lake or . . . marshlands – the joke would have had particular significance for the work's dedicatee, Eugène Rouart, a student of agriculture. 'Polders' was also the title of one of the *Poésies d'André Walter* and therefore was, in one sense, already written. In another sense, the real polders, André Gide's, not the putative *Polders* of the rather ridiculous narrator, was *Les Nourritures terrestres*, a hymn to a barren land made fertile. There is also another 'sequel' to *Paludes*, *Le Prométhée mal enchaîné*, Gide's second *sotie*, written after *Les Nourritures*, in which Tityre and Angèle reappear.

'I am writing *Polders* . . .' brings to an end only the main body of *Paludes*. Gide has not yet finished sending up his own work. There follow an '*Envoi*' (in verse), a short 'Alternative' (in rather poetic prose, ending with the word '*fin*' (end)) and a 'Table of the most remarkable sentences in *Paludes*', which reads as follows:

Page 91. – He said: 'Well, well! Are you working?'
    Page 143. – When one takes up an idea, one must carry it to its logical conclusion.
    Page *

At the bottom of the page a footnote reads: '*Out of respect for personal idiosyncrasies, I am leaving to each reader the task of filling up this page.'

The refusal of authorial omniscience, even of the limited knowledge of a first-person narrator; the rejection of the smooth integrity of the textual fabric in favour of sudden shifts from one narrative mode to another (the narrator's narrative, the narrator's diary, Tityre's journal, verse, etc.); the replacement of any real plot by the progress of the writing of the work-within-the-work; the linguistic circularity effected by almost identical beginning and end; the invention of a comic, satirical form that is philosophically, even theoretically, oriented, but takes as its object, not the universal foibles of mankind, seen from the point of view of an all-knowing, self-confident moral intelligence, but the pitiful, literary enterprise itself, the difficulty of saying anything about anything – all this makes *Paludes* an astonishing work to be written in 1894 by a young man of twenty-four. It is not at all surprising that modern French critics, Sarraute and Barthes *en tête*, whose preoccupations are so similar, have seen it as the first 'modern' novel.

The isolation of La Brévine had enabled Gide to finish *Paludes* – and to continue with other works in progress. Indeed part of the difficulty in writing *Paludes* was keeping at bay a swarm of ideas that could not be contained within its narrow compass. But with *Paludes* finished, Gide could hardly stay a day longer in his Swiss 'hole'. In fact, he was back in Paris by 16 December. André's early return certainly upset Mme Gide's plans. The Rondeaux sisters were expected to spend Christmas at the rue de Commaille – this would be out of the question if André were there. In the end, they did come to Paris for Christmas, staying at their Aunt Claire's. The reunion seems to have been a disaster on all fronts. On Christmas Day, André took the train for Montpellier, travelling overnight: he was to spend the New Year with Uncle Charles. A few days later, he received a letter from Madeleine, now back in Rouen. 'Quel triste revoir,' she began:

You seem to imply that the fault lay with the others, but it lies, half at least, with us, and now I think, I know, my poor friend, that it will always be so. Ah! I beg you, let us not see one another any more. Why that embarrassment, that silence, that sense of being in a false situation, when we have so much to say to one another? Oh! It's unbearable . . .

On Christmas Day evening, when you came over to the sofa where I was sitting . . . to say goodbye, I could hardly get a word out. It was as if my heart had stopped beating . . . I understood, clearly and suddenly, that you were leaving . . .

Madeleine clearly thought that André might put off his departure at the last minute and try to see her again:

Next day, I waited madly all morning for you to come. In the afternoon, I went to the Louvre and it pained me to look at things without you. It was four o'clock, I was with Valentine, we had plenty of time to go to the rue de Commaille – I wanted to so much! I didn't dare to: fear of what others might think, fear of what we might do. And I went home feeling quite desperate, planning a farewell letter in which I would say that I did not want to write to you any more, because I felt too much that our correspondence was merely a great mirage . . . You did not receive that letter, but it was half-written . . .[47]

Gide spent three weeks at Montpellier. He had lunch with Paul Valéry's mother and looked up various young literary acquaintances, one of whom he visited in hospital most afternoons. (Jean de Tinan, the author of three novels, died in 1898, aged twenty-four.) Since the fierce intellectual activity that ended with the finishing of *Paludes*, however, he felt that he was in the grip of his old nervous illness, a depressive, indecisive state of torpor. 'This tiredness paralyses and stiffens my thinking,' he wrote to his mother, 'deadens all sounds, wraps my brain in cotton-wool, so that everything reaches it smothered, diminished, so that it doesn't seem worth the trouble any more.'[48] He could not work; he wanted to write to Madeleine, but had to resort to passing messages of goodwill via his mother; he had difficulty making up his mind as to whether he should go back to Paris or set out for North Africa. In the end, almost incapable of decision, he decided to sail for Algiers.

At Marseille, he took a room in an hotel on the Canebière. It seems as if he was suddenly terrified of the prospect of finding himself alone on the other side of the Mediterranean. Within a few days of sailing for Algiers, he is begging his mother to join him with Madeleine. 'I am so obsessed by the desire to see you ["*vous*", in the plural] that I dare not leave Marseille without knowing whether you would come with me?! . . . Reply quickly, for this waiting is wearing me out . . .'[49] Receiving no telegram next day, he wrote again – in fact, he wrote twice, suggesting other possible places where the three of them could go (Naples, Florence, even Cannes or Menton) if Algeria were rejected. By Sunday, 20 January, his fourth day in Marseille, still no news had arrived from Rouen, where Mme Gide was staying with the *cousines*. In fact, that same day, Mme Gide finally put pen to paper, rejecting the whole idea out of hand, in a letter that André did not see until he was in Algiers. '"I'm waiting for you!" you say. But why!? For what!? . . . And how could you, knowing Madeleine's character and the circumstances of her life, get so carried away with this crazy plan? You must be quite out of your mind! . . .'[50] Mme Gide goes on to say that a certain young man is coming to Rouen, with his sister, to press his suit to Jeanne Rondeaux, and Madeleine would therefore not dream of absenting herself at such a time, 'on any pretext whatsoever'.

The same day Mme Gide wrote this letter, André was writing to her. Quite suddenly, it seems, he had emerged from his depressed state. He was now 'madly happy', as if an operation for cataract had given back his sight or an ear had come unblocked. The day before he had met up with a young poet, Léon Parsons, invited him to lunch, 'baptized with Moët' the literary magazine that he was starting and spent the afternoon at the house of '*une dame . . . qui s'intéresse aux arts*', where he played 'Schumann, Massenet, etc.' on 'an excellent Pleyel grand' and read aloud the first part of *Paludes*. Failing the arrival of a positive telegram, which, he now realized, was 'very unlikely', he would be sailing for Algiers the next day.[51]

André Gide dreamt of seeing an Algiers bathed in sunlight. 'I had looked forward excitedly to finding spring already there; but the sky was overcast; it was raining; an icy wind blowing from the heights of the Atlas Mountains or from the depths of the desert brought with it fury and despair. Jupiter had betrayed me. I was horribly disappointed.'⁵² He found it impossible to find lodgings anywhere but in expensive European quarters – and this further depressed him. But, with Gide the meteorological soon became metaphysical: 'I have the feeling that I am going through a very important *crisis*, and I don't understand anything about it at all – a decisive crisis perhaps, and one from which I shall emerge fully grown: nothing, nothing interests me any more.'⁵³ Meanwhile, he tried to distract himself from his distraction reading *Barnaby Rudge*. Next day the weather had changed and so, too, had his mood. A few hours later he had left Algiers, that 'frightful bazaar', for Blida, a small town some 30 miles away. Three days later, he was leaving the Grand Hôtel de l'Orient (not arriving, as Richard Ellmann has it, in his *Oscar Wilde*), when he happened to notice the blackboard in the entrance hall on which the guests' names were written. Gide left three, subtly different versions of what happened next.

The first, written the following day, is contained in a letter to his mother and, therefore, the most 'edited', though also, in many ways, the most interesting. 'I wanted to leave at four o'clock: my luggage was packed, I was ready . . . What name did I see, on the visitors' board . . . Oscar Wilde! Perhaps he had seen my name; if I left without shaking his hand, I could not avoid the suspicion of wanting to avoid him . . . He had gone out: so, missing my train, I stayed and waited for . . . that terrible man, the most dangerous product of modern civilization.' Giving Gide the charitable benefit of any doubt, it might be argued that he was merely repeating, ironically, sarcastically even, the common *bien pensant* view of Wilde. But then he was writing to his mother, on whom any such ironic intent would be lost: if she had been capable of encompassing the truth about Wilde, she, too, would have judged him no less sternly. Any doubts that Gide was not simply passing moral judgement seem dispelled by his comments on Douglas, 'cette folie de dépravation', whom Wilde 'seems to have corrupted to the core' and who is capable of 'doing anything under the pretext of aestheticism'. The two had now been put 'on the index of London and Paris' and were 'the most compromising company in the world'.⁵⁴ Nevertheless, Gide did wait for Wilde and dined at the hotel with him. They were then joined by Douglas on a tour of the town's night life. 'Un guide bizarre' took them to a number of cafés, in one of which 'a brawl transformed the scene into a Delacroix picture – superb! superb!' Clearly, Gide is anxious, by his moral strictures, to reassure his mother that he himself is impervious to Wilde's evil influence and that his decision to see Wilde stemmed from his own morality, from a rejection of the moral cowardice that spurning an old friend would entail. Equally clearly, Gide is not being hypocritical. He was certainly anxious, confused, divided; part of him still disapproved of 'Wilde's immorality'; yet another part of him was gaining in confidence and was soon to triumph. It is a commonplace that inner division is often manifested in extreme expression of one side or the other. It is also a commonplace that emergent homosexuals, especially those of a 'masculine' cast, are often fearful of where their inclination will take them and are easily set back by the sight of the more flamboyantly effeminate. Indeed Gide's own homosexuality never found room for effeminacy and was always 'Hellenic', in an earnest, idealized way.

The second account, 'In Memoriam', was written in December 1901, just after Wilde's death, and published in *Prétextes*. Seeing Wilde's name on the board, 'next to mine', touching it, Gide picked up the sponge and wiped off his own name. He then set off for the station. On the way, he was 'no longer sure that a little cowardice might not have been hidden in that action', and returned to the hotel. Wilde was no longer quite what he had been in Paris a few years before. A certain coarseness had affected his wit and his charm. 'He seemed at once surer of pleasing and less concerned to be so . . . He pursued pleasure as others perform their duty.'

In the 'In Memoriam' version the names of Wilde and Gide are next to each other, 'touching'. In the third version, in *Si le grain ne meurt*, Gide's is at the top of the list, Wilde's and Douglas's at the bottom. Perhaps the erasing of his name, he suggests, was not so much *mauvaise honte*, self-consciousness, as anti-socialness. No sooner had the three met up than Douglas took Gide's arm and declared: 'I hope you are like me: I hate women. I like only boys. Since you're with us this evening, I'd rather tell you so straight away.' Gide tried to conceal his 'stupefaction' at Douglas's behaviour.[55]

Gide left Blida next morning at 8 a.m., 'almost surreptitiously'. Two days later, he was writing to his mother: 'Algiers is marvellous – I begin with this, because my first impression was so unjust . . .' He is still reading *Barnaby Rudge* and finds that marvellous too – the previous day Wilde had declared that one 'should not read Dickens', but Wilde 'never forgot to be an artist and did not forgive Dickens being human'. He had met up with Wilde again and dined with him: 'Wilde! Wilde!! What life could be more tragic than his!! If only he would take more *care* . . . he would be a genius . . .' He was glad that he had met Wilde 'far away' – even Algiers was not really far enough away. 'I spoke to him very frankly . . . If I met him in London or Paris, I would not acknowledge him . . .' The reason he gives his mother for this verges on hypocrisy: in this way he would be able 'to safeguard our friendship and defend him against those who attack him . . .' He is relieved that Wilde is leaving next day. 'If he comes to Biskra, I shall leave . . . If Wilde's plays did not play for three hundred performances and if the Prince of Wales did not attend his first nights, he would be in prison, and Douglas with him.'⁵⁶ This was to be the year of the Wilde trials, but so far nothing had been set in train.

A few hours after writing that letter to his mother, Gide was sitting at a café table with Wilde. As to what occurred that evening, we have only Gide's version in *Si le grain ne meurt* to go on; the letter that he wrote to his mother the following day does not even allude to it. Suddenly, Douglas burst in, ignored Gide and proceeded to upbraid Wilde, 'in a hissing voice, filled with contempt and hatred', then left. 'He's always making scenes,' a visibly shaken Wilde remarked. Later that evening (not 'another evening', as Gide has it in *Si le grain ne meurt*), Wilde took Gide off to a Moorish café. After a while, 'a marvellous youth' appeared in the doorway. At a sign from Wilde, he came in. He was, Wilde explained, 'Bosie's'; he had hesitated to come in at first because Lord Alfred was not there. The boy, whose name was Mohammed, began to play on a reed flute, accompanied on a *darbouka* by one of the *caouadjis*, or waiters. '*Venez*,' Wilde suddenly said. Outside, in the street, he asked: 'Dear, vous voulez le petit musicien?' This, Gide realized, was the turning-point in his life. Summoning up all his courage, he answered, in a strangulated voice, 'Oui.' Wilde went back into the café to make the necessary arrangements, then, laughing uncontrollably all the way, took Gide off in his carriage to the Hôtel de l'Oasis, where he proceeded to consume several cocktails over the next half-hour. They then moved on to an hotel near the docks, where Wilde had the key to a small, two-roomed apartment, on the second floor. Gide was beginning to wonder whether anything would come of Wilde's proposition, when Mohammed arrived, with the *darbouka* player. Gide went with Mohammed into one of the rooms, Wilde and the *darbouka* player into the other.

'Since then, whenever I have sought pleasure, it is the memory of that night that I have pursued,' Gide wrote, twenty-five years later. Apart from the adventure in the sand dunes outside Sousse and the brief idyll on Lake Como, this had been his only homosexual contact. 'Then nothing; nothing but a frightful desert, full of appeals that found no response, upsurges of emotion that had no object, anxieties and struggles, exhausting dreams and imaginative flights, only to fall back, each time, into abominable depression

. . . Ah! What a hell I was emerging from!' The year before, with Meriem, he had made an 'effort of "normalization"', but it had led to nothing. 'Now, at last, I had found my normality . . . My joy was unbounded and I cannot imagine it greater if love had been added to it.'⁵⁷

It is at this point, in the middle of Gide's thoughts on sex and love, that the second, and longer, cut occurs in the English translation. (It amounts to over two-and-a-half pages, pp. 593–6, in the Pléiade edition.) It begins:

How could there have been any question of love? How could I have let desire dispose of my heart? My pleasure had no ulterior motive and was to be followed by remorse. But what, then, shall I call my transports of delight at holding in my bare arms that perfect, wild little body, so dark, so ardent, so lascivious? . . . After Mohammed had left me, I remained for a long time in a state of quivering jubilation and, although I had already achieved sensual delight [*atteint la volupté*] five times while with him, I rekindled my ecstasy a number of times after he had gone and, back in my hotel room, prolonged its echoes until morning.

The older, more modern Gide then comments: 'I am well aware that such precision may raise a smile; it would be easy to omit it [cf. the English translation] or to alter it in the interests of verisimilitude; but it is not verisimilitude that I am seeking, but truth . . .' Indeed, it was not until Mohammed expressed surprise that Gide realized that his seminal liberality was unusual. It is at this point that the only cut in the much reprinted 1928 Gallimard edition occurs. It consists of a page-and-a-half in the complete 1954 Pléiade edition and recounts another meeting with Mohammed 'two years later'. In fact, it describes Gide's meeting with the boy one year later. We shall return to it in due course.

The morning after the night spent with Mohammed, Gide rose at dawn and went for a long run. He felt no tiredness, but 'an exhilaration, a sort of lightness of the soul and of the flesh that stayed with me throughout the day'.

Wilde left the following morning to attend the final rehearsal of *The Importance of Being Earnest*. Douglas, after his stormy entrance and exit, had gone back to Blida, where he made arrangements for a young *caouadji*, whom he had fallen for, to enter his service. Fired by Gide's promises of Biskra and its oasis, Douglas planned to join Gide there, with the youth Ali. But Douglas found that certain bureaucratic procedures – parents' consent, papers signed at the Arab office and at the commissariat of police – had to be gone through before he could go off with an Arab boy, aged, according to Gide, writing to his mother, '12 or 13'. So Douglas wrote to

Gide asking him to wait for him at Algiers. All three could then go off
to Biskra together. Having Gide as his travelling companion would spare
Douglas the 'mortal tedium' of a two-day journey with Ali, who apparently
spoke neither English nor French. Gide was no more enthusiastic about
travelling with Ali and Douglas. The following day, he left Algiers for Sétif,
which he found covered with snow.

There, half-way to Biskra, he stayed for a few days, waiting for Douglas
and Ali to arrive. He had expected 'some quite ordinary *caouadji*, dressed
more or less like Mohammed'. What he saw getting out of the carriage at
Sétif railway station was

a young prince . . ., wearing dazzling clothes, with a silk sash and a golden turban
. . . How stately his bearing, how proud his glance! What masterful smiles he
bestowed on the hotel servants as they bowed before him! How quickly he had
understood that, however humble he had been the day before, it was now for him
to enter a room first, to sit down first . . . Douglas had found his master and
however elegantly dressed he was himself, he looked like an attendant, awaiting
the orders of his sumptuously apparelled servant. Every Arab, however poor, has
an Aladdin within all ready to blossom forth; all that is needed is for fate to touch
him and he turns into a king.[58]

Ali was, Gide admits, 'very beautiful', yet 'his beauty held no sway over
me'. He disliked the 'cruelty in the disdainful pouting of the lips' and,
above all, his generally effeminate appearance. At Biskra, Gide found that
his old room at the Hôtel de l'Oasis was occupied. Instead the three moved
into rooms at the new Hôtel Royal. Writing to his mother, Gide gave a list
of (more formal) clothes to be sent on, 'so as not to cut too sorry a figure at
the hotel, which naturally requires a different standard of dress' from his
lodgings of the year before.[59] They were soon joined by Athman, who,
hearing of Gide's imminent arrival, gave up his job as a guide to resume
service with him: his main task was to act as interpreter between Douglas
and Ali on innumerable excursions to nearby oases, while Gide insisted on
staying in his room to work.

André had already told his mother, with surprising frankness, that
Douglas had committed 'a veritable abduction' of the Arab boy Ali; he
goes on to admit that he finds Douglas 'absolutely charming'. Although
he spends between 50 and 100 francs a day (to André's 15 to 20), he does
so without causing the slightest embarrassment. Privately, Gide admitted
that Douglas *did* embarrass him: he 'returned incessantly, and with disgusting obstinacy to things I spoke of only with the greatest embarrassment
– an embarrassment that was only increased by his total lack of it'.[60]

Douglas's infatuation with Ali was not to last for long. He accepted that his Arab boy should have sex with others of his kind – he even encouraged it, especially if he himself was present. What he would not tolerate was Ali going with women. The boy was made to confess – and to promise, on pain of dismissal, that he would not do so again. One day, suspicious that Ali was consorting with Oulad-Naïl women, he found a photograph of Meriem in his suitcase. Douglas promptly gave the boy a whipping and, next morning, packed him off on the first train for Blida. Two days later, Douglas himself left Biskra. Athman, with nothing to do all day, returned to his job as a guide; he augmented his 'official' earnings by introducing tourists to Oulad-Naïl women. After work, he returned to Gide and recounted his day. Gide's emotional dependence on Athman was growing, though he denied having any sexual relations with him. This would seem to be confirmed by Gide's claim that he remained 'chaste' during his time in Biskra. When confronted by Douglas's 'dissipation', the surviving puritan within Gide reacted with disgust and turned, with renewed determination, to work – it was during this period that he wrote large sections of *Les Nourritures terrestres*. No sooner had Douglas gone than he took to going on long walks into the desert, 'drunk with the immensity, the strangeness, the solitude, my heart lighter than a bird'.[61]

On 19 February, Gide wrote to his mother: 'I can no longer hide from you my plan to bring Athman back to France. He will lend a hand at La Roque and thus relieve Marie.' André had arranged matters with the boy's parents; the mother, it seems, would not have agreed had she not had particular confidence in André and met his mother. Yet, in a later letter, André refers to 'Athman's abduction', using precisely the same word (*enlèvement*) as he had used of Douglas and Ali.[62] As if this were not bad enough, he was now planning to buy a small plot of land (costing 4,500 francs, £180 or $900 at the time) on the outskirts of Biskra, on which he would build a small house. He had had enough of 'this unbearable hotel life' and would like 'a comfortable pied-à-terre' where he could put up friends and 'who knows? one day, perhaps, Madeleine, with you'. What he did not tell his mother – he had already told her enough to convince her that he had taken leave of his senses – was that he planned to turn the ground floor of the house into a Moorish café, run by . . . Athman.

A few days later, Mme Gide launched her offensive on both of André's plans. What her son was doing in relation to Athman was a form of child abuse. How would such a child react to our grey skies and cold weather? Has he any idea what our cities are like, how miserable he would be living on the sixth floor (that is, in a maid's room)? Far from being a help, he would be a hindrance. 'No, no, let's have none of this whim at the expense of a fellow human being, even if he is black. No more picturesque notions, no more literature with a human creature.' The plan to buy a plot of land fared no better: it was, Mme Gide concluded, after a page of detailed objection, 'premature from every point of view'. André hit back: 'All you say about Athman is INCREDIBLY ridiculous.' Of course Athman would not occupy a maid's room on the sixth floor; he could have the guest room, when it was not in use and, even then, he could have the spare bed in his (André's) room! Meanwhile, André continued with the legal process of buying the land. The correspondence continued around 'the two subjects in dispute'. 'I'm buying my land, and I'm bringing Athman' – and if Mme Gide did not welcome *both* of them at the rue de Commaille, they would go elsewhere. If he married, André expostulated, he could foresee 'a veritable conjugal hell, because of the role of experienced counsellor that you will not be able to give up playing. O terror!! . . . I have obtained many of the best things in my life only by an obstinate resistance to the invasion of your will.'[63] Mme Gide resumed her detailed, well-argued case against both of her son's 'whims'. Claiming that she has no wish to do so, she then adopts precisely the same uncompromising tone as her son: 'Athman will never sleep in the apartment and there is no room on the 6th floor . . . But you're ill, you must be ill . . . Your nerves must be unbalanced . . . Let's hope that it doesn't all end in some disease – cerebral fever, typhoid fever, nervous fever! . . . Ah! André, I beg you, leave Biskra . . .'[64] Having now come round to approving a marriage between her son and her niece, she then turns to what she must have regarded as the supreme argument: how can Madeleine accept as her husband someone who acts so irresponsibly, who reveals such a lack of mature judgement? Is this any way to overcome Madeleine's doubts as to his suitability as a husband?

It was too late to give up the plot of land (he still owned it thirty years later), but, on 19 March, he sent his mother a telegram announcing a change of heart over Athman. In *Si le grain ne meurt*, he attributes this to a letter from Marie Leuenberger: in it she swore that she would leave the house the day his 'nigger' entered it. It is possible that Gide did not take seriously Marie's threat to leave his mother, to whom she had been a devoted servant–companion for twenty-five years. An additional explanation of his change of plan was the direction that the Wilde affair was taking. The preliminary hearings of Wilde's libel action had already taken place and, on 5 April, only two weeks after André's telegram to his mother, the

Marquess of Queensberry was acquitted and Wilde, in turn, arrested. By 25 May, Wilde had been tried, found guilty of 'indecency' and condemned to two years' hard labour. Some indication that, even by 19 March, the general public was beginning to see the reality beneath the newspapers' circumlocutory reporting is that, a day or two after André's telegram to his mother, Wilde and Douglas, who were staying at an hotel in Monte Carlo, were asked to leave at the request of other guests. Even at this early stage, both of the Wilde affair and of his self-awareness as a homosexual, it must have occurred to Gide that, while consorting with a fifteen-year-old Arab boy in Algeria might pass unnoticed, this would no longer be the case in France itself.

Mme Gide wrote off an immediate reply to André's message: 'Your telegram made me very happy, happy that you thought of sending it to me straightaway. Happy that, between me and Athman, you did not hesitate to give up [*renoncer*] one of your wishes [*désirs*], cherished [*caressé*] and enthused over [*exalté*] for some time. Isn't this the *first* time such a thing has happened?' Juliette Gide could not be magnanimous in victory: note the (no doubt unconscious) suggestiveness of the French words and the further 'barb' in the second sentence. As for the 'little difficulty of explaining this change to Athman', this should not prove difficult. Neither for André nor for Athman was this a 'little difficulty'. Gide 'hadn't the heart to demolish in one blow the imaginary edifice' of hopes and dreams that the Algerian boy had built up in his mind. Instead he let the truth dawn on Athman gradually over the next few days.

Often, in the evening, they would be joined by Athman's big brother, Sadek, and a few friends. Gide's hotel room being on the ground floor, they would come in through the window. Sitting on the floor in a circle, sipping cordials and nibbling sweetmeats, they would listen to Sadek play his flute. Sadek spoke little French and André little Arabic, but, 'had we spoken the same language, what more could we have said than was expressed in our looks, our gestures and above all that tender way he had of taking my hands, of holding my hands in his, my right hand in his right hand so that we walked on, silent as shades, with arms intertwined'. On Gide's last night in Biskra, Sadek and he walked, arm-in-arm, around the town, as André said goodbye to their friends: 'Ah! How hard it was to make up my mind to leave! It was as if I were taking leave of my youth.' To soften the blow of parting, André and Athman spent 'two heavenly days together at El Kantara': 'In that Eden . . . spring was coming to birth under the palms; the apricot trees were in bloom and were humming with bees.' On the third morning, André went into Athman's room to say goodbye but found that the boy had already left, without message or explanation. Then, on the train taking him from El Kantara to Algiers, Gide caught sight of him, sitting beside the track in his white burnous, his head in his hands. 'He did not stand up when the train passed; he made no movement. He did not even look as I waved to him; and for a long time, as the train was carrying me away, I watched that small, motionless, grief-stricken figure, lost in the desert, an image of my own despair.'[65] Athman may have entered Gide's life as a servant, but he had soon become a friend and, in a sense, a Platonic lover. His sacrifice of Athman on the maternal altar of common sense, prudence and respectability did not come easy. Nor did Gide give up entirely: five years later, at the time of the 1900 Exposition Universelle, he brought Athman to Paris. Gide spent rather longer in Algiers than he had anticipated. This brought on another attack from his mother:

So conditions at sea were bad enough to keep you another week in Algiers? . . . I no longer dare to give that reason for your delay, having been met with incredulous smiles, full of *sous-entendus* . . . I understood at once the comments that had been made concerning your acquisition of land at Biskra! . . . You, a Gide, whose name has remained pure and unsullied and which I believed you would hold it an honour to pass on as such to your children! . . . Yes, how humiliating! And how bitter I feel when I think of your father! It seems to me that we have both betrayed, forfeited his memory. And when I think of Madeleine! Is that the jewel you want to give her as a wedding present? Is that the past you want to put into your children's cradle? Oh, I feel so bitter . . .[66]

Clearly, Mme Gide imagined – for she could imagine nothing else – that her son had been seduced by the ease with which young women's 'favours' could be obtained on the other side of the Mediterranean. Had she not witnessed, at Biskra, the year before, just such an incident? Some months before, she had dropped her last remaining objections to the cousins' marriage. Now she saw Madeleine as the only hope, the only true moral authority that her son seemed to acknowledge. Yet, just when André was most in need of Madeleine's stabilizing influence, he was squandering what, in her eyes, was his chief attraction: his moral and intellectual integrity as a Gide, as a fearless upholder of Puritan rectitude. Not only was André proving more emotionally unstable than ever, he was now, perhaps months before marrying, consorting with Arab prostitutes. This amounted to a moral collapse; it also put his own health, and possibly that of his wife and children in danger. That, I think, is hinted at in the references to 'wedding present' ('joyau . . . dans sa corbeille de noces') and 'cradle'. As it happens, her son was not leading the life she dimly imagined. Had Mme Gide put two and two together, the mysterious change that had apparently come over her son and the Wilde trials, she would have come up with, for her, an even more disturbing answer, one for which Madeleine would have provided no cure.

Mme Gide unburdened her fears to Charles Gide, her brother-in-law and nominally *in loco patris*. We do not have her letter (she asked its recipient to burn it at once), but we do have Charles Gide's reply, quoted in full in the *Correspondance* between mother and son. He confronts his task in a businesslike way, a plausible performance as moral guardian fully confident in his own understanding and judgement. As chance would have it, André arrived in Montpellier one hour after his mother's letter, so Uncle Charles was also able to make an on-the-spot assessment of his nephew's 'state'. His conclusions must have gone some way to reassure the anxious mother. He finds André's 'confidences on Goethe' (by now, Mme Gide considered Goethe more responsible than Oscar Wilde for the change wrought in her son!) and his comments on the life that he is leading 'fairly innocent'. True, 'last summer at Biskra' André committed 'a deplorable act that I would not have expected of him'. (Mme Gide had obviously recounted to him the incident involving Meriem.) Such an action is more in the nature of 'psychological experimentation' than 'the result of bad instincts'. Observing André in the flesh, he could detect no 'abnormal dispositions' (i.e., such as would lead him to take up with another Meriem!). 'In short,' Uncle Charles declared, with good sense, 'André is an original, he always will be: I would even regret it if he weren't. But so far I have seen nothing to justify the disturbing state in which you seem to be.' Of course, André's not having a career is unfortunate . . . And, if he doesn't marry, this will be another cause of instability. But neither André nor Madeleine should be 'pressed' into a marriage about which he feels less enthusiastic than some. It would probably not be a happy marriage, but both parties would surely be unhappy unmarried.[67]

After three days at Montpellier, André joined his mother in Paris on 19 April. Like Charles Gide, she was reassured by his generally healthy appearance. Madeleine, who was in Paris at the time, also noticed the difference. After her return to Rouen, she wrote to André. She had, she admitted, been 'rather dreading' the meeting, but had spent with him 'the best hours that we have spent for a long time – and something I no longer believed possible. I look forward with pleasure to seeing you again.' A week later, incidentally, she wrote again, asking André if he had read about the final judgment of the Wilde trial and enclosing a newspaper cutting on the subject. Surprisingly, perhaps, that austere Puritan showed more charity than condemnation in her reaction. Paris saw a truce in relations between mother and son:

For no lasting peace between us was possible; the reciprocal concessions that allowed us a little respite could only be temporary and were based on an agreed misunderstanding . . . She had a way of loving me that sometimes made me almost hate her and set my nerves on edge. Imagine . . . the effect of being constantly watched and spied upon, incessantly and harassingly advised as to your actions, your thoughts, your expenditure, as to what you ought to wear, or what you ought to read, even as to the title of a book . . . She disliked that of *Les Nourritures terrestres* and since there was still time to change it, she tirelessly returned to the charge.[68]

Then there were the 'wretched questions of money'. Apparently, Mme Gide had kept her son in ignorance of the extent of the inheritance from his father, allowing him only a fairly modest allowance, in the belief that if he had access to it all he would merely squander it. On 24 May André left Paris to join Eugène Rouart at Grignon, taking with him the advance copies of *Paludes*, which he had collected from the publisher, Edmond Bailly. Mme Gide went off to La Roque, where André planned to spend the summer, joined, in July, by Madeleine. Four days later, he received a letter from Marie Leuenberger, informing him that his mother was suffering from severe migraine attacks. There seemed to be no great cause for concern, but nevertheless André decided to go to La Roque immediately. On arrival at Lisieux, he learnt from the estate manager, who had come to collect him in a barouche, that his mother had had an attack of apoplexy.

'I almost think she recognized me, but she no longer seemed to have a clear idea of the time or the place, of herself or the people around her, for she showed neither surprise nor pleasure at seeing me.' She was holding a pencil and seemed to be writing on an open account-book, but the pencil made no contact with it. When André removed them, her hand continued to move over the sheet, as if writing. Seeing those 'poor hands', he imagined them on the piano. The idea that she, too, strove after 'a little poetry, a little music, a little beauty' overcame him with a sense of veneration. He fell to his knees, burying his face in the sheets to stifle his sobbing. He did not inform his relations of his mother's imminent death. 'I was jealous of watching by her side alone. Marie and I assisted her in her last moments and when at last her heart ceased to beat I felt myself sink into an abyss of love, anguish and freedom.' The funeral service took place in Paris on 4

June at the Protestant church in the rue de Grenelle. Juliette Gide was buried in the Cimetière Montparnasse beside her husband.

The infinite spaces, the freedom for which he had longed during his mother's lifetime, now terrified André. 'I felt dazed, like a prisoner suddenly set free, like a kite whose string has suddenly been cut, like a boat broken loose from its moorings, like a drifting wreck, at the mercy of wind and tide.'[69] The only thing left for him to cling to was his love for Madeleine. Gide's dual nature required, like John Donne's 'stiff twin compasses', a stable, unchanging 'fixed foot' as well as the other that 'far doth roam'. Having lost his mother, he replaced her with the person who most resembled her, another Rondeaux. Juliette Gide had died of a cerebral haemorrhage on 31 May 1895 at the age of sixty. Seventeen days later, on 17 June, André Gide and Madeleine Rondeaux announced their engagement. When, in 1938, forty-three years later, Madeleine died, Gide felt the same sense of 'love, anguish and freedom'. In *Ainsi soit-il*, he remarked how 'subtly, almost mystically', his mother had merged into his wife.[70]

7

Marriage and Nomadism: Les Nourritures terrestres, Saül, Le Prométhée mal enchaîné, Philoctète

(JUNE 1895 – OCTOBER 1898)

I am now astonished at the aberration that led me to believe that the more ethereal my love, the more it was worthy of her – and to be naïve enough never to ask whether she would be content with so disembodied a love. So the fact that my carnal desires were directed towards other objects hardly concerned me. I even arrived at the comfortable conviction that things were better thus. Desires, I thought, were peculiar to men; I found it reassuring to believe that women – except 'loose' women, of course – did not have similar desires.[1]

During Gide's lifetime, the public came to know quite a lot about Gide the homosexual theorist and practitioner: indeed, he had shown great moral courage in making sure that it did. His marriage, however, remained publicly undocumented. *Si le grain ne meurt* takes the story of Gide's life no further than his engagement. When he published the first extracts from his *Journal*, in 1932–3, he deleted most of the references to Madeleine, out of deference to her natural reticence, rather than to protect his privacy. A more appropriate place for a consideration of the Gides' marriage would be 1918, the great half-way turning-point, than 1895, when it began. What concerns us here is rather what each of the partners expected from the union. What is certain is that it remained a *mariage blanc*; it is equally clear, I believe, that, whatever doubts and uncertainties each may have felt, neither side *assumed* that it would be unconsummated. André had no purely physical problem to confront: he had conducted a successful liaison with Meriem at Biskra. But Meriem was, arguably, a special case. She was a 'wild', childlike sixteen-year-old, who showed no emotional attachment to the man she slept with and who was genuinely quite 'unfeminine' in her behaviour. With more mature 'womanly' women, such as the Arab in Biskra or the Italian in Rome, any sexual desire vanished. What is more,

Gide knew where his sexual attraction *did* lie. He must have had serious doubts as to his ability to see Madeleine, who represented for him everything that was pure and spiritual, in physical terms. He no doubt imagined that this problem could be overcome. In any case, there is proof that he did not anticipate an unconsummated marriage. In *Et nunc manet in te*, he describes how, after the engagement, he consulted a doctor. The eminent specialist listened, with a smile, as the young man described his sexual proclivities. These were nothing to worry about, the doctor reassured him: 'You say you love a young lady and yet hesitate to marry her, on account of your other tastes . . . Get married! Marry without fear. And you'll soon see that all the rest exists only in your imagination.' Once married, he would soon rediscover his natural instincts. Gide, he said, was like a hungry man trying to make a meal out of gherkins! 'I am quoting his exact words,' Gide adds.[2] Further proof that Gide hoped to have a normal marriage with Madeleine is cited by Jean Schlumberger.[3] In his *Confidence africaine*, Roger Martin du Gard had depicted the child of an incestuous relationship between brother and sister as necessarily weak in health, doomed by tuberculosis. Gide responded, in a letter dated 11 March 1931, that there was no evidence that the children of healthy blood relations ran any risk of ill-health. He had, he goes on, studied the question prior to marrying his cousin.

If the marriage remained unconsummated, then, it was for psychological, not physiological reasons. One can go further and say that the psychological reasons that precluded consummation were the same that made the marriage possible at all: Gide must have felt, however obscurely, that Madeleine could be his wife, precisely because she was like a sister. It may even be that Madeleine similarly felt that she could marry André, because he was a 'brother'. With the death of Juliette Gide, André's mother and Madeleine's surrogate mother, a further twist seems to have taken place: the sister became a mother, the brother a son. This was made easier by the fact that since the death of her father and the removal of her mother, Madeleine had become a maternal head of her own family. At times, Gide's identification of Madeleine with his mother verged on the hallucinatory. Three months into their marriage, he writes in his journal: 'How often when Madeleine is in the next room, I *forget* that she is not my mother!'[4] It lasted all their lives – and the misapprehension was not always Gide's. In *Et nunc manet in te*, Gide relates how, when he and Madeleine were staying in an hotel at Fécamp, one of the staff remarked to him: 'Madame votre mère vous attend dans la voiture.'[5]

Madeleine Rondeaux was twenty-seven in the year of her marriage. It is unlikely that she was any less innocent of matters sexual than she had been at seventeen: given her class and religious background, her innocence (ignorance) must have been total. When Madeleine was sixteen, her mother had left home to marry the man who had been her lover for some years. Madeleine reacted to her mother's behaviour with shame and horror: it was probably hard for her to regard sex any differently. André had always, until quite recently at least, inspired confidence because he represented all that was moral, devout, respectable in the Protestant Gide–Rondeaux clan. The prospect that he would probably, in the future, be in the public eye could only have been a source of apprehension to this shy, withdrawn young woman, but the idea that their private life could become raw material for his books was deeply disturbing. His North African escapade must have given rise to further doubts, especially in view of Mme Gide's obvious disapproval – though Madeleine would have known nothing of the details. It was only when André's mother abandoned her opposition to the marriage and actually encouraged it, that Madeleine, too, changed sides. She certainly loved André, but she probably had no physical attraction to him – or, for that matter, to any man. 'I am not afraid of death – I am afraid of marriage,' she remarked in a letter to André, dated 25 June, seven days after the announcement of their engagement. Puritan religiosity, combined with disgust for her mother, had surely stifled any sexual stirrings. Had she not married André, she might well have remained unmarried. But, having finally abandoned all her doubts and misgivings, her love for André, much of which she had held back, came flooding out. During the weeks of betrothal, her letters reveal a light-hearted, innocent delight at the thought of the future ahead.

Meanwhile, *Paludes* had appeared in the bookshops – or rather in a few of them, this first edition being of only 400 copies. Letters began to arrive from friends. Pierre Louÿs, who might have taken umbrage at being denied both first sight of the manuscript and the expected dedication, wrote to say that he found it '*épatant*' (terrific). Henri de Régnier was 'wild' about it. Francis Jammes wrote that *Paludes*, together with Gide's earlier work, was forming 'the mysterious avenue of a strangely enchanted garden'. According to Rachilde, *Paludes* was the mirror of 'la jeunesse d'élite présente' and placed him at the head of it. Letters of thanks arrived from Barrès, Huysmans and Maeterlinck. Madeleine, while finding *Paludes* excellent, wondered how anyone, possessed of 'so much faith in life, so much hope, so much love', could write it. Weeks later, she notes that their cousins at Le Havre have all read the book (passing it round in view of its high price) and 'nobody can make head nor tail of it'. The reviews, often written by friends, were largely favourable. In *Mercure de France*, the twenty-three-year-old Camille Mauclair hailed *Paludes* as 'the book of a man *who has had enough*': it spoke for a whole generation that had had enough. The *Figaro* compared *Paludes* to Sterne, but abandoned any attempt at description: 'One can hardly more analyse a book like this than explain a scent.'

Having announced the engagement, André was in a great hurry to get married – or, more probably, to get the wedding out of the way and thus be free to go off on his travels once again, this time with Madeleine. He proposed September for the wedding; the more practical Madeleine, well aware of the preparations involved, declared that November was the earliest possible month. They settled on October. Madeleine stayed at Aunt Lucile's, in Rouen, where the wedding-dress was being made. Then, after a few days' last-minute shopping in Paris, she went back to Cuverville. Meanwhile, André divided his time between La Roque and Paris, with visits to the Laurens at Yport, the Rouarts at La Queue-en-Brie and Uncle Charles's family at Noirmoutier. Except for a couple of weeks at Cuverville in August, the couple saw very little of one another during the engagement period. Without parents, said Aunt Lucile, it was considered improper for engaged couples to be seen together too often; it might even affect adversely the marriage prospects of Madeleine's two sisters.

On 3 October, at a Rouen notary's, the legal contract was signed, placing the parties under 'communauté réduite aux acquets', whereby only acquisitions made after marriage would be held in common. Cuverville, which Madeleine had inherited from her father, remained, therefore, her own property. The civil marriage took place at Cuverville *mairie* on 7 October, the religious ceremony the following day at the Protestant chapel at Etretat. The service was conducted by Pastor Roberty, who, thirty-four years before, had married Paul Gide and Juliette Rondeaux. André's best man was his former tutor, Pastor Elie Allégret. Most of the Rondeaux clan were present. There were no Gides: Uncle Charles declared that travelling disagreed with him, but that the couple were welcome to call on him and his family on their way to Italy. André's witnesses were the Démarest brothers, Maurice and Albert.

The wedding breakfast, at Cuverville, was a short, rather solemn affair. The couple then went by carriage to Le Havre. There they caught the train to Paris, where they spent a couple of days, at the rue de Commaille, before going on to Nîmes, where a carriage was waiting to take them to 'Les Sources', Uncle Charles's property at Bellegarde-du-Gard. After a week, they moved on to Geneva, calling on Mme Charles Gide's sister and brother-in-law, then to Neuchâtel, where they spent ten days. On 1 November, after a train journey to Coire and an exhausting thirteen hours by *diligence*, they arrived at Saint-Moritz. Throughout their five weeks in the Swiss Alps, Madeleine felt weak and quite incapable of anything more than short, slow walks. André tried, not always successfully, to hide his impatience. Occasionally, he went off alone on short excursions. No sooner did Madeleine show signs of improvement than he took her off on a long, arduous walk across the Diavolezza pass. At one point, to ascend a particularly steep incline, the party had to be roped together and use their alpenstocks. To André's exasperation, Madeleine took fright and resolutely refused to follow instructions, thus endangering the whole party.

While at Saint-Moritz, Gide tried to work on *Les Nourritures terrestres*, but without much success. Then, out of the blue, came a letter from Edouard Ducoté, a rich poet who had just taken over the review *L'Ermitage*, asking him, 'as a matter of urgency', to contribute something to the first issue to appear under his editorship. Gide set to work, using odd jottings that he had made for use in *Les Nourritures*. The result, 'Ménalque (a fragment)', occupied the first eight pages of the January number of *L'Ermitage*. In a letter to Marcel Drouin, Gide remarks that 'after three feverish days spent on this work to order, the result seemed so unworthy of my book – of me – that I was absolutely disgusted with it'.[6] The piece would never be reprinted, Gide adds, 'at least in its entirety'. In the event, it was not dropped, but came to form the first section of Book IV of *Les Nourritures*.

The Gides had been at Saint-Moritz for five weeks, waiting in vain for snow: André had wanted to cross the Alps on a sleigh. They had to be content with a carriage, leaving on 5 December for Milan, which André 'already hated'. They went straight on to Bologna, where, André tells Paul Valéry, 'I walked under the arcades . . ., ate mortadella and drank chocolate.'[7] Gide, note, says 'I', not 'we' – there is no mention of Madeleine throughout the letter. Indeed he even fantasizes about how 'at sixteen', we (meaning Valéry and he) might have 'taken to the road together with the sea on our right, the orient desert [an allusion to Racine's "l'orient désert", in *Bérénice*] on our left, and, before us, far off, perhaps, some inn, where we might embark on the adventure of satisfying all our hungers . . . In the morning, before dawn, we would bathe and would not have a headache. Now we drag too many balls and chains around with us . . .'[8] Certainly, he does not sound like a man on his honeymoon: he seems already to be feeling that Madeleine was such a 'ball and chain'.

From Bologna, the Gides went on to Florence, staying at the *pensione* that André had stayed at eighteen months before. The other guests included two 'very beautiful' American women of literary inclinations (one was reading Marlowe, the other Omar Khayyám) and a young Russian orientalist, Fedor Rosenberg, who, as well as being able to read the *Rubaiyyát* in the original Persian, was also a fine pianist. In the evenings, the guests would play games together, Madeleine often retiring early to bed, feeling weak or ill. During the day, André would go off with Rosenberg visiting the churches and museums. They were to meet up again in Naples and North Africa, where they discovered that they had similar sexual tastes.

In *Feuilles de Route* Gide writes of the Florentine treasures that had made a particular impact upon him: a young man in Giorgione's *The Concert*, Ghirlandaio frescoes in the church of Santa Maria Novella, and above all the Donatello *David* in the Bargello, which clearly had special significance for him. Donatello's work, he says, reveals 'an astonishing preference for the male body and a strange understanding of the child's form'. He writes of *David*'s 'delicate little body, graceful in a frail, stiff sort of way': 'I would like to be able to bring him before my mind's eye at will. I observed him for a long time – trying to learn, to memorize those delicious lines, that fold at the belly immediately under the ribs, hollowed by breathing . . . And even that extraordinary flatness of the loins immediately above the sacrum . . .'9 He notes the 'oriental graces' of Donatello's work and goes on: 'Obsessions with the Orient, the desert, its ardour and its emptiness, the shade of the palm gardens, white, loose garments – obsessions in which the senses are thrown into turmoil, the nerves become exacerbated, and which, at the beginning of each night, make me think that sleep will be impossible'.10 Meanwhile, he had to be content with roaming the streets of Florence, following 'a few fellows who intrigue me'. Madeleine having retired to bed early, André goes out on New Year's Eve and tries to abandon himself to 'that dancing and that shouting, that approach of time', but to no avail: his Puritan heart still yearned to celebrate the coming of the New Year with a religious service of prayer. 'The horror of whatever is not serious – I have always had it,' he wrote in his *Journal*, then asks: 'What was Em. thinking about, all alone, during this time?'11

On the way to Rome, the Gides spent a rainy day in Pisa, visiting the garden where Shelley, just before his death, walked one moonlit July night. 'His last letter was written in Pisa. I am more furious than ever that I don't know English,' he wrote to Marcel Drouin. In Rome, they visited 'the horrible enormity of Saint Peter's', the Palatine, the Baths of Caracalla, etc. In the Capitolino Museum, Gide found another 'favourite' among the statuary: the *Spinario*, a bronze statue of a boy removing a thorn from his foot.

By the end of January they were in Naples. A week later, they moved into the Hôtel Quisisana on Capri, where they found an abundance of Americans and a superabundance of Germans. 'Personally, I found Capri unbearable or almost,' he wrote, 'despite its admirable rocks; I would rather see Capri from Naples, floating like a vision on the sea.'[12] André went on excursions into the countryside on the mainland, with or without Madeleine. Together they went to Pesto, the once Greek colony of Paestum, with its three raised Doric temples. For André, it was a 'revelation'. 'To discover such an emotion,' he wrote to Marcel Drouin, 'we must go back to our first reading of the *Iliad*. Paestum is no longer Italy and it is already Greece in its entirety.'[13]

The Gides spent about a month in southern Italy, then travelled along Sicily's eastern coast from Taormina to Syracuse, where they stayed for a few days. Here the Greek spirit seems to have overwhelmed André entirely. They visited the spot, he wrote to Drouin, where Persephone was carried off to Hades. 'We also saw the captive Arethusa weep and we gathered asphodels growing between the stones of the avenue of Tombs; the half-moon rose half-veiled over the theatre where the men from the island of Ortygia recited the verses of Euripides with such perfect languor that, though prisoners, they were not killed, for no one else would have been found to speak those lines . . .'[14] In early March they left Syracuse for Tunis.

Tunis, which Gide had seen two-and-a-half years before, was in the process of being modernized *à la française*, with broad, straight boulevards, avenues of trees, street lamps. Camels and their Arab drivers could no longer sleep out in the place des Moutons. But the old town had preserved its 'incredible taste of the exotic'. Soon after arrival, André made for his old haunts in the souks. There he met up with Fedor Rosenberg, who had arrived in Tunis shortly before. Together they went off to the Caracous (Karagoz), a form of marionette theatre, of Turkish origin, that used only shadows. These entertainments, which always involved the manipulation of a gigantic phallus, were frequented largely by young, unattended boys, who took great delight in their unmitigated obscenity. During one of the interminable intervals, 'a strangely beautiful boy is playing the bagpipes; everyone gathers round him; because of him; the others are his gallants . . .'.

Yet the place was no brothel, 'rather a court of love'.[15] Occasionally, one of the boys got up and danced, accompanied perhaps by another.

After some days in Tunis, the Gides, accompanied by Rosenberg, who got on extremely well with Madeleine, travelled by train to Constantine, then on to El Kantara. There, at the end of a splendid day, a splendidly attired Athman was waiting for them. Now seventeen, he had outgrown the child's simple *chechia* and was wearing 'three burnooses, a white silk gandourah lined with blue silk and edged with pink', a jacket of blue cloth and an 'enormous brown cord turban holding the fine white cloth that falls from it, brushes his cheek and floats loose under his chin'. Athman had bought his new costume in honour of his French friend and had spent all that he had on it. Thus apparelled he had been at the station an hour before the train was expected. It had seemed a long wait, but, he told André, 'I thought to myself: now it is only an hour; before it was a whole year.' They went by carriage on to Biskra as the sun was going down. On the way they stopped in front of a Moorish café.

In the courtyard, near us, some camels in heat were fighting. A keeper was shouting at them. The flocks of goats were turning; their hasty feet made the sound of a sterile shower . . . The sky to the west was a very pure blue, so deep that it still seemed to be saturated with light. The silence became wonderful. You could not imagine any song breaking it. I felt that I loved this country perhaps better than any other . . .[16]

They go for walks, but Madeleine soon tires and André remembers fondly his long excursions out into the desert of the year before. Athman is a constant source of amusement. He 'reads like Bouvard and writes like Pécuchet'. He works hard at educating himself. He considers André's *La Tentative amoureuse* badly written because he uses the word '*herbe*' (grass) too often. André lends him *The Thousand and One Nights*. Next day, Athman comes back and says that he and his friend Bachaga were reading it until two in the morning.

The Gides and Fedor Rosenberg were soon joined, at André's invitation, by Eugène Rouart. Rouart brought with him the young poet Francis Jammes, whom André had not yet met. On seeing Jammes for the first time, Gide was quite disconcerted: 'That bearded, vivacious, little fellow with the strident voice and the piercing gaze' was not at all how he had imagined the Béarnais poet. Things went well at first. Madeleine had a genuine admiration for Jammes' verse and was won over by his natural gaiety and childlike enthusiasm. Athman and he got on extremely well, each presenting the other with his poetic creations, occasionally made up on the spot. The whole party travelled by carriage the 125 miles of desert to Touggourt. By the time they got there, for reasons that are not entirely clear, Francis Jammes had had enough of North Africa and his friends. They were probably all physically exhausted. Jammes, irritated by the delight of his fellow-travellers in the strange sights and sounds of the desert, reacted in the opposite direction: he was in the grip of a profound homesickness for the freshness and green of his native Béarn. He would return to Orthez forthwith. This he did – at Gide's expense and, probably, to his relief. In his letter of thanks, Jammes made it clear that his main quarrel was with Rouart, even going so far as to ask Gide if he would also be willing to repay Rouart for the outward fare.

The rest of the party stayed three more days at Touggourt, then returned to Biskra by a longer route, passing through the oasis town of M'Reyer, where they dined with the officers of the garrison. At Algiers, André met up with Mohammed, the beautiful youth that Wilde had introduced him to the year before. In the last chapter, I referred to various cuts that were made in the English version of *Si le grain ne meurt*. The last of these, which was even cut in the much reprinted French edition, but restored in the Pléiade edition, concerned this reunion with Mohammed. The boy was still attractive, indeed more attractive than ever, but he seemed not so much '*lascif*' ('lascivious', 'sensual'), as '*effronté*' ('shameless', 'brazen'). Gide was with a friend, 'Daniel B . . .'. This was, in fact, Eugène Rouart. The three went up to a room in a shady hotel. Drinks were brought by a waiter and left on a table on which stood a candle, the only illumination. The two men sat in the only two chairs, Mohammed on the table between them.

He lifted his haik, exposing his bare legs. 'One for each of you,' he said, laughing. Daniel then seized Mohammed in his arms and carried him over to the bed at the end of the room. He laid him on his back, on the edge of the bed, crosswise; and soon all I could see of him, on either side of a panting Daniel, were two slender, dangling legs. Very tall, standing against the bed, ill-lit, seen from behind, his face hidden by the curls of his long black hair, still wearing the overcoat that reached to his feet, Daniel seemed huge and, bending over that little body, almost obscuring it, he looked like an enormous vampire feeding on a corpse. I nearly cried out in horror . . .

It is always difficult to understand the way others make love . . .

As for me, I can only understand pleasure face to face, reciprocal and without violence; like Whitman, I find the most furtive contact satisfying. I was horrified not only by Daniel's actions, but also to see Mohammed accept them so accommodatingly.[17]

By 22 April the friends were back in France. The following day, in Marseille, Gide called on a group of young poets, one of whom, Edmond Jaloux, was to be the dedicatee, in 1929, of Gide's *Ecole des femmes*. After a few more days, Rouart and Rosenberg went their separate ways and the Gides went on to Montpellier, where they called on Uncle Charles and his family. After some days in Paris, at the rue de Commaille, they returned to La Roque.

No sooner were the Gides at La Roque than, at the instigation of his estate manager, Armand Desaunez, André was elected municipal councillor (by 28 votes to 8). Two weeks later, he was chosen mayor by his fellow councillors (by 7 votes to 3), becoming the youngest mayor in France and replacing a man who could not even write his name. In a letter to Paul Valéry, Gide presents his electoral triumph as a misfortune brought upon him by people he had never done any harm. 'You can have no idea what it is like. They are all three-quarters lost to alcohol . . . Some of them are so far gone that a glass or two are enough to knock them out; the children are born idiots, nervous, or aren't born at all.' He had hoped to come back to La Roque to rest and to finish *Les Nourritures terrestres* – 'I daren't sing the praises of drunkenness any more'[18] – and found himself caught up in hours of tedious business. Being Gide, he could not carry out his duties other than conscientiously. He remained in his post for close on four years, attending nine of the fourteen sessions, despite his frequent travels abroad. More important, he was unstinting in time and money in the alleviation of innumerable cases of hardship or misfortune.

The Gides spent much of the summer of 1896 at La Roque and at Cuverville. In May, Eugène Rouart stayed for a few days at La Roque – and gave Gide the benefit of his expert knowledge on matters of estate management. André and Madeleine spent ten days at Rouen, prior to the wedding of Valentine Rondeaux to Dr Charles Bernardbeig on 22 May. After a few days in Paris with André, Madeleine returned to Cuverville for the rest of the summer, while André went off to stay with Rouart at his Burgundian farm near Autun, where he spent much of June. André then went off to Paris, where, much to Madeleine's disquiet, he was engaged in negotiations to buy a house in Auteuil. In letters reminiscent of those written to André by his mother, full of practical, detailed advice, Madeleine begged him not to get carried away with enthusiasm. In the end, nothing came of the project. On 20 July, André came back from Paris with Marcel Drouin. During his stay at Cuverville, Drouin and Jeanne Rondeaux fell in love. For weeks the house at Cuverville was filled with friends and relations: in addition to Aunt Claire, Madeleine's brothers and sisters, the Démarests and the Widmers, there were Drouin, Rouart and, for a few days, the Laurens brothers, who arrived on bicycles from Yport. A great deal of reading, much of it aloud, got done: Stevenson (*Dr Jekyll and Mr Hyde*, *Treasure Island*); Balzac (*Les Paysans*); Emily Brontë (*Wuthering Heights*); Dostoevsky (*The Idiot*, *The Brothers Karamazov*), and *Othello*.

In the midst of all this, André continued to work – he finished *El Hadj* and 'Reflexions sur quelques points de la morale chrétienne', which appeared in the September number of *L'Art et la Vie*. In those few pages, Gide pursued his attempts to save Jesus and what he saw as his subversive message from institutionalized religion. More particularly, he used the Christ of the Gospels in a Ménalque-type attack on the family and marriage: 'I have read and re-read the Gospels and have failed to find a single word that might strengthen, or even authorize, the family and marriage. On the contrary . . .' The disciples were enjoined to leave all and follow him, to give away all that they possessed and henceforth to have nowhere to lay their heads. Furthermore, did not Christ say: 'I am come to set a man at variance against his father, and the daughter against the mother'?[19] Again, as in the case of 'Ménalque', it is amusing to note a certain discrepancy between Gide's published views and his actual situation.

El Hadj, a tale of some nineteen pages in the Pléiade *Romans*, first appeared in September 1896 in the second and last number of *Le Centaure*. (It was not published in book form until 1899, when it was included in a single volume with *Philoctète* and two other pieces.) Led by their prince, the men of the city set out on a journey into the desert. The destination and purpose of the journey are as mysterious as the prince, who, unseen and unheard, is carried on a closed litter during the day and sleeps alone in a closed tent at night, guarded by dumb slaves. The narrator, El Hadj, is an itinerant storyteller, taken on to entertain them, singing love songs to console them for the women left behind in the city. (In Arabic, *haj* means 'pilgrimage'. Any Muslim who has made the pilgrimage to Mecca is entitled to assume the title of *haj*.) As the journey progresses, El Hadj becomes more and more obsessed by the person of the prince. At night, he takes to singing what amount to serenades outside the prince's tent. On the third such night, the prince, sumptuously attired, his face veiled, appears at the entrance to his tent and orders him to visit him the following night. The prince then tells El Hadj that, in some far off country in the north, where there are trees and flowers he – the prince – will meet his betrothed. (By a neat reversal of European exoticism, and Gide's, the men of the southern desert are travelling northwards to a mirage-like Eden.) Night after night, the minstrel goes to the royal tent and sings of love. El Hadj himself is consumed by love for the prince, who takes him more and more into his confidence. El Hadj becomes an intermediary between prince and people, an ever more necessary instrument of the prince's authority as the people's unquestioning faith is eroded by hardship. But he also becomes necessary to the prince's belief in himself and his vision: 'El Hadj, you must believe in me with all your strength; the future requires it in order to come about . . . In your belief in me I draw the certainty of my life.' One day the travellers see a lake in the near distance and rejoice in the refreshment promised. After so many mirages, the prince seems unconvinced of its reality and orders El Hadj to go secretly at night and verify its existence. He reaches the 'lake' and walks into it. It turns out to be neither land nor water, but mud covered by a thin crust of salt reflecting the moonlight. He returns to the camp and finds the prince dead. Concealing the truth from the people, El Hadj continues his role as the prince's intermediary and, after much travail, succeeds in bringing them back to the city. 'Prince, you are mistaken; I hate you,' El Hadj exclaims. 'For I was not born a prophet; it was by your death that I became one; it was because you no longer spoke that I had to speak to the people.'[20]

El Hadj belongs, loosely, to the group of texts that Gide called, or came to call, '*traités*', treatises: on its publication in volume form, it was subtitled 'The Treatise of the False Prophet'. Stylistically, however, it marks an advance on the two previous 'treatises', *Le Traité du Narcisse* and *La Tentative amoureuse*. Despite the oriental, potentially exotic quality of its subject, it is written in a beautifully restrained, pure style that has no more than a fleeting resemblance to the Koran or to the Bible (from which the two epigraphs, both referring to prophets, are taken). El Hadj's songs, however, do introduce a properly oriental flavour; they are reminiscent of the great fourteenth-century Persian poet, Hafiz, whose work was introduced to Gide by Fedor Rosenberg. Hafiz's poems are almost entirely in praise of wine and women. Muslim exegetes have traditionally interpreted them as pertaining solely to relations between the soul and God, and it is true that Hafiz was very close to the Sufis. A similar problem arises with Christian interpretations of the Song of Songs. Traditionalists have always interpreted these verses as symbolizing the love of God for his Church; modernists tend to see them simply as erotic poetry, dating as late as the third century BC, wrongly attributed to Solomon (tenth century BC). Few of us are qualified to adjudicate on such matters, but it seems to me that when poetry is so erotically charged, the poet, is, to say the least, having it both ways: the concept can only be added to the image, it cannot be substituted for it. Yet, curiously enough, many of Gide's commentators try to do just that, although, in Gide's case, of course, the eroticism of El Hadj's serenades is homosexual. In her notes to the Pléiade edition of *El Hadj*, Yvonne Davet, for example, declares: 'As for the symbolic meaning of *El Hadj*, God must be substituted for the mysterious prince' and goes on to cite as evidence one of Gide's letters which does refer to God in relation to the story, but certainly does not justify such a 'substitution'.[21]

The most obvious, non-literary source of *El Hadj* was a visit to the *chott*, or salt lake, of El Melrhir, half-way between Biskra and Touggourt, in April 1896. (On that occasion, Gide was with Paul Laurens, to whom the story was originally dedicated – later editions, however, were dedicated to Fedor Rosenberg.) The salt lake is the scene of the story's climax: it is also the central, mirage-like image of a false prophet's 'treatise' on the sustaining and shattering of illusion. When they reach the salt lake, El Hadj convinces prince and people that they are near journey's end, then, with the prince dead, keeps up the illusion that he is still alive and brings them safely home. Verbal illusion is shown to arouse and sustain sexual, religious and political illusion. Not that the listener, the lover, the believer and the political subject are necessarily worse off under the thrall of illusion than if it were shattered. El Hadj, the prince and his subjects are all happier believing in the happiness to come than facing the bleak alternative: no beloved, no other world, no sense of direction; no oasis, no lake, no destination – just sinking into the mud of the *chott*. *El Hadj* is both a hymn to the creative power of verbal art and a diatribe against its deceptive power, while being itself an accomplished piece of verbal art. *El Hadj*, too, is an early example of Gide's self-referentiality, a work meditating on itself, on its means and on its ends.

André Gide was back in Paris on 28 October; Madeleine joined him a week later. In his post he found a volume of verse by Saint-Georges de Bouhélier. Two months before, he had been sent the last two numbers of *Documents sur le Naturisme*, the latest literary enterprise of the twenty-year-old Bouhélier. At seventeen, he and Maurice Le Blond, a fellow-pupil at the Lycée Condorcet, had started a review called . . . *L'Académie française*! In it, Bouhélier declared, 'We are the primitives of a race to come' and cited André Gide as one of the masters of 'the future art'. Bouhélier was now trying to establish a new school around the concept of 'Naturism'. In sum, what Naturism amounted to was a reaction against Symbolism, with its esoteric abstractions and artificial language, and a return to a direct response to nature. Whatever reservations Gide may have had as to the company he would have to keep, he could hardly refuse support to a cause that seemed, at the time, to be so very much his own. He responded enthusiastically to Bouhélier's gesture, ending his letter: 'Croyez-moi votre co-religionnaire.' It was the sort of commitment that did not come easily to Gide, which he was capable of occasionally and on the spur of the moment, but which he always came to regret. This was to be the case with Bouhélier and his Naturism. The breaking-point came some months later over what Gide regarded as the group's meretricious attacks on Mallarmé.

In December, Gide was visited by André Ruyters, a twenty-year-old Belgian writer, with whom he had been in correspondence for a year. During the previous year, Ruyters had sent Gide his first volume of verse and his recently published short novel, *Les Oiseaux dans la cage.* In September, on a visit to Paris, Gide being at Cuverville, Ruyters went to the rue de Commaille: 'I knew you weren't there, but I wanted to know the usual horizon of your private life, the landscape of your everyday life.'[22] In reply, Gide sent him a photograph of himself – Ruyters had earlier asked for such a photograph, declaring 'you are far away and any immediate approach is not possible for us' and he would like to be able to put a face on the 'absolute idea' that he had of Gide. More intrigued than ever, Gide asked for a photograph of Ruyters in return. At first Ruyters was reluctant to oblige, claiming that 'I am still very young and whatever good there is in me has not had time to become exteriorized.'[23] The photograph that he did send shows him to be an elegantly dressed, good-looking young man.

February 1897 found the Gides in the middle of moving. André had finally given up the idea of the 'delightful little house' in Auteuil and took, instead, an apartment a short distance from the rue de Commaille, on the fifth floor of 4 boulevard Raspail. For a few weeks, they were besieged by builders and decorators. 'Sunday! The workers rest and the house becomes quiet again,' Gide wrote to Valéry. 'It was frightful. Six days of restaurants, escapes . . .' He had tried to work 'in vague asylums: libraries, cafés, *mercures* . . .' (the last a reference to the offices of the review *Mercure de France*).[24] It was in such conditions that Gide finally completed *Les Nourritures terrestres.* Having delivered the manuscript to Vallette at the *Mercure*, his mind turned again to travel. Madeleine was not at all well. In addition to her usual 'tiredness', he told Valéry, she had 'an ill-mended tooth, periostitis, adenitis, an abscess and the beginning of a dangerous phlegm'. He himself was 'exhausted, weighed down with family and other concerns'.[25] One such family concern was his wife's sister, Jeanne. That summer, when Marcel Drouin thought that he was finally about to win Jeanne's consent to marry him, he met with stiffened resistance. The truth was that Jeanne had fallen in love with Fedor Rosenberg, an altogether more charming, more attractive, more 'artistic' figure than the rather serious, highly intellectual Drouin. The Gides thought that, if they were to spend the next couple of months in Italy, the best thing for Jeanne was for her to go with them.

The three left Paris on 5 April – André, as he was so often to do, missing the publication of a book. Jeanne was not, however, so easily removed from the attentions of the two suitors. In Marseille, they met up with Rosenberg. Then, at Ravello, near Naples, Gide wrote a long letter to Drouin, inviting him to join them. With truly Gidean prevarication, he referred to himself as Drouin's 'brother-in-law', while urging his friend to come '*in order* to see that Jeanne is not the right wife for you. Jeanne *thinks* that you are very intelligent, but will you ever succeed in making her believe *in* your thought?' Here, of course, Gide was projecting his own problem on to poor Drouin: by now he was all too well aware that his own mind was travelling in directions that Madeleine could not follow. Anyway, Gide concludes, the two of them could leave the women for a few days at Ravello and go off on 'un petit voyage de garçons' to the Vesuvius area.[26] In fact, Gide spent little of those three weeks at the hotel with his wife and sister-in-law. In a high state of nervous excitement, he wandered off to Naples, Amalfi, Minori and La Cava. There can be no doubt that there were sexual encounters on the way, but they are not detailed.

The three travellers left Ravello for Florence; from there, they went on to Geneva, where Madeleine consulted Dr Andreae, who advised her to take a cure at Lostorf-bad, in northern Switzerland. André then went off, alone, to Montpellier, urgently summoned by Aunt Anna: her thirteen-year-old son, Paul, had narrowly escaped death and was still seriously ill. In a letter to Marcel Drouin, André described his five days at Montpellier as 'a frightful Ibsen drama'. Relations between Charles Gide and his wife had deteriorated still further: they were no longer speaking to one another. After a detour to Marseille to see Fedor Rosenberg, André rejoined his wife and sister-in-law. Madeleine began her three-week cure at Lostorf on 24 May. André spent the time reading, writing verse, playing the piano and answering the many letters that arrived on the subject of *Les Nourritures terrestres*, which had just appeared. At Lostorf and over the next few weeks he answered over thirty letters, known to exist, on the subject of *Les Nourritures*. Most were favourable; many testified to the change that the book had wrought in the reader. Gide had had the effect that he had desired.

Les Nourritures terrestres (literally, *Earthly Food*; *Fruits of the Earth* in the English translation) is a work, more than usually with Gide, difficult to classify. The mood that prevails throughout is one of celebration, celebration of all the beauties of the world available through the senses. This can take the literary form of prose that differs little from Gide's journal entries (headed by the places of their writing, if not their dates – Honfleur, Villa Borghese, Fiesole, Amalfi, etc.), more poetically charged, lyrical prose and, occasionally, poems. There are no characters, only three 'figures': the unnamed first-person narrator, the imagined disciple, Nathanaël, to whom the work is addressed and who is constantly addressed by name, and the narrator's teacher, Ménalque. Much is autobiographical: in the sections describing North Africa, Athman and Meriem are even mentioned by name. There is the odd, fleeting reference to experiences with boys and young men, though so phrased that they might be missed by the inattentive reader: 'O little face that I caressed beneath the foliage! No shade could have dimmed your brightness and the shadow of the curls on your brow seemed darker still.'[27] There are the pages describing 'the most beautiful gardens I have seen' (Florence, Seville, Munich, Granada, etc.). Book 5 is a celebration of the very different pleasures of the 'rainy land of Normandy, domesticated land . . .'

The narrative within the narrative, Ménalque's account of his life (the 'fragment' published separately in *L'Ermitage*), occurs near the beginning of Book 4. It falls into three phases. The first, Ménalque between eighteen and twenty-five, is that of the nomad, footloose and fancy-free:

I passed through cities, but stopped nowhere. Happy is he, I thought, who becomes attached to nothing on earth . . . I hated homes, families, all places where man thinks he can find rest; and lasting affections and fidelity in love, and attachment to ideas . . . I slept anywhere . . . In the morning I washed in the grass and the rising sun dried my damp clothes . . . Families, I hate you! Closed homes; locked doors; the jealous possession of happiness. Sometimes, at night, I stood, unseen, leaning by a window, observing . . . The father was there, next to the lamp; the mother was sewing . . . A boy, near the father, was studying; – and my heart swelled up with a desire to take him with me on the road. Next day, I saw him again, as he was coming out of school; the day after that I spoke to him; four days later he left everything to follow me. I opened his eyes to the splendour of the plains . . . I taught his soul to become more vagabond, more joyful – then to free itself even from me, to experience its solitude.[28]

At twenty-five, Ménalque underwent a change. He returned to the apartment that he had abandoned for seven years. 'I surrounded myself with all the precious or delicate objects I could . . . For fifteen years, I hoarded like a miser; I did everything I could to get rich; I educated myself . . .'[29]

At fifty, he sold all he had and invested the proceeds in such a way that he would have whatever he needed for the rest of his life. 'Do you believe that you are able, at the precise moment, to taste the powerful, complete, immediate sensation of life . . .?' he asks a friend. 'The habits of your life prevent you from doing so; you live in the past, in the future and you perceive nothing spontaneously. We are nothing . . . but the instantaneousness of life . . . Each moment of our lives is essentially irreplaceable . . . Without wife and children, you would be alone before God on the earth. But you remember them, and carry with you, as if afraid to lose them, all your past, all your loves . . .' Ménalque has a ship built and, with three friends and a crew, sets sail. He falls for 'the least beautiful' of the cabin-boys. At Venice he has a brief affair with 'a beautiful courtesan'. He lives in turn in a palace overlooking Lake Como, a large property in the Vendée, an Alpine chalet, a palace in Malta, etc. He owes his happiness, he concludes, not to wealth, but to a capacity to enjoy life to the full; unattached to anything, he will die easily.[30]

In a 1935 *Journal* entry, Gide complains that 'Ménalque's ethic' has so dominated people's perception of *Les Nourritures* that it has obscured the book's more important message, the need for *dénuement*.[31] It is not immediately clear what Gide means by this. The French word means literally 'denuding' and usually refers to destitution, poverty. Gide's *dénuement* was rather less literal, more literary, a Lear-like stripping down to essentials, to the 'poor, bare, forked animal'. But, even as a young man, Ménalque never subjected himself to this. Behind his travelling was parents' money or a private income; the spacious family apartment awaited his return. The second Ménalque actually accumulates wealth, while the third does not give it away, but invests it to finance his luxurious, if restless, way of life. The only sense in which *dénuement* can apply to Ménalque – and to do so one must push the word beyond normal usage to a peculiarly Gidean use – is in that of 'non-attachment', an absence of possessiveness towards persons and things, even towards ideas and memories, that would be Buddhistic were it not so strongly imbued with *joie de vivre*. Yet it is in no sense contradictory to what Gide understood by 'Ménalque's ethic'; on the contrary, it provides a justification for avoiding attachments and moving on to other delights. There is, too, something ludicrous about having recently come into a fortune and 'attached' himself to a wife, sitting in the luxury of the Hôtel Kühn at Saint-Moritz, on the first stage of a honeymoon that was to last for seven months, preaching the virtues of *dénuement*, however it is to be understood; and about a Gide, who could hardly have been more attached to his family, even to the extent of marrying his cousin weeks after the death of his mother, declaring, albeit through the mouth of a character, but with unmistakable conviction, 'Families, I hate you!' – words that he was to regret and were to dog him for the rest of his life.

Les Nourritures terrestres is a work of ethical, even pedagogical intent, the moral lesson being that sensual joy is the highest good and that we have to learn (by unlearning much else) to experience it. There is also a more specifically religious dimension to the experience and celebration of earthly delights. The theology of *Les Nourritures terrestres* is pantheistic: we must not seek God, God is not to be found in any one place, He is everywhere. But, in Nietzschean, 'existentialist' fashion, the sermon contains the seeds of its own destruction. In the brief foreword, the author urges Nathanaël, 'when you have read me, throw away this book – and go out . . . Go out from wherever you may be, from your town, from your family, from your room, from your thoughts. Do not take my book with you.'[32] At the very end of the work, the narrator repeats the same injunction: 'And now, Nathanaël, throw away my book . . . Leave me . . . You are in my way . . . I am tired of pretending that I can educate anyone. When did I ever say that I wanted you to be like me? It is because you are different from me that I love you . . . Do not think that *your* truth can be found by anyone else . . .'[33] A child of culture, Gide had had to use culture to achieve communion with nature; the writing of *Les Nourritures* assumes that others are in the same position – this particular piece of culture may help others to do as he has done. In the Preface to the 1927 edition, Gide protests that he has been 'confined' in this 'escape manual'. Yet he had no intention of 'stopping short at this book'. 'I am usually judged by this book of my youth as if the ethics of *Les Nourritures* were the ethics of my whole life, as if I myself had not been the first to follow the advice I gave my young reader: "Throw away my book and leave me." Yes, I immediately left the man I was when I wrote *Les Nourritures*.'[34] All his life Gide was adept at discarding former selves, but he never threw away his books. Even at his most nomadic, he was usually accompanied by crates of them, which he would spend much of the day reading.

Gide had outlived *Les Nourritures terrestres* before he had even finished it.

From the outset, it was a young person's, more particularly a young man's, book. It has found an especially widespread response at times when individual youthful revolt has turned into a broader, social phenomenon: the turn of the century, the early 1920s, the years following the Second World War, the late 1960s. Jacques Copeau, later to become the great modernizer of the French theatre and a lifelong friend of Gide, has described how, in 1901, aged twenty-two, he discovered *Les Nourritures terrestres*. 'When I was shut up in my room, in fierce idleness, rejecting everything, consumed by desires, parched with waiting, this book came to quench my thirst . . . Gide never left my side.'[35] In his *Les Thibault*, Roger Martin du Gard, also a lifelong friend of Gide, has the twenty-year-old Daniel de Fontanin discover *Les Nourritures terrestres* by reading a few lines over the shoulder of a fellow-passenger in a train. After great difficulty, the young man tracks down a copy of the book, reads it through twice and is transformed. Throughout his life, but especially during his last thirty years or so, Gide constantly received letters from young men who had been 'resuscitated' by reading *Les Nourritures terrestres*, as Gide himself had been by his experience in North Africa. From a selection of these, in an appendix to Yvonne Davet's *Autour des Nourritures terrestres*, one might cite one from a patient in a sanatorium: 'I owe you whatever faith in life and hope in the future is left in me . . . You have taught me the beauties of life . . .' A twenty-two-year-old in hospital, expecting to die from tuberculosis, wrote:

You have been the guide and support of the worst hours of pain and suffering in my life. *Les Nourritures terrestres* has not only helped me to live, it has saved me from death. At seventeen, I copied out the most important parts of the book into a little exercise-book that I have always kept on me ever since; it gave me the will to live and, if I am still alive, it is thanks to you, because, through you, I learnt that 'the smallest instant of life is stronger than the death that denies it.'[36]

Publication of *Les Nourritures terrestres* passed unnoticed by the Paris newspapers, but, as usual, quite extensive coverage came from the literary reviews. The most detailed and perceptive accounts of *Les Nourritures terrestres* were by Léon Blum in *La Revue Blanche* and Henri Ghéon in the *Mercure de France*. *Les Nourritures terrestres* was, said Blum, 'a new stage in autobiography, more scattered and poetic, but more serious, more strange . . . There has always been a great writer in M. Gide. Yet each of his books reveals in turn a surer, more secret perfection of form. I could imagine nothing better written than *Paludes*, but I cannot not prefer *Les Nourritures*.'[37] Henri Ghéon, who was just twenty-two, was a poet. Under his real name of Henri

Vangeon, he was a medical student. His first volume of verse, *Chansons d'Aube*, had been published by the *Mercure de France*. He would be doing a short review of *Les Nourritures* for the May number of *L'Ermitage* and a larger essay on Gide's work in general for the June number of the *Mercure*. Alfred Vallette, the *Mercure*'s owner–editor, suggested that he see Gide. This he did, shortly before Gide left for Italy in April. The two got on extremely well: for Ghéon, Gide was something of a hero and Gide responded at once to the younger man's enthusiasm and exuberance. As Ghéon left the Gides' apartment, Gide thrust into his hand a proof copy of *Les Nourritures terrestres*. The *Mercure* essay on Gide, consisting of twenty-six closely printed pages, was to remain for a long time the most thorough study of his work. Ghéon is perceptive about the unity of sensibility that underpins the diversity of the works: 'The dilettante plays with everything and believes in nothing so that he can believe in everything. André Gide's great strength lies precisely in faith: it is this that binds the various works together . . . For he has set out to express himself in his books in all sincerity and each and every one of them marks a stage in his intellectual and moral history.'

In *Autour des Nourritures terrestres*, Yvonne Davet gives a fascinating account of the publishing history of the book. The first printing by *Mercure de France* was for 1,650 copies. In the first year, 329 had been sold; the following year produced no sales, but 119 returns, making a net sale of 210 copies. Over the next nine years, sales ranged from three to ninety, bringing the total sale, in 1908, to 500 exactly. The next seven years, until 1915, produced almost identical sales, bringing the total up to 1,007. When, in 1917, the *Nouvelle Revue Française* wanted to republish the work, the *Mercure* ceded its rights without payment.[38] The tide then turned. The *NRF* had to order a reprint the following year and eight further editions appeared up to 1948. It is now enshrined in the Pléiade edition of the *Romans* (1958) and has never been out of print since.

On 19 June, Gide went to Berneval-sur-Mer, a small Channel resort. There, at the Hôtel de la Plage, he asked to see a 'M. Sebastian Melmoth'. Oscar Wilde had been released from Reading gaol on 19 May and, retreating to France, adopted the name of the Satanic hero of *Melmoth the Wanderer* (1820), by Charles Maturin (1728–1824), his maternal great-uncle. Gide, who had been the last of Wilde's French friends to see him before his imprisonment, wanted to be the first to see him again. He arrived in the early afternoon of a cold, wet day, to find that 'M. Melmoth' had gone off to Dieppe for the day. Gide took a room in the same hotel and waited. Wilde finally arrived at eleven in the evening, shivering with cold, having

lost his overcoat on the way. They sat up, sipping grogs, and talking. Gide
noticed that the skin on Wilde's face and especially on his hands had grown
coarser, but he was wearing the same rings as before. His teeth were in a
shocking state. Observing the Wilde in front of him, Gide was taken back,
'not two years, but four or five': Wilde was no longer the over-confident,
overweening pleasure-seeker he had seen last, but the gentler, more sensitive
man he had first known. Wilde admitted that prison had greatly altered
him: he could not just resume his previous way of life. The following day,
he spoke at length about his prison experiences. Just as Gide was taking his
leave, Wilde finally referred to *Les Nourritures terrestres*: 'It's very good, very
good . . . But, dear, promise me one thing: from now on, never write *I* any
more . . . In art, you see, there is no *first* person.'[39] For Gide, of course, there
was really no other. Wilde had plans to write more plays and thus regain
his literary standing. While at Berneval he wrote *The Ballad of Reading Gaol*,
but little else was to come. Over the next three years, he wandered between
Paris, the South of France and Italy, with or without Douglas, ending in a
room in the Hôtel d'Alsace, rue des Beaux-Arts, where he died on 30
November 1900.

The summer, which began at La Roque and ended at Cuverville, saw
what seemed like an endless stream of visitors. On 2 July, André and
Madeleine arrived at La Roque with Uncle Charles, his somewhat estranged
wife having gone to her sister's in Geneva. They were soon joined by Jeanne
and Georges Rondeaux, Marcel Drouin, Rita Gay, a friend of Madeleine's, and Eugène Rouart; other family friends followed. There were
expeditions into the woods and fishing parties. Gide also had his responsibilities as mayor of La Roque-Baignard: council meetings, visits, assisting
those in difficulties. He tried to write – he was working on two plays, *Saül*
and *Philoctète*, and on the autobiography that was to become, many years
later, *Si le grain ne meurt* – but found it difficult to concentrate. Fedor
Rosenberg, now nicknamed 'Batouchka', arrived for the first two weeks of
August – and Jeanne Rondeaux removed herself to her sister's at Le Havre.
Restless, tiring of the society of friends and relations, Gide would wander
off on his own, '*rôdeur*', 'prowling', as he described himself in an unpublished
journal entry. There were one or two fortuitous encounters, like the Spanish
boy who sold waffles, but nothing came of them. On a trip to Etretat, he
escaped from the others with Rouart and watched the sailors, lying half-
naked on the deck of their ship.

Two or three times, Gide went to stay with the Laurens at Yport. On
one such occasion, he called on Henri Ghéon, who was spending his

summer holidays there, and brought him back to Cuverville for a week. The summer came to an end with the marriage of Jeanne Rondeaux and Marcel Drouin on 14 September. The months leading up to the wedding had not been easy for either party. Certain members of the Rondeaux clan had looked askance at the prospective husband's lack of means. Furthermore, he was a freethinker, which pleased neither the Protestant nor the Catholic wings of the family. More seriously, the heart of the rather frivolous, romantic Jeanne was by no means won over. At the beginning of the school year, the couple moved to Alençon, where Drouin took up his first teaching post at the *lycée*. In November, the Gides spent a week or two with them.

Gide then spent two weeks of feverish social activity, entertaining and being entertained by those of his friends who happened to be in Paris at the time. Exhaustion, boredom, exasperation soon set in, however, and on 12 December the Gides set out on their travels for the second time since their marriage. They were to be away for five months. After five or six days at Neuchâtel, they joined Charles Gide and his wife at Lausanne, where they spent Christmas and the New Year. They then went to Marseille, where Gide met up with Francis Jammes. They were expecting to set sail for Algiers when Madeleine went down with a bad cold. Plans were changed: they rented a villa in Nice and, when Madeleine had recovered, made their way through Italy. 'If you ever marry,' Gide wrote to Valéry, 'marry a colossus.'[40] At Rome, they rented a three-room apartment on the Piazza Barberini.

Over the next six weeks, they visited the usual museums and churches. They attended concerts of music by Palestrina and Bach, and made excursions to Hadrian's Villa at Tivoli. André went several times to the old Protestant cemetery, persuading the caretaker to lend him a key for his own use. There he visited Keats's grave, reciting lines to himself that he barely understood. Madeleine, usually plagued by a series of colds, retired to bed early, leaving André to wander the streets and squares of the city in search of encounters: the Piazza di Spagna and the Borghese Gardens proved particularly fruitful. During the day, he took to photographing the young 'models' who offered their services on the Spanish Steps, taking them back to the apartment, while Madeleine went off 'for long hours' elsewhere. To avert any suspicion on Madeleine's part, he would show her some of the 'academic', very inexpert photographs. The photographs became little more than a pretext: the oldest of the models, Luigi, soon understood

Gide's real predilections and began to procure others on his behalf. 'I was possessed by a demon,' Gide writes. His account of these activities occurs in *Et nunc manet in te*, the almost excessively self-condemnatory work that he wrote soon after Madeleine's death in 1938.[41] As Jean Schlumberger demonstrates, Gide erroneously places them during his honeymoon, two years before. This makes for a more dramatic narrative and, Schlumberger suggests, places Gide in an even worse light.

Their stay in Rome coincided with a new, dramatic turning-point in the Dreyfus Affair. Over three years before, Captain Alfred Dreyfus, serving on the general staff of the French army, had been found guilty of passing secrets to the Germans, stripped of his rank and transported to the penal colony of Cayenne. Prompted by the indefatigable work of Dreyfus' relations and friends, Colonel Piquart, a new head of military intelligence, reopened the evidence and, much against his own preconceptions, decided that the evidence on which Dreyfus had been condemned was a forgery and that the probable forger was a Captain Esterhazy, a distant relation of the Hungarian aristocratic family. On 10 January 1898, Esterhazy was tried by court martial and acquitted. It was this apparent refusal on the part of the military authorities to admit their error (and to overcome their antisemitic prejudices) that led Zola to write his celebrated open letter to the French president, 'J'accuse . . .', published by Clemenceau in his newspaper, *L'Aurore*. Zola was promptly charged with libel, condemned to a year's imprisonment and, pending appeal, took off for London. It was really from this point that the Dreyfus Affair took hold of the public imagination, becoming, for years to come, at least among the higher intellectual echelons of the population, one of the most important topics of conversation. It also divided the French intelligentsia more evenly than might have seemed possible to later generations, such, until relatively recently, has been the hegemony of the left over French intellectual life. Indeed, what troubled many people who might otherwise have kept an open mind was the way in which, in certain quarters, the case seemed to have become a weapon used by the left to attack its targets – the Army, the Church, even the concept of Nation – all of which, of course, were held in great respect by the Dreyfus family, who, though of Jewish extraction and therefore suspected of 'international' allegiances, having, like many French Jews, relations in Germany, were intensely patriotic Alsatians, still smarting under the ceding of their province to the Prussians in 1871. They were also very rich, with absolutely no socialist or radical leanings: in choosing a military career, Alfred Dreyfus himself was moved entirely by patriotic feelings. Gide's Protestant background may be seen as some predisposition to the Dreyfusard side, but, although Protestants may have tended to oppose the usually Catholic anti-Dreyfusards, André failed to convince his Uncle Charles of Dreyfus' innocence. In any case, Gide's own fear of commitment, of certainty, of fanaticism made him as suspicious of Dreyfus' defenders as of his attackers. By the time of 'J'accuse . . .', Gide, in Rome, was reading half-a-dozen newspapers and had come round to the pro-Dreyfus side. When *L'Aurore* began to publish lists of leading intellectuals who pledged their support to the Dreyfus–Zola cause, Gide had his name added. Not all Gide's friends were Dreyfusards, however. Valéry adopted a position of superb contempt for both sides: 'How can these revolutionaries who never make revolution make fun of soldiers who never make war? . . . The humblest Jesuit knows a thousand times more than they do, the humblest wine merchant sees things more clearly . . .'[42] Eugène Rouart was fiercely anti-Dreyfusard. Gide tried to be conciliatory: Dreyfus may well be guilty, Gide had little time for the 'Dreyfusard party', but what matter are truth and justice.

On 25 March, after six weeks at the Piazza Barberini, the Gides left Rome. On medical advice, Madeleine would undergo treatment at Arco, in the Tyrol. They set off, in leisurely fashion, calling at Orvieto, Perugia, Assisi, Ancona, Ravenna and Venice, where they spent a fortnight, before reaching Arco. As always when travelling, Gide spent long hours reading and writing. Arco, with its lack of competing attractions and with much of Madeleine's time taken up undergoing treatment at the spa, was particularly productive. A week after arriving there, Gide finished *Saül*, the five-act tragedy begun the previous summer and largely written in Rome.

'Each of my books turns against those who like the preceding one,' Gide wrote in 1924, criticizing the Dadaists, who, enthusiastic over *Les Caves du Vatican*, sought to encapsulate him in that one book.[43] Certainly *Saül* was intended to distance its author from *Les Nourritures terrestres*. In 1927, Gide wrote to Victor Poucel, a Catholic priest: 'The danger presented by the doctrine [of *Les Nourritures*] appeared so clearly to me that, immediately afterwards, I wrote *Saül* as an antidote to it.'[44] This was not an opinion arrived at with benefit of years. In a letter to Valéry of 1898, Gide refers to *Saül* as 'the negation of *Les Nourritures*'. How, then, did Gide see *Saül* as an 'antidote', a 'negation' of its predecessor? In another letter, this time to a Pastor Ferrari, he rejects the idea that his ethic can be reduced to 'sensualism', as *Les Nourritures terrestres* might suggest. Indeed, the subject of *Saül* was 'the disintegration of the personality' brought about by an over-passive tendency to '*accueil*', to receptiveness, openness, a willingness to welcome almost any experience,[45] the very quality that was urged on the disciple Nathanaël in *Les Nourritures*. In the play itself, the Witch of Endor enjoins Saül: 'Roi déplorablement dispos à l'accueil – clos ta porte!' ('King so deplorably disposed to welcome – shut your door!').[46]

In two aesthetic ways, *Saül* also represents a reaction to *Les Nourritures*. After reading *Les Nourritures*, Oscar Wilde had remarked to Gide that he should not use the first person: it is curious, though no doubt coincidental, that his next work was a play, pre-eminently the form in which the author does not speak in the first person and therefore seems to be less committed to the opinions expressed. This enabled him to speak more openly than ever before of erotic relations between men. Gide took the story of *Saül* mainly from the First Book of Samuel, who, incidentally, appears as a ghost, summoned by the Witch of Endor. Saül, King of the Israelites, is a weak, vacillating, self-preoccupied ruler; his capital is besieged by the Philistines. David, a young shepherd from Bethlehem, appears at the court, answers the challenge of Goliath, the Philistine hero, and kills him with a stone from a sling. Saül grows jealous of David's reputation and tries to kill him. David flees. For dramatic reasons, Gide has David return with an army of Philistines and defeat Saül's forces. Against his strict orders, David's soldiers kill Saül and Jonathan. On Saül's death, David is invited by the Israelites to become their king. But Gide's principal addition to the biblical narrative is to make Saül infatuated with David, the 'Lord's anointed', who is destined to replace him as king. This lends a Sophoclean or Shakespearean irony to his tragedy: Saül is drawn towards the instrument of his own destruction. Saül's wife is also attracted towards David at first meeting and tries, unsuccessfully, to seduce him. This further arouses Saül's feelings of jealousy. And Saül's own son Jonathan conceives for David a love 'passing the love of women' as the biblical writer, in language more Greek than Hebraic, has it. Of David's three royal admirers, only Jonathan has his feelings reciprocated. As portrayed by Gide the relationship between David and Jonathan is clearly eroticized, but there is no suggestion that it is sexual in a physical sense. Saül's infatuation for David, on the other hand, is shown to be self-indulgent, obsessive and destructive.

On a personal level, Gide was obviously drawn to the subject of *Saül* because of the love of David and Jonathan; moreover, he chose to depict Saül infatuated with David. But the play is not *about* homosexuality; its principal theme, as Gide made clear, is Saül's moral (and therefore psychological) disintegration. (Similarly, *Othello*, say, is not about heterosexuality, but about the destructive power of jealousy; no one suggests that

Othello is an argument against marriage.) Gide said as much in a letter to Valéry, who had found Saül's 'violent pederastism' difficult to accept, and suggested that Gide had chosen the subject because it was a ready-made 'vehicle for the thing you wanted above all: the special love that presides over your drama'.[47] Gide replied that Valéry had confused the '*anecdote*' with the true subject of the play. On the other hand, by making Saül's highly erotic infatuation with David reprehensible, while sublimating the potential erotic charge of the Platonic love of David and Jonathan, can Gide be accused of 'bad faith', of letting the homosexual side down? The question has greater actuality today than in Gide's time. It should concern only propagandists, those with an instrumental view of art, those who resent art's ability to elude control, the artist's own control in the first instance. Gide clearly did not *approve* of Saül: what is more interesting is the extent to which his depiction eluded his disapproving grasp. Clearly, the instance of an older man, married to a woman he has come to resent, falling in love with a youth, is one that Gide could not but have feared. His insight into Saül's disintegration stemmed from his insight into his own potential situation, from the tension within him between the moral man, the loving husband, the responsible citizen, on the one hand, and, on the other, the terrifying power, with all its destructive potential, of the search to gratify a desire that could not be socialized.

Valéry was not alone in finding *Saül* disappointing: most commentators see it as morally dubious, aesthetically unresolved or simply untheatrical. Gide himself, however, always had a soft spot for it: as late as 1931, he said that it was one of the best things he had written. More curiously, his friend Roger Martin du Gard admitted that if he had to take one of Gide's works to a desert island, he would have taken *Saül* – surely an incomprehensible judgement. My own feeling is that it is not of Gide's best because the language itself is flat, under-charged, an accusation that might be levelled, too, at Gide's translation of *Hamlet*. Valéry points out *Saül*'s evident debt to Shakespeare, but Gide's language can only rival Shakespeare's in French translation, which seldom amounts to much. One need only compare Shakespeare at his most functional, as in Fortinbras' final words in *Hamlet*, with David's rather similar words at the end of *Saül*:

> Let four captains
> Bear Hamlet like a soldier to the stage,
> For he was likely, had he been put on,

> To have proved most royal: and for his passage
> The soldier's music and the rites of war
> Speak loudly for him.
> Take up the bodies. Such a sight as this
> Becomes the field, but here shows much amiss.
> Go, bid the soldiers shoot.

Come now, let us arise. Carry Saül's and the Prince's bodies back to the palace. Place them on a royal litter. Let the whole people follow in procession; let them accompany my grief with sobs and lamentations! You, musicians, sound a funeral march![48]

Lest it be thought that some untranslatable French essence eluded Dorothy Bussy in her translation, here is Gide's original. It reads, for all the world, like a first-draft prose translation:

Allons! Maintenant, levons-nous! Qu'on apporte au palais les corps de Saül et du prince. Qu'on les pose sur une litière royale. Que tout le peuple forme cortège; qu'il accompagne ma douleur de ses sanglots et de ses lamentations. Vous, musiciens! – qu'une musique funèbre retentisse.[49]

Gide, of course, was as incapable as anyone else of rivalling Shakespeare and he deliberately avoided the kind of third-rate fustian much current on the stages of Paris and London at the time. But he had not found a satisfactory prose for the theatre, as, arguably, Maeterlinck had in *Pelléas et Mélisande*. Yet Gide was adamant that the play had been written for actual performance. It was dedicated to one of the leading actors of the day, Edouard de Max, who had made his name partnering Sarah Bernhardt. De Max was a personal friend and, incidentally, an overt homosexual, whom Gide saw as the ideal Saül. De Max tried to persuade the avant-garde director Antoine to take it on. Antoine seemed enthusiastic, but he could only take on the play if his current production was a financial success. It was not and Antoine withdrew his offer. It was not until 1922, when Jacques Copeau put on the play at the Vieux-Colombier, with himself in the title role, that *Saül* reached the stage, but it was withdrawn after a few performances.

Saül was finished on 30 April. Two weeks later, after an absence of five months, the Gides were back in Paris. There André threw himself into the social–literary whirl, with excursions to Alençon, staying with the Drouins for five days; to Le Havre, where, on 8 June, his sister-in-law Valentine gave birth to a son; to La Roque, for a meeting of the municipal council on 19 June. On 11 July, after a difficult delivery, Jeanne Drouin gave birth to a son, Dominique. A week later, there was anxiety over the mother's health and André rushed over to Alençon to give what comfort he could. Jeanne was confined to bed for weeks afterwards. We learn from a letter to André Ruyters that in August he was frequenting 'a marvellous Turkish bath' that had made an August heatwave bearable – and 'knocked two years off me'.[50] Back at La Roque, Gide escaped to Trouville, where he was met at the station by Ghéon. After spending the day with Ghéon's mother at Criqueboeuf, where the Vangeons *mère et fils* had rented a villa, the friends were back in Trouville by evening. They 'cruised' around the Casino, but saw nothing but 'revolting, elegant riffraff'. A long, complicated account ensues involving three young sailors, which ends, far into the night, with the two friends meeting up again with one of them. They lie down on a jetty. In the moonlight, the sailor, 'radiant with sensuality', undresses. 'It was perhaps the most unalloyed pleasure I have ever experienced; comparable only with that on Lake Como on just such a night.' The sailor leaves them and they walk along the beach back to Trouville. 'My joy is so violent I could weep . . .'[51]

On 3 September, Mallarmé had died suddenly while talking to his doctor: he had been ill with tonsillitis, but was not thought to be in any danger. He was fifty-six. Gide learnt of the news from a 'devastated' Valéry, too late to attend the funeral. A few weeks later, Valéry wrote to Gide describing the financial straits in which Mallarmé's widow and daughter now found themselves. Would Gide agree to contribute towards paying the women's rent of 75 francs a month? Valéry himself could only afford 15 francs a month. In the end, it was agreed that Gide would pay 30 francs, Vielé-Griffin another 30 and Valéry 15 francs.

That summer, Gide had planned a 'great gathering' of his friends at La Roque. However, Jeanne Rondeaux's continuing illness, the baptisms of André's two nephews and the birth of Ruyters' first child had the effect of postponing the gathering to the autumn and, even then, not all his friends could come at the same time. In fact, Valéry could not come at all: with only two weeks' holiday from his office job, he felt that he should spend them with his mother, whom he had not seen for a year. Finally, on 15 September, Gide collected Henri Ghéon, his mother and sister from the seaside resort of Ver-sur-Mer. The two women stayed at La Roque for two days, then returned to Paris; Ghéon stayed for three weeks. Next to arrive was Francis Jammes, to be joined, some days later, by his friend Raymond Bonheur, the composer. No sooner had Ghéon left than Ruyters arrived; Rouart came for a couple of days. Ghéon and Jammes took a great liking to each other; they were both sociable, exuberant, fun-loving men, just the kind of men, in fact, that the more austere Gide took to. The atmosphere was so gay that Gide's elderly Aunt Claire, 'who did not smile easily, sometimes laughed herself sick'.[52] From six to midday, however, Gide wrote. Then the papers would arrive from Lisieux and they would all sit around a table endlessly discussing the latest ramifications of the Dreyfus case: on 30 August, Colonel Henry, who had succeeded Picquart as head of Intelligence, committed suicide, having admitted forging documents unfavourable to Dreyfus. Cavaignac, the War Minister, had resigned: Esterhazy, the real culprit, had fled the country; and, on 27 September, the whole Dreyfus case was referred to the Cour de Cassation; justice and the triumph of the Dreyfusards were at last in sight.

During those three weeks at La Roque, the friendship between Gide and Ghéon took a decisively new turn, as we learn from the exchange of letters between the two after Ghéon's departure. In the first, Ghéon's *lettre de château*, or thank-you letter, he writes: 'Our souls are forever acquainted, they have stripped themselves bare before one another . . . My over-excited imagination conjures up objects with terrible precision and I have spent the whole day picturing to myself what you were doing there . . . what has become of young René . . . and the others.'[53] It was while encountering 'young René', or one of the other young farmhands, on their walks, that Gide and Ghéon discovered that they had the same sexual tastes. Gide did not reply at once and, the following day, Ghéon sent off another, shorter, even more 'over-excited' note: 'Oh! I beg you, my dear Gide, write to me . . . I am in a state of dejection and mad despair . . . I can think of only one thing, only one . . . I am burning my life away . . . I don't know what is to become of me . . . What I write excites me all the more instead of calming me . . .'[54] Gide did not write back at once, pleading obligations to his guests. However, three days after receiving his friend's second letter, he wrote a twenty-page (2,300-word) 'secret history of the farm since you saw it and since you left it'. 'Ah! What events, dear friend! Read quickly and thrust this letter in the depths of your most secret drawer . . . Thanks to me all the farm people are astir; scandal is in the air . . .' What on earth had happened? Gide teases Ghéon with a long parenthesis about Ruyters and his obsession with Baghdad. 'But you are languishing for Boulay, my poor friend – well, well – I'm coming to him [abbreviated to "B." in the published correspondence, Boulay may or may not be the same as "young René"]: the 7th had been devoted to the baptism [of his nephew, Dominique Drouin]; on the 8th, languishing myself for *him*, I *had* to leave Ruyters and go out in the rain to the farm . . .' There follows a complicated narrative far too long to repeat here. In brief, Gide asks Boulay if he is going to the fair that is taking place the following day at nearby Cambremer. Boulay says he has no money to go. Gide offers the boy 10 francs – an enormous sum at the time (8 shillings or $2). 'I talk to him; I don't touch him.' The boy says he will buy shoes with the money. The following day, Gide and Ruyters join the locals at the fair and, despite appalling weather, find its bucolic delights highly amusing. Later, Gide meets up with Boulay and talks about the fair with him: 'My hand stroked his cheek . . . Boulay let my hand play clumsily over him ['Ma main s'amuse gauchement de la complaisance de Boulay']. Gide catches Boulay out lying. Things take a more serious turn when Gide learns from Desaunez, the estate manager, that the boy is going around saying that the master gave him money to speak ill of Lafosse, another worker. Gide denies the story absolutely and, anticipating trouble, warns Lafosse of the situation. Gide fears he may have to dismiss Boulay who, when questioned, denies having said anything to anybody. In a reply, Ghéon takes Boulay's part – it was just Boulay's clumsy way of explaining why he had so much money – and goes on to tell of a fruitless day following around the streets of Reims 'a delicious lad of about fifteen, who worked in some ironmonger's or other, whose long, delicate neck excited me furiously'.[55] As for the 'Boulay affair', there is no real evidence as to what, if anything other than a little stray fondling, took place between Gide and Boulay. The affair blew over and there was no scandal. The longer outcome was that, over the next fifteen years or so, Gide and Ghéon were constant companions, in Paris and further afield, in search of more tangible satisfaction.

During that summer and autumn of frequent comings and goings, Gide did manage to write. He always had the capacity to retreat early in the day to the 'dovecote' at La Roque or, at Cuverville, to the large room over the kitchen. It was during this period that he embarked on his 'Lettres à Angèle' (Angèle was the cultivated literary hostess of *Paludes*). They appeared over the next eighteen months in *L'Ermitage*. (Most of them were collected in volume form in 1900 and appeared in *Prétextes*, 1903.) The first, in the July number, concerned mainly *La Villa sans maître*, the first novel by Eugène Rouart, the dedicatee, it may be remembered, of *Paludes*. As if this were not incestuous enough, Ménalque had managed to escape *Les Nourritures terrestres* and play an important role in Rouart's novel, complete with scarcely disguised quotations from Gide's work, and even the words originally spoken to Gide by Oscar Wilde: 'I don't like your lips; they're straight, like those that cannot lie.' What is more, Rouart kills off Ménalque. As Gide put it in his 'letter': 'I learn of his death in a book by your friend Eugène Rouart, and I am saddened by it, because I was fond of him.'[56] But the intertextuality did not end there. In the November 'Lettres à Angèle' Gide wrote about Ruyters' as yet unpublished novel, *Les Jardins d'Armide*, in which Ménalque also makes a brief appearance.

The October *L'Ermitage* opened with Gide's 'In memoriam' on Mallarmé, a beautifully phrased defence of Mallarmé against enemies and disciples alike. Gide stresses Mallarmé's uniqueness. Something may be learned from 'his patient method', but it is stupid 'to imitate the result of that method in all its bizarre externalities'. 'By a sort of cruel pride', Mallarmé had 'preserved his work from life'. 'For Mallarmé, literature was the end, yes the very purpose of life . . . To sacrifice everything to it, as he did, one had to believe in it in a quite unique way.'[57] During that summer and autumn of 1898, Gide also worked on a new full-length play, *Le Roi Candaule*, and finished two shorter pieces, *Le Prométhée mal enchaîné* and *Philoctète*. As early as December 1895, Gide notes that he is thinking of writing a *Prometheus* 'in the manner of a Voltaire tale',[58] though its inception might date as far back as his reading of Goethe's *Prometheus* in the spring of 1892. However, it was mostly written during the winter of 1897–8, at the same time as *Paludes* and *Les Nourritures*. In style and spirit, it belongs to the Gidean line of *soties* that stretches from *Paludes* to *Les Caves du Vatican*. The title, of course, is a playful allusion to Aeschylus's *Prometheus Bound* and Shelley's *Prometheus Unbound*, and might be rendered as *Prometheus Misbound* or *Prometheus Ill-Bound*: as in the other *soties*, the setting is modern, the tone light-hearted, flippant even, Parisian, while possessing an underlying, very Gidean seriousness of intent. It opens in the manner of a newspaper *fait divers*:

In May 189 , at two o'clock in the afternoon, the following, to all appearances strange incident took place:

On the boulevard leading from the Madeleine to the Opéra, a fat, middle-aged gentleman, whose unusual corpulence was his sole distinguishing feature, was approached by a thin gentleman who, smiling and, in our opinion, without ill-intent, handed back to the first gentleman a handkerchief that he had just dropped. The fat gentleman thanked him briefly and was about to continue on his way, when, changing his mind, he leaned towards the thin man and must have made some inquiry, which the latter must have answered . . .[59]

Taking pen and inkwell out of his pocket, the fat man hands them to the thin man who writes an address on an envelope. 'By way of thanks', the fat man slaps the thin man hard on the cheek and, jumping into a fiacre, disappears. It later transpires that the fat man is 'Zeus, the banker'; the thin man is Coclès and the envelope bears the name of Damoclès. We are then introduced to the character of Prométhée, who, tired of his inactivity at the top of the Caucasian mountains, gets up and takes himself off to Paris where, on the boulevard des Capucines, he enters a café. The waiter, a parody of the loquacious, worldly-wise Parisian waiter, embarks on a pseudo-philosophical discourse about his profession, which he sees as 'creating relationships' between people who would otherwise be unaware of the other's existence. This is what he calls 'a gratuitous action'. The waiter explains: a gratuitous action is one lacking in motivation, a disinterested act, a spontaneous, unpredictable action with no purpose in view. Just such an action took place here a few hours ago and the waiter proceeds to relate, in his own fashion, the incident involving Zeus the banker. We learn that the envelope contained a 500-franc note. But the money brings Damoclès nothing but misfortune; he becomes ill and eventually dies. As it happens, Coclès and Damoclès are also sitting in the café . . . Each has a story to tell. Prométhée seems reluctant to speak. After much persuasion, he admits his occupation: he is a manufacturer of matches . . . He remarks that he has an eagle. His listeners seem unconvinced, so he stands up and summons it. The sky darkens and an eagle comes crashing through the window, puts out one of Coclès' eyes with a beating of its wing and, after Prométhée has undone his waistcoat, proceeds to feed on his liver. This is regarded as impolite, 'not done', by the onlookers. The police are called and Prométhée is jailed as an unlicensed manufacturer of matches. The eagle joins him in prison and, feeding regularly on his master's liver, grows ever stronger as his master grows thinner and weaker. After a time, the eagle is so strong and Prométhée so light that the bird is able to carry its master to freedom. Prométhée gives a public lecture on the subject of his eagle. At Damoclès' funeral a rejuvenated Prométhée, brimming with health, admits that he has killed his eagle – and would be eating it later. He goes on to tell of a certain Tityre, who lived in the middle of marshlands . . . We meet Angèle and Ménalque – another Gidean use of the '*en abyme*' technique and more 1890s' 'intertextuality'.

Gide regarded *Le Prométhée mal enchaîné* as an antidote to *Saül*, which, in turn, had been an antidote to *Les Nourritures terrestres*, itself a reaction to *Paludes*. In style and tone, *Le Prométhée* may be a *sotie*, yet its very choice of subject, the rebel Prometheus, who challenges divine authority and benefits mankind, is a return to some of the Nietzschean concerns of *Les Nourritures*:

the contempt for moral authority coming from above, the cavalier attitude to conscience, the search for a personal, inner-based integrity. *Le Prométhée* appeared in the first three 1899 numbers of *L'Ermitage* and later in the year in volume form, published by the *Mercure de France*. As so often with the younger Gide, there was little general critical notice, apart from that of a few friends and acquaintances in the literary reviews, and poor sales.

In *Philoctète*, Gide takes over the broad outlines of the story from Sophocles. Ten years before the play begins, Philoctetes was stung by a snake; the wound proved incurable and, before long, began to stink so much that his companions decided to leave him on a deserted island. Both plays begin with Odysseus (Ulysse) and Achilles' son, Neoptolemus, arriving on the island with the intention of obtaining Heracles' bow, which is in Philoctetes' possession, and without which, according to the priests, the Greeks will not win the Trojan war. In Sophocles, Odysseus fails to persuade Philoctetes to accompany them to Troy and the sick man agrees to do so only after the intervention of Heracles. Gide's Ulysse wants only the bow and arrows, not their owner, and tries to obtain them by his famous cunning, without benefit of a *deus ex machina*. Philoctète outwits the cunning Ulysse by voluntarily giving the bow and arrows to Néoptolème. The sick hero is left alone, but mysteriously happy, on his island.

Gide began thinking about his own *Philoctetes* soon after reading the Sophocles play in August 1892: the following year, a *Philoctète ou l'immonde blessure* was announced as 'forthcoming' in *La Tentative amoureuse*. Gide worked further on the play at La Brévine in September 1894 and 'two short fragments' from it appeared in *La Revue sentimentale* over the winter of 1894–5. Nevertheless very little of the final version was finished until the summer of 1898, the second act being written in August, the fourth and fifth acts in October. Gide's constantly shifting intellectual development over those six momentous years gives the play what might be called a semantic layering. This surely is why Gide commentators are so curiously at odds as to its 'meaning'. The latest of them, Patrick Pollard, stresses the importance of establishing the play's date of composition, 'since this shows several suggested interpretations to be unlikely or impossible'. On this basis, he dismisses in turn Delay's 'psychobiographical' view of Ulysse as a duty-bound representative of Gide's mother and Philoctète as an idealized self-image, Luria's suggestion that Philoctète, with his unhealthy wound, is a Wilde figure, the notion of Philoctète as a Nietzschean hero (O'Brien, etc.) and *Philoctète* as a 'parable of the Dreyfus case' (Chauffier, etc.). He then proposes his own view that *Philoctète* belongs with the 'Symbolist treatises'.

Pollard is right to see the history of the play's writing as an initial criterion of the possibility of certain meanings, but he is wrong, it seems to me, in his application of it. Indeed, it eliminates only the Luria (Wilde) interpretation and even that one only on the most literal level. Once past the first hurdle, of course, the real criterion has to be a reading of the play. Again Pollard is right to reject any strict notions of 'parable' or equivalence of meaning, but no one is seriously proposing any. A reading does, however, in varying degrees, confirm all the interpretations suggested as semantic elements in the work, with the exception of Delay's 'psychobiographical' one, this being too mythical to be determined either way.

Of the rest, the Symbolist 'semantic' layer is the earliest and, in the final version of the play, the least apparent. *Philoctète* was conceived and begun at the same time as Gide's most Symbolist work, *Le Voyage d'Urien*. It is also true that, in 1899, a year after its appearance in *La Revue Blanche*, it was first published as one of the 'treatises' in volume form, with *Le Traité du Narcisse*, *El Hadj* and *La Tentative amoureuse*. The 'treatises' began as Symbolist works, but they were never termed such by Gide and did not end as Symbolist works. By the time Gide finished *Philoctète* he had long left Symbolism behind. The traces that remain of the Symbolist period are at the very beginning: the description of Philoctète's ice-bound island is straight out of *Le Voyage d'Urien*. Nevertheless, not even in the opening passage is the language in any way Symbolist; on the contrary, it is a model of austere colloquial prose, suited to the conveying of moral argument, with no trace of the exoticisms and poeticisms of the earlier period.

What of the other interpretations? The Wilde hypothesis may be discounted, at least in any narrow sense: Gide chose his original subtitle, with its '*l'immonde blessure*' ('filthy wound'), long before Wilde's disgrace. But this is not the end of the matter. Gide had known Wilde since December 1891. For the rest of Wilde's stay in Paris, the two saw each other almost every day. In the manuscript of the journal, the pages concerning the meetings with Wilde for 1891 have been torn out. Why? We cannot be sure. We do not know how early Wilde and Gide understood each other's sexual orientation (in such matters, there are ways of knowing and not knowing), but, even by 1892–3, Wilde was the subject of gossip and quite blatant in his behaviour. Many must have wondered how long it could last, even the as yet inexperienced twenty-two-year-old Gide, who saw enough of Wilde in himself to be both overwhelmed and terrified. What drew Gide to the subject of Philoctetes if it were not the hero with the '*immonde blessure*' of the original subtitle? He did not have to have Wilde in mind; he had the subject of his deepest, most detailed thought – himself. Could social ostracism come to the likes of himself – or Wilde? Could one be oneself and not live a lie?

By the time Gide was really working on *Philoctète*, the summer of 1898, some five or six years had passed and Gide had found his *modus vivendi*; he no longer saw his sexuality as a wound that could bring ostracism; the wound remained an essential element in the play, but a more pressing question had largely obscured it. Indeed it was precisely the realization that the general moral questions raised by the particular instance of the Dreyfus affair were inherent in the play that gave Gide the impetus to reshape and complete it. This is reflected in the change of subtitle, '*l'immonde blessure*' giving way to '*traité des trois morales*'. Pollard also dismisses the Dreyfus reference on chronological grounds: 'general public feeling reached its climax only when the retrial occured in 1898–9' and cites a letter to Rouart of 24 January 1898 in which Gide expresses some confused doubt on the matter of Dreyfus's innocence. In that letter, Gide was simply trying to keep cool and see the position clearly – and concluded with a plea for the truth to be brought out, whatever the consequences for the State. Again it is misleading to say that the climax of the Dreyfus affair occured in 1898–9: in fact, it occurred in *January* 1898 with Zola's '*J'accuse*'. By the summer and autumn of that year, when *Philoctète* was being written or rewritten, Gide had gone over wholeheartedly to the Dreyfus cause. A second climax in this affair occurred in August, with the flight of Esterhazy and the suicide of Colonel Henry – the following month, at La Roque, Gide and his friends would rush to the newspapers every morning and talk of little else but the Affair.

What, then, were the 'three moralities' represented by the three characters? Ulysse stands for patriotism as supreme moral value: the gods and Greece are indistinguishable. For him, duty is 'the voice of the gods, civic order, the sacrifice of ourselves to Greece'.[60] Néoptolème represents the opposed morality of charity, pity, concern for one's fellow men as individuals, youthful generosity, moral conscience. It is surely inconceivable, given the time of writing and the terms in which their moral views are expressed, that Ulysse did not, in some sense, represent for Gide the anti-Dreyfusards, French Catholicism as a conservative force, and Néoptolème the Dreyfusards, a more genuinely Christian morality, in which human concern veers into social concern and political opposition. Incidentally, Gide chose to publish *Philoctète*, not in *L'Ermitage*, but in *La Revue Blanche*, which had Léon Blum as its literary editor and had come out enthusiastically on the

Dreyfusard side. Gide must have felt that the readership of that review would be particularly appreciative of his piece – this does suggest, though it does not in itself constitute proof, that, for Gide, *Philoctète* did have a certain political import.

The third 'morality', that of Philoctète himself, is more complex, more Gidean, than that of the other two characters. It requires its inverted commas because it is beyond good and evil, beyond morality ('there is no such thing as virtue') but, for Gide, Ulysse's 'morality' deserves inverted commas because it is a travesty of morality. He agrees with Néoptolème that the gods are above the State, but goes further: there is something above the gods. 'What?' Néoptolème asks. 'There is . . . I don't know any more . . . Ah! Ah! Oneself! . . .'[61] This is no mere egoism: this 'self' is above the gods, who are above the State. Philoctète (like Gide) is none too clear about it, but it is evidently Nietzschean in inspiration. Gide rejects Sophocles' *deus ex machina* and allows Philoctète to relinquish the bow as a voluntary act, thus outwitting Ulysse's cunning by rendering it redundant. He chooses to remain on the island and, at the very end, undergoes a kind of apotheosis, becoming himself, by an act of Nietzschean *dépassement*, self-creation, a sort of god. His last words are 'I am happy.' Yet, says Pollard, 'the *direct* influence of Nietzsche's idea of the individual must *probably* be discounted, since although Gide was *to some extent* familiar with these theories by 1895, he had not yet read any of Nietzsche's works'[62] and cites in support a letter to Marcel Drouin of 1895. But, by that time, a Parisian intellectual could know a great deal about Nietzsche (most of them did) and even call himself a Nietzschean (many did) without actually having read a single work by Nietzsche. Nietzsche had spread through the European intelligentsia largely by word of mouth. Gide was a friend of Henri Albert, who, in 1896, for example, published a long article, 'Les dangers du Moralisme', largely concerned with Nietzsche's thinking; Gide read the article voraciously and discussed it with the author. Marcel Drouin, too, of course, was a specialist in German philosophy and Gide's letter to him was in response to a long letter on Nietzsche. Nietzsche's ideas were also being discussed regularly in the literary reviews, which also published extracts from his work. By the end of 1895, Gide had written 'Ménalque', an evidently 'Nietzschean' work, and what Gide had gleaned of Nietzsche's thinking by then would have served his purposes in *Philoctète*, which, after all, is a play, not an academic disquisition on Nietzsche. More importantly, very little of *Philoctète* had been written by 1895. In March 1898, while at Arco, Gide read Henri Lichtenberger's *La Philosophie de Nietzsche*, a thorough, detailed account of the entire Nietzschean *œuvre*. After finishing it, he wrote to Drouin: 'Nietzsche is driving me mad. Why did he exist? I would *madly* have wanted to be him. I am jealously discovering my most secret thoughts, one by one.' During the summer of 1898, when most of *Philoctète* was written, Gide also read Henri Albert's translation of *Also Sprach Zarathustra* and a translation of *Jenseits von Gut und Böse* (*Beyond Good and Evil*). On 28 August, he again wrote to Drouin: 'Only Nietzsche has done me any good in my crisis.' Far from preceding the influence of Nietzsche on Gide, then, *Philoctète* was written at a time when he was at his most Nietzschean.

In December, he was to write an interesting thirty-six-page essay on Nietzsche, discussing two Nietzsche translations and the recently published translation of *Menschliches, Allzumenschliches* (*Human, All-Too-Human*). This appeared the following month in *L'Ermitage* as one of his 'Lettres à Angèle'.[63] It is a perceptive, searching, yet quietly assured piece that shows Nietzsche *working* within Gide's own mind. It provides as much insight into Gide himself as into Nietzsche, who is seen as carrying the Protestant mentality to its logical conclusion. Unlike its modern rival, scepticism, it, too, is a form of belief. Nietzsche's work may be seen as destructive, but it is not negative; it is carried out with passion and joy, and it enables others to create. Indeed Gide sees Nietzsche's tragedy to lie in his inability to create, as artists create, 'the fiction of their passions' and thus undergo a 'continual purgation'. Nietzsche became trapped in a philosophical system, 'a prisoner in his philosopher's cage, in his Protestant inheritance', and went mad – an interesting view of his own prophylactically zig-zag creative course.

Although, unlike *Saül*, *Philoctète* had never been intended for the stage, Jammes' friend, Raymond Bonheur, who had stayed at La Roque that September, planned to write an opera based on it. Gide even began to write the libretto, but nothing came of the project.

8

High Hopes Brought Low: Le Roi Candaule *and* L'Immoraliste

(NOVEMBER 1898 – OCTOBER 1902)

Over the next few weeks, Gide threw himself into a frenetic round of activity. He saw Edouard de Max several times about a possible production of *Saül*. He was deeply involved in the new order at *L'Ermitage* that would begin with the January number. Edouard Ducoté would remain an editorial influence, but he would be only one of a committee of twelve, consisting almost entirely of close friends of Gide: Paul Fort, Ghéon, Jammes, Stuart Merrill, Vielé-Griffin, etc. The new review would not be allied to any specific group, but it would be much less eclectic than before: the committee would be an active one and the contents of the review would reflect its taste. Gide's 'Lettres à Angèle' would continue to be an important monthly event. In the midst of this social and literary whirl came 'a supreme appeal from Rouart'[1]. On 21 November, Gide set off for Rouart's farm in Burgundy. A few hours later, Rouart's fiancée, Yvonne, called on Madeleine, with a woman friend. In a letter to André, Madeleine writes: 'The silent distress of that child is deeply moving. Does Eugène love her enough?'[2] Neither André nor Madeleine gives us any precise notion of the drama taking place between Rouart and his fiancée, but we know from his dealings with Gide that Rouart could be impetuous and aggressive. Two days later, the two friends returned to Paris. Over the next ten days, Gide was caught up in the drama, trying to play the honest broker. On 29 November, there was a violent scene between the engaged couple. 'I have sacrificed my best friends to you!' Eugène yelled at the hapless Yvonne. The following day, Rouart returned to Gide all the books and letters he had received from him. On 1 December, Rouart challenged Gide to a duel: nothing came of it. A few days later the couple were married. Not unnaturally the Gides did not attend either the ceremony or the reception given that evening. A few weeks later, Rouart's brainstorm had subsided, and he and Gide were good friends once more.

*

That winter Gide saw a great deal of Ghéon – in fact, the two met almost every day. They went to plays, concerts and exhibitions together. Ghéon's lust for life was intoxicating. After his death, in 1945, Gide wrote: 'He observed the external world as if caught up in some panic-stricken, but ecstatic devotion . . . "De tout, beaucoup, deux fois" was his motto.'³ He even managed to be one of Madeleine's favourites among her husband's friends. His good nature was evident in his round, highly animated face. His laugh often aroused comment. The best description of it is Maria Van Rysselberghe's: it sounded like the prolonged quack of a duck and it 'would have been intolerable were it not so irresistible'.⁴ In an interview with Léon Pierre-Quint in 1927, Ghéon defines the role that he played in Gide's life during those early years of their friendship: 'I think Gide looked to me for what was lacking in himself: a certain drive, exuberance, strength, health, frankness and, I admit, boldness in satisfying my desires.' He and Gide would 'wander around Les Halles, in small, shady cafés, surrounded by pimps and tarts, with young men, whose youth gave them beauty, drug dealers sometimes or ex-convicts . . . We were excited by the danger . . .' They would often spend the night there, until four or six in the morning, when Ghéon would catch the first train back to Bray-sur-Seine. 'It was a time of dissolution, of crazy, shameful dissipation!'⁵

Gide and Ghéon pursued their 'extraordinary quest for a certain happiness' not only in the streets of Paris: most years, up to the outbreak of war, they would go off abroad together. It was three years since Gide had last seen Africa. The year before, Madeleine's health had forced him to change their plans and opt for Italy. This year, he had an added incentive to reach North Africa: Ghéon would go too. In the event, André – and Madeleine – failed to persuade him to abandon his medical studies. The departure was planned for 4 March, but, as so often, Madeleine felt too ill to travel. They left Paris for Marseille four or five days later. There the roughness of the sea delayed them further: they even considered giving up North Africa yet again and going to Rome. On 13 March, André and Madeleine finally set sail for Bône. By now the sea had almost calmed, but it was a difficult crossing: Madeleine vomited constantly and hardly left her couchette. They spent six weeks in North Africa: it was André's fourth visit, Madeleine's second. They spent a few days at Bône, recovering from the crossing. André at once set about investigating the town. On the steps of the law courts, he was smiled at by one of two drunken youths. Later in the day, he saw the boy again. He was called Ali and offered to take Gide 'to see a Jewish woman'. Before long, Gide was being followed by 'the worst rabble in

Bône'. Later, there were encounters with a 'little Maltese' and a fourteen-year-old called Jean, born in Tunis, of Italian parents. From Bône, the Gides went on to Tunis, where they stayed for nine days.

'Far from distracting me from you, everything here makes me regret you all the more,' Gide wrote to Ghéon. 'Did I have any idea, before meeting you, of all that was still missing in my life?' The cruel absence of 'my friend, my "comrade", in the most Whitmanish sense of the term', meant that each new thing was experienced only half as much as if he had been there. Gide then reminds Ghéon how, in order to appreciate things to the full, he must be able to share them with someone else – 'whether Madeleine or you', he hastily adds. 'Madeleine or you'? Since he was with Madeleine, was not his need served? Obviously not. Gide makes this all too clear by referring to his first visit: 'The memory of my first trip here with Paul Laurens haunts me, triumphs constantly over the present . . . We were born again at each instant . . .' Now only Ghéon would do. Lacking his companionship, Gide wrote long letters to him: indeed they are almost our only information about those six weeks in North Africa. Gide suggests that the fault lies in himself: 'My error here has been to chase after a dead emotion, to seek to revive past moments, as if I had not read my *Nourritures*.'[6] This was no passing mood either. On 11 April, near the end of the trip, Gide was writing to Valéry: 'Of the whole of our trip, five exquisite days at El Kantara are the only ones worth remembering; the rest were enough to put me off travelling . . . [they] made me feel old [he was twenty-nine] . . . I travelled as if in mourning . . .'[7] Yet, some eighteen months later, Gide returned to North Africa, not only with Madeleine, but also with Ghéon. What is more, Ghéon took a great deal of persuading to join the Gides, even though André was paying his expenses. One can only conclude that, for Gide, the trip of 1899 was so dismal a failure because he had no companion but his poor, uncomprehending wife. Ghéon replied in terms similar to Gide's: 'Don't talk about my "youth", I owe it entirely to you; since you left, my life has completely changed. When I go out I ask myself why. The places we went to no longer hold any attraction for me . . . We are too used to one another . . . Your letter overwhelmed me; it's the first time anyone has written to me like that and, really, you are my first friend.'[8]

At Tunis André met up with Athman, who had turned ugly, but was as lovable as ever. He tells André that he has only been with a woman twice over the past eight months and 'almost without pleasure'; next year, he will have a boy of his own. Tunis is famed for 'that': there 'all the boys up to the age of twelve are like girls'. The main cruising ground was the Porte de

France, the gateway aptly dividing (and joining) the Arab from the French city. André makes a few excursions there that lead to nothing; one '*débris*' ('wreck') led him up a sidestreet, 'full of Italians and Maltese', but he took fright and retreated, 'not wanting to be murdered'. Once, when Athman was not there, Gide met up with Azous, who had followed him when he had been with Rosenberg three years before. Gide was taken off to the Moorish baths, where the boy offered to massage him. However, he had to be content with watching 'that charming, brown body being caressed, embraced, cynically pawed by the attendant, who amused himself by taking my place all the time, or Azous's place, when he came to massage me'.[9]

After nine days in Tunis, the Gides and Athman travelled, through Sousse, Kairouan and Batna, to El Kantara, which 'made us forget the mortal tedium of this trip'. There were consolations, however. At Kairouan, a 'delicious' twelve-year-old boy 'laughed voluptuously and pressed his lips against mine'. 'He was called Mohammed, like so many others; elegant and thin, like a mountain kid. When our train was due to leave he was there; the look he gave me promised more than the day before and made me desire his lips all the more; if I had been alone I would not have been able to leave; I would have sacrificed my day for an hour with him. By every possible means and the most charming subterfuges, he tried to touch me, to press himself against me; but the station was full of people!'[10]

The Gides spent five 'delicious days' at El Kantara and set off for Algiers. On the train occurred an incident that, in *Et nunc manet in te*, Gide erroneously places during his honeymoon trip, two years before. The Easter holidays had ended and, in the next compartment, three schoolboys were on their way back to their *lycée*. It was extremely hot and the boys were 'half undressed'. At each stop, one of them leaned out of the window as did Gide out of his. Before long, they were 'playing' at touching each other:

I experienced a torturing delight [*suppliciantes délices*] as my fingers ran along the downy, amber flesh that he offered to my caress . . . At the next station, one of the others had taken his place and the same game began again. Then the train started to move and I sat down in my seat, panting, breathing heavily, pretending to be absorbed in my reading. Madeleine, who was sitting opposite me, said nothing, as if she had not seen me, did not know me . . . In Algiers, when we were alone in the omnibus that took us to the hotel, she finally said, in a tone of voice that seemed to express even more sorrow than blame: 'You looked like a criminal or a madman.'[11]

Algiers found the Gides at a low ebb. Madeleine was 'too ill to move'. As a result, they spent eight days there. André tried to work, but 'I waste a considerable amount of time waiting to be able to work. But no . . . I prowl, prowl, prowl.'[12] From Algiers, the Gides took the train to Oran: after their experience of the long sea crossing from Marseille, they had decided to take the shorter sea route and return home through Spain. On 26 April, they sailed from Oran to Cartagena; from there they endured an eighteen-hour train journey to Madrid, with Madeleine so ill that André thought she might have contracted typhoid fever. Another (nineteen-hour) train journey took them to Biarritz. On 30 April, they arrived at Orthez, where they stayed briefly *chez* Jammes. A further long train journey brought them back to Paris and 'cet exile atroce', as Gide called it in a letter to Jammes, was at an end.

In Paris, much of Gide's time was taken up with *L'Ermitage*. This brought him into more than usual contact with the poet Francis Vielé-Griffin, who had hitherto spent much of his time at his country house at Nazelles, Indre-et-Loire. Vielé-Griffin was the son of Egbert Ludovicus, an American general, architect, politician and writer on things military, and Teresa Griffin, the author of a novel set at the time of the American–Mexican war. On his parents' divorce, when he was nine, he was brought to France by his mother and educated in Paris at the Catholic Collège Stanislas. He now lived, with his wife, Marie-Louise, in an apartment in the rue Hamelin, near the Trocadéro. It was there, in June 1899, that Gide met a couple who were to play a crucially important role in his life. The occasion was a reading, by Gide, of *Saül*: his audience consisted of the host and his wife; Henri de Régnier; Théo Van Rysselberghe, a Belgian painter and his wife, Maria. During the following winter, Théo Van Rysselberghe painted a well-known portrait of the thirty-year-old Gide, who became a frequent visitor to the Van Rysselberghes' flat in the rue Scheffer.

On 17 June, Gide took Francis Vielé-Griffin along with him to La Roque. Griffin wanted to visit the nearby house and estate of Formentin, which he was thinking of buying. In the end, he did not buy Formentin, but Gide's revisiting of the house spurred him on to write *La Mivoie*, Gide's fictional name for Formentin, the story that was to become *Isabelle*. Throughout the summer, there were the usual visits from friends and relations. Finally, in early October, the Gides took themselves off to Cuverville.

'I'm stifling in Normandy, where the moon illuminates nothing but green roundnesses,' Gide wrote to Ruyters. 'I'm afraid I shall be reborn a hyena, so much, prowler that I am, do I love arid places'[13] – Gide was getting itchy feet. For some time, Ruyters had been tempting him with the prospect of a journey to Baghdad: like Gide, Ruyters had a taste for the exotic and was to spend some twenty years in the Far East. Gide might well have given in had not his feelings for Ruyters cooled considerably over the past year or two. In the end, nothing came of the project and Gide, after a week at Cuverville, went no further than Lamalou-les-Bains for his annual *cure*. Madeleine joined André for the last of his four weeks at Lamalou. It was there that he finished *Le Roi Candaule,* and thus brought to an end six months of productive work that also included the first act of a libretto for *Le Retour,* a projected opera by Raymond Bonheur that remained unfinished, an unfinished series of poems, *Proserpine,* and sketches of the future novel *L'Immoraliste,* of the *récit Isabelle* and even of *Les Caves du Vatican* (not published until 1914).

Gide had begun *Le Roi Candaule* in North Africa, but it was written mostly during the summer at La Roque. In a letter to Ghéon, of 19 July, he complains: 'My work irritates and bores me; it's progressing so slowly, my reason alone is at work in it . . . Nyssia [Candaule's wife] gets on my nerves. It's the last time I'll put a woman in a play of mine . . .'[14] Two days later, he had produced the first of the three acts, which appeared in the September number of *L'Ermitage.* The second act appeared in the November number, the third in December. (The play was first performed by the Oeuvre company on 9 May 1901, with Lugné-Poe as Candaule, Edouard de Max as Gygès and Henriette Roggers as Nyssia.) As he explains in his preface to the first edition of 1901, Gide found the story of Candaule (Candaules) in Herodotus' *Clio.* To this he added variants of the story that he had found in Plato's *Republic* (as told by Glaucon) and Théophile Gautier, giving the whole a characteristic twist of his own. The Lydian king Candaule has a wife, Nyssia, whom he regards as the most beautiful of women. None of the courtiers, however, has seen her unveiled. One day, a splendid ring is found inside a fish served up at the king's table. Candaule puts on the ring and immediately becomes invisible to others. Intrigued, the king sends for Gygès, the humble fisherman who supplied the fish. In conversation, it transpires that he was, as he puts it, the possessor of only four things, his hat, his net, his wife and his poverty. The first two he has just lost in a fire; when he discovers that his drunken wife is also little better than a whore, he kills her; he intends to keep his remaining possession, his poverty. (This he will lose, too, by the end of the play.) Candaule proceeds to lavish all manner of gifts and privileges on Gygès. He even proposes, by means of the magic ring, to share the beauty of his wife with his new friend. When

Nyssia discovers what has happened, she gets Gygès to kill her husband and assume his place as king.

In the preface, with an apparent concession to critical fashion, Gide refers briefly to some of the 'ideas' of the play. His commentators do likewise, since there is little else in the play to discuss. As in *Saül*, what, ultimately, robs the play of any artistic interest is the thinness, the lifelessness of the language. Gide was aware of this problem: *Candaule*, he writes, is a drawing, rather than a painting, and he has tried to retain 'its integrity, severity, logic', with no attempt to conceal its faults with 'excessive lyricism'. The reviewer in the newspaper *L'Aurore* remarked of the play: 'It will not need Gygès' ring to pass unnoticed.' Certainly it ended Gide's honeymoon with the theatre. He was not to return to it again until his *Oedipe* of 1930. Yet, as he was finishing *Candaule*, in October 1899, at Lamalou, Gide was also working on his eleventh 'Lettre à Angèle' in which he asserted his faith in a 'rebirth of the theatre', to which he hoped to contribute. 'For a new theatre,' he went on, 'we need a new ethics. Do we have one? I think we do . . . Nietzsche gave us this ethics.'[15]

In January 1900, the editorial committee of twelve completed their promised twelve months' régime at *L'Ermitage*. During that time, much of the editorial work, indeed over half of the writing, had fallen to Gide and Ghéon. Now it was proposed to open up the review to a wider choice of writers.

In February, Gide received a letter from Christian Beck, asking him to contribute to *Vie Nouvelle*, a new review that he was founding in Brussels. Beck, now just twenty-one, had visited Gide four or five years earlier to consult him on a 'school edition' of *Paludes*, which he was preparing for Hachette. The first of the eventual three numbers of *Vie Nouvelle* appeared in March. Its aim was to propagate the celebration of sexual, platonic and divine love; its heroes were Dante, Goethe, Wagner, Maeterlinck, D'Annunzio and 'that tender hero, André Gide, doctor of felicity . . .' Gide's contribution consisted of five 'Paradoxes', the first of which is perhaps the most interesting: 'Intelligence no longer seems to me to be the pearl of great price for which one sells everything else. The vanity of understanding everything is as ridiculous as any other, and more dangerous. After a while, what one understands least well is oneself.'[16]

The health of Valentine Bernardbeig, Madeleine's sister, was giving cause for concern. In February, Madeleine accompanied her and her infant son, Alain, to Pau, in south-west France. There, it was hoped, the climate would be more beneficial than that of Le Havre. (In fact, it was snowing and the temperature was −7°C.) André did not go with them – he was recovering from influenza. Valentine was examined and admitted at once into a sanatorium.

On 29 March, at the instigation of André Ruyters, Gide addressed 'Libre Esthétique', a Brussels literary society. His talk, 'De l'influence en littérature', was later published in the May number of *L'Ermitage* (and placed first in the *Prétextes* collection). It amounts, in sum, to a praise of influence: only the weaker artist fears influence, sees it as an infringement on his originality, precisely because his originality is so insecurely established. The great artist, on the other hand, has only one care: 'To become as human as possible . . . to BECOME ORDINARY [*banal*]'. A Shakespeare, a Goethe, a Molière becomes more individual the more he becomes ordinary. An artist who resists his humanity becomes 'odd, strange, defective'. Finally, Gide makes a very Gidean celebration of friendship, of the group. An artist cannot be self-sufficient: 'A great man . . . not only has *his* mind, but also that of all his friends.'[17]

In April, Gide saw Paul Claudel for the second time. They had first met four years before, at Marcel Schwob's, and Gide had continued sending Claudel copies of his works as they appeared. Claudel was on furlough from his consular duties in China, and Gide, accompanied by Jammes, who was staying with the Gides at the time, called on him at his apartment high up in an old building on the quai d'Anjou, on the Ile Saint-Louis. Claudel had already become deeply religious and, during his time in France, went on retreats at the Benedictine communities at Solesmes and Ligugé. However, the monks persuaded the thirty-year-old poet–diplomat to postpone any decision to join the order.

Easter Saturday saw the opening by the President of the Republic, Emile Loubet, of the Exposition Universelle. Over the next seven months or so, it attracted over fifty million visitors. It occupied much the same area as its predecessor of 1889 – the two large rectangles between the Ecole Militaire and the Trocadéro, and between the Invalides and the Champs-Elysées. Its permanent gifts to Paris were the Pont Alexandre III, the avenue Alexandre III, which linked the bridge to the Champs-Elysées, and the Grand and Petit Palais on either side of it. In contrast with the Eiffel tower of 1889, a masterpiece of modern style and technology, they present an academic, sumptuously neo-Baroque extravagance that has found its advocates at last. In May, Athman arrived in Paris and stayed for two weeks at the boulevard Raspail: Gide had finally done what his mother had prevented him from doing five years before. Athman's presence in Paris is commemorated in a painting by Jacques-Emile Blanche, *M. André Gide and his friends*, set against the background of a 'café maure' at the Exposition. On a more serious level, what gave Gide most pleasure at the Exposition was the kabuki theatre company, led by Sada Yacco, the first woman to appear in a Japanese play. So astonished was Gide by these performances that he returned six times and devoted another 'Lettre à Angèle' to them.[18]

In May André and Madeleine went to Pau to collect Valentine Bernardbeig from her sanatorium. It had been decided to take her to another establishment near Frankfurt. With them was a fellow-patient, Marcel Gilbert – as the Gides were soon to realize, the two had fallen in love. A few weeks later, a double marriage took place between Ernest Rouart (Eugène's younger brother) and Julie Manet (the painter's daughter), and between Paul Valéry and Jeannie Gobillard (the painter's niece). Gide was the *témoin* (witness) at the civil ceremony.

On 18 June, Madeleine was riding in a fiacre across the place de la Concorde when her vehicle collided with a heavy carriage loaded with ice. She was knocked out of the fiacre into the roadway, where she was run over by the wheels of a dray-cart, which narrowly missed her head, but crushed both her arms: both humeruses and one collar-bone were broken. She was taken home to the boulevard Raspail, where André arrived some time later. In fact, they had been about to leave for Cuverville: the luggage was packed, train seats booked and the furniture covered with dust-sheets. In the end, the Gides did not reach Cuverville until 7 August. For five weeks Madeleine had both arms in plaster, the left arm for a further twenty-five days; she did not recover the full use of both arms until mid-September. During the weeks in Paris, André set about sueing those responsible for the accident, but nothing came of it. Recommended by Léon Blum to a lawyer who turned out to be a swindler, Gide even lost the money that he had advanced towards future fees. To escape from such tedious chores and from the oppressive heat of an exceptionally warm summer, Gide paid frequent visits, usually with Ghéon, to a swimming baths at the other end of Paris, in the rue Rochechouart.

The legal wranglings resulting from Madeleine's injuries were not the only distraction from André's work (and pleasure) during those weeks in Paris. Since their marriage the Gides had been the owners of two large country properties, La Roque-Baignard, which André had inherited from his mother, and Cuverville, which Madeleine had inherited from her father. The Cuverville estate and dependencies covered an area more than twice that of La Roque, 17 acres of grounds, plus a total of 327 acres of farmland.

Increasingly, over their five years of marriage, the Gides had felt the burden of managing two such Norman estates. Each was very dear: as cousins, André and Madeleine had known both from childhood. Sooner or later, they would have to give up one of them. By 1900, the matter had become more urgent: André was still dreaming of a house in Paris, where he would have the space to work and entertain his friends – the rented apartment at 4 boulevard Raspail held no attractions for him and he had even rented an attic at No. 10 to work in. He had now decided to have a large house built to his own specifications. This would require more capital than he had readily available. Clearly, this would have to come from the sale of one of the Normandy properties: it was quite clear which one it would have to be. The Paris house was entirely André's pet idea and Cuverville was not only Madeleine's spiritual refuge, but her personal property. This suited André, it must be said. If he sold La Roque, he would give up a host of time-consuming responsibilities, not least that of being mayor. Cuverville, on the other hand, was largely run by Madeleine anyway. Once he had a house in Paris, he would spend more of his time there (when not travelling), while Madeleine would spend much of hers at Cuverville. In the summer, together at Cuverville, they could entertain their friends and relations. There is no evidence that the sale of La Roque caused André any great heartache. This must surely astonish anyone who has seen it. A year after the sale, Jacques-Emile Blanche visited the house. Afterwards he wrote to Gide: 'Why did you not drag me there by force when it was yours, you wretch? If you had, I might be living there now. It is the most delightful thing I have seen in Normandy, and so much my dream made real that I wonder whether it can be true.'[19] Twenty years later, Gide offers none of the practical reasons listed above, but a subtler, more interesting explanation:

When, in 1900, I was led to sell La Roque, I suppressed all my regrets, in a gesture of defiance, in which confidence in the future was backed up by an avid hatred of the past, and in which quite a lot of theory, which we now call futurism, played a part. In fact, my regrets were much less strong at the time than they became later. It was not so much that my memories of the place grew fonder with the passage of time: I had occasion to see it again and, having travelled more widely, was better able to appreciate the captivating charm of that little valley, which, at an age when all too many desires were welling up inside me, struck me by the narrowness of its horizons.[20]

In July 1900, after months of complicated negotiations, the château and most of the woodlands of La Roque-Baignard were sold to the painter Henri Manguin. (The rest of the property, nearly 490 acres, mainly tenant-farms, was sold in 1909 to the popular novelist Charles Mérouvel, for 190,000 francs, £7,600 or $38,000 at the time.) Gide resigned as mayor and was replaced by Armand Desaunez, his estate manager. He remained a councillor, however, until 1903, staying as Jean Schlumberger's guest, at Val-Richer, when he attended council meetings. With the money from the sale of La Roque, Gide bought a plot of land in the avenue des Sycomores, at Auteuil. On it Gide was to build the Villa Montmorency.

The Gides finally took off for Cuverville on 7 August, reading *Our Mutual Friend* aloud, in French, in their first-class compartment. Gide's thoughts were, and were not, back in Paris with Ghéon. 'Why did I fear these first evenings here?' he wrote to his friend. 'My body is no farther from the boulevards than my thoughts are from its festivities; I renounce my debauchery, suddenly, effortlessly, and would no longer think about it were I not writing to you.'[21] Three days later, the weather had changed: the sweltering boulevards were forgotten and fires had to be lit in the rooms. Gide wrote the first pages of *L'Immoraliste*. Ghéon's letters, clearly, continued to be full of 'debauchery', though all of them addressed to Gide from Paris, over a period of four weeks, have disappeared. Similar material was arriving from Fedor Rosenberg, who 'writes me excellent letters that will join yours in the most secret drawer', he writes again on the 25th. 'Fou! ton histoire de la piscine!' ('Your story of the baths is quite crazy!'), Gide writes back on 14 August, adding: 'I'm having safety locks put on the drawers.'[22] Three weeks later, Gide writes: 'Your last letter – the account of the evenings at the baths; the new acquaintances; that conversation with the *faux* Dumas – terrific!!!'[23] '*Piscine*' had become, for the two friends, a euphemism (by metonymy?). 'This morning, received a letter from Rosenberg – wonderful, exquisite and very . . . *piscine*. He "thanked" me for what I have introduced him to and asks anxiously about "Maurice".' Gide, too, is insatiable for more information. 'What has become of all Paris without me? Has Chanvin been in the showers? Have you seen Edgar? Have you met Pedro yet . . .?'[24] Gide, of course, has little of the kind to relate other than the odd, frustrating, incident. There were visits to the coast, once or twice alone, by bicycle, more usually with friends and relations who were staying at Cuverville.

And so the weeks passed with the usual mixture of work (*L'Immoraliste*), playing the piano (he discovers Schubert's sonatas), entertaining (and extricating himself from) house guests. Sometimes, unable to face the conversation of his brothers-in-law, he would claim liver trouble and retreat to his study. Ghéon's mother and sister stayed for a few days, Henri himself having to remain in Paris to look after his sick grandfather. But the great drama, in anticipation at least, surrounded the arrival of Valentine Bernardbeig, from her sanatorium near Frankfurt. Against doctors' orders, but at the insistence of her husband, Valentine would spend two weeks with her family at Cuverville. Knowing only too well how temperamental and impetuous his sister-in-law could be and being fully aware of the liaison between her and Marcel Gilbert, André could not but be apprehensive. In addition to the host and hostess, the household had to accommodate Madeleine's German friend, Emma Siller, and eight relations. Then, when Valentine did arrive, it was with Marcel Gilbert, who spent the whole of the two weeks with her, under the same roof as her husband and child, before returning with her to their sanatorium at Pau. Evening entertainment included the reading aloud of that great family romance, *Le Roi Lear*. As soon after Valentine's arrival as he decently could (two days), André escaped to Cabourg, to join Ghéon, now staying at the country house of Edouard Ducoté, the owner of *L'Ermitage*. After a few days there, the two friends went on to Trouville and Le Havre, before returning together to Cuverville.

For some time, Gide had been planning the next visit to North Africa: this time, there would be no question of Ghéon's not going – at André's expense, of course. Gide arrived in Marseille on 30 October and was joined two days later by a Madeleine exhausted by a week spent in Paris making all the arrangements necessitated by her departure and long absence. Ghéon arrived on 4 November and the following day the three set sail for Algiers. The Gides' last trip to North Africa was so well documented because André felt impelled to write long, detailed letters to Ghéon. This time, Ghéon was with them and the documentation is much sketchier as a result. In particular, we know little of how they spent the first five weeks in Algiers, Constantine and Biskra, where they were joined by Athman. Gide wanted to share with Ghéon the experience of the desert. Madeleine, so easily tired and liable to illness, could not accompany them on so arduous a journey. So, on 14 December, before dawn, the three men set out southwards, leaving her alone at the Hôtel Royal. They spent the night at M'Raier, on the edge of the Chott Melrhir, the original salt-lake of *El Hadj*. They reached Touggourt in the evening of the following day. There they rested for a day, before embarking on the last stretch of the journey, on mule-back, accompanied by a guide. This 'frightful' journey was not at all what Gide had anticipated: we have a long description of it in a letter Gide wrote to Marcel Drouin some two weeks later. 'So much nothingness, so much emptiness, so much gloom, so much hideousness' were enough to cure Gide forever of his obsession with the desert. It consisted of 'ten oases, each separated from one another by two, three, or four leagues of sand . . . On the way out, one is still sustained by the gloomiest curiosity, one anticipates some recompense for one's pains . . . On the way back, one's exhaustion and boredom are made worse by an unparalleled disappointment, the sad realization that one is going to see nothing new.'[25]

Gide and Ghéon arrived back in Biskra on the evening of Christmas Day to a distraught Madeleine. Two days after André's departure, she had suffered something like a mild nervous breakdown. This usually self-reliant, self-possessed woman, well used by now to André's absences, had experienced a sense of terror and depression on being left alone in such an alien environment. During André's twelve-day absence, she wrote him three letters, which, in a sense, tried to conceal her true state of mind, but which also reveal it. They were all cries for help, but, each time, they arrived at their destination after Gide had already moved on. 'This solitude is frightful,' she wrote on 16 December. 'And only two days have gone by. It would be terrible to be without you, if alone, even in Paris – but here, in the midst of all this deadly splendour . . . My dear, my only love, come back, come back.' In the second letter, dated 18 December, Madeleine explains how she had been expecting him to have turned back, until she received his telegram informing her that they had already left on the next stage of their journey, before the arrival of her letter:

I was very disappointed – especially as I was very ill and had to stay in bed. But if I tell you that, it is because I tell you everything, my André . . . I follow your every step – with your eyes I watch the sun rise and the sun set . . . Every evening I go up to the minaret of the Royal. Those are my only little joys – my big ones are your letters. Apart from that the hours drag on. – I read a bit, write a bit, sew on all your buttons – I eat a bit, I go out for a bit . . . And night comes. And I'm with you again. Don't we love one another more than ever, my dear André? My whole life hangs on yours . . . Eight more days to spend like this. But those eight days will pass – and you'll be there, in my arms, against my heart, which loves you so much.

Then, two days later, she thinks of catching the mail-coach for Touggourt, and thus reduce the separation from André by three days, but she cannot bring herself to do so. 'This evening, I daren't do it – there's the expense [!] – my tiredness . . ., the bad weather. You might be angry with me, too? I hope El Oued was worth so much pain and weariness on your part – and mine. *And that a beautiful story like El Hadj will come out of it.*'[26] So Madeleine resigned herself to waiting five more days. Finally, on the evening of Christmas Day, the expedition was back in Biskra. André was as surprised as no doubt Madeleine herself had been by her reaction to his absence. No new *El Hadj* did come out of the expedition, but, as we shall see, it was to suggest an ending for *L'Immoraliste*. Gide was smitten with remorse: leaving his wife alone for eleven days was, he admitted to Drouin, 'an act of cruelty'. It was the last time Madeleine accompanied Gide on his travels in North Africa. The Gides spent a few days in Biskra, recuperating from their contrasting, complementary ordeals, while Ghéon left almost at once for Tunis, where he would be joined by his friends. We know from a page of Ghéon manuscript, dated 20 December 1900, that the friendship between the two men had reached crisis-point:

That's it. Our friendship is over. It couldn't last, based as it was on the *worst things* . . . Lies, lies, lies! We flattered each other's vices as if we *shared* them. *We shared nothing*. What happened today is proof of that . . . Each day we lost another illusion about what we wanted to believe we were. He a born writer, forcing himself, without much difficulty, to live, in the interests of the literature that will come out of it, a born moralist, forcing himself to be immoral . . .; I the pleasure-seeker . . ., the born immoralist, ignorant in action of any morality to be transgressed, incapable of any scruple, any regret . . . And we came to that journey too different, he sated on the country, imposing on me his view, intentionally or unintentionally, by his words as well as his writings, I new, dazzled, wanting to discover things for myself, to see more of them, to see others, as the mood took me, in my own way, stopping or moving on when I pleased . . . Two incompatible oddities of temperament; he indecisive, scrupulous, I all or nothing – yes or no . . .[27]

Five years later, in an article in *L'Ermitage*[28] Ghéon wrote: 'A few days in the desert distilled within me a hatred that an incident, that very evening, was to gush forth against my closest friend . . . Yes, as night fell, . . . I hated my dearest companion as I had never hated anyone.' What incident? Nowhere does either Ghéon or Gide say. In itself it was probably of no great moment. It clearly served as a flash-point in a situation that was ready to explode at any time. Ghéon's own attempt to understand makes it clear that there was an inbuilt problem in their relationship, stemming from an opposition of temperaments. It is a perceptive analysis both of Gide and of himself. It was just such an all or nothing mentality that led to Ghéon's conversion, while Gide's 'indecisive, scrupulous' approach kept him for so long on the brink of such a conversion, but never succumbing to it. The problem between them did not surface in Paris, because they were together for hours, not days, on shared, common ground, not on Gide's elected territory – or at Gide's expense. Jammes, in his own way, had felt a similar sense of alienation, of disorientation, when being shown North Africa by Gide – he, too, had broken off the trip and returned home.

Once back in Paris, on his own, familiar ground, Ghéon seems to have lost all his resentment of Gide and was full of whole-hearted apologies. 'Ah! *Mon vieux! Mon vieux!* Thinking about that journey, I see how odious I was, full of contradictions, whims, madness . . . Our separation has awoken in me the "tender" half of a friendship . . .' As the boat taking him home moved away from the Tunis quayside and Gide's image gradually faded into obscurity, Ghéon wept. 'I am your friend, after all, your friend.'[29] Gide replied in kind: 'You can't imagine what pleasure, what emotion your letter aroused in me . . . I sensed, I knew, that the journey would be a long, dangerous leap for our friendship . . . You now show me that we have found our feet again, hand in hand as before.'[30]

Before receiving Ghéon's letter, Gide was writing to him, retailing his (usually unsuccessful) adventures in precisely the tone of his letters of the year before, as if nothing had happened between them. After seeing his friend off, he had gone back to the hotel, 'put my feet into my slippers' and begun to write. After half-an-hour, however, the urge came upon him. He put his feet back into his boots and, 'against all resolutions (but in Africa resolutions are falling)', went out. Nothing came of it and he returned to the hotel. Another day, there is an incident involving 'le petit Turc' and a masseur. Later, the Turkish boy gives Gide a cigarette, containing 'some strange tobacco' (obviously hashish). After smoking it he felt 'completely, deliciously intoxicated'. 'The vaults of the baths extended before me in a marvellous series of arches – and when, outside, I wandered through the streets, the unexpected lighting of the buildings, their whiteness, the depths of their courtyards, their darkness, everything seemed accentuated, surprising, beautiful, magical . . .' He went back to the hotel and, after dinner, went out again, this time with Madeleine. During that walk he stumbled on the *café louche*, the seedy café, that he and Ghéon had been, unsuccessfully, looking for. He promptly put Madeleine on a tram back to the hotel and went into the café alone. That, he tells Ghéon, is where they should have been going all along. 'Oh, the evenings wasted in the Halfaouine! How can I leave Tunis now?' He writes of 'deux petits danseurs délicieux'. It was after eleven; he should be getting back; Madeleine would be getting anxious. He leaves, but cannot stop himself going back to see the rest. More dancers, 'young, disturbing', appear in the doorway. The audience applauds wildly and some of the spectators set about undressing them.[31]

Ghéon's response is understandable: North Africa had not lived up to his Gide-inspired expectations and now Gide was describing the delights that he had missed in Tunis: 'Enough, for pity's sake. Enough. Your letter is setting my whole body atremble in the most awful way. I won't read your next letter, I'm warning you, if it disturbs yet again the relative peace that I have found here . . . Your dancers were old, ugly, absurd . . . Let me hear no more of them!' To make matters worse, Ghéon had returned to a Paris that had been cleaned up. Police raids on their old haunts had succeeded in depopulating them of their attractions. Rouart had gone to the Piscine Rochechouart and found it closed. Meanwhile, Ghéon was running *L'Ermitage* single-handed. Couldn't André hurry up and get back? Then there was the matter of the wedding on 29 January of Henri's sister: Gide had said that he would be one of the witnesses.

Gide seemed in no hurry to return. He and Madeleine sailed from Tunis to Trápani, in Sicily, went on to Palermo, Taormina, Naples. By 18 January, they were in Rome. There they learnt that Valentine had absconded from the sanatorium at Pau with Marcel Gilbert. After three days in Rome, the Gides left for Nice, where Valentine would meet them. She did not turn up and, meanwhile, Madeleine had caught a bad cold and taken to her bed. Stuck in Nice, André met Vielé-Griffin and went further afield to see Ducoté at Hyères and Jaloux at Marseille. The Gides did not arrive back in Paris until 1 February, having missed the wedding of Ghéon's sister by a few days.

A letter from Marcel Gilbert arrived, informing Madeleine of the 'appalling situation' in which he and Valentine now found themselves. 'Being unable to live without one another, we decided to do anything rather than agree to a separation.' Valentine was now pregnant by him. Ill though they both were, they were determined to remain together and had therefore gone off to a secret destination. Would Madeleine inform Monsieur Bernardbeig of the situation, though without mentioning the child? 'I swear to you, as long as I live, I shall never abandon either of them.' The next day, André, not Madeleine, left for Rouen, where he discussed the situation with Valentine's husband. Madeleine wrote to Valentine, urging her to return to her husband, in order not to bring upon her child, Alain, 'one of the saddest fates on this earth'. André's view seems to have been rather different and the couple were grateful for his support and sympathy. Gide's approval aided the divorce proceedings and, at their wedding, on 28 July 1902, he was his cousin's witness.

On 9 May Lugné-Poe's production of *Le Roi Candaule* opened at the

Nouveau-Théâtre. Gide attended all the rehearsals, after which he and Edouard de Max often went off together to a nearby steam-baths, joined by Ghéon. The play was a critical disaster. A few days before the first night, *La Revue Blanche* had published the play in volume form. But it was to meet with no more understanding or appreciation than the stage version.

Apart from three weeks at Lamalou-les-Bains, the Gides spent most of what was left of 1901 at Cuverville, though André made several trips elsewhere. In August, with Drouin, he visited Ghéon at his house in Bray-sur-Seine, his home town, some 60 miles south-east of Paris, where he had set up in medical practice. A few days later, he accompanied the Van Rysselberghes back to Paris from Cuverville. That night, having booked into an hotel (in those days, a gentleman alone, without benefit of wife and servants, was incapable of staying in his own apartment), he went 'on to the boulevards'. There he met up with a certain Joseph, just out after six months in prison. 'I don't know which of us was the more pleased by our meeting, he having scarcely eaten all day, I suddenly realizing that it was he above all others I wanted to meet.' Joseph had an *interdiction de séjour* that forbade him to enter Paris for five years and so he was anxious every time he saw a policeman and might have to show his papers. His clothes smelled. He also smelled of 'wildness, health, revolt; he may be less graceful, but he's handsomer than ever'.[32] In October, Gide was back in Paris for a few days and, on the boulevards, met up with Joseph again. They tried to find somewhere to go, but it was too early – the two places suggested by Joseph were swarming with 'young maids and apprentice butchers'. They tried a cheap hotel, only to be turned away by the owner. 'Bad evening . . . Next day, I went back to the baths . . . The day after that I went back again; it was Sunday: a crowd – charming but quite impracticable. Monday, a few memories, but crude and of pretty poor quality . . . I returned to Cuverville feeling calmer . . .'[33]

When Gide was at Cuverville, his work was interrupted to some extent by the presence of innumerable house-guests, relations and friends, who, as usual, stayed anything from a few days to several weeks. Not that visitors stopped him retreating to his study for hours on end each day if he wished. His difficulty in returning to *L'Immoraliste* was of a deeper, more mysterious kind, as a passage in a letter to André Ruyters suggests. Gide is urging his friend to come with his wife to stay, but warns him that he will find 'a strangely taciturn, morose bear, between two ages and two moralities, who is no longer satisfied with the past, whom the present does not satisfy, and who is wearing himself out trying to find within himself enough to satisfy the future'. He would willingly go off to Baghdad with Ruyters, were it not for the 'unbearable book', which, he knows, is the sole cause of his tiredness and depression. 'I should have written it two years ago; what I should have written in one go I extract line by line, recomposing it artificially, for the greater benefit of art, perhaps, but also for my greater exhaustion.'[34] In fact, the genesis of the book went back more than 'two years'. To an outraged Francis Jammes, who declared that it should never have been written, Gide wrote: 'It has lived in me for over five years and I have spent over two years writing it. I could no more not write it than today I can not have written it.'[35].

Gide had not touched the manuscript of *L'Immoraliste* for ten months. Then, on 20 July, he took it up, at page 74, where he had left it, and wrote the thirty pages that completed Part 1, just under half of the whole book. As so often, Gide was already somewhere else, had moved on. 'I wrote it in order to get to the other side,' he wrote to Jammes. 'I get through books like one gets through illnesses. Nowadays I only like books that nearly killed off their authors.'[36] By 30 October, he had finished Part 2 – a further 114 pages. The final part was finished on 26 November, though a certain amount of cutting was subsequently made, especially in Part 1. On 29 January, Gide took his manuscript along to the *Mercure de France* offices. Three weeks later, the proofs arrived. Gide then sat on them for over six weeks, making further changes, before handing them over to Drouin for proof-reading. It was, said Alfred Vallette, 'the best title for a book published here for years!' On 20 May the 300 copies arrived from the printer. Why 300 copies? 'To hide from myself as much as possible the bad sales I know I shall have. If twelve hundred were printed, the sales would seem four times worse and I'd suffer four times as much.'[37] However, Vallette insisted on bringing out a cheaper, standard edition in July – which took fifteen years to sell out. As usual, Gide paid the printer's bills.

The 'immoralist' is Michel, who tells the story of his life and of his marriage. But this first-person narrative is preceded by a letter from a friend to his brother, a 'Monsieur D. R.', who happens to be 'Président du Conseil', that is, prime minister, asking him to find Michel some post commensurate with his undoubted talents. The writer of the letter explains how, as schoolboys, he, Michel and two others had made a pact whereby, if ever one of them called for the others' help, they would come to his aid immediately. From his home in North Africa, Michel summons his three friends and recounts his story. This was written down verbatim by one of the friends and appended to the letter, by way of explaining the 'change' that had come over the 'one-time learned puritan'.

Michel owed his 'puritan' temperament to his Protestant mother, who died when he was fifteen; his learning he derived from his father, an eminent ancient historian, with no religious beliefs. By the age of twenty, Michel knew not only Greek and Latin, but Hebrew, Sanskrit, Persian and Arabic. Like his father, whom he assisted in his work, his entire existence was devoted to 'ruins or books'. He knew nothing of life. On his deathbed, his father urged him to marry Marceline, the young relation kneeling beside him. 'Although I did not love her . . ., at least I had never loved another woman.' They marry. Michel is twenty-four, his fiancée twenty. They spend their wedding night in his Paris apartment, 'where two bedrooms had been got ready': 'I had married without imagining that my wife would be anything other than a comrade.' The next day, they set off for North Africa. On arrival at Tunis, Michel is besieged by 'new sensations'. He becomes aware of 'dormant faculties that, being unused, had retained all their mysterious youth'. As they travel inland, however, Michel becomes ever more tired, begins to cough and, one night, wakes to find himself coughing up blood. At Biskra, they rent rooms and Marceline tends her sick husband. One day, she brings in one of the young Arab boys that she has been befriending. Michel notes the 'tender animal grace' of his movements and that he is completely naked beneath his thin, white gandourah. The boy comes each day, transmitting, in some mysterious way, his own health to the sick body of the invalid. Michel is overcome by a determination to live. Gradually, his health improves. He goes out for walks, he meets other young Arabs and, as he gets stronger, goes out alone. Michel and Marceline leave North Africa and return home via Italy. 'After that touch from the wing of Death, what seemed important is so no longer; other things become so that did not seem important or that one did not even know existed. All the accumulation of acquired knowledge that has overlain the mind peels off like a mask of paint and, here and there, exposing the bare skin, the authentic creature that had lain hidden underneath.'[38] He takes to nude sunbathing in Ravello (very much a new fashion in 1901) and, in Amalfi, has his beard and moustache shaved off. Between Ravello and Sorrento, there is an incident in which, summoning up unsuspected resources of strength, he overpowers a drunken, violent coachman, and brings Marceline and himself safely to their destination. There follows a brief single-sentence paragraph: 'That night I possessed Marceline for the first time.'

Part 2 finds the couple in La Morinière, their property in Normandy. A week after their arrival Marceline tells Michel that she is pregnant. Michel settles down to a summer of study, preparing his courses at the Collège de France, where he has been given a chair. Bocage, his estate manager, introduces him to his seventeen-year-old son, Charles, who is studying modern farming methods at a model farm. 'He was a handsome fellow, so brimming over with health, so lithe, so well-made . . . He did not look more than fifteen, his eyes were so bright and childlike . . .'[39] The two take to walking over the estate and tenant-farms, the young man suggesting how much better things might be run along modern, rational lines. In November, Michel and Marceline return to Paris, with its professional and social obligations. Michel had never been 'a brilliant talker'; he did not care for 'the frivolous mentality of the *salons*'. He now felt a new revulsion for a life in which everybody seemed to be saying the same thing: 'The more they resemble one another, the more they differ from me.' He aspired to 'a more spacious, more airy life, one that was less constricted, less concerned about what others thought'. With others, he remained a stranger, 'like someone who had come back from the dead'. The proximity of death had shown him the falseness, the shallowness of people's lives: through death, he had discovered life. He carried this conviction into his lectures on Roman civilization. Culture, he concluded, was born of life, but ended up by killing it. After this first lecture, an old friend, Ménalque, came up to him. This Ménalque is subtly different from the more shadowy figure of *Les Nourritures terrestres*, but corresponds to his third and final stage, as described in the 'Récit de Ménalque'. He has recently been the subject of 'an absurd, shameful trial'. Society has turned against him and he is about to set out on his travels again. Michel tries to explain the change that North Africa has wrought on him. On the eve of Ménalque's departure, he and Michel sit up all night, drinking 'Sheraz wine'. Ménalque makes no attempt to convert Michel to his own way of life, free of all ties and responsibilities: 'Of the thousand forms of life, each of us can only know one. It is mad to envy others' happiness – one could not avail oneself of it. Happiness does not come ready-made, it is made to measure . . . Keep the calm happiness of your home.' Nevertheless, Michel hankers after Ménalque's freedom. He did cut his happiness to his size, but he has now outgrown it: it 'now feels tight, sometimes it almost strangles me . . .'[40] On his return home, he finds that Marceline has had a miscarriage, four weeks before the child was due. As the weather improves, they go to La Morinière, where Marceline makes a fitful and only partial recovery. After a while, Michel becomes ever more restless. Bored with his responsibilities to his property, he decides to sell La Morinière.

Part 3 takes the couple to Switzerland, where the mountain air helps Marceline to recover. When she praises the 'honesty' of the Swiss, Michel responds with a Nietzschean diatribe against a nation 'with no crime, no history, no literature, no art'. He expected to be bored, but, 'after two months, this boredom had become a sort of rage and I could think of nothing but leaving'.[41] He dreams of returning to North Africa and reminds Marceline of how it was there that he recovered his own health. They travel slowly through Italy. In Naples, at night, he goes out and wanders the streets, prowling. ('Je posais ma main sur les choses; je rôdais,' as Gide discreetly puts it.)[42] They reach Tunis and, retracing their earlier itinerary, go on to Biskra. There Michel finds, to his horror, that his young Arab friends have all grown up ('affreusement grandi'), in a little over two years: 'What vile labours have so soon twisted those beautiful bodies?'[43] Michel is possessed of a desire to go even further south, into the desert. Unaware of what lies before her, Marceline agrees to go with him, though she is not well. At Touggourt, at night, Michel is taken on a tour of the town, which he knows well. In a Moorish café, he is approached by an Arab woman – and sleeps with her. On returning to the hotel, he finds that Marceline has coughed up blood . . . Here the narration pauses and jumps: Marceline, Michel tells us, lies in the French cemetery at El Kantara. 'I am still young,' he reminds his friends. 'Get me out of here and give me some reason for living . . . Something in my will has broken . . . I would like to begin anew.' A boy who is 'tender and as faithful as a dog' brings him food for 'a few sous and caresses'. The boy's sister is an Ouled-Naïl, a prostitute. Once, when Michel slept with her, the boy showed every sign of jealousy. 'She says that I only stay here because of him. She may be right . . .'[44]

With these words – and dots – *L'Immoraliste* ends. It does not, I believe, represent a failure to end more conclusively. The apparent petering out of the narrative, the equivocal, open-ended ending, is surely intended. Will Michel finally summon up the will to leave? Will his friends be able to help him? Or will the way of life that the Arab boy-servant represents for Michel be enough to keep him in North Africa? The suggestion that it might does not even come from Michel himself, but from the boy's sister. By this time, the reader may well be questioning the suitability of the title. Michel is more '*démoralisé*' than '*immoraliste*'. Far from being a Nietzschean *Übermensch*, he is almost a warning of what can happen when Nietzschean ideas fall into inadequate hands. In his Collège de France lecture Michel expounds the Nietzschean notion that 'culture, born of life, is killing it'. When Marceline tells him that she now understands his 'doctrine', that 'it may be beautiful . . ., but it does away with the weak,' he replies coldly: 'And so it should!'[45] It 'does away' with Marceline, but, by the end of the book, it looks as if it will soon 'do away' with Michel too. He, for all his fine words, is also one of the 'weak'. Lacking the courage of his immoral convictions, he is unable to summon up the will-power to abandon what has become a monotonous, passive existence. He has to call on his friends to help him do so.

Gide scrupulously refrains from passing overt judgement on Michel. Hence the 'functional' open-endedness of the ending and our own difficulties in assessing the author's 'view' of his 'hero'. Gide, realizing after publication that he was almost alone in not passing judgement, confronts the question in his Preface to the second edition. 'I offer this book for what it is worth,' he begins. 'It is a fruit full of bitter ashes . . .' In *L'Immoraliste*, Gide seems to be saying, the *nourritures terrestres*, the earthly fruits of Ménalque's triumphalist immoralism, have turned to ashes in the mouth. Yet *L'Immoraliste* was intended neither as an indictment nor as an apologia of its hero.

Nowadays the public does not forgive an author who, after depicting an action, does not come out for or against him . . . I am not claiming, of course, that neutrality (I nearly said, *indecisiveness*), is a sure sign of a great mind; but I believe that many great minds [Gide has cited, among others, Shakespeare and Goethe] have been very loath to . . . conclude – and that to pose a problem is not to suppose that it is solved in advance . . .

Michel's 'problem' is that of a man, with wife, means and a career, a man caught up therefore in a complicated network of overlapping relations and responsibilities, who comes to see his whole life as a hypocritical sham and, in pursuit of what he sees as his true, authentic, homosexual self, abandons everything. This was, *in potentia* at least, the central 'problem' or drama of Gide's own life. It must have come as no surprise to him that many readers identified him with his hero. Much of the indignation felt by certain readers towards Michel, he tells us in the Preface, 'spilled over on to me; I was all but confused with him'. Gide's aesthetic problem, the problem that had to be solved in terms of the work, was how the work could draw on, draw life from, the drama of his own life, while acquiring an autonomy, a difference, without which it could not grow into a work of art.

Works of literature originate in their authors' lives, but their publication and reception are also events in those lives. In the first instance, to put it crudely, Gide had to consider what Madeleine, his family and friends would think. Such a work could return to plague its inventor. In freeing his subject from too close an identification with himself, Gide was fulfilling a dual function, one creative, one protective. At its simplest, he did this by a series of changes in the relation between the fictional and the autobiographical, sometimes involving simple reversal. Thus Michel is an academic (not a writer). His mother (not his father) dies during his childhood, it is with him (not her) that he visits Spain and he marries shortly after his father's (not his mother's) death. Marceline is beautiful and fair (Madeleine was rather plain and dark), though their names were perhaps too close for Madeleine's comfort. The route taken by Michel and Marceline on their honeymoon, Michel's illness, recovery and friendship with young Arabs come not from the Gides' honeymoon, but from André's trip to North Africa with Paul Laurens in 1893–4. Gide borrowed the route taken during his own honeymoon for the fictional couple's return journey to North Africa. It is the husband (not the wife) who is ill during the journey. Michel is four years older than Marceline (André was two years younger than Madeleine). Marceline comes from a Catholic background (Madeleine was a Protestant, like André), but their families had always been close (André and Madeleine were cousins). Their Paris apartment is in Passy (not the 7th arrondissement), but La Morinière, the property in Normandy that Michel inherits and then sells, is obviously La Roque. More important than any of these superficial differences and similarities is a comparison of the two marriages. 'I had married,' says Michel, 'without imagining that my wife would be anything other than a comrade' – that Whitmanesque, homophile term again. Yet Michel and Marceline have sexual relations on at least one occasion and Marceline becomes pregnant. Gide always let it be understood that no such relations took place in his marriage. He may have been well aware that his wife should have been more than a 'comrade', but that, as best she could, is what she became. But, given the incident in which Michel 'possesses' his wife, one may wonder whether such an incident took place between André and Madeleine. Perhaps such an attempt was made; perhaps it was not successful and was not renewed. It might be argued that the fictional 'possession' was necessary for Marceline to become pregnant and later lose her child. Yet, in fiction, a wife can be with child, without mention of how it came about – indeed, in those days, it was usually not mentioned. Moreover, although it was essential to the fiction that Marceline die, it was not important that this be preceded by a miscarriage: her death was due to the tuberculosis caught, presumably, from her husband. Whatever the truth of the matter, one may wonder how Madeleine took the sexual experience of her fictional counterpart.

But the central, essential similarity between fiction and autobiography lies in the 'problem' confronting hero and writer; the great, overriding difference in the way they confronted it. Michel took Nietzsche simplistically, absolutely, abandoning Culture for Nature, letting the weak go to the wall, etc. and, in the end, lost everything. Gide knew what to leave as well as what to take of Nietzsche – and when to keep Nietzsche within the bounds of his (Gide's and Nietzsche's) books. While pursuing his natural inclinations, Gide cherished and retained his wife, his independent means (the means of his independence) and his position in the literary world. In working out a *modus vivendi* that could accommodate both his marriage and his homosexual adventures, Gide called on the un-Nietzschean but very Gidean quality of compromise – as also, of course, did Madeleine.

The same qualities, or rather their aesthetic counterparts, equivocation and elusiveness, were essential to Gide's strategy as a writer at this time. Such was the nature of his creativity that he could seldom obey Wilde's injunction not to say 'I'. Gide's response to the reader's tendency to identify a first-person narrator with the writer was to claim (rightly) that his first-person narrators were themselves fictional characters. One means of demonstrating this was the use of various distancing devices whose function was to say '"I" says', rather than 'I say'. The 'letter' with which *L'Immoraliste* opens may seem a rather creaky, old-fashioned convention, but, for Gide, it was just a device, intended to dispel any embarrassing identification of the author with the hero-narrator. If the letter is taken at face-value, Michel, whose story accompanies it, cannot be 'André Gide', since 'André Gide' is presumably the writer of the letter, one of the three friends who witnessed Michel's narration. (Moreover, most readers would have been aware that André Gide did not have a brother who was prime minister.) Yet, on a literal level, such a device lacks conviction: it is no more than a loop-hole, intended to make the author feel more comfortable, rather than a successful attempt to mislead the reader. Few readers would have been misled; most of the small circle of original readers would have assumed there was some essential identification between Michel and the author.

As soon as the book was published, Gide had to continue his disavowals. To Jacques-Emile Blanche, for example, he wrote: 'You must understand that I am not Michel; that if I were Michel, I would not have written *L'Immoraliste* . . .' One might say, with even more plausibility, that, if Gide had not, to some extent, been Michel, he could not have written it. What is unsatisfactory about statements of the 'I-am-not-Michel' kind – as of their obverse, the 'Ménalque is Wilde' (Painter) type – is that, in their absolute simplicity, they foreclose questions of a more interesting, complicated kind. Clearly, we have to begin with the assumption that Michel is and is not André Gide. In a letter thanking Robert Scheffer for his review in *La Plume* (1 July 1902), Gide repeats his usual disavowal: 'It is only because I am not Michel that I was able to recount his story as "remarkably well" as you say.' But he goes on, more interestingly, to berate 'fools' who need to have it explained to them that 'although René is in Chateaubriand, Chateaubriand is not all in René, any more than all Benjamin Constant is in Adolphe or all Goethe in Werther. That a bud of Michel is in me, it goes without saying.'[46] So, on Gide's own admission, André is in Michel, even if not all of him is. Many years later, in 1949, Gide could be franker. 'To what extent did the drama of *L'Immoraliste* have its roots in your own life?' Jean Amrouche asked him in one of his radio interviews. 'It had very deep roots,' he replied. 'It will be almost indiscreet on my part to say too much, but any reader who knows a little about my life must realize this.'[47]

Gide had great expectations for *L'Immoraliste*. It marked a new stage in his literary career: it was the first of his works that could be regarded by the general public as a novel – though, at some 42,000 words, or 100 pages in the Pléiade edition, it was on the short side for this. With it he achieved a quite new classicism of style, austere, unemotional, unemphatic, unhurried, discreet, meticulously chiselled with an art that conceals art. Behind the apparent authorial self-effacement, he had never written a work that was so autobiographical, in detail and essence. Yet, as always, no sooner was it in the public domain than he felt that he had outgrown it: here was the dissatisfaction, the strangeness that always led to the next work, the next rectifying push on the pendulum. In fact, it was to be another seven years before the new work, *La Porte étroite*, conceived at the same time as *L'Immoraliste*, appeared.

When Gide dedicated *L'Immoraliste* 'to Henri Ghéon, his frank comrade', he spoke truer than he knew. A few weeks after publication, at the home of Jacques-Emile Blanche, the conversation turned to Gide's book. Before long, Ghéon was telling Blanche of his – and Gide's – sexual proclivities. 'I would have preferred Ghéon not to have been so frank,' Blanche wrote to Gide on 10 July. 'I am so far removed from that sort of thing! . . . It would have been better if it had remained a purely literary matter.' Blanche, a painter moving in the most exalted bohemian circles in Paris, could not claim to moral disapproval: 'Alas! I understand everything and I would

take offence at nothing.' But he is clearly embarrassed by the revelation –
and concerned for Gide's wellbeing: 'Will you have the physical and moral
courage to confront the dangers that you are piling up on your own head?'[48]
The next day, Blanche, '*bouleversé*', wrote to Ghéon: 'I no longer feel capable
of going to Cuverville just yet, so heavily will the atmosphere weigh upon
me.' One may feel sorry for those born 'abnormal', but 'in our country
and in our time', they cannot lay claim to a 'normal life'. When '*tout cela*'
gets mixed up with 'rapports sentimentaux avec une femme, *qui est la vôtre*
(!)', he can feel nothing but horror. He tells Ghéon, as he had told Gide,
that he has no wish to pass censure, but he is worried by his friends'
'adventurous existence' – apparently, Ghéon had even told a perturbed
Blanche where Gide and he had met the previous Wednesday![49]

Ghéon's 'outing' did not at all accord with Gide's own strategies for
coping with the problem at this time. 'Despite all my friendship for you, I
could have lived through three lives without speaking to you as I am doing
here, my dear Blanche,' Gide wrote back. 'Forgive this letter, and lay all
the blame on Ghéon; yet I can no more blame him for doing so – my
friendship for you . . . has no reason to hide from you what nevertheless I
would not myself have told you. I hope your friendship, which is very dear
to me, will not be affected.'[50] The sensitive phrasing makes it quite clear
that Gide regrets Ghéon's revelations, not because he is in any way ashamed
of them, or embarrassed that Blanche should now be in the know, or
apprehensive that Blanche might now think less of him, but solely because
they had upset his friend and might affect their friendship. The next day,
Gide wrote Ghéon a short letter, enclosing Blanche's letter and a copy of
his reply to it. His only criticism is directed, not at Ghéon, but at Blanche:
'Before ten days are up Blanche will have talked about it to twenty people
– who in a month will have talked . . . too bad.'[51] Eighteen days – and five
letters – later, Gide is telling Ghéon that what he feared has happened.
Before leaving Paris, Blanche has repeated what Ghéon told him 'to anyone
who would listen' and 'shown your letter to anyone who asked to see it'.
Gide had learnt this from Valéry, 'who hardly knows Blanche', but who
knows Régnier, Lebey, Pierre Louÿs, etc. very well and 'who knows me
even better, but learns *that* only after those others, and through them'. Gide
is clearly put out – he has lost the weapon of ambiguity, but he does not
take it too seriously: 'Before, people would say: How could that be possible!
They're such a happy couple! – Now they'll say: how can they be happy!
We know that . . . etc. The lack of understanding is total in both cases, but
before it denied everything and thus permitted everything; now it suspects

everything and will make everything *difficult*.' Again there is no trace of anger against Ghéon. On the contrary, he even manages to feel that Ghéon has injured himself more: 'One of the saddest results of the affair is that, in their amused eyes, you are thought to have betrayed your friend, and your friendship will now seem to them to be as suspect as his morals.'[52] In a letter written some weeks later, Gide puts the situation with La Rochefoucaldian precision: 'C'était si beau de pouvoir être sincère sans être cru!' ('It was so good to be able to be sincere, without being believed!')[53]

On 5 January 1902, Gide took up his journal, which he had abandoned in 1895 – or 1896, if one includes the travel notes, 'Feuilles de Route'. It was only to last for three months, however, before another year's break. The thirty or so pages in the Pléiade edition covering those three months are invaluable, but far more revealing, both of Gide's state of mind and of his activities at this period, is the Ghéon correspondence. We owe it, of course, to the fact that the friends were rarely together: throughout this period, Ghéon was struggling to make a living as a doctor in Bray-sur-Seine and to get up to Paris as often as he could; Gide was either in Paris, from early December to early March, or the rest of the time in Cuverville, making frequent brief trips to Paris. There was a complicity between the two men. Their secret lives were known only to them; each only had the other to confide in; each regaled the other with his adventures. A whole new *dramatis personae*, referred to solely by Christian names, have their exits and their entrances. Gaston, 'very pleasant'; 'the kid Ernest, now taller and exquisite, very butcher's boy'; 'my delicious Henri – not me, the other one' (says Ghéon); 'he's called Henri, like you, like *the other one*, and, if you hadn't seen *the other one*, I would say this one was the handsomest of the Henris' (Gide says in his next letter); 'ended (the said evening) with a certain Georges, whom you must have seen – or touched at least – in the baths'.[54] When Gide and Ghéon did meet up it often seems to have been in the baths in the rue Rochechouart or the Turkish baths in the rue Oberkampf. 'I'm thinking of you reigning today over Mimile, Jalot, Mablouse, etc. in the fabulous clouds of the steam-baths,' Ghéon writes. 'Will you be there again on Tuesday?'[55] Christian names have given way here to rather camp nicknames. 'Wandered around on the boulevards without pleasure or profit until 10 or 11,' Gide writes. 'Before dinner, had the not very good idea of trying the rue O. Full, as it seems, every Sunday, with an army of infants. On the other hand, an admirable Monday, rue Rochechouart. I was so satisfied, so intoxicated that I was even determined to go back next morning . . .'[56] Much of Ghéon's inexhaustible *joie de vivre* spills over into Gide's letters, though, it has to be said, they seldom have Ghéon's mock epic exuberance. Here, for example, is one of Dr Vangeon's trips to Paris. At 5.30 pm he arrives at the baths to find them 'empty and without charms – except those of Laurent, the shoe salesman, whose completely naked form was turning white on the threshold of one of the cabins'. Ghéon takes 'a too anodyne, though crowded métro' and dines with friends. At 9.30, 'I make my escape, without hiding the purpose of my brief visit and the probable use to which my next night will be put.' Near the Madeleine, he bumps into Gaston, 'the young "metal-worker" from the Champs-Elysées'. Without feeling 'any desire of any kind', but afraid that he may not find anybody better, Ghéon invites the young man to go with him. On the way, they meet Joseph: Ghéon agrees to meet him at 12.30 and gives him '20 sols' (i.e., 1 franc). They go 'to the rue Saint-Martin, you know'. Gaston is 'exquisite, but too "*déjà-vu*", *déjà-fait* . . . I'm always tormented by the new. At midnight I was back on the boulevard at Le Pousset [a café] waiting; none of the passers-by aroused me . . . I slept alone that night . . . Satisfied, though, physically at least. I dreamt of the baths: I must go back before leaving! Next morning, I telephoned to Bray; I had to go home in the evening to call on an old lady.' An owner of one of the new-fangled automobiles, he had the pleasure of driving home through the deserted countryside at four in the morning.[57] Ghéon was as much a master of the fleeting pleasure as of its long, laborious quest. One night, before going back to Bray, he was 'opposite the Gymnase [a theatre] – a charming bouquet of blooms, from which I picked a bud and put it in the car, oh young, dark and charming, less than 5 minutes'.[58]

In his letters, Gide never seems to have quite such a good time as Ghéon – perhaps he was more honest. There is, too, a darker side that is quite absent from Ghéon's letters. But, then, he notices things that perhaps Ghéon would not have done – or, at least, would not have pursued. There is the extraordinary scene witnessed by Gide, about midday, in the small garden at the side of the church of Saint-Germain-des-Prés. 'On one of the benches, exposed to the sky, passers-by and policemen three young kids (12, 13 and 14) are abandoning themselves to the strangest frolics. The one lying on his back lifts his legs (he's the youngest one) and the oldest gets into position. The third acts as a screen, hiding, protecting, above all helping – yet doesn't stop me seeing the three bums in the air [les trois Q. à l'air], and all the homage being paid them [tous les cultes qu'on leur rend – wonderful word-play, this, on *cul* (bum), Q and *culte* (worship)]. Gide watches them – in their 'innumerable changes of position' – for twenty minutes, partly hidden behind a newspaper kiosk. 'The amazing thing was', nobody, André Gide excepted, stopped to look. In the end, he went up to them. 'They immediately assumed the most innocent air.' Apparently, they are pupils at the Christian Brothers' school. Gide takes the oldest boy by the arm and asks if they do that every day. No, it was the first time. Gide offers him a cigarette: he's so nervous that he takes the whole packet. 'I could hardly stop myself laughing, offering him my services, inviting him to lunch . . . I repeated a dozen times that they should be careful, then left them with a warm handshake . . . I'm now looking for the Brothers' school . . . I'd love to see him, and them, again.'[59]

In November 1901, Fedor Rosenberg, who had been back in Russia for some months, invited Gide to join him in St Petersburg. Preparations were made and fur clothes ordered. Gide would, as so often, be absent from Paris when one of his books was published. Then, in January, after buying his ticket, he suddenly changed his mind. He would not be going to Russia: no explanation is forthcoming. When *L'Immoraliste* appeared in the bookshops, Gide managed to be no farther away than Cuverville. The Gides considered another trip to Italy, but that, too, was abandoned. In February, André went with his young cousin, Paul Gide, to Brussels for a few days, but not until September, when he went to south-west France for three weeks, did Gide travel farther afield. From Cuverville there were constant visits to Paris. Gide went a couple of times to the Opéra-Comique to see *Pelléas et Mélisande*, Debussy's version of the Maeterlinck play – undoubtedly the musical event of the year. In May, Athman turned up in Paris for a short time. Ghéon suggested that Gide should bring him down to Bray-sur-Seine: 'What an effect he would have on the "rural population"!'[60]

On 28 July, in Paris, Madeleine's sister Valentine, having been divorced from Charles Bernardbeig, married her beloved fellow-consumptive, Marcel Gilbert. From Cuverville, Gide made a few short-distance sorties. He went back to La Roque 'to vote'. While there he saw the parish priest, who apprised him of the terrible news relating to a former employee. Gide passed on the news to Ghéon: 'Gustave – you must remember him . . . has finally got himself thrown out of the seminary; he was corrupting the younger ones, it seems . . . He had an eight-year-old "friend". The priest said: "Ah, Monsieur! When I learnt that, I went and shut myself up in my room and wept all night." Good fellow! What wouldn't I do to see the delinquents again!'[61]

That summer, Jacques-Emile Blanche was at his old family home in Dieppe, organizing an exhibition that would contain 'Monets, Pissarros, etc.' 'My only consolation here is my friend Sickert,' he writes to Gide. 'This immoralist has ended up living alone . . ., so that he doesn't have to do anything that people usually regard as normal and can do whatever he likes, whenever he likes. He manages this, without a sou, having a legitimate family in England and a fishwife in Dieppe, with a swarm of children from every provenance.'[62] Gide joined Blanche for a couple of days. In a long letter to Ghéon, written in the carriage that was taking him back to Cuverville, Gide describes his time there. After lunch, Blanche and Gide set out for Sickert's 'very uncomfortable chalet' just outside the town. Also there were Wilde's friend Reggie Turner and Max Beerbohm (not the German writer Otto Bierbaum, as the editors of the Gide–Ghéon correspondence). 'I don't like having to meet them,' said Blanche to Gide, 'but I thought they would interest you.' Every room in the house was full of paintings. Later, in a letter to Blanche, Gide explains why he did not offer to buy any of them, there and then. He was too embarrassed by the low prices Sickert was asking. He inquires after one – 'the 2nd leaning against the wall in the 1st-floor room, depicting a street, a stretch of wall, a blue poster . . .' – and arranges to buy another. 'I'd be ashamed to offer no more than a poor 50 for that one – and I even find it disagreeable, I admit, to send the 100 enclosed [£4] directly to your friend.'

The Gide–Ghéon correspondence for 1902 reveals a happy, high-spirited Ghéon constantly in the grip of financial problems and a Gide, without a material care in the world, beset by moods of depression and a general lack of direction. After a summer spent travelling constantly between Paris and Cuverville, Gide spent the first three weeks of September in south-west France. It did nothing to raise his spirits: 'At first alone, at Biarritz and Bayonne, with frightful weather, I thought I'd die of boredom; nothing to do, nothing to see and not an idea in my head.' He went on to spend three days with Jammes at Orthez, then three days at Cauterets, 'spent trying to cheer up Rosenberg, who is ill and very depressed'.[63] Back in Cuverville, the sense of depression, of having lost direction, of being unable to work at projects that were already fully formed in his head, such as *La Porte étroite*, deepened. On 23 October 1902, Gide wrote to Ghéon: 'I no longer have any idea where I am – morally, intellectually, physically.'[64]

9

The Barren Years: Le Retour de l'Enfant prodigue *and* La Porte étroite

(OCTOBER 1902 – OCTOBER 1908)

Since 25 October [in fact, 25 November] 1901, the day on which I finished *L'Immoraliste*, I have not worked seriously . . . A dull torpor of the mind has made me vegetate for the last three years. Perhaps I have busied myself too much in my garden and have taken on the habits of the plants. The simplest sentence costs me enormous effort; talking exhausts me almost as much as writing. And I must admit too that I was getting difficult: at the merest suspicion of a thought, a cantankerous critic, who is always lying in wait in the depths of my mind, would rise up and say: 'Are you really sure it's worth the trouble?' And, since the trouble required to express it was enormous, the thought quietly withdrew.[1]

Three years had gone by from the completion of *L'Immoraliste* to that *Journal* entry for November 1904. The same mood, with little more than shorter, occasional pieces written, was to continue for much of the next three years. In November 1902 Gide was thirty-three: he was too old, he felt, to be satisfied with sales of a few hundred to readers of the small literary reviews, with praise from friends in the same reviews, while the wider, newspaper-reading public eluded him. He did not expect, with an initial print-run of 300, that *L'Immoraliste* would be a breakthrough to that wider public, but part of him did just believe that it might be.

Gide's failure in this regard was made all the more mortifying by the phenomenal and quite unexpected success of Pierre Louÿs' *Aphrodite*. A highly laudatory review from François Coppée in *Le Journal* set off an inexhaustible demands for copies. Reprint followed reprint, amounting, after a few years, to sales in excess of 100,000. *Aphrodite* now seemed destined for a theatrical career. There were plans for an opera by Saint-Saëns with the great cabaret star Yvette Guilbert, but nothing came of them. Puccini, Albeniz and Leoncavallo each took out non-exclusive options on the work. In the end, it was the lesser figure of Camille Erlanger who composed the opera, first performed at the Opéra-Comique on 27 March 1906, with

the English soprano Mary Garden, Debussy's original Mélisande. Louÿs
was not, the extraordinary fortune of *Aphrodite* apart, a writer of bestsellers.
Gide's oldest literary friend, he was, like him, an intellectual; they had
pursued similar literary careers, though they had become estranged and
had had no real contact since 1895. Gide was not envious of Louÿs' success,
which, in fact, brought him little benefit: he frittered away his huge earnings
and got into ever greater debt. He was constantly plagued by illness, turned
to drug addiction and, in 1925, at the age of fifty-four, succumbed to tertiary
syphilis. For Gide, *Aphrodite* was scarcely a work of literature at all. Nor did
he envy Louÿs' commercial success: he had more than enough money for
his needs and was still paying for the publication of his works. There was
nothing personal in Gide's low opinion of Louÿs' literary achievement. As
late as June 1907, he was writing in his *Journal*: 'Immense disgust with
almost all the literary production of today and with the public's satisfaction
with it. More and more I feel that to obtain a success *beside* one of those
successes would not satisfy me. Better to withdraw altogether. Know how
to wait, even if it means waiting until after one is dead.'[2]

It is as impossible to explain artistic sterility as it is to give any plausible
account of the origin of artistic creation: it is foolhardy or arrogant to
make anything but hesitant hypotheses in either case. One clue to Gide's
difficulties at this time may lie in his cult of 'sincerity': this had its roots in his
Calvinistic background, but survived his ultimate rejection of Christianity,
becoming an ethical and aesthetic constant for him. Another was his
inability to remain in any one place for long, either physically or mentally.
Put the two together and there is an inevitable conflict. Sincerity is easier
for those who never change; for those who, like Gide, are in a constant
state of flux, sincerity is a hard taskmaster. What may seem true, to oneself
and to others, at the time of utterance may seem false later. During the
years covered by this chapter, the tension within Gide the man must have
been acute. He was finding it increasingly difficult to keep both sides of his
life hermetically sealed off from one another. He was devoted to Madeleine
– and cultivated his garden at Cuverville with ever greater passion,
redesigning it, ordering new plants, spending hours examining them. But,
with erratic frequency, he would have himself driven off to Lisieux, jump
on a train, arrive at Saint-Lazare and spend a few days in Paris, meeting
up with an equally delinquent Ghéon, often in the steam-baths. When
Madeleine was with him in Paris, his sorties became more frequent, daily
even, if shorter. Gide, the man of sincerity, was living a lie.

For Gide the writer, the combination of mutability and sincerity was even more difficult to bear. He was not one of those inventors of stories, who, with an unchanging viewpoint and well-practised technique, turn out a novel every two or three years. Gide invented very little and usually spoke in the first person. Most of his fiction had so far derived from his own life, his family, his marriage, his travels: that life was now riven in two. In *L'Immoraliste*, he had tried to bring the two parts together. But it was an uneven meeting: most of the book concerns Michel's public life (career, marriage); the secret life, though central, being the cause of the hero's downfall, is only hinted at. Gide had said as much as he dared. His new, secret life was no longer something that happened in North Africa, separable off in a circumscribed, exotic frame; it happened in the streets and baths of Paris, its imperious demands requiring daily excursions when he was there and frequent trips to the capital when he was in Cuverville. What had once been on the exotic margin of his life was now at its centre. And it could not, in 1902, 1908 or many years later, be turned into fiction. He was left, as a source of subject-matter, with the rest of his life – and he must have felt that it was a diminishing asset. He had, only with great difficulty, brought *L'Immoraliste* to its conclusion. 'I should have written it two years ago at least,' Gide wrote to Valéry on 5 July 1901. 'One always writes too late; the truth is that this arrests development; there is always something inside one or at one's side that is pulling in a different direction.'[3] Some weeks later, Gide again refers to *L'Immoraliste*: 'I'm dragging it after me like a dead skin; it clings to the past, holds me back, stops me thinking anew and growing.'[4] How much more Gide must have felt that *La Porte étroite*, conceived at much the same time, but not finished until October 1908, was a 'dead skin', clinging to the past, holding him back, actually preventing him from catching up with himself, from creating new work, in response to the new, rapidly changing world in which he was living. Every time he returned to *La Porte étroite* he must have felt that it had receded further into the past, placing a double strain on his sincerity. Not only were the things of which he wrote less and less central to his living and thinking, but he could not sincerely sustain a single view of his material over so long a lapse of time.

A similar loss of direction, a similar inability to work were afflicting Ghéon. His play *L'Eau-de-Vie* remained unfinished and a new novel, *Journal d'un médecin*, never got beyond the first few dozen pages. 'My flourishing health bears no fruit,' he wrote to Gide in December 1902. 'I'm well aware that I'm now "the gentleman who can't finish anything".'[5] Like Gide, he produced little more than articles for *L'Ermitage*. His other profession was going no better: he was losing, rather than gaining, patients. For over a year he talked of giving up Bray and medicine, and starting a new career in Paris. Gide and his other friends did everything possible to help him do so. Once or twice, publishing jobs seemed to open up, only to elude his grasp, then, in November 1903, another doctor left Bray, leaving Ghéon his clientèle. He and his mother then moved into a new house with a 'miraculous garden'. What he continued to call 'work' did not come any easier: before, he could not write because of financial worries and the boredom of provincial life; now the needs of his patients absorbed all his energies.

Gide did begin one work at this time: the curiously inconsequential *Bethsabé*. He had been thinking about the subject, David's infatuation with Bathsheba, Uriah's wife, as recounted in the *Book of Samuel*, since working on *Saül*, of which it is a sort of offshoot. Gide wrote what he calls the first two 'scenes' very quickly; they appeared in *L'Ermitage*, in January and February 1903. The third and final scene appeared much later, first in the March 1909 number of *Vers et Prose* (after the republication of the first two scenes in earlier numbers), then, in volume form, with *Le Retour de l'enfant prodigue* in 1912. The term 'scenes' is misleading: they are really three monologues spoken by David, written in the same kind of free verse as *Le Roi Candaule* (*Saül* was in prose). For Gide, it was 'la moindre des choses'[6] – 'nothing of any importance' – something he turned to *faute de mieux*.

André and Madeleine left Cuverville for Paris on 25 October. Three days later, at midnight, Gide was writing excitedly to Ghéon: 'What have I not seen and heard today . . .' – and this letter does mark in the correspondence a new degree of frankness in revelation and language.[7] On the way back from the Van Rysselberghes', Gide jumped off the omnibus (obviously what is now the no. 63) at the boulevard Raspail and, 'almost by chance', entered the urinal at the corner (with the boulevard Saint-Germain and the rue du Bac), at the same time as 'un type épatant' ('a terrific fellow'). The 'very young' man went out again at once, but hung around near the entrance, just as two policemen arrived, one on either side of Gide, which 'gave me a scare'. Gide's immediate reaction was to get out at once, but he then realized that 'le type était venu branler' (*branler*, literally 'to shake', is slang for 'to masturbate') the two policemen! *Différents pays, différents moeurs!* If it had been Britain, the 'type épatant' might himself have been a (plainclothes) policeman and the two in uniform would no doubt have arrested Gide on a charge of 'soliciting for an immoral purpose', with or without evidence. It should perhaps be explained to the uninitiated that the urinals in question did not provide all the facilities of a public lavatory, but were, literally, urinals. Circular constructions of black-painted sheet-metal, they provided three standing places at an oblique angle to one another. They were politely (and wittily) referred to as '*vespasiennes*', after the Roman emperor Vespasian, who introduced a tax on urinals; more colloquially, and almost as wittily, they were known as '*tasses*', cups, on account of their shape and liquid associations. From well before Gide's day to the 1960s, they were a familiar, not inelegant, vaguely oriental feature of the Parisian boulevards. They began to disappear after the advent of the Fifth Republic. Up till then, they were one of the few places where homosexuals could meet. When Gide and Ghéon talk of going 'on the boulevards', they were certainly participating in that custom of the gay subculture of the time which consisted of walking from one '*tasse*' to another in search of adventure, hoping to get into the middle place, thus doubling one's chances, and being less exposed to the (usually good-natured) expostulations of those waiting outside.

A few weeks later Gide was complaining to Ghéon of the endless chores that beset his working day, seeing 'notary, barrister, solicitor, architect, businessman' about the new house being built in Auteuil, the selling of La Roque, the case following his wife's accident, the will of Marc de La Nux, his old piano teacher, etc. In addition to that, there were 'the continual visits of bores, beggars or friends, life's thousand little cares'.[8] A *rentier*'s work was never done. As a result, Gide had not been to a single concert, hardly seen any of his friends and had even given up going to the baths. Ghéon, struggling to earn a living in his capacity as Dr Vangeon, must, at times, have felt short on sympathy.

Between Christmas and the New Year, Ghéon came to stay with the Gides for a few days: 'I shall try to see Blanche, go to the baths and dine with you ["piscinerai et dînerai avec toi"] and you know whom (if the little combination can be revived!)'[9] The New Year brought Gide some relief from his time-consuming chores. His social life resumed somewhat. There were, for example, the *mondain* Thursday evenings at Blanche's, with their 'conversation de snobs' – and there were the baths. Sometimes the two kinds of activity clash awkwardly: Ghéon is joining Gide on some social event requiring evening dress, but, of course, he will want to call at the baths first. Problem: 'I can't turn up at Oberkampf in tails after all.' Problem solved: he'll leave the baths early enough to call on Gide at home, if Gide is not also in the baths, and change there. One Sunday in January, Gide's and Ghéon's letters crossed excitedly. Both men had read 'two scandalized – and scandalous – columns on the morals of telegraph boys'. Ghéon wondered if Gide had seen the question raised in any other newspaper: 'Let's exchange a few press cuttings . . . It's not going to do anything to rehabilitate the homosexual corporation, is it?'[10]

In April 1903, the Gides moved from 4 boulevard Raspail, where they had lived since March 1897, to a larger apartment at no. 10 in the same street, where André had turned a sixth-floor maid's room into a study. They now retreated to Cuverville. Over the next few weeks, André cultivated his garden, which was an ever-growing source of fascination and pleasure to him, played the piano for hours on end, read, but did little writing. He corrected the proofs for the *Mercure de France* edition of *Saül*. For the same publisher, he prepared *Prétextes*, a collection of articles, lectures and 'Lettres à Angèle'. He also worked fitfully and painfully on a lecture that he was to give at Weimar in August. There were the usual, frequent trips to Paris – to see two new plays by Maeterlinck, *Monna Vanna* and *Joyzelle*, to stay with the Van Rysselberghes (Théo was painting a portrait of him), and to visit Rochechouart and Oberkampf – in June, unknown to themselves, Gide and Ghéon even managed to be in Paris at the same time, one in one establishment, one in the other.

In early July, he participated in what must have been a horrifying experience. Madeleine's sister, Jeanne Drouin, was staying at Cuverville, where she expected to give birth to a child around the middle of the month. By the first week of July, the labour pains began. Gide describes the event in a letter to Ghéon: 'After 60 hours of pain and vain effort, after 3 useless attempts using forceps, the obstetrician could only save Jeanne by sacrificing the child . . . and disfiguring it atrociously. I had to help in this abominable operation; what days and what nights!'[11] Marcel Drouin was not at Cuverville during his wife's ordeal. The next day, Gide set off for La Flèche. 'I hadn't the heart to tell him the sad news by letter.'[12] The two men then returned to Cuverville together.

On 3 August, Gide arrived in Weimar, as a guest of Count Harry von Kessler, diplomat, essayist and admirer of Gide's work. That morning, at 4 a.m., as his train approached Rouen, he noted in his journal the words 'allégresse matinale', the sensations of joy, of exhilaration one might feel as a new day dawns. 'Even at the moment of leaving her, you were unable to hide your joy from her,' he says, addressing himself. 'Why were you almost annoyed that she could not hide her tears?'[13] Madeleine had not accompanied André on his German trip, even though she spoke good

German – Gide's own was rather faltering. From this time on, Madeleine rarely accompanied André anywhere, except to Cuverville and – sometimes – back to Paris. Even when they were both in Paris and André wanted to go to the theatre or to a concert, he often did so with the Van Rysselberghes – Ghéon, not Madeleine, making up the four. Madeleine did not care for the rather bohemian van Rysselberghes – they were among the few of André's friends never invited back to Cuverville.

The train journey to Weimar was not without its 'petite aventure'. No doubt as the result of his usual systematic inspection of the entire train, Gide found himself in a compartment with two German boys, brothers aged sixteen and fourteen. After falling asleep, Gide woke up to find the younger boy standing near him looking out of the window. Gide got up and stood behind him. Wandering fingers were met with encouragement – the elder brother was still asleep. Under a large rug, matters proceeded, further helped when the train entered a long tunnel. The third party awoke and a conversation 'between three extremely polite strangers' ensued. 'Moll, K. Ebing and others maintain that homosexuals tend to exaggerate, to invent such stories,' Gide comments. 'Mind you, I can scarcely believe what happened myself.'[14]

At Weimar, Gide was joined by Marcel Drouin – and by Maria Van Rysselberghe and her friend Aline Mayrisch, nicknamed 'Loup', the wife of a rich Luxembourg industrialist. Our most detailed account of the Weimar visit comes from the draft of a letter, dated 6 August, written by Gide to an unnamed recipient addressed as '*Chère amie*'.

Inside the palace, Gide and his party were received by the Hereditary Grand Duchess of Saxe-Weimar. They were not exactly put at their ease by having been instructed to address the Grand Duchess ('who is enormous and rather red . . . adorned with the largest emeralds you could ever see') in the third person – and to insert the words 'Her Royal Highness' into every sentence. For perhaps obvious reasons, *décolletage* was frowned on by the Grand Duchy's hereditary ruler, so the ladies' dresses were not up to much ('les toilettes étaient peu sensationnelles'). The twenty guests entered the dining-room, situated under the dome: 'One might have thought one was at Sans-Souci' (Frederick the Great's Potsdam palace). As guest of honour, Gide sat next to the Grand Duchess, who threw him into a fit of embarrassment by talking to him about *Le Voyage d'Urien*. However, Gide's conversational skills were not to be taxed for long. 'The dinner, according to the custom here, was dispatched with speed. The lackeys never wait for you to finish before removing your plate; as a result you don't eat very much.' The guests then retired to the Grand Duchess's study to hear Gide's talk.

Gide began by paying homage to Goethe, the *genius loci*, before turning to his subject, 'The Importance of the Public'. His thinking here confirms his movement away from Symbolism ('Art for Art's sake') towards the need to communicate with a wider public:

A public – it has become so rare a thing that nowadays we hardly know what it is. Too often we have to look back to the past to find it . . . A public – the artist, alas!, has had to learn, for better or for worse, to do without it . . . We even go so far as to claim that the artist *must* do without it. That is a dangerous mistake . . . The artist cannot do without a public; and when the public is absent, what does he do? He invents one and, turning his back on his time, expects from the future what the present denies him.

This looks like a criticism of avant-gardism, of the self-consciously modernist artist of the time, but Gide goes on to show that he has no truck either with popular artists, who 'wanting a public at any price, buy a cut-price one from the mob'. As usual, he wants to take a middle way. Later, in his talk, he caused momentary consternation among the ladies when he spoke of Christianity and art. No art has sprung from monotheism – be it Jewish or Arab, he declared. Christianity could only produce art when the 'formless God of the prophets' took on human shape in the Incarnation. Furthermore, it required a host of other human forms – apostles, prophets, saints – before a 'Christian art' became possible. Even then, such art can only become truly art by refusing to conform to religious demands. 'Christian art *qua* Christian art hardly exists; perhaps it is a contradiction in terms . . . Society . . . asked art to be Christian; art pretended to be so and the artist served up what was asked of him.'[15]

Gide and his friends visited the gardens of Oberhof, with its famous waterfalls, and Bad-Kissingen. They then went on to Leipzig, Berlin and Dresden (where they were joined by Rosenberg). Back in Weimar, Gide had tea with Elisabeth Forster-Nietzsche, the philosopher's sister, and, with Maria Van Rysselberghe, returned to Paris on 30 August. The German trip had gone some way to shaking him out of his apathy. Back in Cuverville, the effects soon wore off and Gide sank back into dejection.

I blamed the weather (it rained incessantly that year); I blamed the Cuverville air (and I still fear that it has a soporific effect on me); I blamed my routine (it was very bad, it is true; I never went further than the garden, where, for hours on end, I would *contemplate* each plant, one by one) . . . Eventually, seriously worried, determined to shake off that torpor, to which was added an unhealthy restlessness, I convinced myself and convinced Em. that nothing but the diversion of travel could save me from myself.[16]

In fact, as he corrects himself, Madeleine was not 'convinced': his proposals were met with 'a desperate wall of indifference'. He invented all manner of arguments why he had to go back to North Africa. He had, he said, to do research for a *serious* book on North Africa. (In fact, the resulting work, ironically entitled *Le Renoncement au voyage* (*Giving Up Travel*), is really no more serious than any other of his writings on North Africa and certainly required no more research.) He refused to be swayed by Madeleine's no longer expressed, but all too clearly communicated opposition. She agreed to join him in Algiers after four weeks. He left Paris on 10 October for Bordeaux, where Marcel Drouin had just begun his first term as philosophy teacher at the *lycée*. Gide then travelled by train to Cartagena, where he caught a boat to Oran; from there, he went overland to Algiers: 'Frightful night; air heavy; my sleep, despite my tiredness, torn to shreds by fleas, mosquitoes, bugs and the constant din from the shipyards. In bed by eight, I get up at ten, dying of thirst; . . . I run down to the quay for ice-cream and beer.'[17] Two days later, he retreats to the mountain resort of Tizi-Ouzou, where he meets up with two old friends, Ali and his brother Saïd. Later, Ali takes Gide to meet his family: 'We are in a square room. In one corner a lamb is bleating. On the ground Ali's wife, a child of sixteen, or perhaps less, is suckling a sickly-looking child. In front of the door, Ali's mother is feeding her latest son. In this tiny dwelling, three generations cohabit.'[18]

Three days later, Gide is back in Algiers: the sirocco has ended and the weather turned pleasant. Gide sets off again – this time to Bou-Saada. Near to his destination, the weather changes again, this time in the opposite direction. Grey, overcast skies have their usual effect on him: 'This morning I am full of hate against this country.' He tries to escape back to where he has come from: in his mind he goes over passages from Schumann's Third Symphony and a Beethoven violin sonata, then takes out a Virgil and reads one of the Eclogues. 'But none of that is enough; I would like to be able to go to the Louvre this morning and re-read La Fontaine.'[19] By 28 October, he was back in Algiers, where he saw Jean Coquelin in a production of *Le Bourgeois Gentilhomme*. He also began to learn by heart Bach's *Well-Tempered Clavier* and read Nietzsche's correspondence.

Our main source for this trip being, not letters to Ghéon, of which there are few that have survived, but the published *Le Renoncement au voyage*, we have very little idea of Gide's sexual activities. We may assume that they were no different from on previous visits. As he is about to leave Algiers for Biskra, he hints as much. For years, he has promised himself that he would not go back again. 'But the longing for this garden, in the evening – for this night garden where I come every evening . . . Oh, how shall I bear it?'[20]

At the end of November Madeleine joined André at Algiers and on the 28th they set off by train for Biskra. On arrival, Gide wrote a long letter to Ghéon: 'My head is splitting from the journey and the intoxication of finding myself back here. It's as if my heart beats differently here . . . For the past hour, I haven't been walking, but floating.' He recognizes old friends. There is 'Mohammed in Turkish dress – superb'. There is 'Ahmed, easy Ahmed, whom we took to the old fortress and who took us to the Turkish baths', etc., etc. 'Each of them is charming; I rather feel that they expect to find coins in every hand they shake [*ils comptent sur des poignées de mains argentées*], but that doesn't affect my feelings for them.' Ahmed was at the station when they arrived: he was 'still the same – affectionate, puffy-faced, babbling and not in the least Nietzschean . . . yet charming, accom-modating, open to everything and more a poet in every sense of the word than three-quarters of those who pass as such in Paris'. After dinner – Madeleine presumably having retired to bed – André and Ahmed go out into the town. More old faces: 'Your delicious Mohammed, the younger brother of Madaoui the one-eyed, the one who was washing up in a café when we were here last; he is now serving in the Jardin Landrou and we know what that means.'[21]

At the Biskra hotel Gide is highly appreciative of that other exoticism, the English abroad (that is, the English upper classes of the time). Like the ancient Romans, says Gide, they are never *dépaysés* because they take their customs with them. In Lady W . . .'s room one never feels one is 'in an hotel': she takes with her, wherever she goes, portraits of friends and relations, vases for her mantelpiece, etc. 'She lives *her* life, at ease.' But the most astonishing thing about her is that she has also been able to create a social group for herself. 'There were four of us French couples, each keeping out of each other's way, but living in an hotel as a kind of penance. The English, twelve in number, did not know each other previously, but seemed like people who were expecting one another.' He notes the gentlemen's 'gleaming shoes' and evening dress. 'The conquest of the hotel lounge came easy to them; it would have been presumptuously useless to try to dispute their right to it, so normal did it seem that they should take it over; they knew how to make use of it, we didn't.'[22]

After a month in Biskra, the Gides left for Tunis and, from there, sailed to Sicily, following their now familiar route from Messina, to Sorrento, to Rome. There they met up with Jean Schlumberger and his wife, who, with their two young children and two women servants, were spending the winter and spring of 1903–4 in Rome. Schlumberger, it will be remembered, was the heir of Val-Richer, the property adjacent to La Roque. As a child – he was eight years Gide's junior – he had witnessed young André's passionate attachment to his cousin François de Witt. Like Gide, he had been brought up a Protestant – his family were of Alsatian origin. The two met whenever Gide was at La Roque, then, when Gide sold the property, he stayed at Val-Richer when attending council meetings. Meanwhile Schlumberger, after studying ecclesiastical history at the Sorbonne, had taken up writing: a man of independent means, he had no need of a profession. At twenty-two, he married Suzanne, a painter and also a Protestant. In 1903, he published *Poèmes des temples et des tombeaux*, which he dedicated to Gide, and, the following year, his first novel, *Le Mur de verre*, was published in volume form. The two couples got on extremely well: a strong affection grew up between the two women, and the two men, despite very different temperaments, became close friends.

In the *Journal*, Gide notes that he saw Jean Schlumberger every day and, 'as he confided in me more and more, our friendship soon deepened'.[23] In an unpublished passage, he adds: 'But it was only later, and by letter, that he dared to make his confessions more specific.' Schlumberger had been dropping hints, also by letter, nearly two years before. On 22 June 1902, after reading *L'Immoraliste*, he wrote: 'I was moved, not by a general emotion, but very personally. Did I rediscover too much of myself in it . . .?'[24] A week later, he wrote again: 'I am one of those who have always been interested in Oscar Wilde . . . as victim of the most odious hypocrisy . . . I would be happy to ask you more about him when I see you.'[25] Finally, in early November 1904, during a brief visit that Gide made to Val-Richer, Schlumberger opened his heart to Gide. Afterwards, he wrote: 'As soon as you got off the boat, you were dying to know *if it had happened* [i.e. during Schlumberger's stay in Italy]. A sort of embarrassment did not stop me saying yes, but a cruel sense of shame prevented me from admitting no.' An 'excessive stubbornness', 'a sort of sensual delight in prolonging this fast' had driven him to go on seeking the ideal partner – and failing to avail himself of what was on offer. Now, he confesses, his 'unbearable torture' would make him content with 'the least food'. There follow two paragraphs that are moving enough to be quoted in full:

I am astonished to find myself again, new before life, with furious appetites . . . No doubt later I shall envy this second youth, more truly young than the first, more excessive and more joyful, an opening up and a revenge, the outburst of a life stifled under an unnatural discipline, a gloomy life that despaired of the poverty of its emotions.

I owe you a great deal, my friend. I cannot begin to say how much. I would ask still more of you: practical advice certainly, but, above all, to introduce me to some of your friends, all too aware as I am that I must become stronger through new socal links, if the old, much slackened ones are to be broken.[26]

Gide's reply is affectionate, caring, but astringent: 'For months I have been waiting to hear you say what you have finally made up your mind to say . . . "Practical advice" . . . Alas! I am only too well placed to offer it. (Why: alas? It would take a whole book to explain . . .)' Gide has little patience with 'the sophistical shelter that timidity, whether of the flesh or of the mind' takes in the uncompromising search for an ideal.[27] During a few days in Paris, Schlumberger clearly followed Gide's instructions: 'It isn't peace . . . It's joy . . . A memory that remains all over the skin . . . I, who have always claimed to lead my life, the reins firmly in my hands, now abandon myself to it, eyes closed! . . . Ah, the sensual delight I now feel! . . . I feel I am being born, like Adam, a marvelling adult.'[28]

At the beginning of 1904, the year of the Entente Cordiale, a group of French writers decided to pay homage to Edmund Gosse, a man who had done so much to familiarize his fellow-countrymen with French literature. On 9 February, at the Restaurant Durand, a banquet was given in his honour. Gide was one of some fifty guests. The two men did not meet on that occasion, but, some weeks later, Gide sent Gosse copies of *Saül* and *Le Roi Candaule*. Gosse's reply opened a correspondence that was to last until Gosse's death in 1928.

Soon after his return from North Africa, Gide began work on a lecture that he had been invited to give by the 'Libre Esthétique' society of Brussels where, four years before, he had lectured on 'Influence in Literature'. This time he was asked to speak on 'The Evolution of the Theatre' (previous lectures in the series had dealt with the evolution of poetry, painting and music). There are interesting things in the lecture, not least the fact that he adopts a position in the art/life question that is the opposite of the one he propounded at Weimar only seven months before. The pendulum effect, for long so evident in his fiction, was now operating in his theoretical writings. In Weimar he had declared that contemporary artists should abandon their isolation from their fellow men and express once more the feelings, the preoccupations, the aspirations of their public. In Brussels, he argued that, in the theatre, the new can only be reached by moving away from realism, from the 'anecdotal', by digging a 'moat' between stage and auditorium, actor and spectator, fiction and reality, the hero and 'the cloak of morals'. This last pair is the one that really interests Gide here. It is *mœurs*, conventional morality, that is, the audience, that is holding modern drama back. It should leave familiar social reality behind and embark on what Nietzsche called 'the open sea', 'those unexplored regions of man, full of new dangers'. Yet, paradoxically, this can only be done by returning to such 'constraints' as were accepted by the classical theatre of the past. 'Give us back freedom of morals and the constraint of art will follow; remove hypocrisy from life and the mask will return to the stage.' The lecture was published in a second edition of *Saül* (1904) and again in *Nouveaux Prétextes* (1911).[29]

In Paris and Cuverville Gide worked at writing up the notes that he had taken while in North Africa. As epigraph to *Le Renoncement au voyage*, he wrote: 'I was of an age when life begins to assume a more dubious taste on the lips; when one already feels each moment falling from a somewhat lesser height than in the past.'[30] Nothing had changed; he was back where he had been before setting out. The book ends: 'The squalls from the North beat at my window. It has been raining for three days. – Oh! How beautiful the caravans were at Touggourt, when at dusk the sun set on the salt.'[31] *Le Renoncement au voyage* began to appear with the January 1905 number of the *Mercure de France*, then, the following year, was published by the review in volume form, together with earlier travel writings, under the Virgilian title of *Amyntas*.

Meanwhile, Ghéon found himself in the curious situation of working as never before, but actually having less money than usual. As he explains in a letter to Gide, asking for a loan of 1,000 francs (£40 or $200 at the time), he has had to pay out huge sums to buy his new house and practice. He now earns between 1,200 (£48 or $240) and 1,500 (£60 or $300) a month, but the patients are slow in paying their bills. Needless to say, the sum requested was sent at once – and probably never repaid.

In July, it would seem that Gide's cousin, the twenty-year-old Paul Gide (the 'Gérard' of the *Journal*), was being introduced, with precisely how much personal involvement is left unclear, into the peripatetic ways of his older cousin. 'One of our better evenings,' Ghéon writes to Gide.

Your cousin is charming and born to this kind of adventure. From now on you'll
be able to go roaming the streets [*vadrouiller*, or cruising] together, he'll replace me.
The ease with which he has taken to these promiscuities . . . and his amusement
in taking part in them astonished and delighted me . . . My evening ended *precisely*
where you said it would: on the right, going up the street, just before the rue La
Fayette. I was not disappointed.[32]

Gide replies: 'What pleasure your letter gave me! If it had arrived a day
earlier I could have read to my cousin the passage concerning him. He
would have loved it. He came and spent Saturday night here at Cuverville.'[33]
In the event, nothing was to come of the 'mutual discovery' of the Gide
cousin. Before a year was up, young Paul Gide was to find other objects for
his erotic desires than those sought after by André – in particular, the actress
Ventura. Gide was rather put out, but agreed to introduce his cousin to the
famous interpreter of Racine. When nothing came of it, Gide tried to divert
the young man's attentions to that 'grande horizontale', Liane de Pougy,
'an easier conquest than Ventura'.[34] The indignant Paul remained loyal to
his first infatuation and eventually toppled the actress's defences. He then
went back to his law studies and duly graduated. His youthful rebellion
over, cousin André rather lost interest in him. But he did not live to become,
like his father Charles Gide, a pillar of academic respectability. In 1915, like
so many other young Frenchmen, he was killed in action, aged thirty-one.
(His brother Edouard, five years his junior, lived another fifty years, dying,
in 1975, at the age of eighty-six.)

The 'Paul Gide Affair', then, was a false alarm, a mere prefiguration of
another triangle that began only a few months later. The third party in this
case is referred to, both in Gide's *Journal* and in letters to and from Ghéon,
as 'M'. The *Journal* has a few discreet references to 'M', the first in April
1905, but our main, almost only source is the Gide–Ghéon correspondence.
In their edition of the correspondence, the editors warn us that 'eleven
complete letters and a number of fragments' (in fact no fewer than thirty-
eight) have been omitted on account of 'their references to living persons'.[35]
(Out of a similar 'respect for third parties' proper names were replaced by
initials.) However, they do us the service at least of listing their cuts, with
dates. With the exception of two early fragments, dating from early 1899,
they all cover the period November 1904 – January 1906, precisely the
period of the 'M' affair. None of the material cut differs essentially from
that appearing in the published correspondence; none of it is in any way
shocking. It does, however, give us a fuller, more detailed view of the affair
and the state of mind of the protagonists. 'M' was Maurice Schlumberger,

the younger brother of Jean. Born in 1886, he was eighteen when the affair began. When the Gide–Ghéon correspondence was published in 1976, he was ninety: he was to die the following year. Apparently, the cuts were made at his insistence. It is difficult to imagine why an old gentleman of that age, albeit *père de famille* and founder of the Banque Schlumberger, should care very much if people knew that seventy years before he had been an object of infatuation to André Gide.

Gide first met Maurice Schlumberger at a tennis party. In an unpublished letter to his wife, Jean Schlumberger writes that the party will include 'André, his nephew Paul Gide, M. and Mme Ducoté, the Van Rysselberghes, Jean-Paul Laurens, and others. I am trying to get Maurice to join us, but Maman isn't happy about it. She's afraid of the milieu, though I have described it in the best possible light.' In view of what happened, one is tempted to wonder whether her reluctance stemmed from something rather more like maternal instinct or feminine intuition, than narrow-minded disapproval of what she saw as a suspect bohemian circle. In the event, the fears of Mme Schlumberger *mère* were overcome and Maurice did go to the party. Proof that he was not an innocent falling into the clutches of two older men is that, at first sight, he fell for Paul Gide, now twenty. 'He makes every possible advance to him,' Gide writes to Ghéon, 'and Paul *is quite unaware of the fact*; his mind is elsewhere and he *doesn't see* how immeasurable this excess of tenderness and this sudden friendship can be on the part of someone who has never had a friend before.'[36] 'My mind is inhabited by him,' Gide goes on, in the published correspondence. 'From one end of the week to the other I rush to the day when I may hope to see him again.' For the first time – and there were not to be many more – Gide had succumbed to what, for the generality of mortals, is a common enough event – he had 'fallen in love'; love and sexual passion had converged. As a result Gide is quite disorientated. For Maurice Schlumberger is not an Arab or working-class youth; he is a *fils de famille*, a student, the brother of a close friend and, therefore, in the Gidean scheme of things, a fit object of Platonic, not sexual love. At this stage, indeed, Gide is so confused that he tells Ghéon: 'I don't even have any desires; no, it's something else, something much more overwhelming.' Ghéon has already met Maurice, already fallen in love with him, too, already, it would seem, made physical advances. He told Gide as much as they were coming out of the theatre. 'I would like to have had other details,' Gide writes next day. 'Would he have accepted that from me? The question has obsessed me all day. How far can I go?'[37]

Gide's first reaction after meeting Maurice was to share his experience with Ghéon. This led to their sharing the young man. Gide was not of a jealous disposition. On the contrary, he was, in a sense, so much at one remove from things that he actually needed the collaboration of a third party to experience them himself. Once Ghéon had been introduced into the situation, it became, for Gide, 'literature'. 'I am still lost in *wonder* at the *beauty* of this story' (of the 'story', not of the young man). 'Don't let us lose any of it; everything concurs to make it interesting . . . A mass of tiny details would throw more light on it for you.'[38] The letters are not only a record of the three-sided relationship, an attempt to salvage the details, the words without which this adventure could not become a story, a narrative that could endure long after the adventure itself; they also feed back into it. 'I draw from them the food that sustains my only thought,' Gide writes. 'Nothing can distract me from it; I am obsessed with it every hour of every day; . . . my only source of repose is to speak of it.'[39] All that remained was for Maurice himself to read the letters about him exchanged between his two lovers. 'As we walked along the quays to Passy . . ., what could we talk about, if not you?' Gide writes to Ghéon. The young man then remarks: 'You ought to copy out his letters for me.' (This Gide duly does into a vellum notebook bought in Rome.) 'Yes,' says young Maurice, who certainly seems at home in this erotico-literary game, 'everything in our story is marvellous; yes, every chapter, from the beginning; there's no falling-off of interest at any point.'[40] There are two authors to this real-life fiction: a primary author, Gide, and a secondary author, Ghéon. Given the fiction's epistolary form, the two authors are also the two readers. The central character, the only begetter of this fiction, is Maurice; the two writer–readers also play a secondary role as characters. The moment Maurice reads the letters, he, too, becomes a reader and, judging by his remarks, a born critic. But the character-become-reader can also, under Gide's voyeuristic gaze, become a character again. Maurice and Gide are sitting on a bench in the Louvre, Gide writes to Ghéon, 'he, reading your last letter; I watching him [*l'épiant*, literally, "spying on him"] smile as he reads it'.[41] The situation is spiral: the end of the literary process, the real-life reader (Maurice) is reading about a character (Maurice) in a text written by author 2 (Ghéon), observed by author 1 (Gide). But we do not actually witness this scene, of course. We read a description of it by author 1 (Gide) in a letter sent to author 2 (Ghéon); the end of the literary process, the real-life reader (Maurice), thus returns to the position of character, to begin a new circular movement of the spiral. Of course, Gide himself is the *primum mobile* of the whole structure, the observer–manipulator: it was he who met and became infatuated with Maurice, turned him into a character in his letters to Ghéon, introduced him to Ghéon, showed him Ghéon's letters. We are already in the world of *Les Faux-Monnayeurs*, twenty years before it was possible to write such a work, to bring that world into literature. Gide had to be content with an epistolary non-novel and, of course, it is, as such, in a volume published by Gallimard in 1976, that we become the readers, readers who are not also characters, while the other readers survive only as characters who read.

In the shadows of this real-life adventure, there was another figure. On 17 March 1905, in a letter to Ghéon, Madeleine moves centre-stage. 'André,' she tells him, 'is very tired, not a general, physical tiredness . . . a mental, cerebral tiredness . . . I have no doubt at all that this tiredness has some connection, direct or indirect, with you.' André's 'tiredness' has increased since Ghéon's last visit to Paris. Since then, too, André's activities have taken on an air of secrecy and letters from Ghéon arrive daily. She is, she stresses, making no criticism, no accusation. Nor is she seeking information. She and André have always had a tacit agreement that 'all that part of his life and soul that belonged to his friends remained private ground [*terrain réservé*]'. She has always respected that agreement, though 'not always willingly [*de gaîté de coeur*]'. But she begs Ghéon to remember that although André's 'taste for life', his 'passionate curiosity' about it, is 'one of the causes of his value', it does 'in itself involve great danger'. 'Goodbye, my dear friend,' she ends. 'You are very young . . . be careful . . . Don't give me too much to worry about.'[42] Exit Madeleine: she makes no further appearance in this section of the Gide/Ghéon correspondence. What this letter makes quite clear is that she is, by 1905, well aware of the nature, if not of the details, of her husband's sexual activities.

André was certainly suffering from 'cerebral tiredness'. About the same time that Madeleine was writing to Ghéon, Gide also wrote to him: he was, he said, '*quite aged with happiness*, love and painful anxiety'. He had reached such a stage of 'surexcitation sentimentale' that he would burst into tears in the street at the slightest provocation. He retreated to Cuverville, leaving Ghéon and Maurice behind: 'Yes, my old friend, jealousy is a barbarous feeling, which friendship, love's rival, seems to have eliminated, in all three of us . . . When I left you both, on Monday evening, I was quite uplifted with joy at seeing you together and thanks to me – then suddenly stopped thinking about it entirely, as if, by doing so, I had unburdened on to you, at one go, the agonizing burden of my love.'[43]

Three weeks later, Madeleine had got André further afield: as far from Paris, in fact, as one could go and still remain on French territory. They travelled to Bordeaux, picked up Jeanne Drouin and went on to Hendaye, a resort on the Atlantic coast bordering Spain. From the Grand Hôtel de la Plage, Gide wrote to Ghéon on 17 April: 'Friend of my friend, my friend – how much your last letter moved me. Yes, *that* is how I love him now, how we must both love him at the same time.'[44] Ghéon was in a worse state than Gide:

What a chasm, what a bottomless chasm love is. You think you can feel the ground under your feet, you think you are basing your life and your joy in life on it once and for all . . . Then suddenly the ground gives way beneath you and you fall once more . . . more deeply than before . . . The more I see him, the more I want to see him. The more I have him, the more I desire him, and the more I shall have him, the more times I shall want to have him again . . . And I fear satiety!

A few days later, Gide is admitting: 'I understand nothing of what is happening inside me' – and adds, untypically, 'and I am not trying to understand'.[45]

By June, that particular winter's tale was at an end, clearly at young Maurice's instigation. He replies to one letter from Ghéon, in which he was criticized for his 'new attitude' and reacts sharply to a charge of '*coquetterie*', which he does not think he will ever be able to forgive. A shattered Ghéon went off to Brittany and Gide retreated for the summer to Cuverville, almost with relief; Ghéon felt drained, Gide filled with raw material. 'My affection for him has not diminished,' Gide wrote, 'but my weakness for him has.' Referring to the two friends' last meeting, he adds: 'We should not so much have wept over our love as smiled at our liberation.' Gide, who seems to have recovered his calm more quickly than Ghéon, points out his friend's error: he should not have believed that a friendship could retain its solidity in becoming so amorous ('Quelle confusion de "genres"!'). 'Analyse, analyse, analyse again,' Gide advises. On rereading Ghéon's last letter, one sentence – 'let us hate life' – saddened him. 'No! No! No *rancour*,' Gide exclaims. 'One step more and you'll be a "Catholic writer". May Apollo preserve you from that, *cher vieux*.'[46] Ghéon's reply is unusually bitter and suggests that he was ripe for religion.

Catholic writer, you say, or Catholic cured of writing rather. I move further along that path every day. So far it is the clearest result of this *lamentable* story . . . My past life has certainly sunk into the chasm, with all that is unexpected, all that is temporary about adventurous debauchery . . . Obviously love (and I don't understand your reference to confusion of genres in my case – what has friendship got to do with it?) . . . love cannot give me the guarantees I need to live, any more than the fluctuations of my art can. I say: down with art and down with life! Without the physical curse that weighs upon me my fate would have been to marry, have children, rear them and die. Where shall I find refuge? Reading Claudel's verses, I see clearly enough what religion can do with an admirable mind, animated by a genius that I don't possess . . . A gap has opened up in my life and nothing will ever fill it. I tasted love, and did not know it. And my whole life will be spent, unless some dogma takes care of it, wearing myself out trying to find it: but at our age such beautiful chances are not offered twice! . . . Could I ever believe in nothing? All I need is belief.[47]

This is a very different Ghéon from the exuberant, witty, happy-go-lucky creature we had come to know in his earlier letters to Gide: the term 'physical curse' ('malédiction physique') is particularly shocking. However, he soon recovered his spirits – and concerned himself less with his soul; it was to take another ten years before he finally did take the road to Rome.

As usual, in the summer, Cuverville was full of guests: 'Twelve at table! The Charles Gides, the Drouins, the Albert Démarests . . .' When he could, Gide retired to the loft and worked on what was to become *La Porte étroite*. By late August, he had written about fifty pages of it. Jacques Copeau, his wife and two young daughters were invited to Cuverville for the first time – and stayed for three weeks. Copeau had first come to Gide's notice in 1902, when *L'Ermitage* received some pages on *L'Immoraliste* from an unknown young Frenchman living in Denmark. Gide asked Ducoté not to publish them since they were altogether too laudatory to appear in a review so closely associated with his name. However, more work was forthcoming from Copeau and *L'Ermitage* published some reminiscences of a childhood spent in the rue du Faubourg Saint-Denis. His love of the theatre manifested when he was still a pupil at the Lycée Condorcet. At seventeen, a play of his performed before former pupils of the school received an approving mention from Francisque Sarcey, the eminent critic of *Le Temps*. At twenty-two he married a Danish girl. Soon afterwards, his wife's father died and the young couple went to Denmark where they stayed a year. In July 1902, on a beach in Sweden, Copeau read *L'Immoraliste* and was overcome with enthusiasm – he had already devoured *Les Nourritures terrestres*, *Le Voyage d'Urien* and *Paludes*. In 1903, he returned to France to run the family business, a 'buckles and hooks' factory in the Ardennes. When that failed, he came back to Paris to make a living as a writer. He got a job in an art gallery and

wrote reviews for *Le Théâtre*. He continued to write adulatory letters to
Gide. When Gide and Remy de Gourmont took over the running of
L'Ermitage in December 1904, Copeau was put in charge of the theatre
section. He was then twenty-five, but looked ten years older. At first Gide
was on his guard: 'The gentleness of his voice is sometimes disturbing; he
would be naturally charming, if he did not at times try too hard to charm.'[48]
Madeleine, too, had shown some reticence towards Copeau's easy charm,
but was quite won over by his Danish (Protestant) wife, Agnès, and their
two daughters. Gide and Copeau had long conversations together, but Gide
felt that a certain embarrassment had set in by the end of the stay: 'Perhaps
I began to suffer a little from not daring to say more to him.' However,
when they met up again in Paris, a few days later, Gide confessed all: his
homosexuality, his experiences in North Africa and in Paris, even, finally,
the Maurice Schlumberger affair. Copeau was overcome. He idolized Gide,
but was quite unprepared for *that*: it was all so beyond anything that he
had encountered in his own life. However, he betrayed not the slightest
disapproval: he was all sympathy, indeed, fascination.

Gide's stay at Cuverville was broken by the usual brief visits to Paris and
by a longer stay at Les Sources in September for the wedding of Jeanne
Gide, Charles Gide's daughter and Paul's sister. Meanwhile, Ghéon escaped
from his medical labours in Bray for his annual holiday on the Channel
coast. He had fully recovered from the Maurice affair and was soon regaling
Gide about 'extraordinary Dinard, the even more extraordinary Saint-
Malo today. Five adventures in six hours.' At Saint-Malo, he drags himself
away from 'a swarm of kids' and goes up on to the rocks alone. There he
meets up with a lad of 'fourteen-and-a-half, very proud that I thought
he was sixteen'. After a delightful walk around the ramparts, they go to a
hollow overlooking Chateaubriand's watery grave: 'O great man! And
there, in a deep excavation, like a bed, I half undressed him. He fucks badly
[*il baise mal*], but is quite charming.' He thinks of going back to Dinard for
dinner, but in front of the Saint-Malo cafés there is such 'a crowd of kids'
that he decides to stay, eat there and then 'prowl' around. He talks to a
group of youths. He asks one of them what he does for a living: '"I fuck
gentlemen's arses" [*Je b . . . les q . . . des "Monsieurs"*] Axiom: all Saint-Malo
is willing [tout Saint-Malo marche]. After a few vague caresses, he brings
me an older lad, whom I feel up on the sea-wall.' Ghéon soon leaves him
for a fifteen-year-old, with whom he ends up on the ramparts 'opposite the
same Chateaubriand'. Ghéon goes on to Audierne, on the Atlantic coast,
where a new *embarras de richesses* is on offer. 'But Audierne!!! The best

evenings in Tunis, etc., etc. And what is more, with *satisfaction* . . . Thirty, fifty kids at the station, all as handsome as each other, all fishermen, all *willing!*[49]

Ghéon's letter from Brittany aroused a 'frightful fever' in poor Gide. 'If only an hour's walk from here could take me to Douarnenez or Dinard, instead of Les Loges and Fongueusemare,' he lamented.[50] However, by late October, during a visit to Paris, Gide had had sex with a youth he had picked up and been left with what he thought might be a venereal disease: 'What drove me to that act? A mystery. Tiredness, boredom, the very weakness of my desire and the need to stimulate it . . . When you catch the pox it's always stupidly.' He then gives Dr Vangeon a detailed description of the symptoms adding, 'N.B. The contact only lasted a moment.'[51] Gide's fears were evidently unfounded.

On 30 November, at the house of Arthur Fontaine, a friend of Jammes, Gide read Jammes' latest poem, 'L'Eglise habillée de feuilles'. Present there was Paul Claudel, whom Gide had not seen since 1900, when, persuaded by the Benedictine authorities that he did not have a vocation to the priesthood, he returned to his consular post in China. The monks' percipience was soon borne out. 'Ysé', Rosalie Vetch, a woman of Polish birth whom Claudel had met in October 1899, her husband and children joined the ship that was taking him back to Fuchow. Claudel and Ysé fell hopelessly in love; Ysé, together with husband and children, moved into the French consulate. For four years, this Catholic poet and diplomat 'lived in sin', wrote nothing and risked dismissal from his post – his career was saved only by the intervention of his friend Philippe Berthelot, a senior civil servant. Suddenly on 1 August 1904, Ysé decided to leave her lover – apparently to save his faith, his vocation and his career. (A daughter from the liaison was born shortly afterwards.) Claudel returned to France in the spring of 1905. He visited Francis Jammes at his home in Orthez, finding him in deep depression after a three-year love affair. Hitherto only a moderately practising Catholic, Jammes was inspired by Claudel to a new militancy. They took communion together and went on a pilgrimage to Lourdes. Listening to Gide reading Jammes' poem that evening, Claudel assumed that Gide had acquired a new sympathy for Catholicism and immediately conceived the notion of converting him before his twelve-month furlough was up in the following spring. Gide was fascinated by Claudel's apparent certainty on all matters, so different from his own searching equivocation; but, as he confided afterwards to his *Journal*, he reacted rather unfavourably to Claudel the man: 'As a young man, he looked like a nail,' he wrote, 'now he looks like a sledge-hammer.' When he is discussing something, he 'maintains a hostile tone even when you share his opinion'.[52] A few days later, Claudel came to lunch with Gide and Madeleine. Gide confesses that he did not even try to argue with him and, after the meal, when Claudel spoke 'of God, of Catholicism, of his faith, of his happiness', Gide expressed understanding of his position. Claudel attacked at once: 'But, Gide, why don't you become converted, then?' 'He talks unremittingly; others' thoughts do not stop his for a moment . . . In order to talk with him, to try to talk, you have to interrupt him. He waits politely until you have finished your sentence, then resumes where he had left off, at the very word, as if you had said nothing . . . On leaving, he left me the address of his confessor.'[53]

In January 1906, Claudel left Paris for Lyon, where he had arranged to marry an architect's daughter. The couple left for China on 1 April: having tasted the disruptive power of Eros, Claudel had opted for a marriage of convenience. He had succeeded in one of the aims he had set himself; he had to admit defeat in the other, Gide's conversion. It would, he admitted, have been 'ungracious to ask you to do at once what it has taken me four years to resolve – it is a sort of little death.'[54] Claudel could bide his time: meanwhile, he left Gide with a hand-written 'Summary of all Christian doctrine' some few pages long and continued to bombard him with letters. 'Claudel is blowing on me a sort of religious typhoon that is shaking me from top to bottom, but I find it more exhausting than convincing.'[55]

'Another year! And what a year!' Gide wrote to Ghéon on 31 December 1905. In art, it had been a particularly barren year; in life, he had reached new heights and new depths. The new year, he hoped, would be a new beginning, symbolized by the long-anticipated move to the Villa Montmorency. Sitting in the unfinished house in May, he had written: 'I expect this house to release my ability to work . . . All my hopes dwell here already.'[56] He had come to hate the apartment in the boulevard Raspail. 'I cannot concentrate here; I am defenceless here against everything and everyone; I can hear the slightest noise from the street or from inside the building.'[57]

On 18 January, with Jean Schlumberger, Gide left Paris to attend the final rehearsals of the German version of *Le Roi Candaule* at the Vienna Volkstheater. Gide was particularly impressed by 'the splendour and ingenuity' of the production. He not only attended some ten days of rehearsals, but directed the actors. The first night, on 27 January, was a triumph and an extremely nervous author was summoned several times to take curtain calls.

Finally, on 17 February 1906, the Gides moved into an as yet unfinished Villa Montmorency. The architect, Louis Bonnier, was well known for his rather grandiose, 1900s-style public buildings. Once Bonnier had set to work, Gide was, in a sense, lost: the building took on a character quite alien to its owner – and cost him a fortune. Gide wanted a 'large' house, at least by Paris standards, not to impress, but to accommodate others, one where he could take himself off to some small, quiet room – as he used to do at La Roque and now did at Cuverville – and leave others to their own devices. What he got was a rather pompous, showy building that seemed to begin and end at the enormous stone entrance-hall, cold and unwelcoming, for which Gide commissioned three statues from that most fashionable sculptor of the day, Aristide Maillol. (In the event, the commission did not materialize. Instead Gide bought two other works by Maillol.) At the top of the impressive staircase was hung *Hommage à Cezanne*, a recent work by Maurice Denis. The hall was ill-lit by porthole-windows placed high up in the façade; the kitchen was ill-equipped, the bedrooms small and, in the absence of central heating, impossible to heat adequately in winter. Madeleine never liked the house, the servants hated it and Gide, always susceptible to cold, took to wearing two pullovers, a woollen bonnet and mittens. Once his initial enthusiasm had worn off, he tended to avoid it altogether during the winter months and, at other times, often lived there alone, without a servant.

For Gide, 1905 had been a year of creative drought, but one in which his personal life reached unusual intensity. 1906 was, if anything, to prove even more barren creatively and brought his personal life to new depths of misery and despair. He worked, intermittently, on *La Porte étroite*; he took notes and collected press cuttings for what was already called *Les Caves du Vatican* and had characters called Lafcadio and Burailloul (later Baraglioul). He went to the theatre: he sat in Maeterlinck's box at the first night of his *Mort de Tintagiles*, with Mary Garden opposite and Eleonora Duse to the right; he saw Antoine's productions of *The Wild Duck* and *Julius Caesar*. He went to concerts: Monteverdi's *Orfeo*, given by the Scola Cantorum, and Palestrina's *Missa Papae Marcelli*, sung by the choir of Saint-Gervais in the Sorbonne chapel. Madeleine did not accompany him on any of these outings, though she was often at Cuverville when he was in Paris. More and more, they were to lead their own lives. Each had an abiding sense of being, at some profound level, anchored to the other, yet there were whole areas of Gide's life that he had no wish to share with her – or that she did not wish to share. When in Paris, he continued to haunt '*boulevards*' and '*piscines*', though perhaps less frequently than before. Ghéon had less and less time for such diversions, but, by now, Gide had a new *compagnon de route* in Jean Schlumberger. In a letter to Ghéon Gide recounts an incident in the 'rue O.'. Apparently, one of the attendants ('Jean, the varlet'), 'dressed (of course)', and 'young S. (?), naked' had an argument that developed into a fight. 'In four punches, Jean, his nose broken, was put *hors de combat*, or almost . . . Very Apache. But I'm afraid that that might put an end to the games.' Gide and Schlumberger managed, with great difficulty, to dissuade the owners from calling the police.[58]

Gide knew that he had to finish *La Porte étroite* before he could go on to write *Les Caves du Vatican*; he knew, too, that *La Porte étroite* was about his past, about Madeleine, about a world that retreated further into the past with each year that it remained unfinished. He knew, too, that *Les Caves du Vatican* represented his future, the new 'emancipated' Gide, but, as a work, he could but dimly conceive of it, let alone write it.

'Very depressed for 8 or 10 days,' he wrote to Ghéon. 'Certainly there is something inside me that is not functioning properly – and which is preventing the brain from functioning as it would like.'[59] Over the next few days, he wrote in his journal: 'I must make up my mind and consult a specialist . . . What have I done up till now compared with what I might have done? For the past four years I have been floundering about and getting nowhere . . . It's frightful how I have aged recently. Certainly something is not right inside me.'[60] He was suffering badly from insomnia. Then, the *Journal* breaks off for three weeks with two, very brief entries:

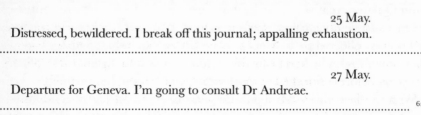

25 May.
Distressed, bewildered. I break off this journal; appalling exhaustion.
....

27 May.
Departure for Geneva. I'm going to consult Dr Andreae.
.... [61]

Those dots are Gide's, an indication of a rare failure to express himself in words: they have their own eloquence. Gide had last seen Andreae in July 1894. This time the good doctor's common-sensical, worldly-wise diagnosis, untrammelled by any theoretical notions as to 'treatment', had the same beneficial results as before. The patient was not suffering from a brain tumour, nor from any identifiable nervous disorder. As before, he was simply the victim of his unstable artistic temperament. The insomnia? Nothing to worry about: read a book or play the piano. This time, Gide told Andreae about his homosexuality. Again the doctor's good sense prevailed: it would not make life any easier, but would not lead to impotence or insanity. Perhaps he should simply take more care whom he consorted with. Andreae prescribed a few weeks' 'hydrotherapy', followed by a holiday in the mountains. This was the placebo: at least the treatment could do the patient no harm and might well 'calm him down'. The real 'cure' lay in the doctor lending his medical authority to what was really no more than a few kind, understanding, reassuring words. Gide set off for Schönbrunn, near Zug, in Switzerland, for his 'water cure'. At the end of the fifth week, Gide was joined by Madeleine. They then went on to Adelboden, in the Bernese Alps, for a couple of weeks.

By mid-August, the Gides were back in Cuverville. André was still suffering from insomnia and depression. After a little more than a week, he was off on his travels again: this time to Brittany, alone. He spent a week or so at Perros-Guirec, where he enjoyed the agreeable company of Maurice Denis, Paul Sérusier, and 'half-a-dozen other rather curious individuals'.[62] He then went on to Angers, where he called on Albert Démarest, who was suffering from what was to be a terminal illness, before moving on to a beach at La Baule, where he spent 'four or five delicious days' with cousins he hardly knew. Back in Cuverville on 15 September, he was met by autumn winds and rain. There he found the Drouins, who were about to leave Bordeaux for an apartment in the rue Jasmin, a short walk away from the Villa Montmorency: Marcel had been appointed to posts at the nearby Lycée Janson-de-Sailly and at the Lycée Saint-Louis, in the Latin Quarter.

On 18 November Albert Démarest died, aged fifty-eight. 'He was my first friend,' Gide wrote to Valéry.[63] The Gides took in his confused widow, the woman whom he had been able to marry only after his mother's death, five years before, until she felt more capable of leading her own life.

With the December number, *L'Ermitage* came to an end. It had lasted for sixteen years, from its foundation by Henri Mazel in 1890. During the last eleven of these years, Edouard Ducoté had provided the funds that kept it going; by the end of 1906, he had decided that he could no longer afford to do so. Its subscribers and most of its contributors were transferred to the Belgian review *Antée*.

The Gides spent New Year's Eve at Charles Gide's: there André learnt from his niece Jeanne that he was being considered for inclusion in the honours list. Apparently, his friend André Fontaine was a friend of the *chef de cabinet* of Aristide Briand, the (then) Socialist, anti-clerical, Minister of Education and Worship. As it happened, Gide had a particular dislike of the *chef de cabinet* in question. Next day, he wasted four hours drafting repeated versions of a letter of refusal, which he then threw in the fire. Presumably, Gide's views on the matter eventually reached the appropriate quarters, through Paul Gide, Fontaine, etc., and nothing came of it.

January brought another brush with the powers that be. For the first time, he attended the inauguration of a new member of the Académie Française. The recipient of the honour, Maurice Barrès, 'wore the frightful costume as elegantly as possible'. 'How I suffered from his cowardice, the flattery, the homage paid to the opinions of his audience . . . Emerged quite demoralized . . .'[64]

A German production of *Candaule* was being prepared in Berlin and Gide was invited to attend discussions and rehearsals. He could not make up his mind whether to go or not: in the end, he was persuaded to do so by Maurice Denis, who went with him. Things were at a much earlier stage than he had been led to believe: rehearsals had not even begun. Indeed the production was not to take place until a year later. Gide and Denis spent much of their ten days in Berlin visiting museums. In the *Journal*, Gide notes particularly an 'excessively youthful' Donatello *John the Baptist*, 'of a mannerism without mawkishness, strangely long neck, frail torso' and a very poorly painted Pollaiuolo *David*: 'The folds of his cloak, the corners of which are stuck into the belt, raised almost immodestly.'[65]

While in Berlin, Gide first conceived of a short prose piece that was to become *Le Retour de l'Enfant prodigue*. Two days after returning to Paris he wrote the first two pages (the story amounts to sixteen in the Pléiade Edition). The writing took two weeks. Another week or so was spent in revision. This rapidity of conception and execution ran quite counter to Gide's normal practice: 'I was afraid that, if I brooded over it any longer, I would see the subject proliferate and become distorted; anyway, I was sick of not writing anything and all the other subjects I am carrying inside me presented too many difficulties to be tackled at once.'[66] What was it about *Le Retour* that so fired Gide's creative imagination? At first it seems, with its choice of biblical subject, like a throw-back to an earlier Gide. Was it not just such a habit of looking back, of coming to terms with his past that, in *La Porte étroite*, had caused him so many months of agonizing inactivity? It was certainly not a breakthrough into a new subject and a new form.

As the title suggests, Gide's tale begins with the return of the Prodigal Son, almost where the parable as recounted in the Luke Gospel ends. Like the biblical younger son, who 'wasted his substance with riotous living', Gide's demands his father's wealth and leaves home. But Gide's Prodigal does not simply return home when he is destitute: he is 'tired of his caprice', 'disenchanted with himself' – and with the *dénuement*, that very Gidean notion again, that he sought. The suggestion is that he acquired his paternal portion, not to indulge himself, but in order to strip himself bare in a reaction against the suffocating luxury of his father's house. He came home when he had outworn that particular intellectual caprice and learned what *involuntary* destitution was really like. After the two introductory pages, the work consists entirely of four dialogues between the Prodigal and, in turn, his father, older brother, mother and younger brother. (The last two characters are Gide's invention.) To the father's question as to why his son left him, the Prodigal replies (in Ménalque-like, pantheistic terms): 'Did I really leave you? Father! Are you not everywhere? I never ceased to love you.' The father then speaks of the House that had been built to shelter his sons. Why did he wish to leave it? 'Because the House was like a prison to me. The House is not You, Father . . . You built the whole earth, the House and what is not the House.' Clearly, 'Father' stands here for God. When the eldest son asks the Prodigal why he left home, he replies: 'I imagined other cultures, other lands . . . roads that had not been trod . . . I imagined inside me the new being that I felt rushing along them.' When the mother asks the same question he replies: 'Nothing . . . myself.' 'Did you think that you would be happy far from us, then?' 'I was not seeking happiness.' 'What were you seeking?' 'I was seeking . . . who I was.' At first, the youngest son is suspicious of the Prodigal, believing him to be in league with the tyrannical eldest son – after all, he has returned home. He then confesses that he, too, intends to leave home. 'You gave up being the man you wanted to be,' he adds contemptuously, but tries to persuade him to go away with him. The Prodigal declines, but wishes him well: 'You take away with you all my hopes. Be strong; forget us; forget me. May you not come back.'[67]

The publication of *Le Retour de l'Enfant prodigue* was as swift as its composition. It appeared in May in the review *Vers et Prose*. (It was published separately in a *de luxe* edition of 100 copies, in 1909, by the Bibliothèque de l'Occident. In 1912, it was republished by the *NRF*, 'preceded by five other Treatises'.) Not surprisingly, the strongest reaction came from Gide's Catholic friends – at greatest length and with greatest vehemence from Francis Jammes.[68] What shocked Jammes most were the Prodigal's words to his young brother: 'Be strong; forget us, forget me. May you not come back.' It meant, of course, that Gide had, at the very end of his tale, reversed the biblical message. The Prodigal may have grown out of his youthful rebellion, tried to persuade his brother not to leave, but, in the end, his heart is with him and he knows that he himself has failed in what he has set out to do. As ever, Gide can see both sides of the argument. In his preface to the work, he even speaks of 'the double aspiration that animates me' and adds: 'I do not seek to prove the victory over me of any God – nor my victory.' Talking to Claudel about his Catholic faith, Gide could give the impression, such was his sympathy, that he was nearly there. Hence the bitterness felt by Jammes – and by Claudel – that Gide had, in some way, duped them. The only way Gide could quietly put his bifocal case was in a work of fiction, stemming directly from and commenting on the Gospels. *Viva voce* Claudel was incapable of listening to him. In the middle of writing *Le Retour*, Gide received another letter from Claudel, written in Tientsin on Christmas Day! Gide comments in the *Journal*: 'This morning, letter from Claudel . . . full of sacred anger, against the period, against Gourmont, Rousseau, Kant, Renan . . .' Such anger, says Gide, is 'as painful to my mind as the barking of a dog in my ear. I cannot bear it.'[69] It is now clear that the immediate source of the tale was the tension set up in Gide by the continual attentions of Claudel, Jammes, etc.

Le Retour de l'Enfant prodigue is a minor masterpiece. It displays all the classical virtues to which Gide still aspired: a beautiful symmetry of form (it begins with a return and ends with a departure), constriction of mode (here the consistent use of the dialogue form) and the often remarked on purity of its language. The speed with which it was conceived and executed is betrayed only in its confident, unhesitant flow. Not surprisingly it also revived Gide's spirits and gave him a new determination and confidence to finish *La Porte étroite* and move on to other things. He wrote the first scene (some six pages) of *Ajax*, a play that he had been thinking about for two years, but which was to remain unfinished. April brought him low for two weeks with typhlitis, though he admitted to Dr Vangeon, who came all the way from Bray to visit him, that he had suffered more from the spartan diet imposed upon him by his local doctor than from the illness itself. This he soon made up for at a lunch at the Tour d'Argent, with the Van Rysselberghes, Harry Kessler and Rodin. But Gide was no gourmet and the *Journal* passes over the meal itself in silence. On 21 May, with Ghéon, he went to Richard Strauss's *Salomé* and hated it: 'Execrable romantic music, his orchestral rhetoric enough to make one like Bellini . . . indiscretion in the means and monotony in the effects, wearying over-emphasis; ceaseless mobilization of all resources.' Ghéon repeats the 'perhaps apocryphal' words of Frau Strauss, who considered that the Paris audience had not applauded her husband enough: 'Well, it's time we came back here – with our bayonets.' The response of this German-loving, quite unchauvinistic Frenchman is untypically fierce: 'Better to condemn the work in its entirety, and wait for the bayonets, because that art really is *the enemy*.'[70] But, in truth, it is really the response of a lover of the classical French virtues of clarity, restraint, etc., who hated what he saw as romantic obscurity and excess, whether it came from Victor Hugo, Wagner – or Strauss. He would certainly have preferred the composer's *Der Rosenkavalier* of four years later.

June brought André and Madeleine to Cuverville for the summer. Gide's patience with Bonnier, the architect of the Villa Montmorency, and with the house itself had reached its limit. 'There are days when I would happily have packed my bags and abandoned unfinished this house, which has consumed so much time, money, patience and enthusiasm . . . I scarcely know how I shall pay for it – or how, after paying for it, we shall live.'[71] A week later, he was back at work on *La Porte étroite*, beginning 'this wretched book' again for the fourth time.

In July, Gide spent three days with Eugène Rouart, at Bagnols-de-Grenade, in south-western France. There, he tells André Ruyters, he led 'a frenzied, ardent, carefree' existence. There, too, Rouart introduced him to François-Paul Alibert, a local poet. (Later, the two discovered their shared sexual tastes and a correspondence began that ended only with Gide's death.) On 12 August, Gide left Cuverville again – this time for a house that Copeau had rented in Saint Brelade's Bay, Jersey. On the way, he met up with Jean Schlumberger and the two travelled the rest of the journey together: neither was joined by his wife. Already in Jersey were the Van Rysselberghes and they were joined later by Ghéon. There Gide posed for the portrait that Théo Van Rysselberghe was painting of him and assiduously bathed three times a day. In the end, he enjoyed himself so much that he spent over three weeks there.

On 8 October, the Gides attended Francis Jammes' wedding at Bucy-le-Long, in the Aisne. A few weeks later, they had to go to Pau, to the funeral of Valentine Rondeaux's second husband, Marcel Gilbert: three daughters had been born to their all-too-brief marriage. After the funeral, Gide went back to Orthez, with Jammes, then on to see Rouart at Bagnols, where he rediscovered 'my restlessness, my curiosity, my transports of delight'.[72]

In November, André Ruyters came to stay for a week at the Villa Montmorency. As a result of complicated machinations involving Gide,

Rouart and others, he had obtained a post with the Banque de l'Indochine. After a probationary period at the Paris headquarters he would be sent out to one of the bank's Far-Eastern branches – for Ruyters, the real attraction of the move. (In the event, he remained in Paris for another two years before leaving for Ethiopia, in the employ of another bank.) 'We shall live *en garçons*,' Gide wrote to Ruyters, 'for my wife is still at Cuverville.'[73] One evening, the two of them joined Ghéon, Copeau and Jean Schlumberger in 'a small room at the back of a very vulgar café near the boulevards'. After some hesitation, Ghéon took out a manuscript and 'despite the din nearby' read what were the first 100 pages of *L'Adolescent*, the 'daring' novel that he had begun at the same time as Gide had started work on *L'Immoraliste*.[74] It tells the story of Guillaume Arnoult, a character based in many ways on Gide (they have the same initials, reversed) and, perhaps even more so, on the hero of *L'Immoraliste*. Guillaume falls in love with a twelve-year-old boy, Marcel, who has a scar on his face. He also becomes attached to the boy's older sister, Cécile. He feels no sexual desire for her, having learnt to dissociate 'reproduction, pleasure and love', but they marry – and Marcel comes to live with them. After a few months, Cécile dies, thus leaving Guillaume and Marcel a *ménage à deux*. Some days later, the same group, minus Copeau, gathered at the Villa Montmorency, where Gide was persuaded to read the first two chapters of *La Porte étroite*. It did not go down well, especially with Ghéon, and Gide felt as dissatisfied with it as his two friends. 'What is making the writing of this book so hard for me is just what made it so hard for them to listen to it: it remains an anachronism beside what we are thinking, feeling and wanting today. Nevertheless, I cannot not write it.'[75] This 'rather bruising trial' was hardly likely to spur him on. He was only too well aware that what Ghéon was doing in *L'Adolescent* was precisely what he himself thought, felt and wanted.

Madeleine returned from Cuverville and life assumed a more regular course. Gide acquired his first typewriter – and, in the person of Pierre de Lanux, the grandson of his old piano teacher, his first secretary: 'Hence discipline, zeal and regularity in work, general raising of moral standards, etc.'[76] But Gide was, if anything, in a worse mental state: 'Again my mind is disjointed, dislocated; my flesh weak, restless, hopelessly distracted. My whole organism is like those over resonant houses, in which, from the attic, you can hear everything that is going on in the kitchen and cellar.'[77]

On 9 January, the Berlin production of *König Candaules* finally opened at the Kleine Theater. The response of the first-night audience was divided, but, the following day, the reviews were all highly critical, comparing Gide's work adversely with Hebbel's on the same subject. There was no second performance.

Three of Gide's oldest friends were now living in Paris. Since the new school year, Marcel Drouin had taken a house in the nearby rue Jasmin. In November, Ruyters left Brussels and now moved into an apartment in the rue du Ranelagh, also quite near Gide. Then Gide learnt that Eugène Rouart had been appointed *chef de cabinet* to Jean Cruppi, the Minister of Commerce in the new Clemenceau government. The future team of the *NRF* was gradually falling into place (though Rouart was never actually a member of the editorial board). On 25 January, Gide attended a dinner organized by Jean Royère, poet and editor of the 'neo-Mallarméan' review, *La Phalange*. Reluctant at first, on the grounds of literary incompatibility, Gide was persuaded to go by Vielé-Griffin. Unlike *L'Ermitage* and *Antée*, which had both disappeared, *La Phalange* was on a sound financial footing. Vielé-Griffin was trying to effect another literary merger and thus find another outlet for his friends' articles. Griffin's ruse worked and *La Phalange* provided a temporary home for Gide and his friends, before the founding of the *Nouvelle Revue Française* later in the year.

In February, Gide spent a few days in Bray. The manuscript of *L'Adolescent* had meanwhile doubled in size and Ghéon read aloud what he had recently written. On the train back to Paris, Gide was in a high state of excitement: 'Stimulated by the reading, sustained by the Chambertin, I didn't stop writing during the whole of the return journey . . . I sketched the *portrait* of "Lafcadio" in *Les Caves* . . .' What he had just heard from Ghéon's novel was even more what he was thinking and feeling than what he had heard before. So much so that he was impelled, if only temporarily, to return to his own book of the present – and future – rather than the 'anachronistic' *La Porte étroite*. But what had excited Gide even more than what he had heard read was Ghéon's description, just before Gide left, of the next chapter. What Gide really wanted to have written was that. What excited Gide so much about those characters, why he felt so personally involved in them was that they described, transposed, the adventure with Maurice Schlumberger. In a will, dated 24 August 1914, Ghéon entrusted to his friends, Vielé-Griffin, Gide, Drouin, Copeau, Ruyters and Jean Schlumberger, the task of examining his manuscripts – among which he specifically refers to *L'Adolescent* – and, where possible, arranging for their publication. Two years later, however, Ghéon was converted and felt compelled to destroy all that he had written of *L'Adolescent* subsequent to the pages read in the Paris café in November 1907. At the bottom of the last of these pages, he wrote: 'Today, 21 March 1919, the rest of the book has been burned as unworthy and bad. Glory be to God! H. G.'

After a few weeks in Italy, alone, Gide was back in Paris by 24 March. In his absence, the group of which he was the acknowledged head had moved further towards the realization of a new review – Vielé-Griffin's notion of a fusion between *La Phalange* and the old *Ermitage/Antée* having foundered. Meetings were held on at least three evenings, culminating in a 'broader' meeting on 18 March. In the absence of Gide himself, Schlumberger (also in Italy) and Ghéon (finishing the paintings to be submitted to the Salon des Indépendants), the 'Gide' group was represented by Copeau and Drouin. A provisional title, *Ulysse*, Copeau's suggestion, had been agreed, financial backing coming from the members of the editorial committee in proportion to their means. There, for the moment, the matter rested.

Gide spent the spring in Paris, lunching with the German poet Stefan George, buying a Bonnard for 500 francs (£20 or $100 at the time) at Drouot's auction house, inspecting Jeanne Drouin's second newborn, Jacques. He returned to Cuverville but after a couple of weeks took himself off to Trégastel, in Brittany. A few more weeks at Cuverville and he was on his travels again – this time to spend most of July with Rouart at Bagnols-de-Grenade. With mounting excitement he read Bergson's *L'Evolution créatrice*. 'It seems to me,' Gide wrote to Ghéon, 'that he is opening a door through which philosophy, held captive for so long, will be able to escape at last.'[78] (Bergson, now at the Collège de France, was already the major figure in French philosophy and the greatest influence upon it since Nietzsche.) But Gide did not go to Bagnols to read Bergson: he had particularly fond memories of his adventures in that part of the world. Of these, Gide has little to say. However, Ghéon, following in his footsteps three months later, tells us, in his exuberant way, all we need to know. On his return to Bray, he wrote to Gide: 'If I didn't write to you from there, it's because at Bagnols one does not write, one lives . . . Where shall I begin? Everything's so mixed up . . . I still haven't recovered from it.' There is Abel, 'a superb sun-tanned youth, with a delicate smile . . . Rouart is already familiar with him, as you can imagine . . .' Then there is the baker's son from Saint-Caprais: 'Fourteen, very developed, very virile, very tall . . .' He has a talent for painting and arrives, complete with portfolio, to ask Ghéon's opinion of his work. At Ghéon's instigation, he gets a place at the Toulouse Beaux-Arts. A few days later, he travels with Ghéon to Toulouse. 'I take my place next to him, and there, quite shamelessly, as the horse trots along, we take our sensual leave of one another . . .' Of the 'others', Ghéon remarks: 'They certainly remember Monsieur Gide! . . . I'm sending the best wishes of Ferdinand, Jean C., *"l'abricot"* ["the apricot"?], young Hippolyte . . .'[79]

Back at Cuverville, Gide set about planning a great summer gathering of all his friends. The Drouins and the Jean Schlumbergers were there most of the time; Ghéon followed, but Copeau did not join them until the beginning of September. The great gathering turned rather into a succession of visits. One splendid day, Gide, Ghéon, Schlumberger and Copeau were lying on the grass when 'someone', according to Copeau, declared that they should all go away on a trip together. It was decided that they would go to England – at once. Timetables were consulted and, on 8 September, the four of them, together with Suzanne, Jean Schlumberger's wife, sailed from Le Havre for England. After two days exploring London, Ghéon returned to Paris, while the others went on to Oxford. Something of the exuberance, the 'excellent comradeship' of this no longer youthful group of friends shines through a letter that Copeau wrote to Ghéon on his return: 'Never have I felt more tempted by the unknown, more ready for adventure, more carefree. That feeling . . . has still not left me.' In the same letter, Copeau notes that, on the boat back, 'Gide shaved again, in the hope of finding the jocundus stewardus on board.' Apparently, on his own return journey, Ghéon had struck lucky with a young steward who had left him 'quite exhausted'.[80]

The two brief trips to Bagnols and to England had stirred Gide into a new burst of literary activity. Back in Cuverville, he began work on the 'Platonic dialogue' *Corydon*, which had been occupying his thoughts for so long. As the editors of the Gide–Ghéon correspondence point out in their introduction, the second of these two dialogues bears, at several points, a striking resemblance to Ghéon's *L'Adolescent*, which, in turn, of course, derived, behind its fictional disguises, from Gide's own life. The interesting point is that Gide used Ghéon's disguises, rather than the literal truth of his own life. Thus the homosexual Corydon recounts his life: 'I loved the woman who was to become my wife tenderly, but with a quasi-mystical love and, of course, in my inexperience, I scarcely imagined that there was another beautiful way of loving. My fiancée had a brother, younger than she by some years, whom I saw often and who acquired the keenest affection for me.'[81] Similarly, Gide and Ghéon both made use of strikingly similar quotations from Montaigne. The epigraph to *L'Adolescent* begins: 'We call *against nature* what runs counter to custom . . .' While, in the second dialogue of *Corydon*, Gide quotes Montaigne to similar effect: 'The laws of conscience, which we say derive from nature, derive from custom.'[82]

Meanwhile, 'with a yawning of my whole being',[83] Gide returned to *La Porte étroite* for the last time, finishing it on 15 October. The next day, in a symbolic break with the past, he shaved off his moustache. A disapproving Madeleine saw this act in aesthetic, rather than symbolic, terms: 'My poor André! . . . You must see your mistake.'[84] Of all Gide's works, *La Porte étroite* proved to be the most difficult to bring to birth. It began, if a work so imbued with Gidean autobiography may be dated so specifically, in 1891, with a project entitled *L'Essai de bien mourir*, a fictionalized account of the lonely death of Anna Shackleton in 1884. By 1894, this had become *La Mort de Mademoiselle Claire*, but was left unfinished. In 1905, Gide took up the work again, the solitary death of the spinster being transferred from the English governess figure to a new heroine, Alissa. This brought with it a new, but not yet definitive, title, *La Porte étroite*. It comes from Luke, 13:24: 'Efforcez-vous d'entrer par la porte étroite', in the French translation. The English translation opted, not for *The Strait Gate*, but for *Strait is the Gate*. This derives, not from Luke, but from Matthew 7:13–14, a passage also quoted by Gide, as the text of a sermon preached by Pastor Vautier. In the Authorized Version, it reads: 'Enter ye in at the strait gate: for wide is the gate, and broad is the way, that leadeth to destruction and many there be which go in thereat: Because strait is the gate, and narrow is the way, which leadeth unto life, and few there be that find it.' The English title is, I think, an improvement on the original, and the biblical quotation more telling. Incidentally, this was the first of Gide's works to be translated into English – by Dorothy Bussy, months after meeting Gide in 1919. However, it had to wait until 1924 to be published in New York, having met on the way rejections from a number of London publishing houses. One of these, Chatto and Windus, turned it down on the charming grounds that the French of the original was not difficult enough to justify a translation.

Like most of Gide's work up to *Les Caves du Vatican*, *La Porte étroite* is a first-person narration that disavows its fictional character. 'Others might have made a book out of it,' it begins. 'But the story that I relate here consumed all my strength, exhausted my store of virtue in the living. So I shall set down my recollections quite simply, and although they are rather tattered in places I shall not resort to invention to patch them up . . .'[85] All this, of course, is yet another play on the eternal contradiction of truth presented as fiction and fiction telling the truth.

We are back in the Protestant upper-middle-class world of Normandy in the 1880s. The narrator, Jérôme Palissier, had been brought up in Le Havre. When he was eleven, his father died, and he and his mother moved to Paris. With them went Flora Ashburton, an English spinster, his mother's former governess, now her friend. All three spent their summers at Fongueusemare, the country house of Jérôme's Uncle Bucolin. In a fit of imprudent infatuation, Jérôme's uncle had married a beautiful Creole from Martinique. For Jérôme, as we saw in a passage quoted in Chapter 2, Aunt Lucile was an object of fear and fascination. She wore 'gaudy' clothes, despite her sister-in-law's bereavement, took no part in the social life of the household and spent the morning before her dressing-table and the rest of the day reclining more or less *en déshabille* on a sofa in the *salon* or in a hammock in the garden, when she was not having one of her *crises*, her 'attacks'. Jérôme discovered, quite by chance, that she had a lover, with whom, shortly afterwards, she absconded, leaving home, husband, a young son and two daughters. Alissa and Juliette Bucolin were devoted to their father; in reaction against their mother's character and behaviour their puritanical outlook grew more pronounced. Alissa and Jérôme were childhood sweethearts; by the time Jérôme is a student, it is assumed that they are, in some unofficial way, engaged. However, when, in a rather confused way, Jérôme proposes to Alissa, she refuses him with a 'not yet'. Unbeknown to Jérôme, but not to Alissa, Juliette, too, is in love with him.

Jérôme arrives with his old schoolfriend, Abel Vautier, a pastor's son. Abel becomes infatuated with Juliette and urges Jérôme to pursue his suit of Alissa so that all four can be married. However, Alissa persists in refusing Jérôme; Abel learns of Juliette's feelings for his friend and abandons his suit. Meanwhile, Juliette is being courted by Edouard Teissières, an unattractive but well-to-do wine grower. Her relations are advising her to accept his advances. Alissa has already rejected Jérôme in favour of her sister. Juliette, not to be outdone in sacrifice, abandons her love for Jérôme and decides to accept Teissières, though she does not love him. Alissa withdraws ever further into a kind of religious fanaticism, replacing the literature on her bookshelves with sectarian tracts, unnecessarily humiliating herself with manual chores about the house. Letters are exchanged between the two cousins. While pursuing a path of sanctity that would seem to preclude it, Alissa claims to love Jérôme as she has always done. 'Ah! Will you ever know how much I love you? . . . Till the end I shall be your Alissa,' she ends one letter. Their last meeting, at Fongueusemare, shows how far Alissa has moved away from her former self. She accuses Jérôme of being in love with a ghost. Jérôme replies that the 'ghost' is not an illusion on his part: 'Alissa, you are the woman I loved ... What have you made yourself become?' Jérôme leaves, 'full of a vague hatred for what I still called virtue'.

Three years later, Jérôme calls, unannounced, at Fongueusemare: he finds Alissa pale and thin, 'extraordinarily changed'. She offers him a small cross, decorated with amethysts, asking him to give it to his daughter – when he marries and has children. Perhaps he will call the girl after her. Jérôme refuses the cross and leaves. A month later, he learns from Juliette that Alissa has died in a Paris nursing home. Ten years later, still unmarried, Jérôme calls on a Juliette settled comfortably into marriage and motherhood, and looking rather middle-aged. She has another child, a girl, whom she has called Alissa, after her sister.

The parallels, general and particular, between *La Porte étroite* and Gide's early life are evident. The members of the related Protestant families, the Palissiers and Bucolins, correspond precisely to the Gides and Rondeauxs. In the case of such minor characters as, say, Flora Ashburton (Anna Shackleton) and Aunt Bucolin (Aunt Mathilde Rondeaux), the identification is total. More interesting, and much more complicated, are the parallels between Jérôme and Gide, Alissa and Madeleine. On this question, Gide seems none too sure himself. Comparing and contrasting *La Porte étroite* with *L'Immoraliste* in his radio interviews, Jean Amrouche suggests that it is Alissa who corresponds to Michel in *L'Immoraliste*. 'Si vous voulez . . .' Gide responds.[86] Justin O'Brien goes further, surely too far. Citing Flaubert and *Madame Bovary*, he declares: 'Obviously Alissa is not Madeleine, because she actually *is* André Gide.'[87] Alissa is André Gide only in the sense that he had no need to go outside himself to find the kind of moral absolutism to which Alissa became drawn: it came from the same puritanical world that he and Madeleine shared. The difference was that André Gide escaped from it. Madeleine did not travel as far down that road as Alissa; she remained, at least for some ten years longer, closer to the younger Alissa than to the later one – after all, she did marry André Gide. Of course, one might argue that an unconsummated marriage to André Gide was enough to drive any such woman into moral disapproval, retreat and rejection. On the other hand, would an ageing Madeleine, spinster, or married to another man, whom she probably could not have loved, have been in any very different state? Such questions are better asked than answered. As well as being a literary work, in the public domain, almost perfect within its own terms and limitations, *La Porte étroite* was also part of a long meditation on

Gide's own personal development and his relationship to Madeleine. In that sense, it is a warning *post factum* to Madeleine of what might have happened if she had rejected him and pursued the path on which she might well have embarked. It was also, in a sense, a prescient insight not only into what Madeleine might have become, but into what she did become. In *La Jeunesse d'André Gide*, Jean Delay relates how he asked Gide whether Madeleine was the model for Alissa. '"No," he, replied, "for a long time I thought she was Alissa, but she wasn't." Then, after a brief pause, he added: "but she became her".'[88] Again, in *Et nunc manet in te*, Gide notes how he had 'anticipated, by a sort of foresight, what reality was later to confirm':

The truth is, she thought I no longer loved her. So what was the point of dressing to please me? . . . What did culture, music, poetry matter any more? She deserted the pathways where we might meet and plunged into devotion. If I were jealous of God, I was quite free to join her on that religious terrain where alone she was still willing to communicate with me.[89]

In *La Porte étroite*, Gide extrapolated a possible alternative future for Madeleine and himself, a future that turned out not to be, after all, an alternative one, but, in a sense, a delayed one. She had protested at André's indiscretion at revealing the secrets of their relationship in *Les Cahiers d'André Walter*: what must she have thought of *La Porte étroite*? Her whole life was there: her appalling mother, whose memory she had tried hard to erase; her beloved father, whose death she could hardly bear to remember; a sister who had also been in love with their cousin; Cuverville, with its 'score of large windows' facing out over the garden, also described in detail, even to the 'secret gate' that led out to the little coppice, with the bench on which they had so often sat together; then, above all, the early travails of their religious aspirations and her love for André. Remarking, in 1928, that he had written *Les Faux-Monnayeurs* to win Marc Allégret's 'attention' and 'esteem', Gide adds that he had written all his previous books 'under the influence' of Madeleine, 'or in the vain hope of convincing her'.[90]

Yet 'meaning', in any form approaching rational argument, is as difficult to extract from this work as from any other of Gide's. Such 'meaning' certainly lies at the origin of the work, but it is something that Gide does his best to occlude, with truly classical reticence and subtlety. Indeed, if that 'meaning' is to be understood in any authentically Gidean way it must be taken with that of its predecessor: 'That book is the twin of *L'Immoraliste* . . . The two subjects grew up concurrently in my mind, the excess of one finding a secret permission in the excess of the other and together achieving a balance.'[91] Yet precisely because of the rule of excess in each, readers have tended to prefer one very much over the other: a reaction that began with Gide's first readers, with Ghéon and Jammes heading the opposed parties. Such reactions stem from a facile identification with the hero or heroine, missing Gide's critical, even ironic view of the excesses indulged in by Michel and Alissa. 'If the author had been able to produce them simultaneously, as they had been conceived,' Gide wrote in *Feuillets*, 'he would no doubt have avoided a rather serious misunderstanding'[92] – the belief that, because *La Porte étroite* was published seven years after *L'Immoraliste*, it represented a profound shift on the part of the author, rather than a change of subject. What had occurred in the intervening years was a slow distancing from the subject of the work, with a corresponding increase in mastery over it. But Gide, being Gide, was still close enough to that subject to be able to identify with it, at least during the writing, and to persuade some readers of his approval of Alissa's moral choices. Hence Gide's embarrassment at Jammes' approval of the first instalment (about a third of the whole) published in the *NRF*. 'I am rather astonished at the extraordinarily favourable reception of the 1st part of my book, for I wrote those first chapters only to make possible what follows, which alone is what matters to me.'[93]

In other words, don't get too carried away by Jérôme's disgusted reaction to his Aunt Lucile, or, like him, see her as the villain of the piece – she is another Immoralist; wait and see what happens to her daughter's truly destructive moralism. Gide was sympathetic towards Michel's immoralism; he was also critical of it and demonstrated its destructive, ultimately futile power. Alissa's rejection of Jérôme, of life, as inextricably connected with evil, in favour of a 'better' life, leads not to a life lived more abundantly in the spirit, but to emptiness, faltering faith and a lonely death. Michel's decision to live life more abundantly here below, ignoring the claims of society, family and morality, is the mirror image of Alissa's and, as such, just as self-destructive.

With that 'anachronism', *La Porte étroite*, despatched, together with his equally anachronistic, though increasingly Nietzschean moustache, Gide felt that he could turn, bare-faced and undisguised, to the new century.

The 'New' Gide and the Founding of the NRF: Isabelle *and* Les Caves du Vatican

(OCTOBER 1908 – AUGUST 1914)

'I cannot wait to write something different! It will be ten years before I dare to use such words as *amour, coeur, âme*, etc . . . again.'[1] The 'something different' would take a fictional form, *Les Caves du Vatican*, and a frankly didactic one, *Corydon*. Meanwhile, Gide's friends had been making progress in their plans for a new literary review. During this crucial period, Gide had been at Cuverville, utterly absorbed in the completion of *La Porte étroite*; Jean Schlumberger's time and energy had been taken up with family affairs, one grandfather taking it into his head to marry a young woman of thirty, the other dying at Val-Richer; Ghéon was fully occupied with his medical (and painterly) activities; Drouin, Rouart and Ruyters, though all now in Paris, had full-time jobs. This left the indefatigable Jacques Copeau and Eugène Montfort, with his indispensable experience of managing such an enterprise. Various titles had been proposed and rejected. Copeau and Montfort agreed on the rather inept, vaguely nationalistic-sounding *Nouvelle Revue française* – the '*nouvelle*' being added to distinguish it from a *Revue française* of the 1830s. The title, clearly Montfort's work, spoke of a renewed pride in the nation's traditions and achievements, and clearly marked it off from the *Revue Blanche*, now dominated by Dreyfusards of a strongly political, leftist inclination. To the title, Copeau added the words '*de littérature et de critique*'. The final editorial committee (and shareholders) now consisted of Gide, Montfort, Charles-Louis Philippe, Copeau, Paul Léautaud, Marc Lafargue, Jean Schlumberger, Michel Arnauld (Drouin), Ruyters, Louis Dumont-Wilden (a Belgian poet and art critic) and Louis Rouart, Eugène's brother. The promotional leaflet spoke of the new review as the rallying-point of 'the generation that, in literary chronology, followed immediately after Symbolism', in particular those writers who 'began together some ten or eleven years ago'.

The first number was planned for 1 November. Last-minute hitches meant a postponement to 15 November. It looked, to the attentive and interested eye, exactly what it was, an amalgamation of the old, Gide-led *Ermitage* team and Montfort's friends from *Les Marges*. Neither side was happy. Gide himself had taken little part in the decision-making process: when, after finishing *La Porte étroite*, he finally arrived in Paris, he fell victim to influenza. He was particularly angered by two items by friends of Montfort: a laudatory study of d'Annunzio by Marcel Boulenger and an intemperate attack by Léon Bocquet headed 'Contre Mallarmé'. There were other complaints: on the back cover, after the names of the members of the editorial committee, appeared a long and heterogeneous list of 'collaborators', followed by a disturbing 'etc.' Clearly two contradictory views of what the review should be were trying to coexist. Montfort would not take responsibility for the opinions of those he published; the review should be as broad in its views as possible, open to an entire generation. Gide's friends did not wish to propagate a particular line on literary matters, but they did have a (largely implicit) sense of the kind of review they wanted: it had to have a certain unity. The break was soon in coming: the planned December number did not appear. Montfort agreed to withdraw, leaving Gide and his friends with the title that he had invented.

For a time, Gide was confronted by a conflict of interests. Louis Ganderax, editor of *La Revue de Paris*, had agreed to serialize *La Porte étroite*. This would give Gide a much wider audience than if he gave his new work to the *NRF.* In the end, Gide opted in favour of the *NRF*, which duly appeared on 1 February 1909, with the first part of *La Porte étroite* as its most substantial contribution (ignoring the false start in November, this issue was also billed as no. 1). Nos 2 and 3 followed, with the rest of *La Porte étroite*, in March and April. No one could have imagined, in February 1909, that this 'little magazine', with a very small circulation, run on a shoe-string by a group of unbusinesslike friends, would still be going strong three-quarters of a century later, would become, for most of its life, the unchallenged centre of Parisian literary activity and give rise, in the house of Gallimard, to the most astonishing concentration of a country's literary talent in the history of publishing.

Gide was now taking a more active, more detailed interest in the affairs of the new review. As he put it to Claudel, 'I am not officially taking over the editorial direction . . . but it amounts to that, and it's better that way . . .'[2] Officially, the editorial committee consisted of Copeau, Ruyters and Schlumberger. In fact, no sooner was the second number on sale than

Gide set off for Rome, though a constant stream of letters and postcards, interrupted only by a French postal strike, passed between Rome and Gide's colleagues in Paris.

During his stay in Italy, Gide made notes for *Les Caves du Vatican* and spent hours correcting the proofs for the volume edition of *La Porte étroite*, which made him more than ever sick of the work. The company being 'too pleasant and idle', he ended up talking more than writing.[3] The 'company' was not, this time, youths from the Spanish Steps – the weather was cold and wet – but his old friends the Van Rysselberghes, Théo, Maria and their eighteen-year-old daughter, Elisabeth. The Van Rysselberghes had left Paris in November and, after spending several weeks in Sicily and Naples, were already in Rome when Gide arrived. Next day, he found a room at 86 Via Sistina, quite close to them, and hired a piano. Gide and Maria were already close friends, but, before the Van Rysselberghes left for Italy, their relationship had taken on a closer, confessional nature. Maria had told Gide of an all-consuming, but unreciprocated love that she felt for a certain person; she was, of course, very fond of Théo, loved him even, but this other love was of a quite different nature. The identity of the person in question was not revealed. Gide repaid this confession by recounting his infatuation with Maurice Schlumberger, for him an altogether exceptional kind of passion, his own tastes leading him much more towards 'pleasure, frenzy, risk, the unknown'. In an entry dated 30 August 1922, Maria notes that, on a certain evening in Rome, 'I felt that Elisabeth was, as it were, enthralled by Gide; she, too, was attracted by a force to which she probably gave no name and which was to blossom later.'[4] This might suggest that the secret object of Maria Van Rysselberghe's affections was Gide himself. Certainly she felt deep love for Gide, but it was of a very calm, unpassionate kind. In fact, the person in question was the Belgian poet Emile Verhaeren. Some fifteen years before, Verhaeren and 'Mme Théo' had fallen hopelessly in love. However, they were both married, both devoted to their spouses and the relationship remained platonic. The story of this intense but unconsummated love affair, *Il y a quarante ans*, was published by Maria Van Rysselberghe under the pseudonym of 'M. Saint-Clair', in 1936.

While in Rome, Gide met up with a group of Florentine intellectuals and artists that had subscribed to the *NRF*. One of them, Giuseppe Vannicola, later to become his first Italian translator, showed him 'more of Rome than I ever dared to see of Paris'. Through them, too, he met an 'adorable monk', who invited him to join him at the monastery of Monte Cassino. There he was treated as an honoured guest: he found the Benedictines' company quite charming. After dinner, a few of them came out on to his bedroom terrace, smoked cigarettes and asked him to tell them all he knew about Oscar Wilde. Gide also got on very well with the abbot, who turned out to be a devotee of Chopin. (When writing to Claudel, on 19 April, Gide teasingly refers to this episode as 'a short retreat'.) Towards the end of March, the Van Rysselberghes left for Florence, where Gide joined them soon afterwards, to return to Paris.

A few weeks later, Gide went with Ghéon to a performance of Diaghilev's Russian company at the Châtelet theatre. Assembling dancers, singers and musicians from the St Petersburg and Moscow Imperial Theatres, in a company that included Ida Rubinstein, Karsavina, Nijinsky and Chaliapin, Diaghilev presented an astonishing programme of ballet and opera. Surprisingly, or perhaps not, Gide was not particularly impressed by what became an event of major importance in the history of the theatre. His 'note' on the evening appeared in the July number of the *NRF.* Earlier in the year, he had attended, on a few occasions, and with greater enthusiasm, another historical event, Isadora Duncan's performance at the Gaîté theatre.

More central to Gide's preoccupations at this time was the question of 'nationalism and literature'. Over the past few years, French nationalism had experienced a resurgence of support, not only among the population at large, but also among respected and talented writers. The main focus of this nationalism was the Action Française movement, which was royalist, conservative, pro-Catholic and generally backward-looking – very different from the later 'revolutionary' nationalisms of Fascism and Nazism, which were strongly influenced by socialist attitudes and thinking. In 1908, the fortnightly *Action Française* became a daily newspaper, edited by the brilliant polemicist Léon Daudet, elder son of the novelist Alphonse. The acknowledged leader of the group, the writer Charles Maurras, contributed an important regular column. The spirit of 'Dreyfusardism' was loosening its hold on French intellectuals, especially writers; nationalism in general, and Action Française in particular, were gaining increasing support from the young. The subject of 'nationalism and literature', then, was very much in the air. From August 1908 to February 1909, the results of an investigation of the opinions of French writers on the subject had been published in the review *La Phalange*. In his reply, Ghéon defined the French genius as: 'Harmony of form and content, beauty and idea, lyricism and reason. Strict artistic and intellectual probity . . . So many classical qualities, so many French qualities . . . And this does not prejudice innovation.'[5] Gide could have said as much. He published his own response to the question of

Gide, aged eight, 1877

Gide's father, Paul Gide

Gide, aged three, with his mother, 1872

La Roque, drawing by Anna Shackleton, 1856

Anna Shackleton,
about 1873

Gide, aged twenty-one, 1891

Gide at Biskra, 1893

Athman, aged fourteen, 1893

Pierre Louÿs, *c.* 1894

Paul Laurens

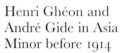

Eugène Rouart

Henri Ghéon and
André Gide in Asia
Minor before 1914

Francis Jammes, 1898

Jean Schlumberger

Jacques Copeau at the Galerie Georges
Petit, 1911

André Ruyters

Gide and Maria Van Rysselberghe at Weimar, 1903

Cuverville, 1923, taken by Roger Martin du Gard

Madeleine Gide in her
bedroom at Cuverville, 1902

nationalism and literature in three articles, published in the June, October and November numbers of the *NRF*. (The first two were republished in *Nouveaux Prétextes*.) Characteristically, Gide sought to demonstrate that every great work of literature was both national and universal: 'What could be more national than Aeschylus, Dante, Shakespeare, Cervantes, Molière, Goethe, Ibsen, Dostoevsky? And what more generally human? And also more individual?'[6]

Gide spent most of July at Cuverville, with the usual round of visitors, then the first two weeks of August in the south-west, mainly with Eugène Rouart at Bagnols-de-Grenade. This time, less time was spent in search of 'adventures': Rouart was not feeling well and Gide was working – on *Corydon*. 'I prolonged until yesterday,' he wrote to Ghéon, 'a state of good behaviour in which I could hardly recognize myself.'[7] Rouart and Gide were joined by François-Paul Alibert, who, 'for the first time . . . except to Eugène', unburdened himself of his secret: he, too, was homosexual. Gide read to them what he had written of *Corydon*, which he hoped to finish before the autumn. Alibert could see no objection to publishing what he had heard, though he wondered what effect it would have on Gide's 'private life', that is, his marriage. Rouart, *chef de cabinet* to a minister and with political ambitions of his own, was all too well aware of the dangers of public scandal. In October, Gide read what he had written to Paul Laurens and, a few weeks later, to Marcel Drouin. He expected disagreement, protest even; he was not prepared for their utter condemnation. If Gide published it, he would be finished, both as man and as writer. Not surprisingly, Gide decided to bide his time.

On leaving Bagnols, Gide went on to Argelès, where he called on the composer Florent Schmitt, who was planning to write an opera on *Proserpine*, a text that Gide had been working on for ten years. (Nothing came of these plans and it was Stravinsky, who, in 1932–3, set Gide's work to music. Renamed *Perséphone*, it was produced at the Paris Opéra in 1934.) Gide called on Jammes at Orthez and on his sister-in-law Valentine Gilbert, who was spending the summer with her children at Mimizan.

La Porte étroite appeared in volume form on 1 July. Vallette of *Mercure de France* had no reason to suppose that this work of 'virtue' would sell any better than its predecessor, that work of 'vice', *L'Immoraliste*. At first reviews and sales were slow in coming. By October, close on forty reviews had appeared and it had won golden opinions from all sorts of critics: 'a complex and profound work'; 'after *Hermann und Dorothea*, this is the finest, the rarest flower of the Protestant spirit'; 'perhaps the most beautiful novel of the inner life in our language'. With such critical attention, in quantity and quality, it was inevitable that sales would improve. After a few months the *de luxe* edition of 300 copies and the cheaper edition of 1,000 were nearly exhausted. Then a long article by Edmund Gosse on Gide's work in general and on *La Porte étroite* in particular appeared in the September number of *The Contemporary Review*. On publication, Gide had sent Gosse a copy of *La Porte étroite*, the only complimentary copy to be sent to England, Gosse being, as he told him, his 'only "correspondent" (and I was going to say: my only reader) in England'.[8] Gosse responded: 'I do not know how long it is since I have read a book which has so profoundly moved me. I can witness to the penetration, the truth, the bitter sweetness of your searching analysis of Calvinistic pietism . . .' Gosse goes on to say that 'for many years past', he has sensed between them 'very close spiritual and intellectual ties'. Gosse had suffered a far worse Calvinistic upbringing at his father's hands than Gide had ever suffered at his mother's, as he was to learn when he read the enclosed copy of *Father and Son*, published the year before. (What Gide was not to know was that his English admirer was also a married homosexual. Over the next twenty years, the two men were to exchange about 100 letters, the last being in the year of Gosse's death, 1928.) Gosse, now sixty, had more or less given up reviewing, so his article in *The Contemporary Review* was a particular compliment. *La Porte étroite*, he writes, is 'one of the most beautiful books which has been printed for a long time' and notes perceptively that Gide's portrayal of an instance of self-destructive Puritanism is both sympathetic and critical. 'No element of Alissa's progress in holiness is caricatured, or exaggerated, while every symptom of it is recorded with a perfect sympathy for herself and recognition of her aims.' Nevertheless, Gide 'entirely appreciates the nature of the error he so closely describes, and regards it with deep disapprobation'. Alissa's sacrifice is 'vain, futile and wretched, a tribute to that religion "against nature, against happiness, against common sense", which is the final outcome of Puritanism'.[9]

The result of Gosse's review was a sudden demand for copies from English bookshops that could not be met – and, since the type had been broken up, the text had to be reset. A second edition of 3,000 copies was produced in November.

When, on 22 November, Gide celebrated his fortieth birthday, he had every reason to feel that success was at last smiling on him. True, he had made little progress with *Les Caves du Vatican*, the novel of the new Gide; success had come with the 'anachronistic' *La Porte étroite*, but it did provide an achievement of recognition from which the future Gide could reach a wider audience. True, too, that *Corydon* had run out of steam in the face of his friends' opposition. On the other hand, the *NRF*, with nine numbers published, was on a sound footing from a financial as well as a literary point of view. In a letter to Jammes, Gide even moots the idea of setting up an *NRF* publishing house. Its aim would be 'to reprint in *perfect editions* the *great works* of our literature (we would like to begin with the complete works of Stendhal)' and to publish the works of '*a very limited group* of contemporary authors . . . Claudel, Jammes, Gide, Philippe, Suarès, Verhaeren, *to the exclusion of all others*'.[10] This very Gidean notion of a publisher's list made up of a small band of like-minded friends, consorting with the French classics, was the first adumbration of what was to become the 'maison Gallimard'.

The *NRF* also brought Gide new, younger friends. There was Jacques Rivière, who, after the war, was to become the managing editor of the review. Having failed his *agrégation de philosophie* examination, he rejected the idea of spending another year studying – against the advice of his mentor, Paul Claudel, who regarded the idea of earning a living as a writer with repugnance. This Rivière set out to do, however, eked out by part-time teaching at the Catholic Ecole Stanislas – obtained on Claudel's recommendation. He was one of many of Gide's friends who had moved, or were moving, in a Catholic direction. That year, 1910, he had married the sister of his best friend, Henri Fournier, the future Alain-Fournier. When Fournier had finished his military service, he, too, moved into the *NRF* orbit, though he was also publishing stories in other, more widely circulating reviews. He was already working on his most famous work, *Le Grand Meaulnes*, which was published in 1913. To make ends meet he gave private French lessons to foreigners, one of whom was T. S. Eliot. Another young friend was Valéry Larbaud, the 'rich amateur' of the *Poésies de A. O. Barnabooth*, which Gide himself had reviewed in the 'first' February number of the *NRF*. Later in the year, the *NRF* published his story 'Dolly' and, in 1910, serialized his novel, *Fermina Marquez*. In his *Journal* Gide notes Philippe's remark to Ruyters concerning Larbaud: 'It is always a pleasure to meet someone beside whom Gide seems poor.'[11] The heir to the Vichy springs, Larbaud had spent his life travelling. He first wrote to Gide in 1905, from Tunis, but the two men did not meet until December 1909. Other young writers, destined for later fame, who also appeared in the pages of the *NRF* during that first year of publication, were Jean Giraudoux and Saint-Léger (the future 'Saint-John Perse').

*

An *NRF* 'banquet' was organized for 21 December *chez* Marguery, a restaurant on the boulevard Bonne-Nouvelle. One expected guest was Charles-Louis Philippe, but, the day before, it was learned that he was ill with typhoid and had been taken to hospital. That morning Gide had visited him and found him gravely ill. The dinner went ahead nevertheless, with a certain apprehension in the air. Philippe died at 9 that evening: he was thirty-five. Gide was profoundly moved by this sudden loss, devoting nine pages of his *Journal* to Philippe, his death and his funeral. Of tiny stature, uncertain health, facially deformed by a large scar partly hidden by a beard, Philippe had emerged, self-taught, from poverty in his native village to a clerk's job in the Paris Hôtel de Ville. He devoted all his spare time to writing. At his death he had already published a number of novels, the best known of which was *Bubu de Montparnasse*. In February, an extra mid-month number of the *NRF* was devoted entirely to his memory.

The Charles-Louis Philippe number brought Gide into one literary–social circle in which he was not an habitué. The Comtesse de Noailles, *née* Anna de Brancovan, like her cousins, the Bibescos, belonged to one of the oldest Rumanian aristocratic families. A poet and a novelist under the name of Anna de Noailles, she had warmly received Philippe's novel *La Mère et l'enfant* on publication. Perhaps, Gide asked her, she would care to write something on the work for the *NRF*. The *Journal* entry for 20 January 1910 reveals a hitherto unsuspected gift for the comic, bravura cameo:

Mme de Noailles is at the hotel (Princess Hôtel), rue de Presbourg; the windows of her room look out on to the Arc de Triomphe. She was expecting us, as is rather obvious: she's lying on a chaise longue consisting of two armchairs and a stool between them, sinuously draped in a sort of Rumanian or Greek shift of black Tussore silk with a broad band of greyish white, that soft white to be found in China paper and certain Japanese felts; this shift floats loosely around her bare arms, which are loaded with Venetian bracelets . . . Her hair is dishevelled, wild and jet-black, cut in a short fringe on the forehead, but falling as if wet on to her shoulders. She introduces us to the Princesse de Caraman-Chimay (?), who trains on me a lorgnette that she doesn't put down during the entire visit.

Impossible to note down anything from the conversation. Mme de Noailles talks with amazing volubility; the sentences rush to her lips, three or four at a time, crushing together in confusion. The result is a very tasty compote of ideas, sensations, images, a *tutti-frutti* accompanied by movements of the hands and arms, and particularly of the eyes, which she turns heavenwards in a swoon that is not too feigned, though rather too emphatic . . .[12]

In late March, Gide and Copeau set off on a few weeks' tour around

Spain. They arrived in Valencia and felt that they had 'done' it in a morning and moved on – to Alicante, Elche, Murcia. 'Half our time is spent travelling; much of the rest brushing down our clothes,' Gide writes to Ghéon. But, he adds, teasingly, 'I wish you were here, *cher vieux*. I regretted your absence a certain evening in Alicante.'[13] (By now, incidentally, Ghéon had abandoned Bray and medicine. With money from an uncle and the proceeds from selling his practice, he had moved, with his mother, to Orsay, in the Chevreuse valley.) The trip was not, on the whole, a success – either for Gide or for Copeau. In a letter, written some months later, Copeau suggests that it was his fault; he had been something of a 'gloomy killjoy' ('morne trouble-fête'), inhibiting Gide's spirit of adventure: 'I desired nothing and I held you back, I broke the spell for you, I diminished you, I encumbered you with my presence.'[14]

On 14 April Gide attended a luncheon given by Jacques Rouché, editor of *La Grande Revue* (and future director of the Opéra), in honour of Gabriele d'Annunzio, who was 'stiffer, more constricted, more contracted, more scaled down, but also more sparkling than ever'. 'He is the epitome of all Italy,' Mme Rouché remarked after the meal. 'Minus Dante,' Suarès responded, with his usual lugubrious acerbity.[15]

It was about this time that Rainer Maria Rilke lunched with the Gides at the Villa Montmorency. Born in Prague in 1875, of German-speaking parents, Rilke was a subject of the Austrian emperor, but the French language and literature represented for him an ideal of elegance and clarity unavailable to a German poet and Paris an earthly paradise, a materialization of the French spirit. In 1900, he had stayed with a friend in an artists' colony near Bremen. There he met and married Clara Westhopf, a pupil of Rodin. A daughter was born to them, but they soon agreed that married life, with little or no material means, would be impossible for them. The child was left with her maternal grandparents and the couple separated. Meanwhile, through his wife's influence, Rilke had come to regard Rodin as the major contemporary artistic figure, the man who had solved the eternal opposition between art and life. In 1902, armed with a commission from a German publisher to write a book on Rodin, Rilke set off for Paris, where he got himself taken on as Rodin's secretary. He had been living largely in Paris ever since. His first collection of poems, the *Neue Gedichte*, was published in November 1909, dedicated 'A mon grand ami Auguste Rodin'. Two years before, Rilke had read the German translation of *Le Retour de l'Enfant prodigue* and had been deeply affected by it (one of the *Neue Gedichte* is 'Der Auszug des verlorenen Sohnes', 'The Departure of the

Prodigal Son'). The shy, withdrawn Rilke had still made no attempt to meet Gide, though the two had a number of mutual friends, including Verhaeren, Hugo von Hofmannsthal, Count Harry von Kessler and Rudolf Kassner. Kassner later introduced Rilke to Princess Marie von Thurn und Taxis, who accommodated Rilke at the Schloss Duino, on the Adriatic coast (the eighth of the Duino Elegies is dedicated to Kassner). Finally, Kassner took Rilke along to meet Gide. The following July the *NRF* published Gide's translation of short extracts from Rilke's prose work, *Die Aufzeichnungen der Malte Laurids Brigge.* Rilke repaid the compliment when, in 1914, his new version of *Le Retour de l'Enfant prodigue* was published in a popular series in Germany. Gide was Rilke's first important French literary influence and it was through him that Rilke met most of his French friends, above all the figure who, for him, was to represent the pinnacle of French poetry and whose work he was to translate, Paul Valéry.

One afternoon, in late May, two days before leaving to spend the summer at Cuverville, Gide called on Anna de Noailles. There he met the widow of Lucien Mühlfeld, former editor of *La Revue Blanche.* (Mme Mühlfeld, the 'Witch of the rue Georges-Ville', as Gide affectionately referred to her in a letter to Valéry, was to be one of their favourite hostesses.) The two women asked Gide to join them that evening at a rehearsal of the Ballets Russes at the Opéra. It was the final rehearsal of Rimsky-Korsakov's *Schéhérazade,* with Ida Rubenstein in the title role and Nijinsky as the slave. Some of the male dancers of the *corps* had not bothered to change into rehearsal clothes, but still wore their usual jackets and trousers, which, Gide tells Ghéon, 'gave a prodigious character to the great orgy scene!' Afterwards, they went back-stage – 'I'd have loved you to be with me . . . it would have given us a few more good memories to share' – and called on Nijinsky in his dressing-room.[16] Gide was completely won over by the Ballets Russes and bitterly regretted the cool welcome he had given them in the *NRF* the year before. He was not alone, of course. The whole *NRF* team had become enthusiasts: Ghéon and Rivière were to pen laudatory reviews over the next few weeks. Gide was to move closer, socially, as well as aesthetically, to the Diaghilev company. Later in the month, he hoped to come back to Paris for the rehearsals of *Firebird,* the new ballet with music by the twenty-eight-year-old Igor Stravinsky.

Gide left for Cuverville, determined to finish 'the very respectable novel' (*Isabelle*) and *Corydon* (in fact, its first half), which he planned to publish at the same time – the respectability of the first offsetting the shock value of the second. By 5 July, he could report to Ghéon that he had finished 'another chapter of my novel and well sketched out the rest'. As for my 'terrible book' (*Corydon*), he had rewritten everything 'from the first word'. He feels 'more and more determined to publish it'.[17]

In July, the visitors came. The Drouins were there, of course. Ruyters arrived and, during his stay at Cuverville, finished his novel *L'Ombrageuse*, which was serialized in the *NRF* from October, in his absence. (On 25 September, he set out for Addis Ababa to take up a French government post, attached to the Franco-Ethiopian Railways Company; he would be away for some eight months.) The young Rivière couple came for a ten-day stay. 'We awoke in a fairy-tale house,' they wrote to Alain-Fournier. 'We have a whole apartment to ourselves. And around us some of the most marvellous countryside in the world . . . I can't tell you how delightful the Gides have been towards us . . . Copeau is coming this evening.'[18] Copeau had just arrived back from Russia, where he had spent several weeks gathering atmosphere for his long-standing project of a dramatized version of *The Brothers Karamazov*.

On 5 August, Gide took the night train for Toulouse, where he was met by Eugène Rouart. They went on together by car to Rouart's property at Bagnols-de-Grenade. After some days, they were joined by Jules Iehl, now a *juge-de-paix* at Fronton, then by François-Paul Alibert. On 18 August, all four set out on 'an impossible expedition' into Andorra, 'one of the least known and mysterious spots on earth'. They travelled by train to Aix-les-Thermes, by carriage to Hospitalet, then on foot 'into the unknown, escorted by a guide, with a horse to carry our provisions'.[19] Gide kept a diary of the 'expedition', which was published in the September and October numbers of the *NRF*. By 25 August, he was at 'Les Sources', Charles Gide's property near Nîmes. From there he escaped for a couple of days to the coast, to Grau-du-Roi, near Aigues-Mortes. A week later, he was at Hyères, again in search of sea-bathing and adventure.

On 10 September, Gide was at Pontigny for the first 'Entretiens d'été'. Pontigny, near Auxerre, in the Yonne, was a former Cistercian abbey, bought and saved from ruin by Paul Desjardins in 1906. Desjardins taught Classics and French at the Lycée Condorcet and wrote literary criticism. He became preoccupied with the need for a general moral reawakening, based on a spirit of disinterested inquiry and international cooperation. In 1892, he founded the Union pour l'Action Morale, later renamed the Union pour la Vérité. In 1904, he began the 'Entretiens d'été', in which intellectuals in various domains might come together in pleasant surroundings, for periods of ten days. These became known as the 'Décades de Pontigny'.

They continued, interrupted only by the First World War, until the outbreak of the Second. In 1910, there were five such 'Décades', dealing in turn with the themes of 'justice', 'art and life', 'the religious life', 'working-class life today' and, finally, from 10 to 19 September, 'contemporary poetry', organized by the *NRF*. The 'Décades de Pontigny' were to become something of an institution and Gide attended several of the *décades littéraires*, including the last in August 1939.

Between Christmas and New Year, Gide spent a few days with Jacques Copeau and his family in their new house at Le Limon, near La Ferté-sous-Jarre, in the Seine et Marne. In February 1910, Copeau had sold the family factory, which produced funds just large enough to allow him to buy a house in the country and give up work at the art gallery. Described by Ghéon as 'a modest house, but large enough and charming in appearance', it had a large orchard, a spring, a pond, 'an old mill, which will be converted into a study' and 'a small, tumbledown outhouse for friends'. Its only disadvantage was its distance from Paris.[20] For Copeau, this was not entirely a disadvantage: it left him free to pursue his extra-marital activities with a series of actresses and occasional visits to favourite prostitutes.

From Cuverville, on 1 October, Gide wrote to Ghéon: 'My book (the novel) is going by leaps and bounds; I hope to have it finished within a fortnight – if I carry on at this rate . . .'[21] In fact, it was finished on 12 October, though he went on making small changes right up to publication. Like so many of Gide's works, it had been long in gestation. In a letter to Valéry, dating probably from 1892, Gide describes the Château de Formentin, near La Roque:

A huge park, completely abandoned, a large house, whose owners we used to know, now locked up after various tragic adventures – heavily mortgaged; everything was sold, all the rooms emptied, the shutters closed and the doors padlocked. I found my way into the park and, after forcing a lock, spent all day wandering through the great empty rooms in which nothing remained on the walls except old panelling and mirrors.[22]

Some six years later, in September 1898, Gide visited Formentin again, this time in the company of Henri Ghéon and Francis Jammes, who were staying at La Roque. This visit inspired not one, but two literary works, the second actually quoting from the first – a delight to modern connoisseurs of intertextuality. Indeed Jammes serves as a frame to the *récit*. In a few introductory pages the unnamed narrator of this outer frame, to be identified by the reader, according to the literary conventions with 'André Gide' (but not by the alert literary critic) describes how, while staying in the country house of their friend Gérard Lacase, he and Francis Jammes were taken by the host to visit a dilapidated property nearby. During the visit, Gérard Lacase relates the 'story' of the deserted Château de la Quartfourche to his two friends – and it is repeated, in writing, for the reader's benefit, by 'André Gide'. This device serves a number of purposes. Its very hackneyed character suits the apparently gothic nature of the tale. The presence of Francis Jammes, an actually existing poet, lends credence to the rest of the account. 'André Gide' is little more than a scribe; the ostensible narrator of the main body of the *récit* is not 'André Gide', but Gérard Lacase. Since the real André Gide is the sole source of the story and Gérard Lacase his created character, this enables Gide to make Gérard Lacase reveal more about himself than about his subject. This filtration of a story through a narrator quite different from himself marks a new departure for Gide. There is a further complication: Gérard Lacase is certainly not André Gide, but 'André Gide' is not exactly André Gide either. Whereas, in fact, it was Gide who invited his two friends, Francis Jammes and Henri Ghéon, to La Roque and showed them the (real) Château de Formentin, in the story it is Gérard Lacase who lives at 'La R. . . .' and invites his two friends, Francis Jammes and the presumed 'André Gide'.

Gérard Lacase is a young scholar doing research on Bossuet. The supervisor of his thesis at the Sorbonne suggests that he visit an old colleague of his, Benjamin Floche, now retired to his country house in Normandy. There he would find primary sources for his work. Gérard Lacase is not only a scholar; he also has literary pretensions: 'At twenty-five I knew nothing [of life] except from books; and that is probably why I thought I was a novelist.'[23] His visit to the Château de la Quartfourche, his expectations aroused and interpretations coloured by books, is not unlike that of Jane Austen's gothic-novel-reading heroine to Northanger Abbey: he 'peopled it with adventures'. Late at night, he is collected from the local railway station by a surly coachman, Gratien, who drives him to the house, where he is received by the housekeeper, an inaptly named Mademoiselle Verdure: his hosts have already retired to bed. The following day he meets his elderly hosts, M. and Mme Floche, their in-laws, M. and Mme de Saint-Auréol, and Casimir, the Saint-Auréols' crippled young grandson. The visitor's flagging interest in the house and its occupants is revived when Casimir shows him a miniature portrait of a beautiful young woman who, the boy says, is his mother. From the priest employed as tutor to young Casimir, he learns that Isabelle de Saint-Auréol comes to the house very rarely, then only briefly and at night. In the grip of 'amorous curiosity', he pieces together the 'truth' about the mysterious beauty. In a derelict summer-house, he finds the letter that she had written to her lover, the Vicomte Blaise de Gonfreville, on the eve of their elopement. He then learns from the priest that the Vicomte was killed, supposedly in a hunting accident, on the same day the letter was written. However, the priest believes, correctly, that it was murder, committed by Gratien, the family servant. Some months later, Isabelle gave birth to a son, deformed as the result of her attempt to conceal her pregnancy. Learning that Isabelle is to visit the house that night, Gérard spies on her meeting with Mme de Saint-Auréol and Mme Floche – she has come for money. Still obsessed by her mystery, he tries, unsuccessfully, to meet up with her as she is leaving. The following year, Gérard returns to Quartfourche to find that three of the old people have died – a sickly Mme Saint-Auréol is being lodged, temporarily she believes, with Gratien and her grandson, Casimir. In fact, the estate is heavily mortgaged and will be auctioned off. Meanwhile, Isabelle is in residence, despoiling it of its trees for whatever money she can get for them. Gérard meets Isabelle in the grounds and, pretending at first to be a possible buyer, gets into conversation with her. The scales fall from his eyes: 'fiction' is finally dissipated by truth. Isabelle emerges as an unfeeling, grasping, pathetic and no longer attractive woman. She even flirts with Gérard: later, he learns that, after the sale of the estate, she went off with the coachman.

Thanks to R.-G. Nobécourt's *Les Nourritures normandes d'André Gide*, we know that what, at first sight, looks like a somewhat far-fetched fantasy, was very largely based on fact. Gide knew some of the inhabitants of the Château de Formentin personally. Their names are only thinly disguised: the 'Saint-Auréols' were the Saint-Albans, their daughter 'Isabelle' Louise, their grandson 'Casimir' Maxime, like his fictional counterpart a cripple. The original of 'Floche' was called Floquet and, like him, was a Bossuet scholar. Many of the original reviews of *Isabelle* criticized it for taking so long in introducing the heroine and even longer in revealing the truth about her. Clearly they considered that Gide had failed to write a traditional novel, with a properly constructed plot. In a letter to Jean-Marc Bernard of 21 September 1911, Gide writes: 'What an admirable book a novelist might have written if he had presented Isabelle at length and directly . . . describing her upbringing, bringing out more clearly the responsibility of her education, her milieu . . . depicting the rapid moral disintegration of an old family. But that was not what I set out to write.' What began as a few historical facts, closely bound up with La Roque and Gide's own past, did not end up as an 'anachronism'. By poking gentle fun at the genre, rather as Jane Austen mocks her heroine's 'gothic' expectations, by making the presumed narrator himself the object of fun, a narrator who does not narrate what he knows, but, in the manner of the thriller, the difficult process of acquiring it, Gide was moving into the world of his literary maturity, the world of *Les Caves du Vatican* and *Les Faux-Monnayeurs*. Lucien Maury, writing in *La Revue bleue* (9 September 1911), places *Isabelle* four-square in the 'modern' movement: 'We are used to appreciating a direct, in some sense rectilinear narration ... André Gide has discerned the possibility of a skilful disorder, a constant imbalance, a constantly shattered harmony, a jerky movement, with stops and starts ... so that the real turns into the fantastic, the free play of a logic-chopping fantasy around a very simple adventure.'

With the end of 1910 and the completion of *Isabelle*, Gide had every reason to feel pleased. Since the foundation of the *NRF*, his health had been uninterruptedly good: constant contact with a group of like-minded friends and public recognition of his talent had done what consulting doctors and taking the waters had failed to do. The *NRF*, too, was in a healthy state. In its second year, it continued to gain in circulation and influence. The headquarters had been removed from Jean Schlumberger's apartment in the rue d'Assas, to the offices of the publisher Marcel Rivière, 31 rue Jacob.

In his first *Journal* entry for 1911 Gide writes: 'I read an hour of English' – *Robinson Crusoe* and Macaulay's *Life of Byron* – 'before going to bed.' Curiously, in view of Anna Shackleton's constant presence throughout his childhood, Gide, who managed very creditably in German, had failed to master English. Though an avid reader of English literature in translation, this is the first time that Gide made a serious attempt to read an English book in the original. It was not the result of any whim: he was taking English lessons every day from a teacher at the Berlitz School. In 1911, the future translator of Blake and Shakespeare regarded his acquisition of English as 'a considerable event in my life'.[24] By February, he was subjecting Madeleine to *viva voce* readings of English works.

On Saturday, 11 February, at Van Rysselberghe's studio in the rue Laugier, a reading took place of Copeau's adaptation for the theatre of *The Brothers Karamazov*. The enterprise was bedevilled by enough complications and obstacles to put a writer off the theatre for life. (Copeau's response, as we shall see, was to found his own 'reformed' theatre two years later.) The first night finally took place on 5 April to great critical acclaim. It effectively launched the career of that great actor Charles Dullin, who was noticed by Copeau during early rehearsals in a minor role and promoted to play Smerdiakov.

In early May, Gide declined a suggestion from Copeau that the two of them should go off to London where Valéry Larbaud had taken up temporary residence in Chelsea. He went instead to Bruges, where, over the next nine days, at the *NRF*'s printers, Verbeke, he corrected the proofs of the review's June number, the first three books to be published by the new *NRF* publishing house – Claudel's *L'Otage*, Philippe's *La Mère et l'enfant* and his own *Isabelle* – and *Corydon*. In fact, *Corydon* was not about to be 'published' and had not even been finished. Giving in to pressure from various sources, most vocally from Marcel Drouin, Gide had decided that perhaps the risks were too great after all. 'Everything convinces me that this book must not be published,' Drouin wrote to Copeau. 'André has forfeited the right to do so by the entire organization of his life, by all those destinies bound up with his.' As Gide's brother-in-law and as a philosophy teacher in a *lycée* (a public servant) his own position was 'very exposed (more than that of any of you)'. Gide was susceptible to such concerns. As late as the 1922 Preface to *Corydon*, he writes: 'My friends tell me again and again that this book is of a kind to do me the greatest harm.' Yet 'I do not believe that it can take from me anything that I hold dear . . . I have never sought to please the public.' However, 'I do place an excessive value upon the opinion of a few people.' If ever he had been accused of 'a certain timidity of thought', it was usually to be explained by 'a fear of saddening those few people; of saddening, in particular, one soul who is dearer to me than any other'.[25] Why, then, did Gide decide, in 1911, to have printed privately, anonymously, without date or place of publication, under the abbreviated title of CRDN, twenty-two copies (or twelve, or twenty, depending on the conflicting evidence) of a book that he himself admitted was only 'three-quarters finished'? Clearly his action was a compromise. *Corydon* was not just any book: for Gide it held a unique place in his œuvre. It lay at the centre of his life – and, for him, sincerity was all. He knew that, sooner or later, the book would have to be published. What is more, he knew that the new Gide, the Gide that would come to birth in *Les Caves du Vatican*, was inseparable from the concerns of *Corydon*. He felt, therefore, that he could not simply put the manuscript away in a drawer and leave it there until a more propitious time. There was a further reason for putting the book, as it were, on record. A year before, while working on *Corydon*, Gide noted in his *Journal*: 'The fear that someone else might get there before me; it seems to me that the subject is in the air.'[26] Then, having had a small number of copies of his work in progress printed, he locked them away in a drawer . . . and went back to work on it.

On 31 May, a contract was signed setting up the *NRF* publishing house as a separate company: Gide, Jean Schlumberger and Gaston Gallimard each contributed a share of 20,000 francs (£800 or $4,000 at the time). At Cuverville, over the next few weeks, Gide worked hard at *Corydon*, but got more and more depressed. Finally, he decided to drop everything and join Valéry Larbaud in London. He sailed from Le Havre to Southampton and arrived in London on 7 July. Larbaud, an English specialist, had already travelled extensively throughout England. He was preparing a doctoral thesis on the poet Coventry Patmore. The subject had had a profound effect on him. Following in the steps of Patmore, who had been received into the Catholic Church in Rome in 1864, Larbaud, brought up by his mother as a Protestant, had been baptized a Catholic on Christmas Eve 1910. He had kept the matter a secret, from his mother and from many of his friends, including Gide. On that visit to London, Gide introduced Larbaud to Edmund Gosse, who had known Patmore well and, in 1905, had published a critical biography of him. Gide lunched with Gosse at the House of Lords (of which Gosse was librarian) and was initiated by him into the mysteries of that most elevated of London clubs, the Athenaeum. It is not clear where, on arrival, Gide stayed. He had been invited to stay with Prince Antoine Bibesco, a cousin of Anna de Noailles, an old schoolfriend of Copeau's at the Lycée Condorcet, now Rumanian secretary of legation and married to Elizabeth Asquith, the Prime Minister's daughter. Gide, however, was 'apprehensive about the elegant society' into which Bibesco might lead him. After a few days, he placed an advertisement in the *Daily Telegraph* for a household to accept a 'French gentleman, wishing to perfect himself in English'. As a result, on 12 July, he moved in with the family of an anarchist teacher at 462 Uxbridge Road, Acton. It is not certain how long Gide bore this arrangement, but, by 21 July, his last day in London, he was writing to Gosse from the Curzon Hotel. During his stay in London, he went with Larbaud and Miss Agnes Tobin, an American Catholic lady of the Alice Meynell circle, to call on Joseph Conrad, near Ashford, and Arthur Symons, who also lived in Kent.

Gide was to meet Gosse and Mrs Gosse again, at Pontigny, for the second *décade littéraire* organized by the *NRF*. This took place on 19–28 August on the subject of 'The Tragic'. Gosse described the situation in a letter to Evan Charteris: 'Well! We sit in a circle, under the elm trees, and we discuss in

libres conversations the Tragic – *Le Tragique, vous savez, non pas la Tragédie.*
Paul Desjardins takes the lead, firmly, modestly, slowly, with beneficence
and gaiety. It is not at all pedantic or scholastic . . . Bursts of laughter
intervene, *calembours, je ne sais quoi!* . . . The new ideas that I have got here,
the new impressions! I could sob with chagrin to think that I am sixty-two,
not twenty-two . . .'[27]

From Pontigny, Gide went straight back to Cuverville, with, he claimed,
'a twenty-day cold'. It was the excuse, if not the reason, for calling off a
trip to Morocco that he had planned to take with Rouart. In any case, he
took the opportunity to return to his desk. He struggled, without success,
to finish *Corydon*. He turned back to the 'almost as dangerous' *Caves du
Vatican*, but made little progress there either. The weather was particularly
fine and he went for long walks. He played the piano and he read – a lot
of English. By July, this amounted to Defoe's *Robinson Crusoe*, Fielding's *Tom
Jones* (which he saw as the nearest thing that he had read to his – barely
begun – *Caves*), Stevenson's *Olalla, The Bottle Imp* and *Weir of Hermiston*,
Lamb's *Essays*, Hardy's *Mayor of Casterbridge*, Conrad's *The End of the Tether*,
Milton's *Samson Agonistes* and Thomson's *Evolution of Sex*. After Pontigny, he
began Edmund Gosse's study of Sir Thomas Browne and Browne's *Religio
Medici*. Between 27 September and 2 October, Jacques Rivière and his
brother-in-law, Alain-Fournier, came to stay. Gide read to them part of *Les
Caves du Vatican*. This cannot have improved what were already rather
strained relations between Gide and Alain-Fournier, who, unlike his brother-
in-law, whose commitment was total, seemed keen to keep his distance
from the *NRF* group. Even Rivière's reaction to a reading was one of '*effroi*'
(terror, fright); for the first time, it seems, Rivière became aware that Gide
was undergoing a kind of sea-change as a writer, one that he found deeply
disturbing.

On 13 October, Gide travelled by overnight train to Nîmes. After a few
days at Les Sources, he went on to Bagnols to stay with Rouart. There he
received a letter from Copeau, written at '114 Grosvenor Road, SW' – the
home of Antoine Bibesco: 'Guess who I have spent all my days and even
part of my nights with? . . . Isadora Duncan.'[28] Clearly, Copeau's week in
London had been a great deal more 'glamorous' than Gide's two in July,
though we have to turn to Copeau's journal rather than his letter to Gide
to discover why. On his first day, he visited Gosse at the House of Lords,
saw a matinée of Shaw's *Fanny's First Play*, dined at Bibesco's and, at
midnight, was taken off by 'Harry Melvil, notorious homosexual', to call
on Isadora Duncan in Cadogan Square. She was wearing a Greek tunic

and sandals. Also there were 'a beautiful American', Mrs Mary Sturges, also dressed *à l'antique*, Isadora's brother Gus and two other men. About one, Mary Sturges decides to take them all off for supper 'at the Savoy, where she lives'. At Covent Garden, Copeau saw both *Walküre* and *Siegfried* (from Isadora's box, with Duse in the neighbouring one). He saw Tree's *Macbeth* and went back-stage to meet the great actor–manager, who expressed interest in *Les Frères Karamazov*. He visited Joseph Conrad and Arnold Bennett. Copeau's wife Agnès was expecting him to be back in Paris on 29 November. In fact, he left four days earlier in order to spend time with the actress Pauline Teillon, sister of Charles Dullin. Back at Le Limon with Agnès, Copeau wrote to Gide what amounts to an *apologia pro vita sua*: 'I'd like you to know, *cher vieux*, what sincerity there is in all my surges of affection [*élans*]. How un-blasé I feel about each and every adventure . . .' With every encounter, 'I take leave of myself', become the other, 'share her feelings and live her life'. It is 'a veritable *passion*', beside which mere pleasure pales into insignificance.[29] Perhaps this gives some indication of Copeau's extraordinary success with women. No photograph can account for this: in 1911, the thirty-two-year-old Copeau, almost entirely bald, looked at least ten years older. His face was neither handsome nor particularly interesting. Nor, at this time, had he either fame or fortune. Despite their very different sexual tastes and a difference in age of ten years, Gide and Copeau had an instinctive sense that they were 'on the same wavelength' – hence the exuberant honesty with which they discussed their most intimate concerns.

The end of 1911 found Gide in one of his periodic fits of depression. The *NRF*, which, at the outset, had given him a new lease of life, now seemed to be an endless cause of distraction from his own writing. *Corydon* had had to be abandoned, if only temporarily, and *Les Caves du Vatican* was making no progress. He felt unsettled by what seemed like the invincible progress of Catholicism in his own circle of friends and felt constantly harassed by Claudel's tireless attentions. On 1 January 1912, in the conservative, Catholic *L'Indépendance*, Georges Sorel launched a vicious attack on Desjardins and the *NRF*. He even, quite gratuitously, but with evident intent, referred to Oscar Wilde, 'whose memory has remained an object of veneration at the *NRF*'. It was not simply an attack from outside: it highlighted divisions and dissensions within the *NRF* group. On 5 January, Copeau wrote to Schlumberger: 'The gravest and terribly delicate question remains that of our relations with Desjardins and with Pontigny.'[30] A key-figure in all this was Claudel, who, though certainly not an inner member of the group, was perhaps the *NRF*'s most highly prized acquisition. His first appearance in the review came in December 1909, with his 'Trois Hymnes'. His play *L'Otage* was serialized in three numbers between December 1910 and February 1911. The September and October 1911 numbers included his translations of poems by Coventry Patmore and the first three numbers of 1912 featured his play, *L'Annonce faite à Marie*. Jacques Rivière, the rising star of the *NRF*, was Claudel's protégé. Gide himself had ambiguous, but (or, perhaps, therefore) very strong feelings about Claudel. Gide found Claudel's single-mindedness and absolute assurance rebarbative, even frightening, but it also held a strange fascination for him. Something of Gide's depression over this period lay in a sense that he was losing control over the intellectual course before him, that Claudel *assumed* that he was ripe for conversion and that such a conversion would not be a free choice, but an invasion from without. Days after the second *Indépendance* attack, Gide wrote to Claudel that he felt 'full of courage and zeal in the defence of ideas that are dear to me', but those of Desjardins were not among them.

The atmosphere of the Union pour l'Action morale is now, for me, quite unbreathable, as is the Protestant atmosphere. Outside Catholicism, I can see only isolation. I am an isolated being, *cher ami*. I take no pride in this, for I need friendship as I need bread – *and servitude* [my italics] – but what am I to do? For of all who practise literature and politics, there is not one whose Catholicism does not take on monstrous forms. (And it is because you are so different from them that I have listened to you so attentively.) They use the crucifix as a truncheon [*casse-tête*] . . . To move towards Christ is, for me, to move away from them.[31]

Claudel wrote back from Frankfurt, where he was now Consul, expressing delight that Gide had distanced himself from Desjardins. 'Obviously the worst trick that could be played on the *NRF* would be to force you to side with a man whom we cannot but regard as an *enemy*.'[32] The tone is typical of Catholic polemics at this period. Desjardins was no anti-Catholic propagandist, but a highly civilized, well-meaning teacher whose misfortune, at this time of partisan extremes, was to try to open up dialogue, to bring people together. Similarly, Claudel was not some ill-informed bigot, but a scholar, poet and diplomat who represented *moderate* Catholic opinion and who had distanced himself from the *casse-têtes* of the Action Française movement. A week later, Claudel returned to the attack: 'It is indisputable that the decadence of Art derives from its separation from what one rather stupidly calls Morality, and which I call the *Life*, the *Way* and the *Truth* . . .

What is the *NRF*'s position on this matter? It is absolutely necessary that France be saved from this literature of libertinage, scepticism and despair, which is exhausting it and which, in any case, is itself rotting away.'[33] Gide's 'official' response to the attacks from *L'Indépendance* (and to Claudel's insistent questions) appeared in the February number of the *NRF*. The review was not 'the organ of an individual, nor of a coterie, nor of a party. It belongs equally to all its contributors. Each of them may express . . . his own ideas and tendencies. All hold firmly to their right to appreciate the value and sincerity of individuals, whoever they may be, without these judgements committing the review in the struggle between parties.'[34] In the privacy of his *Journal*, Gide noted: 'I wish I had never met Claudel. His friendship weighs on my thinking, forces it in a particular direction, impedes it . . . I still can't bring myself to hurt him, but my thinking can only be affirmed by offending his.'[35] Later in the year, on a visit to Paris, Claudel invited Gide to call on him at his sister's. Claudel talked of Rimbaud, whose complete works he was editing for the *Mercure de France*. He cited one or two second-hand anecdotes that, Claudel maintained, were 'enough to demolish the imputations of *mauvaises moeurs* [literally, 'bad morals', but clearly homosexuality] that are still sometimes associated with his name'. When Gide brings up Rimbaud's relations with Verlaine, Claudel 'with a vague look on his face, touches a rosary in a bowl on the mantelpiece'.[36] By the end of the year, Gide had still not brought himself to hurt Claudel. On 27 December, Claudel wrote to say that, on a recent visit to Paris, he had been to see the Abbé Fontaine, who had been Huysmans' last confessor and who was now priest to the working-class parish of Clichy, succouring 'a population of railwaymen, rag-and-bone men, ruffians and whores'.[37] Why doesn't Gide go along and talk over his problems with him? To his *Journal*, Gide made his position quite clear: 'Catholicism is unacceptable. Protestantism is intolerable. And I feel profoundly Christian.'[38]

The early months of 1912 brought changes to the *NRF*. In the midst of mental depression and creative barrenness, the two being, as always, interactive, Gide wished to remove himself as much as possible from the everyday running of the review. Of the editorial committee, Jean Schlumberger was preoccupied with a production of his play, *La Mort de Sparte* (which did not, in the end, take place) and André Ruyters, back from his year in Abyssinia, seemed less interested in matters literary. That left Jacques Copeau, who, discussing the problem with Gide over dinner, proposed that he should take over the editorship alone, assisted by the excellent and hard-working Jacques Rivière. Gide agreed enthusiastically and soon gained the support of the others. He and Schlumberger remained, of course, the actual 'owners' of the review, who regularly covered the gap between income and expenditure, which Schlumberger calculated as being 1,000 francs (£40 or $200 at the time) per month. The year also saw a dearth of contributions from Ruyters, Drouin and Gide himself. This was largely made up by the acquisition of André Suarès and Albert Thibaudet as regular contributors. In October, the review finally severed its connections with the printer Marcel Rivière (no relation to Jacques) and moved to new, larger premises of its own at 35–37 rue Madame, complete with bookshop. This would enable the Editions de la Nouvelle Revue Française to expand under the management of Gaston Gallimard, with Gide, Schlumberger and Copeau as editorial directors. The previous November the new publishing house had brought out its second batch of books: Schlumberger's novel *L'Inquiète Paternité*, and Ghéon's collection of essays, *Nos Directions*, followed, in January, by Rivière's *Etudes*. Some half-dozen more titles were in place for the autumn and there were plans to publish translations of Conrad and Walt Whitman.

On 19 January 1912, Gide left Paris for ten days in Switzerland, stopping off at Vichy to spend a couple of days with Valéry Larbaud. On the way, Gide wrote to Copeau: 'In what a gloomy ocean I am sailing, seeing nothing, imagining nothing but greyness, understanding neither who I am nor what I am doing here, on earth.'³⁹ From Neuchâtel, Gide went on to Zürich and then on to Andermatt, in the Alps. By the middle of February he was in no better state. 'I've been through some appalling days,' he wrote to Alibert. 'One night . . . I wrapped myself in anguish, actually believing I was going mad . . . Sometimes I'm terrified to feel in my heart such a need for love . . .'⁴⁰

On a February day, sitting on a bench in the Bois de Boulogne, he wrote: 'The weather was radiant this morning; that is the secret of my happiness. But already the sky is clouding over again; I need Apollo; I must depart.'⁴¹ Claudel urged him to join him in Frankfurt and to open up his heart to him: Claudel believed that Gide, 'like all those in labour with conversion', was 'under the influence of the Devil, furious to see you escape his clutches'.⁴² Instead of Claudel and Frankfurt, Gide decided on Tunis and the unknown. On 2 March, he took the night train for Marseille. The sea was rough, so he postponed his departure, going instead, via Toulon, to Cannes. There, he knew, he would find Valéry Larbaud and Arnold Bennett. Bennett, Gide notes, 'earns about a thousand francs a day; he is paid at the rate of a shilling a word; he writes without stopping from six to nine every morning, then does his ablutions and doesn't give his work a thought until the following morning'.[43] The three writers were joined in Cannes by the painter Pierre Bonnard, but, despite the pleasure of their company, Gide left on the fourth day, not for Marseille and Tunis, but for Florence.

Gide himself did not seem to know why he had changed his plans. He no doubt felt that at all costs he must get on with *Les Caves du Vatican* and that Italy would be more conducive to the work in hand. If he chose Florence, rather than the more appropriate Rome, it was because he had friends there and happy memories of the city. Indeed, before leaving Paris, he had received 'a charming letter' from Giovanni Papini, telling him of the impoverished, sickly condition of his Florentine friend Giuseppe Vannicola. For 3 francs (2s 5d or 60 cents at the time) a day, he found 'a bedroom that is not at all sordid, with a rather large drawing-room painted in the Italian style, the windows of which look out over the Arno, between the Ponte Vecchio and the Ponte Santa-Trinità . . .'[44] He hired a 'passable' piano, unpacked his books and bought a batch of his favourite paper, made by Fabriano's of Ancona, 'for *Les Caves*'. But he was still not ready for work. Every day, he saw Vannicola – and wrote to Madeleine. Before long, he was hoping to be joined by other friends – Larbaud and Bonnard from Cannes, Ghéon and perhaps Copeau from Paris – and reporting to Copeau that he was coming out of his torpid state: 'Lafcadio is awakening and I fill my pen every day.'[45] Two days later, Gide had reached Section V of Book 2. Copeau, his chief comforter during those first troubled weeks of 1912 and the dedicatee of the novel-to-be, resisted the temptation to join Gide: after all, he was now in sole charge of the *NRF.* Now that he was at work, Gide himself put off Ghéon's arrival for another month, having earlier sent him a card depicting *putti danzanti*, with a tempting greeting: 'Florence and I await you.' Ghéon's presence would be the occasion for debauch, not creative labour. Larbaud arrived from Cannes on 11 April, but he had his own work, finishing his second 'Barnabooth' book and chasing up references to W. S. Landor in the civic archives. On 16 April Gide went to Pisa to meet Ghéon and brought him back with him to Florence: a bed was fixed up for him in the *salone*. For ten days they led 'an amazing, unrecountable life, of incalculable value'.[46] They wandered the streets of the city and walked along the banks of the Arno. Once or twice they went out into the surrounding countryside. It was Ghéon's first visit to Italy; he arrived at its point of greatest aesthetic concentration and he was overwhelmed. He and Gide spent hours in the churches and galleries. Years later, after his conversion, he saw that encounter with religious works of the Italian Renaissance as the beginning of the movement that brought him back to the Church: 'I admired everything, yes! But my choice was made . . . It was Giotto, Angelico and the Masaccio of the Apostle Peter; all the rest gravitated around them. I tried to cling to paganism; but the master of my love was now the Art that was closest to the Faith – so close that it could hardly be distinguished from it.'[47] Ghéon's stay in Florence was cut short by news that his nieces were seriously ill. Gide spent a few days on the Adriatic coast, then he, too, returned to Paris: he had been away for eight weeks.

On his return, he set to work revising what he had written in Florence. One weekend, at the Villa Montmorency, Gide read what he had written to Copeau. Both reader and listener were pleased with the results. A few days later, Gide wrote to Copeau: 'Genius came upon me between 11 and 1 o'clock in the morning and I completely turned *Les Caves* upside down. Nothing is in the same place as before. Everything has become clear, beyond my wildest hopes . . . and grown by a half.'[48] On 12 May he left for Rouen, where he had been summoned to serve as a juryman. The session lasted from 13 to 25 May. Gide wrote up his notes of those two weeks in *Souvenirs de la Cour d'assizes*, published by the *NRF*, in November and December 1913, then in volume form in 1914. The opening paragraph has a certain celebrity: 'Courts have always exercised an irresistible fascination over me. When travelling, four things above all attract me in a town: the public gardens, the market, the cemetery and the Law Courts.' Gide was, as we might expect, an admirably scrupulous juror and reporter of the sixteen or so cases, usually involving theft or rape, that he heard. 'I cannot be persuaded that society can do without courts and judges,' he writes, 'but, during those twelve days, I was made to feel, to the point of anguish, to what extent human justice is a dubious, precarious thing.'[49]

Gide retired to Cuverville for several weeks, determined to make progress with *Les Caves* – and there, except for a few brief visits to Paris, he stayed until his departure for Pontigny in August. 'I must admit,' he wrote to Copeau on 8 June, 'that these *Caves*, though dedicated to you, cannot and must not be a "masterpiece" – but a shocking book, full of holes, gaps, but also entertaining, bizarre, a book of partial successes. Let me write it like that.'[50] In other words, Gide was painfully breaking new ground, not trying to write a vast, nineteenth-century masterpiece. Copeau, always able to raise Gide's spirits, came to stay in July. Less welcome was Marcel Drouin, whose annual visit brought on what seemed like a final break between the brothers-in-law. 'It's over between Marcel and me,' Gide wrote to Copeau, 'and he seems to feel nothing! And he will never know that for months, for years, it will still hurt me as much as it does today!'[51]

Gide was beginning to wonder whether he should not absent himself from the next literary *décade* at Pontigny and distance himself from Desjardins. Another attack on Desjardins in *L'Indépendance* persuaded him that he could not desert his friend – even though he had no wish for Pontigny to be too closely associated with the *NRF*. As late as 9 July, to Copeau, Gide was expressing further doubts: he was afraid that the 'question laïcité' (Desjardins' anti-clerical, secularist tendencies) and the 'question moeurs' (that is, his own 'immoralism') would be conflated to the damage of both. Gide himself did not fear attack ('*I hope* to be attacked'), but he was anxious about the repercussions on the *NRF*.[52] Again, Gide overcame his doubts. The 'English connection' caused a few problems too. Gosse was very happy to come, but not just for that. Could Gide and Vielé-Griffin arrange 'a little trip . . . in the Creuse, for example?' Then, again, he was anxious to be the only English representative there. Two major hurdles disappeared: Conrad wrote to say that he could not come and Galsworthy was not asked. Gosse continued to play hard to get. Gide and Copeau both wrote persuasive letters. A fulsome appeal from Desjardins finally won him over. The subject would be 'Observation and Invention in the Novel', the core of the programme would be the eighteenth-century English novel: it was inconceivable without Gosse's expert contributions.[53] Gosse came, without his wife. He was in his element. 'Twenty people of varied sex and charm, all reading *Father and Son*, in French at once, is rather an intoxicating phenomenon,' he wrote to Robert Ross, a close friend of his Wilde days.

Immediately after Pontigny, Gide set off for Italy. He spent eight days in a Florence almost abandoned by visitors. One day, he walked along the banks of the Arno well out of the town. He met some young fishermen, 'naked or almost'. One was wearing nothing but 'a shirt, pulled in at the waist by a belt and raised a little, as Donatello would have done, just above what it is usual to hide'. Two of them took him out in their boat, so that he could bathe. On returning to the boat, he found the lads entirely naked and promptly took off his new bathing costume. 'The elder one showed me the tattoos on his arms and on his penis.' Gide asked the younger lad if he had any tattoos to show him: the boy suggested that they moor the boat on the other side of the river and find a quiet spot there . . .[54]

Gide spent eight more days on the Adriatic coast, at Grottamare (where, suffering from a cold, he finished *Oliver Twist*), San Benedetto del Tronto and Acquasanta, in the foothills of the Abruzzi. Gide describes those 'fifteen admirable days' in *Acquasanta*, written much later, probably in 1935. He went for long walks, observed the wine harvest, and read *Paradise Lost*. Every morning, he went swimming, in what the locals called '*la piscina*', a pool largely covered by the walls of a cave, into which gushed the glaucous mineral waters of a spring. He noticed a boy of 'fourteen, perhaps fifteen', who was there every day before he arrived. 'He was like a Triton who had escaped from Amphitrite's voluptuous cortège; the water seemed his natural element. His extraordinarily rapid stroke was like a dance, something between a crawl and a mazurka . . .' Gide talked to him in his faltering Italian: he was called Bernardino. He lay in wait for him at the entrance to the pool, but the boy always seemed to leave by some other way. A few days before leaving Acquasanta, he was sitting on the stone bench, almost under the waterfall, when Bernardino came and sat on his knees, 'laid his chin on my shoulder, hid his eyes against my neck and pressed his forehead against my cheek. How light was that tiny body! . . .' Gide's hand roamed over the boy's torso and descended to his thigh, where it came to a stop: 'the slender limb over which my hand was amorously moving was only a stump'. That explained the boy's strange way of swimming and his sense of wellbeing in 'the opaque waters that protected his secret' – and why he had so far eluded Gide's evident desire to be friends with him. With 'many kisses', 'many caresses', Gide convinced the boy that he did not mind his deformity. Having revealed his secret, the boy was happy to leave the pool with Gide; he even took him home to meet his parents and brothers. Thus far, the account has an impossibly innocent quality. However, it gains interest towards the end as Gide becomes aware that his feelings of tenderness towards the boy were interfering with his erotic attraction to him. True to his own split nature, he was creating two Bernardinos. He loved them both, but with a different love. His feelings for the affectionate, *attendrissant*, 'terrestrial' Bernardino had become pure. 'But I think he preferred those I felt for the Bernardino of the pool', a 'laughing, playful, mischievous, liberated creature', who was also more 'lustful and tenderly voluptuous'.[55] Gide left Acquasanta and made his way, via Florence and Paris, back to Cuverville and Madeleine. He had been away for five weeks. He brought with him another chapter of *Les Caves du Vatican* – what is now Chapter 7 of Book 4. By the middle of October, he had written the first chapter of Book 5 – the book was now over three-quarters finished.

There were visits to Paris. A cryptic letter to Ghéon declares: 'Paris welcomes me with the craziest adventures. Dined yesterday with Charley!

[Charles Du Bos] – spent the evening with Cocteau! etc. . . .'⁵⁶ Gide had met the twenty-three-year-old Cocteau earlier in the year and was obviously still under his youthful spell. It was not to last: Cocteau never entered the charmed circle of the *NRF*, but, for Gide, was to remain a frivolous irritation, sometimes too close for comfort. On 31 October, Gide went south, spending three days at Les Sources with the Charles Gides, then going on to Rouart's at Bagnols and Alibert's at Carcassonne. With 'the two C. brothers', Alibert and he went on to Narbonne. There Gide spent a 'wonderful night, which put me back on my feet, physically and mentally. The extraordinary over-exertion of that night left me in a state of radiant equilibrium.' He was back in Paris on 9 November, to be joined a day or two later by Madeleine, who was 'finally putting Cuverville to sleep'. He was in 'an excellent mood for work', but felt more drawn to reading than writing. His reading, as so often at this time, was in English: Spenser's *Faerie Queene*, Marlowe's *Hero and Leander*, Keats's *Endymion*. He also resumed his private English lessons, noting, on 12 November, that his teacher, who now seems 'sinisterly inade-quate', cannot bring himself to believe (understandably, one might think) that he had read the whole of *Paradise Lost*.⁵⁷

About this time, Copeau was told by Antoine Bibesco of a work by their one-time fellow-pupil at the Lycée Condorcet, an as yet little-known writer, Marcel Proust. Proust, who had considerable means of his own, was looking around for a suitable publisher to bring out, at the author's expense, of course, a novel with the unprepossessing title of *Du Côté de chez Swann*. Copeau deflected the inquiry in the direction of Gaston Gallimard, now in charge of the *NRF*'s book publishing. Given that the *NRF* was far from being a 'normal' publishing business, but rather an extension of the review, publishing only books by its contributors, who were, in turn, usually members of its inner circle or friends, it is really quite surprising that Gaston Gallimard did not simply turn down the request. There were other reasons for doing so. What was known of Proust was not encouraging. He was clearly a social-climbing snob who moved in a quite different world from the rather serious-minded *NRF* group. Proust's first letter seemed *calculated* to solicit a rejection, retailing all the reasons why he should not be dealing with the *NRF* and why the *NRF* would not be interested in his work. He was already committed to another publisher, Fasquelle, who was about to deliver the first proofs of his book, which would have to be published in two volumes, each the size of *L'Education sentimentale*, that is, each four times longer than the volumes so far published by the *NRF*. That Proust's badly typed, unrevised typescript ever reached the *NRF* offices was due entirely to Gaston Gallimard's inexperience – and to the fact that he did not really belong to the *NRF* editorial team. Having got that far, Proust laid down a further condition for acceptance: a few extracts must first be published in the review. Proust also warned Gallimard that the work was extremely indecent and dealt, among other things, with homosexuality. (He already knew, from Bibesco, that Gide, Ghéon and Schlumberger were practising homosexuals.) If the shocking revelations of the second volume meant that the *NRF* could not publish it, then there was no point in reading the first. After Copeau's return from London in November, Antoine Bibesco and his brother Emmanuel gave a dinner for Copeau, Gide and Jean Schlumberger, and left the 633-page typescript with Gide. We do not know how much of it Gide read – he probably did little more than leaf through it. The consequent rejection by the *NRF* becomes more understandable. As Auguste Anglès remarks: 'If one is willing to throw off the illusion of retrospection and the presumption that one would oneself be capable, in any circumstances and without prior warning, of detecting the unknown genius, one will have to admit that all the probabilities were *against* acceptance ... It would have been more glorious for the *NRF* to see through appearances and to recognize at once the genius that was there. Of course. But who, among the prophets of the past, would swear that he would have been capable of piercing the celebrated parcel, better protected by prejudice than by Céleste's string, with the eye of a lynx?'[58]

On 22 December, Gide left for England. For reasons that are not clear, Gide spent two nights at the Belvedere Hotel, Brighton, leaving on Christmas Eve for London, where he booked in at the Charing Cross Hotel. He immediately left a visiting card at Gosse's house, bearing the words: 'So impatient to see you again! But where and when?' A message came back, inviting him to spent Christmas Day with the Gosse family. He replied, accepting the invitation and adding: 'Taine did tell me, though, that it is very tactless to come to London at Christmas time. Do forgive me.'[59] Why, then, one wonders, did he run the risk of spending a lonely, inhospitable Christmas in London? To escape from Christmas at Cuverville with Madeleine, the Drouins, etc.? We do not know. Also invited on that Christmas Day was Henry James. On 28 December, Gide went off to Kent to spend two days with Conrad, during which he visited James at his house nearby. Gide was back at the Gosses', 17 Hanover Terrace, Regent's Park, for dinner on 30 December; also present was George Moore, who had been active in Parisian literary circles in the years 1872–82. Through Gosse, Gide was able to enjoy 'the delights and proprieties' ('délices et convenances') of the Athenaeum Club for four days. However, he fell victim to a 'grippe féroce' (given Gallic exaggeration on this matter, a bad cold, rather than influenza) and decided to cut short his visit and, on 5 January, left for home.[60]

In the course of 1913, the new régime at the *NRF* was to undergo a further transmutation, brought about by the opening of the Vieux Colombier theatre under Jacques Copeau. From January onwards, the negotiations and preparations proceeded at an accelerating pace, leaving Copeau with less and less time for *NRF* matters: although he remained *directeur* in name, the *de facto* editor was Jacques Rivière. In the spring of 1912, Copeau had abandoned the project of starting a new theatre in collaboration with Arsène Durec. But the idea would not die. First with Jean Schlumberger, then joined by Gaston Gallimard (whose father owned the Variétés theatre) and the actor Charles Dullin, Copeau had pursued his dream, planning possible productions, gathering around him a team of actors, chasing up financial support. By late January, he had found his theatre, the former Athénée Saint-Germain music-hall, at 21 rue du Vieux Colombier. He was to mark the change in the theatre's fortunes by abandoning the old name for the name of the street, the Athenaeum for the Old Dovecote. Gide, of course, was no stranger to the theatre: two of his full-length plays had been published and performed. Nevertheless, his young friends at the *NRF* kept him in the dark during the earlier stages of the project. There were a number of reasons for this. His ambivalent attitude to the theatre was well known to them: they had no wish to have their (relatively) youthful enthusiasm blunted by Gidean hesitations and doubts. They sensed, too, that Copeau's involvement in the theatre would be seen by Gide as a dereliction of duty towards the review, which he saw as more important. There was, too, an element of filial rebellion on Copeau's part towards his revered and beloved father-figure: he wanted to succeed in his venture, without Gide's help, asking for Gide's cooperation later. Finally, during a dinner at the Van Rysselberghes', Gide was put in the picture. As expected, he was less than totally enthusiastic, but he promised his support.

Gide retired to Cuverville to work on *Les Caves du Vatican*. A week later, he was travelling southwards. After a few days *chez* Uncle Charles, at Les Sources, he was in Florence, later joined by Ghéon, who had just recovered from a short illness and, at a deeper level, was trying to come to terms with the death of his mother, nine months before. The two then moved south to Siena, where they were joined by Mme Mayrisch and her car. The curious, but devoted trio drove in leisurely fashion through Umbria, reaching Rome a week later. There they were joined by Alibert and Rouart. Their lodgings in the Via Sistina overlooked the Spanish Steps. A feverish few days were spent visiting the Forum, the Colosseum, the Vatican, the Villa Pamphili and several churches. There is no evidence that these four still active homosexuals did very much more than 'sightsee' during their weeks in Italy. It is unlikely that the presence of the charming, but no doubt redoubt-able Mme Mayrisch, that *dame-patronesse* of arts and artists, would have had much of a sobering effect. The absence of information may be due simply to the fact that all possible correspondents were all there together.

On 15 May, at the newly opened Théâtre des Champs-Elysées, the new Diaghilev season began with *Jeux*, danced and choreographed by Nijinsky, to music by Debussy. Before long, Paris – or at least, the small part of it that mattered – was in the grip of 'Russian fever'. Rivière, Schlumberger and Ghéon all contributed reviews of the Diaghilev season to the *NRF.* On 22 May, *le tout Paris*, political and literary, was present at the first night of *Boris Godunov*, with Chaliapin. There were revivals, too, of *Khovanshchina* and *Petrushka*, then, on 29 May, the infamous first night of Stravinsky's *Le Sacre du Printemps*, at which the audience broke into such an uproar of disapproval that the dancers could not hear the orchestra. Jacques Rivière, usually so polite, even shy, had to restrain himself from attacking vociferous neighbours with his cane and shouted 'bande de voyous' ('gang of hooligans') at a Rumanian prince and his party. Behind the scenes, things were no calmer: Stravinsky had nearly died of typhoid and relations between Diaghilev and the increasingly unpredictable Nijinsky were reaching breaking-point. On 9 June, Gide was at the Hôtel Meurice, with Misia (*née*) Godebska (the former Mme Thadée Natanson and Mme Alfred Edwards), the Spanish painter José Maria Sert (Misia's future third husband), Harry Kessler, Diaghilev and Nijinsky for a farewell party – the company was about to leave for its London season.

The following day, Gide and Madeleine left for Cuverville. Gide's long-drawn-out labours over *Les Caves du Vatican* were coming to an end. 'My book is finished – at last!' Gide wrote to Gosse on 29 June. 'In a few days I'll be setting out, with light heart, for Constantinople and Bursa, while Cuverville will be overrun with cousins and nephews.'[61] By 2 July, Gide was confiding to his *Journal*: 'The thought of my departure is making me positively ill: sometimes I hope that the situation in the Balkans gets worse, so that it will be impossible for me to go there.'[62] (In June, Greece, Serbia and Montenegro had declared war on Bulgaria, their former ally, joined the following month by Turkey and Rumania.) Eight days later, he was complaining: 'I would like, I *ought* to go away.' But the trip (with Rouart) to Turkey was abandoned – or rather postponed until the following April, when Gide went there with Ghéon and Mme Mayrisch. Instead Gide went back to Italy. Of the five weeks spent there we have only the barest outline. He went first to Tivoli, where he bathed in the sulphurous springs. He worked on *Souvenirs de la Cour d'Assises* and on his translation of the English version of *The Gitanjali* by the Bengali poet, Rabindranath Tagore. He visited the Etruscan tombs at Chiusi and, from the Hotel Paradiso, the Etrurian shades of Vallombrosa. He spent ten days at Santa Margarita, on the Ligurian coast.

Gide had not entirely escaped the summer invasion of 'cousins and nephews'. Marcel Drouin, the main problem, was still in residence. Two weeks later, Drouin was still there and matters were such that the master of the house felt that he ought to make his escape again to avoid 'Marcel and I having to be too close to one another'. Even Cuverville, it seems, was not big enough to contain the two brothers-in-law. Gide took 'infinite precautions' and kept as much as possible to his study in the loft.[63] There he finished *Souvenirs de la Cour d'Assises*, which appeared in the November and December numbers of the *NRF* and in book form in 1914. Spurred on by the awarding of the Nobel Prize for Literature to the Indian poet, Gide also completed his Tagore translations. Twenty-five of the poems appeared in the December number of the *NRF*, followed a few weeks later by all the poems in volume form, under the title *L'Offrande lyrique*.

Gide arrived back in Paris on 15 October, the date on which the new Vieux Colombier theatre was supposed to open. In the event, the opening night did not take place until a week later. The tireless efforts of Copeau and his friends had finally come to fruition. By the end of June, his company was made up, with Louis Jouvey acting as a sort of secretary, logging their progress. Rehearsals began on 1 July at Copeau's house at Le Limon, accommodation being found for the actors in the village. All summer they worked away at exercises of various kinds and rehearsals of the first plays in the repertoire. During the same period, Copeau and his friends were frantically trying to raise the rest of the money needed to proceed. The better-off members of the *NRF* team – Gide, Schlumberger, Gallimard – had contributed to the best of their abilities. More came from Mme Mayrisch, the Bibescos, the Princesse de Polignac, Anna de Noailles. The temporarily rejected Marcel Proust contributed; Arnold Bennett, one of whose stories had been published by the *NRF*, 'shied away' in a 'pitiful letter'. The great Eleonora Duse sent a contribution and Copeau's rival, Antoine, made a generous appeal for help from the stage of his own theatre, the Odéon. More money came from richer, less celebrated individuals. Friends, too, were lavish in their unpaid labours. Gaston Gallimard took over the thankless task of business manager, dividing his day between theatre and publishing house. At a more menial level, there is Roger Martin du Gard's description of his first visit back-stage, shortly before the opening, when he caught sight of Jean Schlumberger, 'hammer in hand and tacks between his lips . . . nailing down numbers in an improvised cloakroom'.[64] The visitor, who had imagined those associated with the *NRF* 'enthroned in intimidating majesty', was struck by the general atmosphere of friendly informality. Certainly, solemnity did not reign there. Rivière would refer to the Vieux Colombier as '*le vieux con*' ('the old cunt') and Copeau himself called it '*le VC*', which, pronounced *à la française*, was how many French people referred to a 'WC'.

The theatre had not only changed its name. True to the new spirit of austerity and simplicity, Francis Jourdain had had the mirrors and gilt ornamentation at the entrance covered over with plywood and smothered in thick layers of his favourite colour, yellow ochre. In the same spirit – and to the horror of the owner – the theatre's accumulation of all-purpose stage sets was dumped in the courtyard and left to rot in the rain: Jourdain's sets were to consist of schematic doorways, curtains, moveable screens and a minimum of props. A certain concordance may well have existed between such scenic minimalism and the theatre's financial straits, but Copeau's theatrical aesthetic was well established at the outset of the project: in none too rigorous or literal a way he hoped to bring about a French equivalent of the work of Stanislavsky, Max Reinhardt and Gordon Craig. He had also been much influenced by William Archer's *Play-making, a Manual of Craftsmanship*, which he had reviewed briefly in the *NRF*. 'We could not,' he declared, 'find a better declaration of principles' and proposed that the book be translated and put on the *NRF* list.

The inauguration of what was to be one of the most celebrated undertakings in twentieth-century theatre took place on 22 October. A lecture by Copeau was followed by a dress rehearsal of his own adaptation of Thomas Heywood's Jacobean tragedy *A Woman Killed with Kindness*. The opening night followed next day. The rue du Vieux Colombier had never seen such a crowd. The *ouvreuses*, who had been forbidden to accept tips, were unable to shut the doors, as people forced their way in and stood at the back of the auditorium. What had set out as an improvised, radical reform of theatrical *mœurs* had turned out to be a social event that was not on any account to be missed. The Prime Minister, Louis Barthou, was there, in Anna de Noailles' entourage. A few days later, a scandalized Arnold Bennett remarked that, at 'one of the most solemn, most Parisian of solemnities' Gide had only risen to the semi-formality of a dinner-jacket, rather than tails.[65] An exceptionally fine cast, led by Roger Karl as the husband and Blanche Albane as the eponymous woman, included Charles Dullin, Louis Jouvey . . . and Copeau himself, who had never before set foot on a stage. Heywood's play, hitherto unknown to the French and rarely played in English, was joined in the repertoire by Molière's *L'Amour Médecin*. Within a few weeks, with Jean Schlumberger's *Les Fils Louverné* and Molière's *L'Avare*, the repertoire had expanded to four plays. The Vieux Colombier also organized a series of lectures under the general title of 'Matinées poétiques'. Gide gave the first of these on Saturday, 22 November, which he devoted to the work of Verlaine and Mallarmé. Twelve weeks later, he gave another lecture, this time on Rabindranath Tagore.

It was during a visit to the theatre that Roger Martin du Gard met members of the *NRF* group for the first time. His first novel, *Devenir*, had been published at his own expense by Ollendorf in 1909. His second, *L'Une de Nous*, had been taken on, again at the author's expense, by a young newcomer to publishing, Bernard Grasset. When, in 1913, Martin du Gard presented Grasset with an extremely long novel, largely in dialogue, which he called *S'affranchir*, the publisher, who had agreed to undertake the costs of the next novel, took fright. Martin du Gard had followed the *NRF* from the beginning and an accidental meeting with Gaston Gallimard, a fellow-pupil at the Lycée Condorcet, persuaded him to submit the manuscript to the *NRF*. It was passed on to Gide, who, three days later, sent a telegram to the *NRF* office declaring: 'To be published without hesitation.' Four months later, as *Jean Barois*, the name of its hero, it was published in volume form by the *NRF*. The character of the hero was partly based on the Abbé Marcel Hébert, the principal of the Ecole Fénelon, where Martin du Gard had studied. A modernist Catholic theologian, he fell foul of the papal denunciation of all modernist thinking; forced to resign his post, he later left the priesthood. Martin du Gard had been brought up a Catholic, but claimed that he was a 'born unbeliever': 'My atheism was formed at the same time as my mind.' The fate of his revered teacher further fuelled his anti-clericalism. He was the most scrupulously fair-minded of men and was genuinely surprised at the virulent reception Catholics gave his *Jean Barois*.

Some days after publication, Martin du Gard attended an *NRF* Sunday 'at home' for the first time. He describes the scene in *Notes sur André Gide*, published in 1951. The atmosphere struck him at first like that of a church youth club: 'a dozen young men' were standing around Gaston Gallimard. Jean Schlumberger, with 'a well-mannered coolness that seemed to intimidate even himself', moved around trying 'to transform it into an appearance of smiling good nature'. In the next room, he found 'a hilarious, uproarious Bluebeard in a state of demonic excitement', who 'spluttered and gesticulated as he talked', punctuating what he said with 'strident whinnyings' (Ghéon). Then 'a man sidles into the shop . . . His eyes are hidden behind the rim of a battered old hat; an all-enveloping cloak hangs from his shoulders. He looks like an old, half-starved, out-of-work actor; or like one of those bohemian wrecks who end up in a doss-house . . .' He takes off his hat and cloak.

His shapeless, outworn, travelling-suit doesn't seem to belong to his awkward limbs; his detachable collar, frayed and hanging loose, reveals a neck like that of some elderly bird . . . The Mongol mask . . . is dotted with a few warts . . . There is no candour in the eyes, as they hover beneath the eyelids, and with the momentary flashing glance there goes a smile that is almost a grimace; a smile that is at once childlike and sly, at once timid and studied. Schlumberger brings him over to me. I am dumbfounded: it is André Gide . . .

Gide takes the young writer to one side and gives him a candid, though on the whole complimentary, view of his book. 'The voice flows easily and naturally; it has an admirable timbre – deep, warm, solemn, a voice that coaxes and whispers, a voice made for confidences, with the subtlest modulations, and just occasionally an abrupt heightening of tone to make way for a rare epithet or an original, meaningful turn of phrase.' Disregarding 'the two-days' growth of beard, the unkempt hair, the rumpled collar', he becomes aware of 'the nobility of the face, instinct with feeling and intelligence, the subtle tenderness of his smile'.[66]

A couple of weeks later, Martin du Gard was invited to lunch at Auteuil. It was probably his second meeting with Gide and certainly the first with Madeleine. A letter to Marcel de Coppet, dated 4 January 1914, shows what a perceptive observer this young man of thirty-three could be. After an excellent description of the 'strange, Anglo-Egyptian fortress', he turns to his hosts. He notes the 'very youthful, smiling expression' on Madeleine's face. Yet, behind 'this welcoming, expansive manner', there is 'great reserve'. 'She seems to worship him [Gide], not as a husband, but as a marvellous cousin, an elusive genius, surprising in everything . . .' Gide seems 'ill at ease, amiable, shy, exaggerating his mannered way of saying certain specific words, twisting his mouth sideways, pursing his lips hard, then releasing them with a slow, pained, ambiguous smile . . .'[67] He compares Gide's gaze to a lighthouse, at times absent, then suddenly turning on one a jet of blinding light.

During 1913, the *NRF* had consolidated its progress: both review and publishing house were in a healthy state. In purely literary terms, it had been an exceptionally fine year. With his *A. O. Barnabooth: Journal d'un milliahdaire*, which had been published by the review in five instalments from February to June, Valéry Larbaud had emerged as a writer of immense, idiosyncratic talent, many would say, of genius. On 18 May, this tireless Anglicist and invincible Anglophile began another leisurely tour of the British Isles, providing regular 'lettres anglaises' for the *NRF,* while continuing with his own writing. In London, he finalized with Macmillan's the agreement that gave Gide the French rights in Tagore's *Gitanjali.* He urged Gide to join him in Cambridge, before the end of term, with tempting images of beautiful young men in boats. 'There one meets Phaidon, Alcibiades and Menexenes, stretched out on velvet cushions, reading – who knows? *Les Nourritures terrestres,* while the oars lie idle in the water.'[68] (Gide did not join him and had to wait until the end of the war before seeing the Cam and its boatmen.) By 3 July, Larbaud was in Scotland. From Greenock, he sailed, not to Iceland, as he had intended, but to Dublin, where he met James Joyce. (He was later to be responsible, in part, for the translation of *Ulysses.*) In July the review published the first of five instalments of a very different work, Alain-Fournier's *Le Grand Meaulnes.* A novel of much broader appeal, it was to acquire an added glamour from the death of its author the following year on active service. By November, the deliberations of the Goncourt jury had reached an eleventh round. Both Larbaud and Alain-Fournier were in the running. If the *NRF* had taken up Proust's offer (*Du Côté de chez Swann* had just been published by Bernard Grasset), it would have had a third candidate in the short-list. It is not often that a single year can boast three fictional works of such unquestionable greatness. True to its usual blend of book-trade politicking and aesthetic myopia, the jury's election lighted on a soon-to-be-forgotten nonentity, Pierre Hamp.

Early in the New Year, Gide did his best to make personal amends to Proust. 'For several days now I have not left your book,' he wrote. 'I am supersaturating myself in it with delight, revelling in it.' Its rejection was 'the *NRF*'s most serious mistake' and, since he admits to being largely responsible for it, 'one of the bitterest regrets of my life'. With a candour that would have been astonishing in most people, but which was entirely natural to Gide, he admits that he had had an image of Proust based on 'a few encounters in "Society" going back about twenty years': for him, Proust was '*un snob, un mondain amateur*'. 'I shall never forgive myself – and it is only to alleviate my pain a little that I am confessing to you this morning – begging you to be more indulgent with me than I am myself.'[69] The *NRF* offered to publish the next and future volumes of *A la recherche du temps perdu*, at its own expense, and republish the first volume when the Grasset edition went out of print. With exquisite hyperbole, Proust replied that he in no way regretted the *NRF*'s initial rejection, since, without it, he would not have received Gide's letter, which gave him infinitely more pleasure than being published by the *NRF*! Proust accepted the offer, but the publication of the second volume had to await the end of the war, when the Goncourt Academy also made its amends. However, extracts from it appeared in the review's June and July numbers.

Since the foundation of the Vieux Colombier, Copeau had had less time to devote to the *NRF*. Though Jacques Rivière was now acting editor, he was not yet editor in name: on matters of policy, Copeau still expected to be consulted. On 21 January Gide had written to Rivière instructing him, on behalf of Ghéon and himself, to include some poems by Jean Cocteau in a forthcoming number of the review. Rivière replied that the poems were 'frankly bad', and should not appear. He also alerted Copeau, who wrote Gide a long, forceful letter, full of new-found self-confidence. The editorship was still in his hands and he should have been consulted. Cocteau's entry into the charmed circle would be 'deplorable'. 'There is perhaps no one in Paris at present more representative of everything we detest, everything that is antagonistic to us. Cocteau will never be one of us . . .' He suggests that Gide has allowed himself to be swayed in Cocteau's favour against his better judgement. This was probably true and it was largely Ghéon's work. Gide cared not at all for what he saw as the frivolous, snobbish, *mondain* society frequented by Cocteau – and his homosexual friends, Lucien Daudet, Marcel Proust, Reynaldo Hahn and Robert de Montesquiou. Nevertheless, Gide had been dazzled by the young man's social charm and not unaffected by his sedulous efforts to win Gide's approval. In the end, Cocteau's poems did not appear in the *NRF*. Indeed, nothing by Cocteau appeared there until 1923, in a special number devoted to Proust, who had died the previous year.

Les Caves du Vatican appeared in the first four numbers of the *NRF* in 1914. The first edition (550 copies in two volumes) followed in the summer of that year. The title was followed by the words 'sotie par l'auteur de *Paludes*'. This seemingly half-hearted gesture towards anonymity was further contradicted by a frontispiece: a portrait of the author by P.-A. Laurens. (The cheaper, 'popular' edition in one volume, which followed some weeks later, did bear the author's name.) It is worth noting the first appearance of the term '*sotie*', which Gide also later ascribed, retrospectively, to *Paludes* and *Le Prométhée mal enchaîné*. The original *soties* were satirical plays put on by law students and clerks in late medieval Paris: a favourite theme was the election of a 'pope of fools'. Gide's *sotie* is shot through with just such youthful irreverence.

Les Caves had been more than usually painful in the writing, though it appears all spontaneity and lightness of touch in the reading. The time that elapsed from its original conception to final birth was so long, even by Gide's standards, that he had forgotten when the idea of the book had first occurred to him. He had to be reminded by Paul-Albert Laurens that he had talked to him about it in Biskra, in 1893, twenty years before. Indeed, it was about this time that a rumour began to circulate that the Pope, Leo XIII, had been taken prisoner by a group of cardinals, working in concert with a Masonic lodge, and an impostor put in his place. (The origin of the rumour was clearly the dismay felt, especially in France, by traditionally-minded Catholics at an apparently liberalizing shift in papal thinking. In 1884, an encyclical urged Catholics to accept the French Republic as the legal state and to respect its laws. Then, in 1891, the encyclical *Rerum Novarum* expressed concern for the condition of the working class and advocated a fairer distribution of wealth.) Taking advantage of the rumour, if they did not actually originate it themselves, a priest, an ex-nun and a crooked lawyer, living in Lyon, set about collecting money for a crusade that would free the 'real' pope. They succeeded in persuading several rich Catholics to part with large sums of money. To this *fait divers*, Gide added another, dating from the same time: the public renunciation of his atheism by a Freemason cousin of Emile Zola in the church of Il Gesù in Rome. The essential role of such *faits divers* for Gide was that they provided him with narrative elements that were not autobiographical: they represented an escape from self and from the history of that self. Gide was quite capable of narrative invention; he was less adept at creating the raw materials out of nothing.

Les Caves du Vatican is divided into five books, each subdivided into numbered sections. Four of them are named after leading characters – the fourth book, named after the criminal gang 'Le Mille-pattes' ('The Millipede'), might also have been called after their leader Protos. The fifth book bears the name of the young hero, Lafcadio. Of course, each book is not devoted solely to one character and, in the final one, all the various roads lead to Rome. As in all farce, it is accident, often of a far-fetched kind, that governs the plot, not action as the expression of character. In fact, the characters – like everything else in the novel – lack 'depth': Gide tried, quite deliberately, to make the characters, other than his hero, two-dimensional stereotypes and, as such, fit objects for the author's ridicule. We are alerted to this by the very names – all unusual and, in varying degrees, ridiculous.

Anthime Armand-Dubois, the character based on Zola's cousin, Free-mason and scientist, materialist and atheistic in outlook, is converted to Catholicism on being cured of his sciatica after dreaming of the Virgin Mary. Julius de Baraglioul, a fashionable writer, a Catholic and a conservative, frustrated of his hopes of being elected to the Académie française, begins to write a 'modern', iconoclastic novel. Amédée Fleurissoire is a provincial nobody. All three are brothers-in-law, husbands of the unhappily named Péterat sisters ('*péter*' means 'to fart'). Protos, the leader of the 'Millepattes', is, as his name implies, a master of disguise and dissimulation: as Father Salus, he extracts a large sum of money from the Comtesse Guy de Saint-Prix, Julius' sister; as Professor Defouqueblize, of the Bordeaux law faculty, he even manages to take in his old schoolfriend, Lafcadio. We do not have to wait until the last book to meet Lafcadio Wluiki: he appears in Book 2 when Julius is sent to call on him by his sick father, the Comte Juste-Agénor de Baraglioul, a former diplomat, with instructions to find out what he can about him. He turns out to be a young man of nineteen, of Rumanian nationality, but with several languages at his command, the son of a courtesan and father unknown. During his childhood, he had a succession of 'uncles', of various nationalities, as his mother travelled with them from country to country. He calls on the dying count, having worked out that he is his father. Soon afterwards, the count dies, leaving Lafcadio a good part of his huge fortune.

The three brothers-in-law are examples of what Protos and Lafcadio, as schoolboys, called 'crustaceans' (*crustacés*), slow-moving minds, protected by shell-like dogmatic systems. Even when such men swap their philosophical systems for diametrically opposed ones, their mode of thinking remains equally dogmatic. Against the 'crustaceans', the young Protos and Lafcadio set the 'subtle' (*subtils*), those, like themselves, quick-witted, fast-moving, chameleon-like.[70]

Lafcadio can be traced to no single original, though aspects of the most varied individuals have been attributed to him. His name, if nothing else, came from the American writer and Japanese scholar, Lafcadio Hearn; his cosmopolitan elegance and linguistic skill from Valéry Larbaud, who may have suggested the surname Wluiki; his physical attraction from any number of young men encountered – 'Alexandre S.', 'Emile X' and, of course, 'M.' (Maurice Schlumberger). Literary antecedents have been suggested: Stendhal's Julien Sorel and Fabrice del Dongo, Dostoevsky's Raskolnikov. One might add the picaresque heroes of Fielding and Smollett, in a more refined, less full-blooded form. Then there are the real-life literary antecedents: Guillaume Apollinaire (the son of a Polish courtesan of noble birth and a father variously supposed to be a bishop's brother, the bishop himself or a grandson of Napoleon), Lautréamont and Rimbaud (both of whom Gide was reading in 1905). There is another literary reference: Lafcadio was born in the Schloss Duino, near Trieste, the property of the Princess Marie von Thurn und Taxis, where Rilke wrote the first of the Duino Elegies.

Clearly Gide conceived Lafcadio *con amore*: a great deal of creative fantasy went into the making of the handsome, fair-haired young man from nowhere and everywhere. A bastard, he is free of family ties and of the morality inculcated by the family. He has loyalty to no one country and has therefore no sense of patriotism. In the social structure, he has no definable place, possessing the style and manners of the aristocracy, but, on account of his illegitimacy, excluded from it. Attractive to everybody, young and old, male and female, he crosses sexual boundaries with as much ease as territorial ones. However, this aspect is handled by Gide so discreetly as to require a particularly attentive reading. In a letter to Gide of 6 April 1914, one, perhaps over-attentive, reader, Proust, remarked, with bitchy hyperbole, that Lafcadio's '*oncles*' were in fact '*tantes*' (i.e. 'queens') and were as interested in the son as in the mother. The German Baron Heldenbruck was much possessed of 'children's hygiene' and himself took on the task of bathing the boy in cold water, winter or summer. The Polish Vladimir Bielkowski, like everyone who wanted to please my mother was most attentive to me; it always seemed as if *I* were the one being courted . . . He always followed his bent . . . and he had more than one . . . I could not but be flattered by the particular attachment he had for me.'[71] The English 'Uncle Faby' (Fabian Taylor, Lord Gravensdale) was 'quite embarrassed at first to feel that he had fallen for me'.[72] He, like his German predecessor, was keen that the youth should benefit from total exposure to air and sunlight – his photograph of the boy, sitting naked on an upturned canoe, is on Lafcadio's mantelpiece. Later, Faby took the sixteen-year-old off on 'a marvellous trip' to Algeria: 'I think it was the best time of my life.'[73] Lafcadio is attractive not only to his mother's lovers: he seduces almost everyone he meets with his charm. Julius de Baraglioul, who turns out to be his half-brother, is attracted by his 'youthful grace':[74] in one of his unused notes, Gide has Julius 'completely concealing his wedding-ring beneath an enormous cornelian ring' and 'he and his wife seem to be wearing the same makeup'.[75] At the end of the book, Lafcadio sleeps with Julius' daughter, Geneviève, but, in the morning, it is clear that the experience will not be repeated and that the young man will be on his way. On the train, Fleurissoire chooses his compartment solely because he is 'attracted . . . by Lafcadio's youthful grace'[76] – and consequently meets his death.

Fleurissoire's death – Lafcadio's *acte gratuit* – is the incident that brings all the book's various strands together. It is also its most famous – and scandalous – moment, the one that brought Gide most praise and blame. It arrives without warning. One minute Lafcadio is thinking of helping Fleurissoire, who is having difficulty doing up his collar; the next, he is saying to himself:

Who would see? . . . The door would suddenly give way and he would topple out; the slightest push would do it . . . A crime without a motive . . . What a puzzle for the police! . . . I'm curious not so much about events, as about myself. Many a man thinks he's capable of anything, but draws back when it comes to the point . . . If one could foresee all the risks, the game would lose all interest![77]

He decides to allow an element of chance to enter the game. If he can count slowly up to twelve before seeing a light out of the window, he will spare the old man. A light appears on the count of ten – and Lafcadio ejects his travelling companion out of the door. Gide is not Dostoevsky; *Les Caves du Vatican* is not *Crime and Punishment*; Lafcadio is not Raskolnikov. Raskolnikov is a depressed, impoverished 'eternal student', with no prospects whatsoever, who murders his unpleasant, avaricious landlady; Lafcadio, attractive, carefree, now rich, seems, at first sight, to be the last person to murder an inoffensive old man of whom he knows nothing. At no point are we allowed to feel sorry for his victim: his exit from the carriage-door is no more *serious* than a character's unexpected entrance in a farce. Lafcadio never feels the slightest remorse, nor is he found out and made to suffer for his actions; he is treated by the author with no more understanding, plausibility or justice than any of his other characters. Like them, he is treated, as Gide himself said, in *ironic* mode: *Les Caves du Vatican* is a *sotie*, not a tragedy or a philosophical treatise.

Lafcadio's *acte gratuit*, which has attracted so much attention, has two, more or less distant ancestors in Gide's work. In *Paludes*, the philosopher Alexandre alludes in passing to what he calls an *acte libre*, 'an act dependent on nothing . . ., detachable . . ., suppressible, valueless'.[78] Four years later, in 1899, the *action gratuite* makes its appearance in *Le Prométhée mal enchaîné*. Again a serious problem in moral philosophy is treated with deliberate lightness, reduced almost to absurdity. This crime is further reduced to absurdity in the next section. Julius is explaining to his new-found brother the new direction that his fiction is taking. Up till now, 'an erroneous ethics' has inhibited the free development of his creativity. His characters had similarly suffered from his insistence that they act logically, in accordance with their natures. In his present novel, a crime is committed 'gratuitously', 'entirely without motive' . . . (Again, as in *Paludes*, Gide places '*en abyme*' a literary miniature of the work in which it appears.) Julius then picks up a newspaper and shows Lafcadio an account of the train murder.

Indeed it was the crucial role played by chance and the *acte gratuit*, as well as the light-hearted, frivolous attitude adopted towards the Church, the family, morality and 'established' intellectual endeavour that endeared this book to the younger avant-garde, especially to the Dadaists and Surrealists. It is a book that has always appealed to rebellious youth: it enjoyed a new lease of life in the years after the Second World War, when it suddenly seemed to readers attentive more to its iconoclasm than to its lightly worn elegance a contemporary of Sartre's *La Nausée* and Camus' *L'Etranger*. The response from the Catholic Right was as strong in the opposite direction. It began, in March 1914, when Claudel read the proofs for the final *NRF* instalment. 'It is with growing unease that I am following Gide's novel,' he wrote to Jacques Rivière.

Finally I was brought to a stop on page 478 by a pederastic passage that throws a sinister light on certain of our friend's previous works. Am I finally to resign myself to believing that he is himself a participant in these frightful practices [*ces mœurs affreuses*], something that until now I have always refused to do? After *Saül* and *L'Immoraliste*, he could not allow himself another imprudence. The one that he has just committed labels him once and for all . . . Is this why he is so anxious to attribute the same morals to Arthur Rimbaud, and no doubt even to Whitman?'[79]

*

Sancta simplicitas! The same day Claudel wrote in similar terms to Gide himself: 'In heaven's name, Gide, how could you write the passage on page 478 . . .? Answer me, you must . . . If you are not a pederast, why this strange predilection for this sort of subject? And if you are one, unfortunate man, then get yourself cured and do not display these abominations. Consult Mme Gide; consult the better part of your heart . . .'[80]

Gide received the letter soon after his arrival in Florence, where he was joined by Jacques Raverat and his English wife. Raverat, an artist, had been living in and around Cambridge, a familiar of the Rupert Brooke circle. Three years before, he had married one of Charles Darwin's grand-daughters. Also staying in the same house was Louis Fabulet, the translator of Kipling, with whom Gide was working on the translation of Whitman. Fabulet, another practitioner of '*ces mœurs affreuses*', was as keen as Gide to espouse the 'cause' by publishing Whitman in unbowdlerized French. On 7 March, Gide replied to Claudel: 'By what right do you issue this summons? In the name of what do you ask these questions?' His main fear is that, in his outrage, Claudel will say or write something that will hurt Madeleine. 'I entreat you only to consider this: I love my wife more than my life, and I could not forgive anything you did or said that would impair her happiness.' He is quite willing to share his thoughts with Claudel, but will only do so as to a priest, under the secrecy of the confessional. 'I have never felt any desire for women; and the great sadness of my life is that the longest, the strongest, the most constant love has been accompanied by nothing of what normally precedes it. On the contrary, it seemed as if love prevented desire.' Far from doing harm, his books have brought relief to many who, 'like me, have been smothered by the lies of morality': 'I find hypocrisy odious and I know that there are those it has killed.'[81] The following day, Gide writes again, apologizing for insulting Claudel by so much as raising the possibility that Claudel might divulge his secret to a third party. (In fact, it was too late: Claudel had already written to Jacques Rivière, Francis Jammes and a priest, Father Fontaine, whom Gide is urged to see.) There is, in any case, he adds, nothing to be done 'to solve this problem that God has inscribed in my flesh. Do you understand? No, you don't, do you?'[82]

'My poor Gide,' Claudel replied the following day, 'I would not have written had I not preserved my friendship for you' – and launched into a 1,000-word sermon. Contrary to natural reason and Revelation (Leviticus, Epistle to the Romans), Gide's *mœurs* are 'neither permitted, excusable nor admissible'. 'Reproduction' is the sole purpose of sexual attraction. If one starts by justifying 'sodomy', one will go on to justify 'onanism, vampirism, the rape of children, cannibalism . . . Despite all the doctors, I absolutely refuse to believe in physiological determinism.' Gide's resort to 'idiosyncrasy' is a result of his 'Protestant heredity'. The first thing Gide must do is 'suppress at once that horrible passage' from the book version of *Les Caves*. 'You are demeaning yourself [*vous vous déclassez*], marginalizing yourself among those on the fringe of society, outside the human pale . . . You will no longer count.' To Gide's request for secrecy, he replies that it is Gide himself, who, by publishing such things, is 'displaying on all the walls of Paris, a text that, for everyone, will be tantamount to a definitive, official admission . . . No writer, even Wilde, has done that.'[83]

Letters go back and forth until the end of March: between Gide and Claudel, Gide and Jammes, Claudel and Rivière. In one letter to Rivière, Claudel urges him to persuade Gide to see a priest or, failing that, at least a certain specialist in nervous diseases. If Gide does not do something about his condition, Claudel concludes, dogmatic as ever, he would decline into a complete 'break-down, a sad end to a man who promised so much'.[84]

Rivière, who admired both men, declined to take sides, his affection and reverence for Gide undiminished. Gide absolutely refused to cut out the offending passage and considered Claudel's suggestion that, if he did, 'people will gradually forget', shameful. Then there was the question of the epigraph to one section of the book, a quotation from Claudel's *L'Annonce faite à Marie:* 'But of which King do you speak and of which Pope? For there are two and one does not know which is the true one.' In 1912, Claudel had given permission for Gide to use the lines, but now fears that, in the context, they might assume 'a heretical aspect'. Claudel insisted that they be removed. Gide agreed to do so in the cheaper, popular edition, but it was too late in the case of the small, *de luxe* edition.

The reactions of Gide's non-Catholic, or at least less bigoted friends, was enthusiastic. From England, praise came from Conrad (who provided, from *Lord Jim*, the epigraph for the last part), Bennett ('full of meat') and Gosse (who noted the affiliation with Fielding and called it 'a *great* novel').[85]

'Le Cinéma des *Caves* m'enchante,' wrote Cocteau with an eye on the future.[86] The naturally backward-looking Proust compared it to 'a rose-window'. Apologizing for being too ill to see Gide he adds: 'Anyway, I'm not very far away. The Baragliouls, Juste-Agénor and Julius, but above all Lafcadio are much more faithful transmitting organs than a telephone.' That was only after reading the first instalment: 'How I wish it were 1 February!'[87] After the third instalment, Proust comes out with the intriguing comment: 'In the creation of Lafcadio, no one has been objective with such perversity since Balzac.' But he has even more exalted comparisons in mind: 'I read your book with passion. It is truly a Creation in the genetic sense of Michelangelo; the Creator is absent, it is he who has made everything and he is not one of the creatures. I see you regulating Fleurissoire's comings and goings like the choleric God of the Sistine installing the moon in the sky.'[88] Friends apart, *Les Caves* was generally either ignored, condemned or misunderstood. It was, Gide himself said, 'one of my biggest "flops"'. The critic of *Les Marges* made the expected, facile remark that *Les Caves* should have been called not a *sotie*, but a *sottise* (stupidity). Another declared that he would not care to share a railway compartment with M. André Gide.

In Gide's absence, the Vieux Colombier devoted one of its 'matinées poétiques' to Gide's work, in particular to a reading by actors (including Copeau) of *Bethsabé*. It was, said Ghéon, 'very successful'. In the same letter, Ghéon speaks of '*mes nouvelles amours*'. Apparently, he had made advances to a young actor in the darkened auditorium, during rehearsals for a revival of *Les Frères Karamazov*. They were to dine together the following day. The Vieux Colombier was also about to begin rehearsals of his own play, *L'Eau-de-Vie*, and the projected *Twelfth Night* was well advanced.

No sooner had Gide arrived back in Paris on 17 March than plans were afoot for a long tour of Anatolia. The party would consist of Gide, Ghéon and Mme Mayrisch, who consulted Cook's and came up with plans for a four-month absence. Ghéon was reluctant to agree to a date, not knowing the fate of his play – or of his affair with the young actor; Gide simply hesitated, as always. *L'Eau-de-Vie* had its first night on 23 April – and was a flop. (It was taken off after ten performances.) Ghéon had no further reason to stay in Paris; he and Gide took the eastbound train from the Gare de l'Est. With them were Thadée Natanson, who left them in Vienna, and Anna de Noailles' brother, Prince Constantin de Brancovan, who was replaced by Loup Mayrisch. At Sofia, Gide posted the proofs of *Les Caves du Vatican*, on which he had been working throughout the journey.

They arrived at Constantinople on 28 April, travelling on by train to Bursa and, by horse-carriage, to Isnic and Konya. 'After dinner, our minds hungry for marvels and ready for all manner of stupefactions', Ghéon and Gide set out on a tour of the town.[89] It was not long before Gide realized that Anatolia was not North Africa: even the people, whatever their mixed ancestry, were 'universally ugly'. 'In the end I have to admit that Konya is by far the most hybrid, the most vulgar, the ugliest place that I have seen since being in Turkey' – and the entire country and its people were far worse than his wildest fears. 'Did I have to come here to realize how pure and special everything I saw in Africa was? Here everything is soiled, warped, tarnished, adulterated.'⁹⁰ Throughout the entire trip Gide is in a decidedly bad mood. They spent a few days at Ephesus and Smyrna (Izmir), then sailed for Greece.

It is better to come from Turkey, rather than from France or Italy, to admire as one should the miracle that was Greece . . . 'Brought me home to the glory that was Greece.' On the ship taking us to the Piraeus, I am already repeating those lines from [Poe's] *To Helen*. My heart is filled with peace, laughter and serenity . . . I am so little surprised to be here. Everything seems so familiar. I seem so natural to myself here . . . I recognize everything; I am 'at home': this is Greece . . .⁹¹

Gide's perversity is seldom so explicit. He escapes from Paris in search of another Islamic world, an attempt to re-create his youthful infatuation with North Africa, and finds instead a kind of Islamic obverse, his paradise turned into an ugly hell. From there he refreshes himself at the source of European, in particular French, civilization. Such sentiments are worthy of Maurras and *Action Française*: written only a few weeks before the outbreak of the 'Great War' – and the flood of patriotic fervour that followed – they assume a certain, unintended, appropriateness. The German-trained Ottoman Turks were, of course, on the other side and were to be one of the war's four great imperial casualties.

Gide left his companions in Greece and was back in Paris by the morning of Sunday, 31 May, in time to see the last two performances, *matinée* and *soirée*, of *La Nuit des Rois*. The new theatre's triumphant season had come to a triumphant end with a universally praised production. (The sets and costumes had been designed – and partly made – by Duncan Grant, the twenty-nine-year-old English artist and former pupil of Jacques-Emile Blanche, who had played an important role in the celebrated 'Post-Impressionist' exhibition in London the year before.) Inspired, in part at least, by Harley Granville-Barker's celebrated production of *Twelfth Night* at the Savoy Theatre the year before, it came as a revelation to French audiences of what the much-vaunted, but generally ill-served Shakespeare could be. The following day, an exhausted Copeau, who, on top of all his other responsibilities, had played Malvolio, set off with a contingent of his actors for Alsace. There, over six days, they performed Molière's *L'Avare* and *L'Amour Médecin*, and *Les Fils Louverné* by their native son, Jean Schlumberger. (*Twelfth Night* had been excluded on the grounds that only French plays should be performed in the province which, since the end of the Franco-Prussian War in 1871, had been German territory.)

Next day Gide was in Misia Sert's box at the Opéra, together with Kessler, Cocteau, Stravinsky and Massine, for performances of *Petrushka* and *Midas*. On Wednesday he lunched with Kessler, who begged him to stay on in Paris for more *délices russes*, but the opening night of the Oeuvre production of Claudel's *L'Otage* would be taking place on Friday, 5 June: Gide left Paris for Cuverville the day before.

Without any enthusiasm whatsoever, Gide worked at the travel notes that were to become *La Marche turque*. (He finished what he himself called 'a mediocre piece of work' three weeks later.) Dedicated 'à Em', to make up for the paucity of letters André had sent her during his absence, it appeared in the August number of the *NRF*. He worked on a translation of Tagore's *The Post Office* and read Clive Bell's recent book *Art*. He revised his Whitman translations and examined the work of the German translator of *Les Caves*, but could not get down to any 'serious' work. On 15 June, Copeau arrived with his wife and three children. Gide felt – and felt that Copeau felt – that their relationship had reached a boundary: there was nothing more to know of one another. A fortnight later, Gide accompanied Copeau back to Paris, leaving Agnès and the children with Madeleine for a few more days. The following day, he called on Ghéon at Orsay and listened to the account of his friend's adventures in Naples and Rome. Back in Cuverville, he called on Jean Schlumberger at Braffye and, next day, the Quatorze Juillet, the two men were in Le Havre. That night, they 'prowled interminably'. At 12.30, they decided to split up and go different ways. Gide got back to the hotel at 1 a.m.; Schlumberger joined him an hour later.

The assassination at Sarajevo, on 28 June, of the Archduke Francis Ferdinand, heir to the Austrian Imperial throne, and his wife passed unnoted by Gide in journal or letters, as it did by most people at the time. Nor, over the next five weeks, is there any mention of the various diplomatic manoeuvres among the European powers until 26 July, when Gide refers to the Austrian ultimatum to Serbia. Over more or less the same period, however, the *Journal* does refer, at length and on an almost daily basis, to a more immediate, if less consequent tragedy. It begins on 22 June, when, Gide notes, 'Yesterday morning, in the avenue, I found a little starling that had fallen from its nest, but was almost ready to fly.'[92] Gide picked it up and took it to the dairy, which it soon made 'uninhabitable'. He fed it (on bread, soaked in milk, with hard-boiled eggs and worms), bathed it, gradually tamed it to the point that it would voluntarily return, after its period of freedom, to the large cage that Gide had set up for it, to protect it from his cats. Eventually, the bird was well enough to be let out at night; each morning it was on the lawn, waiting for Gide and its food. Then, on 19 July, we read: 'This morning, my poor starling let himself be torn to pieces by the cats. They threw themselves on that fearless, defenceless little thing; I was at the piano, but suddenly I recognized its call.' Two days later, Gide writes: 'I didn't think it was possible to miss a bird so much.'[93]

On 22 July, Dieter Bassermann, the German translator of *Les Caves du Vatican*, arrived. He turned out to be 'an enormous young man of 24 or 25 . . . who speaks French perfectly'.[94] Over the next two days, Gide worked with him on various problems in the translation. By 25 July, Gide was with Blanche at Offranville. From there, Blanche drove Gide the few miles into Dieppe to catch the boat for Newhaven. A telegram was sent to Larbaud, who was staying in Hastings to announce his imminent arrival. He then intended to join Jacques Raverat at Royston, near Cambridge, where he hoped to meet Rupert Brooke. That day, Austria declared war on Serbia. Next morning, after reading the newspapers, Gide had second thoughts about crossing the Channel at such a time and returned to Cuverville. The same day, Madeleine's young sister, Valentine, arrived with her two young daughters and a letter from Copeau asking if, given the probability of war, he could send Agnès, her mother and their children to Cuverville – living at Le Limon, they were in direct line of any Franco–German fighting. Gide sent off a telegram urging them to come at once. They arrived on 2 August. Copeau also asked Gide if he could lend him some money – 'not only do I not have *a sou* in prospect to face any crisis . . . But the war might last longer than two months.'[95] Gide was more pessimistic – and more percipient. The *Journal* entry for 31 July reads: 'We are about to enter a long, dark tunnel, full of blood.'[96] On 3 August, Germany declared war on France. Next day, Great Britain declared war on Germany.

The War: De Profundis, Summer's Lease

(AUGUST 1914 – NOVEMBER 1918)

'Before leaving Em this morning, I knelt down next to her (something I hadn't done since . . .) and asked her to recite the Lord's Prayer. I did this for her sake and my pride yielded to love quite easily; indeed I joined her in her prayer with all my heart.'[1]

Gide wrote those lines on 2 August, in a packed train taking him back to Paris. They mark his sense of the gravity of the moment as he and Madeleine entered, with the whole of Europe, the 'long, dark tunnel, full of blood' that the coming war was to turn out to be. They hint, too, at the turn that his own thinking was to take, in response to the horrors of war, though they also bear witness to his continuing ambivalence towards Christianity – he performed that solemn act 'with all my heart', but he did so 'for her sake'.

The train arrived an hour late. There were no taxicabs at Saint-Lazare, motor- or horse-driven. He left his luggage at Uncle Charles' in Passy, then called on Copeau in the rue du Dragon. They went on to the *NRF* offices. There they found Jean-Gustave Tronche, Gallimard's trade manager, who would be joining his regiment next day. 'All are leaving, or have already left,' Gide comments – Ruyters, Rivière, Alain-Fournier, Péguy and Paul Gide, his nephew. Ghéon, declared unfit, got himself attached to an ambulance unit as an army doctor. Gide himself, now nearly forty-five, had been excused military service on health grounds. Schlumberger, also unfit, had been put in charge of an office at the Red Cross headquarters. Gide went along to see what help he could give. There he found Misia Godebska, 'who, here as everywhere else, immediately assumes a role of the first importance'.[2] Her natural authority backed up with the Red Cross insignia, she commandeers the unhappily named Hôtel du Rhin. What, Gide wonders, will happen to the (then German-sounding) Ritz? After unloading several bundles of sheets, Gide goes off to the Quai d'Orsay to call on Philippe Berthelot, by now a very senior official in the Foreign Ministry. At the Red Cross, Gide noted down the details of those offering their services and filed their applications on cards; he then formed the most likely ones into teams of stretcher-bearers. They were then informed that the military authorities could accept none of their applications – all their efforts had been wasted. As there was less and less to do at the Red Cross offices, Gide became more and more dispirited: 'I pretend to be useful, rather than actually being useful.'[3] For company and reasons of economy, Gide and Schlumberger moved into the house of the Van Rysselberghes at 44 rue Laugier, sharing meals and expenditure. Most evenings, after dinner, the three men would sit around the dining-table reading the newspapers and commenting on the news. Once a week, they were joined by the composers Vincent d'Indy and Pierre Onfroy de Bréville. By the end of November, Schlumberger had got himself declared fit for service and joined a heavy artillery unit commanded by his brother Conrad. Another brother, Maurice, the 1905 *amour* of Gide and Ghéon, now twenty-eight, had just married prior to joining up, only to be taken prisoner five months later.

One evening, Gide called on Elie Allégret and told him how much he wished he could find something useful to do. The good pastor offered him a job: 'To register all the boys between 12 and 18 [in the 16th arrondissement] who turn up and think of ways of keeping them occupied!'[4] Gide replied, with a touch of irony, that he did not think that he was quite the man for the job. Meanwhile, Ghéon, too, is complaining of inactivity: 'What a disappointment, *cher vieux*! It's a holiday. A house on the estate of the Duc de Guise, where the manager, a good enough fellow, has taken it into his head to install an ambulance and put me in charge of it! But not a trace of any wounded . . .'[5] A few days later, the irrepressible Ghéon is celebrating the arrival of the British army, 'splendid fellows, who would not for the world leave without properly having their tea . . . Splendid Scotsmen in short skirts, with bare legs . . . and [their] extraordinary negro music, in which the nasal whine of the bagpipes is punctuated with obsessive blows on the big bass drum.'[6]

On 20 August, Gide reluctantly agrees to meet Jean Cocteau at an 'English tea room':

I did not enjoy seeing him again, despite his extreme kindness. He is incapable of seriousness and all his thoughts, his witticisms, his feelings, the extraordinary brio of his conversation shocked me like some luxury article displayed at a time of famine and mourning . . . He has the carefree attitude of the street-urchin; it is when I am with him that I feel most awkward, most heavy, most morose.[7]

Over the next few weeks, Copeau had come to the conclusion that

Cuverville was perhaps not the best place for his family to live out the war. Arrangements were being made to send them to stay with Clive Bell in England – the mother-in-law and a friend had already set off on a long, perilous sea-voyage to Denmark – but the idea was soon abandoned. Instead the Copeaus (and Valentine Gilbert) would go to the Schlumbergers' house at Braffye and Jeanne Drouin to Etretat. In fact, they all returned to Cuverville before long, the Copeaus spending the whole winter of 1914–15 there. On 23 September, Gide met Jacques Raverat off the Channel ferry at Le Havre and brought him back to Cuverville. Over the next few days, they read together Milton's 'wonderful *Ode on the Nativity*' (*sic* for 'On the Morning of Christ's Nativity') and 'several of Shakespeare's *Sonnets*', and talked interminably of morality and religion. 'He believes in the devil,' Gide wrote. 'He even told me that he believed in the devil before believing in God. I said that what stopped me believing in the devil was that I wasn't sure of hating him [a touch of Blake here]. Certainly there will be someone in my novel who believes in the devil.'[8] This is one of the earliest explicit references to what was to become *Les Faux-Monnayeurs*. Gide finished Hardy's *Tess of the d'Urbervilles*, noting that it had taken him a month to read it, that he admired it, rather than liked it, and much preferred *Jude the Obscure*. He read a lot of Browning, remarking (surprisingly, perhaps) that he 'derived more interest and pleasure from him than from any other English poet.'[9]

On 24 August, Jacques Rivière disappeared without trace after the Battle of Eton. Four weeks later, his brother-in-law, Henri Fournier (Alain-Fournier) disappeared on the Hauts-de-Meuse. (It was not until 24 October that Isabelle Rivière learnt that her husband had been taken prisoner – he was not released until 1918 – and a further three weeks before she learnt that her brother had been killed.)

After nearly ten weeks at Cuverville, much of it spent in 'abominable anxiety', Gide left for Paris, where he rejoined 'the colony' at the Van Rysselberghes', now swollen to include Copeau and, since the retreat of the French forces from the Marne, Ghéon. Gide and Maria began helping at the Cirque d'Eté, where refugees from northern France and Belgium were assembled. The organization was put on a more formal footing when it became the 'Foyer Franco-Belge'. A Belgian, M. Delouarmol, was made chairman, and Gide vice-chairman. Before long, the original organizers were joined by André Ruyters' wife, Georgina, Charles Du Bos (with the young composer Darius Milhaud as his assistant) and the American writer Edith Wharton, through whom valuable American funding came to the Foyer. In his interviews with Jean Amrouche, Gide remarked how he

retained 'an exquisite memory of that whole period'. 'Mme Van Rysselberghe and I set out early every morning so as to arrive at the office first.
We would lunch – Oh! I remember very well how we had persuaded
ourselves not to spend more than two francs a day on it – at a little bistrot
near the Foyer and we would get back in the evening, quite exhausted, after
the office had closed.'[10] It was, it has to be said, the only time in his life
that Gide experienced anything approximating the working lives of most
mortals. What is more, he stuck it, week after week, with only a few breaks
to recuperate, for some sixteen months – he had rarely stayed in any one
place, let alone done the same thing, for so long. At Cuverville, during his
first two-day break, he noted: 'My dreadful tiredness was due, I think, to
being exposed to sympathy all day long . . . I felt *drunk dry* by others.'[11] The
work could be 'extraordinarily depressing': they saw nothing but 'human
wrecks' and, however deserving an individual might seem, 'a sort of secret
policing and perpetual examination' had to be gone through to obviate all
too evident abuses of the charity offered. Jean Amrouche asked Gide if he
had given up writing during this period. 'Oh! I completely stopped thinking
about it,' Gide replied. There is even a gap of about a year in the *Journal*:
'My letters to Em. have taken the place of this journal,' he writes on 8
October 1914.[12] Instead he dictated to the Foyer secretary a day-by-day
account of his activities there.

The *Journal* for 1914 ends with a nameless poem: it is as if Gide had some
comment to make on that dreadful year, on the war in general, that
demanded a 'higher' mode of expression. The 'old instrument' is broken;
we should not stoop to pick up the pieces, but seize the opportunity to
speak with a new voice. Our libraries and brains were so full that there was
no room for anything new. 'In the depths of our hearts, we yearned for this
cataclysm, the great gust of wind that blew away what was unclean . . .
This war is like no other war; it is not only a matter of protecting a territory, a heritage, a tradition . . . No! It is a future that is coming to
birth . . .'[13]

In a letter from Jacques Raverat, dated 25 April, Gide learnt of the
death of Rupert Brooke from septicaemia on a French hospital-ship in the
Dardanelles. As chance would have it, Gide was sleeping in the room of
the Van Rysselberghes' daughter, Elisabeth, who was then in Scotland. For
a few months in 1911, in Munich, she had been Brooke's lover. The two
met again briefly in Paris the following year, but, by that time, Brooke's
thoughts were elsewhere. Gide applied to Edward Marsh, Brooke's executor

and Winston Churchill's secretary, for permission to translate some of Brooke's poems, but nothing came of the project. Two months after learning of Brooke's death, Gide was informed of the death on active service of his nephew, Paul. 'Alas!' he wrote to Valéry. 'I am no longer surprised to hear of the death of any of them out there; what will be surprising will be to see a few of them come back.'[14]

Meanwhile, Gide had retreated from the 'colony' in the rue Laugier to the Villa Montmorency, where, he wrote to Schlumberger, he lived as an 'anchorite': 'What I found so wearing, so exasperating, so demoralizing at the Laugier was the endless talk, the immediate release of any thought, any emotion; here I live once again without pressure.'[15] Madeleine would join him for a few days once a month. Otherwise, he was attended only by a charwoman, who came every morning 'to clean my shoes'. 'I leave before nine and get back at night absolutely whacked,' he wrote to Alibert.[16] Meanwhile, Alibert, who had joined the auxiliary services as a nurse, was now in Greece, in the enviable position of having little to do but watch the sun go down over Mount Olympus.

On 26 September, a card arrived from Copeau. It was, Gide wrote, 'strangely *out of time*' [in English]. 'He speaks of Florence, Angelico . . . Does all that still exist?'[17] Copeau had been found unfit for active service, but volunteered for the auxiliary services. However, in February 1915, a medical examination detected infection in both lungs and he was invalided out. He turned at once to his plans for the future of the theatre and won the support of Clemenceau, a former prime minister, but now an out-of-office, though influential senator – he did not resume the premiership until November 1917. Copeau wrote to Edward Gordon Craig, who invited him to visit him in Florence, which he did, largely thanks to financial help from Jean Schlumberger. He stayed there for five weeks, seeing Craig almost daily, discussing his theories and examining his models of stage sets. Craig, he acknowledged, was a genius, but one so radical that he could influence only by his ideas, not by his example – Craig, in fact, was to do little actual work in the theatre. Copeau was tempted by Craig's ideas, but he was a practical man of the theatre, a lover of actors and plays; Craig dreamt of a theatre in which the director would be all, even going so far as to dispense with actors, authors and (one suspects) audiences altogether. Yet the obsessive, unsmiling visionary could also turn into a quite different Craig, captivating and charming, when he abandoned his theories and talked of Irving and Ellen Terry, his mother, acting out whole scenes by way of imitation. Together with the help of a rich American patron,

Robertson Trowbridge, there were plans to reconstitute the Vieux Col-
ombier company and take it to America with a version, staged jointly by
Copeau and Craig, of Bach's *St Matthew Passion*. Later, Copeau and the
Vieux Colombier company did go to New York, but nothing came of the *St
Matthew Passion* project, though Craig's 12-foot-high model set did influence
Copeau's rearrangement of the Vieux Colombier stage and auditorium for
its reopening in 1920.

By September, Gide was not so much physically exhausted by his work
at the Foyer, as morally depressed by it. What had begun as personal acts
of charity had become, almost as a result of its efficiency and success, a
bureaucratic routine. He even planned to leave for England with Edith
Wharton. Raverat – and Henry James and Arnold Bennett – were expecting
him. In the end, he gave up the idea when faced with the endless bureaucratic
procedures required for war-time travel. He settled instead on a week at
Cuverville, but that solved nothing. On his last day there, he wrote: 'Dreadful
torpor. I think with a sort of distress of the life that Cuverville holds in store
for me and from which I don't see how I will be able to escape, except by
breaking bonds and freeing myself from the most revered and cherished
obligations.'[18] He returned to Paris and the Foyer. Three weeks later, he
escaped with Edith Wharton and her car for five days in the South of
France.

'Ghéon writes that he has "taken the plunge" [*sauté le pas*]. He sounds like
a schoolboy who has just plucked up courage to enter a brothel . . .'[19]
Apparently, on Christmas Day, 1915, Ghéon had taken communion, having
previously been to confession – being technically already a Catholic, he did
not have to be 'received' into the Church. In his brief letter, of 8 January
1916, ostensibly a belated communication of good wishes for the New Year,
Ghéon offers no explanation of his statement, assuming, correctly, that
Gide would understand. What had brought Ghéon to this, in many ways
improbable, step? His decision was less the culmination of a long intellectual
process, than an overwhelming emotional reaction to the death of a friend,
earlier in the year.

In 1903, a young man of nineteen, Pierre-Dominique Dupouey, introduced himself to Gide as a devotee of his *Nourritures terrestres*. Gide's 'sensual
hymns' had helped to free him from the Catholicism of his childhood and
spur him on to embark on 'a quest of the world'. Five years later, Dupouey
wrote to Gide again: 'I like you because of all my friends you are the only
one who has been tyrannically haunted by a faith or by regret for the loss

of a faith.'[20] In 1910, under the influence of Mireille de la Ménardière, the woman he was to marry, Dupouey returned to his Catholic faith. On the outbreak of war, he joined the French navy. When Ghéon was posted to Nieupoort, in Belgium, Gide, knowing that Depouey was stationed in the area, suggested that he go and visit him. Ghéon was immediately captivated by the handsome naval officer, with his shining faith in God and Country. They talked at length of the war – and of Gide. They met again, over lunch, at a table so small that their knees touched. Afterwards, Dupouey introduced Ghéon to some of his men. 'Look at *him*,' Dupouey said, pointing out one of them. 'Isn't he handsome?' 'I'd go mad in this place!' Ghéon comments.[21] To his evident surprise, Ghéon then learnt that Dupouey was married. Ghéon left Dupouey heartbroken, 'in a state of strange intoxication'. The day before, Ghéon tells Gide, 'I saw, massacred in front of me, in our courtyard, by a huge shell, two of our best men . . . Back in my room, I started to sob, begging heaven, not for myself, but for them . . . Pity! Pity, Lord . . . They were men – and what have you done to them? . . . After the enthusiasm of war, I now sense all its horror . . . And in this hell, *to whom* can one turn?'[22] Ghéon and Dupouey met again, for the third and last time, at the end of March. On 3 April, Dupouey was killed by a stray bullet to the head. Ghéon did not learn of his friend's death until two weeks later. '*Cher vieux, pauvre vieux,*' he wrote to Gide, 'I have frightful news! Your friend Dupouey, already mine, is no more. I talked to you about him the other day as if he were alive! And already, he lay in the churchyard of a village not three kilometres from here . . .' On hearing the news, Ghéon had rushed over to the grave and tied to the simple wooden cross 'my offering, a branch of boxwood that my sister had sent me for Easter'. 'Did I pray for him? . . . I think so, or it amounted to that. In the exalted state I'm in I'm quite capable of praying without believing . . . Why did I love him so much? . . . He answered so much to what I am disposed to love at the moment.'[23]

Ghéon met the army chaplain, who told him that Dupouey was not only a hero, but also a saint: 'Over the last few months, he rose to the very summit of ecstasy. Totally available, totally ready . . . He had given himself to the Lord. Hence his gaiety and calm.'[24] On Holy Thursday, he had insisted on serving at Mass before going off on a mission. At Gide's suggestion, the widow wrote to Ghéon, expressing her joy at knowing that her husband was with God. 'Pierre is praying for you,' she added. In October, Mireille Dupouey sent Ghéon her husband's private journal. In it Ghéon's suspicions were confirmed: he, too, was attracted to young men.

This revelation was an important stage in Ghéon's spiritual journey: if Dupouey could reconcile his earthly feelings with religious belief, he, Ghéon, could surely reconcile a religious belief with his earthly feelings. He plunged into a reading of Pascal and Bossuet. He got Gide to send him a Bible – a Protestant Bible, as it happened, Gide being unable to find any other. But he still could not bring himself to confide in a confessor: the very thought of doing so terrified him. Nor did he feel any less 'the temptations of the flesh'. When on leave, he gave in to his 'demon', 'for reasons of hygiene and pleasure'. Yet, as if setting himself a challenge were the only way he would ever do it, he promised himself, in mid-December, to take Communion on Christmas Day. He began writing poems again, which, collected as *Foi en la France: Poèmes du temps de guerre*, were published later in the year by the newly reopened *NRF* book publishing house.

Gide's ill-tempered response to Ghéon's announcement – 'like a schoolboy who has just plucked up courage to enter a brothel' – comes as a shock. After all, from Dupouey's death, nine months before, Gide had shown the greatest possible sympathy for Ghéon's emotional and intellectual plight. According to Ghéon, Gide had even suggested that, having got so far, it would be 'unpardonable' on Ghéon's part not to settle the matter once and for all. Gide is responding as much to the style as to the content of Ghéon's announcement: Ghéon is treating the matter altogether too lightly. Oh, yes, Gide seems to be saying, and how seriously am I supposed to take that – and how long will it last? At a deeper level, it may well have expressed a sudden realization that things would never be quite the same again with his 'franc camarade', the companion who had been at the centre of so much of his life; a fear, also, perhaps, that if Ghéon could join the growing cohort of friends who had gone back or gone over to Rome, how long would it be before he, too, would succumb? In the *Journal* entry for 17 January, immediately after his comment on Ghéon's announcement, Gide recounts a dream that he had had, over a year before. Gide was walking, 'or rather floating', with Ghéon through a beautiful wooded valley. Suddenly Ghéon stopped and said: 'No further! Henceforth there is *this* between us.' Gide adds: 'He was not pointing at anything, but, looking down, I could make out a rosary hanging from his wrist, and I suddenly awoke in unbearable anguish.'[25] The following day, while writing back to Ghéon, Gide re-read the following lines from the St John Gospel: 'If a man abide not in me, he is cast forth as a branch, and is withered; and men gather them, and cast them into the fire, and they are burned' (John 15:6). 'Truly was I not "cast into the fire",' Gide asks, 'and already prey to the flame of the most abominable desires? . . .'[26] What, one may wonder, has come over Gide? There is worse to come. The following day, he writes: 'Everything in me calls out to be revised, amended, re-educated. What I find hardest to struggle against is sensual [i.e., sexual] curiosity.' He compares his compulsion to a drunkard's absinthe. He would drop everything to follow certain faces he sees in the street. 'There is a compulsion here that is so imperious, a counsel so insidious, so secret, a habit so inveterate that I often wonder if I can escape it without help from outside.'[27] Gide had entered another dark night of the soul.

In the *Journal*, Gide returns obsessively to talk of God and the devil, sin and guilt, with scarcely veiled references to masturbation and his attempts to resist it: 'Yesterday evening I gave in, as one gives in to an obstinate child, to have some peace';[28] 'Since Saturday I have been assailed again by abominable imaginings, against which I am defenceless; I find no refuge anywhere. At certain moments . . . I wonder if I am not going mad';[29] 'Yesterday, an abominable relapse . . . I get up, my head and heart heavy and empty: full of all the weight of hell';[30] 'Yesterday, abominable relapse that has left my body and mind in a state bordering on despair, suicide, madness',[31] etc., etc. Sometimes, in unpublished entries, such relapses are marked by a solitary 'X'. Throughout this period, Gide certainly addresses God as a believing (and doubting) Christian would: 'Lord! You know that I have given up being in the right against anyone. What does it matter if it is to escape submission to sin that I submit to the Church! I submit! Ah! Untie the bonds that still hold me back. Deliver me from the terrible weight of this body. Ah! Let me live a little! Let me breathe! Snatch me from evil. Let me not stifle.'[32] But Gide's relationship with '*le diable*', '*le Malin*', '*le mal*' is altogether more unusual, interesting and unexpected. Gide's previous 'theology', if it may be so graced, was a simple, personal matter. He was, if anything, a pantheist: God was not so much a supreme, autonomous intelligence as a spirit that may be felt everywhere, but perhaps especially in the beauties of nature. Gide venerated the person of Jesus, whom he regarded as a great teacher, travestied by a Pauline Church. He had as yet no sense of the presence of evil, still less of a personal embodiment of it. In the *Feuillets* of 1916, pages intended for the *Journal*, excluded from its original edition, but included in the later Pléiade edition, Gide comments on the notion of God and devil. It was, he reminds us, Jacques Raverat who 'introduced' him to the devil. In May 1914 (not 1910, as Gide claims here), Raverat and he had been reading Milton. Raverat talked of Satan. 'It was believing in him, *whose presence I actually felt*, that led me to believe in God.'

Gide's reaction was one of amusement. After all, Raverat may have been a Catholic, but he had spent a number of years in England, studied mathematics at Cambridge, married into the Darwin family, frequented the agnostics of Bloomsbury and the neo-pagans of the Brooke circle. Gide had great respect for Jacques Raverat, but he could not take his words entirely seriously. Nevertheless, he carried them inside him 'like seeds'; they germinated during that terrible year of the war, when, 'against a background of philanthropy' (the Foyer), 'the face of the Evil One stood out all the more clearly'. In the *Journal*, Gide *addresses* God, in the form of prayer; the absent God does not reply. With the devil, Gide enters into *conversation* and the last page of the *Feuillets* is a dialogue with him. The devil, with splendid displays of sophistry, answers back: 'This is all a comedy that you are acting out to yourself. With the first blush of spring, you will go over to the enemy lock, stock and barrel. The enemy? What enemy? You have no other enemy than your fatigue.'[33] Of course, the accents were familiar from *Paradise Lost*, where, as Blake points out, Satan is the star of the show: 'The reason Milton wrote in fetters when he wrote of Angels and God, and at liberty when of Devils and Hell, is because he was a true Poet and of the Devil's party without knowing it.'

Curiously, Gide had first really encountered Blake in August 1914, while leafing through Elisabeth Van Rysselberghe's books in her bedroom in the rue Laugier. *The Marriage of Heaven and Hell*, which he was to translate, was also to act as a seed that later germinated in his mind. Had he been ready to avail himself of it in 1916, that extraordinary work, written a century or more before Nietzsche's *Beyond Good and Evil* or Freud's formulation of 'super-ego' and 'id', might have provided a more healing mythological structure than the Catholic one that was tormenting him. For Blake, the human soul was not a battleground in which Good had to conquer Evil, but a conjunction of forces, in which what official religion calls 'evil' is what provides energy and creativity. Some of the 'Proverbs of Hell', in particular, must have fallen on fertile soil: 'The road of excess leads to the palace of wisdom'; 'He who desires but acts not, breeds pestilence'; 'Prisons are built with stones of Law, Brothels with bricks of Religion'; 'Sooner murder an infant in its cradle than nurse unacted desires'. In 1916, however, 'the devil' was still there, assuming the guise of rationalism! 'He is much more intelligent than we are and above all hides behind reasoning . . . If we were humbler, we would recognize him in the *Cogito ergo sum*. That *ergo* is the devil's ergot.' (Ergot is a disease affecting grain.) 'You know very well I don't exist,' the devil whispers in Gide's ear, 'but you probably needed me

. . . to believe in God . . . You created me in order to saddle me with your doubts, your disgust, your boredom.'

There is a problem here. Did Gide really believe in the devil? We cannot answer such a question. What, after all, is belief? Perhaps no more than the willing suspension of disbelief, 'God' or 'the devil' appearing in the mind like characters on a stage. The more plausible the dialogue Gide attributes to the Evil One, the more we suspend our disbelief, but the less likely we are to place on the same level of reality what is happening on the stage and what is happening in the auditorium. Verisimilitude undermines verity. When Gide writes, 'Yesterday, abominable relapse . . . Lord, . . . Deliver me from the terrible weight of this body,'[34] we at least feel that we are being given the bare, unvarnished truth, what a journal entry should give us. When he makes the devil speak, his language becomes literature, mounts the stage. Occasionally, Gide shows that he is well aware of the problem. Having just referred to 'le Malin', he adds: 'I am consciously using here, as I did earlier, a vocabulary and images that imply a mythology in which it is not absolutely necessary that I believe. It is enough that it is the most eloquent in explaining an inner drama to me.'[35]

On 4 October 1915, Gide had written to Arnold Bennett, thanking him for putting him on to 'Rutherford'. Mark Rutherford was the pseudonym of William Hale White (1831–1913), a would-be Congregationalist minister who found refuge among the Unitarians. Gide read *The Autobiography of Mark Rutherford* and went on to *Mark Rutherford's Deliverance*, from which he quotes 'a passage on the devil and hell that has been of great help in my thinking'. It begins: 'The shallowest of mortals is able now to laugh at the notion of a personal devil. No doubt there is no such thing existent; but the horror at evil which could find no other expression than in the creation of a devil is no subject for laughter . . .'[36] Gide was so taken by the two Rutherford books that, at one stage, he intended translating them himself and publishing them at the *NRF*. Clearly, they arrived in Gide's life at precisely the right time, recommended by an unsuspecting Bennett, who simply thought that Gide, with his Calvinist background, would find them interesting. In his fifth Vieux Colombier lecture on Dostoevsky, Gide quotes from Rutherford again, this time to suggest that the Englishman had also assisted Gide out of the slough of despond: 'As I grew older, I understood how crazy was this perpetual running after the future, this postponement of happiness to a later date. At last I learnt, when it was already almost too late, to live in the present moment . . .'[37]

In addition to the *Journal* and the *Feuillets*, Gide began making observations on his religious quest in what he called his '*cahier vert*', a notebook that happened to have a green cover. All except the last two (20 June 1917 and 15 June 1919), the entries date from 1916. Most of them are comments on specific quotations from the Gospels, sometimes comparing the Latin Vulgate with different French translations and, occasionally, with the Greek originals or the English Authorized Version. Gide was in no hurry to publish his *cahier vert*, now called *Numquid et tu . . .?* (The words are from the Vulgate version of the St John Gospel: 'Numquid et vos seducti estis? . . . Numquid et tu Galilaeus?' The Authorized Version renders them: 'Are ye also deceived? . . . Art thou also of Galilee?' – John 7:47 and 52). In 1922, a limited edition, bearing no author's name, was printed by the Sainte-Catherine press in Bruges. A second, also limited, edition appeared in 1926 in Jacques Schiffrin's Editions de la Pléiade. In his preface, addressed to the dedicatee, Charles Du Bos, Gide explains how he has agreed to the reissue of *Numquid et tu . . .?* as part of a small collection of *Ecrits intimes*. While accepting that 'nothing worth knowing should be kept secret', he feels that 'intimacy cannot bear the full light of day' and has therefore insisted on the limited edition. 'I am neither a Protestant, nor a Catholic; I am quite simply a Christian . . . Written during the war, these pages retain a certain reflection of the anguish and disarray of that time; and although I can still bring myself to sign them, I would probably not write them now.'[38]

On 9 January, Gide received a letter from Romain Rolland, then working for the International Red Cross in Geneva, asking him to do what he could on behalf of their mutual friend Rilke. Apparently, the outbreak of war had found him in Munich, unable to return to his beloved Paris. Since he had failed to contact his landlord or to make any arrangements for the payment of rent, his apartment in the rue Campagne-Première had been sequestrated and its contents auctioned off. With Copeau, who had received a similar letter, Gide went round at once to Rilke's old apartment. There he learnt from a tearful concierge that she had managed to keep two chests of personal papers, but that Rilke's furniture, books and other possessions had indeed been auctioned off. Gide then chased up the booksellers who had acquired Rilke's library. He found that 'a quantity of rare and valuable books, dedicated first editions, a collection of engravings, original works of Rodin, eighteenth-century furniture and other, objets d'art, etc.' had been sold off for the derisory sum of 538 francs (some £21 or $100 at the time), that the auctioneer had not advertised the sale, and that three bookshops and antique dealers had bought everything in job lots. Gide readily admitted that, since Rilke had failed to make the necessary arrangements, everyone had acted within the law. Nevertheless, he felt impelled to do everything he could to help a friend, even if that friend happened to be an Austrian citizen, engaged on the other side in the war.

At the end of February, Gide left the Foyer Franco-Belge, after a kind of coup d'état. Soon afterwards, Edith Wharton became its president, its name was changed to the 'Foyer Américain' and, by 1918, it was taking care of 5,000 refugees, and running four shelters for the aged and two sanatoriums for women and children. Before leaving Paris for Cuverville, Gide 'ended the evening' with Marcel Proust, whom he had not seen since 1892. He promised himself 'to recount that visit at length', but did not do so.[39]

A party consisting of Gide, Madeleine, two maids, two dogs and five cats set out from the Gare Saint-Lazare early on the morning of 29 February and, severely delayed by a train crash resulting in 'four or five dead and some twenty hurt', arrived at Cuverville eighteen hours later. Later, they were joined by Madeleine's sister Valentine and her two daughters. At Cuverville, Gide was to be, if anything, more depressed than he had been in Paris, with sleepless nights and a recurrence of the headaches that had plagued him up to the age of twenty. He felt quite incapable of pursuing the great fictional work that was already taking shape in his mind. To fill the long hours, he wrote more than usually long entries in the *Journal*, and continued with *Numquid et tu . . .?* and a work on Chopin. He also began what he called his '*mémoires*', which, by the following January, had found a title, *Si le grain ne meurt*, taken from a text commented upon in *Numquid*: 'Except a corn of wheat fall into the ground and die, it abideth alone: but if it die, it bringeth forth much fruit' (John 12:24). By the end of the year, 'with such palpitations of the heart that, at times, I have to break off', he read the first four chapters to Madeleine. He then gave her to read the first few pages that he had written of the fifth chapter – ending with his 'furtive visit' to the Rondeaux house in Rouen, the scene described, with some changes, in *La Porte étroite*. *Si le grain ne meurt* is undoubtedly one of the great, classic autobiographies. With the begun and temporarily abandoned *Corydon*, it marks a new stage in the process by which Gide came to terms with himself (in the writing) and (in the publishing) made the world come to terms with him as he was. Neither came easily: *Corydon* was not published until 1924 and *Si le grain ne meurt* not until 1926.

In April, after six weeks at Cuverville, Gide went to Paris for a few days. He stayed at the house of Octave Maus, the Belgian writer, where the Van Rysselberghes were also staying: they had left their villa in the rue Laugier and had not yet moved into the new house, which they were having built in the rue Claude-Lorrain. He lunched with Copeau and Ghéon (who was on leave). Contact with his 'vaillants camarades' did him some good, but, five days later, he was writing: 'The last few days at Cuverville have been horrible . . . What is the cause of this strange *withdrawal of sap* that afflicts my mind so often, leaving it cluttered with dead wood?'[40] There is a gap in the *Journal* between 6 May and 15 June. On 15 June, Gide writes: 'I have torn up about twenty pages of this notebook . . . The pages I tore up read like the pages of a madman.'[41] The destroyed pages covered, at the outside, a period of four weeks. There is then another, longer gap in the *Journal* until 15 September, when Gide writes of the destroyed pages: 'They reflected a terrible crisis involving Em. Or, to be more precise, of which Em. was the cause. I wrote them in a sort of despair and, since they were really addressed to her, I tore them up at her request after she had read them.' Or rather, Gide adds curiously, Madeleine did not actually ask him to destroy them, but he was aware of how relieved she would be if he did destroy them. Yet he regrets that he did so: 'I don't think I ever wrote any like them . . . They might have helped me get out of an unhealthy state of mind of which they were a sincere reflection.'[42]

What happened between Gide and Madeleine? In his *Madeleine et André Gide*, Jean Schlumberger recounts how Gide had told him that Madeleine had opened a letter from Ghéon addressed to him. In normal circumstances, says Schlumberger, it would have been 'inconceivable' that Madeleine would have done such a thing. But Ghéon, an army medical officer at the front, was constantly exposed to danger and Madeleine was anxious to have news of him. What, Schlumberger asks, could the newly converted Ghéon have revealed of Gide's life? 'Perhaps not very much, no more than allusions, exhorting his old fellow-traveller in adventure to throw off the old Adam and change his way of life.'[43] In their introduction to the Gide–Ghéon correspondence, the editors argue that the opening of a letter from Ghéon occurred not in May–June 1916, but in December 1917: what probably happened in May or June 1916 was that Madeleine, seriously disturbed about her husband's mental state, fell upon something that he had been writing. (He was in the habit, it must be remembered, of writing in every part of the house or apartment, and leaving his work open where he left it.) What Madeleine had probably read was some of the pages from the *Journal* that Gide later destroyed. As for the opening of one of Ghéon's letters, eighteen months later, we shall return to it in due course.

In July, Gide returned to Paris and moved in with the Van Rysselberghes at their new house, 14 rue Claude-Lorrain, in Auteuil. The house had been designed by three of Théo's architect friends, who had committed 50,000 francs (£2,000 or $10,000 at the time) of their own money to the building. When they asked Théo to repay the money, he could not do so – he also owed the Banque de France a further 25,000 francs (£1,000 or $5,000). The Van Rysselberghes were saved by friends, including Gide (20,000 francs (£800 or $4,000)) and Conrad Schlumberger, Jean's brother (10,000 francs (£400 or $2,000)).

At the beginning of August, Gide went to spend a week at Bagnols with Rouart, then accompanied him to Mas, Amélie-les-Bains, Perpignan and Banyuls. After another week in Paris, he returned to Cuverville. Gide suggested to Madeleine that they should spend the winter at the Van Rysselberghes' house in the South, at Saint-Clair, in the Var. '"*I certainly owe you that*," she said with an effort of her whole being, which at once made her face so sad, so serious, that I immediately thought only of giving up this plan, like so many others, since it costs her so much and I would have to buy my happiness at the expense of hers – so that it could no longer be my happiness.'44 So Gide stayed at Cuverville – until the second week of November, when he went to Paris to see Jean Schlumberger, who was back on leave. Since March, Schlumberger had been transferred from the front and was working in the army information service, selecting and translating extracts from the German press. The week that Gide had intended staying turned into a month, brought to a sudden end by the death of his old friend Emile Verhaeren: the poet had been hit by an oncoming train while trying to cross to the other side of a platform at Rouen station. Verhaeren had also been a close friend of the Van Rysselberghes – indeed, as we have seen, he and Maria had had a passionate but platonic affair twenty years before. With Maria and her daughter Elisabeth, Gide travelled to Belgium for the funeral. (Théo was already there, working on a commission.) In her *Cahiers de la Petite Dame* (her friends called her, on account of her diminutive size, 'la Petite Dame'), begun the following year, 1918, Maria Van Rysselberghe recounts an incident that took place in the corridor of the train that was taking them back to Paris. Gide passed a note to her daughter on which was written: 'I shall never love any woman except one [Madeleine], and I have true desire only for young boys. But I find it hard to resign myself to seeing you without a child and not to have one myself.' 'This extraordinary, stark declaration,' the Petite Dame continues, 'untangled an unbearably tense situation, brought about by two exhausting days of exhilarating and painful emotions.' But what, she asks, brought Gide and Elisabeth to that point? During the trip to Italy in 1909 (not 1907 as she says), she sensed that 'Gide felt drawn to Elisabeth [then nineteen] other than by friendship and interest.' For her part, Elisabeth seemed to be 'subjugated' by Gide, drawn to him by 'a force to which she could probably not give a name and which was to blossom later'. The following year, in Munich, Elisabeth had met and fallen in love with Rupert Brooke. At the time of Brooke's death, in 1915, Maria remarked to Gide: 'I know Elisabeth very well. I'm sure she'll never get over not having had a child by Brooke.' 'What would you have done if that had happened?' Gide asked. 'I'd have been delighted to bring the child up,' she replied. She felt sure that Gide had remembered her words when he made his 'declaration'. Elisabeth, apparently, was deeply moved by it and, afterwards, looked 'radiant'. Gide 'certainly withdrew somewhat, full of fears and apprehensions' – and the moment passed.[45]

Since July 1916, Copeau had been trying to organize a tour of the Vieux Colombier in the United States. This involved official permission and support, and, not least, the demobilization of many members of the company. The French government was certainly interested: America had not yet entered the war and a successful French presence in New York would help to counter the strong German presence of the actor and director Max Reinhardt and his company. (There were, of course, many more German-speaking people in New York than French-speaking, but it would be a useful propaganda exercise.) Negotiations dragged on interminably and Copeau was, momentarily, tempted by a lucrative offer to be 'artistic adviser' to the Gaumont film company. However, on 21 January 1917, Copeau set sail from Bordeaux alone, leaving Agnès and the children with the Van Rysselberghes at Saint-Clair. It was no ordinary crossing: it was a French ship and the Atlantic had its share of German submarines. None the less, the ship landed safely in New York harbour on 30 January. Copeau was met by the secretary of the Marquis Melchior de Polignac, who had been sent to New York to superintend French cultural activities there. (He was also head of the Pommery champagne business.)

Copeau was installed in the Hotel Brevoort, on Fifth Avenue. A letter was waiting for him from his old (and continuing) flame, the actress Suzanne Bing, with whom he had a child. He then called on the composer Edgar Varèse – husband of Suzanne Bing and father of another of her children – who was living at the same hotel. Varèse was 'horribly cordial' and talked about Suzanne. Copeau dined at the palatial home of Otto Kahn, banker, patron of the arts and, among other things, chairman of the Metropolitan

Opera Board and part-owner of the Théâtre Français in New York City. At the Met he saw *Carmen*, finding Caruso 'grotesque' and the production 'sickening'. Over the next two months, Copeau gave lectures and made a lot of useful contacts. By the time he left New York, Otto Kahn had given him a free hand and financial support for a season at the Théâtre Français, to begin in November. Armed with a cheque for $1,800, to cover rehearsals in Paris, Copeau set sail on 9 June and landed back in Bordeaux on 19 June.

Gide spent most of the winter in Cuverville with Madeleine. Much of his time was taken up with Conrad translations: he was still revising Isabelle Rivière's version of *Victory* and working on *Typhoon*. He was also writing *Si le grain ne meurt*: by mid-February he had finished Chapter 4, bringing him up to the age of thirteen. On 20 February, he went to Paris, initially to attend to *NRF* business. The situation at the office was 'not brilliant', as he put it to Valéry. Copeau was in America; Schlumberger was mobilized; Rivière was a prisoner-of-war and Gallimard was ill in hospital at Saint-Mandé, though he had put Berthe Lemarié, his assistant, in charge of the book publishing business and kept in constant touch with her.

During that week in Paris, Gide stayed, for the first time, with the Allégrets. In 1914, Pastor Allégret had signed on as an army chaplain. Nevertheless he was able to get home on leave. On 28 January, however, he left France for the Cameroons, which had been recently captured from the Germans: his task was the reorganization of the French Protestant missions and the setting up of the French educational system. He did not return to Paris until May 1919. During his absence, 'Uncle' André assumed the role of unofficial guardian. The four resident children were André (now eighteen), Marc (seventeen), Yves (twelve) and Valentine (eight) – the two oldest sons, Jean-Paul (twenty-three) and Eric (twenty-one) were on active service. Elie Allégret had played a not dissimilar role, it will be remembered, in Gide's education: he had first been employed by Gide's mother to assist her son in his studies – and to serve as moral guide in the absence of a father. The friendship between the two men grew and, in 1895, Allégret was one of André's *témoins* at his wedding. In 1908, Elie Allégret was made pastor to the Protestant church in Passy, thus becoming a neighbour of the Gides. When Pastor Allégret left for Africa, his wife was very grateful for 'Uncle' André's constant support and advice. Gide, of course, had a magical effect on children and, in the eyes of the Allégret children, especially the two older, more difficult adolescent boys, he enjoyed great prestige and respect, with none of the stern, puritanical authority of the '*gouverneur*', as they called their father. Uncle André was associated with treats, such as taking them to the Médrano Circus every year and, later, to the Vieux Colombier matinées – this despite the parents' disapproval of the theatre in general. For his part, Gide was only too delighted to have such close and constant contact with what, for him, were, in many ways, surrogate children. So, from February 1916, Gide often stayed with the Allégrets, at 74 avenue Mozart, when in Paris. He found this arrangement altogether more enjoyable than staying with the Charles Gides or Marcel Drouins. (Given scarcity of fuel during wartime, Gide did not open up the Villa Montmorency when alone, on short visits). The arrangement also provided Gide with an excuse to give the hard-pressed Suzanne Allégret extra money.

Back in Cuverville, Gide felt that he was 'passing through another desert region'. 'Awful, idle days, occupied solely with ageing,' he confided to the *Journal*. 'With enormous effort, I managed to extract from myself in a few hours a new page of the Memoirs, which would have taken only a few minutes in happier times . . . The thought of death did not leave me all day. It seems to be right here, close beside me.'[46]

On 23 March, Gide left Cuverville for Paris. From there, he went south, to meet Alibert, who was on his first home leave for over two years. Alibert was waiting for him at the Rouarts', outside Bagnols-de-Grenade. Then, after some days in the company of Eugène and his family, the two went on to Alibert's home in Carcassonne. In an article[47] written in 1952, but unpublished in his lifetime, Alibert recalls their 'long, confidential conversations' there. To his astonishment, Gide spoke at length of the devil, 'or, to use his own term, the Evil One [*le Malin*]', and of the influence that he could have on our most secret thoughts. And in what was clearly, in view of its subsequent developments, a transitional stage in his thinking, Gide linked these diabolical preoccupations with 'a certain liaison that he had just embarked upon and which, I believe, had a greater influence on his life than any other'. (From this we may conclude that the 'liaison' with Marc had already begun during Gide's stay with the Allégrets in February.) Alibert, a once-believing, no longer practising Catholic (now a believing and, when possible, practising homosexual), must have found the conjunction very odd indeed. He knew nothing of Gide's strange mental state throughout 1916, assumed that he had left his earlier Protestant beliefs behind and had always seen Gide at his most relaxed during, for example, sexual escapades instigated by Eugène Rouart.

Back in Greece, Alibert wrote to Gide, recalling his time on leave: 'Certain springtime nights in Marseille, extraordinary nights, so hot and so frenetic in debauchery' and a 'last adventure that had only just begun and which was fully consummated the very evening I left'. He also remembers 'our conversations at Bagnols and above all at Carcassonne, when I felt closer to you than ever'.[48] Comparing Catholicism to an unbroken chain, 'always all or nothing', in which one is obliged 'to accept it in its entirety, from its first principle to its most extreme consequence, metaphysical and moral included', he points out that Gide, by his very selectivity, is acting like a Protestant: he simply cannot reconcile his sexual practice with the Church's teaching. To his 'amazement', Gide wrote back to say that at present he was 'not particularly concerned with the devil'. This letter has not survived, but we can guess its tenor from Alibert's next letter (27 July), in which he guesses at the curative effect that Marc Allégret was having on Gide: 'Don't you realize that what you took to be self-hatred and self-disgust was merely your inability to renew your joy and happiness . . . that what is called repentance or rather remorse is merely a sense of that inability, a sense of having missed, of letting slip a happiness that will not return . . . that pleasure is an antiseptic, our joy our justification?'[49]

From Carcassonne, Gide travelled to Nîmes and spent some days at Les Sources, before returning to Paris on 11 April. A few days later, he called on the Allégrets, who had just got back from their country house, La Sapinière, in the Haute-Marne. Gide notes of André Allégret: 'The most *born-in-exile* [in English] child I know. Forced into hypocrisy. The School of Falsehood. How much about him I still find mysterious! I asked him what he wanted to be when he grew up. With deep conviction he replied: "An ambassador." I'm afraid my ill-concealed surprise hurt him.'[50] Gide has clearly observed the ingrained hypocrisy that, like its obverse, the sincerity that he so much esteemed, derived from a puritanical upbringing. For both André and Marc, Uncle André was to be the crucial influence in their emancipation from the values inculcated in them by their family. Clearly, the enterprise was a delicate one, one requiring diplomatic skills of a high order – together with the necessary admixture of conscious hypocrisy.

On 28 April, the *NRF* publishing house brought out Paul Valéry's *La Jeune Parque*, a poem of some 500 lines in Alexandrines. (The French *Parques* are the Latin *Parcae*, the Greek *Moirae*, the English Fates.) It was Valéry's first publication of any length since the short prose work *La Soirée avec Monsieur Teste* of 1896 and his first verse publication in volume form. Addressing André Gide in his dedication, Valéry declares: 'For many years I have deserted the art of poetry: in an attempt to subject myself once more to its discipline, I have composed this exercise, which I dedicate to you.' *La*

Jeune Parque was recognized at once as a masterpiece; soon its author would be hailed as the greatest French poet since Mallarmé. Yet, until the poem's appearance in 1917, Valéry, now forty-five, had been a little-known, largely forgotten figure.

'I have not known such calm for months, for years,' Gide wrote in his *Journal* on 5 May, the evening of his return to Paris after two weeks at Cuverville. 'It would require a great deal of reasoning not to call this happiness.'[51] Over the next two months, Gide saw Marc a great deal, spending with him most Thursdays and Sundays. As the summer holidays approached, the two saw more and more of each other, spending evenings together, with Gide sleeping at the Allégrets' or Marc with Gide at the Villa Montmorency. 'I refrain from speaking of the sole preoccupation of my mind and flesh . . .', he wrote on 19 May.[52] Two days before, he had been thinking about Ghéon, who, he knew, would soon be on leave, when his old friend arrived at the door. Gide was expecting Madeleine to arrive that afternoon, so Ghéon stayed on to see her. Afterwards, Gide notes how much Ghéon had come to resemble 'le brave curé de Cuverville': 'the same intonations, the same rather abstracted, benevolent attention . . . the same indefinable absence'. Ghéon stayed the night and, next day, for over an hour, Gide did his best to administer 'artificial respiration' to their friendship, trying to persuade Ghéon, and himself, that they still shared the same views, but to no avail. 'At times it seems that Ghéon is more lost to me than if he were dead. He is neither changed, nor absent; he has been confiscated.'[53]

On 11 July Gide left for Cuverville, seen off from Saint-Lazare by Marc, who had spent the previous night at the Villa Montmorency. A few days later, Marc and his brother André went to Switzerland, dividing their time between their maternal grandparents in Basle and family friends, the Breitensteins, in Geneva. (Jules Breitenstein, a Protestant pastor, was professor of theology at the University of Geneva and, like Suzanne Allégret, a native of Strasbourg.) André and Marc would then spend ten days at a lakeside students' camp at Chanivaz. Gide was already scheming frantically to join Marc Allégret in Switzerland – with a sufficiency of excuses to assuage suspicion on both sides, the boy's mother and his wife. As early as June, in an entirely 'loving' letter, Madeleine had dropped the words: 'Don't devote yourself too excessively to the Allégrets. I think there is some danger there.' She was later to admit that her grief at the direction her husband's life was taking really began in the summer of 1917. For Gide, one capital pretext was to hand: Jacques Rivière had recently been transferred, on grounds of poor health, from a prisoner-of-war camp in Germany to a camp at Engelberg, in Switzerland, on condition that he remained there until hostilities ceased. What could be more natural than Gide going to visit Rivière, whom he had not seen for three years? While in Switzerland he could also call on Stravinsky with a view to persuading him to compose the incidental music for a production of *Antony and Cleopatra* that Ida Rubinstein was planning, in a translation by Gide. This could coincide with the end of the Chanivaz camping holiday; Uncle André could then take both boys, thus diverting suspicion, on a trip to the Swiss mountains.

'I am jealously counting the hours that separate me from M.,' Gide wrote on 6 August.[54] This is the first *Journal* reference to Marc. There was, of course, another 'M.' (Maurice Schlumberger) in 1905–6. The new 'M.' soon becomes 'Michel' and, for some time, as if by a further precaution, Gide writes of himself in the third person, as 'Fabrice'. After calling on the Allégret brothers at Chanivaz, Gide went to see Jacques Rivière at Engelberg. Of his two days with Rivière, the *Journal* tells us nothing: the entry headed 'Engelberg' is concerned entirely with 'Michel'. At first sight, he had hardly recognized the boy: 'The fear of seeing the adolescent grow up too quickly constantly tormented Fabrice.' What he found most endearing in him were the childlike qualities that he still retained. Back in Geneva, Gide stayed for two days with the Breitensteins. Then, with André and Marc, he went the short distance to Les Diablerets, where Stravinsky, who was spending the war in Switzerland, had taken a house for the summer. The three spent six days there, seeing Stravinsky almost every day and, once, being presented with a 'performance' of *Renard*, in which the composer not only played the piano transcription, but acted out the parts for fox, cock, cat and goat. It was, says Gide, in a letter to Sarah Breitenstein, 'the most frightening thing I have ever heard; a sort of clowning that, in its very intensity, attained the tragic at certain moments'.[55] Commissioned by the Princesse de Polignac, *Renard*, a 'chamber cantata' for four voices and sixteen instruments, with the singing parts to be mimed by dancers, was first staged at the Paris Opéra on 18 May 1922, by the Ballets Russes. *Antony and Cleopatra* was discussed, but Stravinsky did not, in the end, provide the incidental music.

On 18 August 'Uncle André' and his two 'nephews' set out for Saas Fee, where they spent a week mountain climbing. The *Journal*, again, is devoted almost entirely to Marc. Some days, he seemed 'clothed in grace', his skin emanating 'a sort of blond radiance'. 'Nothing can describe the languor, the grace, the sensuality of his eyes.' Observing him, 'Fabrice' lost 'all sense of time and place, good and evil, of the proprieties and himself'. Remembering Ghéon, who had once 'accompanied and preceded him in pleasure', he doubted whether his friend's 'religious calling' would have resisted 'such a flagrant invitation', or whether 'to worship such an idol' he would not have become a pagan once more. At other times, the sun was obscured by cloud and Marc revealed 'a refractory, argumentative nature, always ready to rebel. It is difficult to obtain from him what he doesn't give spontaneously and lovingly.'[56] After two more days at the Breitensteins' in Geneva, the trio travelled back, on 29 August, to La Sapinière. There they stayed until 9 September, when they went on a short trip to Montbéliard to meet Schlumberger, who had obtained a twenty-four-hour pass from his army barracks. They then caught the Paris train – the brothers getting off at Chaumont to catch a connection for La Sapinière. After a week in Paris, Gide finally returned to Cuverville on 18 September, after an absence of six weeks. Two days later, he is writing: 'What is the point of resuming this journal if I dare not be sincere in it and have to conceal my heart's secret occupation.'[57] And the next day: 'Ah! How little my desires have diminished and how hard it would be to reduce them! I cannot consent to put my happiness in the past . . . I never felt younger or happier than I did last month.'[58] Ten days later, he was at the Gare de l'Est to meet the Allégrets, back from La Sapinière for the beginning of the new school year – André and Marc were at the Lycée Janson-de-Sailly. 'Glorious weather today,' he notes. 'My inner sky is even more splendid; an immense joy . . .'[59]

From his return to Cuverville on 18 September until 1 January 1918, Gide made in all eight journeys to or from Paris spending a week or two each time at the Allégrets' house in Passy. He finds in Keats's letters a man after his own heart, delightedly quoting: 'Better be imprudent movables than prudent fixtures.' 'Never have I aspired less to rest,' he goes on, 'never have I felt more uplifted by that excess of passion that Bossuet regards as the privilege of youth . . . Age is unable to empty sensual pleasure [*volupté*] of its attraction or the whole world of its charm. On the contrary, disgust came more readily at twenty and I was less content with life. I embraced more timidly; I breathed less deeply and I felt less loved. Perhaps, too, I wanted to be melancholy; I had not yet understood the superior beauty of happiness.'[60] He turned to the *Journal* only when he was not in Paris. 'I have lived through the last few months,' he wrote on 22 October, 'dizzy with happiness; hence the long empty space in this notebook. It reflects only my clouds.'[61] One such cloud darkened the sky on 16 November: 'The thought of death pursues me with strange obstinacy. With each gesture I make, I calculate: how many times have I done that already? I compute: how many times more? And, full of despair, I feel the turn of the year rushing towards me. As I measure how the water is withdrawing around me, my thirst increases and, the less time that remains for me to feel it, the younger I feel.'[62] Six days before his forty-eighth birthday, Gide would no doubt have been surprised to learn that death would stay his hand for a further thirty-four years. Letters arrived from Marc ('yesterday, a letter full of exquisite fantasy and grace') or did not ('For the past week I have been waiting in anxious impatience for a letter from M.'). (On 28 October, that earlier 'M.', Maurice Schlumberger, now thirty, interned in Switzerland after being a prisoner-of-war in Germany, became a father, with the birth of a daughter, Odile.)

On 31 October, Jacques Copeau and the Vieux Colombier company sailed for New York. This time, Copeau took his wife and children with him. Somewhat to Gide's annoyance, Gaston Gallimard, who had recovered from illness, also went, leaving the *NRF* publishing house without its head. After a dangerous twelve-day journey, the company reached New York and took up its occupation of the Garrick Theater, on 35th Street. Despite enormous practical difficulties, the season opened on 27 November, with Molière's *Les Fourberies de Scapin*. Copeau – and indeed his company – had never enjoyed such financial reward for their work. But, after the initial excitement had worn off, most of the company felt homesick.

On 22 November, at Cuverville, Gide finished his translation of *Antony and Cleopatra*. Next day, he set off for Paris, where he gave a reading of it to Ida Rubinstein at the home of Léon Bakst.

Gide was not easily given to jealousy. He had felt none over Maurice Schlumberger, his first great love; indeed Ghéon's role in the relationship was almost integral. But, then, at that time Ghéon was Gide's closest companion, one whom he loved, respected, trusted. It is an indication of the nature and degree of his feelings for Marc Allégret that he felt jealousy for the first time. 'The day before yesterday,' he wrote on 8 December, 'and for the first time in my life, I knew the torment of jealousy. I tried in vain to defend myself against it. M. did not come back until 10 p.m. I knew he was at Cahé's. I couldn't bear it any more . . . and measured the depth of my love by the anguish I felt.'[63] (The earlier published versions of the *Journal*[64] have only 'C.', which everyone assumed referred to Cocteau, as it later did. We now learn from Eric Marty's new, uncut version that the manuscript has 'Cahé'. Cahé was Catherine Krüger, Marc's cousin and a pastor's daughter, who had been in Switzerland with the Allégret brothers that summer. Next day, Gide called on Cahé, who reassured him by recounting at length everything that was said or done throughout the entire evening. In the *Journal*, Gide claims that his mood of jealousy did not last, but he did not forget it. The incident reappears in *Les Faux-Monnayeurs*.

The attraction of the forty-eight-year-old Gide for the sixteen-year-old Marc Allégret is entirely understandable. But what of the counter-attraction of Gide for Marc? That is, naturally, much more difficult to elucidate. It is much less documented and, in any case, a sixteen-year-old boy is unlikely to be sure what he feels from one week to the next. But, equally, the relationship that acquired an amatory, a sexual character in May 1917 was not, as one had every reason to expect, doomed to an early end, broken off, as in the case of Maurice Schlumberger, by the rapidly changing younger man. It continued, at the same degree of intensity, indeed deepening, over the next few years at least. In 1918, Gide and Marc spent three-and-a-half months together in England; then, in 1925–6, they travelled together for a year in Africa; Marc accompanied Gide on other journeys and, in Paris, lived with him, first at the Villa Montmorency, then in the rue Vaneau. He was to make a highly successful career for himself as a film director. In 1938, aged thirty-seven, he married and, in 1942, had a daughter. He had innumerable affairs with women before, during and after his marriage, but Gide was the most important, most influential person in his life and they remained close friends, bound by an unbreakable bond of mutual love and respect. Relationships do not endure so long, in a world so besieged by change and decay, unless the earliest foundations are of the strongest. In many respects, of course, 'Uncle André' represented for the young Marc Allégret an ideal mentor, one who possessed true authority rather than the mere image of it offered by the narrow, puritanical father. He enjoyed immense intellectual (and moral) prestige. He led a life, moreover, that must have seemed highly enviable to a boy still at school. At the same time, the youth's natural rebelliousness found a sympathetic ally in the eternally young Gide. Marc seems to have taken to the situation in the most natural way in the world. We are not entirely devoid of evidence on his side. There is a rather laconic and sometimes cryptic diary and there are letters. Nowhere is there any trace of the panic felt by many young homosexuals, who do not yet see themselves as such, that they are being drawn into a frightening world of effeminacy from which they will not be able to escape. Marc had no sense that what he did with André made him anything or did anything other than add more abundantly to whatever it was that he already had. In true Socratic fashion, Gide was teaching his young lover how to use his body as well as his mind. Again, Socratically, and in the spirit of *Corydon*, this was not, in any final or exclusive sense, a homosexual initiation. It was made clear that, at some future date, Gide would initiate the young man into heterosexuality – a promise that Marc did not forget. From Grantchester, in August 1918, Gide wrote to Jean Schlumberger: 'The girls and the maids are crazy about him . . . From time to time, he asks me if I have forgotten that I promised him his first mistress; but he has already taken so many small payments on account that this first mistress will not exactly be a novelty.'[65] Naming oneself, and acknowledging it with pride, has undoubtedly brought liberation to many. But one advantage of those linguistically innocent days was that people often felt things and did things without naming them or without being named, and therefore regarded them as quite normal as, in some more 'primitive' societies, they still are. Nor, perhaps surprisingly, in view of Marc's puritanical background, is there any trace of guilt. This was undoubtedly helped by adolescent rebellion, but also encouraged perhaps by attending an excellent *lycée*, Janson-de-Sailly, rather than a private, religious school. Much of Marc's *insouciance* must have come naturally to him; much, too, must be attributed to Gide's personality and deftness in such matters.

Little direct evidence of all this can be found in Marc's diary or letters; it is more a question of deducing it from the overall picture emerging from these documents. For example, during the weeks preceding and following the May event, Marc is clearly much more concerned with his courtship of Antoinette Lederlin, the sister of one of his schoolfriends. Nothing came of this and, with the new school year, in October, Marc found that the girl had dropped him. He was devastated, retired to his bedroom and sobbed his heart out. He had only one friend, Uncle André, and felt he had to talk to him at once. He wrote him a short letter, but tore it up. But, as Gide discovered in a long letter from Marc, dated 2 May 1918, Antoinette Lederlin was not his first 'petit amour'. Apparently, during the summer of 1916, while staying at the Breitensteins', near Geneva, he and his hosts' daughter, Sarah, would often go on long walks together. The girl clearly flirted with the then fifteen-year-old boy. The following summer, Marc and his brother André made several visits to the Breitensteins'. Sarah and Marc renewed their mild infatuation: André got jealous and, with the bravura of a boy one year older, made a successful bid for her. Marc withdrew, again heartbroken: 'You can't imagine how I suffered in Switzerland, how I suffered whenever I had to lie to you, because above all I didn't want you to know about my love [for her] . . . Since then I have not wanted to love bad girls any more – and when I have thought about them, it has been in the flesh and, for a long time now, I have concentrated my spiritual affection on you . . . Oh! My dear friend, you know how horrible it is to suffer all alone . . .' On the one hand, Gide was there when Marc needed him most, but, on the other, it was a situation that required all Gide's skill, not only to enable the relationship to continue and thrive, but also to watch over the boy's wellbeing and to preserve the trust placed in him by the boy's mother. Though exultant with passion, Gide was at all times clear-sighted: 'I am under no illusion,' he wrote on 25 October. 'Michel [Marc] loves me not so much for what I am as for what I enable him to be. Why should I ask for more? Never have I enjoyed life so much, or found the taste of life so delicious.'[66]

And Marc? As we have seen, the letter from Ghéon to Gide that Madeleine opened 'in error' was one dated 13 December 1917. It is clearly a response to a (lost) letter from Gide in which he writes of his relationship with Marc Allégret:

If I were really your friend, and not an indulgent comrade, do you know what I would dare to do? Not only pray for you, which I do every day, with more tears since I received your letter and consider the abyss in which you say you have found happiness, but reprimand you with all the vehemence of a prophet and remind you of certain of Christ's words that would make you shudder with shame . . . I guessed what is going on . . . If atheists are shocked by it, what will a Christian say? 'Whoso shall offend one of these little ones . . .' But no, I shall say nothing. I am only your friend. I still love you too much, even in evil, and I have too much to blame myself for when I think of our past together. I did too much to encourage your present to assume the right to blame . . . When I think that I had begun to write a book with the aim of rallying the world to the cause of my sin![67]

The reading of this letter certainly marked an important stage in Madeleine's understanding of her husband's sexual tastes and practices. It could not, however, have come as a revelation; it was more in the nature of a confirmation of suspicions. Those suspicions must have taken root during their early visits to North Africa and Italy. Later, she became anxious about André's 'abnormal' interest in various young boys on the Cuverville estate and surrounding countryside. In 1905, her letter to Ghéon, ending 'you are very young . . . Be careful . . . Don't make me worry too much', shows that she had a good idea of what he and her husband were up to. All this must have received further confirmation in some of her husband's writings, *L'Immoraliste* and *Les Caves du Vatican* in particular. Ghéon's letter confirmed that Gide was now involved in a sexual relationship with a young man of not yet seventeen, the son of close family friends, who, in the absence of his pastor father, had been placed under André's unofficial guardianship. There was no more for her to learn; her relationship with her husband was now irreparably poisoned. When, in June of the following year, Gide confirmed that he was leaving for England with Marc, it was merely the last straw. Gide's response to the letter of 13 December does not attempt to answer Ghéon. It is short and attends only in passing to the main point at issue. It has brought him physical health and mental wellbeing and, far from sinking into a pit of iniquity, he is sitting at his desk in Cuverville, working as hard as he has ever done. He had recently finished his preface to the Dupouey letters. This was more obviously 'anachronistic' than his works usually were. Nevertheless, he does not allow the later Dupouey, the convert revealed in the letters to Ghéon, to obscure the earlier Dupouey, the reader of *Les Nourritures terrestres*, the seeker after personal liberation, as revealed in the letters to Gide himself. As soon as Gide had written the preface, he finished 'at one go' and 'by way of reaction' to it, the opening pages of a revised *Corydon*.

After spending Christmas and New Year's Eve with the Allégrets, Gide returned to Cuverville on 1 January. 'What a state I am in!' he wrote to Jean Schlumberger. 'I don't recognize anything in myself any more. Sometimes it seems that all the years of my life are mixed up and that only now am I entering adolescence . . . after which it will suddenly be decrepitude and the grave.' In the same letter, Gide tells Schlumberger that, during the week just spent at the Allégrets', he slept in Jean-Paul's bedroom. Jean-Paul, the eldest of the Allégret children, then twenty-four, was home on leave. He was, says Gide, 'un charmant compagnon de chambre' and, 'providing you don't scare him, I think you'll succeed in taming him completely. His rather sad, winning tenderness is exquisite. He has a prodigious need of affection.'[68] Schlumberger was already making moves to have the young man transferred to his information unit at Réchésy near the German border. When this was achieved, at the end of the month, Schlumberger discovered that young Allégret's German was 'terribly poor' and his typing non-existent. Meanwhile, to the despair of his mother, who already had two sons at the front, André Allégret signed up in an artillery regiment.

In Cuverville, Gide worked on *Corydon*, which, by 14 January, he considered 'more or less finished' – it was to be another false ending. He turned back, with delight, to Meredith's *The Shaving of Shagpat*. On 25 January, he went to Paris, ostensibly to sign the *Antony and Cleopatra* contract with Ida Rubinstein. This was not done until 10 February: he came back to Cuverville the next day. There he helped Madeleine to serve soup to some twenty village children in a deserted house. She did this every lunch-time, lit the fire and put flowers on the table. Their charity went further than an improvised soup-kitchen. One day, they went over the Cuverville accounts together: gifts took up almost a quarter of annual expenditure, itself well exceeded by income. 'Happy to see Em. approve that expenditure as much as I do. I know that if she let herself go, she would give even more – to the point of depriving herself completely – Ah! I would like to be able to bring myself to give more . . . to give everything away, to enjoy only what I give and receive from others.'[69] Yet such aspirations towards a form of Tolstoyan Christian socialism were accompanied by what might well seem to be inappropriate political views. When, over lunch, Lucien Maury expressed anxiety over 'the wave of socialism' that he thought would submerge Europe after the war and the inevitability of revolution, Gide declared his support for the kind of active resistance being put up by Action Française, the extreme right-wing Monarchist group. Whatever their faults, they were the only opposition.

In February, Gide began a new work of fiction, his first since *Les Caves du Vatican*, published before the outbreak of war. He called it *L'Aveugle*. By the end of the month, he had written forty-five pages of it, which he read aloud to Madeleine. *La Symphonie Pastorale*, as it was to become, was to be another 'anachronism': 'I already wish I were finished with it . . .'[70]

In the middle of an extended stay in Paris, in March–April, Gide spent a week with Marc at Carantec, in Finistère, with his friends the Godebskis. (Cipa Godebski, a painter, was Misia's brother.) About that time, the German bombardment of Paris increased in severity and Suzanne Allégret took her remaining family first to Poitiers then to Limoges, where her brother-in-law, Paul Allégret, was a law professor at the university. Meanwhile, Marc's education was the subject of a four-sided discussion involving, in addition to 'Uncle André' and the boy's mother, Uncle Paul and Aunt Léonie, her husband's formidable sister, one of the first women teaching graduates and, since 1912, headmistress of the Lycée Victor Duruy. Intent on spending the summer with Marc in England, Gide not unnaturally advocated a course that would include English. His view prevailed. However, although Marc had quite a good knowledge of German, he hardly knew a word of English. Arrangements were made and Marc took up the study of English. 'Doing without M. is already out of the question,'

Gide noted on 4 May. He could not, he confessed, resist trying to improve those he loved. Yet it was often Marc's 'faults' – his carefree attitude, his boisterousness, his unconcern for the time – that he found most attractive. They met as best they could, in Paris, if Marc could get there, or in Limoges, if not. They wrote to one another frequently. Marc read Gide's works in rapid succession. 'Lafcadio, Nathanaël, Immoralist, all three of you are within me,' he wrote to their creator on 21 April. Three weeks later, Gide addressed him as '*Mon Cadio bien aimé*'. 'I'm reading *Les Caves*, it gets more and more terrific [*épatant*] as it goes on,' Marc writes on 29 May. 'You're the swellest [*le plus chic*] of Lafcadio's uncles, quite the best, the only one. But when I think that you once called me "Cadio", I faint with shame to think how little I deserve it. But I was devilishly pleased [*sacrément content*] . . .'

'I was already imagining the little English house where, for the first time, we would live together, alone. It was so beautiful, so unhoped for,' Gide later told Roger Martin du Gard. Meanwhile, he was fighting the endless-seeming battle with bureaucracy over passports and visas. He wrote letters off to England: to Gosse, to use his influence with the authorities over visas; to Raverat, regarding tuition for Marc in Cambridge and for possible accommodation there; and to Paul Wenz, a writer friend and translator, about accommodation in London. 'I'm ready,' he writes to Marc on 1 June. 'I'm so tense I cannot even be happy any more. Thanks to you I live more intensely than ever before. My Cadio, whom I was always waiting for.' But, fearful that he might turn out to be some kind of sorcerer's apprentice, Gide does not entirely forget that he is the 'uncle' *in loco parentis*. He points out that Lafcadio's principal quality is his 'disinterestedness'. 'I want to teach you many more things,' he goes on. 'In particular (but you know this already, don't you?) that the best is not always to be found in the *laisser-aller*, and that one must be very demanding of oneself.'

When in Paris, on his way back to Cuverville from Limoges, at the end of May, Gide stumbled on 'Douglas's abominable book', *Oscar Wilde and Myself*. It was, Gide realized, a hypocritical tissue of lies, 'a monstrous travesty of the truth'. Gide had been an eye-witness to acts that Douglas now claimed never happened. 'He even claims that he was unaware of Wilde's morals! And that he supported him at first only because he believed him to be innocent.' Gide hoped that he would live to unmask Douglas.[71]

By the end of May, a new German offensive brought the enemy to Château-Thierry, within 50 miles of central Paris. For a time, it looked as though Gide and Marc would have to give up their trip to England. The danger passed and Gide got ready to leave. In his *Cahier bleu* (reproduced in part in Jean Schlumberger's *Madeleine et André Gide*), Roger Martin du Gard recounts a conversation with Gide on 19 December 1920. In it, Gide describes the last night he spent in Cuverville before leaving for England.

'You aren't going away alone, are you?' [Madeleine asks].
    'No . . .,' I stammered.
    'You're going with X?'
    She stopped me short with the terrible words: 'Don't say anything. Never tell me anything again. I prefer your silence to your deceit.'
    I went up to my room, shattered. All night, I paced up and down . . . I was mad. I was leaving next morning, at dawn, everything was ready. And, suddenly, I asked myself if I ought to leave, if I really wanted to go on that trip. I didn't any more. But it was too late . . .

Next day, Gide tells us, before leaving, he handed Madeleine a letter that he had written that night. In it, he told her that he could no longer stay in Normandy with her, 'that I was rotting away there . . ., that all my vitality was ebbing away there, that I was dying there and that I wanted to live, that I had to live and that meant escaping from there, travelling, meeting new people, loving people, creating!'[72] As Jean Schlumberger has established, this is not quite what happened. Gide omits to say that Madeleine wrote him a sort of reply, which he read before leaving. He cannot therefore have given Madeleine the letter just before leaving. Schlumberger 'cannot forgive' Gide for not reproducing it in his own account of events:

André dear,
    You are mistaken. I have no doubts as to your affection. And even if I had, I would have nothing to complain of. *Ma part a été très belle* [untranslatable – let us say, 'I have had the best of you']. I have had the best of your soul, the tenderness of your childhood and your youth. And I know that, living or dead, I shall have the soul of your age.
    I have always understood your need of travel and freedom. How often in your moments of nervous pain, which are the ransom of your genius, the words nearly rose to my lips: 'Why don't you go away, you're quite free, there's no door on the cage to keep you in.' (I didn't say them for fear of hurting you by seeming to acquiesce too readily in your absence.)
    What does cause me worry – and you know it, though you don't admit it to yourself – is the way of life that you have taken up, and which will lead to the perdition of others, as well as yourself. Don't think that I say this with any feeling of condemnation. I feel sorry for you as much as I love you. A terrible temptation has been put before you, armed with every attraction [*toutes les séductions*]. Resist.
    Adieu, au revoir.
        Your Madeleine.

Gide caught the train to Paris, where, at the Van Rysselberghes', he was joined by Marc. 'I am leaving France in a state of inexpressible anguish,' he noted. 'It seems to me that I am saying goodbye to my whole past.'[73]

Gide and Marc arrived in London on 20 June and moved into rooms at 9 Lancaster Gate. Next day, Gide dashed off a note to Arnold Bennett, announcing their arrival: 'This *we* means my nephew Marc Allégret and I.'[74] Bennett responded at once from the Ministry of Information, where he had been put in charge of British propaganda in France by the newly ennobled minister, Max Aitken, Lord Beaverbrook, a close friend. Gide and 'Monsieur le neveu' were invited to dinner at the grill-room of the Café Royal. They saw Jacques Raverat's paintings, then on view at the New English Art Club, in Suffolk Street. On 27 June, they left London for the Raverats' home at Weston, near Stevenage, in Hertfordshire. Next day, they visited Cambridge and called on Simon Bussy, a French painter, married to Lytton Strachey's sister, Dorothy, to whom Gide had a letter of introduction from an old mutual friend, Auguste Bréal. The Bussys were out, but responded with an invitation to lunch, at Lady Strachey's. Meanwhile, Gide and Marc moved into Byron's Lodge, Grantchester, the house of Louis de Glehn, a French teacher at the Perse School, who also took charge of Marc's English lessons.

The Cambridge of the long vacation was not the arcadia of beautiful young men in boats, held out so temptingly for him by Valéry Larbaud in 1913, but 'the course of the Cam is charming', he wrote to Jacques-Emile Blanche. 'I am inconsolable that I did not taste this life thirty years ago; one is particularly sensitive here to "getting old" [English in the original] and Marc Allégret's presence makes it all the more bitter.'[75] Marc's presence, 'l'aspect glorieux de son corps', as he enthused to Jean Schlumberger, was more than a mere compensation. Cambridge had other attractions, too: it was a paradise for the book-browser and collector. Writing to André Ruyters, that other bibliophile, Gide refers to 'a prodigious bookshop; three floors to rummage through'.[76] (This is the old Heffer's in Petty Cury.) By 21 August, Gide had already amassed sixty books.

Lady Strachey, the imposing widow of General Sir Richard Strachey, the great Indian administrator, had taken a house, 27 Grange Road, for the summer. There Gide met innumerable members of the 'Strachey clan': as well as Lytton, Philippa, an activist in the cause of women's suffrage; Pernel, a French supervisor at Newnham College and its future Principal; and James, the future psychoanalyst and Freud's English translator. He also met their eldest sister, Dorothy, who was to become his English translator. Then fifty-three and married, rather improbably, to a Frenchman five years her junior, Dorothy Bussy fell at once hopelessly in love with Gide. Gide asked if she could recommend an English teacher and she offered her services at once. He arrived punctually each morning by bicycle from Grantchester, his homework scrupulously done. Dorothy Strachey soon realized that, despite his poor, rather antiquated spoken English, he read English fluently, indeed had read the English poets and novelists voraciously. When the lesson was over, they would chat for another hour or so in French. Writing to Gide from Venice, a year later, she remembered those

happy Cambridge days, when I was just your dictionary and your grammar, convenient and helpful. And you had the same kind of friendly feeling for me that one has for a dictionary. I understood *that* perfectly. And you didn't notice – you were too much engrossed by other things – that your dictionary had eyes and a heart, was watching you and wondering at you, was charmed and thrilled and shaken by you. I couldn't help it. Gide, I couldn't help it really. Aren't you the strangest and loveliest and the most disturbing thing I have ever come across in my life?[77]

In another letter, she remembers Gide's voice, 'so pure, so true, so thrilling', a voice that 'ravishes me', 'pierces me through', 'makes me melt' and 'fall upon my knees'.[78]

Through the Stracheys Gide met other Cambridge *illuminati*, many of them, unbeknown to him, more or less homosexual: A. E. Housman, poet, Professor of Latin and Fellow of Trinity, Maynard Keynes and Goldsworthy Lowes Dickinson, both Fellows of King's. Dickinson, a close friend of Lytton's, offered Gide his rooms in College for the rest of the summer, but, for reasons that remain obscure, the Provost refused the necessary permission. Instead, at the end of July, Gide moved into more spacious quarters at Grape House, in Grantchester. Later, on 18 August, in order to avoid the daily 2-mile bicycle ride into Cambridge, he accepted an offer to take over Merton House, in Queen's Road, while its owner, Harry Norton, was away. Norton, a mathematics don at Trinity, was also a man of considerable private means. He, too, had been introduced to Gide by Lytton Strachey, who had dedicated his recently published *Eminent Victorians* to him. Merton House was a fine building, set in its own beautiful garden, and came complete with two female servants. Norton clearly had tastes to match his means. The house was filled with works of art, though Gide mentions only two: a Picasso 'of the latest period' and 'an admirable Persian vase'. The library was 'inexhaustible' and the cellar was no less well endowed: as a matter of course, Gide was served with a 'Mouton-Rothschild '78 that would delight Rouart'.[79] Rouart? And what of Gide? The poor man's limitations where the art of the table were concerned seem to have prevented him from appreciating to the full a forty-year-old Mouton-Rothschild of an exceptionally good vintage.

There were country weekends. William Rothenstein, painter and one-time Parisian, invited Gide and 'nephew' to his farmhouse in Gloucester-shire and Roger Fry received them in his art-filled house in Guildford, which he had designed himself. Fry and Gide, who had a common friend in Harry Kessler, talked of art and literature, discussing in particular Mallarmé's poetry, which Fry was translating. During that first weekend, Gide impressed the company by playing 'all the old Italian things' on the virginals, 'as no one has ever played them before and as I have always dreamt they might be played'.[80] Later, Fry painted Gide's portrait. There were trips to London, where Gide and Marc were guests of the Stracheys. They dined with the Bennetts. They saw Rimsky-Korsakov's opera, *The Golden Cockerel*, given by Beecham's company at Drury Lane, where an elegant Englishman flirted with Marc. They attended the first night of Bennett's new play, *The Title*. They were taken by Roger Fry to a performance of Borodin's *Prince Igor* by the Diaghilev company. Afterwards, in the dressing-room of Lydia Lopokova (the future Mrs Maynard Keynes), Gide met up again with Diaghilev and Massine. Also there were Lady Ottoline Morrell, Aldous Huxley and Mark Gertler.

Before leaving England, Gide and Marc paid a brief visit to Drummeldrie, a village in Scotland, where Elisabeth Van Rysselberghe and Ethel White-horn ('Whity') were working on a farm. Marc got on extremely well with the two women. Gide told Elisabeth's mother that 'sympathie spontanée' sprang up between Elisabeth and him and a 'grande camaraderie', between Whity and him. According to the 'Petite Dame', Gide said to her: 'Marc was perfect. I think he put all his coquetry into it. He must have felt that, for me, Elisabeth is not just an ordinary friend . . .'[81] By the time the two were due to leave England, Marc had fallen victim to the influenza epidemic that was raging in Europe at the time. He would stay in Grantchester for a few more weeks. When he had recovered, he tried to get himself accepted by the British forces. He applied to a recruitment office in Cambridge and passed all the necessary tests. Eventually, Marc joined the Royal Flying Corps and stayed on in England until Christmas.

On 28 September, Gide was back in Cuverville, where he spent a few days before moving on to Paris for a week. 'Home in port', he noted in the

Journal, unaware of the storm brewing, for all the world as if things at Cuverville could return to the *status quo ante.* Already the English summer was taking on an unreal quality. 'The three months I spent in England passed in so strange a way,' he wrote to Copeau, 'that I could hardly convince myself that they actually took place in my life.'[82] He began what was to become Book 2 of *La Symphonie Pastorale,* but found it hard to revive his interest in 'the state of mind of my pastor' and feared that the end of the work might suffer as a result. In an attempt to reanimate the pastor's thoughts, he went back (for the first time for months) to the Gospels and to Pascal. But, while trying to re-create a state of religious fervour, he did not want it to take him over: 'I pull on the reins and wield the whip at the same time.'[83]

News of two young deaths brought their own gloom. Paul Desjardins' son, Michel, had been killed on active service and Valentine's epileptic son from her first marriage, Alain Bernardbeig, had died from meningitis. Both were twenty. 'Obsessive fear of death,' Gide writes in the *Journal,* 'and that the ground may suddenly open up under my feet. I love life passionately; but I don't trust it. One should, though.'[84] One morning, Gide and Madeleine were pleasantly surprised by the unannounced arrival of Eric Allégret and Domi Drouin, both on convalescent leave.

Maria Van Rysselberghe returned to Paris after a stay in Lausanne with Aline Mayrisch. From 29 October to 4 November, Gide and she lived alone in the house in the rue Claude-Lorrain. It was during those days together, spent 'in a lack of comfort that soon became amusing', that the Petite Dame began work on her 'Cahiers'. It was to be not so much an autobiography as a biography of Gide, which ended only with Gide's funeral in 1951. With tact, understanding and gentle persistence, she got Gide to talk about his relationship with Marc. The months in England had not been entirely idyllic. Marc was subject to violent swings of mood – one moment he could be charming everyone around him, then, suddenly reveal 'l'accent aigu des Allégret' (their acute accent, their sharp tone). '*Petites tyrannies*' would be followed by '*délicatesses infinies*'.[85] Gide returned to Cuverville for another week, but was back again in Paris for the Armistice celebrations on 11 November. 'It was splendid, we spent three days in a state of inexpressible exaltation,' Gide wrote to Dorothy Bussy. But his 'exaltation' was short-lived. Marc was still ill, confined to bed, and the only actual news from him was 'brief reassuring notes to his mother . . . I would so much like to be with him!'[86]

Gide was back in Cuverville by 13 November. While working on his memoirs, he wanted to check a date in one of his letters to Madeleine. He asked his wife for the key to the desk in which his letters were kept. She went very pale and, her lips trembling, said that the drawer was now empty and that the letters no longer existed. This résumé of the bare bones of the incident occurs in a footnote in *Et nunc manet in te*, a meditation on Madeleine and their relationship, written after her death in 1938. It was largely in response to *Et nunc . . .*, which he regarded as both excessively self-accusatory and an over-gloomy evocation of Madeleine, that Jean Schlumberger wrote his *Madeleine et André Gide*, published in 1956. (The inversion in the title is clearly intended to place the retiring, self-effacing Madeleine to the fore. One might add, for what it is worth, that it also leaves the label-signifier of the literary *œuvre* intact, unsplit.) The destruction of the letters is, in many ways, the climax, the heart even, of Schlumberger's book. He uses as evidence three versions of the incident, written down by three different people, based on conversations with Gide. In chronological order they are Schlumberger's own (2 December 1918), Maria Van Rysselberghe's (between 10 and 17 January 1919) and Roger Martin du Gard's (22 December 1920, the longest and most detailed, taken from his *Cahier bleu*). Gide takes up the story (in RMG's account):

'I don't have your letters any more. I've burnt them all.' I thought I was dying . . . But you must understand what those letters were. I had written to her from my early youth, which was already dominated by that only love of my life. I did not spend a day away from her without writing to her [an exaggeration this, especially in more recent years]. Those letters were the treasure of my life, the best of me: certainly my best work . . . Suddenly there was nothing: I had been stripped of everything! Ah, I can imagine what a father might feel on arriving home and being told by his wife: 'Our child is dead. I have killed him.'

'But why?' I asked her. 'How could you do that? Our dear love, all our past destroyed by you! By you?' . . .

Poor creature, she, too, had suffered terribly. I could not, for a moment, hold it against her. When she was once more alone, with the appalling certainty that I was going away, far from her, a smile on my lips, a gleam of joy in my eyes, to betray our love; and when she read my words that, with her I was *rotting away*, she must have felt that it was all over. Nothing of the past must survive. She wanted to break all ties, leave me to my crazy, disordered life . . . So she burnt everything![87]

The image of the child crops up again in the Petite Dame's account: 'When I think of the mother that she could have been, the lover even! I had been odious . . . But what could I do? She said: "If I were a Catholic, I'd enter a convent . . . I was suffering too much . . . I had to do something

... I reread them all beforehand; they were the most precious thing I had ...'"[88] For Gide, she had murdered their child; for Madeleine, they were the most precious thing she had, *because* he had not given her a child. Days later, Gide repeated to Madeleine that she had destroyed 'the best of me', adding, rather foolishly, that it was 'all the rest that she should have destroyed'. 'The rest' could not be destroyed, of course, because it was in the public domain, even things that she saw as a breach of privacy. It might even have crossed her mind that, as her husband's fame grew, even those letters might one day enter the public domain – if only after their deaths.

Madeleine was intensely reserved, even shy; never very attractive, she had aged markedly over the past few years and, at fifty-one, seemed older; intellectually insecure, while having no reason to be, her moral sense, based on impregnable, if narrow certainties, was unshakable, and she clung to it desperately as to a lifebuoy – she had never recovered from seeing her mother sink into the sea of 'immorality'. Her life at Cuverville was already nun-like, even to secular equivalents of poverty, chastity and obedience (abstemiousness, an unconsummated marriage, the tyranny of routine chores). The more she felt impelled to withdraw from the world, the more her husband was becoming a public figure. And the more he did so, the more his work moved further and further away from anything she could approve of: 'with all her heart and soul she disapproved of my conduct and the direction of my thinking'.[89] The burning of the letters was not an impulsive act: it takes time and patience to read twenty years' correspondence before destroying it. It sprang, not from the heat of the moment, but from quiet, determined calculation. She never expressed regret for it. It was no mere act of revenge: it was a ritual cleansing of the body domestic, a self-inflicted surgical excision, without which the doctor–patient would not live, but which did not guarantee survival.

The Post-War Years: La Symphonie Pastorale

(NOVEMBER 1918 – DECEMBER 1921)

For a whole week, I wept; I wept from morning till evening, sitting in front of the fire in the room in which our life together was concentrated; and even more, at night, when I had retired to my bedroom, where I always hoped that she might come in and see me; I wept without stopping, without trying to say anything to her other than my tears, and always waiting for a word, a gesture from her . . . But she continued to busy herself with petty household chores, as if nothing had happened, passing to and fro, indifferent to my presence, as if she did not even notice that I was there. I hoped that the constancy of my pain would triumph over that apparent insensitivity; but no; and she doubtless hoped that my despair would bring me back to God, for she admitted of no other outcome.[1]

These words were written in February 1939, twenty years after the event and almost a year after Madeleine's death. After quoting them, Jean Schlumberger comments that Gide had 'reversed the roles' that should have existed between husband and wife. Why should he have expected Madeleine to make the first move of reconciliation? Why did he suppose that Madeleine had done what she did? If her actions seemed monstrously out of character, how much more monstrous must have been his treatment of her to drive her to such an act? She had burnt twenty years of letters, but had he not reduced to ashes twenty years of love? Even after twenty more years, in a book written in her honour, says Schlumberger, Gide is incapable of seeing things from any other point of view but his own. This is not entirely fair. 'I am now convinced that I have warped her life much more than she may have warped mine,' he wrote on 25 November 1918, four days after he had learnt of the destruction of the letters. 'For, to tell the truth, she has not warped my life . . . My love for her has dominated my whole life, but suppressed nothing in me: it merely added conflict.'[2] Indeed Schlumberger himself quoted such passages, only to accuse him of exaggerated self-criticism.

Schlumberger's own book, also written in Madeleine's honour, is dedicated 'to the memory of two of Madeleine's friends, Agnès Copeau and Suzanne Schlumberger'. Of the three wives, Suzanne Schlumberger undoubtedly had the happiest marriage. As usual in such matters, the credit for this must be given to both parties – and to their inherent compatibility. The husband's homosexual adventures were not of a kind, or so pressing, as to affect the marriage adversely. But the wife, too, facilitated matters: she was an artist and moved easily in the same circles as her husband. Agnès Copeau fared much less well: her husband's innumerable affairs, usually with actresses, some of which remained intermittently active over many years, and therefore overlapping, were a constant source of pain to her – all the more so in that she, too, like the others, was devoted to him. In a romantic whirlwind, she had had Copeau's youth and, as he went into premature decline, she had his age; throughout, she had his children, though not all of them. Madeleine had no children to bind her to her husband and to compensate for his failings. Moreover, by temperament and religious conviction, she found that she could share her husband's life less and less. 'The love I have for my wife,' Gide told Roger Martin du Gard, 'is like no other, and I believe that only a uranist [a homosexual] can give a creature that total love, divested of all physical desire . . .: an integral love, in all its limitless purity. When I compared my marriage to the wretched, discordant marriages of those around me, I considered myself privileged; I thought I had built the very temple of love.'[3] This is not an intelligent man of 1998 speaking, but it doesn't sound like an intelligent man of 1919 either. Such a love the troubadours had for their inaccessible muses, Dante for Beatrice. A love – let alone a marriage – based on 'limitless purity' could hardly be 'integral'. Gide, with his 'other' life, may have considered himself 'privileged' to have such a marriage. Madeleine, with nothing else, could hardly be expected to. Yet, for most of the time, she probably did – such were her particular nature, inexperience and Christian indoctrination. Christianity has at best a grudging attitude to human sexuality, seeking, ideally, to reform it altogether. Gide's marriage was only made possible by a shared endorsement of the Christian view. Madeleine could hardly abandon it, having early renounced any possibility of sexual experience, however limited or legitimate. André was nearly fifty before he finally emerged from its thrall and, even then, as the passage above shows, he was still using its language.

A week after his discovery of the destruction of the letters, Gide wrote to Jean Schlumberger, asking to see him as a matter of urgency. They met on 2 December and sat through a performance of *Le Dit des Jeux du Monde*, a dramatic poem by Paul Méral, a Belgian protégé of Lady Rothermere's, with music by Arthur Honegger, recited by actors wearing masks, speaking in unison. Schlumberger, who had witnessed the final battles of the war, taken part in the triumphal entry of French troops into Alsace (after twenty-five years' exile from his native province) and, furthermore, whose wife had just undergone a serious operation, was 'irritated in the extreme' by what was no doubt 'a very original experiment'. Nor was he, afterwards, in any mood to share Gide's grief to the degree expected of him.

Apparently Gide had concluded an agreement with Lady Rothermere and Jacques Doucet, a rich *couturier* and book collector, for a new, enlarged edition of *Corydon*, for which they would cover the costs. In the course of their discussion, Schlumberger persuaded Gide to go back on the agreement. It is not clear precisely what his objections were, whether they concerned the commercial transaction itself or his possible fears (as a homosexual himself) that the time had not yet come for Gide (and his friends) to expose themselves to the inevitable attacks that would ensue on the publication of what would be seen as a piece of homosexual propaganda on the part of one of France's most eminent literary figures. As a result, Gide decided to go back to a work that had already caused him several rewritings and extensions – not to mention the private printing in 1911 of a version corresponding to the first half. There were also discussions between the two men as to the future of the *NRF* book publishing business, in view of growing disagreements and antagonisms between Gide and Gaston Gallimard. With wisdom and tact, Schlumberger defended Gide's right to override Gallimard on matters of major policy (for example, the choice of books, as witness the Dupouey letters), but felt that Gallimard should be given a free hand in the firm's day-to-day management. This, after all, Schlumberger implied, was the least Gallimard might expect, having sunk his entire fortune in the firm and, illness and the American trip apart, devoted his entire time to it – neither of which Gide and Schlumberger had been willing or able to do. (Indeed Gallimard was to obtain further capital investment in the publishing house from his younger brother Raymond and from one of his best friends, Emmanuel Couvreux, resulting in the formation, in July, of a new company, the 'Librairie Gallimard–Editions de la Nouvelle Revue Française'.) Moreover, the new publishing business had been a great success, not only publishing books during the war, but expanding from a few books to over 100 titles published or forthcoming by 1918.

After four or five days, Schlumberger joined his wife and two daughters at the Van Rysselberghes' house at Saint-Clair, in the South of France. In addition to Théo and Maria, their daughter Elisabeth was also there with her English friend Ethel Whitehorn. Gide had expected to join them, but now felt that he had to return to Cuverville. There 'frightful days' awaited him.

I am a broken man . . . I no longer have any heart for anything and all the light in my heaven has gone out . . . I can feel this too calm life closing over me again. I could only escape from it by wrenching myself free. Extreme weakness and a sense of growing old. Whatever would make my heart beat again could only be a cause of pain and horror for her. I can affirm nothing of myself without hurting her and it is only by suppressing myself that I could ensure her happiness.[4]

Even in those days of unprecedented mutual hurt, Gide still tried to bring Madeleine round to his point of view. He even, foolhardily, tried to read extracts from *Corydon* to her, anxious to show her that it was not the terrible advocacy of evil that she suspected. Even then Madeleine seemed more concerned about the harm it would do André than the harm it might do to others. 'Don't you realize how many people will turn their backs on you?' she asked. 'Yes,' he replied, with the fearlessness of the true puritan, 'but I consider that it would be cowardly to retreat.'[5]

Gide escaped to Paris for Christmas week, staying at the Allégrets'. Marc had just returned from England: Gide and he had not seen each other for nearly three months. 'I'm certainly more in love with him than ever,' he told Maria Van Rysselberghe. Gide spoke of the boy's 'acts of kindness', something 'lyrical', 'poetic' about him; and he was still very attracted to him physically.[6]

Gide returned to Cuverville on New Year's Day, but, between then and Easter, he spent all but two weeks in Paris, first at the Allégrets', then, from 7 March, at the Villa Montmorency. He saw Jacques Rivière, back from 'exile' in Switzerland. They discussed plans for the resumption of the *NRF*, but Rivière was not yet free to work full-time on the review, having been drafted to a post at the War Ministry.

On 16 April, Gide and Marc left for Dudelange, the Mayrischs' property in Luxembourg. There they found Maria and Elisabeth Van Rysselberghe, and Ethel Whitehorn. For Gide and his young friends it was a great reunion, the first since their days in Scotland and London. Over the next two weeks, hostess and guests went for walks and motorcar rides, read aloud together and talked a great deal. 'How can I convey the exaltation, the effervescence he provokes in our minds, in our hearts,' writes the spellbound Petite Dame. One afternoon, he read aloud from the proofs of *La Symphonie Pastorale*. Alone with Loup Mayrisch, Gide talked of Marc. 'We can never spoil Marc enough,' said Loup Mayrisch, 'for this balance, this fulfilment he has brought you.' Gide looked overcome with emotion: 'That's just it, you see. For Madeleine, that is precisely the most painful thing about it.' They talked of a post-war 'change in morals', of the desire of many young people to have done with marriage, of young women to have children without benefit of husbands. 'Youth,' said Gide, 'always has truth on its side; it mustn't believe in experience; what is called experience, wisdom, is usually nothing but exhaustion, a repudiation of the best that one once had; one must refresh oneself in the company of the young if one is to keep going.'[7] They visited Emile Mayrisch's factory and the Institute that he had founded for the education of his workers. In the library reading-room, filled with books and magazines, Gide was moved to tears. 'I was thinking of Jude [the hero of Hardy's *Jude the Obscure*],' he explained, 'of those who wanted to educate themselves and couldn't.'[8]

On 27 April, Marc had to leave for Paris – the new term at the *lycée* was about to begin. Later, the conversation turned to his future. He was not academically inclined, said Gide, but he had 'an extraordinary quality of judgement where art was concerned'. Gide himself left Dudelange a few days later. After a week spent in Cuverville, he returned to Paris, where he found the Bussys, en route from their house at Roquebrune-Cap-Martin, on the Côte d'Azur, to England. All that Dorothy managed to extract of Gide's time was 'one or two hours' on each of her remaining four days in Paris. An offer arrived from the New York publisher, Alfred Knopf, to publish the translation of *La Porte étroite* that Dorothy had done, uncommissioned, simply for the pleasure of it. Apart from Lady Rothermere's *Prometheus Illbound* of 1919, it was to be the first published English translation of any of Gide's works. However, this was only the first move in a tortuous, long-drawn-out process: publication did not take place until 1924 – and it took another twenty-four years for the translation to appear in London. Dorothy Bussy found it hard to confine her letters to such business matters. For her, those four days in Paris had been more than a meeting of minds. 'I suppose you don't know,' she wrote from Cambridge, 'how beautiful your face is – a *mille* times more beautiful than Marc's.' (It is difficult to imagine whether Gide would be more gratified or terrified by this avowal.)

'Ah! My friend, I am not like you. Never in all my life has my soul been tempted by youth and its bloom. I have never loved a face that had not the visible marks of thought and suffering upon it . . .' Occasionally, the poor woman's measured prose broke down under the pressure of her feelings: 'You are my Kingdom of Heaven – something outside me – a vision – a glory – a despair.'[9]

Gide had a long conversation with André Ruyters, whom he had not seen since the end of the war and who 'criticized me for flaunting my affair with Marc'. Ruyters, of course, was 'speaking on behalf of others, others made more prudent with age, who thought only of not being compromised'. One such was Eugène Rouart, now embarked on a political career. In a 'revealing' letter, Rouart declares how delighted he is that 'Ghéon, though lacking any close family ties, has been able to rediscover the tradition of his fathers . . .' 'How sad all this is!' Gide comments. 'What sophistry to hide one's failure from oneself! God preserve me from the wrinkles of the mind!'[10] Considering the influences that an older lover might have on someone as young as Marc, such people can only think in terms of corruption. They always compare the present situation with the *status quo ante*, ignoring what might have happened if the two had not met. Gide believed that he had done Marc a lot of good, saved him from '*influences médiocres*, etc.'. As for the effect of Marc on him, it had been 'incalculable'. 'It is all my youth! Without him, I would be my age!'[11]

In June, Jacques Copeau and his family landed at Le Havre. They had been away for twenty months. The Vieux Colombier season had come to an end in New York on 7 April and the company had sailed for home soon afterwards. To raise more money, however, Copeau decided to stay on several more weeks and embark on a lecture tour that took him to Boston, Chicago, Cleveland and Detroit. Jean Schlumberger, his wife and two daughters had joined Gide at the harbour to meet them. In the afternoon, the whole party arrived at Cuverville. During the week that Copeau stayed at Cuverville, he and Gide had much to talk over, but the general impression is rather of a lack of communication between the two men. It was as if some barrier had come between them. Copeau still felt that he had 'not *come back* yet, as it were'.[12] Gide – and other friends – seemed insufficiently curious about his American experiences, too absorbed in their own affairs. This was probably inevitable. Copeau's friends had just emerged from four years of war, much of which Copeau had missed, and were acutely aware that they were entering a new, exciting, but largely uncharted time. What

Copeau had to recount about America must have seemed of little interest by comparison. Copeau had decided to relinquish his editorship of the *NRF*, which, for a time, Gide himself had thought of taking over. Claudel got wind of this and wrote to Jacques Rivière, who was about to resume his job as editorial assistant: 'I am told that Gide is going to take over the editorship of the *NRF* officially. If that is the case, you may rest assured that I shall not give a line to that periodical. The name Gide signifies pederasty and anti-Catholicism. It is a banner under which I have no intention of marching.'[13] Whether or not he was influenced by Claudel's opposition, Gide bowed out in favour of Rivière as editor.

On 1 July, Gide and Copeau left Cuverville for Paris. Two days later, the original founders of the *NRF* and Jacques Rivière met at the Van Rysselberghes'. Many of the participants expected a violent clash of opinion, but, as the Petite Dame comments, 'reasons of friendship won out'.[14] Given that the June number of the *NRF* was the first to appear for close on five years, and the first under his editorship, Rivière thought fit to preface it with a brief 'manifesto', in which he called for 'the liberation of intelligence', which had been put into the nation's service during the war, and the '*gratuité*' of all creative action. The manifesto had not been seen, prior to publication, by the review's 'founding fathers'. Gide himself would have preferred to have no such manifesto, but he felt that the new editor should be given his head. Copeau, when he saw it, also gave it his approval, though he admitted that it was 'clumsy' and 'inopportune'. The opposition came from Drouin, Schlumberger and Ghéon, '*les anciens*', 'the old guard'. Rivière arrived and offered his resignation. It was refused and, as a result, he emerged stronger than before. Sooner or later, 'the old guard' (all of whom were younger than Gide) would be eliminated, wrote Martin du Gard, and Rivière, 'under Gide's great wing', supported by Copeau and Gallimard, would open up the review to younger elements, thus saving it from the 'fossilization' that had overtaken the *Mercure de France*.[15] This is what happened: for different reasons, to different degrees and at different times, the '*anciens*' did withdraw from active participation in the *NRF*, which did, to some extent, open up to 'younger elements' (Rivière was sympathetic, no more, to the Dadaists, for example). However, the situation was not a simple opposition between new and old, old and young. What Rivière was doing was reviving the spirit of the pre-war *NRF*: openness to the new, while maintaining a certain elusive cohesion of spirit, a certain fastidiousness in expression. In the case of Rivière, the war had merely reinforced him in these values. He had had his fill of conflict: it had robbed him, among others, of his best friend and brother-in-law, Alain-Fournier. Less dramatically, but more profoundly, it had debased language and sincerity. Rivière once remarked to Gallimard: 'I want to say and can say only what I see, not what "must" be said, precisely because, while a prisoner in Germany, I lived among people who said only what "must" be said.'

Drouin rejected the idea that for thought to remain dominated by the experience of the war was tantamount to 'intellectual slavery'. Schlumberger was as anxious as anyone to get back to his desk, but could not agree that 'those four years had been a sterile enclave in my life'. He could not forget the '*élan de fraternité*', 'the presence of our "neighbour" in the thousands of faces that we had never taken the trouble to look at'. But it was Ghéon, 'the man born of the war', as the title of his war memoirs had it, who was most violent in his opposition. No, the war was not 'over', in the sense that we can take up where we left off. It did not 'vitiate' our thinking, but gave it *meaning*, which is what it had most lacked. The difference that existed between the two groups within the editorial committee could not be resolved simply by the undoubted friendship that linked them together. The whole question had to be discussed and decided upon collectively. Meanwhile, Ghéon had signed a manifesto, emanating from Action Française, that referred to the movement as 'le Parti de l'Intelligence' and declared 'the Catholic alliance' to be 'indispensable to the fate of civilization'. Rivière wrote a scathing note in the *NRF* on the so-called 'Party of Intelligence'. And so, for the moment, the dissensions within the *NRF* team rumbled on.

Another stage passage of arms, remarkable more for feints than palpable hits, was taking place at this time. It reached the public with the first postwar number of the *NRF*, which contained a 'Lettre ouverte à Jean Cocteau'. The 'open letter' was not necessarily an occasion for public controversy, still less of abuse. In Gide's, and others', hands it was a literary form, from which both parties gained. It was couched in terms of the most exquisite politeness and contained enough praise or flattery to please the recipient. The writer, however, dissented on one or two points that he considered of public interest (hence an 'open', rather than a private letter). Even the dissensions, of course, provided good publicity for the recipient – especially if the writer was an older, more celebrated figure than he. If there were a published response, it, too, had to obey the same rules of polite exchange. Gide's open letter concerned Cocteau's *Le Coq et l'Arlequin*, which consisted largely of a series of aphorisms on art and a defence of his *Parade*. The style was brilliant, self-conscious, luxuriating in artifice, very Cocteau. Gide was quite prepared to respect their difference: what irritated him was that Cocteau was preaching a 'classical' aesthetic of simplicity and purity of style that was essentially his, Gide's, and consorted ill with Cocteau's own practice. It related 'not so much to the writer you are as to the writer you would like to be thought to be . . . What I reproach you with is sacrificing your most charming, your most brilliant qualities to the benefit of other, heavier ones that, perhaps, you do not have.'[16]

The question that naturally arises is whether, in his open letter to Cocteau, Gide was motivated solely by questions of literary politics or whether more personal matters entered into it. For Gide the two could not really be separated. Cocteau's style as a writer and his style as a man were one, as they were in his own case. For Gide, with his cult of sincerity, Cocteau represented cultivated insincerity, outward show, showing-off, *parade*. It was morally dangerous in life as well as in art. It was not to be confused with the kind of 'immoralism' that he had himself entertained (without entirely adopting): such a post-Protestant, Nietzschean 'immoralism' was, effect-ively, a 'higher' morality, one that must be preached with all the ardour of the Protestant missionary. Gide was afraid that Cocteau might give Marc Allégret something that he himself could not give him, something, moreover, that would be corrupting, that would undermine all the patient Socratic education that he had lavished on the boy. Cocteau knew this, of course, and teased Gide unmercifully. Léon Pierre-Quint remembered a conversation dating from 1926, in which Gide confessed that 'my hatred for C . . . . . . derived from C . . .'s moral influence, his brio, which had dazzled, spellbound a still childish mind . . . I was like Pygmalion finding his statue damaged, his work vandalized; all my effort, all the care that I had expended as an educator . . . had been sullied by someone else, the "nice" C . . . It was not jealousy, it was something else.'[17] Cocteau's version, published after Gide's death, speaks of Gide's 'quasi-feminine' jealousy: 'he had put in my charge one of his young disciples, who, finding it amusing to tease Gide, had so praised me to him that Gide had taken it into his head to want to kill me'.[18] Cocteau's feline remarks, keeping the revelations respectable (just) with euphemisms like 'quasi-feminine' and 'one of his young disciples', which informed readers would see through, while keeping himself clear of any such implications, are not to be taken as unadorned truth. But, in 1939, Gide himself confessed to Claude Mauriac that his jealousy over Marc was such that he 'would have gone as far as to kill Cocteau', who had employed 'a Satanic coquetry' to attract [*séduire*, to seduce?] Marc. He felt that, under Cocteau's influence, Marc was moving away from him. 'It was horrible.

Jealousy is horrible.'[19] Throughout this affair – indeed, for the rest of their lives – Gide and Cocteau managed to maintain relations on a perfectly cordial level. This no doubt had much to do with Cocteau's gift for the social graces, or two-facedness, depending on one's point of view. He was much in awe of Gide's power and influence. Many of the posthumous barbs that Cocteau directed at Gide derived from the resentment he must have felt, Gide *vivant*, at having to practise such two-facedness. However, this did not prevent him, in his letter to Gide, from concealing the odd barb beneath a covering of flattery. Thus, on 24 August 1918, he writes to thank Gide for sending him a copy of his translation of Conrad's *Typhoon*. The tale is fine enough, but, he adds, 'I suppose your style has added a special relief to it.' Then Cocteau slips in: 'And how is your wild foal? What is he doing with his strong ties and "his unruly hair"? I'd like to see him again, to see you again, to enrich more and more our friendship [with Marc, Gide, or both?], which consoles me in my sad hours.'[20]

Having got wind of Gide's open letter, Cocteau wrote to Gide asking to see him: 'It is indispensable, if our friendship is to be maintained, that I read your open letter before the *NRF* prints it.' Even then he cannot resist adding: 'Tell our Marc that I often think of him.'[21] Gide invited Cocteau to come and see him, and read him the open letter. Cocteau declared it to be 'unfriendly', then replied by letter: 'You had to choose between the public and me. You have chosen . . . I simply demand the "right to reply".'[22] Gide wrote back the same day that he had re-read the letter and could not find anything in it that could be called 'unfriendly'. However, he had added a few lines and changed a word that Cocteau had disliked. He had also read it to Gallimard, Rivière and Du Bos, who had found it entirely reasonable. Gide had no desire to hurt Cocteau, but there was 'something more important than that, and friendship is ill-nourished with reticence'.[23] Cocteau lunched with Gide and told him of the planned reply. Gide was very taken by the notion of a duel that would revive 'a literary chivalry'. Cocteau duly submitted his reply. It is too personal, too anecdotal, too unfocused in its attack to summarize adequately. A short quotation may give some notion of its style: 'You have, Gide, a whole system of mysteries, reservations, imperfect subjunctives, alibis and imbroglios . . . Does Gide like X . . .? Does he admire Y . . .? people ask him. He sniffs, leans forward, shrugs his shoulders . . . Is not uncertainty the charm of your works and your style? One thinks of a woman by the water who daren't jump in and who just wets her breasts, uttering little cries . . .' That implication of femininity again – rich coming from Cocteau. 'There is inside you the pastor and the bacchante' – again, not, this time, Gide's own 'little boy amusing himself'. Then, turning Gide's words back on to himself: 'It is not that I do not recognize the grace of your imprudent intoxications, but certain of them seem to concern not so much who you are as the person you would like people to believe you to be.'[24] Not surprisingly, Jacques Rivière took exception to the personal tone of Cocteau's reply. 'Instead of *replying* to any of the criticisms,' Rivière told Gide, 'he throws at you whatever spiteful remarks occur to him.'[25] Rivière wrote back, refusing to publish it. It narrowed the debate, rather than widened it and 'went beyond the bounds of the literary'. He had shown it to Gide, who, 'very generously' wanted Rivière to publish it, but Rivière, as editor, could not contemplate doing so – and Gide felt that he could not intervene further. Cocteau's response was that 'the right of reply is a legal right'. On 20 June, a bailiff arrived at the *NRF* offices, armed with a writ, a letter to Gide recounting Cocteau's version of events, a copy of his open letter and a demand that it be published, 'according to article 13 of the law of 29 July 1881'. Nothing came of this dramatic gesture, the open letter was published elsewhere and the affair fizzled out.

Elie Allégret arrived home from Africa in May, astonished by the state of open rebellion among his sons. Gide had 'several serious conversations' with him about how to handle them, then went off to counsel them as to the best way of dealing with him. For example, the father's idea of a good Whit Sunday was a family reunion in the country, featuring a religious talk, given, naturally, by himself. Marc declared that he would not go. Gide persuaded him that a better strategy would be to attend, then, later, take his father to one side and explain his feelings on the matter. In one sense, Gide, ever able to see both sides of any question, was ideally cast in the role of mediator. In another, the situation was fraught with delicious irony, in so far as he had been chief nourisher of the sons' rebellion. What Pastor Allégret would have thought – even done – had he known this is scarcely imaginable, if an entry in the *Journal des Faux-Monnayeurs* is to be believed:

The pastor, learning that his son, at 26, is no longer the chaste adolescent that he had believed him to be, cries: 'Would to heaven he had been killed in the war! Would to heaven he had never been born!' What judgement can an honest man bring to bear on a religion that puts such words into a father's mouth? It is out of hatred for this religion, this morality that oppresses all young people, out of hatred for an austerity that he had never been able to throw off himself, that he worked to debauch and pervert the pastor's children.[26]

*

There is no evidence that Pastor Allégret actually said what Gide attributed to 'the pastor'. Nevertheless, the *Journal des Faux-Monnayeurs* is a journal, not just working notes for a novel; indeed his entries are often indistinguishable from those of the *Journal* proper. Gide's comment, too, seems to be a shocked response to words actually spoken. A week later, in the *Journal* proper, the last entry for 1919, he comments on the 'drama at the Allégrets': 'I had to open his eyes; his blindness was such . . . To what extent things suprasensible can blind you to everyday realities!' . . . The pastor is suffering from 'a gradual numbing of the critical faculties'.[27]

Meanwhile, Gide hung on in Paris, unable to drag himself away to Cuverville to work, yet appalled by the time and energy expended on his 'passion'. 'I'm jealous of his pleasures,' he told the Petite Dame. 'I need to be there, yet am afraid of boring him.'[28] He spent the first post-war celebration of the Quatorze Juillet with Marc and the Van Rysselberghes *mère et fille*. The Petite Dame noted how concerned Gide was to maintain his position in the Allégret family – and to rescue Marc from his family during the summer holidays. On 26 July, he left for Dudelange, soon to be joined by Maria Van Rysselberghe and her daughter. There, during his eight-week stay, he worked at *Les Faux-Monnayeurs* in Loup Mayrisch's library, 'one of the most exquisite laboratories imaginable'.[29] As usual, the writing did not come easy: when the problems became intractable, he resumed work on his memoirs. But there were diversions, too. The Petite Dame recounts how, while walking in the woods, he had stumbled on an old quarry, in which the boy goat-herds met in the afternoon. There they played at 'Red Indians', or, when the weather was bad, retired to a hut, which they called '*le Club*', and played cards. Gide was delighted by the 'truly Virgilian' quality that he found among those charming young goat-herds, aged between seven and sixteen. Next time, he took 'Schnouky', the Mayrischs' daughter Andrée, along, 'to some extent to keep an eye on him', but also for the pleasure it would give him to watch her trying to take part in their games, to be like them, to speak their dialect, to 'fraternize' with them, as he did.

On 22 August Marc arrived, accompanied by father and eldest brother. However, Elie and Jean-Paul left two days later. Marc, Gide told the Petite Dame, was 'prodigious, irresistible: wild, charming dances, excitement, fun, indecency, lyricism, such an appetizing mixture!'[30] One evening, Gide, Marc, Schnouky and the Petite Dame took the kids of the 'Club', some forty of them, to the local cinema. On 2 September, Marc had to return to his family. Visits to the 'Club', continued. Gide and Schnouky being joined occasionally by Beth. Gide, says the Petite Dame, trailed the lads after him 'like the worker of miracles that he is'. He bought a knife for one of the older ones who seemed particularly fond of him. Then, a few days before leaving for Paris, he had 'the little adventure he'd been hoping for', though, next day, he was not sure which of the lads it had been with. 'You two,' he told the Petite Dame and Loup, 'are about the only people I can still recount my adventures to – my other friends have renounced their youth.' It was that youthfulness that everyone found so attractive. 'He'll be fifty in November,' the Petite Dame noted. 'Although it sometimes shows in his face, it never does in his walk, so imbued is it with youthful enthusiasm and vivacity.'[31] On his last day at Dudelange, Gide wrote in his journal, referring to himself in the third person:

Every day, he spent long hours with them there. When he was with them, he forgot time and place, his age, social rank, all cares and proprieties. He looked around at them, among their goats, as they played games that could not have been very different, he thought, from those played by Theocritus' shepherds. He kept one of them snuggled up against him, and sometimes it was the ugliest, the puniest or most wretched of them, but the beauty, health, joy of some of them exalted his spirits like a hymn.[32]

After two weeks at Cuverville, Gide left for Paris, where, until the end of October, he stayed with the Van Rysselberghes. He then moved into the Allégrets' new house at 122 avenue d'Orléans (now the avenue du Général-Leclerc), near the Porte d'Orléans. Of an evening he and Marc would sit opposite one another at a table in one of the bedrooms, the writer writing, the schoolboy doing his philosophy homework (having passed the first part of the baccalauréat that summer, he was now in the final class at the *lycée*, the *classe de philo*').

The November number of the *NRF* published the second and last instalment of *La Symphonie Pastorale* (the publication in volume form did not take place until July 1920). Though not a full-length novel, this *récit* of some 21,000 words (fifty-two pages in the Pléiade edition), represented Gide's return to fiction after *Les Caves du Vatican* of 1914. The past couple of years had seen new editions of *L'Immoraliste*, *Les Nourritures terrestres*, *Le Retour de l'Enfant prodigue* and *Le Voyage d'Urien*. Gide had also published a few short, non-fictional pieces: a preface to an edition of Baudelaire's *Les Fleurs du Mal* (reprinted in *Incidences*, 1924); seven 'Fragments', from that work-in-progress *Les Nouvelles Nourritures*, which he gave to the first number of *Littérature*, a review run by the young Dadaists, Louis Aragon, André Breton and Philippe Soupault; three shorter pieces published in the *NRF* since its June reopening.

The new work had been awaited with some excitement, not least by the young Dadaists, for whom the character of Lafcadio had become something of a mascot. 'You can't imagine how much André Gide is on our side,' André Breton wrote to Tristan Tzara on 18 February 1919. 'He's prodigiously interested in modern experiments in literature and painting.'[33] It would not be the first (or last) time that Gide's sympathy for the young, his openness to new ideas, his ability to entertain the point of view of almost anyone he was speaking to were misinterpreted as agreement and support. In the first post-war number of the *NRF*, he wrote a short, sympathetic article on 'Dada'.[34] In April 1920, Gide returned to the questions raised by the Dadaists; four months later, Breton was given space in the *NRF* and, in the same number, Jacques Rivière included an article entitled 'Reconnaissance à Dada' ('Thanks to Dada'). Both Gide and the *NRF*, then, were regarded by the Dadaists as essential allies – much to the annoyance of others associated with the review, in particular, Jean Schlumberger. What the young Dadaists wanted from Gide was a sequel to *Les Caves du Vatican*, complete with Lafcadio – the novel that was to become *Les Faux-Monnayeurs*, without Lafcadio. What they got was *La Symphonie Pastorale*, an inexplicable throw-back, it seemed, to *La Porte étroite* and *Isabelle*. After reading the first instalment in June, Breton wrote to Tzara of Gide's 'involuntary senility'.[35]

The story is set in the small, isolated Swiss village of La Brévine. It takes the form of a journal, written by the Protestant pastor. The first entry describes an event that took place two-and-a-half years before. Called to the deathbed of an old woman, the pastor finds, cowering in a dark corner of the room, a girl of about fifteen. She is, he learns, the old woman's niece: the girl is blind, covered in vermin and apparently an idiot. Concealed from the outside world, treated like an animal, she has never learnt to speak. In an upsurge of Christian love (*agape*), the pastor decides to care for the poor creature. His wife, Amélie, takes a dim view of what she sees as her husband's misguided charity: there are 'already enough in the house'. The pastor responds with the parable of the lost sheep and proceeds to lavish all his attention on the girl. Martins, a doctor friend, shows interest in her and tells the pastor of the case of Laura Bridgeman, which Dickens used in his story 'The Cricket on the Hearth': born blind and dumb, she had been taught to speak. Over the next year or so, the pastor uses the same methods on the girl, whom he calls Gertrude: she makes rapid progress. The pastor extends the girl's education. He takes her to a concert at Neuchâtel, where they hear Beethoven's Pastoral Symphony: this, more than anything previously, enables her to imagine the world that she cannot see.

At the beginning of the summer holidays, the pastor's eldest son, Jacques, comes home from university and falls in love with Gertrude. Still blind to his own feelings, for he is as blind mentally as Gertrude is physically, the pastor accuses his son of disturbing 'the purity of Gertrude's soul' and insists that he spend the holidays away from home, as he had originally planned. The pastor is reassured when Gertrude tells him: 'You know very well that it is you I love . . . Do you think there is anything wrong in that?' 'There is never anything wrong in love,' comes the reply, *eros* acquiring, by a pastoral sleight of hand, all the virtue of *agape*. The next stage in Gertrude's education entails her leaving the pastor's house and lodging at La Grange, the home of Louise de la M . . . There, in an altogether more elegant setting than the pastor's house, she acquires the finer social graces – it also makes it easier for the pastor to spend time with her, away from his wife's critical gaze, for he makes a point of calling in on her during his pastoral round.

The following Easter Jacques comes home for a week. To the father's surprise, he does not attend the Easter communion service. Later, in a theological discussion with his son, the pastor propounds the view (very much Gide's own) that 'many of the notions that make up our Christian faith derive not from Christ's words, but from St Paul's commentaries'. Jacques accuses his father of 'picking and choosing' from Christian doctrine the bits that suit him. 'Souls like his think they are lost when they no longer feel protected by props, hand-rails and fences,' the pastor comments. They cannot tolerate in others 'a liberty that they have renounced'. When the pastor accuses his son of wanting the submission of souls, rather than their happiness, his son replies: Happiness is only to be found in submission.[36] The pastor pursues the ethical debate with Gertrude. After a conversation about the nature of love, *agape* and *eros*, in which Gertrude runs logical rings around the professional moralist, they agree, tacitly, that their love permits of physical expression. Dr Martins examines Gertrude's eyes with an ophthalmoscope. According to a medical friend in Lausanne, the condition is operable. The pastor hesitates to pass on the good news to the girl and decides to reflect on the matter. One evening, while visiting La Grange, he goes up to Gertrude's room: the two make love. The following day, they go to Lausanne, where Gertrude is operated on. Three weeks later, Martins brings the now seeing Gertrude back to La Brévine. Soon after her return, she narrowly escapes drowning in a stream nearby and, for a few days, remains unconscious. She later confesses to the pastor that her near-drowning had not been accidental – she had tried to kill herself. When she had seen the unhappiness on Amélie's face, she could not bear the thought that it was her work. Her eyes had been opened not only to the beauties of the world, but to all the unhappiness on men's faces – and to the reality of sin. Jacques, too, has been seeing her and together they have read passages of the Bible that she had never heard before, in particular St Paul's epistles. For the pastor, there is worse to come. On seeing the faces of both father and son, Gertrude realized that Jacques had the face that she imagined that the pastor had; it was Jacques she loved. It is too late – Jacques, now a Catholic, has decided to become a priest. Gertrude has a relapse and dies. Jacques tells his father that he owes his conversion to him, to the example of his error and that, while at Lausanne, Gertrude, too, had become a Catholic. 'I wanted to weep,' says the pastor, 'but my heart felt more arid than the desert.'[37]

From the age of twenty, Gide writes in his unpublished 'preface', 'my books were there, lined up in front of me; all I had to do was write them'.[38] This *boutade* is not to be taken too seriously. The timing is somewhat exaggerated, but, more important, the writing of the books 'in front of me' entailed considerably more than mere transcription. Often a book was little more, at this stage, than an idea, a title or a character. The idea for *L'Aveugle (The Blind Girl)*, as *La Symphonie Pastorale* was called until well into the final writing, dated at least from 1893 – a germination lasting twenty-five years. It is set in the small Swiss village of La Brévine, where Gide spent the last few months of 1894. (It was not, as the editors of the Pléiade edition have it, written there – nor finished at Cambridge, as Painter has it. Gide did not revisit La Brévine until 1947 and the *récit* was written at Cuverville, before and after the English visit of 1918.) The French Swiss setting was important: the isolated, desolate village, with its wholly Calvinist community, bigoted, narrow-minded, joyless, provided a perfect foil for both the pastor's 'sin' and his son's conversion to Catholicism. The pastor arrives at Gide's view of Christianity as a humane, loving creed that had been perverted, in similar and in different ways, by both Protestantism and Catholicism. Gide's religious views may be put into the pastor's mouth, but the character is not simply a vehicle for the author. The pastor is not so much Gide as an example of what could happen if Gide's views were accepted uncritically and used by a 'blind' puritan as an excuse for selfish behaviour. Moreover, the criticism of these views is put into the mouths of Jacques, the Catholic convert, and Gertrude herself, also now speaking as a Catholic. But Gide, as author, in turn criticizes the Catholic view. The pastor is shown trying, under the onslaught of his love for Gertrude, or rather of his belated acknowledgement of that love, to argue his way towards a new Christian view, based on the sanctity of love. He fails because he is too much the old unregenerate puritan, his moral reflexes shot through with self-delusion. The Catholic view, on the other hand, may have the virtue of rigour and consistency, but the price paid for it is the death of love (Jacques) and spiritual destruction, followed by actual death (Gertrude).

The story, then, is itself a 'pastoral symphony', a disquisition on pastoral care, an orchestration of religious themes and moral questions. The narrative is generated by a play on the word 'love', one constantly on the pastor's lips. It was ostensibly Christian love (charity, *agape*) that led the pastor to take the blind girl home in the first place. The blind girl 'sees' this turning into sexual love (*eros*) and accepts it; the professional moralist is 'blind' to this until it is too late. The pastor's self-delusion brings him a kind of self-fulfilment that he has never known; nor must it be forgotten how much it brings to Gertrude. Tragedy comes when her eyes are, literally, opened and the pastor loses his delusions. As well as being a pun on 'love', *La Symphonie Pastorale* is also a pun on 'blindness'. The link between the two is a quotation from the St John Gospel: 'And Jesus said, For judgement I am come into this world, that they which see not might see; and that they which see might be made blind . . . If ye were blind, ye should have no sin: but now ye say, We see; therefore your sin remaineth.'[39] By 1894, Gide had read the works that provided him with his 'research material' on blindness: Dickens's *American Notes*, with its account of the case of Laura Bridgeman (1829–89), and 'The Cricket on the Hearth', in which the father of a blind girl, Bertha Plummer, does everything possible to make his daughter's life happy, while concealing from her the ugliness and unhappiness in the world. (Later, Gide read the French translation of *The World I Live In* by Helen Keller, who was blind, deaf – and therefore dumb – from the age of nine months.)

La Symphonie Pastorale was in many ways, another 'anachronistic' creation. Yet it, too, was written under the pressure of the present and the recent past. The final configuration of the religious themes, for example, would have been different without the personal crisis of 1916 and *Numquid et tu . . .?* Indeed whole arguments from that work are inserted into *La Symphonie Pastorale*. When Gide began writing the story in February 1918, he did so in the shadow of a crisis from which he had emerged only eighteen months before. It is even possible that, without that crisis, the story would never have got written at all. That, in itself, may not have been enough. What really spurred Gide on was the realization of the parallels to be found between the characters and relationships in the story and those in his own life at that time. Moreover, the division into two *cahiers*, the first being an account of the past, the second bringing us up to the present, relating events immediately after they have happened, corresponds to the crucial break in Gide's life before and after the visit to England. In the second we find a sharpening of the criticism directed at Pauline Christianity, Protestant and Catholic, and an acceleration of the narrative, deriving, as Gide himself admitted, from a desire to have done with the work. By 1918, the theme of innocence and experience, of an older man initiating sexual experience with a young person, while opening that person's eyes to the beauties of the world and the splendid creations of the human mind, had taken on a particularly powerful significance for him. Certainly, while the work still lay dormant, there had been an earlier case of master–pupil relations with Elisabeth Van Rysselberghe, to whom *L'Aveugle* was originally to be dedicated. If Gide altered the dedication, it was because Marc was far more potently present in Gertrude than Beth – and, since he could hardly dedicate it to him (even in 1925, he did not dare to dedicate *Les Faux-Monnayeurs*, which was much more his book, to the then twenty-five-year-old Marc), he made over the dedication to Jean Schlumberger, a suitably 'Protestant' dedicatee.

The portrayal of Amélie, the pastor's wife, too, bears the mark of recent experience. There is much of Marc's mother, an actual pastor's wife, in this, but there is even more of Madeleine, Madeleine as Gide saw her during the crisis in their relations brought on by the English visit of 1918 and the burning of the letters. The pastor and his wife have 'remained (or become) an enigma for one another, as if locked away behind walls'. 'The only pleasure I can give Amélie,' writes the pastor, 'is to refrain from doing the things she dislikes.' For her, the spiritual life has no other aim than the 'domestication of the instincts'.[40] Hitherto Gide had always tried to justify himself to Madeleine, even, against all the odds, to bring her round to his point of view. But, ironically, in view of the criticisms levelled at the work by Gide's younger and more 'progressive' admirers, *La Symphonie Pastorale* represents a watershed in this at least, that it is actually directed against the kind of person that Madeleine was and against the values that she represented. Probably because of misunderstandings as to its 'meaning', it was an immediate success and went on to be one of Gide's most 'successful' works, in terms of sales and world-wide translations. In Japan it has always been particularly successful – and it was there, in 1938, that the first filmed version of any of Gide's works was made. The only other film of a Gide work was also of *La Symphonie Pastorale*: in 1945, Jean Delannoy directed a version of the story, starring Michèle Morgan as the heroine.

*

Early in the New Year, Gide went to Bruges to see the *NRF* printer Verbeke regarding two books that he was having printed '*clandestinement*', one of which was 'of a kind to have me thrown into prison'.[41] The two books were Volume I of his 'memoirs', *Si le grain ne meurt*, and *Corydon*, a completed and revised version of the dialogue on homosexuality printed privately as *CRDN* in 1911. Both were printed without author's or publisher's name, the first in an edition of twelve copies, the second in an edition of twenty-one copies. Neither book was intended for publication ... yet. He will, Gide tells Dorothy Bussy, send her a copy of *Corydon*, but asks her to speak to no one about it. He does not intend 'to keep it a secret forever – or even for long'. However, it is still 'premature' and it would be 'pointlessly impudent to throw it at the public now'. He is concerned less about himself than about 'certain people who are dear to me'. 'I see before me a terrible landscape that I must enter and cross.'[42]

Gide left Bruges with a bad cold and took refuge at Dudelange, where he stayed with Loup Mayrisch for ten days. Back in Paris, he moved in with the Allégrets. However, he found it difficult to work there. Marc was developing a great love of painting: 'His greatest pleasure is going from one exhibition to another, or to the Louvre – and mine, to go with him.'[43]

On 9 February, Gide attended the reopening of the Vieux Colombier. With *Twelfth Night* the theatre had ended its pre-war season in triumph. Thanks again to Shakespeare, it entered the post-war years with another, *Winter's Tale*, in a translation by Suzanne Bing and Copeau himself. It was an ambitious production, employing twenty-eight actors and walk-ons, as well as the choir of Saint-Gervais and dancers. But Copeau was already elaborating his theory of minimal staging: 'Unencumbered, as bare as possible, waiting for something, ready to receive its form from the action that takes place on it, that stage is never so beautiful as in its natural, primitive, vacant state.'[44]

Gide spent about two weeks at Cuverville, then escaped back to Paris. On 17 March, he lunched with John Maynard Keynes and Duncan Grant: the *NRF* was about to bring out a translation of Keynes's *The Economic Consequences of the Peace*, a book that, with its criticism of French policy at the Versailles conference, did not go down well in France.

Gide and Marc spent Easter in Florence. Elisabeth Van Rysselberghe and Andrée Mayrisch were already there, having spent the winter in Rome. Ethel Whitehorn joined them from London. 'One cannot imagine a more joyful reunion,' the Petite Dame notes in her *Cahiers*. The friends met up again at Saint-Clair. Gide 'never looked younger'; he was 'sparkling', 'indescribably funny, as if intoxicated'; 'he has a reserve of joy that comes out in everything he does'.[45] Over lunch, next day, they were all in high spirits, recounting their time in Florence and laughing at the '*odieux trucages*' required to get Marc's parents to agree to his spending the Easter holidays away from home (he was now nineteen). Before Marc returned to Paris, Gide and he visited Loup Mayrisch at her house at Bormes, nearby in the Var. On the way back to Saint-Clair, Gide shared his anxieties about the future with the Petite Dame. How would everything turn out? Marc would have to leave his parents before long – a responsibility that Gide was only too delighted to take over. Then, before too long, *Corydon* would be published and he would be 'compromised' forever. In a few months, Marc would have to do his military service: that would mark a break with his parents and give Gide a respite. What would Marc do in life? He seemed drawn to a bohemian kind of existence, if a *bohème de luxe*. 'He must help me carry out an experiment that has not yet been done. We are adventurers, *chère amie*. We are embarking on something new. How will it all end?' After a long silence, Gide, overcome with emotion, blurted out that, in Florence, Beth had told him that the thing that they had both wanted so much was now possible. In other words, Elisabeth might have a child and the father would be Marc. Gide, the Petite Dame notes, is 'really radiant, overcome with elation and joy. He speaks of Elisabeth and Marc with passionate tenderness.' A few days later, Gide and the Petite Dame were on the train from Saint-Clair to Paris. Gide returned to the subject of Marc, *qua* ephebe, rather than expectant father:

Marc is being led on by a group of young men [Cocteau, etc.]; they certainly want to avail themselves of him, in order to hurt me, open up doors for him, then shut them in my face. My position isn't always easy, and neither is his. He mustn't feel that I am holding him back in any way. I try to show him how best to approach things . . . He really shows very little curiosity about my literary work; there's a whole part of its content that cannot be of interest to him, and he doesn't understand yet that what attracts him most, a whole aspect of modernism, I refuse to avail myself of.

He then talked of Marc and Beth. He is moved by their 'boldness', their 'generosity'. 'Ah! *chère amie*, we are making possible a new humanity. That child must be beautiful.'[46]

On her return from Florence, Beth informed her father of her decision to have a child outside marriage. It is difficult not to admire, with Gide, the 'boldness' and 'generosity', in 1920, of this woman of thirty: there was nothing inevitable about her motherhood; she was not yet pregnant. For her, motherhood was not a means of strengthening a relationship with a man: Marc was not yet twenty, still, technically, a schoolboy, would soon be doing his military service, had no career prospects whatsoever and no fortune. His role in the matter was simply, in the most natural way possible, to impregnate her. She was, of course, very fond of him, found him attractive, but she had no intention of spending the rest of her life with him. The true intent of this earth-mother was to run a farm: for her, motherhood was an essential means of participating in the natural process. Of course, she could not have arrived at this degree of liberation from the usual *mores* of her society without benefit of certain influences. She had been given no religious upbringing (her mother regarded Gide's lingering religious preoccupations as incomprehensible); the liberated views of her 'godmother', Loup May-risch, had given even greater validity to her mother's; at an earlier stage, Rupert Brooke and his 'paganism' had been another influence; so, too, more recently, had been that of her female friends, 'Schnouky' Mayrisch and 'Whity'. Opposition came, as Beth expected, from her father, who felt only 'blame, disapproval, sadness'. The support that her 'bohemian' artist father refused was provided by the industrialist husband of her mother's best friend: Emile Mayrisch bought a farm, 'La Bastide Franco', near Brignoles, in the Var, and set her up as its manager.

For a couple of hours on a May afternoon, Gide met Dorothy Bussy, at her insistence, alone. This wife and mother of fifty-five, four years his senior, had been hopelessly in love with him, that lover of young men, since their first encounter in Cambridge in 1918 – and remained so to the end. In many of her letters, especially in the early years, she made no secret of her feelings – not the most endearing tactic when love is not requited. Dorothy Bussy knew that the situation was hopeless, but that made no difference. Usually, Gide postponed replying to her letters until a second or third had arrived. Her self-abasement is total: 'There's no need for you to take such trouble to explain to me so gently that your life and heart are full and that I "mustn't count" on your finding time or room for me. I don't count on anything but having to spend the rest of my life wanting things I can't have. It doesn't matter. What matters is you.'[47] On the whole, Gide handled this difficult situation with gentle tact, his irritation only rarely getting the better of him.

The Bussys spent the winter at their house, La Souco, at Roquebrune-Cap-Martin, 3 miles west of Menton. On their way to and from England they passed through Paris. For one reason or another, Gide had managed to avoid a meeting. Then, in April, while staying with Marc at Saint-Clair, Gide and some of his friends motored over to Roquebrune and called on the Bussys. They spent a couple of hours with them, and then left. At no time could Dorothy get Gide on his own and unburden her heart to him. 'I can't bear that memory of you to be my last for another year, perhaps for ever,' she wrote a few days later. They would be spending two days in Paris on their return in May. She insisted that Gide see her alone, 'for just a few minutes, for just once'.[48] During those few hours in Paris, Gide told Dorothy the story of his life, ending with the final breakdown with Madeleine and the burning of his letters. She returned to England in a state of ecstasy verging on the mystical. She had been granted, as if in response to a magic wish, the very thing she most craved: 'The clouds of darkness and doubt and ignorance have rolled away and I now stand in the light . . . It seems at times as though that vision and that glory were just *You* – your irradiated face, your irradiated spirit.' She now felt that she had a total knowledge of Gide, 'the motive of all your acts, the subject of all your books, of all your thoughts'. She had understood what was 'the single passion' of his life – and it was neither Madeleine nor Marc, not Art, Beauty, Truth, Love, Life . . . nor even God. It was 'the purest, the divinest, most mysterious of all the idols . . . and oh! the cruellest [by now, Gide's suspense must have been unbearable] . . . Virtue.'[49] Of course, their relations were not to remain for long on that exalted plane – especially when competition was suspected. Madeleine, she knew, had a prior claim, but was no rival. Marc she positively liked and she knew that she and he would necessarily occupy different regions of Gide's affection – in any case, the sister of Lytton Strachey and an habituée of what was becoming the 'Bloomsbury group' found such male relationships entirely normal. No, the real rival was a woman of her own age, born within a few months of her and, curiously, to die within a few months of her too. Maria Van Rysselberghe, the Petite Dame, was also, in a very relaxed, unpossessive way, in love with Gide. But because that love was, to all outward appearances, indistinguishable from deep affection, it was one that Gide could reciprocate without the slightest fear. 'How lucky I am that I live not very far from the Van Rysselberghes; otherwise . . .' Dorothy Bussy was writing to Gide as late as 1927. 'Oh, the irony of fate!'[50] The irony was that, had she not lived so close to her 'rival', she would have seen less of Gide.

On 13 June, Gide attended the dress rehearsal of his translation of *Antony and Cleopatra*, with his friends Edouard de Max and Ida Rubenstein in the title roles. Box 22 at the Opéra was occupied by Jeanne Mühlfeld, Aline and Andrée Mayrisch, Maria and Elisabeth Van Rysselberghe and, at the back, Gide and Marc. Gide, notes the Petite Dame, was 'the picture of happiness'. 'How beautiful everything is!' he said. 'What?' Loup Mayrisch asked. 'Mais nous, chère amie!' What indeed was making Gide feel so happy was not the occasion or pride in his own achievement, but having around him, in that tiny space, what amounted to his surrogate family. 'Marc held my hand during the whole performance,' he told Maria afterwards.[51] Next day, there was the 'princely gala' of the opening night. According to Roger Martin du Gard, 'Gide, at the back of a box, wearing white tie and tails, an old grey trilby stuck on his head, laughing like an idiot . . . exclaiming: "But I don't recognize the play at all! I don't recognize a word they're chanting out there!"'[52] Many of the critics, too, complained that they could not hear the words over Florent Schmidt's incidental music. Four more performances of the production were given.

Gide spent the next few weeks at Cuverville, returning to Paris for a few days before he and Marc set off for London on 30 July – the Allégrets being under the misapprehension that their son was taking up a post as French teacher with an English family. Some weeks before, Gide had written to Dorothy Bussy asking for her help in arranging a stay in England of some five or six weeks. What he had in mind was 'some picturesque spot', preferably near the sea, an inn where we can live cheaply and freely; in Wales, perhaps . . .'[53] She came up with just such a place: Llanberis, in the foothills of Mount Snowdon, in north Wales. It was on the edge of a lake and about 8 miles from the sea. On arrival in London, Gide and Marc were entertained at Lady Strachey's, 51 Gordon Square. They were then joined by Beth, who had been staying with Ethel Whitehorn in Oxford. The travellers set out for the *terra incognita* of Wales, Gide entering into the spirit of the thing by reading Peacock's *Nightmare Abbey* on the train. Gide wrote several letters to Dorothy Bussy from Llanberis, usually enclosing other letters to be posted from London – clearly, traces were being covered up. Enchantment with the charm of Snowdonia did not last long. By the third day, Gide is noting that the weather is hideous but, he adds, essaying his idiosyncratic English, 'exactly what suits us . . . The trial is sometimes so cruciating for me that I believe that I can bear it no longer more. Yet it must be so, and I willed it.'[54] A week later, Gide reported that it had stopped raining for the first time since they had arrived. He was sitting on a bench, facing the lake, and admiring the view: 'To my right: Snowdon and slate; behind me, before me, slate. There's enough here to cover a continent. It is of an indefinable tone, not at all blue like our own slate, but rather the colour of rhinoceros (belly of).'[55] While he took advantage of the bad weather to work, Marc and Beth went rowing in the rain. They looked 'the picture of happiness', Gide reported to the young woman's mother.[56] In the evenings, round a fire of slate and coal, they read Sterne's *Tristram Shandy* and James's story, *The Lesson of the Master.*

Meanwhile, poor Dorothy was having doubts about her (very perceptive and intelligent) comments on *Corydon*: 'I always feel in such a fearful panic after I have sent you a letter. I want to go and drown myself . . . I thought of you – goodness! how I thought of you, how I think of you!' The previous weekend the Bussys had gone to Garsington Manor, Lady Ottoline Morrell's house near Oxford. As they left, the hostess had asked for Gide's address: she wanted to invite 'us' (i.e. Gide and Dorothy) to spend a weekend there. 'If you go I should like to go too, but it would probably be impossible to speak to you alone and I should be dying to.'[57] Gide and Marc arrived back in London on 27 August – Beth rejoining Whity before returning to London. As arranged, Gide, Marc and the Bussys spent the weekend at Garsington. No sooner back in London, they set out for Arnold Bennett's country house, Comarques, at Thorpe-Le-Soken, in Essex, where they spent the night. They also found time to stay with the Bussys at Fernhurst, in Surrey. On 3 September, they were invited to dinner at the Gosses'. A day or two later, they set sail for Antwerp. They probably parted in Brussels, Marc returning home and Gide going on to Rochefort, en route for Luxembourg, to spend three days with a young Belgian poet, René Michelet, whom he had met in Brussels. Gide then went on to the Château de Colpach, the Mayrisches' new property. Already there, from England, was Beth. Later, Walther Rathenau, a colleague of Emile Mayrisch, arrived at the house. Rathenau, head of AEG, the vast German engineering firm, had been largely responsible, during the war, for Germany's economic policy. In one of the early post-Armistice German governments, he was Minister of Reconstruction. At the time of his visit, he was not in government, although, later in the year, he was to become Foreign Minister. He was anxious to meet Gide. Gide, too, was interested and quite willing to give him a cordial welcome. What he was not prepared for was a display of extravagant enthusiasm, entailing an arm around his shoulder as they walked in the grounds, a hand on his knee as they sat together talking. Their conversation got little further than a discussion of national and racial characteristics, American, French, German, Jewish – Rathenau was Jewish.

On 30 September, Gide left Colpach for Paris. He spent six days at the Villa Montmorency, 'playing at Robinson [Crusoe]', leaving early in the morning, arriving back at night only to sleep, eating out every day. Whether by accident or design, Gide managed to miss Dorothy Bussy as she passed through Paris on her way South – a farcical episode involving letters left in drawers and keys being in the wrong place. Poor Dorothy was accustomed to rejection by now: 'So, Thursday night, I make a tryst with you,' she had written from London a few days before. In a final, ill-chosen metaphor, she became Mary Magdalen, pouring 'my box of ointment over your feet'.[58] Roger Martin du Gard has left a delicious impression of the Gide–Robinson of this time and his 'cabin', that 'strange, fabulous house where he seems so little at home – indeed, where it doesn't seem possible that anyone could feel at home':

He guides me impatiently through the circumlocutions of the staircase whose preposterous design might have been intended to illustrate a tale by Edgar Allan Poe. It's like the staircase of a lighthouse, stuck on to the inside wall of some enormous, terrifyingly empty cage . . . On the first floor, I follow him along a corridor; through a wide-open door I glimpse a ship's cabin, with the bed unmade. We climb a few more steps. Another corridor, half blocked with suitcases. We pass a rickety folding table, heaped high with papers; a kitchen stool stands against a big radiator. 'This is where I usually work, but you'll be more comfortable up here' . . . more steps. Eventually we enter a sort of tiny loggia, with windows everywhere, overlooking . . . a dark hall, in which I can make out tables, bookcases, chairs covered with dust sheets and piles of books on the floor . . .[59]

There Gide read to his guest the opening pages of Part 2 of *Si le grain ne meurt*, describing his journey to Biskra with Paul-Albert Laurens. They talk of 'the eternal drama' of Gide's life, how everything that he had so far written had been intended for Madeleine. Suddenly Gide decides that he must go to Cuverville – at once. Martin du Gard accompanies him in a taxi to the Gare Saint-Lazare. Apparently, it was the Gides' wedding anniversary, 8 October, a day when, in spite of everything, he tried to be with his wife. 'I don't know which is more awful: not to be loved any more, or to see the person you love, and who still loves you, cease to believe in your love,' he confided in the *Journal*. 'What is the use of protesting that I love her more than anything in the world? She would not believe me.'[60] Ten days later, he was back at the Villa. Again his time was frittered away on 'errands, visits, etc.'. 'Impossible to find a servant,' he wrote to Dorothy Bussy. 'Between six and seven in the evening, a charwoman comes and cleans my bedroom. I bring back a bit of *charcuterie*, which I eat sitting on the corner of a table. The day before yesterday I spent three hours cleaning my stove . . .'[61]

On 25 October, Gide received a letter bearing the address 'Hôtel Foyot, Paris'.

My dear André Gide,

Four days ago, at Basle, I found this beautiful, conscientious book that you intended for me; I think it had been waiting there a long time for me, and I am angry with chance for persisting in postponing my joy for so long . . . Nevertheless, that envious chance worked with a certain precision: the same day I decided to come to Paris . . . I am too moved to say more. Just think that – since yesterday – I have been wandering through the Luxembourg and the streets of Paris; I mean, I am so attached to so many well nigh indispensable places, and sometimes the contact is so flagrant that I have to shut my eyes . . .

I shall only be here for a few days this time, but I shall take away with me, I am sure, a strong conviction of continuity; indeed it was you who first helped to give me back that feeling by sending me your *Symphonie Pastorale*.

Grand merci! Et merci encore.

Rilke

For Rilke, the war and the nationalism that had given birth to it and fed fat on it represented a terrible force that had shattered his personal, inner world from the outside. He probably assumed that his French friends felt the same. But, since they and he had become more or less unwitting instruments on opposing sides of the conflict, he no doubt felt that an actual encounter with his friends would be too embarrassing so soon after the end of hostilities. Not for him the insouciant bonhomie of Walther Rathenau.

Since 27 October, Gide tactlessly told Dorothy Bussy, 'Elisabeth Van Rysselberghe shares my solitude';[62] her mother would be arriving four days later, 'to help me keep house'[63] – and to help him arrange the mass of books and papers that had accumulated, in quite disorderly fashion, at the Villa. Dorothy Bussy pounced on the information: 'I was very glad you have got Mme Van Rysselberghe and Elisabeth with you . . . I have always thought that one of my occupations in heaven (if I were allowed to go there) would be arranging a library with a friend . . . When will you invite me to stay in your house? . . . Am I not quite as respectable as Mme Van Rysselberghe? Or perhaps respectability is not the passport? What then?'[64] Tantalizingly polite, Gide replied: 'What! You'll agree to stay at the Villa when passing through Paris! . . . That would be simply marvellous.'[65]

Marc took the second part of his baccalauréat (for the second time) and, that very night, left for Strasbourg, where he began his military service. Gide would see him again four weeks later. Next day, Gide went to meet the Petite Dame at the Gare du Nord. They soon settled into a regular routine, Gide looking after the stove and doing the shopping, she 'seeing to the rest'. At 11 o'clock in the evening of 27 November, Marc arrived, late but expected, on his first twenty-four-hour leave. The Petite Dame improvised a little supper. 'He looks well; his attitude is exquisite; he talks well of everything around him,' she noted.[66]

On 22 December, the Petite Dame travelled South to Saint-Clair and Gide made the much shorter (one-hour) journey to Clermont, in the Oise, where Roger Martin du Gard had acquired a small country retreat. Gide spent two nights there. His host outlined his plan for *Les Thibault*, the vast series of novels that he had begun and read aloud to him the first six chapters. Gide was all enthusiasm: 'He walked about me like a caged lion, laughing that infernal laugh of his, rubbing his hands, interjecting, making noises of approval, getting me to re-read certain paragraphs, saying: "I see, I see . . . Ah, *mon vieux*, I'll have it in for you if you don't pull all that off!"'[67] On another occasion, Gide talked about his own long, involved novel, which was still at an early stage, and contrasted the two different 'aesthetics' at work. Martin du Gard's was strictly chronological, linear, accumulative; *Les Faux-Monnayeurs* would be more like a spotlight moving backwards and forwards, illuminating first this episode then that. He compared his friend's method to Tolstoy's ('I admire Tolstoy profoundly'), his own to Dostoevsky's.[68]

Gide celebrated the arrival of 1921 at Cuverville, arriving there on New Year's Eve. The night before he had finally gone along to the Diaghilev company's revival of *Parade*. As was only to be expected, he found it pretentious and vacuous. Gide went back-stage afterwards. Cocteau was looking 'older, tense, unhappy': 'he knows very well that the sets and costumes are Picasso's, the music Satie's, but he wonders if Picasso and Satie are his too'.[69] The waspish Cocteau always managed to bring out a certain waspishness in Gide, not usually noted for it.

'Dreadful days. Insomnia; relapses into the worst; bad work' – by 3 January Cuverville had exerted its usual spell over Gide. 'If only I could believe that she found my presence here agreeable . . .' Madeleine seemed only to tolerate it; her attitude to him was made up of 'incomprehension, misjudge-ment or, which is worse, indifference'. But, Gide asks himself, what if the misunderstanding is on his side? 'If only we could talk it over!' But, he admits, he no longer knows *how* to speak to her. It seems as though she were deliberately doing everything she could to make herself unattractive in the hope that he would leave her. 'Nothing of me interests her any more.'

In a copy of the latest *NRF*, he finds the pages containing an extract from *Si le grain ne meurt* uncut, but she has clearly read Claudel's *Saint Martin*.[70] They said little to one another. If they did speak, it was *par personne interposée*, as it were: during their four weeks together they read aloud to one another nineteen of Chekhov's stories, in Constance Garnett's English version. A depressed Gide arrived back in Paris on 27 January.

On 9 February, Gide attended a banquet given in honour of Copeau, who had been decorated with the Légion d'honneur. He took Duncan Grant, who was staying at the Villa, along with him. There were plans for a production of *Saül* towards the end of the Vieux Colombier season and Grant had come over to Paris to discuss the costumes, which he had been asked to design. In the event, the production was postponed until June 1922 – and Grant did not design the costumes. Meanwhile, Marc arrived back in Paris, where he was attached to the army staff headquarters. Gide noted how much less 'wild' he was, how much he had 'developed'. 'He is one of those,' he remarked to the Petite Dame, with great percipience, 'who find the events that draw their faces [*dessiner leurs figures*].'[71] A week or so later, at Saint-Clair, Gide and the Petite Dame talked of Marc, of Madeleine, of whether *Corydon* should be published sooner or later, of plans to sell the Villa Montmorency and find some new Paris home that he could share with Marc, the Van Rysselberghes and, possibly, the Schlumbergers. Five days later, he travelled along the coast to Roquebrune, where, at last, Dorothy Bussy would have the pleasure of his company, not for a few fleeting, tantalizing hours, but for some five weeks. He even hired a piano for the duration of his stay. Dorothy was more than satisfied. After he had gone, she began to count the 'treasure' that she had accumulated during those weeks: a whole life would not be long enough to exhaust it.[72]

Gide spent a few days with the Raverats at Vence, before going back to the Var, this time to Beth's new farm, near Brignoles, arriving there on 2 April. Gide was immersed in a reading of *Le Côté de Guermantes*. 'It's so successful in what it does, it rather demoralizes me,' he confessed to the 'Petite Dame'. 'I feel crude beside him.'[73] A few days later Gide read them a piece on Proust that would appear as a 'Lettre à Angèle' in the May number of the *NRF* (and be included in *Incidences* of 1924). Though less than half-a-dozen pages in length, it goes to the heart of Proust's achievement, with great perception and generosity.

You seem to be speaking only of yourself, yet your books are as peopled as [Balzac's] *La Comédie humaine*; your narrative is not a novel, you do not tie and untie a plot, yet I know of none that one follows with more lively interest; you present your characters to us only incidentally, as if by chance, but we soon know them as deeply as we know Cousin Pons, Eugénie Grandet or Vautrin. Your books do not seem to be 'composed' and you lavish your profusion apparently at random, but I postpone judgement until I have read the books to follow, when, I suspect, all the elements will turn out to have been deployed according to some hidden ordering . . .[74]

Gide goes on to praise Proust for the 'gratuitousness' of his work. Gide has recognized, behind Proust's apparent nostalgia, his obsession with a declining class and a rapidly disappearing way of life, the essentially 'modern' artist, the kind that he himself, since *Les Caves du Vatican*, had been striving to become. He compares Proust, intriguingly, with Montaigne. Both produce '*œuvres de long loisir*', forcing the reader to an 'extreme' slowness, robbing him of any wish to move faster, such is the 'continuous satisfaction' produced in the process of reading. While at La Bastide, the company spent the evenings reading aloud – Stevenson's *The Pavilion on the Links* and *New Arabian Nights*. During the day, Gide read Meredith's *Harry Richmond*. There were visits, too, from friends; Eugène Rouart called briefly and Charles Du Bos stayed for two days. Gide and the Petite Dame left La Bastide together on 21 April and parted at Toulon: he for Paris, she for Saint-Clair.

The evening of his arrival in Paris, Gide went to the Vieux Colombier to see the last performance of Jean Schlumberger's play, *La Mort de Sparte*. It had not been much of a success either artistically or commercially. Next day, he had lunch with Rabindranath Tagore ('Il est EXQUIS').[75] After lunch at Martin du Gard's, Gide read to his friend the latest chapter from *Si le grain ne meurt*, the one recounting his second visit to Algeria, his meeting with Wilde and Douglas. In the ensuing conversation, Gide described, in some detail, the peculiar form that masturbation took with him. Without the least trace of boastfulness, indeed with some embarrassment, he explained how he always felt the need of 'a total expulsion of sperm' and that this could only be achieved by 'coming' six or seven times consecutively. He regarded this phenomenon not as an 'exploit', but as a 'monstrosity' of his nature. At first, he came twice, in rapid succession – a fact that often astonished his sexual partners. Then, shortly afterwards, he came again, but he could seldom come more than three times with the same person. So, if circumstances permitted it, he would come again with someone else or, more usually, retire and masturbate alone, coming three or more times before he felt satisfied. The amount of sperm produced with each ejaculation did diminish, but not by very much. On ejaculation, he fell into a 'swoon' (*pâmoison*), almost to the point of losing consciousness. He had no other explanation for this sexual 'abnormality' than the guilt inculcated in him by his religious upbringing.[76]

The following week, Gide spent an hour with Proust. For four successive days, Proust had sent a car to collect him, missing him each time. On arrival, Gide was shown into a stiflingly warm room, in which his host was shivering with cold – he had just got up and left an even hotter room. His life, he complained, was a long agony. No sooner was Gide in the room than Proust began to talk about homosexuality. Gide had brought with him a copy of *Corydon*, getting Proust to promise to speak of it to no one. Some days later, he was about to go to bed when the bell rang. It was Proust's chauffeur, returning the copy of *Corydon*, and asking Gide if he would be so kind as to go back with him. M. Proust was feeling a little better and would like to see him. The chauffeur's sentence was so long and so complicated that Gide felt that the poor man had repeated it to himself over and over again as he drove the few miles from the rue Hamelin. Similarly, says Gide, when Céleste, Proust's housekeeper and the chauffeur's wife, opened the door to him a few days before, apologizing that her master did not feel well enough to receive him, she had added, in very Proustian fashion: 'Monsieur prie Monsieur Gide de se convaincre qu'il pense incessamment à lui' (Monsieur begs Monsieur Gide to be in no doubt that he thinks of him constantly). On this second occasion, they talked of little else but homosexuality. Proust admitted that he felt some regret that he had transposed all his most 'gracious, tender and charming' homosexual memories to the '*jeunes filles en fleur*', leaving only the 'grotesque' and 'abject' for *Sodome et Gomorrhe*. When Gide objected that he seemed to be stigmatizing homosexuals, Proust protested that he personally was not attracted to youthful beauty, that, in any case, beauty had little to do with desire. Gide 'understood at last that what we find ignoble, an object of laughter or disgust, does not seem so repulsive to him'.[77]

Madeleine arrived at the Villa Montmorency. Two days later, Dorothy Bussy came for tea, thus meeting Madeleine for the first time. What might have been a risky undertaking seems to have passed off well. Back in England, Dorothy wrote to Gide that 'it wasn't hard meeting your wife. I thought it was going to be, but it wasn't. She looked at me with such beautiful eyes and such a beautiful expression that things seemed easy. And how happy she seemed . . .'[78]

Gide was getting more and more interested in Freud, though 'he doesn't tell me anything I haven't already thought myself'. Freud did, however, clarify 'a series of thoughts that remained in me in a floating state'. Gide felt that he had to make contact with Freud: he even thought that Freud might write a preface to a German translation of *Corydon*. (Nothing came of this.) Dorothy Bussy made the necessary introductions through her brother James Strachey, who had now embarked on his life's work of translating Freud into English. The following year, the *NRF* brought out a French translation of *Three Essays on the Theory of Sexuality*.

Madeleine left the Villa for Cuverville – she had spent eleven days there. On 10 June, the 'Petite Dame' left for Brussels – her mother was ill – and Gide decided to go with her. He stayed with Jan Vanden Eeckhoudt, a painter friend of Simon Bussy. His main reason for going to Brussels, as the 'Petite Dame' knew, was to see René Michelet, a young (twenty-one-year-old) poet – and paedophile – whom he had met on an earlier visit. 'It's incredible how widespread pederasty is here,' he confided to her, 'in the schools, among the boy-scouts, everywhere.' He was very struck by Michelet's 'boldness', an utter lack of precaution, which was soon to attract the attention of the Belgian police, and by the 'trembling lyricism' he displayed with his young friends. 'I cannot believe he depraves them,' Gide comments.[79] On 18 June, he was due to go on to Colpach, but was feeling liverish, after too much bicycling, swimming and bad chocolate – the ill-effects, clearly, of consorting with those a quarter his age. One night, Michelet took him to see one of his young friends, Charlot (Charles Brunard, then fifteen). With the 'amused complicity' of the concierge at the Brunards' magnificent townhouse, they go into a storeroom in the basement. Charlot apologizes for receiving them so badly. They sit on a bench and the boy kisses Gide with '*précipitation frémissante*', trembling haste. Before long, Charlot's mother calls her son and he has to go upstairs. Gide's last view of the boy is of a half-dressed figure on a second-floor balcony, waving them goodbye. (Gide and the boy remained friends. In 1974, Brunard published their correspondence.)

At Colpach, Gide met Ernst Robert Curtius, a German scholar and critic who taught French history and literature successively at Bonn, Marburg and Heidelberg. The two got on extremely well and remained lifelong friends, right through and beyond the terrible years of Nazism and the Second World War. Curtius spoke excitedly of the Wilde case and Gide read to him the most recently written part of *Si le grain ne meurt* (presumably the North African section of Book II, involving Wilde), 'which transported him'. He told Gide that, in Berlin, since the war, homosexuality had become widespread to a degree that could not be imagined and those who practised it did so without let or hindrance. Curtius went on to speak of the poet Stefan George, who had established a sort of 'Hellenic cult of beauty', complete with rituals and adepts, in honour of a young lover who had died.

On 27 June, much to Maria Van Rysselberghe's surprise, Gide, whom she believed to be at Colpach, turned up at her mother's house in Brussels. 'Something extremely serious is happening here,' he began. 'In which you are involved?' the Petite Dame asked. 'No, but something in which I want to get involved. Young René Michelet has been arrested . . .' Apparently, he had been denounced by persons unknown and released on bail. Fearing that his copy of *Corydon* and letters from Gide would fall into the hands of the police, Michelet had asked Gide to help him leave the country. The plan failed and Michelet was rearrested. After a few weeks, however, the parents of his 'victims' withdrew their charges for fear of 'gossips'[80] and Michelet was released. He remained, however, under constant police supervision for several weeks.

Gide arrived back in Paris on the morning of 29 June and saw Marc, who was on short leave, very briefly before going on to Cuverville. There he was able to work well and, by the middle of the month, had finished the second part of *Si le grain ne meurt*, which was all he intended to have published for the time being. He even doubted whether he would continue writing his memoirs – and he did not. He returned instead to *Les Faux-Monnayeurs*.

He spent the first week of August at La Sapinière with the Allégrets. He described to the Petite Dame 'the tragic atmosphere' that hung over the Allégret family and the 'curious psychology' of the mother, who has 'views of life that we cannot even imagine', and who has no idea of what is going on behind her back. Gide then went on to Colpach, where a card arrived for him from Fedor Rosenberg. He had heard nothing from him since the Bolshevik revolution and assumed that he was dead. Another day, 'Schnouky' Mayrisch brought into lunch two boy scouts, 'The Thinking Lion' and 'The Blue Jaguar', who had been camping in the park. 'Of course, this aroused him no end,' the Petite Dame observed, 'and he didn't fail to prowl around their tent.'[81] In the evening, the scouts 'invited' the Mayrisches and their guests to a magnificent bonfire in their honour. A week later, Marc arrived on a two-day leave. Jean Schlumberger turned up to spend ten days with the Mayrisches; a slight improvement in his wife's condition had allowed him to get away for a short break. (Suzanne Schlumberger was to have another operation, for cancer, a month later.) There was much talk about *Corydon* (whether or not Gide should publish it), Proust's *Sodome et Gomorrhe* (admiration tempered with irritation at its wholly negative portrayal of homosexuals), *Si le grain* . . . (the Petite Dame suggested that Lord Alfred Douglas might sue Gide; Gide hoped that he would) and Freud (against the overriding primacy that he accords to sexuality, Gide would set a universal, generalized *volupté*, what, in fact, Freud would stigmatize as 'polymorphous perversity'). The day before Gide left Colpach, a bus arrived carrying the 'Club' from Dudelange, now transformed into a football team, and their young supporters. They were to play a game against the home Colpach team. Schnouky and Gide immediately took charge of the situation. The Petite Dame admired the way in which Gide 'merged with them quite naturally, with an evident wish to be one of them' – he had quietly changed into old clothes and sandals. On the way back from the match, he said: 'We were born too early, *chère amie*. We're witnessing a great transformation of the world of youth; and I think that's even more true for the girls than for the boys.'[82]

After a few weeks wandering along the Mediterranean Coast, from Hyères to Grau du Roi, near Aigues-Mortes, Gide was back in Paris on 21 September, staying, for ten days, in the 'deserted, dusty, already freezing' Villa Montmorency, impatiently awaiting the departure from Cuverville of the Drouins. Once there, he stayed barely two weeks, trying to work on *Les Faux-Monnayeurs*, but 'floundering about in it as in a bog, a quagmire, from which I despair of ever extricating myself'.[83] To avoid working on it, he 'welcomes every distraction', including spending three or four hours a day at the piano. Then, suddenly, without difficulty, he writes two pages of dialogue, with which he thinks he will begin the novel (in its final version, it opens with no such dialogue). He will be satisfied only if he manages to 'move away even more from realism'.[84]

By the middle of October Gide was back in Paris, where he was joined at the Villa Montmorency by Marc, who had just had a small operation that would keep him in bed for a week. Marc had forty-five days convalescence leave and they left for the South, Gide spending three days at Roquebrune with the Bussys, Marc at La Bastide with Beth, before joining up for a three-week stay in Italy. At Orvieto, Gide was arrested and taken off to a police station, on account of his 'conspirator's cloak' and 'mysterious air'[85] – the atmosphere of fear and suspicion aroused by Mussolini's destabilizing tactics was already evident. The March on Rome was still a year away, but the city itself was already in Fascist hands. 'A great chaste wind has blown over Italy since the war,' Gide wrote to Valéry Larbaud on 10 November, 'sweeping the models from the Spanish Steps and cleaning the streets. Everything has become noble, martial, frowning.' Gide and Marc had arrived the day before in the middle of a general strike. The train, already five hours late, stopped short of the city centre and they had to cover the remaining few miles on foot. Troops were everywhere; the shops were shut and the hotels full. 'It is difficult to understand what is going on, but people in the streets are over-excited; flags and banners are saluted and cheered . . .' Later, Gide described the trip as 'a complete fiasco': you can now 'cross Italy off your diary – for some time at least'.[86] For their first three days, Gide and Marc had to be content with 'a space behind a screen in a public corridor by way of a room . . . and don't imagine there were any compensations! Nothing is left of the pre-war attractions.'[87] To Alibert, however, Gide described the holiday as 'a month of cloudless felicity'[88] and, to Dorothy Bussy, Marc as 'the best and most delightful companion who has ever followed me'[89] – though to both he complained that he had done no work. On 22 November, Gide's fifty-second birthday, Beth arrived. Next day, he left for Paris, leaving his young friends in Rome for a few more days. On arrival in Paris, Gide went straight on to Cuverville, where he stayed for three weeks, during which he managed to write thirty pages of *Les Faux-Monnayeurs*.

The November number of the nationalist *Revue universelle* carried a long article by Henri Massis attacking Gide as a 'public danger'. It used as evidence an amalgam of quotations, many inaccurate, that made no distinction between Gide's own views, views attributed to characters and views ascribed to him by hearsay. This was no isolated attack. Leafing through clippings sent by a press agency, Gide notes:

I have received nothing but violent attacks . . . Three-quarters of the critics, and almost all those in the newspapers, form their opinions, not from the books themselves, but from café chit-chat. I know that neither the cafés, nor the salons, nor the boulevards are on my side; and these are what make successes. That is not the kind of favour I seek, or have ever wanted. I shall let my books patiently choose their readers; today's small number will form tomorrow's opinion.[90]

About the same time, in an article in *Action Française*, Ghéon attacked the notion of '*gratuité*' in literature: every work of art worthy of the name has been created to serve a particular point of view. This was, by implication, a criticism of Gide. Thus Gide was being attacked by a Catholic nationalist enemy for doing the devil's work and by a Catholic nationalist friend for trying to remain above the battle. 'Ghéon's desertion causes me almost unbearable, constantly renewed pain,' Gide commented.

Gide returned to Paris and moved into a room on the sixth floor of the

Lutétia, a fairly luxurious hotel at 45 boulevard Raspail, opposite the Bon Marché department store. He could not face all the problems entailed in reopening the Villa Montmorency in mid-winter; he also wanted 'to enjoy the neighbourhood', that is, the area centred on the Jardin du Luxembourg, in which so much of *Les Faux-Monnayeurs* is set. A few weeks later, however, he was back in Auteuil.

13

Gide, Homosexual Theorist and Father: Corydon *and* Les Faux-Monnayeurs

(JANUARY 1922 – JULY 1925)

Gide spent the morning of New Year's Day correcting proofs and reading; he lunched alone, 'a little sad; let's say, serious'. The following day, a message arrived from Walther Rathenau, who wanted to see him before he left Paris. He spent an hour with the German Foreign Minister in his private drawing-room at the Crillon. As at Colpach, Gide found it difficult 'not to be embarrassed by his over-friendly way of seizing hold of your person; his hand hardly left my arm once during the whole conversation'. 'Europe is rushing to the abyss,' said Rathenau. 'It's too late to stop it . . . The abscess has formed: it must burst, yet again.'¹ Europe, if not 'rushing' towards the abyss, was certainly moving towards it. Rathenau himself would not take so long; six months later, he was assassinated by a right-wing extremist.

Gide, too, was not immune to thoughts of danger. Madeleine wrote from Cuverville that she was very worried about 'the campaign of vilification' being waged against him: 'If you were invulnerable, I wouldn't tremble with fear. But you *are* vulnerable, and you know it; and I know it.' Gide comments: 'Vulnerable . . . I am, I was, only because of her. Now I don't care and I'm afraid of nothing . . . What have I to lose that is still dear to me?'² At the heart of the 'campaign of vilification' against Gide was the extreme right-wing Catholic, Henri Massis. In 1914, in a review of *Les Caves du Vatican*, he had attacked the 'diabolical role' played by Gide in French culture. The publication of *Morceaux choisis* was the occasion for a fresh onslaught on Gide's 'influence' in the *Revue universelle* (15 November 1921). There were exceptions to the almost total condemnation of Gide by Catholic and extreme right-wing intellectuals. Léon Daudet, the brilliant polemicist of *Action française*, always defended Gide, only too well aware, perhaps, of his brother Lucien's homosexuality. Defence also came from a young, liberal Catholic writer, François Mauriac, who, in the review *Université de Paris*, published an article, 'A propos d'André Gide, réponse à M. Massis'. Mauriac became and remained a faithful friend; he, too, was not immune to the attractions of younger members of his own sex.

It was precisely at this time of increasing demonization by the Catholic Right that Gide was planning to publish not only *Corydon*, his theoretical defence of homosexuality, but also *Si le grain ne meurt*, the autobiographical work that would serve as a personal plea on behalf of his own homosexuality. Unlike most people in a similar position, Gide's response to notoriety and attack was to rip away the last vestiges of pretence and fight back. Roger Martin du Gard, himself homosexual and, in his way, no more happily married than Gide, counselled caution. Scandal would be inevitable and would serve no useful purpose. It would put 'decisive weapons' into the hands of his many enemies. 'It will cut you off from two-thirds of your friends – I mean those who accept your private life for as long as it is discreet, more or less veiled, as long as appearances are kept up . . .' Not only would Gide suffer terribly, at a personal level: it would also impede the full flowering of his talent. Gide would have none of this: 'I can't wait any longer. I must obey an inner necessity, one more demanding than any other . . . I must, absolutely *must* lift this cloak of lies that has sheltered me since my youth . . . I'm stifling under it!' Martin du Gard wondered whether Gide, inspired by the tragic fate of Oscar Wilde, was actually seeking martyrdom in the cause of some higher mission; was being over-affected by his re-reading of Dostoevsky, acquiring a 'Slav intoxication' with public confession; or was still unconsciously in the grip of his inherited 'puritan atavism', seeking 'expiation' for his sense of guilt. Gide believed that the time had come 'to strike a great blow' on behalf of homosexuality.[3] Since the war, the whole climate had altered concerning sexual matters: people's attitudes were changing under the impact of new ideas, notably Freud's, and young people were leading their lives in open disregard for the old ways. In the event, Gide stayed his hand for two more years.

About this time, approaches had been made to Gide regarding a candidature for a vacant seat in the Académie Française. Martin du Gard advocated a principled refusal to compromise with the powers that be. This lent support to Gide's instinctive repugnance for an institution that embodied all that he most despised. Two days after their conversation, Martin du Gard wrote to Gide: 'I have a profound feeling that the day you accept the compromises entailed by a candidature to the Académie . . . something will have changed . . . You belong to the race of those who are not *of* it, Molière, Rousseau, Stendhal, Baudelaire and so many others.'[4]

In January, Charlie Du Bos had sent Gide a copy of Blake's *The Marriage of Heaven and Hell*. He had browsed through a copy in Beth's room in the rue Laugier in 1914 and had recognized at once a fellow soul. 'Like an astronomer calculating the existence of a star whose rays he cannot yet perceive directly, I sensed Blake's existence, but had as yet no idea that he formed a constellation with Nietzsche, Browning and Dostoevsky. The most brilliant star, perhaps, of that group; certainly the strangest and most distant.' Almost at once, Gide set about translating *The Marriage of Heaven and Hell*; by early June the work was done; a year later, it was published by the *NRF*.

Freud, too, came upon Gide with a sense of recognition, but Freud was no star, to dazzle, to illuminate, rather a systematization of insights and notions that had been his for a long time. 'Freud, Freudianism . . . For the past ten or fifteen years, I have been practising it without knowing. Many ideas of mine, if expounded and developed at length in a thick book, would have been highly successful . . . It is high time I published *Corydon*.'⁵ About this time, Gide and a number of *NRF* friends invited Eugenia Sokolnicka, a Czech doctor who had studied with Freud, to talk to them about psycho-analysis. At one such meeting, the speaker described homosexuality as 'a substitution of direction'. Gide opposed what she said in an intelligent, if brutal manner. 'Everybody talked at once and no one could hear what anyone else was saying; the things one manages to say in the simplest way imaginable is incredible. A certain impropriety in the terms used by Mme Sokolnicka had us constantly on the edge of giggling.'⁶ However, Gide decided to try psychoanalysis himself, but, finding Mme Sokolnicka's obser-vations '*fastidieuses*' (tedious), he did not pursue it beyond the fifth session. This was, however, enough for Gide's creative purposes and the analyst turns up in *Les Faux-Monnayeurs* as Sophroniska.

Meanwhile, Gide was much possessed of that other great star of his personal constellation, Dostoevsky. After the celebratory address on the occurrence of the centenary in December, he undertook to deliver six lectures on the great Russian. Beginning on 17 February, they were given at weekly intervals in the actors' library at the Vieux Colombier theatre. Together with Gide's 1908 essay on the correspondence, his 1911 essay on *The Brothers Karamazov* and the centenary address, they were published in 1923. In these lectures, especially the earlier ones, Gide is anxious to let Dostoevsky speak for himself and there are long extracts from the work, the correspondence and the journals. His comments are always intelligent, often brilliantly incisive; they are also, as Gide admitted at the opening of his last lecture, 'a pretext to express my own thoughts'.

Gide had not been entirely alone at the Villa Montmorency during those early weeks of the year. Marc, back briefly from Berlin or Warsaw, was a frequent visitor and, for a time, Beth stayed with him. In February, the Petite Dame arrived in Paris from Saint-Clair and stayed for six days, before going on to Colpach. By late March, Marc was back in Paris, living at the Villa. He had been transferred from his post as military envoy to the office of the War Minister's *chef de cabinet*. His main task was translating extracts from British and American newspapers relating to French policy. Most Sundays, the two would lunch *en famille* with the Allégrets. Gide could not get over how much Marc had changed in the past few years: the once shy, withdrawn, rather sullen boy had acquired 'a sort of comic lyricism, a quick-wittedness, a resourcefulness, a sense of fun! He's inventing a whole new genre.'[7]

Gide was feeling more than usually depressed by the calls on his time. On top of his usual complaints, tiredness, apathy, insomnia, he was now suffering from dizzy spells. With him, no single mood lasted for long, however. One evening he got the Petite Dame and Marc to swallow their dinner in ten minutes and dragged them off to a gymnastics demonstration organized by Raymond Duncan, Isadora's brother. It was 'gloomy and rather grotesque' and they did not stay for long. Not wanting to waste their evening, they went off to see Georges Pitoëff's company in Gorky's *The Lower Depths*. During one of the intervals, Gide and Pitoëff met and got on extremely well. On the spur of the moment, Pitoëff asked Gide to translate *Hamlet* for him. A week or so later, they went back to the Théâtre des Champs-Elysées to see Pitoëff's company in *Uncle Vanya*. After the play, they met up with Pitoëff in a nearby café and Gide agreed to start work on *Hamlet*. About this time another of Gide's English translations, Rabindranath Tagore's *Post Office*, finished just before the outbreak of war, was published as *Amal et la lettre du Roi*.

At Jacques Rivière's, Gide met 'two gentlemen sent to him by Rilke', Jean Strohl, a Swiss biologist, and Erik Klossowski, a Polish painter and critic. Klossowski was anxious to bring his two highly talented sons, Pierre and Balthasar (Balthus, for short), then aged seventeen and fourteen, back to Paris, where they had been born and brought up, so that they might both enter the Vieux Colombier school. Arrangements to this end dragged out over the next year, with Gide providing invaluable, indeed financial help. Pierre Klossowski still speaks of Gide with devotion and gratitude. In the event, neither boy made a career in the theatre, Pierre becoming a writer and Balthus (using his shortened Christian name only) a painter.

Plans for the Vieux Colombier's production of *Saül* were maturing. During early discussions, Gide had begun to think that the history of his relations with the theatre was now taking a better turn. By the first read-through of the play on 28 April, all his old fears had revived. Gide sat there, flanked by Marc and the Petite Dame, who noted his nervousness and irritation. Afterwards, over tea at Martin du Gard's, Gide exploded: 'That's not it at all! Copeau is totally changing the whole tone of the play. He's turning Saul into a senile, dirty old man. The whole moral side of the drama has been missed . . . I'll go to the theatre every day. I won't let Copeau get away with it.' Gide did attend rehearsals every day, but his critical sense was worn down in the end – 'one gets used to actors' ways'.[8] The first night took place on 16 June. Gide, Beth and Marc dined with Loup Mayrisch before the performance – the Petite Dame was at Saint-Clair. Afterwards Copeau came up with, on his arm, 'a wonderful old ruin', who proceeded to express her admiration of the play. 'Imagine my feelings! It was Duse!'[9]

Gide wrote to Martin du Gard, whose enthusiasm for the play had done much to persuade him to get it staged: 'I expected hostility, indignation, protests . . . – there was only incomprehension and boredom.' Of the reviews, Gide remarks: 'The curious thing is that the *mœurs* question [homosexuality] was scarcely raised at all. They preferred not to understand; pretended not to understand; . . . or, quite simply, didn't understand.'[10] *Saül* was given ten performances, to fairly full houses – it was not, therefore, quite the flop that Gide claimed.

The Martin du Gards were staying in an hotel on the island of Porquerolles, near Toulon. In the late afternoon, they were sitting under the pine-trees when they noticed the little boat that made the daily run to the island bringing food supplies. Roger turned his binoculars on to it and was astonished to see Gide, 'standing alone at the prow, his cape floating in the wind, very Lohengrin'.[11] He had arrived a day earlier than expected. Next morning, Gide rose at dawn and

went off at random, tearing across the island like a drunken savage, half naked, scratching himself on arbutus and tamarisk, chasing after butterflies, picking flowers and berries, plunging into every creek to find which was the warmest, jumping from rock to rock and fishing, in the narrow clefts, for seaweed, shells and tiny sea-monsters, which he brought back in his handkerchief. It was past twelve when he reappeared in the hotel dining-room, with sand in his ears and bits of sea-wrack stuck all over his body, laughing, wild-eyed, drunk with light and heat and joy, reciting intoxicatedly Heredia's lines:

Le soleil, sous la mer, mys-té-ri-euse aurore,
Eclaire la forêt des coraux abyssins . . .!¹²

On 3 July, the Petite Dame and Beth arrived to spend a few days with them, before going on to La Bastide. A week later, Gide and Martin du Gard left Porquerolles for the mainland, Gide deciding to stay at Hyères-Plage for a further three weeks. Gide divided his time between bathing, sunbathing and, inappropriately, translating *Hamlet* – transporting himself from a summer's day by 'the blue Mediterranean' to a 'bitter cold' winter's night by the Baltic. He found many of Shakespeare's sentences 'retorses comme l'enfer', 'tricky as the devil'. On 14 July, he finished Act I, admitting defeat. He sent the manuscript off to Georges Pitoëff, expressing regret that he could not go on. *Hamlet* had presented problems that were 'infinitely more insuperable' than *Antony and Cleopatra*.

One can tackle them only by performing veritable verbal acrobatics, dislocating one's brains in the process . . . How, without betraying Shakespeare, without *leaving him behind*, is one to write a French text that is clear, at once easy on the ear and easy to understand (for it is not intended to be read, but to be heard from the stage), and whose superabundant, inconsequent images do not shock too much the French mind's insistence on logic?¹³

This is a perfect summation of the difficulty of translating Shakespeare into French at all, indeed of the incompatibility of the two languages at their characteristic best.

Gide had no more reason to remain in isolation at Hyères-Plage. Beth, on her way back to La Bastide from Saint-Clair, called to collect him. Early next morning, 16 July, a Sunday, they went for a walk and, in a deserted spot by the sea, the child that Beth had wanted for so long was conceived. As her mother put it, with the elegance and charm, at once abstract and sensuous, of which French is pre-eminently capable in these matters, Gide had rediscovered with Elisabeth 'toute la liberté qui favorise les dispositions amoureuses'¹⁴ – a phrase, incidentally, that is well nigh untranslatable, though the words themselves are almost English, the obverse of Gide's problems with *Hamlet*.

The morning after their arrival at La Bastide, Gide and Beth set about doing odd jobs around the farmhouse, taking off squeaky doors and oiling hinges, repairing oil-lamps, etc. In the evening they went over the *Hamlet* translation, Gide reading it aloud, Beth following the English, the Petite Dame comparing both with the versions of François-Victor Hugo and Marcel Schwob. Pitoëff found Gide's version 'very beautiful' and was bitterly disappointed that it would not proceed. 'Perhaps one day you will take it up again,' he wrote. In 1926, he put on *Hamlet* at last, using the old Schwob–Morand version. Gide's Act I was published in the December 1929 number of the review *Echanges* and, in 1930, in a bilingual edition by the Editions de la Tortue.

On other evenings, Gide and his friends read other things: an old favourite, *The Ring and the Book*, by one of Gide's constellation, Browning, then, almost by chance, *The Devil's Disciple*, by Shakespeare's self-appointed rival, Shaw. All three were overcome with admiration and enthusiasm. 'Why doesn't Copeau put it on?' the Petite Dame asked. 'He wouldn't dare to, wouldn't want to,' Gide replied, adding, with prescience, 'I tell you, Copeau is moving more and more towards Catholicism.' The shared passion for English spread beyond reading aloud: they decided to talk only in English during meals. Why, they wondered, had Gide not yet been published in English, when he had already appeared in German, Spanish, Danish and even Japanese? Gide was both indignant and amused.

The Pontigny *décades* had resumed after an interruption of eight years. The title of the *décade littéraire*, which opened on 14 August, was 'Miroir de l'honneur: culture de la fierté par la fiction'. 'I'm no good in this kind of gathering. I hate declarations and am terribly bad at consecutive argument,' Gide told the Petite Dame, who commented: 'He brings neither *amour-propre* nor obstinacy to it. He is so concerned to hear everything that is said, to miss nothing important that he never really manages to gather his thoughts.'[15] Gide was attended by his trio of close women friends, Maria and Elisabeth Van Rysselberghe, and Loup Mayrisch. Also there were Martin du Gard, Jean Schlumberger, Jacques Rivière and Charles Du Bos. There were representatives from Switzerland, Italy, Holland and Germany (Curtius, but not Rilke). Lytton Strachey did not come (though he came the following year), England being represented solely by his sister, Dorothy.

In their first conversation, Gide and Dorothy talked about Marc Allégret, who was also there – Gide had not seen him for six weeks. When she first met Marc, at Cambridge, she did not particularly like him. She felt, she said, that he did not love Gide as much as he should have done. Now she found him 'quite the most exquisite person' there, not excluding Gide himself. He had acquired a quality of grace, over and above natural beauty. 'Now he loves you,' she told Gide. 'Do you think so?' Gide said, sadly. 'I don't know. I daren't believe it. I never ask myself if he does. Anyway, he's delightful [*exquis*] with me – perfect.' Gide went on to tell Dorothy how, some days before, Madeleine had written to him to say that she was giving the gold necklace with an emerald cross to Jean Schlumberger's daughter, Sabine, who was her god-daughter. For Gide, this cross had special significance: it was a present from him, the 'original' of the amethyst cross that Jérôme gives Alissa in *La Porte étroite*. Apparently, Madeleine had wanted to 'dispose' of it while she was still alive, lest it fall into uncaring hands. 'How could she do such a thing? How could she be so cruel?' a distraught Gide asked. 'Either she is quite unaware of my feelings or she doesn't care.' Then, 'with indescribable bitterness', he added: 'Even if I went to see her on her deathbed, she would say: "Go away! You're *disturbing* me!"'[16] But the emerald cross was merely the most cherished item. About the same time Madeleine also gave a small ivory crucifix, a wedding present, to Copeau's daughter Edi. (Eight years later, Edwige Copeau became a Benedictine nun and missionary.) Madeleine gave away other presents from her husband to friends and servants.

On 22 August, two days before the end of the Pontigny *décade*, Elisabeth informed her mother, Gide, Loup Mayrisch and Marc that she believed that 'her wish to have a child had at last been granted', and that the 'miracle' child was undoubtedly Gide's. She seemed 'borne up by extraordinary happiness'. Gide seemed both 'intoxicated with pleasure and disconcerted'. But so, too, are they all, Maria observes, 'happy and confused, absorbed in all the possibilities, all the complications opened up by this reality that was coming to birth'.[17] Gide confided the news to Martin du Gard, now his closest friend/colleague and a man whose discretion he could rely on absolutely. With most of his friends he would have to keep up the story of 'father unknown' in order to protect the feelings of 'Cuverville'. After Pontigny, the Petite Dame drove to Colpach with 'Schnouky' (Andrée Mayrisch); they would be joined, in a few days, by Gide and Beth, who went first to Paris. There Beth saw a doctor, who confirmed that she was pregnant.

Gide and Beth went on to Colpach. Two days later, Whity came over from London to be with her friend. Gide admitted to the Petite Dame how difficult he found it to get used to the idea of his forthcoming fatherhood. He was making progress, however, though he compared the process to forcing open a locked door. 'He is astounded at the quiet efficiency with which Elisabeth is approaching the matter.' There was the problem of her employees at La Bastide: it was decided that the best story would be that she had adopted a child, 'whether they believed it or not'. Loup Mayrisch would be the godmother, Gide the godfather, which would explain his interest in the child. The legal situation was not as simple as Gide had thought. He could not give the child his name, nor even adopt the child before the age of twenty-one and, even then, he would require his wife's consent to do so. (In fact, Gide acknowledged his daughter only after Madeleine's death in 1938.) Then there were the financial arrangements to be made: these would have to be met from his earnings as a writer which, fortunately, were now sufficient, since Madeleine managed all their other income and expenditure. He also intended to go on supporting Marc. Before long, Elisabeth would have to leave La Bastide: Whity agreed to manage the farm in her absence. It was suggested that she spend her last months of pregnancy in Italy, though she would have to return to France for the birth, in order to safeguard the child's French nationality. Gide would not be able to spend much of that time with her: he would have to retreat to Cuverville for most of the winter and work. There was a general feeling among the friends that something very modern was taking place. Loup Mayrisch, the wife of a pillar of Luxembourg industry, even went so far as to declare that 'the institution of marriage is mainly of an economic order and inseparable from the capitalist constitution of society', that marriage suited men much more than women, who were 'much better at doing without it . . . Man's reign is over, something else will come about.' Gide added: 'We are all such exceptions that some new arrangements will have to emerge.' Gide was already imagining his son-to-be: 'the charming smile', the voice, his physique . . .[18] Names were discussed: Gide favoured Nicolas. Not only he, but Elisabeth, too, laughed at the idea that the child might be a girl. The name of Catherine was held in reserve, just in case. The *Journal*, however, reveals a darker side to Gide's feelings in that haven of friendship and liberty: 'Awful days of idleness and listlessness . . . Each day I wake up with a heavy head, duller than ever. Forced to act out a comedy of joy and pleasure in front of the others – while I feel all real joy slowly cooling in my heart.'[19]

A party of scouts arrived and set up camp in the park. Their arrival came as no surprise to Loup Mayrisch – or to Gide. Back in June Gide had asked his friend if she could accommodate, in August, a party of scouts under the orders of Faustin, a close friend of René Michelet's. In the evenings, Gide and Schnouky joined them around the camp fire. When the Petite Dame advised Gide to be careful, he replied: 'What I find so attractive is a sort of sensual gluttony, almost an appeal, that I sense in some boys. That's why I've rarely made a mistake and, so far, avoided scandal.'[20]

On 13 September, Gide left Colpach to spend a week with the Allégrets at La Sapinière, before returning to Paris. Between then and the end of the year he spent more time in Cuverville than in Paris, travelling between the two half-a-dozen times. He arrived in Cuverville to find the house still full, but, over the next few weeks, he worked 'fairly well': he read the proofs for the book of Dostoevsky lectures and for the translation of Blake's *Marriage of Heaven and Hell*. He revised *Corydon* and wrote a preface for it. The visitors left on 7 October and Gide got down to work more seriously: by mid-November, he had written about thirty more pages of *Les Faux-Monnayeurs*. Soon he noticed that Madeleine was, quite unnecessarily, devoting more and more of her time to humble household tasks: 'I don't think she has opened a book during the entire holidays,' he wrote to Martin du Gard, meaning their guests' holidays, not Madeleine's. 'One of these mornings I expect to wake up and see that she has turned into an ant.' More seriously, she 'constantly acts as if I didn't love her any more and I act as if she still did'.[21]

In October, Gide spent six days in Paris, during which he saw the Bussys on their way back to Roquebrune. He spent most of a day alone with Dorothy. The poor woman was as much as ever at sea about the emotional as well as the sexual promiscuity of her soul's idol. What did Marc think about the whole business? Gide: 'Oh, he's so mysterious. It's difficult to guess what he thinks!' Is it just a quite superficial affair, then, in which no one feels anything? Gide: 'Oh, no, not at all!' Later, by letter, Dorothy asked Gide: 'Are you saying good-bye to Marc? Are you looking into the future with Elisabeth?'[22] It is odd that Dorothy Bussy, with her free-thinking background, with Lytton Strachey as her brother, married to a French painter, was not more subtle in her views on human relationships. The fact is that, in various ways and to various degrees, Gide loved and was loved by many people, of both sexes. At this time, he loved Madeleine, Marc, Beth, her mother – even, in a way, Dorothy Bussy, and told her so towards the end of his life, when he felt confident enough that he would not be misunderstood. Of course, Marc did not say what he thought – he probably didn't know himself. He was, in any case, going his own way to some extent – as, clearly, was Gide . . . Of course Gide's relationship with Beth was not 'superficial', but the fact that she was going to bear his child did not mean that either wanted to repeat the experience by the sea at Hyères, still less set up house.

On 18 November, like everyone else, Gide was shocked to hear of the death of Marcel Proust, at the age of fifty-one. Proust had been at death's door for so long that it seemed he might stay there forever. 'Proust died yesterday,' Gide wrote to Dorothy Bussy. 'I saw him again, his face very thin and blue from the cold of the grave. I am very heavy at heart.'[23] The last three volumes of *A la recherche du temps perdu* were to appear in 1923, 1925 and 1927. Five days later, Gide attended the performance of a work by Darius Milhaud based on *Le Retour de l'Enfant prodigue*. Composed in Rio de Janeiro and dedicated to Paul Claudel, whose secretary Milhaud then was, the 'cantata' for five voices and twenty-one instruments was given by the Concerts Wiener, under the composer's baton.

Gide spent Christmas at Cuverville. On 27 December, he left for Paris, where he stayed at the Lutétia for ten days. He spent 'one of the dullest possible evenings' with Marc and 'sa petite amie B.' at the Casino de Paris, 'where everything struck me as frightful. Silliness, vulgarity, bad taste.'[24] 'B.' is clearly the 'Bronja' mentioned in the *Journal* six days later. On 30 December, Gide called on a 'very gloomy' Copeau, who felt abandoned by all his friends, having done everything possible to lose them. Martin du Gard, who had been Copeau's closest friend at one time, saw less and less of him. As much to reassure Copeau as anything else, Gide accepted an invitation to lunch with him *en famille* on New Year's Eve. Afterwards he retired to his room at the Lutétia to rest, but deciding that the Turkish baths would be more relaxing, spent over an hour there. He called on Uncle Charles, then on the Drouins, in Passy. He dined alone in Montparnasse, then called on Paul Laurens and his wife. After an hour with them, he moved on to the Allégrets' – and so ended a rather *mouvementé* New Year's Eve.

On 5 January, Gide called on Loup Mayrisch, who had just arrived at her usual Parisian *pied-à-terre*, the Grand Hôtel, on the boulevard des Capucines. They were joined for lunch by Martin du Gard. Gide propounded his theory that those who dissociated love from sex were more likely to find happiness. Loup Mayrisch very sensibly assured him that she knew of 'dissociaters who weren't at all happy, and the contrary'. She noted, too, that Gide was very anxious that Beth should have a boy. 'If it were a girl, he wouldn't have any idea how to bring her up, how to interest himself in her; he realizes that he hasn't even thought about it . . .'[25] Next day, Gide took RMG off on his first visit to Cuverville. In his *Notes sur André Gide*, Martin du Gard devotes twenty pages[26] to his three days at Cuverville – two of them to the train journey. The account begins at Saint-Lazare, with Gide, who had made the journey hundreds of times, wandering hither and thither, not seeming to know where the ticket office was, how to get on to the platform, the time of departure for the Le Havre train or whether there was a connection at Criquetot. Once on the train, Gide began his '*étrangetés*':

Swathed in an overcoat that he'd thrown across his shoulders, with a furry black hat perched on the top of his head, his arms piled high with books and magazines, with a wild inquisitive gleam in his eye (and that winning, undecided smile, that spuriously natural air that he assumes on such occasions, under the illusion that a free-and-easy manner will enable him to pass unnoticed), he made his way along the train, dragging me behind him along the ice-cold and largely deserted corridors. We did the whole train several times, from the guard's van to the front carriage, and back. He scrutinized each compartment in turn, pausing at those with more passengers in them, trying first one then another, abandoning this one for some mysterious reason, that one on some excuse or other . . .

Throughout the journey, Martin du Gard felt a mingled sense of insecurity and responsibility, 'as if I had charge of a child who was about to commit the most imprudent acts'. At Cuverville he detected similar 'signs of distress' on the face of Gide's wife. She, too, he thought, felt that same 'insecurity' that he had experienced on the train, except that in her case it was a lifetime's experience: 'How can one believe that this timid, sensitive, fearful woman, with her conservative, austere tastes, has ever found the least support in her capricious companion – that perpetual fugitive, with his disconcerting whims and his inability to resist temptation . . .' He notes their 'odd behaviour' to one another, the 'attentive politeness', the 'tender affability', the 'smiling watchfulness', with, underneath it all 'an impenetrable coldness', 'a sharp fall in temperature in the depths'. Martin du Gard describes the 'romantic little park', with its splendid trees, the plants that Gide seems to know and care for individually and the house, with its magnificent panelled drawing-room, with windows on both sides, unused in winter, the study, also unheated and unused, and the dining-room, presided over, from the only three chairs, in front of the blazing fire, by three huge, majestic Siamese cats. Beyond this room lay 'the sanctuary of the mistress of the house': there, hour after hour, Mme Gide toiled away, 'among the heady smells of petrol and beeswax and turpentine. For the tyranny of spit and polish is absolute at Cuverville. Everything that can possibly be polished is mirror-bright. Flagstones, tiled floors and parquets are perilous skating rinks.' Martin du Gard contrasts this with the Villa Montmorency, 'the dust, the unmade bed, the sink full of dirty china'.

At nightfall, on his third day at Cuverville, Gide took Martin du Gard on a long, wet walk to the village. They stopped at a dilapidated thatched cottage. Inside was 'a spindly boy of ten or eleven', doing his homework, a girl, who could be anything from fifteen to twenty-five, and, on a couple of filthy mattresses, three flea-ridden children, the youngest not more than a year old. Gide went up to the boy and stroked his head 'as if he were a little dog' and talked to him about his school work. 'We were just passing, Barnabé, my friend and I . . . and thought we'd pay you a little visit . . .' Afterwards Gide told Martin du Gard that the mother had died of tuberculosis years ago, that the daughter, now six months pregnant, was thought to sleep with the drunken farm-worker father, that, although that man earned a good wage, they never had any money and Madeleine brought them something three times a week.

Gide broached the subject of Elisabeth and her child to Madeleine. What had happened to Valentine, Madeleine's sister, had happened to Elisabeth. She, too, was expecting a child outside wedlock. 'I always thought it was a mistake to raise her without religion,' Madeleine commented, illogically, given Valentine's upbringing. 'And, of course,' she added, 'people will hold you morally responsible.' This was exactly the response Gide wanted. He fully acknowledged this and made it the reason why he would take a particular interest in the matter. He then reminded Madeleine of the happiness that Valentine had found in her two daughters. With a mysteriousness that may have marked an intuitive insight into the truth of the matter, she said: 'Yes, you have a right to that happiness.' Later, she wrote to her husband, saying how she blamed the sin, but felt pity for the sinner, who had been 'the victim of sophistry'.[27] She is clearly blaming her husband, but deliberately refraining from doing so directly, still less inquiring too closely into the extent of that blame.

Gide left Cuverville on 14 January, arriving a few days later at Roquebrune. Reading Dorothy Bussy's account of those ten days, one is surprised that she and Gide were able to stay in the same house for so long. 'I didn't think I'd lose you like that,' Dorothy complained. Uncomprehending as ever of Gide's emotional and sexual complexities, she meant by way of Elisabeth Van Rysselberghe. 'But why must you lose me?' an equally uncomprehending Gide asked. 'Why should my affection for you change? It isn't the kind of affection that changes, since it is without passion, without ardour and leaves no burn.'[28]

Half-way through his stay at Roquebrune, Gide escaped to meet the Petite Dame at Menton station, on her way to join Beth, who was staying in Rapallo. In fact, he travelled with her the 6 or 7 miles across the border to Ventimiglia and returned later that day. She told him how she had written to several women friends telling them the news of Beth's pregnancy and in 'quelle façon exquise' they had all responded. This was in marked contrast with her husband's angry disapproval. On that subject, Gide gave her a letter that he had supposedly written to Jean Schlumberger and which she was to show Théo. In it, Gide admitted part of the moral responsibility for Elisabeth's child on the grounds that when she had told him of her wish to have a child outside marriage he had given her support and encouragement. He intended therefore to give her whatever help he could and would make financial provision for her and the child if necessary.

On 29 January, he left Roquebrune and joined Beth and her mother at the luxurious Hôtel Bristol, Rapallo. He turned up, 'of course', the Petite Dame notes, at a time when he was not expected, tired, looking like a vagabond. Next day, he arrived in the hotel dining-room, 'fresh, dashing, dressed like Lafcadio himself'. He made it quite clear that his stay at Rapallo would depend entirely on whether he was able to work there: *Les Faux-Monnayeurs* had reached a decisive point. In a letter to Martin du Gard, he complained of 'the huge hotel with its uncomfortable luxury and hideousness'. Then there was the noise: trains passing, dogs barking, convent bells at all hours of the day and night, the coughing and snoring of neighbours. He had tried to work, but without much success. He yearned to be alone: he was forced 'to make conversation' just when his mind was on the novel. Moreover, the town was rather less endowed with 'amusements' than he had hoped.[29] After two weeks, he had had enough and took himself off to Portofino. There he found quiet, but no heating. A few days later, he was back at the Hôtel Bristol.

To ensure the French nationality of her child, Beth would return to France in time for the birth. Gide considered it unwise to be with her then but did not want her to travel alone. They therefore left Rapallo on 24 February for Annecy, a lakeside town in the Haute-Savoie. There they passed the time, when Gide was not working or walking, reading English together: *The Merry Wives of Windsor*, Goldsmith's *The Vicar of Wakefield* and Keats's 'Endymion'. Alone, Gide continued to read George Eliot's *Middlemarch*, 'with an admiration so keen,' he wrote to Dorothy Bussy, 'that it almost makes me look with hostility at my *Faux-Monnayeurs* – I can now see only its thinness and "deficiencies" [in English].'[30] Gide spent ten days with Beth at Annecy, then returned to Paris, where he spent another three before going on to Cuverville.

Earlier in the year, Gide had been invited by Paul Desjardins to join him on a semi-official visit to Morocco as guest of Marshal Lyautey, the senior administrator of the French protectorate. At the time, he had declined, but, after seeing Desjardins in Paris, had changed his mind: apparently, the redoubtable Lyautey had expressed a particular wish that Gide join the party. On 24 March, the Petite Dame drove Gide to the Gare de Lyon, where they met Martin du Gard and had dinner. Later, they joined up with Gide's fellow-guests on the Moroccan trip: Desjardins, Pierre Hamp, a novelist of working-class life, whom Gide did not particularly care for, and Henry Bidou, a critic and historian. The ship left Marseille next day, putting into Tangier three days later. It was Gide's first visit to Morocco, now a French protectorate. Despite 'tremendous joy at being back on Arab soil', Gide felt some disappointment. He soon became irritated by his companions' unwillingness to expose themselves to the alien. Hamp, ever ready to protest at the trials and tribulations inflicted on the working class, could not conceal his impatience with 'Muslim nonchalance', with people who 'do damn all'; he seemed afraid to make contact with the local people, to sit down in a Moorish café and eat Moroccan cakes.

The following day, the ship took them on to Casablanca. From there the party went inland to Marrakesh, where Gide had his first 'adventure'. In a café he caught the eye of the younger of two impeccably well-mannered Arabs. He met up with the youth later, in the street, and was taken by him to a walled garden, scented with orange blossoms. A few Arabs were walking about. It was raining lightly. Nevertheless, they sat down on a damp bench and the boy let Gide take his hand. After a while, it rained more heavily and they left. Another day, Gide got talking to a youth with 'marvellous lips' and the two ended up in a particularly sordid 'Jewish bathhouse'. This time Gide was luckier: 'an admirable body and most accommodating'. Back in Casablanca, Gide met up with Loup Mayrisch, who had arranged to join the party later. They then drove on to Rabat, where, next day, the French visitors were Lyautey's guests at a dinner. On 15 April, Desjardins and his friends joined their home-bound ship. Gide and Loup Mayrisch had decided to travel by car to Oran, where they would catch a boat to Marseille. On the way, they stopped off at Fez, where they moved into the French official residence. Over the next few days, Gide would be receiving a telegram from Annecy. This duly arrived, announcing the birth of a daughter on 18 April. The child was registered under the name of Catherine Elisabeth Van Rysselberghe. Gide's reactions were carefully observed and noted by Loup Mayrisch, who passed them on to her friend for inclusion in her *Cahiers*: 'Great disappointment at first that it was a girl; complete and utter confusion in the face of this unexpected thing . . . visibly disconcerted, so much so that he doesn't really know what he is saying. The devil has played a trick on him . . .'[31] The two parted in Marseille. Gide was back in Paris by 21

April – he had decided that it would be unwise to go straight to Annecy. He spent a few days with Marc then, on 26 April, went on to Cuverville, where he set to work correcting the proofs of *Corydon, Si le grain ne meurt* and his Dostoevsky book.

During his absence, the attacks by right-wing critics had resumed. Using Gide as a pretext, Henri Béraud launched a scurrilous and quite absurd attack on the *NRF*, 'not a little chapel, but a little bank, for they are much richer in cash than in faith'. This group of 'clergymen' and *'fils à papa'* ('rich kids'), these 'Latter-day Saints', with 'their long faces, their Bibles, their sermonizing and their sobriety' have banished all laughter and made sure that 'literature goes to bed at ten'.[32] In fact, the *NRF* was, if anything, more and more Catholic in its religious allegiance (Jacques Rivière, its editorial director, was a Catholic) and its only (ex-) 'Huguenots' were Jean Schlumberger and Gide.

After the birth, Beth, the baby Catherine and the Petite Dame had left Annecy for Talloires, a small resort also on Lake Annecy. On the morning of 17 May, they were sitting in brilliant sunshine on the lakeside. Beth was testing her mother on a Keats poem that she had learnt by heart. They could see the boat from Annecy appearing. 'Just think, one of these days we'll be here waiting for Bypeed,' said Beth. 'But no, he's bound to come when least expected.' ('Bypeed', from *bipède*, biped, was the Van Rysselberghes' nickname for Gide, deriving from his love of walking.) That very moment, Beth caught sight of two figures standing on the ship's prow. Even at that distance, she was certain that they were Gide and Marc. They ran down to the landing-stage. It was a strange, moving, but quite unsolemn reunion. They all went in to look at the baby, who was lying in her cot on the large covered terrace in front of their room. Gide insisted on seeing the baby alone. He then unpacked the many presents that he had brought back from Morocco: a necklace, a little djellaba, sandals, tiny green boots, an amulet, etc. Over the next few days, he paid close attention to the child, watching her being bathed, weighed, put to sleep. Once, he gently moved his hand over the child's head and said: 'I would so much like her to be intelligent, yet we're already happy that she has five fingers on each hand!'[33]

He returned to Paris on 20 May. A few days later, the Bussys arrived on their way back to London. He saw Dorothy briefly, with the usual emotional mismatch. 'Yes, our meeting – or rather our separation – in Paris left me with a very sad heart and eyes too easily filled with tears,' Dorothy wrote.[34] Meanwhile, however, there was one gleam of light on the horizon: Alfred Knopf had finally agreed to publish her translation of *La Porte étroite*. Thus encouraged, Dorothy went back to work on *Les Caves du Vatican*, which she had abandoned dispiritedly.

It had finally been decided that the people of Brignoles would be given the version of the 'adopted child'. It was important therefore that Beth return to La Bastide a few months before Catherine made her appearance. So, on 17 June, Beth left Catherine with her grandmother and a nurse at Saint-Martin-Vésubie, a small mountain township 30 miles north of Nice. This had the advantage of being accessible for Beth from Brignoles, yet far enough away to avoid any unwanted contact between the two places. Beth then left for La Bastide, to resume her management of the farm. Gide arrived at Saint-Martin a few days later. He set to work on *Les Faux-Monnayeurs* – as so often, a slow painful process. At night he slept badly, then, during the day, suffered from 'incomprehensible torpor'. Partly to tire himself, he would sometimes get up at dawn and go out for long hikes in the mountains, following flocks of sheep in the hope of meeting the shepherd boy. Occasionally, his perseverance paid off, there was an 'adventure' and he came back, glowing with health and ready to work.

In July, Gide set off to spend a couple of weeks at Hyères. As always, swimming and sun-bathing soon brought him back to the peak of physical and mental wellbeing. He was then joined by Beth and André Allégret and the three went off on a short visit to Corsica. From Vizzavone, they set out on an exhausting climb of Monte d'Oro, refreshing themselves in deep pools at the foot of waterfalls. 'Ah!' Gide exclaims. 'I felt less young at twenty!'

The title of the 1923 *décade* was 'Le Trésor poétique réservé, ou de l'Intraduisible', itself verging on the untranslatable. (Let us say, 'Poetry as a private treasure, or the untranslatable'.) The French contingent was much as before. The German-speaking lands were represented by Heinrich Mann and Rudolph Kassner – Rilke had again declined. From England, Dorothy Bussy had persuaded her brother, Lytton Strachey, to accompany her. Oddly, for someone not noted for his lack of opinions and possessing excellent French, he contributed very little to the discussions, other than witty epigrams delivered in his 'bleating falsetto'. The New World was represented by Gide's old friend from Foyer Franco-Belge days, Edith Wharton. On the last day, Marc arrived and they set out that evening for La Bastide. Beth and the baby had arrived on 19 August, with a new nurse, who knew nothing about the situation. The local people had accepted the official version of Catherine's provenance (adoption) without question.

On 4 September, after two days at La Bastide, Gide and Marc set sail for Tunis. There is little information about their four weeks' stay in Tunisia. After his return to Cuverville, Gide wrote to Dorothy Bussy, of all people, that he had come back 'replete with sun, heat and sensuality'. He is all praise for Marc: his kindness 'did not falter a single day, a single hour. Unadulterated bliss.'[35] This, knowing Gide, did not mean that they confined their attentions to one another.

Back in Cuverville, Gide found the garden devastated by a cyclone that had struck the week before. A dozen of the oldest trees near the house had been uprooted or blown over, in addition to several of the beech-trees bordering the avenue and apple-trees in the orchard. He had not seen Cuverville since May, or Madeleine since June, but things fell back into place soon enough. They started reading aloud Hawthorne's *The Scarlet Letter*; he read Browning and Marvell, Logan Pearsall Smith's *History of the English Language*, William James's *Psychology* and Bossuet's *Histoire des Variations*; but most of his time was taken up dealing with neglected correspondence. The 'Cuverville mood', too, was not slow to return: 'Some days, at certain moments, I completely lose all sense of reality. It is as if, at the slightest wrong step, I shall pass through to the other side of the scenery.'[36]

On 16 October, he left for Paris and the Lutétia, returning twice more to Cuverville before Christmas. He saw the Petite Dame on her way back from Colpach to Saint-Clair. During her stay in Paris, she received a letter from her husband, who, on a visit to La Bastide, had seen his granddaughter for the first time. 'There is no point trying to conceal the child's paternity,' he wrote. 'It is written all too clearly over every feature of that little face. I had my suspicions: now I'm sure.' Gide was highly amused that Catherine already resembled him so much. He felt sure that Théo would not abuse the truth and gave the Petite Dame *carte blanche* to tell him whatever she thought would be for the best. She wrote back to her husband saying how relieved everybody was that he had learnt the truth, but she felt sure that he would understand the importance of not letting it spread any more widely.[37]

By the time of his second stay in Paris, Gide was back at the Villa Montmorency. Marc was living there and so, too, was the eighteen-year-old Pierre Klossowski. Over the previous two weeks, the correspondence between Gide and Rilke, who was acting as an intermediary on behalf of the boy's parents, had increased in frequency. Could Gide find somewhere for the young man to live? What studies should he undertake? How much allowance would he need to live on? Gide was lavish in help and advice.

He put the boy up at the Villa, then took him off for a week at Cuverville. On their return to Paris, he arranged for Pierre to use a two-roomed apartment on the boulevard Saint-Michel, overlooking the Luxembourg, belonging to a friend, the writer André Rouveyre. He provided sheets and blankets, arranged with the concierge to have the flat cleaned every morning and kept in constant touch with him. Pierre Klossowski stayed there for five months. Gide also introduced him to a number of friends, so that the boy would not be left too much on his own, and advised him to complete his education, rather than seek some badly paid work. As a result, he became a full-time student at the Lycée Janson-de-Sailly. Gide was also in correspondence with the boy's mother, Balladine Klossowska. Some weeks later, her younger son, Balthus, arrived in Paris, followed in May by Madame Klossowska herself.

Earlier in the year, Gide had been subjected to a scurrilous, disreputable and quite indefensible attack from the journalist Henri Béraud. In the 1 November number of the *Revue universelle*, a far more formidable enemy, enri Massis, turned the full force of his attack on Gide. The article, 'André Gide et Dostoïevski', was ostensibly a review of Gide's lectures. A second article, 'La Confession d'André Gide', appeared in the 15 November number. Massis declared that he had no intention of attacking Gide on the grounds of immorality. This was to be a trial for heresy: Gide was to be attacked as a Protestant, as a thinker who, by placing value upon individual idiosyncrasy, on individual witness, was undermining theological order and authority. For Massis, Gide was using Dostoevsky to preach the diversity, the polymorphism of truth, a kind of spiritual anarchy, while the truth could only be the Truth, a God-given unity. Because Gide was using his influence in this direction, he was a serious moral danger to an already disintegrating Europe, to *Latin* civilization, represented at its peak by the Church, Roman *and* universal. These attacks did have one effect that was not anticipated by either Gide or his critics: the sales of all Gide's books suddenly increased. Within weeks, *Les Nourritures terrestres*, *Les Caves du Vatican* and *Le Retour de l'Enfant prodigue* were out of print.

Massis knew that there was worse to come from Gide's pen. His November articles were, in a sense, pre-emptive strikes. Another tactic was tried: Jacques Maritain arrived at the Villa Montmorency, by appointment, charged with the task of persuading Gide not to publish *Corydon* or, failing that, at least to postpone publication. Professor at the Institut Catholique in Paris, Maritain was already, at forty-one, one of France's leading theologians. He is usually described as a 'neo-Thomist', but the 'neo-' represents very little compromise with the modern world. He was a convert from Protestantism and therefore a peculiarly suitable advocate to confront Gide. Martin du Gard urged Gide to write down an account of their interview as soon as Maritain had left: it occupies three pages of the *Journal*.[38] Gide took an instant dislike to his visitor's way of holding his head and body, 'the clerical unction of his gestures and voice'. Maritain came straight to the point: he had come to ask Gide not to publish 'a certain book'. Gide replied that he had no intention of defending his course of action, but that there were no reasons that Maritain could adduce not to publish that he had not himself considered beforehand; that ten years before, he had read the first two chapters to a friend (Marcel Drouin) and, on his advice, had put the book to one side. In the end, however, he had come to the conclusion that it had to be written, that it was his duty to write it. The heritage of his Protestantism was that he hated lies: Catholics could not understand that. Maritain asked Gide whether he did not think that the truth, which he claimed was contained in his book, could be dangerous. No, Gide replied, if he did think that, he would not publish it. Lies, however, are dangerous. 'And don't you think that it could be dangerous for you to say so?' It was a question Gide refused to consider. Maritain said how concerned he was for the salvation of his soul. 'I can see,' Gide replied, smiling, 'that you are much more concerned about the salvation of my soul than I am myself.' Maritain tried a last throw: he asked Gide to pray to Christ and ask him 'directly' if he was doing the right thing in publishing the book. Would Gide promise to do that when he was alone? 'No,' Gide replied. 'I have lived too long, too intimately, with the thought of Christ, to agree to call him today as one might call someone on the telephone.'

A week later, Gide left Paris to spend Christmas at Cuverville. On 26 December, he wrote to Dorothy Bussy: 'This time, silence = work. I have shut myself away with my characters and my dog in the big bedroom over the kitchen . . . and tried to make the inner voices prevail over all the noises of the house.'[39] Next day, Jacques Rivière came to spend two days and Gide read to him the first seventeen chapters of *Les Faux-Monnayeurs*.

On 11 January, Gide returned to Paris to attend rehearsals of *Amal et la lettre du Roi*, the translation that he had made in 1914 of Tagore's *Post Office*, for a Vieux Colombier production that, as we shall see, was not to take place. Apart from two short visits to Cuverville, Gide spent the next nine weeks in Paris. Marc, now a student at one of the *grandes écoles*, the Ecole des Sciences Politiques, known colloquially as 'Sciences Po', was living with him at the Villa. Much of the time they would quietly work away, Gide in the drawing-room, Marc in the 'gallery'. 'Knowing that he is working near me,' Gide wrote to Dorothy Bussy, 'gives me moments of perfect happiness.'[40]

On 14 March, Gide left for six weeks in the South, the first two at Beth's farm. The following day, the Petite Dame, who was at Saint-Clair, went over to Hyères, to collect Martin du Gard, who was on holiday there. Gide had already arrived that morning; also there was Beth's English friend, Whity. In his *Journal*, Martin du Gard describes his three days there, the company and the beautiful setting: 'La Bastide is a farm, with a small house attached, on a hillside, overlooked by the wooded hill that follows the valley of the Carami. Four splendid plane-trees rise above the kitchen garden, which goes right up to the windows of the house.' He has nothing but admiration for the life that Beth has made for herself. She was a genuine farmer, with no trace of play-acting, working every day, side by side with her tenant farmers. What she had done was the result, not of a 'feminist or rebellious gesture', but of a 'serene decision' that had brought her, with motherhood, perfect satisfaction. RMG was amused by Gide's manner of observing his daughter, like an entomologist observing some rare specimen that had cost him dear in the capturing.[41] During those few days, Gide read aloud several extracts from *Les Faux-Monnayeurs*. With a sudden lurch into post-modernist 'self-referentiality', the Petite Dame comments: Gide 'is writing a working journal of *Les Faux-Monnayeurs*. Edouard [the novelist character] is keeping another; there is something rather breathtaking at the idea that I, too, can take notes about it. It's a telescoping, a complication worthy of the subject! For him, the whole of this game is only a reflection of sincerity. However contorted it may seem, his sole aim is to show things as they really are.'[42] After two weeks, Gide left La Bastide to spend a few days with the Raverats at Vence. From there he went on to Roquebrune, staying most of April at the Bussys', which he hoped to find less distracting, more conducive to work.

On 28 April Gide left for Paris. At the Villa, life with Marc was not to be as idyllic as it had been earlier in the year. Marc had become involved in running a more or less avant-garde theatre group, 'Les Soirées de Paris'. This was the brain-child of the Comte Etienne de Beaumont, a rich patron of the arts and, in January, rehearsals for the opening show had begun in his townhouse in the rue Duroc. Marc Allégret soon got taken on as the count's secretary, which turned out to be an excellent apprenticeship in human organization and diplomacy. Beaumont then took a short lease on a music-hall in Montmartre, the Cigalle, brought up to date by a new curtain designed by Picasso. The enterprise began well, with an interesting mixture in the audience of the fashionable and the youthful avant-garde. Nor was there any shortage of artistic talent. The programmes, which had a strong emphasis on ballet, with Leonid Massine as choreographer, included *Gigue*, with music by Bach and Handel, and costumes by Derain; *Salade*, with music by Darius Milhaud and costumes by Braque; and *Mercure*, with music by Satie and costumes by Picasso. A more avant-garde contribution was *Mouchoir de nuages*, a 'tragedy in fifteen acts', none lasting longer than three minutes, by the chief Dadaist, Tristan Tzara. Gide, who at first had welcomed Marc's initiative, soon became concerned about how much of the boy's time and energy it was taking up. His studies would surely suffer – and Gide himself was seeing less and less of him. Gide saw the Beaumont circle as 'dubious, snobbish', 'a deplorable example'.[43] Before long, the whole enterprise began to fall apart, with desertions (Cocteau), dissensions (the split in the Dadaists and the founding of the Surrealist group under André Breton) and falling box-office receipts.

One day, Marc had to vacate the Villa. Madeleine was making one of her ever rarer visits to Paris: her nephew Jacques Drouin, Marcel's younger son, was being confirmed. On the day, a Sunday, she let both maids have the morning off. When they showed no sign of returning in time to serve lunch, she decided to stay and serve it herself. Half-way through the meal Gide remembered that she was supposed to have gone to the confirmation service. 'Yes,' she said, 'but there wasn't time, so I prayed alone.' 'But that isn't the same at all!' he expostulated. 'No,' came the blank reply, 'it wasn't the same.'[44] Gide recounted this incident over another lunch at the Schlumbergers', where the Petite Dame was staying. With tears in his eyes, he explained that Madeleine was so used to being alone that she had become quite incapable of a normal, social existence; every problem, every obstacle, assumed gigantic proportions, leaving her resigned in advance to failure.

At this time, Gide was in an anxious, uneasy mood on another account: the publication date of *Corydon* was approaching. He had warned Madeleine, indirectly, that the book that was about to come out might make him a social outcast. 'The idea of your great journey [to Africa] frightened me enough already,' she replied, 'but this frightens me much more.' As Gide said goodbye to her at Saint-Lazare, she said: 'You know, whatever happens, I'll be with you.'[45] Marc returned to the Villa, the two friends had a long talk and all Gide's fears about him were dissipated. 'I saw Marc again yesterday,' he wrote to Dorothy Bussy. 'I hadn't seen him for ten days and thought I'd lost him, perhaps forever. He came back to me more exquisite than ever, dismissing to the world of chimeras the hideous fantasies created by my imagination.'[46]

'*Corydon* emerged from its cage last Friday,' Gide wrote to Dorothy Bussy on 25 June.[47] As so often with Gide's works, the idea of *Corydon* had been with him a long time. As early as 1895 he was collecting press cuttings in a file labelled 'Pédérastie' for use in a work on the subject. By 1908, he was writing what were to become the first two dialogues of *Corydon*. In 1911, he placed his work on 'record' by having what he had already written – the first two dialogues and part of a third – printed privately (and anonymously) in a very small edition. However, the question of Madeleine's reaction was still the major stumbling-block to publication: the dozen or so copies remained locked in a drawer. At the end of the war, Gide's relationship with Marc Allégret gave an altogether new, more personal impetus to the subject and, by January 1918, the first full-length version of the book was written. Moreover, relations with Madeleine, especially after the burning of the letters, were now such that publication could at last be contemplated. Yet Gide still hesitated. He hit on a compromise solution: on 5 March 1920, a limited (and, again, anonymous) edition of twenty-one copies was printed and distributed among friends. In this way, the existence of the book became well known before it was available to the general public and Gide could assess the likely reaction to publication. Then, finally, in 1924, *Corydon* 'came out'.

The work consists of 'four Socratic dialogues', but unlike, say, *The Symposium*, Plato's dialogue on the subject, there are only two speakers. It is 'the year 190–', soon after a 'scandalous trial' (an oblique reference to the Eulenburg scandal of 1907, in which the homosexual activities of a number of high-ranking German officials and a French diplomat were exposed). The conversation in cafés and salons is of little else. The first-person narrator (and as such, by the fictional game invoked, to be identified with the author, 'André Gide'), unsympathetic to homosexuality, but anxious to be better informed on the subject, calls on an old schoolfriend, Corydon, whom he has not seen for ten years – since, in fact, Corydon publicly acknowledged his sexual nature. The classically educated public of the time would know that Corydon was a shepherd, celebrated both by Theocritus and Virgil for his love of the handsome youth Alexis. The use of the name also removes any naturalistic dimension to the dialogues, stressing their artificial literary form and thus enabling Gide to concentrate on the arguments. By making the first-person narrator Corydon's opponent, the conventional, *bien pensant* heterosexual, Gide not only avoids too automatic, too total an identification between Corydon and himself, but also allows an additional dimension of irony: Corydon can win the argument, convincing the reader, if not his interlocutor, even as reported by his opponent, while the narrator can condemn himself out of his own mouth. The irony is at work from the outset. On entering Corydon's apartment, the visitor is surprised by its 'correct' style; it even 'affected a certain austerity'. He looks around in vain for the expected 'signs of effeminacy'. True, there is a large reproduction on the desk of Michelangelo's *Creation of Man*, with its naked figure of Adam, but there is nothing specifically homosexual about that. More surprising, the visitor thinks, is the photograph of an old white-bearded gentleman, whom he happens to know is Walt Whitman – surprising, since as everyone knows since Bazalgette's recent biography, Whitman was not the homosexual that some had rumoured him to be. The visitor asks Corydon how he now views Whitman in the light of Bazalgette's work. Corydon replies that one's view of Whitman should be unaffected by his sexual orientation, but, as a matter of fact, Bazalgette has deliberately distorted the truth. In his translation of the work, for example, he translates 'love' as '*affection*' or '*amitié*' (friendship), 'sweet' as '*pur*', where the love-object is clearly male, and, where ambiguity is just possible in English, as in the word 'friend', it is feminized as '*amie*'. Bazalgette's view of Whitman is based on the following syllogism: homosexuality is unnatural; Whitman is the most perfect representative in literature of the natural man; therefore Whitman was not a homosexual. Corydon, who is writing a *Defence of Pederasty*, believes, on the contrary, that homosexuality is perfectly 'natural'. 'And you dare to publish such a thing?' 'No,' Corydon admits, 'I daren't.' Thus Gide introduces one of his favourite technical devices: within André Gide's *Corydon*, a defence of pederasty, finally published after much hesitation, the character Corydon is writing a *Defence of Pederasty* that he dare not, for the time being, publish. The book we are reading is reduced to the status of mere talk about the 'real' book, placed *en abyme*, which, of course, is actually a fiction.

'You're all the same,' the visitor retorts, on hearing that the book is not to be published, and accuses Corydon of moral cowardice. Corydon admits that homosexuals lack (willing) martyrs, though there are plenty of 'unwilling' victims. By way of excusing his own 'cowardice', he cites the feelings of his mother and the situation of an as yet unmarried sister – equivalent to Gide's own wish not to expose Madeleine to any more pain than he could help. For the rest of the first 'dialogue', Corydon recounts his own slow, painful discovery of the nature of his sexuality: inability to participate in the escapades of his fellow medical students, 'almost religious' devotion to a young woman he hoped to marry, the approaches made to him by his fiancée's young brother, Alexis, which, in his lack of self-knowledge, he spurned, the boy's suicide, etc.

On successive days, Corydon plans to discuss homosexuality from three main points of view: natural history; history, literature and the arts; sociology and ethics. Armed with quotations from Montaigne and Pascal, Corydon is anxious to draw a distinction between nature and custom: much of what we regard as 'natural' behaviour is socially acquired. The social pressures to conform to heterosexual behaviour are so strong in our society that it is surprising that homosexuality survives at all: 'Everything teaches hetero-sexuality, everything urges it upon us, everything provokes us to it: plays, books, newspapers, the flaunted example of elders . . .'[48] If, despite all this, a young man does end up with homosexual tendencies, society concludes that he must have been subject to some undesirable influence, rather than admit the naturalness of that tendency. The truth is that homosexuality has necessarily existed in every human society; all that changes is the way society encourages, tolerates or represses it.

If proof were needed of the 'naturalness' of homosexual behaviour, one need only turn to the animal kingdom. Most of the second dialogue is taken up with a long, complicated discussion of homosexuality among animals, with much citation of scientific authorities. It is largely the result of a disparity between the super-abundance, not only of males over females in many species, but also of male sexual energy and the seasonal sexual instincts of the female. The lack of interest shown by the female in sex for most of her existence leaves males to satisfy their sexual demands with each other, thus diverting sex from a blind imperative of the species to individual play. In the human being, as the sexual desire becomes less and less seasonal in the female, heterosexuality, too, takes on the form of play – and there is an accompanying growth of female homosexuality.

The third dialogue concerns the greater prevalence of homosexuality, not only in those civilizations most noted for their artistic excellence (fifth-century Athens, Renaissance Florence, Elizabethan and Jacobean England, etc.), but also in those societies that exalted the 'manly', soldierly virtues (Sparta, imperial Rome, modern Germany). Again a range of authorities is cited: Goethe on *Knabenliebe* ('boy love'), Diodorus Siculus, Aristotle, etc.

The fourth dialogue brings us to modern society, with a certain recapitulation of arguments expounded earlier. Léon Blum's *Du mariage* is discussed: his solution to the problem of excessive male sexual energy is the promotion of prostitution and adultery. This brings on an anti-semitic attack on Blum from the narrator: the Jew as agent of moral and social disintegration. Corydon, too, deplores Blum's programme and prefers homosexuality, especially pederasty, as a far more moral course – and one, incidentally, that maintains respect for women. The adolescent male's sexual instincts are in a 'floating', unfocused state; how much better for him to be initiated into adulthood by an older friend, who can also act as a guide and educator, than by a prostitute or married woman.

It is difficult, at this remove in time, and more difficult the younger one is, to comprehend why this patently sincere, scrupulously researched and argued defence of homosexuality so horrified 'well-thinking' minds – and made Gide's friends so fearful for his survival in what, in the 1920s, must have been one of the most liberal milieux on earth. Ironically, in a way, we owe this first serious study of homosexuality by a self-confessed homosexual to a mind stubbornly loyal to all that is most admirable in the Protestant ethic, a burning desire to vindicate the truth as one sees it, an abhorrence of lies and hypocrisy. In recent years, the public had become aware of the existence of sexual practices that it had once preferred to ignore, or remain ignorant of. The general awareness of sex and of its fundamental importance in human life was due as much to Freud as to any other single writer, but there was also a plethora of less well-known works on sexual theory and practice. Where they concerned homosexuality, however, they were written 'from the outside' by doctors and other 'professionals', who, coming into contact only with 'pathological' cases, tended to see homosexuality in general as pathological.

Gide was particularly concerned that homosexuality might be narrowly identified with Magnus Hirschfeld's notion of *sexuelle Zwischenstufen*, or intermediary state of sexuality *between* male and female. In a passage from the *Feuillets*, or 'detached pages',[49] written in 1918 and headed '*Corydon*', Gide tries to work out his own taxonomy of homosexuals: *pederasts* ('of whom I am one') love young boys; *sodomites* address their desires to mature men; *inverts* assume the woman's role when making love and desire to be possessed. While noting that the three categories 'are not always distinct' and admitting the inadequacy of his treatment of both 'sodomites' (to his surprise, they have turned out to be 'much more numerous' than he had supposed at first) and 'inverts' (whom he has 'hardly frequented at all'), he is still trying to understand homosexuality in the terms inherited from the 'human sciences'. The pederast may seem, *to some extent*, to be an identifiable category. The pederast's sexual attraction is for 'young boys' ('jeunes garçons'), says Gide. This is ambiguous. Gide himself was drawn sexually to adolescent boys, that is, boys who were already biologically men. At first sight, these words could be interpreted to include male children – this, not without its own ambiguities, is what we usually call paedophilia. Gide was a great lover of children and was immensely successful with them, but he was not, as far as we know, sexually attracted to them, or, at least, could not admit of such attraction, still less act on it. As for the other two categories, they are a classificatory nonsense. 'Sodomites' here are not those who practise anal penetration, 'actively' or 'passively' (many, perhaps most, doing both), but those who desire 'mature men'; inverts those who want to be penetrated anally. According to these definitions, almost all 'inverts' would also be 'sodomites' – and a very large proportion of 'sodomites' would also be 'inverts'. In view of this terminological and categorial confusion, it is odd that Gide should go on to claim that each category usually feels for the others 'a profound disgust . . . accompanied by a retribution that in no way yields to that which you (heterosexuals) fiercely show to all three'. The final perfidy is when he turns on the poor 'inverts', declaring that 'it has always seemed to me that they alone deserved the reproach of moral and intellectual defamation, and were guilty of some of the accusations levelled at all homosexuals' – this, though he claims to have hardly 'frequented' them at all. This is Gide at his weakest. Again, in a footnote to the 1922 preface, Gide states that *Corydon* is not concerned with 'cases of inversion, effeminacy, sodomy' and admits that this is one of its great shortcomings.[50] The subject of *Corydon* is 'pederasty', 'Greek love', in which neither party is effeminate. If it were the case that *Corydon* was solely about 'pederasty', as against other forms of homosexuality, this would have been more than a 'shortcoming'. It would have lacked any relevance to most homosexuals and would have concerned a form of homosexuality that, in its narrow sense, had a declining future. It is difficult to imagine today, with our 'youth culture' and 'peer-group' pressure, many male 'teenagers' placing their bodies and minds at the disposal of older men with a view to their intellectual, artistic, moral, sexual education – indeed, the sexual might be the least difficult hurdle. By purporting to be dealing only with pederastic homosexuality, associating it with the manly virtues and artistic excellence, *Corydon* is not simply ignoring other forms of homosexuality, it is actually excluding them. By claiming that the pederast, far from being effeminate, presents the zenith of maleness, Gide is justifying homosexuality in the terms of a largely heterosexual society and therefore, by implication, lining up with that society against other homosexuals.

Because *Corydon* is not a treatise, in which a clear definition of terms might be regarded as essential, but takes the form of a dialogue between two men, there is a natural slipping and sliding of terminology. Gide uses the older '*uranien*' (uranian) and the newer '*homosexuel*' more or less interchangeably. By *pédéraste* Gide usually means an adult male lover of adolescent boys but, for the French reader, this term, too, was synonymous with 'homosexual', being its current, colloquial equivalent. Until fairly recently all homosexuals were referred to as '*pédérastes*' – '*pédés*', for short, with a touch of contempt. (The term has now dropped out of use and been replaced, under the hegemony of American gay culture, by the anglicism *gai*.) This terminological confusion makes possible a reading of *Corydon* that is more persuasive, because closer to the truth of the situation, than Gide intended.

This certainly accounts for *Corydon*'s success with the more or less homosexual public. Most of those reading it would be less affected by the detailed argument than by the sheer fact of someone of Gide's literary standing writing and publishing, under the imprint of the *NRF*, a book that claimed a place for them, not only as part of nature, but also at the centre of man's greatest achievements. This is borne out in the hundreds of letters that Gide received over the years from readers of *Corydon*. It is why, too, writing near the end of his creative life, in Tunis, in 1942, Gide noted in his *Journal*: '*Corydon* is still, for me, the most important of my books.' It was a view that none of Gide's friends or admirers could comprehend. Klaus Mann, for example, son of Thomas, homosexual and friend of Gide, writes: 'If I had to sacrifice one of Gide's major works, I would choose *Corydon*, without hesitation.'[51] Gide's friends did not need *Corydon* – so they read it as a text and found it wanting. But it was not written for them. Even as early as 1918, Gide noted that he no longer felt any need to write it. As far as he himself was concerned, he had found 'a practical solution', the 'problem' no longer tormented him. If he went on writing it, 'out of season', it was because he believed that it might be of service to others. By 'important', Gide did not mean greatest, best, most finely written. He goes on to say that it is the book that, if he were to rewrite it, he would change most. It was, in fact, 'the least successful', but it was 'the one that it was most important to pull off'.[52] All books are acts in the world as well as texts with a literary textuality. Works like *Corydon*, while necessarily 'texts', are above all 'acts', which explains why *Corydon*, for all its faults as text, had such an impact as act –

and why it was so commercially successful. Still fearful of the public's response, Gide sent out no review or complimentary copies, and copies were sent to bookshops only on request. He expected abuse, but he did not intend to invite it. Despite this, 3,000 copies were sold in the first few weeks. Before many weeks had passed, the first edition (5,500 copies, Gide's largest initial print-run so far) was almost exhausted and, in August, a new impression, of 8,000 copies, was printed. A number of subsequent editions and reprints followed over the years.

One of the earliest responses to *Corydon* came out in the form, not of a letter, but of a book. Exactly twenty days after publication, *L'Anti-Corydon*, by a 'Docteur François Nazier', a friend of Gide's old Catholic enemy Henri Béraud, appeared. Hearing that it had been written in three days, Gide commented that if Nazier had spent as much time reading *Corydon* attentively, he would not have published his book. Of course, polemicists like Nazier are interested in making their own points, not in understanding their opponents' but, when one considers the length of time it took to write and publish *Corydon*, Nazier's three days in the writing and the Editions du Siècle's further seventeen days in bringing to press a book of 20,000 words, two-thirds the length of *Corydon* itself, one is caught between disbelief and hilarity.

Eventually, letters arrived from friends and acquaintances, usually mentioning that they had not received a complimentary copy – and had gone out and bought one. One of the first was from François Mauriac, thanking Gide for sending him *Incidences*, a new collection of essays, and a new edition of *Souvenirs de la cour d'assises*. 'I have read the other one, too – the one you didn't send me – what can I say?' Always the 'liberal' Catholic – and, at that time, there seemed to be few of them – blame is tempered by compassion. 'If there existed only desperate homosexuals, on the verge of suicide, I could see the need to show them that there is nothing in nature that is not natural and that it may be good to accustom them to contemplating their bodies and their hearts without disgust . . . But there are all the others, more numerous with each day that passes – who show no embarrassment at being what they are.'[53] Another friend who had every interest to go out and to buy the book was the seventy-five-year-old, and soon to be knighted, Edmund Gosse. Quite as discreet as Mauriac about himself, though he had, in the past, more to be discreet about, Gosse's heartfelt, unqualified understanding must have come as a great balm to Gide:

You did not send me 'Corydon', so I had to buy it. Perhaps you thought I should be 'shocked'. But that is not my way. There is nothing in the whole diversity of life which serious men cannot seriously discuss. I think you show great courage in writing this book . . . No doubt, in fifty years, this particular subject will cease to surprise anyone, and how many people in the past might wish to have lived in 1974.[54]

Two months later, Gosse got Gide elected to the 'honorary fellowship', left vacant by the death of Anatole France, at the Royal Society of Literature, of which he was chairman. Given Gide's growing ill-fame and the conservative nature of the institution, this was a considerable achievement. When the Society asked Gide what titles or letters were to follow his name on the list of fellows, Gide replied: 'Honours began by fleeing me. Later I fled honours. On the list of Honorary Fellows of the Royal Society my name is not to be followed by any title. The FRSL will only stand out the better.'[55]

After two weeks at Cuverville, Gide spent a couple of days in Paris before going off with Marc to Coxyde-les-Bains, on the Belgian coast, where Beth and her friend Marie-Thérèse Muller, now married and a mother of two sons, had rented a villa. The Petite Dame arrived a week later. In the crowded little house, surrounded by friends and children, it would have been impossible to work. So Gide rented a seaside hut, but, in the end, did rather more swimming than writing. On 19 July, he and Marc left Coxyde for Paris. After a few days, Marc went off to England, and Gide returned to Cuverville, where, over the next three weeks, he tried to work on *Les Faux-Monnayeurs*. On 17 August, he met up with the Petite Dame and Enid McLeod, now head of the British Council in Paris, and the three went off to Pontigny.

Gide had thought seriously about not going to Pontigny, fearing the interruption that it would bring to work on the novel. In the end, he could not bring himself to tell Desjardins of his decision. In fact, Gide's presence was a disturbing factor to some: a number of members of the organizing committee had protested against an invitation to the author of *Corydon* being sent at all and at least ten subscribers had declared that they would not come, alleging Gide's presence as the reason. Desjardins himself confessed to Loup Mayrisch that he had not read *Corydon* and had no wish to do so. With such reactions from such people one begins to get the measure of Gide's audacity in publishing the book. The title of the *décade littéraire* that year was 'The achievement of the nineteenth century in the order of intelligence'. As always, Gide was not at his best in intellectual discussions where any degree of formality was present. Everyone expected him to give a lead, but he would not be drawn, could not be pinned down to any one point of view. He came into his own in the informal conversations in the evening and in readings: to universal acclaim, he read extracts from *Les Faux-Monnayeurs*.

Gide and his friends travelled back to Paris, where they met up with Beth and Catherine, who had come from Coxyde and were on their way back to La Bastide. Gide was highly amused by how much his daughter had changed in so short a time – and by how much she resembled him. The Petite Dame, her daughter and grand-daughter stayed at the Schlumbergers' apartment in the rue d'Assas, the Schlumbergers being at Saint-Clair. Jean Schlumberger had not gone to Pontigny that year, having decided to stay with his wife, whose condition seemed to be deteriorating. On 6 September, Gide spent the day at Chartres with Roger Fry, artist, art theorist and early member of the Bloomsbury Group. Then, after a couple of days with André Maurois and his family at Elbeuf, near Rouen, Gide was back in Cuverville on 9 September. On arrival, he heard that Suzanne Schlumberger had died two days before at Saint-Clair, finally defeated by cancer. Madeleine, who had been particularly close to her, was deeply distressed.

On 19 September, Gide spent the day at Le Havre with Marc, who had arrived back from England after an absence of two months. Of the many things they had to talk about, the most important was certainly the projected trip to Africa. Plans for a long journey through Central Africa had been maturing for months. A meeting with Marcel de Coppet, a close friend of Roger Martin du Gard and his future son-in-law, had suddenly given reality to a dream that Gide had had since he was twenty. Since June 1923, Coppet had been on a twelve-month furlough from his post as *chef de cabinet* to the governor of Chad. Prior to his return he was appointed acting governor, before taking up the governorship officially. Coppet had tried, without success, to persuade Martin du Gard to visit 'Black Africa'. Gide lent a more pliant ear. By the time of Gide's meeting with Marc, a detailed itinerary had been worked out, officials contacted and even passages booked. Why, one may ask, did Gide take it into his head to go off on a long, possibly dangerous journey, at this particular time? Dorothy Bussy asked precisely this:

I very much doubt whether you have the moral right to go for your trip across Central Africa before [*Les Faux-Monnayeurs*] *is* finished. Whatever your friends Coppet and Martin du Gard may say, it will certainly be more dangerous than going to Cuverville or Brignoles or Roquebrune. And moreover the kind of experience with which it is likely to enrich you is not the kind that will be useful in *Les Faux-Monnayeurs*. On the contrary, it is one more likely to alter the focus of your mind irretrievably, so that you won't ever be able to find your point of view again or the things that you saw from it.[56]

Where *Les Faux-Monnayeurs* was concerned, Gide had reached a stage when he would welcome a complete, extended break. He felt that he was getting stale, going through the motions, forcing himself to continue. He would come back from Africa, he felt sure, a changed man and polish off the book in less time than if he had stayed in France. He had even decided to publish it in two parts and had sent off the manuscript of the first part to Gallimard. He was concerned, too, about Marc, after the 'Soirées de Paris' débâcle. He wanted to have him to himself, over several months, away from the temptations of Paris, and try to influence his future in the right direction. Marc was keen on photography – through Cocteau, he had met Man Ray – and the cinema. Gide bought him a good cine camera and he began to take lessons in how to use it. Their journey through Black Africa would provide excellent material for a film.

Gide left Cuverville on 3 October. To his surprise and delight, he was met at Saint-Lazare by Marc and the Petite Dame. Over the next few days, he and Marc began to think seriously about the expedition that they were undertaking. It soon became clear that they were quite incapable of making the necessary preparations in the four weeks remaining; it would be much better to postpone the trip until the following June. Gide abandoned any idea of publishing *Les Faux-Monnayeurs* in two parts: instead long extracts from the parts already written would be published in the *NRF* (March–August 1925). Marc threw himself into his studies at 'Sciences-Po', with the result that he did 'very brilliantly' in three of the autumn examinations.

On 23 October, Gide went back to Cuverville, where, apart from four days in Paris in November, he stayed for the next six weeks. He had written what was to become Chapter 9 of the third part (Olivier's attempted suicide). In other words, he was almost four-fifths of the way through the book. On 3 December he returned to Paris: 'joy at finding Marc at the Villa', he noted in the *Journal*.[57] The stove was lit and tea ready. Within days, he had succumbed to the *grippe*: confined first to the house, then to the bedroom, he nevertheless continued to read and to write: 'Not too painful a confinement, thanks to M., who has come to live here in the Villa . . . My soul was wrapped in a fog that his good humour, his good grace and his light touch barely managed to pierce.'[58] But Gide's condition seemed to worsen rather than improve. A doctor was called and chronic appendicitis was diagnosed. On Christmas Eve, he entered a nursing home. For two days, Gide lay in bed, under observation, an ice-pack on the appendix area. He wrote to Madeleine, who had a bad cold, telling her not to come and visit him. Friends called: Du Bos, Rivière, Schlumberger. RMG came and spent long hours with him. Preparing for the worst eventuality, Gide discussed his testamentary arrangements with him. He appointed Madeleine his sole legatee, having assigned the ownership of *Les Faux-Monnayeurs* to Catherine and of *Corydon* to Marc. He also left the sum of 200,000 francs (£8,000 or $39,000 at the time) to Jean-Paul Allégret, Marc's permanently incapacitated elder brother, who was to die in 1930, aged thirty-six.

RMG called on the morning of 26 December, hours before the operation, and noted a Gide 'very changed, clear of complexion, his face curiously rejuvenated, more beautiful, his eyes an extraordinarily pure pale blue, a fine smile on his lips . . .' They shook hands and Roger kissed André on the forehead: 'My stay here is one of my best journeys,' Gide then remarked. 'Charles-Louis Philippe said that illness is how the poor travel. If nothing happens, I'll leave here very changed. I feel it already. And my book, too, might be very different as a result.'[59] His appendix did not cost him his life, but things might have been very different if he had found himself in the middle of equatorial Africa at the time. It turned out to be have been a chronic condition that had possibly existed for years and on which, rightly or wrongly, Gide blamed his persistent tiredness and giddiness. Over the next week, Gide whiled away the time, between visits, with a copy of Gibbon's *Mémoires littéraires de la Grande Bretagne* (written in French, in Lausanne, with his young Swiss lover Georges Deyverdun), which Dorothy Bussy had given him as a present.

After Gide's seventeen-day stay in the nursing home, Martin du Gard came and collected him in his car and took him back to the Villa, where he stayed for two weeks. After a fortnight at Cuverville, he arrived at the Bussys' house at Roquebrune on 12 February. There, in the southern sun, he had hoped to convalesce – and make progress with *Les Faux-Monnayeurs*. A few days later, a telegram from Jean Schlumberger announced that Jacques Rivière had just died of typhoid fever. He was thirty-eight. Gide left Roquebrune and, the following day, attended the funeral in Paris. Rivière's had not been a quiet death. Jacques Copeau left a graphic account of his last days. In pain and delirious most of the time, he had terrifying moments of relative lucidity, as when he cried out: 'If I go back into that little hole, which, it has to be said, is a hole of pederasts, I'll be lost . . . [Was Rivière in his delirium, identifying the *NRF* with a homosexual hell?] All the ways out are blocked . . . Don't you understand, it's terrible what is happening to me? . . . Oh! The end of my life . . . My life! My life! My life!'[60] The burial took place at Bordeaux, both sides of the *NRF*'s activities being represented by Gaston Gallimard and Jean Paulhan, Rivière's assistant, who, in 1934, became editor of the review, a post that he held until his death in 1968. Rivière's friends did what they could to help his widow and children. A number of them, with the Mayrisches contributing most, organized a regular income for them. As Isabelle Rivière began to recover from the original shock, she assumed the role of sanctifying her husband's reputation: he was now 'with Henri' (her brother, Alain-Fournier). In fact, as everyone but she seemed to know, Rivière's Catholic faith had declined over the years, his thoughts being much more taken up by extra-marital affairs. Loup Mayrisch told the Petite Dame that, some weeks before his death, Rivière had confessed to her: 'I am very far from God at the moment; the only two things that interest me are love and Freudianism.'[61] In a letter to Mauriac, of 1947, Gide has a racier – and curiously divergent – version: 'I now pride myself on two things, Jacques said just before his last illness, lying well and fucking well.'[62]

Gide spent five days in Paris, then went back to the South, not, this time, to Roquebrune, but to La Bastide. On the way, he stopped off at Marseille, spending 'a frightful number of hours' that brought 'neither profit nor pleasure'. In search of the latter, he wandered through the Arab quarter, finding nothing but 'sordid poverty and sadness'.[63] He spent the next two months at La Bastide, with Beth and Catherine, who was coming up to her first birthday. For much of the time, the Petite Dame and Whity were also there.

One April day, Loup Mayrisch arrived with her daughter and a carload of guests from her house at Bormes: Jane Harrison, the eminent Hellenist from Newnham College, Cambridge, and her young lover, the writer Hope Mirrlees, and Ernst-Robert Curtius: 'La Bastide had never seen such a gathering round its table. The kitchen garden was a mass of colour and scent from the first flowers. We spent the afternoon there, some of us sitting in the shade, others walking endlessly round the garden in pairs . . . Marc was trying to make a film and Catherine, rather put out by all the visitors, shyly stroked her first rocking-horse.'[64] Alone, Gide talked to the Petite Dame about the forthcoming journey to Africa, now booked for 19 July. He was aware that it could prove a severe test for a man of his age. But he felt an overwhelming need to go, to confront something absolutely new, though he would not have considered going without Marc. Several times he repeated: 'Ce qu'il peut être gentil, ce petit!' ('He can be so nice, that lad!')

An offer arrived of 16,000 francs (£634 or $3,044 at the time) for the manuscript of the first part of *Les Faux-Monnayeurs*, the first of five extracts having appeared in the March number of the *NRF.* Gide suggested that Beth should buy a little car with the money. So he, Beth and Whity went off to Marseille and bought one, which Whity drove back. At this time, Gide was also planning a huge sale of part of his library, including complimentary copies, complete with fulsome dedications, from men such as Henri de Régnier, who now claimed that he had 'never been able to take an interest in either the work or the person of André Gide'.[65] Gide left La Bastide for Paris on 21 April. The sale took place at the Hôtel Drouot (the Parisian equivalent of Christie's and Sotheby's combined). It comprised 405 books and manuscripts, including rare editions of his own work, and fetched 123,000 francs (£4,877 or $23,400 at the time). The sale of complimentary copies also brought Gide a lot of ill-will. The Petite Dame was afraid that it might look like a vindictive attack on former friends and, in the wake of the publication of *Corydon*, this was not a time to make more enemies. People would have difficulty believing Gide's proffered reason for the sale: to raise money for his trip to Africa. 'The sale has taken place,' Gide wrote to Martin du Gard. 'None of my books has ever caused so much ink to be spilled.'[66]

On 30 April, Madeleine arrived at the Villa for a ten-day stay, while Gide threw himself into an apparently endless round of appointments and shopping expeditions. In an attempt to amuse the rather withdrawn, sombre Madeleine, he and the Petite Dame took her off to see Buster Keaton's film *Our Hospitality*. 'During the showing,' the Petite Dame notes, 'Madeleine smiled with good grace, rather embarrassed at not being able to share our amusement.' She seemed more at home with the scientific documentary on submarine life that followed.[67]

At the end of May, Gide joined Madeleine at Cuverville for two weeks. There he learnt of the death, on 4 June, of Pierre Louÿs, his oldest, but long since estranged literary friend. Four days later, he noted in the *Journal*: '8 June. Finished *Les Faux-Monnayeurs*.' On the same page of the *Journal*, he notes a weakening in his sight and his need of spectacles. 'Would that the brain could wear them too! Difficulty my mind has in "focusing" on the idea it is examining ... The outlines remain blurred.'[68]

On 18 June, Gide attended a lecture on the Russian theatre by Jacques Copeau. Copeau was only in Paris for a few days and Gide agreed to call on him the following week at Morteuil. Since February 1924, when it looked as if the Vieux Colombier would not be able to continue, Copeau had been looking for a country house, with grounds, where, with a small group of actor friends, he could at least continue the work of the drama school attached to the theatre. Over recent years, as we have seen, Gide and Copeau had moved ever further apart, each deeply regretting the fact, neither being able to alter it. Both men had reached decisive moments in their lives. Yet the difference could not have been greater. Gide had just finished his greatest work and, at fifty-five, with a friend thirty years his junior, was about to embark on a year-long, perhaps dangerous expedition into darkest Africa. 'Where do you get that insane strength?' asked a puzzled forty-five-year-old Copeau, tired, disillusioned, visibly ageing. Career and life were unravelling before him. He yearned for security and stability, a yearning that, over the next few months, would bring him back to the Church of his childhood. It was now over a year since the Vieux Colombier had finally closed its doors – or rather, the theatre opened again, but Copeau and the company that he had founded were no longer there. Overwhelmed by financial difficulties, Copeau had been made to see that he would have to choose between the theatre and the school. His financial partners wanted the school to go. For Copeau, already bored and depressed by what even as uncommercial a theatre as his own could do, the school was all that mattered: there the future, his own and the theatre's, lay. Copeau left, taking with him the theatre's artistic identity. The rest, the Vieux Colombier as legal and financial institution, was merged with Louis Jouvet's company. (The casualties of the early closure were a version of a Japanese Nō play and Gide's translation of Tagore's *Post Office*, *Amal ou la lettre du Roi*.) It was the end of one of the century's legendary theatrical undertakings, France's equivalent of Russia's Moscow Arts Theatre or England's Vedrenne-Barker management of the Court Theatre in Sloane Square. Seeing the break coming, Copeau had already been looking for premises in the country where his nephew Michel Saint-Denis, his daughter Marie-Hélène, Suzanne Bing and a few other colleagues could reopen the school. Their choice fell on the Château de Morteuil, 10 miles outside Beaune. There the teaching continued, interspersed with short visits to villages in the area, where the 'Copiaus', as the locals called them, per-formed a programme of short pieces, together with songs accompanied by mime and dance.

On 24 June, a 'very young, sprightly' Gide joined Copeau for two days at his Burgundian retreat. 'I felt older than he,' Copeau later wrote to his wife. Gide enjoyed himself immensely and was a great success with the young actors and students. Days later, Copeau was still under the spell of the reunion, speaking of their 'very strong, ancient, deep, male tenderness'. While in Paris, desperately seeking financial support for his school, Copeau attended high mass with Isabelle Rivière at the chapel of the Benedictine nuns. There he felt a '*delicious* transport': his soul 'was taking off at last'.[69] During the summer, he was in constant touch with Claudel. On 2 September, he visited the Benedictine abbey of Solesmes for the first time. On 18 November, Suzanne Bing, Jewish by birth, was received into the Church by baptism at the church of Saint-Sulpice, by the Abbé Altermann, himself a convert from Judaism. Finally, on 6 December, at Solesmes, Copeau confessed and took communion. Meanwhile, further financial difficulties arose with his school, which he more or less disbanded. He gave up his lease of Morteuil and bought a large house at Pernand-Vergelesses, also in the Beaune area, to which he retired with a smaller contingent of followers. But there, too, there were problems, not least those caused by the double 'conversion' of Copeau and Suzanne Bing. One entry in Copeau's *Journal* presents the tragi-comic spectacle of Copeau arriving back from Paris, where he had been to mass at the Benedictine convent feeling 'full of grace', until, that is, he set eyes on Suzanne, when he was overcome by 'a terrible desire'. She responds. Then both remember their new-found religion and manage, just, to resist the temptations of the flesh.[70]

From Morteuil, Gide went to Chartres, where he had arranged to meet Martin du Gard, thus avoiding farewells on a station platform. 'That may have been our last conversation,' RMG wrote in his journal on 1 July. But, he goes on, there was nothing planned or solemn about the meeting: Gide treated the whole affair as if they might meet again the next day. They spent the evening at the cinema, where Gide committed 'mille extravagances' with 'incredible skill'. After a long conversation, RMG saw Gide off on the train for Paris.[71] Over the past six months, Marc had had rather more to occupy his time than his studies at Sciences-Po. He had been appointed 'secretary' to Gide for what had become a semi-official expedition. From the outset he had taken charge of the entire planning of the itinerary, spending his afternoons poring over maps at the French Geographical Society headquarters or reading up in libraries a vast amount of literature on Africa – political, anthropological, literary and medical. He had done all this with great enthusiasm and assiduity. He was also continuing with his lessons in photography and film-making, and already planning to sell photographs to magazines such as *L'Illustration* and *Illustrated London News*.

The Petite Dame arrived in Paris two days before Gide and Marc were due to leave. That evening she went to the Villa for dinner and found René Michelet there – he had probably been on the same train as she from Brussels and had come especially to say good-bye to Gide. She found that Gide had a bad cold, 'or fears that he has, which is worse', and, despite the intense heat, had an overcoat round his shoulders. The hall was in 'an indescribable mess': 'one didn't know where to put one's hat'. In the drawing-room, 'Marc reigns over the objects and organizes the parcels'. Engrossed in his work, he 'doesn't waste a minute', but occasionally 'corrects what Gide says' about the expedition. On the floor, a dozen tin trunks were arranged in a semi-circle: one was for Gide's personal belongings, another for Marc's and one each for cooking equipment, photographic equipment, provisions, books, etc. Seeing the quantity of books – French, English and German – competing for entry, the Petite Dame remembered Gide telling her that he would be taking only a copy of the *Aeneid* and a Latin dictionary. Next day, the Petite Dame arrives to find that 'the mess has increased, if that's possible'. Also there are the two Klossowski brothers, Pierre and Balthus, helping Marc pack. An astonished, incredulous Valéry arrives to take his leave. Jean Schlumberger is there most of the time. The telephone never stops ringing. Various Allégrets and others are invited to dinner, but told to bring some ham. Dinner turns out to consist of eggs, fruit, champagne and a vast pile of ham. At one point, Gide takes the Petite Dame to one side and gives her a box, in which he has put all his 'secret papers': manuscripts, notes, letters. It is to be given to Martin du Gard and she is to keep the key. Next morning, Marc and his brother André load the luggage on to a lorry, while Gide stands, 'dressed as in mid-winter, checking a list'. They have lunch in a brasserie opposite Auteuil station, sitting at a long table, as if celebrating the Quatorze Juillet, which it happens to be. A slightly different contingent returns there for dinner, after which they set out in two taxis for the Gare d'Orsay. The quai is a mass of coloured lights and crowds of celebrating people. 'We couldn't leave on an ordinary day,' Gide comments. At the station are Marcel Drouin and his son Domi, the Klossowski brothers and, with their mother, Rilke, who has been in Paris since January. (Gide and Rilke were not to meet again. Rilke left Paris a month later, taking with him the precious relics of his pre-war Parisian days, which had been sitting in the cellars of the *NRF* bookshop in the boulevard Raspail for close on twelve years. Rilke returned to Switzerland and died eighteen months later, aged fifty.)

'The leave-takings are rushed, done any old how, as best we can. It's horrible. I have only one idea in my head: I wish it was all over,' the Petite Dame concludes. Gide, standing in the carriage doorway, is 'wearing his most frozen smile, like a Japanese mask and says "yes, yes", with a nod of the head. At last the train moves off. What a relief! How right Elisabeth and Martin du Gard were not to come!'[72]

When Gide and Marc left Paris on 14 July, the final extract of *Les Faux-Monnayeurs* was still to appear (in the August number of the *NRF*). The novel did not appear in volume form until February 1926, by which time author and companion were in the wilds of Chad. In a short text, probably written in 1919, Gide described *La Symphonie Pastorale*, his most recent fictional work, as 'the last of my youthful projects'. Since then he had felt able to work freely at last, without a preconceived plan. The result of that freedom was *Les Faux-Monnayeurs*, a work that, in so many ways, marked a break with his own past and literary practice. Though dedicated to Roger Martin du Gard, the 'onlie begetter' of *Les Faux-Monnayeurs* was Marc Allégret. It had been written 'to win his attention, his esteem'.[73] At the time when he began the actual writing of the book, Gide felt that Marc did not really appreciate him as a writer, *Les Caves* excepted, and was more drawn to the work of the younger avant-garde. From the formal point of view, too, Gide put *Les Faux-Monnayeurs* in a class on its own. It was, he said in the dedication, 'my first novel'. Though not conceived, however imperfectly, in the author's 'youth', *Les Faux-Monnayeurs* was not of recent origin. The book sprang, so to speak, from the conjunction of two quite unrelated *faits divers*. The first described a case in which children of good family were involved in the circulation of counterfeit 10-franc gold coins, which they obtained for 2 francs 50. The second concerned a fifteen-year-old *lycée* pupil who, following the rules of a secret society to which he belonged, had been drawn by lots to be the first to kill himself. Gide had kept press cuttings of these two incidents, dating from 1906 and 1909. In 1914, the first edition of *Les Caves du Vatican* announced a 'forthcoming' work by Gide entitled *Le Faux-Monnayeur*, a sort of sequel in which Lafcadio would again be the central character. However, the novel was abandoned for the duration of the war. It was not until 1919 that Gide began work on the new *Les Faux-Monnayeurs* – and on the *Journal des Faux-Monnayeurs*. It was then that he decided to merge the two *faits divers* into the same plot. The actual writing took six years but, as always with

Gide, he worked at it erratically, inconsistently, interrupted by other projects.

Until 1921, the novel still had only two characters: the novelist Edouard, engaged, unsuccessfully, in writing a novel called *Les Faux-Monnayeurs*, and Lafcadio. Gide abandoned any idea of making Lafcadio the first-person narrator: to do so would limit and unbalance the novel. In the end, there was an unnamed narrator (assisted by Edouard's journal, which, in all, amounts to about a third of the book), while Lafcadio survived, in a paler form, in the less conspicuously named Bernard. Other shadowy figures appeared in the *Journal des Faux-Monnayeurs*, referred to simply as X, Y and Z. Eventually, a large cast of characters emerged, many having, to a greater or lesser degree, their origin in individuals known to Gide. Few novels of merit are actually *romans à clef* and few consist of totally invented characters. Even Edouard, in so many ways Gide himself, living in Passy and having a house in Normandy, is not entirely Gide, who distances himself from him in a number of ways. Thus an example of Edouard's work is provided, written in an un-Gidean, high-flown style, with characters bearing preposterous names such as Audibert, Eudolfe, Hildebrant (a satirical throw-back to Gide's own 'Symbolist' *Le Voyage d'Urien*) which concludes that he is 'an amateur, a failure' who will never finish his book.[74]

Edouard is one of the poles of the book; the other, less dominant one, is the Comte Robert de Passavant, like Edouard, a writer, but a modish, superficial one, for whom Edouard feels nothing but dislike and distrust. In name and character, he is reminiscent of that other literary count, Robert de Montesquiou, one of the models for Proust's Baron de Charlus. His name is even identical with Charlus' family motto, 'Passavant', meaning 'Press on!', though it could also be construed as 'passe avant', get ahead. More importantly, Passavant is based on Cocteau: his novel *La Barre fixe* (*The Horizontal Bar*) is an amusing transformation of Cocteau's *Le Grand Ecart* (in gymnastic parlance, 'the splits').

Edouard has a nephew, Olivier, now eighteen. He is very attracted by the boy's good looks, his shy manner, his tendency to blush, his guileless enthusiasms. On his side, Olivier has great affection and admiration for an uncle who seems to lead an altogether more interesting life than that of other members of his family. (Clearly, Olivier has much in common with Marc Allégret.) However, each interprets the other's timid, diffident approach as indifference. Olivier is the son of a judge, Oscar Molinier; his mother, Pauline, is Edouard's half-sister. He has an older brother, Vincent, now a doctor, the lover of a rich American, Lady Lilian Griffith. Into Vincent's character and his affair with Lady Griffith went much of Gide's cousin Paul and his liaison with the actress Ventura. Olivier also has a younger brother, Georges, who, unknown to all until near the end, is associated with a gang of counterfeiters. Olivier is a member of a group of students who meet regularly in the Jardin du Luxembourg to discuss literary and intellectual matters – and has a youthful infatuation for one of the group, Bernard. While studying for his '*bachot*', Bernard discovers some old love letters of his mother's, which show that he is her illegitimate son by a former lover. (Lafcadio, his earlier incarnation, was also illegitimate, of course.) Realizing that he never believed he had anything in common with his 'father', Albéric Profitendieu, an examining magistrate, he leaves home. Through Olivier, Bernard meets Edouard, who offers him the post of secretary.

Edouard, Bernard and Laura Vedel go off to Switzerland for part of the summer, to Saas-Fée (where Gide and Marc spent some time in 1917). Mention of Laura Vedel introduces the novel's third family group. At its head is the grandfather Azaïs, a former Protestant pastor. His son-in-law Prosper Vedel, also a pastor, and his wife run a private boarding-school. The Vedels' daughter, Laura, is married to a French teacher living in Cambridge. She has a rather platonic relationship with Edouard and has just been jilted by Vincent Molinier, Olivier's elder brother, by whom she is pregnant, in favour of Lady Griffith. At Saas-Fée, Bernard falls in love with her. (The Vedels are more or less based on the Bavretels, mentioned in *Si le grain ne meurt*.) The ostensible purpose of the Saas-Fée visit is for Edouard to collect young Boris La Pérouse, a disturbed youth who is staying there in the care of a Polish psychoanalyst, Madame Sophroniska. Long before *Les Faux-Monnayeurs* was conceived, Gide referred in the *Journal* to his old piano teacher Marc de La Nux as 'Lapérouse'. In the novel, he becomes 'La Pérouse'. Boris, his grandson, is based partly on Pierre de Lanux, once Gide's secretary, partly on his friend Emmanuel Faÿ, but also on the adolescent Gide himself. From Saas-Fée, Bernard writes to Olivier, announcing his changed circumstances. Aggrieved, not only at losing Bernard, but at being replaced in his uncle's affections by him, Olivier gives in to Passavant's blandishments. The Count makes his protégé editor of a new review that he plans to set up and the two go off on a holiday to Corsica. (An exaggerated, fictionalized version, this, of Marc's encounter with Cocteau and his susceptibility to Cocteau's flattery.)

With the *rentrée* all the characters find themselves in Paris again. The plot takes a decisive turn at a 'banquet' given by a literary review, *Les Argonautes*, at which the four main protagonists – Edouard and Bernard, Passavant and Olivier – are also present. The real-life Alfred Jarry, author of *Ubu Roi*, makes a scene. Olivier gets drunk and asks Edouard to take him back with him to his house. Ashamed of his behaviour and disgusted by his relationship with Passavant, Olivier makes a bungled attempt to commit suicide. Edouard looks after him as he recovers. Each realizes the love felt for him by the other. In the Jardin du Luxembourg, Bernard is 'visited' by an angel, who takes him first to the Sorbonne chapel, then to a right-wing political meeting (of the Action Française type) and, finally, to the poor quarters of the town, 'inhabited by disease, prostitution, shame, crime and hunger'. Olivier's elder brother, Vincent, in Africa with Lady Griffith, goes mad and, believing himself to be the devil, murders her. His younger brother, Georges, learns that Judge Profitendieu's investigations are about to close in on the counterfeiting gang. The gang is led by the sinister Strouvilhou, a friend of Passavant's and a former boarder at the Vedels' *pensionnat*. The other members are all young boarders at the Vedels': one is the curiously named Léon Ghéridanisol (the first three syllables are a near-anagram of Radiguet, a lover of Cocteau's and author of two remarkable works, *Le Diable au corps* and *Le Bal du Comte Orgel*, before his death in 1923 at the age of twenty). The gang ceases its activities. On the fringe of the gang is Boris La Pérouse. He is persuaded by his young friends to undertake a test of his courage: this consists of pointing a revolver at his head and pulling the trigger, a form of mock Russian roulette, since he is told that the gun is not loaded. It is, and Boris blows his brains out. Gide's *Les Faux-Monnayeurs* comes to an end, but Edouard's is no nearer completion.

What did Gide mean by the phrase 'my first novel'? When Jean Amrouche remarked that he could not see why *Les Caves du Vatican*, too, could not be called a novel – what 'essential difference' was there between the two? – the Gide of 1949 confessed that there might not be one. In the preface to *Les Caves*, where he introduces the term '*sotie*', the Gide of 1913 is no more enlightening. 'Why do I call this book a *sotie*? Why *récit* the three preceding ones? To make clear that they are not strictly speaking *novels*.' To the 'three preceding ones', *L'Immoraliste*, *La Porte étroite* and *Isabelle*, one may add, among the *récits*, the following one, *La Symphonie Pastorale*, while the ancestors of *Les Caves*, as *soties*, are *Paludes* and *Le Prométhée mal enchaîné*. The *récits* belonged to a long French tradition of first-person narrative fiction, epitomized by Madame de La Fayette's *La Princesse de Clèves* and Constant's *Adolphe*, with their predilection for stylistic purity, narrative economy and psychological subtlety. Against the 'serious', backward-looking *récits*, the *soties* represent Gide's comic, irreverent, inventive, fantastic, innovative side. *Les Faux-Monnayeurs* clearly began as a *sotie*, a sequel to *Les Caves*. The fantastic, the frankly unrealistic, was to be its dominant mode. As late as 27 December 1923, Gide was writing: 'It will be as well to introduce, from the first chapter, a fantastic, supernatural element that would later make possible certain deviations in the narrative, certain unrealities.'[75] Gide thought of setting the atmosphere of fantasy from the outset, in the first chapter, by making the Jardin du Luxembourg 'as mythical a place' as Shakespeare's Forest of Arden in *As You Like It*. For thousands of people the Luxembourg is, in any case, a 'mythical' place, the still centre of a turning Latin Quarter, crammed with France's most celebrated institutions of higher education (Sorbonne, Ecole Normale Supérieure, Ecole des Beaux-Arts, Collège de France, Ecole Polytechnique, etc.), four of its greatest *lycées* and other institutions of secondary education, all within 1,000 metres of its railings, and many much closer. The Luxembourg plays a similar role in *Les Faux-Monnayeurs* and did so from the beginning. The newspaper cutting kept by Gide concerning the gang of young counterfeiters described how one of them corrected the judge who referred to them as the 'bande du Luxembourg': call us rather the 'cénacle du Luxembourg', he said. (Not a 'gang', but a 'literary club' – only in France, only in the Latin Quarter . . .) In *Les Faux-Monnayeurs*, Bernard, Olivier and their friends also meet in the Luxembourg, as a sort of *cénacle*. Apart from Edouard, who lives in Passy, and the La Pérouses, the four main families of characters all live around the Luxembourg.

The 'fantastic' or 'supernatural', however, was to be more than an atmospheric halo cast over the Jardin du Luxembourg. 'I would like one character (the devil) to move incognito through the whole book,' Gide notes in the *Journal des Faux-Monnayeurs* on 13 January 1921. His reality would become more apparent the less people believed in him. Gide then quotes one of his own declarations from *Numquid et tu* of 1916: 'Why should you be afraid of me? You know very well that I don't exist.' This, Gide adds, is the keystone of the book.[76] In the end, the devil did not appear as a character, even incognito, though he remains as a circumambient presence, a hypothetical explanation for some of the characters' actions, for some of the plot's 'inexplicable' twists and turns. The sole survivor of the supernatural as character, is the angel: he cannot be dismissed as a figment of Bernard's imagination, though he alone sees him. The angel's arrival is described in the most natural, down-to-earth way in the world and, when he speaks, he does so like any other of Gide's characters. He does not appear mysteriously: he arrives, in angelic fashion, like some aerodynamic creature, 'gliding on so light a foot that one felt that it might have rested on the waves'.[77]

If *Les Faux-Monnayeurs* began as a *sotie*, it also contains much of the *récit*. In the end, it became a unique blend of Gide's hitherto separate modes. In September 1919, he was still thinking of dividing the material that he had accumulated into two books, 'one in the manner of *Paludes*, entirely critical and disconcerting, the other a novel of life'.[78] Later, as the material prolifer- ated, Gide began to doubt his ability to weave together a number of different plots and a large number of characters, and was tempted to separate off each of the 'stories' into different *récits*. It was Martin du Gard, constantly urging him on to write a 'great novel', who was responsible for persuading him to keep the various narrative strands together. Again, Gide's final decision to reduce the supernatural presence in the book may well owe something to Martin du Gard's pleadings, but that would seem to be the extent of his influence. Even then Bernard's angel stayed – to RMG's horror, an offence equally to human reason and to narrative credibility. Post-modern readers (especially critics), who would not, except in the course of professional duty, plough through RMG's family saga, are delighted by such instances of 'magical realism' *avant la lettre*.

Les *Faux-Monnayeurs* was not only Gide's attempt to write a 'modern' novel, one whose form and style would appeal to the young, it was also a novel about contemporary youth. Olivier, Bernard and their friends are all about eighteen; Georges, Boris and their friends are younger; even Edouard and Passavant are in their mid-thirties; the older characters are of no more than secondary importance. There are what look like a couple of contemporary allusions to Dada: the title of Armand Vedel's poem 'Le Vase nocturne' (The Chamber Pot) is clearly suggested by Marcel Duchamp's notorious *Fountain* (a simple mass-produced urinal) of 1917 and his review publishes the same artist's *Tableau Dada* (*Mona Lisa* with moustache) of 1919. Again, psychoanalysis (in the person of Madame Sophroniska, the fictional counterpart of Eugenia Sokolnicka, who arrived in Paris in 1921) had not become fashionable in France until the early twenties. More generally, many readers, at the time and since, have noted an indefinable feel of the 1920s about the book. By the time Gide came to write *Les Faux- Monnayeurs*, as early as 1919, he wrote: 'The future interests me more than the past and even more what belongs neither to tomorrow nor to yesterday, but which in all times can be said to belong to today.'[79] The trouble was that Gide began collecting his press cuttings about the young counterfeiters in 1906. More specifically, what they counterfeited were 10-franc gold coins, which had gone out of circulation by the end of the war. At one stage, Gide contemplated writing the book in two parts, corresponding to the pre-war and post-war periods. Contrary to received notions of how the war had transformed everyone's outlook, he would pick characters of different religious and political persuasions, and show how each had been reinforced in his views by the war. Such a programme would have appealed to Martin du Gard, with his predilection for the *longue durée*. Gide, on the other hand, though a man who, through art, music and, above all, literature, lived very largely in the past, actually had little historical sense, still less any notion of all the data required to evoke a past period. For him human artefacts existed only at the point of reception, in an eternal present. In the end, Gide made a virtue of the twin necessities imposed by his material and his own limitations. Chronology would be ignored: pre-war and post-war indicators would exist side by side in an anachronic state, capable of accommodating not only a moustachioed *Mona Lisa* and 10-franc gold coins, but also the presence of Alfred Jarry (d. 1907) at the literary banquet, soon after the première of his *Ubu Roi* (1896), a bottle of Montrachet 1904 and a character reading a copy of *Action Française* (a periodical since 1899, not a daily newspaper until 1908). Even within the time-scale of the novel itself, time eschews the chronological straight line, jumping backwards and forwards, going over the same incident from the point of view of different characters.

This cavalier attitude to chronology is pursued in the working out of the plot. Over against the traditional novel's concern to depict character through action, and action flowing necessarily from character, Gide makes great play with two notions: *inconséquence*, acts committed by individuals 'out of character', unpredictably, and *coincidence*, an arbitrary linking together of two unrelated actions. This rejection of logical development, this refusal, as he puts it, to 'profiter de l'élan acquis', to exploit the narrative momentum already achieved, certainly made the writing of the novel arduous. Beginning a new chapter became like beginning a new book: 'Sometimes, for days on end, I have wondered whether I would be able to get the machine going again.'[80] Just as each chapter starts anew, so the novel as a whole does not come to a 'satisfying' close. Gide has Edouard note in his journal: 'X . . . maintains that, before beginning his book, a good novelist ought to know how it will end. Personally, I let mine wander at will [*à l'aventure*]. I believe that life never offers us anything that may not be regarded as much as a fresh start as an end. "Might be continued" – it is with these words that I should like to end my *Faux-Monnayeurs*.'[81] Gide did as much with *his*

celebrated ending: 'I am very curious to know Caloub',[82] Caloub being
Bernard's younger brother. In the *JFM*, he noted, a few months before he
finished the novel, that it 'will end suddenly, not with a thorough exhaustion
of the subject . . ., but on the contrary with its expansion, a sort of blur-
ring of its outline. It must not be neatly rounded off, but rather disperse,
disintegrate.'[83]

As with chronology and plot, so with the characters. In the *JFM*, Gide
notes: 'Make Ed say perhaps: "The bore, you see, is having to condition
one's characters . . . As soon as I have to put clothes on them, establish their
position in the social scale, their careers, the amount of their income . . ., find
them neighbours, invent friends and relations for them, I pack it in."'[84]
Gide himself did not pack it in: on the contrary, he ended up, by dint of
hard work and over-compensation, relating practically every character to
every other character. But the insight certainly applied to Gide himself. He
could 'make out the slightest intonation' of his characters' voices,[85] the
result no doubt of his innate and cultivated musicality, and hours spent
reading aloud. But he had difficulty imagining their physical appearance
in detail and therefore refused to build up descriptions of them in words.
He has Edouard declare that 'novelists, by too precise a description of their
characters, hinder the reader's imagination, rather than assist it' and 'they
ought to allow each reader to imagine them as he wishes'.[86]

Gide's various technical departures from 'realism' do not, of course,
represent a flight from reality. On the contrary, the traditional, Balzacian
novel, with its carefully researched background, its consistent characterization, its complicated, but clearly worked plots, does not ring true for Gide,
as an accurate mirror of reality, as he sees it. Edouard has come to realize
that the '*sujet profond*', the underlying subject of his book, is 'the rivalry
between the real world and our representation of it', between the world of
appearances and our interpretations of it.[87] The 'representation' shared by
the realistic novelist and his public is merely a set of agreed conventions, the
realist novel an aesthetic form, in itself no truer, nor less codified, than, say,
the strict conventions of French classical tragedy. The 'modern' novelist's
task is therefore to find other aesthetic forms, other equally artificial
conventions, but ones that express more truly his vision of the world. This
was precisely the view held by those two great modernist writers of English
fiction, James Joyce and Virginia Woolf. Like the advanced painters of the
1920s, who believed that photography relieved them of the duty of literal
representation, Gide believed that the depiction of external events could
better be left to the cinema: 'Purge the novel of all the elements that do

not belong specifically to the novel.'[88] Gide also strove to remove 'everything that someone else might just as well have written'. This meant avoiding 'those neutral passages' that 'lull, reassure, tame the reader' and so ran the risk of alienating many.[89]

The abandonment of pseudo-objective representation gives a new validity to the novelist's subjectivity, thus opening up a new world to be explored. On the same page of the *JFM* on which Gide notes that he has finished his novel, he quotes a few lines from his friend Albert Thibaudet: 'The authentic novelist creates his characters out of *the infinite directions of his possible life*; the factitious novelist creates them from the single line of his real life. The genius of the novel brings the possible to life; it does not revive the real.'[90] Not unsurprisingly, such a view had a radical effect on the character of the narrator. In the traditional, realist novel, the narrator was, like God, omniscient, omnipresent, omnipotent – but also totally absent. Gide's narrator is not only less than all-knowing; he also makes his presence felt, commenting from time to time on the action, very much in the manner of his beloved English eighteenth-century novelists, Fielding and Sterne. Often the narrator interjects in order to admit this lack of knowledge: 'I should have been curious to know what Antoine could have told his friend the cook; but one cannot listen to everything. This is the time when Bernard is supposed to meet Olivier. I am not sure where he dined that evening, or even whether he dined at all.'[91]

The undisputed authority of the narrator is further weakened by the role played by Edouard's journal, even if it is the narrator who transmits its contents to us by, for example, having Bernard read them and comment on them. As Gide noted in 1921, the book did not really have 'a single centre', but 'two foci, as in an ellipse'. Around the first is focused the 'innocent' narrative of events, around the second the struggle of the novelist character Edouard to turn them into a book. And it is really the second that is the book's 'principal subject, the new focus that throws the narrative off centre and draws it towards the imaginative'.[92] This is the most highly developed instance of composition '*en abyme*', the term derived, it will be remembered, from heraldry. Gide had described its significance for him as early as 1893, while working on *Paludes*: 'In a work of art I rather like to find transposed, on the scale of the characters, the very subject of that work.'[93] Gide cites as examples certain of Memling's paintings, Velásquez' *Las Meniñas* and the play-within-the-play in *Hamlet*. As in *Paludes*, a writer-character is writing a novel with the same title as the book in which it appears. Moreover, he is writing a *Journal des Faux-Monnayeurs*, just as Gide wrote his. In it, like Gide, he jots down ideas for his novel and comments on the progress of the work. Gide even has Edouard remark in conversation with his friends: 'Just think how interesting such a notebook kept by Dickens or Balzac would be; if we had the journal of *L'Education sentimentale* or *The Brothers Karamazov*! – the history of the work, of its gestation! It would be quite fascinating . . . More interesting than the work itself . . .'[94] However, and here Gide marks a distance between himself and Edouard, Gide would not have found such a journal more interesting than the work itself. Edouard's great limitation is his excessive interest in theory, to the detriment of practice; so much so that he will never write the book he is forever talking and writing about.

The self-referential structure of the novel is most elegantly encapsulated in its title. It occurs first with Edouard thinking that it may not be such a good title after all: unlike the narrator, he knows nothing as yet of the actual counterfeiters. Typically, he is giving the word a general, metaphorical implication. Though hints are dropped throughout the narrative, the identity of the actual counterfeiters, Strouvilhou and his gang, is revealed only towards the end of the novel. But, as we read, we become aware that almost all the characters are more or less moral counterfeiters. The most obvious haven of moral counterfeit, hypocrisy, is the Vedels' home and school, based on 'sound' puritanical principles. Significantly, Strouvilhou is an ex-boarder and it is the young gang of boarders who circulate the false coins – and drive young Boris, tortured by religion-induced guilt over masturbation, to death. Everyone in the house, from the old patriarch Azaïs, through Vedel and his wife, to the children, is acting out a hypocritical lie. Armand Vedel, one of the pastor's sons, is a literary con-man, a parody of the modish, superficial avant-gardist, contemptuous of those he takes in. That other literary *faux-monnayeur*, Passavant, steals others' ideas, as Gide believed Cocteau did, and produces a slick, elegant confection at the behest of fashion. Lady Griffith, herself a past mistress in the art of dissimulation, says to Passavant's face: 'You have all the qualities of a man of letters – you are vain, hypocritical, fickle, selfish . . .'[95] Even Edouard, another former boarder of the Vedels, struggling so hard to understand himself and the world, so preoccupied with the problem of sincerity, is not immune to the charge of falseness: when confronted by Boris' death, he chooses to exclude it from the novel because it does not fit into his view of things, as he tried to ignore it in real life. For Gide the title has both a literary and a metaphorical sense – just as the novel is an intriguing, entertaining story, as well as a fascinating philosophical investigation into the process of literary creation. *Faux-monnayeurs* are literally those who produce false currency. Currency and language are both abstract systems of human exchange, in which one thing stands for another. The notion of literary counterfeiters plays with the paradox of how literature can speak truth about the world while 'telling stories', saying something is the case when it is not.

The novel's critical reception was much as one might have expected: a few intelligent reviews, often by sympathetic friends, a great deal of mindless abuse. An example of the first, by Henry Bidou, noted acutely that beneath the novel's 'continuous, spontaneous movement', its 'exuberant, relaxed, natural' air, the impression of 'disorder and confusion *à la russe*', there was 'a concealed, but very strong infrastructure'.[96] (Henry Bidou, it may be remembered, was among Gide's party on his visit to Morocco in 1923.) But, at this remove at least, it is the stupid, abusive reviews that are the more entertaining and, in a sense, revealing. André Billy, later to become a minor pillar of the French literary establishment, recoiled before the task of describing, 'in a paper such as this one, so disagreeably immoral a work'. The vice depicted in this 'hateful book belongs rather in the criminal court than in a work of literature'.[97] Others had no such inhibitions, whatever their view of the book. The improbably named Fortunat Strowski declared that it should have been called *Les Nouvelles Liaisons dangereuses*, the liaisons being 'between cynical youths and mature men, some of whom are intelligent and corrupt, others stupid and selfish. A few women pass by, but they don't count. We watch this world descend from depravity to crime. And the author's implacable *sang-froid* leaves us, simple readers, embarrassed and rather ashamed of ourselves.'[98] The following year, in 1927, the book appeared in New York and London in Dorothy Bussy's translation. This resulted in one of the most intelligent and favourable reviews, by Louis Kronenberger. This 'magnificent book . . . restores the novel to us in all its native freshness'. Like *Hamlet*, '*The Counterfeiters* was made for re-reading, and nobody can get all the rich compensations of its art . . . by reading it once.'[99] In *The Nation*,[100] Clifton Fadiman placed Gide's novel with 'the three other masterpieces of the genre in the twentieth century' (Thomas Mann's *Der Zauberberg*, Joyce's *Ulysses* and Proust's *A la recherche du temps perdu*). In London, Cyril Connolly gave a favourable (and amusing) review in *The New Statesman*.[101] This 'excellent book,' he concluded, 'will not influence English intellectual life in any way', but 'it does help us to understand the kind of revolution that is going on in France'. Gerald Gould, in the *Observer*,[102] concluded rather differently: 'The main impression is of a dreary and confused unpleasantness. Schoolboys, one knows, *can* be unpleasant: but surely they do not often engage in the circulation of false coin!'

Gide was well aware, as never before, that he was taking risks with the reading public: 'Too bad for the lazy reader: I want a different kind of reader. My role is to disturb people. The public always prefers to be reassured. There are those whose job it is to do just that. There are all too many of them.'[103] That he did not at first get the readers he wanted, or in large enough numbers, is shown by a remark in the *Journal* two years after he had finished the book: 'Before twenty years are up it will be recognized that what people now hold against my book are precisely its qualities.'[104] The prediction was borne out. In 1947, in a preface to *Portrait d'un inconnu*, by Nathalie Sarraute, that first practitioner of the *nouveau roman*, Sartre included *Les Faux-Monnayeurs* among what he calls the '*anti-romans*', which he defined with his usual intransigence: 'It is a matter of making the novel challenge itself, destroying it while one seems to be building it, writing the novel that does not make itself, cannot make itself.' Sartre seems to be describing the more unrelenting, the more arid of the *nouveaux romans*, rather than Gide's scintillating story, told with the mercurially light touch we have come to know in, say, the music of 1920s' Paris, of Ravel and Poulenc.

14

Heart of Darkness: Voyage au Congo *and* L'Ecole des femmes

(JULY 1925 – DECEMBER 1930)

'It was imposed upon me by a sort of ineluctable fatality, like all the important events of my life,' Gide wrote on the first page of his *Voyage au Congo*. It was 'a project made in youth and realized in maturity', a project first conceived when he was twenty, thirty-six years before.[1] Then, in 1889, the twenty-four-year-old Elie Allégret had set off on his first visit to the Congo. Now, with delicious symmetry, Gide was embarking on his own voyage there, with Elie Allégret's twenty-four-year-old son. (One is reminded of that other symmetry: in 1888, the eighteen-year-old Gide was taken on his first visit to England by the same Elie Allégret; thirty years later, Gide took the seventeen-year-old Marc on *his* first trip to England.) It is significant that Gide calls his book *Voyage au Congo*, for, by 1925, the one-time 'French Congo' had long since been merged in the larger French Equatorial Africa. For Gide, 'the Congo' was a country of the mind, nourished by reading, pre-eminently, *Heart of Darkness*: it was to Conrad, who had died the year before Gide's expedition, that he dedicated his own *Voyage au Congo*. Unlike Pastor Allégret, Gide set out not to teach, but to learn, or, rather, to discover a form of humanity that had not been 'deformed by clothes, civilization, laws, the usual morality'. Part of this attraction, he admitted to Jean Amrouche, was that he was 'very attracted, if I might dare to say, in a sensual way as well, by the negro race'.[2] This 'free, natural humanity' he did find, to some extent, in the more 'primitive' areas. But 'the Congo' turned out to be a very different place from his country of the mind. On 10 December, he wrote to Jean Schlumberger: 'Everything that I expected to give me delight and which . . . persuaded me to undertake this journey has disappointed me – but out of that very disappointment . . . I have acquired an unexpected education.' He had always maintained that, in order to understand France, one must go abroad. He is struck by the formlessness of the landscape, which achieves its uniformity, not, like the Sahara desert, by absence of life, but by its very 'profusion, prolixity, superabundance'. He now sees the enemy of culture to be not the desert, or even barbarism, but *indifférence*, lack of differentiation.[3] In his travel journal, he noted 'the absence of individuality, of individualization, the impossibility of achieving differentiation', not only in the landscape, but also in the identical configuration of villages and houses, in the physical appearance of members of the same small tribal community, in their tastes and outlook: 'This notion of differentiation that I have acquired there, on which depends the exquisite and the rare, is so important that it seems to me to be the principal lesson to bring back from this country.'[4]

The *Asie* left Bordeaux on 18 July. Apart from Gide and Marc, the ship's passengers seemed to be made up entirely of colonial officers and tradesmen. When asked what he hoped to find out there, Gide replied: 'I shall see when I get there.'[5] The ship made its first call at Dakar (Senegal), 'a gloomy town': 'one cannot imagine anything uglier or less exotic'. Three days later, they arrived at Conakry (Guinea) in the middle of driving rain and fog. The weather cleared and they went on land. 'Everything here seems to promise happiness, voluptuousness, oblivion,'[6] but they have only half-an-hour to enjoy it. Over the next two weeks, they called at several ports before leaving ship at Matadi and taking the Belgian railway to Kinshassa.

On 14 August they reached Brazzaville and made several excursions out of the town, notably to the Congo waterfalls. Gide went butterfly-hunting; Marc took film footage and photographs. They witnessed the trial of a colonial official, who, promoted too young, compensated for his lack of natural authority by waging a reign of terror on those under him: he was condemned to a year's imprisonment. 'The less intelligent the white man is,' Gide comments, 'the more stupid he thinks the black.'[7] They take on a 'hideous' cook, bearing the 'ridiculous name of Zézé', and two 'boys', Adoum and Outhman, both Arabs. With them and their porters, each carrying a load of 20–25 kilos, they embark on their journey up the Congo, the river forming the boundary between the French and the Belgian colonies. On the boat, they are joined by Yvonne de Lestrange, a cousin of Antoine de Saint-Exupéry, who is doing research for the Institut Pasteur into the effectiveness of a vaccine against the sleeping sickness.

On 12 September, they arrive at Coquillatville (now Mbandaka), on the Belgian side, having crossed the Equator a few miles before. There the governor puts a car and a senior official at their disposal. They visit the botanical gardens at Eala, where its director shows them some of his prize exhibits: 'Cocoa-palms, coffee-trees, bread-trees, milk-trees, candle-trees, loin-cloth trees' and the extraordinary 'traveller's tree', which contains in each of its leaves a cupful of pure water.[8] They leave their ship for a smaller boat. No sooner have they moved off than 'three negroes start a deafening tam-tam on a calabash and an enormous wooden drum'. Gide takes refuge in Bossuet's funeral oration for Anne of Austria (wife of Louis XIII). At Irebu, they change boats again, this time for a whale-boat. At Liranga, they spend two days awaiting the arrival of yet another boat, this time a larger one, with pleasant cabins, saloon and dining-room. With the captain, they are the only whites on board. The monotony of the landscape encourages reading. A short textbook on contemporary philosophy convinces Gide that he has always been a Bergsonian without knowing it. He then turns to Molière's *Le Misanthrope* and Stevenson's *The Master of Ballantrae*.

At Bangui, they are met on board by the governor's *chef de cabinet* – they have now left the Middle Congo and are in Ubangi-Chari, almost 1,000 miles up river from the coast. They lunch with the governor, Auguste Lamblin. The following day, they borrow the governor's Citroën and set off on a two-day visit to the M'bali falls. If this were Switzerland, Gide writes, 'huge hotels would have been built all around. Here, solitude; a couple of huts with straw roofs, in which we are to sleep, do not spoil the wild majesty of the scene. Fifty yards from where I'm writing, the cascade falls in a great mighty curtain, silvered by the light of the moon between the branches of great trees.'[9] They return in a tornado. They take their leave of Yvonne de Lestrange, though they meet up again later.

On 1 October, they leave Tabou, for a three-week tour of Ubangi-Chari. Their car is a none too healthy-looking Ford without headlights; a van brings up the rear with their luggage. At Sibut, they attend the monthly rubber auction at which a cartel of whites buys up the rubber brought by the blacks, then, in a private, all-white auction, distribute it among themselves. The merchants then go to Kinshassa, where they sell the rubber at about seven times what they paid for it. At Mobaye, Gide and Marc visit a hospital, where men come from miles around to have an operation on elephantiasis of the sexual organs, a common condition of the area: 'one is dumbfounded, without at first understanding what the huge bag can possibly be that the native is dragging along underneath him.' These protuberances weigh anything up to 82 kilos. That morning, Dr Cacavelli operated on a young man from whom he removed 30 or 40 kilos of 'a sort of bloody, whitish substance'. The operations are invariably successful and the patient recovers his virility. In three years, the doctor had performed 136 such operations.[10]

At Foroumbala, they visit a school, where they are regaled with a 'chorus by Gounod', followed by a football match, in which Gide and Marc take part, an orange serving as the ball. They reached the most easterly point of their journey at Rafai, the last remaining sultanate in the colony. What autonomy it had left was no more than show, like 'the fine operetta uniform' invented for the sultan by the French authorities. They made their way back to Bangui, which they reached on 18 October.

'The image that I had of this country,' Gide notes, 'was so strong . . . that I wonder if, later, that false image will not struggle for dominance over my memory of it.'[11] Five days later, they left Bangui, on a fifteen-week journey northwards that would take them to Lake Chad, some 1,600 miles away. They would be accompanied most of the way by some fifty or sixty porters, replaced every few weeks by others. On a typical day, Gide notes that 'we did a ten hours' day – including a two hours' halt and an hour and a half of *tipoye* – six-and-a-half hours on foot at about 6 kilometres an hour.'[12] The *tipoye* was a chair, raised on poles and carried by porters. Gide and Marc often refused the luxury of the *tipoye* for several hours, in order to rest the porters and share their experience of the journey. They consistently treated their African servants far better than they were used to being treated – either by the employees of the rubber companies or by their native superiors – and were rewarded with smiles, gratitude and a remarkable degree of honesty. Once, Gide notes, Marc gave a splendid 'ticking off' to one of the local 'guards' who had dared to strike their cook.[13] Both Gide and Marc used what medical knowledge and supplies they had to treat their porters when ill – and whoever needed treatment in the villages they passed through. In the evening, Gide often read to his boy Adoum, who also acted as their interpreter. They were both kept busy writing their accounts of the journey and letters home. They found time for reading: on 21 November, Gide finished *The Master of Ballantrae* – more than usually inappropriate reading for Gide – and gave it to Marc to read, Gide swapping Stevenson for Goethe.

On 27 October, at Boda, they lunched with Georges Pacha, the local French administrator. They were no sooner on the second day of their journey than they became embroiled in what turned out to be a major incident. At N'Goto they were awoken at two in the morning by a man who turned out to be Samba N'Goto, chief of the Bofi tribe. It was clear that the man had a long and terrible tale to tell, but, since neither side could understand the other very well, he was told to come back in the morning when they would have an interpreter. It transpired that six days before Pacha had sent a Sergeant Yemba to punish the inhabitants of the next village, Bodembéré. He had ordered them to remove their huts from their native village, where they cultivated their fields, and to live with people of a different tribe along the new roadway. Sergeant Yemba had set out with three guards, requisitioned two or three more men in each village that he passed, then, on arrival, had twelve men tied to a tree and shot. They then set about the women, Yemba wielding a machete. Five young children were shut up in a hut and set alight. There were, in all, thirty-two victims. At great risk to himself, Samba N'Goto had called on Gide, thinking him to be an important French official and convinced that the white man would see justice done. His account, carefully written down by Gide and Marc, took over two hours. 'For me, it is not good enough to say, as many do, that the natives were even more wretched before the French occupation,' Gide comments. 'We have taken on responsibilities towards them that we have no right to ignore. I know things that I cannot be reconciled to . . . Now I know, I must speak out . . . I want to go back-stage, behind the scenery, and to find out at last what is hidden there, however horrible it may be.'[14]

Gide was presented with 'a strange little animal' that looked like a sloth. It was, more specifically, a *perodictique potto*. It was about the size of a cat, moved extremely slowly and ate anything it was offered, 'jam, bread, honey', but had a particular liking for concentrated milk. Once befriended by Gide it could hardly be separated from him, spending most of the day round his neck, looking very like a woman's fur stole, and sleeping with him at night. Gide called him Dindiki, the native name for that species of animal.

They arrived at Fort Archambault, where Marcel de Coppet was awaiting them, a little after midnight on 26 December. After several hours of talk, they retired to bed. Two days later, Gide wrote to Dorothy Bussy, declaring that, in spite of the monotony of their fifty days of trudging through 'this shapeless, enormous land', he had experienced 'some of the most intense joys of my life'. He had never felt better and had taken quite easily to covering over 40 kilometres on foot each day, for several days at a stretch, almost without stopping, 'and at my age!'[15]

Gide and Marc had hoped to spend several weeks at Fort Archambault, recuperating from their exertions. However, Marcel de Coppet had been appointed acting-governor of Chad and would have to leave Fort Archambault for the colony capital, Fort-Lamy, in a week's time. Gide and Marc decided to accompany him. On the morning of 17 January, Marc shot 200 metres of film before they boarded the boat, the *Jacques d'Uzès* (as chance would have it), that was to take them on their journey down the Chari. On the way, they went antelope hunting: Coppet killed three huge ones. Another day a crocodile was killed; on yet another, Coppet brought down what he called an 'aeroplane bird' for Gide to take to the Muséum de Paris; later, more practically, succulent guinea fowl and wild duck.

They arrived at Fort-Lamy on 26 January. For a small consideration, Marc found a young girl, Hamra, to share his bed, after rejecting the advances of an older, less attractive girl. This was not Marc's first experience of young native girls: in November, at Baya Yangéré, there had been Mangua, 'about fourteen', who had joined him in his siesta[16] and, shortly after arrival in Fort-Lamy, there had been 'la petite Titiani'. Gide, too, had 'adventures'. Later in the year, while writing up his travel notes, he read extracts to the Petite Dame, who commented: 'On the few occasions when he referred to an adventure with one of the boys, he broke off and said: "Would you leave that in? You don't think it will discredit the rest . . .? Oh, well, too bad. It all happened so naturally, so easily. It would be puerile to cut it out."'[17] In the end, he did take a more cautious line: there are no such explicit references in the published version, though the description of his feelings for Adoum may be taken to imply a liaison. Marc Allégret's *Carnets*, on the other hand, were private notes, often written in telegraphic style, never intended for publication. They could afford to be quite explicit: what emerges from them is that Marc's sexual preference (for young girls) was now firmly established – and that the relationship with Gide was as close, as loving, as ever.

After four days at Fort-Lamy, they took a boat northwards to Lake Chad, which they crossed to Bol. From there, they ventured out into the surrounding villages, where Marc found good film material. They went back to Fort-Lamy and stayed there a further ten days before beginning the return journey. It is at this point that Gide's *Voyage au Congo* ends. The narrative of the eleven-week journey back to the coast, first through Chad and the Logone river, then the longer, more arduous stage overland through Cameroon, is taken up in *Le Retour du Tchad*. They left Fort-Lamy in three whale-boats on 20 February. By 1 March, Marc had a fever, his temperature staying around 40°C for a few days. Then Gide fell ill, quite suddenly while reading Goethe's *Faust*. Gide notes that the ship's 'boys', no longer content with calling him 'Commander', had promoted him to 'Governor'. During his illness, they begin to chant: 'The Governor is ill. / Row, row, that we may go quicker than the illness, / And take him to the doctor at Logone.'

It was, he added, the most extraordinary chant that he had heard so far. He wished that Stravinsky could have heard it and proceeds to a musical analysis of it.[18] Later, 'Governor' was not good enough and Gide was given the ultimate title of 'Government'. They received a ceremonial visit from the local sultan, who arrived in 'a marvellous *boubou* of white broché silk with portraits of Edward VII scattered over it'.[19] From a purely human point of view, the second book is less interesting than the first, though Gide is lavish in his observations of fauna and flora. Marc misses killing a lion, but shoots a hippopotamus, which surfaces several hours later, to be expertly butchered, an operation that takes two hours. Later, Gide declared a steak from the enormous beast 'fort bon'. Away from the river, the temperature rose into the upper 40s and the air was so dry that the soft leather binding of his beloved *Concise Oxford Dictionary* began to curl up. Presumably with its help, Gide continued to read Milton's *Paradise Lost* and *Samson Agonistes*.

With great sorrow on both sides, Gide said good-bye to his Arab boy, Adoum. At all hours of the day, he used to go off on his own and learn by heart the short sentences that Gide had written down for him in his exercise book, 'so strong was his wish to educate himself and so come closer to us'. He had originally joined the party seven months before at Brazzaville, with the idea of leaving them at Fort-Lamy and returning to his family in the Ouaddai, some 500 miles to the north-east. Now, every mile of the journey back to the coast was taking him further from his destination. Gide arranged for the young man to go to Fort-Lamy, armed with a letter to Coppet. The acting-governor then made sure that Adoum was reunited with his mother, whom he had not seen for two years. Gide also sent money to the mother on behalf of her son. 'Such devotion, such humble nobility, such a childlike desire to do things well, so much capacity for love – all of which, as a rule, meets with nothing but rebuffs . . .' There was, he believed, nothing unusual about the boy. 'Through him, I have come to feel a whole race of suffering humanity . . . whose beauty, whose worth, we have failed to understand . . . I wish it was in my power never to leave him . . . The death of a friend would not grieve me more, for I know that I shall never see him again.' Each turned away to hide his tears, Adoum muttering, in a sorrowful voice: 'Merci . . . merci . . .' Later, Gide notes: 'I have never seen anything more moving than that poor boy's unhappiness. Perhaps he was surprised to see me so unhappy myself . . . What an abominable crime it is to repulse, to prevent love.'[20]

At Rei Bouba the sultan added two 'pages' to their cortège. Their sole function was decorative. They were the most handsome young men Gide had so far seen, 'créatures de luxe'. Each kept to himself, as if forming part of the party, but not deigning to mix with its members. Each had a bow slung round his shoulders and 'on his back, like Cupid, a quiver of arrows . . .' They 'looked as though they had stepped out of the Campo Santo fresco at Pisa, ready to take part in Benozzo Gozzoli's *Wine Harvest*'. Their walk, especially that of the young one, was like dancing: 'He was Nijinsky.' 'It is certain,' Gide adds, 'that it was for the pure joy of looking at them that the sultan had lent us his two pages . . . I think it is hardly possible that he would have been apprised of my tastes.'[21]

On the morning of 1 May, almost at journey's end, Gide discovered that his beloved Dindiki was dead. The poor creature had not taken kindly to the drier climate they had encountered since leaving the area around the river Logone. It suffered from constipation and finally refused to eat. Over two pages Gide describes the endless attempts he made to experiment with different kinds of food – all to no avail. They reached Douala and a week later they set sail: 'The ship has weighed anchor and Mount Cameroon is disappearing slowly in the fog.'[22] They were back in Bordeaux, seventeen days later, on 31 May.

The Petite Dame and Beth were there to meet them. Beth had arrived the day before, but her mother had been there for the past two weeks, not waiting for Gide and Marc, but because her husband was undergoing an operation on his sinuses at the hands of a well-known surgeon who specialized in such operations. The Petite Dame and Beth stood on the quayside as the *Asie* moved slowly to shore. Suddenly Beth cried out: 'I can see Bypeed. Yes, yes, it can only be him – and Marc's beside him.' Eventually, the Petite Dame caught sight of Gide's broad-brimmed hat; Marc was bareheaded and seemed to be shivering in a big overcoat.

The friends had been together exactly fifty weeks before. The Petite Dame scrutinized Gide's face for signs of change: 'He is much thinner and the skin around the eyes is very wrinkled . . .' He didn't really look older and, as soon as he spoke, all the old vitality was there. Marc 'looked a splendid colour'. They talked of Catherine. 'So she's talking,' said Gide in wonder. 'I simply cannot imagine it. She really speaks? She has things to say? It's incredible!' Beth asked what had happened to Dindiki. Gide recounted Dindiki's sad death, but announced that, on board ship, he had bought a civet cat and a little monkey. They grabbed a few things to take to the hotel: the rest they would come back for the next day. Very hungry, they went out for a meal at 'the big tavern opposite the theatre'. Joy reigned supreme: 'I notice that they haven't lost the capacity to laugh at one another, which is a very good sign. No, nothing has become tarnished in our hearts and we are there, all four of us, just as before. Happiness makes Elisabeth very beautiful.' When Gide left the dining-room for a time, Marc asked his friends how they thought he looked. On the way back through Cameroon, they had had a terrible time: the heat had never been less than 45°C during the day and 39°C at night. They could only move at night and, during the day, it was impossible to sleep. Gide was really at the limit of his endurance, exhausted. There had been times when they wondered if they would ever reach the coast and their ship home. They ended their meal with strawberries: ecstatic, Gide and Marc agreed that they had never eaten anything like them when away.

The following morning, Gide and Marc dealt with their luggage. The monkey, they were told, had escaped through a porthole. Suspecting a trick, Gide decided to visit a dealer in animals whose name he had been given. He described what he wanted. The dealer had just the thing, but unfortunately it had already been sold: it was, of course, the same monkey that Gide had bought. An altercation ensued, but Gide, shouted down, retreated, 'outraged, disconsolate, angry'. They were left with the civet cat, which the Petite Dame found 'a terrible nuisance'. Gide prepared for it 'a banana, some cream cheese and milk, but to no avail'. Eventually, it was discovered that it would drink milk out of a baby's bottle.[23]

Gide and Marc left Bordeaux for Paris, where Gide spent the next two months, broken only by two week-long visits to Cuverville and Madeleine. He had not been back four days when he was writing: 'Once again I feel that numbing of my mind, my will, my whole being that I feel hardly anywhere else but at Cuverville. Writing the briefest note takes me an hour, the slightest letter a whole morning . . . A few days ago I was still full of enthusiasm; I felt I could move mountains; today I feel quite dragged down.'[24]

Roger Martin du Gard, who had an equal detestation of arrivals and departures, wrote a letter of welcome to Gide to be handed to him by the Petite Dame. Gide tried to get him to join him at Cuverville, but RMG felt that he could not get away from Le Tertre for more than a couple of days. (Le Tertre was the seventeenth-century house and its grounds that RMG had bought from his father-in-law in 1924 for 200,000 francs – £8,000 or $39,000 at the time. It is situated at Bellême, in the Orne, 100 miles or more south-west of Paris.) He was still supervising the work of four painters, six labourers, two upholsterers, three masons and a joiner. The two friends finally met at the Villa Montmorency on 21 June: RMG left a long account in his journal. Pushing the half-opened door, he entered the dusty, echoing hall, full of luggage – tin trunks, chests and 'strange, battered packages, giving off a very exotic smell, sweet and strong'. He called out and Gide came running and the two fell into each other's arms. In the dining-room, a fire was burning in the hearth, 'despite the season'. Gide seemed nervous: he got up, lit a cigarette, put it out, got up to shut the door and to poke the fire. Then he began to speak, not of Africa and the journey back, but of the 'petite cuisine littéraire', the journalistic campaign being waged against him, the reviews of *Les Faux-Monnayeurs*, the inner politics of the *NRF*. Then, eventually, he talked about the report that he was writing for the government. He picked up an official report of 1902 describing the ill-treatment of an African tribe by the French companies and began to read. At one point, he broke down and began to sob. RMG noted a 'disproportion' between the report, dealing with events a quarter of a century before, and Gide's emotional response. He realized that the experience of Africa had left his friend in a state of extreme nervous sensitivity: he was '*vibrant comme un disque de microphone*'.[25]

On 11 July, Gide went to stay for a few days at the Château de Chitré, near Châtellerault, the country house of Yvonne de Lestrange, whom, it will be remembered, Gide had met in Africa. Usually referred to, democratically, as Mme de Lestrange, she was the dowager Duchesse de Trévise and Vicomtesse de Lestrange in her own right. Known familiarly to her friends as 'Pomme', she is referred to in Gide's *Journal* as 'P.'.

At the beginning of August, Gide dined with Edouard Herriot, then Prime Minister and Foreign Minister. Herriot, leader of the Radical party, was a former *professeur de rhétorique* (*lycée* classics teacher) and a writer. In the course of the conversation, Herriot asked Gide to sound out whether Martin du Gard would accept the 'red ribbon' (of the Légion d'honneur). If so, he was to send a telegram to the Prime Minister stating simply '*Volontiers*' (willingly). Somewhat to Gide's surprise, RMG did accept: unlike Valéry, who had recently joined the 'Immortals', he had previously rejected overtures to join the Académie française. RMG seems to have found the idea rather amusing: he had always considered that the only way to show 'how little value one placed on that distinction was to accept it, *without having solicited it*, to say thank you with a smile – . . . *and never to wear it!*'[26]

On 7 August Gide arrived at La Bastide and saw his daughter for the first time since his return. 'He is very moved that she isn't afraid of him,' wrote the Petite Dame. 'She takes his hand and leads him off to inspect all her treasures . . . He didn't expect that at all.'[27] Later, Gide talked to the

Petite Dame about Marc. The only influence exercised by the Allégret parents over their children had been by reaction. He had noticed this 'contrariness' in Marc from the beginning: indeed, at first, Marc had tended to take the opposite view to anything he said. Gradually, Gide was able to overcome this automatic response and begin Marc's true education. In their life together, at the Villa, Marc was 'marvellous'. He has a wonderfully light touch and is 'full of an exquisite sense of fantasy that makes everything delightful and amusing'.[28]

On 17 August, Gide, Marc and Beth set out for Pontigny. On the way they called on Copeau at Pernand-Vergelesses. At Chablis, they set up house, together with Catherine and her Danish nurse. From there Gide could attend proceedings at Pontigny, some 10 miles away, whenever he wanted to. The Petite Dame and Loup Mayrisch were already installed in the 'abbey', attending a *décade* on 'The Christian imprint. How can we recognize it? Is it disappearing?' One highlight of that *décade* was the presence of Tolstoy's eldest daughter, then sixty-two. Gide attended two of the lectures, one on Kierkegaard by his French translator and one on Nietzsche by the head of the Nietzschegesellschaft. The *décade littéraire*, on 'Humanism. Its essence. Is a new Humanism possible?' began with Desjardins doing his usual expert *tour d'horizon* of the question, moving from Petrarch, through Erasmus, to the present. Gide felt that the *décades* were becoming too dominated by academic philosophers. In one discussion, he gently suggested that he did not believe that Montaigne would have understood a word of what had just been said about him. Gide was not a professional, reading Montaigne with a view to teaching it. He had lived with Montaigne intimately over a period of forty years and treated him like a dear old friend, constantly sharing his thoughts with him. Even in 1926, it seems, Gide was aware of belonging to a declining race of 'common readers', however 'uncommon' some of them might be. Often, in the evenings, Youra Guller, a concert pianist and wife of the publisher Jacques Schiffrin, would play for the assembled guests. When she played Chopin, Gide was critical, as he invariably was of Chopin's interpreters: 'It's always the same: personal interpretation in order to show off, never a pure, honest presentation.' He was happier when Mme Schiffrin played C. P. E. Bach, Scarlatti or Stravinsky.[29]

After Pontigny, Gide and Marc made for Marseille, sailing from there to Tunis on 13 September. Things went badly from the first day. 'Indescribable boredom,' Gide wrote in his *Journal*. 'Everyone is ugly. I would give this whole trip for a few hours of practice at a good piano ... Terrible waste of time, at an age when . . .' Indeed, a few days later, he was writing that his best memory of Tunis was of 'a few hours spent in front of the excellent little Pleyel belonging to Tournier, the bookseller'.[30] Disgusted with Tunis, they moved on to the seaside resort of Hammamet, which turned out to be worse. Gide had clearly fallen out of love with his Tunisians, who, he wrote to Alibert, were 'hideous, vile, abject', such a contrast with his 'good blacks in the Congo'.[31] The truth is, Marc had fallen sick, with violent vomiting, and remained more or less indisposed for the rest of their time in Tunisia. They decided to cut their visit short: however, they would stay at Hammamet for a few days in order to meet René Michelet and friends, who would soon be arriving from Tunis. Gide had hoped to work while away, but had done nothing but bathe and rest. They were back in Marseille by 30 September.

After a week in Cuverville, Gide returned to Paris. A few days later, the Petite Dame arrived, staying, as usual, at Jean Schlumberger's flat in the rue d'Assas. On a visit to the Villa, she noticed that it was in even greater disorder than ever – nearly four months after the return from Africa. The trunks and wooden chests were still lying around, open, part of their contents strewn over several rooms. On top of all that, there was all Marc's cinema equipment: 'Everywhere, on everything, were reels, wheels and files, and still nobody to do the cleaning!' 'When will you have a proper home?' she asked Gide. '*Chère amie*, I don't think I ever will,' Gide replied. 'Unless I had somewhere of my own in Paris that you could use,' said the Petite Dame. 'Yes,' said Gide, 'that's what I say to myself sometimes.' Two days later, the Petite Dame called again, bringing cakes for tea. Marc and his youngest brother, Yves, were busy preparing Marc's film – Yves was later to become Marc's assistant in a number of films. A despairing Petite Dame looked around the dining-room. There was something 'diabolical' about the confusion of 'exotic things' and yards of film. There was no fire in the grate and the fireplace was full of waste paper, stretching out to the middle of the room. The room was lit by a single lamp, which was constantly being moved from one part of the room to the other: the cord was so long that one tripped over it wherever one went. She found just enough room to rest her elbow on 'a little table, transformed into a laboratory', but had nowhere to put her ashtray except on her knees.[32]

The following day, the Petite Dame and her husband went to spend a few days with Roger Martin du Gard at Le Tertre. Théo was not well and his condition grew worse on the journey back to Saint-Clair. Nevertheless, his death, on 13 December, came as a shock to his wife. 'The divergences between Théo and me,' she wrote, 'never prevailed over the tenderness we felt for one another.'³³

On 15 December, Gide was in Paris, seeing Dorothy Bussy on her way back to London for Christmas. An afternoon spent together seems to have gone well – for once. Gide, she tells him, was 'full of kindness and friendship'. She had been approached by Virginia Woolf on behalf of the Hogarth Press, concerning Gide's Africa book. Gide was 'flattered' by her interest, but felt that Knopf had the prior claim. (Dorothy Bussy's translation of *Voyage au Congo* and *Le Retour du Tchad* was published by Knopf as *Travels in the Congo* in 1929.)

After spending the New Year at Cuverville, Gide went South to commiserate with the bereaved wife and daughter at Saint-Clair. 'I'm glad he only came yesterday,' the Petite Dame noted next day. 'Earlier his presence would have embarrassed my pain. Now he is doing us nothing but good . . . He is there, silent, with his work, full of little, discreet attentions and showing a real interest in everything concerning Théo.'³⁴ They went to the studio and Gide helped her to decide which of his paintings should be included in a group show planned to take place at Druet's. They talked of the future. La Bastide, Beth's farm, had already been sold and she was thinking of converting her father's studio at Saint-Clair into accommodation for herself and Catherine. Gide had already offered to put up the money needed for the conversion. The Petite Dame could then sell the house itself and find an apartment in Paris, where they could come and stay whenever they liked. Gide was pleased with the idea that he would still have somewhere in the South to stay, as well as seeing the Petite Dame, Beth and Catherine in Paris.

They all went over to Bormes to visit the Mayrisches. Staying there were Bernard Groethuysen, a German-born, but French-naturalized philosopher, who had been one of the speakers at Pontigny that year, and his lover, Alix Guillain, a woman whom the Petite Dame had known as a child. Both were ardent Communists. Two days later, Loup Mayrisch and her guests came over to Saint-Clair for lunch and questioned Gide intently about his experiences in the Congo. Alix Guillain said she would contact *L'Humanité*, the Communist newspaper, on the subject. Gide talked of his wish to go back there, perhaps in September. Meanwhile, he was already at work on a new work of fiction, *L'Ecole des femmes*, begun a few weeks before at Cuverville. After a week at Saint-Clair, Gide decided to spend a couple of weeks at Roquebrune with the Bussys.

Apart from one afternoon in Paris, two weeks before, Dorothy had not seen Gide since his return from Africa: 'we talked as we hadn't talked for many years,' she noted on one of his letters.[35] One day, they were walking down to the village, when they met 'a very good-looking boy of about sixteen or seventeen'. On seeing Gide, the boy's face lit up, 'a wonderful expression of joy and affection'. Because he was with her, Gide obviously did not acknowledge the boy's look, but the boy's face remained 'radiant' throughout.[36] It was probably during that stay at Roquebrune that Gide met Raymond Poincaré. The current Foreign Minister, Hanotaux, an historian and *académicien*, had a house very close to the Bussys'. That January, Poincaré, who had returned to office as Prime Minister six months before, was staying with him and asked to meet Gide. 'I only had to read a few pages of your *Voyage* [which had appeared in the last three numbers of the *NRF*] . . .,' the great man declared. 'Monsieur Gide, it is a book written in good faith.' In the last session of the Chamber, Poincaré had defended Gide's case against the big concessionary companies. On 9 February, Gide left Saint-Clair for Paris.

Back in Paris, Gide and the Petite Dame attended a private screening of Marc's film at Léon Poirier's apartment in the rue Vignon. Poirier, nephew of the painter Berthe Morisot, was a film director and had himself made a documentary in Africa, *Croisière noire*. The film, which the Petite Dame found 'very uneven in interest', though some of the shots 'admirable', lasted an hour.[37] Poirier declared that Marc's inexperience was as self-evident as his gifts and promptly offered him the post of assistant director for a long film about the battle of Verdun. It would take a year to eighteen months to shoot. This seemed to put paid to any idea of Gide's to set out for Africa again in October.

Two days later, the Petite Dame arrived at the Villa: Gide was about to go off to spend a week with Martin du Gard at Le Tertre. 'Ah! When will we emerge from this temporary state!' Gide sighed. During his absence, the Petite Dame had been looking for somewhere to live. On his return, she showed him plans for the fifth floor of a new building then being completed at 1 bis rue Vaneau, on the corner with the rue de Varenne, overlooking the Prime Ministerial gardens. The floor consisted of two apartments that could be made communicating and two studios, one of which could be a large library, the other accommodation for Marc, with separate entrance. Gide was excited by the whole idea and wanted to go and inspect the site at once. They made their way through the rubble to the fifth floor and agreed that it would suit them very well. Over tea in the café of the Gare d'Orsay, they discussed the question. Both felt enthusiastic – and apprehensive. Perhaps they ought not to rush into anything. 'And anyway,' Gide added, 'I have an indefinable sense that I'm not made to settle down anywhere.' Then he at once saw the other side of the argument: 'There is the practical side of life to take into account: not to catch cold, to be sure one is properly cared for when one is ill and, above all, the best background for work.' The Petite Dame said that she could always offer him a bed under her stairs, with radiator.[38]

At this time, Gide had left Marc at the Villa and accepted an invitation from Yvonne de Lestrange to stay with her at the quai Malaquais. It was a ridiculous situation, but he had come to regard the Villa as a botched mess and it demoralized him. He was anxious, too, about Marc. It looked as though he would make a career in the cinema, but he seemed to live from day to day, awaiting events. Tempting offers had already come his way – like 750,000 francs (about £30,000 or $150,000 at the time) to make a film of *Les Caves du Vatican*.

On 4 April, the Petite Dame had dinner with Martin du Gard, who was in Paris for a few days. She talked about 'ce projet de vie un peu en commun', which seemed to be taking shape. She realized what she would lose in terms of peace, but also that what she would gain would be priceless. More important, it would be the best solution for Beth and Catherine, the best way of giving them continuing, but discreet contact with Gide, without restricting his freedom. RMG completely agreed with her analysis of the situation and thought that the rue Vaneau offered the best solution. He would visit the apartment next day. On arrival, RMG suggested that they ought also to see the floor above, the sixth and top floor. They both thought it much more tempting, with its balcony, extreme brightness and irregular ceilings, than the one below. RMG thought that they should not hesitate, but secure it at once. The following day, Gide, suddenly bedridden at Yvonne de Lestrange's, could not join them on a further exploration of the site. Marc, however, was with them, 'with his quick, steady eye' and, despite his usual reticent manner, seemed to approve of everything. They all went back to the quai Malaquais and, over tea, made their report. Gide was enthusiastic. 'If we don't make such experiments,' he asked, 'who will? And even if we're making a mistake, let's do it with joy. But I don't think it is a mistake. On the contrary, I think it's a very wise move. For my part, I can see nothing but advantages and I'm very grateful.' They agreed to ask an architect friend to make further inquiries. Two days later, the architect reported: he had visited the site, studied the papers and gave his wholehearted approval. The day after that, Gide was well enough to go to the rue Vaneau himself. On 9 April, he gave his formal approval to the contractors and left for a few days at Cuverville. 'You don't seem to realize how incredible all this is,' said the Petite Dame. 'And you don't seem to realize that I always expect the incredible,' Gide replied. In Cuverville, Gide had shown Madeleine the plans, but found it difficult to get any opinion out of her: 'She is so withdrawn from everything!'[39] Back in Paris, he found that the Petite Dame had arranged everything with the contractor and all that was needed was his signature and a cheque for 100,000 francs (£4,000 or $20,000 at the time). On 15 April, contracts were exchanged and, two months later, the sale was completed. But it was to be over a year before they could move into their apartments and live, as Loup Mayrisch called it, 'in symbiosis'.

On 15 April, Gide left Paris for three weeks in Switzerland. 'I'd be very happy to live in Neuchâtel, where the memory of Rousseau still roams,' he writes. But Rousseau was not the only writer roaming the streets and, for Gide, the main attraction of the town was not so much the lingering presence of Rousseau as the fact that 'the children are more beautiful than anywhere else' – though, unfortunately, not admitted to the cinemas under the age of sixteen.[40] At Zürich, where he spent about ten days, he saw Jean Strohl, the biologist, and was shown the university's 'various collections of shells, shell fish, corals, insects – of the greatest interest'. Strohl also took him out on 'a wonderful car ride, into a landscape extraordinarily full of flowers'. Meanwhile, Gide was correcting the proofs of *Voyage au Congo* and working on a new play, *Oedipe*. But he was missing Marc: 'With M. all my youth has left me; I am half-asleep waiting for his return and waste my time, as if I still had a great deal to waste. I sleep too much, smoke too much, digest badly and hardly notice the spring. A human being gives up when he has no one to think about but himself.'[41] On 11 May, Marc joined him at Basle. Next day, he was in Heidelberg having 'endless conversations' with Ernst-Robert Curtius. 'I find in him, in his eyes, in the tone of his voice, in his gestures, a gentleness, a graciousness, a kindness that are almost evangelical.'[42]

Soon after Gide's return, Madeleine made one of her few, brief visits to Paris. She would, Gide wrote to Copeau, have 'just enough time to clean the Villa and go back worn out, having seen just enough of Paris to make her a little more disgusted with it'.[43] On 3 June, the Petite Dame, back in Paris after three weeks at Le Tertre, met the Gides at a private showing of Marc's Congo film, given at the Vieux Colombier. It was the first time for some years that the two women had seen one another. 'I found Madeleine rather changed, her walk much stiffer,' the Petite Dame notes. 'Her face is sweeter than ever, of a trembling tenderness that is quite moving. It took me some time to realize that it was her false teeth that had robbed her smile of its peculiar quality: a slow, sad, rather oriental smile . . . Gide was most attentive towards her; he was afraid she might get too tired or bored!' Afterwards they went off, with a few friends, for tea at the Lutétia. Madeleine talked to the Petite Dame about the new apartment in the rue Vaneau: 'She does everything with great delicacy, seizing on any opportunity to express approval and doing so consciously and with apparent conviction.' Madeleine asked to see the Petite Dame again and, three days later, invited her to tea at the Villa. The Petite Dame was astonished to find the house completely transformed: 'It was unrecognizable, everything in perfect order, smelling of polish.'[44]

One day, Marc narrowly missed being seriously injured in the place de l'Alma. It was pouring with rain. Gide and he were looking for a taxi to take them to the Vieux Colombier, where they had arranged to meet Picasso. Suddenly an '*auto-bolide*' (Gide's word: a racing-car, sports-car?) was bearing down upon them. It tried to avoid them, skidded and knocked Marc over. 'I saw him disappear under the car, which finally stopped, after dragging him along in the mud for ten metres,' Gide wrote to RMG. 'It was wonderful to see him get up on his own.' He had a few bad bruises on his legs, but little more.[45] In July, Gide went to Cuverville and was joined there, for three days, by Curtius. At the beginning of August, he spent three days with RMG at Le Tertre, then, on 7 August, went South with Marc to join the Petite Dame, Beth and Catherine at Peïra-Cava, a hillside village north of Nice. Gide and Marc put up at a 'Russian pension', where, over the next ten days, they all had lunch together. While at Peïra-Cava, he and Marc worked on a long article, 'The Distress of our Equatorial Africa', for the *Revue de Paris*. For Gide, this was merely the latest – and not the last – chore in his campaign to expose the role of the rubber companies in the French equatorial colonies. Since his return, he had not only written up *Voyage au Congo* and worked on *Le Retour du Tchad*, but had been in communication, by letter and in person, with various officials and politicians, right up to the Prime Minister, Poincaré. His principal demand was that the companies' 'concessions', which included political, judicial and police powers, should not be renewed. These powers were 'purchased' from the government by the companies in exchange for a tax levied at 15 per cent of their net profits. Gide demonstrates, in great detail, official statistics to hand, that the system provides a poor financial return to the French state, while reducing the native population to 'a condition that does not differ from slavery'. The 'concessions' had often been condemned by French government officials, but such were the power and influence of the companies that they could ignore any complaints. If threats did not have the desired effect – and the governor-general himself had been threatened – the companies knew that no official would remain long enough in his post to be of any serious consequence.

On 16 August, the Petite Dame notes that Gide has shown her a letter from 'that young pupil of Jouhandeau's who has thrown himself violently on him and writes such touching letters'. This was the beginning of a relationship with Robert Levesque, then seventeen, who was to become and remain to the end one of Gide's closest friends. Levesque, who was attending a boarding-school in Passy, was in the middle of a passionate infatuation with one of his teachers, Marcel Jouhandeau, a Catholic and a novelist, and with a fellow-pupil. To complicate matters further he also wanted to become a priest. In desperation, the boy wrote long letters to Gide, pouring out his troubles and seeking advice. In Paris, Gide had agreed to meet him. The conversation got on to the subject of hell. Levesque told Gide how he had been to see Max Jacob, the Surrealist poet and painter, originally a Jew, but now converted to Catholicism. Jacob, said Levesque, 'prays a lot, I know he regrets becoming converted, but he prays because he is afraid of hell; Jouhandeau, too, is afraid of hell'.[46]

That year, Gide had decided not to accompany the Petite Dame to Pontigny: he pleaded over-work, but, clearly, the charm had worn off. Instead he and Marc would go back to Paris and, from there, to Arcachon to spend some time with Marc's eldest brother, Jean-Paul, who was in a sanatorium there. Gide met his old friend, Fedor Rosenberg, who had managed to arrange an official visit to Paris from the Soviet Union, and took him off to Cuverville for a few days. They had not seen one another since before the war.

On the morning of 2 October, an official car arrived at the Villa to take Gide to a meeting at the Colonial Ministry. There he was told that, at the International Conference in Geneva, during a discussion of the regulations concerning 'native' labour, *Voyage au Congo* had been cited in evidence. It was also referred to at length in the Minister's report, which was read to him. Afterwards, he was amused to note that the window of Rasmussen's in the boulevard Saint-Germain was filled entirely with a display of his books and Marc's photographs, with, at its centre, a large map of the Congo, with their itinerary marked on it.

The Petite Dame spent all of November in Brussels organizing an exhibition of her husband's work at the Galerie Giroux. She was joined by her daughter and grand-daughter a few days before the exhibition opened. Towards the end, Whity and Enid McLeod arrived from London. Then, on 4 December, the last day of the exhibition, Gide arrived, twenty minutes before the gallery closed at 1 p.m. – it was a Sunday. The management agreed to remain open an extra half-hour. 'What vitality, what fraternity his presence exudes,' the Petite Dame noted. She was delighted to be able to tell him that she had sold her house at Saint-Clair, though she would continue to use it for some weeks. She hoped to be in her new apartment by the end of January.

On 14 December, they went off to the rue Vaneau to inspect progress. Marc took methodical notes. Gide shivered at the sight of the windows, which he could see only as cooling surfaces: 'If he could have done so, he would have had some of them walled up.'[47] On 20 December, the Petite Dame, Beth and Catherine went South, to spend their last Christmas and New Year at Saint-Clair. The sun-loving Gide went north, to Cuverville.

There the cold was such that Gide hardly left the house. When he did, it was to perform acts of charity: to visit an old labourer on the estate, 'who is never free of the most appalling pain', and to give 'the three little orphans who had greeted me in such a friendly way on the road . . . something to help them celebrate the New Year a bit more gaily'. 'I find more and more incomprehensible,' Gide comments, 'the indifference of some rich people, or their selfishness, when faced with the enormity of human misery.' All those young writers, suffering from the *mal du siècle*, religious aspirations, *angst* or mere boredom would be cured at once if they tried to care for or relieve the real sufferings of those around them. 'The more fortunate have no right to complain. If we cannot be happy, it is because we have failed to understand that the secret of happiness lies not in possessing, but in giving.'[48]

The following day, Gide was back in Paris, staying at an hotel, unable to face the Villa Montmorency until Marc was back to join him. A fortnight later, the two went off to Berlin. Their guide was Gide's old friend Count Harry von Kessler. Gide, who was supposed to have given a lecture, found that the distractions of the city were such that he did not have time to prepare it: the lecture was replaced by a 'reading-talk'. In Berlin, Marc made valuable contacts in the burgeoning film industry. On their way back, they called in at Colpach on Loup Mayrisch and her daughter. Back in Paris, Gide wrote to Martin du Gard that their two weeks had been 'exhausting, but extremely interesting and profitable from every point of view except that of the purse'. Marc had decided that RMG *must* go to Berlin, but suggests that he should not go without them: 'I think that we could show you the underside of the city and spare you innumerable useless gropings.'[49] Clearly, Harry Kessler had initiated their guests into what, by now, was the sex capital of Europe.

Gide attended a big family dinner at the Allégrets' to celebrate, as he put it, '*le retour du père prodigue*' from missionary work in Africa. Soon afterwards, Madeleine arrived in Paris, very briefly, for the wedding of her niece, Françoise Gilbert, the eldest daughter of her sister Valentine's second marriage. On 10 February, the Petite Dame arrived at the Villa to find Gide and a secretary confronting a quantity of letters to answer, many from total strangers, requesting help for one reason or another. Gide was sure that 'not one out of ten was genuine', but dared not risk deciding which nine were unworthy of consideration – so he felt obliged to answer them all.[50]

Gide went to spend two weeks at Beth's new house (her father's converted studio), at Saint-Clair. Beth reported back to her mother:

He arrived tired, oppressed, but nevertheless *in high spirits* [English in the original], delighted with the new house . . . He has spent the day in bed, letting himself be looked after like a good boy. He is the most unburdensome, the most lovable, the easiest of patients, but, at the same time, he is most difficult to deal with . . . His tyranny is delightful and life with him is very pleasant . . . Curiously, he does all that one might expect: he spends hours at the piano . . . He writes at my big desk, takes his siesta in my bedroom . . . Goes in and out of his room fifty times a day and decides to have a bath just when a meal is ready.[51]

On 5 March they learnt that Emile Mayrisch had been killed in a car crash near Châlons-sur-Marne. The Petite Dame joined her friend Loup at Colpach, where the great Luxembourg industrialist was buried in the gardens of his house.

At the end of March, before going off to Cuverville for a week, Gide met Dorothy Bussy in Paris. On her side, the result was, as so often, disastrous. On the night of her arrival, Gide was on his way back to the Villa, intending to practise the piano and, after dinner, to work. But, realizing how lugubrious it must be to arrive in Paris alone on a cold, wet evening, he decided to go and meet her at the station. His kindly intention seems to have misfired: 'T.V. [his code for D.B.] would like love; I can only give her friendship.

However great this may be, her hopes of greater tenderness distort every-thing I say and do, almost to the point of insincerity.'[52]

Advance copies of *Le Retour du Tchad* arrived from the printers and Gide set about signing a, for him, unprecedented number of complimentary copies. No fewer than 600 were sent out, many of them to politicians, in the hope of spurring them into action. The Petite Dame arrived in Paris and she, Gide and Marc visited the rue Vaneau, then sat around, talking endlessly of 'painting, joinery, the delays in the work'.[53]

Madeleine spent the first two weeks of May at the Villa, helping her husband organize the removal to the rue Vaneau – not that this was a single, simple operation. Gide did not finally move into 'the Vaneau' until August, with innumerable partial removals taking place in the intervening months. Meanwhile, Marc had left the Villa and was camping in his new studio, supervising the final works. The arrival of Madeleine and 'two Luxembourgeoises' made short shrift of 'the formidable disorder, dust and filth'.[54] The Petite Dame, who saw Madeleine twice while she was at the Villa, noted:

How life in that house has a different tempo when she is there! Everything becomes serious, discreet, quiet. One is invited to come in and say hello, to have a cup of tea with her, to rest for a moment. And yet one can sense what her determination to welcome one, that shy friendliness, costs her . . . I admire Madeleine's sweetness, her good grace at being faced with all this chaos, which must be so repugnant to her! . . . I am deeply touched by the trust that she has shown me. She took me to one side and said: 'I'd like you to try and stop André going to great trouble and expense over the little sitting-room he's planning for me. Kind as ever, he wants to make it too pretty; but, you see, I'm so seldom in Paris! All I want is for that apartment to be as comfortable as possible for him. I'm depending on your influence. But he'll never settle down anywhere – he's a vagabond and no doubt that's the price one has to pay for his gifts.' Yes, I was deeply touched and just as deeply embarrassed . . .[55]

On 7 May, an offer was accepted for the Villa from a prospective buyer: it was less than Gide had been hoping for, but it came as a great relief nevertheless.

Plans were already afoot for another big voyage: Borneo was mentioned. Gide and Marc would leave in November and be away for about six months. Everyone was saddened, even horrified. An already rather hesitant Gide confessed to the Petite Dame that 'this desire to travel has much more to do with being with Marc than with seeing something new. It's even rather frightening! And Marc is terribly keen to go there . . . I admit I need someone to take the lead. If it were left to me, I'd go back again and again to the places I know.'[56] Ten days later, the trip was off. He was concerned about the moral effect on Marc, who had done hardly anything since their return: he feared that Marc's tendency to take the easy way out might make him lose the habit of work altogether. Then, too, Gide himself had only just recovered from the effect of the Congo expedition. He reluctantly admitted that he should take cognizance of his age. In the end, he played safe: on 30 June, Gide set off, alone, for Tunisia. He spent the next few weeks by the sea, at Hammamet. There he hoped to finish *L'Ecole des femmes*, in time to keep to a deadline laid down by an American magazine, *Forum*, which was paying extremely well for a translation of it, but would brook no delay. Dorothy Bussy was working away at the translation as Gide wrote the original – in fact, he did not finish this relatively short work (fifty-eight pages in the Pléiade edition) until October, while staying with the Bussys at Roquebrune.

Gide was back in Paris on 21 July and, for the next few days, moved into Marc's studio in the new apartment. A few days later, he was back in the Villa supervising the packing of his library. Much of August was spent 'moving in'. 'Gide's good humour makes everything charming,' the Petite Dame writes. The new arrangement was 'like a renewal for him'. The three, juxtaposed installations were very different. Marc's studio was all light, an austere temple to modern activities: 'typewriter, cinematic equipment, negro woodcarvings, big maps, primitive necklaces . . . and the charming untidiness of a life lived from day to day, as in a camp'. A total contrast with this was Gide's library, 'serious, heavy with culture, books, books, every book, a grand piano, nothing belonging to the taste of the day'.[57]

Gide spent the first half of September alone at Saint-Clair – Beth and Catherine were still in England. There he worked at *L'Ecole des femmes* and finished re-reading all Montaigne's essays. This was for an *Histoire de la littérature*, conceived and edited by Malraux, in which various writers would be asked to contribute articles on some French writer of his (and Malraux's) choice. Jean Schlumberger was to do Corneille, Giraudoux Racine, Mauriac Pascal. They would be, not works of scholarship, but 'dialogues' between a living writer and a writer of the past. In the end, nothing came of the project, or, rather, something was to come of it thirty-four years later. (The first volume of *Tableau de la littérature française*, 'De Rutebeuf à Descartes', appeared in 1962, although volume 2, 'De Corneille à Chénier', appeared in 1939.) Gide's essay on Montaigne was published separately in 1929. True both to his own temperament and to Malraux's brief, Gide allowed, by constant quotation from the *Essays*, a genuine meeting of minds to take place.

'Our relations at the Vaneau are working themselves out, quite effortlessly,' the Petite Dame notes on 10 October. It is agreed that Gide must let her know by 10 a.m. if he intends eating with her. Usually, he says that he won't be having lunch, then, a little later, reappears, saying: 'I hope the maid hasn't gone out yet because . . .' – and lunches with the Petite Dame after all. Breakfast is the 'most typically funny' meal:

It is impossible to predict what Gide will decide to do, and it is better not to ask him, because to his own indecisiveness is to be added that of Marc, who is not up yet, or not ready yet; the piano is very tempting; on the other hand, perhaps he *is* hungry and, since breakfast is ready in my apartment . . . he wanders around from one apartment to the other, carrying teapot, jam, *biscottes*, his little remedies, begins his breakfast in one place, finishes it in another, opens his post here and leaves it here, etc.[58]

On 20 October, Gide set off for a week at Roquebrune, where he finished *L'Ecole des femmes* and worked with Dorothy Bussy on the translation. On his way back, he stopped off for one day at Saint-Clair to see Beth and their daughter, and another at Carcassonne, to see Alibert.

Apart from two brief stays at Cuverville, he remained in Paris until the end of the year. Jean Schlumberger, who had had an operation for appendicitis and a hernia, came to stay with the Petite Dame after leaving the nursing-home. On 3 December, Beth and Catherine arrived: they were to spend two months in Paris. Catherine was very struck by the hustle and bustle of Paris: 'It's like an accident all the time,' she said. Gide spent the last few days of the year with Madeleine at Cuverville, returning to Paris on the evening of New Year's Day.

On 11 January, scarcely recovered from a bad cold, Gide set out for Algiers. After dining at the Gare de Lyon, with Marc and Jean Schlumberger, he caught the night train for Marseille, to be greeted next morning by 'a nasty fine rain, grey and cold'. There was not a 'ray of sunlight in the whole sky, nor in my heart'. The following morning, 'the passengers, the appearance of the sea and sky, everything seemed so unappetizing' that he withdrew to his cabin to read Goncharov's *Oblomov* – and sleep.[59]

By the fourth day in Algiers, Gide's mood had not improved: 'Slept, since yesterday, an unbelievable number of hours . . . A real orgy of nothingness, brought on by the cold, ugly weather, my utter lack of curiosity with regard to Algiers and a complete absence of all desires.'⁶⁰ He left the hotel and moved into a small apartment that had been sublet to him by Henry de Montherlant. Nearby, he found a very good bookshop and bought, among other things, with his usual genius for the inappropriate, Jane Austen's *Pride and Prejudice.* 'A perfect achievement,' he later notes. 'An exquisite mastery of what can be mastered . . . What a charming woman she must have been!'⁶¹ He wandered around the Kasbah, unable to summon up his old 'intoxication'. 'Had I lived less chaste at twenty, I should find it less difficult to give up now,' he notes bitterly.

Which is worse? To reject pleasure when young or to go on seeking it when old? There are certain felicities of the flesh that the ageing body pursues, ever more vainly, if it were not sated with them in youth. Too chaste an adolescence makes for a dissolute old age. It is no doubt easier to give up what one has known than what one has imagined. It is not what one has done that one regrets here, but what one has not done and might have done . . . Young hands are made to caress and to sheathe love; it is a pity to make them join too soon . . . That gesture of prayer enacts the religious embrace of the impalpable after loving arms have closed on absence and the flight of what is real.⁶²

Montherlant's apartment turned out to be freezing cold: Gide could keep warm only by staying in bed, covered with a pile of blankets and overcoats. He decided to go back to the hotel. He writes to Marc: 'Out of fear of living too much through you, I wanted to get along without you for a while; I'm not alive any more.'⁶³ It was a disastrous visit, the cold, inhospitable weather mirroring, as so often, his own inner state. He was back in Paris by 24 June. He had intended staying for two months, taking with him no books, but a lot of paper that he intended to cover. He spent nine days in Algiers and wrote nothing.

Apart from a visit of a few days to Cuverville and another to Brittany, Gide spent the next four months in Paris. The day of his arrival, he insisted on joining the Petite Dame and Beth on Catherine's first visit to the cinema, to an afternoon showing of *Uncle Tom's Cabin.* Next day, the five-year-old Catherine was full of questions about the technology of cinema: why did the people move? Were the pictures at the front or behind the screen? That evening, Gide and Beth dined alone *chez* Foyot, the celebrated restaurant near the Odéon. They talked a lot about Marc. Beth's account of the conversation confirmed her mother's suspicions about relations between Gide and Marc. Beth, too, was 'disappointed in Marc'. She found him 'lacking in friendship'; he was 'nice enough', of course, but there seemed to be no 'depth' to his feelings. 'Yes, I must admit,' said Gide, 'there is something in that. Sometimes I even wonder if Marc has not had a bad influence on me.' 'I think he has been both an excellent and a deplorable one,' Beth replied. 'He has helped you to stay young, but he stops you concentrating on what you should be doing.'[64]

On 2 February, Beth and Catherine left for Saint-Clair. The Petite Dame left for Colpach on 11 February and came back, with Loup Mayrisch, a week later. In April, Gide and Marc went off by car to Brittany for a few days. In mid-May Gide spent some days at Roquebrune with the Bussys, who had recently returned after several weeks in the Middle East and Greece. He then joined Marc, who was making a documentary film of a gypsy festival at Les Saintes-Maries, in the Camargue, and paid his annual visit to Alibert, at Carcassonne, before returning to Paris.

After a fortnight at Cuverville, and another at Gréoux-les-Bains, the spa in the Basses-Alpes, recommended by a Paris doctor, Gide arrived back to find Paris in the middle of a July heatwave – with much use being made of their latest modern acquisition, a refrigerator. While he was away, Andrée Mayrisch had married Pierre Viénot, 'from my apartment,' writes the Petite Dame, 'without the slightest ceremony, as the merest formality!' Schnouky had told the Petite Dame that the reason why, despite her advanced views, she had married was that, as a married woman, she would have more influence over the young. The Petite Dame believed that it would have the opposite effect: her influence would have been greater if she had followed her convictions. Gide agreed.[65] Next day, Gide suddenly showed the Petite Dame four photographs of a boy. 'What do you see?' Gide asked, with an irrepressible smile. 'Seventeen, sensitive, affectionate, bright, intelligent rather than interesting,' the Petite Dame pronounced. 'Fifteen, precocious, loveable, Levantine! A type for which, in principle, I feel no attraction.'[66] Gide had never set eyes on the boy, who wrote him long, passionate love letters from Constantinople. His name was Emile Dana.

Over dinner in a restaurant, Copeau revealed that Gide was one of the main characters in *Les Jeux de l'enfer et du ciel*, Ghéon's new 900-page novel, in three volumes, his first for twenty-six years. A rather embarrassed Copeau admitted that it was dedicated to him. Gide, who had already read an extract from it in *La Nouvelle Revue des Jeunes*, and considered it 'abject', remarked that the character must be pretty odious. Not really, Copeau replied, the character in question is called 'The Sage' and is converted at the end. Next day, Gide and Marc set off for a few days in Baden-Baden, where Marc had film business.

On 2 August, Gide, Marc and the Petite Dame drove off to join Martin du Gard at Le Tertre, where they would work on Coppet's translation of Arnold Bennett's *The Old Wives' Tale* – Coppet himself arrived the following day, with Christiane Martin du Gard. They had hoped that Bennett himself might have joined them, at least for part of the time, but he was unable to. What took place over the next two weeks must have been rare in the history of modern translation. The procedure consisted of Coppet reading the translation aloud, while the others followed in the original – except, that is, for RMG, who just listened to the French. Often the proceedings turned into a seminar on translation theory, the two writers holding opposite views on the art. RMG was resistant to anything that seemed 'awkward, anti-French, blaming both original and translator'. Gide was 'conscientious, meticulous', trying at all times to miss nothing of the distinct flavour of the English, even if, at times, the result seemed, to RMG, 'unFrench'. 'I'm the only one here to preserve any sense of the French language,' an exasperated RMG exclaimed on one occasion. 'I sincerely hope that I'm never translated into any language by the likes of you. You're just hypnotized by this text . . .'[67] Each day, there were three working sessions. Between times, Gide attended to his ever-increasing correspondence – some letters, of course, not requiring answers. Some were not even read: such were the fifteen-page 'incredibly boring' screeds that arrived twice a week from the woman he called 'la folle de Saint-Etienne'. Gide also brought with him two separate manuscripts on which he was then working: one, on green paper, was his play *Oedipe*, the other, on orange paper, *Les Nouvelles Nourritures*. They were soon to be joined by a third, a sequel to *L'Ecole des femmes*, provisionally called *L'Ecole des maris*, which Gide began one night at Le Tertre.

On 22 August, the *décade littéraire* began at Pontigny, with the title: 'Sur la réussite classique dans l'art'. The day before, Gide and the Petite Dame met up over lunch at the Gare de Lyon with the Bussys and Malraux, who had just returned from Persia. 'Malraux's conversation leaps over the centuries, history, religions,' the Petite Dame noted. 'The proposition presented by his thought is always so stark, so simplified, so clear that one would feel rather ungracious if one did not accede to it at once, and so one finds oneself agreeing to things one had never thought about before, without ever finding an opportunity of asking a question or raising an objection.'[68]

Gide spent most of September in Paris, with two visits to Cuverville. The Petite Dame, who was at Saint-Clair, did not hear from him for some time and even supposed that he might have gone off to Constantinople to see Emile Dana. On two occasions at Pontigny she had handed him thick envelopes bearing the boy's handwriting, which he had taken from her 'with visible impatience'. She hoped that he had embarked on 'a great new adventure'. He needed 'contact with youth in order to exhaust all his own'.[69] Gide did not go to Constantinople – but he did finish *Robert, Supplément à l'Ecole des femmes.*

L'Ecole des femmes itself had appeared early in the year, in two numbers of the *Revue de Paris* and in volume form from the *NRF* in June. It begins with the now well-worn Gidean device of a letter from an unknown woman, Geneviève D . . ., accompanying a journal, written by her mother in two parts, in 1894 and 1914, with a short epilogue dating from 1916. The first part recounts how the writer, Eveline, a rather simple, shy, trusting soul, is looking forward to a future in which Robert will guide her 'towards the beautiful and the good, towards God'.[70] She has only one talent to her name: a former student at the Conservatoire, she is an accomplished pianist. Robert, however, does not care at all for music, so Eveline soon abandons her daily practice. Her self-confidence is further undermined by Robert's habit of constantly correcting infelicities in her French. For reasons that are not entirely clear, Eveline's parents have reservations about Robert: we later learn that most of the couple's fortune is on Eveline's side. Robert gets Eveline to agree to keep a journal of their life together and he agrees to do the same; only the survivor will ever read what the other has written. 'I find it quite natural,' she writes, 'that, in marrying Robert, I should give up my independence (I already acted independently in marrying him despite papa), but each woman ought at least to be free to choose the servitude that suits her best.'[71] Her disillusion is not long in coming. Her eyes are first opened, when, one day, Robert comes in while she is writing her journal and asks to read what she has written. She reminds him of their agreement, but is eventually talked into handing over her journal on condition that she can read his. When he returns hers, he is forced to admit that he has not kept one himself. 'I am stopping this journal here,' Eveline writes, 'since it no longer serves any purpose.'[72]

The journal resumes twenty years later, in 1914. Now the mother of two children, Gustave and Geneviève, Eveline has become possessed by an overwhelming desire to leave her husband. It is not that she has a lover; her husband is not unfaithful to her; it is just that she has acquired, over the years, an intense revulsion for him and everything he stands for. Robert's display of religious zeal has made her doubt the authenticity of her own:

'His ostentatious genuflections stop dead the prayer in my heart . . .'[73] She confides in a priest friend, who is scandalized by her ideas. Even her father, who seems to have seen through Robert at the outset, counsels caution: if she deserts her husband she will lose all access to her children. Robert is involved in a car accident and is slightly injured. Her immediate response is to rush to his side and to abandon all ideas of leaving him. Over the next few months, however, she is sickened by his histrionic pretence of being at death's door. She then realizes that, although her son is the image of the younger Robert, her daughter has nothing but contempt for him. The story ends with Eveline going off to work as a nurse in a hospital dealing with dangerous cases of infection, leaving her journal to her daughter, 'in case I do not come back'. It is clearly suggested that she will not.

The origin of *L'Ecole des femmes* goes back to June 1919. On the second page of the *Journal des Faux-Monnayeurs*, Gide refers to a projected 'novel of two sisters' and goes on to recount the story of the elder one, which corresponds at every point to that of Eveline in *L'Ecole des femmes*. (No mention is made of the situation of the younger sister and, in the end, Eveline did not have one.) Gide did not begin work on the 'new novel' until December 1926, when, at Cuverville, he wrote 'the first pages so gaily and easily . . . almost without erasures'.[74] In the spring of 1928, he read what he had written to Martin du Gard, who urged him to go on with it. As we know, the American magazine *Forum* had commissioned a translation of it, at a temptingly high fee, which, very generously, Gide decided to halve with the translator. By September, Gide concluded that he would not finish the story on time – and wrote to New York, asking for a postponement. The reply came back that it was out of the question and that, if the text were not delivered on time, there would be a penalty to be paid. As much for Dorothy's sake as his own, he set to work and polished off the novel in time: 'Perhaps the insistence of the Americans was necessary to make me finish this book, which ceased to interest me a long time ago.'[75]

The truth is that Gide had never recaptured the 'ease' and 'pleasure' that he had felt when writing the first few pages. It had become something of a drudge. Certainly, it was astonishing for a writer, even one as unpredictable and inconsistent as Gide, to write such a work after the major achievement of *Les Faux-Monnayeurs*. (But he had also written *La Symphonie Pastorale* in the wake of *Les Caves du Vatican*.) It may be argued that *L'Ecole des femmes* is a more modern work than may at first appear. It can certainly be read as pro-feminist, as an example of what married women had to put up with in the days before emancipation had opened their eyes – as it clearly had done for Eveline's daughter, Geneviève. Eveline is an uneducated, conforming woman, born too early to rebel effectively. Unfortunately, Eveline's limitations do nothing for Gide's prose. On the first page, we read: 'That sentence, which I have just written, with tears in my eyes, strikes me as frightful . . . I don't know if I will ever learn to write well.'[76] Given the constrictions that he has encumbered himself with, Gide performs his task with his usual skill and accomplishment. But there is a dull, depressive quality about the writing. Marc, with his modernist tastes, disliked it intensely. So, interestingly, did Beth, the modern woman personified. The appropriation of Molière's title, too, however ironically meant, seems to verge on the pretentious.

Nevertheless, Gide felt impelled to write a sequel, *Robert*, in which the husband tells his side of the story (to be completed, as we shall see, by Geneviève's version). The idea of *Robert* seems to have originated while Gide was staying at Le Tertre. On 9 August, Gide received a letter from Ernst-Robert Curtius. After making a number of intelligent remarks about *L'Ecole des femmes*, it went on: 'It's a pity that we don't have a page or two from Robert's journal. We know him only from the outside.'[77] Gide was already contemplating an *Ecole des maris*: Curtius' letter pointed him in the direction to follow. The following day, Gide wrote the opening of Robert's letter to him (Gide), protesting at his late wife's version of events. 'You may be surprised to learn that I am not alone in refusing to recognize myself in the irresponsible, vain, insignificant individual portrayed by my wife,'[78] Robert writes. Gide took up the story a few weeks later and completed it in about a week. He dedicated *Robert* to Curtius and prefaced it with a brief letter to him recalling his role in its inception. *Robert* is half the length of *L'Ecole des femmes* and cannot really be regarded as an autonomous work. As one might expect, it does not do much to rectify the version of events recorded by Eveline. *Robert* first appeared in two numbers (11 and 18 January 1930) of the *Revue hebdomadaire* and in book form later in the year by the *NRF*, first on its own, then together with a new edition of *L'Ecole des femmes*.

One September morning, Yvonne de Lestrange arrived at the Vaneau. Since her meeting with Gide and Marc in Africa, she had become a close friend of both men. She was also the mother of a son, Michel, who at this time was not yet two years old: his father was Marc Allégret. She and Gide set off for Brussels, where, for the past two weeks, Marc had been making a film for Belgian railways. Marc would be there for another ten days, but Gide and Yvonne de Lestrange would be staying for only four of them. Marc arrived back from Brussels and, on 7 October, Gide dined with him and Yvonne. The relationship of his two friends seems to have been in crisis: Yvonne wanted Marc either to marry her or to leave her (a similar situation arose in 1933). Meanwhile, Gide was in the midst of his own emotional crisis. In October, 'Emile D.' makes four appearances in the *Journal*. 'I cannot write . . . anything about what is dearest to me,' he writes on 7 October. 'No trace will be found here of the Constantinople adventure, which, during the last three months, has so preoccupied me and which I cannot yet accept is over. I think about it every day and cannot pass the concierge's door without looking anxiously to see whether a letter has arrived at last . . . I cannot believe that Emile D. would accept being forbidden to write to me.' The following day, he is worrying that the boy's 'sudden silence' might mean that he has killed himself. Two days later, he is asking: 'What has become of him? Where is he? Is he thinking about me? Is he telling himself perhaps that I have forgotten him?' Five more days passed, then a letter arrived from Emile. He was in Paris. A few days before he had walked down the rue Vaneau. He had nearly rung the bell, but was now glad that he hadn't. He says that he still loves Gide, but also declares that he will give up loving him. He asks Gide not to try to contact him, but to forget him. He leaves no address. 'It seems to me,' Gide concludes – and this is the last we hear of 'Emile D.' – 'that I let myself be taken in – in the most ridiculous fashion . . . We are half cured of a love affair when we are able to convince ourselves that the person with whom we are in love is, after all, quite an ordinary creature. The strength of an attachment lies in the gnawing conviction that there is something exceptional, unique, irreplaceable in the beloved that we will never find again.'[79]

In November, Gide, the Petite Dame, Groethuysen and Alix Guillain worked on Hans Prinzhorn's German translation of *Les Nourritures terrestres*. Almost every day, for over three weeks, they began work after lunch and continued on until eleven in the evening. By 17 November, the Petite Dame was noting how 'the corrections are getting ever more numerous, ever more radical'. Sometimes, when forced to clarify what he meant, Gide chooses to change the original – and thus the translation – completely. 'What a good job Prinzhorn is in Honolulu!' the Petite Dame adds.[80] The translation appeared in Germany at the end of the year, twenty years before its English equivalent. The Deutsche Verlags-Anstalt had already published translations of *Les Faux-Monnayeurs* and the *Journal des Faux-Monnayeurs* and, more recently, of *L'Ecole des femmes* and *Si le grain ne meurt* and, in 1930, was to bring out *Voyage au Congo*, *Les Caves du Vatican*, *La Porte étroite* and *Isabelle*, followed by *Corydon* in 1932. For Gide's sixtieth birthday, on 22 November, the same publishing house was to distribute a small pamphlet in his honour. No one around him, notes the Petite Dame, was in the habit of celebrating his birthday. When scores of telegrams arrived from Germany and flowers from Poland and America, the residents of the Vaneau and their friends decided, at the last moment, on a rather better dinner than usual, ending with a dessert of exotic fruits, 'specially dedicated to the author of *Les Nourritures terrestres*'.

A few days before, Gide had seen his American publisher, Mrs Knopf. 'Tea was enough,' he wrote to Dorothy Bussy. 'I recoiled before the prospect of dinner.' Afterwards, at Lady Ottoline Morrell's request, he called on Siegfried Sassoon, the English poet, now forty-three, at his hotel. Gide found him 'a very pleasant gentleman'. In the room next door, lying in bed, recovering from an operation for pneumothorax, was 'a very young, very charming (too charming)' young man, and a splendid, uncaged parrot, with whom he always travelled.[81] They were on their way to Sicily, where Sassoon hoped that his friend, Stephen Tennant, would recuperate.

On 18 December, the residents of the Vaneau gave a party to celebrate the engagement of Marcel de Coppet and Roger Martin du Gard's daughter Christiane. The young woman's father was too upset to attend. Coppet and RMG were the same age – forty-eight – and had been best friends since they were twenty. Coppet's career in the colonial service had meant long periods of separation. RMG had been at Bordeaux to meet his friend off the boat on 6 May. 'What solid bonds twenty-five years of exceptional friendship have forged between us!' he wrote to Gide.[82] They saw much of one another in Paris; their friendship, RMG noted in his journal, was 'intact' on both sides. There were times when RMG was 'seized with despair at the idea that his presence was only temporary, that he will escape again, disappear, plunge into some inaccessible distance'.[83] They planned to spend October and November in Tunisia together. They spent two weeks in August at Le Tertre, going over Coppet's Bennett translation, and ten days at Pontigny – Christiane being there on both occasions. On 6 and 7 September, from Quiberville, her Uncle Marcel's seaside house in Normandy, Christiane wrote to her father two charming, sensitive letters broaching the subject of her feelings for Marcel de Coppet. He was 'one of those very rare men whom one can respect unreservedly . . . He was the kind of man I would like to marry.'[84] Her father's immediate reaction was confided to his journal: 'Coppet has *fallen* for Christiane, and he has *let* Christiane *fall* for him. I am appalled. I never suspected for a moment that such folly was possible.' His confidence, his friendship had been betrayed. What had developed between them was a 'sentiment monstrueux et ridicule'. That night he couldn't sleep, every now and then breaking down into tears. Their 'happiness' was a chimera. There was a twenty-five-year difference in their ages; he was tubercular and had never been fully cured; he had a serious heart condition; he was an alcoholic (2 litres of wine a day, plus whiskies and brandies); a divorcé, he was a lady's man and quite incapable of a steady, still less a permanent relationship. They could not have children and, if they did, they would surely be diseased. This pathetic old man (his best friend and, like him, under fifty) had taken advantage of an innocent 'child' of twenty-two.[85] When RMG consulted his embittered Catholic wife, Hélène, she replied that such behaviour was only to be expected of a child imbued with her father's free-thinking principles. By 10 November, RMG was admitting (to himself) that the intensity of his feelings was such that it was as if he were 'being driven crazy by a sort of jealousy': 'I am suffering from not loving Christiane as I used to. Of not loving Coppet as I used to. I am suffering from a lack of love . . . The warmth of tenderness and friendship that I have carried inside me for twenty years has suddenly undergone a terrible drop in temperature. I am suffering from the cold.'[86] On 30 December, the day before the wedding, a terrible dialogue took place between father and daughter. He refused magnanimity in defeat. He repeated all his fears, all his accusations, regarding Coppet's mental and physical state. Christiane gave a terrible laugh and repeated his words, imitating his voice, apparent hatred written all over her face. Hours after the marriage, the couple left for Africa. (In fact, RMG's fears were as unfounded as his reactions had been pathological. The tubercular, alcoholic, philandering Coppet gave his young wife two healthy children and outlived his old friend by ten years, dying in 1968, at the age of eighty-seven.)

Gide, RMG's other 'best friend', knew little of what was going on in the Martin du Gard family. RMG avoided Gide all summer and, when they did finally meet, avoided the subject. Clearly, RMG was unwilling to expose his views of the situation to someone who not only saw both sides of any question, but who had every reason to sympathize with Coppet's. Gide did not wait for the wedding, but left for Roquebrune on 26 December, although, before leaving, he witnessed an event to which he attached 'particular importance': Catherine and Michel, the baby son of Yvonne de Lestrange and Marc, were 'introduced to one another'.

By 30 December, his thoughts were already elsewhere: 'Why, how did I let myself be held back for so long in my youth? . . . Why did I not meet, when I was twenty, the man who would have taken me off with him? The man whom I would have followed to the ends of the earth! But no one talked about travelling then; to have been to Algeria was quite an achievement.'[87]

Gide saw in the New Year – and the new decade – with his friends Simon and Dorothy Bussy. He left Roquebrune on the morning of 3 January. The same day an enflamed Dorothy was writing off to him: 'Last night you were here. Five minutes after you'd gone up, I had such a desire to knock on your door, go in and throw my arms around your neck . . .' Everyone was in bed and she had stood for a few minutes outside Gide's door, 'burning to go in'. She had not dared to. 'I know it is no use knocking on heaven's gate. You have to wait for it to open of itself – as it sometimes, mysteriously, does. And then one has to step in on tiptoe, pretending not to notice the miracle.'[88] Reading such effusions, it is hard to remember that this is a sixty-four-year-old woman addressing a sixty-year-old man.

Gide called on the Vicomte Charles de Noailles and his wife Marie-Laure at their villa at Hyères. There he found Marc, Cocteau and the composer Georges Auric. He had intended staying only for lunch, but ended up staying for three days. He was so impressed by the 'prodigious ingenuity of the comfort', the 'perfect functioning of everything' that, when the English butler arrived in his room with his breakfast, on a tray 'loaded with delicacies and fruit', but minus a knife to butter the toast, he used a spoon to do so rather than summon the servant back and thus create a situation that would rapidly assume the proportions of a domestic catastrophe. Host and guests swam in the pool, and did gymnastics with 'a very agreeable' teacher. There were a lot of new games, involving 'shuttlecocks and balls of all sizes', which they played 'more or less naked, then, sweaty all over, ran and plunged into the lukewarm water of the pool'.[89]

At Toulon, Gide met up with the writer Jacques de Lacretelle and the two travelled by Pullman back to Paris. Gide arrived at the Vaneau at eleven, to find the Petite Dame getting ready for bed. They began to chat, as Gide went through his voluminous correspondence, including seven letters from 'la folle de Saint-Etienne', the last accompanying 'photographs, drawings, theatre tickets, at least thirty letters addressed to her'. There was also a photograph of her 'that must be quite old'.[90] 'Really! This time the *folle* has gone too far!' the Petite Dame expostulates on 28 January. A new parcel containing some thirty old photographs, pictures of famous people cut out of newspapers, innumerable letters addressed to her, including two from Jacques Rivière, who was not the only writer to respond to her. 'One can imagine a man going mad receiving such things,' Gide commented, 'drowned, submerged by the banality of it all.'[91]

For much of January, the residents of the Vaneau were assailed, to various degrees, successively or simultaneously, by the *grippe*. Gide, disinclined to work, whiled away the time playing *crapette* (Russian bank), a game introduced to him by Beth, who was staying there with Catherine. *Crapette* soon became a passion, indulged in at all hours of the day. On 26 January, Gide went out for the first time, 'after twelve days of limbo'. He got back exhausted and coughing. He had planned to go to Cuverville, but could not face the prospect of the weather there: instead he would go South. He left Paris on the night of 1 February, for Nice. Next day, he moved into a room at Vence, which he had booked for a fortnight, but soon decided that he needed 'more comfort' than was on offer at a *pension*, and, hiring a taxi, left for Roquebrune and the Bussys. There the weather did not raise Gide's spirits: 'Grey, rainy, cold, monotonous days,' he wrote to Martin du Gard.[92] For ten days, he did not even go out. He began to take notes for '*Geneviève* or *La Nouvelle Ecole des femmes*'. In it, he hoped 'to tackle head on the whole question of feminism'.[93]

On 8 March, he was met at the Gare de Lyon by Marc. Over lunch with the Petite Dame, he confessed that he had just spent one of the gloomiest periods he had ever experienced: 'thirty days that might be cut out of his life'.[94] A week later, Gide was in Cuverville. There he set to work, with great difficulty at first, but he had soon written thirty pages of *Geneviève*. In early April, he was back in Paris for a few days. He saw the Petite Dame off to Saint-Clair: they would not meet again until June. Gide was anxious to get back to Cuverville to work, before the arrival of the Drouins and other relations over Easter. With Madeleine in Cuverville, he was more than ever possessed by death, though realizing that it was a 'vain preoccupation': what saddened him most was the thought of what he had not done in his life. Madeleine told her husband that she had 'long since doubted whether she had ever occupied any place whatever' in his life. Gide was at a loss to say anything by way of response to such 'monstrosities', his silence being interpreted no doubt as 'confirmation of her fears'.[95]

Gide was back in Paris on 12 April. Twelve days later he set off for Berlin to join Marc, who was working for several weeks on a film at the giant VFA studios. This visit was not entirely in the interests of pleasure. Over the past six months, Gide and his friends had been much occupied with matters cinematic. In October 1928, the first public showing of a 'talking' film had taken place in Paris. However, it soon became clear that the French public would no longer go to American films once sound was added. This situation offered what seemed like a golden opportunity to French writers to step in. Prompted by Marc Allégret, who was already working as a director for the young, up-and-coming film producer, Pierre Braunberger, Gide assembled a group of writers, whose task would be to provide scenarios. In December 1929, a company was formed, the Film parlant français (FPF), with the playwright Jules Romains as chairman, Gide, Jean Giraudoux, Martin du Gard, André Maurois, Paul Morand and Jean Schlumberger as 'writer' directors, and Marc Allégret as technical director. In the end, nothing came of these plans and the invention of 'dubbing', whereby American films could be given sound-tracks in any language, soon put paid to European dreams of rivalling Hollywood.

Gide returned to Paris, after two weeks in Germany, during which he had seen very little of an over-worked Marc. On 12 June, the 'folle de Saint-Etienne' actually appeared. She rang on the Petite Dame's bell, then, realizing that it was the wrong door, beat a hasty retreat. Soon afterwards, Gide arrived, announcing that he had just spent a quarter of an hour talking to the '*folle*' in the street. Over the past month, she had written to him every day. She then came to Paris, staying at a *pension* in the rue Vaneau. 'When she met me,' said Gide, 'she told me everything I'd done the day before. She must follow me everywhere . . . She's convinced that I write everything that is published in the *NRF* . . . Yes, yes, she said, I understand this is a round-about way of replying to my letters. I understand all your allusions!' Asked for his advice, Gide told her to learn English. When, trying to get away, he offered her his hand, she replied, with a wriggle: 'No, the elbow, it's more pointed!'[96]

Gide had intended going back to Cuverville, but Madeleine wrote to say that she would prefer him not to come before 16 July. So, after three days in Paris, he went back to Berlin, where, he knew, he would find the Bussys: Simon was spending several weeks there, painting the animals in the zoo. After hardly a week in Berlin, Gide made straight for Cuverville. By the second day he was complaining that the weather was 'frightful' and that there was 'not a single handsome young man to smile at'.[97] Before long, however, the *Journal* is full of 'le petit François Déhais', who, if not handsome, certainly appealed to the pedagogue in Gide. One of eight children of a farm labourer who had died of cancer the year before, François was an excellent pupil at the local school and wanted to continue his education and become a teacher. Gide made inquiries: the boy could attend a certain school that took in boarders. It would be too late to get a scholarship for the first year, but Gide would cover the expenses incurred. The boy was delighted – until his younger brother pointed out that he ought to be supporting the family by working. We do not know how the story of François Déhais ended.

On 5 August, Gide and the Petite Dame, who had been on a *cure* at Marienbad with Loup Mayrisch, both arrived at the Vaneau, neither expecting the other to be there. They had a quick snack and went off to the cinema. Three days later, Gide left Paris for Chitré. From there, Yvonne de Lestrange drove him to La Rochelle and then on to Arcachon, to see Jean-Paul Allégret, whose tubercular condition had worsened: 'Spent six frightful days with him, encouraging him, helping him to suffer, lying to him, trying to hide death from him.'[98]

After a day spent with Alibert at Carcassonne, Gide sailed for Corsica. At Calvi, Gide congratulated himself on being alone – and free. The following day, he was rhapsodizing about 'the admirable flight of the palm trees, in the night, along the quay', under which 'a half-naked people circulates, the high society from several pleasure yachts mingling with the fishermen . . .; everywhere a sense of carefree joy. The atmosphere is an invitation to brief encounters, games, debauchery . . . I don't think my joy has ever been deeper or keener . . . I did not feel any younger at twenty . . . I owe a great sense of calm to my excesses at Calvi.'[99] An unpublished passage in the *Journal* is more explicit:

At Calvi, the entire male population, young and older, prostitutes itself. Yet that's not quite the word, for it seems to be not so much a matter of money as of pleasure. Women are closely guarded, unapproachable; a girl is compromised if a young man speaks to her too often . . . He would have to marry her . . . In the dance-halls men only dance with each other – and in a very sensual way. The little boys, from the age of eight, witness the sexual activities of their older brothers with the strangers they take down to the beach, among the rocks or under the pines; they keep a look out, even offer themselves and enjoy being voyeurs . . .[100]

In this southern, sensual paradise, he read . . . Hardy's *The Woodlanders*.

Gide was back in Marseille on 30 August. Next day, he was in Briançon. Why Briançon? In July 1929, while taking a *cure* at Gréoux, Gide had become very friendly with a boy of thirteen. 'Néné' (Antoine Brun, referred to in the published *Journal* as 'le petit Henri B.') was also there on account of his health, accompanied by his mother. The father worked on the railways. Gide had kept in touch, calling on the family when he was in

Marseille just after Christmas that year and, again, on his way to Corsica. Gide went to Briançon, in the Alpes-de-Haute-Provence, because Néné was on holiday there with his family. On arrival, he took the boy to the cinema and, afterwards, put him up at his own hotel. But, Gide had told RMG, 'nothing but what was perfectly honest took place': Gide was content just to watch the boy sleeping. This put Gide 'in an extraordinary state of tenderness and exaltation'. When RMG's reaction seemed rather to be one of amusement, Gide replied: 'Yes, absolutely, *mon vieux*, if that is all I want!' He was already planning the boy's future. He would help him to get trained as a mechanic. Later, he would employ him as a chauffeur. 'One felt that he could stop at no manoeuvre, no trick, to get what he wanted,' writes the Petite Dame. The fact was that Gide's sexuality, while 'so profound, so demanding, so irresistible', could be satisfied 'so easily, so lightly and turn so quickly into exaltation'. It was hardly surprising if people found this improbable and assumed a 'depravity equal to the duplicity into which his desire led him'. Nevertheless, these 'very special sexual dispositions' were, she believed, 'an important key in understanding Gide'.[101]

He returned to Cuverville, where, by the end of the month, he had 'more or less' finished *Oedipe*. On 8 October, he was back in Paris, where Jean Schlumberger collected him by car and took him off to Braffy. The Petite Dame, who had been staying there for four weeks, noted how 'splendid' Gide looked, 'the features firmer, the skin clearer and exuding an extraordinary vitality'. Officially a farmhouse attached to the property of Val-Richer, Braffy was, thought the Petite Dame, 'some family paradise in a picture-book, bathed in a sea of orchards and on the edge of a wood, as if in a fairy-tale'.[102] That evening, Schlumberger read from his current novel, *Saint-Saturnin*. The following day, at his friends' insistence, Gide read them what he had written of *Oedipe*, though he was far from satisfied with it. Schlum found it too skeletal, too lacking in flesh. Gide agreed that it was a natural shortcoming on his part to err on the side of 'thinness': he had such a horror of stylistic inflation.

After a few days at Cuverville, Gide returned to Paris, where, on 24 October, Marc learnt that his brother Jean-Paul had taken a serious turn for the worse. Gide was getting ready to go and visit him, when a telegram arrived announcing his death. Gide left instead for the South, breaking his journey at Pernand-Vergelesses. Copeau was at Dijon station to meet him, having offered up that morning's mass in the local church for his guest's conversion. Earlier Gide had tried to resist a meeting with him. 'The pain

I feel at having to think *against* you is already bad enough,' Gide wrote.[103] Gide relented on receiving a letter from Copeau 'so plaintively sentimental, so insistent' that not to go would amount to a break in their friendship. Gide spent two nights at Pernand, something of their conversations finding their way into both men's journals. Copeau tried to engage his friend in theological argument. Gide refused: 'I consider all argument useless. One can go on arguing forever. It's pointless . . . I'm not out to prove that I am right or that they are wrong . . . What he has not considered is the extent to which "faith" can, and must of necessity, distort the integrity of thought, which then becomes so easily reconciled to lies.'[104] Copeau noticed that Gide was no longer interested in arguing against Catholicism from a Christian standpoint: 'For him, that is no longer the problem . . . It is the act of believing, Faith itself, that he is now down on. He has ended up with *atheism*. He preaches it.'[105] Of their two wives, Gide remarked, interestingly, that Madeleine was closer to Copeau's position, Agnès to his. Agnès could not accept her daughter's decision to become a Benedictine nun as God's will: firmly Protestant to the end, she believed that Edi 'had made a mistake and would regret it'.[106] Madeleine Gide, on the other hand, now almost on the verge of conversion to Rome, wrote to Agnès: 'I know in my heart that she is right to follow the master wholly and entirely.'[107]

From Dijon, Gide went on to Marseille, where he called on Auguste Bréal and, no doubt, his young friend Néné. By 2 November, Gide was at Saint-Clair. Beth wrote to her mother to report that Bypeed had given Catherine her first piano lesson and, each evening, by the fire in the library, he told her a story from *The Thousand and One Nights*. 'Sitting in front of him, she listens with both eyes and both ears, and interrupts him quite a lot! They're getting on famously.' In the morning, he would sit at the piano for three hours or more. Two days later, he announced that *Oedipe* was finished and that they were leaving for Marseille and Tunisia the following day.

Gide, Beth and the car landed in Tunisia on 14 November. 'Despite a little nettle-rash and a capricious stomach, Bypeed is remarkably well,' Beth wrote to her mother.

I don't think I have often seen him so even-tempered, so communicative, so continuously happy and amused. We are getting on terribly well and are having a wonderful time. He is at his most delightful all the time and, when he is like that, I don't think there is a greater pleasure on earth than to travel with him. I feel that I'm not at all in his way; on the contrary, despite his well-established principle of absolute freedom, he seems to take pleasure only in doing things with me, for me. No one will ever know how young, unpredictable, tender and charming he can be.

All Beth's letters from Tunisia were 'hymns of joy, with no cloud on the horizon', her mother comments.[108] Not, of course, that Beth was the sole object of Gide's attentions. Later, the Petite Dame reports a conversation with her daughter in which Beth describes how she had come to understand 'the powerful charm' that a group of young Arab boys could exert over Gide and the kind of spell that he exercised over them when he spoke. Just the company, in all innocence, of 'those laughing, trusting, familiar lads, with their direct sensuality, plunges him into a sort of drunkenness', quite apart from 'the pleasure he might seek with some of them'.[109] They drove south, calling at Zaghouan, Kairouan, Sousse and Sfax. On little more than dust tracks, they moved inland, westwards, through the Chott el Fedjadj and Chott Djerid to Tozeur and Nefta. Between driving, they worked together, revising a translation of Bennett's *The Old Wives' Tale*, read or played *crapette*. From Nefta, they travelled north, through the Seldja gorges and the oasis of Chibika.

They left Tunis on 18 December, having spent five weeks on Tunisian soil. They spent two or three days in Marseille, as they had done on the way out, Gide being very concerned to spend some time with young 'Néné'. Beth casts interesting light on this particular adventure, one whose significance for Gide was beyond her comprehension. The boy in no way resembled the type that usually aroused his desire: 'Imagine a somewhat heavily built, rather fat boy, with a quite ordinary, if quite pretty, face, fine features, blue eyes . . . A well-behaved boy, with nothing unusual about him, no sensuality, no wildness, no strangeness, a child who could have no special feeling for Bypeed, for whom he is simply Monsieur Gide, who is very nice to him and takes him to the cinema . . .' On their first evening in Marseille, Gide had warned Beth that he would be collecting Néné from his parents, take him to the cinema and ask their permission to bring him back the following morning, as he had done before. Naturally, Beth made plans to spend the evening on her own. Gide, however, insisted that she meet the boy and have dinner with them. Afterwards, Gide talked about Néné 'with all the emotion of a lover'. The night spent with him was of 'an inexplicable enchantment'. Gide had spent much of the night watching the boy sleep in his arms. 'Weren't you taking a lot upon yourself not to caress him?' an astounded Beth asked. 'No,' Gide replied. 'Not really.' 'Nevertheless,' the Petite Dame comments, 'given his reputation, he's playing a dangerous game, not that that will stop him, and the last thing anyone will believe about it all is how innocent it is.'[110]

A telegram arrived at Saint-Clair, warning of their arrival. The car drove in at Le Pin on 22 December, 'all grey with dust, looking like a tired beast and crammed with trunks and parcels'. Only later did the Petite Dame learn that it had also contained a huge Christmas tree, bought in Marseille: Beth had left it in the care of the village shop, so that it could be a surprise on Christmas Eve. 'With some difficulty, Gide extricated himself from the car, so covered was he with shawls and coats.' Despite his horror of public holidays, Gide threw himself into the celebration of Christmas and New Year, 'submitting in the nicest possible way to all our little family traditions and went to bed very late, long after the warm wine at midnight'.[111]

Gide, 'Fellow-traveller': Oedipe, Perséphone, Les Nouvelles Nourritures

(JANUARY 1931 – JUNE 1936)

Gide, the Petite Dame, Beth, Catherine and maid were back in Paris on 8 January. Over the next few weeks, they saw little of Marc. Though living at the Vaneau, he was working enormously hard: 'His day begins at 9.30 in the Billancourt studios and almost every day he works there until two or three in the morning.'[1] In the course of 1931, Marc was to direct no fewer than three full-length films (*L'Amour à l'américaine, Mam'zelle Nitouche, La Petite Chocolatière*) and four shorter films. On 13 January, Gide saw Arnold Bennett, who was staying in Paris. It was to be their last meeting. Some ten weeks later, Bennett died in London of typhoid fever.

Gide left for Cuverville, where, over the next three weeks, he 'dabbled' in his *Notes sur Chopin, Geneviève* and *Les Nouvelles Nourritures*, but felt unable to work in any sustained fashion. As so often, he turned to his piano 'as to an opium, in which my thoughts are calmed and my restless will finds peace'. He practised for four or five hours a day – transcriptions of some of Mozart's piano concertos, Busoni's arrangement of Bach's chorale preludes and Granados' *Goyescas*. And he read: Curtius' book on France and, with ever-increasing passion and admiration, Richardson's *Clarissa Harlowe*, finding it superior to Laclos' *Les Liaisons dangereuses*. He arrived back in Paris, suffering from *la gratte*, an itching like that caused by nettlerash, which was to plague him on and off for the whole year. The following day, Beth and Catherine left for Saint-Clair.

On 20 February, Gide, too, left for the South, arriving the following morning at Marseille. There he saw Néné, although, before he left Paris, the Petite Dame had noted: 'I don't know quite why, but I feel that the Marseille adventure is fading away.'[2] But the *Journal* recounts at some length a meeting with a certain 'B.', who took Gide into his confidence over a drink in a café. 'B.' it seems, was having an affair with a woman other than his wife, but was in the grip of jealousy about another man that this woman was seeing. 'B.' was planning to arrive at the woman's home unannounced and, if he found her with the other man, to kill them both. Gide did his best to let 'B.' talk out his fury and counselled caution. In fact, 'B.' was Néné's father, which goes some way to explain the parents' *insouciance* regarding Gide's relations with their son. From Marseille, Gide went on to Toulon, where he saw his young friend Robert Levesque, then twenty-one and doing his national service in the navy – 'a charming companion, for whom my affection becomes deeper month by month. Nothing is more trusting, more naturally joyous and *good* than his smile.'³ Gide then spent a week with the Bussys at Roquebrune, another at Vence and another at Grasse.

On 8 April, Gide was back in Paris, where he stayed, apart from a week in Cuverville, until 3 June. One day, he was sitting over breakfast with the Petite Dame and Marc, when he suddenly mentioned an article he had been reading. It was the first article about Russia that had really excited him. It consisted largely of statistics covering the Soviet Five Year Plan. 'It's quite simply prodigious,' said Gide, as naïvely trusting as millions of others. 'Really, after everything that the Russians have had to listen to! What a triumph! The whole of Europe will be at their feet.'⁴ A letter from Beth announced that Pierre Herbart, whose first novel, *Le Rôdeur* (*The Prowler*), had just appeared had moved into Le Pin, her house at Saint-Clair.

In June, Gide spent three days in Munich with Thomas Mann, whom he had met in Paris in May, and his family. With Klaus, the eldest son, whom he already knew slightly, and the two 'gloriously beautiful' younger children, the Manns took Gide on a car outing to the Starnberger See. The following day, Gide attended a reading by Mann of his then work-in-progress, *Joseph and his Brothers*, in the University. At the dinner afterwards, Gide was the guest of honour. He then moved on to Berlin, where, over the next two weeks, he worked on the German translation of *Saül*, with Stoisy Sternheim, who was revising the original translation by Félix-Paul Grève and Bernard Groethuysen.

On 21 August, he arrived at Toulon, met from the Paris train by Beth. Gide arranged at once to meet Robert Levesque at the gate of the Arsenal, where he was stationed. Robert, it was agreed, would join them for a few days at Saint-Clair at the end of the month. He arrived with 'a young vagabond from Mauritius' called John, whom he had met in Toulon. Over the past week, Gide had not been idle in this direction either. With him, at Saint-Clair, was 'a certain Paul Verbrughe, who comes from Buenos Aires'. Gide had first met this young Belgian through Charles Brunard, another

Belgian whom Gide had first met in Brussels in 1922, as a sixteen-year-old
friend of René Michelet. Also present in this motley gathering was Prince
Mirsky, now teaching Russian literature at London University, accompanied
by 'a rather strange young Russian woman called Véra'.[5] (A twenty-seven-
year-old officer of the Imperial Guard in 1917, Mirsky left Russia soon after
the Bolshevik revolution. Perhaps uniquely among members of his caste,
he became a Communist sympathizer. His biography of Lenin, first published in English, was brought out by the *NRF* in 1935. Returning to Russia
a few years later, he was arrested and ended his days in the Gulag.)

On 22 August, the Petite Dame, who was at Pontigny, received a letter
from her daughter. Beth and Pierre Herbart were to marry: 'It would
simplify the situation and legitimize the child that I hope, that I am certain,
will come.' The Petite Dame was not really surprised, but she did wonder
why they were bothering to get married. She also felt some apprehension
as well as joy for her daughter. There was the difference in their ages: she
was then forty-one, he only twenty-eight.[6] Later, Gide set her mind at rest.
The difference in their ages would not matter in the sense that the Petite
Dame feared. 'Women are not very important for him, you know,' said
Gide.[7] Yet another man of varied sexual tastes was to be introduced into
the network of relationships. In his journal, Levesque notes that he is not
alone in coming under Herbart's spell: 'he bewitched the youth of Vence
and Cabris'. Herbart had confessed to him that he understood women
much better than boys; he had never lusted after them, they had come to
him.[8] The wedding would take place at Le Lavandou on 15 September.
Two weeks later, Herbart would be leaving for Japan, with Andrée Viollis,
a journalist and wife of the novelist Jean Viollis, and for whom he was
working as secretary.

On 1 September, Gide decided that he would go back to Cuverville and
work. The following day, Beth and Herbart drove him and Levesque to
Toulon, where the sailor reported back for duty and Gide caught the train
to Paris. That evening, Gide arrived, unannounced, at the Vaneau, just as
the Petite Dame was going to bed: the following day, she was leaving for
Colpach. They talked for an hour or two, then, again, next morning, and
over lunch at the Gare de l'Est – especially of Herbart, about whom the
Petite Dame knew very little. Gide had first met him in 1927, through
Cocteau, and took to him at once. At the time, he was completely under
Cocteau's sway and, like him, addicted to opium. He seemed determined
to consume his life as fast as possible and toyed with the idea of suicide. He
had literary ambitions and, in an attempt to save him from Cocteau and

opium, Gide had encouraged him in his writing. The result was *Le Rôdeur*, which, with Gide's support, was published by the *NRF.* Gide believed, wrongly, that Herbart was now cured of his addiction. 'I think he is very gifted,' he went on. 'He has a sort of demonic genius and the form of his writing is much better than I thought it might be. He is completely detached from Cocteau's influence, and his critical spirit detected all the weakness of Cocteau's latest books.' His father had had a fairly important job, then, after sixteen years of peaceful family life, set off, one fine day, without a *sou*, leaving everything to his wife, in order to become a tramp. Many years later, Pierre was called by the police to identify his father's corpse, which had been found in a ditch. People found Pierre quite irresistible: 'He has nothing, lives on nothing . . . His wardrobe could be put into a pocket handkerchief, but he always manages to appear extraordinarily elegant . . . Politically, he tends to Communism.'[9]

On 12 September, Gide was sitting in the Gare de Lyon, waiting for the train to Marseille. 'I am leaving Paris reluctantly,' he noted in his *Journal*. 'But I'm afraid I haven't had enough sun . . . I have never set out with so little enthusiasm. It's raining. I have a headache. My heart is beating feebly. I feel old.'[10] He arrived in Marseille the following morning and took the boat to Bastia. Next day, he was at Calvi, where he hoped to find young Paul Verbrughe, who had gone there, a week or two earlier, with John (the Mauritian) and Véra. For two days he wandered around, but saw none of them. He had no sooner booked a cabin to leave than he finally bumped into Paul Verbrughe, feverish from sunstroke. Not wanting to leave him alone, Gide took the boy with him to Saint-Clair, where he left Paul in the no doubt capable hands of Miss Todd, Catherine's English nanny, while Beth and Herbart, who had been married for a fortnight, left for Cabris, near Grasse, where they rented a small house.

After two weeks at Cuverville, Gide was back at the Vaneau on 2 October. The following day, Gide, the Petite Dame and Schlumberger were invited by Martin du Gard to dinner in his apartment in the rue du Cherche-Midi. It was the first time these old friends had met since January. (On New Year's Day, the Martin du Gards' car had overturned in a ditch inside the grounds of Le Tertre. Quite badly injured, they had spent the next ten weeks in hospital.) 'The pleasure of finding ourselves together again, in such a fraternal atmosphere, made me completely forget, for a time, that I ought to be listening to what everyone was saying, playing my role [as diarist],' noted the Petite Dame. They talked of RMG's play, *Un Taciturne*, then in rehearsal; of the financial crisis; of the progress of Communism in Russia.

Gide talked again about the Five Year Plan, 'with great enthusiasm'. Schlum remarked dryly: 'But you seem to have just discovered things that have been occupying people's minds for a long time now.' Undeterred, Gide went on lyrically to speak of 'the suppression of the family' and 'that drive, that sort of joy, that feeling of solidarity' being produced in the USSR by the changes in education. Schlum and RMG agreed that nothing of the kind could ever happen in France, 'where people are quite uninterested in the public good', 'too individualistic'. RMG could not understand why Gide advocated such a large role for the state: 'in France, the state only has to meddle in something for it to stop working'.[11]

On 26 October, Gide, the Petite Dame and Robert Levesque attended the final rehearsal of Martin du Gard's *Un Taciturne*, in a production by Louis Jouvet's company. Thierry, the 'taciturn', aged forty-seven, married, a rich industrialist, falls in love with a young man, Joë, without realizing it. When, finally, he does understand what is happening to him, he commits suicide. There was also the suggestion of a lesbian relationship between Isabelle (Thierry's wife) and a certain Wanda. At first, the audiences were quietly receptive. The critics invariably followed the same line: a genuflection to *Les Thibault*, another to the play's formal expertise, followed by disapproval, even outrage, that the author should have treated the subject of sexual aberration with such apparent *insouciance*. At later performances, very vocal, orchestrated disturbances broke out among sections of the audience. On no more evidence than a review in *Le Temps*, Paul Claudel wrote from Washington, where he was French ambassador, a long letter to Jouvet, couched in the most violent, undiplomatic terms. Claudel declared that he could no longer respect anyone who had dealings with a 'disgusting [*immonde*] writer whose name he did not even wish to recall' and could not contemplate allowing Jouvet to produce his play *L'Annonce faite à Marie*.[12]

On 12 November, Gide attended the first rehearsal of *Oedipe*, which was to be produced by Georges Pitoëff's company. Pitoëff thought *Oedipe* a little on the short side and wanted a one-act play to precede or follow it. Gide set to work on an idea that was to become *Le Treizième Arbre*: an obscene drawing was found on the thirteenth tree on the avenue leading up to a château. The play would describe the effect of the discovery on the various stylized characters: countess, parish priest, young man, teacher, doctor, governess, children. (In the event, Gide persuaded Pitoëff not to use *Le Treizième Arbre* and *Oedipe* was followed instead by Maeterlinck's *Le Miracle de Saint-Antoine*.) In the first week of December, Gide was in Berlin. From there he went to Antwerp for the first night of *Oedipe*. More performances

followed at Brussels, Geneva, Lausanne, Montreux. The plot follows Sophocles, though in a rather simplified way. The characters are the same, with
the addition of Oedipus' three children Ismene, Antigone and Polynices,
from *Oedipus at Colonus*, and a second son, Eteocles, not in Sophocles. But
if the characters are Sophocles', the characterization is not. Oedipe, an
assertive, 'self-made man' type, has less depth, less mystery. Tirésias has
none of the reluctance of Sophocles' blind prophet to reveal the truth, but
is an authoritarian, vindictive figure, very much the Catholic prelate. On
the other hand, Gide's Créon is more sympathetic than his Sophoclean
counterpart, an easygoing political trimmer, a sort of right-wing parliamen-
tarian. The language of the play is unambiguously modern, Gide's most
austere, pared-down prose. The play begins well, theatrically speaking, in
the best modern self-referential way:

Oedipus. Here I am, all present and correct in this moment of eternal time; like
someone who might walk up to the front of the stage in a theatre and say: I am
Oedipus. Forty years of age, twenty years into his reign. By brute force I have
attained the greatest happiness. A lost child, found, no identity, no papers. My
greatest happiness is that everything I have I owe to no one but myself.[13]

On Christmas Day, Gide left Paris for Cuverville to spend the festive
week with Madeleine. 'The cold, the fog, the lack of comfort' soon got the
better of him – he was already in the grip of a cold – and he was back in
Paris by 31 December. He spent New Year's Eve with Robert Levesque.
'We'll try and have a good evening, but I'm not feeling on top form. Public
holidays always make me sad . . .' he warned his young friend. He talked
of a letter that he had just received from Curtius, describing the situation
in Europe in general, and in Germany in particular: hundreds of thousands
of young intellectuals not knowing if they will eat next day and for whom
a piece of soap is a luxury. They went off for dinner at the Lutétia, followed
by a play.

On 7 January, Gide left Paris for the South, spending the first day with
Alibert at Carcassonne. On the train between there and Marseille, he read
Andromaque, with 'indescribable delight', confessing nevertheless that in his
current state of mind things like Racine's 'exquisite games' have no place.
He keeps telling himself, as if needing to convince himself, that 'the age in
which literature and the arts could flourish is past'.[14] This was to be a
recurrent theme throughout this year of ever-increasing awareness of social
and political realities – an ever-greater commitment to the cause of

Communism and the new Soviet state, which seemed to offer the only hope for the future. He spent six days with the Bussys at Roquebrune, then returned to Paris. There he suffered again from insomnia and general 'nervousness'. Time was wasted eating out – the Petite Dame was not in residence – and the mornings were 'completely devoured by correspondence, telephone calls, etc.' On 22 January, he learnt that Lytton Strachey, who had been suffering from stomach cancer for some time, had died the day before. The eleventh of the thirteen Strachey children, he was not yet fifty-two. (Three weeks later, Lytton's friend Dora Carrington shot herself dead, having tried unsuccessfully to kill herself from the fumes of her car the day that Lytton died.)

On 18 February, the Paris opening night of *Oedipe* took place. The Petite Dame did not care at all for Pitoëff's interpretation of the title role and thought that Gide's language had been 'massacred'. A by now tired and indifferent Gide could only murmur acquiescence: 'It's always the same . . . there's nothing to be done about it.' A week later, Gide had lunch with Robert Levesque at the buffet of the Gare Saint-Lazare, before catching the train for Cuverville. There, his thoughts were very much elsewhere: 'I read with the greatest interest Stalin's new speech, which exactly answers my objections and fears.' He approved of the Leninist notion that 'humanity can change, that a society can take shape on different foundations . . ., that the future need not be a repetition and reproduction of the past.'[15]

After four days, Gide was back in Paris, to visit his dying Uncle Charles. Later, he saw Martin du Gard, who was spending a short time in the capital. RMG, feeling ever more isolated at Le Tertre, ever more alienated and bounded by the life of a country squire, invited the whole of the 'Vaneau' to join him there for a week. So, on 3 March, Gide, the Petite Dame and Whity, who had arrived from Saint-Clair the day before, set out for Bellême. There, too, politics was much to the fore. RMG, not unsympathetic to socialist ideas in general or to the Soviet Union in particular, was none the less too sceptical to give them his unqualified support. Detesting what he called the 'ant-hill mentality', he still found the problem of individualism and the state unresolved. Gide replied that Stalin's last speech, 'enthralling in its lucidity and good faith', had satisfactorily addressed that very question.[16] For all his 'individualism', RMG, like Gide, was finding it ever more difficult, in the prevailing political situation, to concentrate on his work: 'Reading the newspapers has taken on an interest that novels no longer have. It requires a lot of courage and perseverance and illusion to take our little "stories" seriously.'[17] He also had serious financial worries: a man of property in an economic slump, he was faced with the curious situation whereby he would be better off if he owned less. He never expected to cover any of the 'two million' (about £80,000 or $400,000 at the time) sunk in Le Tertre. Indeed, 'if some splendid fire or some harmless revolution removed Le Tertre from our lives', he concluded, they would have an annual surplus of 80,000 francs (£3,200 or $18,000 at the time), instead of expenditure in excess of income. 'We could live in Paris for three months in the spring, spend the winter in the South, in good second-class hotels, or in small furnished villas, with local charwomen. We would suddenly feel unburdened, rejuvenated, free and rich.'[18] 'As we said goodbye, we were all aware of our tender feelings for one another,' the Petite Dame noted[19] – this did not include Hélène Martin du Gard who, beneath her impeccable manners, harboured deep disapproval of the Vaneau and all its works.

On 12 March, Gide learnt that his Uncle Charles had died: he was eighty-five. The following day, he took the Petite Dame and Whity off to see Marc's film *Mam'zelle Nitouche*. On their return, the concierge called out: 'Ah! So you aren't dead, then, Monsieur Gide! Journalists have just been here, wanting information about your death!'[20] Writer nephew and economist uncle were to be confused to the last. After the burial at Nîmes, Gide went on to Saint-Clair, where he spent about a week. Pierre Herbart read him what he had written of a new novel, *Contre-Ordre*. (Dedicated 'To Elisabeth Van Rysselberghe', it was published by the *NRF* in 1935.) On 27 March, Easter Sunday, Gide arrived at a medical establishment at Valmont, near Montreux, Lake Geneva. 'I scarcely leave my (very pleasant) room and my meals are brought to me,' he wrote to Dorothy Bussy. 'After each meal I lie down for an hour with a hot-water snake in my abdomen . . . Yesterday, by means of a rubber pipe inserted into my oesophagus, and which had to be kept there between 8 a.m. and noon, the gastric juices were extracted, then, by inserting the pipe further, three kinds of bile were extracted, from my duodenum.'[21] A few days later, an unusually inactive Gide received a letter from an unusually active Martin du Gard, who had just returned from Berlin, ecstatic about 'the beauty of the young people', 'the simplicity of their [sexual] morals': they had replaced 'the costly pleasures of the old bourgeoisie' with 'natural, gratuitous pleasures, sport, bathing, free love, games, a truly pagan, Dionysiac freedom'. On the political side, he noted how the young were attracted by Communism, but it was counterbalanced by 'an irrepressible individualism'.[22] He 'spent most of his time wandering around the less salubrious districts of the city', drinking in bars and cafés, talking to anyone willing to talk to him – and everyone seemed to be. In his *Journal*, he notes a prevalence of 'prostitution of both sexes' in Berlin, but is even more struck by 'the sexual relations, at once light-hearted, serious and free, without flirting or vulgarity', operating between people, especially the young. Pornography, too, is everywhere and delighted in, without shame or hypocrisy. By comparison, the French seem like 'a puritan people, still buried beneath moral principles inherited from Christianity'.

While in Switzerland, Gide looked into the matter of a boarding school for Catherine, now nine. He visited a number of establishments, his eventual choice falling on La Pelouse, at Bex, in the canton of Vaud. It was progressive in spirit, with plenty of sport, as well as a serious attitude to education. Living at Saint-Clair, Catherine complained that she had no friends of her own age and was very excited at the prospect of going away to school.

In April, Beth gave birth, a month prematurely, to a son. Three days later the child died. A few days later, the Petite Dame found her daughter in a state of despair, 'as if haunted by a nightmare'. Beth felt that she could not bear to remain in Saint-Clair, where she had looked forward to bringing up her child. She would try and sell Le Pin.[23]

Meanwhile, Gide had met up with Robert Levesque, whose description of Fez and its attractions excited his interest – Gide decided to go there himself. On 8 May, he landed at Tangier; next day, he called on Haddou, his host in Fez, an Arabophile Frenchman who had 'gone native'. Gide hardly knew him, but he was a friend of Eugène Rouart, who, when he wished to escape the sexual bonds imposed on him by a wife and a political career, went over to stay with him. In 'that tiny Arab dwelling', Gide wrote to Dorothy Bussy, 'one enjoys a perfect lack of comfort. One lives in the Arab style, eats in the Arab style. But will I be able to work in French?? If not, I shan't stay long . . . I brought with me the first four volumes of *Capital* (there are fourteen altogether!) and am plunging into them with the greatest interest.'[24] Martin du Gard was treated to a rather different version: 'I gorged myself on Fez, for seven days on end – till I was thirsty no longer.'[25] 'It's a pity Fez is so far away,' he told Levesque on his return, 'one ought to be able to go and spend three days there every fortnight to purge one's mind and body.'[26]

A few days later, Gide was in Cuverville, making a great effort to get back to *Geneviève*. 'Do I not have any creative power left in me?' he asks. Neither his own fiction nor anyone else's seems to interest him any more. 'How can one still write novels, when our old world is crumbling around us, when a new society is coming to birth that will take its place?'[27] He had hoped to spend some weeks at Cuverville, trying to work, but Madeleine, expecting him a fortnight later, had made plans to come to Paris and help Charles Gide's daughter in the removal of his things from the apartment. He was excluded, too, from the Vaneau, where decorators were at work painting walls and ceilings. He therefore set off for Berlin.

Meanwhile, Jenny de Margerie, the daughter-in-law of the French ambassador, took Gide and Harry Kessler on a tour of a splendid new workers' housing estate, which Mme de Margerie called 'la cité magique'. Gide was very impressed and lamented French backwardness in modern architecture. Kessler countered that to regard such a project simply as architecture was to miss the point: 'It has to be understood as a new way of living, a new assessment of what life is for and how it should be lived.' Similarly, the 'hideous, fussy and ostentatious building' at the turn of the century reflected precisely 'the vulgar ideals of the time'.[28] It is all too easy, with hindsight, to see these intellectuals' attempts to understand the world around them as tragi-comic. Six months later, Hitler became German Chancellor, invited by Hindenburg in an attempt to tame him with the responsibilities of office. On his way back to Paris, Gide stopped off at Darmstadt to attend the opening night of his *Oedipe* (in Curtius' translation). All the anachronisms that had shocked Paris were taken in its stride by the German audience. Between ancient Greek arches could be seen a backdrop depicting Notre-Dame-de-Paris. Créon wore white tie and tails, a monocle and, instead of a cloak, rags.

Gide spent a week at Cuverville, then, after a few days back in Paris, went South again. At Marseille, he called on Marc Allégret, who was directing a film based on Marcel Pagnol's play *Fanny*. He then went on to Saint-Clair, to see his daughter and to commiserate with the bereaved parents of her infant half-brother. At the beginning of July, he spent a couple of days with Martin du Gard, now alone at Cassis-sur-Mer, near Marseille: Hélène Martin du Gard was in Paris, supervising the removal of their possessions from the rue du Cherche-Midi flat, the lease on which they were giving up as an economy measure. Gide seemed more than usually obsessed with death: 'the *leitmotif* of everything he says'. When urged to explain further, Gide spoke of 'the rapid changes taking place in the world . . . He is well aware that he will not live long enough to see the realization of the social progress for which he longs with all his heart; and it is partly this uncertainty that is detaching him from life . . .' After a pause, Gide added, 'That is why I am involving myself so deeply, so *imprudently* . . . in Communism.' Martin du Gard's gloss on Gide's 'imprudently' was that, had he been younger, with time to judge the outcome, Gide would have approached Communism more cautiously, but that he was now 'an old man in a hurry'.[29]

Gide spent most of the next five weeks in Cuverville, with three brief stays in Paris. Copeau, who arrived for a two-day visit, noted that their conversations had been 'better than for several years'. He puts Gide's political concerns down to 'a certain mental restlessness', a preoccupation with youth. He praises Madeleine's 'admirable tact'; she 'knows him, loves him, follows him, adapts to his mood, never clashes with him, yet never abdicates her feelings before his'.[30] Some weeks before, Madeleine had written to Agnès Copeau: 'The spirit of your friend Gide, so noble, so concerned to be fair . . . is more and more in thrall to the slavery of Bolshevism.'[31] Gide was soon complaining that he felt no urge to write at all, but had read 'a lot of books, almost all dealing with economic and social questions, and with the current crisis'.[32] Later, he admitted: 'If social questions are occupying my mind so much now, it is partly because the creative demon is withdrawing from it.'[33] But the 'political question' was causing him some doubts. Over dinner at the Vaneau, he had asked Alix Guillain to explain what she understood by 'Trotskyite' in the present situation. There was, she said, 'a Trotskyite wave' because many intellectuals had allowed themselves to be seduced by Trotsky's 'brilliant intelligence', by the 'individualist' and 'opportunist' aspects of his thinking. She, of course, deplored 'all these separatist movements, which could only harm the Communist cause'. The trusting Gide acquiesced, at the time. Later, he describes the 'terrible confusion' he felt after reading some Trotskyite manifestos that Pierre Naville, Yves Allégret's brother-in-law, had given him. 'Dismayed at being forced to think that all is not for the best in the USSR,' he wrote to Dorothy Bussy. 'The Trotskyite party is taking a terrible advantage of it and I don't really know what to think. It was so restful fully approving of something.'[34] But he was not looking to have his new-found faith shaken: 'However well-founded certain criticisms might be, it seems to me that nothing could be more prejudicial than divisions within the Party.'[35] When in Paris, he was also meeting from time to time that at best ambiguous, at worst time-serving, literary figure, Ilya Ehrenburg. Ehrenburg had lived in Paris before and after the Revolution, only gradually making his peace with the Bolsheviks. By 1932, however, he was securely (as securely as anyone could be at that time) ensconced in the Party's hierarchy, as unofficial cultural representative of the Comintern. In exchange for services rendered, he was allowed to live comfortably in Paris.

During and after the Second World War, he lived in the Soviet Union, a pillar of the Writers' Union under Stalin and the author of a bestseller, *The Thaw* (1954), when, under Khrushchev, things were beginning to change. In the 1930s, Ehrenburg played a key role in the Party's 'wooing' of the French intelligentsia.

On 7 August, Gide left for Berlin. He spent 'six marvellous days' there, going around the city and the surrounding countryside with a young German who had a car, but no money. He got back to Paris, 'drunk with sun, adventures, pleasure'. He had intended staying for three weeks, but, after six days, he had only one idea in his head: to get back to Cuverville and work. 'A typical reaction,' the Petite Dame commented. But, once at Cuverville, Gide was besieged again by a desire to be in Berlin and set off again. Back at the Vaneau, he confessed to Robert Levesque that Paris seemed to him to be taking on some of the qualities of Berlin. 'This summer it has been prodigious,' he said. 'I've been living here as if I were on holiday.' The young man agreed: he could no longer recognize Paris. 'Tanned skins, abandon, nonchalance. The passers-by have an excited air about them. In the evenings, amorous strollers. It's like a foreign, southern city . . .' Gide told Robert that he had just been awarded the Goethe Medal by the German government, which seemed unaware that he had just published pro-Communist statements in the German press and that *Corydon* was about to appear in German.[36]

Gide went back to Berlin on 17 October, this time with Marc and by car. Some days before, Martin du Gard and Pascal Copeau, Jacques' son, had also set out for Berlin. Gide was to stay for a little over two weeks, RMG for over five, which did not prevent him from complaining that he could hardly go anywhere without having his footsteps dogged by Gide. Understandably, he had not gone to Berlin to spend his time with him. They were together at a 'very brilliant luncheon' given by the Margeries on 21 October. A week later, they were both guests at a dinner given by the Bärmann-Fischers at their 'very elegant villa in Berlin's Neuilly', RMG wrote to his wife. 'All that is rather entertaining and enables me to see Berlin from both ends: the distress of the unemployed in the clandestine bars and the exceptional luxury of the haute bourgeoisie . . .'[37] (Bärmann was the son-in-law and partner of Samuel Fischer, the publisher. Within months, both families had left Germany.) On their explorations of the other end of the social scale, Gide and RMG seem to have gone their separate ways – which did not prevent them comparing notes and arguing over their findings. RMG was convinced that only one-tenth of the male prostitutes in Berlin were in fact homosexual. Gide disagreed profoundly, claiming that his friend was merely looking for proof of a preconceived theory and that the young men would say whatever was expected of them. RMG also pursued his investigations by visiting Magnus Hirschfeld's Institut für Sexualforschung and, purporting to be a French specialist, sat in on a number of interviews with patients. RMG also took in a number of night-clubs, his favourites being the lesbian Monokel and the male homosexual Hollandais.

Gide's stay was cut short by the news that Marc, who had returned to Paris some days before, was to be operated on for appendicitis. On arrival in Paris, he went straight to the hospital, arriving back at the Vaneau only late in the evening. The following day, Marc's appendix was removed, with no ensuing complications. A few days later, Gide went into the Petite Dame's apartment and, almost overcome with embarrassment, showed her three photographs of 'a really exquisite young boy, of about thirteen or fourteen'. 'Ah!' said Gide. 'He was the great love this summer. It was to see him again that I didn't hesitate to go back to Berlin . . . but, then, I wonder if I should go back and see him again, or whether I am attaching too much importance to him.' The Petite Dame noted 'that mixture of joy, fire and mystery' on her friend's face as he showed her his mementos.[38] On 11 November, Gide left for Cuverville after lunching with Robert, who was shortly to go off on an eight-month trip to Ibiza and Morocco. He urged Robert to go and stay with Haddou in Fez. Apparently, Rouart, now a senator, would be there at the same time. 'He was one of those who dropped me when *Corydon* was published,' said Gide. 'When he saw that I was not, after all, to be cast out of society, he came back, nicer than ever . . . It's astonishing how, with him, everything is subordinated to politics.'[39] 'I do envy you,' Gide added. 'There are so many things I ought to have done and didn't . . .' He said how he intended visiting the Soviet Union. Then, displaying his misunderstanding of Soviet thinking, he added: 'I'd like them to have *Corydon* translated. It seems to me to have been written for them . . .' By 23 November, Gide was back in Berlin for two weeks. It was his fifth visit to the city that year. On 21 December, Beth arrived with Catherine, whom she had collected from her school in Switzerland. Gide spent Christmas Day with them and the Petite Dame, then, the following day, set off for Cuverville.

Gide was back at the Vaneau on 6 January. Over lunch, there was much talk of Russia and of the possibility of an eventual visit. Whity, who had arrived in Gide's absence, described her own visit as a tourist the previous autumn. A few days later, Martin du Gard arrived and the subject of a Russian visit arose again, Gide trying hard to urge his undecided friend to join him on a tour, lasting three months, in the company of some eight or nine companions, including Marc. It was to be organized by the magazine *Vu* and take in the Caucasus, Turkestan, Siberia and Manchuria. In the end, neither Gide nor his friend took up the offer and the project was abandoned. Pierre Herbart spent a few days at the Vaneau – he would shortly leave for Spain as correspondent for *L'Humanité*. Yves Allégret and his wife had just returned from Spain and, now convinced Communists, were able to give him valuable information. 'Les Groet' often called. The question of Trotsky arose more than once. It was always left to Alix Guillain, 'unshakeable in the purity of her convictions', to deliver the 'correct' view: the Trotskyites were 'tainted with personal ambition and defeatist tendencies'.[40] A few days later, Beth took Catherine back to school in Switzerland.

Gide spent the first four days of February in Wiesbaden, discussing with Stravinsky and Ida Rubinstein the possibility of an opera-ballet based on his thirty-year-old text *Proserpine*. Rubenstein, once one of Diaghilev's star dancers, had already produced his translation of *Antony and Cleopatra* with herself as the serpent of old Nile; she now saw herself performing her swansong as Gide's Proserpina. Stravinsky seemed excited by the idea and agreed to write the music. Gide went South to work on the text, taking up residence at the Grand Hôtel, in the Mediterranean resort of Le Lavandou. On 2 March, Paul Vaillant-Couturier, the editor of *L'Humanité*, telephoned asking Gide to send a telegram protesting against the 'provocative' burning down of the Reichstag. Gide's immediate reaction was to refuse: could he protest against something about which he knew nothing? Eventually, he agreed: a long, tortuous text was composed, full of qualifications, and sent off. The following day, Gide left for Marseille, where he was to meet Marc, Yvonne de Lestrange and their young son Michel. Gide and Marc spent some days in Marseille working on a project for a film that Gide had suggested, a version of Zola's novel *La Bête humaine*, which was to be backed and produced by Philippe de Rothschild. After some time, Gide decided that, although he would be available to give advice, he did not want to write this scenario and offered the job to Martin du Gard. Spurred on by a fee of 30,000 francs (about £1,200 or $6,000 at the time), RMG agreed. Four-and-a-half months later, forever disabused of his cinematic ambitions, Martin du Gard produced a typescript weighing '3 kilos 800'. His fee was paid in full, but the film was never made.

Gide was asked by Vaillant-Couturier to chair an anti-Nazi meeting of the 'Association des Ecrivains et Artistes Révolutionnaires', a Communist front organization. 'It's quite ridiculous,' he confessed to the Petite Dame. Nothing could be less his style than chairing such a meeting. He would try to persuade Vaillant-Couturier to let him off the hook: there were far better qualified people than he. There were, of course, but the Communists were intent on capturing the biggest possible name. The fastidious Gide was no match for Vaillant-Couturier's conviction and charm. When Gide telephoned, the Communist editor 'protested violently that it was too late, all the posters had been printed. It would look like desertion, treachery even.'[41] Gide capitulated.

On 19 March, Gide visited Harry Kessler, who was trying to persuade him to write a preface to his life of Rathenau. Kessler had arrived in Paris eleven days before on what he thought would be a short visit. A mere week before, the Reichstag had been burnt down and a Dutch Communist, Van der Lubbe, had been arrested and confessed to the act. The following day, Goering had declared the Communist Party guilty and the Socialists suspect. The entire Communist membership of the Reichstag, as well as hundreds of thousands of Communists in the country, were arrested. A complete ban was imposed on the left-wing press, lasting four weeks for the Communists, two weeks for the Socialists. A week later, hastily called elections resulted in a resounding Nazi victory, with great losses sustained by the left-wing parties. Though uncommitted to any political group, Harry Kessler, a liberal-minded aristocrat, was sufficiently known to have socialist sympathies for his position in Germany to be endangered. It was not until he was in Paris that he learnt, in a letter from Roland de Margerie, that his name was on a list of future SS victims. (Still later, he learnt that he had been betrayed to the Nazis by his manservant, who later ransacked his Berlin flat.) 'Sometimes I seem to be going through an evil dream from which I shall suddenly awake,' he wrote in his journal.[42] He made arrangements to dispose of his house in Weimar and never returned to Germany: he died in Paris, where he was born, in 1937, aged sixty-nine. Kessler was not, of course, the only one of Gide's friends who left Germany in 1933. A week later, Klaus Mann arrived in Paris from Munich – his uncle, Heinrich, was already there and his parents had left for Zürich. Gide's translator, Stoisy Sternheim had been in Paris for the past nine months. Before long, the publisher Hugo Simon had been removed from the chairmanship of S. Fischer Verlag. Even the most eminent non-political figures were already under threat, simply by being Jews: the great Bruno Walter, Mahler's assistant and successor at the Vienna Philharmonic, had been summarily dismissed from the Berlin Philharmonic and Albert Einstein had lost his university post. Gide set about getting the authorities to offer Einstein a chair at the Collège de France. The proceedings took time and, to Gide's mortification, Madrid got in its offer of a chair more rapidly. 'The whole of the Kurfürstendamm is descending on Paris,' Kessler noted a few weeks later.[43]

In the end, the anti-Nazi protest meeting proved not to be the trial that Gide had feared. His brief opening address, reprinted in his *Littérature engagée*,[44] begins with the self-deprecating admission that 'no one could be less qualified to preside over anything than I'. He would like, after speaking, to leave the platform and 'merge into the mass of mere listeners'. He spoke of the tragic events taking place in Germany, how, if allowed to continue, they would lead inevitably to a new war, thus betraying those who had died in 'the war to end all wars'. He referred to the motion passed by 'the courageous students of Oxford' in their Union (not 'in any circumstances to fight for King and Country'). He sympathized with their loathing of war, but could no longer accept their position. Nazism had to be opposed by force. He referred to the recent crushing of opposition in Germany and admitted that people might object that opposition is crushed in the Soviet Union also. He then becomes uncharacteristically 'jesuitical' – if not intellectually shabby. How can he approve one and disapprove of the other, he asks. 'In German terrorism I see a resumption of the most deplorable, the most detestable past. In the establishment of Soviet society, an unlimited promise of the future.' He was not alone, of course, in justifying those particular means by far-off, quite unobtainable ends. His closest friends were divided on the matter of Gide's 'conversion': 'Les Groet', Malraux, Pierre Herbart and Beth pushing him towards commitment; Jean Schlumberger, Martin du Gard, Dorothy Bussy, trying to pull him back. Like Gide, the Petite Dame could see both sides and shared his indecision. From his brother's house in Cassis RMG wrote Gide a long critical letter on the matter.

It is painful to see a life, whose finest achievement has been to struggle, with the weapons of the critical sense, against the dogmas of religious and moral conformity, end in an 'act of faith'. The argument whereby the sacrifice of reason, of the critical spirit, is seen as a proof of selflessness and courage is specious. And this defence seems to me no better from your lips than from those of Claudel or Copeau . . . The Gide of twenty years ago would be pitilessly severe on the Gide of today . . . What terrifies me is that it is too late for you to take a grip on yourself and to think freely. Little by little you have already been pushed so far that the slightest failure to demonstrate fanaticism would make you look like a coward and a renegade. They've got you, the 'ungraspable' Gide![45]

On 8 April, Gide left for Roquebrune – he had long promised the Bussys to visit them. There he would work on *Perséphone*, as he was calling *Proserpine* in its new version, and intended staying in an hotel. However, after an attack of pharyngitis, he decided to move into the Bussys' house. As a result, little work got done. He arrived back in Paris three weeks later to find an urgent message from his old friend Fedor Rosenberg, in hospital in Leningrad. It was, says the Petite Dame, 'a pathetic, rather incoherent letter, as if from someone with a fever, an urgent request for help and a last farewell'.[46] Gide sent 3,000 francs (about £120 or $600 at the time), though Rosenberg had asked for only 200 francs, through a Scandinavian commercial bank. Rosenberg lived on another year, dying in June 1934.

One day, as he was leaving the Soviet embassy, Gide felt a tap on his shoulder. It was Louis Aragon, one-time Surrealist poet, now a devout Party member, which he remained until the end (1983). Gide was rather surprised to be accosted by quite so voluble an Aragon: in his Surrealist days, he hardly deigned to speak a word. The Soviet authorities, he told Gide, were very keen to make a film of *Les Caves du Vatican*, for which he, Aragon, would prepare the scenario. It was important, however, to make certain changes to the book. For example, in order to increase its anti-Catholic impact, the swindlers who disguised themselves as priests would be actual priests. 'I just can't see how I can agree to that,' Gide later told the Petite Dame. She shared his disgust at what would, apart from anything else, be a dishonest attack on the Catholics, something he had never descended to.[47] He wrote to Aragon, declining the offer, 'with great regret, for I would have been happy to work for and with the USSR'.[48]

On 30 May, Gide chaired another political meeting, again very much against his will. In the taxi taking them to the meeting, Gide told the Petite Dame that Vaillant-Couturier was trying to persuade him to allow a serialization of *Les Caves* in *L'Humanité*. A dubious Gide had suggested *Souvenirs de la Cour d'assises* instead, a much more suitable choice for the Party daily. The meeting had been organized by another Communist front organization, the Friends of the USSR. It consisted largely of French workers giving accounts of their visits to the Soviet Union before an audience of 4,000. A rather puzzled Petite Dame notes: 'Whenever they wanted to pay homage to a name that was mentioned, an idea, or just to show their enthusiasm, they all stood up, right arm bent, clenched fist at

shoulder height and loudly intoned the first couplet of the *Internationale*.'⁴⁹ [49]
On 1 June, *L'Humanité* appeared with a large photograph of Gide and
announcing the forthcoming publication of 'a work by Gide'. In other
words, the announcement had appeared on the same day that Gide had
received the official request. It was also the day that Gide had left Paris for
Cuverville – the Petite Dame cut out the relevant extract and sent it on to
him. Gide responded at once, refusing permission. Vaillant-Couturier sent
off a telegram, informing him that it was too late, that the issue announcing
the serialization of *Les Caves* had already gone to press. The first instalment
of the novel appeared in the Communist daily three days later on 12
June.

On 15 June, Gide, now to all appearances a convinced Communist, left
Paris for a *cure* at Vittel. Some weeks before, his doctor, Sourdel, had
diagnosed 'low blood-pressure, swollen liver, congestion of the kidneys',
and ordered his patient to take the waters – and submit himself to the
attendant medical rigours. Gide, as susceptible to his doctor's persuasions
as he had been to those of the editor of *L'Humanité*, did as he was told. He
stayed for three weeks at the Vittel Palace, complaining of 'the lamentable
hideousness of this petty-bourgeois crowd' – 'not a single creature whose
existence one would want to prolong'. Moreover, he could not convince
himself that he was suffering from anything that could be treated there.⁵⁰ [50]
In fact, the contradiction between Communist fellow-traveller and elderly
gentleman taking the waters was not as absurd as it might seem: acting out
the role of the second provided an escape from the first. 'To achieve peace
of mind, one has to break off contact with the outside world,' he wrote to
Dorothy Bussy. 'People just overrule my abstention, or even my refusal,
and enrol me in a lot of organizations, where I look like a shirker if I don't
agree to be in the front row, in full view. The only remedy: flight.' He was,
he said, 'very depressed by the rather disturbing news from the USSR',
but preferred to keep his counsel 'until more fully informed'.⁵¹ [51] But, away
from the importuning and 'explanations' of Vaillant-Couturier, Alix Guillain, etc., doubts were coming to the surface. ' . . . In this sense one is quite
right to speak of a "conversion". For just as in a conversion to Catholicism,
conversion to Communism involves an abdication of free inquiry,
submission to a dogma, recognition of an orthodoxy. I find all orthodoxies
suspect.'⁵² [52]

Gide left Vittel on 7 July and, passing through Paris to Cuverville, saw
his doctor, who was pleased to see that the liver and kidneys were now
functioning normally, but surprised and rather concerned that his blood-

pressure was lower than ever. At Cuverville, Gide completed his transformation of *Proserpine* into *Perséphone* and, back in Paris, saw Stravinsky and Ida Rubinstein. Production was planned for the following March or April. Robert Levesque, back after his eight months in Morocco and Spain, came to dinner. As he approached the Vaneau, he felt, he writes, like a lover going to 'un rendezvous tendre'. The young man felt closer to Gide than ever, 'as I do to our classics when I re-read them'. They talked of North Africa and Spain. Gide, too, was dreaming of escape: 'I've been absolutely snowed under with distractions since I made my Communist declarations. They use me, chase me, manipulate me. There are always papers to be signed . . . They sometimes put my name to things without even asking my opinion on the matter . . . Next year, I'll have to get away, to Africa or Tahiti, who knows?'[53] In the short term, Gide escaped for 'a week of licence in the Belgian Ardennes' (camping with René Michelet and his boy scouts), which seems to have benefited him more than six (expensive) weeks at Vittel – a fact medically confirmed a few days later, when Dr Sourdel found his patient in excellent condition – and his blood pressure normal.

Gide returned to Paris to find the Petite Dame already in residence. 'I've been leading such a life of pleasure and am so intoxicated by it,' he told his old friend, 'that, as always in these cases, I have only one wish: to go back to Cuverville and work.'[54] In the end, he decided to stay in Paris. On 12 August, he saw the Petite Dame off to Pontigny at the Gare de Lyon, preceded by the traditional lunch at the buffet. The following day, he did leave for Cuverville, but what he found there was not a haven of peace, but a battlefield of family conflict. Jacques, Marcel Drouin's second son, had become engaged to a certain Ghisa Soloweitchik. The Drouin parents were not pleased by their son's choice. His Aunt Madeleine was horrified: 'She loved Jacques as if he had been her own son and now regards him as lost,' Gide wrote to Martin du Gard. For him, the marriage was 'in no way disastrous . . . The young Lithuanian Jewess turns out to be highly intelligent, of excellent family (good families are not only to be found in France) and not without fortune.'[55] Indeed, Ghiza Soloweitchik came from a family of brewers and financiers in the Lithuanian town of Kaunas. At the young couple's wedding on 18 September, Gide was one of the few of Jacques' relations to attend the ceremony.

A letter arrived from Yvonne Lartigaud, organizer of a Communist amateur theatre group, 'Art et Travail', proposing to stage an adaptation that she had made of *Les Caves du Vatican*. (The Party, decidedly, was tireless in its schemes to exploit Gide's name – and the 'anti-Catholicism' of *Les*

Caves.) Gide tried to put her off as best he could, but 'she was so insistent that, in the end, I gave in', while declining any responsibility for the outcome. Yet, as Gide now realized, it was impossible *not* to become involved in such an undertaking. So, on 10 October, he was back in Paris to meet Mme Lartigaud and her 'young comrades'. Yvonne Lartigaud had prepared the script, but did not, it seems, have overall control of the group. This she shared with a Louise Lara and, in the background, her husband, Autan. Gide soon realized that he would have to be unstinting in his time and fully exploit his authority if disaster were to be avoided. Most of the dialogue had been left intact, but Mme Lartigaud had introduced two clowns, who provided a sardonic and often politically pointed commentary on the action. Anything relating to Catholicism was made to look quite ridiculous. 'It was as if I were trampling everything underfoot,' said Gide, 'whereas I was ridiculing only religious hypocrisy, like Molière in *Tartuffe* . . . It's quite intolerable . . .' Worst of all was the ending, in which all the characters come on and describe what they later become – Protos a banker, Julius an Academician, etc. The following day, Gide took Mme Lartigaud to one side and insisted that she remove the ending. 'If you refuse, I shall have no alternative but to protest in the press and, if necessary, cause a scandal.'[56] The question was postponed.

One day, Gide moved from one end of the theatrical spectrum to the other: the contrast could hardly have been starker. After a rehearsal with 'the little red company', as the Petite Dame called Art et Travail, he went on to Ida Rubinstein's, where he joined Stravinsky, Copeau (who was now more or less directing *Perséphone*) and André Barsacq, Copeau's choice as designer. After dinner, Stravinsky and his youngest son, Sviatoslav Soulima, played a piano transcription of the first two parts, with the composer singing along and commenting on the work.

The following day, it was back to the Studio des Champs-Elysées – though, even there, greatness was heard, if only in passing: Toscanini was rehearsing a concert in the big theatre. In the Studio auditorium, they found Robert Levesque, Julien Green and a young man from Lausanne, Daniel Simond, who wanted Gide to give permission for his students' group, Les Bellettriens, to put on a version of *Les Caves*. Next day, tension mounted as Mme Lara launched into a tirade, in which she recited her devotion to her art, her understanding of Gide's work, her disappointment at his excessive caution, his reluctance to accept the implications of his own work. She saw how things were going when he tried to cut the ending. It was clear that she (and probably most of her colleagues) now regarded Gide

Breakfast at Pontigny, 1923. Left to right: Roger Martin du Gard, Gide, and Dorothy Bussy

Marc Allégret, aged seventeen, 1917

Pontigny, 1923. Left to right, standing: Lytton Strachey, Maria Van Rysselberghe, Loup Mayrisch, Boris de Schloezer, Gide, André Maurois, Johan Tielrooy, Martin du Gard, Jacques Heurgon, Funck-Brentano, Albert-Marie Schmidt. Left to right, sitting: Pierre Viennot, Marc Schlumberger, Jacques de Lacretelle, Pierre Lancel

Villa Montmorency, interior (left), exterior (below)

Gide at Villa Montmorency, 1908

Elisabeth Van Rysselberghe

Gide and Marc Allégret in the Congo, 1925

Jef Last

Robert Levesque,
Ibiza, 1933

Gide and Pierre Herbart in Moscow, 1936

Gide at the rue Vaneau, 1929

Gide and Maria Van Rysselberghe, rue Vaneau, 1938

Gide speaking in Red Square, Moscow, 20 June 1936, on the occasion of Gorky's funeral. Left to right: Gide, Bulganin, Molotov, Stalin and Dimitrov

Gide and his daughter, Catherine Lambert, Lake Maggiore, 1947

Gide, his daughter Catherine, her husband Jean Lambert (standing), their children and Marc Allégret, at La Mivoie, 1951

as a coward. In present company, he realized, it was no use pleading in favour of good taste. 'Don't you understand,' he protested, 'that if I want to cut something, it's not because it's too bold, but simply because I think it's bad!' 'But you're castrating your work!' said Autan. 'No,' Gide replied. 'I'm simply rejecting the papier-mâché balls [*couilles en carton*] you're trying to give me!'⁵⁷ The play finally opened on 24 October.

Meanwhile, Beth arrived. It had been agreed that she would come and try to put some order into the proliferation of books and correspondence that always accumulated around Gide. It was felt that she needed something to occupy her mind while her husband was away and could be of real service to Gide. On 2 November, Alix Guillain asked Gide if he would lend his attic room (which she herself had occupied for a time) to a German refugee, Ludwig Tureck, 'a printer and proletarian writer'. He agreed. The following day, the great-nephew of Rabindranath Tagore called, hoping to persuade Gide to become president of a new political movement that would be Communist, but anti-Stalinist and anti-Gandhian. Gide was affected by the young man's fanatical enthusiasm, but refused. Such requests arrived with almost every post: requests to join this movement or to chair that meeting, to support this cause or to protest against that action. In September, he had been billed, against his will, as one of five 'honorary presidents' of a World Conference of Youth Against War and Fascism, organized by the 'Revolutionary Students' International', yet another Communist front organization.

The October Revolution celebrations were not over yet. With the Petite Dame and Beth, Gide attended a reception at the Soviet embassy. Afterwards, they went off to see a film version of Eugene O'Neill's play *Emperor Jones*, starring Paul Robeson. The following day, with Alix Guillain, they were at a big public meeting organized by the Party at the Salle Bullier. Gide was on the platform. 'It was a meeting much like any other,' comments the Petite Dame, though marked by 'the moving presence of Dimitrov's mother'. (Dimitrov, a founder member of the Bulgarian Communist Party and head of the European section of the Comintern in Berlin, was being held by the German authorities, accused of complicity in the Reichstag fire.)

Gide's Communist sympathies had been noted in a surprising quarter. On 10 November, he received a letter from the Royal Society of Literature, which in its bald entirety reads:

Dear Sir,

I am instructed by my Council to inform you that the Honorary Fellowship of this Society, which was conferred upon you in 1924, has now terminated.

Yours faithfully,

W. H. Wagstaff

Hon. Secretary

'Have I been sacked?' a puzzled Gide asked Dorothy Bussy, quoting the letter. 'I imagined one was immortal for life! As at the Académie Française.'[58]

Next day, Gide and Beth left for Lausanne. Gide had agreed to go and work with the 'Bellettriens' on their production of *Les Caves du Vatican*, thinking that, with them, he stood a better chance of achieving a satisfactory result than with Art et Travail. He and Beth would call at Catherine's school and take her back with them for a couple of days. 'This simple, familiar resumption of contact between Bypeed and Elisabeth pleases me enormously,' the Petite Dame wrote, 'and, to my mind, this represents as many good marks for Pierre. In exceptional situations, exceptional natures are required. I also recognize in this the superior wisdom with which Bypeed is capable of carrying through something that seems at first sight to be insane.'[59] For several weeks, rehearsals proceeded, with none of the dramas that Gide had known with Art et Travail, the students showing all possible goodwill in trying to achieve what was wanted of them. For this production, he had prepared a new version, much closer to the novel than Yvonne Lartigaud's tendentious one. The Petite Dame arrived in Lausanne for the opening night on 14 December.

On 4 January 1934, Gide and André Malraux took a plane to Berlin. Their intention was to call on the Propaganda Minister, Goebbels, and lodge a protest against the continued imprisonment of Dimitrov and his two Bulgarian Communist associates. Their trial, on a charge that they were the instigators of the Reichstag fire, had begun on 21 September in Leipzig. It lasted three months, but, despite pressure from the government, the court found the defendants innocent – at this stage, the courts still retained some independence of the political authorities. Nevertheless, the prisoners had not been released. At the end of December, Gide had been to see his old friend Léger (the poet Saint-John Perse) at the Quai d'Orsay and been assured that pressure from Britain and France had played a large part in Dimitrov's acquittal. On arriving in Berlin, Gide and Malraux found that Goebbels was in Munich and left a letter[60] addressed to him, expressing, in polite terms, the concerns of many people, throughout the world, that men found innocent were still being held in custody; they flew back to Paris the next day. Meanwhile, the efficient Communist organization had arranged for public meetings to take place throughout the world (thirty-two in France alone). On 31 January, a large meeting was held in Paris at the Salle Wagram, for which, *in absentia*, Gide acted as 'honorary chairman': a letter from him[61] was read out to the gathering. Dimitrov was deported to Moscow on 27 February, probably as part of a secret deal between the German and Soviet governments, rather than as a result of international protest. (He became Secretary-General of the Comintern and, in 1945, returned to Bulgaria as head of government. Although he carried out the 'Sovietization' of the country, he fell out of favour with Stalin on account of his close links with Tito. He died in Moscow, in 1949, while undergoing medical treatment.)

A week later, Gide was in Cuverville, reading a manuscript that had arrived from Dorothy Bussy. Four weeks before, Dorothy had added, as a postscript to another letter and almost in passing: 'A *deadly* secret. I have written a book! A very short one but I'm dying to show it to you. No one else in the world knows nor probably ever will . . .'[62] The typescript arrived, accompanied by a more than usually self-abasing letter: 'I'm absolutely disgusted with it – poor, meagre, inadequate thing . . . At any rate, it isn't long and won't take you half an hour to read. For heaven's sake, don't think it necessary to write to me about it. Drop it into that friendly, comfortable gulf of silence and oblivion that swallows up all my letters. It is less important . . . *Strictly anonymous* . . .'[63] This story, entirely about women and girls, was not likely to elicit much response in him. On 15 January, Gide wrote: 'Yes, I read Olivia's story with the keenest emotion . . . How little ash even today covers so much flame! And how readily the breath of my attention rekindles them . . . And constantly, as I read, it was your voice I heard.'[64] A tactfully warm, if noncommittal response.

In an article '*Olivia*, roman à clefs', published in two numbers of the *Bulletin de l'Association des Amis d'André Gide* in 1983,[65] the German scholar Harald Emeis expounds the thesis that *Olivia* is not fundamentally the story of a schoolgirl infatuation, but a transposed account of the author's relationship with Gide – and a disguised love letter to him. Olivia was Dorothy herself. Gide appeared not as the 'hero' of the novel, but as the heroine, Mlle Julie; the withdrawn, distant Mlle Cara ('the beloved') was Madeleine. Olivia's great rival in Julie's affections, Laura, was Elisabeth Van Rysselberghe, and so on. Over and above the plausibility of one-to-one substitutions of real persons for characters, support for Emeis' thesis is to be found in comments made at various times by Gide and the author. In the Introduction to *Olivia*, Dorothy Bussy writes: 'Its truth has been filtered, transposed and, maybe, superficially altered, as is inevitably the case with all autobiographies.' A month after sending the manuscript, Dorothy tried again, nudging him in the right direction: 'I hope you didn't think the whole of my story *true*. A good deal of it was, but still more wasn't. But of course you saw through it all. I don't know whether you will believe me, but I think it is true to say that I sent it to you grudgingly, reluctantly, even painfully, but as a matter of conscience.'[66] If the real subject of *Olivia* were not Gide, why would its author feel it a 'matter of conscience' to send it to him? Gide did not take up the bait and Dorothy said no more of *Olivia*. Then, in February 1948, half-way through a letter, she wrote: 'I think it must be 15 years ago that I showed you a MS of a short story. Oh how could I be so idiotic?' Recently, she had shown it to three women friends: 'They astonished me by the – almost – violence of their approval.' One of them, Rosamund Lehmann, called it 'a work of literature, far too good to lose. It *must* be published.' At her insistence, Dorothy showed it to John Lehmann, Rosamund's brother, who, in turn, got Leonard Woolf to publish it under the Hogarth Press imprint. 'So now, dear friend,' Dorothy added acerbically, 'perhaps you will have the glory of having rejected two bestsellers – Proust and yours truly! But you won't write me such a nice letter as you wrote him. P.S. My book is to be anonymous and *please don't mention it to anyone* . . .'[67] It appeared as '*Olivia* by Olivia' in 1949, dedicated 'To the beloved Memory of V.W.' (Virginia Woolf, who, back in 1933, had urged Dorothy to write an autobiographical work). A few days later, Gide replied that he 'had *no memory of* reading' such a manuscript.[68] Dorothy Bussy hit back: 'The little work that you have so completely *refoulé* [repressed], when you come to re-read it, as I hope some day you will, will make only too clear a) the reason you disliked it and b) the reason why I wish it to be anonymous.'[69] Gide read the manuscript and responded by telegram: 'As repentant and embarrassed as with Proust.' A letter followed. He had 'devoured the whole thing . . . hungrily, delightedly, with anguish, intoxi- cation . . . At one and the same time I recognized it all and discovered it all . . . Freud alone could say and perhaps explain what scales covered my eyes the first time I read it. For it's not at all comparable to my earlier mistake concerning Proust (despite what my telegram says). I had done no more than "scan" – and with a hostile eye – a few pages of the *Temps perdu*.'[70] 'I am glad that Olivia after so many years of patience has at last succeeded in touching you, as she would have wished,' Dorothy wrote back.

'Do you recognize, I wonder, that it is your presence in my life, your teaching, your example that brought her to life?'[71]

To return to 1934. On 24 January, Gide wrote to Dorothy Bussy: 'I don't belong to myself any more. I shall try to escape.'[72] Three days later, he saw Robert Levesque briefly, before leaving for Syracuse. 'I'm telling everyone that I am going for three months,' he told his friend. 'I'd like to be able to, but I'll be needed, in Paris or Cuverville. I'll be called back. Anyway, I know what I'm like . . . But I feel a great need to be alone.'[73] Life in Paris had become quite impossible, an endless round of telephone calls, visits, mountains of correspondence to be dealt with. He spent two days at Marseille, with Martin du Gard, who was there to see off the Petite Dame and Loup Mayrisch, about to leave on a trip to Cairo. He then set out on an almost unbroken, forty-eight-hour journey to Syracuse, stopping for a few hours in Rome and Naples to change trains. At Syracuse, he found the hotel where he had intended to stay 'mediocre, stupidly situated, ugly, vulgar, with pretentious, shoddy furniture, an unheatable room'. He took himself off to the Villa Politi and found a room for 50 lire. Realizing who he was, the *padrone* begged him to accept, for the same price, 'an enormous room, with bathroom, a superb view and all manner of useful things: two tables, sofa, armchairs, etc., etc.' The weather, however, was 'frightful': 'Thunder hasn't ceased shaking my windows since eight this morning . . . A continual downpour of rain; icy wind; a sky the colour of soot.'[74]

Gide set to work on *Geneviève* which he hoped to finish before leaving Syracuse. Given the weather, which remained bad for three weeks, he also read a lot: Dos Passos's *Manhattan Transfer*, which, though recommended by Yves Allégret, irritated him; *Othello*, 'for the sixth time', with ever-growing admiration; Goethe's *Faust*, Part 2; Voltaire's *Contes*; Hölderlin; Racine's *Iphigénie* and *Phèdre*.

By 21 February, Gide could report that the weather had been 'splendid' for the past two days and that he had been working better than he had done for months. He had finished what he calls the 'third chapter of *Geneviève*' – the final work does not have 'chapters', but is divided into two 'parts'.

By the end of February, Gide realized that he had got nowhere with *Geneviève*: it ended, as he noted in the *Journal* years later, in a 'fiasco'.[75] He tore up what he had written of 'Chapter 3' and returned to Paris. While away, trying to escape day-to-day involvement in the political situation, Gide missed an event that was seen by many as the beginning of a possible breakdown in France's political institutions, leading to an extreme

right-wing coup d'état or a Communist revolution. In January, the unex-
plained suicide (or murder) of Alexander Stavisky, a Russian émigré 'con-
man', embroiled in widespread corruption, involving deputies and even
ministers, brought down Chautemps' centre-left coalition government. It
was succeeded by a similar government under Daladier, which sacked
the Paris prefect of police, Chiappe, a Corsican of extreme right-wing
sympathies. On 6 February, the war veterans' organization and various
extreme right-wing groups staged a demonstration in the place de la
Concorde. A smaller counter-demonstration, led by the Communists,
turned to violence. A contingent of right-wing demonstrators broke through
the police lines and entered the Chambre des Députés, which was in session.
Daladier resigned and was replaced by a centre-right coalition under
Doumergue. Six days later, Communists, Socialists and other sympathizers
staged a protest in the place de la Nation, draping the statue of the Republic
in the Red Flag. It was one of the first instances of the Communist Party
having anything to do with those outside its own ranks. The Party line had
always been that the biggest traitors in the class war were those who were
close to them, but not of them: Party organs regularly referred to democratic
socialists as 'social fascists'. Many had long come to see that it was divisions
on 'the left' that had been responsible for the triumph of Mussolini's Fascists
and Hitler's Nazis. The following year, 1935, the Comintern line had
changed, the Party believing that more was to be gained by manipulating
other left-wing parties than by opposing them: the Popular Front was born.
Needless to say, the February events, and their implications, were to occupy
a large place in the conversation of Gide's circle over the next few months.

After a week in Cuverville, Gide was back in Paris. On 22 March, he
had a long lunch with Robert Levesque at his favourite restaurant, Lesur,
on the *quais*. Afterwards, they called in at the *NRF* offices, then walked to
the rue Montmartre, where Gide had arranged to meet Aragon. 'He
frightens me,' Gide confessed. 'He is full of hate, a terrorist.'[76] Gide did not
get back to the Vaneau until midnight, where he was met by an excited
journalist, who seemed astonished to see him. Apparently, a rumour had
spread some hours before, that Gide had committed suicide. About the
same time, Madeleine had been awoken from her sleep by a reporter from
the *Journal de Rouen* informing her that her husband had been 'the victim
of an accident'. An hour before, a press agency had telephoned the Vaneau
and informed Marc of Gide's death. The telephone continued to ring until
two in the morning.

Early in the year, Martin du Gard had come to the realization that he owned, leased or rented so much property that he and his wife did not have enough to live on. He was not unaware of the 'absurdity' of his situation. With his brother, he was co-owner of a garage, a block of flats and a building in the rue du Dragon, none of which yielded a profit, while Le Tertre cost him 40,000 francs a year to run even if he didn't live in it. At that time, furthermore, it was impossible to sell any property except at a considerable loss. He and his wife had already decided to give up any idea of living at Le Tertre or in Paris. They took a lease on a flat in Nice, of modest size, running costs and rent (500 francs per month (£20 or $100 at the time)). The flat was on the sixth floor, with a splendid view over Nice and the sea.

On 28 March, Gide escaped southwards. After spending a few days in Marseille and Manosque, he turned up, 'glum and with a cold', in Nice. Two days after Gide's arrival, the Petite Dame, who had been staying with her daughter at Cabris, also decided to call on 'Martin', as she always refers to him, on her way back to Paris, not knowing that Gide had anticipated her. The following day, Gide read her what he had written at Syracuse. In that third chapter, Geneviève becomes involved with a character based on Charles Du Bos and an institution like the Foyer Franco-Belge. The Petite Dame was 'appalled by the result: under the pretext of situating Charlie, he recounts the whole story of the Foyer Franco-Belge, from notes that I had already found too boring to be included in a journal . . . Geneviève drops into the background!' RMG, to whom Gide had earlier read the same material, had reacted similarly. Gide himself agreed: 'In fact, it's all very poor stuff . . . and I don't mean just this latest part, but almost all of it. In fact, I'm not very good at dealing with real things, documentation. I'm much better when I invent. I'm writing all that against my natural bent. I know too well how good books are born not to know how bad ones are too . . . No, I'm giving up *Geneviève*. If she has to live, she will come back in a different way.'[77]

On 9 April, all three of them went over to Roquebrune to lunch with the Bussys. A few days later, Gide and Beth took Catherine back to her school at Bex, then spent ten days driving through the Italian Tyrol. Gide returned to Paris, in order to see the third and last performance of *Perséphone*. On the same day, Gide had been asked to co-chair a meeting, with Malraux, to protest against the continued imprisonment of the German Communist leader, Ernst Thaelmann. He chose the public meeting: so he never saw *Perséphone*, except in rehearsal. (Despite a long, intensive campaign, organized by the Party and its sympathizers, Thaelmann was not released: he died in Buchenwald, probably by execution, in 1944.)

In early June, Gide attended a meeting of the AEAR (Association des Ecrivains et Artistes révolutionnaires). At some point in the proceedings Aragon read out a letter that Gide had addressed to 'the students of the USSR', which was enthusiastically applauded. (The text was used as a preface to an edition of Gide's *Collected Works*, then appearing in Russian translation.) Later, Aragon, who had been instructed by Vaillant-Couturier to deliver a 'correct' response to views expressed by another speaker, Drieu La Rochelle, did so in such a venomous way that many of the 'fellow-travellers', including Gide, were shocked. Ramon Fernandez even handed in his resignation to the AEAR, returning, before long, to his earlier extreme right-wing views. Drieu, too, moved to the right. In fact, both men collaborated with the Germans during the Occupation, Drieu taking over the running of the *NRF.* Both men, too, died in 1944, before post-war retribution could take its toll.

On 6 June, Gide set out with Marc and Yves in their new Chrysler for the South, where they hoped to find a suitable setting for a film to be made of Hector Malot's novel *Sans Famille*. On his return, a fortnight later, Gide also found a card from Robert praising a youth hostel at which he was staying. The hostel was at Boissy-la-Rivière, near Etampes, about 40 miles south of Paris, on land owned by Marc Sangnier, a rich, socialistically inclined ex-deputy and a paedophile, who also organized camping holidays for boys and youths on his estate. A few days after sending the card to Gide, Robert caught sight of the Allégret Chrysler pulling up, with Yves at the wheel, and his wife and Gide with him. They went into the hostel and were almost deafened by the noise. 'What's happening?' a rather startled Gide asked. 'Oh, a whole crowd of campers has just arrived,' Robert told him. 'And another fifteen or twenty kids are expected tomorrow.' 'Then I'm staying!' said Gide. 'I've brought my suitcase.' Renée Allegret was so enthusiastic about the hostel that she would like to have stayed, too, but she and Yves had to be back in Paris that evening. Robert drew the line at letting Gide sleep in the dormitory and took him off to a nearby inn. After dinner, they went off into the woods in search of the young Communists they had seen arriving earlier. They stumbled upon 'a very elegant tent', in which three scantily clad boys and three girls were finishing their dinner. Robert went up to them and said: 'Comrades, André Gide would like to say good evening.' Gide and Robert moved on and found a group of German émigrés, whom Robert had already met. Gide spoke to them in German. 'Let's make a fire,' said one of them. So they all set to work gathering wood, Gide included. The flames spread and rose upwards, illuminating their young faces and bright red scarves. One of the Germans took out his mandolin, another a harmonica. They started singing the *Internationale* and other songs. Gide was delighted: as luck would have it, it was Midsummer's Night, St John's Eve. Back at the inn, they went off to their rooms to sleep. At five, Robert woke up and couldn't get back to sleep. He went into Gide's room and got into bed beside him. Gide woke up, but soon they both went off to sleep again. 'Never have I known that sort of pleasure, one that I would give for any other,' Levesque wrote. 'I understood then that Gide was my best friend, the person for whom I had felt the greatest affection for years, which replaced *love* in my life (without anything sexual).' Next morning, it was raining. Before leaving for Paris, Gide said to Robert, who was staying on for another five days: 'I shall always remember that early morning with great fondness. I feel happy, at peace, quite calm . . . It was perhaps the first time. I don't think I ever experienced it before.' 'I felt the same,' said Robert. 'It wouldn't have been the same otherwise.'[78]

Some days later, over dinner with Stoisy Sternheim, the conversation drifted to the subject of Gide's health and whether or not he should go to Vittel. Stoisy strongly recommended 'Karlsbad' (officially Karlovy Vary and now part of the Czech Republic). On 8 July, the Petite Dame was leaving for her own *cure* at Bex, close to Catherine's school in Switzerland. Gide decided to travel with her as far as Lausanne and to go on from there to Karlsbad. On the train from Lausanne, Gide met a Swedish rabbi, on his fifth *cure* at Karlsbad, who had met his Uncle Charles in Jerusalem. He was soon joined by Stoisy Sternheim. Before long, Gide noticed that most of the staff and patients were Jewish. This had the advantage that he could practise his German, which was spoken much more in the town than Czech. The day after his arrival, he found that bookshops in the town were displaying notices that read: 'André Gide ist gekommen!' (André Gide has arrived). One woman came up to him and, mixing up her Beethoven with her Schubert, declared that she was a great admirer of his *Symphonie inachevée*! One day, he entered a synagogue, where he heard 'a very beautiful concert' and a 'rather stirring sermon' on the theme 'Ein Gott, ein Volk, ein Land', whose implied exclusivity he detested. ' "Kein Gott, Kein Volk, Kein Land" [no God, no people, no country] is the still Utopian programme that tomorrow may save the world and to which I already subscribe.'[79]

The anecdote and its wider context are fraught with irony, an irony of the most tragic kind, but one, too, that has its comic side. Gide, still quite capable of addressing vast meetings, organized by representatives of a 'dictatorship of the proletariat', as 'comrades', was spending four weeks in a luxury hotel. Most of his fellow-residents were rich, German-speaking Jews, attended by Jewish doctors, in a German-speaking town 15 miles from the German border, in 1934, a year and a half after the rise to power of a German (ex-Austrian) determined to remove a whole race of 'aliens' from the midst of the Master Race, five years before the Germans of lands Czech since the Treaty of Versailles were 'liberated' by their fellow-Germans, thus precipitating the eventual Second World War. There he was listening to a sermon, in German, in which members of a race about to be exterminated in their millions were being addressed as representatives of a Chosen People, who, under the one God, who is their God alone, will eventually inherit the Earth. Furthermore, two years from then, that Georgian ex-seminarian Stalin, representative of the Utopia to come, would embark, in the name of an ideology bearing the name of a German Jew, on the extermination of even more millions of people than Hitler, disproportionate numbers of whom would be Jewish, and therefore suspected of 'international' loyalties – or sympathy for his great (Jewish) rival, Trotsky.

On 4 August, Gide left Karlovy Vary for Thun, in Switzerland, where he was joined by Robert Levesque, hot from Pontigny. Gide had already written to Martin du Gard, asking him to take Robert under his wing at Pontigny. 'We talked about love . . . [RMG] seems to have an extraordinary understanding of sexual adventure. He enjoys the deep, though rapid, knowledge that one acquires of individuals in such sexual encounters. Intimate revelations about his own sexual nature, his fear of death, his need of tenderness, his curiosity about *everyone* . . .'[80] They took their leave of Stoisy Sternheim and her daughter, Nouki, and set out for Lake Maggiore. Near Locarno they took a room at a 'wonderful hotel' on the Monte Verità overlooking Ascona. It belonged to a German friend of Harry Kessler's, an art collector, and was filled with antique furniture. The whole length of the dining-room looked out over the lake, while the other walls were covered with works by 'Picasso, Gauguin, Matisse, etc.' Other rooms were hung with tapestries or lined with books. 'In the great silence,' Robert noted, 'Gide began to sleep well and to work, which he had not done for a very long time.' He bought exercise-books and began to make notes for the play that he was writing, having abandoned, yet again, *Geneviève*. The play later acquired a title, first *L'Intérêt général*, then *Robert, ou l'intérêt général*. This, too, was to be abandoned and resumed several times. Gide worked in the morning. In the afternoon, he and Robert had a one-hour siesta in their room. 'To tell the truth,' Robert wrote, 'it was perfect happiness. Weather and natural scenery were extraordinarily beautiful. My intimacy with Gide quite admirable. Without in any way being exclusive, I experienced a tender pleasure in feeling that he was mine alone. I would not have wanted to impede him in his work, but I found his mere presence so satisfying that my desire to go off and wander about by myself was much diminished . . .'[81] One morning, Robert received a letter confirming that he had been offered a teaching post at the French *lycée* in Rome. Overcome with delight, he rushed up to tell Gide, who took him in his arms and said: 'It's quite the best thing that could have happened to you . . . You were born under a lucky star . . . At Rome, one always works very well. Rome was always good to me. One feels surrounded by labouring ghosts, Goethe, Stendhal . . .'[82]

They stayed at the hotel above Ascona for five days. They then took the boat and sailed the length of the lake, crossing the Swiss–Italian frontier on the way. After dinner, they walked along the quayside: 'Quite a lot of young men, looking quite excited, like all Italians, but also "healthy" looking,' Levesque notes. The following morning, with unerring instinct, Gide found a group of young boys to befriend. As their train left the station, two of them ran along the platform waving and shouting *'Addio!'*[83] On the train, 'studious as ever', Gide set to work on a pile of German books and newspapers, dictionary to hand. As they approached Turin, they were both moved at the thought of Nietzsche's final breakdown in the Piazza Carlo Alberto in 1889.

In Nice, they found a quiet hotel to spend the night, then, next day, got a bus to Cabris. On the way, Gide said to Robert: 'I'm looking forward to seeing little Catherine again . . . We'll also see a charming boy, Elisabeth's godson. The Herbarts took him in as a lodger because his parents couldn't do anything with him. He's fourteen, I think, quite marvellous. But we'll have to be careful. Herbart is bound to have fallen in love with him and he gets terribly jealous. For a long time, you know, he didn't want me to come to Cabris. He first settled there to be near his friend Marius. He met him when he was thirteen . . . He was killed in a car accident recently, as Herbart looked on. Herbart's fate really is tragic. He doesn't believe in anything, but is very superstitious. "I kill everything I touch," he says. When his son died – he only lived a few days – it was a terrible shock to him. He swore that he would not try and have a child again . . .' While Gide had a siesta, Pierre took Robert into his study. Robert noticed that there was a photograph of young Marius on the desk. The conversation soon took on an intimate character. 'Since he asked me questions about myself,' Levesque writes, 'I told him that I lose in depth what I gain in extent. But what can

I do if love never knocks at my door? He replied (rather sadly) that it was an illusion to believe that life spent with just one person deepens anything. Was he referring to Marius or his wife? Both, perhaps . . . Several times I got the impression that Herbart and his wife were both unhappy.'[84]

They spent two nights in Cabris, then took buses along the coast to Le Lavandou. On the way, Gide said to Robert: 'I'm always afraid you might get bored when you're with me, afraid that I'm not being nice enough to you . . . Not taking enough notice of you . . .' Robert whispered back: 'I was thinking just now that never in my whole life have I been so pampered as I am with you . . .'[85] They arrived at Le Lavandou, had lunch, then got a taxi to take them the few miles inland to Bormes, where they called on 'les Groet'. The following day, they left Bormes, spent a night at Hyères-Plage and another at Toulon. They woke next morning to find it raining: 'And so,' said Gide, 'this extraordinary summer has come to an end.' 'I don't regret not having travelled with Gide before now,' Robert wrote. 'It needed these eight years for our friendship to reach this perfection. How much we are at one now! The difference in age [forty years] does not matter. We understand one another without having to say a word . . .'[86]

Gide spent three days in Paris, he and the Petite Dame bringing each other up to date: they had not seen one another for eight weeks. She read to him her *Il y a quarante ans*, the account of her passionate, but platonic affair – both were deeply attached to their spouses – with Emile Verhaeren of forty years earlier. (It was published by the *NRF* in 1936.) Shortly afterwards, they discussed the problem posed by those parts of Gide's journal that concerned Madeleine. She thought that he should cut out all references to Madeleine in the published version. He argued that if he did so, Madeleine would conclude that she had played no part in his life. In the end, he agreed to follow the Petite Dame's advice, and have published what related to his wife separately, only after her death. (This material was finally published in 1951, the year of his own death, as *Et nunc manet in te*.)

Back in Paris, after three weeks in Cuverville, assailed once more by telephone, correspondence and visitors, Gide decided to spend some days *incognito* at Yvonne de Lestrange's, working on his play. On 23 October, a few days after leaving the Vicomtesse de Lestrange's 'princely residence', Gide was chairing a meeting at the Palais de la Mutualité, at which various speakers gave their impressions of the recent Congress of Soviet Writers before 4,500 people. Gide himself opened the meeting, managing better than usual to overcome his shyness and find the right tone. The 'Association of Soviet Writers' had been formed in 1932, replacing the Association of

Proletarian Writers (RAPP). The change of title reflected a change in the Party's cultural policy, itself a side-product of the new political line. RAPP was essentially a Bolshevist/Leninist creation, based on the notion of intensifying and widening the gap between genuinely 'revolutionary' writers and unredeemably 'bourgeois' writers, as part of the international struggle leading to world revolution. Such a line offered no comfort to fellow-travellers like Gide. With the adoption of the 'United Front' line, however, cultural policy was also changed. Agitprop-type literature, what Bukharin, the leading patron of the new line, called 'the mere paraphrasing in verse of political slogans' was dropped, but so, too, was 'modernism' in the arts. The new doctrine was 'socialist realism', seen as a natural successor, rather than an antagonist, to the critical 'bourgeois' tradition (Dickens, Balzac, etc.) Paradoxically, the change in cultural policy, hamfistedly implemented by bureaucrats, brought less, not more freedom for artists. It was against this background that Gide's speech is to be understood:

There is a bourgeois conventionality that I personally have always struggled against. But let us not be afraid to say it here: there can also be a Communist conventionality. I believe that any literature is in great danger when the writer feels that he must obey some slogan. That literature and art can serve the revolution goes without saying; but they should not try to serve it. It never serves it better than when it is concerned only with the truth. It does not have to place itself at the service of the Revolution. In this it differs essentially from the fascist, Hitlerian, imperialist productions of every country, which respond to slogans; their task it not to speak the truth, but to conceal it . . . If the USSR triumphs – and triumph it must – its art will soon disengage itself from the struggle; I mean: free itself.[87]

Malraux, improvising, was, as always, dazzling, though his thinking, too, was 'rather too subtle for that audience'. He achieved eloquence without detriment to intelligence. The only other speakers of any note were Ilya Ehrenburg and, 'through impossible French', Jef Last, 'Dutch sailor and writer'. Two days later, Jef Last came to see Gide. Before long, the conversation wandered from politics to the situation of homosexuals in the Soviet Union. Last, who had been in Russia for the Writers' Congress, had noted a distinct difference in official attitudes, since his earlier visit two years before. In earlier years, despite the harsh material conditions, people had been buoyed up by a kind of joyful confidence in the future, one result of which was a widespread freedom of sexual morals. This had now gone and a kind of official puritanism was being imposed, together with a new law against homosexual acts. Last also told Gide that he had been a close friend of Marius Van der Lubbe, who had been accused of the Reichstag fire. He was, said Last, a very remarkable man and not at all like the pathetic creature who had appeared in court after treatment at the hands of the Nazis.

On 22 November, the Petite Dame and Beth 'discreetly celebrated' Gide's sixty-fifth birthday, with a quiet, but 'amusing' dinner. By the end of the month, Gide had finished working on a version of some of Pushkin's stories, from a literal translation provided by Jacques Schiffrin. On 7 December, 'taking advantage of the suddenly milder weather', Gide left to spend two days at Cuverville. On his return, everyone was talking about the murder of Kirov on 1 December. Kirov, a leading member of the Politburo and Party head in Leningrad, had assisted Stalin in his struggle against his rivals. However, earlier in the year, he had led the opposition in the Central Committee against Stalin's personal rule. The murder was declared to be the work of a young Communist, who seems to have left a statement of the reason for his action, before 'committing suicide'. Fourteen of the young man's Party associates were immediately shot. Kirov's murder, which, it is generally believed, was the work of Stalin himself, was used, over the next few years, as a pretext for the 'trial' and execution of all the Old Bolsheviks, those who had worked with Lenin and could be regarded by Stalin as potential rivals. Eventually, the Great Purge was extended to include some ten million victims including a majority of the Party's Central Committee, the commanders-in-chief of the Red Army and Red Navy, together with a large section of their officer classes – not forgetting the head of OGPU, the secret police, Yakhov himself. Of course, Gide and his Communist or fellow-travelling friends had only the official version of Kirov's death to go on: hence their perplexity. Many were beginning to have doubts about what exactly was going on in the Soviet Union, but it was only later that the true horror of the situation dawned on them.

On 21 December, Catherine, now eleven, arrived back from her school. The following day, Gide took her and two children of friends to the Jardin des Plantes, then to the cinema. Christmas Day was spent *en famille*, Catherine surrounded by her parents, grandmother and stepfather. On 28 December Gide packed his bags and set off for Rome and Robert Levesque.

Gide arrived on the evening of 29 December and he and Robert spent the night at the Hôtel Hassler at the top of the Spanish Steps. 'Ah!' said Gide, as they descended the steps again. 'You can't imagine what it was like when all the artists' models plied their trade here. It was swarming with them from morning till night!' There were other changes, too, in Mussolini's cleaned-up capital: Gide regretted the passing of 'Goethe's squalid Rome' and remembered how, in 1922, with Marc Allégret, he had wandered the tiny streets around the Forum in search of 'adventure'. As they walked the streets after dinner, Robert was subjected to 'a sort of examination' on what he had seen in Rome. He was amazed at how well Gide knew the city: for him, each street, each square was imbued with a mass of historical and literary reference.

Next morning, they caught the train to Naples, and on to Salerno, spending the night at the Hôtel Astoria in nearby Cava. The following morning, they hired a carriage, which took them to the ancient town of Paestum, with its three temples. The grass around was full of faded asphodels. When Shelley came there, said Gide, it was full of violets. 'You must read Burkhardt about this place . . . He speaks about it lovingly, stone by stone.' The conversation moved on – to Swinburne, Keats, Leopardi. After a night accompanied by the sound of fireworks welcoming the New Year, they left Cava next morning for Rome, arriving there at night ('on Lafcadio's train!').

Later in the day, they called on the poet Giuseppe Ungaretti, whom Gide had met in Paris and put in touch with Robert. Also there were some young poets and Arduini, a close friend and antique dealer in his thirties. There was much talk of Gide's works, until Gide himself shifted the conversation to Caravaggio, who, he knew, was of great interest to all present. The following day, it was decided, Arduini, with Ungaretti, would collect Gide and Robert and take them on a tour of the Caravaggios in and around Rome. In the French church, Saint-Louis-des-Français, they saw Caravaggio's St Matthew triptych – and unerringly picked out those figures that gave the painter (and them) greatest pleasure: 'an adorable kid, with chubby cheeks and big, sad eyes', 'a tall, naked executioner (who obviously had the painter's sympathies)', 'a very beautiful angel'.[88] They moved on to *The Madonna of the Pilgrims* (which Levesque calls *The Adoration of the Virgin*) in San Agostino. At the Villa Borghese were *St Anne and the Virgin holding the Child* and a young *David*. They lunched at Samuele's in the old Jewish ghetto, before returning to the hotel for the mandatory siesta. Next day, the same party drove to Palestrina, where, in the Barberini Palace, an unfinished *Pietà* by Michelangelo was to be seen. They returned to the car, to find a drawing of a large phallus on one of the seats. The square was 'full of kids and young men looking very excited . . . The whole town seemed lubricious.'[89] Back in Rome, after dinner, Gide went off alone to a small local cinema to see *42nd Street* and Robert went off, also alone, to wander the streets.

The following Sunday Arduini took Gide and Robert out to see the

Etruscan tombs near Tarquinia. They saw ten such tombs or chambers, each decorated with elaborate mural paintings, glorifying some form of sensual delight: one depicted horse-riding, another the pleasures of the table, but their interest was particularly aroused by the second, which depicted sexual orgies between men. 'What a love of life they had!' Robert exclaimed. 'Everything in their tombs speaks of festivities and pleasures. Joy in death.' 'Ah!' said Gide 'How far away they seem from us, yet how well we would have got on with them!' The following day, Gide left for Paris. In his journal Robert notes that Gide had admitted that he was beginning to lose his curiosity. 'Yet, beside other men,' he adds, 'how vibrant he still is, his antennae all alert, interesting himself in everything and constantly discovering things!'[90]

On 26 January, a debate entitled 'Gide and our time' took place at Paul Desjardins' Union pour la vérité. Over 200 people crowded into the premises in the rue Visconti. Gide had insisted that his adversaries, as well as his friends, should be invited to contribute, including Henri Massis, his most virulent (and most competent) ideological opponent, whom he had not seen for twenty-three years. Massis had got up from his sickbed to represent his Church, unaware until he arrived at the hall that no fewer than three other, in many ways more eminent, Catholics would be taking part: Jacques Maritain (France's leading theologian and a convert from Protestantism), Gabriel Marcel (a convert from Judaism, later to be labelled a 'Catholic existentialist') and François Mauriac.

The discussion was opened and guided in its course by Ramon Fernandez, author of an *André Gide*, published in 1931. Gide's influence, said Fernandez, had been stronger and more durable than that of any contemporary French writer. That influence had been 'liberating', an attempt to free the 'natural' man from the shackles of family and society. This was not disputed by Gide's Catholic critics, but they did deplore it. 'The drama of our civilization,' said Massis, 'is being played out, as in a microcosm, in the person of André Gide who . . . brings into question the human values on which our entire civilization is based.' With some subtlety, Massis went on to explain Gide's influence by 'his extreme impressionability', an 'extraordinary plasticity': 'No one has been more finely attuned to the ideological currents, the moral atmosphere of the period.' Later, Massis compared Gide with Proust, to Gide's detriment. While describing 'the successive circles through which he leads us down to his hell, Proust . . . does not destroy our moral universe. I even believe that you are secretly irritated that Proust accepts the laws of the universe, or rather does not *deny* them.'

'That is precisely what I reproach him with,' Gide snapped back. 'Proust is a master-camouflager.' The neo-Thomist Maritain declared that such Communist ideals as the dignity of labour and the rejection of exploitation of man by man had been borrowed from Christianity, that 'our present civilization is the corpse of medieval Christianity', which represented as ideal a form of society as was likely to be realized here below. The discussion continually returned to the apparent contradiction between Gide the apostle of moral and aesthetic individualism and Gide the fellow-travelling Communist. When one speaker suggested that the value that Gide cherished more than any other was 'the freedom of his person', Gide replied: 'What I cherish more than anything else is my art.' He would like to believe that art and Communist doctrine were not incompatible, but personally, his growing social awareness and political commitment had meant that he had written practically nothing over the past four years. A sacrifice was involved here. The question he asked himself was whether the sacrifice was justified. He had always opposed all orthodoxies and, today, the Marxist orthodoxy was as dangerous as any other, at least as far as the work of art was concerned: 'The work of art cannot obey orders.' He could follow the Party line in political matters, not in artistic ones. It was not that he didn't *want* to write, rather that he *couldn't*. He could not toe the Party line, but did not want to oppose it either. Throughout, Gide had been treated with politeness and respect, even by Massis. In particular, he had been moved by the sympathy and understanding shown him by the other three Catholics. Afterwards, Gabriel Marcel even went up to him and said: 'For ten years, I admit, I was wrong about you.' The proceedings of the conference were published by Gallimard later in the year as *André Gide et notre temps*.

Early in February, Gide set off with Yves Allégret, in Marc's car, for ten days in Belgium (Marc having gone to the Tyrol for winter sports). Gide met up with Jef Last in Antwerp, which, Last had promised him, was like the old pre-Nazi Berlin. Gide also saw a lot of Louis Gérin, the young miner with literary ambitions who had already gone to see him in Paris a few times. Gérin was now doing his military service and, during a twenty-four-hour leave, took Gide and Yves down a mine. 'I couldn't help but admire myself,' Gide wrote to Martin du Gard, 'for being able, at my age, to play the earthworm for three-quarters of an hour on end, along an airless little tunnel 2 feet high, in suffocating coal-dust, at a temperature of close on 35 degrees, at a depth of 17 metres.'[91]

On 19 March, he and Jef Last left Paris for Spain and Morocco; Gide hoped to spend two months away – and work. In Paris, sustained work was impossible and he needed 'somewhere more exalting than rainy, gloomy Normandy',[92] where he had just spent two weeks. 'If I did not constantly remind myself of my age,' Gide wrote on the way from Tangier to Fez, 'I would hardly be aware of it. And even repeating to myself, like a lesson one has trouble learning *by heart*, I am over sixty-five, I find it hard to convince myself.'[93] At Fez, they spent three glorious weeks, installed *à l'arabe*. However, the catarrh that had affected his sinuses for three months turned into earache and, on 18 April, leaving Jef Last in Fez, Gide set off for home. He spent four days at Algeciras, on the Spanish coast, mostly lying in bed, in pain. After his previous experience of earache, which turned out to be a serious abscess, he resisted calling a local doctor. He would wait until he got to Madrid. On the train to the Spanish capital, the abscess burst, fortunately draining out of the ear.

Over the next two weeks, Gide was preoccupied with preparations for the forthcoming International Writers' Conference in Defence of Culture, which was to take place in Paris in June and of which he and Malraux would be honorary joint-chairmen. The initiative for the conference had, of course, come from Moscow. Since the Party line had shifted from a sectarian to a 'broad front' line, there had been many such initiatives. The Party's role in these was to retain control, while appearing to take a back seat. Where the forthcoming conference was concerned, Gide's instinct was not to confine participation to those on the left, however broadly defined, but to take in the full spectrum of French opinion prepared to unite on an anti-fascist stance. He wanted, for example, to invite an agnostic, non-political, but implicitly 'conservative' figure like Valéry and, perhaps, some Catholics. This was seen to go well beyond the parameters laid down by Moscow and Gide's plans had to be subtly deflected. Over dinner, he, the Petite Dame and 'les Groet' discussed the latest developments in the Soviet Union. Bernard and Alix 'talked freely', the Petite Dame notes, of Stalin's rather 'disconcerting' new line. They did not question the 'purity' of Stalin's intentions, or the necessity for a more 'moderate' approach, but feared that the Party line was being watered down to accommodate non-Communist elements. Five days before the Congress, Malraux telephoned to tell Gide that he had just heard from the Soviet embassy that Gorky would not be coming. This was a terrible blow. Malraux and Gide went straight to the Soviet embassy and insisted on Boris Pasternak and Isaac Babel as replacements. The Soviet authorities acquiesced and the two astonished writers were bundled on to Paris-bound planes, unaccompanied, of course, by any members of their families.

'The First International Congress of Writers for the Defence of Culture' began, in sweltering heat, on Friday, 21 June in the Palais de la Mutualité and lasted four days. Some 230 official delegates arrived from thirty-eight countries, sixty-one 'reports' being delivered, usually followed by translation, to audiences of around 2,000, many more listening over loud-speaker systems in adjoining halls and cafés. Gide, as 'honorary chairman', opened proceedings with a short address of welcome, then handed over the actual chairmanship of the meeting into the more capable hands of André Malraux.

Gide was followed by E. M. Forster, leading a British delegation that included Aldous Huxley. Forster's timid, dry, very English, very liberal contribution was given a rather lukewarm reception, and was actually mimicked and ridiculed by some of the younger, more extreme members of the audience. In addition to those already mentioned, the better-known speakers at the Congress included Heinrich Mann, Brecht, Musil, Tristan Tzara, Ehrenburg, Henri Barbusse, Aragon. Malraux, ever the brilliant demagogue and histrionic manipulator, was a great success. But so, too, was Gide, with his major speech on the second day. 'How bashful and yet haughty, how movingly isolated and out of place he appeared among all those glib and violent agents of a powerful party machine!' Klaus Mann wrote some years later. 'The speakers preceding and following him recited their perfunctory variations of current Party-line slogans. He said simple and serious things, in a simple and serious manner . . .'[94] Gide began by noting how nationalists had managed to assimilate internationalism with denigration of one's own country. Yet he himself had always been profoundly internationalist, while remaining profoundly French. He noted how, unlike the Tsarist empire, the USSR was a genuine union, which respected each people's language, customs and culture. (In this, of course, he was deluded. There is more to independence than subsidized folk dancing: behind each 'autonomous republic' there was only one power, that of the same monolithic Party.) It was in a Communist society, achieved by common efforts, that the individualist could best fulfil himself. On the argument being waged in the Soviet Union between proponents of the new orthodoxy of 'socialist realism' and its opponents, he sided with the opposition. It was no use factory workers complaining that writers did not describe *their* lives: literature is more than a mirror, 'it is not content to imitate; it informs; it proposes; it creates'. The true writer will create his own (perhaps future) audience, rather than confirm readers in their present view of the world. At present, 'in the capitalist society in which we are still living', 'literature of value' cannot be other than a 'literature of opposition'. It is not hard to imagine how Gide's contribution must have shone like true metal amidst the surrounding dross. Yet, with greater hindsight than Klaus Mann enjoyed in 1948, a reading of Gide's text today suggests rather how little true Gidean metal is to be found in it and how much naïve, self-deluding, if well-meaning alloy.

The Congress ended by deciding to set up an 'International Association of Writers for the Defence of Culture', with a permanent International Bureau of 112 members, headed by a praesidium of twelve: Henri Barbusse, Romain Rolland, André Gide, Heinrich Mann, Klaus Mann, Maxim Gorky, E. M. Forster, Aldous Huxley, Bernard Shaw, Sinclair Lewis, Selma Lagerlöf and Ramón Valle-Inclán. The Congress had been a huge success. The Party had got what it wanted, or almost. A small group of Trotskyites were determined to raise the question of repression in the Soviet Union and, in particular, the case of Victor Serge, a Belgian writer. Serge had been a fervent Communist and had gone to live in Russia. In 1928, however, increasingly dissatisfied with many aspects of the regime, he asked for a passport to return to France. This immediately aroused suspicion: he was refused work, boycotted by all his fellow-writers and, in 1933, arrested, charged with Trotskyite activities and banished to 'internal exile' at Orenburg, near the Urals. Henry Poulaille and André Breton tried to raise his case at the Congress but, under pressure from Ehrenburg and Aragon, were refused permission to speak. In the afternoon of the last day, however, in a smaller hall, Magdeleine Paz managed to deliver a detailed report on Serge's case. Vaillant-Couturier and Aragon rose to their feet and protested, the Communists in the hall took their cue and shouted her down, but Malraux, who was chairing the meeting, insisted that she be allowed to continue. Malraux's action was all the more laudable in that, personally, he believed that the Trotskyites were expoiting the Serge case in order to sow dissension. Later, when Gide demanded an explanation of Serge's fate, the Soviet case seemed to him to be so feeble that, during a reception at the Soviet embassy, the day after the Congress ended, he tried, in vain, to speak to the ambassador about it. Later, he drafted a letter, which he and Malraux took round to the embassy, insisting that it be sent to the highest authority. The letter is couched in the most fulsome, uncritical terms: the USSR is, for many of us, 'an ideal fatherland; *we are part of it* and would be ready to fight for it, were it physically attacked'. *In its own interests*, the Soviet Union should release Serge, thus setting an example of magnanimity to less happy lands.[95] Martin du Gard was scandalized by

Gide's *tone*, 'the ever so humbly respectful form of this timid approach. One wrote thus to the Grand Roy at the time of the Monarchy by Divine Right . . . Your tone is that of a neophyte, the tone of a man who has "submitted". I find it irritating when that man is André Gide.'[96] Gide, pliant as ever, accepted the criticism, claiming that it was necessary if any result were to be obtained, thus implicitly admitting the similarity between absolute monarchy and Stalin's régime. 'Les Groet' did their best to persuade Gide to drop the matter. 'Alix is in quite a state about it,' writes the Petite Dame. 'She says she knows that gang of so-called seekers after justice' – they are simply using the affair to damage the Soviet Union.[97] While conceding that this might be so, Gide distinguished between what looked like injustice and the use that might be made of a protest against it – and went on doggedly. His persistence (and perhaps diplomacy) were rewarded: later that year, Serge was released and allowed to leave the country by a government that realized that it now had less to lose by doing so than by holding on to him.

On 30 June Gide had to preside over the renaming of a street in the Communist-controlled Parisian suburb of Villejuif, to be known hereafter as the 'boulevard Maxime-Gorki'. Gide got back to the Vaneau feeling 'rather disgusted' with the proceedings. The Communists there had treated him with embarrassing adulation and Aragon had made a speech praising him in exaggeratedly fulsome terms. He *knew* that Aragon was not so kindly disposed towards him: he was merely obeying orders. Next day, Gide had to see the Soviet ambassador in the morning (to hand him the letter concerning Serge); he lunched with Pasternak and Ehrenburg (Pasternak had no need of a translator, so we may assume that Ehrenburg was there to keep an eye and ear on the poet–linguist). The following day, Gide escaped to Cuverville for a few days.

Gide joined the Petite Dame at Bex to attend the annual open day of Catherine's school. He arrived at about four in the afternoon, in the middle of a performance of *Robin Hood*, in English, slipping in unobtrusively among the audience. Afterwards, with Catherine, they all went to Montreux, where they stayed for five days. 'Gide is a born educator,' the Petite Dame notes. 'He is careful not to influence the child in any one direction. He lets her approach him, he's very indulgent, observing everything, correcting without seeming to, leaving her the maximum of responsibility.' She and Gide, she adds, acted very like grandparents! Again the Petite Dame notes the very special affection between Catherine and her father. On their last day at Montreux, Gide asked the Petite Dame: 'What effect do you think it would have on her if she learnt the truth? Do you think it would come as a terrible shock?' She replied that she thought Catherine would be very touched. 'I think so, too,' said Gide. 'Perhaps we shouldn't delay for too long telling her. I think she'll be able to keep it a secret . . . and understand.'[98]

On his way back to Paris, Gide spent a few days with Robert Levesque and his brothers, Michel and Jacques, at a farmhouse outside Lyon. (Michel was now working in a factory near the city.) Robert, he learnt, had decided not to go back to Rome, but to study philosophy for a year at Lyon University, where a friend of Gide's, Jean Wahl, had taken up a post teaching philosophy. Gide spoke of his forthcoming visit to the Soviet Union. He had just received a letter from Ehrenburg, saying that he had learnt of Gide's plans and, as it happened, he too would be going back to the Soviet Union in September and could act as a guide, etc. Gide was clearly irritated by Ehrenburg's attentions. He was still working on *Les Nouvelles Nourritures* and wanted to finish it before going to Russia. That would be October at the earliest.

Gide was back in Paris on 15 August, staying only two days at the Vaneau before going on to Cuverville, where he found almost the entire family – with fourteen round the table at mealtimes. 'Perfect harmony, providing one does not talk about religion, politics, tastes, colours, or recipes. I'm spending almost all my time, between meals, shut up in the big room over the kitchen.'[99] A long letter arrived from Martin du Gard, who had been seeing a lot of Catherine at Nice – and getting on very well with her. He was, however, concerned about how the girl was being brought up by her mother and, more particularly, by Pierre Herbart.

This child is being reared in the strait and narrow path of the communist *faith*. And, for me, this is a form of education *quite* as prejudicial for the development of judgement as if she were being brought up by some bigoted, churchy old spinster . . . *Thought only begins with doubt.* Any upbringing that systematically sets doubt aside – and which encourages in a child . . . that blind, contemptuous confidence, whatever that faith might be – not only deprives the intelligence of healthy nourishment, but distorts it from the outset . . . Catherine is being reared in an atmosphere of sectarian fanaticism.[100]

Gide replied that he fully agreed with his friend's 'wise' remarks. That was why he intended taking Pierre Herbart with him to Russia – in the hope that he might stay there. Apparently, he had been offered a job as editor of the French edition of the *International Review*, a Comintern organ published in Moscow in many languages. Jef Last would be going with him too. 'He knows Russian and Moscow well enough to be passed off as our interpreter-guide. He has promised to show me a lot of things that one is not usually allowed to see.'[101]

The day before, Gide had written to Jean Schlumberger confessing that 'this trip, for a number of reasons, terrifies me'. A week later, Schlum wrote back, expressing his own fears about it. He had attended only the last day of the Congress, but had read Gide's speech in the newspaper. In it, says Schlumberger, Gide had carefully marked out the 'very personal role' that he wanted to play, 'while accepting the Communist framework'. If he went to Russia, however, 'all the distinctions that you have so far taken great care to maintain' would be blurred. 'You will no longer be in charge of your own strategy. You will resist on one point, only to have to give in on others . . . The Propaganda Ministry will lead operations . . . What you say will be translated tendentiously. You will not be able to make corrections and what will go out will not be your carefully phrased words, but terrible approximations . . .'[102] Gide wrote back to say that he agreed with every word that his friend had written: he would grab at the slightest indisposition not to go. Schlum's letter was probably the last straw as far as Gide's doubts were concerned. No, he would not go. He wrote to Jef Last to tell him so. The letter is lost, but we have Last's astonishing reply, dated 25 September: 'If you go to the USSR on an official visit, as a famous man, you will be used in the most stupid way . . . You will never see the USSR as it really is . . . It will be nothing but a series of receptions, speeches, car drives, surrounded by the authorities, interviews in which you will be compromised and praise that will be extracted from you in one way or another for the glory of the regime.'[103] Strange words from a committed Communist and friend of the Soviet Union to a fervent fellow-traveller! On 2 October, the Petite Dame, who had just arrived back from Brussels, learnt for the first time that Gide had abandoned his plans to go to the USSR. His criticism of the Soviet Union seems, for the time being, to come from a 'leftist' ('Trotskyite') position rather than from a 'rightist' ('social democratic') one. What concerns him most about new developments in the USSR is not Stalin's personal dictatorship, the activities of the secret police, the concentration camps, the stifling of all opposition, or the complete loss of civil liberties, but the growing '*embourgeoisement*' of the country, a process that, presumably, narrowed the differences between the Soviet Union and the capitalist West.

On 14 October, Gide arrived back from Cuverville. In the afternoon, he went to the *NRF* offices, where he met Malraux, who told him of Ehrenburg's fury at his decision not to go to the Soviet Union. Poor health, he had said, should not be allowed to damage the interests of the Party, the general political situation, the consolidation of the Franco-Soviet alliance, etc., etc. It was clear that Ehrenburg's anger had more to do with self-interest: accompanying the greatest fellow-travelling figure to the socialist fatherland would no doubt have raised his own status in the eyes of the Party authorities at home. When Ehrenburg finally realized that his persuasions had failed, he got Gide to write 'a sort of address to Russian youth', which he would translate and take back with him.

Pierre Herbart arrived in Paris to sign copies of his novel, *Contre-Ordre*, which was about to be published. He was, of course, very disappointed by Gide's decision about the Soviet visit. Jef Last, escaping 'the Amsterdam hell' of his marriage, turned up. There was much talk of the new Soviet legislation against homosexuality. Suspects were being sent off to a particular town, where they would be free to practise their vice and where, since there were no women, they could not perpetuate their own kind!

On 5 November, Gide had lunch alone with Marc, who was in excellent spirits, happy at last that he could make the films he wanted in the way that he wanted to make them. There was a possibility that he might move out of the Vaneau; he needed a larger place to accommodate the accumulating mass of film equipment, documentation, etc.; he also felt that he could no longer subject his friends to the constant comings and goings of visitors. That evening, Gide and Jef Last left for Roquebrune, where over the next month, they worked on a French translation that had been made of Last's novel *Zuyderzee*. (It was published by Gallimard, with a preface by Gide, in April 1938.)

Les Nouvelles Nourritures was published while Gide was at Roquebrune. The title is first mentioned in a journal entry for 1 February 1916, in which Gide speaks of a 'book of meditations that would serve as a pendant to *Les Nourritures*'.[104] Most would agree that it is not a fit pendant to that work of 1897, so much of its time and yet so far in advance of it, a major work that had had an incalculable influence on succeeding younger generations. By comparison, *Les Nouvelles Nourritures* is a slight, very hybrid work. Gide was taking some risk in evoking comparison: the new work's relative feebleness is indicative of a decline, not only from the youthful figure of 1897, but, by implication, from the heights of *Les Faux-Monnayeurs* of 1925. Many of Gide's works were written over a long period of time, but they do not usually reveal their long gestation in internal heterogeneity. If any unity at all is to be ascribed to *Les Nouvelles Nourritures* it is that of autobiography: in its lyrical, allusive way, it follows Gide's intellectual progress from early, late-

Romantic verses written in the first decade of the century; to passages contemporary with *Numquid et tu* and his 'dark night of the soul' in 1916; to fragments written in 1917–18, at the beginning of the relationship with Marc, and published in the *Morceaux choisis* of 1921; to three sections called *Rencontres* (Encounters), dating from 1922–3, and another *Rencontre*, describing Gide's visit to the dying Jean-Paul Allégret in 1930; to, lastly, the very different passages written during Gide's Communist phase between 1931 and 1935. The work opens very much in the style of the earlier *Nourritures*: 'You who will come when I shall no longer hear the sounds of the earth, when my lips will no longer drink its dew – you, who may read me one day – it is for you that I write these pages.'[105] It ends: 'I have lived; now it is your turn. It is in you that my youth will live on . . . Find happiness in increasing others' happiness . . . Accept no evil that can be changed . . . Comrade, do not accept the life that is offered you by men. Always tell yourself that life might be better – your own and others'; not a future life that might console us for this one and help us accept its wretchedness, but this one of ours.'[106]

Gide's friends were as kind as they could be. Jean Schlumberger compared the sudden shifts to a lift stopping unexpectedly at a floor other than one's own, but found that the work had unity all the same.[107] Martin du Gard, as one might expect, was less reverent. He admired 'unreservedly' the less 'poetic' passages – the philosophical argument and the 'Rencontres' – but admitted his dislike of 'exclamation marks and the vocative case'. He also noticed the reference to '"Marc" on page 28': 'It would have been so easy to call him Daphnis or Valentin! . . . This really is a prime example of *useless indiscretion*. But, wretch that you are, you have become so accustomed to leading your private life on the public stage, that such nuances escape you . . .'[108] Gide's own view of the book came to be quite harsh. In Tunis, in 1943, he re-read it in Gallimard's new, combined edition of the two *Nourritures* and admitted that he could hardly recognize himself in it. 'Of all my books, it is the most uneven, the least good.'[109]

Gide arrived back at the Vaneau on 6 December with Beth, who had managed to let the house at Cabris to English acquaintances. She would later be joining her husband in Moscow. On 21 December, Catherine arrived for Christmas. On 23 December, Gide spoke at a huge meeting at the Salle Wagram organized to celebrate the release of Dimitrov and to demonstrate against the continued imprisonment of Thaelmann, the German Communist leader. Catherine, now twelve, went along with her mother and grandmother. She could hardly fail to be impressed. She had never seen so many people (4,000) in one place, such a noisy, excited, enthusiastic crowd.[110]

In the first week of 1936, Gide was visited by two delegates from the local branch of the Young Communist League asking for his support (moral and financial) in starting a Youth Club for the 7th arrondissement. (They were not, presumably, working-class youths, genuine proletarians being thin on the ground in the Faubourg Saint-Germain, that most aristocratic of Paris districts.) He agreed to be its honorary president. They also asked him for a signed photograph and a brief message for inclusion in their next magazine. The photograph was inscribed: 'To the young people of the 7th, their comrade-friend, André Gide.'

'To escape! To inhabit for a time some abstract, hollow, unfurnished region or other, where I can abstain from living and judging, yet without betraying or deserting any cause,'[111] Gide wrote 'at sea', on 12 February. The day before he had left Marseille with Marcel de Coppet, by then Governor-General of French West Africa, and his wife Christiane, Roger Martin du Gard's daughter. They arrived at Dakar on 19 February. From there, Gide and the Governor-General's party travelled by train to Saint-Louis, a seven-and-a-half-hour journey in appalling heat, only made bearable by the luxury of the official carriage. The *Journal* says little of what Gide did or saw during his seven or so weeks in Senegal. He worked on *Geneviève* (again and, this time, or so he thought, finished it). He read the whole of Shakespeare's historical cycle from *Richard II* to *Henry VIII*, 'in all, nine plays', interrupted only by Mark Rutherford's *Catherine Furze*, which Christiane de Coppet was thinking of translating.

On 14 April, the Petite Dame and Catherine (it was her Easter holidays) arrived at Nice, where Martin du Gard had booked them rooms at the 'Petit Palais', close to his own apartments. Gide would join them three days later, from Marseille. The mere mention of Gide's imminent arrival was enough to bring on in Hélène what, in RMG's journal, reads like a minor nervous breakdown. The Petite Dame and Catherine were invited to tea and, 'as always', Hélène adopted an unnatural, *mondaine* attitude, with 'that false, smiling amiability that makes the atmosphere quite unbreathable for everyone'. Next day, she handed her husband a sealed envelope, containing changes to her will. She had taken it into her head that Roger was showing an unhealthy interest in Catherine, who responded by calling him 'Uncle Martin'. Hélène had no intention of allowing any of her personal effects to pass on to Catherine after her death. She then launched into a whole series of accusations, all false. She was clearly ill. 'That very honest, very frank woman,' RMG writes, 'incapable of lying, is fabricating, unconsciously, at a distance, in the past, fictitious episodes that are pure invention, but which she certainly sees as true, incontrovertible, self-evident.' For her, Gide was 'Satan, the Evil Genius, who creates disorder and disunion everywhere, etc.'

Gide arrived on 17 April. The following day was Catherine's birthday. Gide and the Petite Dame had a serious discussion about her future. Gide thought it might be better if she went to a *lycée* in Paris. In this way, he hoped to counteract Herbart's too exclusively political influence. In any case, none of them knew how long Pierre would remain in Moscow. Beth, it seems, wanted Catherine to join them there as soon as possible. Gide, who had now decided to go to the Soviet Union at the end of June, did not want Catherine to go before he did: he would be jealous if she saw 'so many extraordinary things, without his being there to share them with her'. Two days later, on a wet afternoon, Gide read the revised second part and the new last part of *Geneviève* to the Petite Dame and RMG. They both found the second part 'delicately moving', but 'straight away, from the beginning of the third part, we were ill at ease; it's clumsy, quite uninteresting . . . Her first sexual experience, which should have been very important, is completely evaded in a short, boring passage . . . It soon becomes terribly . . . mediocre. He senses this and reads badly, hesitantly.' Half-way through, Gide stopped reading. What was the point of going on? Yet again, *Geneviève* had ended in an impasse.

Ironically, the upheaval in Martin du Gard's conjugal life coincided with a moment of great happiness in his life as a writer. He had finished the last of three books that were to conclude the Thibault cycle. For several days, he went over to his friends' rooms and read extracts from it, to their great satisfaction. Clearly, given her attitude to Gide and the Petite Dame, there could be no question of inviting Hélène to the reading, but not inviting her would merely inflame her animosity. When Gide suggested that she might be asked to join them over tea after the reading, RMG explained that this would be taken amiss: she would see it as a slight, a demotion. For all this, Martin du Gard's account of Gide's visit has its lighter moments: 'He walks around Nice in a cream tweed suit, with scarlet socks and a light felt hat . . . I feel some embarrassment at being seen with him in the town I *live* in and try to pass unnoticed. I'm the one who looks like a "comrade", he like a nabob of the grand hotels! His presence causes me innumerable little expenses that will exhaust my month's pocket money in five days. But the incomprehension of the rich for those who are not is unfathomable and incorrigible.'[112]

Gide took Catherine to Monaco to see the aquarium. Later, in their rooms in Nice, Gide and Catherine were alone, drinking tea, and Gide decided to broach the 'big question'. He asked her if she ever wondered what her father was like? 'No,' she replied. Had she believed it when told that her father was dead? 'No.' 'Well, weren't you curious about him?' 'I didn't want to ask questions.' Gide went on to to say that she was a big girl now and ought to know the truth. Would she be surprised, he asked, if she were told that he was her father? By now, there were tears in the girl's eyes. She suddenly put her arms around him and kissed him. Gide related the incident to the Petite Dame next morning. 'We went on talking for some time,' he continued. 'I explained to her that it was because I was married that she didn't bear my name. For the same reason, it must be kept a secret, though all our close friends know the truth . . .' The Petite Dame wondered if it might have been a little premature, but, on balance, approved. Later, she took Catherine to one side, told her how pleased she was that Bypeed had been able to tell her at last and that if there was anything she wanted to talk about she had only to ask. The response was a broad smile 'that seemed to be beyond that of a thirteen-year-old child'.[113]

On 24 April, Catherine's last night with them, Gide took her, the Petite Dame and the Martin du Gards to see Chaplin's latest film, *Modern Times*. The following morning, Catherine caught the train to Bex and school. During his last evening in Nice, Gide discussed with RMG his plans to include Catherine in his will, without hurting Madeleine – on the assumption that Madeleine would outlive him. Next morning, 1 May, Gide took the train to Marseille, where he called on his old friend Auguste Bréal. The following day, he was joined by the Petite Dame and the two travelled together to Paris.

They arrived at the Vaneau to find that the decorators had several days' work before them – in the end, they were still there three weeks later. Over the next few days, Gide was still trying to make the final arrangements for his visit to the Soviet Union. He told a half-astounded, half-amused Ehrenburg that he intended speaking to Stalin about the legal position of homosexuals in the Soviet Union. 'I tried politely to dissuade him, but he was adamant,' Ehrenburg writes. 'He was a Protestant, even a Puritan – not only by upbringing, but by nature – and yet he had become a fanatical moralist of immorality.'[114] Paul Claudel could hardly have put it better: Ehrenburg chose not to see the difference between a concern to remove an unjust, discriminatory law and being a fanatic. Gide had won one concession from the Soviet authorities: he could now take whomever he liked. Jacques Schiffrin, the founder and editor of the Editions de la Pléiade, now published under the Gallimard imprint, had asked to go with him. He was Russian by birth, but had not been back to Russia since before the war. Though not a Communist, he was sympathetic to the new régime. Gide would probably also take two friends, both left-wing novelists of working-class origin, Eugène Dabit and Louis Guilloux, and, of course, Jef Last – providing he recovered from illness in time. Relations between Last and his wife had reached a deeper crisis than usual: in fact, he was now living, not in Amsterdam with his family, but in Antwerp, with Gide's young Belgian friend and literary miner Louis Gérin and *his* family. While in Nice, Gide had received a desperate letter from Last asking for 'a few hundred francs' to pay for medical treatment recommended by a doctor. Gide had told him to ask if he ever wanted help; he had never done so until now, but his 'last resources' were almost exhausted. Gide rushed to the post office with a cheque.

On 12 May, Gide escaped the decorators' reign of terror at the Vaneau for two weeks at Cuverville. After a few days, he reported in the *Journal* that he had torn up all the work done in the Senegal on *Geneviève*, just as he had previously done with what he had written of it at Syracuse. That last chapter was worthless; it would be quite pointless to spend more time on it. Gide decided to end the *récit* with the end of the second part, cutting out the wretched third chapter altogether. He now set about trying to finish his play, *Robert ou l'Intérêt général.* 'If, according to Marx,' Gide wrote, 'the labour expended on a work is the measure of its value, this play would certainly be my masterpiece.'[115]

Gide was back in Paris on 29 May. The plans for the Russian trip were getting complicated. A second 'International Congress of Writers for the Defence of Culture' was to take place in London in June and Gide had been asked to act as honorary chairman, but the organizers kept changing the dates proposed. Beth wanted to come back to France for Catherine's summer holidays, but did not want to leave Russia before seeing more of it. However, she did not think that she could stay there until Gide arrived. It seemed impossible to reconcile every part of the jigsaw and settle on a date for the visit. On 30 May, a telegram arrived from Herbart announcing his arrival that evening. Gide, intrigued and a little anxious, decided to meet him at Le Bourget: Marc offered to drive him there. Apparently, he had come back to sort out certain 'difficulties' regarding Gide's trip and wanted, in any case, to talk to Gide before he left for Russia. It seemed that the authorities were objecting to Schiffrin's presence in the party. As a Russian émigré, he was suspect, however left-wing his sympathies might be. Apparently, Aragon had not helped by referring to Schiffrin as Gide's interpreter – that task would have to be carried out by a trusted Soviet official. Herbart had tried to smooth matters over by explaining that Schiffrin would not be Gide's interpreter, that he was going solely as a friend and would not be at Gide's side throughout. In any case, he would be arriving a week after Gide. It was now up to Aragon to sort things out with the authorities.

The Petite Dame was getting more and more intrigued by her son-in-law's incommunicability about his experiences in the Soviet Union. When questioned, he was evasive. Gide got no more out of him. Then, one day, provoked perhaps by the presence of Alix Guillain, with her uncompromisingly pro-Soviet views, he began to criticize the lack of competent, properly trained staff in every area of Soviet life. On his own review, for example, there was an official censor, who was quite out of his depth and who, terrified of making a mistake, which would cost him dear, stupidly censored the most inoffensive things. In order to reverse the decision, Herbart had to go to higher authority, create a scandal and threaten to leave – something no Russian could do. Herbart's friends were left with a strong impression that he would not want to stay in the Soviet Union for much longer. Herbart also revealed, in passing, that the Soviet government had had printed 300,000 postcards bearing Gide's portrait to be released on his arrival. 'But everyone will recognize me!' said a horrified Gide. Later, the conversation turned to a very moving 'Letter to André Gide' by Victor Serge, published in *Esprit*. Pierre admitted that everything Serge had said about the Soviet Union was true. Gide was more than ever determined to see Stalin and confront him with a whole lot of his regime's shortcomings! Pierre said that the Left should regard the Soviet Union as an experiment, not as an example. We should learn its lessons now and not make the same mistakes: later, it will be too late. The situation of artists in the USSR had become 'intolerable, subject to all manner of petty controls'. Left-wing artists in the West should take up a clearly critical position on the matter of artistic freedom.[116] By way of distraction from those distracted times, they all went off one afternoon to see the Marx Brothers' *A Night at the Opera*: 'We laughed like kids.'[117]

On 6 June, the inaugural session in the Chambre des Députés of Léon Blum's new government took place. The previous month's elections had resulted in a substantial shift to the left, giving the new 'Popular Front' a majority of forty-three seats in the Chamber. Blum, as the leader of the Socialists, the middle party in the coalition, formed a new government, though the Communists, while giving it their support in carrying out its new 'social policies', the forty-hour week, holidays with pay, etc., preferred not to take up ministerial posts. A few days later, Gide, the Petite Dame and Alix Guillain were strolling down the Champs-Elysées after seeing an American film. It was a beautiful evening. Though many of the cafés were shut – the waiters were on strike – there was a sense of excitement in the air. Groups formed spontaneously around speakers, 'holding forth on the situation, expounding theories, sometimes very intelligently'. They did not feel like going home at once: 'Life was in the street.' They sat down in a café at the Rond-Point (apparently quite happy to patronize non-striking establishments) for a snack. 'It seemed,' wrote the Petite Dame, 'that we were living through historic days without being quite able to see what was happening.'[118]

At last, on 16 June, after several changes of plan and date, Gide left Paris for Russia. At one o'clock, two cars drew up outside 1 bis rue du Vaneau: Marc's convertible and Yvonne de Lestrange's. During the drive to Le Bourget, Gide seemed depressed. He took the Petite Dame's hand and said: 'We get on well together the two of us.' A German plane would take Gide and Pierre to Berlin, where they would change on to another plane for Moscow. (Schiffrin, Dabit, Guilloux and Last would be going via London, leaving on a Leningrad-bound Soviet ship on 20 June.) At Le Bourget, thanks to Yvonne de Lestrange's cousin, the aviator and writer Saint-Exupéry, Gide's party were given special treatment. The Petite Dame went into the plane to look around: it was the first time she had been near one. Marc and Yves took photogaphs of Gide standing in front of the plane, taking care not to include a large swastika in the shots. 'At last the pilot arrived, a handsome giant of the North,' wrote the Petite Dame. 'We kissed each other goodbye. The noise of the engine drowned our final words. We waved to one another and the machine took off, gleaming in the sunlight. I suddenly felt a pain deep down inside. They'll be in Moscow tomorrow.'[119]

Retreat from Moscow, a Sense of Ending: Retour de l'U.R.S.S. *and* Geneviève

(JUNE 1936 – SEPTEMBER 1939)

Gide's plane landed in Moscow at six o'clock on the evening of 17 June. A triumphal welcome awaited him. He was carried shoulder-high by airport employees to the official reception committee led by Mikhail Koltzov. Koltzov was a a senior editor of *Pravda*, the official Party newspaper, and, when he cared to be, its correspondent in Paris (he was arrested in 1942 and executed). Aragon and his Russian-born wife Elsa Triolet, Gide and Herbart were driven to the Metropol Hotel, where Gide, an official guest of the Soviet Writers' Union, moved into a six-room suite. That evening, he saw Pasternak, whom he had met and liked during the Writers' Congress in Paris the year before. Next morning, he was informed by Koltzov that Maxim Gorky had died: it was in order to see the dying writer that Gide had decided not to go to the London conference, but to fly straight to Moscow. He tried to go to Gorky's villa, but his car was stopped at the gates and he was refused entrance. That evening, he and Herbart attended a performance of Gorky's *Mother*. In the middle of the play, the writer's death was announced. The audience stood in silence as an invisible orchestra played funeral music, after which the play continued.

Opinion is divided as to whether Gorky died of natural causes. He was sixty-eight and had a record of tuberculosis. On the other hand, political history may have made him more vulnerable than did his medical history. The year before, he had been expected as the guest of honour of the Writers' Congress in Paris and, at short notice, had been declared unfit to travel. Rumour had it that he had fallen out of favour with Stalin. He had been an early supporter of the Bolsheviks and, during the 1905 uprising, their chief source of income. In 1906, he went to live on Capri, returning to Russia only in 1914. During that period he had been involved in anti-Leninist activity within the Bolshevik group. He opposed the Bolshevik seizure of power in 1917 and, in 1922, took up residence in Italy once more.

In 1928, he made his peace with Stalin and returned to the USSR. In 1932, he became head of the new monolithic Soviet Writers' Union and presided over the doctrine of 'socialist realism'. It is quite likely that this blunt-spoken 'man of the people', with his foreign experience and a sense of his own impregnability, was becoming too critical of the régime: certainly Gorky, a beloved 'proletarian writer', would be more useful dead than alive. The causes of Gorky's death were left uncommented on. People could presume natural causes until such time as it suited Stalin's purposes to blame someone else. This duly arrived. During the 'show trials' of 1938, Gorky's death was blamed, preposterously, on 'the bloc of Rightists and Trotskyites'.

On 19 June, Gide went to see the body of Gorky lying in state in the Hall of Columns of the House of Unions and, for a time, joined the guard of honour, as thousands of Muscovites filed past. Afterwards, in a smaller room, Gide met a number of the senior Soviet figures, including Dimitrov, for whose release he had campaigned. Gide's impression of the man was one of insincerity, 'like all politicians' (manuscript of *Retouches*, not in published version). With him was Bukharin, who, as soon as Dimitrov's back was turned, took Gide's arm and said: 'Can I see you at the Metropol in an hour's time? I want to talk to you.' Koltzov, who had noticed Bukharin speaking to Gide, came up, then took Bukharin to one side and said something to him. Pierre Herbart, who had better reason than most to know what was happening behind the scenes, said to Gide: 'I bet he won't come.' He did not, and Gide did not see Bukharin again.[1] Called by Lenin 'the darling of the Party' and quite the most attractive of the Communist leaders, Bukharin was, nevertheless, a Bolshevik and therefore a supporter of most of what his Party had done to Russia since the Revolution. A close friend of Stalin, he was still, to all appearances, a considerable figure in the Soviet hierarchy. In fact, his slow decline had already begun. In 1938, Bukharin was to be the central figure of the 'show trials', in which he and twenty other leading Communists were accused of collaborating with foreign powers to dismember the USSR, overthrow socialism and restore capitalism. They all made abject confessions, obviously after torture and threats to their families, and were executed.

On 20 June, Gide was on the podium overlooking Red Square, flanked by Stalin, Molotov, Bulganin, Mikoyan, Zhdanov (the dreaded and obtuse 'cultural commissar') – and Dimitrov. A funeral oration, three days after his arrival, with Stalin at his side and a potential audience of millions, was not perhaps an occasion to express doubts about the latest developments in the Socialist Fatherland. But Gide may certainly be criticized for trying to win the approval of his hosts. He even managed to slip in the obligatory quotation from Stalin – the meaningless tag about the future literature of the world being 'national in form, socialist in content'. Hitherto, says Gide, writers 'of value' have always been 'revolutionary', combatants against 'something'. They brought into people's hearts and minds 'a ferment of insubordination, of revolt'. This, from so informed a twentieth-century writer, is preposterous. In fact, it is arguable that a sizeable majority of the great writers of our time have been politically conservative, if not extreme right-wing – one thinks of Valéry, Proust (even, at an earlier stage, Gide himself); Joyce and Faulkner; Eliot and Pound; Rilke and, before real politics caught up with him, Thomas Mann (his less talented brother Heinrich was the left-wing one). Moreover, in the USSR, thanks to the Revolution, says Gide, reaching new depths of wilful naïvety, 'for the first time . . . the writer, by virtue of being a revolutionary, is no longer in opposition'. Here Gide adds a footnote to the later published version: 'Here I was wide of the mark, as, alas!, I was soon to realize.'

That evening, Gide dined with Babel in his dacha outside Moscow; afterwards the two men called on Pasternak and Pilnyak. All three had ceased having their work published. Babel, a protégé of Gorky's, was arrested months later and died in a concentration camp in 1940 or 1941; Boris Pilnyak was arrested in 1938 and is thought to have died shortly afterwards. Only Boris Pasternak survived, saved perhaps by his self-protective servility towards Stalin, who clearly enjoyed tormenting him, and his role as Shakespeare's Russian translator. (His *Zhivago* was banned in the Soviet Union, even under the relatively 'liberal' Khrushchev; after its publication in the West, he was expelled from the Writers' Union and forced to refuse the 1958 Nobel Prize for Literature.) At Babel's dacha, Gide also met Eisenstein, who was making a film about a boy who denounces his own parents: it was easier for a film director to toe the line than for a writer. But the great Eisenstein seemed incapable of repressing his 'formalist' tendencies: later, he had to give up the film, on which he had spent two years and two million roubles, and acknowledge his 'errors'.

Like all important visitors, Gide was taken to Bolshevo, a model prison colony, now a sizeable town, with its own factories. There the prisoners worked while undergoing a thorough education in good Soviet behaviour. Gide was duly 'reassured' and 'encouraged' by the visit, though his suspicions were aroused by the fluency with which the prisoners would recite their former crimes on demand. He later learnt that only criminals who had denounced others were admitted to this 'show' prison colony.

On 27 June, Gide addressed the students of the Bubnov Institute of Education (not the Chemistry Faculty, as *Littérature engagée* has it – I am indebted to Rudolf Maurer's *André Gide et l'U.R.S.S.* for this correction and for other details concerning Gide's visit). The text of the speech shows that, in spite of his growing fears and reservations, shared and encouraged by Pierre Herbart, Gide was still, in terms of his public statements, an ardent fellow-traveller: he still wanted to believe that mankind's future lay with Communism in general and Soviet youth in particular. He told the students how he had always written for a future, not a present public. His *Nourritures terrestres* sold 500 copies during the first twenty years of its life. It had, he told them, been written for them: 'For you carry the future within you. The future will not come from anywhere else . . . And not only the future of the USSR, for on the future of the USSR will depend the destiny of the rest of the world. You will make the future.'[2]

A stone's throw away from the luxury of the Metropol Hotel was the Lubyanka, the secret police headquarters, with its miles of personal files, its interrogation rooms and torture chambers. Gide knew nothing of this, of course. But his forays into the street, unattended by officials, did help to sow his doubts. He notes the 'extraordinary uniformity in people's dress'. No doubt, he adds, 'it would be equally apparent in their minds, if one could see them'.[3] Near the Metropol he sees a queue of people outside a state store; the queue reaches into the next street. Three-quarters of an hour later, the queue is still there and the store has not opened yet. It seems that a newspaper has announced the arrival of a consignment of cushions. Towards the end of their two weeks in Moscow, Gide and Herbart were joined by Beth, who had been visiting the southern republics of the Soviet Union. On 1 July, the three travelled by train, in a special, luxurious carriage, which effectively isolated them from other passengers, to Leningrad. There they met the other three members of Gide's party off their ship.

On his first day in Leningrad, Gide was to have addressed a meeting of writers and students. In Moscow he had shown the three-page text of his proposed address to a couple of Party acquaintances (Koltzov, Aragon?). He was told at once that the text did not follow the Party line and would be 'most unsuitable'. He did not therefore deliver the address, but included it instead in his *Retour de l'URSS*. 'The majority,' he writes, 'never applauds what is new, virtual, unconcerted and disconcerting in a work, but only what it can *recognize* in it, that is to say, the commonplace. Just as there were

bourgeois commonplaces, there are now revolutionary commonplaces . . .'
The enduring value of a work of art is to be assessed 'not by the degree to
which it conforms to a doctrine, but the extent to which it proffers new
questions, questions that anticipate those of the future'. A successful revolution runs the danger, 'almost as great as under the worst fascist oppression',
of establishing an artistic orthodoxy. What the artist requires from a revolution is 'above all, freedom. Without it, art loses significance and value.'[4]
Gide was still innocent enough of Soviet ways to believe that the creatures
of Stalin and Zhdanov would tolerate such 'friendly criticism'.

Two days later, Gide addressed the Leningrad section of the Writers'
Union. This time, the text met with the approval of the cultural police,
though it was pointed out to Gide that the words 'future of the USSR'
should be preceded by 'glorious' and that, in an allusion to the 'great
Monarch' (Peter the Great), the adjective 'Great' should be omitted as
inappropriate to a monarch. Gide avoided the contentious matter of literary
theory and spoke instead of 'the charm, the beauty, the historical eloquence
of Leningrad', of how redolent the city was of 'the most cordial and fruitful
intellectual relations between Russia and France'. But, whereas in the
past, their relations were conducted between 'monarchs', they could now
embrace the entire people in each country. Indeed he was expressing not
only his own feelings, but those of 'the immense French working masses'.[5]

During their four days in Leningrad, Gide and his friends were accommodated in the luxury of the Astoria Hotel. After one lunch, Gide congratulated
their hosts on the excellence of the food. 'The remarkable thing, Comrade
Gide,' said one of the Russians with them, 'is that all our people eat like
this nowadays.' Afterwards Herbart made a rapid calculation, menu in
hand, of the price of such a meal for one and concluded that it would be
equivalent to what an average worker would earn in a month. Gide and
his friends went to the theatre (a play by Bulgakov, Stanislavsky's assistant
at the Moscow Arts Theatre) and the opera. They spent several hours in
the Hermitage museum. They visited St Isaac's Cathedral, now an anti-
religious museum. They went out to Detskoye Zelo, where 2,500 Pioneers
organized a parade, waved flowers and shouted 'Vive André Gide!' Gide,
who did not respond to humanity (even male youth) organized en masse,
was not impressed.

Herbart had an 'adventure' with a charming, fair-haired, blue-eyed boy
called 'Vova' (short for Volodin), who waited for him every day outside the
Astoria Hotel, offering his services as a guide, but asking for nothing in
exchange. He was very badly dressed and there were holes in his trousers.

The boy, it seems, was as much enamoured of Herbart's French clothes as of the handsome Frenchman himself. One day, Herbart asked him to take him to a public baths. On the way, Vova took to talking at great length of Herbart's clothes, detailing every item. The cloth of his suit struck the boy with 'amazement and admiration'. He lovingly stroked a sleeve; he kissed the hem of the jacket; kneeling down, he stroked the leather of Herbart's shoes and then laid his cheek against them. His face betrayed no sense of envy, just sheer joy at the beauty of the thing before him. He was *drunk* with enthusiasm. Vova then stood up and looked down disdainfully at his own poor shoes. 'Now that I have seen yours!' he exclaimed dramatically and flung his own into the river. One morning, Vova was not at his post: later Herbart learnt from Guilloux that 'a very badly dressed, barefoot boy had been brutally chased away' by the splendidly attired hotel porter.[6] But the friends did meet up again. Before leaving Leningrad, Herbart took Vova to a big store to buy him some new shoes. Blushing with pleasure, the boy tried on the shoes, putting a piece of paper into them so that they would not be soiled by his bare feet. The best available cost 60 roubles (Vova had already told Herbart that his mother, who worked in the post office, earned only 200 roubles a month), but they were of very poor quality.[7] What, one cannot help wondering, happened to Vova? Did he die, as thousands did, during the terrible siege of 1941–43? Did he become a soldier and get killed towards the end of the war? Is he alive today, in his seventies, unaware that he had once been the friend of a friend of André Gide's?

In the special carriage, Gide and his friends returned by train to Moscow. 'Coming back from Leningrad, Moscow strikes one as being all the more ill-favoured,' Gide wrote. 'It has an oppressive, depressing effect on one's spirits.'[8] The seemingly endless round of endless dinners and receptions resumed. Gide was easily bored on such occasions: once he managed to slip out undetected. Guilloux remembered 'the horrified faces of the officials when they realized that Gide was no longer there'. When Gide left the hotel in the morning, he made great efforts to throw off the OGPU plainclothesmen employed to follow him. Before leaving Moscow Gide learnt that Eugène Rouart had died on 6 July, at his property in Bagnols-de-Grenade: three years Gide's junior, Rouart was one of his oldest friends and the dedicatee of *Paludes*. Gide and his party also learnt that on 18 July part of the Spanish army had mutinied, under General Franco, and was trying to remove the Republican government: the Spanish Civil War, which was to serve as a prelude to the Second World War, had begun.

On 12 July, the six men – Beth had already left for Paris – set out on the thirty-six-hour journey southwards. With them was their interpreter-guide, Bola Boleslavskaya. Their luxury Pullman provided separate cabins for each of the travellers and a splendid sitting-dining-room. The luxurious comfort was not an unmixed blessing: it isolated them from the other Russians travelling on the train. This they intended to overcome. At the first stop, they got out on to the platform and inspected their fellow-travellers. To Gide's (and Herbart's and Last's) delight, they found that the next carriage was occupied by a group of Komsomols en route for a climbing holiday in the Caucasus. The young Russians knew at once who the distinguished foreigner was – his photograph had been in all the papers, together with translations of his speeches and details of his itinerary. One or two claimed to have read *Voyage au Congo*. (By the end of Gide's visit, his *Collected Works* in Russian translation had reached Volume 4. Volume 5, with *Si le grain ne meurt*, was to appear at the end of the year, but fell foul of the new cultural line and the publication of Gide's *Retour de l'U.R.S.S.*) The communicating doors between the two carriages were opened and the Komsomols joined the visitors; Gide got out the toys that he had brought from Paris and others that he had got Last to buy in London.

On 15 July, they arrived at Ordzhonikidze, formerly Vladikavkaz, renamed in 1932 after the one-time Party boss in Caucasia, now Commissar for Heavy Industry. (In 1937, this Old Bolshevik was 'purged' and died the same year, in the usual mysterious circumstances.) They visited a Pioneers' Camp outside the town and were regaled with the usual banquet by the local worthies. They then crossed the Caucasian mountains, to Tiflis (Tbilisi), by car. Gide took more than usual pleasure in the natural scenery; here, at least, was something that the Party had been unable to infiltrate. They drove through the splendid forests and called at 'a strange little village' that is covered in snow nine months of the year.

Oh! If only I'd been there as a mere tourist! Or as a naturalist, delighted at recognizing on those high plateaux the Caucasian scabius in his own garden! . . . But this is not what I came to see in the USSR. What matters to me here is man, men – what can be done with them, and what *has* been done with them. The forest that drew me here, the frightful tangle in which I am lost, is the forest of social questions. In the USSR they solicit you, weigh down on you, oppress you on every side.[9]

At first, they were disappointed with Tiflis. However, on their first day in the Georgian capital, Gide discovered the celebrated sulphur baths – and they stayed for over a week. When the opportunity arose, the group split into two trios (according to sexual tastes), 'Dabit, Schiffrin and Guilloux going their own way or, to be more precise, Pierre Herbart, Jef and I leave them and go on the hunt . . .'[10] There were also, of course, the usual, more serious activities: they visited a factory and a collective farm; they attended meetings and banquets. The patience of Gide and his friends was often sorely tried. 'Gide's fame doesn't help,' Herbart noted, 'he's an official guest and we know what that means in the USSR. Addresses, poems read by a Pioneer, speeches, toasts and banquets.' As they leave a town, they are asked to say something for the local paper. They thank their hosts and admire this or that. 'The French writers praise our achievements,' the paper reports. 'They have nothing of the kind in their country. Long live our great Comrade Stalin, leader of the peoples!' Herbart felt sad and disgusted: 'This is all very far from what I hoped for before I came to the USSR, but it is what I expect after six months living in Moscow.'[11] 'It was only in Tiflis that our eyes really began to be opened,' Gide wrote.[12] Two of the party, Schiffrin and Guilloux, had certainly had enough and decided to cut short the visit, take a train from Tiflis to Moscow and another from there to Paris, passing through Berlin.

On 18 July, in the hottest weather that Tiflis had seen for twenty years, the remaining visitors took the train to Batumi and the Black Sea. On the way, they stopped off at Gori, the native village of Iosif Dzhugashvili, better known as Stalin. Gide, courteous as ever, took it into his head to send the Soviet leader a telegram, thanking him for the splendid welcome that they had been given by the Soviet peoples. He jotted down a few words: 'Passing through Gori in the course of our wonderful journey, I felt a need to express our cordial feelings . . .' The translator objected: 'You' was not enough when addressing Stalin. 'You, chief of the workers' or 'You, master of the peoples' would be more in keeping. Gide protested that Stalin was quite above such nonsense. Translator and post office were adamant. Gide made a scene, declaring that he recognized nothing that had been attributed to him during his stay in the USSR.[13] In a footnote, Gide quotes one statement attributed to him in the Soviet press. He was, Russian readers were told, neither understood nor loved by French youth and had decided, henceforth, to write only for the people. 'Stalin's effigy is met with everywhere,' Gide adds, 'his name is on every tongue, his praises are sung in every speech. In Georgia, particularly, I did not enter a single room, even the humblest and most sordid, without noticing a portrait of Stalin hanging on the wall, in the very place no doubt where the icon used to be.'[14]

They arrived in Batumi late in the evening. The hot, dark atmosphere reminded Herbart of Saigon. They visited an excellent botanical gardens and an oil refinery, where they noted that there were two restaurants, with two prices, for two different classes of employee. On the way back to the train, by bus, they passed the shacks where most of the workers lived. A few days later, they caught a boat for Sukhumi, further along the Black Sea coast, where they visited the mandatory collective farm. They were guests at the inevitable banquet, with the usual round of toasts. Jef Last proposed a toast to the Red Front in Spain. There was restrained applause: the Party line on the Spanish situation had not yet been announced. (In fact, Stalin was initially quite uninterested in saving the Spanish republic: such action would have smacked of Trotskyite internationalism at this time. Only after the Germans and Italians had given substantial support to Franco and the rebels did the Soviet Union, too late and too half-heartedly, assist the Spanish government.) One of the hosts countered by a toast to Stalin. Gide proposed a toast to the political prisoners in Germany, Yugoslavia and Hungary. This was enthusiastically applauded. Then ... another toast to Stalin was proposed. One night, they stayed out later than usual, bathing in the warm sea. On returning to the hotel, they were met by an armed guard who, at first, refused them entrance. 'In no country,' Herbart notes, 'have I seen so many barricades, barbed-wire fences, "no entry" signs, special passes, guards and sentry-huts.'[15]

After several days in Sukhumi, they took to the boat again for the 100 miles along the coast to Sochi. There they visited the 'rest houses' for the élite of the skilled workers, the very few whose exceptional output had earnt them such a reward. After a few days at Sochi, they took the ship for the 350-mile trip across the Black Sea to Sevastopol in the Crimea. At Artek, outside the town, they visited a rather special holiday camp for the crème de la crème of Soviet youth: Stalin, they were told, took a special interest in the place. Here the visitors were surrounded by the most talented children of the most privileged parents: they heard an 'amazing' thirteen-year-old boy play virtuoso pieces by Paganini on a Stradivarius. These young people had a blind, unshakeable faith in the superiority of all things Soviet, an illusion carefully fostered by the propaganda machine. When the visitors dared to contradict any of their cherished beliefs, they were simply not believed: these young people *knew* that Moscow was the only city with a métro, that in a country like France everybody except a few capitalists lived in misery and poverty, that Russian films were forbidden in France. When Gide dared to suggest that Soviet people were less well informed about France than the French were about them, there was a murmur of disapproval. '*Pravda* provides adequate information about everything,' said one. Then another declared: 'To describe all the new, great, beautiful things being done in the USSR, there would not be enough paper in the whole world.'[16]

After the visit to Artek, Dabit complained of a sore throat and said that he would not go down for dinner with the others. In the night – he and Herbart were sharing the same room – he woke Herbart up to ask him to get him a glass of water. Herbart took his temperature – it was 40° C. In the morning, a doctor was called. Angina was diagnosed. They were planning to catch the boat to Odessa the following day; instead, they stayed on. By the third day, the doctors diagnosed scarlet fever and immediately took him to a hospital. Forbidden access to the patient and assured that he would be better in a few weeks, his friends decided to take the next train to Moscow, rather than going on, by boat, to Odessa. On arriving in Moscow, they learnt that Dabit had died: had he left with Guilloux and Schiffrin, he might never have caught the haemolytic streptococci.

Gide and his friends found a Moscow obsessed with the 'Trial of the Sixteen' (all leading Party figures). The newspapers published the statements for the prosecution in full (there was no defence) and were whipping up a frenzy of public outrage against the accused. Former friends and colleagues publicly expressed regret that they had ever consorted with such 'bandits'. In 'spontaneous' public meetings, workers cursed the 'mad dogs' and, fists raised, demanded their death. On the day that Gide, Herbart and Last caught the train back to Paris, *Pravda* announced that Zinoviev and Kamenev had been executed. (The careers of these two men had followed parallel courses: born in 1883 to Jewish parents, they joined the Social Democratic Workers' Party in 1901 and its Bolshevik faction in 1903. They were Lenin's most senior collaborators in the leadership of the faction until 1917, when they opposed Lenin's policy of a seizure of power. After Lenin's death, they sided with Stalin against Trotsky, but later led a Left Opposition against Stalin. Gradual demotion followed until 1935, when they were accused of complicity in Kirov's murder and sentenced to ten and five years' imprisonment respectively. A year later, while Gide and his friends were in the Soviet Union they were retried, becoming the star defendants in the Trial of the Sixteen.)

As the plane crossed the frontier, Gide sent a telegram of thanks to the Soviet people. Translated, and suitably embellished, it appeared in *Pravda*, next day, 25 August: 'After our unforgettable journey to the great country of victorious socialism, I send from the frontier a last cordial salute to my wonderful friends whom I leave with regret, saying to them, and to the whole of the USSR, au revoir.' Hours later, the 'sixteen' were all shot. The charges had been based entirely on the 'confessions' of the accused, who had 'declined' the assistance of lawyers. The accused appeared before three military judges, approved by the Politburo, that is to say, Stalin. No verbatim reports of the trial were made: instead 'summaries', purely for propaganda purposes, were published.

Just the sight of the illuminated Paris boulevards with their shop windows was enough to raise the spirits of those two Communist Party members and their still fellow-travelling friend. Here one could actually sit at a café terrace, drink a beer, order a meal, take an hotel room and even, if one wanted to, travel to Bordeaux, London or Rome. Of course, it required some money, but in Moscow one could not do anything without money either. Travelling abroad, for pleasure, was out of the question – one could not even travel freely within the Soviet Union.[17]

That was one side of the emotional coin, joy at finding oneself in a sane, normal, pleasurable world. The other was desperation at the realization of the form that their political dreams were taking in Stalin's Socialist Father-land. Herbart and Last were still Marxists, still loyal to their Communist beliefs (it was Stalin's Russia that was betraying them), still loyal even to the Party (it would, it must inevitably survive the Stalinist episode). Before many weeks were out, both men would be in Spain, fighting to defend the Spanish Republic against the Fascists: there at least their loyalties and energies would go to real working-class people, with whom they felt an immediate emotional bond, rather than to lifeless, grey-suited Soviet bureaucrats. Unfortunately, the Spanish working-class did not, on the whole, support the small Communist Party, but the Socialists and, to a lesser degree, indigenous anarcho-syndicalist parties such as the POUM (Partido Obrero de Unification Marxista, the Workers' Party of Marxist Unification). The role of the Communists increased with the formation of the International Brigades (not entirely manned by Communists, but always under their control) and the decision by Moscow to support the Popular Front of parties to their right, Socialists and Liberals, *against* other extreme left-wing parties. Stalin was not interested in saving socialism in Spain, which would remain outside his control, but in the defence of the Soviet Union. By supporting 'moderates' against 'extremists', he hoped to earn the support of France and Great Britain against Germany. (When this failed, he engin-eered the German–Soviet pact of August 1939.) By 1937, there were *two* Spanish Civil Wars: one between the government forces and Franco's, the other a reign of terror practised by the Communist Party against the other extreme left-wing groups. As many came to realize, Communists were fighting not for Spanish workers, but for the grey-suited bureaucrats in the Soviet Union.

Gide was neither a Marxist nor a Party member. As a fellow-traveller of indomitable individuality, disengagement was easier and more rapid, though his sense of despair and betrayal was no less intense. 'Everything seems frightful. Everywhere I feel the catastrophe coming . . . We are plunging into a tunnel of anguish, the end of which cannot yet be seen.'[18] After a short visit to Cuverville, he was back in Paris by 2 September, when he dined with Schiffrin. Schiffrin spoke of the 'disappointment' that he and Guilloux had felt after the Soviet trip. The following day, he saw Malraux, who was in Paris for a few days before going back to Spain. With Schiffrin, he went to see Marc Allégret's new film, *Les Amants terribles*, an adaptation of Noël Coward's play *Private Lives*, and found Robert Levesque there. Meanwhile, Gide was reading the official account of the Trial of the Sixteen, which had just ended in Moscow: 'What is one to think of those sixteen men under indictment accusing themselves, and each one in almost the same terms, and singing the praises of a régime and a man that they risked their lives to eliminate?'[19] Gide, like most people at the time, was unfamiliar with the techniques employed to get men to say whatever one wanted them to say.

Gide called on Dabit's parents at the hotel they ran in Montmartre, the Hôtel du Nord, which their son celebrated in his novel of the same name. Next day, he called on Clara Malraux and went with her to Père Lachaise. He was very moved by the funeral, for him, spoilt only by the 'political' speeches of Vaillant-Couturier and Aragon, claiming the dead man's 'complete moral satisfaction in the USSR'.[20] Gide knew better: his response, to the comrades' outraged fury, came with the dedication of *Retour de l'U.R.S.S.* 'To the memory of Eugène Dabit, I dedicate these pages, reflections of what I lived and thought beside him, with him.' In his *Retouches*, Gide recounts how Dabit had told him 'more than once that it was up to me to speak out'.[21]

The following day, Schiffrin came to lunch and the Petite Dame guessed from the gloom that hung over them how disappointed and worried they were by what they had seen in the Soviet Union. Who or what was at fault, the Petite Dame asked. 'Communism, the Russian temperament, Stalin, or man himself?' Gide said that it was all these things, because they could not be disentangled.[22] On 10 September, Gide received a 'desperate letter' from Jef Last. At a party organized by his wife, he had been bombarded with questions about the Soviet Union in general and the Moscow trial in particular. His answers had not pleased his Communist friends and he had been summoned to Party headquarters for interrogation. He now had a disgust for political discussion entirely and wanted to throw himself into action – in Spain.[23]

On 11 September, Gide set out for Cuverville, where he worked with unaccustomed speed on his 'little book' about the Soviet Union. By 20 September, he was back at the Vaneau to welcome Jef Last, who stayed for three days on his way to Spain. With Last was a curious German, Harry Domela, a Communist activist who, in 1926, had passed himself off as a Prussian prince and had been received in the highest aristocratic circles in Germany. The following year he published an account of his adventures as a 'false' prince (*Der Falsche Prinz, Leben und Abentauer*). The day that Last and Domela left for Spain, the Petite Dame arrived back after spending ten days with Jean Schlumberger at Braffy. Gide told her about Last's visit: 'He has just left for Spain, where he may get himself killed! He is so bewildered, he feels that his position with regard to the Party is so false, so intolerable that he thinks this is the only way to get a certificate of purity.'[24] When the Petite Dame inquired about the book, she was astonished to learn that a first version was finished and in the process of being typed. Later that evening, Gide read extracts from it to her, Guilloux and the Schiffrins. 'We were very worried,' the Petite Dame noted afterwards. 'One cannot conceive what the consequences might be. Guilloux looked winded . . . That little book will be a bombshell. One tries to imagine the reactions: the rage of some, the triumph of others, generally blame from friends and enemies.'[25]

On 26 September, at dawn, Gide caught the train for Marseille. From there he made his way to Cabris and the Herbarts – Catherine had already left for Paris, where she was to attend the Ecole Nouvelle de Bellevue. Ironically, one of the reasons why Gide had arranged for his daughter to come to Paris was to free her from what he regarded as Pierre Herbart's excessively extreme, dogmatic influence. Since their visit to the USSR, he now found that Herbart shared all his views on Soviet society, the Party, Stalin, etc. The very warm, almost collusive feelings the two men had always had for one another were now unimpeded by any ideological baggage. Indeed, over the next ten days or so, they worked together on Gide's book – Herbart, with his longer experience of the Soviet Union and his better grasp of Marxism and Party practice, offering invaluable help. As Rudolph Maurer demonstrates, in a comparison between the original manuscript and the final version, Gide was acutely concerned to be *fair* to the Soviet Union. The *Retour* was certainly not to be a polemical attack: many of the changes made by Gide were intended to soften the criticisms that he had made. On 1 October, the two men went to Nice to spend a couple of days with Roger Martin du Gard. There they found Marc. Gide noted in his *Journal* how delighted he was that RMG had 'adopted to such a degree Pierre Herbart and Marc, both of whom get along with him famously'. These four men, all in different ways, at different times and to varying degrees bisexual, spent their first evening together discussing the new Soviet laws against homosexuality, their possible motivations and implications.

Gide was back in Paris on 21 October. The same day, he took his corrected typescript to the printer's (finished copies were ready by 5 November). A few days later, a letter arrived from Jef Last. He was on leave in Madrid, staying at the 'Alliance of Intellectuals against Fascism and for the Defence of Culture'. There he had been asked to try to persuade Gide to come to Madrid. It would, he said, be a 'testimony of trust and friendship' that would have 'a great influence on world opinion and on the morale of Spanish intellectuals'. A week later, another letter from Last arrived. The Spanish government would be sending Gide an official invitation to go to Spain. It would, he remarked, be an opportunity 'to testify once again to your absolute fidelity to the revolutionary, socialist cause'. Last was beginning to sound like a ventriloquist's dummy. The impression that he was being 'used' was not dispelled by the next sentence: 'Moreover, I believe that it is now no longer possible to publish a book on the USSR without dealing with the Spanish question and without taking into account the effect that this book will have on the struggle.'[26]

On 23 October, the Soviet government announced that henceforth it would reserve the right to supply arms to the Spanish government. In other words, it was leaving the Committee of Non-Intervention formed with Great Britain and France. This, of course, was what the Republicans in general and the Communists in particular had been pleading for. At last they would have the arms necessary to counteract the support given to the insurgents by Germany and Italy. The following day, Ehrenburg telephoned, asking to see Gide. He was about to go back to Spain and was so insistent that Gide found it difficult to refuse. Clearly, he was trying to sound Gide out about his book and, if necessary, would alert the Soviet government. Gide decided to be evasive about the book's contents and to shift the conversation on to the subject of the Moscow trial, then, in order to reassure him, tell him that there was no mention of the trial in the book, which was true. Ehrenburg arrived two days later. He was, says the Petite Dame, 'consummately skilful'. He tried to find out exactly what was in the book. Yes, he had a good idea of the criticisms that Gide was making, indeed, he agreed with most of them himself and could, if he wanted to, provide further material along those lines. But the Soviet Union was now making an immense effort to assist Spain: it really wasn't the right time to attack her. He really should postpone publication until the Spanish civil war was over. That evening, Gide and the Petite Dame began correcting the proofs of *Retour de l'U.R.S.S.*

Two days later, a telegram arrived from Last begging Gide to postpone publication until he had spoken to him in Madrid. Gide found the telegram very disturbing. It showed that Last had learnt, probably from Ehrenburg, both of the imminent publication of Gide's book and of his probable arrival in Spain. He decided to consult Magdaleine Paz. Her view was that the truth about the USSR should be published as soon as possible. The longer it was delayed, the more difficult it would be to say it. She urged him to meet Victor Serge, who would provide him with a great deal more information about the Soviet Union. On 29 October, Gide and the Petite Dame had just finished correcting the proofs of the book when Aragon telephoned. He had just got back from Spain and had a letter to Gide that Last had given him to deliver personally. So Aragon, too, had been 'working' on Last. In the letter, Jef declared: 'I am convinced that it is our absolute duty at this time to avoid anything that might in any way shake people's resolve or serve, even against one's will, the cause of Fascism. At present, the only true ally of the heroic Spanish people is the Soviet Union and we must avoid by all means anything that might tarnish the prestige of that ally'.[27]

On 30 October, Jean Schlumberger and Harry Kessler came to lunch with Gide and the Petite Dame. Kessler had had to give up his house in Spain and was now living in Paris. He had managed to sell his 'beloved Weimar house' four months before. 'How many memories and how much of my life vanished with it,' he wrote in his diary on 6 July.[28] He was to die just over a year later, at the age of sixty-nine; he thus avoided the greater horror of living in a France occupied by his own compatriots.

The following day, Gide lunched with Léon Blum, still Prime Minister: Gide found his old friend 'very calm, firm, lucid', exasperated by the Communists' attacks, but determined to do all he could to maintain the Popular Front. Gide went on to meet Victor Serge, whom Gide had helped to free from 'internal exile'. The previous June, he had published an 'open letter' to Gide, in *Esprit*, in which he described the intellectual terrorism at work in the Soviet Union (a single, imposed 'aesthetic' theory, rigid censorship, the re-writing of history, the removal of thousands of books from libraries, etc.) and the appalling character of social life (low wages for the working masses, internal passports, the death penalty, even for children). Much of this must have alerted Gide to the gap between Soviet propaganda and reality before his visit. Gide was 'favourably impressed' by Serge. Gide then found time to see Pierre Naville, the leading French Trotskyite, whose sister was married to Yves Allégret. Gide found the Trotskyites in general 'rather terrifying', determined to prevent Stalinism from taking root in Spain at all costs. One failed revolution was enough, they believed. Defeat in Spain would be preferable to a false victory. All this made Gide wonder whether he ought to go to Spain. What sort of a mess would he be landing himself in? The Spanish Popular Front was obviously even more divided than the French. How would he be able to maintain a position of independence and integrity?[29]

On 4 November, Pierre Herbart arrived. He read them part of an article that he was writing on his impressions of the Soviet Union. In it, he declared that Marxist socialism had not been established in the Soviet Union: this would be enough to get him expelled from the Party. Nevertheless, he tended to side with those who favoured postponing publication of Gide's book; he was even thinking of going to Spain to fight. Gide telephoned Aragon, out of courtesy, to warn him that publication was going ahead. 'I am saddened not so much by the probable reaction of our enemies,' Aragon declared, 'as that of our friends.' Later in the day, Aragon rang again: the news from Spain was very bad, Madrid looked like falling to the rebels. He wanted to organize a delegation of French intellectuals, from many political persuasions, to go to Madrid and to try, by their presence, to prevent a bloodbath. Aragon's voice was becoming ever more emotional, 'as if he were haranguing a crowd' – sitting a couple of feet away, the Petite Dame could hear every word. He then played his last card: Jef Last had telephoned him from Madrid, asking him to try once again to dissuade Gide from publishing his *Retour*. Herbart decided to go over and see Aragon, hoping to get more information about the situation in Spain. When he had gone, Gide said to the Petite Dame: 'I get on very well with Pierre, very well. The only point on which we disagree, of course, is the Party – he remains very attached to it. I don't really know what to think . . .' He thought that his book might encourage a section of the Party membership to break with Moscow, or join the Socialists.[30] Herbart persuaded Gide to take up the idea of a deputation to Madrid. A week later, after scores of telephone calls and hours of meetings, they had to admit that the project had failed: no one could agree as to how 'broad' the group should be, many of those approached backed down and no list could be found that was agreeable to all. On 9 November, Herbart left for Toulouse, where he hoped to get a plane for Spain. Six days later, they finally learnt (from Clara Malraux) that Herbart had at last reached Madrid.

Retour de l'U.R.S.S. appeared in the bookshops on 13 November. It is not a travel book in the sense that Gide's two African books are: there are hardly any dates and the exact chronology of the tour is left vague. There are good reasons for this. In Africa, with little to do for long stretches of time, Gide kept a copious diary, while Marc left a meticulous report of all their movements. In the Soviet Union, he and his friends were bombarded with time-consuming hospitality and tours of inspection. They were, too, actually afraid to make detailed notes, knowing that these might well fall into the hands of the secret police. Gide was less concerned to make a tourist's observations than to come to a fair assessment of Soviet society. If the book seems a mass of unresolved contradictions, it is to some extent because it was written and published in haste by a confused man whose mind was not yet made up. Yet the book's apparent confusion may mask three possibly linked strategies: first, the progress from delighted approval to bitter criticism follows the actual progress in Gide's mind over the nine weeks he spent in the Soviet Union; second, it shows that Gide is a reluctant critic, not one looking for material to make an attack; third, it lulls the pro-Soviet reader into a false sense of security, gradually exposing him to doubts that, in more hostile hands, he would not have entertained. The book's last sentence contains a truth of which Gide could not have been aware: 'The USSR will go on instructing and astonishing us.'[31]

The reactions of Gide's friends to the *Retour* are fascinating in their variety. Chronologically, the first was Herbart's 'open letter', and based on a reading of the proofs, unaffected therefore by any other published reaction. It appeared in the fellow-travelling weekly *Vendredi* on 20 November.[32] Herbart expresses great concern about the effects of such a book, appearing at a time when, 'once again, the enemies of the Revolution are unleashing a furious campaign against the Soviet Union', but his main concern is to place the question of the present state of Soviet society on a more 'theoretical' level. He summarizes Gide's criticisms: 1) The formation of classes in the USSR, a privileged bureaucracy, wide differences in earnings and 2) the dictatorship of the proletariat has become the dictatorship of Stalin, or at least of a very small group of men. Are we to conclude from this, Herbart asks, that the Soviet Union is not on the road to Communism? His ingenious argument is that the Soviet Union *is* moving towards Communism (the final stage), but has not *yet* reached *socialism* (the intermediate stage between capitalism and Communism), this for the good reason that the Revolution occurred only in one, backward country, instead of in an advanced Germany, followed by the other advanced capitalist countries. This is not a view that was ever propounded by the Party, of course, and, as Herbart realized, might lead to his expulsion: it came perilously close to Trotsky's attack on the possibility of 'socialism in one country'. Over the next six months or so, Herbart, sickened by the actions of the Party in Spain, was to move towards Gide's view.

Jef Last, too, was changing his mind. With the book now published, he was no longer under pressure from 'comrades'. 'Generally speaking, I think you are right after all. This propaganda must end – it's based only on lies. Even the heroic tragedy here serves . . . the greater glory of the leader [Stalin]. But I'd like to see the [Soviet] weapons we've been told so much about. I'm entirely on your side . . .'[33] Martin du Gard showed his usual percipience. 'I still don't find this book satisfying,' he wrote to the Petite Dame. 'I feared that the inadequacy of content would compromise the book's success and Gide's reputation. I was completely wrong on that score. I thought only about the book itself, its content. By a marvellous stroke of luck, public opinion seems to take account only of the *gesture*. I was aware of the *gesture*, of course, and was moved by its honesty, its courage, its greatness. But I thought that this gesture would be compromised by the book's inadequacy. But not at all. Alleluia!'[34] A reading of the *Retour* led Jean Schlumberger to write one of his longest, frankest and most perceptive letters to Gide. Over the years, he said, Gide may have felt that he had been 'rather distant, rather absent, not in heart, but in thought'. What was taking place inside Gide was not susceptible to argument; one could only wait and let it take its course. 'You have been so cruel towards "converts" that you provided against yourself a terrible arsenal of disagreeable terms – mysticism, the obliteration of the critical sense, the abandonment of art (they too thought they had something more important to do) – for the day when you, too, adopted the position of a convert.' Gide would simply brush away 'the imperfections of Communism in the same off-hand way in which Catholics view the shortcomings of the Church'. Schlumberger understands the attractions of feeling oneself to be 'a man in the herd of men': he had felt the same during the War. He applauds the 'generosity of spirit' that

had thrown Gide into the 'Soviet adventure', but it was based on a fatal
confusion of the personal and the political, of the needs of Gide's soul with
'the real needs of the people'.[35]

For nearly three weeks, the PCF and its ideologues maintained a studied
silence, waiting for the 'line' to arrive from Moscow. Gide was not a Party
member and therefore could not be summoned to Moscow, disciplined or
expelled. Then, on 3 December, *Pravda* launched a campaign of vilification.
Gide was, quite simply, 'the victim of anti-Soviet agents', 'a kind of Judas'.
Later, two great artists, Eisenstein and Pasternak, who had entertained
Gide in the Soviet Union and tried, as much as they dared, to alert Gide
to what was happening there, were forced, at the risk of their own skins, to
make public attacks on Gide. Eisenstein, at least, saved his self-respect by
using language that was manifestly not his own, calling Gide a 'lackey of
the fascists and Trotskyites'. The text reappeared, almost word for word,
in *L'Humanité* a few days later. The world's Communist press followed suit:
Gide was a traitor, a fascist agent, an impostor, a hypocrite, a degenerate.
Ehrenburg, who had been entertained by Gide on several occasions, called
him a 'vieillard infâme' (which might be Englished as 'dirty old man').
Klaus Mann had just published in an Amsterdam review an article by
Ehrenburg praising Gide in glowing terms. One attack that Gide found
particularly poignant came from the Young Communists of the 7th arrondissement: 'At a time when we must defend the Soviet Union more than
ever, we note with disgust your volte-face and the praise lavished on you in
the fascist press . . . We can only conclude that your book was written to
make money. We now regard you as unworthy of being our "Honorary
President".' Gide replied that the letter came as no surprise and pointed out
that, in financial terms, what he had lost in Soviet royalties far outweighed
anything to be earned by his *Retour*: 'When you take on such absurd
accusations so lightly, I am less surprised that you allow yourself to be taken
in by the rest.'[36]

The *Retour* is a short book, was given a large initial printing and,
consequently, a low price. In ten months, it was reprinted eight times
and sold 146,300 copies. None of Gide's book had ever had such an
immediate success. By the end of 1937, it had been translated into fourteen
languages. The Communist, Nazi and Fascist dictatorships avoided it. The
Spanish and Portuguese editions came from South America, the German
from Switzerland; there was no Italian edition until after the War.

Geneviève and *Pages de Journal* were published on the same day as the *Retour*.
Geneviève, as a character, first appears as the author of the covering letter

to Gide, dated 1 August 1928, enclosing her mother's journal which, she suggests, he might be able to get published: *L'Ecole des femmes* might be a good title. *Robert*, second panel of the triptych, is the widower's response to his dead wife's version of events: neatly, Gide allows him to be condemned a second time, this time out of his own mouth. *Geneviève*, the last panel, takes the form of a long letter to Gide, in which the daughter recounts her adolescent years and provides a third view of her parents' marriage. Most of it concerns Geneviève's obsessive, unrequited infatuation with a schoolfriend, Sara Keller, the beautiful daughter of a successful painter. Geneviève's parents do all they can to prevent a friendship from developing between the two girls. The fact that the Kellers are Jewish does not *necessarily* rule Sara out as a suitable friend for their daughter, though it probably would as far as the father is concerned. The mother takes a more pragmatic line: 'Jews have a great many qualities and some of them are very remarkable people.'37 Eveline takes it upon herself to investigate: the results are not favourable. Keller, though obviously successful, is nevertheless an artist and leads a bohemian way of life. But the *coup de grâce* comes when it is discovered that Sara's mother was her father's model and that the parents are not actually married. Geneviève has already been forbidden to see Sara outside school; she is now summararily removed from the *lycée* (which Robert had never approved of in any case, being against too rigorous an education for women). Geneviève prepares for the *bachot* on her own, with the help of private lessons. One of her tutors is Dr Marchant, physician and family friend. Under his wife's watchful eye he gives Geneviève an hour's science lessons every evening. One day, Mme Marchant is away. It is the moment Geneviève has been waiting for. After approaching the question of why the Marchants do not have any children, Geneviève finally blurts out: 'I would like to have a child.' Marchant handles the situation with great delicacy: you are only seventeen, you have plenty of time before you have to think about marriage. 'Perhaps,' says Geneviève, 'but I don't want to marry.' By now quite worried, the doctor pursues his questions. 'Are you in love with someone?' Geneviève answers that she is well aware that love is not necessary to have a child. Has she anyone in particular in mind as the prospective father? 'Yes, you.' With as much composure as he can muster, Marchant makes it clear that such an idea is out of the question, he and his wife, etc.

In the *récit*, this conversation does not seem quite as improbable as it may in this necessarily truncated summary. Geneviève hates her father, has seen what marriage has done to her mother and, at school, under Sara's inspiration, founded with her and another girl, a 'league for women's independence'. And this improbable event had happened to Gide himself. There are many parallels in the two situations, real and fictitious. Gide and Marchant are both married and childless. There is the same difference in age between the man and the woman in each case – about twenty years. Both men are friends of the women's parents, especially of the mother. The motive of the two women in wanting a child, outside marriage, even outside a continuing sexual relationship, is the same. But, as the real woman's mother told Martin du Gard in August 1936, 'in fact, Elisabeth and his [Gide's] heroine have nothing in common – neither in character, milieu, circumstances, friends, events'.[38] The Petite Dame does not mention the most important difference: the age of the two women at the time. It was one thing for Elisabeth Van Rysselberghe, aged thirty-two in 1922, sexually experienced, brought up in a bohemian world, with an enlightened, independent mother, surrounded by women friends, all feminists and many of them lesbian, to have approached a man like Gide. It is quite another for a seventeen-year-old virgin in 1914, with highly conventional parents, very limited experience, none of it sexual, even lesbian, to approach a happily married family doctor in his late forties. Of course, there is another, crucial difference, one that the Petite Dame pointed out to Gide himself: Dr Marchant refused the proposition, Gide did not.

The conversation between Marchant and Geneviève takes place just before the outbreak of the First World War. The narrative jumps forward to 1916, to the point at which *L'Ecole des femmes* breaks off. Geneviève goes to see her mother at the military hospital where she is working as a nurse. In the course of their meeting, Geneviève recounts her conversation with Dr Marchant two years before. Eveline, who is to die a few days later, hints that the reason for the doctor's rejection of Geneviève's proposition was not so much loyalty to his wife as respect for her, Eveline. They had been in love, but never lovers, feeling unable to break their marriage vows.

There *Geneviève* ends. Gide explains its 'unfinished' character in a preparatory note:

Shortly after the publication of *L'Ecole des femmes* and *Robert*, I received, in manuscript form, the beginning of what was in some way a complementary account, one that might, taken with the other two, be regarded as the third panel of a triptych. After long waiting in vain for the rest of the story, I decided to publish what follows as it stands . . .[39]

Short of putting the entire manuscript in a drawer and leaving it there, this was Gide's only option, far-fetched as the 'explanation' might be. In fact, of course, a great deal of a Part 3 had been written – rewritten and rejected. 'I spent as much time . . . making a failure of *Geneviève* (most of which I tore up) as I did making *Les Faux-Monnayeurs* a success,' Gide noted in 1949.[40]

On the morning of 16 November, Léon Blum telephoned. He had a little time, in his prime ministerial schedule, for a chat. Could Gide come for lunch? They discussed the 'delegations' to Madrid (Blum doubted if they would do any good). Gide brought up the question of Trotsky, who was in Norway, but only temporarily. Blum thought that he might be able to act on Trotsky's behalf in a personal capacity. (A few days later, the French government allowed Trotsky to cross France on his way to Mexico.)

On the 17th, Beth arrived from Cabris: she had had no news from Pierre and was very worried. Later in the morning, Clara Malraux telephoned to say that Pierre had telephoned her from Madrid. Pierre would be returning to Paris shortly and hoped to see Last before leaving Spain. The following evening, 'les Groet' came to dinner with the Petite Dame and Beth – Gide arrived back at the Vaneau later in the evening. Throughout they had, rather artificially, avoided 'the burning question' (what was happening in the Soviet Union, Gide's book, etc.) and talked about Herbart's return from Spain and the suicide that day of Blum's Interior Minister, Salengro.

Pierre Herbart had been expected to arrive on 21 November. Over the next few days, anxiety at the Vaneau rose. Then Clara Malraux telephoned: for three days, bad weather had stopped any planes flying between Alicante and Toulouse. An Italian friend of hers had just returned from Spain, where he had been fighting on the Republican side. In Barcelona, he said, 'the Stalinist propaganda is quite shameless, worse than in Russia' and the Communists' 'reign of terror' against other non-Party republicans was in full swing. He himself had been refused permission to go to Paris and had only got there through Malraux. Anxiety about Herbart rose even more and Gide was determined to get Jef Last out of Spain.

Three days later, a telegram arrived from Pierre: he had been unable to leave Alicante by air. He finally arrived on 26 November. In Valencia, he had met Malraux and the German poet Gustav Regler, a Communist in the International Brigade. Since he had on him an advance copy of Gide's book, he read them extracts from it. They both urged him to take it back to Madrid and show it to the Russians – the Soviet embassy was now in charge there, in the absence of the Spanish government. It was better for the Russians to face the truth, they said. In Madrid, Herbart met Koltzov and lent him the book. Later he was summoned by Koltzov and other

Russians; their reaction to Gide's book was violent in the extreme and they refused to give it back. Herbart was told that accommodation would be found for him in Madrid's best hotel, which had been taken over by the senior Russians in the city. Pierre soon realized that he was under surveillance and would find it difficult to get back to France: he was now guilty by association with Gide. Meanwhile, Koltzov learnt of the publication of Gide's book and the initial reaction to it from Aragon, his 'eyes and ears' in Paris: as yet, there was no official line from Moscow. Herbart reckoned that if he were ever to get back to France he would have to do so by deception. He told Koltzov that he wanted to go to Barcelona to report on the situation there. Koltzov would make the necessary arrangements (including surveillance) and gave Herbart a 'pass' for Barcelona. Suddenly, Herbart announced that he had got a lift by car to Albacete and that he could catch a plane from there to Barcelona. At Albacete he saw Malraux, who arranged for him to fly to Toulouse. It was, said Herbart, out of the question that Gide should go to Spain. He had not been able to see Jef Last, but knew that he was well: he should, however, be got out of Spain as soon as possible. Even Malraux, who had served the Republican side so brilliantly, was under the surveillance of the Communists: he was altogether too popular, too independent. He had been deliberately removed to Albacete, away from the front line. Herbart then launched into a long diatribe against Aragon, whom he accused of turning the Russians against him. He telephoned Aragon and went off at once to confront him. With great suavity, Aragon denied all Herbart's charges.

Gide was reading *Le Livre rouge du procès de Moscou*, an account of the Trial of the Sixteen, published by a Trotskyite publishing house, and was overcome with grief and despair. Pierre and Beth were 'feverishly' reading Trotsky's *The Revolution Betrayed*. 'Until now,' said Pierre, 'I was careful not to read Trotsky's books, for . . . religious reasons, as it were, as one avoids bad books . . .'[41]

Over the previous few months, Catherine, it seems, had been going through a kind of adolescent crisis: inexplicable moods, surliness, refusal to say what was wrong, etc. In an attempt to liven her spirits, Gide decided to take her to Switzerland over the Christmas holidays. 'He is certainly the one who is the more innocently excited,' the Petite Dame notes. He was very concerned about wearing the right clothes, appropriate to the holiday spirit. The holiday appears to have been disastrous. 'The gloomiest days of my whole life,' Gide wrote to Dorothy Bussy. 'Only fifty-two hours (I counted them) of purgatory . . . I've done nothing, couldn't do anything here . . . My mind dulled to the point of imbecility, old, useless . . . It's what is called "resting in Switzerland"!' Catherine was 'unbearable', though he excused her on account of *her* being bored too. It had been too late to book rooms near the skiing-slopes and they had ended up at an *'hideux palace'*, from which they managed to escape for the last few days to a 'modest pension'. There they found a schoolfriend of Catherine's age and the two girls were able to go off skiing together.[42]

Gide and Catherine arrived back on 3 January, preceded by a few hours by the Petite Dame, who had spent the holidays with Loup Mayrisch at Colpach. Over the next few weeks, minds in the Vaneau were much exercised by the announcement of a new 'trial' in Moscow, in which Radek would be the star. He and his 'accomplices' would be charged with 'Trotskyite terrorism'. This 'trial', of course, was only the tip of the iceberg, useful for propaganda purposes. Millions of more humble individuals were not given even the semblance of a court appearance: they just disappeared, either shot or deported to labour camps. Meanwhile, Gide was planning a second book on the Soviet Union, in which he would answer criticisms made of the first and provide further documentation. He already had the title: *Retouches à mon Retour de l'U.R.S.S.* On 20 January, Robert Levesque left for Moscow as tutor to the son of the counsellor at the French embassy. He was to stay for about five months.

Gide left for Cuverville and Herbart for Cabris. Beth had finally sold her house at Saint-Clair, which had been let since their removal to Cabris – and Loup Mayrisch had sold her house at Bormes, also in the Var. The Petite Dame went off to remove the owners' personal effects – both houses had been sold with their furniture. At Cuverville, Gide worked on *Retouches* and sat by the fire with Madeleine, reading aloud Tocqueville's *Mémoires*, Gogol's *Dead Souls* and Racine's *Athalie*. At the end of March, Gide left Cuverville – 'The presence of the second of my sisters-in-law [Valentine] rather scared me off' – and took refuge at Fontainebleau, where, for ten days or so, he found 'perfect peace and quiet, comfort and everything to facilitate work'.[43]

On 7 April the Petite Dame woke up to find Last's friend, Harry Domela, 'der Falsche Prinz', sitting with Gide at the breakfast table. He had just come back from Spain. Jef was well, but his situation was extremely dangerous. Those in charge in Valencia (German Communists) regarded him as a Trotskyite: Domela had been warned not to see him. However, his men worshipped him and he himself seemed quite unconcerned about the dangers he ran. Gide went along to the Spanish embassy and saw the ambassador's wife. She agreed that the rivalries between the various Republican groups were terrible and that they must try and get Last out of Spain. Gide later learnt from a Dutch friend that all Jef's letters to his wife were intercepted by the Party's political police.

Gide spent ten days in the South. At Vence, he and Herbart read each other's books on the Soviet Union. He also called on the Bussys at their new home, 40 rue Verdi, in Nice (with great regret they had let La Souco, at Roquebrune).

He was back in Paris on 30 April to attend the wedding of his Uncle Charles' grand-daughter: he would not normally have made the effort, but 'to the great consternation of her relations, she is marrying a Jew' and he felt that she needed all the support she could get.[44] He did have another reason, however: he wanted to meet his 'petit protégé de Marseille', Néné Brun, who had three days' leave from the Navy. To the young man's great delight, Marc was able to use him for two days (and 160 francs) as a sailor extra in a film, *La Dame de Malacca*, which he had just started directing. (In the same film, Jacques Copeau, also short of money, if at a different level, was playing an English major.) On 3 May, Gide took the manuscript of his completed *Retouches* to Gallimard's. Next day, the manuscript of Herbart's book arrived and Gide took it along to the publisher's. On 11 May, Gide left for four days at Cuverville. Between February and July, Gide went no fewer than six times to Cuverville. Madeleine's health seemed to be deteriorating. She was now blind in one eye and could not see well out of the other; her varicose veins, too, had got worse and had to be bandaged each day, a task that Gide himself did when at Cuverville.

During a few days in Paris, in May, he had lunch with the Bussys, who were passing through on their way to London, and took Catherine to the Exposition Universelle, which was to be the last of a series that had begun in 1878. On 14 June, Gide called on Copeau at the studios at Epernay and the two old friends dined together. 'Gide was absolutely exquisite,' Copeau wrote to Agnès. 'In the taxi that brought us back to the rue Vaneau, he said: "Give me your hand." And he held it in his.'[45] The following day, Gide left for Carcassonne, to spend a couple of days with Alibert. On his return, he learnt of the collapse of the Blum government.

Gide had held back publication of *Retouches à mon Retour de l'U.R.S.S.* so that it could appear on the same day, in late June, as Pierre Herbart's *En U.R.S.S. 1936*, dedicated to 'M. Saint-Clair', the pseudonym that his mother-in-law had used for her *Il y a quarante ans*. Gide's *Retour* had been criticized on all sides for its lack of documentary evidence. His indictment of the Soviet Union had been largely a moral one. During the months after his return, he had had time to reflect on the nature of the Soviet experiment and on his own feelings towards it. He had also taken the trouble to read the massive documentation that was building up about it, much of it, but not all, from Trotskyites and disillusioned Communists. One valuable witness, who was not an ex-Communist or a Trotskyite, but a leading trade unionist and socialist of evident honesty, was Walter Citrine, General Secretary of the British Trades Union Congress. Citrine's book, packed with information, was not overtly anti-Soviet. Indeed, as late as May 1936, he was being referred to with approval in the Soviet press. In November 1936, Gide also read Trotsky's *The Revolution Betrayed* in Victor Serge's French translation! Gide had also been provided with copious extracts from the Soviet press in translation by Serge, whom he saw during a visit to Brussels in January.

There were, of course, limits to the truth of the statistics provided, above all when they concern the number of 'political offenders' imprisoned and executed. Stalin's best-informed, most avowed enemies fell far short of what we now know were the *minimum* figures. Gide, anxious to err on the side of caution, referred to people 'deported in their thousands'.[46] The reaction of the Party was, of course, even more vehement than it had been to the *Retour*. Soon after publication, the Second International Congress of Intellectuals for the Defence of Culture took place in Madrid. Stephen Spender, a member of the British delegation, recounts how, beneath the ostensible subject of the Congress, the attitude of the 'intellectuals of the World' to the Spanish war, 'there was also a hidden theme constantly discussed in private and almost as often dragged on to the open platform. This was: the Stalinists versus André Gide.'[47] From Spain, Ilya Ehrenburg ended an article in *Izvestiya* by referring to Gide as 'the new ally of the Moroccans and Black Shirts'.[48] For Jef Last this situation was intolerable. 'I have just spent a few days, more terrible than those of the bombardments, at the Congress of Writers. Both the Russians and the French have been putting enormous pressure on me to make a statement condemning your book, which, as luck would have it, I haven't read . . . Many of the comrades are very angry with the book and I'm afraid it won't help my already difficult position. Fortunately, I'm not afraid of facing bullets, even those that might come from behind.' It was right to criticize the Soviet Union for many things, but only on condition that one 'does not shake the confidence of the masses in the salutary strength of the revolution'. Whatever disagreements they might have, these have 'no influence on the love and esteem that I will always feel for you. Your friendship has always been the best thing in my life and I shall never repudiate it.'[49]

Sales for *Retouches* did not quite reach the heights for those of the earlier book. German and English translations (by Ferdinand Hardekopf and Dorothy Bussy) appeared rapidly, followed by others in Spanish, Portuguese, Czech, Japanese and Chinese.

On 10 July, Gide accompanied Catherine to the station on her way to England, where she was to spend a few weeks improving her English. A week later, he, too, left for London, where he spent a week with the Bussys and worked with Dorothy on his revised and expanded translation of *Antony and Cleopatra*. That same day the Bussys' young friend Julian Bell, Virginia Woolf's nephew, was killed in Spain, where, less than three weeks before, he had gone to serve in the Red Cross as an ambulance driver: originally, he had wanted to go and fight in the International Brigades, but had been dissuaded from doing so by his mother.

At the end of July, Robert Levesque arrived back from Moscow. A few days later, he and Gide set off for Sorrento, arriving there on 2 August, after a night in Rome. They made excursions to Naples and Amalfi, went to a performance of *La Traviata* and were visited by their old Italian friends Barbieri and Arduini. They visited friends at La Consuma, a villa outside Sorrento, owned by Bernard Berenson. After a visit to Pompeii, they left Naples on 18 August for Rome, where they spent about a week, San Gimignano and Florence. Italy found Gide at his most expansive. 'Nobility, grace and sensuality . . . *Nobility*; that word haunts me in Italy – where the most sensual caress merges into spirituality . . . I have never managed to express all I owe to Italy or how much I was and remain in love with her.'[50] As one might have guessed, behind his paean to beauty and sensuality, lay something more specific. He had, he wrote to Martin du Gard, 'things to recount; a prodigious adventure, which has probably only begun and promises, on my return to the North, to lead on to marvellous things . . . I try not to think about it too much, or to tell myself that it has come too late . . .' RMG adds a footnote in his edition of the correspondence: 'Prodigious adventure? I don't remember anything about it.' (Perhaps out of discretion, Levesque makes no mention of it either in his detailed account of their Italian holiday.[51]) Poor Gide! It clearly *had* come too late for him, a few months off his sixty-eighth birthday. The suffusion of some complaisant young Italian's 'sensual caresses' with something that he took for 'spirituality' had led Gide to exaggerate the moment's capacity to endure. It was a lesson that he had to learn each time over again; it did not embitter him or make him inaccessible to other such moments; he simply added them to his collection of memories and gratefully passed on. If a small consideration oiled the wheels of *social* intercourse, it was a small price to pay for the young man's greater consideration. 'The weather is ineffably beautiful; everything floats in the azure, seems unreal, imponderable,' Gide writes, adding, as the northern puritan looks on: 'I shall probably not be able to bear more than a fortnight of this plunge into Nirvana.'[52]

In his euphoria, Gide is not unaware that he is in Mussolini's Italy. He notes the presence everywhere of slogans: 'Believe. Obey. Fight', etc. The Fascists, at least, are being honest. What is chilling is how similar they are to the slogans to be seen all over the Soviet Union.[53]

Gide decided that, after an absence of eight years, he would attend that year's *décade littéraire* at Pontigny. On 20 September, he, Martin du Gard and his daughter Christiane, the Petite Dame, Dorothy Bussy and Enid McLeod met at the Gare de Lyon and, in accordance with tradition, lunched together in the buffet. There were more people than ever attending the *décade*, over fifty, to discuss 'The Social Vocation of Art in periods of mental turmoil and despair'. There were, the Petite Dame noted, 'a majority of women, a lot of young people, very few of the old habitués, and yet the usual atmosphere prevailed'.[54]

On 5 October, Curtius and his wife, on a visit to Paris, called for tea. 'It is fairly difficult to know how much Curtius is suffering under Hitler's régime,' the Petite Dame notes, 'but suffer he must. With obvious pain, he recounts how the teaching of French has been abolished in Germany and other disturbing things.' She remarks on his 'passivity', his 'fatalism' and a certain intolerance of Thomas Mann's stand against the Nazis. A week later Curtius and his wife came to lunch and gradually 'he allowed his distress to show'.[55] After two weeks in Cuverville, Gide was back in Paris on 3 November. Madeleine, he told the Petite Dame, had attained 'real serenity', but she had become 'a very old woman' (she was seventy): her sight was bad, her hands shook and were deformed by rheumatism, she was clumsy to the point of being dangerous to herself.[56] In contrast to his poor wife, Gide did not feel his age: in fact, he was thinking of going on another long trip, perhaps to Mexico or Africa again, with Pierre Herbart.

Jef Last turned up: after being slightly wounded, he had been given leave to go back to Holland and carry out a propaganda tour. He had called on Gide 'in secret': he was expected to go at once, on arriving in Paris, to the apartment of a friend called Ryn, a Croat and '100 per cent Communist', who now regarded Gide as a traitor and even to see him as a crime.

Although he would be in Paris for the next few days, he would not be able to see Gide again and asked him to meet him later in Brussels. Two days later, however, Last did turn up again: he had given his friend the slip. He had left Spain because he couldn't take any more, sickened by the cold, inhuman application of abstract ideas by the Party leadership. He now regarded Russia as a counter-revolutionary force, but believed that, until the Spanish republic was victorious, one must not turn on her ally. He had come to an agreement with the Party: on condition that he did not criticize the Soviet Union and the Party, he would not be forced into making a public condemnation of Gide. Some days later, he wrote to Gide from Holland. He was being attacked on all sides: the Trotskyites criticized him for not coming out against Stalin, the Communists for not turning against Gide. He was being followed everywhere – by the Communists. He also learnt that none of his letters from Spain had arrived at their destination and that material left with his Dutch publisher had been stolen. Moreover all his proposals for lecture tours had been turned down.

On 11 November, Gide and the Petite Dame learnt, to their great delight, that Martin du Gard had just been awarded the Nobel Prize for Literature. RMG's *Journal* has a thirty-page account of the experience, from being summoned by his Nice concierge to answer a telephone call (he had no telephone of his own), through the journey to Sweden, the proceedings in Stockholm and the beginning of a two-month journey through Germany.[57] His immediate reaction was one of terror: he jumped on the first train for Cannes and booked into an hotel under an assumed name. Next day, he returned to Nice, where, on his instructions, the concierge directed all reporters and photographers to another apartment, which happened to be empty. After a few days, his friends (and his publisher) persuaded him that he must emerge from hiding and confront the press: 'France expects a public gesture from him . . . Sweden is getting irritated . . .' Finally, on 25 November, he arrived in Paris, gave a few interviews, went along to the Quai d'Orsay, etc. Hélène, his cold, embittered, cantankerous wife, was in her element. He found her 'radiant, uplifted by events, delighted at the prospect of the glorious journey to Sweden, rejuvenated'.[58] They moved into the Lutétia, with a room each, plus a study for Roger, where Pascal Copeau, Jacques' son, helped him with the mountains of correspondence that arrived each day. He was offered the *rosette* of the Légion d'honneur. When he refused, the nonplussed Education Minister pointed out that he had accepted the *ruban* (the ribbon, a lower grade). RMG replied that he had done so only on condition that he never wore it: there was therefore no point in accepting another. On 6 December, the Martin du Gards and the Gallimards left Paris for Stockholm. It was the culmination of an extraordinary year for Roger Martin du Gard. The three latest volumes of *Les Thibault*, published simultaneously, had sold well, but he still owed Gallimard more money than he was earning. Then, in October, he was awarded the Prix de la Ville de Paris; to his relief, Gallimard allowed him to keep the 25,000 francs (£1,000 or $5,000 at the time), rather than pay off the debt to his publishers. Now, with the £8,000 from the Nobel Prize, and the ensuing world sale of books, his financial troubles were over.

On 10 December, Gide and Maria went to hear Valéry's inaugural lecture at the Collège de France, where he had been given a Chair of Poetics. Two weeks later, the Petite Dame left for Colpach and Loup Mayrisch, leaving Gide to spend Christmas at the Vaneau with Beth and Pierre.

The Petite Dame arrived back on New Year's Eve, Catherine, from a holiday in the Alps a few days later. On 10 January, Gide and Herbart left on a trip to West Africa. This undertaking, commissioned by the French government, formed part of a 'Commission of Inquiry into the Colonies'. They set sail from Bordeaux on the *Asie*, the same ship on which Gide had travelled to the Congo thirteen years earlier. They arrived at Dakar on 19 January. After spending a few days with Governor-General de Coppet and his wife, they set off inland. A journey of some 400 miles took them out of Senegal to Kayes, in what is now Mali. They pressed on to Bamako, a distance of over 300 miles. Gide notes the 'admirable' work done by many of the French *colons* and regrets that, in *Voyage au Congo*, he had not paid sufficient tribute to the 'endurance, patience, courage, initiative and virtue' shown by many of them: 'There were a few heroes among them; one would wish them to be less rare.' At Bamako, Gide suffered a bad attack of nephritis: it was fortunate that this occurred while they were in a large town, with adequate medical facilities. They decided to cut short their journey and, instead of going further inland, turned south-westwards back to the coast, through Guinea. A ship took them from Conakry to Casablanca. There, on 5 March, they caught a plane to Marseille, arriving in Paris the following day.

On the journey home, Gide had learnt that the condition of his sister-in-law, Valentine, had taken a turn for the worse. On arrival at the Vaneau, he telephoned Cuverville and learnt that Valentine had died during the night. The following day, Gide went to Cuverville to comfort Madeleine in her distress.

Gide arrived back in Paris on 9 March, met at Saint-Lazare by Marc, who had not seen him since his return from Africa, and the two friends dined out together. Next day, Gide went over to the Lutétia, where, in unaccustomed luxury, Martin du Gard had set up residence since his return to Paris four weeks before. That evening, Jean Schlumberger came round. At this time, Gide and his friends talked of little else but the latest news and its implications for the future. In Moscow, a pathetic, almost unrecognizable Bukharin was on trial and rumour had it that, at one point, he went back on his confession and denied his guilt. The latest French government fell and it looked as though Blum would form another Popular Front ministry. On 11 March, the German army marched into Austria, to the apparent jubilation of its people.

Gide spent Easter with Yvonne de Lestrange at Chitré. By this time, her relationship with Marc Allégret had come to an end. (Their son, Michel, then aged nine, remained with his mother.) Marc had already embarked on an affair with Nadine Vogel, a twenty-one-year-old actress and daughter of the art publisher, Lucien Vogel. On Easter morning, Gide received a telephone call from his nephew Jacques Drouin: Madeleine had died. About two o'clock in the morning, she had woken her niece, Odile Drouin, who was sleeping in the next room, complaining of pain in her chest. 'Go and tell your mother, and telephone the doctor,' she said. 'Here's his number and put on a shawl so that you don't catch cold.' Those were almost her last words. When the doctor arrived, she was already dead. During his previous visit to Cuverville, Gide and Madeleine had talked of death: Valentine had died only a month before. 'If ever I become really sick and you are called, I hope that you will arrive . . . too late,' Madeleine had said. 'I'd like to spare you that pain.'[59] They had talked of the last sacraments and Gide said that he was aware of how much Madeleine was drawn to Catholic practices: if ever she wanted him to call a Catholic priest, not only would he have no objection, it would give him great satisfaction to do so. She declared that she would have no wish to see a priest. Yvonne de Lestrange drove Gide straight to Cuverville.

When I approached the bed on which she was lying, I was surprised by the gravity of her face. It was as if her grace and charm, which gave her goodness such radiant strength, dwelt entirely in her gaze; now that her eyes were closed, nothing but austerity remained in the expression of her features; my last sight of her recalls, not her ineffable tenderness, but the severe judgement that she always felt obliged to pass on my life.[60]

The funeral took place the following day. Gide had been unable to get Martin du Gard on the telephone in time; Jean Schlumberger was in Morocco; the Copeaus were in Naples, but their children, Maïene and Pascal, came. Henri Ghéon rushed to Cuverville at once. The body was carried by farm-workers on the estate from the house to the little churchyard. In this way, Gide told the Petite Dame, they avoided 'all the awful pomp and circumstance one usually has at funerals'.[61] According to the Gides' marriage settlement, Madeleine's property remained hers, rather than becoming her husband's. Cuverville, therefore, went to her next of kin, Dominique Drouin, the eldest son of her sister Jeanne, although, in her will, she left her husband the 'usufruct', the use, of the estate for life.

The Petite Dame arrived back at the Vaneau, in Loup Mayrisch's car, half-expecting to find Gide there. She was met by her maid, who told her the news. Gide had already telephoned twice. About nine, she finally brought herself to call Cuverville. Gide admitted that it was a 'blessing' that Madeleine had gone before him, thus avoiding the 'moral suffering' that discovery of Catherine's real parentage would have caused her. Then, given her declining physical powers, she had become almost incapable of real life. But the Petite Dame knew that such practical considerations, concerning the *real* Madeleine and her relations with Gide, would not play much part in his future mental state: 'I think his memory of her will grow stronger and, who knows?, she may come to occupy a larger part in his life than when she was alive.'[62] Over the next few months, Madeleine was to be very much in the forefront of Gide's thoughts. Her death also gave rise to, or revived, a problem relating to the publication of his works. In 1932, Gallimard had decided to republish all Gide's works in several large volumes, arranged in chronological order. These also contained large extracts from the journal, following the same chronological sequence. By 1937, the *Œuvres complètes* had reached Volume XII (there were to be three more). Jacques Schiffrin now proposed to publish a single Pléiade edition of the whole of the journal to date. Hitherto, Gide had adopted the policy, after much heart-searching, of excluding from the published extracts all references to Madeleine. Should he restore those references in a new, complete edition of the journal, since they were excluded in the first place to spare Madeleine's feelings? The Petite Dame suggested another solution: to gather them together, with suitable commentary, and publish them in a small volume devoted to her memory in a limited edition, perhaps even privately. In this way, he would preserve the full picture for posterity, while respecting what would have been Madeleine's wish, at least during the lifetimes of her husband, friends and immediate relations. Gide accepted the argument: the 'mutilated' edition of the *Journal* appeared in 1939, but what was to become *Et nunc manet in te* did not appear until 1947 and then in an edition of thirteen copies, normal publication taking place shortly after Gide's death. The title, meaning 'And now she [or he] remains in you', is borrowed from Virgil's *Culex*. Over the few months following Madeleine's death, Gide wrote the first ten pages, beginning with a simple, moving encapsulation of the phenomenon of mourning: 'Yesterday evening, I was thinking about her; I was talking to her, as I often did, more easily in imagination than in her real presence, when suddenly I said to myself: but she's dead . . .'[63] The work ends with a line of dots, the representation of the 'hole' (the last word in the book) left in the writer's life. On 21 August, he wrote: 'Since Madeleine left me I have lost all taste for life . . . I have only pretended to live, taking no interest in anything or in myself, lacking appetite, taste, curiosity, desire . . .' He was in 'a disenchanted world, with no hope of escape'.[64] 'Isn't Gide over-dramatizing his situation?' we are tempted to ask. Their marriage was a sad mismatch in any of the matters that normally make up a human life. She was an austere, reserved, devout Christian, of 'conventional' views (in full reaction against her mother's transgressing sexuality), devoted to family and to a home that she left less and less; he a restless soul, physically incapable of staying in one place for very long, equally restless and searching in the world of the mind. As a young man he had preached salvation through sensual pleasure; in his middle age he published a defence of homosexuality; as if that were not enough, he then became a Communist fellow-traveller. For the last twenty years of her life, Madeleine had read her husband's writings very selectively. In almost every real sense, Gide's life was elsewhere. He spent relatively little of his time at Cuverville with her; when he did go back, there was little of substance that they could talk about other than the French and English classics. He even had, in his own singular way, an alternative ménage at the Vaneau: a former boyfriend in his own studio and, next door, the Petite Dame, with whom he usually ate, from breakfast, through lunch, tea and dinner, to nightcaps before retiring, with whom he discussed everything in complete freedom, with whom he would entertain friends and with whom friends would entertain him, with whom he often went to the theatre and even more often to the cinema, with whose daughter, too, he had a child. Could Madeleine have meant *so* much to him and, if so, what *did* she mean to him? Towards the end, she had told him what he had meant to her: 'My greatest joys . . . and also my greatest sorrows: the best and the bitterest.'[65] In the first nine or so pages of *Et nunc manet in te*, written during the first few months after Madeleine's death, Gide meditated on the tragic misunderstanding that lay beneath their love:

Latterly I came to understand her much better, I think; but how wrong I had been about her at the height of my love for her! For all the effort of my love was employed not so much in coming closer to her, as in bringing her closer to that ideal figure that I had invented . . . My childish love was indistinguishable from my earliest religious fervour . . . It seemed to me, too, that, in coming closer to God, I was coming closer to her . . .

Today I am astonished at this aberration, which led me to believe that the more ethereal my love, the more worthy I was of her – my naïvety was such that I never wondered whether she would be content with so disembodied a love. The fact that my carnal desires were directed towards other objects scarcely concerned me. And I even managed, conveniently, to convince myself that this was all to the good. Desires, I believed, were proper to men; I found it reassuring not to accept that women could feel the same; or, at least, only women of 'ill-repute' . . .

What I fear that she could not understand was that it was precisely the spiritual power of my love that inhibited any carnal desire. For I was able, elsewhere, to prove that I was not incapable of making love with a woman, providing nothing intellectual or emotional came into it . . . It was only later that I began to realize how cruelly I must have hurt the woman for whom I was ready to give my life . . . In fact, I could only develop, as an individual, by hurting her.[66]

Gide's profound sense of loss was out of all proportion to what Madeleine *qua* real person had brought him. The disproportion of Gide's reaction to that loss can only be explained by her symbolic role. Maria Van Rysselberghe understood this perfectly: 'He has been touched in the most vulnerable part of his heart. The principal figure in the play of his life is no more. He has lost his counterpart, the fixed measure with which he confronted his actions, his true tenderness, his greatest fidelity: in his inner dialogue, the other voice has fallen silent.'[67] Moreover, as a 'symbolic' figure, Madeleine represented all that was best, in some mystical, eternal, immutable form. Although Gide had witnessed the decline of that symbol's earthly remnant, its death was inconceivable: eternal symbols do not die. Once Gide had recovered from the immediate shock of Madeleine's death, with its inevitable, if deferred summons of his own demise, she became again what she had always been, a symbol: *et nunc manet in te*. For Gide, she had always resided more in him than outside him.

Gide left Cuverville for Paris on 24 April. Two days later, he was already thinking of escaping the demands that Paris placed on him. He decided to spend a few weeks with the Desjardins at the Foyer, at Pontigny, and left Paris on 1 May. Some days later, he wrote to Martin du Gard: 'I had hoped to work' [he had taken his new secretary, Lucien Combelle, with him]. 'I don't have the heart for anything any more. I'm just pretending to be alive.'[68] He also tells RMG that the 'commission of inquiry' into the West African colonies seems to have wound up. He had already written two chapters (of the five planned) and submitted them to Coppet, but, given the political situation, there seemed no point in going on with his report.

Gide left Pontigny on 16 May, had lunch in Paris next day with Dorothy Bussy, then went on to Le Tertre. During the week he spent there, Martin du Gard wrote in his *Journal*, 'I "belonged" to Gide, from ten in the morning until eleven in the evening.' RMG also makes some perspicacious remarks on Gide's mental state at this time: 'It is the first *great* sorrow in his life. He bears it in silence, without display of emotion. He is like a convalescent after an amputation, who knows that he will have to live in this new state, and who makes brave efforts to get used to the mutilation.'[69]

On 10 June, Gide left for Amsterdam to see Jef Last, who, as a result of irregularities in his official papers, had been in prison for a time. Gide had intended to go on from there to Norway, but was back in Paris, after 'six days shivering in Holland' (in mid-June). He saw a lawyer about recognizing Catherine officially as his child. However, because, according to French law, she was the child of an adulterous relationship, 'recognition' would have no legal binding. The curious solution arrived at was for the child's father to adopt her as his daughter. For this, two witnesses would be required. So, on 26 July, Gide, with Martin du Gard and Jean Schlumberger, appeared at the *mairie* of the 7th arrondissement and the necessary papers were signed. RMG notes laconically in his *Journal*: 'The declaration that Jean and I signed stipulated that we testified to the good living and "morals" of M. Gide . . . and considered that he had everything required to become an adoptive father.'[70] At the signing, the latest recipient of the Nobel Prize for Literature wished to be described as '*rentier*' (of independent means), rather than as '*homme de lettres*'.

About this time, Marc moved out of his studio at the Vaneau into an apartment at 11 bis rue Lord Byron, near the Etoile, with Nadine Vogel. This meant that Gide had much more peace and quiet in his own part of the apartment, but, as he wrote to Dorothy Bussy, 'I'm taking his absence quite hard.' He then adds, curiously, that he doesn't think that Marc is very happy, with no explanation other than that he is 'overworked'.[71] On 14 July, Gide and the Petite Dame saw Catherine off to Vienna, where she was to spend a month in a school: Austria had been annexed by Germany four months before. War, which would bring an end to all such movements, was over a year away. Indeed by September and the Munich conference, it seemed further away.

After two weeks at Chitré with Yvonne de Lestrange, Gide was back in Paris on 18 August. The Petite Dame, who had been at Pontigny, had arrived back the day before. Next morning, over breakfast, Gide 'unburdened himself of all that was oppressing him': 'I'm going through a real depression at the moment. How can I put it? I'm getting into the habit of speaking of myself in the past tense.' To cheer him up, the Petite Dame recounted how, at Pontigny, an old friend of hers told her of a sort of opinion poll that he had carried out among the young people there. Gide, he told them, had been the major literary figure for his own generation, as Barrès had been for the previous one. Who, for you, holds that position today? he asked. Several had said: 'Nobody.' But far more had said 'Mais encore, Gide!'[72] Later that day, the Petite Dame left for her annual *cure* at Mondorf, followed by a stay at Colpach.

The following day, Gide saw a young German painter, called Kurt Erichson, who for two years had been writing passionate letters to which he had responded with 'calculated moderation'. In each letter, the young man had said how he would leave Riga (Latvia), where he was 'vegetating miserably' as a political exile and come to Paris, simply to be near Gide and to see him from time to time. Gide had rehearsed all the arguments against such a move. What could he find in Paris other than unemployment, poverty and despair? Rejecting his advice, Erichson had arrived in Paris unannounced, while Gide was at Chitré, and moved into an hotel. What little money he had saved, enough to live on moderately for two years in Latvia, was now almost spent. Gide talked to him at length, explaining to him that he would not be able to see him again because he was leaving Paris next day. He found that he could not help thinking about the young man, who knew no one else in Paris, and felt that he should have done more for him. Two days later, Gide was again accosted by Erichson, who protested that he 'worshipped' Gide 'as a god'. Gide was put off by the German's professions of love: 'Faced with excessive effusions I become like ice and feel like thumbing my nose at anyone who declares that he "worships me as a god".' The young man begged Gide to live with him for a fortnight. Gide protested: he was an old man, his time was not his own, etc. Kurt

had come too late. The German laid his head on Gide's shoulder and
began to sob uncontrollably. And what, one may be wondering, did this
sorry figure look like that Gide, lonely, sixty-eight and surely the world's
best-known living homosexual (there not being, it is true, many known to
be such at the time), was trying so hard to get rid of? He was twenty-six,
'a very handsome fellow who looks like one of the athletes I admired so
much yesterday in the film of the Berlin Olympics'. Kurt Erichson called
on Gide again the following morning, begging for only ten minutes of his
time. Gide ended up 'wasting two hours with him'.[73] Gide then took him
off to see Louis-Daniel Hirsch, sales director at Gallimard, to see if he could
suggest a gallery where Erichson might exhibit his paintings. That was the
last we hear of Kurt Erichson.

On 24 August, Gide finally left Paris for Cuverville. Jacques Schiffrin
came to stay for a couple of weeks and, with Drouin, they went over Gide's
translation of *Antony and Cleopatra*. (It was to be published in Schiffrin's
Pléiade complete Shakespeare.) 'Certain passages are giving a lot of trouble,'
he writes in the *Journal*. 'They are usually Shakespeare's least good ones.'
The first week in September produced day after day of splendid weather:
'Everything that breathes should feel happy, it seems. And, before this
display of beauty, my heart remains indifferent, almost hostile . . . What
divine indifference to man's infinite misery!'[74]

Gide then went to Braffy to stay with Jean Schlumberger for a couple of
weeks. On 13 September, they listened on the radio to Hitler's Nuremberg
speech. 'The call to arms permits a facile eloquence,' Gide notes, 'and it is
easier to urge men to fight and to stir up their passions than it is to temper
them and to perform the patient labours of peace . . . The affirmation of
strength contains a permission to be stupid.'[75] On 23 September, Gide
drove to Lisieux station to meet Dorothy Bussy and bring her back to Braffy.
Next day, Gide took Dorothy to see the Schlumberger family house, Val
Richer. That evening, Dorothy was invited to comment on various points
in the *Antony and Cleopatra* translation. But it was difficult to keep their minds
on such things, listening to every news programme on the radio, as the
Anglo-French negotiations with Germany seemed to be collapsing and war
imminent. The Petite Dame, who was back in Paris, had been expected at
Braffy next day. But, given the uncertainty of the political situation, it was
felt that the Braffy party should be called off. The Petite Dame would stay
in Paris and, the following day, Gide and Dorothy Bussy would go to
Cuverville for a few days, before travelling back to Paris, Dorothy going on
to Nice as soon as possible. Before leaving Braffy, however, Gide took

Dorothy through the woods to La Roque, which he had not seen since he sold it. He showed her the various things that she already knew from his books: the postern, the waterfall, the tower where Jammes and Ghéon had stayed. He enumerated all the changes brought about by the new owners and was visibly disturbed by his memories, almost to the point of remorse. Next day, he was showing Dorothy the literary sights or, perhaps, 'sites', at Cuverville: the *porte étroite*, the path by which Jérôme came back to the house, the beech grove, now without Alissa's bench. Indoors again, he took Dorothy to Madeleine's (Alissa's) room.

On 29 September, Gide and Dorothy arrived at the Vaneau, to be joined a little later by Janie Bussy, who had come from Scotland to join her mother in Nice. The news seemed to worsen every day. A week before, at Godesberg, Chamberlain had been presented with a memorandum from Hitler, in which Germany increased its demands concerning Czechoslovakia. The British fleet had been mobilized. The day before Gide's return, Jean Schlumberger had arrived with a suitcase in which he took away all the Petite Dame's *Cahiers*, to be kept, in greater safety, at Braffy. The Petite Dame herself was very touched that everyone seemed to think that these were the most important things in the apartment to be saved. She and Gide wondered whether they should cut short Catherine's stay in Austria. They decided to wait and see how the situation developed. (In the event, she arrived back a few days later.) That evening, Gide's German translator, Ferdinand Hardekopf, called. The poor man felt doubly threatened, by the Nazis, because of whom he had left Germany and now, with war imminent, by the French authorities. Hardekopf was, said the Petite Dame, a 'terrified wreck' and had come to get Gide to give him a testimonial without which, he feared, he would end up in a French concentration camp. On 30 September, after an intervention from Mussolini, the Munich accords were signed and war, it seemed, had been avoided. In fact, it had been postponed – by eleven months.

On 17 October, Marc, who had just arrived back from London, informed Gide that he was getting married the following day. Only a small number of relations and friends had been asked to attend the ceremony. Gide counted himself out, but, in order not to appear disapproving, agreed to attend a small party that evening. At the end of October, Jef Last came to stay and, very soon, became great friends with Catherine. He even suggested that Catherine go back to Holland with him in the holidays, believing that she would have a good influence on his own daughter, who was the same age, and thus counteract his wife's 'mystico-Communist influence'. On 3 November, Gide learnt of Francis Jammes' death. Asked to speak about his old (former) friend on the radio, he declined. He sent a conventional telegram to the widow. November saw a reopening of diplomatic relations between Gide and Marcel Jouhandeau, Catholic writer, one-time teacher, lover of adolescent boys – and Robert Levesque's teacher and mentor. This reunion, after decades, had been brought about, engineered almost, by François Mauriac's son, Claude, a close friend of Jouhandeau's and, for some weeks now, a friend of Gide's. In his *Conversations avec André Gide*, Claude Mauriac devotes several pages to the reunion and subsequent meetings in November 1938. The Petite Dame accompanied Gide to the dinner at the Jouhandeaus' (the writer had a stormy, but longstanding marriage to a rather ridiculous woman who acted under the stage name of Caryathis) and left a pithy, acerbic account: 'I left quite worn out, drunk with the picturesqueness of it all. Caryathis talks a lot, talks all the time. Seeing them together, one would never guess how badly they get on. He seems filled with admiration for her, as if under a spell. Their comments on politics and social matters are of the most utter, unbelievable stupidity . . . [Their] anti-semitic attitude so brutal, so unjust . . .'[76]

By the end of December, the temperature had dropped to −15°C and rain was coming in through the roof of the studio. Gide expended all his ingenuity in keeping warm and avoiding draughts, covering himself in a varied assortment of clothes. On 23 December, the Petite Dame left for Colpach (Catherine had already joined her mother at Cabris a few days before) and Gide moved over into the Lutétia, where Martin du Gard was also staying. The two old friends had 'endless conversations' and were joined every day by Jean Schlumberger.

The Petite Dame arrived back at the Vaneau on 2 January, Catherine from Cabris the following day. Gide arrived a couple of days later – and promptly plunged into a dozen Simenon thrillers that he had not yet read. One day, the Petite Dame observed Gide 'sitting on a low chair, jammed up against a radiator, his knees under his chin, all huddled up, wearing a brown house suit, with every button done up, a great black felt hat on his head. He looked like some big, expensive, fluffy toy, a bespectacled monkey.'[77] His thoughts were on Egypt and the sun, but it was with some apprehension that he contemplated travelling alone: his first choice of companion, Pierre Herbart, had already agreed to supervise the building of Loup Mayrisch's new house at Cabris and he would not be free for another nine months or so. In the end, Gide did set out alone, joining Robert Levesque at the end for a week or two in Greece. 'I haven't travelled alone for a long time,' he confided, rather apprehensively, to his *Journal*. 'I always needed a younger companion, someone to set the pace; his pleasure would be catching.'[78] He set sail on 26 January, arriving in Alexandria four days later. From there, he was given a lift by car to Cairo by the director of excavations at Luxor, Alexandre Varille. An after-dinner walk produced not a single face that gave him any pleasure. Later, 'to break the boredom', he set out, 'my pocket full of baksheesh, and my heart full of undistributed smiles'.[79] Gide was feeling old and lonely, but his depressed mood was not to last. Guiraud, one of the directors, took him on a two-hour tour of the Cairo Museum. Then, in the afternoon, Louis Massignon, Melchite priest and orientalist, whom he had already met in Paris, drove him to a monastery on a hill outside the city, from which he had a splendid view of Cairo's mosques and, in the distance, 'in a luminous dust haze', the Pyramids. That same evening, he took the night train to Luxor, where he arrived, refreshed from the comforts of the *wagon-lit*, early next morning. By four o'clock that first afternoon, the old incorrigible was writing:

No, I no longer have any great wish to fornicate; at least it is no longer a need as in the great days of my youth. But I have a need to know that, if I wanted to, I could . . . I mean that I like a country only if it offers many opportunities for fornication. The most beautiful buildings in the world cannot replace that; why not admit it frankly? This morning, at last, walking through the native quarter of Luxor, I was well served. I caressed with my eyes ten, twelve, twenty charming faces. It seemed that my look was understood at once; the response was a quite unmistakable smile. There are places, whole countries, where the most desire-laden looks get no response at all; others, Russia, for example, where the slightest wink comes back, like the dove, bearing its olive branch. The laws of the country have nothing to do with this . . . assent is there and that sort of amused connivance that needs only a few words to be expressed . . .[80]

If Gide had a problem during his six weeks at Luxor, it was that practically every adolescent male Egyptian appeared, not only to be available, but in competition with the others for the attention of men like him. Everyone seemed to regard this as entirely normal. So much so that, most of the time, he felt little desire to take advantage of the situation: it was all too easy, too superficial. No doubt, too, as he suggests, age was finally taking its toll: the heyday in the blood was tame. The pursuit of Gide the pursuer by the youth of Luxor began that first day. He wandered out of the town and looked at a boy walking in the opposite direction carrying salad vegetables, obviously on his way home. Gide responded to his 'playful greeting' as he passed. Ali was 'not more than fourteen, hardly fifteen', 'very handsome . . . perhaps no more handsome than many others, but strong-looking, radiating health and joy'. The boy offered Gide some of the best leaves, carefully picking them out of the heart of a lettuce. As they walked, Ali never stopped talking, though Gide had some difficulty in knowing 'whether he was trying to speak Arabic or English', but he could tell, by the boy's smiles and gestures, that he was making 'obscene' proposals. They reached a gate, which Ali opened with a huge key. They passed first through one courtyard, then another. After what seemed like an argument with some people in one building, he took Gide into another. In the semi-darkness, Ali lifted his long tunic and dropped his trousers and, without more ado, offered his behind. This was not, as we might say nowadays, Gide's 'scene': 'That was enough for me. I had no wish to pursue the adventure further.' He was suspicious of what the people in the other shed might do – and he was carrying all his money on him. He moved to the door. At first, Ali tried to stop him leaving, then walked back with him to his hotel. Gide gave him two piastres.[81]

Over the next few weeks, Gide looked out for Ali, without success. Then, a few days before leaving, he noticed him amongst a group of boys talking to an Englishman, whom he had seen the day before watching some young Arab men bathing. He called him over and the two went off in a boat and, under a blazing sun and the indulgent eye of the oarsman, they lay down, arm-in-arm. Seldom, said Gide, had he experienced 'such reciprocity, such amused, unhurried caresses'. There was 'not a single defect in that body, so young, but already as muscular as an athlete, supple and hard'. This time, the boy struck just the right chord with him, treating him with tenderness, but also in a boyish, light-hearted way.[82]

Between the two meetings with Ali, Gide discovered the gardens that separated the Luxor Hotel from the Winter Palace: 'At the end is an orangery, in which a large number of young gardeners work, rather indolently. When I pass, they stop working and try, by gestures and exhibitions, to get me to go into the shade. One might well believe that they had been chosen on purpose.'[83] Four weeks later, he returned to the subject of the gardeners, none of whose many solicitations he had taken up: 'When one of them fails to attract, another offers himself, quite shamelessly . . . The youngest of them may not be more than ten, but he is already being trained by the others. I circulate among all that, amused, but more or less insensitive to it, but I give them each a half-piastre, so as not to discourage them. What I'd like to know is how the English behave when faced with these offers. The insistence of the propositions can only be explained by the fact that they are not always rejected.' For perhaps the first time in his life, however, Gide did reject such propositions. One afternoon, as he was leaving the hotel, the head waiter, 'a tall, most dignified negro', presented him 'the most modest, most decently dressed, most beautiful boy (he was probably thirteen) I had seen since my arrival in Egypt.'[84] At first, he thought he was the head waiter's son, then, with a broad smile, the waiter stroked the boy's cheek and pushed him towards Gide, who took the boy's hand. The boy smiled back. The waiter discreetly withdrew. Subsequently, the boy came back several times, looked at Gide and smiled.

The six weeks at Luxor were not entirely spent walking around and rejecting attractive propositions. Apart from writing a large part of *Et nunc manet in te* and the part of the journal that became *Carnets d'Egypte*, he worked on *Thésée*, and turned, yet again, to *Robert ou l'intérêt général*. He visited the Ancient Egyptian and Greek sites at Karnak and Thebes and, accompanied by archaeological experts, went farther afield to the Valley of the Kings. On 16 March, he took the overnight train to Alexandria, where he stayed for a few days. With a group of French people, including the head of the French Lycée, he went out to Rosetta. Before leaving Alexandria, he 'handed out, here and there, a few piastres and half-piastres, to the most wretched children, overcome by the look in their eyes and their smiles of gratitude'.[85]

Gide boarded a ship that took him to Athens. There he sent a telegram announcing his arrival to Robert Levesque, who got the first available boat from Spetsai, where he was teaching in a school. Of the week spent in Greece, Gide tells us little; what we know of it we owe to some twenty pages of Levesque's journal.[86] After climbing up to the Acropolis and back, they set off on a tour of mainland Greece, travelling by a combination of train, bus, hired car and horse-drawn carriage, visiting ruined temples and crowded churches, pursued, wherever they went, by crowds of boys, none of whom seemed willing or able to be separated from his friends. On Good Friday, they learnt that Italy had attacked Albania. The Greeks felt that they might be next: everywhere they went there was great hatred of the Italians – and great love of the British and French. Robert returned to his school on Spetsai and Gide embarked on a sixty-hour train journey across Europe, arriving in Paris on 17 April, suffering from catarrh, laryngitis and coughing fits.

While Gide had been away, Jef Last had written to him from Norway, desperately asking him 'to do what he could' for his friend Domela, who, like thousands of other refugees from Germany and Austria, had now been interned by the French government. This blanket policy of interning all German citizens or ex-citizens, most of them being either the bitterest opponents of the Nazis (Communists or democrats) and/or their greatest victims (Jews), as Europe moved towards war, was particularly heavy-handed – and it was carried out by the French police, who had no liking for either category and who, of all French people, later collaborated most willingly and assiduously with the German occupiers. Domela's situation was made even worse in the camp by being regularly persecuted by his Communist fellow-inmates, alerted to his critical, independent stance in relation to the Party and the Soviet Union. (Jef Last, though at liberty, was also suffering at the hands of 'comrades', finding all outlets for his work being closed to him, as the word went round that he was no longer to be regarded as 'sound'.) On his return to Paris, Gide began at once to try and get Domela – and others – released. On 1 May, he spent several hours seeing officials at the Ministry of the Interior. Next day, he left for Perpignan, where he believed Domela was being held. Domela was released four weeks later, with a two-month permit to stay in Luxembourg, where Loup Mayrisch organized his welfare.

Back in Paris, Gide took the Petite Dame and Catherine to see a new Japanese film version of *La Symphonie Pastorale* (Yamamoto Satsuo's *Den'en Kōkyōgaku*), being shown privately. It seemed a very good piece of cinema, though it was difficult for the author to recognize his own work in it: 'The pastor has become a teacher, his son a younger brother . . . etc. etc.'[87] Catherine said that she would now like to read the book: she had previously never read any of her father's works and he seemed rather unwilling that she should.

One May evening, Gide dined at the Mauriacs'. Not only had Claude brought about a revival in the friendship between his father and Gide, put under some strain in recent years by the ideological gap between them, but Claude had, on his own account, established a developing, if cautious, friendship with Gide. Over the next few weeks, they were to see quite a lot of one another. Claude was working on an investigation into the condition of foreign refugees in France for the journal *La Flèche*. To help him in his work, Gide introduced him to André Dubois, assistant *chef de cabinet* to the Interior Minister, who had already responded to Gide's pleas on behalf of refugees. A pleasant, intelligent young man, Dubois later confided to Claude Mauriac how much Gide had meant to him in his youth. 'The marvellous thing about him,' he said, 'is that *he doesn't know who he is.*' He felt quite overcome by Gide's shy, embarrassed manner as he apologized for taking up his time – he a man who would have counted it a privilege merely to meet Gide.[88]

The end of June saw the appearance in the Bibliothèque de la Pléiade of the first volume of the complete *Journal*, covering a period of about fifty years, from autumn 1889 to 26 January 1939. Hitherto the journal had appeared only in selected sections placed, chronologically, at the end of each volume of the *Œuvres complètes*. This had brought the journal only up to 1932. In addition, two more volumes, *Pages de Journal* and *Nouvelles Pages de Journal* had brought the entries up to 1935. From then on, all the entries in the Pléiade edition were previously unpublished. Gide approached the prospect of publication with some trepidation: 'I'm expecting a great outcry . . .', he wrote to Martin du Gard.[89] RMG himself had often criticized Gide for his appalling indiscretions in the *Journal* and, over the next few weeks, the protests from old friends were not slow in coming.

On 27 June, Gide left Paris to join the Mauriacs, father and son, at their country house at Malagar, near Bordeaux. Over the two weeks, each of the three men spent part of most days alone, writing, but much of the time was spent together, making excursions by car to Bordeaux and the surrounding countryside, talking and reading aloud. They paid two visits to a camp set up for Spanish refugees. The two older men talked of the literary figures they had known – Wilde, Verlaine, Jammes, Proust, Cocteau, Rivière. They read to each other from Racine and Corneille. They read from the Bible. Gide, 'in that voice of his, which is both diabolical and divine', as Claude described it in a letter to his mother,[90] read little-known, highly equivocal passages concerning the incest of Amnon, son of David, and Abraham's attempt to bargain with God in order to save Sodom from destruction. They talked a great deal about religion, always, it seems, at Gide's instigation, as if he were obstinately obsessed with religious questions, never content with his host's defence of his Catholic beliefs. During Gide's stay, both Mauriacs were avidly reading Gide's *Journal*. One night, François said to his son: 'I've just read the passages in his *Journal*, from 1917, in which he's dying of love for Marc Allégret. What heartrending and often magnificent cries they are! And what courage to publish that . . . He's a man who cannot bear lies. He is determined that nothing about him will be hidden. That insistence, one has to admit, gives him back a sort of miraculous virginity, a certain purity . . .'[91] 'It's curious,' Claude Mauriac later wrote, 'to read fifty pages of a *Journal*, whose author is with one throughout the day. My father and I emerged from reading Gide only to speak to Gide.'[92]

Gide had arranged with Yvonne de Lestrange for his hosts to spend a few days with him at Chitré on their way back to Paris. They left Malagar early on 11 July. On the way, they paid homage to the great essayist at the Château de Montaigne. After lunch, they drove on through Angoulême, arriving at last at Vouneuil-sur-Vienne and the imposing Château de Chitré.

'That poor Mme de Lestrange is bored,' Gide had said at Malagar. 'We must go and see her.' They found a clearly unhappy Yvonne de Lestrange, living with Michel, her ten-year-old son by Marc Allégret, a New Zealand nanny and servants in the 'boring sumptuousness' of a huge, ugly château, cut off from all signs of life. The *châtelaine*, Claude Mauriac writes, was 'still young, almost beautiful, silent, absent . . . beyond life'. This 'extremely polite', 'conventional' woman was the same, Claude Mauriac notes with some astonishment, as the younger, emancipated woman who had cared for lepers when 'in revolt against her class'.[93] The Mauriacs had no wish to stay longer than one night – despite François' bed, which reminded him of Louis XIV's. For Gide's sake, and his alone, they stayed for three nights in all.

A few days later, Gide left for Mont-Dore, a resort in the hills south of Clermont-Ferrand, for treatment to his throat. He stayed there for three weeks, leaving on 10 August, with Robert Levesque, who had come to join him, for Pontigny. Paul Desjardins' wife, who was now running the *décades*, was particularly anxious that Gide should attend the second *décade* on the problem of refugees in France (14–24 August), which Claude Mauriac was helping to organize. During the few days before the opening of the *décade*, Gide made the first draft of a preface for an English translation of *Les Liaisons dangereuses* (*Dangerous Acquaintances*, London, Nonesuch Press, 1940). On 22 August, everyone sat around the wireless listening to the news; to their astonishment, a non-aggression pact had been signed between Germany and the USSR. The third *décade*, 'Intellectual, Moral and Spiritual Relations between England and France', organized jointly with the *Times Literary Supplement*, was due to start on 26 August. It had hardly begun, when it was decided, in view of the obvious imminence of war and the poor attendance, to bring it to an abrupt end. It was also the last of the *décades* at Pontigny. Paul Desjardins died the following year, aged eighty-one. On 1 September, Germany invaded Poland. On 3 September, Great Britain and France declared war on Germany, thus honouring their treaty with Poland. Gide was expected at Cabris the following day. Finding that the trains were not working normally and those that were were full, he accepted a lift in the car of Aline Lion, reputedly an illegitimate daughter of Edward VII. The two embarked on what turned out to be a complicated odyssey that same day, 3 September, arriving at Cabris just after midnight on the morning of 5 September.

Gide was one of the generation of Frenchmen to have lived through three wars with Germany: when the Franco-Prussian war broke out, he was not yet one year old; the First World War had occurred in his late forties; now, at a few months away from seventy, he saw France yet again at war with its great neighbour.

17

Another War: Retreat and Exile

(SEPTEMBER 1939 – MAY 1945)

Yes, all that might well disappear, that effort of culture that seemed to us so admirable (and I am speaking not only of French culture). At the rate at which we are going, there will soon not be many who feel the need of it, who understand it; not many left to realize that it is no longer understood.

Strive as we may to shelter those treasures from destruction, no shelter is safe. A bomb can get the better of a museum. There is no acropolis that the flood of barbarism cannot reach, no ark that it cannot sink.

We cling to wreckage.[1]

So Gide confided in his *Journal*, a week after the declaration of war. In fact, since the collapse of Poland, occupied by the Germans from the West and by the Russians from the East, there were no further hostilities for another six months; it was the period of the so-called 'phoney war'. Young Frenchmen, including Gide's Drouin nephews, the Allégret brothers, Claude Mauriac, had been called up – although Marc Allégret, 'vaguely "secretary to the general staff"',[2] was continuing to live, with his young wife, in their apartment near the Etoile. For everyone else, life continued much as before, though with a great question-mark hanging over the future. Those who had any choice in the matter did not know what to do for the best. Gide and the Petite Dame would, normally, have gone back to Paris, but felt that it might be safer if, for Catherine's sake, they stayed in the South, well away from German bombs (everyone knew what had happened to Warsaw) and even, perhaps, a German invasion. Les Audides, Beth's house in Cabris, was already housing Beth, Pierre, Catherine and the Petite Dame. There was no room to accommodate Gide as well, so he took a room at the village inn, but had his meals at Les Audides. A week later, he moved into La Messuguière, the large house that Loup Mayrisch had just had built in Cabris. There Gide passed the time reading – Cyril Tourneur's two tragedies and Proust (he had reached *La Prisonnière*). The two Vaneau maids arrived and were put up in a small house nearby.

On 5 October Gide accepted an invitation to go and stay with the Bussys in Nice. Astonishing as it may seem, given his and Dorothy's troubled relations, he stayed there for the next seven months, making only brief visits to Cabris – age and the war had obviously appeased old yearnings and healed old wounds. The Petite Dame spent the first week of November in Nice, staying at the Petit Palais, but seeing Gide every day over meals at the Bussys'. 'He seems to be very happy at the Bussys',' she wrote, 'their studious side leaves him free and he's practising his English with ardour and tenacity.'[3]

For some weeks, Gide had been very concerned about Stoisy Sternheim, who, like almost all the German émigrés in France, had been put in an internment camp. His other German translator, Ferdinand Hardekopf, and his wife, the former actress Sita Staub, were still at Pontigny, living, at Gide's expense, in the village. During the First World War, Gide had worked on behalf of refugees, mainly Allied Belgians; now he found himself caught up in a long, time-consuming campaign to help those Germans, who, though technically France's enemies, were, in fact, the Nazis' greatest enemies. These camps were often referred to as 'concentration camps', which, given the connotations that the term later acquired, is misleading. Nevertheless, conditions in the camps were extremely harsh. Gide frequently complained that the French authorities, unlike the British, were treating these friends of France like prisoners of war. Through his friend André Dubois, at the Interior Ministry, he was able to effect improvements in their conditions and the release of many of the interned whom he could guarantee to be neither dangerous nor suspect. These included Franz Pfemfert, a former publisher, whom Gide had met in Prague; Valeriu Marcu, a German writer of Rumanian Jewish origin, an early Communist who had known Lenin, but who had later moved away from left-wing politics altogether; Franz Schoenberner, writer and editor of the pre-Nazi satirical paper *Simplicissimus*; and Walter Hasenclever, playwright. The first three escaped to make a new life in the New World; the last committed suicide in June 1940. Gide made frequent visits on their behalf to the Fort d'Antibes. One day, he thought he recognized one of the internees. 'Where have I met you before?' he asked. 'At Pontigny, Monsieur Gide!' the man replied. 'We spent ten days together at the *décade* on the refugees.'[4]

Much against his own inclinations, Martin du Gard had given in to his wife's wish to return to France as soon as possible. On 11 November, they left Martinique by plane for San Domingo. From there they took an American boat that brought them to a freezing New York on 19 November. All voyages by American ships to Europe had been suspended, but the

Martin du Gards were able to get places on the *Conte di Savoia*, 'the Italian *Queen Mary*', which landed them at Genoa on 5 December. (Italy had not yet declared war on France and Great Britain: this was to come the following June.) They were back in Nice a couple of days later. Before long, RMG left Hélène in Nice and took off for Paris, where he moved into the Lutétia, nursing a bad cold, 'for the whole of Paris has a bad cold, the métro is a concert of coughing, people *freeze everywhere*; a frozen bouillabaisse in the streets, deserted by the road-sweepers'. Paris is 'gloomy by day, sinister by six in the evening'.[5] By Christmas, he was at Le Tertre, where he hoped to resume his life as 'gentleman-writer'.

On 14 February, the Petite Dame and Beth came to spend a week at the Petit Palais. They saw a lot of Gide, usually over meals at the Bussys'. Jean Schlumberger arrived on the same day and also moved into the Petit Palais, so there was another reunion of old friends. Before leaving, the Petite Dame was able to have lunch alone with Gide and discuss matters of a personal nature. Much to her surprise, Gide seemed to feel quite at home with the Bussys – as she did with Beth and Pierre. Nevertheless, she regarded these arrangements as only temporary: she had every intention of renewing her 'vie en commun' with Gide at some future date. It would be better, not only for them, but also for Catherine. Gide agreed entirely: when the political situation looked clearer and more stable, they would either return to Paris or find somewhere to live in Nice.

One day, the Petite Dame went into Nice to call on her old friend, to find that he had now recovered enough from a bout of renal colic to get up and go off to the cinema. Gide was contemplating going back to Paris. In the end, he gave up the idea – he was not to see Paris again until the end of the war. Perhaps he and the Petite Dame should go and spend a week or two at Vence. Using Loup's car, they investigated the hotel at Vence, the Domaine de la Conque, found it excellent, then drove down to Nice to collect Gide's things. Before long, they had resumed all their old habits. Like everyone else, they discussed the news, 'fulminating' against the pusillanimity of Chamberlain, Pius XII and practically all the French politicians. On 10 May, they were shocked to learn of the invasion of Holland, Belgium and Luxembourg; the same day, German troops entered France near Sedan, in the Ardennes. On 26 May, the British began to ship their troops back from Dunkirk. (Denmark and Norway had already fallen to the Germans a month before.) Gide was particularly concerned about the fate of Jef Last, from whom he had heard nothing for weeks: the success of his most recent book, on Van der Lubbe, the supposed instigator of the Reichstag fire, would have endeared him to the Germans even less than before. In fact, he was to spend the war in Amsterdam. The Bussys arrived in Vence, having decided to leave their house in Nice, in view of Mussolini's claim on the once-Italian 'Comté de Nice': Italy declared war on France three weeks later. They moved into a rented villa that the Petite Dame had found for them. While in Vence, the Bussys (and consequently Gide) saw a great deal of their friend Henri Matisse, a long-time resident of the township.

Roland Cailleux, Gide's doctor, had accepted a lift in the car of a young Belgian refugee and patient, Vezal, to his family property at Saint-Genès-la-Tourette in the Puy-de-Dôme, in central France. Gide expressed interest and was asked to join them: from Saint-Genès, he would go on to Vichy, where he would see an old Swiss friend and financier, Arnold Naville, who was there at the time, supervising the affairs of the Banque Ottomane. The three set out at 7 p.m. on 4 June, arriving next day at 5 p.m. The journey of 600 kilometres (375 miles) had taken them twenty-two hours, the two young men sharing the driving. Apart from a two-hour break at Puy for a meal, they were frequently stopped by police checking people's papers. The roads were also heavily congested, even at night, by army movements and civilians more than usually on the move. On arrival at Vichy, Gide found a message from Cabris with news of his nephew, Domi Drouin: for the past month nothing had been heard of him. Apparently, he had joined the British troops at Dunkirk and was now in London.

On 14 June, the day that the French government left Paris for Bordeaux, Gide wrote:

How can one deny that Hitler has played the game in masterly fashion, not allowing himself to be bound by any scruple, by any rule of a game that, after all, has none . . . In the tragic light of events there suddenly appeared the profound dilapidation of France, which Hitler was only too well aware of. Everywhere incoherence, indiscipline, the claim to chimerical rights, the repudiation of all duties . . .

We shouldn't have won the other war. We were taken in by that false victory. The relaxation that followed was our undoing. (On this subject, Nietzsche spoke words of gold. *Thoughts out of Season*.) Yes, we were ruined by victory. But will we learn from our defeat? The sickness has gone so deep that it may well be incurable.[6]

Gide saw Arnold Naville and, on 16 June, left Vichy with Naville's wife and younger daughter Dora, bound for Alet-les-Bains, a small spa town in the Pyrenees. On the way, they picked up Naville's elder daughter, Renée, who was married to Yves Allégret. If Gide had stayed at Vichy a few more days, he would have been joined by the German army, the French government, which had already been in Bordeaux for a week, and Marshal Pétain, recalled from his embassy in Madrid. The signing of an armistice on 22 June divided the country into two zones, the north and west under German occupation, the south and east under a puppet, fascist-type régime headed by Pétain.

Meanwhile, at Le Tertre, the Germans were approaching rapidly and Martin du Gard set about burning compromising documents, including the entire 'German' section of his journal for 1938. His friends the Emmanuel Berls buried their dollars, sterling and diamonds in the garden. At 5 p.m. on 24 June, there was 'a sudden invasion of the park and house by officers, men, motorbikes, armoured cars, tanks . . . Swastika on the roof. Feeling of servitude.' The Germans wanted to take over the whole house. A polite discussion took place, after which the officer in charge gave in, saying: 'Difficile d'être vainqueur!'[7] (RMG left Le Tertre a few days later for Lyon, then Vichy, arriving in Nice on 3 August.) On the same day, at Carcassonne, Gide wrote in his *Journal*: 'Yesterday evening we listened, astonished, to Pétain's latest broadcast. Can it be? Was it Pétain himself speaking? Freely? . . . How can he speak of France as intact after handing over more than half the country to the enemy? . . . How can one not agree with Churchill? [Who had become Prime Minister on 10 May.] Not give one's wholehearted support to General de Gaulle's declaration? Is it not enough for France to be beaten? Must she also be dishonoured?'[8]

The government was not the only French institution to burn 'incriminating' documents and to leave the capital. The Librairie Gallimard/*NRF* did likewise, moving first to a couple of country houses owned by Gaston Gallimard and his mother near Avranches, on the Channel coast, then to a house near Carcassonne owned by Joë Bousquet, a poet paralysed by a bullet in his spine in 1918 and a friend of Alibert's. It was there that Gide called on the '*treize épaves*' (thirteen pieces of wreckage) of the *NRF*,[9] headed by the Gaston Gallimards and the Jean Paulhans. (The Gallimards, incidentally, had heard nothing of their son Claude since May. He had, in fact, been taken prisoner by the Germans during the Belgian campaign and spent much of the war in Germany. He was to head the publishing house from 1976 to 1988.) Gide began his *cure* at Ginoles-les-Bains, where he stayed for about three weeks. He read a lot of Goethe (the supreme symbol of that *other* Germany) and meditated on the state to which their two countries had come. What did France have to set against the Germans, with 'the superiority of their armaments, their numbers, their discipline, their impetus, their trust in their leaders, their unanimous faith in the

Führer', but 'disorder, incompetence, negligence, internal divisions, decay'?[10]

By July, Gide was back in Cabris, where he moved into La Messuguière. Gide and the Petite Dame were both struck by the changes, physical and psychological, that seemed to have occurred in their friend Loup Mayrisch since they saw her last. Her state was not improved when she learnt that her son-in-law, Pierre Viénot, deputy and former Under-Secretary of State for Foreign Affairs in the Popular Front government, had been arrested in Morocco, after arriving with other parliamentarians, following the removal of the government from Bordeaux. Because, legally, he was in the army at the time, he was charged with desertion. (He was then brought back to France and, in December, given an eight-year suspended sentence. He then joined the Resistance, was arrested, escaped and, in April 1943, joined de Gaulle's Free French government in London.) Some days later, Gide left Cabris to spend some time with Marc Allégret and his wife at Cap d'Antibes, where they had gathered round themselves a group of friends from the world of the cinema, with a view to setting up new studios in the so-called 'Free Zone'.

Gide's efforts on behalf of his refugee friends were beginning to bear fruit. Stoisy Sternheim was released from internment in early August, as was Sita Staub, the German actress who had left Germany with Ferdinand Hardekopf. Hardekopf himself was released a couple of weeks later. That, of course, was not the end of the matter: they then had to be found accommodation and helped financially. They could also be very time-consuming: the Hardekopfs, in particular, were in a bad way psychologically, requiring great sympathy and understanding. Martin du Gard's patience was sorely tried at times; Gide's seemed endless. Gide was even getting attentions from those, nominally, on the other side. He was deeply moved by a letter from a young German lieutenant who had met him a few years before in Berlin, probably, though this is not made clear, in one of the homosexual nightclubs. He had arrived in Paris, 'the city of his heart', and found it empty and gloomy, 'its soul torn from it'. The first thing he did was to try to find Gide: he had gone to the offices of the *NRF* for news of him, only to discover that Gide had deserted Paris.

On 23 September, Valeriu Marcu came for lunch. He had just seen Heinrich Mann off from Marseille, on a boat bound for New York, and had a message from Thomas Mann, who was working for a committee organizing refuge in the United States for European intellectuals who felt threatened. If Gide so wished, the necessary papers would be sent him.

Gide replied that, at present, he had no wish to leave France. Some of his acquaintances did leave, including some who had less to fear than he: Julien Green and his friend Robert de Saint Jean, Stravinsky, André Breton, Jacques Maritain, even Jules Romains, who in the immediate pre-war period had accepted German patronage. Gide did all he could to help those most vulnerable to get out. Within weeks, he took up Mann's offer in order to get the Hardekopfs and four other German refugees to the United States. Many of Gide's most virulent critics, those who, from a nationalist or Catholic point of view, had attacked his internationalist spirit and 'immoral' influence, rushed to collaborate with the Nazis, those upholders of true patriotism and uncompromising morality. Henri Béraud wrote for the fascist weekly *Gringoire*, heading one of his articles: 'Great Britain must be reduced to a state of slavery!'; Henri Massis wrote for the *Revue des Deux Mondes*, now a semi-official mouthpiece of Vichy; Charles Maurras and *Action Française* found Pétain under the Germans the next best thing to a restoration of the Bourbons. Some of Gide's acquaintances, too unpolitical to soil their hands with propaganda, such as Cocteau and the composer Georges Auric, stayed on in Paris, exploiting German patronage to the full, frequenting the best *salons* and attending first nights in the company of the German High Command. Gide, like his closest friends, Martin du Gard and Jean Schlumberger, went into 'internal exile', in and around Nice, doing what they could, refusing to compromise, but willing, where appropriate, to write articles that were quietly subversive, risking censorship.

Gaston Gallimard, pre-eminently, steered an even subtler, more sinuous course, negotiating a limited freedom with the German authorities, publishing authors at their 'request' that he would not normally have published, in exchange for others, which the Germans would not normally have approved, while producing splendid editions of the German classics (above all Goethe, with a preface by Gide) that could not, by any stretch of the imagination, be considered as proto-Nazi, but which, as part of their national heritage, the Nazis wanted to see glorified.

In October, Gallimard returned to Paris, determined to reopen the publishing business on the best possible terms. He believed, not unreasonably, that if he did not, the Germans would reopen it on *their* terms, thus compromising the firm's entire spirit. On the other hand, resuming its management would involve Gallimard in compromise in any case. It was a question of pursuing the lesser of two evils. German cultural policy in occupied France was in the hands of the ambassador, Otto Abetz, who had been given instructions from Hitler sufficiently ambiguous to allow a wide range of discretion. The general line seemed to be: forbid anything that might stir up French political opinion or threaten the security of the occupying forces, but do not interfere in small matters. All books censored in Germany itself, including the works of the émigrés, Thomas Mann at their head, would be forbidden, as would all works critical of the Nazi or Italian Fascist régimes. An initial list of 153 forbidden titles had been issued: it included Gide's two books on the USSR and his *Journal*. Self-regulation would be preferable to a heavy-handed, bureaucratic censorship. The Germans, as Gallimard realized, were well aware of the importance of the *NRF*. (It is said that Abetz once remarked: 'There are three powers in France: Communism, the big banks and the *NRF*.') Gide was often tempted to join Gallimard in Paris and exert whatever pressure he could in the direction of a more liberal regime. The Petite Dame succeeded in persuading him of the folly of such a move. Instead, Gallimard came to see Gide, explaining the conditions in which, under the German occupation, the publishing house and review could continue. Jean Paulhan would be replaced, as editor of the *NRF*, by Drieu La Rochelle, a fascist-inclined writer, acceptable to the Germans, but the editorial committee could include Eluard, Giono, Malraux, Saint-Exupéry and Gide. Gide was non-committal. Over the next few weeks, the Germans played a waiting game with Gallimard: first closing down the offices and removing their contents, then quietly negotiating terms with the firm's principal owner. Agreement was reached, Drieu La Rochelle would be in over-all control and Gallimard would return to 5 rue Sébastien-Bottin. The *NRF* reappeared on 1 December, containing an 'avant-propos' by Drieu La Rochelle and one of Gide's 'Feuillets', ending with the words '*à suivre*' ('to be continued'). Armed with a copy, Gallimard went back to Cabris to win Gide's continued cooperation. Gide refused to have his name appear in any advisory or editorial capacity, but agreed to provide occasional 'Feuillets'.

In November, Malraux came to Cabris and spent the night at Les Audides. He had been taken prisoner, then, realizing that he and his fellow-prisoners would all be sent off to Germany to work, escaped. During the twenty-four hours spent with his friends, only sleep stopped the machine-gun-like outpouring of 'implacable logic', delivered with 'vertiginous rapidity', fuelled, it seemed, by a never-ending chain of cigarettes. 'The only human contact one has with Malraux is a slight, fleeting smile, which consents to set aside for you the world of thought; and that smile is his only form of politeness,' wrote the Petite Dame.[11] A few weeks later, Malraux, his new young wife Josette Clotis, and his brother Roland rented La Souco, the Bussys' house at Roquebrune. On 23 December, to Loup Mayrisch's enormous relief, the Viénots arrived safely at La Messuguière. On Christmas Day, the whole of the Cabris 'clan' were Loup's guests.

On 17 January, Gide had news at last of Cuverville and the Drouins in a letter from Domi. At Cuverville, being in the country, food supplies were not too bad, 'but for the last five days, at Auteuil, we have been unable to find meat, potatoes, butter or eggs, and yesterday I queued in the snow in order to bring home *one* huge fetid swede'.[12] Professionally, things were no better for Domi. He had arrived back in Paris in the New Year to take up a post at the Comédie-Française under Copeau, only to find that the German authorities had gone back on their approval of Copeau as director. The reason, it seemed, had less to do with Copeau's own views (he was, after all, a Catholic and, therefore, not *a priori* suspect in their eyes) than with the overtly anti-German views of his son, Pascal. (In June 1940, the Vichy government removed Pascal Copeau from his post at French Radio. In January 1941, he reached North Africa, hoping to join up with British troops. Failing to do so, he returned to France. He then tried to get to London, by crossing Spain, on foot, to Portugal, but was arrested by the Spanish police and interned, first in Spain, then at Pau. Released in September 1941, he joined the 'Gaullist' Resistance movement.)

Within a few days of each other, Gide received several letters criticizing him for continuing to publish articles in the *NRF* since the review had been placed under the direction of Drieu La Rochelle. As so often, Gide could see both sides of the argument. Gallimard had negotiated back his imprint and review to prevent them falling into pro-German hands. He had had to hand over the review to the fascist Drieu, but, it seems, Drieu had done much to protect the *NRF*'s relative freedom and won an assurance from the authorities that they would not lay a finger on Gallimard and the *NRF* team, which still included Paulhan and, more surprisingly, Groethuysen, ex-German and still very much a Communist, running the firm's German list. Gallimard, who had already visited Gide in October and December, called twice more. By the end of March, Gide's patience was exhausted and his doubts dissipated. The catalyst was the arrival of a book by Jacques Chardonne, a close collaborator of Drieu La Rochelle's and, by the same post, a letter from Drieu asking him, in strong terms, to come to Paris. Gide sent off a telegram asking for his name and any announcements of future contributions to be removed from the review. Later, Gide made it plain to a hurt, aggrieved Gaston Gallimard that his withdrawal applied only to the review, under Drieu's editorship, and did not extend to the book-publishing side of the business. (At the Liberation, the French authorities made a similar distinction: the review was closed down as 'collaborationist', but the publishing house allowed to continue. Drieu La Rochelle himself committed suicide in 1944.) Nor did Gide give up publishing articles in the occupied zone altogether. It was in the *Figaro*, which, for all its conservative, *bien pensant* image, or perhaps because of it, was allowed a certain independence, that Gide published his *Interviews Imaginaires*. Here, usually in the person of a young, brash interviewer, he poked gentle, subversive fun at 'modish', Pétainist views. (From February 1942, Gide's *Figaro* articles became less frequent, ending altogether on 29 August. Soon afterwards, the newspaper ceased publication.)

There were plans for sending Catherine to the United States. A friend of her mother's had offered hospitality at her house in Atlanta, Georgia. Beth made several visits to the appropriate offices in Nice to get the necessary transit visas for Spain and Portugal. The plan was that Catherine would leave Nice with the Marcus for Lisbon, then sail with them to New York. Suddenly, the Marcus' visas arrived, with their departure fixed for five days later (being Jewish, they had every reason not to postpone their escape). Catherine's visa for Portugal had still not arrived when, on 17 February, the Marcus left. Secretly, all concerned – Gide, the Petite Dame, Beth and even Catherine herself – breathed a sigh of relief. One reason for Catherine's change of heart was a new-found love of the theatre. She had had some success at acting in her school play, and had become friendly with Claude Francis, a young actress of English descent, who coached her and gave her acting lessons. Seizing on her interest, Gide read scenes from Racine with her, explaining in detail how he thought the speeches should be rendered. Catherine began to attend classes at the Nice Conservatoire three times a week.

On 21 May, Gide was to have given a talk to a literary society in Nice, followed by another a few days later in Cannes. Gide chose a subject that was quite uncontroversial and non-political, the work of his friend, the Belgian poet Henri Michaux. On the same day that the talk was due to take place, he received a letter from members of the Légion d'Anciens Combattants, the official veterans' organization, notorious for its extreme right-wing, now Pétainist views. Gide, the letter said, would not be allowed to speak: if he did not withdraw, the Légion would make sure the meeting was broken up. Other, anonymous letters arrived, threatening violence and even death if he turned up. The offence was not, of course, the subject of the talk, but the speaker. True to character, and in the spirit of his 'imaginary interviews', Gide chose neither confrontation nor retreat, but defused the situation with gentle ridicule. He did arrive, got up and addressed a packed audience. He had, he said, received a letter from the Anciens Combattants threatening violence if he spoke. Not wishing to be the cause of any disorder, he had chosen to remain silent. A young man (whom Gide knew) then got up and read out the offending letter, which condemned itself by its own inappropriate violence. With hardly a word, Gide had a minor triumph. It was later learnt that 160 veterans had resigned from their organization in protest. The text of Gide's 'talk' was published later in the year by Gallimard as *Découvrons Henri Michaux*.

In early June, Jacques Schiffrin and his family had managed to get out of France and were already bound for New York, when their ship was turned back at Casablanca. Schiffrin sent off a telegram pleading for the 30,000 francs necessary for them to complete the journey: Gide and Loup Mayrisch each sent 15,000 francs. The Schiffrins reached New York, where, in due course, Jacques set up a French publishing business. (This became Pantheon Books and, under Jacques' son, André, was absorbed into Random House.)

On 21 June, in the depths of wartime tragedy and deprivation, Gide could still, at seventy-one, respond to a natural world that ignored man's doings, yet of which he knew himself to be, through the decline of his body, a part:

The last four days have been more beautiful than I can say; more beautiful than I can bear. A sort of call to happiness in which the whole of nature concurred . . . On such a night one wants to kiss the flowers, stroke the bark of trees, embrace any young, ardent body, or prowl in search of it until dawn. Going off to bed alone, as I must nevertheless make up my mind to do, seems blasphemous.[13]

Before long, the miracle of nature had receded and nature the destroyer was apparent in Gide's mind: 'The end of life . . . A rather flagging last act; reminders from the past; repetitions.'[14]

Gide, the Petite Dame, Beth, Pierre and Catherine spent most of August at the seaside resort of La Croix-Valmer. They moved into Les Palmeraies, a large house, only half-full, in charming, rather run-down grounds, in which palms had once been grown commercially. Gide was taking his daughter's histrionic ambitions seriously. The day after arrival, he read them, over tea, the first two acts of *Bajazet*, making innumerable comments for Catherine's benefit. That evening, after dinner, came the third act, the final two being read the following afternoon. Throughout the three weeks, the weather was splendid and their time was devoted to other things than reading Racine: swimming, walking, bicycle riding . . . Catherine returned to Nice, her mother and grandmother to Cabris. Gide, after visiting a dermatologist in Nice for his recurrent eczema, moved into the Grand Hôtel at Grasse, where he stayed for some five or six weeks.

Early in September, Gide was visited by Sartre, whom he regarded as 'a commercial traveller in ideas', though the ideas that Sartre peddled were 'of the greatest interest . . . of the most subversive, of the most dangerous kind'.[15] Sartre had been released from a prison camp a few months before and, with Maurice Merleau-Ponty, had formed 'an intellectuals' resistance movement' called 'Socialisme et Liberté'. By the end of the month, however, Sartre had taken up a post as senior philosophy teacher at the Lycée Condorcet. 'Socialisme et Liberté' was wound up and, henceforth, Sartre's Resistance activity consisted entirely of writing, among other things, *L'Etre et le Néant*. He constantly referred to his work as a 'Resistance activity' and, at the Liberation, passed himself off as a leading light of the Resistance. He was not, of course, alone in this.

Gide found the comfort of the hotel, the beauty of the surroundings and his relative isolation conducive to work. For several days, he went to the local library to read translations of Goethe's plays, while working on his preface to the Pléiade edition. He continued to write his *Interviews Imaginaires*. Stimulated by his work with Catherine on the interpretation of Racine, he wrote 'Conseils à une jeune actrice: notes sur l'interprétation de Phèdre'. (It appeared in *Le Figaro* on 25 and 28 July, and 4 and 8 August of 1942.) At the same time, Gide had started a new fictional work, 'Mané Thékel Pharès', which was left unfinished. (Claude Martin included its eight or so pages, preceded by a detailed commentary, in an appendix to his *La Maturité d'André Gide*.) It is a fictionalized, but close transformation of the Rondeaux family drama of 1900–1, when Madeleine's younger sister, Valentine, deserted her husband and infant son for Marcel Gilbert, a fellow-patient at her sanatorium. The curious title comes from Chapter 5 of the Book of Daniel, which recounts Belshazzar's feast. The words are written by a disembodied hand on the wall of Belshazzar's palace in a language that he does not understand. They occur in Gide's story during a Sunday Bible reading.

By the end of September, Gide was thinking of moving to Nice. One reason was to be nearer Catherine: he had no wish to live with her, but he wanted to be on hand, to supervise her progress and give her the benefit of his tuition. His decision was somewhat accelerated by the arrival, in the same hotel, of Loup Mayrisch, who was escaping builders and their works at La Messuguière. 'I can't decently refuse her my company, at least at table,' he wrote to Martin du Gard. But it would be 'the end of my quiet, fruitful meals. And I was getting on so well!'[16] Helped by the Petite Dame and Loup's chauffeur, Gide packed up his things and moved into the Hôtel Adriatic in Nice. The Petite Dame, the Herbarts and Catherine took rooms at a 'pension scandinave, 3 rue des Ponchettes', at the other end of the town.

Gide received his first letter from Robert Levesque since the German invasion of Greece in April, though he had had news of him through his brother Michel. Robert had joined a group of Englishmen trying to reach Crete in a caïque; from there, they hoped to reach Egypt and, eventually, Britain. They reached Milos, where they stayed for a week. They were about to set sail again, when they were arrested: they had been betrayed to the Germans. Robert lost all his belongings, including his journal, covering the period from June 1938 and Gide's last letter. The prisoners were transferred to a barracks at Piraeus, near the foot of Mount Hymettus. In June, his British companions were transferred to Germany, but he was released, by mistake, being taken for a Greek. He now settled in Athens, where he gave talks on French literature to private gatherings of rich friends. At the beginning of the new academic year, he took up a post at the French Institute, where he remained until the end of the war. In a letter dated 15 November, he writes to Gide: 'If only, just for a few minutes, I could come and warm myself near you, and bring you a little of that fire whose exchange has made all the strength and joy of our friendship! I have found no one with whom it is sweeter, more intoxicating even, to be oneself, and your absence is for me a mourning.'[17]

By the end of October, Gide was beginning to feel the cold: heating in the hotel was restricted. On one visit, the Petite Dame found him wearing pyjama trousers outside his ordinary trousers. 'How can anyone who feels the cold as you do not have a dressing-gown?' she asked. 'I've been studying the question for the past twenty years,' he replied.[18]

On New Year's Day, Gide turned to his *Journal*: 'I have aged terribly of late. It's as if I were moving away from myself. Oh! I'm not too sad about it. I think I shall take leave of myself without regret.' Catherine 'might have been able to attach me to life', but 'she is interested only in herself' and, he admits, with disarming honesty, 'that doesn't interest me'.[19] In other words, one might say, the daughter was behaving like the father, and the father didn't like it. Catherine interested Gide to the extent that she showed a desire to be educated by him: the pedagogue/pederast would make allowances for her sex. The eighteen-year-old Catherine was now a *jeune fille en fleur*, one who showed no interest whatsoever in her father's work and only perfunctorily in matters intellectual. That was the only way in which she could discover and protect her own identity. Gide had little idea what she was interested in. When she did show interest in a book, an exhibition, a piece of music, Gide seized the opportunity with intimidating enthusiasm and Catherine's interest waned.

One January afternoon, a cold, underfed Petite Dame – her room was unheated and her weight had shrunk to under 6½ stone (88 lbs) – was invited by Gide for tea at the Hôtel Adriatic. There, beside the radiator in his huge room, he regaled her with treasures from his cupboard, including 'a certain American tin of tiny Vienna sausages, which seemed the height of luxury!' On another occasion, the *pièce de résistance* was 'some unctuous strawberry jam, with a scent that one had almost forgotten . . . It's frightful the place that food is taking up in our conversations,' the Petite Dame remarked. 'There we were, quite delighted because there was some good, real cheese and jam on the table.'[20]

Some days later, Martin du Gard called on the Petite Dame and told her of a conversation that he had had with Catherine – she often confided in 'Oncle Martin'. She was reading *Les Faux-Monnayeurs* and liked it enormously, whereas she had found many of her father's books, *La Symphonie Pastorale*, for example, 'unreadable'. RMG's response was that she should tell her father of her enthusiasm: 'you can't imagine how much pleasure it would give him'. 'Never,' Catherine replied. 'I just couldn't.' 'Be careful you don't regret it when it's too late,' said RMG. She seemed stopped in her tracks, then went on: 'It's very annoying being the daughter of a great man sometimes. As soon as someone hears my name, he always says the same old things about my father, about his books . . . There are times when I've really had enough.'[21] Meanwhile, Catherine was pursuing her theatrical interests. At the end of February, Copeau came to Nice for a few days and had a long talk with her about her future. She should, he confided in his *Journal*, go to Paris and get a basic training at the Conservatoire – to counteract the eccentric, over-critical influence of her father and grandmother. Of the 'ex-Vaneau' set, only Elisabeth, he believed, had any semblance of common sense. Next day, Copeau's daughter, 'Maiène', Marie-Hélène Dasté, came to Nice with a company headed by Gaston

Baty and Marguerite Jamois. Maiène, too, took an interest in Catherine's budding career, even proposing that, parents willing, she come to Paris, live there as her lodger, attend courses at the Conservatoire and join a small 'company-school' that she and Jean-Louis Barrault were thinking of starting. In the end, nothing came of these plans. It was decided that it would be better for Catherine to stay in the relative safety of Nice.

By April, Gide was planning to move to Tunisia for a time. The idea had first come to him during a visit from Marcel Tournier, a Tunis bookseller and old friend. 'Where did I get the idea that it was all over, that spring didn't interest me any more and could no longer take possession of me?' Gide wrote in his *Journal* on 11 April. 'For days now, ever since the fine weather returned and the air became warm, I have felt like a migratory bird and think only of leaving . . . Ah, would that I were already there. Everything will have started. I shall miss the overture again.'[22]

Gide arrived in Marseille on 30 April. He set about at once going through the bureaucratic mill, 'running from office to office to get the necessary visas, identification marks and stamps'. 'All very Kafka,' Gide notes, in the company of thousands of others since, in similar situations.[23] His few days in Marseille were lightened by two meetings. Paul Valéry, whom Gide had not met since he was last in Paris, long before the outbreak of war, happened to be there. To his *Journal*, he confessed: 'Never have I felt my friendship and admiration for that incomparable personality to be keener and more unreserved. I experience nothing but joy in feeling his unquestionable superiority . . .'[24] They were not to meet again until 1945, the year of Valéry's death. Also in Marseille Gide met Jean-Louis Barrault, who urged him to continue his translation of *Hamlet*. Gide took up the challenge and worked on the translation during his first year in Tunisia. He set sail on 4 May and was met at Tunis by Tournier, who booked him into the most expensive hotel, the Tunisia Palace – the city was full of refugees and accommodation difficult to find – and kept a constant watch over his well-being. 'Oh! The food!' he wrote to RMG:

That's the great surprise here. Yet I was warned. It goes beyond all expectation, all hope. Three meals already, at which I stuffed myself to a degree you wouldn't believe possible . . . And no coupons required! Ten sorts of hors d'oeuvres, ten, I say! I counted them. And everything of prehistoric quality, beginning with the bread. I eat with fury, ferocity, lyricism. I eat for the Petite Dame, for the Bussys, for Catherine, for all of you. I'd forgotten how good it is to eat.[25]

The Tunisia Palace was less prodigal in peace and quiet. 'Three weeks at

Tunis were a sore trial,' Gide wrote to Dorothy Bussy. 'Endless din, stifling heat . . . work and sleep almost impossible.'[26] Despite Tournier's friendship, Gide would have left Tunis for some coastal or mountain resort, had it not been for a meeting with a Dr Ragu, a Parisian exile and specialist in dermatology at the Hôpital Saint-Louis, who had taken it on himself to cure him of his *gratte*, which was proving particularly bothersome at the time: 'Every morning a charming young Russian nurse comes and takes charge of my legs and feet for an hour or more, while I plunge into my reading.'[27] He had other consolations, too. In the *Journal*, he describes 'two nights of pleasure such as I did not think I would be able to experience at my age':

Both nights were marvellous, the second even more surprising than the first. F. [probably an employee of the hotel] came to my room at curfew . . . He said that he was fifteen, but looked younger. His body was even more beautiful than his face. I noticed him on my first day here, but he seemed so wild I hardly dared to speak to him. He brought to pleasure a sort of joyful lyricism, an amused frenzy, which probably had about as much to do with inexperienced surprise as sensuality. There was no question of compliance on his part, for he took as much initiative as I. He seemed to care so little about my age that I came to forget it myself, and I don't remember ever experiencing pleasure so fully or so strongly. He left me in the early hours of the morning, and then only because I asked him to leave me so that I could get some sleep. That night, he had come at my invitation. The second night, four days later, he came of his own accord. A third night, some days later, he again knocked on my door . . . How I regret now that I did not let him in; probably out of fear that I might not rediscover such perfect joy and spoil, by superimposition, such a memory . . . Many people, when still young, have no need of youth and beauty in their partners to attain with them, thanks to them, the height of ecstasy – to which their own youth and beauty invite us.[28]

Gide accepted an invitation to move to a villa at Sidi-bou-Saïd, on the hills outside Tunis, belonging to a couple with whom he had become good friends: Théo Reymond was an architect, now without work, his wife an ophthalmologist at the hospital. The villa turned out to be a large house, with a superb view from terrace and windows of the bay, the city below and the mountains in the distance. There he lived entirely alone, attended only by an Arab woman, who spoke no French. She cleaned his room and brought him a breakfast of 'café au lait and two Arab pancakes' every morning. Towards the end of June, he was joined at the villa by its owners, but, since they left for Tunis first thing each morning and returned only quite late, he saw little of them.

Gide set to work on the translation of *Hamlet* that he had abandoned twenty years before. He was assisted in his work by the excellent public library in Tunis, which had commentaries on the play and earlier translations. 'Every day, I spend four or five hours with *Hamlet*,' he wrote to Dorothy Bussy. 'There are infernal difficulties . . . Ah! Would that I were near you to talk to you about them!'[29] Failing that, letters passed back and forth between Nice and Tunis with greater frequency than would otherwise have been the case. Many of the knottiest problems came not in the more famous speeches, but in Hamlet's responses to others in rapid conversation, where his speech is on the verge of rational discourse. By the end of August, the translation was finished and a typescript sent to Dorothy Bussy. It is, she responded, lapsing into French, 'absolutely *étourdissante* [astounding, staggering] and shows your extraordinary mastery of language . . . It has left me with increased admiration and respect for you . . . *and* Shakespeare. Many things strike me afresh, or at any rate, as they have never done before.'[30] (The translation was first published in New York, in 1944, by Jacques Schiffrin–Pantheon Books.)

During the still burning heat of a Tunisian September, which Gide feels 'ashamed to endure so badly', he begins to feel, 'probably for the first time in my life . . . what is known as nostalgia'. It is almost a mirage:

My thoughts go back to the mysterious undergrowth of the woods at La Roque, where, as a child, I could not venture without trembling; the edges of the pond thick with flowering plants; the evening mists over the little stream. I remember the beech grove at Cuverville, the great autumn winds carrying away the russet leaves; the rooks' calls; dreaming by the fireside of an evening . . . I think of everything I owe to Em. I have thought of her constantly over the past few days, with regret and remorse for having so often fallen short. How often I must have seemed harsh and insensitive! . . . For a smile from her today, I think I would quit life . . .[31]

Meanwhile, the Côte d'Azur had its wonderful summer, if little else. The Martin du Gards had decided to rent a villa for several months at Cap d'Antibes. RMG thanked Gide on Hélène's behalf for a parcel containing all her favourite things. He had even sent packets of shampoo with some books from Tournier's. RMG reported on the plight of his friends: the Bussys were 'skeletal' and he feared that, during the coming winter, the food restrictions would end up killing off the Petite Dame. (They did not: she outlived Martin du Gard, fifteen years her junior, by a year, dying, in 1959, aged ninety-three.) Others had more to worry about than the next meal. In that summer paradise, the authorities, French and German, were rounding up Jews 'in huge, brutal deportations, children separated from their parents, etc., under the eyes of an indignant, but powerless and passive population . . . It's all so moving, so hopeless.'[32]

In September, Gide left Sidi-bou-Saïd for a flat in Tunis, which he shared with Mme Reymond's mother, Mme de Gentile, and two children, a twenty-year-old daughter and an impossible, 'uncontrollable' fifteen-year-old son, François (the 'Victor' of the *Journal*). Gide and François seem to have had a feeling of mingled dislike and fascination for one another. The young man claimed to be a Communist and, 'after reading Freud, was convinced that his mother was in love with him'.[33] With his *Figaro* articles becoming less frequent and the *Hamlet* translation finished, Gide turned more often than of late to the journal. He saw his friends the Ragus, the Tourniers and Jean Amrouche, with whom he often played chess. (Amrouche, a poet and teacher of Kabyl origin, had edited *La Tunisie française littéraire*. Later, in 1949, he made the French radio interviews with Gide.)

On 30 November, Gide witnessed the German and Italian occupation of Tunis: 'In the streets, endless movement of trucks, armoured cars, tanks and anti-aircraft guns. With every day, new ships are unloading fresh munitions and troops.'[34] To the inhabitants of Tunis it must have looked as though the war had taken a turn for the worse. In fact, the German–Italian occupation of Tunis was a retreat westwards under the thrust of Montgomery's British Eighth Army from Egypt, planned to precede the Anglo-American landings in Morocco and Algeria. At the same time, the Germans entered the formerly 'unoccupied' zone of France, thus effectively bringing the charade of Vichy government to an end. In May 1943, Rommel's famous Afrika Korps, the German reinforcements under Von Arnim and the Italians were all to be caught in an Allied pincer movement from east and west, thus freeing the whole of North Africa from Axis control. To Gide and the inhabitants of Tunis, it did not look as though they would be free so soon. Over the next few days, Gide noted a marked difference in the behaviour of the German and Italian troops: 'The Germans, one has to admit, are behaving here with remarkable dignity, which makes the undisciplined swaggering of the Italians even more scandalous.' Moreover, it was quite clear to all that the Germans had nothing but contempt for the Italians, who, in turn, hated the Germans. Of course, the Germans, the Afrika Korps in particular, were élite troops, motivated more by the Prussian warrior spirit of its officer class than by the Nazi mentality.

Within days, Tunis was being subjected to heavy Allied bombing. On 14 December, Gide wrote: 'Three times I went over to the drawing-room

window to watch the strangely illuminated sky ... A huge fire at La
Goullette lasted almost until dawn: an Italian munitions-ship, it is thought.
Such destruction awakens all that is darkest and most primitive in us, a
savage, elementary state of excitement, at once irrepressible and unacceptable.'[35] By 19 December, the electricity supply was cut off, for lack of fuel.
All communications were broken. After five o'clock, it was no longer light
enough to read. In desperation, Gide turned to the Reymonds' piano, only
to find that he could no longer remember completely any of Bach's preludes
and fugues, and could only come up with odd bits of Chopin and Schumann.

Over Christmas, posters in French, Italian and Arabic appeared in the
city, announcing that before the end of the year the Jews of the city would
have to pay 20 million francs as aid to the victims of the Anglo-American
bombings, 'for which they are responsible', 'international Jewry' having,
as everyone knows, 'wanted and prepared for the war'. 'The Jewish victims,'
Gide adds, 'are naturally excluded from those to receive help.'[36] His friend
Dr Reymond was already working twice as hard as usual after all Jews had
been sacked from the hospital where she worked. On 31 December, he
noted:

The last day of this year of disgrace ... I may no longer cling to life as I did, but I
have this *idée fixe*: *to last*. To make myself and my appurtenances last a little longer:
linen, clothes, shoes, hopes, trust, smile, good will; make them last until it is time
for them to go. In view of this, I am becoming thrifty, parsimonious with everything,
so that none of this will wear out before its time, out of fear that this war may drag
on, out of a great desire, a great hope, to see the end of it.[37]

On New Year's Day, Gide lunched with his friends the Ragus at the Hôpital
Civil. Two other guests, Gérard Boutelleau and his English wife, Hope,
arrived late, a bomb having just fallen on the building in which they lived.
At this time, there were constant Allied air raids, often missing the port and
other strategic targets, and landing on civilian buildings. Gas and electricity
were often cut off, with the result that people dined early and then went to
bed. It also meant that they were deprived of the radio and news, true or
false. Gide imagines how his friends would react to the bombing-raids: 'I
think of them, each in turn ... and feel lonely.'[38] A few days later, he is
thinking of them again: 'Ah! If only I knew how Dorothy's eyes were, and
Madame Théo's knee, Roger M. du G.'s kidneys, Jacques' liver, Marcel's
asthma? ... Are they still alive? Which of them will I see again over there,
and in what state? ...'[39] Earlier, he had sent a few letters to them, but all
communications with mainland France were now broken off.

One day, he got talking to a young German army officer who turned out to be a friend of Curtius and a student of art history. With some hesitation, he agreed to meet him again: 'We did not mention the war. He told me quite simply at the beginning of our conversation how embarrassed he felt by his uniform.' He was a great admirer of Thomas Mann's *Lotte in Weimar* and showed Gide a tiny copy of Goethe's *Divan*, which he always kept in his breast-pocket: 'The war can never make me regard such representatives of Germany as enemies; but he knows and feels himself to be an exception and expects to be crushed in a world in which he will be unable to find a raison d'être.'[40]

By the end of March, the British Eighth Army had captured Gabès, about 200 miles to the south of Tunis. On 1 April, it was announced that postal services had been resumed with mainland France: many pointed out that it was April Fool's Day. Nevertheless, Gide sent off cards to a number of friends and letters, by diplomatic bag, to the Petite Dame and Dorothy Bussy. The British were advancing rapidly up the Tunisian coast. Day by day, the bombing of the city increased: by 6 May, the anti-aircraft guns had fallen silent. Next day, Tunis enjoyed its own liberation, fifteen months before Paris.

It is still hardly believable that what we have so long waited for has happened; *they* are here; we hardly dare believe it. What! With no resistance, no fighting? . . . Our astonishment is all the greater when we learn . . . that these tanks, these soldiers are those of the Eighth Army . . . that glorious army that had come from the Egyptian frontier, after sweeping through Libya, Tripolitania . . . It was like a miracle.[41]

Gide went down into the street: everyone was kissing each other, laughing, weeping with joy. He went further afield. A district in which everyone spoke Italian was suddenly displaying French flags at every window. That evening Tunis celebrated its liberation in darkness: before leaving, the Germans had blown up the electricity generators. A few days later, Gide writes:

A sort of exhilaration is floating in the air. We can breathe freely. The daily bread ration has just been increased from two to five grams per person. Milk is reappearing on the market. Since people are expecting plentiful supplies to arrive and restrictions are to be lifted, they are finally taking their reserve supplies out of cupboards and daring to eat their fill. Packets of American and English cigarettes rain upon us, and bars of excellent chocolate. Each meal becomes a feast.[42]

Next day, Gide dined with his friends the Ragus, Hope Boutelleau and Mrs Sparrow, who, despite her married name, was a distinguished Polish doctor. With them, as guests of honour, were two British army officers, Captain Chadburne and Dr Gidal, the Eighth Army photographer. To Gide's surprise, Gidal turned out to be a lover of German poetry, much preferring Rilke to Stefan George.

On 17 May, back in Nice, an excited Martin du Gard telephoned the Petite Dame to tell her that he had just heard the following announcement on the BBC: 'The Allied troops have found in Tunis André Gide, who had gone there from the Free Zone long before the German occupation. He is seventy-four and in perfect health.'[43] Gide decided that he would go to Algiers. He took a sad farewell of his many Tunis friends and boarded a plane for the Algerian capital. There he was met by his old friends the Heurgons. Later, he would be joined by Jean Amrouche. Also in Algiers was Antoine de Saint-Exupéry. Before long, the three of them were planning a literary review, which was to appear the following year with the title *L'Arche*. At the Heurgons', he yielded to 'the intoxication of a new library, reading, one after another, a little Leopardi, then some Dante, then some Stendhal, then some Virginia Woolf'.[44]

On 25 June, Gide was invited to dine with General de Gaulle. With him was Jean Hytier, an academic and author of a book on André Gide, published in 1938: they sat on either side of the General. It was a quite intimate occasion, there being eight diners in all, including Gaston Palewski, soon to be de Gaulle's *chef de cabinet*, and René Pleven, politician and, in July 1950, Prime Minister.

De Gaulle's welcome was very friendly and very simple, almost deferential towards me, as if the honour and pleasure of the meeting were entirely his. People had told me of his 'charm'; they were quite right ... The General remained very dignified, even somewhat reserved, it seemed, as if elsewhere. His great simplicity, the tone of his voice, his attentive but not inquisitorial eyes, filled with a sort of affability, put me at ease at once. And I would have been completely so did I not always feel with men of action how remote the world I inhabit is from that in which they operate.

Before meeting de Gaulle, Gide had taken the trouble to read some of the General's published writings. They were 'excellent, even capable of making one like the army, presenting it not as it is, alas, but as it ought to be'. Gide reminded the General of a reference that he had made to the effect that Jellicoe had all the qualities of Nelson save that of knowing how *not* to obey. How and when, Gide asked, approaching the heart of de Gaulle's career, should an officer take it upon himself to disobey an order?

De Gaulle replied, with great conviction, that this could only occur at a time of great events and when an order was contradicted by a sense of duty. After dinner, de Gaulle invited Gide to take a walk with him around the garden. Gide notes in the *Journal*: 'He is certainly called to play an important role and he seems "up to it". He has no pomposity, no self-importance, but a sort of profound conviction that inspires confidence. I shall not find it hard to pin my hopes on him.'[45]

By the end of August, the residents of Les Audides in Cabris had decided to return to Paris. Catherine, it was decided, would enter the Conservatoire in November. Pierre Herbart went off to do a reconnaissance operation, joined by Beth on 1 September. They found the Vaneau in such a mess that they got the Petite Dame to postpone her arrival by another three weeks: 'My apartment has resumed an almost normal appearance,' she wrote, after arriving there on 21 September, 'but my neighbour's is still in an indescribably messy and filthy state.' When the cleaning was finished, Catherine would move into Marc's old studio, and Beth and Pierre into Gide's apartment. 'Gide's absence here is more poignant, more obsessive than I can say,' she adds.[46] In September, Gide went to Rabat, in Morocco, where he stayed with his old friend Jean Denoël. There the plans for the launching of *L'Arche* took shape. Gide then moved on to Fez, where he found his old friend Si Haddou (Guy Delon, before his conversion to Islam) living in a villa owned by a Swiss friend. Gide moved in with Haddou (and his servant, Mohammed). The villa was hidden in a series of gardens below the Medina, filled with orange-trees and olive-trees. These months in Fez are thinly documented: correspondence with France was intermittent and Gide neglected the journal, save to note his reading: Webster's *The White Devil* and *The Duchess of Malfi*, Ford's *The Broken Heart*, Schiller's *Don Carlos*, stories by Gottfried Keller, *David Copperfield*, Stevenson's *Kidnapped*, a lot of Conan Doyle's stories.

Gide, though an intermittently fastidious eater, was never really much of a gourmet, at least by the French norms of yesteryear. Surprisingly, then, and it says much about the privations of the day, he opens his *Journal* for 1944 with a menu: 'Rillettes; pâté; salade de choux-fleurs; unlimited butter. Alose [shad, a fish]; spinach purée with hard-boiled eggs; boiled potatoes. Knuckle of ham (excellent). Jam and "cake" [a French version of English fruitcake, pronounced, more or less, "keck"].' Supply and demand are the ultimate determinants of value – so the 'menu' is worth recording. 'This (or the equivalent) is what I find served on my table every day,' Gide adds, but he is not one to luxuriate in his good fortune, or to abandon a lifetime's abstemiousness: 'A third of all that would be enough for me.'[47] Gide eats the fish and saves the ham for the evening. Early every morning, his host leaves for the centre of town, where he runs a veterinary clinic. At this time, Gide was preparing *Pages de Journal*, which were to appear in *L'Arche* in three instalments, beginning in March, the first number of which had just appeared. (They were published in volume form, later in the year, both in Algiers, by Charlot, and in New York, by Jacques Schiffrin.)

On 6 February, a mysterious telegram arrived from the Ministry of the Interior, instructing Gide to go at once to Algiers – an earlier telegram from Amrouche had also requested his presence, but he had not taken it seriously. Gide called on General Suffren, who, the following morning, informed him that all the necessary arrangements had been made. His own car would collect him and take him to Meknès, where a plane would be waiting for him. Gide could not imagine why the authorities required his presence in Algiers. It turned out that he had been called on to settle a dispute between Amrouche and Robert Aron, co-editors of *L'Arche*, as to the future policy and running of the review: 'First I must collect information, listen to the disputants, read copies of their letters to one another, consult various third parties.'[48] One could hardly have a more dramatic instance of the seriousness with which French politicians take cultural matters. During their walk in the gardens of the Maison-Blanche, some seven months before, Gide had spoken to de Gaulle of his plans to help found a review in Algiers that would represent Free France in the cultural domain: at the time, de Gaulle appeared not to be listening. Clearly he had been listening: he was not a man to ignore the wishes of France's greatest living writer. (In 1960, the same de Gaulle, now back in power, called on France's greatest living writer of *that* day, André Malraux, to be his Minister of Culture, with unprecedented funds at his disposal.)

On 3 April, for reasons that are not at all clear, Gide boarded an official plane in the grounds of the Maison-Blanche bound for Gao, in Mali. The *Journal* recalls his pleasure in the scenery, but little else – except, that is, for a single 'adventure', due to a plane break-down at the end of his stay, 'around which all my memories of Gao radiate'.[49]

Gide was back in Algiers at the end of April. He took up his notes for *Thésée*: this reworking of the story of Theseus was Gide's first fictional work since the ill-starred *Geneviève*, published in 1936, and was to be his last. It was to wait another two years for publication. 'There are still large sections to rewrite . . . For a month now, I have worked at it every day, almost without stopping, in a state of joyful fervour that I've not experienced for a long time and thought I should never know again.'[50]

On 6 June, news of the long awaited Allied landings in Normandy marked the most dramatic turning-point of the war. Over the next few months, under the influence, perhaps, of his host, Jacques Heurgon, professor of Latin at Algiers University, he set about re-reading the Latin classics to be found in Heurgon's well-stocked library. He did so 'with much more pleasure and less difficulty than I would have thought possible'.[51] He devoted three hours a day to Virgil's *Aeneid*. Most days, he played chess with Jean Amrouche.

In July, Gide got a foretaste of *épuration*, a phenomenon instigated and concerted almost entirely by the Communist Party in the months after the Liberation – the Communists were rather given to and expert at purges. It began at a meeting of the 'Provisional Consultative Assembly', a proto-parliamentary body set up by de Gaulle in Algiers, consisting of members of his own 'government in exile' and representatives of the various Resistance groups ('Gaullist' or Communist-dominated). On 7 July, a Communist representative, Giovoni, asked: 'Is it possible in Algiers to print remarks such as the following . . .' and proceeded to quote, out of context, a few sentences from Gide's *Journal*, reprinted in the April-May number of *L'Arche*: 'It is through the privations it entails . . . that the great majority will be affected by the defeat. Less sugar in one's coffee and less coffee in one's cup . . . Which of them [the farmers] would not willingly agree that Descartes and Watteau were German . . . if, by doing so, he could sell his wheat for a few *sous* more? Patriotic sentiments are no more constant than our other loves.' These words were written four years before, in the aftermath of France's rapid, ignominious collapse. They are a lucid critique of a certain craven defeatism that was soon to turn into collaboration. They were written in the name of what Gide saw as a more valorous, less corrupt France – precisely the France that de Gaulle had come to embody. For the Communists, they were merely a pretext to whip up animosity against France's best-known literary figure, their former friend, now their enemy, who had the temerity to be living in the same city as the future French government and lending his name and prestige to a new review that lay outside their influence. A furious Giovoni went on:

André Gide . . . has insulted the patriotism of the French and has misjudged the peasants of France, as he once did those of the USSR. In short, this tainted writer, who has exerted such a murky influence over young minds, indulges in defeatism in wartime. His mania for originality and exoticism, his immorality and perversion, make him a dangerous individual. Today, literature is a weapon of war. That is why I demand prison for André Gide and the prosecution of the managing editor of *L'Arche*.

Nothing, of course, came of the demand: that was not the point of the speech. Ironically, two months before, the German authorities in Paris had announced officially that, henceforth, all Gide's works were banned. As usual, totalitarianism of left and right had much in common. Meanwhile, the fifth number of *L'Arche*, in August, featured the first instalment of *Robert, ou l'intérêt général*. Over the next twelve months, three more instalments appeared.

On 26 August, de Gaulle led his Free French army into Paris, the bulk of the Allied force, mainly American, keeping, at his insistence, a discreet distance. That film director *manqué* was not to be cheated of his big scene: indeed, the most enduring image of the Liberation of Paris is of the tall general, standing in his car, accepting the acclamation of the fickle crowd below him as he moved down the Champs-Elysées. Also back in Paris was Maurice Thorez, the Communist leader. When war broke out he had been conscripted, but deserted and made his way to Moscow, where he stayed throughout the war. Stalin and Thorez had their own plans for France. They were not de Gaulle's. In the end, de Gaulle outwitted them; his first move was to bring the Communists into government.

The exaltation did not last long; recriminations, justified in principle, often unjust in practice, were not long in coming. The eighty-eight-year-old Marshal Pétain, 'hero of Verdun' in the First World War, German-backed head of state in the Second, was arrested in Germany, tried and found guilty of treason; his death sentence, commuted to life imprisonment, expired with him, seven years later. His hated assistant and rival, Laval, one-time socialist politician and Vichy's Prime Minister, escaped to Germany, then to Spain. Brought back to France, he was tried, found guilty of treason and condemned to death. The night before his execution he tried to kill himself with poison. Next morning, half-unconscious, he was hanged.

The purge extended to the smaller, but no less self-important circle of Paris literary politics. The 'literary Pétain', the seventy-seven-year-old Charles Maurras, founder of Action Française, was brought to trial and, on 27 January 1945, sentenced to life imprisonment. (He was released, on medical grounds, in 1952, just before his death.) Drieu La Rochelle, the 'literary Laval', in role if not at all in character, took his own life after being summoned to appear in court. A far greater figure, Céline, fled to Denmark and was condemned to death *in absentia*; however, his verdict was later reversed and he returned to France, to die there in 1961. Gide's old Catholic enemy, Henri Béraud, was condemned to death in December 1944. Defended by François Mauriac (now known as 'Saint-François des Assises') in the *Figaro*, his sentence was commuted to forced labour. He was released in 1950. Robert Brasillach was less fortunate. Despite a petition for clemency organized by his mother and signed by fifty-nine intellectuals, including Mauriac and Schlumberger, he was shot on 6 February 1945. The *épuration littéraire* did not stop there. A Comité d'Épuration de l'Édition was set up. In due course, it considered the complicated case of Gaston Gallimard. Sartre and Paulhan (published author and employee of the house, respectively) pleaded his cause. Vercors, of the clandestine Editions de Minuit, argued that all publishers who had accepted German control should be purged. In the end, nothing came of it – the Committee had no official jurisdiction in any case and could hardly resort to shaving heads.

'Having nothing to do, my mind empty, my eyes tired,' Gide wrote in early September, 'never has a wait seemed so long.' He had been asked to head a mission to Italy, but refused. 'It's in France I'd like to be . . . I fear I may not have enough strength at the last moment to climb that final slope, nor have time left to embrace those few whom I would like to see again before closing my eyes forever. Six times a day, I listen on the wireless to the news that I have already read that morning in the newspapers, as if my impatient attention could hasten events.'[52]

Gide arranged for a parcel to be taken to Jean Schlumberger containing letters to all his friends. It was the first news that many of them had had from him for a long time. Gide mentioned plans to return to Paris. The cautious Jean Schlumberger thought a brief exploratory visit might be wiser: 'You should resume contacts and find out what is happening. The ground is shaky; each step has to be taken with care. The hypocrisies of the new patriotic vocabulary conceal many a trap.'[53] As autumn approached, Gide began to have second thoughts: in October, postal services between Algiers and France had been resumed and he learnt more of the deprivations and unpleasantness of life in Paris. He decided that he could not face an unheated winter there and postponed any decision to return until the spring. In the letters that flooded back he learnt what had been happening to his friends over the past year. Catherine, now twenty-one, a drama student and lodging with friends, was pregnant. The Petite

Dame had left the Vaneau for Villars-de-Lans to stay with Loup Mayrisch, whose condition was worsening: though in fact, she was to survive another three years. Loup's daughter, Andrée, was in hiding, moving around constantly to avoid arrest. Her husband had joined de Gaulle in London. They were not to be reunited: Viénot died of a heart attack on 20 July, at the age of forty-seven. Pierre Herbart was deeply engaged in underground activities and was about to take up a position in Rennes: in fact, it later transpired that he had been put in charge of the Mouvement de Libération Nationale (MLN) in the entire Brittany region, where he was known by the *nom de guerre* of Le Vigan. Beth went out to join him. It was decided to let the Groethuysens, who felt at risk since their concierge had been arrested by the Gestapo, take over the Petite Dame's apartment. A young writer from Algeria, Albert Camus, took over the studio in Gide's apartment. On 26 August, Herbart entered Paris with Leclerc's French division. In October, the Petite Dame arrived back in Paris, 'indescribably disappointed not to find Gide at the Vaneau'. 'Great emotion at seeing Catherine again,' she writes. 'She seems happy and one senses that she is entirely focused on expecting the child, with disarming sweetness, so perfectly simple, not seeming to realize that it commits her for a lifetime or to concern herself with all the problems that the future will bring; more than ever disconcerting.'[54]

The Martin du Gards had decided, in May, to join their daughter, Christiane, and her husband Coppet in Figeac, in the Lot. When they tried to get back to a liberated Nice, they found that no transport was available. Eventually, in a van hired for them by the Bussys, at enormous expense, they set out on 30 December, at a temperature of −6°C. They reached Nice three days later. The Bussys had survived the war, although, on 30 October, a seventy-nine-year-old Dorothy wrote to Gide: 'It is no use telling you that I'm growing very old, that my hair and teeth are falling out, my eyes, my ears, my memory failing, that I hardly dare walk without a stick, that perhaps you wouldn't recognize me.'[55] Cuverville, after six months of German occupation, was now housing a company of Scottish Highlanders, who turned out to be 'most attentive and respectful' towards Jeanne Drouin: Marcel Drouin had died in the previous July, while their daughter, Odile, had died in childbirth seven months before. Henri Ghéon had died on 13 June, aged seventy-nine, alone and much diminished in his faculties. In June 1945, Gide published an obituary of his early companion:

No; there was no break between us. We simply stopped seeing one another; that constant companion . . . was 'converted' during the last War. From then on he walked in the shadow of the cross and I refused to follow him. God confiscated him for me. I did not try to divert him from his new route . . . As a sceptic, I could have continued the dialogue; but we were both convinced of our rightness and could not, after living in such intimate communion for close on twenty years, have been content with relations in which nothing of our secret concerns could be discussed . . . I missed him enormously.[56]

Maurice Schlumberger, Jean's younger brother, now, at fifty-eight, an eminent banker, but, in 1904, the eighteen-year-old paramour of both Gide and Ghéon, had lost two sons at the end of the war. Both had fought in the Free French forces; Georges was killed in action in October in his ancestors' Alsace; Xavier was arrested in Paris in June, deported to Germany in August and died at Ellrich in January 1945. Copeau was in very poor health, deteriorating mentally and physically. His son Pascal had been active in the Resistance and edited the underground newspaper *Libération*. After the war, he was elected a deputy to the Constituent Assembly. Jacques Copeau's son-in-law, the actor Jean Dasté, was arrested by the Gestapo in 1944 and was about to be transported to Germany when he and his fellow-prisoners were liberated by American troops. (He died in 1994, aged ninety, seven weeks after his wife, Maïene.) Fearing the worst, Gide did not write to one of his oldest friends, Alibert, until May 1945. Alibert replied at once: thanks to an operation for cataract, his sight had not deteriorated any further and, apart from a recent prostate operation, his health was tolerable. The two friends had last met, briefly as usual, at Carcassonne in July 1940; it was to be their last meeting. (He outlived Gide by two years, dying in 1953, aged eighty.) A more recent friend of Gide's, Antoine de Saint-Exupéry, disappeared during a reconnaissance mission over Corsica on 31 July 1944.

On 20 October, Jean Schlumberger wrote to Gide: 'There is a rumour that you would be willing to be academized . . .' Mauriac and Valéry, together with Georges Duhamel, whom they had got appointed 'temporary perpetual secretary' of the Académie Française in 1942, were trying to bring new life to that dusty old body by persuading the best writers of the day to submit themselves for election. Two days later, Gide wrote back:

As for the Académie . . . *quae te dementia cepit* ['What madness has got hold of you?' – Virgil, *Bucolics*, II, 69]. To my astonishment, I learnt from a Paris newspaper that I was submitting my candidature; I know absolutely nothing about it . . . If the chair were put under my backside, I wouldn't sit on it. But I shouldn't want my Immortal friends, or you, to see this as expressing any contempt on my part for the venerable institution. I simply don't think I'm made to sit there or that the seat suits me.[57]

Martin du Gard had also been approached by Duhamel. He, too, had found it difficult to refuse, without hurting the feelings of those who were members of the Academy: he pleaded that all he wanted was to retire to a quiet life and write. 'I think you are quite right to stay over there,' he wrote to Gide. 'The climate in Paris is not ready for the likes of us yet . . . They are purging, purging. The "Republic of Left-Wing Writers" (to which we belong, it goes without saying) is practically a totalitarian police state, in which one gets rid of enemies, and even rivals, by prison or death . . . It was necessary no doubt; but it didn't have to become an institution.'[58]

Typical of this atmosphere was the decision by the Comité d'Epuration de l'Edition, instructing Jean Paulhan, that *éminence grise* of the house of Gallimard: '1) To proceed with the liquidation of the *Nouvelle Revue Française* [it had not appeared since 1942] in order that it cannot appear from the Editions Gallimard, either under that name or under another; 2) To take all steps to ensure that the words "Editions de la Nouvelle Revue Française" do not appear either on works published by the Editions Gallimard, or advertising in periodicals, or elsewhere.' (When the review did reappear, in January 1953, it had to assume the title of *La Nouvelle Nouvelle Revue Française*, which it kept until February 1959.) However, in a way, its place was taken almost at once, if with a radically different tone, by *Les Temps modernes*, which appeared from Gallimard in October 1945, under a team headed by Sartre. The order concerning the *NRF* appeared on 25 November in *Les Lettres françaises*, the organ of the Comité National des Ecrivains, now in the hands of Communists and fellow-travellers. The same number of *Les Lettres françaises* carried an attack on Gide by Louis Aragon, protesting against the publication in the previous number of unexceptionable extracts from Gide's *Délivrance de Tunis*, which had previously appeared under the imprint of the underground press Editions de Minuit. Aragon's argument in objecting to Gide's presence is a particularly devious one. It begins by saying that he noticed Gide's name in the review 'with a certain amazement'. He goes on to say, with evident irony, that he is not opposed to Gide applying 'from Italy or North Africa' for membership of the Comité, or to its being granted, but he cannot forget that Gide is the author of *Retour de l'URSS*, which, by attacking our heroic ally, gave succour to the enemy; that, leafing through his journal for 1940, he notes that Gide seems to have spent his time 'studying German', 'reading and re-reading' Goethe; that 'people coming back from North Africa recount a lot of unpleasant things about M. Gide', but, of course, they may be gossips, so he will confine his attentions to Gide's writings, etc. Gide, of course, was tempted to reply. His friends urged him not to: Aragon had really made himself look ridiculous and, anyway, if that was all he could come up with against Gide, Gide had nothing to worry about. In a letter to Jean Schlumberger, of 7 December, Gide noted that Ehrenburg, now in Moscow, was constantly making attacks on him in American periodicals. 'This quarrel goes well beyond my own case,' Gide went on. 'It is a sort of "terror" that they want to reign over our letters and thought; a "totalitarianism" similar to that of the Nazis, which they claim to oppose, but is as much to be feared and even more perfidious, in that it is dressed in the colours of Liberty.'[59]

'I work away at my Latin, with rather ridiculous obstinacy. Every day I spend between four and six hours on it, sometimes more,' Gide notes. If he had a good master to teach him, he adds, he would learn in an hour what now took him two weeks.[60] Unfortunately, Jacques Heurgon had left Algiers, appointed attaché to the French embassy in Rome. Gide's thoughts were returning more and more to the prospect of a return to France and his friends. He toyed with the idea of going first to Nice, where the weather would come as less of a shock than in Paris, and seeing Martin du Gard and the Bussys. RMG warned him, however, of the still quite appalling food situation in Nice and lack of heating. He would, of course, like nothing better than to see Gide again, but, in all honesty, he had to counsel against his coming back so soon: 'It would, quite simply, be *to risk your skin* . . . At Nice, where the climate is incomparably more clement than elsewhere, the complete and utter absence of any heating . . . is decimating the "retired" of our age.'[61] In the course of his masterly sixteen-page letter, RMG meditates on the past six years, the present situation and the prospects for the future. Despite the hardships of his life in Nice, he is well aware that his lot has been preferable to that of almost anyone in the war-ravaged Europe of the day. He cannot bring himself to feel any pity for Germany: 'At no point during the other war did I feel any feeling of hatred for Germany. *I can't say as much today.* For in two years, in Nice and, this summer in the Lot, I witnessed too many atrocities. If one has any idea of what took place in the Gestapo's cellars in every town in France, in every town of every country occupied by the Germans, one cannot "understand", one cannot forgive!' The vast majority of the German people followed Hitler, passively, if not enthusiastically. Yet, despite his outraged feelings, he could clearly see that it would merely be sowing the seeds of future destruction to repeat the mistakes of the Treaty of Versailles. 'We saw the wretched poverty of Berlin in 1929, 30, 32 . . . Hitlerism was possible only as a result of that material misery, that moral humiliation . . . Everywhere one meets peace-loving people who have become enraged, who want to smash Germany into pieces, sterilize all the males, take them off into slavery to rebuild the countries that they have devastated!' He distances himself from such feelings of revenge, 'not out of a sense of justice or charity', but because such measures would be 'a terrible mistake'. The only way to change Germany, he concludes, is '*to make it happy*': 'I believe in the deleterious power of wellbeing, of prosperity. I imagine a Germany *blunted by happiness*.'[62] That, of course, is what the Allies, led by the Americans, did. There could have been few Frenchmen, in 1945, capable of such sentiments.

So Gide decided to postpone any return to France until the spring. Could not Pierre Herbart bring the Petite Dame to Algiers instead? 'Normal' transport was still impossible: any journey required an *ordre de mission*, which entailed days of waiting in freezing offices. One then had to spend a night in the station entrance to queue for tickets next morning – only the first arriving would get them. The journey, on unheated trains, many with windows missing, would take four or five hours, the nights being spent in unheated waiting-rooms en route. However, Gide had enough influence in Algiers and Paris to arrange for the Petite Dame to fly direct, but even that would take time. Pierre Herbart, who, with Camus, was now coediting the newspaper *Combat*, which had emerged from the underground press, was too busy to go with her: Camus was now seriously ill and all responsibility for the paper had fallen on him.

Meanwhile, on 9 February, the Petite Dame's seventy-ninth birthday, Catherine gave birth to a daughter, Isabelle. A week or two later, the Petite Dame was called on by Pierre Reynaud, a pilot who had become close friends with Gide. He had, he said, a letter from Gide to Gaston Palewski, de Gaulle's *chef de cabinet* and a great admirer of Gide, asking him to obtain an *ordre de mission* for Algiers. The plane would leave five days later. On the afternoon of 26 February, the Petite Dame landed in Algiers airport: 'We were so moved, so happy to see one another at last that we could only find smiles and nothing to say.' Gide had wanted to put the Petite Dame up in an hotel, but Anne Heurgon had insisted that she stay with them. She had thought that they would not stop talking for days. It was not like that: 'too many things to say, things that were heavy to raise and would cast a shadow over our joy at being reunited'. 'Later, later, fortunately we have the time,' Gide would say.[63] In the evenings, they all sat around the one fire in the house. During the day, however, if the sun was out, it got quite warm out of doors. They discussed Catherine, her daughter and what was to be done about them. They were living with the father, whom Gide later, in a letter to Jef Last, described as 'the Stalinist Communist who gave her a child, without being married to her . . . I don't care for him much.'[64] He was full of praise for the way Pierre and Beth had handled the situation. While Gide worked on an essay on Poussin, the Petite Dame caught up on the reading of his journal – and wrote her own *Cahiers*. On 20 March, he wrote to Beth asking her to arrange for flowers to be sent to Marie Bell for the opening night of *Antoine et Cléopâtre*, in Gide's revised translation, and to Jean-Louis Barrault, asking him to send tickets to Beth for the dress rehearsal.

On 1 April, Gide, the Petite Dame and a friend, Marcelle Schveitzer, were taken to Biskra, in the personal car of General Duval, the local commander. 'I can just see Gide,' writes the Petite Dame,

dressed as if he were going to the North Pole: two overcoats, a silk scarf, a woollen scarf and his black woollen cap . . . Suddenly, before the huge rocks of El Kantara, he stops the car; he says he wants to show me, on foot and with me alone, the enchantment of the great oasis. In the twinkling of an eye, he takes off one pair of underpants (he was wearing two), a coat, the silk scarf and cap, and emerges from all these skins slim and light, wearing a light suit and one of those hats – one may well wonder where he gets them. At a brisk pace, without hesitation, as if he had forgotten no twist or turn of the road in forty years, he took me into the verdant oasis, and I rediscovered it all, everything that sang in my memory, all that his fervour had been able to create and give such a prodigious existence.[65]

They were picked up by the car further along the road. At Biskra Gide took her to the Hôtel de l'Oasis and showed her the room that he had occupied on his first visit in 1893. He made inquiries about Athman. He had, it seemed, died about fifteen years before. 'All those who went with me to Biskra, or who joined me there, are dead,' he wrote to Copeau. 'Laurens, my mother and our old maid Marie; then Madeleine, Ghéon, Rouart, Jammes; my faithful Athman, in the grip of an attack of religious mysticism (and, moreover, driven batty by *kiff*) set out, one night, and got lost in the immensity of the desert.'[66]

Back in Algiers, Gide received a call from Camus, who had come home to recuperate after his illness. He was already known to the Heurgons, having been a student of Jacques' at the university. On 3 May, the rumour ran that Hitler was dead and the whole city threw itself into celebrations. The following day, they were informed that a plane would be ready to take them to Paris on 6 May.

'The End of Life . . . A Rather Dull Last Act': Thésée *and* Ainsi soit-il

(MAY 1945 – FEBRUARY 1951)

Gide had last seen Paris almost six years before. He and the Petite Dame arrived at Le Bourget and took the Air France bus to the air terminal in the rue La Fayette, where they had expected to be met by the Herbarts – a telegram had been sent warning of their arrival. The telegram had not yet arrived and no one was there waiting for them. So, with no taxis or porters to be seen, this elderly pair in their late seventies left their heavier suitcases at the left-luggage office and set off, 'burdened like donkeys: appallingly heavy bags, overcoats, umbrellas, walking-stick, shawls, and heaven knows what else', in search of the nearest métro station. The journey to Solférino-Gare d'Orsay station required two changes, then, on arrival, there was a further long walk to 1 bis rue Vaneau. 'But we managed it, and very well, too!' a triumphant Petite Dame exclaims. 'We must have looked like a couple of old provincials, just arrived in Paris, who hadn't taken the métro since before the war.'[1]

What was uppermost on Gide's mind was the reunion with Catherine. She came to lunch next day, 'full of grace and kindness', and Gide 'immediately melted in front of her, very sensitive to her charm'. They went up to Marc's old studio, now Camus', to hear the broadcast of de Gaulle's proclamation of victory in Europe – presumably, the only radio in that conjunction of apartments was to be found *chez* Camus. The next few days were a turmoil, inwardly and outwardly, at home and in the street. 'What emotions! What people! What *Marseillaises*! What flags! What marches!' the Petite Dame notes after abandoning her *Cahier* for a week. The day after Victory in Europe day, the Bussys arrived from Nice, making the Vaneau even more 'overpopulated'.[2] Simenon turned up. Gide attended a luncheon given by the *Figaro* in honour of T. S. Eliot. On 13 May, he attended a performance of *Antoine et Cléopâtre* and called on Barrault backstage. There was a succession of callers: Malraux, Copeau, Jean Schlumberger, Coppet and Domi Drouin, who brought Gide up to date with Cuverville and its inhabitants. Dorothy returned to London, but there were still bureaucratic problems about allowing her French husband to join her in England.

It was not all euphoria, of course: 'The war has left us in such a moral and material turmoil, and the accounts of the repatriated are so appalling that our conversations are rather sombre.'[3] One of the 'repatriated' was Louis Martin-Chauffier, the editor of Gide's fifteen-volume *Œuvres complètes*. Pierre had heard that he was in Belsen and took steps to have him flown to Paris. On 9 June, he called at the Vaneau: 'It was the first time that we saw someone we knew well come back from the hell of the German camps. He was extraordinarily changed – almost another person. I would not have thought that a face could change so much: his excessive thinness changes the proportion of his features; his forehead seems higher, his eyes bigger, his hair is white.' In fact, the Petite Dame thought that he looked 'infinitely better than before . . . a sort of nobility is imprinted on his face'. He recounted 'frightful things', which, when he had recovered, he would try to write about.[4] (His memoirs were published by Gallimard in 1948 as *L'Homme et la Bête*. Martin-Chauffier survived his ordeal, physically at least, dying in 1980, aged eighty-six.) Some weeks later, Gide and the Petite Dame dined at Stoisy Sternheim's. Also there was her daughter, who, a month before, had been released from Ravensbrück camp. She had spent a few weeks in Sweden and had therefore recovered somewhat from her ordeal. 'She spoke without hatred, without exaggeration, but her simple account sent shivers down our spines.' As a result of 'the ordinary brutalities', the young woman had lost her front teeth.[5] Gide was tempted by the idea of going to Germany with Pierre Herbart, but was soon dissuaded from doing so.

Valéry was ill: stomach ulcers had been diagnosed. Throughout June, Gide visited him several times. With his usual clarity and lack of emotion, Valéry 'talked very simply about his illness, not recoiling before the hypothesis of a cancer'.[6]

On 21 June, 'le Vaneau' attended a Stravinsky concert at the Théâtre des Champs-Elysées that included Gide's *Perséphone*. Afterwards, Keeler Faus, an American diplomat friend of Gide, took them off to dinner at the Hôtel Wagram, which was occupied by Americans: a meal of 'pre-war luxury and refinement', the Petite Dame comments. Afterwards they went up to Faus's seventh-floor rooms, from which they had a splendid view of the Tuileries.

Next day, Martin du Gard arrived at the Vaneau, having travelled from Nice the previous day. After long conversations with Gide, Pierre and the Petite Dame during the day, he came back for dinner in the evening: they rediscovered their friendship 'like the most well-fitting of garments . . .'⁷

On 23 June, driven by Simenon, Gide left for Cuverville. It was the first time that he had been there since Madeleine's death in 1938. He had only intended to spend two nights there, but, in the event, spent only one, arriving back 'very sad and upset'. He had found Jeanne Drouin 'aged, tired, almost blind'; her brother, Georges Rondeaux, then seventy-three, was 'completely deaf, with no teeth'. Gide was particularly depressed by the state of the house and its gardens; everything seemed dilapidated and uncared for. It 'smelled of death and neglect'; he had only one idea in his head, to get back to Paris as soon as possible.⁸ He was not to return alive.

On 3 July, Gide and Catherine went to see a performance of *Richard III*, given at the Théâtre-Français by the Old Vic company, led by Laurence Olivier. Also there were François Mauriac and his son Claude, who left an amusing account of the evening. The theatre was full of 'the eternal faces of the Tout-Paris de toujours' going through their mutual recognition ceremonies. Claude Mauriac then noticed Gide in the circle, obviously sitting in an uncomfortable position, 'in order to facilitate the work of a photographer taking pictures, not of him, André Gide, but of the box of Lady Diana Cooper, the wife of the British Ambassador, Sir Alfred Duff Cooper, currently known in Paris as "le Duff sur le toit"'. Beside Lady Cooper, Cocteau sat enthroned, obviously as much at ease with the British embassy as he had been, a short while before, with high-ranking Germans. During the interval, Jacques Duchesne, who had worked for the BBC French Service during the war, came over and insisted that Gide and François Mauriac should go with him to meet Laurence Olivier in his dressing-room: it was a fitting occasion for two great French writers to meet the great English actor. Afterwards, a rather shamefaced Gide, constant reader of English literature, translator of *Antony and Cleopatra* and *Hamlet*, admitted that, apart from a word here or a phrase there, he had understood nothing of 'the Chinese of these British actors'!⁹ Clarity of diction would not, of course, have been a problem with Olivier and his 1945 actors. The truth is that Gide's acquaintance with the language was almost entirely from books and when he read aloud, it was his English that sounded, if not like Chinese, like nothing on earth.

On 20 July, Paul Valéry died. Four days later, Gide and Martin du Gard were the guests of Simenon at the Hôtel Claridge. RMG was as enchanted by their host as Gide: 'He writes his books in ten or twelve days, typing them himself from six in the morning', prior to which he always makes love with his wife or his maid, Boule, who had been in the house for years. 'He now earns millions of francs, *per month*, since many of his novels have been turned into films.'[10] Afterwards, they went to the Trocadéro to await the arrival of Valéry's coffin: a funeral service was taking place at the church of Saint-Honoré-d'Eylau (though Valéry was an unbeliever) and the hearse would be carried in a torch-lit procession from the place Victor-Hugo to the Trocadéro, where it would be placed on the central area facing the Eiffel Tower and overlooking Paris. There students would keep watch all night. When the three writers arrived there was already a large crowd waiting. A policeman told them that the procession would not be arriving until the early hours of the morning. After waiting a while, the friends decided that they had better leave. An official ceremony took place in Paris and, two days later, Valéry's body was buried in the 'Cimetière marin' of his best-known poem, in his native Sète.

About this time, Gide received a letter, quite out of the blue, from Amsterdam. It was the first he had heard from Jef Last, whom he had feared dead, since 1940. Jef had spent most of the war in hiding from the Gestapo editing an underground monthly, *De Vonk* (*The Spark*), produced by a non-Communist extreme-left group. Two of his daughters, too, had served in the underground, the eldest being sent to a German concentration camp for ten months. He was thinking of going to China. He had had enough of Europe (but clearly not of politics and war) – why didn't Gide join him?

On 1 August, Gide left for three weeks at Le Mont-Dore. The weather was appalling: cold, rain, fog, wind. When he was not subjecting himself to treatment for his 'vocal cords', he was working on a long article about Valéry.[11] It would, he wrote to Martin du Gard, 'horrify Mauriac, Duhamel and many others, but too bad: what matters is fidelity to . . . the most irreverent, most irreligious, most free-thinking mind this century'.[12] He read, too, of course: Simenon, Virgil, Xenophon ('not alas!, in the original'), Jane Austen's *Emma* and Robert Graves's *I, Claudius*.

Back in Paris, Gide found a Vaneau occupied by Pierre Herbart alone. The Petite Dame had left for Belgium, Beth for Cabris, Simon Bussy for London. 'How well we get on together!' Gide wrote to RMG. 'Pierre is exquisite, pleasant and complaisant, amusing and amused, bringing his humour and intelligence to everything. Not a moment of lassitude or boredom.'[13]

In early September, Robert Levesque arrived back from Athens, the

proud author of two books: translations, with long introductions, of
the Greek poets Seferis and Solomos. There were already plans for Gide
to go back to Greece with him at the end of October and then to go on to
Egypt. (Referring to these plans, almost in passing, brought on a response
from London of a kind that Gide might have thought a thing of the past.
'The old familiar physical sensation of a knife being plunged into the heart
on reading . . . that you are going to Greece with Robert Levesque in
October (next month!),' Dorothy wrote. 'Tell Robert Levesque that I envy
him.'[14] Did the poor, crazed eighty-year-old woman imagine that she was
a fitter travelling companion to the seventy-five-year-old Gide than the
placid thirty-six-year-old Levesque, who, in any case, had spent the war in
Greece? On the evening of his return, Robert telephoned Gide and went
round to the Vaneau the following day. That same evening, they met up
again, this time with Pierre Herbart, and the three men compared notes
on the difficulty of sexual 'adventures' in Paris, Italy and even North Africa.
Perhaps Egypt . . . They discussed Roger Peyrefitte's recently published
Les Amitiés particulières, now a classic of adolescent homosexuality. Robert
doubted whether schoolboys nowadays thought so much about purity, still
less talked about it so much. They discussed mutual acquaintances: Aragon
and his new attack on Gide in Les Lettres nouvelles; Montherlant, now trying
to pass himself off as anti-German; Jouhandeau, whose hand Robert would
never shake again after his wartime anti-semitic statements, made, Pierre
claimed, under the influence of his wife, who was mad with jealousy when
her husband fell in love with a young Jew.

Gide was approached by the Société Gibé, in which his cousin Edouard
was an executive producer, to write a scenario for a film based on his
Symphonie Pastorale: Michèle Morgan had already been signed up to play the
blind heroine and was planning to come back to France from the United
States. In the end, Gide could not get on with the film people and abandoned
the project. The film was finally made by Jean Delaunay, with a scenario
by Jean Aurenche and Pierre Bost. Presented at the Cannes Festival in
1946, it won the Grand Prix; Michèle Morgan was awarded the Prix de
l'Interprétation féminine and Georges Auric the Prix de la Musique.

Gide had better luck with his translation of Hamlet and Jean-Louis
Barrault, who came to the Vaneau several mornings in September to work
on his planned production. At this time, Barrault was still at the Comédie-
Française, but was planning, with his wife, Madeleine Renaud, and with
several of the sociétaires, to set up a new company at the Théâtre Marigny.

Beth arrived back from Cabris on 8 October and set about rearranging the 'studio', which she and Pierre would soon take over – the Camuses had already left. The Petite Dame returned a few days later. She noted that, about this time, there was much talk of Sartre and 'Existentialism'. Gide was 'very resistant to this new philosophy' – though one side of him, the younger, 'Nietzschean' Gide, might have been expected to be more sympathetic to it: 'I'm willing to be an Existentialist, providing I'm not aware of the fact.'

Meanwhile, de Gaulle's unelected Consultative Assembly had drawn up a referendum asking the electorate (including women for the first time) whether or not it wanted to return to the constitution of the Third Republic. In October, an overwhelming majority rejected the proposition. At the same time, elections produced a new, heavily left-inclined Constituent Assembly. The old Third Republic groupings, the Modérés (Conservatives) and the Radicals, were reduced to 10.4 and 4.9 per cent of the deputies respectively. With 27.3 per cent of the seats, the Communists were the largest party. Together with the Socialists' 24.2 per cent, they had 51.5 per cent of the seats, a working majority of eighteen seats. The strategy of Moscow and the PCF leadership was to create first a Popular Front government and then, once the Allied armies were off French soil, a 'Socialist Unity' party of the type later set up in Eastern Europe. The principal obstacle to this plan was de Gaulle himself. The second was the unexpected success of the MRP (Mouvement républicain populaire), a broadly-based centrist party, largely Catholic and 'Gaullist', stretching from Christian socialists to conservatives, that had emerged from the Resistance; with 24.2 per cent of the deputies, the MRP was the second largest party. The third, almost as unexpected, was the decision of the Socialists, by a narrow majority, to seek a more broadly based alliance, rather than work exclusively with the PCF; this decision owed much to their leader, Léon Blum, recently back from Buchenwald, where he had continued his education in the ways of Communists (who, under the SS, ran the camp). Having failed to get their own candidate elected to the premiership, the Communists threw their support behind the rest of the Constituent Assembly. On 13 November, de Gaulle was elected Prime Minister unanimously and formed an MRP/Socialist/PCF government, while refusing Thorez's demands for one of the great portfolios, Foreign Affairs, Defence or Interior. Malraux became Information Minister.

On 15 November, Robert Levesque, accompanied by his friend John, called. Gide told them of a schoolboy, then about seventeen, who had written him a few enthusiastic letters from Bordeaux, then came to Paris to see him and 'threw himself into his arms'.[15] Over the next few weeks, Gide and Robert saw a great deal of one another. They went to the cinema together – a film of Malraux's *L'Espoir* and Jean Vigo's *Zéro de Conduite*, in which Gide was 'very excited by the schoolboys'.

On 5 December, Martin du Gard came to lunch. The conversation reverted to the subject of the Académie Française. De Gaulle himself, it seemed, had decided to renovate the old institution: he found it absurd that a body that, abroad, represented French culture, should not include so many of its best literary talents. To begin with, Gide, Claudel, Jules Romains and Martin du Gard should be approached and they should consider it their duty to accept. They would have to be elected together, without going through the traditional procedures. RMG was determined to refuse, not out of contempt for the Academy's membership, but because he did not want to end his days 'in an official's skin'. What was Gide's attitude? 'In half an hour,' writes the Petite Dame, 'he had adopted every position in turn, however contradictory.' They agreed that the General's proposition did rather alter the situation. Other names, too, had been mentioned: Aragon, Paulhan, Eluard, Malraux. Gide admitted that he felt rather attracted by the idea of the author of *Corydon* entering the Academy. In the end, turning to RMG, Gide said: 'I'll join if you do.'[16] Neither did: as so often, it was left to lesser men to do so.

Early on 10 December, Gide went into the Petite Dame's bedroom to say goodbye. In a few hours, he would be flying in an RAF plane to Naples with Robert Levesque, on the first stage of their journey to Egypt. He had found time, he said, to light the fire in her sitting-room (as he did every morning, there still being no central heating in the building). At ten o'clock, he reappeared: the plane would not be leaving that day on account of repairs. They finally left Paris on 14 December, arriving in Naples next day. They met up with Professor Caccioppoli, with whom they had spent an 'unforgettable evening at Sorrento, in 1937', and were invited to 'a veritable feast of a dinner' at his mother's (she was Bakunin's daughter).

On 20 December, they flew to Cairo, where they spent 'an exhausting week' and 'where the marvellous Abbé Drioton', an eminent Egyptologist, took them round the museum.[17] Gide tried to think about the lecture that he would have to give in March, in Cairo: the prospect 'terrified' him. Robert was working harder: each week he produced an article for *La Marseillaise*, a French-language Cairo newspaper. By the end of the year, they were at Luxor, where, as we learn from an unpublished letter to Arnold Naville, Gide had 'almost daily adventures'.

*

On New Year's Day, they were invited to lunch by the Chevriers, a French couple Gide had met in Egypt in 1939. They took to the Nile again, arriving at Aswan on 4 January. There, at the Cataract Hotel, they were joined for a few days by Etiemble, a young scholar who was now running the Amitiés Françaises in Alexandria, and a woman friend, Yassu Gauclère. Étiemble had first met Gide in 1933, when, as a besotted young man, he had burst into tears during a visit to the Vaneau. They had last met in Algiers in the summer of 1944. At Aswan, too, there were 'adventures', though we learn nothing of them in either man's journal. However, in a letter written a few weeks after Gide's return to Paris, Robert asks in passing: 'Could the square Boucicaut [near the Sèvres-Babylone métro station] replace the municipal garden at Aswan?' Clearly, the implication is, not. On 30 January, Gide and Levesque embarked on the long journey southwards, on the Nile, to Wadi-Halfa on the Sudanese border. Their boat was 'escorted on each side by a supplementary boat, one serving as the second class, the other full of Egyptian scouts'. They visited the temple of Abu Simbel and returned to Aswan, where they collected their mail. For Gide, there was a letter from André Ruyters, whom he had not heard from since October 1939. He was in what had been, until recently, a Japanese internment camp at Hué, in Indochina, awaiting repatriation. In 1936, he had been awarded the Légion d'honneur, for services not to literature, but to banking. The following year, he retired from the Banque de l'Indochine. Unfortunately, he and his wife happened to find themselves in Indochina in 1940 and could not get back to Paris.

On 9 February, they were back in Luxor, from where, over the next couple of weeks, they made explorations of the Valley of the Kings and other sites. A letter from Martin du Gard recounted the celebrations, on 9 February, of the Petite Dame's eightieth birthday. On 7 March, Robert Levesque gave a lecture at the French Lycée. Introduced by Gide, it concerned the work of the Greek poets Sikelianos, Seferis and Kazantzakis. Gide's own lecture, 'Souvenirs littéraires', devoted mainly to the Symbolists, was on 12 March. The two spent a week in Alexandria, where Levesque repeated his Cairo lecture, again introduced by Gide, before a distinguished audience, including the governor of the city, the French and Greek consuls, etc. Gide's own lecture, on 'Youth and its problems', was given before a packed audience, ranging from local dignitaries to students. At the Amitiés Françaises in Alexandria, Gide met up with Etiemble, who was organizing a Gide exhibition. A dramatization of *Le Retour de l'Enfant prodigue* was also given. At the unlikely-sounding venue of the Roxy Cinema, Gide gave his

'Souvenirs littéraires et problèmes actuelles', which, with its attack on the Jesuits and on Barrès, caused something of a stir. One day in Beirut, as they were sitting at their desk, Gide put down his pen and said:

Mon petit, there is a secret between us. Everything I have seen of you over the past month has convinced me that I am not wrong . . . In my will, I have left you the rue Vaneau apartment and everything in it. I thought it would be nice for you to own a library and that the apartment would be useful for you and your brothers . . . I can't bear the idea that Catherine's fiancé, a Communist, will inherit anything of mine. The Party would put its hand on everything . . . I'm very fond of you, *mon petit* Robert. Let's hope this journey won't be the last! You've always been . . . a marvellous companion. Of course, nothing is changed between us and we won't talk about all this again.[18]

Before leaving Paris, Gide had written a codicil to his will, put it in an envelope marked 'To be opened after my death by Roger Martin du Gard' and slipped it into a drawer. He had previously discussed the matter with RMG, who approved of the change. However, a few weeks after her father's return to Paris, Catherine left her Communist lover in favour of Jean Lambert, who fully met with her father's approval. (Lambert, an academic specialist in German and English, had first met Gide – and an eighteen-year-old Catherine – in Cabris in 1941.) Gide now felt that he no longer had any reason to deprive his daughter of what was rightfully hers and, on 15 July, wrote to RMG to this effect. To Robert Levesque, Gide was as good as his word in only one respect: he never spoke to him again about the matter. Levesque did not learn of the further change in the will, in which he was left a number of books, until after Gide's death. By way of explanation, one might cite nothing more dramatic than embarrassment on Gide's part, and fear perhaps that Robert's attitude to him might change.

They left Beirut for Cairo on 16 April. The following day, Gide caught a plane back to Paris, accompanied by Amrouche, Robert staying on a few days more, before making his way back to Athens.

Jean-Louis Barrault arrived at the Vaneau to work on the adaptation that Gide had made of Kafka's *The Trial*. This was to continue several days a week for several weeks. In June, *Thésée* was published at last in the Gallimard edition – it had already appeared in April in the first issue of Jean Paulhan's *Cahiers de la Pléiade* (Gallimard's house review, replacing the proscribed *NRF*) and, in a *de luxe* edition, from Jacques Schiffrin's publishing house in New York. *Thésée* beats Gide's record in the time elapsing between a work's first conception and its completion. There are references to the legend of Theseus as early as 1897, in *Les Nourritures terrestres* and *Le Promethée mal enchaîné*. By 1911, a *Thésée* was already being planned. In the undated notes jotted down in that year, we read: 'Similarly, Ariadne makes Theseus go back to the point from which he started after he has killed the Minotaur ... In *Thésée* this must be brought out – the thread, to put it crudely, is the apron-string.'[19] A fragment, 'Monologue de Thésée', written in 1924–5, was placed in Volume 13 of the *Œuvres complètes* and described as 'a fragment of a play or novel planned by Gide, but never written'.[20] Only in 1944, in a sudden, excited burst of energy, with peace in sight, did *Thésée* finally emerge, a *récit* of some 16,000 words (or thirty-eight pages in the Pléiade edition).

Like all Greek myths, the story of Theseus is to be found in innumerable versions, each repeating much, omitting some things and introducing others. Gide's main source was Plutarch's *Life of Theseus*, with hints from Racine's *Phèdre*, but he felt quite free to rearrange the usual sequence of events, stressing some, underplaying others. It is a first-person narrative, in which a now elderly Thésée tells the story of his life. His carefree adolescence is evoked in terms reminiscent of *Les Nourritures terrestres*: 'I was the wind, a wave. I was a plant, a bird ... I stroked fruit, the bark of young trees, smooth pebbles on the shore, the coats of dogs and horses, before my fingers ever touched a woman's skin. At the sight of all the charming things presented to me by Pan, Zeus and Thetis, I got an erection.'[21] Thésée then sets out on his adventures: 'Where women are concerned I have never been able to settle down.'[22] When not breaking hearts, he was slaying monsters. He insists on joining the seven young men and seven maidens sent each year as tribute to Crete, 'to satisfy the appetite*s* of the Minotaur'.[23] (Note the plural. Traditionally, the Minotaur killed and devoured the young people, to satisfy his appetite. By writing 'appetite*s*', Gide is suggesting, rather, a sexual appetite.) It was the practice, when the ship returned empty-handed from Crete, for the black flag to be raised. Thésée promised his father, Egée, to hoist a white flag if he was successful in killing the Minotaur and thus bringing an end to Attica's subjection to Crete. On their victorious return, Thésée 'forgot' to hoist the white flag and, thinking that he had lost his son, Egée threw himself off a cliff into the sea. 'One can't think of everything,' Thésée adds. 'But to tell you the truth ... I can't swear that it was really forgetfulness – Egée was in my way ...'[24]

The narrative returns to the Cretan expedition. Here Gide's innovations are at their most obvious. During a dinner given in honour of the Greek hostages, the women, especially the queen, Pasiphaë, and her eldest daughter, Ariane (Ariadne) cannot keep their eyes (or hands) off Thésée.

He, however, is more taken by the younger Phèdre (Phaedra). The queen manages to get Thésée up to her bedroom. Protesting that she has no designs upon his person, 'attractive as that may be', she slips her hand under his leather jerkin and fondles his pectorals. 'Please try to understand me: I am of a religious temperament. I have love only for the divine. The problem, you see, is knowing where the god begins and where he ends. I've had a lot to do with my cousin Léda. For her, the god hid himself in a swan . . . But how is one to know how much of the animal remains in the seed of the gods?' She had, she admits, been wrong about that bull. But, make no mistake, 'my bull was no ordinary beast'. It had been sent by Poséidon . . . And, then, her mother-in-law, Europa, was carried off by a bull. But, of course, that time, Zeus was in the bull . . . Very well, then, she did not, on that occasion, consort with a god. People may call her son a monster, but he is after all her son. She begs Thésée not to harm him. Couldn't he make friends with him?[25] He leaves the mother and goes and meets Ariane, as previously arranged, on the terrace. She tells him to take no notice of what her mother has told him. Thésée is in great danger: she alone can help him. She tells him about the labyrinth: tomorrow she will introduce him to Dédale (Daedalus), who built it. 'Only thanks to me, by me, in me, will you be able to find yourself again. Take it or leave it . . . You can start by taking me.'[26] Thésée obliges.

Dédale turns out to be a silver-haired old man, who, unknown to Minos the king, is of Greek origin. He will help Thésée escape. He recounts why and how the maze was constructed. In the first chamber, Thésée will be overcome by the fumes of a hallucinogenic drug that will rob him of any desire to leave: 'they induce a delicious intoxication that arouses flattering delusions', beside which 'reality seems unappealing'. But the drug acts differently on each person: 'each, according to the tangled web of his own brain, becomes lost, if I may say so, in his own labyrinth.' Thus his son Icare (Icarus) became embroiled in metaphysical speculation. Thésée, too, might become a victim of his own brain, but, if he has sufficient will-power, he will go forward until he meets the Minotaur. To ensure that he is then able to find his way back, Ariane must remain at the entrance, out of range of the fumes, and Thésée must be linked to her by a thread (the 'umbilical' apron-string), 'the tangible symbol of duty . . . your link with the past. Go back to it. Go back to yourself.'[27]

Thésée's thirteen companions enter the maze first. By the time Thésée himself joins them, armed with the thread and holding an antidote-impregnated cloth over his face, they are already under the influence of the drug. He makes his way through the various chambers until he arrives at a garden. Here, again, Gide departs from, even reverses, the received version of the myth. The 'monster' is not ugly and terrifying, but young and beautiful, lying asleep on a bank of flowers: 'As with centaurs, there was about him a harmony of the human and the animal.' With the 'confrontation', too, Gide performs a skilful reversal. There is no feat of arms, no scene of slaughter. In fact, Thésée cannot remember what happened, his brain obviously affected by the drugged fumes. It is clear that the encounter was, initially at least, sexual: 'If I did overcome the Minotaur, my recollection of the victory is confused, though, on the whole, rather erotic . . . the charm of that garden was so alluring I thought I could never drag myself away.' But, '*quitte du Minotaure*', he did. Brilliantly laconic and indeterminate that '*quitte du*'; it means, literally, 'quit of', or 'after settling with' (Russell's version), almost the old-fashioned 'having settled his hash'.[28] Later, Thésée remarks: 'Although a Greek, I am in no way inclined to those of my own sex, however young and charming they may be. In this I differ from Hercules. As far as I'm concerned, he can keep his Hylas.'[29] Yet, when confronted with the (male) Minotaur, this bluff, unreflecting, 'virile' man admits that youth and beauty are, for him, 'weapons stronger than strength'. He thinks that he 'overcame' the Minotaur, but the Minotaur 'overcame' him, too – as did his mother and as his half-sister will do. Thésée is in some confusion as to where his inclinations lie: in this case, the experience is 'unforgettable', but one that he cannot quite remember. But, afterwards, did he kill the Minotaur? We are never told that he did, but can only assume that he did. If he did, he would have no idea why he did. We are in no better position to know. It might be tempting to invoke a particular kind of 'sex murder': the man who murders his male sexual partner out of shame. We must resist such an interpretation, I think. Shame is quite foreign to Thésée. He has nothing against homosexuality, what was good enough for Hercules . . . It's just that he doesn't fancy men. He has quite enough on his hands with women. Of course, if anything did take place, it was the drug . . . He probably killed the Minotaur because that is what he had set out to do: he was a killer of monsters and the Minotaur was just one more; the fact that his victim was beautiful, stupid and quite harmless was beside the point.

Following the thread, Thésée makes his way back through the maze and finds his companions, still luxuriating in the delights of the first chamber. He forces them, much against their will, to leave. His next problem is to abduct Phèdre, while letting Ariane believe that he is leaving Crete with her. Phèdre is dressed up as her brother Glaucos and, as such, leaves with Theseus. Ariane goes with them: though fiercely jealous of her sister, she would not take Thésée's attraction towards her younger brother seriously. On Naxos, Thésée ditches Ariane, leaving her to the delights of Dionysos, 'in other words, she found consolation in wine'.[30]

On his return to Greece, a change comes over Thésée. He becomes at once king and husband, what is more a just king and a faithful husband. He has reached mature manhood. He sets about uniting Greece under the hegemony of Athens, but refuses all royal privileges. He then divides up the land equally among the peasants. 'The accursed love of money that torments you does not bring you happiness, for it is insatiable,' he tells the landowners.[31] With this form of primitive communism, Thésée also introduces democracy. Attica will be ruled not by a tyrant, but by a government of the whole people: each citizen will have a right to sit on the Council.

In the final section, the blind, wandering Oedipe arrives at Athens seeking refuge. Thésée recognizes in the former Theban king 'a nobility equal to mine'. In one sense, he regards Oedipe as his superior: 'He had stood up against the Sphinx; he had set Man up against the riddle and dared to oppose the gods.' What he cannot understand is why Oedipe accepted defeat and then blinded himself. He finds Oedipe's explanation, that he had burst his eyes in order to prevent them from seeing what should not be seen, unsatisfactory. Nor can he understand Oedipe's cry at the time: 'Oh darkness, my light!'[32] Thésée and Oedipe pursue their discussion. In the radio conversations, Jean Amrouche tried to get Gide to come down on one side or the other of the argument, between 'the mystic, the man who chooses darkness as the sole, definitive, absolute light' and the man 'who opts for an earthly destiny'. Gide replied: 'I choose as little as possible, and I'm really quite unable to say to which side my preference goes.'[33] *Thésée* ends with a brief *apologia pro vita sua*:

I have built my city. My thought will live on there, immortal, after I have gone. It is with a consenting heart that I approach a solitary death. I have tasted the good things of the earth. It is sweet to think that after me, thanks to me, men will see themselves as happier, better, freer. What I have done I have done for the good of mankind in the future. I have lived.[34]

There is a testamentary air about those lines. The author, in many ways so different from his Thésée, seems now to be speaking for himself: for 'city' read 'œuvre'. Gide said that this would be his last work of fiction and it was. It was a fitting end, a minor masterpiece in the French neo-classical mode, wittily updating older versions of the myth, written in French of impeccable style, yet unflinchingly modern in idiom, occasionally encompassing the colloquial and risqué. Written by a man of seventy-five, *Thésée* has the serenity of old age, but it also has the lightness of touch, the irrepressible fantasy of the thirty-year-old Gide of *Le Prométhée mal enchaîné*.

Gide raised the question of whether or not Dorothy Bussy should translate *Thésée*: 'I'm convinced, rightly or wrongly, that it really isn't for you [ce n'est pas du tout votre affaire].'[35] This, understandably, elicited an outraged response: 'Now, dear Gide, do tell me the *truth* about *Thésée*. What is there in it so different from the style of all your other books that makes it not my "affaire"? . . . You may perhaps think that, considering my age and years of wear and tear, my capacity has in all probability diminished . . . but I can't understand that *Thésée* is not my affair.'[36] Gide wrote back to say that he had entrusted the translation to no one: 'Your amiable jealousy is totally wasted. It simply seemed to me that a woman's vocal cords were inappropriate for so deep a voice. But rest assured that there is still time to prove me wrong.'[37] Dorothy replied that she found Gide's opinion of the qualities required of a translator 'absolutely fantastic', but now that she knew his reasons, she would not, could not translate *Thésée*. She then points out, quite devastatingly: 'How can you, who pride yourself particularly in imitating a woman's, a young girl's voice, think that the opposite impersonation, especially in a translator, who has nothing to invent, is impossible?' If Gide agrees, she will happily set about finding for him 'a male translator with a bass voice'.[38] (The translation, by John Russell, was published by Horizon in 1948.) By August, Dorothy Bussy had read *Thésée* and collected her thoughts on the matter. She now understands 'why you didn't want to offer it to me . . . You were quite right. It isn't the tone of voice (I think) nor the language that is too masculine for me to find words for – it is the spirit that I don't like or, more probably, don't understand. I don't like your Thésée.' So Gide had been right all along: his antennae had told him that Dorothy would interpret *Thésée* too literally, see its narrator-hero as a mouthpiece for the author. Her next words, by their very absurdity, proved this: 'I don't want the coming generations to learn and follow his lesson. So, Hitler might have advised and written, if Hitler had known how to write, which, fortunately, he didn't . . . Thésée's misogyny (and you pretend that he is *not* a misogynist!) I find very hard to forgive and almost impossible not to impute to you.'[39]

In July, the Petite Dame, Gide and Jean Lambert visited a small apartment in the rue Chanoinesse, near Notre-Dame, on the Ile de la Cité. It had originally been offered to Julien Green, who decided that it would be too small for him; it was to become the Lamberts' first home. In August, Gide and Pierre Herbart set off for Pertisau, near Innsbrück, where Gide had been asked to participate in an international gathering of teachers and students. There he gave a revised version of his Beirut lecture. They then went on to Zürich, Herbart returning to Paris, Gide going on to Lausanne. On the way, Gide caught a bad cold in the train and was besieged by toothache. He decided to go and stay with Richard Heyd, a Swiss publisher, in Neuchâtel, 'who smothered me with kindness'.[40] (Heyd ran the firm of Ides et Calendes, which, in 1946, published Gide's *Le Retour*, and was to publish the posthumous *Et nunc manet in te*.)

Gide turned up at the Vaneau on 16 September. A few hours before, Enid McLeod had arrived; a few hours later, Jean Lambert and Catherine, who had been married at Cabris a few weeks before and would soon be moving into their new apartment. Gide's absence from the wedding in no way expressed disapproval. On the contrary, he approved entirely of Jean Lambert. He just thought that things would be better for all concerned if he were out of the way. Anyway, he cared as little for weddings as he did for funerals. Next day, the Petite Dame received a telegram, announcing Bernard Groethuysen's death: he had been suffering from lung cancer and had gone to Luxembourg to be treated and to stay with Loup Mayrisch.

On 26 September, 'the Vaneau' attended a gala showing of the film of *La Symphonie Pastorale*. 'An incredible deployment of police, lights, carpets, palms and dresses,' wrote the Petite Dame. 'I imagine a reception at the Elysée would be like that.'[41] Gide decided to attend in order not to hurt the feelings of his cousin Edouard Gide, the film's executive producer. The Lamberts sat in pride of place in the circle, next to Michèle Morgan. Gide wandered about. Back at the Vaneau afterwards, they all agreed that it was, all in all, a good film, but retained of the original only the basic human story – the pastor might just as easily have been a doctor. Later, Catherine asked her father what he had talked about to Maurice Chevalier. He looked puzzled: had he been talking to Maurice Chevalier? That day, a letter arrived from Maurice Chevalier, apologizing that he had not realized the man he had been talking to was André Gide.

Jean-Louis Barrault had now acquired a lease on the Marigny Theatre, the charming octagonal building in the middle of the gardens of the Champs-Elysées. The new Renaud-Barrault company was to open its season with Gide's translation of *Hamlet*. Gide attended many of the rehearsals, still, apparently, failing to understand the ways of actors. The semi-public dress rehearsal took place on 16 October. In Gide's box were the Petite Dame, Pierre Herbart, Stoisy Sternheim, and Dorothy and Janie Bussy, who had arrived at the Vaneau the day before. Barrault's performance and the production in general met with no one's full approval, but, a few days later, Gide went again, with Pierre and Martin du Gard, and found everything much more to his satisfaction. Madeleine Renaud was not in the production, but Copeau's daughter Marie-Hélène Dasté played the Queen. The sets were designed by André Masson. The music, by Honegger, was played by two young music students destined for higher things: Maurice Jarre on percussion and Pierre Boulez, playing the ondes Martenot (an instrument particularly associated with his teacher, Olivier Messiaen). *Hamlet* was joined in the company's first repertory season by Marivaux's *Les Fausses Confidences* and *Baptiste* (the complete pantomime from the film *Les Enfants du Paradis* danced, of course, by Barrault himself).

One day, Gide suggested that he and the Petite Dame went to Brussels for a week: he had earned Belgian francs from a lecture that he had given earlier in the year, but could not take them out of the country. They left Paris on 6 November: 'It was a real success. We were like two kids on holiday, determined to have a good time, even when things went wrong'[42] – like when they arrived at the frontier to find that Gide had forgotten his passport: 'Fortunately, miraculously, his name settled the matter.' What would have happened, the Petite Dame wonders, if they had had to deal with a more ignorant official? In Brussels, they moved into well-heated, inter-communicating rooms at the Hôtel Métropole. They had breakfast together in the Petite Dame's room, then went their separate ways until the evening. By an odd coincidence, a visiting English company was playing *Hamlet*: 'Curious to compare it with Barrault's interpretation.' The English Hamlet was 'irresistibly likeable', 'an exquisite voice', 'very much a prince and with surprising naturalness, less authority than Barrault, less intellectual, less nervous'. The Ophelia was 'prodigious'.[43] (Though neither seemed aware of the fact, they had witnessed performances by the greatest Hamlet and Ophelia of their day, John Gielgud and Peggy Ashcroft.)

They came back to the Vaneau to find Beth there. The servant problem had not been solved. Gide now lit fires for both of them. On 22 November, they celebrated Gide's seventy-seventh birthday. The event was also cele-brated on French radio, the day before, in a broadcast organized by Jean Amrouche, almost against Gide's will. Malraux, Schlumberger, Paulhan,

Camus and Martin du Gard all spoke. Gide recorded the last few sentences of *Thésée*. A wireless set was borrowed and fixed up in his apartment, but reception was so poor that they could hear practically nothing. Martin du Gard came to see them. The conversation got on to the recent elections. 'No, I didn't vote,' said Gide, 'I never vote. I'm against universal suffrage.'[44] On 30 November, Gide, RMG, the Lamberts and Enid McLeod went to see Laurence Olivier and the Old Vic Company in *King Lear*. 'As for Olivier, he is without any doubt a great actor. The fact that he can, with the same success, play one after the other the dashing young officer of Shaw's *Arms and the Man* and old Lear is amazing.'[45] Meanwhile rehearsals had started for Barrault's production of *Le Procès*, Gide's version of Kafka's *The Trial*.

In September, while still in Athens, Robert Levesque had written in his journal: 'Curious to know Gide's plans. I would drop everything to follow him, for I know that nothing more exciting could happen to me than to live near him.'[46] By the time Levesque came back to Paris, in November, Gide's 'plans' had expanded to a tour across the world, ending in Tahiti, 'which he finds very tempting'.[47] By the end of the year, however, his mighty plans had shrunk to the little measure of another trip to Switzerland.

Gide, the Petite Dame and Beth celebrated New Year's Eve with a dinner, followed, at midnight, by the traditional Van Rysselberghe warmed wine. On 4 January, Tania Lvoff, Tolstoy's grand-daughter, arrived from Cabris with bad news of Loup Mayrisch: she was paralysed in her left leg, could hardly speak or see, but, fortunately, was now in a comatose state. On 19 January, they learnt that Loup had died. The body was cremated privately in Paris and the ashes taken to Luxembourg, where they were placed in her husband's grave. On 9 February, the Vaneau celebrated the Petite Dame's eighty-first birthday and her great-grand-daughter's second. They had a 'sumptuous tea' at the Lamberts', at which Gide took great delight in playing the benevolent grandfather, followed by dinner at the Vaneau; the evening ended with a Humphrey Bogart film at the local cinema.

On 21 March, Gide left for Ascona, a resort near Lugano, on Lake Maggiore; the Lamberts had already gone there two days before. He arrived to find it pouring with rain, rain that did not let up for several days. They were staying in the annexe of the Casa Tamaro, a former monastery, turned hotel, at the lakeside. They were later joined by Richard Heyd. On the top floor of the hotel was a well-furnished library, to which Gide was allowed access. There he finished the preface to his anthology of French verse and, in consultation with his companions, made last-minute changes to the choice of poems.

Heyd returned to Neuchâtel and, on his recommendation, the others moved to an hotel at Ponte-Tresa, on Lake Lugano. After a few days, the Lamberts went off to spend Easter in Venice, leaving Gide alone. On their return, the weather had improved and they thought they would go back to Ascona. Before doing so, they decided to call on Hermann Hesse, who lived in a village nearby. Gide first wrote to Hesse in 1933, expressing a keen interest in his work. Over the next few years, they corresponded occasionally and exchanged publications. Now the previous year's laureate of the Nobel Prize for Literature was to meet the man who was to be that year's. Gide and the Lamberts arrived one afternoon, without warning. Leaving his wife to entertain the visitors, Hesse rushed upstairs to shave and to change out of the old clothes he wore about the house. For two hours, the five of them sat over tea; also in the room was a cat, with a kitten that had been born a few days before. As Lambert discussed with Hesse various points that had arisen in his translation of *Morgenlandfahrt* (*Journey to the East*), Gide's attention was absorbed by the spectacle in the basket on the floor. Hesse, clearly, was as fascinated by Gide:

His was the tranquil gaze of a disciplined face, at home in the world, a polite face, but, in that gaze and in the persistence with which it always returned to its object, there was the great strength that governed his life, a life that had taken him to Africa, to England, to Germany and to Greece. That gaze, that ever open receptivity, that ability to submit to the attractions of the wonders of the world, was capable of love and compassion, but had nothing sentimental about it and, fervent as it was, retained something objective about it, finding its original source in its thirst for knowledge.[48]

Gide and the Lamberts returned to Ascona. There Jean finished his Hesse translation and Gide wrote a preface for it. They benefited from the now splendid weather to sail on the lake and to go for long walks in the surrounding hills. One day, Gide said: 'When it's fine like this, I want to kiss everyone!' Lambert notes that he and Catherine exchanged anxious looks: Gide was already well equipped with his usual collection of toys and gadgets. 'We daren't get in his way too much,' Lambert notes, 'but we knew what temptations we were sometimes leaving him prey to . . . in a country with vigilant police and very concerned about respectability.'[49] However, they all returned to Paris on 28 April without mishap.

A few days later, Gide learnt that, at the instigation of Enid Starkie, the

French don at Somerville College, Oxford, moves were afoot to award Gide the University's honorary doctorate. (Enid Starkie had called on Gide in Paris, in 1938.) Gide wrote what was to be the Bryce Memorial Lecture, only to decide that it was unworthy of the occasion and wrote to Enid Starkie withdrawing. She responded at once that such a thing was out of the question: one could not refuse such an honour and the Public Orator had already written his Latin oration (a translation of her own, English original). Dorothy Bussy, who was to put Gide up at 51 Gordon Square, pursued a similar line, holding out temptations of varying allure: would he like to see E. M. Forster?; perhaps he would like to discuss an English production of *Saül* with Laurence Olivier and Michel Saint-Denis (Copeau's nephew); or meet 'a ravishingly beautiful youth lately picked up by Duncan Grant and preparing to be a monk'?[50] Gide gave in. In Paris, Gide met Cyril Connolly, who invited him to lunch with John Lehmann. Other invitations arrived, including one from the critic Raymond Mortimer and another from the composer, Lord Berners, which Gide left Dorothy Bussy to accept or refuse, as she thought fit – though, he warned her, he did not have '*un smoking*' (dinner jacket). On 31 May, Jean Schlumberger celebrated his seventieth birthday at the home of his son Marco, in Auteuil. On the way back, the car carrying Gide and the Petite Dame passed the Villa Montmorency and Gide insisted on stopping and calling on the present residents. The owner, an architect, was highly flattered by Gide's visit and showed him and his friends round. 'Curious to see that familiar place, inhabited in such a bourgeois style, cluttered up with luxurious, heteroclite things in deplorable taste,' the Petite Dame notes sharply.[51] The following day, Gide left for London, with Beth.

They were met at Victoria in the middle of a heatwave, by the Lamberts. After a few days in London, Gide set off for Oxford, accompanied this time by the Lamberts and Dorothy Bussy – Beth seems to have stayed in London. Enid Starkie was waiting to meet them. She dropped the Lamberts at the Maison Française, then took Gide and Dorothy Bussy to the Principal's house at Somerville, where they had lunch. After the mandatory 'nap', Gide was ready for the lecture. 'The Hall at Somerville was crowded to overflowing and the Reading Room next to it and all the passages,' Enid Starkie remembered.

There were people massed all the way up the stairs hoping to get a glimpse of him as he passed above on his way to the Hall. The people were even packed in the quad outside . . . Hundreds were turned away . . . He chose as theme the lines in which Virgil describes Aeneas fleeing the burning city of Troy with his father on his shoulders . . . This may be interpreted symbolically, that Aeneas was not merely bearing his father on his shoulders, but the whole weight of his past. We too, were fleeing from the burning city of our civilization with the whole weight of our Christian past on our shoulders. He spoke of romanticism, surrealism, existentialism, all the 'isms' that must disappear, leaving only the individuals influenced by them. He protested against literature that was 'committed' to ideology, whatever it might be. 'The world will be saved by the few,' he added.[52]

Next day, Gide was the guest at a lunch given by the Modern Languages Faculty at the Randolph Hotel. Afterwards Enid Starkie took Gide on a tour of the colleges. He was particularly interested in the gardens, naming many of the plants as they passed. In Broad Street, she showed him the 'Gide window' that Blackwell's bookshop had arranged, complete with photographs and piles of books. On Saturday, Gide was awarded the degree of Doctor of Letters (D. Litt.) *Honoris Causa*. He took a great interest in the whole ceremony and evident pleasure in the Public Orator's address about him: he was amused to hear that to translate the title of *L'Immoraliste* recourse was had to a Greek word. 'He must be one of the few honorands to understand the Latin,' Enid Starkie notes. Gide received his degree first, followed by several MAs, who, he noticed, were tapped on the head with a Bible by the Vice-Chancellor. He inquired of the Principal of Somerville sitting next to him whether it was in deference to his reputation as a free-thinker that this gesture had been omitted in his case. 'She reassured and comforted him as one might a child from whom some treat had been withheld': no, doctors did not receive the tap on the head with the Bible. Janie Bussy, who came to Oxford for the day with her father, leaves a delicious (French, rather than English) view of the proceedings in a letter to Martin du Gard: 'It was incredible [*inouï*] as a spectacle – both impressive and . . . killingly funny [*tordant*]. The ceremony clearly dates from the twelfth century. Beadles, mace, scarlet robes, ermine, Bibles, speeches in Latin – nothing was spared.'[53] Gide and his followers emerged from the Sheldonian to 'a crowd such as there is only in the case of kings and marshals or admirals'. Every newspaper had its photographer there. Gide took evident pleasure in his scarlet and grey gown. 'He was one of the few foreigners not to look in fancy dress in his academic robes,' Enid Starkie remembers. 'He might easily have been an Oxford don.'[54] At Magdalen, he asked to see Oscar Wilde's rooms. There he and his companions found a cricket team having a party. The undergraduates watched in silence as Gide, clearly moved, looked round.

Gide and the Lamberts caught the Golden Arrow at Victoria, only to find, on arrival in Calais, that French Railways was on strike – as they and the other public utilities were, intermittently, over the next few months. However, a diplomatic car, sent by Enid McLeod from the British Council in Paris, awaited him.

On 20 June, Gide and Jean Lambert left for Germany. The main occasion for the visit was a *Jugendtreffen* or 'youth rally' in Munich, organized by Last's friend Harry Domela, at which Gide would be joined by Last and Pierre Herbart. Before that, however, Gide and Lambert went to Tübingen as guests of General Widmer, a distant relation of Gide's and military governor of Würtenberg, then part of the French-occupied zone. They visited the old quarter of the town, mercifully intact, including the two rooms overlooking the Necker occupied by Hölderlin, but, as in Oxford, Gide showed more interest in plants (in the botanical garden) than in buildings. He had wanted to go to Berlin and the General offered to have him taken there. He was afraid, however, that the Russians might seize him, Last and Herbart, and gave up the idea. From Munich, Gide went on to Frankfurt, Bonn (where he met up with Ernst-Robert Curtius) and Cologne, arriving back in Paris on 12 July.

On 10 October, the opening night of *Le Procès* took place at the Théâtre Marigny. In Gide's box were the Petite Dame, Pierre Herbart and Richard Heyd, who had arrived from Neuchâtel the day before. The audience, hesitant at first, became ever more enthusiastic. A critical success, too, followed.

On 16 October, Gide learned that Catherine had given birth to a son, Nicolas. Two weeks later, he joined mother and child at Neuchâtel. In a letter asking if he might take over Gide's apartment for a time, Jean Lambert had said, in passing: 'I hope I won't have to see Mme D. I have particular reasons for not wanting to meet her.'[55] Naturally, both Gide and the Petite Dame were intrigued as to why Jean so wanted to avoid Yvonne Davet, Gide's new and almost over-devoted secretary. This requires, by way of explanation, a series of parenthetical flashbacks. Yvonne Davet first came into Gide's consciousness ten years before, when, as a very young woman in Avignon, she wrote Gide passionately admiring letters. 'Two letters from *La petite D.*', the Petite Dame notes on 5 December 1937. She 'grabs any opportunity to insinuate herself into his life'.[56] Six months later, the Petite Dame returns to the subject: 'La petite D. . . . continues to poison him with her attentions, her assiduities; he doesn't know what to do, no treatment seems effective, neither affectionate interest, nor brutal frankness. This lamentable affair might very well end badly.'⁵⁷ In December 1937, Yvonne Davet went to Nice to stay with her father and, in a mixture of solicitude, insensitivity and, perhaps, perverse curiosity as to what the encounter might produce, Gide asked Dorothy Bussy, that other Gidean obsessive, to 'look after her'. As a result, Dorothy Bussy was drawn into Yvonne Davet's own Gidean hell. A rather apprehensive Gide told Dorothy to try to keep Davet on the subject of Communism and not to let her get too 'emotional'. Dorothy invited Davet to tea. 'Your young friend Mme Davet came to see us two or three times,' Dorothy replied. 'She's very pretty and emotional, but too obviously interested in only one subject in the world – and by communism only in so far as it relates to that subject.'⁵⁸ The war came, Gide went to North Africa and that seemed to be the end of the matter. However, Davet kept in touch with Dorothy Bussy. In the winter of 1942–3, against all advice, Davet volunteered to join a scheme whereby French men and women could go to Germany to work, where, they were told, they would enjoy wonderful working conditions, work an eight-hour day, have a room of their own, etc. Yvonne Davet ended up in what was effectively a labour camp run by the Zeiss glass firm in Jena. On arrival, she realized what a terrible mistake she had made. She remained there, a prisoner, until the end of the war. Throughout this time, Dorothy Bussy continued to write to the poor creature, through the Red Cross. 'Pauvre, pauvre, pauvre petite Davet!' Gide wrote to Dorothy Bussy. 'She really didn't deserve that awful fate.'⁵⁹ Later, the Petite Dame notes: 'He has just taken on as secretary la petite D, whom he has done so much to avoid. It strikes me as incomprehensible and, to say the least, imprudent.' Yvonne Davet turned out to be an incomparable secretary, intelligent, efficient, only too delighted to work all hours. 'Yes, she works like an angel, because everything she does is an act of love.'⁶⁰ There were, however, regular scenes and outbursts of jealousy directed at any of the women who had anything whatever to do with Gide, from the Petite Dame downwards. 'I see, all I am for you, all I'll ever be, is . . . a secretary,' she would sob. 'A perfect secretary,' Gide would reply, 'and that's already quite something. I've never had that before.'⁶¹ By May 1947, 'her passion, always ready to explode, is beginning to wear Gide down quite absurdly,' the Petite Dame notes.⁶²

But why, particularly, did Jean Lambert not want to have to see her? It seems that, while working for Heyd in Neuchâtel, where Gide had sent her in order to get a breathing-space, she had given Gide's friend the 'inside story' of life at the Vaneau. Jean Lambert, she maintained, had originally been Jean Schlumberger's 'friend' (that is, lover), then Gide's, which was why he married Gide's daughter. Catherine hated her father. All this was accompanied by an endless stream of anecdotal 'evidence'. Heyd had decided to take Lambert and Gide into his confidence. However, this did not terminate Davet's employment. The affair blew over and she remained Gide's secretary almost to the end, even, in 1948, publishing her own book on Gide, *Autour des Nourritures terrestres. Histoire d'un livre* and editing a collection of his political pieces, *Littérature engagée.*

On 13 November, at Neuchâtel, Gide learnt that he had been awarded the Nobel Prize for Literature. Not over-impressed, he went to see a Fernandel film. Meanwhile, the poor Petite Dame was besieged by journalists and photographers, in search of information, an address, a picture. The telephone never stopped ringing, telegrams arrived from all over the world and from every part of France, sacks of letters arrived. Martin du Gard, who had arrived back in Paris the day before, was similarly besieged: 'Journalists and radios, frustrated at not finding you at the Vaneau, came and hammered on the Dragon [rue du], and yesterday I had to barricade myself in against their indiscreet assaults,' he wrote to Gide. 'I feel great joy, *cher grand ami*, to feel both of us isolated together in this rare privilege! (It's like a symbolization, on the world scale, of our exceptional understanding and affection which have continued to grow over thirty years.) I feel very embarrassed at having been the first of us to receive this consecration, but it wasn't my fault . . .'[63] RMG begs Gide to go along with the whole business; he must not look for excuses not to go to Stockholm, but just sit back and enjoy it. Of course, when *he* was awarded the Prize he was twenty-two years younger than Gide was now. Gide, who had been suffering from what he calls 'an ailing heart', quickly decided that he would not be up to the journey, still less to all the hullabaloo that it would entail. Gide saw a doctor, who confirmed that he should not go.

Gide's selection by the Nobel committee did not, of course, proceed without violent opposition. In the end, the official statement did not read too much like a compromise. Gide had been named 'for the importance and artistic value of a body of work in which he has expressed the problems of human life with an intrepid love of truth and great psychological penetration'. Gide's official reply was reprinted in the *Figaro*, 21 November:

I have never sought honours; and yet from an early age, I was much concerned with fame [*gloire*]. For a long time, my books had no success. This hardly bothered me, for I was never in any doubt that they deserved to be read . . . The fame of which I dreamt was that of Keats, Baudelaire, Nietzsche, Kierkegaard and so many others who were scarcely listened to until after their death. The eminent distinction accorded me by Sweden has made me realize that I miscalculated; I did not expect to live so long . . .

If I have represented anything it is, I believe, the spirit of free inquiry, independence, insubordination even, protest against what the heart and reason refuse to approve. I firmly believe that the spirit of inquiry lies at the origin of our culture. It is this spirit that the so-called totalitarian regimes, of left and right, are trying to crush and gag . . . There can be no question here of frontiers, geographical or political, racial or national. Sweden, at the balcony of Europe, takes no account of these; what matters here is the protection, the safeguarding of that spirit that is 'the salt of the earth', and which can still save the world . . . the struggle of culture against barbarism.[64]

'I have not kept my journal for over a year,' Gide wrote on 5 January. (This is not strictly true, but the entries for 1947 amount to less than two pages.) 'I have lost the habit.' Feeling quite incapable of anything more arduous, he will, he says, try at least to keep it up. (The result was a mere seventeen pages.) Next day, he begins: 'Interrupted yesterday by the arrival of the mail. That's my morning done for. And every day it begins all over again.' He remembers Valéry once saying that he would like as his epitaph: 'Here lies P. V., killed by others.' 'Ah!' says Gide. 'If only I could manage to concern myself a little less with them! And yet I usually reply to hardly more than one in six (some of them are incredibly absurd!). But, if I do write a letter, I cannot do so uncaringly; and so it takes time.'[65] Many of the letters included requests for money. Most, of course, had to be ignored, but Gide could be very generous to friends or to those who, in some way, belonged to his past. Edi Copeau wrote from Madagascar congratulating him on the Nobel Prize and asked him if he could contribute to a fund for the building of a convent for her order of Benedictine nuns: in all 800,000 francs were required. Astonishingly, given Gide's views on the Catholic Church and his treatment by Catholics, Gide offered 100,000 francs (£4,000, or $20,000). 'This is typical of his generosity,' wrote the Petite Dame, 'and of his lack of moderation . . ., of realism in questions of money.'[66] What lay behind this particular act of generosity was the deep friendship that Madeleine had had for Edi Copeau. Jef Last asked for help to the extent of 10,000 francs: Gide responded with an offer of '100 or 200,000' to help Last go away and work, with his new young lover, Jacques, while leaving enough to support his wife and children. (By July, Jacques was in prison and Jef in the midst of an 'aventure amoureuse' with a boy in Zürich.) To his credit, Last replied that 10,000 would be quite enough. Where others were not concerned, Gide was capable of extremes of parsimony. Pierre

Herbart recalled an occasion when, in an hotel lobby, Gide remembered that he had left a partly smoked cigarette in his room and wanted to go back for it. Only when he saw Herbart's horrified expression did he think better of it. During those weeks of illness, Gide's reading had suffered. Virgil, which, since Algiers, he had read every single day, 'washing my mind' of the day's accumulated dirt, 'drawing from it a sort of calm, comfort and ineffable serenity', had been reduced to a small 'dose' of some fifty or a hundred lines before going to sleep.[67]

Meanwhile, the Vaneau was showing concern for Gide's health. Pierre Herbart made a flying visit to Neuchâtel on 20 January and reported back that Gide 'did not look too bad; he hasn't got thinner and his eyes are bright; obviously, he's looking older . . . he walks slowly, with short steps, and is glad to take my arm.' 'Until now, I didn't feel my age,' he told Pierre, 'but now I do.'[68] This was all the more unfortunate in that he had received a tempting offer from the United States. Through Saint-John Perse, poet and, as Alexis Léger, diplomat, Gide had been invited to participate in an international conference on literary criticism at Johns Hopkins University, Baltimore. It would not only be well paid, but would be followed by an extended stay in a villa in Florida. Pierre Herbart had agreed to go with him, at least for the first part of the trip. Gide confessed to Dorothy Bussy, however, that 'this swerve into the New World terrifies me'.[69] He was never to see the 'New World', though he sent a contribution to the organizers and, at the instigation of Justin O'Brien, translator of the *Journal* and professor of French there, Columbia University awarded him an honorary doctorate. 'All this has come when it can no longer give me any pleasure,' he complained.

Marc Allégret arrived in Neuchâtel and brought Gide up to date with his 'lamentable conjugal situation'.[70] Some weeks later, in a letter to RMG, Gide returns to the subject: 'I am no less astonished than you by the Marc–Nadine conjugal shipwreck.'[71] Later in the year, Marc and Nadine were divorced. Gide's puzzlement probably stemmed from the fact that everyone, including Nadine, knew that Marc had had relations with many other women, before and during their marriage. Only the long absences, caused by war and Nadine's illness, had postponed a breakup of their marriage.

On 3 March, Gide was back in Paris. He saw Dr Laubry, a heart specialist, who forbade the American trip, recommended rest and restricted the smoking to six cigarettes a day. 'It's as if he had suddenly become older, more dependent,' the Petite Dame noted. She, Pierre and Beth discussed Gide's condition and decided that he ought to give up his 'rather Bohemian life' and employ a *valet de chambre* who could travel with him and look after him.[72]

Beth reminded Gide of a conversation they had had at Neuchâtel, when he had said how much he would like to have a garden again, observe the plants, prune the roses. His idea was to use some of the Nobel Prize money to buy a house near Paris for the Lamberts, who wanted to live in the country, a house where he would have his own, independent part. There he could escape Paris in the summer, though, of course, he would keep his apartment at the Vaneau. Had he given the matter any more thought, Beth asked. He said that he had, but feared that no one would get round to doing anything about it. Beth said that she would look into the matter at once. Eventually, their choice fell on a house in the Chevreuse valley, at Lévis-Saint-Nom, near Dampierre, 35 kilometres (19 miles) from Paris. On 10 May, Catherine signed the necessary papers and the house was theirs. Gide already had a name for it: it was to be called La Mivoie, after his grandparents' property near Rouen. There was a good-sized garden, with pond, leading out into a wood. The house, though charming, was not large enough to accommodate the Lamberts and Gide: a wing would be built providing Gide with a study, a bedroom and a servant's room. The servant had not yet materialized, though he was much talked of. What Gide had in mind was a young Black African, rather like his beloved Adoum, in the Congo, over twenty years before. An understanding colonial administrator had offered to send Gide a batch of eight, from which he could choose whichever one took his fancy . . . On the other hand, the ideal manservant would combine the abilities of a valet, a chauffeur, a cook, perhaps even a nurse . . . As to the extension, Gide had commissioned plans without having any idea how much it would cost or what his financial situation was. When he saw the estimates, he took fright and abandoned the idea, still with no clearer idea of his assets than when he proposed it. He would leave the house to the Lamberts.

On 20 May, there took place an open-air performance of Jef Last's adaptation of his own translation of Gide's *Le Retour de L'Enfant prodigue*. It had been commissioned for the annual Whitsuntide festival of the Dutch Liberal Protestant Youth organization. Last tried to tempt Gide with the prospect of 5,000 young people assembled to watch his 'play', but to no avail. The weather was kind and the production a great success, even to the point of arousing controversy among the Protestant clergy about the way Gide had re-interpreted the Bible story. A week later, Last was in Paris and called on Gide with his daughter. Afterwards he complained that Gide had seemed cooler towards him, preoccupied. Gide was desolate: he was so overcome with correspondence and visitors that everyone was suffering. 'The worst thing is letting people think: "Yes, since the Nobel Prize, he has *become distant.*"' If the *Journal* is to be believed, Gide had even contemplated suicide, an astonishing development: 'After that, nothing is left but to go and drown or hang oneself. Yet, since the warm weather has returned, I no longer have any wish to do so. But, before that, on certain days, I already felt quite unhinged. What held me back was the impossibility of getting anyone to understand, to accept, the real reason for a suicide.' Now, with summer beginning, he yearns to go away: 'As soon as my foot is on the carriage step, what relief to feel out of reach, freed.' But he has no definite plans and 'I constantly hear the Fate, the old one, whispering in my ear: you haven't much time left.'[73]

One day, an excited Gide showed Robert Levesque a copy of the recently published Kinsey Report (*Sexual Behavior in the Human Male*), 'an investigation carried out in America on 12,000 men'. Gide had asked an American friend if he thought the time was right for the English translation of *Corydon*. It was, he said, 'indispensable and urgent'. When the book was first published in France, in 1924, Gide had tried to reduce the scandal as far as possible, not least to spare Madeleine's feelings. This time, he wanted to create as much scandal as possible and to bring to the ensuing debate all the authority of his Nobel Prize and doctorates from Oxford and Columbia.[74]

Beth left to spend the summer in Cabris; Pierre, who had resigned from *Combat*, joined her a week later. Soon afterwards, the Petite Dame left on a two-week trip to Belgium: 'I have things to see there, old friends to meet and an irrepressible desire to see the country once more . . . At my age, one mustn't put off things. Gide, very touched by my wish, insists on paying for my trip.'[75] In July, Gide, too, left Paris, with Marc Allégret, in the Hudson car that Marc had bought from Pierre Herbart. At Torri del Benaco, a small resort on Lake Garda, they worked on the project for a film based on *Isabelle*. In early August, Marc left and was 'replaced' by Herbart, who was also working on the film script. (Nothing came of this project; later, Jean Cocteau became interested in the idea, but nothing came of that either; the scenario, by Gide and Herbart, was finally brought to the television screen by Jean-Jacques Thierry on 24 February 1970.) Marc went back to Paris and, at some point, Herbart was joined by Claude Mahias, friend and 'secretary'. On 16 August, Gide had to be operated on for otitis, after hours of excruciating ear-ache. During the operation, there was some concern for Gide's heart, which seemed weak. 'Condemned to almost absolute rest, incapable of any effort,' he wrote to RMG. 'I live almost "by proxy" . . . in the detailed accounts that Pierre gives me of his extraordinary adventures.'[76] Claude Mahias has also left an account of Gide's 'life by proxy':

From eight in the morning, Gide was on his feet, wandering the corridors, waiting for one of us to leave his room. Over breakfast, as he read his correspondence, he asked us, almost off-handedly, what we had been doing the night before, coming back so late. He was dying to know, but didn't want to ask. With astonishing roundabout questions, feints and diversions, he finally approached the subject. But we amused ourselves by prolonging the game . . . Then, with a disarming smile, he asked: 'Well, go on, what were you doing?'[77]

Marc arrived in a splendid sky-blue De Soto convertible, which he was transferring to Gide. With him, Gide wrote to Martin du Gard, was 'Vadim (the young Russian actor on whom his life has been centred over the last ten months or so)'.[78] Marc had first encountered Vadim Plemianov two years before, when the sixteen-year-old actor was working as an extra on Marc's film, *Pétrus*. Marc took him under his wing and he became, in turn, *répétiteur*, secretary, script-writer, assistant director, before making films of his own. There was between the two men a platonic love, at least. Gide, in the letter quoted, seems to imply more, probably wrongly. Certainly they shared a taste for beautiful young, sometimes very young, women – and a love of photography. For Marc Allégret, the meeting with Vadim was like a rediscovery of his own youth: in a way, he could do for Vadim what Gide had done for him. In each case, there were about thirty years between the two.

Gide was still in a convalescent state: for a time, he had four or six injections a day to assist his heart. Marc and Vadim left Torri del Benaco on 4 September, having been 'replaced' once more by Pierre Herbart and Claude Mahias. 'These last days of life seem the most difficult to live through,' Gide wrote in the *Journal*, 'but this must be an illusion, for all one can do is let time and gravity do their work . . . I think I am sincere when I say that death holds few fears for me (I think of it all the time); but I watch the summer go with a sort of despair . . . To the daily splendour is added a constant feeling that death is very near and that makes me say over and over that these beautiful days are my last. I write this without bitterness.'[79] Gide, Pierre and Claude Mahias left Lake Garda on 13 September, the two younger men taking turns driving the splendid De Soto. They broke their journey at Genoa, Gide retiring early, leaving Pierre and Claude to cruise the port. 'I wonder if it's like it used to be,' said Gide. 'Well, you'll tell me all about it.'[80] At Grasse, Gide booked into the Parc Palace hotel, leaving Pierre and Mahias to go on to Cabris, where Beth awaited them.

The valetudinarian mood returns: death is seen not only as imminent, but as already at work. 'The pleasures of seeing people and things again; but already death has slipped between me and things (people a little less) and the join has come unstuck. I have taken leave; I'm on leave; there is no going back on it.'[81] After about a week at Grasse, Gide and Herbart moved into an hotel at Mougins, just inland from Cannes. By the middle of October, Gide had decided that he wanted to go back to Paris, citing as reasons the opening of Simon Bussy's new exhibition and the need to see Edouard Gide about the projected film of *Isabelle*. Gide and the Petite Dame moved into the Hôtel d'Angleterre at Nice. There he spent most of his time reading in the public gardens opposite the hotel. On 23 October, they both got into the De Soto, with Claude Mahias at the wheel, picked up Pierre Herbart at Cabris, took their leave of Beth, who would soon be joining the Lamberts at Ascona, and set off for Paris. Gide and the Petite Dame sat in the back of the car, 'buried in shawls and coats', with Beth's cat among the luggage.[82]

The three Bussys arrived: the opening of Simon's exhibition provided a reunion of old friends, Gide and 'the Vaneau', the Bussys, Martin du Gard, Jean Schlumberger, etc. The Petite Dame noted how different Gide seemed from his former self. Instead of moving around among the guests, 'he sat in an armchair, wrapped in his great cape, with his cap on his head . . . suddenly older'.[83] By mid-November, Gide's condition seemed to be worsening. He slept most of the day and found any effort exhausting; he felt nauseous and was more than usually sensitive to cold and noise. Nevertheless, by the end of the month, his health was improving again. On 19 December, they learnt that Catherine had given birth to a daughter, Dominique.

At the Vaneau the New Year was celebrated by the return of central heating – the first time since the end of the war. It also saw the publication, by *L'Arche*, of Gide's *Notes sur Chopin*. It consisted largely of the section published in *La Revue musicale*, of December 1931, with the addition of fragments of the journal and unpublished *feuillets*. The volume was dedicated to the Abbot of Monte Cassino, who, in 1909, had welcomed him into the monastery and discussed Chopin with him. In January, Gide recorded the seventeen interviews with Jean Amrouche, broadcast between 10 October and 30

December. Nobody, including Gide, seemed to think very highly of them. The general view was that Amrouche dominated the proceedings too much, making Gide seem not far off his dotage. Occasionally, when Gide was given the opportunity to speak about something that interested him, they came alive. Despite Amrouche's urgings, Gide refused to have the interviews published. (They were finally published in 1987, preceded by a long essay on Gide by Eric Marty.)

The servant problem returned. Gide had been told of an 'Annamite' (Vietnamese), who would shortly be completing his military service at Fréjus. The poor man turned out to be not an Annamite, a type that Gide found attractive, but a Cambodian, which he did not. When Gide asked him what his driving was like, he recoiled in horror: 'Non, non, moi pas chauffeur, moi coiffeur!' A valet–chauffeur was found: he was not a latterday Adoum nor an Annamite Adonis, but a properly trained, forty-two-year-old Frenchman, Gilbert Sellier, on secondment from Jean Schlumberger, to whose service he returned after Gide's death.

At eight o'clock on 19 February a perturbed Pierre Herbart woke the Petite Dame. 'I think Gide has just had a little attack,' he said. Gide had rung him and Pierre had found him trying to get dressed, almost unable to speak clearly, his mouth twisted to one side. Drs Delay and Thiroloix arrived at ten. Gide was thoroughly examined. By now, to the astonishment of his doctors, he had apparently recovered completely, his appearance and speech quite normal. He was simply put on a regime and told to rest. His convalescence was used as a means of limiting Yvonne Davet's presence to mornings. Chess with Amrouche and Yvonne de Lestrange, *crapette* with Beth, patience with the Petite Dame resumed. By 20 March, he was well enough to be driven out to Jouy-en-Josas to see Léon Blum, who was recovering from an operation (and soon to undergo another) for a tumour. The two old friends talked about the past, exchanged memories and views on literature. The former Prime Minister showed no interest in current political events, but wanted to talk about Shakespeare and Montaigne, his present reading. 'Yesterday I said farewell to Blum,' Gide wrote to Martin du Gard. 'I'm very much afraid I won't see him again. And I'm sure that he is under no illusions about his state.'[84] Blum died a year later.

Jean-Louis Barrault called, with ideas for a production of *Saül* and, unaware that preparations were already well advanced, for a film of *Isabelle*. He even mooted the idea of a film based on *Corydon*. Nothing came of any of these projects. About the same time, Yves Allégret revived the idea of making a film of *Les Caves du Vatican*. Over the next year, much work was put into the preparation of a script by Gide and Herbart, but nothing came of this project either. On 21 August, Herbart drove Gide to Nice, where he moved in with the Bussys. The following day, RMG was astonished to see Gide looking so well. In the autumn, he had left 'a Gide aged, always lying down, breathing with difficulty, tired, irritated by everything, pernickety and tyrannical, a real invalid': he had left Paris convinced that he would not see his friend again. In Nice, he found 'a Gide rejuvenated, resuscitated, on his feet, wearing new clothes, his eyes bright and alert . . . his body supple and agile, exuding health and incredible youth':[85] Gide was seven months short of his eightieth birthday. It was not to last. Within a few days, he had been taken into the Clinique du Belvédère, after 'a liver attack, with possible blood poisoning from bile, which could be fatal'. He was given intensive penicillin treatment. He did not leave the clinic until the end of May. Each day, at some risk to an already fragile domestic harmony, RMG paid long visits to his friend. 'Despite the hours of anxiety that I lived through on several occasions,' notes the ever-generous Martin du Gard, 'I have kept an unforgettable memory of that month of daily intimacy.'[86] In his *Notes sur André Gide*, he writes: 'He knows that his heart may stop beating at any moment, that, in a few days, he might be carried off by an attack of uraemia . . . He hardly gives it a thought! And, when he does, it is with a sort of curiosity, as if it were an adventure like no other: his last . . .' Would Gide find any consolation in the idea of an immortal soul? 'Certainly not! Neither old age, nor illness, nor the proximity of death has any effect on me . . . I don't dream of survival at all . . . On the contrary: the farther I go, the more unacceptable I find the hypothesis of a Beyond . . . *instinctively* and *intellectually*!'[87]

Gide and his friends learnt of the suicide at Cannes, on 22 May, of Klaus Mann, aged forty-two. Gide had had ambiguous feelings about Thomas Mann's son and did not approve of his *André Gide and the Crisis in Modern Thought*, of 1943. Jef Last, only a qualified admirer, wrote to Gide: 'He never hesitated to oppose Hitler, and he never betrayed [homosexuals] in the way Proust did.' In a still repressive Holland, he had addressed a homosexual society with great courage. He liked working-class men, but always showed them 'human respect', introducing them to his friends 'without shame', helping them to find them work. 'I've heard that drugs had something to do with it. That's very possible . . . Hearing of his suicide, I felt that, for each of us, at certain moments, that may be the only way out.' Last then goes on to say that Gide should write something about Klaus Mann, 'clearly accusing Society of murdering him'. He recalls the 'hundred thousand homosexuals exterminated by Hitler in special camps, to whose memory no monument has been erected'. He then makes the rather surprising confession: 'There are times when I have felt overshadowed by you, rather as Klaus Mann felt overshadowed by his father. This is because you are leaving unfinished a mission that I feel unfitted to take up.' Gide managed to write a short letter by way of reply. He mentions the forthcoming American edition of *Corydon* and its new preface, which he hopes will 'provoke some protest'. 'You know that I have never recoiled before scandal,' he adds in true Gidean fashion, 'but I think that it would be extremely clumsy to seem to be looking for it.'[88]

'Do I dare to confess now that I hardly expected to leave the clinic alive?' Gide wrote.[89] On 31 May, joined by Pierre Herbart and Gilbert, he moved into the Hôtel de la Colombe, at Saint-Paul-de-Vence. A month later, they moved to the Villa Joyeuse, at Juan-les-Pins. There was, it seems, nothing 'joyful' about this villa, put at Gide's disposal by Florence Gould, multi-millionairess and patron of the arts. (Florence Gould, née Lacaze, daughter of a French publisher, but born in San Francisco, had married into the Gould American railway fortune.) The villa, writes Claude Mahias, was 'fairly comfortable', but furniture and decoration were 'awful'. 'Gide, sitting in an armchair in the middle of the drawing-room, pointed a dismissive finger at each item that had to go. Not much was left . . .'[90] In addition to many other things that she lavished on Gide, Florence Gould presented him with a black poodle bitch, which he adopted at once and called Xénie (a botanical allusion to its colour). Later, the Petite Dame noted that Gide 'brushed and combed her with incredible patience and application'.[91]

July brought the publication of Gide's *Anthologie de la poésie française* and (anonymously) the French translation of *Olivia*. Originally, Dorothy Bussy had submitted her own translation to Martin du Gard for his comments. To his surprise, he concluded that Dorothy could not write French and offered to rework it himself, though his English was poor. The process nearly brought their friendship to an end: the classic situation, author pleading that her work had been traduced, translator pleading for the rights of his own language. It was a great success, as it had been in England earlier in the year. French film rights were sold for £3,000, 'which seems to us an enormous sum,' Dorothy wrote to Gide.[92] The film appeared in 1950, with the great Edwige Feuillère as Mlle Julie. On 21 July, Gide attended a performance of his *Oedipe*, given by Jean Vilar and his company at the third Avignon Festival. Gide was very pleased with the production.

In August, Martin du Gard came and spent ten days with Gide at Juan-les-Pins. 'Incapable of listing the many, profitable memories that I have brought back of those fraternal têtes-a-têtes,' RMG wrote to Gide after-wards. 'How heavy, apathetic, dawdling one feels in daily contact with your octogenarian intelligence, still so agile, so very articulate in its uninterrupted exercise, ever full of surprises! . . . And you complain of intellectual fatigue . . . Cher Phénomène!!'[93]

On 1 September, Gide was at Cannes station to meet the Petite Dame: they had not seen one another for four months. Claude Mahias drove them, in the De Soto, to Cabris, where they were joined by Pierre and Beth for lunch. 'You're looking very well,' the Petite Dame told Gide, when they were alone. Gide replied that some days he was better than others; that he always felt 'tired, deep down'. He had lost all real appetite for life. He had, he said, discovered a word in Littré that described exactly what he felt: anorexia, an absence of desire, of appetite, not to be confused, says Littré, with disgust. At Juan-les-Pins, he had found peace and quiet, and had been able to work well, then 'suddenly I learned I'd been put on the Index', which meant, and this seemed to be his main concern, that the producers were withdrawing their support from the film of *Les Caves du Vatican*, on the grounds that it would be banned in all Catholic countries.[94] In fact, the mills of the Vatican bureaucracy grind even more slowly than most, presumably having eternity on their side, and Gide expired before his *opera omnia* were placed on the *Index Librorum prohibitorum* by the Holy Office on 24 May 1952.

The Petite Dame joined Gide at Juan-les-Pins on 15 September. Next day, Mrs Gould came and took them to Cannes, for a private screening of a documentary film on Morocco. The Petite Dame's appraisal of the millionairess was that she was 'very approachable, pleasant in appearance, full of natural kindness, but really very ordinary [*d'une grande banalité*].'[95] They discussed when they would be going back to Paris. It was decided that they would spend the first few weeks of October in Nice, long enough for Gide to see the Bussys on their return from England. So, on 3 October, Gide collected the Petite Dame at Cabris in the car and took her on to Nice, where they put up at the Hôtel d'Angleterre. Martin du Gard arrived to welcome them that same day – and continued to call every day. Once, Gide came back to the hotel all excited. In the street, he had been stopped by a splendid young man, with a pair of elk horns round his head (he had just killed the animal in Finland). He was Italian and was hitching his way home across Europe. He asked Gide if he would sign one of his books. He opened his bag and there, among socks and handkerchiefs, were a Rimbaud, a Kafka and a copy of *L'Immoraliste*. Gide signed his book and watched the young man stride off, delighted by the encounter.

On 10 October, they listened to the first of the Gide–Amrouche interviews on the radio in the hotel smoking-room, which fortunately they found empty. For Gide, it was a rather embarrassing experience, but he was not too displeased by the result. A few days later, Gide suggested that they take the car and go and visit Matisse at the Hôtel Régina, just above the town. They arranged with Matisse to arrive at eleven. They found him in bed, which, he said, he left only for a few hours a day to go and work in the Dominican chapel at Vence. Around him were the cartoons for the chapel. 'He talked for an hour . . . only about himself, displaying a monstrous egotism with the utmost self-satisfaction,' the Petite Dame commented. 'He talked of everything: his illness, his doctors, the treatment, the diet, entirely absorbed in himself in cynical joy, rather curious and comforting to see.'[96]

On 19 October, Gide, the Petite Dame and Xénie were seen off at the station by RMG and Janie Bussy: 'Xénie was charming the whole of the journey.'[97] They were met in Paris next morning by the Lamberts and their son Nicolas. Next day, they learnt that Jacques Copeau had died in the Hospice de Beaune. The funeral took place at Pernand-Vergelesses on 24 November. Jean Schlumberger and Martin du Gard attended – and were glad that they had taken the trouble to do so, there being very few mourners there: a mere half-dozen in addition to the family. Michel Saint-Denis and Maïène's daughter had flown in from London. At the end of the mass Bernard Bing, Copeau's son (by Suzanne Bing, who, under Copeau's influence, had been converted from Judaism), now a Dominican friar, gave an address and read St Francis's 'Canticle to the Sun'.

Preparations were being made to celebrate Gide's eightieth birthday on 22 November. It was decided that this would take place at the Lamberts' at La Mivoie, out of reach of press and radio, where Jean Schlumberger, Stoisy Sternheim and the Petite Dame arrived for a celebratory lunch. That morning, Gide wrote to Martin du Gard: 'My thought goes out to you particularly, on the threshold of this eighty-first year of my "employment" on this earth, which, thanks to you and a few more friends, seems less desolating and desolate.' On reading the letter, RMG wrote in the margin: 'The expression *"employment" on this earth* did not come from Gide's pen by chance: it expresses the feelings that made him publish *Corydon* and *Si le grain* and the correspondence with Claudel – namely, that he has a role, a mission to fulfil; that his talent, the authority that he has acquired, must, above all, serve in the struggle against the prejudices of a conformist morality, to remove homosexuals from the iniquitous condemnation that weighs on them.'[98]

On 29 November, Jean Schlumberger telephoned the Vaneau with news of the death of Hélène Martin du Gard. Next day, Gide sent his friend a telegram: 'Avec vous de tout coeur et profondément votre ami. André Gide.' Martin du Gard replied: '*Bien cher ami*, we have no need to write to one another, have we? We understand one another, in silence. I'm as well as can be expected. Calm and self-controlled, providing I'm *alone* . . . It isn't the solitude that is terrible, on the contrary, it's the *absence*, which is very different.'[99]

Throughout December Gide and his friends continued to listen to the broadcast interviews, noting their ups and downs. Gide's health and moods also had their ups and downs. On 24 December, the Petite Dame left to spend Christmas with the Lamberts and Beth at La Mivoie. Gide, '*qui a horreur des fêtes*' and felt too tired to join in, decided to stay at the Vaneau. The Petite Dame telephoned every day to make sure he was all right, returning on 27 December. On New Year's Eve, Gide, the Petite Dame, Beth and Pierre dined at the Vaneau, after listening to the last of the broadcast interviews. The Petite Dame was glad that they were over: 'there was little in them that I did not find exasperating'.[100]

The New Year brought increasing incursions from outside and a heightening of tension within the Vaneau. Since her presence had been reduced, Yvonne Davet had become 'more and more impossible' and was constantly 'playing the martyr, the overworked, sick woman', using every possible trick to be the centre of attention. Gide told the Petite Dame of a scene of 'incredible violence'. Davet tried to get Gide to give her exclusive permission to consult the Gide archives in the Bibliothèque Doucet. When Gide refused, she screamed: 'Then my work no longer has any meaning!'[101] In an attempt to assuage her violent feelings, he had told her that he would leave her the income from *Les Nourritures terrestres* (in acknowledgement of her *Autour des Nourritures terrestres*). The Petite Dame and Pierre were horrified to learn this, not because Gide had given her something, but because this particular gift seemed to make her his spiritual heir, which, given their relations, was ludicrous. Gide was soon persuaded of his folly and changed his mind.

One day a man arrived to take a moulding of Gide's hands. The Petite Dame asked him who had sent him. 'Some museum, I think . . .' The Petite Dame laughed: the sheer vagueness of the situation was so typical of anything concerning Gide. On another occasion, two different photographers and their assistants arrived, unbeknown to each other. One had been sent by Amrouche, the other from somebody they had not heard of. Innumerable shots were taken, in Gide's and the Petite Dame's apartments. Gide was photographed in all manner of places and positions, sitting in different chairs, looking through books, at the piano. 'I don't really mind,' says Gide, 'but I only want one thing: to be left in peace.' 'We are witnessing not only the ageing of a man,' said Pierre, 'but the ageing of a great man. For a long time he was not aware of his importance; even now he has no real notion of it.'[102]

On 25 January, Gide took up his journal, which he had not kept for seven months and wrote: 'These last lines date from 12 June 1949.' He crossed out 'last' and wrote 'insignificant'. He then added: 'Everything leads me to believe that they will be the last of this *Journal*.'[103] They were.

An invitation arrived from Florence Gould, offering Gide the use of a villa at Juan-les-Pins. On 4 February, Gide and Beth took the train for Cannes, where Gilbert collected them with the car and took them to L'Oiseau Bleu, on the road leading to Cap d'Antibes. Behind the house, a garden led down to the sea. A few days before, while visiting Agnès Copeau, who was staying at Saint-Cloud with her daughter, Gide and the Petite Dame had seen Madeleine Renaud and Jean-Louis Barrault, who had said how much he would like to put on *Oedipe*. Gide had to admit that he had already given permission to Jean Vilar. And what about *Antoine et Cléopâtre*? That had been given to the Comédie-Française. Barrault expressed interest in a Gide translation of *Arden of Faversham*: an earlier project that Gide had left unfinished in 1932. So Gide and Beth set to work to complete the abandoned translation of *Arden of Faversham*.

But another theatrical project was in view. In February, Gide received a letter from Pierre-Aimé Touchard, the administrator of the Comédie-Française, expressing interest in an adaptation of *Les Caves du Vatican*. Jean Meyer, one of the company's senior actors and directors, had read the Lausanne Bellettriens' version included in Gide's *Théâtre complet*, published by Heyd. Meyer was immediately excited by the idea of directing it at the Théâtre-Français, himself playing the role of Protos. He put the idea to the company board, which approved it unreservedly. Gide wrote back expressing his 'amused surprise': he would be delighted to accept, and invited Touchard and Meyer to come to Juan-les-Pins to talk it over. The news met with varying degrees of disapproval from Gide's friends and relations. This would be the third theatrical version of the novel. Gide was now an eighty-year-old semi-invalid, regularly attended by two physicians,

Dr Mattei of Vence and Dr Augier of Nice, and, as unpaid nurse, Beth. Such an enterprise would make inordinate demands on his declining energies and, anyway, Gide's experiences of theatrical cooperation had rarely been good. RMG had gleaned one possible reason why Gide found the idea so amusing: *Les Caves* would enter the Comédie-Française repertoire immediately after Claudel's *Le Soulier de Satin*. Claudel would now feel that Molière's company was also his and could not, therefore, abide having to share it with Gide: Gide's very presence, above all under the infernal species of *Les Caves du Vatican*, would demean his own success. Claudel, too, would have been aware that the process to forbid Catholics to read any of Gide's published works was under way. Gide told Jean Lambert the story of how one of Francis Jammes' sons, a godson of Claudel's, had told him of an incident at table when Claudel had held a *crêpe flambée* on the end of his fork and cried: 'And that's how Gide will burn in hell!' It was then that Jammes *fils* realized, he told Gide, that he was on his side and not theirs. It was a story that Gide liked to repeat, always with delight at Claudel's expense. When one of Claudel's grandsons brought a copy of the Gide–Claudel correspondence for Gide to sign, Gide saw that Claudel had already signed it with the words: 'With my regret at being found in such bad company'. Gide signed it, adding: 'Ditto'.

On 13 March, Touchard and Meyer arrived. Meyer had a whole list of suggestions regarding changes to the published text, which Gide welcomed. In his *Six années de la Comédie-Française*, Touchard writes of Gide's 'admirable lucidity, his intellectual agility and the childlike pleasure he took in this experiment'.[104] He set out to work at once with enthusiasm, but his health was not good. Sometimes he would sleep through most of the day, then get up in the middle of the night and start working. Once, at three o'clock in the morning, Jean Lambert found him lying on the tiled floor, his spectacles a few feet away, in what looked like, but obviously was not, a drunken stupor. Gide had a new medical problem: his legs had swollen up. He was also getting shorter of breath and his heart was getting weaker. On days when his general condition improved, he became 'unbearable', Beth wrote to her mother. 'He isn't always *easy to manage* [in English], dear Bypeed.'[105] By the end of March, Gide moved out of 'L'Oiseau Bleu' into what he and his friends referred to as 'the Garage'. This was a large house that gave on to a terrace, which was, in fact, the roof of a garage. Here, away from the house in which she lived with her husband Frank Jay Gould, Mrs Gould could entertain her friends for days, weeks on end, constantly supplying them with every possible delicacy. The champagne flowed and, when Gide did not feel up to champagne, Mrs Gould herself would serve him with the even more bubbly Eno's Fruit Salts. This was certainly a *mode de vie* quite unfamiliar and, generally, unsympathetic to Gide. However, in his present relative helplessness, he quite enjoyed, for a time at least, being 'spoilt'. He also had the additional interest of the endless permutations and intrigues of Florence Gould's guests, the terrace being the stage on which the human comedy was played out, Gide observing and participating at will. When he felt well enough, Jean Lambert would take him off to the cinema in Antibes. After one visit to the 'Garage', an outraged Martin du Gard did not spare his friend:

Seeing you beatifically imprisoned in that millionaire's ostentation, smothered with puerile attentions and expensive presents, stuffed with preserved fruit, watered with champagne, lodged, heated, fed, laundered, served and, what is more, basely fawned upon, what I felt was something very near to *shame*! And I trembled at the idea of some young man, fervently drawn to you, suddenly appearing and catching Gide in that willing abandon, and recounting that inverted apotheosis to his friends . . . I spent two *distressing* hours there – the only two atrocious hours that our friendship has inflicted upon me in thirty years! . . . Gide, dear Gide, . . . make room for the other familiar parasites, those who at least have the excuse of going there . . . that their means do not permit them to indulge in such things at home.[106]

Gide understood RMG's reaction all too well and approved of it: he was already planning his retreat. On 5 April, Pierre Herbart flew to Rome, from there travelling to Sicily on a reconnaissance expedition. He came back five days later: they would move into the Hôtel Timeo, at Taormina, as soon as Pierre could leave. Meanwhile, to everyone's astonishment, Gide extricated himself as Yvonne Davet's employer. It was not, of course, to be the end of her impingement on Gide's life and works. She was now working for the review *La Table Ronde* and had assembled a sizeable group of allies. 'Her erotic insanity is obvious only to those who have frequented the Vaneau,' the Petite Dame writes. 'Gide has gathered around him the shady and the suspect in a way that is enough to make one's hair stand on end. I take a very gloomy view of the situation after his death.'[107]

On 20 April, Gide and Pierre travelled by train to Rome, where they met up with Gilbert and the De Soto. Pierre then saw Gide on to the train for Taormina and joined Gilbert in the car, believing his presence to be 'indispensable' if car and chauffeur were ever to reach their destination. At Taormina, Gide and Pierre worked on the new version of *Les Caves*. As usual, the two got on particularly well. There was also 'a superabundance of other joys', but, Gide adds, 'I'm speaking of Pierre, for I am withdrawing more and more and am quite willing to stand down.'[108]

On 11 May, the universally loved Agnès Copeau died suddenly. 'Yet another witness of a disappearing past and so charming, so faithful a witness – and when will our turn come?' asks the eighty-four-year-old Maria Van Rysselberghe.[109] Pierre left for Paris and his role was taken over by the Lamberts. By the end of May, Gide and the Lamberts were in the delicate situation of having hardly any money left and fresh supplies had failed to arrive. They decided to leave very soon, persuading the Sicilian hotelier that a Nobel Prize winner could be trusted to pay the bill at the earliest opportunity. Before leaving Taormina, Gide and the Lamberts drove up to inspect Etna, but heavy rain spoilt the view from that 'belvedere of Sicily'. They arrived at Palermo in scorching heat. A few hours later, they were on the boat bound for Naples. There, through the good offices of the French Institute, where Gide was to give a lecture, money could be obtained. Gide and the Lamberts then moved out to an hotel at Sorrento. After a few days, Catherine left for Paris: she was expecting the imminent arrival at La Mivoie of Beth, Ethel Whitehorn and Enid McLeod. Jean Lambert stayed on a few more days, awaiting the arrival of Pierre Herbart. Almost every evening, they went to the cinema and Lambert became acquainted with Gide's habit of constantly moving around, from seat to seat, in the interests, he claimed, of avoiding draughts, though Lambert noted that many of the boys in the audience did the same. At the end of his stay in the Naples area, Gide gave a lecture in the fine terraced gardens of the French Institute. It was intended, he said, as an expression of gratitude for everything that he and his work owed to Italy, its writers and its landscapes.

Jean Lambert left, Pierre Herbart arrived and the new trio proceeded up the coast to Rapallo. On 30 June, Pierre went back to Paris, leaving Gide for about a week in the sole care of Gilbert, who took his employer out for long rides in the countryside: the weather was splendid, but, without Pierre's constant stimulation, Gide felt gloomy. On 4 July, at Portofino, he was introduced to 'a very agreeable, half-naked, athletic' Englishman who lived on a boat. He turned out to be the author of *I, Claudius*. (Gide seems unaware that, in certain circles, Robert Graves was better known as a poet.) They finally arrived in Paris on 13 July.

During the week Gide spent in Paris, he was brought up to date with the machinations of Yvonne Davet. While Gide had been in Taormina, Jean Schlumberger had written to him that 'all Paris is buzzing' with the gossip being spread by Yvonne Davet.[110] Jean Amrouche, who was already thoroughly disliked by everyone at Gallimard's (and by most of Gide's friends) was now trying to pass himself off as Gide's literary representative on earth, on the basis of some piece of paper that Gide had hastily and innocently scribbled authorizing him to consult certain documents. Only a rather stern letter to Amrouche from Gide, at the instigation of Schlum and Martin du Gard, made him act more circumspectly. Gide now discovered, not only that Davet had been asked to Amrouche's house in the country, but that François Reymond, his Tunis hosts' adolescent horror of a son, the 'Victor' of the *Journal*, was also there. (He had just published, under the pseudonym of François Derais, his own version of Gide's Tunis residence, *L'Envers du Journal de Gide*, although, on publication in 1950 of the last volume of Gide's *Journal*, for the years 1942–9, François' mother had written to Gide agreeing with his comments on her son.) A secretary spurned, a would-be representative reprimanded were now joined by a vindictive 'victim', all three with literary careers parasitical on Gide.

Gide left to spend two weeks at Chitré with Yvonne de Lestrange. After this there was some question of the Petite Dame's joining Gide for a *cure* in the Bayonne region. In the end, Gide changed his mind and suggested that they spend a few months at their old resort, the Hôtel d'Angleterre, in Nice. On 4 August, they were on the road southwards. From Nice, they went for long car rides out into the mountains: there were frequent visits to Cabris. One day, Gide took it into his head that he would like to visit the Monte Carlo casino. It was, the Petite Dame writes, fifty years since they had last been there. Gide bought 1,000 francs-worth of chips and gave half of them to the Petite Dame. He went up to one table and put 100 francs (£4, or $20) on the 13 (his lucky number) and promptly won 3,200 francs. He tried a second and third time, without success. The Petite Dame lost 300 francs and decided to stop. They left 3,000 francs the richer.

Domi Drouin arrived in Nice and, over dinner, outlined a project for a documentary film about Gide's life. The film would be directed by Marc Allégret, with Domi as his assistant. Work would really begin when Marc got back from England, where he was filming. Visits would be made to various places associated with Gide: La Roque, Cuverville, the Vaneau, Gallimard's offices, Cabris, La Mivoie, perhaps even certain places in Africa. Pierre suggested a conversation with Sartre, who happened to be at Juan-les-Pins at the time. Domi agreed and Pierre made the necessary arrangements. The car was sent to bring Sartre to Cabris, where the conversation took place in the garden. Both men showed endless patience with the 'bad preparation, often defective or inadequate equipment, the time wasted setting up the equipment, endless reshootings, which brought out, in the most comic way, the artificiality of scenes that were supposed to have happened by chance! – and it has to be admitted, the mediocrity of what was said'. Sartre, who had some notion of the dangers involved, had suggested that they try to keep to one or two topics, but Gide preferred to say the first thing that came into his head. When it was all over Sartre confessed that he 'had never said so many stupid things in so short a time'.[111]

On 13 September, accompanied by Pierre, Gide was back at the Vaneau, ready to begin work with Jean Meyer and the *comédiens français*. Over the past seven months, he had spent only eight days in Paris and, apart from about three weeks at Chitré, his time had been spent on the Côte d'Azur or in Italy. On the evening after the first rehearsal, Robert Levesque called. The year before he had left his dreary Ecole Industrielle at Casablanca and moved to the Lycée Mixte at Fez. When he could, he escaped to Tangier. His letters to Gide speak eloquently of the town's attractions:

A very indecent town, and that's why I went there. I was guided, or rather welcomed, by a curious collector who, as one might photographs or books, collects boys. They crowd into his bachelor flat; it's on the ground floor and they come in at all hours to drink or offer their services. Sometimes one is in bed with one of them, when one sees peeping through the curtains the very charming face of another who would like to join in. So one chases out the other; one delight is linked to another . . . But I still put Marrakesh at the top of the list . . . This is because, despite its extreme facility, sex [*la volupté*] there has maintained its idyllic charm: one breathes it everywhere; one meets it at every step; gloomy days are unknown; every moment is adorned with caresses . . . Everyone is on the prowl, offering himself; in the torchlight, eyes and lips shine; the movement of bodies outlines an embrace [*une étreinte*, that is, a sexual act].[112]

That summer Robert Levesque had spent a couple of months of debauchery, travelling from Morocco, to Algeria and Tunisia. He came back to Paris to spend a little time with his family, before returning to Fez. He no doubt whetted Gide's appetite for Marrakesh even more *viva voce* than by his letters. That was Robert Levesque's last meeting with Gide. As winter drew in, Gide's thoughts turned to Marrakesh: he would go there in January. Gide never got to Marrakesh. In fact, he never left Paris, alive. Yet the months of sun, combined with the stimulation of working with actors on *Les Caves du Vatican*, brought Gide to a new plateau of good health, for a time at least.

Yvonne Davet appeared, by appointment. She had, she said, something of the utmost importance to impart to him. It transpired that *La Table Ronde* was planning a special number on him and had put her in charge of it. Fortunately, noted the Petite Dame, he refused absolutely to have anything to do with it. 'You'll never get rid of her,' she said. 'No, never,' Gide agreed, 'and even after my death, she'll go on harassing those who are left.'[113] Later that morning, Marc Allégret and Domi Drouin arrived, variously attended, to start the filming of 'Gide at Home'. On 22 November, he celebrated his eighty-first and last birthday. He and the Petite Dame were joined at lunch by Catherine, her young son Nicolas and Domi Drouin.

Over the next few weeks, Gide's time was almost entirely taken up with Marc's film: Gide lying on his bed reading, Gide on the telephone, Gide shaving, Gide having a meal with the Petite Dame, Gide giving a piano 'lesson' to a girl playing Chopin. For some days, he stopped going to rehearsals at the Français, and Jean Meyer telephoned him in the evening with a progress report. 'What luck to escape our apartments these last two afternoons,' the Petite Dame noted on 9 December. 'They are prey to Marc's cameramen: six men, cumbersome and terrifying equipment, long black wires one constantly trips over and which wind their way around the whole place. Fortunately, they're packing up this evening.'[114]

For three months, Gide had attended most of the rehearsals. Pierre-Aimé Touchard notes how Gide was 'unanswerably demanding about the slightest details . . . He meticulously explained each role to the actor who had to play it, and the subtle precision of his thinking amazed all those who heard him.'[115] On 12 December, the last rehearsal took place. Afterwards, Touchard asked Gide to accompany him to his office. There, surrrounded by the cast, he gave a moving speech in his praise and presented him with two leather-bound volumes, 'in affectionate memory of all the actors who will not forget the joy of having worked with Gide'.[116] The two volumes were the *Registre de La Grange 1659–1685*, a complete account of Molière's company. Gide was so overwhelmed he could hardly speak. That evening, Enid and Whity arrived by plane from London.

Next day, 13 December, an official gala performance of *Les Caves du Vatican* took place. When, about seven, Jean Lambert went into Gide's room to dress, he found him sitting on his bed, resplendent in his unaccustomed white tie and tails: he was even wearing white gloves and sat there, hands on knees, quite immobile, 'hieratic', 'like some Egyptian sage waiting to be embalmed'.[117] It was a 'glittering' occasion, attended by the President of the Republic, Vincent Auriol, the entire diplomatic corps and a bewildering array of uniformed men. By the interval, Gide was getting tired and Touchard got a sofa brought into his own box, where Gide could rest, if he wanted to, out of sight. Every now and then, he dozed off. Once he woke up suddenly and exclaimed, quite audibly: 'It's too long! Too long!' Yet he must have been paying more attention than he seemed. Back at the Vaneau, he immediately set to work cutting and rearranging the last scene, which he had not been satisfied with. Next day, he spent several hours with Herbart and Meyer making the desired changes. Fortunately, there was a final dress rehearsal before the first night. (The gala performance had not been open to the public or to the critics.) On that first night, the Petite Dame writes, 'The audience was quite different from the other evening, less decorative, more lively, with more spontaneous reactions.' During the interval, too, the audience showed its appreciation; everywhere there was a buzz of excited chatter and laughter. With each scene the applause seemed to increase and, at the end, Gide took a bow from the front of the stage. Next morning, the critics were less enthusiastic. The influential and merciless Jean-Jacques Gautier of the *Figaro* slated it. Others were kinder, praising the actors and the production, showing deference towards Gide himself, but finding various faults with the play.

His work on *Les Caves* over, Gide returned to what was to be his last work. He had abandoned his *Journal* eighteen months before. Since then he had taken to jotting down his thoughts, as they occurred to him, but they concerned not so much the present as the past. Odd incidents in his life are recounted, with no respect for chronology, yet following an apparently seamless web of free association: episodes from his childhood, his honeymoon in Italy, his travels in Africa, his visit to Russia, right up to the rehearsals of *Les Caves*. He was to call this book *Ainsi soit-il, ou les Jeux sont faits* (*So Be It, or the Chips are Down*). He kept adding to it almost right up to the end. By the end of December, plans had been made for a trip to Marrakesh in January with Beth, but Gide's health fluctuated wildly. The Petite Dame and Beth spent Christmas at La Mivoie, with the Lamberts and their children, leaving Gide at the Vaneau. They came back on 26 December, bringing young Isabelle with them. The weather got colder; there was even a little snow. And so Gide saw in his last New Year.

On 21 January, Gide received an 'exquisite letter' from the Indian Prime Minister, Jawaharlal Nehru, who had once visited him when a young law student at the Inner Temple. Gide's health began, gradually, but relentlessly, to decline. By the beginning of February, Beth, who had carried the burden of looking after Gide and whom he constantly said looked after him better than anyone, had had enough. Her nerves were at breaking-point, as a letter to Martin du Gard of 12 February makes clear:

It's unspeakably painful! I'm the only one to be with him almost all the time . . . All this is so recent, yet it seems to have been going on for centuries . . . That he should show no sign of pleasure seeing Pierre again and never asks after him is for me the most terrible sign . . . He doesn't ask after *anyone*. The Petite Dame, I fear, has now been pushed to one side – I do all I can – I tell him, *ad nauseam*, about the slightest incident . . . It's *frightful*. There are hours of complete senility, wandering – there are others of some lucidity, when I read to him what he has just written, but perhaps these are the more painful. There are hours of *emptiness* . . . As you know, he's an *impossible* invalid, to an unimaginable degree . . . He now demands constant surveillance. Fortunately, since yesterday, I've a perfect nurse . . . he isn't in pain and feels that he's going . . . But how long can he go on?[118]

Next day, Gide wrote the last lines of *Ainsi soit-il*. They are oddly Beckettian, a moving testimony to the breakdown, here syntactical and intellectual, described by Elisabeth Herbart:

No! I cannot maintain that, at the end of this notebook, everything will be finished . . . Perhaps I shall want to add something else. Add something or other. Add something. Perhaps. At the last moment, add something else . . . I'm sleepy, it's true. But I don't want to sleep. It seems to me that I could be even more tired. I don't know what time of the night or morning it is . . . Have I anything more to say? Still something or other to say?

In a final sentence, Gide reaches poetry: 'My own position in the sky, in relation to the sun, must not make me find the dawn any less beautiful.'[119] Whether or not Gide had anything more to say or knew what it was sufficiently to write it, he did not add any more. During the hours of torpor, he had minutes of lucidity. He was amused that the nurse was called Saint-Just and was a descendant of the man who presided over the Reign of Terror. On 15 February, the doctor found 'a little infectious bronchitis'. The patient 'sulked a little' because the day before Beth had not been with him the whole time. To keep her, he said: 'I don't want to die without your being in the room.' In the afternoon, he emerged from a long sleep to remark: 'Oh, so I'm still here.'[120] All day, he refused any food. During the night, despite the presence of Nurse Saint-Just, he thought fit to wake up the Herbarts and Gilbert. Catherine spent the night at the Vaneau, but little sleep was had.

On 16 February, Dr Delay arrived, accompanied by his wife. Delay noted that an unopened half-bottle of champagne lay on the bedside table, together with Virgil's *Georgics* and an almost full packet of Camel cigarettes. Breathing heavily, Gide said: 'I'm afraid my sentences might become grammatically incorrect.' 'It was the old fear that he had confided to me two years ago, in February '49: the fear of losing his command of language, words, syntax, an eminently respectable concern on the part of an old worker of letters who feels that the tool that he has so patiently forged and has given him his power was deserting him.' Gide seemed to go off into sleep, then opened his eyes and said: 'It's always the struggle between the reasonable and what is not.'[121] During the day, Yvonne de Lestrange passed by a few times. Jean Lambert came back from Souvigny, where he had been visiting his convalescent mother. In the afternoon, Pierre Herbart said to the Petite Dame: 'Don't you think, if this is really the end, you ought to try and get him to understand that for thirty years you have been keeping a journal of everything that he has said and done? It would bring him great joy at the end.'[122] At five o'clock, Jean Schlumberger arrived from Rome, having been previously warned that the end was near. Dr Martin prescribed penicillin and, hearing that the injection of Spasmalgine tended to keep him awake, doubled the dose, but he could not see how Gide would survive the following day. At ten o'clock, Martin du Gard, who had telephoned each day for a progress report, arrived and spent the night on the sofa in the studio. Next day, he wrote to Janie Bussy, to keep 'Nice' informed: 'His eyes are closed; he sleeps for hours, then he opens his eyes, very slowly recognizes those around him, makes a friendly sign, smiles and plunges back into sleep.' To the doctor who asked him if he was in pain, he replied very distinctly: 'Ab-so-lu-ment pas.' 'No fear, no rebellion, no trace of anxiety or regret: total serenity, a sort of abandonment to the laws of nature. One could not imagine a sweeter, less emotional death. (One would like to bring the Mauriacs and Massis before this bed of *repose*, where there is no sign of fear . . .)'[123]

'No one really slept last night . . . Fortunately, he did,' the Petite Dame notes, next day. On waking, Gide said, 'Tout est bien' and asked for coffee. Nobody had expected to hear his voice again. Later, he said to Beth: 'It's difficult going.' A sort of family council was formed of Maria Van Rysselberghe, the Herbarts, RMG and Jean Schlumberger – the Lamberts had gone out. What should they do if the government proposed a state funeral? They unanimously rejected the idea. Gide had consistently declined all state honours: to collude in a state funeral would be a contradiction of everything that he had stood for. Beth, who was familiar with his latest writings, confirmed that he had nowhere specified what kind of funeral he wanted. They decided that the best thing would be for Gide to be buried at Cuverville, near Madeleine, with the ceremony restricted to a few friends – the old, 'true' friends, Roger, Schlum and Marc – and the family. The Petite Dame thought it better, in order 'to profane as little as possible the memories that haunt Cuverville', that she and the Herbarts should not go. About seven in the evening, Pierre Herbart fetched the Petite Dame and told her that it would be a good moment for her to talk to Gide. She went in and told him of her thirty-three-year-old *Cahiers*. He murmured: 'Au revoir.' A rather sad Petite Dame wondered if he had understood. A little later, Pierre came out. Gide had told him: 'I fully understand what the Petite Dame said to me, excellent, excellent.'[124]

Sunday, 18 February passed without incident or apparent change in Gide's condition. In the morning, Catherine, Beth and the nurse bathed the protesting patient and changed his clothes. The young doctor arrived at eight and gave the usual injections. Dr Martin arrived at ten. Marc Allégret came and stayed overnight. The nurse sat up at the bedside and Pierre Herbart was in the small room next door. The Petite Dame came in to see Gide first thing in the morning. 'His immobility is impressive . . . The atmosphere is already that of a house in mourning. We speak quietly, walk without making a sound. One ceaselessly crosses the same shadows in the hall and in the long corridor . . . In my memory, that day seems an eternity measured against that terrible immobility already so near to annihilation . . . One goes off alone when one cannot bear it any longer.' Visitors arrived: Gaston Gallimard and his son Claude, Yvonne de Lestrange, Mme Delay. The telephone never stopped ringing. The Petite Dame wandered in and out of the bedroom; Martin du Gard never seemed to move from the bedside, attentive, 'as if he did not want to lose anything of that sacred moment'; on the other side of the bed, Beth held Gide's hand. Just after ten in the evening, Gide's breathing became very intermittent. With him were Beth, Marc and Pierre, who went off to get the others, who were with the Petite Dame in her apartment. Gide lay there, his mouth wide open; Beth was still holding his hand. There were now ten of them, plus the nurse and Gilbert. 'For a few minutes time seemed to stand still . . . The nurse leaned over and felt the heart – it was over. No gesture, no fussing disturbed the extraordinary peace that followed . . . The silence was unbearable and seemed to become infinite. Suddenly, Elisabeth broke it, she kissed his hand and went out, Catherine and I followed her.'[125]

Martin du Gard ends his *Notes sur André Gide*:

Paris, Monday, 19 February 1951.
It was exactly 10.20pm.
Since yesterday, I have not seen his eyelids open.
Not grief: a quiet sadness, rather.
The calm of that end does one good; that renunciation, that exemplary submission to the laws of nature, are contagious.
We must be infinitely grateful to him for knowing how to die so very *well*.[126]

Next morning, news of Gide's death appeared in all the newspapers. From nine o'clock, people came and signed the register left with the concierge or another register left in the hall of the apartment. It was announced that the body would be available for viewing from two o'clock: it would be laid out in the small room near the entrance, to provide easy access to visitors. The body was brought, in its iron bed, and the head unwrapped: it had been left wrapped overnight in order to keep the mouth closed. The freshly washed corpse was then dressed in Gide's white flannel suit. Martin du Gard had commissioned an artist to make a death mask of the face and observed him throughout. (Later, he took it back with him to Le Tertre, where it was displayed in his study.) 'No face of a dead person gave me such an impression of "eternal sleep". *Requies aeterna.*'[127] Another artist, Berthold Mahn, came and did a drawing of Gide's face, which he did not finish until two in the morning.

Visitors began to arrive: the Mauriacs, the Gallimards, the Paulhans, Jean Meyer and some actors from the Comédie-Française, Florence Gould and Julien Green. Yvonne Davet also turned up and was 'thrown into confusion at being so politely received by Elisabeth, who let her stay'. Two priests came and the Petite Dame was 'particularly moved by the respectful, entirely secular attitude of one of them'. Richard Heyd arrived from Switzerland in the morning and stayed for lunch with the 'family'. Flowers and telegrams arrived *en masse*. From two o'clock, a constant stream of visitors passed through the apartment, 'well-known people, unknown people, a lot of young men and women, too, timidly laying a few flowers . . . Messages from all over the world, from officials and from the very humble.'[128]

The following day, 21 February, the body was put into the coffin: visitors kept coming. Only in the evening was the coffin-lid closed and relations and friends finally took their leave. Everyone at the Vaneau was stifled with emotion and physically exhausted. Beth was on the verge of collapse and Pierre took her out for a meal. The Lamberts, Heyd and RMG stayed with the Petite Dame. At ten o'clock the following morning, the coffin was collected and those who were going to Cuverville left with it. 'Suddenly, what a void, what silence . . .' the Petite Dame writes. 'Elisabeth and I were suddenly snatched from the element in which we had bathed for so many days . . . The day dragged on – our minds were out there'. That evening, they were given a detailed account of the day's events by Jean Lambert and Catherine. They had arrived at Cuverville to be met on the steps by Domi Drouin and Amrouche ('who, of course, was with the first arrivals'). They went into the big drawing-room, where they found the coffin draped in blue velvet. A pastor then appeared holding a Bible and said: 'It is with some emotion that I open this book, which served Mme Gide so often for her daily worship.'[129] After reading a few extracts from the Bible, the pastor gave a short address, followed by a reading from Gide's *Numquid et tu . . .?* It was the same passage quoted by François Mauriac in his obituary: 'Lord, I come to you like a child; like the child that you want me to become . . . I renounce everything that made up my pride and which, in your presence, would make up my shame. I listen and submit my heart to you.'[130] It is difficult to imagine a more tendentiously untypical quotation from Gide's entire works, a more desperate attempt to bridge the gulf between André Gide and a Protestant pastor (or Catholic 'friend'), than those words, written in 1916, in the midst of Gide's Christian dark night of the soul. The procession of relations, friends and local people then formed, followed by a group carrying the flag of the Anciens Combattants (the veterans' organization, which, ten years before, in Nice, had threatened his life). The coffin, borne by four farmers from the estate, made its way to the grave. There the pastor spoke again and again read passages from the Bible. Domi Drouin, the present *châtelain*, then addressed the local people, on the theme 'Monsieur Gide was very fond of you all'.

The gathering then broke up. As he passed in front of Domi Drouin, Martin du Gard rejected the outstretched hand and launched into a furious protest. He was outraged, revolted by the participation of a pastor; it was a betrayal of everything that Gide had stood for. There followed an argument that lasted an hour, according to RMG. He was supported vigorously by Jean Schlumberger. Marc and the Lamberts agreed that it was unfortunate, but did not think that it really mattered and was not worth making a fuss over. The poor pastor, whom RMG agreed was quite charming, was highly embarrassed. 'It is neither the time nor the place to create such a scandal!' he said. RMG replied: 'The scandal, Monsieur le Pasteur, is your presence here!'[131] Domi protested that he had consulted Catherine about the suitability of reading some extracts from her father's works and she had agreed. She had, Domi protested lamely, not made it clear that no religious ceremony was wanted. She had, of course, not been asked: its very possibility was unthinkable. As RMG put it, 'Dominique Drouin, flanked by the "family", had managed bit by bit to preserve tradition.'[132]

When, in Paris, that evening, Pierre Herbart heard what had happened, he declared: 'We must act at once, make a public protest. We certainly haven't heard the last of this business of the pastor.' He got up and disappeared. A quarter-of-an-hour later he came back with a text headed 'Families, I hate you . . .', which he then read out to the others: 'I write these lines in the room in which an emotional crowd passed yesterday before André Gide's little iron bed. Here, only his death mask recalls his eternal absence. Our friend is sleeping his first sleep in the earth. His daughter and his oldest friends accompanied him to that final resting-place. They thought that they were simply entrusting him to "that earth that he so much loved", as Albert Camus said in his farewell to Gide. Some thought that they were not betraying the memory of the great man by suddenly calling in the assistance of a pastor. No matter. P. H.'[133] They all agreed that Pierre had hit exactly the right note: cutting, but discreet. He then telephoned *Combat* and dictated his statement: it appeared the following morning, with accounts of the funeral.

The Petite Dame could not wait to see Martin du Gard next day. She feared that he would already be regretting his outburst and, when he arrived, she was full of praise for his action. 'Yes, I'm glad I protested,' he said, 'but was it really necessary to be so angry, so dogmatic about it?' He then laughed, realizing that he had reacted exactly as his anti-clerical hero Jean Barois would have done. He was delighted by Pierre's impertinent, disdainful intervention. That evening, Jean Schlumberger arrived and stayed for dinner: he revealed that Domi had telephoned him on 20 November, asking him if he thought it would be appropriate to have a pastor there. Schlumberger had replied: 'Certainly not.' Domi then said that he would consult Catherine's wishes. If she opposed the idea of a pastor, no part of the ceremony would take place in the house. Clearly, Domi Drouin had tricked everyone into having the funeral that he wanted. The following day, Jacques Drouin, Domi's brother, telephoned Lambert and excitedly asked if he had read Herbart's 'incredible outburst' in *Combat*. 'No,' said Lambert. Jacques Drouin read out the statement. 'It's absolutely incredible!' he expostulated. 'By what right does this Herbart . . .' Lambert cut him short: 'Be careful, we all have the greatest esteem and affection for Pierre Herbart, we will be with him.'[134]

On 31 March, Maria Van Rysselberghe, the 'Petite Dame', wrote the last paragraph of her *Cahiers*:

I shall not write anything more in this notebook – I shall no longer have anything to say. How happy I feel today to think that this task, which weighed so heavily upon me in recent days, was his final joy . . . This long work is my own thanks for everything that he has so generously given me: joy, broadening of mind and above all that absolute confidence that fortifies my conscience. How beautiful it could be to live at his side! . . .[135]

Gide's posthumous existence continued at its most intense in the memories of those who had 'lived at his side', who were also with him when he died. Most of them followed in due course. First to go, in 1958, was Roger Martin du Gard, Gide's closest 'literary' friend and an honorary Vaneau member, aged sixty-seven; Maria Van Rysselberghe died in 1959, aged ninety-two; Jean Schlumberger, the other 'honorary member', in 1968, aged ninety-one; Marc Allégret in 1973, aged seventy-two; Pierre Herbart in 1974, aged seventy; Elisabeth Van Rysselberghe in 1980, aged ninety. Catherine Gide and her first husband, Jean Lambert, are still with us. Beyond 'the Vaneau', other close friends followed. Dorothy Bussy died in 1960, aged ninety-three; Stoisy Sternheim in 1971, aged eighty-seven; Jef Last in 1972, aged seventy-four; Robert Levesque in 1975, aged sixty-six; Yvonne de Lestrange in 1977, aged seventy-seven. Then there was the 'other' family, relations by blood and marriage, and therefore not of Gide's choosing. After Madeleine's death, he had had little to do with them – except with Domi, who worked with Marc. Madeleine's only surviving sister, Jeanne Drouin, died a year after Gide in 1952, aged eighty-four; her son Domi died in 1969, aged seventy-one; her other son, Jacques, died in 1995, aged eighty-six.

For each of these people, Gide survived, or has survived, as a remembered presence. Their pictures of Gide are of a different order from that of a biographer, but they are also necessarily more partial, in both senses of the word, than that of the assembler and interpreter of all the evidence. But a writer has, or can have, another posthumous existence in the experience and memories of readers. For a writer like Gide, that readership is incalculable, but, taken in its entirety, it is neither stable nor static. A writer who 'survives', becomes a 'classic', does not undergo apotheosis and take his place on Olympus, even if his works remain set texts for not entirely willing readers. On a different time-scale and with no end in view, a body of writing is as subject to time's fell hand as the body of its creator. Beyond the accidents of availability, educational imperatives, fortuitous publicity from adaptations in other media, its reception is affected by subtle cultural shifts. Readers are lost, others gained; parts of the *œuvre* gain at the expense of others; under critical attention, works appear to become different works. To end this strange, eventful history of a life and its works, there follows a summing up, however provisional, an *aide-mémoire*, a memorandum, to the several hundred preceding pages.

Conclusion

'The future interests me more than the past, but what interests me even more is what belongs neither to tomorrow, nor to yesterday, but to what, at all times, has been called today.'[1]

This book is 'a life in the present' because it was written in our present, not Gide's. More importantly, though, it is the story of a life lived in the present. Such propositions are fraught with danger: they may seem like word-play and soon collapse into metaphysical confusion. Anything said about Gide, even when he is saying it himself, is, as Maurice Blanchot remarked, necessarily unjust: it usually requires counter-balancing with its opposite. To begin with, one might deny that the 'future' interested Gide more than the past. Few people have spent more hours reading the literary works of the past (including the Latin classics), playing on his piano the music of the past, observing and pondering the art of the past. Much of his own work is a meditation on his own past. As for the 'future', it caused him, like everyone else, altogether too much trouble: the chimera of a future Communist solution for the injustices of the present stifled his creativity for several years. The present is a more complicated matter. The notion of some mindless sensibility responding unreflectingly to the moment's passing sensations could hardly be less like Gide. But, at the time of writing, 1919, he was at the height of his personal happiness and artistic creativity: his relationship with Marc Allégret was at its most satisfying and he had embarked on *Les Faux-Monnayeurs*. The present was exhilarating, the future propitious, the past more than ever an impediment in his life and in his art. But the statement may be given a more subtle reading: the past is valuable only in so far as it is made present, the present must be lived in such a way that it is enriched by the works of the past. This requires experiencing them anew, again and again, not treating them as inherited monuments, symbolic of a nation's values and achievements. Gide read the classics, in four languages (one 'dead'), over and over, often aloud to others, noting how the works *changed* each time. Paintings, for him, were not items in a tourist's itinerary or things seen, years ago, in the Louvre, but acquaintances, endlessly renewed, almost conversed with. Music was not, for him, something captured and repeatable at will by the pressing of buttons, but pieces worked at, day after day, in an endless struggle of hands and brain. For Gide, the past was the present, living past and only out of that past-enriched present could any future worth having come to birth.

Another aspect of Gide's 'life in the present' was suggested by one of his favourite words, '*disponibilité*', the capacity to be 'available', receptive to whatever life brings one's way. 'Work' was not some sacred activity, performed at prescribed hours, in some private sanctum. It was done anywhere and everywhere, when life did not present more pressing or alluring alternatives: hence the constant need to escape Paris – and to return to it.

Nine months after Gide's death and as a special honour to its founder, the *NRF* was allowed, once, to emerge from the outer darkness to which it had been banished at the Liberation. In a 400-page special number, sixty contributors, a third of them, appropriately, from abroad, paid 'Hommage à André Gide'. Many of the contributors remarked on Gide's 'curiosity'. John Steinbeck wrote: 'Gide was curious about everything, each leaf, each insect, the colour of a curtain . . . Our ideas are born of our curiosities.'[2] Thomas Mann speaks of the curiosity that Gide shared with Goethe. One might add that Gide ends his greatest work, *Les Faux-Monnayeurs*, not with a rounded, enclosing conclusion, but with an opening up to the world 'outside' the fiction, a hint of other stories to come: 'I am very curious to meet Caloub.'[3] At the other end of life's scale, the same insatiable curiosity would lead Gide to walk the entire length of a train and back in search of the ideal travelling companion. That great poet Saint-John Perse wrote his *hommage* from his Washington embassy. Gide, he said, had always been ready to look to the younger generations, 'for a genuine curiosity drew him towards all living springs – a curiosity that was never abstract, but personal, fraternal and he knew how to communicate it as such, without any wish to dominate.'[4]

That outward-turned curiosity also became sympathy, identification even with the other. This began very early. In *Si le grain ne meurt*, Gide describes his reaction on learning that 'Mouton', the little friend he played with in the Luxembourg, was going blind. Gide – he would be six or seven – went up to his room and burst into tears: 'for several days I would keep my eyes shut for long periods and move around without opening them, trying to feel what Mouton must have been feeling'.[5] Curiosity and sympathy lay at the base of Gide's genius for friendship. It also had a deeper, more emotional source: 'An extraordinary, an insatiable need to love and be loved. I believe this is what has dominated my life and driven me to write,' he wrote in 1948.[6] That need was never focused on one person solely and, as we know, sex, with Gide, was usually divorced from love. His 'love', therefore, became polymorphous, distributed with prodigality to his friends. That genius for friendship, that generosity of spirit, that absence of envy, jealousy or resentment, undoubtedly set the tone for his circle of friends. It made possible and assured the continuation of the *NRF.* Whatever their differences of temperament and outlook, the group remained friends: there were no 'splits', no setting up of alternative seats of literary power. When friends moved away, as in the case of Jammes, Claudel and, above all, Ghéon, it was because their new-found religion made true dialogue impossible. For Gide, dialogue was of the essence of human life. He was so good a listener, he identified so completely with his interlocutors, that he often adopted their point of view, only to revert back to his own later. The same style in personal relations brought about and made possible 'the Vaneau'. That experiment in human living entailed a *mode de vie* freed of the demands, duties and restrictions imposed by marriage or stable, monogamous relationships – it necessarily lacked the deeper rewards and compensations of such relationships, and their consequent perils and dangers. It was a situation of precisely the right degree of complication and flexibility to accommodate the very different needs of a group of very different and complicated people. The residents came and went as they pleased, joined, for longer or shorter periods, by others. Friends dropped in at all hours, often stayed for meals, which were usually improvised and stronger on conviviality than gastronomy – when neither servants nor women were present, they were taken in restaurants. Presiding over all, in their two intercommunicating apartments, were the dual monarchs, the Petite Dame and Gide himself.

Curiosity and empathy certainly came into Gide's relations with adolescent boys and young men. His devious cunning was untiring in the pursuit of his object. Surprisingly, no complaint was ever made against him, either by a boy or by parents. He was, of course, protected by the innocence of the time. But he never forced his attentions on anyone, nor did he do with his 'partners' anything that they would not have been doing themselves. None seems to have suffered from the experience. Maurice Schlumberger soon turned to women, married, had several children: he almost certainly grew out of any homosexual feelings that he might have had and he moved out of Gide's life. Those who remained his friends never ceased to benefit from his friendship. Marc Allégret also turned to women, but remained for several years part of Gide's loose *ménage* at the Vaneau, a lifelong friend who was with him at the end. Without Gide's guidance and encouragement, he would not have escaped sufficiently from his family to find his vocation. Gide was the single greatest influence on his life and a wholly beneficial one.

Gide's capacity for love was not confined to his friends: it spilled over into a concern for others less fortunate than himself. Undoubtedly, much of his success with Arabs and black Africans was due to the way he treated them: they were not used to such consideration from Europeans. And it was not confined to those whom he found sexually attractive. He was curious about their difference, and respected it; but he also refused to abide by the usual distinctions concerning them. Hence his mother's outrage when he tried to bring Athman to Paris and put him up, not in a sixth-floor maid's room, but in the apartment itself – this in 1895! Gide was not sexually attracted to Athman and he was acting, not out of any political conviction, or moral principle, but simply because he found it the most natural thing in the world and could not understand others' objections. He showed a similar concern for the unfortunates living in hovels around Cuverville, giving help (and money), going to inordinate trouble to try to get the orphaned son of one of his labourers a decent education. During the First World War, he worked all day and every day, for a year, helping to run the Foyer Franco-Belge, offering sympathy and practical help to thousands of refugees. He showed the same compassion for his African 'boys' on his long, arduous expedition in West Africa. When one of the Africans in their convoy was injured, Gide and Marc themselves gave him medical treatment, cleaning and binding his wounds. When he parted from his beloved Adoum, he made sure, by giving him money and a letter to the colony's governor, that he would be able to return to his mother. Back in France, he spent untold hours in laborious research, correspondence and lobbying: he did not let up until his efforts were rewarded with legislation limiting the free rein of the rubber companies.

Gide's curiosity about how others lived, his sympathy for others' misfortune, his natural optimism and, undoubtedly, his susceptibility to the enthusiasm and unshakeable conviction of young friends, led him in the direction of Communism. Deluged with correspondence from all over the world, with requests to chair this meeting and sign that petition, he battled on, because he believed the cause to be just, and sacrificed his own work. The same curiosity and the same sympathy, combined with an acute moral sense of what was right, opened his eyes, in the Soviet Union, to the realities of Communist rule. Although, in 1936, he had little notion of the extent of the Soviet horror, he had seen enough and it was more than most people managed to see. His outrage was far greater than the one that he had felt in Africa. He had not expected rubber companies to behave correctly to black Africans, but the Communists had set themselves up as the saviours of the underprivileged: he had come to regard them as the true heirs of Christ. They had turned out to be the jailers and torturers of 'the poor in spirit', 'the weak', those who 'hunger and thirst after righteousness'. With the coming of the second war, he was tireless in trying to free German émigrés – Jewish, left-wing or both – from French internment. He then helped several of them to get to the United States.

In the matter of human relations, there was, of course, one great failure: his marriage. Its failure was the *fault* of neither party, in the sense that neither had it in his or her power to make it more successful than it was. In all conscience, it could have been much worse. Madeleine retained a semblance of sweet serenity to the end, but only at the cost of an ever-growing withdrawal from her husband's concerns. Gide had no alternative to pursuing his life elsewhere, but he always returned to Cuverville, especially when Madeleine, through illness, needed him. In one sense, his feelings of devotion for her never altered: he would sooner have killed himself than abandon her. Nowadays, no such marriage would ever have come about, still less lasted a lifetime. It would surely have been better for both had it never come about, or been dissolved at some early stage. But, given the time and characters of the two parties, there was no alternative but to make the best they could of it. Gide always attracted women, sometimes, as in the case of Dorothy Bussy and Yvonne Davet, with tumultuous results: in both cases, Gide displayed endless endurance and patience. Any other man would have got rid of them at the outset. Generally, Gide's relationships with women were of the best. He was on excellent terms with that English couple, Enid McLeod and Ethel Whitehorn; he was on intimate terms with those two *grandes dames*, Yvonne de Lestrange and Loup Mayrisch. But his closest women friends were Maria Van Rysselberghe and her daughter Elisabeth, with whom he set up his alternative, very original 'household'.

In his 'Hommage', Ernst Jünger spoke of Gide's charm and went on: 'He was, on the one hand, a young person, playful . . . and, on the other, could assume the features of an ancient sage, one of those kindly Chinese, a learned Mandarin, commenting on some ideogram with his guests, over tea.'[7] That 'little boy amusing himself' again, the Protestant pastor having turned into a learned, but charming old Mandarin. In his introduction to the 'Hommage', Jean Schlumberger also spoke of Gide's youthfulness and quotes Gide's own views on the subject. There are those, said Gide, who, at a certain age, cease to acquire experience and are content to exploit what they have already acquired: 'they live henceforth on their capital'. 'They reproach me for eternally running after my youth: but what they don't understand is the rejuvenation that is brought about through sympathy. They are incapable of sympathy. I'm not a man in his fifties trying to be young; others' youth passes into me.'[8]

If Gide acquired his youthfulness from the young, what made him attractive to the young was that he preached a way of life that they found attractive. He gave expression and authority to a freedom of action and thought that they aspired to: he was a moralist who was seen by their elders as an immoralist. He made himself the spokesman of rebellious youth, exploited Africans, the 'proletariat', the victims of Soviet Communism and Nazism, but he belonged to none of those categories. He knew himself to be protected by wealth and position, but millions of homosexuals were not so protected – and he was a homosexual. He owed it to himself and to them to speak out. What remained in him of the Protestant pastor had to preach in defence of the little boy amusing himself. Assuming the role of immoral moralist was not without risk: by publishing *Corydon* he carried that role to the limit. All his friends had tried to dissuade him from doing so: it would help no one and might destroy the author's life. Whatever the book's shortcomings, *Corydon* was important because it was the first serious attempt by a homosexual to defend the practice of homosexuality to the general public. That was why Gide called it 'my most important book'. It did not change matters overnight: it was merely one step in a long progress. Many contributors to the 'Hommage à André Gide' testified to the change that *Les Nourritures terrestres* had brought to their lives: no contributor made such a claim about *Corydon*, though it must have changed the lives of untold thousands. The time was not yet ripe. Like Socrates, Gide was a 'corrupter of youth'. To its credit, the Swedish Academy observed that Gide had often been accused of 'depraving and disorienting youth' and added: 'This is an old accusation addressed to all emancipators of the mind.' In his *Spectator* obituary, Harold Nicolson referred to the same charge:

The accusation levelled against Gide is that, with tranquil and demonic subtlety, he destroys the valuable certitudes of the young. Such a charge was brought . . .

against the veteran Socrates two thousand three hundred and fifty years ago. I am angered by such an imputation . . . Am I conscious that the *Nourritures terrestres*, or even *L'Immoraliste*, seared the spring buds of principle or withered my young concepts of the beautiful and the good? Not in the very least . . . The effect upon me was not negative but positive. His writings enhanced my curiosity and my zest; from them I derived a distrust of pragmatic injunctions and a delight in the variety of human life. I am certain that they did me not harm but good . . . I became one of the band of his Nathanaels; my gratitude and my esteem for the modern Socrates are neither sporadic nor faint.

Raymond Mortimer, like several others, refers to the effect on him of reading *Les Nourritures terrestres*: 'no book had so profound an influence on me or, I would even dare to believe, more salutary'.[9] Enid Starkie was another. As a schoolgirl, she had stumbled on *Les Nourritures* in a bookshop. She read a few lines at random and it was 'like a thunder clap, a sudden revelation. In Gide I found at once the explanation of my adolescent *malaise*, the justification of my rebellious desires.'[10] For Jacques Brenner, the *coup de foudre* came with *Si le grain ne meurt*. It was 'the eruption of literature into my life. Or rather the end of the separation between life and literature.' Gide's book not only spoke to him of 'the world in which I lived, explained it to me, exposed it to me', but it also 'gave me a lesson in writing. I experienced the delight of reading a fine sentence. Literature became an art, as well as an instrument of knowledge.'[11]

In his introduction to the 'Hommage', Jean Schlumberger noted that Gide was not one of those writers who 'transfuse all their blood into their work', leaving nothing for their private lives, who, 'outside what they publish are insignificant and empty'. Such writers are literature's 'drudges'; they lack 'the true aristocracy, which can be madly prodigal of its wealth and blood, but which nonetheless preserves a margin of inalienable freedom'.[12] During Gide's life, so insistent were the demands of his 'life', of others' needs, responsibilities that he had assumed, causes that he had espoused that the 'margin of inalienable freedom' was often eroded still further. The biographer–critic may sometimes be tempted to reverse the Latin tag: *Vita longa, ars brevis*. For, not only did the demands of the life constantly interrupt the writing, his curiosity and concern about the world and his fellow human beings were such that only a relatively small proportion of his total output may be given the highest appellation of 'art'. The writing most immediately caught up in the life and the world, and the most voluminous section of the *œuvre*, is the correspondence. His curiosity took its toll here, too. Just as he would leap up from his desk at the sound of the door-bell, too curious to let someone else answer it, so he would never sit down to work before opening all his letters and replying to as many of them as he thought fit. The surviving letters alone run into thousands; over forty volumes of the correspondence have so far been published. They cost him a good slice of most working days.

Then there is the *Journal*. In 1946, Pierre Herbart asked Gide which of his books he would choose if only one were to survive. 'I think it would be my *Journal*,' he replied. Neither Herbart nor the Petite Dame agreed. Gide is, as they say, entitled to his opinion. Coming from anyone else it would sound very '*parisien*', an attempt at originality by provocation, rather than a considered judgement. It is also a way of cutting Gide – and literature – down to unthreatening size. As the Petite Dame rightly remarked, the *Journal* would not seem so important were it not from the same pen as the fictional work.[13] Yet the *Journal* is the pre-eminently Gidean mode of expression. The first work, *Les Cahiers d'André Walter*, is not only in journal form, it emerged out of Gide's own journal. Many of the first-person *récits* read more or less like journals, while in *Les Faux-Monnayeurs* Edouard's journal provides an alternative voice to the narrator's. The role of the journal in Gide's life and work creates what looks like a characteristic Gidean contradiction. Many, if questioned as to the most marked feature of Gide's character, as man and as writer, would choose, not curiosity, the mind directing itself outwards, but subjectivity, a certain self-awareness, self-consciousness, self-absorption even. Various causes may be adduced for this: the solitary childhood of an only child, an authoritarian mother, the early death of a beloved father, etc. If it were not an actual cause, Gide's Calvinist upbringing must surely have strengthened that subjective tendency. For the older Gide, the *Journal* became an examination of conscience by other means; but it soon grew out of the adolescent introspection of the André Walter variety, becoming as much turned outwards as inwards.

The *Journal* leads naturally to the autobiographical works (*Numquid et tu, Si le grain ne meurt, Et nunc manet in te, Ainsi soit-il*) and the travel books (the two African and two Soviet volumes). Moving from the more personal to the more social life, there are the three works with 'legal' themes, collected in *Ne Jugez Pas* (*Souvenirs de la Cour d'assises, L'Affaire Redureau, La Séquestrée de Poitiers*), the political articles and speeches collected in *Littérature engagée* and, in a class of its own, *Corydon*. Then there are the critical works, from full-length books like *Oscar Wilde, Dostoïevski* and *Montaigne*, to collections of essays (*Prétextes, Nouveaux Prétextes, Morceaux choisis, Incidences*) and innumerable uncollected prefaces and articles.

The translations of others' literary works include Shakespeare's *Antony and Cleopatra* and *Hamlet*, Blake's *Marriage of Heaven and Hell* and Rabindranath Tagore's *Gitanjali*. *Le Procès* is part translation, part adaptation for the theatre of Kafka's *Prozess* (*The Trial*). The theatre brings us at last to Gide's own creative works. The plays span almost the whole of his literary career, so many repeated attempts, never entirely successful: *Philoctète* (1899), *Le Roi Candaule* (1901), *Saül* (1904), *Oedipe* (1930), the unperformed one-act play *Le Treizième Arbre* and *Robert, ou l'Intérêt général* (1944). Then there are the theatrical adaptations of his own works: *Perséphone* and *Les Caves du Vatican*.

It is the fiction that lies at the summit of Gide's work. Here, as in the *œuvre* as a whole, what strikes one first is the variety. Here, too, we see Gide's curiosity, his youthfulness, at work: a refusal to mine only one seam, to repeat successful formulas. Whereas the output of most prose writers consists largely of a series of novels, often of little else, fiction is a relatively small part of Gide's *œuvre*. What is more, he applies the term *roman* (novel) to only one work (*Les Faux-Monnayeurs*). It is true that, with this one exception, his fictional works tend to be on the short side. As a stylist, he is at the opposite pole to Proust. To present-day readers, under the spell of Proust's long, sensuous, endlessly qualifying sentences, it may come as a surprise to learn that, in France, Proust was not always regarded as a great *stylist*, in the 'classical' sense, whereas Gide, with his clear, succinct, spare, deliberately, subtly phrased sentences, was. Proust always wants to say more, Gide less.

Although Gide's fictional works are very different from one another, they also fall into broad categories. First come the early, rather 'poetic' works written under the influence of Symbolism: *Les Cahiers d'André Walter* (1891), *Le Traité du Narcisse* (1892), *Le Voyage d'Urien* (1893), *La Tentative amoureuse* (1893). (Gide's only published collection of poems, *Les Poésies d'André Walter*, also dates from this period.) These are youthful works, with many of the shortcomings, but some of the consolations, of juvenilia.

With *Les Nourritures terrestres*, Gide moves out of Symbolism into a work that belongs to no very definable genre. It is loose in narrative, vague in characterization, with something of the old Symbolist style about it, complete with episodes in verse. But the spirit, the message, it would not be too strong to say, is life-affirming in a Whitmanesque way. This is very much a young man's book and it has always appealed to the young, often coming to the rebellious young, as we have seen, like a revelation. It is no small achievement for a man of twenty-seven or so; what is quite astonishing is that it was published in 1897. Arriving thirty-eight years later, the only purely literary product of Gide's *communisant* years, *Les Nouvelles Nourritures* is not a success, as Gide soon came to realize.

From now on, two broad categories of works, the 'serious', heavily autobiographical, first-person *récits* and the comic, more 'inventive', even fantastic '*soties*' more or less alternate through Gide's working life, with a third, less homogeneous category, works having a biblical or mythological subject, intervening occasionally.

All 'creative writing', as they still say in circles untouched by critical theory, has an equivocal relation to the 'truth'. By definition, it creates, miraculously, 'out of nothing'; it 'tells stories', that is to say, tells lies. And yet these 'lies' would not be accorded the value that they are if they did not, in some mysterious way, 'tell the truth'. But in the *récits*, Gide reduces the fiction/truth opposition, in the interests of truth, to an apparent minimum. *Récit*, meaning, literally, an account of events, is one of a number of French terms used to describe what in English are called short stories. Others are *nouvelle* (related to the Italian *novella* and, though only etymologically, to our 'novel'), and *conte* (roughly equivalent, with its less realistic, more fantastic connotations, with our 'tale'). Clearly Gide chose *récit* as being the most seemingly 'truthful' of the terms available. Like the early practitioners of the novel in the eighteenth century, he is at pains to establish his alibis as a recorder of the truth. The epistolary novels of Laclos and Richardson lay claim to truth simply by being composed of 'found' documents, of letters. If the narrator speaks in the first person, he can be held to 'account' for the truth of his statements: a third-person narrator is obviously assuming knowledge that he does not have, for only God can be omniscient. *L'Immoraliste* (1902) is the first-person narration of Michel, spoken to a group of friends, written down by one of them and sent as a document, with covering letter, to his brother. In *La Porte étroite* (1909), Jérôme Palissier eschews any ambition to write a book and has tried to set down his account of events as best he can. Towards the end, his narration is interrupted by long extracts from 'Alissa's journal'. In *Isabelle* (1911), Gide turns the first-person/second-person relation around: the whole story, apart from a few introductory pages in Gide's own voice, is attributed to 'Gérard Lacase', a fictitious narrator, who recounts it to Gide and the unfictitious Francis Jammes. *La Symphonie Pastorale* (1919), takes the form of a journal in two '*cahiers*', written by the pastor. Here, for the first time, Gide uses a voice very different from his own and thus has to have his narrator condemn himself, to some extent, out of his own mouth. The late trio of stories, *L'Ecole des femmes*, *Robert* and *Geneviève*, are first-person narratives by a wife-mother, a husband-father and their daughter respectively, each purporting to have reached André Gide, at different times, through the post. Not only do the *récits* all make claims to truth, they are all more or less autobiographical (the final trio less so). *La Porte étroite* is the almost untransposed story of his and Madeleine's lives, and the lives of their families, stopping short of marriage, showing what might have happened had they not married. The *récits* are all imbued with the Protestant spirit of Gide's childhood, even though, implicitly or explicitly, they are critiques of that Protestantism. The oppressive atmosphere is never quite lifted: the Protestant pastor may have lost his faith, seen through the human consequences of his beliefs, but he is still, up to a point, 'boring'. We glimpse nothing of a more joyful, still less more amusing life. For that we have to turn to the *soties*, where no Protestant pastor is allowed to spoil the little boy's games.

The *soties* are Gide at his most inventive, furthest removed from autobiography. In his 'Hommage', Thomas Mann makes a link between Gide's curiosity, his moral concern and his powers as 'an audacious experimenter'. It is perceptive to observe that Gide the man is being most himself in works in which he seems to be furthest removed from his personal life. Astonishingly, the first of the *soties*, *Paludes* (1895), appeared not only seven years before *L'Immoraliste*, but also two years before *Les Nourritures terrestres*. (Gide is no respecter of chronological consistency, a fact partly explained by the extraordinarily long gestation of many of his works and his practice of working on two or three very different ones simultaneously.) *Paludes* is a work of quite astonishing originality, arguably the first 'modernist' novel. This brittle, but gentle 'send-up' of the Paris literary world of the 1890s, was followed, in 1899, by the second *sotie*, the brilliant, exuberant *Le Prométhée mal enchaîné*. The full-length, more ambitious and gloriously successful *Les Caves du Vatican* appeared in 1914. *Les Faux-Monnayeurs* (1925), even more ambitious and equally successful, is too complex, too differentiated a work to be subsumed under the rather self-deprecatory term of *sotie*. Nevertheless, it has much in common with the *soties*, especially *Les Caves*, and, most of the time, breathes their light-hearted spirit. It is also a *locus classicus* of 'modernist' narrative technique, incapable of simply telling a story, or telling a story simply; it displays the utmost contempt for the 'traditional' novel's 'psychological analysis', its linear, 'orchestrated' plots, its carefully built up descriptions of scene and character and, above all, its moral preoccupations. As if all this were not enough for critics who, sixty or seventy years later, with none of Gide's lightness of touch, busy themselves with such matters, Gide followed the publication of his masterpiece of now modish self-referentiality with his *Journal des Faux-Monnayeurs*, extracts from his journal, written over the long period of the novel's gestation, in which he *reflects* on the work as it progresses. *Les Faux-Monnayeurs* was not the work of a man in his mid-fifties who, turning his back on his past, had caught the 'modernist' spirit of the 1920s, under the influence perhaps of his young friends. It was rather the *summum* of a lifetime's struggle against fiction: in 1895, at the age of *twenty-five*, Gide published *Paludes*, a work that is every bit as self-referential, decentred, deconstructed, disrespectful of fictional conventions, 'modern' as *Les Faux-Monnayeurs*. One of its characters is even writing, or claims to be writing, a work called *Paludes*. It is a much shorter, slighter work altogether than its great successor, but, if one were foolish enough to make formal innovation one's sole criterion of excellence, *Paludes* would have to be regarded as the superior of *Les Faux-Monnayeurs*.

My third category comprises *El Hadj* (1899), the 'biblical' *Bethsabé* and *Le Retour de l'Enfant prodigue* (1907), and Gide's final work, *Thésée* (1946), which also has much of the *sotie* about it.

In the past fifty years, such is his protean nature, Gide has never gone out of fashion, in France at least. In Paris, no fashion lasts for long. When the change comes, it is total and receives well-nigh total support. (Elsewhere change is more partial, and slower. Some 'new' something that was wont to set the Parisian tables on a roar, but has since bitten the dust, sweeps across the American universities as some new orthodoxy and, eventually, reaches the British ones, as one-time rebellious research-students acquire their Chairs. None of these successive waves disappears; each survives, another layer in the academic archaeology.) As intellectual fashions change, the new Parisian intellectuals turn their attention to some other aspect of Gide's *œuvre*. In his age, Gide had come to be revered as a French stylist, of classical virtues, and a moralist – or execrated as an 'immoralist'. In the late 1940s, young Parisian 'existentialists' had time neither for style nor for morality, but they discovered that Gide's Lafcadio (of 1914), with his '*acte gratuit*', had been an existentialist all along. (In fact, Gide had a Parisian waiter – in a café on the boulevard des Capucines, not the boulevard Saint-Germain – discoursing on the '*action gratuite*' in his *Prométhée* of 1899.) As the reign of the 'subject' and its 'freedom' receded, with the advent of the *nouveau roman* and the *nouvelle critique*, to be replaced by the 'object' and its 'structures', the *soties* were again in fashion, this time, not as examples of existential freedom from moral norms, but as self-referential linguistic structures, narratives that fail to tell their stories and avoid the messy, subjective world of motive and psychology. Barthes singled out *Paludes* for attention presumably because, of all the *soties*, it was the most 'radical', the one offering fewest of the novel's traditional pleasures. That period of 'structure' also saw the return to fashion of two systems of thought: Marxism and psychoanalysis. In terms of their subject-matter, human history and the human psyche, neither might have seemed to suit the prevailing mood. But what excited the followers of the new fashion was neither history nor psyche, but the structures applied to them. In the hands of Lacan and Althusser, their application became ever more abstract, ever more full of neologisms borrowed from linguistics. It would be a fair assumption, I believe, that both men were more interested in their own ideas than in the woes of patients or proletariat.

With the collapse of the French intellectual's belief in Marxism, all theory fell into disfavour, though, for a time, the French intellectual retained a rather abstract, theoretical style of argument, even when arguing against theory. In the 1980s, the French press was full of another novelty, the '*nouveaux philosophes*', four or five young intellectuals, extreme leftists in 1968, now right-wing propagandists. Even religion was back, after decades of absence among the intelligentsia, though, this time, what attracted was not the 'cold' authority of a self-contained system, theology, but the stress on the subjective, the 'warm' emotional drama of Christian life. History was no longer the movement of anonymous forces: political history was back, with named individuals. The French rediscovered biography.

Autobiography is all the rage in Paris. Gide's *Journal* and *Si le grain ne meurt* are to the fore again. And so we return to Gide, the man. A few weeks after Gide's death, Martin du Gard received a letter from a priest, a certain Father Mondel, who raised the subject of Gide's sincerity. Like its grander, older sister, Truth, sincerity is one of the notions that suffered most during the ascendency of 'critical theory', yet it is one that most of us feel the need for in everyday life. Sincerity is not a quality the educated French feel particularly proud of. They would much rather be considered intelligent or witty: in no other city in the world does one feel that one is living at Court more than in Paris, for all its official republicanism. (For many of us, this is its charm.) Sincerity carries no glamour: Gide's cult of sincerity was untypically French, undoubtedly inherited from his Huguenot forebears. In his 'Hommage', Saint-John Perse said as much: 'The literary France of 1909. Academicism, Parisianism, opportunism . . . A man of his time: like one of those cultivated Huguenot gentlemen of the time of the Leagues, who, having one day shortened his beard and abandoned the Court doublet for some free cloak of plain homespun, went off to live on his estate.'[14]

To end, let us leave the final word to Roger Martin du Gard, Gide's closest and dearest *confrère*, in his reply to Father Mondel:

Gide was a human specimen, typically exceptional, unclassifiable. To call him complex falls short of the truth: he was, in the most authentic way, from birth, an inextricable entanglement of *contradictions*, physical and moral. He devoted his life to taking stock, to seeking the guiding thread in that inner labyrinth. He clearly perceived the secret unity of his being; and he knew, from an early age, that his flagrant contradictions were only apparent contradictions, that it was a profound, unjust error to judge him according to the norms. Hence his perpetual need to plead, to justify what he did. He set out to find the link, the *raison d'être*, the psychological explanation of his inconsistencies (of what seemed to others to be inconsistencies or pretence); and, in that search, he was moved by a wish for total, exclusive, courageous *sincerity*, to the point of heroism. And that search was not in vain: gradually, step by step, with halts, diversions and retreats (of which the *Journal* and his works are the living testimony; and that slow, groping progress is the best proof of his sincerity), he arrived at a sort of miracle, at the co-ordination of all those opposed elements that he carried inside himself; and he was rewarded for that patient, painful effort towards *his sincerity*, by the serenity of his last fifteen years, a serenity of which I was a witness, which was profoundly authentic, which remained unalterable to the end; which had its last, prodigious radiance in that conscious death, consented to without fear, without struggle, without any need of hope, in that lucid abandonment to annihilation, in that acquiescence of his whole being to the laws of nature.[15]

Notes and References

Page references are given, first to the French edition and second, where available, to the English translation. The following abbreviations of titles have been used (full bibliographical details are given in the Bibliography):

A	*Amyntas*
AS	*Acqua Santa*
AW	*Cahiers d'André Walter*
BAAG	*Bulletin de l'Association des Amis d'André Gide*
Bl	Jacques-Emile Blanche. *Nouvelles Lettres à André Gide (1891–1925)*
BU	*Back from the USSR* (with *Afterthoughts on the USSR*)
C	*Corydon*
CAG	*Cahiers André Gide*

    1 (1969): *Les Débuts littéraires. D'"André Walter" à "L'Immoraliste"*

    2 (1970): *Correspondance André Gide – François Mauriac (1912–50)*

    3 (1971): *Le Centenaire*

    4–7 (1972–1975): *Les Cahiers de la Petite Dame, I (1918–1929), II (1929–1937), III (1937–1945), IV (1945–1951)*

    8 (1978): *Correspondance André Gide – Jacques-Emile Blanche (1891–1939)*

    9–11 (1979–1982): *Correspondance André Gide – Dorothy Bussy, I (1918–1924), II (1925–1936), III (1937–1951)*

    12–13 (1989): *Correspondance André Gide – Jacques Copeau, I (1902–1913), II (1913–1949)*

    14 (1989): *Correspondance André Gide – Valéry Larbaud (1905–1938)*

    15,16 (1992): Jean Claude, *André Gide et le théâtre*, I and II

CC	Marc Allégret, *Carnets du Congo*
Cf	*The Counterfeiters*
CJ	Jacques Copeau. *Journal*, 1 (1901–1915), 2 (1916–1948)
EN	*Et nunc manet in te*
FE	*Fruits of the Earth*
G/A	André Gide. *Correspondance avec François-Paul Alibert*
G/Ben	Arnold Bennett, André Gide. *Vingt ans d'amitié littéraire*
G/Bus	*Selected Letters of André Gide and Dorothy Bussy*
G/Cl	Paul Claudel, André Gide. *Correspondance 1899–1926*
G/Coc	Jean Cocteau. *Lettres à André Gide*
G/Gh	Henri Ghéon, André Gide. *Correspondance*

G/Gos	*The Correspondence of André Gide and Edmund Gosse 1904–1928*
G/J	Francis Jammes, André Gide. *Correspondance 1893–1938*
G/Las	André Gide, Jef Last. *Correspondance 1934–1950*
G/Lev	André Gide, Robert Levesque. *Correspondance (1926–1950)*
G/M	André Gide. *Correspondance avec sa mère 1880–1895*
G/MG	André Gide, Roger Martin du Gard. *Correspondance*. 1 (1913–1934), 2 (1935–1951)
G/P	Marcel Proust, André Gide. *Autour de La Recherche*
G/Ruy	André Gide, André Ruyters. *Correspondance. I (1895–1906), II (1907–1950)*
G/S	André Gide, Jean Schlumberger. *Correspondance 1901–1950*
G/V	André Gide, Paul Valéry. *Correspondance 1890–1942*
HAG	*Hommage à André Gide*
I	*The Immoralist*
IID	*If It Die . . .*
J 1, 2	*Journal* (French: Pléiade)
J I, II, III, IV	*Journal* (English)
J² I, II	*Journal* (French: 2nd Pléiade edition, 1996 and 1997)
JFM	*Journal des Faux-Monnayeurs*
LC	*Logbook of the Coiners*
LE	*Littérature engagée*
M	*Marshlands* (with *Prometheus Misbound*)
MGJ	Martin du Gard. *Journal. I (1892–1919), II (1919–1936), III (1937–1958)*
NAG	Martin du Gard. *Notes sur André Gide*; *Notes on André Gide*
R	*Romans* (Pléiade)
Riv/A-F	Jacques Rivière, Alain-Fournier. *Correspondance 1905–1914*, IV
RP	*Return of the Prodigal* (with *El Haj, Saul, Philoctetes*)
RT	*Le Retour du Tchad*
RU	*Retour de l'U.R.S.S.*
SBI	*So Be It*
SG	*Strait is the Gate*
SW	*School for Wives*
TC	*Travels in the Congo* (with *Return from Lake Chad*)
TL	*Two Legends* (*Theseus* and *Oedipus*)
TS	*Two Symphonies* (*Isabelle* and *Pastoral Symphony*)
UV	*Urien's Voyage*
VC	*Vatican Cellars*

CHAPTER 1: *Two Stars, Two Races, Two Provinces, Two Faiths*

1. J 1, 959; J III, 84.
2. G/J, 199.
3. J 2, 358; IID, 14.
4. J 2, 372; IID, 32.

5. Unpublished letter to Maurice Démarest.
6. J 2, 364; IID, 22.
7. J 2, 365; IID, 23.
8. J 1, 250; J I, 217.

CHAPTER 2: *Schooldays and Holidays*

1. J 2, 349–50; IID, 3–4.
2. J 2, 350; IID, 5.
3. J 2, 422; IID, 94–5.
4. J 2, 800; J II, 365.
5. J 2, 352–3; IID, 7–8.
6. J 2, 353–4; IID, 9.
7. J 2, 355–6; IID, 11–12.
8. J 2, 389–90; IID, 54–5.
9. J 2, 391; IID, 56.
10. Boisdeffre, 64–5; italics in the original!
11. J 2, 400; IID, 67.
12. J 2, 404; IID, 71–2.
13. J 2, 406–7; IID, 73–5.

14. J 2, 407; IID, 75–6.
15. J 2, 407–8; IID, 76.
16. J 2, 393–6; IID, 58–62.
17. R, 499; SG, 11.
18. R, 500; SG, 11–12.
19. J 2, 415; IID, 85.
20. J 2, 411; IID, 80–1.
21. J 2, 370, 381; IID, 29, 43.
22. J 2, 378–80; IID, 40–2.
23. J 2, 382; IID, 44.
24. J 2, 415–16; IID, 85–6.
25. J 2, 367; IID, 26.
26. J 2, 370–1; IID, 30.

CHAPTER 3: *Youth: God and Love*

1. J 2, 409; IID, 78.
2. R, 495; SG, 5.
3. J 2, 419; IID, 91.
4. J 2, 422–4; IID, 95–6.
5. J 2, 424–5; IID, 98–9.
6. J 2, 427; IID, 101–2.
7. J 2, 429; IID, 104.
8. J 2, 430; IID, 105.
9. J 2, 434; IID, 109–10.
10. R, 503–4; SG, 16–17.
11. J 2, 435; IID, 111.
12. J 2, 435; IID, 111.
13. J 2, 466; IID, 149–50.
14. J 2, 474; IID, 158–9.
15. J 2, 478; IID, 164.

16. J 2, 507; IID, 200.
17. J 2, 480–1; IID, 167.
18. J 2, 481–4; IID, 169–71.
19. J 2, 486; IID, 174.
20. J 2, 442; IID, 119.
21. G/M, 42–3.
22. J 2, 1190–1; SBI, 61–2.
23. J 2, 468; IID, 152.
24. J 2, 498; IID, 188.
25. J 2, 500; IID, 191–2.
26. J 2, 506; IID, 199.
27. J 2, 1126; EN, 25–6.
28. AW, 77–8.
29. J 2, 518; IID, 214.

CHAPTER 4: *André Walter: Puritan and Narcissist*

1. J 1, 13; J I, 3.
2. Louÿs, *Œuvres complètes*, ix, 300–2.
3. G/M, 53.
4. G/M, 91.
5. Iseler 18.
6. J 2, 523; IID, 220.
7. Iseler, 96–7.
8. Iseler, 23.
9. AW, 64–5, my italics.
10. AW, 167–8.
11. AW, 64, 79, 128, my italics.
12. J 2, 522; IID, 219.
13. AW, 133.
14. AW, 164–5, my italics.
15. AW, 179.
16. Marty, 145.
17. AW, 9–10.
18. Marty, 144.
19. R, 179; FE, 55–6.
20. Valéry, *Lettres à quelques-uns*, 21 December 1890.
21. G/V, 68.
22. G/V, 69.
23. G/V, 102.
24. Iseler, 30–1, 27.
25. G/V, 99.
26. G/V, 46.
27. *Prétextes*, 258.
28. 'Saint Mallarmé l'esotérique', *Interviews imaginaires*, 174.
29. J 2, 532–4; IID, 251–3.
30. G/V, 64.
31. J 1, 26; J I, 16.
32. J 2, 545; IID, 247.

CHAPTER 5: *The Ironic Narcissist*

1. Unpublished letter, 9 May 1891, Bibliothèque Doucet.
2. J 1, 22; J I, 12.
3. R, 7; RP, 10.
4. R, 9; RP, 13.
5. R, 8–9; RP, 12.
6. Schlumberger, 75.
7. Mallarmé, *Correspondance*, V, 80.
8. *Prétextes*, 277.
9. *Prétextes*, 273.
10. G/V, 144.
11. J 1, 27; J I, 16.
12. J 1, 28; J I, 18.
13. J 1, 29; J I, 19.
14. G/V, 157.
15. G/M, 145–6.
16. G/M, 147.
17. G/M, 153–4.
18. Unpublished journal, 11 June 1892.
19. J 2, 593; IID, 307.
20. G/V, 169–70.
21. Pierre-Quint, 486.
22. G/M, 168–9.
23. G/M, 169.
24. Schlumberger, 81–5.
25. R, 21; UV, 26.
26. R, 44; UV, 61.
27. J 2, 1132.
28. R, 56; UV, 93–4.
29. R, 60; UV, 85.
30. R, 64; UV, 91.
31. Marty, 160.
32. R, 66–7; UV, 94.
33. Mallarmé, *Correspondance*, VI, 102.
34. Unpublished letter, 18 March 1893.
35. R, 178; FE, 54.
36. J 1, 293–4; J I, 255.
37. J 1, 34–5; J I, 24.
38. R, 81–2; RP, 35.
39. J 1, 40; J I, 29.
40. J 1, 41–2; J I, 30.
41. J 2, 552; IID, 257.
42. J 2, 550–1, 554; IID, 255, 259.

CHAPTER 6: *Liberation and . . . Engagement*

1. J 2, 554; IID, 259–60.
2. J 2, 561.
3. G/M, 306.
4. G/M, 247.
5. G/M, 260.
6. G/M, 283.
7. G/M, 266.
8. J 2, 567; IID, 275–6.
9. J 2, 568; IID, 277.
10. J 2, 569; IID, 278.
11. J 2, 570; IID, 279.
12. J 2, 572; IID, 281.
13. G/M, 362.
14. G/M, 377–8.
15. G/M, 382.
16. G/M, 412–13.
17. G/M, 417.
18. G/M, 415.
19. G/M, 421.
20. G/M, 433–4.
21. G/M, 420.
22. G/M, 437–8.
23. G/M, 465–6.
24. J 2, 593; IID, 307.
25. Davet, 55–6.
26. G/M, 472.
27. G/M, 475.
28. G/M, 489.
29. J 1, 48; J I, 35.
30. J 2, 578–9; IID, 289–90.
31. J 2, 578; IID, 289.
32. G/M, 512.
33. G/M, 529.
34. G/M, 503.
35. R, 1473.

36. R, 1474.
37. J 2, 575–6; IID, 285–6.
38. Marty, 167.
39. R, 89; M, 13.
40. Mallarmé, *Correspondance*, VII, 241.
41. R, 91; M, 15.
42. J 1, 41; J I, 30.
43. R, 116–17; M, 50.
44. R, 1477.
45. R, 115; M, 48.
46. R, 146; M, 90.
47. G/M, 553.
48. G/M, 567.
49. G/M, 570.
50. G/M, 574.
51. G/M, 576–7.
52. J 2, 579; IID, 290–1.
53. G/M, 579.
54. G/M, 587–8.
55. J 2, 581–5; IID, 290–8.
56. G/M, 588–90.
57. J 2, 586–93; IID, 303–8.
58. J 2, 597; IID, 309.
59. G/M, 602.
60. J 2, 599; IID, 311.
61. J 2, 600; IID, 313.
62. G/M, 606.
63. G/M, 627–8.
64. G/M, 635–6.
65. J 2, 602–4; IID, 315–17.
66. G/M, 656–8.
67. G/M, 658–9.
68. J 2, 607–8; IID, 322–3.
69. J 2, 610–12; IID, 324–7.
70. J 2, 1213; SBI, 106.

CHAPTER 7: *Marriage and Nomadism*

1. J 2, 1128; EN, 28–9.
2. J 2, 1130; EN, 32.
3. Schlumberger, 121.
4. J² I, 208.

5. J 1, 1139; EN, 45.
6. R, 1484.
7. G/V, 254.
8. G/V, 254.

9. J 1, 63; J I, 49.
10. J 1, 64; J I, 50.
11. J 1, 64–5; J I, 51.
12. J 1, 67; J I, 52.
13. Unpublished letter, 11 February 1896.
14. Unpublished letter, 10 March 1896.
15. J 2, 72; J I, 57.
16. J 1, 74; J I, 58–9.
17. J 2, 594–6.
18. G/V, 265.
19. J 1, 96–7; J I, 78–9.
20. R, 343–63; RP, 41–68.
21. R, 1508.
22. G/Ruy 1, 9.
23. G/Ruy 1, 8.
24. G/V, 286.
25. G/V, 288.
26. Unpublished letter, 5 April 1897.
27. R, 176; FE, 52.
28. R, 184–6; FE, 65–7.
29. R, 189; FE, 71.
30. R, 189–91; FE, 65–74.
31. J I, 1222; J III, 317.
32. R, 153; FE, 13.
33. R, 248; FE, 163.
34. R, 249–50; FE, 10.
35. In O'Brien, 135.

36. Davet, 230–4.
37. *La Revue Blanche*, June 1897.
38. Davet, 156–7.
39. *Prétextes*, 287–99.
40. G/V, 305.
41. J 2, 1133–4; EN, 36–8.
42. G/V, 308.
43. J 1, 787; J II, 352.
44. *NRF*, XXXI, July 1928, 41.
45. *NRF*, XXXI, 46.
46. *Théâtre*, 99; RP, 246.
47. G/V, 323, 337.
48. RP, 303–4.
49. *Théâtre*, 151.
50. G/Ruy 1, 93.
51. J² I, 284–8.
52. *NRF*, December 1938, 898.
53. G/Gh, 168–9.
54. G/Gh, 169–70.
55. G/Gh, 170–6.
56. *L'Ermitage*, July 1898, 54–5.
57. *Prétextes*, 251–9.
58. J² I, 201.
59. R, 303; M, 101.
60. REP, 124–5; RP, 78–9.
61. REP, 150; RP, 94–5.
62. p. 324, my italics.
63. *Prétextes*, 116–82.

CHAPTER 8: *High Hopes Brought Low*

1. *Le Retour*, 44.
2. Unpublished letter.
3. Hommage à Henri Ghéon, In Memoriam, *Gavroche*, 14 June 1945.
4. *NRF*, August 1956, 308.
5. Pierre-Quint, 416.
6. G/Gh, 189.
7. G/V, 344.
8. G/Gh, 192.
9. G/Gh, 184.
10. G/Gh, 184.
11. J 2, 1134; EN, 38.

12. G/Gh, 201.
13. G/Ruy, 1, 118.
14. G/Gh, 280.
15. *L'Ermitage*, November 1899, 411–12.
16. J 1, 105; J I, 85.
17. *Prétextes*, 21, 33.
18. *Prétextes*, 135–41.
19. CAG 8, 106.
20. J 2, 392; IID, 57.
21. G/Gh, 277.
22. G/Gh, 283.
23. G/Gh, 295.

24. G/Gh, 282.
25. Unpublished letter, 30 December 1900 – 4 January 1901.
26. Schlumberger, 164–7.
27. G/Gh, 316.
28. *L'Ermitage,* January 1906.
29. G/Gh, 315.
30. G/Gh, 321.
31. G/Gh, 317–19.
32. G/Gh, 354.
33. G/Gh, 367.
34. G/Ruy 1, 136.
35. G/J, 199.
36. G/J, 189.
37. J 1, 111; J I, 91.
38. R, 398; I, 39.
39. R, 412; I, 60–1.
40. R, 435; I, 91.
41. R, 458; I, 122.
42. R, 461.
43. R, 466; I, 132.

44. R, 471–2; I, 139–40.
45. R, 459–60; I, 124.
46. R, 1514–15.
47. Marty, 208.
48. CAG 8, 118.
49. CAG 8, 318–19.
50. CAG 8, 120.
51. G/Gh, 445.
52. G/Gh, 453.
53. G/Gh, 461.
54. G/Gh, 475.
55. G/Gh, 397.
56. G/Gh, 412.
57. G/Gh, 368–9.
58. G/Gh, 400.
59. G/Gh, 379–80.
60. G/Gh, 431.
61. G/Gh, 421.
62. CAG 8, 122–3.
63. G/Gh, 465–6.
64. G/Gh, 476.

CHAPTER 9: *The Barren Years*

1. J 1, 144; J I, 121–2.
2. J 1, 247; J I, 214.
3. J/V, 385.
4. J/V, 389.
5. G/Gh, 483.
6. G/Gh, 484.
7. G/Gh, 476–7.
8. G/Gh, 485–6.
9. G/Gh, 488.
10. G/Gh, 694–5.
11. G/Gh, 532.
12. G/V, 399.
13. J 1, 135; J I, 114.
14. J² I, 359–60.
15. The lecture, dedicated 'au comte Harry de Kessler', was published in the October number of *L'Ermitage* and included in *Nouveaux Prétextes* of 1911, 28–44.
16. J 1, 144–5; J I, 122.

17. A, 89–90; 46.
18. A, 96; 50.
19. A, 117; 63.
20. A, 158; 90.
21. G/Gh, 554–5.
22. A, 174–5; 100.
23. J 1, 146; J I, 123.
24. G/S, 5.
25. G/S, 7–8.
26. G/S, 44–5.
27. G/S, 45–6.
28. G/S, 47–8.
29. *Nouveaux Prétextes,* 7–27; Pretexts, 59–73.
30. A, 85; 44.
31. A, 120; 128.
32. G/Gh, 565–6.
33. G/Gh, 566.
34. J 1, 152; J I, 128.
35. G/Gh, 129–30.

36. 9 December 1904, unpublished.
37. G/Gh, 581.
38. G/Gh, 581.
39. G/Gh, 589
40. G/Gh, 590.
41. G/Gh, 591.
42. G/Gh, 594.
43. G/Gh, 596.
44. G/Gh, 597.
45. G/Gh, 600–1.
46. G/Gh, 602–3.
47. G/Gh, 604.
48. J 1, 167; J I, 142.
49. G/Gh, 611–14.
50. G/Gh, 615.
51. G/Gh, 618.
52. J 1, 186; J I, 159.
53. J 1, 189–91; J I, 162–3.
54. G/Cl, 59.
55. G/Gh, 622.
56. J 1, 156; J I, 132.
57. J 1, 185; J I, 158.
58. G/Gh, 641.
59. G/Gh, 640.
60. J 1, 215, 220; J I, 186, 190.
61. J 1, 222; J I, 192.
62. G/Gh, 652.
63. G/V, 412.
64. J 1, 234; J I, 202.
65. J 1, 235–6; J I, 203–4.
66. J 1, 240; J I, 208.
67. R, 475–91; REP, 127–49.
68. G/J, 248–9.
69. J 1, 237; J I, 205.
70. J 1, 245–6; J I, 213.
71. J 1, 248; J I, 215.
72. J 1, 254; J I, 220.
73. G/Ruy 2, 47.
74. J 1, 254–5; J I, 220.
75. J 1, 255; J I, 221.
76. J 1, 254; J I, 220.
77. J 1, 256; J I, 222.
78. G/Gh, 695.
79. G/Gh, 705–8.
80. G/Gh, 699–700.
81. C, 26; 14.
82. C, 39; 27.
83. G/Gh, 700.
84. J 1, 270; J I, 234.
85. R, 495; SG, 5.
86. Marty, 212.
87. O'Brien, 216.
88. Delay, 501–2.
89. J 2, 1137; EN, 43.
90. J 1, 881; J III, 15.
91. J 1, 365–6; J I, 318.
92. R, 1549.
93. G/J, 258.

CHAPTER 10: *The 'New' Gide and the Founding of the* NRF

1. J 1, 276; J I, 240.
2. G/Cl, 93.
3. G/Gh, 717.
4. CAG 4, 150.
5. *La Phalange*, 15 December 1908, 542–3.
6. *Nouveaux Prétextes*, 74; Pretexts, 109.
7. G/Gh, 726.
8. G/Gos, 47.
9. *The Contemporary Review*, September 1909, 342–50.
10. G/J, 263, my italics.
11. J 1, 269; J I, 234.
12. J 1, 291; J I, 253.
13. G/Gh, 747–8.
14. CAG 12, 393.
15. J 1, 296; J I, 257.
16. G/Gh, 752.
17. G/Gh, 754.
18. Riv/A-F, 208–14.
19. G/S, 305.
20. G/Gh, 748.
21. G/Gh, 761.
22. R, 1560.

23. R, 603; TS, 11.
24. G/A, 5.
25. C, 7; ix.
26. J 1, 306; J I, 266.
27. G/Gos, 65.
28. CAG 12, 521.
29. CAG 12, 523.
30. Unpublished letter.
31. G/Cl, 189.
32. G/Cl, 190, my italics.
33. G/Cl, 192.
34. *NRF*, February 1912, 322.
35. J 1, 359; J I, 313.
36. J 1, 384; J I, 335.
37. G/Cl, 208.
38. J 1, 367; J I, 319.
39. CAG 12, 555.
40. G/A, 61.
41. J 1, 369; J I, 321.
42. G/Cl, 194.
43. J 1, 378; J I, 329.
44. CAG 12, 579.
45. CAG 12, 583–4.
46. J 1, 379; J I, 330.
47. *L'Homme né de la guerre*, 27.
48. CAG 12, 605.
49. J 2, 619.
50. CAG 12, 622.
51. CAG 12, 659.
52. CAG 12, 646.
53. Unpublished letter, 24 July 1912.
54. G/Gh, 805, the dots are Gide's.
55. J 2, 1106–12.
56. G/Gh, 809.
57. J 1, 381–3; J I, 331–3.
58. Anglès 2, 390–3.
59. G/Gos, 87.
60. G/Gos, 74–5; following Gide's own New Year negligence, Linette Brugmans dates this letter '11 January 1912' and places it accordingly; it should, quite clearly, be dated 1913.
61. G/Gos, 102.
62. J 1, 389; J I, 340.
63. G/Gh, 831.
64. Anglès 3, 183.
65. G/Ben, 70.
66. NAG, 9–16; 11–17.
67. G/MG 1, 649.
68. *Correspondance André Gide–Valéry Larbaud*, 141.
69. G/P, 9–11.
70. R, 855; VC, 216 – Dorothy Bussy incomprehensibly renders the two French words as 'the crusted' and 'the slim'.
71. R, 738–9; VC, 75–6.
72. R, 824; VC, 179.
73. R, 741–2; VC, 79.
74. R, 732; VC, 68.
75. R, 1573.
76. R, 824; VC, 179.
77. R, 828–9; VC, 184–5.
78. R, 115; M, 48.
79. G/Cl, 216.
80. G/Cl, 217.
81. G/Cl, 217–18.
82. G/Cl, 219.
83. G/Cl, 220–2.
84. G/Cl, 232–3.
85. G/Gos, 111–12.
86. G/Coc, 43.
87. G/P, 18.
88. G/P, 26.
89. J 1, 410; J II, 15.
90. J 1, 411; J II, 15–16.
91. J 1, 416; J II, 20.
92. J 1, 424; J II, 27.
93. J 1, 440, 442; J II, 42–3.
94. J 1, 443; J II, 44.
95. CAG 13, 68.
96. J 1, 449; J II, 48.

CHAPTER 11: *The War*

1. J 1, 452; J II, 51.
2. J 1, 454; J II, 53.
3. J 1, 463; J II, 60.
4. J 1, 462; J II, 59.
5. G/Gh, 854.
6. G/Gh, 855–6.
7. J 1, 473; J II, 69.
8. J 1, 491–2; J II, 84.
9. J 1, 497; J II, 89.
10. Marty, 232.
11. J 1, 500; J II, 91.
12. J 1, 498; J I, 90.
13. J 1, 505–6; J II, 95–7.
14. G/V, 444.
15. G/S, 585.
16. G/A, 133.
17. J 1, 507; J II, 99.
18. J 1, 511; J II, 102–3.
19. J 1, 527; J II, 117.
20. Unpublished letter.
21. G/Gh, 877.
22. G/Gh, 878.
23. G/Gh, 883.
24. G/Gh, 886.
25. J 1, 528; J II, 117.
26. J 1, 528; J II, 117.
27. J 1, 528; J II, 117.
28. 23 January – J 1, 530; J II, 119.
29. 25 January – J 1, 531; J II, 120.
30. 19 September – J 1, 560; J II, 146.
31. 15 October – J 1, 572; J II, 156.
32. 15 October – J 1, 573; J II, 156.
33. J 1, 539; J II, 127.
34. J 1, 572; J II, 156.
35. J 1, 541; J II, 129.
36. J 1, 531; J II, 120.
37. *Dostoïevski*, 148.
38. J 1, 606; J II, 186.
39. J 1, 543; J II, 130.
40. J 1, 554; J II, 140.
41. J 1, 556; J II, 142.
42. J 1, 557; J II, 143.

43. Schlumberger, 179.
44. J 1, 569; J II, 153.
45. CAG 4, 149–51.
46. J 1, 620; J II, 199–200.
47. G/A, 477–81.
48. G/A, 159.
49. G/A, 168.
50. J 1, 623; J II, 203.
51. J 1, 626; J II, 206.
52. J 1, 626; J II, 206.
53. J 1, 627; J II, 206–7.
54. J 1, 628; J II, 207.
55. BAAG 88, 448.
56. J 1, 630; J II, 209.
57. J 1, 631; J II, 210.
58. J 1, 632; J II, 211.
59. J 1, 634; J II, 212.
60. J 1, 635; J II, 214.
61. J 1, 634; J II, 212.
62. J 1, 638; J II, 217.
63. J² I, 1049.
64. J 1, 640; J II, 218.
65. G/S, 686.
66. J 1, 634; J II, 213.
67. G/Gh, 929–30.
68. G/S, 647–8.
69. J 1, 650; J II, 228.
70. J 1, 648; J II, 226.
71. J 1, 655; J II, 232.
72. Schlumberger, 189–90.
73. J 1, 656; J II, 233.
74. G/Ben, 90.
75. Bl, 139.
76. G/Ru II, 183.
77. CAG 9, 153; G/Bus, 35.
78. CAG 9, 156.
79. G/Ru II, 191–2.
80. *Letters of Roger Fry*, vol. II, 433.
81. CAG 4, 8.
82. CAG 13, 196–7.
83. J 1, 659; J II, 235.
84. J 1, 657; J II, 234.

85. CAG 4, 6.
86. CAG 9, 101.
87. pp. 192–3.

88. pp. 196–7.
89. J 2, 1147; EN, 61.

CHAPTER 12: *The Post-War Years*

1. Schlumberger, 212.
2. J 2, 1148; EN, 63–4.
3. Schlumberger, 186.
4. J 2, 1149; EN, 65.
5. Schlumberger, 198.
6. CAG 4, 13.
7. CAG 4, 23.
8. CAG 4, 19.
9. CAG 9, 123; G/Bus, 20.
10. J 1, 678; J II, 253.
11. CAG 4, 25.
12. Unpublished letter to Agnès, 9 July.
13. Unpublished letter, 8 March 1919.
14. CAG 4, 27.
15. MGJ II, 15.
16. G/Coc, 78–9.
17. HAG, 263.
18. *Gide Vivant*, 210–11.
19. Mauriac, 88.
20. G/Coc, 71.
21. G/Coc, 76.
22. G/Coc, 82.
23. G/Coc, 83.
24. G/Coc, 90, 92.
25. G/Coc, 98.
26. JFM, 19–20.
27. J 1, 680; J II, 254.
28. CAG 4, 27.
29. JFM, 21–2.
30. CAG 4, 31.
31. CAG 4, 33, 39–40.
32. J² I, 1104.
33. Sanouillet, 441.
34. *NRF*, June 1919, 479.
35. Sanouillet, 446.
36. R, 914; TS, 154–5.
37. R, 930; TS, 174.
38. HAG, 377–8.

39. St John: 9, 39 and 41.
40. R, 898; TS, 135.
41. CAG 9, 168.
42. CAG 9, 169.
43. CAG 9, 169.
44. CJ 2, 180.
45. CAG 4, 41.
46. CAG 4, 41–4.
47. CAG 9, 175–6; G/Bus, 47.
48. CAG 9, 180–1; G/Bus, 49.
49. CAG 9, 183–4.
50. CAG 10, 123.
51. CAG 4, 44.
52. G/MG 1, 655–6.
53. CAG 9, 191.
54. CAG 9, 198.
55. CAG 9, 201.
56. Unpublished letter, 15 August.
57. CAG 9, 202–3; G/Bus, 52–3.
58. CAG 9, 218.
59. NAG, 24–5; 21–2.
60. J 2, 1150; EN, 66–7.
61. CAG 9, 230; G/Bus, 60.
62. CAG 9, 230.
63. J 1, 685; J II, 258.
64. CAG 9, 232–6.
65. CAG 9, 238.
66. CAG 4, 61.
67. G/MG 1, 46.
68. NAG, 33–9; 27–32.
69. J 1, 688; J II, 261.
70. J 2, 1151–2; EN, 67–9.
71. CAG 4, 67.
72. CAG 9, 245.
73. CAG 4, 71.
74. *Incidences*, 46–7.
75. CAG 9, 253.
76. MGJ II, 232–3.

77. J 1, 693–4; J II, 266–7.
78. CAG 9, 261; G/Bus, 70.
79. CAG 4, 86–7.
80. Sic, unpublished letter, Gide to Maria Van Rysselberghe, 15 July 1921.
81. CAG 4, 92.
82. CAG 4, 105–6.
83. CAG 9, 303.
84. J 1, 699; J II, 271.
85. CAG 9, 312; G/Bus, 80.
86. CAG 14, 197–9.
87. G/S, 746.
88. G/A, 225.
89. CAG 9, 315.
90. J 1, 703; J II, 275.

CHAPTER 13: *Gide, Homosexual Theorist and Father*

1. NAG, 43; 34.
2. J 1, 727; J II, 296.
3. NAG, 44–7; 35–7.
4. G/MG 1, 179–81.
5. J 1, 728–30; J II, 297–9.
6. CAG 4, 110.
7. CAG 4, 113–14.
8. CAG 4, 124–5.
9. CAG 4, 133.
10. G/MG 1, 183,
11. NAG, 54; 41.
12. NAG, 54–5; 41.
13. Letter to Pitoëff, 26 July 1922, in CAG 15, 116.
14. CAG 4, 151.
15. CAG 4, 146.
16. CAG 9, 518–19.
17. CAG 4, 145–6.
18. CAG 4, 148–54.
19. J 1, 742; J II, 310.
20. CAG 4, 151.
21. G/MG 1, 193, 197.
22. CAG 9, 378.
23. CAG 9, 382.
24. J 1, 748; J II, 316.
25. CAG 4, 160–3.
26. NAG, 58–77; 42–58.
27. CAG 4, 165–6.
28. CAG 9, 527.
29. G/MG 1, 206–7.
30. CAG 9, 414.
31. CAG 4, 178–9.
32. *Les Nouvelles littéraires*, 31 March 1923.
33. CAG 4, 179–81.
34. CAG 9, 423.
35. CAG 9, 437.
36. J 1, 770; J II, 337.
37. CAG 4, 189.
38. J 1, 771–4; J II, 338–41.
39. CAG 9, 448.
40. CAG 9, 454.
41. MGJ II, 413.
42. CAG 4, 191.
43. CAG 4, 195.
44. CAG 4, 195–6.
45. CAG 4, 198.
46. CAG 9, 467–8.
47. CAG 9, 469.
48. C, 41; 29.
49. J 1, 670–3; J II, 245–8.
50. C, 8–9; xx.
51. *André Gide and the Crisis of Modern Thought*, 105–6.
52. J 2, 142; J IV, 130.
53. CAG 2, 71.
54. G/Gos, 169–70.
55. J 1, 824; J II, 387.
56. CAG 9, 480.
57. J 1, 797; J II, 362.
58. J 1, 798; J II, 363.
59. G/MG 1, 670.
60. CJ 2, 222.
61. CAG 4, 228.
62. CAG 2, 113.

63. J 1, 804; J II, 369.
64. CAG 4, 222–3.
65. G/MG 1, 260.
66. G/MG 1, 259.
67. CAG 4, 231.
68. J1, 806; J II, 371.
69. CAG 13, 274.
70. CJ 2, 232.
71. G/MG 1, 672 and MGJ II, 477.
72. CAG 4, 231–9.
73. J 1, 881; J III, 15.
74. JFM, 59; LC, 33.
75. JFM, 69; LC, 40.
76. JFM, 32; LC, 15–16.
77. R, 1208; Cf, 302.
78. CAG 4, 38.
79. JFM, 15; LC, 4.
80. JFM, 84; LC, 49, 50.
81. R, 1200–1; Cf, 294.
82. R, 1248; Cf, 345.
83. JFM, 83–4; LC, 49.
84. JFM, 51–2; LC, 27–8.
85. JFM, 51; LC, 27.

86. R, 989; Cf, 70.
87. R, 1096; Cf, 183.
88. JFM, 57; LC, 31.
89. J 1, 1068; J III, 181.
90. JFM, 86–7; LC, 51, my italics.
91. R, 950; Cf, 29.
92. JFM, 45; LC, 23.
93. J 1, 41; J I, 29.
94. R, 1083; Cf, 170.
95. R, 968; Cf, 48.
96. *La Revue de Paris*, 15 May 1926, 211–17.
97. *L'Œuvre*, 16 February 1926, 4.
98. *La Renaissance*, 6 March 1926, 12–13.
99. *New York Times Book Review,* 2 October 1927.
100. 26 October 1927.
101. 18 February 1928, 595–6.
102. 25 March 1928.
103. JFM, 85; LC, 50.
104. J 1, 832; J II, 395.

CHAPTER 14: *Heart of Darkness*

1. J 2, 683; TC, 4.
2. Marty, 263.
3. G/S, 799.
4. J 2, 799; TC, 137–8.
5. J 2, 683; TC, 3.
6. J 2, 685; TC, 6.
7. J 2, 692; TC, 14.
8. J 2, 704; TC, 27.
9. J 2, 716; TC, 42–3.
10. J 2, 723–4; TC, 49.
11. J 2, 733; TC, 60.
12. J 2, 780; TC, 114.
13. J 2, 771; TC, 102.
14. J 2, 745; TC, 72–3.
15. CAG 10, 53.
16. TC, 108.
17. CAG 4, 258–9.
18. J 2, 892; TC, 232.

19. J 2, 899; TC, 241.
20. J 2, 941–4; TC, 293–6.
21. J 2, 1221–2; SBI, 124.
22. J 2, 1009; TC, 374.
23. CAG 4, 244–52.
24. J 1, 816; J II, 380.
25. MGJ II, 512–14.
26. G/MG 1, 297.
27. CAG 4, 255.
28. CAG 4, 260.
29. CAG 4, 272.
30. J 1, 826; J II, 389.
31. G/A, 302.
32. CAG 4, 292, 295–6.
33. CAG 4, 296.
34. CAG 4, 296.
35. CAG 10, 85.
36. CAG 10, 630.

37. CAG 4, 307.
38. CAG 4, 307, 309–10.
39. CAG 4, 313–16.
40. J i, 834–5; J II, 397.
41. J i, 835; J II, 398–9.
42. J i, 841; J II, 403.
43. CAG 13, 304.
44. CAG 4, 324–5.
45. G/MG I, 313.
46. CAG 4, 332.
47. CAG 4, 339.
48. J i, 867–8; J II, 3.
49. G/MG i, 326.
50. G/MG i, 329.
51. CAG 4, 343–4.
52. J i, 878; J III, 12–13.
53. CAG 4, 354.
54. G/MG i, 342.
55. CAG 4, 357.
56. CAG 4, 360.
57. CAG 4, 364.
58. CAG 4, 371.
59. J i, 903–4; J III, 35.
60. J i, 906; J III, 37.
61. J i, 910; J III, 40.
62. J i, 909; J III, 39.
63. J i, 908; J III, 39.
64. CAG 4, 399.
65. CAG 5, 20.
66. CAG 5, 21.
67. CAG 5, 25–6.
68. CAG 5, 42.
69. CAG 5, 49.
70. R, 1253; SW, 6.
71. R, 1276; SW, 34.
72. R, 1278; SW, 37.
73. R, 1287; SW, 49.
74. J i, 828; J II, 391.

75. J i, 890; J III, 23.
76. R, 1252; SW, 5–6.
77. CAG 5, 34.
78. R, 1314; SW, 83.
79. J i, 939–44; J III, 66–71.
80. CAG 5, 64.
81. CAG 10, 249, 251–2.
82. G/MG i, 367.
83. MGJ II, 718.
84. MGJ II, 731.
85. MGJ II, 734–5.
86. MGJ II, 799, 814.
87. J i, 962; J III, 87.
88. CAG 10, 257–8.
89. J i, 963–4; J III, 88.
90. CAG 5, 72.
91. CAG 5, 80–1.
92. G/MG i, 392.
93. J i, 972; J III, 95–6.
94. CAG 5, 83.
95. CAG 10, 270.
96. CAG 5, 92.
97. J i, 997; J III, 118–19.
98. J i, 1007; J III, 127.
99. J i, 1008–12; J III, 128–31.
100. J² II, 233–4.
101. CAG 5, 114.
102. CAG 5, 101–2.
103. CAG 13, 344.
104. J i, 1015; J III, 133.
105. CJ 2, 307.
106. CJ 2, 313.
107. Unpublished letter, 8 November 1930, Bibliothèque Nationale.
108. CAG 5, 119.
109. CAG 5, 127.
110. CAG 5, 127–8.
111. CAG 5, 120, 123.

CHAPTER 15: *Gide, 'Fellow-traveller'*

1. CAG 10, 322.
2. CAG 5, 139.
3. J i, 1049; J III, 164.
4. CAG 5, 143.

5. CAG 5, 157.
6. CAG 5, 152–3.
7. CAG 5, 156.
8. BAAG 59, 331–3.

9. CAG 5, 155–6.
10. J 1, 1072–3; J III, 185.
11. CAG 5, 162–5.
12. *Cahiers Paul Claudel* 6, 212–13.
13. *Théâtre*, 253.
14. J 1, 1100; J III, 211.
15. J 1, 1117; J III, 224.
16. CAG 5, 221–2.
17. MGJ II, 935.
18. MGJ II, 938.
19. CAG 5, 234.
20. CAG 5, 235.
21. CAG 10, 416–17.
22. G/MG 1, 517–18.
23. CAG 5, 240.
24. CAG 10, 424.
25. G/MG 1, 521.
26. BAAG 61, 57.
27. J 1, 1128–9; J III, 234.
28. Kessler, 417.
29. NAG, 99–100; 72–3.
30. CJ 2, 343.
31. CAG 13, 384.
32. J1, 1136–7; J III, 241.
33. J 1, 1139; J III, 243.
34. CAG 10, 431.
35. J 1, 1142; J III, 246.
36. BAAG 61, 70.
37. MGJ II, 989.
38. CAG 5, 261.
39. BAAG 61, 73.
40. CAG 5, 281.
41. CAG 5, 292.
42. Kessler, 452.
43. Kessler, 460.
44. LE, 22–5.
45. G/MG 1, 555–8.
46. CAG 5, 302.
47. CAG 5, 305.
48. LE, 31–2.
49. CAG 5, 312.
50. J 1, 1174; J III, 275.
51. CAG 10, 477–8.
52. J 1, 1175; J III, 276.
53. BAAG 62, 324–5.
54. CAG 5, 321.
55. G/MG 1, 576–7.
56. CAG 5, 329–30, 332.
57. CAG 5, 339.
58. CAG 10, 507–8.
59. CAG 5, 354.
60. LE, 41–2.
61. LE, 43–4.
62. CAG 10, 511–12; G/Bus, 153.
63. CAG 10, 515–16; G/Bus, 154–5.
64. CAG 10, 517; G/Bus, 155.
65. BAAG, 57, 58.
66. CAG 10, 524; G/Bus, 157.
67. CAG 11, 482–3; G/Bus, 277–8.
68. CAG 11, 484.
69. CAG 11, 489; G/Bus, 279.
70. CAG 11, 497–8; G/Bus, 283–4.
71. CAG 11, 499; G/Bus, 284–5.
72. CAG 10, 520.
73. BAAG 62, 254.
74. G/MG 1, 592–3.
75. J 2, 95; J IV, 83.
76. BAAG 63, 430.
77. CAG 5, 371–2.
78. BAAG 63, 451–7.
79. J 1, 1209; J III, 304.
80. BAAG 63, 467–8.
81. BAAG 63, 464.
82. BAAG 63, 475.
83. BAAG 64, 565–6.
84. BAAG 64, 567–71.
85. BAAG 64, 572.
86. BAAG 64, 578.
87. LE, 57–8.
88. BAAG 64, 603–4.
89. BAAG 64, 607.
90. BAAG 64, 611, 613.
91. G/MG 2, 15.
92. G/MG 2, 21.
93. J 1, 1221–2; J III, 316.
94. *André Gide and the Crisis of Modern Thought*, 158–9.
95. LE, 96–9.
96. G/MG 2, 37–8.
97. CAG 5, 469.

98. CAG 5, 473–4.
99. CAG 10, 587.
100. G/MG 2, 45.
101. G/MG 2, 48.
102. G/S, 867–8.
103. G/Las, 26.
104. J 1, 534; J II, 123.
105. R, 253; FE, 169.
106. R, 299–300; FE, 256.
107. G/S, 870.
108. G/MG 2, 54.
109. J 2, 220; J IV, 196.

110. Gide's speech is included in LE, 113–21.
111. J 1, 1243; J III, 336.
112. MGJ II, 1178.
113. CAG 5, 522–3.
114. Ehrenburg IV, 70.
115. J 1, 12512; J III, 343.
116. CAG 5, 545.
117. CAG 5, 543.
118. CAG 5, 546–7.
119. CAG 5, 548.

CHAPTER 16: *Retreat from Moscow, a Sense of Ending*

1. RU, 178–80.
2. LE, 135–8.
3. RU, 33–4; BU, 33–5.
4. RU, 78–80; BU, 80–2.
5. LE, 138–41.
6. Guilloux, 136.
7. Herbart, 79–81.
8. RU, 33; BU, 33.
9. RU, 31; BU, 30–1.
10. G/MG 2, 75.
11. Herbart, 85–6.
12. RU, 182.
13. RU, 64–6; BU, 66–8.
14. RU, 64; BU, 66.
15. Herbart, 102.
16. RU, 50; BU, 51.
17. Herbart, 69–70.
18. J 1, 1256; J III, 347.
19. J 1, 1254–5; J III, 345–6.
20. J 1, 1256; J III, 347.
21. RU, 183.
22. CAG 5, 553–4.
23. G/Las, 30–1.
24. CAG 5, 558.
25. CAG 5, 559.
26. G/Las, 33–4.
27. G/Las, 35.
28. Kessler, 477.
29. CAG 5, 570.

30. CAG 5, 574–5.
31. RU, 83; BU, 85.
32. The letter is reproduced as an appendix in Herbart, 153–60.
33. G/Las, 36.
34. MGJ II, 1204–5.
35. G/S, 874–7.
36. LE, 146–7.
37. R, 1357; SW, 136.
38. CAG 5, 551.
39. R, 1347; SW, 125.
40. J II, 333; J IV, 297.
41. CAG 5, 608.
42. CAG 11, 13–14.
43. G/MG 2, 96.
44. G/MG 2, 105.
45. Unpublished letter, Bibliothèque Nationale, Fonds Copeau.
46. LE, 171.
47. *World Within World*, 240.
48. LE, 197.
49. G/Las, 41–2.
50. J 1, 1267; J III, 358.
51. In BAAG 100 and 101.
52. G/MG 2, 110–11.
53. J 1, 1267; J III, 358.
54. CAG 6, 32.
55. CAG 6, 38, 42.
56. CAG 6, 43.

57. MGJ III, 91–123.
58. MGJ III, 93, 95.
59. CAG 6, 80.
60. J II, 1125; EN, 24.
61. CAG 6, 80–1.
62. CAG 6, 78.
63. J 2, 1123; EN, 21.
64. J 2, 1309–10; J III, 393–4.
65. J 2, 1128; EN, 28.
66. J 2, 1124–30; EN, 22–31.
67. CAG 6, 78.
68. G/MG 2, 138.
69. MGJ III, 152–3.
70. MGJ III, 166.
71. CAG 11, 84.
72. CAG 6, 99–100.
73. J 1, 1311–12; J III, 395–6.
74. J 1, 1318; J III, 401.
75. J 1, 1319; J III, 402.

76. CAG 6, 112–13.
77. CAG 6, 127.
78. J 1, 1331; J III, 413.
79. J II, 1049.
80. J 2, 1052–3.
81. J 2, 1053–4.
82. J 2, 1072–3.
83. J 2, 1056.
84. J 2, 1070–1.
85. J 2, 1076.
86. BAAG 90–91, 313–35.
87. CAG 6, 136.
88. Mauriac, 53–4.
89. G/MG 2, 169.
90. Mauriac, 153.
91. Mauriac, 173.
92. Mauriac, 187.
93. Mauriac, 179–80.

CHAPTER 17: *Another War: Retreat and Exile*

1. J 2, 9; J IV, 3.
2. CAG 13, 479.
3. CAG 6, 160.
4. Mauriac, 250.
5. G/MG 2, 190.
6. J 2, 28–9; J IV, 23.
7. MGJ III, 343.
8. J 2, 29; J IV, 24.
9. G/S, 291.
10. J 2, 43; J IV, 36.
11. CAG 6, 204.
12. G/MG 2, 227.
13. J 2, 80; J IV, 69.
14. J 2, 90; J IV, 79.
15. CAG 6, 272.
16. G/MGR 239.
17. G/Lev, 348.
18. CAG 6, 280.
19. J 2, 104; J IV, 96.
20. CAG 6, 290, 291, 298.
21. CAG 6, 293.
22. J 2, 115; J IV, 106.

23. J 2, 116; J IV, 107.
24. J 2, 116; J IV, 107.
25. G/MG 2, 243–4.
26. CAG 11, 207.
27. G/MG 2, 246.
28. J 2, 128–9. (This passage is absent from the original edition of the translation.)
29. CAG 11, 219.
30. CAG 11, 240; G/Bus, 220–1. (The translation was first published in New York, in 1944, by Jacques Schiffrin-Pantheon Books.)
31. J 2, 131; J IV, 120.
32. G/MG 2, 264.
33. G/MG 2, 269.
34. J 2, 146–7; J IV, 134.
35. J 2, 153; J IV, 139–40.
36. J 2, 158; J IV, 144.
37. J 2, 159–60; J IV, 145.
38. J 2, 164; J IV, 149.
39. J 2, 167–8; J IV, 152.

40. J 2, 213; J IV, 190.
41. J 2, 235–6; J IV, 210.
42. J 2, 238; J IV, 211.
43. CAG 6, 309.
44. J 2, 246; J IV, 218.
45. J 2, 247–9; J IV, 219–21.
46. CAG 6, 312.
47. J 2, 257; J IV, 229.
48. J 2, 265; J IV, 236.
49. J 2, 268; J IV, 239.
50. J 2, 269–70; J IV, 240.
51. J 2, 273; J IV, 243.
52. J 2, 276; J IV, 246.
53. G/S, 956.

54. CAG 6, 319.
55. CAG 11, 275; G/Bus, 231.
56. G/Gh, 1005–6.
57. G/S, 956, 958–9.
58. G/MG 2, 287.
59. G/S, 966–7.
60. J 2, 284; J IV, 253.
61. G/MG 2, 303.
62. G/MG 2, 306–7.
63. CAG 6, 323–4.
64. G/Las, 114.
65. CAG 6, 343.
66. CAG 13, 519–20.

CHAPTER 18: '*The End of Life . . . A Rather Dull Last Act*'

1. CAG 6, 353–4.
2. CAG 6, 353.
3. CAG 6, 357.
4. CAG 6, 358.
5. CAG 6, 364.
6. CAG 6, 358.
7. CAG 6, 361–2.
8. CAG 6, 362.
9. Mauriac, 283–4.
10. MGJ III, 753–4.
11. Published in *L'Arche*, 10 October 1945.
12. G/MG 2, 329.
13. G/MG 2, 331.
14. CAG 11, 360.
15. Levesque, unpublished journal.
16. CAG 7, 19–20.
17. J 2, 286; J IV, 255.
18. Levesque, unpublished journal.
19. J 1, 347; J I, 301–2.
20. *Œuvres complètes*, XIII, x.
21. R, 1415; TL, 1.
22. R, 1416; TL, 3.
23. R, 1420; TL, 7.
24. R, 1416; TL, 3.
25. R, 1426–7; TL, 16–18.
26. R, 1429; TL, 20.

27. R, 1433; TL, 25–7.
28. R, 1439; TL, 35–6.
29. R, 1441; TL, 39.
30. R, 1444; TL, 43.
31. R, 1446; TL, 45.
32. R, 1451; TL, 52–3.
33. Marty, 312–13.
34. R, 1453; TL, 56.
35. CAG 11, 376.
36. CAG 11, 377; G/Bus, 246–7.
37. CAG 11, 387.
38. CAG 11, 389, 393; G/Bus, 249–50.
39. CAG 11, 417–18; G/Bus, 256.
40. CAG 11, 420.
41. CAG 7, 38.
42. CAG 7, 49.
43. CAG 7, 50.
44. CAG 7, 52.
45. J 2, 302; J IV, 269–70.
46. G/Lev, 387.
47. G/Lev, 388.
48. HAG, 20.
49. Lambert, 103.
50. CAG 11, 457.; G/Bus, 264.
51. CAG 7, 66.
52. HAG, 47.

53. G/MG 2, 553.
54. Richardson, 175.
55. CAG 7, 76.
56. CAG 6, 59.
57. CAG 6, 88.
58. CAG 11, 65.
59. CAG 11, 298, 381.
60. CAG 7, 24, 29.
61. CAG 11, 403–4.
62. CAG 7, 62.
63. G/MG 2, 385.
64. G/MG 2, 554–5.
65. J 2, 315–16; J IV, 282.
66. CAG 7, 82.
67. J 1, 316; J IV, 282.
68. CAG 7, 80.
69. CAG 11, 480.
70. CAG 11, 486.
71. G/MG 2, 402–3.
72. CAG 7, 87.
73. J 2, 326; J IV, 291.
74. Levesque, unpublished journal, 3 June.
75. CAG 7, 101.
76. G/MG 2, 423–4.
77. HAG, 316.
78. G/MG 2, 425.
79. J 2, 330–1; J IV, 294–5.
80. HAG, 316.
81. J 1, 331–2; J IV, 295.
82. CAG 7, 112.
83. CAG 7, 113.
84. G/MG 2, 450.
85. MGJ III, 876–7.
86. MGJ III, 882.
87. NAG, 146–51.
88. G/Las, 144–7.
89. J 1, 342; J IV, 304.
90. HAG, 317.
91. CAG 7, 141.
92. CAG 11, 522.
93. G/MG 2, 459.

94. CAG 7, 136.
95. CAG 7, 141.
96. CAG 7, 152–3.
97. CAG 7, 157.
98. G/MG 2, 468–9.
99. G/MG 2, 469–70.
100. CAG 7, 166.
101. CAG 7, 167.
102. CAG 7, 169–70.
103. J 2, 343; J IV, 306.
104. *Six années de la Comédie-Française*, 135.
105. CAG 7, 172.
106. G/MG 2, 479.
107. CAG 7, 179.
108. G/MG 2, 485.
109. CAG 7, 180.
110. G/S, 1077.
111. CAG 7, 195.
112. G/Lev, 423–4, 427.
113. CAG 7, 210.
114. CAG 7, 216–17.
115. Touchard, 144.
116. CAG 7, 218.
117. Lambert, 174–5.
118. G/MG 2, 568–9.
119. J 2, 1243; SBI, 166.
120. CAG 7, 239.
121. Delay, HAG, 370.
122. CAG 7, 240.
123. G/MG 2, 569–70.
124. CAG 7, 241–2.
125. CAG 7, 244–5.
126. NAG, 152; 107.
127. MGJ III, 942.
128. CAG 7, 246.
129. CAG 7, 247–8.
130. J 1, 588; J II, 170.
131. MGJ III, 941.
132. G/MG 2, 571.
133. CAG 7, 249.
134. CAG 7, 250–1.
135. CAG 7, 252.

Conclusion

1. 19 June 1919, *Le Journal des Faux-Monnayeurs.*
2. HAG, 30.
3. R, 1248; Cf, 345.
4. HAG, 79.
5. J 2, 353; IID, 8.
6. J 2, 330–1; J IV, 295.
7. HAG, 22.
8. HAG, 7.
9. HAG, 34.
10. HAG, 41.
11. HAG, 149.
12. HAG, 6.
13. CAG 7, 28.
14. HAG, 75.
15. MGJ III, 942–3.

Bibliography

Even a bibliography of this length, on the subject of Gide, is necessarily incomplete. Of Gide's own works, I have noted only published volumes, not uncollected reviews and articles. Under 'Works on Gide' I have included books that, though not exclusively on his life and work, relate partly or indirectly to them. I have included only books written in French or English. While including 'special numbers' of reviews and other periodicals, I have excluded isolated articles. Readers wishing to pursue bibliographical questions further are referred to the following works on the matter:

Naville, Arnold. *Note bibliographique sur l'œuvre de André Gide.* Paris: 1930 (pub. author).
Catalogue des Fonds spéciaux de la Bibliothèque Littéraire Doucet à [et manuscrits d'] André Gide. Boston: G. K. Hall, 1972.
Cotnam, Jacques. *Bibliographie chronologique de l'œuvre d'André Gide (1889–1973).* Boston: G. K. Hall, 1974.
Martin, Claude. *La Correspondance générale d'André Gide. Répertoire chronologique.* Lyon: Centre d'Etudes Gidiennes, 1991 (rev. ed., 1996). (This supersedes Martin's own *Répertoire des lettres publiées d'André Gide.* Paris: Minard, 1971 and his *La Correspondance générale d'André Gide,* published by the Centre d'Etudes Gidiennes in six volumes in 1984–5.)
Martin, Claude. *Bibliographie chronologique des livres consacrés à André Gide (1918–1995).* Lyon: Centre d'Etudes Gidiennes, 1995. (This supersedes an earlier edition published in 1987.)

A. WORKS BY ANDRÉ GIDE

I Collections

Oeuvres complètes, 15 vols. Paris: Gallimard, 1932–39. This edition, left unfinished and now largely unobtainable, contains works in chronological sequence published up to 1929, together with letters, articles, prefaces, extracts from Gide's journal and short, unfinished works not published elsewhere. Where possible, my references are to the Pléiade editions of the *Romans* and *Journal,* which have superseded it.
Journal, 1889–1939. Paris: Bibliothèque de la Pléiade, Gallimard, 1939. New ed. 1951.

Includes *Littérature et morale, Morale chrétienne, La Mort de Charles-Louis Philippe, Voyage en Andorre, La Marche turque, Numquid et tu* and various undated '*feuillets*'.

Journal, 1939–1949. Souvenirs. Paris: Bibliothèque de la Pléiade, Gallimard, 1954. Includes *Si le grain ne meurt, Souvenirs de la Cour d'assises, Voyage au Congo, Le Retour du Tchad, Carnets d'Egypte, Feuillets d'Automne, Et nunc manet in te, Ainsi soit-il.*

(*The Journals of André Gide*, trans. Justin O'Brien, 4 vols. London: Secker and Warburg; New York: Knopf, 1947–51. Vol. I (1889–1913) includes: *Literature and Ethics, Christian Ethics, The Death of Charles-Louis Philippe, Voyage in Andorra*; vol. II (1914–1927) includes *The Turkish Journey, Numquid et tu . . . .?*; vol. III (1928–1939); vol. IV (1939–1949).)

Journal, ed. Eric Marty (contains all the material omitted in the earlier edition). *Vol. I, 1887–1925; vol. II, 1926–1949.* Paris: Bibliothèque de la Pléiade, Gallimard, 1996 and 1997.

Romans, récits et soties, œuvres lyriques. Paris: Bibliothèque de la Pléiade, Gallimard, 1958. Includes *Le Traité du Narcisse, Le Voyage d'Urien, La Tentative amoureuse, Paludes, Les Nourritures terrestres, Les Nouvelles Nourritures, Le Prométhée mal enchaîné, El Hadj, L'Immoraliste, Le Retour de l'Enfant prodigue, La Porte étroite, Isabelle, Les Caves du Vatican, La Symphonie Pastorale, Les Faux-Monnayeurs, L'Ecole des femmes, Robert, Geneviève, Thésée.*

Théâtre. Paris: Gallimard, 1942. Includes *Saül, Le Roi Candaule, Oedipe, Perséphone, Le Treizième Arbre.*

II Single Works

1891 *Les Cahiers d'André Walter.* Paris: Librairie de l'Art Indépendant. *Les Cahiers et les Poésies d'André Walter.* Paris: Gallimard, 1952.

1892 *Le Traité du Narcisse.* Paris: Librairie de l'Art Indépendant. (*Narcissus*, trans. Dorothy Bussy, in *The Return of the Prodigal.* London: Secker & Warburg, 1953.)
Les Poésies d'André Walter. Paris: Librairie d'Art Indépendant.

1893 *La Tentative amoureuse.* Paris: Librairie de l'Art Indépendant. (*The Lovers' Attempt*, trans. Dorothy Bussy, in *The Return of the Prodigal.* London: Secker & Warburg, 1953.)
Le Voyage d'Urien. Paris: Librairie de l'Art Indépendant. (*Urien's Voyage*, trans. Wade Baskin. London: Peter Owen; New York: Philosophical Library, 1964.)

1895 *Paludes.* Paris: Librairie de l'Art Indépendant. (*Marshlands*, trans. George D. Painter, with *Prometheus Misbound.* London: Secker & Warburg; New York: New Directions, 1953.)

1897 *Réflexions sur quelques points de littérature et de morale* (Anonymous). Paris: Mercure de France.
Les Nourritures terrestres. Paris: Mercure de France. (*Fruits of the Earth*, trans. Dorothy Bussy, with *Later Fruits of the Earth.* London: Secker & Warburg; New York: Knopf, 1949.)

1899 *Le Prométhée mal enchaîné.* Paris: Mercure de France. (*Prometheus Misbound*, trans. George D. Painter, in *Marshlands and Prometheus Misbound.* London: Secker &

Warburg; New York: New Directions, 1953; also trans. Lady Lilian Rother-mere, as *Prometheus Illbound*. London: Chatto and Windus, 1919.)

Philoctète. Paris: Mercure de France. (*Philoctetes*, trans. Dorothy Bussy, in *The Return of the Prodigal*. London: Secker & Warburg, 1953; also trans. Jackson Mathews, in *My Theater*. New York: Knopf, 1951.)

El Hadj, in *Philoctète*. Paris: Mercure de France. (*El Hadj*, trans. Dorothy Bussy, in *The Return of the Prodigal*. London: Secker & Warburg, 1953.)

1900 *Lettres à Angèle. 1898–1899*. Paris: Mercure de France.

De l'influence en littérature. Paris: L'Ermitage.

1901 *Le Roi Candaule*. Paris: Revue Blanche. (*King Candaules*, trans. Jackson Mathews, in *My Theater*. New York: Knopf, 1951.)

Les Limites dans l'Art. Lecture. Paris: L'Ermitage.

1902 *L'Immoraliste*. Paris: Mercure de France. (*The Immoralist*, trans. Dorothy Bussy. London: Cassell; New York: Knopf, 1930.)

1903 *Saül*. Paris: Mercure de France. (*Saul*, trans. Dorothy Bussy, in *The Return of the Prodigal*. London: Secker & Warburg, 1953; also trans. Jackson Mathews in *My Theater*. New York: Knopf, 1951.)

Prétextes. Réflexions sur quelques points de littérature et de morale. Paris: Mercure de France. (*Pretexts*, selections from *Prétextes*, *Nouveaux Prétextes* and *Incidences*, trans. Justin O'Brien. London: Secker & Warburg; New York, Meridian, 1949.)

De l'importance du publique. Paris: L'Ermitage.

1906 *Amyntas*. Paris: Mercure de France. (*Amyntas*, trans. Villiers David. London: Bodley Head, 1958; Chester Springs, Pa: Dufour, 1961.)

1907 *Le Retour de l'Enfant prodigue*. Paris: 'Vers et Prose'. (*The Return of the Prodigal*, trans. Dorothy Bussy. London: Secker & Warburg, 1953.)

1909 *La Porte étroite*. Paris: Mercure de France. (*Strait is the Gate*, trans. Dorothy Bussy. New York: Knopf, 1924; London: Secker & Warburg, 1953.)

1910 *Oscar Wilde*. Paris: Mercure de France. (*Oscar Wilde*, trans. Bernard Frechtman. New York: Philosophical Library, 1949; London: Kimber, 1951.)

1911 *Nouveaux Prétextes. Réflexions sur quelques points de littérature et de morale*. Paris: Mercure de France. (Selection trans. Justin O'Brien, in *Pretexts*. London: Secker & Warburg; New York: Meridian, 1959.)

Charles-Louis Philippe. Conférence prononcée au Salon d'Automne, le 5 novembre 1910. Paris: Eugène Figière.

Isabelle. Récit. Paris: NRF. (*Isabelle*, trans. Dorothy Bussy, in *Two Symphonies*. London: Cassell; New York: Knopf, 1931.)

1912 *Bethsabé*. Paris: Bibliothèque de l'Occident.

1914 *Souvenirs de la cour d'assises*. Paris: NRF. (*Recollections of the Assize Court*, trans. Philip A. Wilkins. London: Hutchinson, 1941.)

Les Caves du Vatican. Paris: NRF. (*The Vatican Swindle*, trans. Dorothy Bussy. New York: Knopf, 1927; and as *The Vatican Cellars*. London: Cassell, 1952.)

1919 *La Symphonie Pastorale*. Paris: NRF. (*Pastoral Symphony*, trans. Dorothy Bussy, in *Two Symphonies*. London: Cassell; New York: Knopf, 1931.)

1921 *Morceaux choisis*. Paris: NRF.
 Pages choisis. Paris: G. Crès.

1923 *Dostoïevski*. Paris: Plon-Nourrit. (*Dostoevsky*, trans. anon. London: Dent, 1925; New York: Knopf, 1926; London: Secker & Warburg, 1949; New York: New Directions, 1949.)

1924 *Incidences*. Paris: Gallimard. (Selection, trans. Justin O'Brien, in *Pretexts*. New York: Meridian, 1949; London: Secker & Warburg, 1959.)
 Corydon. Paris: Gallimard. (*Corydon*, trans. Hugh Gibb. New York: Farrer Strauss, 1950; trans. P.B. London: Secker & Warburg, 1952; trans. Richard Howard. New York: Farrer, Strauss & Giroux, 1983; London: Gay Men's Press, 1983.)

1925 *Caractères*. Paris: A l'Enseigne de la Porte étroite.

1926 *Les Faux-Monnayeurs*. Paris: Gallimard. (*The Counterfeiters*, trans. Dorothy Bussy. New York: Knopf, 1927; as *The Coiners*. London: Cassell, 1950.)
 Numquid et tu . . .? Paris: Editions de la Pléiade. (*Numquid et tu . . .?*, trans. Justin O'Brien, in *The Journals of André Gide*, vol. II.)
 Si le grain ne meurt. Paris: Gallimard. (*If It Die . . .*, trans. Dorothy Bussy. New York: Random House, 1935; London: Secker & Warburg, 1951.) *Lettre sur les faits divers*. Paris: Gallimard (lim. ed.).

1927 *Voyage au Congo*. Paris: Gallimard. (*Travels in the Congo*, trans. Dorothy Bussy. New York: Knopf, 1929; London: Secker & Warburg, 1930.)
 Seconde lettre sur les faits divers. Paris: Gallimard (lim. ed.).
 Dindiki. Liège: Ed. de la Lampe d'Aladin.
 Joseph Conrad. Liège: Ed. de la Lampe d'Aladin.
 Emile Verhaeren. Liège: Ed. de la Lampe d'Aladin.
 Faits divers. Paris: Gallimard (lim. ed.).

1928 *Le Retour du Tchad*. Paris: Gallimard. (*Return from Lake Chad*, trans. Dorothy Bussy, in *Travels in the Congo*. New York: Knopf, 1929; London: Secker & Warburg, 1930.)
 Feuillets. Paris: Gallimard.
 Lettres (Marcel Proust et André Gide). Paris: Gallimard (priv. ed.)

1929 *L'Ecole des Femmes*. Paris: Gallimard. Also with *Robert* and *Geneviève*. Paris: Gallimard. (*The School for Wives*, trans. Dorothy Bussy, with *Robert* and *Geneviève*. London: Cassell; New York: Knopf, 1950.)
 Pages retrouvées. Paris: Gallimard (priv. ed.).
 Suivant Montaigne. Paris: Gallimard (priv. ed.).
 Essai sur Montaigne. Paris: Jacques Schiffrin, Ed. de la Pléiade. (*Montaigne. An Essay in Two Parts*, trans. Stephen H. Guest and Trevor E. Blewitt. London: The Blackamore Press; New York: Horace Liveright, 1929 – lim. ed.)
 Dictées. Paris: Gallimard (priv. ed.).
 Un esprit non prévenu. Paris: Kra.

1930 *Robert*. Paris: Gallimard. (*Robert*, trans. Dorothy Bussy, in *The School for Wives*. London: Cassell; New York: Knopf, 1950.)
 Lettre. Paris: Gallimard (priv. ed.).

Deux Préfaces. Paris: Gallimard (priv. ed.).

La Séquestrée de Poitiers. Paris: Gallimard.

L'Affaire Redureau. Paris: Gallimard.

1931 *Oedipe.* Paris: Gallimard. (*Oedipus,* trans. John Russell, in *Two Legends, Theseus and Oedipus.* London: Secker & Warburg; New York: Knopf, 1950.)

Jacques Rivière. Paris: Ed. de la Belle Page.

Divers. Paris: Gallimard.

1932 *Goethe.* Paris: Gallimard (priv. ed.).

1934 *Perséphone.* Paris: Gallimard. (*Persephone,* trans. Jackson Mathews, in *My Theater.* New York: Knopf, 1951.)

Pages de Journal (1929–1932). Paris: Gallimard.

1935 *Les Nouvelles Nourritures.* Paris: Gallimard.

1936 *Nouvelles Pages de Journal (1932–1935).* Paris: Gallimard.

Geneviève. Paris: Gallimard. (*Geneviève,* trans. Dorothy Bussy, in *The School for Wives.* London: Cassell, 1950; New York: Knopf, 1950.)

Retour de l'U.R.S.S. Paris: Gallimard. (*Back from the USSR,* trans. Dorothy Bussy. London: Secker & Warburg; New York: Knopf, 1937.)

1937 *Retouches à mon 'Retour de l'U.R.S.S.'.* Paris: Gallimard. (*Afterthoughts on the USSR.* trans. Dorothy Bussy. London: Secker & Warburg; New York: Dial Press, 1937.)

1938 *Deux récits (Jeunesse* and *Acquasanta*). Paris: J. Schiffrin.

1939 *L'Evolution du Théâtre.* Manchester University Press.

1941 *Découvrons Henri Michaux.* Paris: Gallimard.

1942 *Interviews imaginaires.* Yverdon and Lausanne: Ed. du Haut Pays.

Interviews imaginaires. La Délivrance de Tunis. New York: Ed. Jacques Schiffrin.

Attendu que . . . Algiers: Charlot.

1944 *Pages de Journal 1939–1942.* New York: Jacques Schiffrin.

1946 *Thésée.* New York: Jacques Schiffrin; Paris: Gallimard. (*Theseus,* trans. John Russell, in *Two Legends, Theseus and Oedipus.* London: Secker & Warburg; New York: Knopf, 1950.)

Souvenirs littéraires et problèmes actuels. Beirut: Les Lettres françaises.

Journal 1939–1942. New York: Jacques Schiffrin.

Lettres à Christian Beck. Brussels: Ed. de l'Altitude.

1947 *Paul Valéry.* Paris: Domat.

Poétique. Neuchâtel and Paris: Ides et Calendes.

Le Procès (play adapted from Kafka's *Der Prozess* in a French translation by A. Vialatte, in collaboration with Jean-Louis Barrault). Paris: Gallimard.

1948 *Notes sur Chopin.* Paris: L'Arche. (*Notes on Chopin,* trans. Bernard Frechtman. New York: Philosophical Library.)

Théâtre complet IV. Translation of 'Amal', *Oedipe, Perséphone, Proserpine.* Neuchâtel and Paris: Ides et Calendes.

Préfaces. Neuchâtel and Paris: Ides et Calendes.

Rencontres. Neuchâtel and Paris: Ides et Calendes.

Théâtre complet V. *Les Caves du Vatican, Le Treizième Arbre.* Neuchâtel and Paris: Ides et Calendes.

Eloges. Neuchâtel and Paris: Ides et Calendes.

1949 *Théâtre complet* VI. *Robert ou l'Intérêt général.* Neuchâtel and Paris: Ides et Calendes.

Feuillets d'Automne. Paris: Mercure de France.

Anthologie de la poésie française. Paris: Bibliothèque de la Pléiade, Gallimard.

Interviews imaginaires. Paris: Gallimard. (*Imaginary Interviews,* trans. Malcolm Cowley. New York: Knopf, 1944.)

1950 *Littérature engagée.* Paris: Gallimard.

Les Caves du Vatican. Farce en trois actes. Paris: Gallimard.

1951 *Et nunc manet in te.* Neuchâtel: Ides et Calendes. (*Madeleine,* trans. Justin O'Brien. New York: Knopf, 1952; as *Et nunc manet in te.* London: Secker & Warburg, 1953.)

1952 *Ainsi soit-il, ou les Jeux sont faits.* Paris: Gallimard. (*So Be It, or the Chips are Down,* trans. Justin O'Brien. New York: Knopf; London: Chatto & Windus, 1960.)

1972 *Le Récit de Michel.* Neuchâtel: Ides et Calendes.

1993 *A Naples. Reconnaissance à l'Italie* [address, Institut Français, Naples, June 1950]. Fontfroide: Fata Morgana.

Le Grincheux. Fontfroide: Fata Morgana.

1995 *L'Oroscope ou Nul n'évite sa destinée.* Scenario ed. Daniel Durosay. Paris: Jean-Michel Place.

1996 [with Pierre Herbart] Le Scénario d'*Isabelle.* Edited by Cameron D. E. Tolton. Paris: Lettres Modernes.

Entretiens avec Jean Amrouche (1949). Vol. I: *Les Jeunes Années* (1891–1909). Des *Cahiers d'André Walter* aux débuts de la *NRF.* 2 compact discs. Paris: INA/Radio France. [Vol. II: La Maturité, forthcoming.] For text of interviews, see Marty, under 'B. Works on Gide'.

III   Translations

1911 R. M. Rilke. *Les Cahiers de Malte Laurids Brigge* (fragments). Paris: *NRF,* juillet.

1914 Rabindranath Tagore. *L'Offrande lyrique* [*Gitanjali*]. Paris: NRF.

1918 Joseph Conrad. *Typhon* [*Typhoon*]. Paris: NRF.

Walt Whitman. *Oeuvres choisis.* Paris: NRF.

1921 Shakespeare. *Antoine et Cléopâtre.* Paris: Lucien Vogel.

1922 Rabindranath Tagore. *Amal et la lettre du roi.* Paris: Lucien Vogel.

1923 William Blake. *Le Mariage du ciel et de l'enfer.* Paris: Claude Aveline.

A. Pouchkine [Pushkin]. *La Dame de Pique,* with J. Schiffrin and B. de Schloezer. Paris: Editions de la Pléiade.

1928 A. Pouchkine [Pushkin]. *Nouvelles,* with J. Schiffrin. Paris: Editions de la Pléiade, J. Schiffrin.

1930 Shakespeare. *Hamlet* (Act I), bilingual ed. Paris: La Tortue; Brussels: Ed. de la Décagone, 1944.

1933 Goethe. *Le Second Faust* (fragment). Paris: Cahiers du Sud.
Arden of Faversham. Paris: Cahiers du Sud.

1935 A. Pouchkine [Pushkin]. *Le Marchand de cercueils*, with J. Schiffrin. Paris: *NRF*, janvier.
A. Pouchkine [Pushkin]. *Récits*, with J. Schiffrin. Paris: Gallimard.

1944 Shakespeare. *Hamlet*, bilingual edition. New York: J. Schiffrin; Paris: Gallimard.

1950–51 Goethe. *Prométhée*. Paris: Jonquière et Nicaise.

IV   Correspondence

André Gide, François-Paul Alibert. *Correspondance 1907–1950*. Presses Universitaires de Lyon, 1982.

Henri Bachelin. *Correspondances avec André Gide and Romain Rolland*. Brest: Centre d'Etude des Correspondances, 1994.

André Gide, Christian Beck. *Correspondance*. Geneva: Droz, 1994.

André Gide, Arnold Bennett. *Correspondance. Vingt ans d'amitié littéraire, 1911–1931*. Paris and Geneva: Droz, 1964.

André Gide, Félix Bertaux. *Correspondance (1911–1948)*. Lyon: Centre d'Etudes Gidiennes, 1995.

Correspondance André Gide – Jacques-Emile Blanche 1892–1939. *Cahiers André Gide* 8. Paris: Gallimard, 1979.

Jacques-Emile Blanche. *Nouvelles Lettres à André Gide (1891–1925)*. Geneva: Droz, 1982.

André Gide, Rolf Bongs. *Correspondance (1935–1950)*. Lyon: Centre d'Etudes Gidiennes, 1991.

[Correspondance André Gide – Raymond Bonheur] André Gide: *Le Retour*. Neuchâtel: Ides et Calendes, 1946.

Charles Brunard. *Correspondance avec André Gide et Souvenirs*. Paris: La Pensée universelle, 1974.

Correspondance André Gide – Dorothy Bussy. I juin 1918 – déc. 1924; II jan. 1925 – nov. 1936; III jan. 1937 – jan. 1951. *Cahiers André Gide* 9, 10 11. Paris: Gallimard, 1979, 1981, 1982. (*Selected Letters of André Gide and Dorothy Bussy*, ed. Richard Tedeschi, intr. Jean Lambert. Oxford University Press, 1983.)

Paul Claudel, André Gide. *Correspondance 1899–1926*. Paris: Gallimard, 1949. (*The Correspondence between Paul Claudel and André Gide*, trans. John Russell. London: Secker & Warburg; New York: Pantheon Books, 1952.

Jean Cocteau. *Lettres à André Gide avec quelques réponses d' André Gide*. Paris: La Table Ronde, 1970.

Correspondance André Gide – Jacques Copeau. I déc. 1902 – mars 1913; II mars 1913 – oct. 1949. *Cahiers André Gide* 12, 13. Paris: Gallimard, 1987, 1988.

Deutsch-französische Gespräche 1920–1950: La Correspondance de Ernst-Robert Curtius avec André Gide, Charles Du Bos et Valéry Larbaud. Frankfurt am Main: Klostermann, 1980.

'Quatorze lettres et billets inédits de Lord Alfred Douglas à André Gide 1895–1929', in *Revue de littérature comparée* 3, juill.–sept. 1975, 483–502.

Lettres de Charles Du Bos et réponses de André Gide. Paris: Corrêa, 1950.

Charles Du Bos. Jacques et Isabelle Rivière. *Correspondance (1913–1935)*. Lyon: Centre d'Etudes Gidiennes, 1990.

André Gide, *Correspondance avec Louis Gérin (1933–1937)*. Lyon: Centre d'Etudes Gidiennes, 1996.

Henri Ghéon, André Gide. *Correspondance* 1897–1903; 1904–1944. Paris: Gallimard, 1976.

Correspondance André Gide et Jean Giono. Paris: Centre d'Etudes Gidiennes, 1984.

Correspondence of André Gide and Edmund Gosse 1904–1928. New York University Press, 1959; Westport, Conn.: Greenwood Press, 1977.

Francis Jammes, André Gide. *Correspondance 1893–1938*. Paris: Gallimard, 1948.

Marcel Jouhandeau. *Correspondance avec André Gide*. Paris: Santier, 1958.

Claude Foucart. *D'un monde à l'autre: La correspondance André Gide – Harry Kessler (1903–1933)*. Lyon: Centre d'Etudes Gidiennes, 1985.

Correspondance André Gide – Valéry Larbaud 1905–1938. Cahiers André Gide 14. Paris: Gallimard, 1989.

André Gide, Jef Last. *Correspondance 1934–1950*. Presses Universitaires de Lyon, 1985.

André Gide, Robert Levesque. *Correspondance (1926–1950)*. Presses Universitaires de Lyon, 1995.

André Gide, Roger Martin du Gard. *Correspondance 1913–1934; 1935–1938*. Paris: Gallimard, 1968. (See also: Susan M. Stout. *Index de la Correspondance André Gide – Roger Martin du Gard*. Lyon: Centre d'Etudes Gidiennes, 1979.)

Correspondance André Gide – François Mauriac 1912–1950. Cahiers André Gide 2. Paris: Gallimard, 1971.

'Quatorze lettres d'André Gide à Mme Emile Mayrisch (1911–1922)', in *Colpach*. Luxembourg: Amis de Colpach (priv. ed.).

André Gide. *Correspondance avec sa mère 1880–1896*. Paris: Gallimard, 1988.

André Gide, Albert Mockel. *Correspondance (1891–1938)*. Geneva: Droz, 1975.

André Gide, Anna de Noailles. *Correspondance 1902–1928*. Lyon: Centre d'Etudes Gidiennes, 1986.

André Gide, Justin O'Brien. *Correspondance 1937–1951*. Lyon: Centre d'Etudes Gidiennes, 1979.

André Gide, Charles Péguy. Correspondence, in *Feuillets de l'Amitié Charles Péguy*, no. 65, 1958.

André Gide. *Correspondance avec Charles-Louis Philippe et sa famille (1898–1936)*. Lyon: Centre d'Etudes Gidiennes, 1995.

Marcel Proust, André Gide. *Autour de La Recherche. Lettres*. Neuchâtel: Ides et Calendes, 1949; Brussels: Ed. Complexe, 1988.

André Gide, Henri de Régnier. *Correspondance (1891–1911)*. Presses Universitaires de Lyon, 1997.

Rainer Maria Rilke, André Gide. *Correspondance 1909–1926*. Paris: Corrêa, 1952.

Rilke, Gide, Verhaeren. *Correspondance inédite*. Paris: Messein, 1955.

André Gide, Isabelle Rivière. 'Un débat passioné. 1914–1932'. *Bulletin de Jacques Rivière et d'Alain-Fournier* 34, 1984.

Correspondance André Gide – Jacques Rivière. Paris: Gallimard, 1996.

Correspondance André Gide – Jacques Rivière. Supplément. Lyon: Centre d'Etudes Gidiennes, 1979.

Romain Rolland et la NRF.: correspondances avec Jacques Copeau, Gaston Gallimard, André Gide, Roger Martin du Gard, Jean Paulhan, Jean Schlumberger et fragments du Journal. Paris: Albin Michel, 1989.

Correspondance André Gide – Jules Romains, L'Individu et l'unanime. (1908–1946). Paris: Flammarion, 1976.

André Gide and André Rouveyre. *Correspondance 1909–1951*. Paris: Mercure de France, 1967.

Andre Gide and André Ruyters. *Correspondance 1895–1906; 1907–1950*. Presses Universitaires de Lyon, 1990.

André Gide. *Lettres au docteur Willy Schuermans, 1920–1928*. Brussels, priv. ed., 1955.

André Gide, Jean Schlumberger. *Correspondance, 1901–1950*. Paris: Gallimard 1993.

André Gide – Thea Sternheim. *Correspondance 1927–1950*. Lyon: Centre d'Etudes Gidiennes, 1986.

André Gide – André Suarez. *Correspondance 1908–1920*. Paris: Gallimard, 1963.

André Gide – Paul Valéry. *Correspondance 1890–1942*. Paris: Gallimard, 1955.

André Gide. *Correspondance avec Francis Vielé-Griffin 1891–1931*. Presses Universitaires de Lyon, 1986.

La Tristesse d'un automne sans été . . . correspondance de Gabrielle Vulliez avec André Gide et Paul Claudel (1923–1931). Lyon: Centre d'Etudes Gidiennes, 1981.

B. WORKS ON GIDE

Ahlstedt, Eva. *André Gide et le débat sur l'homosexualité. De 'L'Immoraliste' (1902) à 'Si le grain ne meurt' (1926)*. Göteborg: Acta Universitatis Gothoburgensis, 1994.

Albérès, René-Marill. *L'Odyssée d'André Gide*. Paris: La Nouvelle Edition, 1951.

Alblas, Anton. *Le Journal de Gide: le chemin qui mère à La Pléiade*. Nantes: Centre d'Etudes Gidiennes, 1997.

Alibert, François-Paul. *En marge d'André Gide*. Paris: Les Oeuvres représentatives, 1930.

En Italie avec André Gide. Impressions d'Italie (1913). Voyage avec Gide, Ghéon et Rouart, ed. Daniel Moutote. Presses Universitaires de Lyon, 1983.

Allégret, Marc. *Carnets du Congo. Voyage avec Gide*. Paris: Presses du CNRS, 1987.

Amoudru, Bernard. *De Bourget à Gide. Amour et Famille*. Paris: Ed. Familiales de France, 1946.

Angelet, Christian. *Symbolisme et invention formelle dans les premiers écrits d'André Gide*. Ghent: 'Romanica Gandensia' XIX, 1982.

Anglès, Auguste. *André Gide et le premier groupe de 'La Nouvelle Revue Française'*. Paris: Gallimard. 1 (1890–1910), 1978. 2 (1911–1912), 1986. 3 (1913–1914), 1986.

Apter, Emily S. *André Gide and the Codes of Homosexuality*. Saratoga, Calif.: 1987.

Archambault, Paul. *L'Humanité d'André Gide*. Paris: Bloud et Gay, 1946.

Ascarza-Wégimont, Marie. *Regard et parole dans 'La Porte étroite' d'André Gide*. Lyon: Centre d'Etudes Gidiennes, 1994.

Assouline, Pierre. *Gaston Gallimard*. Paris: Balland, 1984.

Aurégan, Pierre. *Gide*. Paris: Nathan, 1994.

Ausseil, Sarah et Jacques Drouin d'après ses souvenirs. *Madeleine Gide ou De quel amour blessé*. Paris: Laffont, 1993.

Babcock, Arthur E. *Portrait of Artists: Reflexivity in Gidean Fiction, 1902–1946*. York, SC: French Literature Publications, 1982.

Barrault, Jean-Louis. *Souvenirs pour demain*. Paris: Seuil, 1972.

Bastide, Roger. *Anatomie d'André Gide*. Paris: Presses Universitaires de France, 1972.

Beigbeder, Marc. *André Gide*. Paris: Ed. Universitaires, 1954.

Belgion, Montgomery. *Our Present Philosophy of Life [According to Bernard Shaw, André Gide, Sigmund Freud and Bertrand Russell]*. London: Faber, 1929.

Benda, Julien. *La France byzantine ou le triomphe de la littérature pure. Mallarmé, Gide, etc.* Paris: Gallimard, 1945.

Bendz, Ernst. *André Gide et l'art d'écrire*. Paris: Messageries du Livre, 1939.

Bennett, Arnold. *Journal 1896–1928* (3 vols.). London: Cassell, 1932–3.

Béraud, Henri. *La Croissade des Longues Figures*. Paris: Ed. du Siècle, 1924.

Bertalot, Enrico Umberto. *André Gide et l'attente de Dieu*. Paris: Minard, 1967.

Bettinson, Christopher D. (ed.). *Gide, 'Les Caves du Vatican'*. London: Arnold, 1972.
    A Student's Guide to Gide. London: Heinemann, 1977.

Blanche, Jacques-Emile. *Mes Modèles. Barrès – Hardy – Proust – James – Gide – Moore*. Paris: Stock, 1928.

Blanchot, Maurice. *La Part du Feu*. Paris: Gallimard, 1949.

Boisdeffre, Pierre de. *Vie d'André Gide (1869–1909)*. vol. 1. Paris: Hachette, 1970.

Boros Azzi, Marie-Denise. *Problématique de l'écriture dans 'Les Faux-Monnayeurs' d'André Gide*. Paris: Lettres Modernes, 1990.

Braak, Sybrandi. *André Gide et l'âme moderne*. Amsterdam: H.J. Paris, 1923.

Brachfeld, George I. *André Gide and the Communist Temptation*. Paris: Minard, 1959.

Brée, Germaine. *André Gide l'insaisissable Protée. Etude critique de l'œuvre d'André Gide*. Paris: Les Belles-Lettres, 1953. English revised version: *Gide*. New Brunswick, NJ: Rutgers University Press, 1963.

Brigaud, Jacques. *Gide entre Benda et Sartre. Un artiste entre la cléricature et l'engagement*. Paris: Minard, 1972.

Broome, Peter. *Gide: 'Les Caves du Vatican'*. London: Grant & Cutler, 1995.

Cabanis, José, *Dieu et la NRF, 1909–1949*. Paris: Gallimard, 1994.
    Le Diable à la NRF, 1911–1951. Paris: Gallimard, 1996.

Cancalon, Elaine Davis. *Techniques et personnages dans les récits d'André Gide*. Paris: Minard, 1970.

Chadourne, Jacqueline M. *André Gide et l'Afrique. Le rôle de l'Afrique dans la vie et l'oeuvre de l'écrivain*. Paris: Nizet, 1968.

Chartier, Pierre. *'Les Faux-Monnayeurs' d'André Gide*. Paris: Gallimard, 1991.

Ciholas, Karin Nordenhaug. *'Les Faux-Monnayeurs'*. Chapel Hill, NC: North Carolina Studies in the Romance Languages and Literatures, 1974.

Claude, Jean. *André Gide et le Théâtre*, 2 vols. Paris: Gallimard, 1992.

Clive, H. P. *Pierre Louÿs 1870–1925. A Biography.* Oxford University Press, 1978.

Cocteau, Jean. *Gide Vivant. Paroles de Jean Cocteau.* Paris: Amiot-Dumont, 1952.

'André Gide Vivant', in *Poésie critique*, I. Paris: Gallimard, 1959.

Combelle, Lucien. *Je dois à André Gide.* Paris: Chambrand, 1951.

Copeau, Jacques. *Journal 1901–1948* [2 vols.: 1901–1915, 1916–1948]. Paris: Seghers, 1991.

Cordle, Thomas. *André Gide.* New York: Twayne 1969; London: Macmillan, 1976 (updated ed., 1993).

Crossman, Richard (ed.). *The God that Failed. Koestler, Wright, Fisher, Silone, Gide and Spender.* New York: Harper, 1949.

Cunningham, Joyce and William Donald Wilson. *A Concordance of André Gide's 'La Symphonie Pastorale'*. New York, London: Garland, 1978.

Dabit, Eugène. *Journal intime 1928–1936.* Paris: Gallimard, 1989.

Dällenbach, Lucien. *Le Récit spéculaire.* Paris: Seuil, 1977.

Dambre, Marc. *'La Symphonie Pastorale' d'André Gide.* Paris: Gallimard, 1991.

Dauvigny, Alain [Maurice Delmas]. *André Gide ou l'impossible morale.* Bordeaux: Samie, 1954.

Davet, Yvonne. *Autour des 'Nourritures terrestres'. Histoire d'un livre.* Paris: Gallimard, 1948.

Davies, John C. *Gide, 'L'Immoraliste' and 'La Porte étroite'*. London: Arnold, 1968.

Delay, Jean. *La Jeunesse d'André Gide*, I (1869–1890), II (1890–1895). Paris: Gallimard, 1956, 1957.

Delmas-Marsalet, Dr Maurice. *La Culpabilité morbide d'André Gide.* Bordeaux: Samie, 1954.

Derais, François et Henri Rambaud. *L'Envers du Journal de Gide.* Paris: Le Nouveau Portique, 1951.

Deschodt, Eric. *Gide. Le 'contemporain capital'*. Paris: Perrin, 1991.

Didier, Béatrice. *Un Dialogue à distance: Gide et Du Bos.* Paris: Desclée de Brouwer, 1976.

Drain, Henri. *Nietzsche et Gide. Essai.* Paris: Ed. de la Madeleine, 1932.

Du Bos, Charles. *Le Dialogue avec André Gide.* Paris: Au Sans Pareil, 1929; Paris, Corrêa, 1947.

Journal, 9 vols. Paris: Corrêa (La Colombe from vol.V), 1946–61.

Dubourg, Maurice. *Eugène Dabit et André Gide* (with eighteen letters from Gide). Paris: Maurice Pernette, Plaisir du Bibliophile, 1953.

Ehrenburg, Ilya. *Truce: 1921–1933.* London: MacGibbon & Kee, 1963.

Falk, Eugène H. *Types of Thematic Structure: The nature and function of motifs in Gide, Camus and Sartre.* Chicago University Press, 1967.

Fayer, Mischa Harry. *Gide, Freedom and Dostoevsky.* Burlington, Vt.: The Lane Press, 1946.

Fernandez, Ramon. *André Gide.* Paris: Corrêa, 1931.

Gide ou le courage de s'engager. Paris: Klincksieck, 1985.

Ferrari, Eugène. *André Gide. Le sensualisme littéraire et les exigences de la religion.* Lausanne: Association Chrétienne d'Etudiants, 1927.

Fillaudeau, Bertrand. *L'Univers ludique d'André Gide. Les Soties.* Paris: Corti, 1985.

Fonvieille-Alquier, François. *André Gide.* Paris: Charron, 1972.

Fortier, Paul A. *Décor et Dualisme. 'L'Immoraliste' d'André Gide.* Saratoga, Calif.: ANMA Libri, 1988.

Foucart, Claude. *André Gide et l'Allemagne: A la recherche de la complementarité (1889–1932).* Bonn: Romantistiche Verlag, 1997.

Fowlie, Wallace. *André Gide. His life and art.* New York: Macmillan, 1965.

La pureté dans l'art. Le Secret du chant – Mallarmé – T. S. Eliot – Gide – Le roman français. Montréal: Ed. de l'Arbre, 1941.

Freedman, Ralph. *The Lyrical Novel. Studies in Hermann Hesse, André Gide and Virginia Woolf.* Princeton, NJ: Princeton University Press, 1963.

Freyburger, Henri. *L'Evolution de la disponibilité gidienne.* Paris: Nizet, 1970.

Fryer, Jonathan. *André and Oscar. Gide, Wilde and the gay art of living.* London, Constable, 1997.

Gabory, Georges. *André Gide. Son œuvre.* Paris: Ed. de la Nouvelle Revue Critique, 1924.

Gagnebin, Laurent. *André Gide nous interroge. Essai critique sur sa pensée religieuse et morale.* Lausanne: Cahiers de la Renaissance Vaudoise, 1961.

Gavillet, Marcel. *Etude sur la morale d'André Gide* [with two letters from Gide]. Lausanne: Ed. du Revenandray, 1977.

Geerts, Walter. *Le Silence sonore. La poétique du premier Gide: entre intertexte et métatexte.* Presses Universitaires de Namur, 1992.

Genova, Pamela Antonia. *André Gide dans le labyrinthe de la Mytho-textualité.* West Lafayette, Ind.: Purdue University Press, 1995.

Ghéon, Henri. *L'Homme né de la guerre. Témoignage d'un converti.* Paris: NRF, 1919.

Got, Maurice. *André Gide – une expérience spirituelle.* Paris: CDU, 1962.

Got, Olivier. *André Gide: Les Faux-Monnayeurs.* Paris: Nathan, 1991.

Gouiran, Emile. *André Gide. Essai de psychologie littéraire.* Paris: Crès, 1934.

Goulet, Alain. *'Les Caves du Vatican' d'André Gide. Etude méthodologique.* Paris: Larousse, 1972.

Fiction et vie sociale dans l'œuvre d'André Gide. Paris: Minard, 1986.

Giovanni Papini juge d'André Gide. Lyon: Centre d'Etudes Gidiennes, 1982.

André Gide, 'Les Faux-Monnayeurs', mode d'emploi. Paris: SEDES, 1991.

Lire 'Les Faux-Monnayeurs' de Gide. Paris: Dunod, 1994.

Green, Julien. *Journal 1928–1955,* vol. IV. *Oeuvres complètes.* Paris: Gallimard, Pléiade, 1975.

Grenier, Fernand. *Réponses à André Gide.* Paris: Ed. des Amis de l'Union Soviétique, 1936.

Guerard, Albert J. *André Gide.* Harvard University Press, 1951; New York: Dutton, 1963.

Guérin, Daniel. *Shakespeare et Gide en correctionelle? Essais.* Paris: Ed. du Scorpion, 1959.

Guilloux, Louis. *Carnets 1921–1944*. Paris: Gallimard, 1978.

Guise, René. *Pour une étude du 'Journal des Faux-Monnayeurs' d'André Gide*. Nancy: Université de Nancy II, 1972.

Harris, Frederick John. *André Gide et Romain Rolland: Two Men Divided*. New Brunswick, NJ: Rutgers University Press, 1973.

Herbart, Pierre. *A la recherche d'André Gide*. Paris: Gallimard, 1952.

  En URSS 1936. Paris: Gallimard, 1937.

  Le Même. La Ligne de force. Paris: Gallimard, 1958.

Holdheim, William Wolfgang. *Theory and Practice of the Novel: A Study on André Gide*. Geneva: Droz, 1968.

Houssiau, Bernard J. *Marc Allégret. Découvreur de stars*. Paris: Cabédita, 1994.

Huddleston, Sisley. *Bohemian, Literary and Social Life in Paris. Salons, cafés, studios*. London: Harrap, 1928.

Hytier, Jean. *André Gide*. Algiers: Charlot, 1945.

Idt, Geneviève. *'Les Faux-Monnayeurs'. Analyse critique*. Paris: Hatier, 1970.

Ireland, George William. *Gide*. Edinburgh and London: Oliver & Boyd, 1963.

  André Gide. A study of his creative writings. Oxford: Clarendon Press, 1970.

Iseler, Paul. *Les Débuts d'André Gide vus par Pierre Louÿs. Avec une lettre d'André Gide et de nombreuses lettres inédites de Pierre Louÿs à André Gide*. Paris: Ed. du Sagittaire, 1937.

Jadin, Jean-Marie. *André Gide et sa perversion*. Paris: Arcanes, 1995.

Jammes, Francis. *L'Antigyde ou Elie de Nacre*. Paris: Mercure de France, 1932.

Jean-Aubry, G. *André Gide et la Musique*. Paris: Ed. de la Revue Musicale, 1945.

Jules-Romain, Lise. *Les Vies inimitables*. Paris: Flammarion, 1986.

Kaplan, Carol L. *Narcissistic Optics in André Gide's 'Récits': Configurations of Imagery and the Reception of the Text*. Ann Arbor, Mich.: University of Pittsburgh Press, 1985.

Kessler, Harry. *The Diaries of a Cosmopolitan 1918–1937*. London: Weidenfeld & Nicolson, 1971.

Keypour, N. David. *André Gide: Ecriture et réversibilité dans 'Les Faux-Monnayeurs'*. Presses de l'Université de Montréal; Paris: Didier, 1980.

Khélil, Hédi. *Sens/Jouissance. Tourisme, erotisme, argent dans des fictions coloniales d'André Gide*. Tunis: La Nef, 1988.

Klossowski, Pierre. *Un si funeste désir*. Paris: Gallimard, 1980.

Lacouture, Jean. *Une adolescence du siècle* [biography of Jacques Rivière]. Paris: Seuil, 1994.

Lafille, Pierre. *André Gide romancier*. Paris: Hachette, 1954.

Laidlaw, G. Norman. *Elysian Encounter. Diderot and Gide*. Syracuse, NY: Syracuse University Press, 1963.

Lalou, René. *André Gide*. Strasbourg: Heissler, 1928.

Lambert, Jean. *Gide familier*. Paris: Julliard, 1958.

Lang, Renée. *André Gide et la pensée allemande*. Paris: LUF, 1949.

  Rilke, Gide et Valéry. Boulogne-sur-Seine: Ed. de la revue *Prétexte*, 1953.

Larina, Anna. *This I cannot forget: The Memoirs of Nikolai Bukharin's Widow*, trans. Gary Kern. London: Hutchinson, 1994.

Last, Jef. *The Spanish Tragedy*, trans. David Hallet. London: Routledge, 1939.

Mijn vriend André Gide. Amsterdam: Van Ditmar, 1966.

Lejeune, Philippe. *Exercises d'ambiguité. Lectures de 'Si le grain ne meurt'.* Paris: Minard, 1974.

Lepage, Pierre. *André Gide Le Messager.* Paris: Seuil, 1977.

Lepoutre, Raymond. *André Gide.* Paris: Richard-Masse, 1946.

Lerner, Anne Lapidus. *Passing the Love of Women. A study of Gide's 'Saül' and its biblical roots.* Lanham, MD: University Press of America, 1980.

Lesage, Laurent. *Marcel Proust and his Literary Friends.* University of Illinois Press, 1958.

Levesque, Robert. *Lettre à Gide et autres écrits.* Lyon: Centre d'Etudes Gidiennes, 1982.

Levy, Zvi H. *Jérôme 'agonistes'. Les structures dramatiques et les procédures narratives de 'La Porte étroite'.* Paris: Nizet, 1984.

Lévy, Jacques. *Journal et Correspondance. Fragments précedés d'une étude sur 'Les Faux-Monnayeurs' d'André Gide et l'expérience religieuse.* Grenoble: Cahiers de l'Alpe, 1954.

Lièvre, Pierre. *André Gide.* Paris: Le Divan, 1927.

Lime, Maurice. *Gide tel que je l'ai connu.* Paris: Julliard, 1952.

Lindegger, Max. *L'Hésitation chez André Gide.* Zürich: Juris Druck, 1972.

McLaren, James C. *The Theater of André Gide. Evolution of a Moral Philosopher.* Baltimore: Johns Hopkins University Press, 1953.

Maeder, Lilian. *Les premières apparitions du thème de la libération dans l'oeuvre d'André Gide.* Zürich: Juris Druck, 1972.

Mahias, Claude. *La Vie d'André Gide* [preface and commentary by Pierre Herbart]. Paris: Gallimard, 'Les Albums photographiques', 1955.

Maisani-Léonard, Martine. *André Gide ou l'ironie de l'écriture.* Presses de l'Université de Montréal, 1976.

Mallarmé, Stéphane. *Correspondance,* vols. V, VII, ed. Henri Mondor and Lloyd James Austin. Paris: Gallimard, 1981, 1982.

Mallet, Robert. *Une mort ambiguë.* Paris: Gallimard, 1955.

Mann, Klaus. *André Gide and the Crisis of Modern Thought.* New York: 1943; London: Dobson, 1948.

   The Turning Point. An autobiography. London: Serpent's Tail, 1987.

March, Harold. *Gide and the Hound of Heaven.* Philadelphia: University of Pennsylvania Press, 1952.

Marchand, Max. *L'Irremplaçable mari.* Oran: Fouque, 1955.

   Le Complexe pédagogique et didactique d'André Gide. Oran: Fouque, 1954.

Marcelet, Maurice [Maurice Delmas]. *André Gide l'enchaîné.* Paris: Piquot, 1955.

Martin, Claude. *Gide par lui-même.* Paris: Seuil, 1963 (new, revised ed., 1995).

   La Maturité d'André Gide, de Paludes à l'Immoraliste (1895–1902). Paris: Klincksieck, 1977.

Martin du Gard, Roger. *Notes sur André Gide (1913–1951).* Paris: Gallimard, 1951. (*Notes on André Gide,* trans. John Russell. London: Deutsch, 1953.)

   Journal [3 vols.: I 1892–1919; II 1919–1936; III 1937–1949, with 'textes autobiographiques 1950–1958']. Paris: Gallimard, 1993.

Martinet, Edouard. *André Gide, l'amour et la divinité.* Paris, Neuchâtel: Victor Attinger, 1931.

Marty, Eric. *L'Ecriture du jour. Le 'Journal' d'André Gide.* Paris: Seuil, 1985.

André Gide. Qui êtes-vous? Avec les entretiens André Gide – Jean Amrouche. Lyon: La Manufacture, 1987.

Massis, Henri. *Jugements*, vol. 2. Paris: Plon, 1929.

D'André Gide à Marcel Proust. Lyon: Lardenanchet, 1948.

Masson, Pierre. *André Gide. Voyage et écriture.* Presses Universitaires de Lyon, 1983.

Lire 'Les Faux-Monnayeurs'. Presses Universitaires de Lyon, 1990.

Index des noms et des titres cités dans 'La Jeunesse d'André Gide' de Jean Delay. Nantes Centre d'Etudes Gidiennes, 1997.

Maucuer, Maurice. *Gide, l'indécision passionée.* Paris: Ed. du Centurion, 1969.

Maurer, Rudolf. *André Gide et l'URSS.* Berne: Tillier, 1983.

Mauriac, Claude. *Conversations avec André Gide.* Paris: Albin Michel, 1951. (New expanded edition: *Le Temps immobile. Conversations avec André Gide.* Paris: Albin Michel, 1990.)

Hommes et idées d'aujourd'hui. Paris: Albin Michel, 1966.

Maurois, André. *Mémoires* I. Paris: Flammarion, 1948.

De Gide à Sartre. Paris: Perrin, 1965.

Maurras, Charles. *Réponse à André Gide. Lettre à Monsieur le directeur de 'La Gazette de Lausanne'.* Paris: Ed. de 'La Seule France', 1948.

Mercier-Campiche, Marianne. *Retouches au portrait d'André Gide jeune.* Lausanne: L'Age d'Homme, 1994.

Meter Ames, Henry. *André Gide.* Norfolk, Conn.: New Directions, 1947.

Meyer, Jean. *Place au théâtre.* Paris: Fallois, 1991.

Michaud, Gabriel. *Gide et l'Afrique.* Paris: Ed. du Scorpion, 1961.

Millot, Catherine. *Gide, Genet, Mishima. Intelligence et perversion.* Paris: Gallimard, 1996.

Mondor, Henri. *Les Premiers Temps d'une Amitié. André Gide et Paul Valéry.* Monaco: Ed. du Rocher, 1947.

Morelle, Paul. *Gide, maître à contester.* Paris: *Tendances*, 57, fév. 1969.

Morino, Mlle L. *La Nouvelle Revue Française dans l'histoire des lettres.* Paris: Gallimard, 1939.

Mouret, François et Paul Phocas. *Jean Ghéhenno et Monsieur Gide* [play]. Nantes: Ouest Editions, 1991 (new ed. 1993).

Moutote, Daniel. *Le Journal de Gide et les problèmes du moi (1889–1925.)* Paris: Presses Universitaires de France, 1968.

Les Images végétales dans l'oeuvre d'André Gide. Paris: Presses Universitaires de France, 1970.

Egotisme français moderne: Stendhal – Barrès – Valéry – Gide. Paris: Sedes, 1980.

Index des idées, images et formules du 'Journal 1889–1939' d'André Gide. Lyon: Centre d'Etudes Gidiennes, 1985.

Réflexions sur 'Les Faux-Monnayeurs'. Paris: Champion, 1990.

André Gide: l'Engagement (1926–1939). Paris: Sedes, 1991.

André Gide: Esthétique de la création littéraire. Paris: Champion, 1993.

Naville, Arnold. *André Gide.* Geneva: Kundig, 1952.

Naville, Claude. *André Gide et le communisme.* Paris: Librairie du Travail, 1936.

Naville, Pierre. *Mémoires imparfaites*. Paris: La Découverte, 1987.

Nazier, François. *L'Anti-Corydon. Essai sur l'inversion sexuelle*. Paris: Ed. du Siècle, 1924.

Neilson, Francis. *André Gide, Individualist*. Brooklyn, N.Y.: Revisionalist Press, 1979.

Nersoyan, H. J. *André Gide, The Theism of an Atheist*. Syracuse, NJ: Syracuse University Press, 1969.

Nobécourt, René-Gustave. *Les Nourritures normandes d'André Gide*. Paris: Ed. Medicis, 1949.

    Madeleine et André Gide à Cuverville-en-Caux. Rouen: Académie des Sciences, 1970.

O'Brien, Justin. *Les Nourritures terrestres d'André Gide et les Bucoliques de Virgile*, trans. Elisabeth Van Rysselberghe. Boulogne-sur-Seine: Ed. de la revue *Prétextes*, 1953.

    Portrait of André Gide. A Critical Biography. New York: Knopf; London: Secker & Warburg, 1953.

Oliver, Andrew. *Michel, Job, Pierre, Paul: Intertextualité de la lecture dans 'L'Immoraliste' de Gide*. Paris: Lettres Modernes, 'Archives André Gide' 4, 1979.

O'Neil, Kevin. *André Gide and the 'Roman d'Aventure'. The History of a Literary Idea in France*. Sydney University Press, 1969.

Painter, George D. *André Gide. A Critical and Biographical Study*. London: Arthur Barker, 1951; revised as *André Gide. A Critical Biography*. London: Weidenfeld & Nicolson, 1968.

Pell, Elsie. *André Gide. L'évolution de sa pensée religieuse*. Paris: Didier, 1936.

Pénault, Pierre-Jean. *Du Val-Richer à La Roque-Beignard. François Guizot, André Gide, Jean Schlumberger*. Pont-l'Evêque: Ed. du Pays d'Auge, 1962.

Perry, Kenneth I. *The Religious Symbolism of André Gide*. The Hague and Paris: Mouton, 1969.

Peters, Arthur K. *Jean Cocteau and André Gide: An Abrasive Friendship*. New Brunswick, NJ: Rutgers University Press, 1973.

Phocas, Paul. *Gide and Ghéhenno polémiquent*. Presses Universitaires de Rennes, 1987.

Pierre-Quint, Léon. *André Gide. Sa vie, son oeuvre*. Paris: Stock, 1932 (new ed. 1952).

Planche, Henri. *Le Problème de Gide*. Paris: Tequi, 1952.

Pollard, Patrick. *André Gide, homosexual moralist*. New Haven, London: Yale University Press, 1991.

Porché, François. *L'Amour qui n'ose pas dire son nom*. Paris: Grasset, 1927.

Poucel, Victor. *L'Esprit d'André Gide*. Paris: A l'Art catholique, 1929.

Privaz, Etienne. *Un malfaiteur: André Gide*. Paris: Albert Messein, 1931.

Pruner, Francis. *'La Symphonie pastorale' de Gide: De la tragédie vécue à la tragédie écrite*. Paris: Minard, 1964.

Putnam, Walter C., III. *L'Aventure littéraire de Joseph Conrad et d'André Gide*. Saratoga, Calif.: ANMA Libri, 1990.

Richardson, Joanna. *Enid Starkie*. London: Murray, 1973.

Rivière, Jacques. *André Gide*. Paris: Ed. de la Chronique des Lettres françaises, 1926.

Robidoux, Réjean. *'Le Traité du Narcisse' (Théorie du Symbole) d'André Gide*. Ottawa: Ed. de l'Université d'Ottawa, 1978.

Rossi, Vinio. *André Gide. The Evolution of an Aesthetic*. New Brunswick, NJ: Rutgers University Press, 1967.

André Gide. New York: Columbia University Press, 1968.

Rousseaux, André. *Le Paradis perdu*. Paris: Grasset, 1936.

Rouveyre, André. *Le Reclus et le retors. Gourmont et Gide*. Paris: G. Crès, 1927.

Sachs, Maurice. *André Gide*. Paris: Denoël et Steele, 1936.

Sacken, Jeannée P. *'A Certain Slant of Light': Aesthetics of first-person Narration in Gide and Cather*. New York, London: Garland, 1985.

Saint-Clair, M. [Maria Van Rysselberghe]. *Il y a quarante ans*. Paris: Gallimard, 1968.

San Juan, Epifanio. *Transcending the heroic. An Essay on Gide's Theater*. Lanham, MD; University Press of America, 1988.

Sanouillet, Michel. *Dada à Paris*. Paris: Pauvert, 1965.

Sartre, Jean-Paul. *Situations* IV. Paris: Gallimard, 1964.

Savage, Catharine H. *André Gide. L'Evolution de sa pensée religieuse*. Paris: Nizet, 1962.

Schildt, Göran. *Gide et l'Homme. Etude*, trans. from German. Paris: Mercure de France, 1949.

Schlumberger, Jean. *Madeleine et André Gide*. Paris: Gallimard, 1956.

Oeuvres, VI (1940–1944), VII (1944–1961). Paris: Gallimard, 1960 and 1962.

In Memoriam, suivi de Anniversaires. Paris: Gallimard, 1991.

Schnyder, Peter. *Pré-textes: André Gide et la tentation de la critique*. Paris: *Intertextes*, 1988.

Schveitzer, Marcelle. *Gide aux Oasis*. Nivelles: Ed. de la Francité, 1971.

Schwob, René. *Le Vrai drame d'André Gide*. Paris: Grasset, 1932.

Segal, Naomi. *André Gide: Pederasty and Pedagogy*. Oxford: Oxford University Press, 1998.

Sherard, Robert Harborough. *Oscar Wilde twice defended from André Gide's wicked lies and Frank Harris's cruel libels*. Chicago: Argus Book Shop, 1934.

Souday, Paul. *André Gide*. Paris: Kra, 1927.

Spender, Stephen. *World Within World*. London: Hamish Hamilton, 1951.

Starkie, Enid. *André Gide*. Cambridge: Bowes & Bowes, 1953.

Stéphane, Roger. *Fin d'une jeunesse*. Paris: La Table Ronde, 1954.

Stocker, Dr A. *L'Amour interdite. Trois anges sur la route de Sodome. Etude psychologique*. Geneva: Ed. du Mont-Blanc, 1943.

Stoltzfus, Ben. *Gide's Eagles*. Southern Illinois University Press; London and Amsterdam: Feffer & Simons, 1969.

Gide and Hemingway. Rebels against God. Port Washington, London: Kennikat Press, 1978.

Strauss, George. *La part du diable dans l'œuvre d'André Gide*. Paris: Les Lettres Modernes, 1985.

Tachot, Jacques. *André Gide et la Cour d'Assises*. Rouen: Poullard, 1957.

Teppe, Julien. *Sur le purisme d'André Gide*. Paris: Pierre Clairac, 1949.

Teuler, Gabriel. *Après Gide*. Paris: Debresse, 1959.

Thierry, Jean-Jacques. *Autour de Lafcadio Wluik: Essai, avec une lettre et un hommage à André Gide*. Aurillac: Clairac, 1951.

André Gide. Paris: Hachette, 1962. (Revised, shorter version: Paris: Gallimard, 1968.)

Thomas, D. Lawrence. *André Gide. The Ethic of the Artist.* London: Secker & Warburg, 1950.

Thwaite, Ann. *Edmund Gosse.* London: Secker & Warburg, 1984.

Tilby, Michael. *Gide. 'Les Faux-Monnayeurs'.* London: Grant & Cutler, 1981.

Tolton, C. D. E. *André Gide and the Art of Autobiography. A Study of 'Si le grain ne meurt'.* Toronto: Macmillan of Canada,1975.

Touchard, Pierre-Aimé. *Six années de la Comédie Française.* Paris: Seuil, 1953.

Tournier, Michel. *Le Vol du Vampire.* Paris: Gallimard, 'Idées', 1983.

Trahard, Pierre. *'La Porte étroite' d'André Gide. Etude et analyse.* Paris: Ed. de la Pensée Moderne, 1968.

Tribouillet, Paul-Henri. *André Gide. Introduction critique à son œuvre.* Hué, 1940.

Ullmann, S. *The Image in the Modern French Novel. Gide, Alain-Fournier, Proust, Camus.* Cambridge University Press, 1960.

Vadim. *Le goût de bonheur.* Paris: Fixot, 1993.

Van Rysselberghe, Maria. *Les Cahiers de la Petite Dame. Notes pour l'authentique histoire d'André Gide. Cahiers André Gide* 4, 5, 6, 7: I 1918–1929. II 1929–1937. III 1937–1945. IV 1945–1951. Paris: Gallimard, 1973, 1974, 1975, 1977.

Veyrenc, Marie-Thérèse. *Genèse d'un style. La phrase d'André Gide dans 'Les Nourritures terrestres'.* Paris: Nizet, 1976.

Vier, Jacques. *Gide.* Paris: Desclée de Brouwer, 1970.

Vulliez, Wanda. *La Tristesse d'un automne sans été . . . Correspondance de Gabrielle Vulliez avec André Gide et Paul Claudel (1923–1931).* Lyon: Centre d'Etudes Gidiennes, 1981.

Walch, C. *André Gide et notre temps (Entretient tenu au siège de l'Union pour la Vérité, le 23 janvier, 1935).* Paris: Gallimard, 1935.

Wald Losowski, Patrick and Roman. *André Gide. Vendredi 16 October 1908.* Paris: Lattès, 1992.

Walker, David H. *Gide, 'Les Nourritures terrestres' and 'La Symphonie Pastorale'.* London: Grant & Cutler, 1990.

André Gide. London: Macmillan, 1990.

Walker, David H. and Catharine S. Brosman (eds). *Retour aux 'Nourritures Terrestres'.* Amsterdam and Atlanta, GA: Editions Rodopi B.V., 1997.

Watson-Williams, Helen. *André Gide and Greek Myth.* Oxford: Clarendon Press, 1967.

Weinberg, Kurt. *On Gide's 'Prométhée'. Private Myth and Public Mystification.* Princeton University Press, 1972.

West, Russell. *Conrad and Gide. Translation, Transference and Intertextualité.* Amsterdam: 1996.

Wharton, Edith. *A Backward Glance.* New York, London: D. Appleton-Century, 1934.

White, William Hale. *The Autobiography of Mark Rutherford.* London: Kegan Paul, 1885.

Wilson, W. Donald. *A Critical Commentary on André Gide's 'La Symphonie Pastorale'.* London: Macmillan, 1971.

Yang Tchang-Lomine. *L'Attitude d'André Gide. Essai d'analyse psychologique.* Lyon: Bosc frères et Riou, 1930.

Yaari, Monique. *Ironie paradoxale et ironie poétique. Vers une théorie de l'ironie moderne sur les traces de Gide dans 'Paludes'.* Birmingham, Ala.: Summa Publications, 1988.

Family Trees

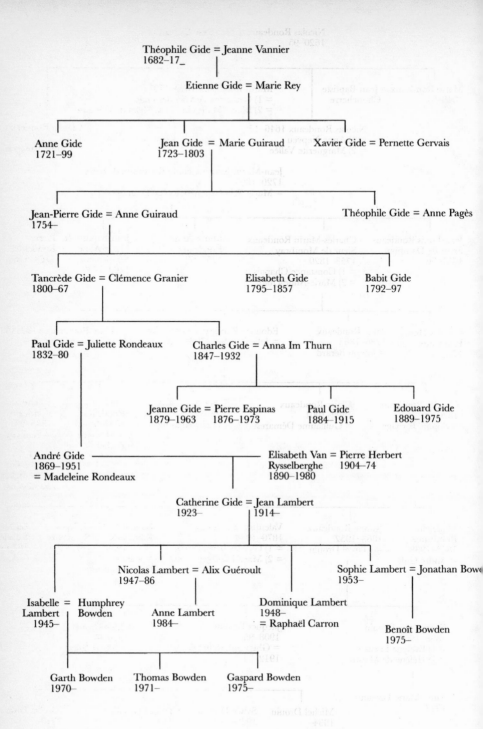

The Gide Family

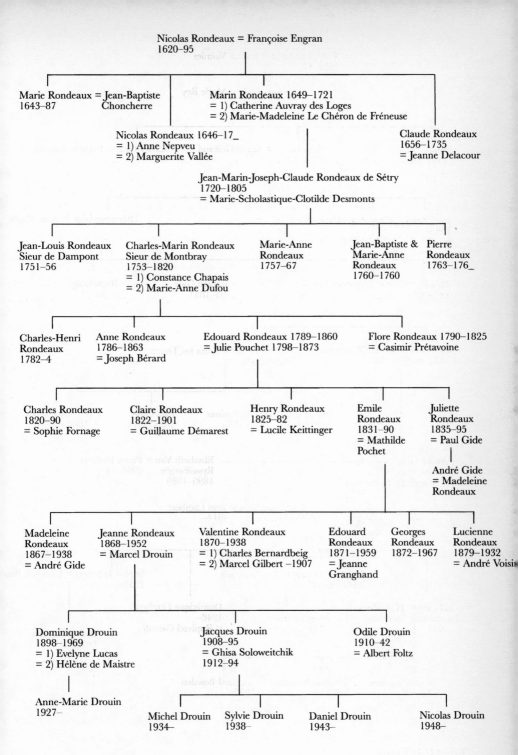

The Rondeaux Family

Index

Italicized page numbers refer to analysis of the works in question.

Abetz, Otto, 544–5
Abu Simbel (Egypt), 577
abyme, en ('in abyss'), 111, 159, 397
Académie Française, 220, 352, 462, 565–6, 576
Acquasanta, 258
Action Française, 236, 252, 277, 307, 323 and 349 (and Ghéon), 351, 359 (and *Faux-Monnayeurs*)
'*acte gratuit*' (and 'gratuitous action'), 159, 272–3, 632
Adelboden (Switz.), 219
Adoum, 402, 406–7, 595, 624
Aeschylus, 60, 158 (*Prometheus Bound*), 237
Ahmed (Biskra), 204
Aitken, Max, Lord Beaverbrook, 310
Aix-les-Thermes, 243
Alain-Fournier (*né* Henri Fournier), 239 (*Le Grand Meaulnes*), 243, 250, 267, 280, 282 (killed), 323, 384
Albéniz, Isaac, 195
Albert, Henri (on Nietzsche), 163
Alençon, 149, 154–5
Alet-les-Bains, 541
Alexandria, 531, 533, 577
Algiers, 96, 107, 115–16, 136, 149, 168–9, 176, 203–4, 423–4, 558–61, 577
Ali (Algiers), 119–21
Ali (Bône), 166–7, 203
Ali (Luxor), 531–3
Ali (Sousse), 94
Alibert, François-Paul (and Carcassonne), 223, 237, 243, 259, 262, 284, 297–8, 349, 423, 425, 436, 446, 542, 565
Alicante, 241

Allégret, André (Marc's brother), 296, 298–9, 306, 367, 388
Allégret, Pastor Elie (Marc's father), xiv, 43 (takes G to London), 131 (G's best man), 281, 296, 326 (returns from Africa), 327–8, 334, 347, 359, 361, 401, 411, 420
Allégret, Eric (Marc's brother) 296, 313
Allégret, Jean-Paul (Marc's brother), 296, 306, 327, 383, 418, 436–7, 485
Allégret, Léonie (Marc's aunt), 307
Allégret, Marc, xiv–v, 82, 231, 296–310, 310–13 (in England with G), 319, 326–8, 333 (and *Symphonie Pastorale*), 334–5 (and G), 335–6 (and Beth), 337–9 (in England and Wales), 341–3, 347–8, 348–9 (with G in Italy), 354 (lives with G at Villa Montmorency), 357–8 (and G), 359, 361 (and Bronja), 366–8, 370–3 (at 'Sciences Po'), 380–5, 387–91, 401–6, 406 (*Carnets*), 408–9, 411–12, 414 (G on African film), 415, 416 (showing of African film), 417, 419–20 (to Berlin with G), 421–6, 430 (and Yvonne de Lestrange), 432–5, 437, 441 (directing films), 442, 448 (*Mam'zelle Nitouche*), 450 (*Fanny*), 453–4, 468, 474, 484, 489, 491, 503 (*Les Amants terribles*), 505, 522 (and Nadine Vogel), 526 (leaves Vaneau), 529 (m. Nadine Vogel), 536, 538, 543, 570, 594 (divorce), 596 (to Lake Garda with G), 597 (and Vadim), 609 and 611 (film on G), 615, 619 (d.), 621, 624
Allégret, Paul (Marc's uncle), 307
Allégret, Suzanne (w. of Elie), 297, 299, 307
Allégret, Valentine (Marc's sister), 296

Allégret, Yves (Marc's brother; and wife Renée), 296, 451, 454, 468 477, 507, 538, 541, 599 (projected film of Les Caves)

Altermann, Abbé, 387

Althusser, Louis, 48, 633

Amalfi, 142, 143 (in Les Nourritures), 183 (in L'Immoraliste), 518

Ambresin, Emile (Armand Bavretel in Si le grain), 38–9, 43

Amélie-les-Bains, 294

Amiel, Henri-Frédéric, 47

Amrouche, Jean (and broadcast interviews with G), 598–9, 603, 605, 608–9, 617

Amsterdam, 72, 526

Anciens Combattants (veterans' organization), 547–8 (and G at Nice), 617 (at funeral)

Ancona, 151

Andermatt, 254

Andreae, Dr, 100–1, 105–6, 142, 218–19

Angelico, Fra, 256, 284

Angers, 219

Anglès, Auguste, 260

Annecy, 364, 366

Antée, 219, 225–6

Antoine, André, 154, 217 (G sees his Wild Duck and Julius Caesar), 264

Antwerp, 72, 339, 445, 477

Apollinaire, Guillaume (né Wilhelm Apollinaris Kostrowitzky), 271 (and Lafcadio)

Arabian Nights (Thousand and One Nights), 13–14, 33, 84, 88, 93, 135, 438

Aragon, Louis, xv, 328, 457, 466, 468, 479–80, 492, 495, 503, 506–7, 566–7, 574, 576

Arcachon, 62, 418, 436

Arche, L', 559, 561–2, 598 (Notes sur Chopin)

Archer, William, 264 (Play-making, a Manual of Craftsmanship)

Arco, 151, 163

Arden of Faversham, 605

Arduini, 475–6, 518

Arezzo, 100

Argelès, 237

Aristotle, 375 (and Corydon)

Art et la vie, L', 138

Artek (élite holiday camp, USSR), 500–1

Ascona, 586–7

Ashcroft, Peggy, 585 (Ophelia, Brussels)

Asquith, Elizabeth, 249

Assisi, 100, 151

Association des Ecrivains et Artistes Révolutionnaires, 455

Astier, Marie-Hélène d' (née Copeau), 523, 586

Aswan (Egypt), 577

Athenaeum Club, London, 249, 260–1 (G stays)

Athens, 533

Athman, 95, 101, 106, 121–4, 135, 143 (in Les Nourritures), 167–8, 172, 176, 193, 569 (d.), 624

Audierne, 214–15

Augustine of Hippo, St, 44

Aurenche, Jean, 574 (film of Symphonie Pastorale)

Auric, Georges, 433, 544, 574, (music for Symphonie Pastorale)

Auriol, Vincent, 611

Aurore, L', 150, 171

Austen, Jane, 245–7 (Northanger Abbey and Isabelle), 424 (Pride and Prejudice), 573 (Emma)

Avignon, 601 (Vilar's production of Oedipe at Festival)

Azous, 168

Babel, Isaac, xvi, 478, 494

Bach, J. S., 45, 56, 77, 106 (Well-Tempered Clavier, Art of Fugue), 149, 203 (Well-Tempered Clavier), 285 (St Matthew Passion), 372 (ballet Gigue), 441 (chorale preludes)

Baden-Baden, 425

Bad-Kissingen (Ger.), 202

Bagnols-sur-Grenade (Rouart's property), 223, 226–7, 237, 243, 250, 259, 294, 297–8

Bailly (Fr. publisher), 62, 108 (Paludes), 126

Bakst, Léon, 302

Ballets Russes, see Diaghilev

Balzac, Honoré de, 71, 81, 82 (Le Cousin Pons), 138 (Les Paysans), 276, 343–4

(Proust compared with *Comédie Humaine*), 398, 473

Bamako (W. Afr.), 521

Bangui (Equat. Afr.), 403–4

Banyuls, 294

Barbey d' Aurevilly, Jules, 96

Barbieri, 518

Barbusse, Henri, 479–80

Bärmann-Fischers (Samuel Fischer), 452

Barnabé (child on Cuverville estate), 363

Barrault, Jean-Louis, 552, 569 (*Antoine et Cléopâtre*, G's trans.), 578 (*Le Procès*, G's trans. of *The Trial*), 584 (opens at Marigny with G's trans. of *Hamlet*), 586 (*Le Procès*), 590, 599 (projects), 605

Barrès, Maurice, xiii, 3, 67–8, 72, 105, 130, 220 (enters Acad. Fr.), 527, 578

Barsacq, André, 460 (*Perséphone*)

Barthes, Roland, 48, 113, 632

Barthou, Louis, 265

Bassermann, Dieter, 278–9

Bastia, 444

Batna (Tunisia), 168

Batumi (USSR), 499–500

Baty, Gaston, 551–2

Baudelaire, Charles, 69, 72, 328 (G's preface to edition of *Les Fleurs du Mal*), 352, 592

Bauer, Abel (son of Henry), 37–8

Bauer, Henry (G's tutor, 'M. Richard' of *Si le grain*), 37–41, 44, 47–8

Baya Yangéré (Equat. Afr.), 406

Bayonne, 194

Bayreuth, 101

Beaumont, Comte Etienne de, 371–2 ('Les Soirées de Paris')

Beck, Christian, 171

Beerbohm, Max, 194

Beethoven, Ludwig van, 45, 96, 203, 329 (in *Symphonie Pastorale*)

Beirut, 578, 584

Bell, Clive, 278 (G reads *Art*), 282

Bell, Julian (Virginia Woolf's nephew), 518 (killed in Spain)

Bell, Marie, 569 (Cléopâtre)

Bellelettriens, Les (Daniel Simond and *Les Caves*), 460, 462, 605

Bellini, Vincenzo, 222

Belsen, 571

Ben Barka (Meriem's cousin), 98

Bennett, Arnold, 251 (Copeau sees), 254–5, 263, 265, 275 (on *Les Caves*), 285, 290, 310, 312, 339, 426 and 439 (*Old Wives' Tale*), 441 (d.)

Béraud, Henri, 366 (attack on G and *NRF*), 369 (attack on G), 379, 544, 563 (executed)

Berenson, Bernard, 518

Bergson, Henri, 226 (*L'Evolution créatrice*)

Berl, Emmanuel (and wife), 542

Berlin, 202, 224 (production of *König Candaules*), 346–7 (and homosexuality), 419–20 (with Marc), 434–5 (with Marc), 445, 450, 452–3, 462 (to see Goebbels), 568

Bernardbeig, Alain (G's nephew), 171, 180, 313 (d.)

Bernardbeig, Charles (Valentine Rondeaux's first husband), 137, 180

Berners, Gerald (Lord), 588

Berthelot, Philippe, 280

Biarritz, 194

Bibesco, Prince Antoine, 249–50, 259, 263

Bibliothèque de l'Occident, 221 (pub. *Le Retour de l'Enfant prodigue*)

Bidou, Henry, 365, 399 (on *Faux-Monnayeurs*)

Billy, André, 399 (on *Faux-Monnayeurs*)

Bing, Suzanne, 334, 386–7 (conversion), 603

biography, xvii, 633

Biskra (Algeria), 93, 95–6, 101, 107, 120, 122, 124–5, 128, 135–6, 176–8, 183 and 185 (in *L'Immoraliste*), 204–5, 269, 340, 569

Blake, William, 247 (G translator of), 282 and 289 (the devil and *Marriage of Heaven and Hell*), 353 (G's trans. of *Marriage of Heaven and Hell*), 360, 629 (translations)

Bizet, Georges, 296 (*Carmen*)

Blackwell's bookshop, Oxford, 589

Blanche, Jacques-Emile, 173 ('André Gide and his friends', Exposition Universelle, 1900), 174, 180, 189–90, 194, 199, 279

Blanchot, Maurice, 621

Blida (Algeria), 116, 121

Blum, Léon, 51, 54, 70, 146 (on *Les Nourritures* in *Revue Blanche*), 162–3 (literary editor of *Revue Blanche*), 173, 490–1 (forms Popular Front govt), 506 (govt falls), 513, 516, 522 (forms new govt), 575 (back from Buchenwald), 599

Bocquet, Léon, 234

Bodempéré (Equat. Afr.), 405

Boileau, Nicolas, 29

Boisdeffre, Pierre de, xviii, 17

Boleslavskaya, Bola, 498

Bologna, 132–3

Bolshevo (model prison, USSR), 494–5

Bône (Algeria), 166–7

Bonheur, Raymond, 155, 164, 170 (projected opera of *Le Retour de l'Enfant prodigue*)

Bonn, 590

Bonnard, Pierre, 226 (G buys one of his paintings), 255

Bonnier, Louis (architect of Villa Montmorency), 217, 223

Bordeaux, 203, 212, 219, 295, 384, 402, 408–9, 521, 541

Bormes, Var (Mayrischs' property), 335, 384, 413, 472, 515

Borodin, Alexander, 312 (*Prince Igor*, Diaghilev, London, 1918)

Bossuet, Jacques, 44, 245, 287, 301, 368 (*Histoire des Variations*), 403

Bost, Pierre, 574 (scenario for film of *Symphonie Pastorale*)

Boulay (farm-hand at La Roque), 156–7

Boulenger, Marcel, 234

Boulez, Pierre, 585

Bou-Saada (Algeria), 203

Bousquet, Joë, 542

Boutelleau, Gérard (and wife, Hope), 556–7

Brahms, Johannes, 79, 96

Brancovan, Prince Constantin de (brother of Anna de Noailles), 276

Brandes, Georg, 68

Braque, Georges, 372 (ballet *Salade*)

Brasillac, Robert, 563 (executed)

Braunberger, Pierre, 435

Brazzaville (Equat. Afr.), 402, 407

Bréal, Auguste, 438, 488

Brecht, Bertolt, 479

Breitenstein, Jules, 299

Breitenstein, Sarah, 300, 304–5

Breton, André, 328–9, 372, 480, 544

Briançon, 436–7

Briand, Aristide, 219

Bridgeman, Laura, 329 (and *Symphonie Pastorale*)

Brighton, 260

Brontë, Emily, 138 (*Wuthering Heights*)

Brooke, Rupert, xiv, 274, 279, 283–4 (affair with Beth), 289 (and Raverat), 295 and 336 (and Beth)

Browne, Sir Thomas, 250 (*Religio Medici*)

Browning, Robert, 282, 353, 357 (*Ring and the Book*), 368

Bruges, 72, 248, 291, 334

Brun, Antoine (Néné, 'le petit Henri B.'), 436–7, 439–40, 441–2

Brunard, Charles ('Charlot'), 346, 442–3

Brussels, 72, 339, 346, 419, 446 (*Oedipe*), 585 (G and Petite Dame, 1946)

Buchenwald, 575 (role of Communists in)

Buffon, George-Louis, 29

Bukharin, N. I., xvi, 473 (and United Front), 493 ('show trial'), 522

Bulgakov, M. A., 496

Bulganin, Nikolai, 493

Bursa, 276

Busoni, Feruccio, 441

Bussy, Dorothy (*née* Strachey; and husband Simon), xiv, xviii, 94, 154 (trans. of *Saül*), 228 (and *Strait is the Gate*), 310–11 (G meets), 313, 320–1, 334, 336–41, 343, 345–6, 349, 357–8, 360 (and G's sexuality), 361, 364, 366–8, 370–1, 373, 381–2, 399 (trans. of *Faux-Monnayeurs*), 405, 413–14, 420–2, 425–6, 428, 431, 433–4, 442, 447–9, 451, 456, 458, 462, 463–5 (and *Olivia*), 467, 514, 516, 518–19, 526, 528–9, 538–9, 541, 553–4, 556–7, 564, 567, 570–1, 573–4, 583 (and *Thésée*), 585, 588–9, 594, 598, 600–1 (pub. of French trans. of *Olivia*; French film of, with Edwige Feuillère), 602, 619, 625

Bussy, Janie (d. of Simon and Dorothy), 585, 589, 598, 603, 614

Cabris (nr Grasse), 443–4, 467, 471, 485, 504, 513, 515, 530, 536–9, 543, 545–6, 549, 559, 574, 578, 584, 596, 598, 602, 609
Cacavelli, Dr, 403
Caccioppoli, Prof., 576
Café Royal, London, 310
Café Voltaire, Paris, 67
Cahiers de la Pléiade, 578
Cailleux, Roland, 541
Cairo, 576
Calvi, 436, 444
Cambridge, xiv, 267, 274, 279, 289, 308, 310–12, 320, 331, 336
Camus, Albert, 273, 564, 568–9, 570 (at Vaneau), 585, 618
Cannabis indica (and hashish), 100, 179
Cannes, 36, 115, 254–5
Cap d'Antibes, 543
Capri, 134
Caracous (Karagoz, marionette theatre, Tunis), 134
Caraman-Chimay, Princesse de, 240
Carantec, 307
Caravaggio, Michelangelo, 475 (paintings in and around Rome)
Carrington, Dora, 447
Cartegena, 169, 203
Caruso, Enrico, 296 (in Carmen)
Casablanca, 365, 521
Céline, Louis-Ferdinand, 563
Cellini, Benvenuto, 100 (Perseus, Florence)
Centaure, Le, 138 (pub. El Hadj)
Cervantes, Miguel de, 237
Chablis, 411
Chad, Lake (Equat. Afr.), 404
Chadburne, Capt., 558
Chaliapin, F. I., 236
Chamberlain, Neville, 529 (Munich accords)
Champel (Switz.), 101–2
Chardonne, Jacques, 546
Charing Cross Hotel, London, 260

Chartres, 387
Chateaubriand, F. R., 189, 214 (grave at Saint-Malo)
Chatto & Windus, 228 (and La Porte étroite)
Chauffier, Martin, 160 (on Philoctète)
Chautemps, Camille, 466
Chekhov, Anton, 343 (G reads stories in Eng.), 354 (G sees Uncle Vanya)
Chevalier, Maurice, 584
Chiusi, 263
Chopin, Frédéric, 45–6, 56, 59, 96, 106, 236, 292, 411, 556, 611
Churchill, W. S., 542
Citrine, Walter, 517 (on USSR)
Claudel, Paul, 456, 488, 576, 603, 606 (G and), 623
Clemenceau Georges, 150 (editor L'Aurore during Dreyfus Aff.), 284
Clementi, Muzio, 96
Clermont (RMG's property), 342
Cocteau, Jean, 259, 268, 275 (on Les Caves), 278, 281, 302, 323–6 (G's open letter to and Marc), 335 (and Marc), 342 (Parade), 372, 390, 433, 443, 544, 596
Collège de France, 184–5 (in L'Immoraliste), 226
Cologne, 590
Colpach, Château de (Mayrischs' property, Luxembourg), 339, 346–7, 351, 354, 358, 368, 420, 521, 530
Columbia University (USA), 594 and 596 (G and honorary doctorate)
Combat, 568, 596, 618
Combelle, Lucien, 526
Comédie-Française, 546 (and Copeau), 574 (and Barreau), 605–6, 616
Communism (and Marxism, USSR), xv–xvii, 444–7, 450–9, 461 (World Conference of Youth Against War and Fascism, Revolutionary Students' International, meeting Salle Bullier, 1933), 463 (meeting, Salle Wagram, 1934), 466 (birth of Popular Front), 467 (and Thaelmann), 468 (meeting of Association des Ecrivains et Artistes révolutionnaires, 1934), 468–9 (at holiday camp), 472–3 (meeting, Palais de

la Mutualité, 1934 and change of line), 473 (Soviet régime and homosexuals), 477 (G as Communist attacked by Catholics), 478–81 (International Writers' Conference in Defence of Culture, Paris, 1935 and United Front; G's speech), 481 (boulevard Maxim-Gorki, Villejuif), 482–4 (Soviet legislation on homosexuality), 485–6 (meeting, Salle Wagram, 1935), 486 (Young Communists of 7th arrondissement), 488 (USSR and homosexuality), 490 (life in USSR), 492 (and Gorky), 502–3 (Stalin and Spain), 503 (Trial of Sixteen), 505 (G, USSR and homosexuality), 506 (USSR and Spain), 508–10, 513, 516–17 (*Retouches*), 522 (Bukharin trial), 534 (Ger. Communists in France), 561–3 and 566–7 (*épuration*), 575 (Soviet post-war strategy), 624–5, 628 (*Littérature engagée*), 633

Concise Oxford Dictionary, 407

Condorcet, Lycée (Paris), 213, 249, 259, 549

Connolly, Cyril, 399 (*Faux-Monnayeurs*), 588

Conque, La, 70

Conrad, Joseph, 249, 250 (*End of the Tether*), 251 (Copeau sees), 254, 257, 260 (G visits), 275 (on *Les Caves*), 296 (G trans. of *Victory* and *Typhoon*), 401 (*Heart of Darkness*)

Constant, Benjamin, 189, 392 (*Adolphe*)

Constantine (Algeria), 135, 176

Constantinople, 276, 427, 430

Contemporary Review, The, 238 (Gosse's rev. of *Porte étroite*)

Cooper, Sir Alfred Duff and Lady Diana, 572

Copeau, Edwige (Edi, d. of Jacques and Agnès), 358 (and Madeleine G), 593

Copeau, Jacques (and wife Agnès), xiii, xix, 79, 88, 146 (and *Les Nourritures*) 213–14, 223–7, 233–4, 240–1, 243–4, 247–51, 253, 255–7, 259–60, 261 (starts Vieux Colombier), 263–5 (VC opens), 268, 276–80, 282, 284–5, 291, 293, 295–6 and 300 (in New York), 313, 317 (the marriage), 321–2 (return from USA), 334, 343, 355 (and *Saül*), 357 (and

Catholicism), 361, 383–4 (on Rivière's death), 386 (end of VC), 387 (return to Catholicism), 411, 416, 425, 437–8, 451, 456, 460 (and *Perséphone*), 516, 523, 546 (Com.-Fr.), 551, 556, 565, 570, 603 (d.)

Copeau, Pascal (s. of Jacques and Agnès), 520, 523, 546, 565

Coppée, François, 195

Coppet, Marcel de, 266, 381, 405–7, 426, 431–2 (relations with RMG), 486, 521, 564, 571

Coquelin, Jean, 203

Coquillatville (Mbandaka, Belg. Congo), 402

Corneille, Pierre, 422

Couperin, François, 45

Couve, Pastor, 46

Couvreux, Emmanuel, 318 (and *NRF* book publishing)

Coward, Noël, 503 (*Private Lives*)

Coxyde-les-Bains (Belg.), 380

Craig, Edward Gordon, 264, 284–5

Crès, G., 64

Cruppi, Jean, 225

Curtius, Ernst Robert, 346–7, 357, 384, 416–17, 429, 441, 446, 450, 519, 590

Curzon Hotel, London, 249

Cuverville (see under Gide, André, homes)

Dabit, Eugène, 489, 491, 499, 501, 503 (Hôtel du Nord and funeral)

Dadaists, 151 and 273 (and *Les Caves*), 372 (split, Surrealists)

Daily Telegraph, 249 (G advertises for room in London)

Dakar (Senegal, Afr.), 402, 521

Daladier, Edouard, 466

Dana, Emile, 425, 427, 430

D'Annunzio, Gabriele, 171, 234, 241

Dante Alighieri, 56, 171, 237

Darmstadt, 450 (*Oedipe*)

Dasté, Marie-Hélène ('Maiène', *née* Copeau and husband Jean), 551–2 (and Catherine G), 565, 585

Daudet, Léon, 236, 351

Daudet, Lucien, 268, 351

Davet, Yvonne, 140 (notes on *El Hadj*),

146–7, 590–2 (*Autour des Nourritures terrestres*), 599, 604, 607–11, 616, 625

Debussy, Claude, xii, 49, 68, 86, 101 (*Les Chansons de Bilitis*), 193 *Pelléas et Mélisande*), 262 (*Jeux*, ballet, Diaghilev)

Defoe, Daniel, 247 and 250 (*Robinson Crusoe*)

Degas, Edgar, 102

de Gaulle, Charles, 542–3, 558–9 (meets G in Algiers), 561, 562 (Liberation of Paris), 570 (victory broadcast 1945), 575 (prime minister)

Déhais, Francis, 435–6

Delacroix, Ferdinand, 45, 116

Delaunay, Jean, 333 (*Symphonie Pastorale*)

Delay, Jean, xviii, 2, 31, 160–1 (on *Le Prométhée*), 231 (on *Porte étroite*), 599, 613

Delouarmol, M., 282 (Foyer Franco-Belge)

Démarest, Albert (G's cousin), 18, 41–2, 45, 52, 57, 77, 94, 98, 102, 131, 138, 213, 219 (d.)

Démarest, Claire (*née* Roundeaux, G's aunt), 18, 37–8, 41–2, 114, 138, 156

Démarest, Isabelle (G's cousin, m. Edouard Widmer), 102

Démarest, Maurice (G's cousin), 5, 56, 131, 138

Denis, Maurice, 84 (illustrates *Le Voyage d'Urien*), 217 (his *Hommage à Cézanne* in Villa Montmorency), 219

Denoël, Jean, 559

Derain, André, 372 (ballet, *Gigue*)

Derrida, Jacques, 48

Desaunez, Armand (estate manager, La Roque), 137, 157, 175 (replaces G as mayor)

Descartes, René, 51, 561

Deschodt, Eric, xviii

Desjardins, Paul (and wife), 243, 250, 252, 257, 313 (s. killed), 364, 411, 476, 526, 536 (d.)

Detskoye Zelo (USSR), 496

Deyverdun, Georges, 383

Diaghilev, Sergei (and Ballets Russes), 236 (Paris, 1909), 242 (Paris, 1910), 262 (Paris, 1913), 278 (Paris, 1914), 300, 312 (London, 1919), 342 (*Parade*)

Dickens, Charles, 82 (*Martin Chuzzlewit*), 88 (*Little Dorrit*), 104, 116–17 (*Barnaby Rudge*), 175 (*Our Mutual Friend*), 257 (*Oliver Twist*), 329 (*Cricket on the Hearth* and *Symphonie Pastorale*), 332 (*American Notes* and *Cricket. . .*), 398, 473, 559 (*David Copperfield*)

Dickinson, Goldsworthy Lowes, 311 (G meets, Cambridge, 1918)

Dieppe, 194

Dietz, M., 53, 70

Dimitrov, Georgi, 461–3 (protest meeting against arrest), 485, 493

Dinard, 214–15

Dindiki (sloth), 405, 408

Diodorus Siculus, 375 (and *Corydon*)

Domela, Harry, 504 (*Der Falsche Prinz*), 515–16, 533–4, 590 (Munich youth rally, 1947)

Donatello, 133 (*David*, Florence), 133, 220 (*John the Baptist*, Berlin), 257

Donne, John, 127 ('A Valediction: Forbidding Mourning')

Dos Passos, John, 465 (*Manhattan Transfer*)

Dostoevsky, Fyodor, 71, 138 (*Idiot, Brothers Karamazov*), 237, 243 and 247 (*Brs Karam.*), 251 (Copeau's version of *Brs Karam.*), 271 (Raskolnikov and *Les Caves*), 272, 276 (Copeau's version of *Brs Karam.*), 342 (and G), 352–3, 360, 369, 398 (*Brs Karam.*)

Douala (Equat. Afr.), 408

Douarnenez, 215

Doucet, Jacques, 318 (and *Corydon*), 604 (Bibliothèque D)

Douglas, Lord Alfred, 1, 76, 100, 116–20 (at Blida), 148, 308 (*Oscar Wilde and Myself*), 344, 348

Doumergue, Gaston, 466

Doyle, Arthur Conan, 559

Dresden, 202

Dreyfus Affair, 3, 78, 150–1, 156, 162 (and *Le Prométhée*), 236

Drieu La Rochelle, 468, 545–7, 562–3

Drioton, Abbé, 576

Drouin, Dominique ('Domi', G's nephew), 154–6 (b.), 313, 388, 523 (inherits Cuverville), 538 (called up), 541, 546, 571,

609 (film about G), 611, 617–19 (G's funeral)

Drouin, Jacques (G's nephew; and wife Ghisa), 226 (b.), 459 (engaged), 522, 618–19 (G's funeral)

Drouin, Jeanne (née Rondeaux, G's cousin and sister-in-law), 23–4 (and G), 34, 52, 115, 137–8 (and Marcel Drouin), 142, 148, 149 (m. Marcel Drouin), 154–5 (birth of Dominique), 212–13, 219, 226 (birth of Jacques), 243, 282, 434, 546, 564, 572 (sees G again, 1945)

Drouin, Marcel (G's brother-in-law), 51–2, 54 (Journal des Inconnus), 70 (La Conque), 73, 79, 87, 91, 102–3, 132–4, 137, 142, 148–9 (marries Jeanne), 154, 163–4 (and Nietzsche), 176, 178, 181, 201 (at Weimar), 213, 219, 225–6 (and Ghéon), 233, 237 (and Corydon), 243, 254 (and NRF), 256–7 (strained relations with G), 260, 263, 297, 322–3 (and NRF), 348, 370 (and Corydon), 388, 434, 528, 546, 556, 564 (d.)

Drouin, Odile (G's niece), 564

Dubois, André, 534, 539

Du Bos, Charles, xiv, 258–9, 282, 291, 325, 344, 353, 357, 383, 467

Duchamp, Marcel, 394–5 (and Faux-Monnayeurs)

Duchesne, Jacques, 572

Ducoté, Edouard, 132, 165, 176, 219

Dudelange (Mayrischs' property, Luxembourg), 319–20, 327 ('le club'), 334, 348

Duhamel, Georges, 565–6, 573

Dujardin, Edouard, 68

Dullin, Charles, 248, 261, 265

Dumas, fils, 81

Dumont-Wilden, Louis, 233

Duncan, Isadora, 236 (Paris, 1909), 250 (London, 1911)

Duncan, Raymond, 354

Dupouey, Pierre-Dominique, 285–7 (and Ghéon), 306 (G's preface to Letters of), 318 (NRF pubs. letters)

Durec, Arsène, 261

Duse, Eleonora, 217, 251, 264 (and NRF)

Eala (Belg. Congo), 402–3

Echo de Paris, L', 72

Ehrenburg, Ilya, xv, 451–2, 473, 479–80, 482–4 and 488–9 (and G's Soviet visit), 505–6 (and Retour de l'U.R.S.S.), 517 (condemns G), 567

Einstein, Albert, 456

Eisenstein, Sergei, xvi, 494 (meets G in USSR)

Elche (Sp.), 241

Eliot, George, 81, 90, 104, 364 (Middlemarch)

Eliot, T. S., 239 (French lessons from Alain-Fournier), 494, 570

El Kantara (Algeria), 123–4, 135, 167–8, 185 (in L'Immoraliste), 569

Ellmann, Richard (Oscar Wilde), 116

El Melrhir (chott or salt lake, Algeria), 140 (El Hadj)

Eluard, Paul, 545, 576

Emeis, Harald, 463 (Dorothy Bussy's Olivia)

En Barka, 98

Entretiens politiques et littéraires, 75

Ephesus, 277

Erasmus, 411

Erichson, Jurt, 527–8

Erlanger, Camille, 195

Ermitage, L', 132, 143, 157–8, 160–2 (Le Prométhée), 165, 169–72, 176, 178, 180, 197–8, 214 (G and Gourmont take over), 219, 225–6, 234

Etiemble, 577

Etretat, 131 (G's wedding), 148

Eulenburg Scandal, 373

Euripides, 134

Exposition Universelle, 124 and 172–3 (1900), 516 (1937)

Fabulet, Louis, 274

Fadiman, Clifton, 399 (on Faux-Monnayeurs)

Fascism, see Mussolini

Fasquelle (Fr. publishers), 259

Faulkner, William, 494

Faus, Keeler, 571

Faustin, 359

Fayette, Mme de la, 392 (Princesse de Clèves)

Fernandez, Ramon, 468

Ferrari, Pastor, 151 (on Les Nourritures)

Feuillère, Edwige, 601 (*Olivia*)
Fez, 449, 478, 559
Fichte, J. G., 81, 104
Fielding, Henry, 250 (*Tom Jones*), 271 (heroes
and Lafcadio), 397 (and *Faux-Monnayeurs*)
Fiesole, 143 (in *Les Nourritures*)
Figaro, Le, 131, 592
Film Parlant Français (FPF), 435
Flaubert, Achille (Gustave's b.), 7
Flaubert, Gustave, 53, 56–7, 259, 398
(*L'Education sentimentale*)
Florence, 100–1, 115, 133, 142, 143 (in *Les
Nourritures*), 236, 255–6, 258, 261, 274,
284, 334–5, 518
'Folle de Saint-Etienne', 433, 435
Fongueusemare, 215
Fontaine, Abbé, 253, 274
Fontaine, Arthur, 215, 219–20
Fontainebleau, 515
Ford, John, 559
Formentin, Château de (Normandy), 169,
244–5 (Château de la Quartfourche in
Isabelle)
Foroumbala (Equat. Afr.), 404
Forster, E. M., 479, 588
Forster-Nietzsche, Elisabeth (Nietzsche's
d.), 202 (meets G, Weimar, 1903)
Fort, Paul, 165
Fort Archambault (Equat. Afr.), 505
Fort d'Antibes, 539
Fort-Lamy (Equat. Afr.), 405–6
Forum, 422 and 428 (trans. of *Ecole des femmes*)
Foucault, Michel, 48, 110
Foyer Franco-Belge, xiv, 282–3, 285, 367,
467
France, Anatole, 68, 380
Francis, Claude, 547
Francis Ferdinand, Archduke, 278
Franc-Nohain, Maurice, 52
Franco, General Francisco, 497
Frankfurt-am-Main, 590
Freemasons, 269 (and *Les Caves*)
Freud, Sigmund (and psychoanalysis), 289,
345–6 (*NRF* pubs. *Three Essays on the
Theory of Sexuality*), 348, 353 (G and), 633
Friends of the USSR, 457
Fromentin, 81

Fry, Roger, 312 (G meets), 381 (G meets at
Chartres)
Fuchow, 215 (Claudel and Ysé)

Gallimard (publishing house), *see under
Nouvelle Revue Française*
Gallimard, Claude (s. of Gaston), 542, 615
Gallimard, Gaston, 249 (founding of *NRF*
book publishing company), 254, 259–60
(and Proust), 261, 263–4 (founding of
Vieux Colombier), 266, 296, 318
(disagreements with G), 322 (internal
divisions in *NRF*), 384 (Rivière's
funeral), 542, 544, 546–7 (under Ger.
occupation), 615–16 (G's death)
Gallimard, Raymond, 318 (and *NRF* book
publishing)
Galsworthy, John, 257
Ganderax, Louis, 234
Garden, Mary, 196 (Mélisande), 217
Garnett, Constance, 343 (Chekhov's stories)
Gauclère, Yassu, 577
Gauguin, Eugène, 53, 470
Gautier, Jean-Jacques, 612 (on *Les Caves*)
Gautier, Théophile, 170
Gay, Rita, 148
Geneva, 100, 106, 132, 142, 446 (*Oedipe*)
Genoa, 100, 597–8
Gentile, Mme (and son François, 'Victor'
of *Journal*), 555
George, Stefan, 68, 226, 347, 558
Gérin, Louis, 477
Gertler, Marc, 312 (G meets)
Ghent, 72
Ghéon Henri, xiii (and G), 146 (on *Les
Nourritures*), 147 (*Chansons d'Aube*), 155–7
(at La Roque), 165–7 (*L'Ermitage; aventures
with G*), 170–1 (*L'Ermitage*), 175–6 (*piscines
and aventures with G*), 176–8 (with G in
N. Afr.), 189 (dedication of *L'Immoraliste
to*), 189–94 (*aventures with G*), 197 (*L'Eau-
de-Vie, Journal d'un médecin*), 198–201
(*aventures with G*), 204, 207 (medical
practice), 208–12 (G/Ghéon
correspondence and Maurice
Schlumberger 'affair'), 212–13
('Catholic writer'), 214–15 (*aventures on*

Channel coast), 218 ('rue O' baths),
222–3 (sees Strauss's *Salomé* with G),
224–5 (*L'Adolescent*), 226–7 (*aventures* at
Bagnols), 227–8 (*L'Adolescent* and *Corydon*),
232–3, 236 (on 'French genius'), 241–2,
244–5 (visits Formentin with G, *Isabelle*),
254 (*Nos Directions*), 255–6 (Florence),
258, 260, 261 (joins G in Florence),
262–3, 266 (RMG describes), 276
(*L'Eau-de-vie* at Vieux Colombier), 278,
280–2 (in ambulance service), 285–8
(conversion), 293, 299, 301, 305–6
(reaction to G and Marc Allégret),
321–3, 349 (in Action Française), 425 (*Les
Jeux de l'enfer et du ciel*), 523 (Madeleine
G's funeral), 529, 564 (d.), 569, 623 (his
Catholicism and G)
Ghirlandaio, Domenico, 133
Gibbon, Edward, 383 (*Mémoires littéraires de
la Grande Bretagne*)
Gidal, Dr (photographer, 8th Army), 558
Gide, André:
    ancestors, 3–5, 7–8, 20–2
    anorexia, 602
    appendicitis, makes will, 382–3
    Association des Amis d'Andre' Gide, xvii
    astrology, 1–2
    Bible, xvi, 13–14, 59–60, 63, 81, 91–2,
        138–9 (*Songs of Songs*), 152 (and *Saül*),
        198 (and *Bethsabé*), 220–2 (*Retour de
        l'Enfant prodigue*), 228 (and *Porte
        étroite*), 274–5 (Claudel on
        homosexuality), 287–8 (and
        Ghéon), 290–1 (*Numquid. . .*), 313
        and 330–3 (and *Symphonie Pastorale*),
        535, 595 (and *Retour de l'Enfant. . .*)
    birth, 7
    compassion, 624–5
    curiosity, 622, 627–8
    death, on, 600
    'dualism', 1–3, 7–9, 66
    eightieth birthday, 603–4
    films, and, 475 (*42nd Street*), 488 (*Modern
        Times*), 490 (*A Night at the Opera*),
        576 (*L'Espoir, Zéro de conduite*), 585
        (*Les Enfants du Paradis*)
    homes: Commailles, 6 rue de (Paris), 37,

54, 80, 91, 114, 131, 137, 141;
    Cuverville (family property in Caux
    – La Morinière in *Porte étroite*), 21–2,
    91, 131, 137, 141, 149, 157, 169, 173–6,
    181, 191, 197–8, 201–2, 208, 211–14,
    219, 223–4, 226–7, 231, 237, 242–4,
    250, 256, 258, 260, 262–3, 278–9,
    282–3, 292–4, 296–7, 299, 301,
    305–8, 312–15, 319–22, 331, 334,
    338, 340, 342, 346–9, 351, 359–60,
    361–3 (RMG's visit), 366, 368, 370,
    380–1, 385, 409, 413, 416–20, 423–6,
    428, 434–5, 437, 441, 444, 446–7,
    449–53, 458–9, 463, 465–6, 472,
    474, 482–3, 489, 503–4, 515, 521–4,
    526, 528–9, 546, 554, 564, 572 (last
    visit 1945), 609, 615–17, 625; La
    Roque-Baignard, Château de
    (family property, Calvados – La
    Morinière in *L'Immoraliste*), 5, 20–2,
    29–30, 38, 50, 57, 66, 73, 75, 81–2,
    91, 102–3, 111, 126, 137 (G elected
    mayor), 148, 154–6, 164, 169–70,
    173–5, 184, 187, 193, 205, 217, 244,
    529, 554, 609; Médicis, rue de
    (Paris), 10; Raspail, 4 boulevard
    (Paris), 141, 172–4, 198, 200, 216;
    Raspail, 10 boulevard (Paris), 200;
    Salle-L'Evêque, rue (Montpellier),
    30; Tournon, rue de (Paris), 12–13,
    37; Vaneau, 1 bis rue (Paris), 303,
    414–16, 419, 421–3, 430–1, 433, 435,
    441, 444, 450, 453–4, 466, 481–2,
    484–5, 488–9, 513, 515, 521, 524,
    529–30, 559, 564, 570–3, 577–8,
    584–6, 591–2, 594–5, 598, 604,
    609–10, 612, 623–4; Villa
    Montmorency (avenue des
    Sycomores, Auteuil), 175 (buys land
    to build on), 199 (plans building),
    216, 217 (G moves in), 219, 223, 241,
    256, 266–7 (RMG's description of),
    284, 297, 299, 303, 319, 339–40
    (RMG describes), 341, 343, 345,
    348, 350, 354, 362, 368–9, 371–2,
    382–3, 288, 409, 411, 414–22, 588
    (G revisits)

'Index, the', xi, 602
letters, Madeleine's burning of, 314–15
moustache, shaving of, 228, 332
Nobel Prize for Literature, xi, 16, 592–3,
    595–6, 608, 626
Oxford honorary doctorate, 587–9
piano playing, 15, 56, 59, 96, 99, 115, 175,
    203, 218, 235, 255, 420, 438
    (teaches Catherine), 556, 621
'the present', and the (past and future),
    621–2
religion, xi, xiv–xv, xvii, 7–9, 31, 35, 39,
    46, 59, 61, 64–5, 76, 78, 82, 88–9,
    91–2, 103 (Madeleine on *Cahiers
    d'André-Walter*), 104–5, 130, 138, 183
    and 187 (in *L'Immoraliste*), 196, 202
    (and art), 215–16 (and Claudel),
    221–2 (*Retour de l'Enfant prodigue*),
    237–8 (Gosse and *Porte étroite*),
    251–3, 256 (Ghéon in Florence), 273
    (Catholic reaction to *Les Caves*), 275
    (and *Les Caves*), 282 (J. Raverat and
    the devil), 285–8 (and Ghéon),
    288–91 ('dark night of the soul'),
    290–1, 297–8 (and devil), 305
    (Ghéon), 322–3 (Catholic attitude to
    G), 329–33 (*Symphonie Pastorale*),
    369–70 (Massis, Maritain), 376 (and
    Corydon), 438 (and Copeau), 457
    (Catholics), 458 (Catholic Church
    compared with CP), 476–7 (debate
    at Union pour la Vérité), 522
    (Madeleine and Catholicism), 535
    (with François Mauriac), 628, 631
    (Protestantism and *Porte étroite*), 637
    (and sincerity)
return to Paris, 570–1
rumour of death, 466
sale of signed copies of books, 385
schools: Mlle Fleur's, 15; Mlle
    Lackerbauer's, 15; Ecole
    Alsacienne, 16, 27–8, 33, 39, 44,
    47–50, 52; Lycée Henri IV, xiii,
    50–1; Lycée de Montpellier, 30–2;
    Pension Keller, 44, 46–7
sexuality (and love), 10–12, 16–17, 19 (the
    'Russian'), 35, 41, 44, 46, 50, 55,
59, 61–5, 66, 76, 81 (sexual
liberation in N. Afr.), 83
(Madeleine), 88 and 91–2 (and N.
Afr.), 94–5 (Ali), 96–8 (Mériem), 99
('la dame', Rome), 103 (Madeleine
on marriage), 103–4 (It. boatman,
Lake Como), 114 (Madeleine),
116–25 (at Blida, Algiers,
Mohammed), 128–30 (and
Madeleine), 131 (marriage), 152–3
(*Saül* – David and Jonathan), 155
(Trouville), 183 and 187 (in
L'Immoraliste), 196, 198–9 ('on the
boulevards'), 201, 208–13 (Maurice
Schlumberger), 214 (G 'confesses' to
Copeau), 217–18 (*piscines* and
boulevards), 218–19 (G sees Dr
Andreae), 238, 253 (and Claudel),
255 and 257 (in Florence), 258
(Bernardino, Acquasanta), 259
(Bagnols), 260 (homosexuality at
NRF and in Proust's work), 262
(Rome), 274 (Claudel on G's
homosexuality), 305 (Ghéon on G
and Marc), 309 (Madeleine on G),
309–13 (in Eng. with Marc), 314–15
(and Madeleine), 327 ('le club'),
335 (and Marc), 344–5 (G and
masturbation), 346 (paedophilia),
346–7 (Berlin and homosexuality),
347 (Boy Scouts at Colpach), 352
(and *Corydon*), 355 (Freud and
homosexuality), 355 (homosexuality
and *Saül*), 356 (Beth pregnant by
G), 359–60 (Scouts at Colpach), 360
(loved different people), 373–80
(*Corydon*), 420 (Berlin), 425 and 427
(Emile Dana), 436 (Corsica), 436–7
(Néné), 448–9 (RMG in Berlin), 459
(with Michelet's Boy Scouts), 474–5
(Rome), 488 and 505
(homosexuality in USSR), 531–3
(homosexuality in Egypt), 553 ('F'
in Tunis), 574 (post-war in Paris, It.
and N. Afr.), 576–7 (Egypt), 600–1
(Last on Klaus Mann and
homosexuality), 603–4 (RMG on

G's championing of homosexuals),
610 (Levesque on Morocco), 623,
626–7 (G's 'public' homosexuality)
sincerity (and Protestantism) and
contradictions, 633–4
travels (*see also under individual place names*):
Corsica, 367 (1923), 436 (1930), 444
(1931); Czechoslovakia, 469–70
(Karlovy Vary, 1934); Egypt, 531–3
(1939), 576–8 (1945–6, with
Levesque); England, 43 (1888,
with Elie Allégret), 227 (1908), 249
(1911, with Valery Larbaud), 260–1
(Christmas 1912–13), 308–13 (1918,
Cambridge, etc., with Marc),
338–9 (1920, and Wales, with Marc
and Beth), 401, 488–9 (1947,
Oxford); Equatorial Africa, 381–2,
385, 387–9, 401–10 (1925–6, with
Marc), 486 (1935, with Coppet), 521
(1938), 560 (1944, Gao, Mali);
Germany, 77–80 (1892, Munich), 91,
200–2 (1903, Weimar, etc.), 224–5
(prod. of *König Candaules*), 416 (1927,
Heidelberg), 419 (1927, Berlin, with
Marc), 425 (1929, Baden-Baden),
430–1 (Ger. trans. of works), 434–5
(1930, Berlin), 442 (1931, Munich,
Berlin), 445 (1931, Berlin), 450
(1932, Berlin), 452–3 (1932, Berlin),
590 (1947); Greece, 277 (1914), 533
(1939); Italy, 18, 99–101 (1894), 132–4
(1895–6, honeymoon), 142 (1897,
with Madeleine), 149–51 (1898 with
Madeleine), 235–6 (1909), 257–8
(1912), 261–2 (1913), 263 (1913), 274
(1914), 334–5 (1919, with Marc,
etc.), 348–9 (1921), 364 (1923), 465
(1934, Sicily), 467 (1934, It. Tyrol),
474–7 (1934–5), 518–19 (1937, with
Levesque), 576 (1945, Naples, with
Levesque), 596–8 (1948, Lake
Garda), 607–8 (1950, Taormina,
etc.); Netherlands, 72 (1891), 526
(1938, Amsterdam); North Africa,
93–9 (1893–4, with Paul Laurens),
104 (1894), 107–8 (effect of), 115–25

(1895, Algeria), 130, 134–6 (1896,
honeymoon), 143 (in *Les Nourritures*),
166–9 (1899, Tunisia, Algeria, with
Madeleine), 176–80 (1899–1900,
Algeria, Tunisia, with Madeleine
and Ghéon), 183–7 (in
L'Immoraliste), 203–5 (1903, partly
with Madeleine), 207 (*Renoncement
au voyage*), 364–6 (1923, Morocco),
367–8 (1923, Tunisia, with Marc),
411–12 (1926, Tunisia with Marc),
422 (1928, Tunisia), 423–4 (1929,
Algiers), 438–9 (1929, Tunisia, with
Beth), 449 (1932, Morocco), 552–8
(1942–3, Tunisia), 558–9 (1944,
Algiers), 559–60 (1944, Morocco),
560–9 (1944–5, Algiers); Spain, 88
(1893, with mother), 240–1 (with
Copeau), 243 (1910); Switzerland,
100–7 (1894), 132 (1896,
honeymoon), 142 (1897), 149 (1898),
185 (in *L'Immoraliste*), 219 (1906),
254 (1912), 416 (1927), 448 (1932,
Valmont), 462 (1933), 470 (1934,
Locarno, etc.), 514–15 (Christmas
1936–7, with Catherine), 584 (1946,
with Herbart), 486–7 (1947); Turkey,
276–7 (1914); USSR, 488–502
(1936)
women, G and, 625
works: *L'Affaire Redureau*, 628; *Ainsi soit-il*,
xviii, 43, 127, 612–13, 628; *Ajax*
(unfinished play), 222; *Amyntas*, 207;
Anthologie de la poésie française, 601;
Bethsabé, 198, 276, 632; *Cahier bleu*,
308–9; '*Cahier vert*' (*see Numquid et
tu*); *Les Cahiers d'André Walter* (*Alain,
Allain*), xii, 23, 35, 47, 50, 57–65, 67–8,
71–3, 85, 90, 103, 231, 628–9; *Carnets
d'Egypte*, 533; *Les Caves du Vatican*,
xii, 2, 109, 158, 170 (first sketches),
217 (makes notes for), 218, 225, 228,
233, 235, 238, 247–8, 250–1, 255–6,
258, 261, 269–76, 278–9, 305,
307–8, 328–9 (and Dadaists), 344,
351, 367, 369, 389, 392–3, 415, 428,
457 (projected Soviet film), 458

(serialized *L'Humanité*), 459–61
(dramatized by 'Art et Travail'),
599–602 (projected film), 605–7
and 610–12 (Com.-Fr. production),
631; *Corydon*, xv, 1, 10, 71, 227–8
(begins), 233, 237, 239, 242–3,
248–51, 292, 304, 306, 318–19,
334–5, 343, 346–7, 352–3, 366,
371–80, 385, 431, 452 (in Ger.), 576,
596 (Eng. trans. and Kinsey
Report), 599 (Barrault's idea for
film), 601 (Amer. ed., 1949), 603,
626, 628; *Découvrons Henri Michaux*,
548; 'De l'influence en littérature'
(lecture), 172; *Délivrance de Tunis*,
566; *Dostoïevski*, 366, 628; *L'Ecole des
femmes*, 137, 413, 422–3, 426, 427–9,
511–12, 630; *Ecrits intimes*, 291; *El
Hadj*, *138–40*, 161, 176–8, 632;
L'Essai de bien mourir (early version
of *La Porte étroite*), 228; *Et nunc manet
in te*, xviii, 47, 85, 129, 149, 168, 231,
314, 472, 524–5, 533, 584, 628; *Les
Faux-Monnayeurs*, xii, 39, 45, 111, 211,
231, 247, 282, 303, 327, 329, 333
(and Marc), 342 (compared with
RMG's *Les Thibault*), 347–50, 353,
360, 364, 367, 370–1, 380–3, 385
(pub. in *NRF*), *389–400*, 410, 428,
484, 513, 551 (and Catholics), 621–2,
628–9, 631–2; *Feuilles de Route*, 133,
191; *Les Feuillets*, 232, 288–90;
Geneviève, 434, 441, 449, 465, 467,
470, 487, 489, *510–13*, 560, 630;
L'Immoraliste, 21, 170 (first sketches),
175 (begins), *181–90*, 193 (pub.), 195,
197, 205, 213, 224, 230–2, 237, 273,
305, 328, 392, 603, 627, 630–1;
L'Importance du Public (Weimar
lecture, 1904), 202; *Incidences*, 328,
343, 379, 628; 'In Memoriam'
Mallarmé, 158; *Interviews Imaginaires*
(in *Le Figaro*), 547, 549; *Isabelle*,
169–70, 242, *244–7*, 248, 329, 392,
596 and 599 (film of), 630; *Journal
des Faux-Monnayeurs*, 326–7, 396–7,
428, 631–2; 'Lettres à Angèle',

157–8, 165, 171, 173, 200, 343 (on
Proust); *Littérature engagée*, 456, 628;
'Mané Thékel Pharès', 549; *La
Marche turque*, 278; *Montaigne*, 422,
628; *Morceaux choisis*, 351 (pub.),
485, 628; *La Mort de Mademoiselle
Claire* (early version of *La Porte étroite*),
228; *Notes sur Chopin*, 45–6, 441, 598
(pub.); *Les Nourritures terrestres*, xii, 65,
99, 101, 104, 112–13, 121, 132
('Ménalque, a fragment'), 137,
141–8, 151–2, 158–9, 167, 184, 213,
267, 285 and 306 (and Dupouey),
328, 369, 431, 485, 495 (sales),
578–9, 626–7, 629, 631; *Les Nouvelles
Nourritures*, 328, 426, 441, 482, *484–5*,
630; *Les Nouveaux Prétextes*, 207, 237,
628; *Numquid et tu*, xiv, 290–2, 332,
393, 485, 617, 628; *Oedipe*, 171, 426,
437–8, 445–7 (prod. by Pitoëf), 450,
601 (Vilar's prod., 1949), 605;
L'Offrande lyrique (trans. of Tagore's
The Gitanjali), 263; *Oscar Wilde*, 628;
Pages de Journal, 510, 560 (pub. 1945,
Algiers and New York); *Paludes*, 21,
90, 99, 103–4, *107–15*, 126, 130,
(pub.), 131 (compared with Sterne),
146, 157–8, 171, 213, 269, 273, 392,
394, 397, 497, 611–13; *Philoctète*, 104,
138, 148, 158, 160–4; *Les Poésies
d'André Walter*, 59, 75, 108, 629; *La
Porte étroite*, 5, 21–3, 29, 34–5, 47,
104 (*La Mort de Mademoiselle Claire*),
189, 194, 197, 213–14, 218, 222–5,
228–32, 233–4, 235, 237–8 (pub.),
329, 358, 366 (A. Knopf accepts),
392, 630–1; Preface to Eng. trans.
of *Les Liaisons dangereuses*, 536;
Prétextes, 117, 157, 172, 200, 628; *Le
Prométhée mal enchaîné*, 113, *158–60*,
269, 273, 320 (Lady Rothermere's
trans.), 392, 578–9, 583, 631–2;
Proserpine (*Perséphone*), 104, 170, 237
(opera), 457, 459–60 (Stravinsky
opera), 467 (prod.), 571 (Stravinsky);
'Réflexions sur quelques points de la
morale chrétienne', 138 (pub. in

L'Art et la Vie); Rencontres, 485; Le
Renoncement au voyage, 203, 207;
Retouches à mon Retour de l'U.R.S.S.,
503, 515, 516–18; Le Retour, 170
(projected opera), 584; Le Retour de
l'Enfant prodigue, 198, 220–2, 328, 361
(and Darius Milhaud), 369, 577
(dramatization, Alexandria), 632;
Retour de l'U.R.S.S., xi, xvi, 495, 498,
503–7, 508–10, 513–14, 566; Retour
du Tchad, 406–8, 417, 421; Robert
(L'Ecole des Maris), 426–7, 429,
511–12, 630; Robert, ou l'intérêt
générale (play), 470, 489, 533, 562; Le
Roi Candaule, 158, 170–1, 180–1
(prod. by Lugné-Poe), 198, 206, 216
(at Vienna Volkstheater, 1906), 220
and 224–5 (prod. Berlin); Saül, 148,
151–4, 159, 164, 165, 169, 198, 200,
206–7, 273, 355 (prod. at Vieux
Colombier), 442 (Ger. trans.), 599
(projected prod.); La Séquestrée de
Poitiers, 628; Si le grain ne meurt, xviii,
10–12, 21, 23–4, 29, 36, 44, 47, 54,
61, 91, 95, 103–4, 106, 108, 117, 122,
128, 292 (begins), 296–7, 334, 340,
343 (in NRF), 344, 346–8, 352, 366,
498, 603, 622, 627–8, 633; Souvenirs
de la Cour d'assises, 256, 263, 379,
457, 628; La Symphonie Pastorale
(L'Aveugle), 307, 313, 320, 328 (pub.
in NRF), 329–33, 389, 392, 428, 534
(Jap. film), 551, 574 and 584 (Fr.
film), 630; La Tentative amoureuse,
89–90, 91, 135, 139, 160–1, 629;
Thésée, 560, 578–83, 586, 632; Le
Traité du Narcisse, 71, 73–5, 109, 139,
161, 629; Voyage au Congo, xv, 401–6,
414, 417–19, 498, 521; Le Voyage
d'Urien, 71, 81 ('Voyage sur l'océan
pathétique'), 84–7, 108, 161, 201,
213, 328, 390, 629

youthfulness, 625–6

Gide, Anna (G's aunt, née Im Thurn), 149,
213

Gide, Catherine (G's daughter; m. Jean
Lambert), 365–7 (b. 1923), 366–8, 371,
381, 384, 408, 410–11, 413, 415, 417, 419,
422–5, 432, 438, 441, 444, 449, 453–4,
459, 467, 469, 471, 474, 481–2, 485–7,
489, 504, 514–16, 521, 523, 526, 527–9
(to Vienna, 1938), 530, 534, 538, 540,
547–51, 559, 563–4, 568–9 (b. of
Isabelle), 570, 578, 584 (m. J. Lambert),
586–7, 590 (b. of Nicolas), 592, 595, 598
(b. of Dominique), 603, 608, 611–13, 615,
617–19

Gide, Charles (G's uncle), 25, 30, 64, 77–8,
91, 114, 125, 131, 149, 208, 213, 219, 243,
259, 261, 280, 297, 447–8 (d.), 469

Gide, Clémence (G's grandmother, née
Granier), 25–6, 76, 92

Gide, Edouard (G's cousin), 208, 574, 584,
598

Gide, Jeanne (G's cousin), 214, 219,
619

Gide, Juliette (G's mother, née Rondeaux),
2, 4–7, 22, 24–5, 28–30, 32–3, 35–8,
40–2, 45, 50, 55–7, 61, 78, 80, 83, 88
(Seville), 91–2, 93, 96, 98, 102–3, 105,
107, 114–16, 118, 121–5, 126–7 (d. and
funeral), 129, 131, 569, 624

Gide, Madeleine (G's wife and cousin), xiii,
xv, 23–34, 46–7, 50, 52, 55, 57, 59, 62–3,
75, 77, 80–3, 85–7 (Emmanuèle in Cahiers
d'André Walter, Ellis in Voyage d'Urien), 91,
102–3, 107, 115, 121, 124–7, 128–30, 131–7
(G marries), 138, 140–1, 148–9, 150 (G's
reaction to death of), 165–70, 173
(accident), 176–80 (with G in N. Afr.),
183–8 (Marcelline in L'Immoraliste), 190,
196, 198, 201, 203–5, 211–12, 216–17,
219, 228, 231, 247, 255, 258, 260, 262,
274, 278–80, 283–4, 292–4, 296, 299,
305, 307, 313–14 (burns G's letters),
316–17, 319–20, 333, 337, 340, 342–3 (and
G), 345–6, 351, 357–60, 362–3 (G tells of
Beth's pregnancy), 368, 372–4 (and
Corydon), 381, 383, 385, 409, 416–17,
420–1, 434–5, 438, 446, 450–1, 459, 466,
472, 488, 519, 522–3 (d.), 524–5, 529, 549,
569, 572, 596, 615, 617, 619, 625, 631

Gide, Paul (G's father), 3–4, 6–7, 10, 13–15,
25–7, 28 (d.), 131

Gide, Paul (G's cousin, 'Gérard' of *Journal*), 193, 207–9, 220, 280, 284 (killed)

Gielgud, John, 585 (Hamlet, Brussels)

Gifford, Adrien, 40

Gilbert, Marcel (Valentine Rondeaux' second husband), 176, 193 (m. Valentine), 223 (d.), 549

Gilbert (Sellier, G's chauffeur), 599, 601, 605, 613, 615

Ginoles-les-Bains, 542

Giono, Jean, 545

Giorgione, 133 (*The Concert*)

Giotto, 256

Giovone (Communist, Algiers), 561

Giraudoux, Jean, 239, 422, 435

Godebska, Misia (m. 1. Thadée Natanson, 2. Alfred Edwards, 3. José–Maria Sert), 262, 278, 280, 307

Godebski, Cyprien ('Cipa'), 307

Goebbels, Joseph, 462

Goering, Hermann, 455

Goethe, J. W. von, 48, 50, 53, 79, 81, 87 (*Roman Elegies*), 91 (*Elective Affinities*), 96, 104–5, 110 (*Wilhelm Meister*), 125, 158 (*Prometheus*), 171–2, 186, 189, 202, 237 (*Hermann und Dorothea*), 375 (on *Knabenliebe*), 404, 406 (*Faust*), 452 (Goethe Medal), 465 (*Faust*, pt 2), 471 (and Rome), 542, 544, 549, 622

Gogol, N. V., 515 (*Dead Souls*)

Goldsmith, Oliver, 364 (*Vicar of Wakefield*)

Goncharov, I. A., 423 (*Oblomov*)

Goncourt, Prix, 267

Gori (USSR, Stalin's birthplace), 499

Gorky, Maxim, xv, 354 (G sees *Lower Depths*), 478, 480, 492–3 (G sees *Mother*, d.)

Gosse, Edmund, 206, 238 (reviews *Porte étroite*), 249–50, 257 (at Pontigny, 1912), 260 (G in London, 1912–13), 275 (on *Les Caves*), 308, 339, 379

Gould, Florence (and husband Frank), 601–2, 605–7, 616

Gould, Gerald, 399–400 (on *Faux-Monnayeurs*)

Gounod, Charles, 404

Gourmont, Remy de, 63, 214, 222

Gozzoli, Benozzo, 408 (*Wine Harvest*)

Granada (Sp.), 143 (garden in *Les Nourritures*)

Granados, Enrique, 441 (*Goyescas*)

Grant, Duncan, 214, 334, 343, 588

Granville-Barker, Harley, 277 (prod. *Twelfth Night*, 1913)

Grasse, 442, 598

Grasset, Bernard, 267

Grau du Roi, 243, 348

Graves, Robert, 573 (*I, Claudius*), 608

Green, Julien, 460, 544, 584, 616

Grenoble, 4

Gréoux-les-Bains, 425

Greve, Felix Paul, 442 (Ger. trans. of *Saül*)

Groethuysen, Bernard (and wife, Alix Guillain, 'les Groets'), 413, 430 (Ger. trans. *Les Nourritures*), 442 (Ger. trans. *Saül*), 454 (on Trotsky), 456 and 458 (urging G towards Communism), 461, 478, 481 (and Victor Serge), 490–1, 546 (ran Gallimard's Ger. list during war), 564, 584 (Bernard d.)

Grottamare, 257

Guilbert, Yvette, 195

Guilloux, Louis, 489, 491 (to USSR with G), 497, 499, 503–4 (and *Retour de l'U.R.S.S.*)

Haddou, Si (Guy Delon), 449, 559

Hafiz, 139 (and *El Hadj*)

Hague, The, 72

Hahn, Reynaldo, 268

Hammamet (Tunisia), 412, 422

Hamp, Pierre, 267, 365

Hamra (Equat. Afr.), 406

Handel, G. F., 372 (*Gigue*, ballet)

Hanotaux, Gabriel, 414

Hardekopf, Ferdinand (and Sita Staub), 518 (trans. of *Retouches*), 529, 539, 543–4

Hardy, Thomas, 250 (*Mayor of Casterbridge*), 282 (*Tess*, *Jude*), 320 (*Jude*), 436 (*Woodlanders*)

Harrison, Jane, 384

Hasenclever, Walter, 539

Hauptmann, Gerhart, 78

Hawthorne, Nathaniel, 368 (*Scarlet Letter*)

Hearn, Lafcadio, 271 (and *Les Caves*)

Hebbel, Friedrich, 225
Heffer's bookshop, Cambridge, 310
Heidelberg, 416
Heine, Heinrich, 48, 77
Hendaye, 212
Herbart, Pierre, 441–2 (moves in with Beth), 442 (*Le Rôdeur*), 443–4 (Cocteau and opium), 448 (*Contre-Ordre*), 456 (and Communism), 471–2 (and Marius), 482 (in Moscow, *International Review*), 484 (*Le Rôdeur* pub.), 489–502 (to USSR with G), 504–5 (changing views on USSR), 507–9 ('open letter' to G *re Retour de l'U.R.S.S.*), 513–15 (in Spain), 516 (*En U.R.S.S. 1936* pub.), 519, 521 (with G to W. Afr.), 540, 548, 550, 559 (returns to Paris), 564 (in Resistance), 568–9 (co-edits *Combat* with Camus), 571–5, 584–5 (at Barrault's *Hamlet*), 590, 593–4, 596 (leaves *Combat*, works on scenario of *Isabelle*), 597 (in Italy with G), 598–9 (at Vaneau), 600–2 (with G in S. of Fr.), 604–5 (on G, 'ageing of a great man'), 607–8 (in Sicily with G), 612–16 (G's last weeks), 618–19 (reaction to G's funeral), 628
Heredia, José Maria de, 67 and 69–70 (Saturday *salon*), 76, 79, 355–6
Herodotus, 170 (*Clio, Roi Candaule*)
Hérold, Ferdinand, 101
Herriot, Edouard, 410
Hesse, Hermann, 587
Heurgon, Jacques (and wife Anne), 561, 567, 568–9
Heyd, Richard, 584, 586–90, 952, 605, 616
Heywood, Thomas, 264 (*A Woman Killed with Kindness*, at Vieux Colombier)
Hindenburg, Paul, 450
Hirsch, Louis-Daniel, 528
Hirschfeld, Magnus, 376 (*sexuelle Zwischenstafen*), 453
Hitler, Adolf, 450, 528 (Nuremberg speech, 1938), 541 (G on, 1940), 542–4, 567–9, 600–1 (and homosexuals)
Hofmannsthal, Hugo von, 242
Hölderlin, Johann, 590 (G visits rooms, Tübingen)

Homer, 56, 81 (*Odyssey*)
Honegger, Arthur, 318, 585 (G's trans. of *Hamlet*)
Honfleur, 143 (in *Les Nourritures*)
Hospitalet, 243
Housman, A. E., 311 (meets G)
Huard, Monsieur (tutor to G, 'M. Hubert' in *Si le grain*), 29
Hugo, Victor, 81, 223
Hugo, François-Victor, 356 (trans. of *Hamlet*)
Humanité, L', xv, 413, 454, 458
Humboldt, Friedrich von, 81
Huret, Jules, 72 ('Enquête sur l'évolution littéraire')
Huxley, Aldous, 312 (G meets), 479–80
Huysmans, Joris Karl, 130, 253
Hyères (-Plages), 35–6, 243, 348, 356, 360, 367, 371, 433, 472
Hytier, Jean, 558

Ibsen, Henrik, 70, 78, 87, 104, 217 (G sees *Wild Duck*), 237
Iehl, Jules ('Michel Yell'), 243
Illustrated London News, 388
Illustration, L', 388
Indépendence, L', 251 and 253 (attacks Desjardins and *NRF*), 257
Institut Pasteur, Paris, 402
Irving, Henry, 43, 284
Isnic (Turkey), 276

Jacob, Max, 418
Jaloux, Edmond, 137
James, Henry, 260 (G visits), 285
James, William, 368
Jammes, Francis, xiii, 3, 130 (on *Paludes*), 135–6 (in N. Afr.), 155–6 (and Ghéon), 165 (*L'Ermitage*), 169 (G stays with), 172, 178–9, 182 (on *L'Immoraliste*), 194 (G stays with), 215, 221–2 (on *Retour de l'Enfant prodigue*), 223 (wedding), 232 (on G's works), 239, 244 (stays at La Roque), 245 (as character in *Isabelle*), 274–5, 529, 530 (d.), 569, 623 (separated from G by religion)
Jamois, Marguerite, 552

Janson-de-Sailly, Lycée (Paris), 50, 219, 301, 304

Jarre, Maurice, 585

Jarry, Alfred, 392 and 395 (*Ubu Roi* and *Faux-Monnayeurs*)

Jellicoe, Lord, 558 (and de Gaulle)

John (Levesque's Mauritian friend), 442, 444

Joseph, 181

Jouhandeau, Marcel, 418, 530, 574

Jourdain, Francis, 264

Journal, Le, 195

Journal des Inconnus, Le, 54

Jouvet, Louis (previously Jouvey), 263, 265, 386, 445

Joyce, James, 267 (*Ulysses*), 396, 399 (*Ulysses* and *Faux-Monnayeurs*), 494

Juan-les-Pins, 601–2, 605–6, 609

Jünger, Ernst, 625–6

kabuki theatre, 173

Kafka, Franz, 586, 590 and 629 (*Le Procès*, G's dramatic version of *The Trial*)

Kahn, Otto, 295–6

Kairouan (Tunisia), 93, 168, 439

Kamenev, L. B., 501

Kant, Emmanuel, 85 (*Prolegomena to all Metaphysics* in *Voyage d'Urien*), 222

Karl, Roger, 265

Karnac (Egypt), 533

Karsarvina, Tamara, 236

Kassner, Rudolf, 242, 367 (at Pontigny)

Kazantzakis, Nikos, 577

Keaton, Buster, 385 (*Our Hospitality*)

Keats, John, 149 (G visits grave, Rome), 259 (*Endymion*), 301 (letters), 364 (*Endymion*), 366, 592

Keller, Helen, 332 (*The World I Live In* and *Symphonie Pastorale*)

Keller, Gottfried, 559

Kempf, Roger, 575–6

Kessler, Count Harry von, 200 (Weimar, 1904), 222, 242 (and Rilke), 262, 278, 312, 419–20, 450 (in Berlin with G), 455–6 (leaves Ger.), 470, 506 (d.)

Keynes, John Maynard, 311 (meets G), 334 (*Economic Consequences of the Peace*)

Kierkegaard, Sören, 411, 592

Kinsey Report, 596

Kinshassa (Equat. Afr.), 402–3

Kipling, Rudyard, 274

Kirov, S. M., 474 (murdered), 501

Klossowsi, Pierre, 354, 368–9, 388

Knopf, Alfred, 320 and 366 (*Porte étroite*), 413 (*Travels in the Congo*), 431

Koltzov, M. Y., 492–3, 495, 513–14

Konya (Turkey), 276

Koran, 139

Khrushchev, Nikita, 452

Krafft-Ebing, Richard, 201

Kronenberger, Louis, 399 (on *Faux-Monnayeurs*)

Krüger, Catherine ('Cahé'), 302–3 ('C' of *Journal*, 1917)

La Bastide Franco (Brignoles, Beth's farm), 336, 343–4, 348, 356, 358–9, 367–8, 371, 381, 384, 410

La Baule, 219

La Brévine, 103, 105–6, 113, 329–33 (in *Symphonie Pastorale*)

Lacan, Jacques, 633

La Cava (It.), 142

Laclos, Pierre Choderlos de, 441 (*Liaisons dangereuses*), 630

Lacretelle, Jacques de, 433

Lafargue, Marc, 233

La Fontaine, Jean de, 203

Laforgue, Jules, 68, 71–2

Lagerlöf, Selma, 480

Lamalou-les-Bains, 32–3, 170–1

Lamb, Charles, 250 (*Essays*)

Lambert, Jean (Catherine G's first husband), 578, 583–4, 584 (m. Catherine G), 586–7 (calls on Hesse with G), 588 (with G in London), 590–2 (and Yvonne Davet), 595 (La Mivoie), 598, 603 (G's 80th birthday, La Mivoie), 606–8 (with G in S. of Fr.), 611–12 (with G at *Les Caves*, Com.-Fr), 614, 616–19 (G's last weeks)

Lamblin, Auguste, 403

La Mivoie (Lamberts' house), 595, 603, 608–9, 612

Lamoureux, Charles, 78

Landor, W. S., 255

Lanux, Marc de (G's piano teacher, Lapérouse in *Journal*, La Pérouse in *Faux-Monnayeurs*), 45, 199

Lanux, Pierre Combret de (s. of Marc), 224

La Pelouse (Catherine's school, Bex, Switz.), 449

Lara, Louise (and husband Autant), 460–1

Larbaud, Valéry, 239, 248, 249 (in London with G), 254–5, 267 (meets Joyce in Dublin), 271 (and Lafcadio), 279, 348

La Roque-Baignard (*see under* Gide, André, homes)

Lartigaud, Yvonne (and 'Art et Travail'), 459–62

Last, Jeff, 473 (meets G after political meeting), 477–8 (with G in Morocco), 482–4 (*Zuyderzee*), 489, 491, 498–502 (in USSR with G), 504–7 (in Spain), 509 (changing views on USSR), 513–14, 516–17 (under Party pressure to condemn G), 519–20 (gets out of Spain), 526 (G visits in Amsterdam), 529 (stays at Vaneau), 533–4 (in Norway), 540–1 (book on Van der Lubbe), 569, 573 (in Dutch Underground), 590 (at Munich youth rally with G), 595–6 (perf. of his Dutch trans. of *Le Retour de l'Enfant prodigue*, 1948), 619 (d.)

Laubry, Dr, 594

Laurens, Jean-Paul, 52, 89

Laurens, Paul (-Albert) (s. of Jean-Paul), xiii, 52, 84, 88–9 (G stays with at Yport), 91, 92–100 (in N. Afr. and Italy with G), 138, 140, 148 (G stays with at Yport), 187, 237 (and *Corydon*), 269 (his portrait of G on frontispiece of *Les Caves*), 340 (in *Si le grain*), 361, 569

Laurens, Pierre (s. of Jean-Paul), 84, 102, 138

Lausanne, 446 (*Oedipe*), 462, 469, 584

Lautréamont, Comte de (Isadore Ducasse), 271 (and Lafcadio)

Laval, Pierre, 562

Lavigerie, Cardinal, 95

Léautaud, Paul, 233

Le Clerc, Jacques, 564

Lecomte de Lisle, Charles Marie, 45, 68, 70

Lederlin, Antoinette, 304

Le Havre, 249, 282, 321 (Copeau returns from USA), 381

Lehmann, John (and sister Rosamund), 464 (and Dorothy Bussy's *Olivia*), 588

Le Houlme (nr. Rouen), 29 (Henry Rondeaux's cloth-printing factory)

Leibnitz, G. W., 51, 81, 85 (*Théodicée* and *Treatise on Contingency* in *Voyage d'Urien*), 104–5

Leipzig, 202, 462 (Reichstag Fire trial)

Le Lavandou, 443, 454, 472

Lemarié, Berthe, 296

Lenin, V. I., 443

Leningrad (*see* St Petersburg)

Leo XIII, Pope, 269 (and *Les Caves*)

Leoncavallo, Ruggiero, 195

Lepape, Pierre, xviii

Lessing, G. E., 79 (*Nathan der Weise*, Munich), 104–5

Lestrange, Michel de (s. of Yvonne by Marc Allégret), 432, 454, 522, 536

Lestrange, Yvonne de (Duchesse de Trévisse; and Château de Chitré), 402–3 (meets G and Marc in Africa), 410 (G stays at Chitré), 415 (G stays at house, quai Malaquais), 429–30 (m. of Marc's son), 436, 454, 472, 491, 522 and 527 (G at Chitré), 536 (G at Chitré), 599, 609 (G at Chitré), 614–15, 619 (d.), 625

Lettres Françaises, Les, 566

Lettres nouvelles, Les, 574

Levesque, Robert, xix (journals), 418 (meets G, 17), 442–3 (at Saint-Clair), 445–7, 449 (and Morocco), 452, 459 (and N. Afr.), 460, 465–6, 468–72 (at Boissy-la-Rivière), 474–6 (It. with G), 482 (brothers), 503, 515 (to Moscow), 518–19 (It. with G), 530, 533 (G joins him in Athens), 536 (at Pontigny), 550 (brothers), 573–4 (trans. of Seferis and Solomos), 575–6, 567–8 (with G to Egypt, etc.), 586 (and G), 596, 610 (and Morocco), 619 (d.)

Levi, Hermann, 78–9

Lewis, Sinclair, 480

Librairie de l'Art Indépendant, 75, 84

'Libre esthétique' (Brussels literary society), 172 and 206 (G lecture: 'Influence en littérature'), 206 (G lecture: 'L'Evolution du théâtre')

Lichtenberger, Henri, 163–4 (*La Philosophie de Nietzsche*)

Ligugé (Fr. Benedictine community), 172 (and Claudel)

Lion, Aline, 536

Liranga (Fr. Equat. Afr.), 403

Littérature, 328

Llanberis, 338

Logique de Port-Royal, La, 91

London, 43 (1888), 227 (1908), 249 (1911), 260–1 (1912–13), 310–12 (1918), 338 (1920), 488–9 (1947)

Lopokova, Lydia (later Mrs Maynard Keynes), 312

Losdorf-Bad, 142

Loti, Pierre, 81

Loubet, Emile, 172

Louis, Georges (elder b. of Pierre Louÿs), 49

Lourdes, 215

Louvre, Musée du, 210

Louÿs, Pierre (*né* Louis), xii, 48–50 (at Ecole Alsacienne with G), 54–8 (friendship with G), 64–7 (L–G–Valéry 'triangle'), 69–70 (at Heredia's with G; *La Conque*), 75 (and *Traité du Narcisse*), 78 (Wagnerite), 101 (*Les Chansons de Bilitis*), 107–8 (and *Paludes*), 190, 195–6 (*Aphrodite*), 385 (d. 1925)

Lugné–Poe, Aurélien, 170 (as Candaule), 180 (puts on *Candaule*)

Lutétia, Hôtel (Paris), 349–50, 361, 368, 417, 446, 530

Luxembourg, Jardin du, 12–15, 19–20, 391–3 (and *Faux-Monnayeurs*)

Luxor (Egypt), 531, 577

Lvoff, Tania (Tolstoy's granddaughter), 586

Lyautey, Louis, 364–5 (invites G to Morocco)

Lyon, 216, 482

Lyon, M. (philosophy teacher, Lycée Henri IV), 51

Lytton, Lord, 75–6

Macauley, Thomas, 247 (*Life of Lord Byron*)

McLeod, Enid, 380, 419, 519, 586, 590, 608, 625

Madrid, 169, 517 (2nd International Congress of Intellectuals for the Defence of Culture, 1937)

Maeterlinck, Maurice, 67–8, 70, 72, 86 (*Pelléas et Mélisande*), 130, 154 (*P. et M.*), 171, 193 (*P. et M.*), 217 (G sees *Mort de Tintagiles*), 445 (*Le Miracle de Saint-Antoine*)

Magdalen College, Oxford, 589 (G visits Wilde's rooms)

Mahias, Claude, 596–8, 601–2

Mahn, Berthold, 616

Maillol, Aristide, 217 (two works at Villa Montmorency)

Mallarmé, Stéphane, xii–xiii, 53, 64, 67–70, 72, 75, 79, 81, 84, 86–7, 109–10 (on *Paludes*), 155 (d.), 265, 299, 312

Malraux, André, 422, 426, 456, 462 (with G to Berlin, 1934), 478–80, 483, 513–14, 545, 570, 575–6, 576 (film of *L'Espoir*), 585

Malraux, Clara (André's first wife), 503, 508, 513

Malraux, Clotis (André's second wife), 545

Manet, Edouard, 102

Mangua (Equat. Afr.), 406

Manguin, Henri, 174 (buys La Roque)

Mann, Heinrich, 367 (at Pontigny), 455 (leaves Ger.), 479–80 ('Writers in Defence of Culture'), 494, 543

Mann, Klaus (son of Thomas), 378 (on *Corydon*), 442 (meets G), 455 (leaves Ger.), 479–80 (on 'Mutualité' meeting, 'Writers in Defence of Culture'), 600 (suicide; G and Last on; homosexuality)

Mann, Thomas, 399 (*Der Zauberberg* and *Faux-Monnayeurs*), 442 (G visits, Munich), 455 (leaves Ger.), 494 (and politics), 519 (and Nazis), 543–5 (in US, helping European intellectuals to escape), 622 (on G and Goethe), 631 (on G's curiosity)

Marcel, Gabriel, 476

Marcu, Valeriu, 539 (G gets out of internment), 543, 547 (leaves for USA)

Marcus Aurelius, 72
Margerie, Diane de (wife of Roland), 450, 452
Margerie, Roland de, 455
Marges, Les, 234, 276 (rev. of *Les Caves*)
Marie (Leuenberger, Gs' Swiss maid), 11, 18, 25, 30–2, 55, 98–9, 122 (and Athman), 126, 569
Marienbad (Czecho-Slovakia), 436
Maritain, Jacques, 369–70 (and *Corydon*), 476–7 (Union pour la Vérité debate), 544
Marius (Herbart's friend), 471–2
Marivaux, Pierre, 585 (*Les Fausses Confidences*)
Marlowe, Christopher, 133, 259 (*Hero and Leander*)
Marrakesh, 365
Marseille, 91–2, 115, 137, 142, 149, 176, 254–5, 297, 365, 384–5, 411, 423, 436, 438–40, 441–2, 444, 446, 450, 454, 465, 467, 487–8, 504, 521
Marsh, Edward, 283–4
Martin, Claude, xviii, 549 ('Mané Thékel Pharès')
Martin, Dr, 614–15
Martin-Chauffier, Louis, 571 (in Belsen, *L'Homme et la Bête*)
Martin du Gard, Christiane (RMG's d.), 426, 431–2, 486, 519, 564
Martin du Gard, Hélène (RMG's w.), 432, 448, 450, 486–7, 520, 539–40, 564, 604 (d.)
Martin du Gard, Roger ('RMG'), i, xix (journals), 129 (*Confidence africaine*), 146 (*Les Thibault* and *Les Nourritures*), 153 (on *Saül*), 264 (backstage Vieux Colombier), 265 (*Devenir* and *Jean Barois*), 266–7 (description of Vieux Colombier and of Villa Montmorency), 308, 317, 322, 338, 340 (on Villa Montmorency), 342 (and *Les Thibault*), 344, 352 (and Académie Française), 357 (at Pontigny), 360, 361–3 (visits Cuverville with G), 371, 381 (at Hyères), 383 (visits G in hospital), 387–8 (on G in cinema; and G's 'secret papers'), 394–5 (and *Faux-Monnayeurs*), 409–10 (sees G after return from Afr.),

410 (and Légion d'Honneur), 412, 414–15 and 417 (G at Le Tertre), 420, 426 (and translation), 428 (and *L'Ecole des Femmes*), 431–2 (relations with Coppet), 434–5 (and FPF), 444–5 (*Un Taciturne*), 447–8 (Berlin), 449–50, 452–4 (in Berlin), 456–7 (on G's Communism), 465–7 (leaves Paris for Nice), 470 (and Levesque), 477, 480–1 (G on Serge), 485–8 (on *Nouvelles Nourritures*; G in Nice), 505 (and Herbart and Marc), 509 (on *Retour de l'U.R.S.S.*), 512, 518–19 (Pontigny), 520 (Nobel Prize), 522 (at Lutétia), 526, 530, 539–40 (return to Fr.), 542–4 (Germans at Le Tertre, moves to Nice), 551 (and Catherine), 554, 556, 558, 564, 566–8 (on *épuration*; attitude to the Germans), 572–3 (on Simenon), 576–8 (and Académie Française; G's will), 585–6 (G's 75th birthday), 592 (G's Nobel Prize), 597, 600 (*Notes sur AG*), 601–4 (with G at Juan-les-Pins; Copeau's funeral), 606, 609 (and Amrouche), 613–19 (G's d. and funeral), 633–4 (on G)
Marty, Eric, 599 (Amrouche interviews with G)
Marvell, Andrew, 50, 368
Marx, Karl, 449 (*Capital*)
Mas, 294
Masaccio, Tommaso, 256 (*Apostle Peter*)
Massenet, Jules, 115
Massignon, Louis, 531
Massine, Leonid, 278, 312, 372 (*Gigue*)
Massis, Henri, 349, 351–2 (attacks on G), 369 (attacks on G), 476–7 (attacks G at Union pour la Vérité debate), 544, 614
Masson, André, 585
Matadi (Equat. Afr.), 402
Matisse, Henri, 470, 541, 603
Mauclair, Camille, 70, 131 (on *Paludes*)
Maupassant, Guy de, 68
Maurer, Rudolf (*André Gide et l'U.R.S.S*), 495, 504–5
Mauriac, Claude, 324, 530 (*Conversations avec André Gide*), 534–6, 572
Mauriac, François, 351–2 (defends G), 379

(on *Corydon*), 384, 422, 476–7, 530, 534–6, 563, 565, 572–3, 614, 616–17

Maurois, André, 381, 435

Maurras, Charles, 68 (at Mallarmé's *Mardis*), 236 (and Action Française), 277, 544 (and Pétain), 562 (trial and condemnation)

Maury, Lucien, 307

Maus, Octave, 292

Max, Edouard de, 154, 165, 170, 181 (in *Candaule*), 337 (in *Antoine et Cléopâtre*)

Mayrisch, Aline ('Loup', w. of Emile), 201 (at Weimar with G), 261–2 (joins G in Florence), 263, 276 (with G in Turkey), 313, 320 (on G and Marc), 327–8, 334–9 (G at Dudelange; in It. with G; G at Bormes; G's trans. of *Antony and Cleopatra*; G at Colpach), 357–9 (Pontigny; godmother of Beth's child), 361, 365 (in Morocco with G), 380, 384 (and Rivière), 411 (Pontigny), 413, 416 (G etc. to Bormes), 420 (G at Colpach), 425, 436, 465 (to Cairo with Petite Dame), 515 (G at Colpach), 521, 530, 534 (and Domela), 540, 543 (decline begins), 546, 548–9 (help to Schiffrins), 550, 564, 586 (d.), 625

Mayrisch, Andrée ('Schnouky', d. of Emile and Aline), 327, 334, 336, 338, 347–8, 358–9 (G and the Scouts), 425 (m. Pierre Viénot), 564 (in Underground)

Mayrisch, Emile (Luxembourg industrialist), 201, 320 (G visits factory), 336 (and Beth), 339, 384, 413, 420 (d.)

Mazel, Henri, 219

M'bali Falls (Equat. Afr.), 403

Melvil, Harry, 250

Memling, Hans, 110, 397 ('*en abyme*')

Ménardière, Mireille de la (Dupouey's fiancée), 286

Mendès, Catulle, 68

Menthon, 56–7

Menton, 115

Méral, Paul, 318 (*Le Dit des Jeux du Monde*)

Mercure de France, 63, 131, 141, 146–7, 160 (pub. *Le Prométhée*), 182 (pub. *L'Immoraliste*), 200, 207, 237, 253, 322

Meredith, George, 70, 306 (*Shaving of Shagpat*), 344 (*Harry Richmond*)

Meriem Ben Atala, 97–9, 101, 121, 125, 128, 143 (in *Les Nourritures*)

Merleau-Ponty, Maurice, 549

Mérouvel, Charles, 175 (bought remainder of La Roque estate)

Merrill, Stuart, 165

Messiaen, Olivier, 585

Messina, 99, 205

Metzys, Quintijn, 110

Meurice, Hôtel (Paris), 262

Meyer, Jean, 605, 610–12, 616

Meynell, Alice, 249

Miard, M., 96

Michaux, Henri, 547

Michelangelo, 276, 374 (*Creation of Man*), 475 (*Pietà*, Barberina Palace, Palestrina)

Michelet, René, 339, 346–7, 359 (and Boy Scouts at Colpach), 388, 412, 443, 459 (and Boy Scouts)

Mikoyan, Anastas, 493

Milan, 132

Milhaud, Darius, 282, 372 (*Salade*, ballet)

Milton, John, 250 (*Samson Agonistes*), 259 (*Paradise Lost*), 282, 288, 289 (*Paradise Lost*), 407 (*Paradise Lost* and *Samson Agonistes*)

Minori, 142

Minuit, Editions de, 566

Mirrlees, Hope, 384

Mirski, Prince Dimitri, 443

Mobaye (Equat. Afr.), 403 (elephantiasis of sexual organs)

Mohammed (Algiers, 1894), 97, 104

Mohammed (Algiers, 1895, 1896), 118–20, 136 (with G and Rouart)

Mohammed (Kairouan), 168, 204

Molière, 172, 203 (*Bourgois Gentilhomme*), 237, 265 and 277–8 (*L'Amour Médecin*, *L'Avare*, at Vieux Colombier), 302 (*Fourberies de Scapin*, New York), 352, 403 (*Misanthrope*), 460 (*Tartuffe* and *Les Caves*), 611

Molotov, V. M., xv, 493

Monaco, 488

Mondel, Father, 633–4

Monet, Claude, 194

Montaigne, Michel de, 227–8, 344 (G

compares with Proust), 375, 411, 422–3 (G's essay on), 536 (G visits Château de M.), 599 (and Blum)

Mont-Dore, Le, 536, 573

Monte Carlo (casino), 609

Monte Cassino (It. Benedictine community), 235 (G's visit, 1909), 598 (*Notes sur Chopin* dedicated to Abbot)

Montesquiou, Robert de, 268, 390

Monteverdi, Claudio, 217 (G sees *Orfeo*)

Monte Verità (nr Locarno), 470–1

Montfort, Eugène, 233–4

Montherlant, Henry de, 424, 574

Montpellier, 25, 30, 32, 64, 73, 75, 77, 114, 125, 137

Montreux, 446 (*Oedipe*), 481

Moore, George, 68, 260

Morand, Paul, 435

Moréas, Jean, 67–8, 70, 72

Morgan, Michèle (in film of *Symphonie Pastorale*), 333, 574, 584

Morisot, Berthe, 414

Morrel, Lady Ottoline, 312, 339, 431

Morteuil, Château de (nr. Beaune), 386–7

Mortimer, Raymond, 588

Moscow, 492–5, 497, 501–5 and 514 (Trial of Sixteen), 515 (new trial of Radek)

Moscow Arts Theatre, 386, 496

Mougins, 598

Mozart, W. A., 79, 441

M'Raier (oasis town, Algeria), 136, 176

MRP (Mouvement Républicain Populaire), 575

Mühlfeld, Jeanne, 242, 337

Muller, Marie-Thérèse, 380

Munich, 77–80, 442 (Thomas Mann), 590 (youth rally, 1947)

Murcia, 241

Musil, Robert, 479

Mussolini, Benito (and Fascism), 348–9, 474–5, 502, 506, 519, 529

Mussorgsky, Modest, 262 (*Boris Godunov*, Diaghilev, 1913)

Nancy, 73, 79

Naples, 99, 107, 115, 134, 142, 180, 185 (in *L'Immoraliste*), 465, 475, 518, 576, 608

Natanson, Thadée, 276

Naturism, 140–1

Naville, Arnold, 541, 576

Naville, Pierre, 57, 451, 507

Nazism, 346, 455–6, 545

Nazier, François, 379 (*L'Anti-Corydon*)

Nehru, Jawaharlal, 612

Nelson, Horatio, 558

Néné, 'le petit' (*see* Brun, Henri)

Neuchâtel, 105–6, 132, 149, 254, 416, 584, 587, 590, 592, 594–5

New York, 285 (visit of Vieux Colombier)

Nice, 180, 467, 487–9, 539, 542, 549–50, 598, 600, 602, 609

Nicolson, Harold, 626–7 (on G as 'corruptor' of youth)

Nietzsche, Friedrich, 51, 78, 86 (*Übermensch* in *Voyage d'Urien*), 159–60, 163–4 (and *Le Prométhée*), 171, 185–6, 188 (and *Übermensch* in *L'Immoraliste*), 203 (G reads correspondence), 207, 226, 232, 289 (*Beyond Good and Evil*), 324, 353, 411, 471 (madness and Turin), 541 (*Thoughts Out of Season*), 592

Nijinsky, Vaslav, 236, 242, 262, 408

Nîmes, 91, 448

N'Goto (Equat. Afr.), 404

Nō theatre, 386

Noailles, Anna de (*née* Brancovan), 240, 242, 249, 263, 265

Noailles, Vicomte Charles (and wife Marie-Laure), 433

Nobécourt, R.-G. (*Les Nourritures normandes d'André Gide*), 6, 35, 246

Norton, Harry, 311

'nouveaux philosophes', 633

Nouvelle Revue Française (*NRF* and Gallimard publishing house), xiii–xiv, xviii (and G's correspondence), 64, 147, 211, 225, 232 (*Porte étroite*), 233–4, 236–7, 239 (maison Gallimard), 242–4, 247, 249–50, 252–3, 254 (moves rue Madame), 255–7, 259 (and Cocteau), 259–60 (and Proust), 261–8, 269 (*Les Caves*), 278, 280, 287, 290, 296, 298, 318, 322–3 (division within), 325 (and Cocteau), 328–9 (*Symphonie Pastorale*), 334, 343, 346 (pub.

Freud), 353, 378 (*Corydon*), 382 (*Faux-Monnayeurs*), 384, 385 (*Voyage au Congo*), 435, 443, 448, 466, 468, 472, 483, 521 (and RMG), 523 (G's Oeuvres complètes), 542 ('treize épaves' at Carcassonne), 543, 544–6 (Ger. censorship), 548, 566, 578, 609, 622–3

Novalis, 104

Oberhof (gardens, Ger.), 202
Oberkampf, rue (baths, *see also* Rochechouart), 191, 199, 218
O'Brien, Justin, 160 (on *Le Prométhée*), 230 (on *Porte étroite*), 594
Odessa, 501
Œuvre, Théâtre de l', 170
Olivier, Laurence (and Old Vic company, Paris), 572 (*Richard III*, 1945), 586 (*Lear, Arms and the Man*, 1946), 588
O'Neill, Eugène, 461 (*Emperor Jones*)
Onfroy de Bréville, Pierre, 281
Oran, 169, 365
Ordzhonikidze, 498
Orvieto, 100, 151, 348
Oulad Naïl, 97, 121, 185
Outhman, 402
Oxford, 227 (1908), 456 (Union motion), 588–9 and 596 (G's honorary doctorate)

Pacha, Georges, 404–5
Paestum (*see* Pesto)
Pagnol, Marcel, 450 (*Fanny*)
Painter, George, xviii, 189, 331
Palermo, 180, 608
Palestrina, Giovanni, 149, 217 (G hears *Missa Papae Marcelli*)
Palewski, Gaston, 558, 568
Papini, Giovanni, 255
Parsons, Léon, 115
Pascal, Blaise, 44, 51, 287, 313, 375 (*Corydon*), 422
Pasternak, Boris, xvi, 478, 494 (translator of Shakespeare, *Doctor Zhivago*)
Patmore, Coventry, 249, 252
Paulhan, Jean, 384, 542, 545–6, 575, 585, 616
Paz, Magdeleine, 480, 506

Peacock, Thomas Love, 338 (*Nightmare Abbey*)
Péguy, Charles, 280
Peïra-Cava (nr. Nice), 417
Pernand-Vergelesses (Burgundy), 387, 411, 437–8
Perpignon, 294, 534 (internment camp)
Perrin, Didier, 57, 62, 67
Perrog-Guirec, 219
Pertisau (Switz.), 584 (G lectures)
Perugia, 100, 151
Pesto (Paestum, It.), 134, 575
Pétain, Henri, 542, 562
Petite Dame (*see* Van Rysselberghe, Maria)
Peyrefitte, Roger, 574 (*Les Amitiés particulières*)
Pfemfert, Franz, 539
Phalange, La, 225–6, 236
Philippe, Charles-Louis, 233, 239–40 (d.), 248 (*La Mère et l'enfant*), 383 (on illness)
Picasso, Pablo, 327, 342 (*Parade*), 417, 470
Pierre-Quint, Léon, 81, 166 (interview with Ghéon), 324
Pilnyak, Boris, 494
Pisa, 100, 133, 255, 408 (Campo Santo fresco)
Pitoëf, Georges (and wife Ludmilla), 354 (commissions G to translate *Hamlet*), 356 (and *Hamlet*), 445–7 (prod. *Oedipe*)
Plato, 28 (*Symposium*), 56, 105 (*Symposium*), 170 (*Republic* and *Roi Candaule*), 373 (*Symposium* and *Corydon*)
Pleven, René, 558
Plume, La, 189 (rev. of *L'Immoraliste*)
Plutarch, 579 (*Life of Theseus* and *Thésée*)
Poe, Edgar Allan, 72, 81, 82 (*Fall of the House of Usher*), 110
Poincairé, Raymond, 414, 417
Poirier, Léon, 414
Polignac, Marquis Melchior de, 295
Polignac, Princesse de (*née* Singer), 263, 300
Pollaiuolo, Antonio, 220 (*David*, Berlin)
Pollard, Patrick, 160–3 (on *Le Prométhée*)
Pompeii, 99, 518
Ponte-Tresa (Switz.), 587
Pontigny (décades de), 243–4, 249–50 (1911), 256–7 (1912), 357–8 (1922), 367 (1923), 380 (1924), 411 (1926), 418 (1927), 426–7

(1929), 431, 443 (1931), 459 (1933), 470 (1934), 519 (1937), 536 (1939), 539
Porquerolles, 355–6
Portofino, 364, 608
Potsdam, 201
Poucel, Victor, 151 (on *Les Nourritures*)
Pouchet, Georges, 208
Pougy, Liane de, 208
Poulaille, Henry, 480
Poulenc, Francis, 400 (and *Faux-Monnayeurs*)
POUM (Sp. Trotskyite party), 502
Pound, Ezra, 494
Poussin, Nicolas, 569
Pravda, 501, 510
Proust, Marcel, i, 10, 36, 70, 259 (and *NRF*), 263, 267–8, 275–6 (on *Les Caves*), 292, 343–4 (G on *Guermantes*), 345 (discusses homosexuality with G, *Sodome et Gomorrhe*), 346–7, 360–1 (d.), 390, 399 (*A la recherche* and *Faux-Monnayeurs*), 464, 476–7, 494, 538 (G reads *A la recherche*)
Prinzhorn, Hans, 430 (Ger. trans. of *Les Nourritures*)
psychoanalysis (*see* Freud)
Puccini, Giacomo, 195
Pushkin, Alexander, 474 (G trans. stories)

Quai d'Orsay (Fr. Foreign Ministry), 462
Quillot, Maurice, 52, 70, 105

Rabat, 559
Rabelais, François, 30
Rachilde (Mme Alfred Vallette), 130
Racine, Jean, 51, 105 (*Phèdre*), 132 (*Bérénice*), 208, 422, 446 (*Andromaque*), 465 (*Iphigénie*, *Phèdre*), 515 (*Athalie*), 548–9 (*Bajazet*), 549 (*Phèdre* and Catherine), 579 (*Phèdre* and *Thésée*)
Radiguet, Raymond, 392 (*Diable au corps*, etc.)
Rafai (Equat. Afr.), 404
Ragu, Dr (Tunis), 553, 556
Rapallo, 363–4, 608
Rathenau, Walther, 339 (meets G), 341, 351, 455
Ravel, Maurice, 400 (and *Faux-Monnayeurs*)
Ravello, 142, 183 (in *L'Immoraliste*)

Ravenna, 151
Raverat, Jacques, 279, 282 (existence of the devil), 283, 285, 288–9 (devil), 308, 343, 371
Regler, Gustav, 513
Régnier, Henri de, 67–70 (and Verlaine, Mallarmé, Heredia), 72, 75 (and *Traité du Narcisse*) 79, 81–2 (in Brittany with G), 85, 107 and 130 (*Paludes*), 169, 190, 385
Rei Bouba (Equat. Afr.), 407
Reichstag Fire, 455, 461–2, 473, 541
Reinhardt, Max, 264, 295
Renan, Ernest, 56–7, 222
Renard, Jules, 76
Renaud, Madeleine, 574, 585, 605
Ravensbrück, 571
Revue Blanche, 108 (*Paludes*), 146, 161–2 (*Le Prométhée*), 233
Revue bleue, 247
Revue de Paris, 417 ('Distress of our Equatorial Africa'), 427 (*Ecole des Femmes*)
Revue hebdomadaire, 429 (*Robert*)
Revue musicale, 598
Revue sentimentale, 160
Revue universelle (Massis' attacks on G), 349, 351–2, 369
Reymond, Théo (and wife), 553, 556, 609
Reynaud, Paul, 568
Richardson, Samuel, 441 (*Clarissa Harlowe*), 630
Rilke, Rainer Maria, 241–2 (trans. *Retour de l'Enfant prodigue*; G trans. *Malte Laurids Brigge*), 271, 291–2, 341 (and Paris), 357, 368, 388–9 (d.), 494, 558
Rimbaud, Arthur, 55, 253, 271 (and Lafcadio), 273, 602
Rimsky-Korsakov, N. A., 242 (*Schéhérazade*, Diaghilev, 1913), 26 (*Khovanschina*, Diaghilev, 1913), 312 (*Golden Cockerel*, Beecham, 1918)
Rivière, Isabelle (wife of Jacques, *née* Fournier), 243, 282, 296, 384, 387
Rivière, Jacques, 239, 242–3, 250, 252, 254 (*Etudes*), 261–2, 268, 274, 280, 282 (taken prisoner by Germans), 299–300, 319, 325, 354, 357, 366, 370, 383–4 (d.), 434
Rivière, Marcel, 247, 254

Roberty, Pastor, 6, 82, 131

Robeson, Paul, 461 (*Emperor Jones*)

Rochechouart, rue (baths, *see also*
Oberkampf), 173, 175, 191

Rodin, Auguste, 222, 241, 291

Roggers, Henriette, 170

Rolland, Romain, 291, 480

Romains, Jules, 435, 544, 576

Romard, M. (M. Gallin of *Si le grain*), 29

Rome, 99–100, 121, 128, 133–4, 143 (Villa
Borghese, in *Nourritures terrestres*), 149–51,
180, 205, 235, 249, 255, 262, 465, 471,
474–5, 518, 607

Rommel, Erwin, 555

Rondeaux, Emile (G's uncle and father-in-
law), 55

Rondeaux, Georges (G's cousin), 148, 572

Rondeaux, Lucile (G's aunt), 34, 131

Rondeaux, Mathilde (G's aunt, Aunt Lucile
in *Porte étroite*), 22–3, 34–5

Rondeaux, Valentine (G's cousin and sister-
in-law, Louise in *Journal*), 23–4, 34, 57,
138, 154 (first son, Alain), 171–2, 176, 180,
193 (m. Marcel Gilbert), 223 (Marcel
Gilbert d.), 237, 282, 292, 313 (son d.),
363, 420, 515, 521–2 (d.) 549 ('Mané
Thékel Phares')

Roquebrune-Cap-Martin ('La Souco',
Bussys' house), 320, 336–7, 343, 363–4,
371, 383–4, 413–14, 422–3, 425, 432, 434,
442, 447, 457, 467, 484, 545–6

Rose (grandmother's maid), 25

Rosenberg, Fedor, 133–5 (in Florence, meets
G), 137, 139–40 (and Hafiz), 142 (Jeanne
Rondeaux in love with), 168, 175 (*piscines*),
193–4 (back in Russia), 202 (sees G in
Dresden), 347 (first news from since
Revolution), 418 (to Cuverville), 457 (in
hospital, Leningrad)

Rosetta (Egypt), 533

Ross, Robert, 257

Rothenstein, William, 312

Rothermere, Lady, 318 (and *Corydon*), 320
(trans. *Le Prométhée*)

Rothschild, Philippe, 454

Rouart, Eugène, 102, 109 (and *Paludes*), 112,
126, 131, 136 ('Daniel B. . .' in *Journal*),
137, 148, 151 (anti-Dreyfusard), 155, 157–8
(*La Villa sans maître*), 223–6 (G at Bagnols;
chef de cabinet to minister), 233, 237 and
243 (G at Bagnols), 250 and 259 (G at
Bagnols), 262 (joins G in Rome), 294
and 297 (G at Bagnols), 312, 321 (on
Ghéon), 344, 449 (and Tangier), 497 (d.),
569

Rouart, Louis (Eugène's brother), 233

Rouart, Yvonne (Eugène's wife), 165

Rouché, Jacques, 241

Rouen, 5–6, 24, 29, 34, 55, 114–15, 125, 131,
137 (Valentine Rondeaux m. Charles
Bernardbeig), 180, 256 (G juryman)

Rousseau, Jean-Jacques, 57, 106 (*Confessions*),
222, 352, 416

Rouveyre, André, 369 (and Pierre
Klossowski)

Royal Society of Literature, London, 380
(G elected to), 461–2 (Fellowship
withdrawn)

Royère, Jean, 225

Rubaiyyát of Omar Khayyám, 133

Rubinstein, Ida, 236, 242, 300, 302, 307,
308 (in *Antoine et Cléopâtre*), 454 (*Proserpine*
and *Antoine et Cléopâtre*), 459–60
(*Perséphone*)

Russell, John, 581 and 583 (Eng. trans. of
Thésée)

Rutherford, Mark, 290

Ruyters, André (and wife Georgina), 141
(and *Les Oiseaux dans la cage*), 155–7 (at
La Roque), 158 (*Les jardins d'Armide*),
169–70, 172 (and G's lecture to 'Libre
Esthétique'), 181–2, 223–5 (moves to
Paris), 233–4 (and the *NRF*), 239, 243
(at Cuverville), 253–4, 280 (called up),
282 (Georgina joins Foyer Franco-
Belge), 321 (attitude to G's relationship
with Marc), 477 (interned by Japanese at
Hué, Indo-China)

Sadek (Athman's elder brother), 123

Saint Brelade's Bay, Jersey (Copeau's
holiday house 1907), 223

Saint-Clair (Van Rysselberghes' house),
295, 318, 334–5, 337, 342, 344, 354–6,

368, 371, 413–14, 419–20, 422–3, 426, 434, 438, 440–2, 444, 447–9, 515
Saint-Denis, Michel, 386, 588, 603
Sainte-Beuve, Charles, 20, 96
Sainte-Catherine Press, Bruges, 291
Saintes-Maries, 425
Saint-Exupéry, Antoine de, 545, 565
Saint-Georges de Bouhélier, 140–1
Saint-Gervais (Paris church and choir), 234 (in *Winter's Tale*)
Saint-Jean, Robert de, 544
Saint-John Perse (Saint-Léger), 239, 462, 594, 622, 633
Saint-Juste (nurse), 613
Saint-Martin-Vésubie, 367
Saint-Moritz, 132, 145 (in *Nourritures terrestres*)
Saint-Paul-de-Vence, 601
St Petersburg (Leningrad), 193, 495–7
Saint-Saëns, Camille, 195
Saint-Sulpice (Paris church), 387
Salerno, 475
Samba Nigoto, 404–5
San Gimignano, 518
Sangnier, Marc (and Boissy-la-Rivière), 468 (holiday camp)
Sans-Souci Palace, Potsdam, 201
Santa Margarita, 263
Sarajevo (assassination of Archduke Francis Ferdinand), 278
Sarcey, Francisque, 213
Sarraute, Nathalie, 113, 400 (*Portrait d'un inconnu* and *Faux-Monnayeurs*)
Sartre, Jean-Paul, 273, 400 (on *Faux-Monnayeurs*), 549 (*L'Etre et le Néant*), 566 (*Les Temps modernes*), 575 (and existentialism), 609–10
Sassoon, Siegfried, 431
Satie, Eric, 342 (*Parade*), 372 (*Mercure*)
Savonarola, Girolamo, 100
Savoy Hotel, London, 251
Saxe-Weimar, Hereditary Grand Duchess of, 201–2
Scarlatti, Domenico, 411
Scheffer, Robert, 189 (rev. of *L'Immoraliste*)
Schiffrin, Jacques (and w. Youra Guller), 291, 411, 474 (trans. Pushkin stories with

G), 489–91, 499, 503–4, 523 (Pléiade ed. of G's *Journal*), 528, 548 (to USA and Pantheon Books), 554 (pub. of G's trans. of *Hamlet*), 560, 578
Schiller, J. C. F. von, 77, 559
Schlumberger, Conrad (Jean's b.), 281, 294
Schlumberger, Jean (and Braffy), xiii, xix, 82 (*Madeleine et André Gide*), 129, 150 (*Mad. et A. G.*), 175, 205–6 (his homosexuality; *Poèmes des temples et des tombeaux*, *Le Mur de verre*), 209, 216 (to Vienna with G, 1906), 218, 223–4, 225 (and Ghéon), 233–4 (and *NRF*), 247, 249 (shareholder of *NRF* publishing house), 251, 253 (*La Mort de Sparte*), 254 (*L'Inquiète Paternité*), 260, 261 (and Vieux Colombier), 262–4 (and *NRF*), 265 and 277 (*Le Fils Louverné* at Vieux Colombier), 266, 278, 280–2, 284 (and E. G. Craig), 293 (*Mad. et A. G*), 296 (mobilized), 301, 304, 306, 314, 316–18 (*re* Madeleine's burning of G's letters), 321–3 and 329 (and *NRF*), 333 (*Faux-Monnayeurs* dedicated to), 343, 344 (*La Mort de Sparte*), 347, 357 (at Pontigny), 364, 366 (and *NRF*), 383, 388, 401, 412, 422–3, 435 (and *NRF*), 437 (*Saint-Saturnin*), 444–5, 483 (and G's Communism), 485 (and *Nouvelles Nourritures*), 504, 506, 509 (and G's Communism), 522–3, 526, 528–30, 544, 563, 565, 567, 570–1, 585, 588, 591, 598–9, 603–4, 608–9, 614–15, 617–18 (G's funeral), 619 (d.), 627 (on G)
Schlumberger, Marco (Jean's s.), 588
Schlumberger, Maurice (Jean's b., first 'M' of *Journal*), xiii, 208–14 ('affair' with G and Ghéon), 225, 235, 271 (and Lafcadio), 281, 300, 302, 565, 623
Schlumberger, Suzanne (Jean's w.), 205, 317 (her marriage), 321, 343, 347, 381 (d.)
Schmitt, Florent, 237, 338 (and *Antoine et Cléopâtre*)
Schönbrunn (Switz.), 219
Schoenberner, Franz, 539
Schopenhauer, Artur, 51, 56–7

Schubert, Franz, 79, 175 (G discovers piano sonatas)

Schumann, Robert, 45, 56, 59, 96, 106, 115, 203 (Third Symphony), 556

Schveitzer, Marcelle, 569

Schwob, Marcel, 68, 70, 87, 172, 356 (trans. *Hamlet*)

Seferis, 574 (Levesque's trans.), 577

Serge, Victor, 480–1, 490, 506–7

Sérusier, Paul, 219

Sevastopol, 500

Seville, 88, 143 (gardens in *Nourritures terrestres*)

Shackleton, Anna, 5–6, 17–18, 27–8, 35, 39–40, 42–3, 77, 247

Shakespeare, William, 59–60, 71, 79 (*Richard III*, Munich), 82 (*Richard III*), 110 (*Hamlet*), 138 and 152–3 (*Othello*), 153–4 (*Hamlet*), 172, 176 (*Lear*), 186, 217 (G sees Antoine's *Julius Caesar*), 237, 247, 276–7 (Vieux Colombier *Twelfth Night*), 282 (sonnets), 300–2 and 307 (G's trans. *Antony and Cleopatra*), 337 (G's trans. *A. and C.* at Paris Opéra), 356–7 (G's trans. Act I *Hamlet* and *A. and C.*), 364 (*Merry Wives*), 393 (*As You Like It*), 397 (*Hamlet*, play-within-the-play, *en abyme*), 399 (*Hamlet* and *Faux-Monnayeurs*), 465 (*Othello*), 486 (history plays), 518 and 528 (rev. trans. of *A. and C.*), 554 (trans. *Hamlet*), 570 (*A. and C.*, prod. of G's trans.), 572 (Olivier and Old Vic *Richard III*), 574 (Barrault prod. of G's trans. of *Hamlet*), 585 (Gielgud's *Hamlet*, Brussels), 586 (Olivier and Old Vic *Lear*, Paris), 599 (and Blum), 605 (trans. of *A. and C.*), 629 (G's trans.)

Shaw, G. B., 87, 250, 357 (*Devil's Disciple*), 480, 586 (Olivier and Old Vic *Arms and the Man*, Paris)

Shelley, P. B., 133, 158 (*Prometheus Unbound*), 475

Sickert, Walter, 194

Siena, 261

Sikelianos, 577

Siller, Emma, 176

Simenon, Georges, 530, 570, 572–3

Simon, Hugo, 455

Smith, Logan Pearsall, 368 (*History of the English Language*)

Smollett, Tobias, 271 (heroes and Lafcadio)

Smyrna (Izmir, Turkey), 277

Sochi (USSR), 500

Socrates, 626

Sofia, 276

Sokolnicka, Eugenia (*née* Kutner), 353

Solesmes (Fr. Benedictine community), 172 (and Claudel), 387 (and Copeau)

Solomos, 574 (Levesque's trans.)

Somerville College, Oxford, 588–9

Sophocles, 81, 160, 163 (*Philoctetes*), 446 (and *Oedipe*)

Sorel, Georges, 251 (attack on Desjardins and *NRF*)

Sorrento, 183 (in *L'Immoraliste*), 205, 518, 576, 608

Soupault, Philippe, 328

Sources, Les (Charles G's property nr Nîmes), 91–2, 131, 214, 243, 250, 259, 261, 298

Sourdell, Dr (G's physician), 459

Sousse (Tunisia), 94–5, 97, 168, 439

Spanish Civil War, 497, 502–8, 513, 517, 520

Sparrow, Mrs (Tunis), 557

Stalin (Josif Dzhugashvili), xv, 463, 474 (and great Purge), 478, 481, 483, 488, 492–4, 496, 499–503, 508–9, 517, 562

Spender, Stephen, 517

Spenser, Edmund, 259 (*Faerie Queene*)

Spinoza, Baruch, 51, 56

Stanislas, Ecole (Paris), 239 (Rivière)

Stanislavksy, Konstantin, 264, 496

Starkie, Enid, 587–9

Starnberger See (Ger.), 442

Stavisky, Alexander, 466

Steinbeck, John, 622

Stendhal (Henri Beyle), 70–1, 239, 271 (Julien Sorel, Fabrice del Dongo and *Les Caves*) 352, 471 (and Rome)

Sterne, Laurence, 397 (and *Faux-Monnayeurs*)

Sternheim, Thea (Stoisy), 442 (works on Ger. trans. of *Saül*), 455 (leaves Ger.), 469–70 (with G at Karlovy Vary, 1934),

539 (interned), 543 (released from internment), 571, 585, 603, 619 (d.)
Stevenson, R. L., 70, 138 (*Dr Jekyll and Mr Hyde, Treasure Island*), 250, 344 (*Pavilion on the Links, New Arabian Nights*), 403–4 (*Master of Ballantrae*), 559 (*Kidnapped*)
Strachey, James, 310, 346
Strachey, Lytton, xiv, 310, 311 (*Eminent Victorians*), 337, 357, 360, 367, 447 (d.)
Strachey, Pernel, 310
Strachey, Sir Richard and Lady, 310, 312, 338
Strasbourg, 79, 341
Strauss, Richard, 222–3 (*Salomé, Rosenkavalier*)
Stravinsky, Igor, 237 (*Perséphone*), 242 (*Firebird*), 262 (*Petrushka, Sacre du Printemps*), 278 (*Petrushka*), 300 (*Renard*), 407, 411, 454 (and *Proserpine*), 459–60 (*Perséphone*), 544, 571 (*Perséphone*)
Strindberg, August, 104
Strohl, Jean, 354
Strowski, Fortunat, 399 (on *Faux-Monnayeurs*)
Sturges, Mary, 251
Suarès, André, 239, 241, 254
Sue, Eugène, 57
Sufis, 139 (and *El Hadj*)
Suffren, General, 560
Sukhumi (USSR), 500
Surrealists, 372
Symbolism, xii, 86–7, 89, 109–10 (and *Paludes*), 140, 160–1, 202, 233, 629
Symons, Arthur, 68, 249
Syracuse, 99, 134, 465

Tagore, Rabindranath, 263 (G trans. *Gitanjali*; Nobel Prize), 265 (G lectures on), 267, 278 (G trans. *The Post Office*), 344, 354 (*Amal* – G trans. of *The Post Office* – pub.), 370 (rehearsals for *Amal*), 386, 461 (nephew sees G), 629 (trans.)
Taine, Hippolyte, 57, 70
Talabart, Charles (Mathilde Rondeaux's second husband), 59
Talloires, 366
Tangier, 365, 449, 478

Taormina, 134, 607–8
Tarquinia (Etruscan tombs, nr Rome), 476
Teillon, Pauline, 251
Temps, Le, 213
Temps modernes, Les, 566
Tennant, Stephen, 431
Terry, Ellen, 284
Tertre, Le (Bellême, RMG's country property), 409–10, 412, 414, 416–17, 426, 431, 447–8, 467, 526, 542
Thaelmann, Ernst, 467, 485
Théâtre, Le, 214
Thebes, 533
Theocritus, 373
Thibaudet, Albert, 254, 397 (on *Faux-Monnayeurs*)
Thierry, Jean-Jacques, xviii, 2, 596
Thiroloix, Dr, 599
Thorez, Maurice, 562, 575
Thousand and One Nights, see *Arabian Nights*
Thurn und Taxis, Princesse Marie von, 242, 271 (and *Les Caves*)
Tiflis (Tbilisi, USSR), 498–9
Times, The, 75
Tinan, Jean de, 114
Tissaudier, Bernard, 40–1, 43
Titian, 406
Tito (Josip Broz), 463 (and Dimitrov)
Tivoli, 149, 263
Tizi-Ouzou (Algeria), 203
Tobin, Agnes, 249
Tocqueville, Alexis de, 515 (*Mémoires*)
Todd, Miss (Catherine's Eng. nanny), 444
Tolstoy, Leo, 57, 71 (*Anna Karenina*), 73 (*War and Peace*), 81 (*Power of Darkness*), 342
Torri del Benaco (Lake Garda), 596–7
Toscanini, Arturo, 460
Touchard, Pierre-Aimé, 605–6, 611
Touggourt (Algeria), 136, 176–7, 185 (in *L'Immoraliste*), 207
Toulon, 254, 442, 472
Toulouse, 226, 243
Tour d'Argent (Paris restaurant), 222
Tourneur, Cyril, 538
Tournier, Marcel, 552, 555
Trápani, 180
Trarieux, Gabriel, 70

Trégastel, 226

Tree, Herbert Beerbohm, 251 (*Macbeth*)

Triolet, Elsa, 492

Tronche, Jean-Gustave, 280

Trotsky, Leon (-ites, -ism), 451, 454, 480, 493, 500–1, 507, 509, 513–14 (*Revolution Betrayed*), 515, 517, 520

Trouville, 155, 176

Trowbridge, Robertson, 285

Tunis, 93, 134–5 (honeymoon), 167–8, 178, 180 and 183–5 (in *L'Immoraliste*), 205, 214, 255, 485, 552

Tureck, Ludwig, 461

Truin, 100, 471 (and Nietzsche's madness)

Turner, Reggie, 194

Tzara, Tristan, 329, 372 (*Mouchoir de nuages*), 479

Uzès (Fr., home of G's paternal grandparents), 24–7, 72, 76–7, 92

Vadim (Plemianov), 597

Vaillant-Couturier, Paul, 454–5, 458, 468, 480, 503

Valencia, 241

Valéry, Paul, 296, 298–9 (*La jeune Parque*), 410 (and Académie Française), 478, 494, 521 (Chair, Collège de France), 552, 565, 571–3 (d.)

Valle-Inclán, Ramón, 480

Vallette, Alfred, 141, 147, 182

Valley of the Kings (Egypt), 577

Vallombrosa, 263

Valmont (nr. Montreux), 448

Val-Richer, Le (property of Guizot de Witt-Schlumbergers, Blancmesnil in *Si le grain*), 21, 43–4, 175, 205, 233, 437, 528

Vanden Eeckhoudt, Jan, 346

Van der Lubbe, 455, 473–4, 541

Vaneau, rue (*see under* Gide, André, homes)

Vannicola, Giuseppe, 235, 255

Van Rysselberghe, Elisabeth (Beth, d. of Théo and Maria, m. of Catherine (G), xiv–xv (and G), 235 (in It.), 283 (affair with Rupert Brooke), 294–5 (and G), 312 (works on Scottish farm), 319, 327, 333–6 (and *Symphonie Pastorale*; in It.), 338–9 (in

Eng. and Wales with G and Marc Allégret), 341, 348–9 (in Rome with G), 353–6 (at Villa Montmorency), 356 (conceives d. by G), 357–9 (Pontigny), 363–4 (and G), 366–7 (b. Catherine), 371, 380–1, 384–5 (G stays at La Bastide), 408–9 (meets G and Marc back from Afr.), 411 (Pontigny), 415, 417, 419–20 (at Saint-Clair), 422–5 (in Eng.), 438–40 (to Tunisia with G), 441–3 (Herbart moves in with), 448–9 (Herbart's *Contre-Ordre* dedicated to; birth and death of second child), 453–4, 456 (and G's Communism), 462–3 (to Lausanne with G), 467, 471 (and Marius), 474, 495 (joins G, etc. in Moscow), 497, 504, 512 (and *Geneviève*), 513–14 (reads Trotsky), 521, 530, 540, 547–8, 550, 559 (in Nice), 569, 573, 575 (takes over studio at Villa Montmorency), 586–7 (to Venice), 594–6, 598–9, 602, 606 (nursing G), 608, 612–16 (G's last weeks), 617 (day of G's funeral), 619 (d.), 625 (G and the Vaneau)

Van Rysselberghe, Maria (the 'Petite Dame', w. of Théo), xiv (Foyer Franco-Belge), xviii (the *Cahiers*), 166, 169 (meets G), 181, 201–2 (with G to Weimar), 222–3 (with G in Jersey), 235 (love for Verhaeren), 236, 261, 281–3 (G moves in with the Van Rs, rue Laugier), 292–5 (G moves into the Van Rs' new house, rue Claude-Lorrain, Auteuil), 310, 312, 313 (begins *Cahiers*), 318–19, 322, 327–8 (intimacy with G), 334–5 (G on Marc and Beth), 337 (and G), 337–8 (G's trans. *Antony and Cleopatra* at Opéra), 341–4 (on Marc), 346–8 (with G in Brussels and Colpach; G on the Allégrets), 354–8 (with G at rehearsals of *Saül*; Pontigny with G), 363–8 (G on Beth's child), 371, 380–1 (Pontigny with G), 384–5 (sees Buster Keaton film with G and Madeleine), 388–9 (G and Marc leave for Afr.), 406, 408 (meets G and Marc on return from Afr.), 415 (and the Vaneau; on Madeleine), 419 and 421–13 (the Vaneau), 426 (with G to Le Tertre;

trans. of Bennett's *Old Wives' Tale*), 430 (works on Ger. trans. of *Les Nourritures*), 433, 435 (on the 'folle de Saint-Etienne'), 436 (with G at Marienbad), (on G and Néné), 441–5 (on Marc; on G and USSR), 447–9, 452–3 (on G), 455–60 (G and the CP), 465 (with Loup Mayrisch to Egypt), 467, 472 (*Il y a quarante ans*), 474 (G's 65th birthday), 478 (G and USSR), 481–3 and 487–8 (on G and Catherine), 490–1 (Herbart and USSR), 504, 506–7 (on G and CP), 512–14 (on *Ecole des Femmes*; on Herbart in Spain), 516 (Herbart's *En U.R.S.S. 1936* dedicated to), 519–21 (Pontigny; RMG's Nobel Prize), 524–5 (relationship with G; G and Madeleine), 527–30 (Schlum hides *Cahiers* at Braffy), 534 (Japanese film of *Symphonie Pastorale*), 538–40 (outbreak of War, to Cabris and Nice), 543 (on Loup Mayrisch), 545, 547–8, 550–1 (moves to Nice with Herbarts), 554, 556–9, 563–4, 568–9 (reunited with G in Algeria), 570 (returns to Paris with G), 571–3, 575, 577 (80th birthday), 584–6 (G's trans. of *Hamlet*, with Barrault; to Brussels with G, sees Gielgud *Hamlet*), 588 (visit to Villa Montmorency), 590 (G's trans. of *Trial*, with Barrault), 592–4 (G's Nobel Prize; G 'older'), 596, 598–9 (moves to Nice with G), 601–3 (on Florence Gould; visits Matisse), 605, 607–9 (on Davet; on death; to Monte Carlo Casino with G), 611–16 (on Davet; on Com.-Fr. *Les Caves*; G's last weeks), 617–19 (day of G's funeral and reaction; d.), 623 (G and the Vaneau), 625, 628 (on G's *Journal*)

Van Rysselberghe, Théo, 169 (meets G), 181, 201, 222–3 (paints G's portrait), 235–6 (in Rome with G), 247, 261, 281–2 (G moves into Van Rs' house, Auteuil), 292–5 (G moves into Van Rs' house, rue Claude-Lorrain), 310, 318–19, 322, 327–8, 343, 364 and 368 (and Beth's child), 401 (and Africa), 412–13 (d.), 419 (exhibition of works, Brussels)

Varèse, Edgar, 295

Vedel, Monsieur (teacher, Ecole Alsacienne), 16, 20, 27, 29

Vedrenne-Barker season (Court Theatre, London), 386

Velásquez, 110 and 397 (*Las Meniñas* and *en abyme*)

Vence, 434, 442–3, 516, 540

Venice, 151

Ventura, 208

Véra, 443–4

Verbeke, Edouard, 248, 334

Verbrughe, Paul, 442–4

Verdi, Giuseppe, 518 (*La Traviata*)

Verhaeren, Emile, 235, 239, 294 (d.), 472 (and Maria Van Rysselberghe)

Verlaine, Paul, 55, 67–8, 70, 72, 253, 265

Versailles, Treaty of, 567

Vers et Prose, 198 (pubs. part of *Bethsabé*), 221 (*Retour de l'Enfant prodigue*)

Vespasian (Roman emperor), 199 ('vespasiennes')

Vetch, Rosalie (*see* 'Ysé')

Vichy, 254, 541–2

Vielé–Griffin, Francis, 72, 155, 165, 169, 225–6, 257

Viénot, Pierre, 425 (m. Andrée Mayrisch), 543, 546, 564 (d.)

Vie Nouvelle, La, 171

Vieux Colombier, xiv, 154, 261 (founding), 263–5 (opens), 268, 276–8, 285, 290 (G lectures on Dostoevsky), 295 (in New York), 297, 321 (return from USA), 334 (*Twelfth Night* and *Winter's Tale*), 343 (*Saül*), 344 (Schlumberger's *La Mort de Sparte*), 353, 355 (*Saül*), 370, 386–7 (end of), 416 (Marc's film shown), 417

Villa Medici, 99

Villa Montmorency (*see under* Gide, André, homes)

Villiers de l'Isle-Adam, Comte Auguste de, 68, 72

Viollis, Andrée (and h. Jean), 443

Virgil, 71, 108 (*Bucolics*), 203 (*Eclogues*), 373, 388 (*Aeneid*), 524 (*Culex* and *Et nunc*), 561 (*Aeneid*), 565 (*Bucolics*), 573, 589 (*Aeneid*), 594, 614 (*Georgics*)

Vittel, 458–9

Vogel, Nadine (m. Marc Allégret), 522, 526, 529

Volkstheater (Vienna), 216 (*König Candaules*)

Voltaire, 81, 465 (*Contes*)

Vova (Volodin, Leningrad), 496–7

Wadi-Halfa (Egypt), 577

Wagner, Richard, 78–9 (*Parsifal*, Bayreuth; *Lohengrin*, Paris Opéra; Mahler's Wagner season, Covent Garden, London), 171, 223, 251 (*Walküre, Siegfried*, Covent Garden, 1911)

Wahl, Jean, 482

Walckenaër, André, 54, 70

Wallonie, La, 81

Walter, Bruno, 455

Watteau, Antoine, 561

Webster, John, 559

Weimar, 200 (visit to 1903), 206, 455 (Kessler's house)

Wenz, Paul, 308

Westhopf, Clara (Rilke's w.), 241

Wharton, Edith, 282, 285, 292, 367

Whistler, James, 68

White, William Hale (*see* Mark Rutherford)

Whitehorn, Edith (Whity), 312 (worked on Scottish farm with Beth), 319 (at Saint-Clair), 334 (joins G etc. in Rome), 338–9, 371, 384–5, 419, 447–8, 453–4 (visit to USSR), 608, 625

Whitman, Walt, 70, 136, 187, 254, 273–4, 278, 374

Widmer, General (G's cousin), 590

Wiesbaden, 454

Wilde, Oscar, xiii, 1, 68, 75–7, 100, 116–20 (at Blida), 125–6, 147–8 (G sees after prison), 148 (d. Paris, 1900), 152 (on first person in literature), 157–8, 160–2 (on *Le Prométhée*), 188–9 (and 'I' in *L'Immoraliste*), 205, 236, 251, 257, 275, 344, 346, 352, 589 (G visits rooms at Oxford)

Witt-Guizot, François de, 43–4, 46 (Lionel of *Si le grain*), 205

Woolf, Virginia (and h. Leonard), 396, 413, 464

Xénie (G's black poodle bitch), 601, 603

Xenophon, 573

Yacco, Sada, 173

Yakhov, 474

Yemba, Sergeant, 405

Young, Edward, 65

Ysé (Rosalie Vetch, Claudel's mistress), 215

Zaghouan (Tunisia), 93, 440

Zézé (cook), 402

Zhdanov, Andrei, 493, 496

Zinoviev, G. E., 501

Zola, Emile, 150 and 162 (J'accuse. . .), 454 (*La Bête humaine*)

454 (*La Bête humaine*)

Zürich, 254, 416, 584